Storage Design and Implementation in vSphere 6

A TECHNOLOGY DEEP DIVE

VMware Press is the official publisher of VMware books and training materials, which provide guidance on the critical topics facing today's IT professionals and students. VMware virtualization and cloud infrastructure technologies simplify IT complexity and streamline operations, helping organizations of all kinds and sizes to become more agile, efficient, and profitable.

VMware Press provides proven, technically accurate information that will help you achieve your goals for customizing, building, and maintaining a virtual environment—from the data center to mobile devices to the public, private, and hybrid cloud.

With books, certification and study guides, video training, and learning tools produced by world-class architects and IT experts, VMware Press helps you master a diverse range of topics on virtualization and cloud computing and is the official source of reference materials for preparing for the VMware Certified Professional certifications.

VMware Press is also pleased to have localization partners that can publish its products into more than 42 languages, including, but not limited to, Chinese (Simplified), Chinese (Traditional), French, German, Greek, Hindi, Japanese, Korean, Polish, Russian, and Spanish.

For more information about VMware Press, please visit **vmwarepress.com.**

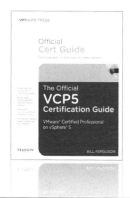

Storage Design and Implementation in vSphere 6

A TECHNOLOGY DEEP DIVE

Mostafa Khalil

vmware® PRESS

Hoboken, NJ • Boston • Indianapolis • San Francisco
New York • Toronto • Montreal • London • Munich • Paris • Madrid
Capetown • Sydney • Tokyo • Singapore • Mexico City

Storage Design and Implementation in vSphere 6

A Technology Deep Dive

ISBN-10: 0-13-426810-5
ISBN-13: 978-0-13-426810-1

Library of Congress Control Number: 2017941457

Printed in the United States of America

1 17

Warning and Disclaimer

Special Sales

For information about buying this title in bulk quantities, or for special sales opportunities (which may include electronic versions; custom cover designs; and content particular to your business, training goals, marketing focus, or branding interests), please contact our corporate sales department at corpsales@pearsoned.com or (800) 382-3419.

For government sales inquiries, please contact governmentsales@pearsoned.com.

For questions about sales outside the U.S., please contact intlcs.@pearson.com.

EDITOR-IN-CHIEF
Mark Taub

PRODUCT LINE MANAGER
Brett Bartow

EXECUTIVE EDITOR
Mary Beth Ray

VMWARE PRESS PROGRAM MANAGER
Karl Childs

DEVELOPMENT EDITOR
Christopher Cleveland

TECHNICAL EDITOR
Jonathan Van Meter

MANAGING EDITOR
Sandra Schroeder

PROJECT EDITOR
Mandie Frank

COPY EDITOR
Kitty Wilson

PROOFREADER
Christopher Morris

INDEXER
Erika Millen

EDITORIAL ASSISTANT
Vanessa Evans

DESIGNER
Chuti Prasertsith

COMPOSITOR
codeMantra

To my wife, Gloria, for her unconditional love and tireless efforts in helping make the time to complete this book.

In loving memory of Mary, my mother-in-law

About the Author

Mostafa Khalil is a senior staff engineer at VMware. He is a senior member of the VMware Engineering team and has worked for VMware for more than 18 years. Prior to joining VMware, he worked at Lotus/IBM. A native of Egypt, Mostafa graduated from the Al-Azhar University's School of Medicine and practiced medicine in Cairo. He became intrigued by the mini computer system used in his medical practice and began to educate himself about computing and networking technologies. After moving to the United States, Mostafa continued to focus on computing and acquired several professional certifications, including VCDX (3, 4, 5, and 6), VCAP (4, 5, and 6)-DCD, VCAP4-DCA, VCP (2, 3, 4, 5, and 6), MCSE, Master CNE, HP ASE, IBM CSE, and Lotus CLP.

As storage became a central element in the virtualization environment, Mostafa became an expert in this field. He has delivered several seminars and troubleshooting workshops at various VMware public events in the United States and elsewhere around the world.

About the Reviewers

Jonathan Van Meter has more than fifteen years of experience in enterprise infrastructure design and engineering for large enterprise, financial, and service provider customers. He is currently working as a solutions architect for Red Hat focusing on automation and cloud application services delivery. Jonathan has been an early mover in virtualization, converged infrastructure, and software defined networking production deployments. He holds multiple industry certifications including several VMware advanced professional certifications in data center virtualization and network virtualization and ISC2 CISSP. Jonathan is an active emerging tech community contributor in the Washington, D.C. metro area.

Acknowledgments

I would like to acknowledge the endless support I got from my wife, Gloria, without whom this book would not have been possible.

Also, I would like to thank my colleagues at Dell PS Series®, David Glynn and Jason Boche, and at Dell-EMC®, Bill Whitney, for their valuable input and help with loaner storage arrays and assistance with Unity® Virtual Appliance.

In addition, special thanks to my colleague Jeffrey Taylor for sharing his knowledge with various teams at VMware.

One last acknowledgement is to all who have taught and mentored me along the way throughout my journey. Their names are too many to count. You know who you are. Thank you, all!

Contents at a Glance

Contents

We Want to Hear from You!

As the reader of this book, *you* are our most important critic and commentator. We value your opinion and want to know what we're doing right, what we could do better, what areas you'd like to see us publish in, and any other words of wisdom you're willing to pass our way.

We welcome your comments. You can email or write us directly to let us know what you did or didn't like about this book—as well as what we can do to make our books better.

Please note that we cannot help you with technical problems related to the topic of this book.

When you write, please be sure to include this book's title and author as well as your name, email address, and phone number. We will carefully review your comments and share them with the author and editors who worked on the book.

Email: VMwarePress@vmware.com

Mail: VMware Press
         ATTN: Reader Feedback
         800 East 96th Street
         Indianapolis, IN 46240 USA

Reader Services

Visit our website at www.pearsonitcertification.com/title/9780134268101 and register this book for convenient access to any updates, downloads, or errata that might be available for this book.

Introduction

This book is a major update to its predecessor, *Storage Implementation in vSphere 5.0*. I expanded the scope to include new features included with vSphere 6.0 through 6.5, along with vSAN 6.0 through 6.6. I share with you in-depth details of how things work so that you can identify problems if and when anything goes wrong. I originally planned to put everything in one book, but as I wrote, the page count kept growing, partly due to the large number of illustrations and screenshots that I hope will make the picture clearer for you. As a result, I had to split this book into a two-volume set so that I don't have to sacrifice quality at the expense of page count. I hope you will find this content as useful as I intended it to be and that you'll have a clearer picture of the wealth of storage features vSphere 6.x has to offer.

The book starts with a brief introduction to the history of storage. It then provides details of the various storage connectivity choices and protocols supported by VMware: Fibre Channel (FC), Fibre Channel over Ethernet (FCoE), and Internet Small Computer System Interface (iSCSI). This transitions us to the foundation of vSphere storage, which is Pluggable Storage Architecture (PSA). From there I build upon this foundation with multipathing and failover (including third-party offerings) and ALUA. I then discuss storage virtualization devices (SVDs) and VMDirectPath I/O architecture, implementation, and configuration. I also cover in intricate detail Virtual Machine File System (VMFS) versions 3 and 5 and how this highly advanced clustered file system arbitrates concurrent access to virtual machine files as well as raw device mappings. I also include an overview of VMFS version 6. I discuss the details of how distributed locks are handled, as well as physical snapshots and virtual machine snapshots. I share extensive details about Network File System (NFS) versions 3.0 and 4.1. Next, I cover vStorage APIs for Array Integration (VAAI) architecture and interactions with the relevant storage arrays. In addition, I explain how Storage vMotion works and its application in various scenarios. After that, I demystify the ESXi boot image's file system VisorFS, followed by vSphere APIs for Storage Awareness (VASA), which is the foundation for storage policy–based management (SPBM), which play a major role in vSAN and vSphere Virtual Volumes (VVols), along with object store file system (OSFS).

This book is a how-to implementation guide as well as a vSphere 6.x storage design reference.

I would love to hear your opinions or suggestions for topics to cover in future publications. You can leave me a comment at my blog, http://vSphereStorage.com, or a tweet @mostafaVMW.

Thank you and God bless!

Mostafa Khalil, VCDX

Who Should Read This Book?

This book is intended for anyone who wants to gain in-depth knowledge about storage technologies supported by vSphere 6.x. It is also beneficial for storage administrators who configure and support storage resources to vSphere 6.x environments.

While the content of this book is a deep dive, it can aid vSphere architects in making informed design decisions that will meet business requirements. This book can be a great resource for architects preparing for VMware Certified Design Expert (VCDX) certification and design defense.

Book Organization

This book contains 23 chapters. The topics all focus on storage design and implementation details with deep coverage of those topics.

The book's topics are organized into two major parts. The following list outlines the organization of this book:

- **Part I: "Storage Protocols and Block Devices":** This part includes 11 chapters, which focus on storage protocols for block devices:

  - **Chapter 1: "Storage Types":** This introductory chapter provides a brief history of storage and introduces various types of block storage devices.

  - **Chapter 2: "Fibre Channel Storage Connectivity":** This chapter deals with Fibre Channel (FC) protocol and FC SAN. I discuss how to design Fibre Channel connectivity without single points of failure. I also explain in detail FC initiators and targets and how to identify each.

  - **Chapter 3: "FCoE Storage Connectivity":** This chapter covers the details of the FCoE protocol and its architecture and how it is implemented in vSphere 6. It also provides details on configuring software FCoE adapters on vSphere 6. I share some sample logs and familiarize you with how to interpret them. Finally, I discuss a potential *gotcha* when using Network I/O Control and FCoE.

  - **Chapter 4: "iSCSI Storage Connectivity":** This chapter provides details of the iSCSI protocol, connectivity, and iSCSI implementation on vSphere 6. I also covered iSCSI initiators (both hardware and software) as well as iSCSI targets and how to identify them. I walk you through gradually building up a logical iSCSI network diagram based on commands available on ESXi 6. Finally, I provide details of iSCSI architecture and the flow of communication between its components.

- **Chapter 5: "vSphere Pluggable Storage Architecture":** This chapter covers Pluggable Storage Architecture (PSA) components. I show you how to list PSA plug-ins and how they interact with vSphere ESXi 6. I also show you how to list, modify, and customize PSA claim rules and how to work around some common issues. This chapter also covered how ALUA (Asymmetric Logical Unit Access)-capable devices interact with Storage Array Type Plug-in (SATP) claim rules for the purpose of using a specific PSP.

- **Chapter 6: "ALUA":** This chapter covers the ALUA standard, including how it is implemented in vSphere 6. I show you how to identify various ALUA configurations and how they affect the hosts.

- **Chapter 7: "Multipathing and Failover":** This chapter covers multipathing and failover algorithms and provides details about failover triggers as well as factors affecting multipathing and failover. It also covers improvements introduced in vSphere 6 to better handle the APD state. Finally, this chapter covers the little-known path ranking feature, including how it works and how to configure it.

- **Chapter 8: "Third-Party Multipathing I/O Plug-ins":** This chapter provides details of VMware partner-developed MPIO software for use on ESXi 6.x. It covers three products from Dell EMC, Hitachi Data Systems, and Dell EqualLogic. This chapter provides details about installing these MPIO software packages and what changes they make to the ESXi host.

- **Chapter 9: "Using Heterogeneous Storage Configurations":** This chapter covers heterogeneous storage environments supported by VMware to expand your storage environment while preserving your existing investment.

- **Chapter 10: "Using VMDirectPath I/O":** This chapter covers VMDirectPath I/O, which you can use to pass through physical storage or network devices, which expose the physical I/O card to the guest OS.

- **Chapter 11: "Storage Virtualization Devices (SVDs)":** This chapter covers SVDs, which present older back-end arrays' LUNs to initiators as if they were physically located within the SVDs themselves.

- **Part II: "File Systems":** This part includes 12 chapters, covering all file systems supported by vSphere 6 and related APIs:

  - **Chapter 12: "VMFS Architecture":** This chapter covers VMFS, including version 5, which introduced several scalability and performance enhancements. VMFS6, introduced in vSphere 6.5, adds support for 512e devices and automatic deleted space reclamation. In this chapter I share with you the file system history, architecture, and recovery tips.

- **Chapter 13: "Virtual Disks and RDMs":** In this chapter, I introduce the basics of virtual disks and RDMs, including structure, layout, and type; and which are eager zeroed thick, zeroed thick, and thin. I also explain the various virtual disk types from the file system's perspective. I discuss RDMs (both virtual and physical modes) in detail. I explain virtual machine snapshots and how they affect their virtual disks. In addition, I cover deleting, going to, reverting to, and consolidating snapshots. I give you a quick glance at linked clones and how they correlate to certain snapshot hierarchies.

- **Chapter 14: "Distributed Locks":** In this chapter I cover details of how distributed locking is done on file systems shared by ESXi hosts. I also discuss perennial device reservation, which helps improve boot and rescan time for hosts with RDMs reserved by MSCS/WSFC nodes on other ESXi hosts.

- **Chapter 15: "Snapshot Handling":** This chapter provides an overview of storage snapshots, replication, and mirroring. It explains the effects of these storage features on VMFS datastore signatures and how vSphere handles them.

- **Chapter 16: "NFS":** This chapter provides details about Network File System (NFS) architecture, implementation, and design tips. It covers examples from NetApp Clustered ONTAP and EMC Unity 4.0.x. NFSv3.0 and NFSv4.1 are covered in detail, along with detailed configurations on vSphere 6.x as well as NFS servers. This chapter also provides details of configuring and implementing Kerberos authentication, where supported.

- **Chapter 17: "VAAI":** This chapter provides details about VAAI, which provides block device primitives, thin provisioned primitives, and NAS primitives. It also covers the details of how to enable and disable VAAI primitives as well as how to identify the various devices' support for each primitive.

- **Chapter 18: "Storage vMotion":** This chapter provides details about the Storage vMotion feature, which facilitates migration of VMs and their files between datastores on the same hosts or across different hosts, with and without shared storage.

- **Chapter 19: "VisorFS":** This chapter covers VisorFS, which is a memory-based file system. An ESXi host boot image is installed on two boot banks, bootbank and altbootbank. This chapter also explains how the system state is saved to the local.tgz file and then added to the state.tgz file hourly and upon shutdown. Finally, this chapter explains how the state gets loaded from the bootbank upon booting the host.

- **Chapter 20: "VASA":** This chapter provides details about VASA, which provides APIs for storage vendors to expose the physical storage capabilities as well as monitor certain storage events. I explain how SPBM is leveraged to create VM storage policies, which are used to simplify the placement of VMs' virtual disk on datastores that meet the virtual disks' I/O and availability requirements. This chapter also provides detailed procedures for creating and utilizing the storage policies while deploying new virtual machines.

- **Chapter 21: "vSAN Core Features":** This chapter provides details about vSAN basic features and vSAN software architecture, requirements, and file system details. I explain how vSAN storage policies affect placement of vSAN objects' components on disks in vSAN disk groups. In addition, I cover RAID 5 and RAID 6 erasure coding (EC), which are new in vSAN 6.2 and later. I also cover how to apply a new storage policy to a virtual disk and the effect on storage.

- **Chapter 22: "vSAN Advanced Features":** This chapter provides details about vSAN advanced features and takes a deep dive into some complex tasks and object property inspections. The skills you gain in this chapter should help you in maintaining and troubleshooting vSAN cluster configurations and data. This chapter also covered creating and configuring vSAN stretched clusters for additional levels of availability. It also discusses remote office/branch office (ROBO), which is a subset of vSAN stretched cluster configuration. Finally, this chapter provides details on deduplication and compression, as well as vSAN iSCSI targets (VITs).

- **Chapter 23: "Virtual Volumes (VVols)":** This chapter provides details about Virtual Volumes, which separate the storage data paths from the management out-of-band path. I explain how VVols represent VMDKs as abstract objects, VVols, managed by the storage arrays that enable the storage array to gain full control over VMDK content, layout, and management. I cover the concepts of storage containers (SCs) that are also managed by the storage array. I show you how access to VVols is done via one or more protocol endpoints and how VVols enable data services like native snapshots at the individual VMDK level. I provide details on how SPBM enables creating policies for initial placement of VVols on SCs according to capability profiles (CPs) associated with the SCs. This chapter also covers sample configurations from a block device storage array and a NAS server.

## Chapter 1

Storage Types

History of Storage

The concept of storage goes as far back as the ancient Egyptians (my ancestors), who built silos to protect grain from moisture and to store it for use when a famine hit. In the well-known example of that, Joseph oversaw the rationing and storage of grains, and he kept records of the stored amounts. Storage has evolved over the centuries, and today we store not just grain and dates (palm dates, that is) but data. Enough ancient Egyptian history for now; let's get down to the wire or, in other words, the bits of computer storage history!

From a computing perspective, the smallest unit of data is a *bit*, whose value is either a 0 or a 1. As you might already know, bits trace their roots back to the very early minicomputer architecture, where toggle switches could be in one of two positions, off (0) or on (1), which means this is binary data. The number of bits that made up one character was eight; eight bits are a *byte* of data.

Figure 1.1 shows an early model computer that utilized dip switches to program the bit digital values 0 or 1.

(Trivia: Data General Corporation was the creator of EMC's CLARiiON family of storage arrays.)

So, any data handled by a computer is simply a sequence of zeros and ones. I discuss the units of measuring data and address spaces in the "Units of Measuring Storage Capacity" section, later in this chapter.

Data is stored on both volatile and permanent media forms.

Figure 1.1 This photo of Data General's Nova 1200 minicomputer shows a 16-bit design (16 toggle switches).

(Photo credit Arnold Reinhold, used under GNU free license)

Volatile data storage is also known as volatile memory, or random-access memory (RAM). Reading data from RAM is a lot faster than reading it from most other forms of memory/ storage because there are no moving parts. Computers use this type of memory/storage to load programs and data for runtime use. Modified data in RAM is written to permanent storage at certain intervals and prior to shutting down the computer system.

Permanent data storage media types vary by the type of data to be stored or retrieved and the type of controllers to which they are attached. The earliest form of data storage was the *magnetic tape* used by mainframe computers. Data is written onto the tape in tracks more or less like the old 8-track audio tape format made popular by car stereo players in most American automobiles in the 1970s. These tracks run parallel for the length of the tape and are read back by heads matching the number of tracks. Mainframe computers in the 1950s used 10.5" magnetic tape reels that were 0.5" wide. These have evolved into *quarter-inch* tape cartridges used with modern personal computers for data backup.

Later forms of removable permanent data storage were the *floppy disks* that ranged from 8" all the way down to 2". The surviving most popular form factors were 5.25" and then later 3.5" floppy disks.

(Trivia: DOS 1.0 [disk operating system] used by the first model of IBM PC was shipped on both *compact cassette* and 5.25" floppy disks.)

IBM PC model 5150 shipped with two 5.25" floppy drives (see Figure 1.2). Later models (models 5160 and XT) shipped with a 10MB MFM hard disk. This hard disk's form factor was 5.25" full height (that is, it occupied the full slot) and replaced the second floppy disk drive. Full height slot actual height is 3.25". I still have a couple of these systems in my collection, and I think you can see one or more of them on display at the Computer History Museum in Mountain View, California.

Figure 1.2 IBM PC model 5150 shipped with two 5.25" floppy drives

Source: Wikipedia (retired document)

Birth of the Hard Disks

As programs and applications grew larger in size, the need arose for larger internal forms of permanent storage, which came to be known as *hard disks* or *hard disk drives*. The term *hard* was used because the disks were inflexible compared to floppy disks and tapes. They first appeared in the IBM PC/XT (model 5160) mentioned in the previous section. That model's hard disk was a whopping 10MB in data size and 5.25" in diameter, with an average 150-millisecond seek time. This was improved to one-tenth of the old seek time, to about 15 milliseconds, near the latter half of the 1980s.

The IBM PC/XT referenced in the previous paragraph was configured with a modified frequency modulation (MFM) ST-506 interface. The run length limited (RLL) ST-412 interface was also used in the late 1980s and early 1990s. The latter type required installing special software that provided a BIOS extension for expanding the logical block addressing (LBA).

There were other forms of persistent storage and hard disk drives, such as enhanced small disk interface (ESDI), which was rather common with early versions of AT&T UNIX and XENIX operating systems on Intel platforms in the late 1980s.

Along Comes SCSI

The need for larger, faster, and more numerous disks in a PC begat the *Small Computer System Interface* (*SCSI*, pronounced "scuzzy"), which has proven to be the most successful and reliable interface and protocol to date. SCSI became an industry standard for attaching all sorts of I/O devices, including scanners, printers, tape drives, and storage devices, including large sets of disks in disk array enclosures (DAEs). The most commonly used SCSI devices these days are disks and tape drives or libraries. The SCSI protocol and standards are covered in the "SCSI Standards and Protocols" section of Chapter 2, "Fibre Channel Storage Connectivity"; Chapter 3, "FCoE Storage Connectivity"; and Chapter 4, "iSCSI Storage Connectivity."

SCSI disks, as well as their buffers, grew larger and faster. The interface also evolved from *parallel* to *serially attached SCSI (SAS)*. Here's an oversimplification of the SAS concept: Instead of daisy-chaining the disks between the controller and the power termination, they are now attached to dedicated channels on the controller or plugged into an external SAS disk enclosure connected to the computer's external SAS controller channels.

PATA and SATA—SCSI's Distant Cousins?

After the introduction of IBM PC/AT computers, disks commonly known as IDE disks were the next generation of disks to arrive. The Integrated Drive Electronics (IDE) interface for these disks was actually AT Attachment (ATA) and AT Attachment Packet Interface (ATAPI), which was later renamed Parallel ATA— (PATA)— to differentiate it from its new sibling, Serial ATA— (SATA).

PATA was limited to two drives per controller interface (master and slave), whereas SATA is limited by the number of channels provided by the controller.

The following are some differences between SAS and SATA:

- SCSI drives are more expensive and faster than SATA drives because of the design and performance achieved with this technology.

- SCSI uses a tagged command queuing implementation that allows many commands to be outstanding. This design provides significant performance gains for the drives/controllers to be able to reorder these commands in the most optimal execution manner possible.

- SCSI drives also use a processor for executing commands and handling the interface, while a separate processor handles the head positioning through servos.

- SCSI disks certified for use with storage arrays include ECC (error checking and correcting) buffers. This is critical for the integrity of the data, especially in the vSphere environment.

- SATA 1.0 used Tagged Command Queuing (TCQ), a queuing technology that was intended to help bridge the gap between SCSI and PATA/SATA drives; however, the overhead was fairly high, and TCQ wasn't efficient enough. TCQ is also referred to as *interrupt queuing*.

- SATA 2.0 introduced Native Command Queuing (NCQ), which is very similar to the outstanding request queuing that SCSI uses. This technology drastically reduces the number of interrupts that TCQ uses due to the integrated first-party direct memory access (DMA) engine and the intelligent ordering of commands and interrupting when it is most optimal to do so.

- Buffer size has grown in newer SATA disks; however, most do not provide ECC capability.

Table 1.1 lists various storage buses and their performance characteristics.

Table 1.1 Storage interface characteristics

Interface	Raw Bandwidth (Mbps)	Max Transfer Speed (MBps)	Devices per Channel
ESATA	6,000	600	1
eSATAp	3,000	300	1
SATA 3.2	16,000	1,970	1
SATA 3.0	6,000	600	1
SATA 2.0	3,000	300	1
SATA 1.0	1,500	150	1 per line
PATA 133	1,064	133.5	2
SAS 600	6,000	600	1 (more than 65,000 with expanders)
SAS 300	3,000	300	1 (more than 65,000 with expanders)

Interface	Raw Bandwidth (Mbps)	Max Transfer Speed (MBps)	Devices per Channel
SAS 150	1,500	150	1 (more than 65,000 with expanders)
SCSI Ultra-640	5,120	640	15 (plus the HBA)
SCSI Ultra-320	2,560	320	15 (plus the HBA)
10G Fibre Channel	10,520	2,000	$126\ 256^3 =$ 16,777,216 (switched fabric)
4G Fibre Channel	4,000	400	$126\ 256^3 =$ 16,777,216 (switched fabric)
InfiniBand	10,000	1,000	1 (point to point)
Quad Rate			Many with switched fabric

Source: http://en.wikipedia.org/wiki/Sata#Comparison_with_other_buses

Based on the performance characteristics of the various disk interfaces, capacity, and cost, storage can be grouped in tiers that meet relevant service level agreements (SLAs). Table 1.2 lists common storage tiers and their pros and cons.

Table 1.2 Examples of storage tiers

Tier	Storage Type	Pros	Cons
0	Solid state drive (SSD)	Highest raw bandwidth and transfer speed, fastest reads and writes, both sequential and random, no moving parts	Very expensive, lower capacity, life span measured in write operations
1	SCSI/SAS—Fibre	Higher raw bandwidth and transfer speed than tier 0	Expensive, lower capacity than tier 2
2	SCSI/SAS—Copper	Average transfer speed, less expensive than tier 1	Somewhat expensive, lower capacity than tier 3
3	SATA 2 or 3	Least expensive, higher capacity than the other tiers	Slower transfer rate than the other tiers

The concept of storage tiers plays an important role in the Storage DRS feature introduced in vSphere 5.0 and continues in vSphere 6.x.

Measuring Storage Capacity

From a hardware perspective, storage capacity (binary) is measured in orders of magnitude of a bit, where the smallest unit is 2^0 (1 bit), and a byte is 2^3. The next unit is 2^{10} (kibibyte [KiB]), then 2^{20} (mebibyte [MiB]), and so on in the increment of 10 powers of base 2. These units are based on International Electrotechnical Commission (IEC) binary units. The units' prefixes are derived from the binary and decimal unit prefixes. For example, *kibi* is a combination of *kilo* and *binary*, *mebi* is a combination of *mega* and *binary*, and so on. The actual storage capacity is based on SI (*Système international*) units, which are decimal in increments of 1000 when you count from a kilobyte onward. The IEC standard is commonly used to represent RAM capacity, whereas SI is used for disks. Table 1.3 compares the units of storage capacity based on IEC and SI units.

Table 1.3 Comparing IEC and SI units of storage capacity

Binary (IEC Prefix)				Decimal (SI Prefix)			
Unit	Abbreviation	Binary	Value	Unit	Abbreviation	Decimal	Value
Bit	Bit	2^0	1 bit	Not applicable			
Byte	Byte	2^3	8 bits				
Kibibyte	KiB	2^{10}	1,024 bytes	Kilobyte	KB	10^3 ($1,000^1$)	1,000 bytes
Mebibyte	MiB	2^{20} ($1,024^2$)	1,024KB	Megabyte	MB	10^6 ($1,000^2$)	1,000KB
Gibibyte	GiB	2^{30} ($1,024^3$)	1,024MB	Gigabyte	GB	10^9 ($1,000^3$)	1,000MB
Tebibyte	TiB	2^{40} ($1,024^4$)	1,024GB	Terabyte	TB	10^{12} ($1,000^4$)	1,000GB
Pebibyte	PiB	2^{50} ($1,024^5$)	1,024TB	Petabyte	PB	10^{15} ($1,000^5$)	1,000TB
Exbibyte	EiB	2^{60} ($1,024^6$)	1,024PB	Exabyte	EB	10^{18} ($1,000^6$)	1,000PB

NOTE

The units of measurement for bandwidth are based on bit count per second, in increments of 1000, with a lowercase b to represent bits and an uppercase B to represent bytes. For example, the bandwidth 10 megabits per seconds is written 10Mb/s or 10Mbps. It is a common oversight to use b and B interchangeably. You must be careful not to specify the wrong one, though, or you might end up getting eight times less or more than you bargained for!

Permanent Storage Media Relevant to vSphere 6

ESXi 6 is installed on local disks, storage area network (SAN)–presented LUNs, or iSCSI storage–presented LUNs (see Chapters 2 through 4).

(Trivia: Boot from iSCSI is not supported by ESX/ESXi releases prior to 4.1.)

Supported Local Storage Media

Supported local storage media can be the following types:

1. SCSI disks (parallel)

2. Serial SCSI disks (SAS)

3. Serial ATA disks (SATA)

4. SD flash drives and USB keys (This applies to versions as early as ESXi 3.5 embedded/installable configurations.)

5. Solid state drives (SSDs)

Shared Storage Devices

vSphere 6.0 requires shared storage for certain features to work—for example, High Availability (HA), Distributed Resource Scheduler (DRS), vMotion, Storage vMotion, Storage DRS, and so on.

Such shared storage, both network-attached storage (NAS) and block devices, must be on VMware's Hardware Compatibility List (HCL). Being listed there means that the devices have been tested and certified to meet minimum performance criteria, have multipathing and failover capability, and also have possible support for certain VMware APIs, such as vSphere Storage APIs for Array Integration (VAAI) and vSphere Storage APIs for Storage Awareness (VASA).

A typical block storage device meeting VMware's HCL requirement is composed of the following:

- It has one or more storage processors (SPs)—also referred to as storage controllers.

- Each SP has two or more ports of varying connectivity types and speeds (for example, Fibre Channel, iSCSI). See Chapters 2 through 4 for further details.

- Some EMC storage arrays provide multiple SPs (referred to as *directors*) with multiple ports on each director. (For example, EMC DMX arrays provide multiple FA directors with four ports on each.)

- The back end of an SP connects to one or more DAEs that house disks of various types, as listed in Table 1.2.

- Some storage arrays connect the SPs to the DAEs via Fibre Channel loop switches.

Tips for Selecting Storage Devices

When you design a vSphere 6 environment, the choices you make in selecting storage components are crucial to successful design and implementation. The following guidelines and tips will help you make the right choices:

1. Identify the list of applications to be virtualized.

2. Identify the disk I/O criteria of these applications.

3. Identify the bandwidth requirements.

4. Calculate the disk capacity requirements for the applications' data.

5. Identify the service level agreements (SLAs) for these applications.

6. Identify the best RAID type for the identified I/O criteria.

Keep in mind that it is often more important to design for I/O peaks than for capacity. Inadequate storage architecture is one of the most common sources of performance problems for virtualized environments.

Summary

This chapter has introduced you to storage, storage types in general, and storage used by vSphere ESXi 6. Further details are provided in the next few chapters.

## Chapter 2

Fibre Channel Storage Connectivity

In the field of diplomacy, protocols are defined as "the set of rules that guide how an activity should be performed." Protocols in the field of technology are similar, also guiding how certain activities are performed.

This chapter provides an overview of the Fibre Channel (FC) storage protocol and connectivity, and the subsequent two chapters cover the Fibre Channel over Ethernet (FCoE) and Internet Small Computer System Interface (iSCSI) protocols.

SCSI Standards and Protocols

SCSI (Small Computer System Interface) is a set of standards for physically connecting and transferring data between computers and SCSI peripheral devices. These standards define commands and protocols.

SCSI-2 and SCSI-3 Standards

SCSI-2 and SCSI-3 standards are governed by the T10 Technical Committee (see www. t10.org/drafts.htm).

SCSI-2 is the name given to the second-generation SCSI standard, and SCSI-3 is the name for the third-generation SCSI standard. However, the subsequent generations have dropped the "-3" from the SCSI standard. When the SCSI-3 Architecture Model (SAM) was revised, it became SCSI Architecture Model–2 (SAM-2). In other words, there is no SCSI-4 standard. Rather, revisions of SAM are used, and the subsequent generations are named SAM-2, SAM-4, and so on.

The chart in Figure 2.1 shows the SCSI standards architecture and related protocols.

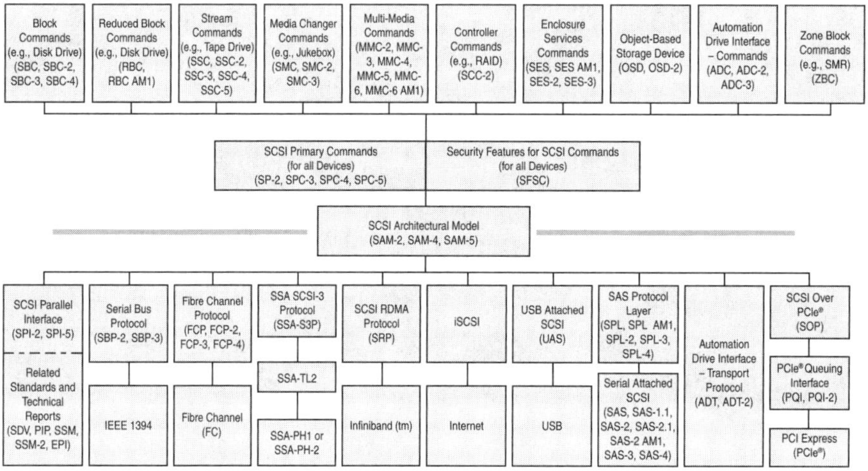

Block Commands (e.g., Disk Drive) (SBC, SBC-2, SBC-3, SBC-4) | Reduced Block Commands (e.g., Disk Drive) (RBC, RBC AM1) | Stream Commands (e.g., Tape Drive) (SSC, SSC-2, SSC-3, SSC-4, SSC-5) | Media Changer Commands (e.g., Jukebox) (SMC, SMC-2, SMC-3) | Multi-Media Commands (MMC-2, MMC-3, MMC-4, MMC-5, MMC-6, MMC-6 AM1) | Controller Commands (e.g., RAID) (SCC-2) | Enclosure Services Commands (SES, SES AM1, SES-2, SES-3) | Object-Based Storage Device (OSD, OSD-2) | Automation Drive Interface – Commands (ADC, ADC-2, ADC-3) | Zone Block Commands (e.g., SMR) (ZBC)

SCSI Primary Commands (for all Devices) (SP-2, SPC-3, SPC-4, SPC-5) | Security Features for SCSI Commands (for all Devices) (SFSC)

SCSI Architectural Model (SAM-2, SAM-4, SAM-5)

SCSI Parallel Interface (SPI-2, SPI-5) | Serial Bus Protocol (SBP-2, SBP-3) | Fibre Channel Protocol (FCP, FCP-2, FCP-3, FCP-4) | SSA SCSI-3 Protocol (SSA-S3P) | SCSI RDMA Protocol (SRP) | iSCSI | USB Attached SCSI (UAS) | SAS Protocol Layer (SPL, SPL AM1, SPL-2, SPL-3, SPL-4) | Automation Drive Interface – Transport Protocol (ADT, ADT-2) | SCSI Over PCIe® (SOP)

Related Standards and Technical Reports (SDV, PIP, SSM, SSM-2, EPI) | IEEE 1394 | Fibre Channel (FC) | SSA-TL2 / SSA-PH1 or SSA-PH-2 | Infiniband (tm) | Internet | USB | Serial Attached SCSI (SAS, SAS-1.1, SAS-2, SAS-2.1, SAS-2 AM1, SAS-3, SAS-4) | PCIe® Queuing Interface (PQI, PQI-2) / PCI Express (PCIe®)

Figure 2.1   SCSI standards architecture

ESXi 6 mostly uses the SCSI-2 standard. It also uses SCSI-3 with certain operations and configurations. Throughout this book I call out which standard is used with various vSphere 6 functions.

Fibre Channel Protocol

Fibre Channel Protocol (FCP) is governed by the T11 Technical Committee. (See www.t11.org/t11/stat.nsf/fcproj?OpenView&Count=70 for a list of current drafts.)

FCP is used on Fibre Channel networks of varying line ratings (currently ranging between 1 and 16Gbps, but higher ratings are in the works, such as 32 and 128Gbps). The basic element of a Fibre Channel connection is a *frame*. Figure 2.2 shows the structure of the FC frame, which is somewhat comparable to Ethernet frames or IP packets.

It is important to understand the FC frame structure as it aids you in interpreting storage-related messages listed in various ESXi logs discussed later in this book.

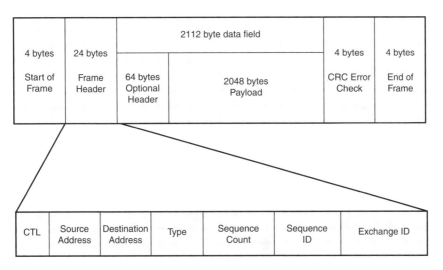

Figure 2.2 Fibre Channel frame architecture

Each frame contains 2KB of data being transmitted, surrounded by fields that guarantee the integrity of the frame as well as information that helps the targets (that is, destinations) and initiators (that is, sources) reassemble the data at either end of the connection. These fields are as follows:

- Start of Frame (4 bytes)
- End of Frame (4 bytes)
- Frame Header (24 bytes)
    - CTL (Control field)
    - Source Address
    - Destination Address
    - Type
    - Sequence Count
    - Sequence ID
    - Exchange ID

The communication between the different entities in the FC network occurs in *exchanges*, each of which is a number of sequences. Each sequence is a number of frames. To transfer information, FCP follows this process:

1. FCP checks the address of the destination port. (You'll learn more about port types and addresses later in this chapter.)

2. It checks the possibility of connection between the *source* and *destination* ports, using *logins*.

3. It breaks down protocol information (referred to as *exchanges*) into information units (referred to as *sequences*).

4. It breaks down sequences into parts small enough to fit into FC frames.

5. It labels each frame with the following (refer to Figure 2.2):

   - Source port address

   - Destination port address

   - Sequence number

   - Protocol

   - Exchange ID

6. It moves sequences of frames to the destination port.

7. At the destination, based on the frame labels, it reassembles the frames data to re-create the *information units* (also known as the *sequences*).

8. Finally, based on the protocol, it puts the sequences together to re-create the protocol information (also known as the *exchange*).

The basic elements of storage can be grouped as *initiators*, *targets*, and the *network* that connects them. That network is also referred to as the *fabric* in certain configurations. These elements vary based on the storage protocol in use.

This chapter covers Fibre Channel (FC) initiators, targets, and fabrics. Chapters 3, "FCoE Storage Connectivity," and 4, "iSCSI Storage Connectivity," cover FCoE and iSCSI.

Fibre Channel (FC) Initiators

Initiators are the endpoints on a storage network that initiate SCSI sessions with the SCSI targets. Examples are SCSI HBA (host bus adapter), FC-HBA, iSCSI hardware initiator, and iSCSI software initiator configured or installed in each ESXi host. I cover iSCSI initiators in Chapter 4.

FC initiators are the FC HBAs that are available in 1, 2, 4, 8, and 16Gbps port speeds and can be a single port or dual port. Higher speeds are planned as well but have not yet been released as of this writing.

Some FC HBAs are in the form of mezzanine cards in blade servers. A variety of this is the Fibre Channel Flex-Connect technology from HP.

FC-Port Identifiers

FC ports have unique identifiers referred to as worldwide port names (WWPNs). A WWPN is an assigned ID that is guaranteed to be unique in the fabric and is based on an organizationally unique identifier (OUI), which is assigned by the Institute of Electrical and Electronics Engineers (IEEE) registration authority (see https://regauth.standards. ieee.org/standards-ra-web/pub/view.html#registries). Each FC HBA manufacturer registers its own OUI and generates the WWPN based on that OUI. In the following WWPN example, the highlighted bytes are the OUI:

```
21:00:00:1b:32:17:34:c9
```

To identify the registered owner of a OUI, first select **MAC Address Block Large (MA-L)** and then enter that OUI (without the colons) in the Filter field at the IEEE URL; for example, searching for 001b32 should return a match to QLogic Corporation.

FC-Node Identifiers

FC nodes have unique identifiers referred to as worldwide node names (WWNNs). These IDs are generated by the HBA manufacturer using their unique OUIs in the same fashion just described for WWPNs. This WWNN example is from the same HBA used in the WWPN example in the previous section:

```
20:00:00:1b:32:17:34:c9
```

Notice that the OUI is identical. In this example, the HBA is the QLogic QLE2462 model. The following sample WWNN was taken from a CLARiiON or VNX SP port:

```
50:06:01:60:c1:e0:65:22
```

Notice that the target OUI bits are in a different position than in the initiator WWNN. This difference in positioning the OUI bits could be inherent to the designation as target or initiator.

Locating an HBA's WWPN and WWNN in ESXi 6 Hosts

In the process of troubleshooting storage area network (SAN) connectivity or mapping out an existing ESXi 6.0 host's SAN connectivity, you need to identify the installed HBAs' WWPNs and WWNNs. In this section I show you how to do that via the user interface (UI) as well as the command-line interface (CLI).

Locating an HBA's WWPN and WWNN Using the UI

To locate an HBA's WWPN and WWNN, follow these steps (see Figure 2.3):

1. Log on to the vCenter server that manages the host by using the VMware vSphere 6.0 Web Client as a user with Administrator privileges.

2. While in the Inventory—Hosts and Clusters view, locate the ESXi 6.0 host in the inventory tree and select it.

3. Navigate to the **Manage** tab.

4. Click the **Storage** button.

5. Select **Storage Adapters** section.

6. Locate the HBAs with the **Type** column showing **Fibre Channel**.

7. Select one HBA at a time and then, in the Adapter Details pane, select the **Properties** tab. There, you see the WWNN followed by the WWPN fields on separate lines.

8. Also look in the **Identifier** to see the WWNN and WWPN, separated by a space.

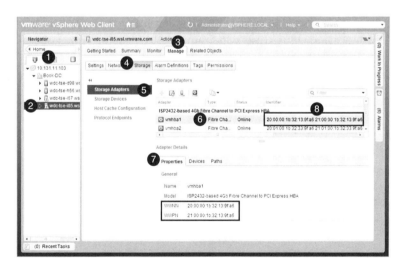

Figure 2.3   Locating an HBA's WWNN and WWPN by using the UI

Locating an HBA's WWPN and WWNN Using the CLI

You can also identify storage adapter properties by using the CLI. The CLI is available via multiple facilities, including SSH, vMA, and vCLI:

- **SSH**—SSH access to the host is disabled by default. To enable it, you can follow the procedure in the "Enabling SSH Host Access" section. If you do not wish to do so, follow one of the next two options: vMA or vSphere CLI (vCLI).

- **vMA**—vSphere Management Assistant version 6.0 is a SUSE Linux Enterprise Server 11 virtual appliance that is preinstalled with all you need to remotely manage one or more ESXi 6.0 hosts, including vCLI. For more information, see www.vmware.com/go/vma.

- **vCLI**—vCLI is available for both Windows and Linux, and you can install it on your management workstation. The syntax for using the Linux version is the same as that for the Windows version. Keep in mind that additional OS-specific commands and tools available on Linux might not be available on Windows. I cover the Linux version only, and you may apply the same procedure on Windows substituting non-ESXCLI commands with relevant ones that are available on Windows. For example, on Linux I might infrequently use `sed` and `awk`, which are not available on Windows by default. You can find a Windows version of `sed` at http://gnuwin32.sourceforge.net/packages/sed.htm and a Windows version of `awk` at http://gnuwin32.sourceforge.net/packages/gawk.htm.

The following section shows how to use SSH. However, due to space constraints, I do not show vMA and vCLI examples in this edition.

Enabling SSH Host Access

SSH access to the ESXi 6.0 host is not enabled by default. To enable it, follow this procedure:

1. Log on to the vCenter server that manages the host, using the VMware vSphere 6.0 Web Client as a user with Administrator privileges. Navigate to the **Hosts and Clusters** view.

2. Locate the ESXi 6.0 host in the inventory tree and select it.

3. Navigate to the **Manage** tab.

4. Click the **Settings** button

5. Select the **Security Profile** option, as shown in Figure 2.4.

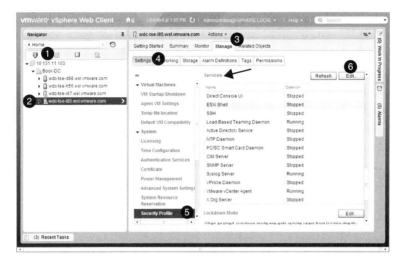

Figure 2.4   Modifying the security profile

6. Click **Edit** in the Services section in the right-hand side pane. The dialog shown in Figure 2.5 appears.

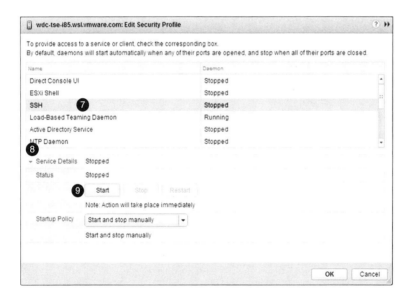

Figure 2.5   Modifying the service properties

7. Select **SSH** under the list of services displayed.

8. Expand the Service Details section if it's not already expanded. Figure 2.6 shows the possible Startup Policy options. The default Startup Policy option is **Start and stop manually**.

Figure 2.6   SSH startup policy options

9. To temporarily enable SSH access to the host, click the **Start** button and then click **OK and stop here**.

10. To permanently enable SSH access to the host, select the **Start and stop with host** option, click the **Start** button, and then click **OK**.

11. Alternatively, if you want to enable SSH access to the host when the SSH port is enabled on the ESXi firewall without having to manually start the SSH service, select the **Start and stop with port usage** option and then click **OK**.

> **NOTE**
>
> You may need to enable **ESXi Shell**, if it is not already enabled, and start it before SSH can start.

Locating an HBA's WWPN and WWNN Using SSH

ESXi 6 uses native drivers whenever possible. Native drivers are developed to run directly on vmkernel rather than the vmklinux-based drivers that have been in use since ESX/ESXi 3.5. Native drivers do not have Linux style `proc` nodes.

To locate an HBA's WWPN and WWNN using SSH, follow these steps:

1. Connect to the ESXi 6.0 host, using an SSH client.

2. Log on as root or another user with root privileges.

3. Run the following command if you are using QLogic FC-HBAs:

```
esxcfg-scsidevs -a |less -S |grep Qlogic
```

This returns output similar to the output shown in Figure 2.7.

```
wdc-tse-i85.wsl.vmware.com - PuTTY                                    —  □  ×

[root@wdc-tse-i85:~] esxcfg-scsidevs -a |less -S |grep -i qlogic
vmhba1  qlnativefc          link-up  fc.2000001b32139fa6:2100001b32139fa6   (0000:06:00.0)
vmhba2  qlnativefc          link-up  fc.2001001b32339fa6:2101001b32339fa6   (0000:06:00.1)
[root@wdc-tse-i85:~] █
```

Figure 2.7   Locating WWPN/WWNN via the CLI

TIP

To preserve the tab formatting of the output so that columns are displayed aligned correctly, I piped the output to the command `less -S`.

The output includes the adapter's vmbha number, driver name, WWNN and WWPN separated by a colon, the adapter's PCI bus location, and description.

The first line shows the first HBA's WWNN after the `fc.` prefix and before the colon. In this example, the WWNN is 2000001b32139fa6.

The first HBA's WWPN is after the colon. In this example, the WWPN is 2100001b32139fa6.

The second line shows the same information for the second HBA.

If you are using Emulex HBAs, substitute `QLogic` with the name relevant to your HBA's driver —(for example, `lpfc`).

Alternatively, you can run this command, which provides the output shown in Figure 2.8:

```
esxcfg-mpath -b |grep WWNN |sed 's/.*fc //;s/Target.*$//'
```

```
wdc-tse-i85.wsl.vmware.com - PuTTY                                    —  □  ×

[root@wdc-tse-i85:~] esxcfg-mpath -b |grep WWNN |sed 's/.*fc //;s/Target.*$//'
Adapter: WWNN: 20:00:00:1b:32:13:9f:a6 WWPN: 21:00:00:1b:32:13:9f:a6
Adapter: WWNN: 20:00:00:1b:32:13:9f:a6 WWPN: 21:00:00:1b:32:13:9f:a6
Adapter: WWNN: 20:01:00:1b:32:33:9f:a6 WWPN: 21:01:00:1b:32:33:9f:a6
Adapter: WWNN: 20:01:00:1b:32:33:9f:a6 WWPN: 21:01:00:1b:32:33:9f:a6
```

Figure 2.8   Alternative command to identify an HBA's WWPN and WWNN

This truncates the output up to the first occurrence of the string `fc` and removes the trailing text starting with `Target`. (I discuss identifying the targets IDs in the next section.) The output shows the HBA's (adapter's) WWNN and WWPN associated with all paths to the attached storage devices. (You'll learn more about paths and multipathing in Chapter 7, "Multipathing and Failover.")

In this example, we have two HBAs with the following names:

First HBA:

WWNN: 20:00:00:1b:32:13:9f:a6

WWPN: 21:00:00:1b:32:13:9f:a6

Second HBA:

WWNN: 20:01:00:1b:32:33:9f:a6

WWPN: 21:01:00:1b:32:33:9f:a6

FC Targets

Targets are the SCSI endpoints that wait for the initiator's commands and provide the required input/output (I/O) data transfer to/from them. This is where LUNs (logical units) are defined and presented to the initiators.

Examples of SCSI targets are storage array controller (also known as processor) ports. These ports can be FC, iSCSI, FCoE, or serial attached storage (SAS) ports. I discuss FC targets in this chapter and cover FCoE and iSCSI targets in Chapters 3 and 4, respectively.

FC targets are the FC ports on one or more storage array controllers/processors (SPs). These ports have globally unique identifiers like those discussed earlier in this chapter, in the "Fibre Channel (FC) Initiators" section. In most configurations, a given storage array uses a single WWNN, whereas each SP port has a unique WWPN.

Most storage vendors' FC ports are from an original equipment manufacturer (OEM), which assigns the WWNNs and WWPNs using its own registered OUI in a similar fashion as those assigned to FC HBAs (see the "Fibre Channel (FC) Initiators" section).

Storage array vendors have different algorithms for generating the WWPNs of their SP ports. Table 2.1 lists some of the patterns that I have identified over the years of reading through hundreds of ESXi logs and with help from storage partners. The table lists the WWPNs of the SP ports with the insignificant bytes replaced with the letter X in order to show the pattern (with the exception of IBM DS4000 family, where I masked the insignificant bytes as zeros).

Table 2.1 Identifying SP port associations with SPs

Array Family	SP Port ID	WWPN
EMC VNX or CLARiiON CX	SPA0	xx:xx:xx:**60**:xx:xx:xx:xx
	SPA1	xx:xx:xx:**61**:xx:xx:xx:xx
	SPA2	xx:xx:xx:**62**:xx:xx:xx:xx
	SPA3	xx:xx:xx:**63**:xx:xx:xx:xx
	SPA4	xx:xx:xx:**64**:xx:xx:xx:xx
	SPA5	xx:xx:xx:**65**:xx:xx:xx:xx
	SPA6	xx:xx:xx:**66**:xx:xx:xx:xx
	SPA7	xx:xx:xx:**67**:xx:xx:xx:xx
	SPB0	xx:xx:xx:**68**:xx:xx:xx:xx
	SPB1	xx:xx:xx:**69**:xx:xx:xx:xx
	SPB2	xx:xx:xx:**6A**:xx:xx:xx:xx
	SPB3	xx:xx:xx:**6B**:xx:xx:xx:xx
	SPB4	xx:xx:xx:**6C**:xx:xx:xx:xx
	SPB5	xx:xx:xx:**6D**:xx:xx:xx:xx
	SPB6	xx:xx:xx:**6E**:xx:xx:xx:xx
	SPB7	xx:xx:xx:**6F**:xx:xx:xx:xx
Array Family	**SP Port ID**	**WWPN**
HDS Lightning (95XXv)	SP0A	xx:xx:xx:xx:xx:xx:xx:90
	SP0B	xx:xx:xx:xx:xx:xx:xx:91
	SP0C	xx:xx:xx:xx:xx:xx:xx:92
	SP0D	xx:xx:xx:xx:xx:xx:xx:93
	SP1A	xx:xx:xx:xx:xx:xx:xx:94
	SP1B	xx:xx:xx:xx:xx:xx:xx:95
	SP1C	xx:xx:xx:xx:xx:xx:xx:96
	SP1D	xx:xx:xx:xx:xx:xx:xx:97
HP EVA	SPA1	xx:xx:xx:xx:xx:xx:xx:x9
	SPA2	xx:xx:xx:xx:xx:xx:xx:x8
	SPB1	xx:xx:xx:xx:xx:xx:xx:xD
	SPB2	xx:xx:xx:xx:xx:xx:xx:xC
IBM FAStT/DS4000 family	See note	20:0X:00:00:00:00:xx
	See note	20:0Z:00:00:00:00:zz

Decoding an EMC Symmetrix WWPN

Decoding an EMC Symmetrix/DMX/VMAX WWPN is a bit tricky. Figure 2.9 helps explain this process.

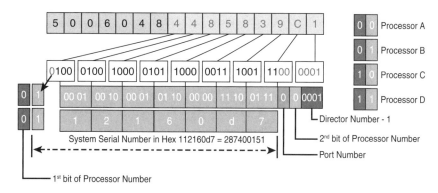

Figure 2.9   Decoding an EMC Symmetrix WWPN

The Symmetrix/DMX/VMAX FA director port WWPN begins with 5006048 (because EMC's OUI is 006048). Each word in Figure 2.9 is converted from hex to decimal in the box directly connected to it. For example, the first word after the OUI has a value of 0x4 hex, which translates to 0100 binary.

The first bit combined with the bit labeled "2nd bit of Processor Number," is used to identify which processor it is on the FA director.

When the first bit (or first half) of the processor number is not set (that is, the value is 0), the processor ID is A or B, and when it is set (that is, the value is 1), the ID is C or D. The second bit differentiates which processor of the pair it is.

The identification of the processors is shown in the top right-hand side of Figure 2.9, and is also listed in Table 2.2.

Table 2.2 Calculating FA director processor numbers

First Bit (First Half of ID)	Second Bit (Second Half of ID)	Processor Number
0	0	Processor A
0	1	Processor B
1	0	Processor C
1	1	Processor D

Locating a Target's WWNN and WWPN Seen by ESXi 6 Hosts

You can locate a target's WWPN and WWNN by using approaches similar to those described in the "Locating an HBA's WWPN and WWNN in ESXi 6 Hosts" section, earlier in this chapter.

Locating a Target's WWNN and WWPN by Using the UI

To locate a target's WWNN and WWPN by using the UI, follow this procedure:

1. Log on to the vCenter server that manages the host, using the VMware vSphere 6.0 Web Client as a user with Administrator privileges.

2. While in the Inventory—Hosts and Clusters view, locate the ESXi 6.0 host in the inventory tree and select it.

3. Navigate to the **Manage** tab.

4. Click the **Storage** button.

5. Select the **Storage Adapters** section.

6. Select one of the HBAs whose Type column is Fibre Channel.

7. In the Adapter Details pane, select the **Paths** tab.

8. Click the **LUN** column to sort by the LUN number. The UI should look similar to Figure 2.10:

- The target column shows the WWNN and WWPN separated by a space.

- Each row lists the target ID for a separate path from the selected HBA to a LUN.

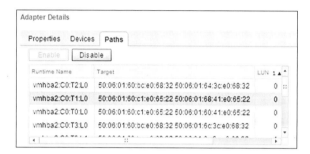

Figure 2.10   Locating a target's WWPN and WWNN

9. Repeat steps 5 through 8 for each HBA.

Locating a Target's WWNN and WWPN by Using the UI

To list all targets accessible by all HBAs in the ESXi 6.0 host, you can use the following procedure, which lists all paths to a given LUN and then identifies the target IDs:

1. Log on to the vCenter server that manages the ESXi 6.0 host, using the VMware vSphere 6.0 Web Client as a user with Administrator privileges.

2. While in the Inventory—Hosts and Clusters view, locate the ESXi 6.0 host in the inventory tree and select it.

3. Navigate to the **Manage** tab.

4. Click the **Storage** button.

5. Select the **Storage Devices** section.

6. In the Storage Devices pane, select one of the SAN LUNs (see Figure 2.11). In this example, its name starts with DGC Fibre Channel Disk.

7. In the Device Details pane, select the **Properties** tab.

8. Scroll down and click the **Edit Multipathing** button (see Figure 2.11).

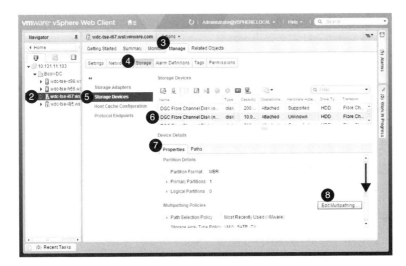

Figure 2.11   Listing LUN paths

Figure 2.12 shows the LUN multipathing details. Note that when Path Selection Policy (PSP) is anything other than **Fixed**, the path listing is grayed out. So, for visibility in this example, I temporarily changed it from **MRU** to **Fixed**. I will discuss PSP choices in Chapter 5, "vSphere Pluggable Storage Architecture (PSA)."

Figure 2.12   Listing paths to the SAN LUN

In this example, I sorted on the Runtime Name column in ascending order. Figure 2.12 shows the following:

- **Runtime Name**—vmhbaX:C0:Ty:Lz, where X is the HBA number, y is the target number, and z is the LUN number

- **Target**—The WWNN followed by the WWPN of the target, separated by a space

In this example, the targets have the IDs listed in Table 2.3.

Table 2.3 List of target IDs

HBA Number	Target Number	Target WWNN	Target WWPN
2	0	50:06:01:60:c1:e0:65:22	50:06:01:60:41:e0:65:22
2	1	50:06:01:60:c1:e0:65:22	50:06:01:68:41:e0:65:22
3	0	50:06:01:60:c1:e0:65:22	50:06:01:61:41:e0:65:22
3	1	50:06:01:60:c1:e0:65:22	50:06:01:69:41:e0:65:22

Notice that in this example, the WWNN is the same for all targets, whereas the WWPNs are unique.

Using Table 2.1, we can identify which WWPN belongs to which SP port on the CLARiiON/VNX array, as shown in Table 2.4.

Table 2.4 Mapping targets to the SP ports

HBA Number	Target Number	SP Number	Port Number
2	0	A	0
2	1	B	0
3	0	A	1
3	1	B	1

SAN Topology

SAN topology is a term that refers to how objects are connected in a storage area network.

Fibre Channel (FC)

FC is the infrastructure and the medium that connects storage devices, utilizing FCP.

FC Layers

Fibre Channel is composed of five layers, as shown in Figure 2.13.

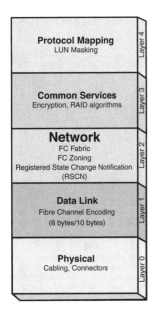

Figure 2.13   Fibre Channel layers

FC Ports

FC ports vary based on their function in an FC network. They can be any of the types listed in Table 2.5.

Table 2.5 FC port types

FC Port Type	Expanded Name	Description
N-Port	Node port	Node port that connects nodes with each other using point-to-point topology, and also connects nodes to the fabric via FC switch ports
NL-Port	Node loop port	Node that connects via arbitrated loop (FC-AL) topology
F-Port	Fabric port	Switch port that connects to a node's N-Port in a point-to-point topology
FL-Port	Fabric loop port	Switch port that connects to a node's NL-Port in an FC-AL topology
E-Port	Expansion port	Switch port that connects FC switches to form an ISL (inter-switch link)
TE-Port	Trunking E-port	A port on a Cisco switch that connects FC switches and routes between VSANs (that is, Cisco VSANs, not VMware virtual SANs)

An FC network connects ports with or without FC switches. The way the ports are connected with each other is defined by the *topology*.

FC Topology

The FC topology describes how the various ports are connected together. There are three major FC topologies: point-to-point (FC-P2P), arbitrated loop (FC-AL), and switched fabric (FC-SW).

FC-P2P (Point-to-Point)

In FC-P2P topology, two devices are connected directly to each other, as shown in Figure 2.14.

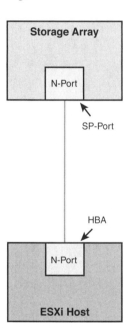

Figure 2.14   Point-to-point topology

An example of FC-P2P topology is connecting an ESXi host's FC HBA directly to a storage array's SP port. VMware supports some storage arrays with this topology. Check the HCL for the Array Test Configuration option **FC Direct Attached**. When you configure FC-HBA BIOS, this is the setting to select regardless of whether you're using this topology or switched fabric.

FC-AL (Arbitrated Loop)

Arbitrated loop topology is similar to Token Ring networking, in which all devices are connected in a loop or a ring, as shown in Figure 2.15.

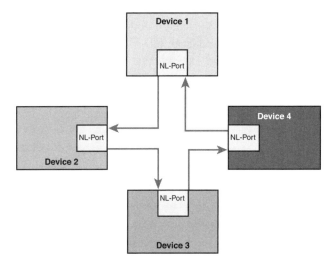

Figure 2.15   FC-AL topology

Adding or removing any device breaks the loop, and all devices are affected. VMware does not support this topology.

Some models of HP EVA arrays use FC loop switches to connect the SPs to the disk array enclosures (DAEs), as shown in Figure 2.16.

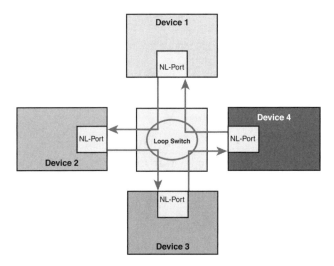

Figure 2.16   FC loop switch

This solution helps avoid breaking the loop when adding or removing devices.

FC-SW (Switched Fabric)

With switched fabric configuration, nodes (N-Port or NL-Port) connect to FC switches (see Figure 2.17).

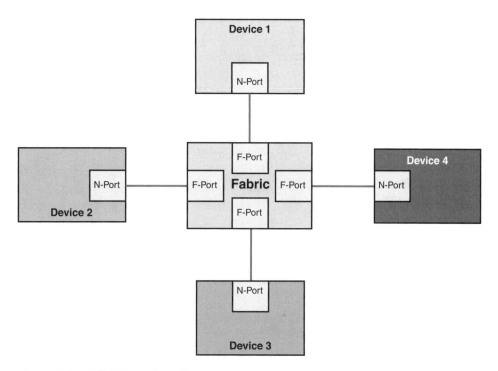

Figure 2.17   FC-SW configuration

In this configuration, switches are connected to each other via Inter-Switch Link (ISL) to form a *fabric*. Design decisions for switch connectivity are covered later in this chapter, in the "Designing Storage with No Single Points of Failure" section.

Fabric Switches

The FC fabric is composed of one or more interconnected FC switches that share a set of services provided by the switches' fabric OS. Some of these services are the Name Server, RSCN, FDMI, and FLOGI services.

Name Server

The Name Server service maintains a list of attributes of all hosts and storage devices that are currently connected to the fabric or that were connected to it sometime in the past and have successfully registered their own port information.

Examples of attributes maintained by the Name Server service are WWPN, WWNN, and port aliases.

Registered State Change Notification

Registered State Change Notification (RSCN) is a Fibre Channel service that informs hosts about changes in the fabric.

State change notifications are sent to all registered nodes (within the same zone) and reachable fabric switches in the event of major fabric changes. Such a notification refreshes the nodes' knowledge of the fabric so that they can react to the changes.

RSCNs are implemented on the fabric switches. This is part of *Layer 2* of the Fibre Channel model (network layer).

The following events trigger RSCN:

- Nodes joining or leaving the fabric
- Switches joining or leaving the fabric
- Switch name changes
- New zone enforcements
- Switch IP address changes
- Disks joining or leaving the fabric

Fabric-Device Management Interface

Fabric-Device Management Interface (FDMI) is a Fibre Channel service that enables management of devices such as Fibre Channel HBAs through in-band (via the storage network) communications. This service complements Name Server service and management service functions of the fabric switch. This service extracts information from connected nodes and stores it in a persistent database.

The following are examples of FDMI extracted information:

- Manufacturer, model, and serial number
- Node name and node symbolic name

- Hardware, driver, and firmware versions

- Host operating system (OS) name and version number

Fabric Login

The Fabric Login (FLOGI) service receives and executes login requests from nodes connected to the fabric.

FC Zoning

FC fabric can experience large numbers of events that can be disruptive to entities not involved in those events. In addition, a certain level of security must be considered while designing an FC SAN (storage area network). Main elements of FC SAN security are *zoning* and *LUN masking*.

Zoning enables you to partition the FC fabric into smaller subsets for better security and easier management. In addition, fabric events occurring on one zone can be isolated to that zone only, sparing the rest of the zones from the noise.

Zone Types

Zoning is available in two types: soft zoning and hard zoning. Zoning combines the following attributes:

- **Name**—The name given to the zone

- **Port**—The initiator, target, or switch port that is a member of the zone

Fabric switches group multiple zone definitions into one or more *zone sets*. However, only one zone set can be active at a time. Figure 2.18 shows a logical representation of two zones with separate members. In this example, Node 1 and Node 2 can only access SPA on the storage array, whereas Node 3 and Node 4 can only access SPB of the same storage array. Depending on the entities that make up the zone definition, zone types can be classified as soft or hard zones.

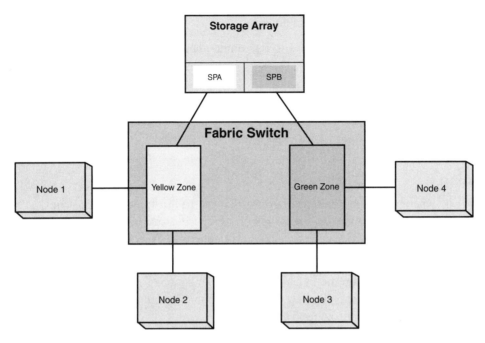

Figure 2.18   Zoning logical diagram

Soft Zoning

The fabric Name Server service allows each device to query the addresses of all other devices. Soft zoning restricts the fabric Name Server service so that it shows only an allowed subset of devices. Effectively, when a node that is a member of a soft zone looks at the content of the fabric, it sees only the devices that belong to that soft zone.

The addresses listed in the soft zone are any of the following:

- Initiator's WWPN
- Target's WWPN
- Aliases of the initiators' or targets' WWPNs

Using aliases simplifies identification of the various WWPNs by providing descriptive names to the complex WWPNs. Using aliases therefore makes it easier for SAN admins to select the correct members of the zones.

In the event of a switch port failure, reconnecting the affected node to another port in the switch or the fabric allows the node to reconnect to the rest of the zone members.

However, if the node's HBA fails, replacing it requires a zone modification to use the new HBA's WWPN instead of the WWPN of the failed HBA. Figure 2.19 shows a logical representation of soft zones. Here, you see that the members of the zone are defined by the aliases assigned to the initiators' ports and the target ports.

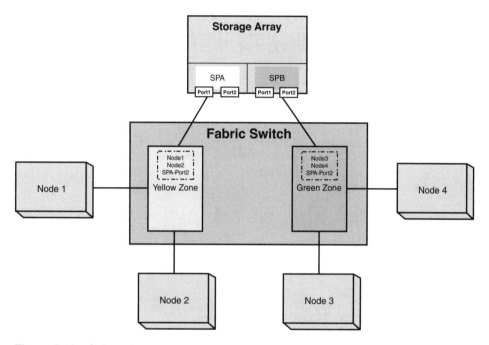

Figure 2.19   Soft zoning

Hard Zoning

Hard zoning is a similar concept to soft zoning, but the difference is that switch ports are used as members of the zones instead of the nodes' WWPNs. This means a node that is connected to a switch port in a given zone can access devices connected to any of the ports that are members of that zone. Disconnecting that node from the switch port and connecting a different node to that port permits the latter node to access all ports in that zone without any zone modifications.

Figure 2.20 shows a logical representation of hard zones. Here, you see that the members of the zone are defined by the physical switch ports to which the initiators' and target ports are connected.

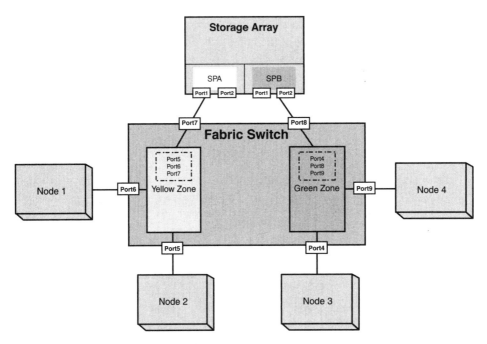

Figure 2.20   Hard zoning

Multi-Initiator Zoning Versus Single-Initiator Zoning

Based on the entities included in a zone configuration, zones can be grouped as follows:

- **Single-initiator/single-target zones**—This zone type includes two nodes only: an initiator and a target. It is the most restrictive type and requires the most administrative efforts. The advantage of this type is limiting RSCN to a single target and a single initiator and the fabric in between. It results in less disruption to other initiators due to events originating from members of the zone. Using this type of zone is recommended by most of VMware's storage partners.

- **Single-initiator/multiple-target zones**—This is similar to the previous type but with more targets in the zone. Using this type of zone is recommended by some of VMware's storage partners.

- **Multi-initiator zones**—This zone type includes multiple initiators and multiple targets. This is not recommended by VMware as it exposes all nodes in a zone to RSCN and other events originating from any of the nodes in the zone. Although this has the least effect on administrative efforts, it is the most disruptive configuration and must be avoided in production environments.

NOTE

VMware recommends single-initiator/single-target zoning, but single-initiator/multi-target zoning is also acceptable and easier to maintain unless the storage vendor does not support it.

Designing Storage with No Single Points of Failure

Storage is a critical element of the vSphere 6.0 environment. If storage becomes unavailable, all vSphere 6.0 virtual machines residing on that storage suffer outages that can be very costly to your business. In order to avoid unplanned outages, you must design your storage to have no single points of failure, as described in the following sections.

Additional aspects of business continuity/disaster recovery (BC/DR) are covered later in this book.

SAN Design Guidelines

The basic Fibre Channel SAN design elements include the following:

- FC host bus adapters
- FC cables
- Fabric switches
- Storage arrays and storage processors

I share some sample design choices over the next few pages and point out the points of failure in a gradual fashion in order to build the best environment possible.

Design Scenario 1

In the scenario shown in Figure 2.21, each ESXi host has a single HBA with a single port. These ports along with a single port from one of the two SPs are all connected to a single fabric switch.

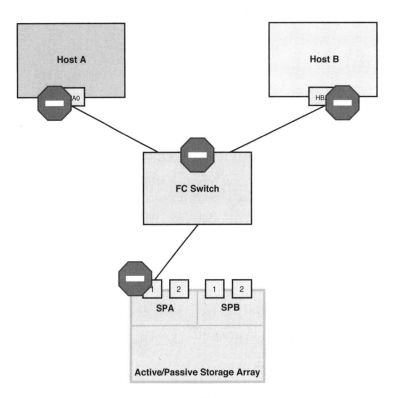

Figure 2.21   Design 1: All points of failure

This is the worst design that can possibly exist. Every element in the design is a single point of failure. In other words, I would call this *all points of failure*!

These are the points of failure in this design:

- If the FC switch fails, both hosts lose access to the storage array.

- If the HBA in one of the hosts or its cable fails, that host loses access to the storage array.

- If the cable connecting SPA Port 1 to the FC switch fails, both hosts lose access to the storage array.

- If any of the connected ports on the FC switch fails, the node connected to that port loses access to the FC switch.

- If SPA fails, both hosts lose access to the storage array.

Design Scenario 2

As shown in Figure 2.22, this scenario is the same as Design Scenario 1 (refer to Figure 2.21) with the addition of a link between SPA port 2 and the FC switch.

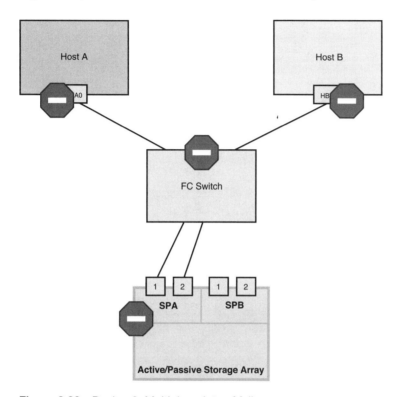

Figure 2.22   Design 2: Multiple points of failure

There are redundant connections to the fabric switch from SPA. However, SPA itself is a point of failure. All other components are still points of failure, as described in Design Scenario 1.

Design Scenario 3

In this scenario, the storage array is no longer a point of failure because there is a link from each SP to the fabric switch. The remaining elements are still points of failure, however.

Each host now has a path to each SP, for a total of two paths (see Figure 2.23).

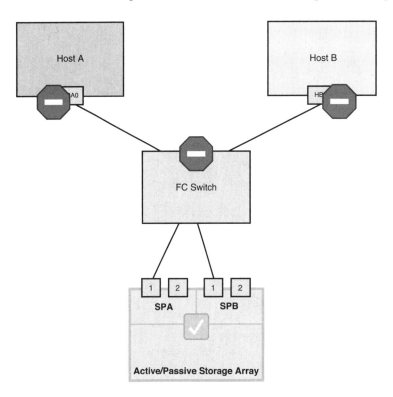

Figure 2.23   Design 3: Fewer points of failure

Design Scenario 4

In this scenario (see Figure 2.24), each host has a dual-port HBA, but everything else remains the same as in Design Scenario 3. Even though there is redundancy on the HBA port level, the HBA itself can still fail, and with it, both HBA ports would fail, leaving the host with no SAN connectivity. The fabric switch is still a point of failure.

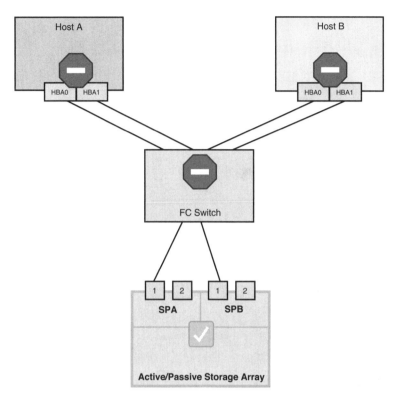

Figure 2.24   Design 4: Still a few points of failure

Design Scenario 5

Now, in this design, each host has two separate single-port HBAs (see Figure 2.25). This eliminates the HBAs and the storage array's SPs as points of failure, leaving us with the fabric switch as the only remaining point of failure.

Each host still has four paths to the storage array because each HBA can access SPA1 and SPB1.

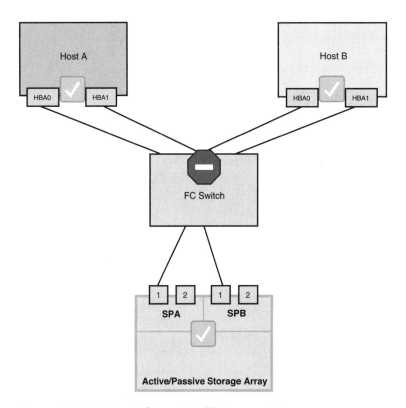

Figure 2.25   Design 5: One point of failure remaining

Design Scenario 6

This design has fully redundant fabric because we've added a second FC switch (see Figure 2.26). Each host still has four paths to the storage array. However, these paths have no single points of failure.

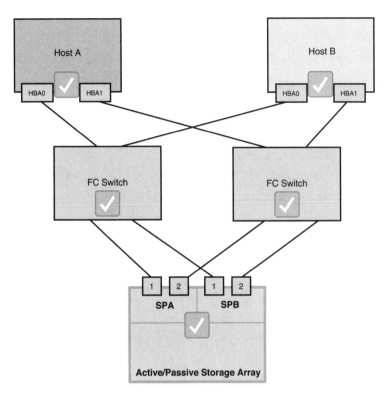

Figure 2.26   Design 6: Fully redundant fabric

NOTE

Design Scenarios 1–6 are logical and overly simplified for the purpose of illustrating the various combinations. Actual physical FC fabric design would include multiple FC switches connected to form two separate fabrics. Furthermore, switches in each fabric would be connected as edge switches and core switches.

Summary

vSphere ESXi 6.0 utilizes SCSI-2 and SCSI-3 standards and supports the block storage protocols FC, iSCSI, and FCoE. This chapter deals with FCP and FC SAN. I discussed how to design Fibre Channel connectivity without single points of failure. I also explained in detail FC initiators and targets and how to identify each. The next two chapters cover the FCoE and iSCSI protocols.

## Chapter 3

FCoE Storage Connectivity

FCoE (Fibre Channel over Ethernet)

Fibre Channel over Ethernet (FCoE, pronounced "ef-see-oh-ee"), is an encapsulation of FC frames over Ethernet networks. The spec is governed by the T11 Technical Committee, which is part of the InterNational Committee for Information Technology Standards (INCITS). FCoE is defined in T11 FC-BB-5 standard (Fibre Channel BackBone—5), available at www.t11.org/ftp/t11/pub/fc/bb-5/09-056v5.pdf. (Later revisions might exist by the time you read this book.)

FCoE maps FC directly over Ethernet but is independent of the Ethernet forwarding scheme. The spec replaces Layers 0 and 1 of the FC stack (see Chapter 2, "Fibre Channel Storage Connectivity"), which are the physical *and the* data link layers, with Ethernet. Simply put, FCoE utilizes Ethernet (10GigE or faster) as a backbone for FC. It provides lossless transport over Ethernet even though Ethernet itself is prone to errors and dropped frames.

The FCoE encapsulation (see Figure 3.1) is somewhat like Russian nesting (matryoshka) dolls, where a figurine is nested within another, which is nested in a third, and so on. Here, the FC frame is encapsulated within the FCoE frame, and the FCoE frame is encapsulated within an Ethernet frame. (The encapsulated FC frame architecture is similar to what I covered in Figure 2.2 in Chapter 2.)

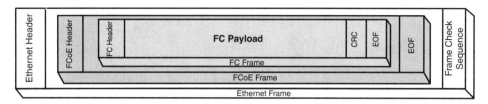

Figure 3.1   FCoE encapsulation

Figure 3.2 shows the architecture of the FCoE frame within an Ethernet frame. It starts with the Destination and Source MAC Address fields, followed by IEE 802.1Q Tag (more on VLAN requirements later). Then an Ethernet Type field with a value of FCoE (hex value 0x8906) followed by the Version field. The Start of the Frame (SOF) field follows some reserved space, and then there are Encapsulated FC Frame and End of Frame (EOF) fields. Ethernet FCS (Frame Check Sequence) is at the end of the FCoE frame.

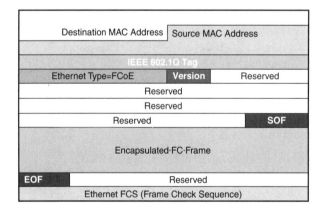

Figure 3.2   FCoE frame architecture

Because the encapsulated FC frame payload can be as large as 2.2KB, the Ethernet frame has to be larger than 1500 bytes. As a result, Ethernet mini jumbo frames (2158 bytes) are used for FCoE encapsulation.

NOTE

FCoE runs directly on Ethernet (not on top of TCP or IP, as iSCSI does) as a Layer 3 protocol and cannot be routed. Therefore, both initiators and targets (native FCoE targets) must be on the same network.

If native FC targets are accessible via FCoE switches, the switches must be on the same network as the FCoE initiators.

FCoE Initialization Protocol

FCoE Initialization Protocol (FIP) is an integral part of the FCoE protocol. It is used to discover FCoE-capable devices connected to an Ethernet network and to negotiate their capabilities and MAC addresses for use for further transactions.

The FIP header has its own Ethernet Type FIP (0x8914) as well as an encapsulated FIP operation (for example, Discovery, Advertise). This is different from the FCoE Ethernet Type listed earlier. Compared to FCoE frames, FIP frames describe a new set of protocols that do not exist in native Fibre Channel, whereas FCoE frames encapsulate native FC payloads.

There are two types of FCoE endpoints:

- **End nodes (ENodes)**—FCoE adapters are the FCoE endpoints on the hosts' side. I expand on this further in the "FCoE Initiators" section, later in this chapter.

- **FCoE Forwarders (FCFs)**—As shown in Figure 3.3, FCoE Forwarders are dual-stack switches (that is, they understand both FC and Ethernet). These switches connect to FC switches by using an E_Port type (expansion port), with ISL (Inter-Switch Link). In addition, they connect to other Ethernet switches and routers natively.

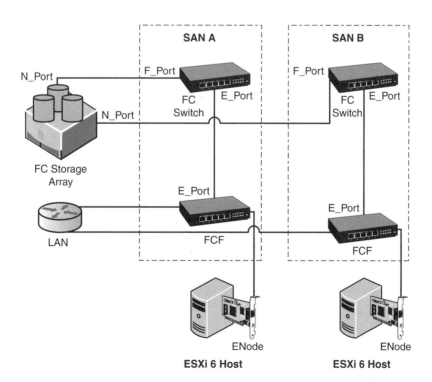

Figure 3.3 FCoE endpoint connectivity

FIP is a control protocol that is designed to establish and maintain virtual links between pairs of FCoE devices: ENodes (FCoE initiators) and FCFs (dual-stack switches). The process of establishing these virtual links is outlined in the following steps and illustrated in Figure 3.4:

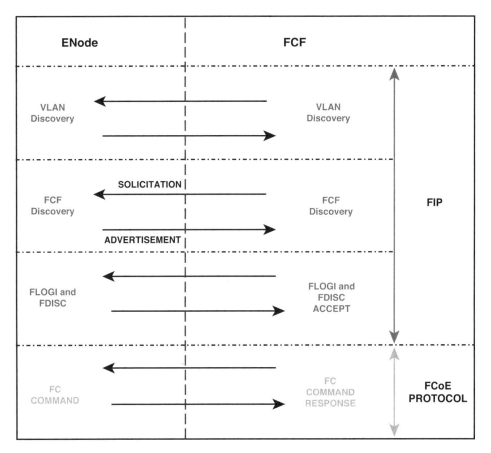

Figure 3.4   Establishing virtual links (Image courtesy www.cisco.com/en/US/prod/collateral/switches/ps9441/ps9670/white_paper_c11-560403.html)

1. FIP discovers FCoE VLANs and remote virtual FC interfaces.

2. FIP performs virtual link initialization functions (similar to native FC equivalents):

   a. FLOGI (fabric login)

   b. FDISC (fabric discovery)

   c. ELP (exchange link parameters)

After a virtual link is established, FC payloads can be exchanged on that link. FIP remains in the background, performing virtual link maintenance functions. It continuously verifies reachability between the two virtual FC interfaces on the Ethernet network. It also offers primitives to delete the virtual link in response to administrative actions.

FCoE Initiators

To use FCoE, your vSphere host should have an FCoE initiator. FCoE initiators are of two types: hardware and software FCoE initiators.

Hardware FCoE Adapters

A hardware FCoE adapter is an I/O card that is usually available as a CNA (converged network adapter). This class of adapters combines different types of I/O cards that utilize Ethernet as a backbone—for example, network interface card (NIC) and iSCSI initiator or FC HBA (using FCoE). An example of such CNAs is Emulex OneConnect OCe10102 (rebranded by HP as NC551i) and Emulex OneConnect OCe11100.

Figure 3.5 clarifies how FCoE and CNAs fit into vSphere 6.0 configurations.

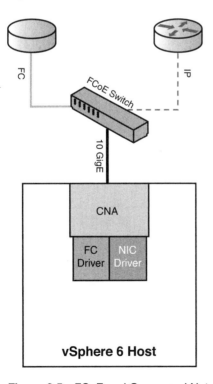

Figure 3.5   FCoE and Converged Network Adapters (CNAs)

This diagram shows an FC driver and a NIC driver both loaded for the CNA. The latter connects to an FCoE switch via a 10GigE connection. The FCoE switch unencapsulates the FC frames and sends them via the FC connection to the storage fabric. The switch also receives regular Ethernet frames sent by the NIC driver and sends them, unmodified, to the Ethernet network.

Software FCoE Adapters

You can use a software FCoE adapter if your ESXi 6 host is equipped with a software FCoE–enabled NIC that is certified for use with vSphere 6. An example of such a NIC is the Intel 82599 10 Gigabit adapter. Several NICs on the VMware HCL are based on the Intel 82599 chipset, such as Cisco M61-KR, Dell X520, and IBM X520.

TIP

To search the VMware HCL for 10GigE NICs supported for use with software FCoE adapters, go to www.vmware.com/resources/compatibility/search.php?deviceCategory=io and use the **Search Compatibility Guide** field, instead of the search criteria, to search for **Software FCoE Enabled**, which gives you matches to the footnotes of the device listings.

The software FCoE adapter in ESXi 6 is based on Intel's Open-FCoE software. Figure 3.6 shows how a software FCoE adapter runs on top of the NIC driver side-by-side with TCP/IP.

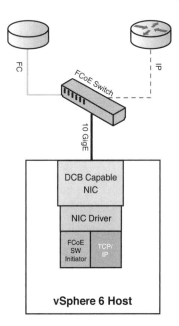

Figure 3.6   Software FCoE and a DCB-capable NIC

In Figure 3.6, *DCB* stands for data center bridging. I will provide more details on DCB later in this chapter.

The transmit and receive queues of the NIC are split between the stacks sharing the NIC.

Overcoming Ethernet Limitations

For Fibre Channel to work reliably over Ethernet, several limitations of Ethernet must be overcome first:

1. **Packet/frame loss**—Making sure that no packets are dropped is the most critical aspect of using FCoE. If the traffic were TCP/IP, retransmits would take care of this. However, FCoE does not run over TCP/IP, and it is necessary to ensure that it is *lossless*!

2. **Congestion**—As you might have noticed in Figure 3.5, the FCoE interface and the Ethernet interface share a 10GigE link. In some blades, there might be a single CNA in each blade. This means that FCoE, VM, vMotion, management, and FT traffic share the same 10GigE link, which might result in congestion (I/O bottleneck).

3. **Bandwidth**—Sharing a 10GigE pipe with everything else might necessitate dividing that pipe among the various types of traffic. However, this is not generally possible without specialized technology like HP Virtual Connect Flex-10 and similar technologies from other vendors.

Flow Control in FCoE

Fibre Channel has flow control using buffer-to-buffer credits (BBC), which represents the number of frames a given port can store. Every time a port transmits a frame, the port's BBC is decremented by one. Conversely, for each R-RDY received, the port's BBC is incremented by one. If the BBC reaches zero, the port cannot transmit until at least an R-RDY is received back.

However, Ethernet does not have such a function. Therefore, FCoE requires an enhancement in Ethernet to support flow control and prevent packet loss. This flow control also helps Ethernet handle congestion and avoid packet drops that result from such congestion. The solution was to implement a flow control PAUSE mechanism to be used by FCoE. This PAUSE mechanism works in a fashion similar to FC's BBC, "telling" the sender to hold off on sending frames until the receiver's buffer is cleared.

Because the PAUSE mechanism does not have the same intelligence provided by FC's BBC, the QoS priority bit in the VLAN tag (refer to Figure 3.2) is used to ensure that the most important data is delivered to its destination first and is not affected by congestion. Using this mechanism, Ethernet is divided into eight virtual lanes according to the QoS priority bit in the VLAN tag. Each of these virtual lanes can be subject to different policies, such as *losslessness*, *bandwidth allocation*, and *congestion control*. This mechanism is referred to as *priority-based flow control (PFC)*.

Protocols Required for FCoE

FCoE depends on a set of extension protocols that enhance Ethernet for use to bridge data centers. This set of protocols is referred to as data center bridging (DCB).

DCB is a standard term that Cisco refers to as Data Center Ethernet (DCE) and IBM refers to as Converged Enhanced Ethernet (CEE).

vSphere 6 supports the DCB set of protocols for FCoE that are described in the following sections.

Priority-Based Flow Control

Priority-based flow control (PFC) is an extension of the current Ethernet pause mechanism, sometimes called per-priority PAUSE. To emulate losslessness, per-priority PAUSE frames are used. This pauses traffic with a specific priority and allows all other traffic to flow (for example, pausing FCoE traffic while allowing other network traffic to flow).

As mentioned in the previous section, PFC creates eight separate virtual links on the physical link and allows any of these links to be paused and restarted independently from each other, based on the flow control mechanism applied to each of these virtual links. This allows multiple traffic types to share the same 10GigE link with separate flow control mechanisms. It is advantageous to have different types of traffic classes with PFC (for example, FCoE, vMotion, and VM traffic) because vMotion is not used most of the time; the virtual link it uses is available until vMotion traffic starts again. When needed, some of the traffic on other virtual links may be paused if there is congestion and the QoS priority for one of the virtual links is higher than for the rest. See the section "802.1p Tag," later in this chapter, for further details on how QoS priority tags work.

Enhanced Transmission Selection

Enhanced Transmission Selection (ETS) provides a means to allocate bandwidth to traffic that has a particular priority. The protocol supports changing the bandwidth dynamically. PFC creates eight different lanes with different traffic classes/priorities, and ETS allocates the bandwidth according to the assigned priorities.

ETS is a means to provide traffic differentiation so that multiple traffic classes can share the same consolidated Ethernet link without impacting each other.

Data Center Bridging Exchange

Data Center Bridging Exchange (DCBX) exchanges the PFC and ETS information with the link peers before an FCoE link is established. This management protocol uses specific Type-Length-Value (TLV) in the Link Layer Discovery Protocol (LLDP) to negotiate values.

DCBX handles the following functions:

1. **Discovery of DCB capability**—DCB-capable devices can discover and identify capabilities of DCB peers and identify non-DCB-capable legacy devices.

2. **Identification of misconfigured DCB features**—DCBX can discover misconfiguration of features between DCB peers. Some DCB features can be configured differently on each end of a link. Other features must match on both sides to be effective. DCBX allows for detection of configuration errors for these symmetric features.

3. **Configuration of peers**—DCBX passes configuration information to DCB peer. A DCB-capable switch can pass PFC information to a converged network adapter (CNA) to ensure that FCoE traffic is appropriately tagged and that PAUSE is enabled on the appropriate traffic class.

   DCBX relies on LLDP to pass this configuration information. LLDP is an industry standard version of Cisco Discovery Protocol (CDP).

> **NOTE**
>
> Any link that supports DCBX must have LLDP enabled on both ends of the link for transmit/receive (Tx/Rx). If LLDP is disabled on a port for either Rx or Tx, DCBX TLV in received LLDP frames are ignored.
>
> This is why the NIC must be bound to a vSwitch. Frames are forwarded to the data center bridging daemon (DCBD) to DCBX via the CDP vmkernel module. This module does both CDP and LLDP. I discuss the DCBD later in this chapter.

10GigE—A Large Pipeline

The bandwidth provided by 10GigE accommodates several types and classes of traffic (see Figure 3.7).

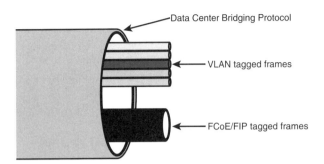

Figure 3.7   10GigE pipeline (Image courtesy http://nickapedia.com/2011/01/22/
the-vce-model-yes-it-is-different/#more-1446)

For example, voice over IP (VoIP), video, messaging, and storage can travel over a common
Ethernet infrastructure. With faster Ethernet under development at the time of writing
this, 100GigE is imminent, and it will make for even better convergence of these various
types of traffic.

802.1p Tag

802.1p priority is carried in the VLAN tags defined in IEEE 802.1Q/p (802.1p).

A field in the 802.1Q tag carries one of eight priority values (three bits in length), which
is recognized by Layer 2 devices on the network. This priority tag determines the service
level that packets receive when crossing an 802.1p-enabled network.

Figure 3.8 shows the structure of a frame tagged with the 802.1p tag for Ethernet frames.

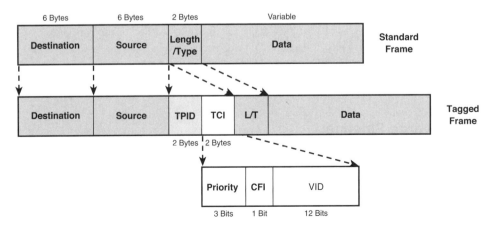

Figure 3.8   802.1p tag

The 802.1p tag includes the following fields:

- **TPID—(Tag Protocol Identifier)**—two bytes long and carries the IEEE 802.1Q/802.1P tag when the frame has an EtherType value of 0x8100

- **TCI—(Tag Control Information)**—two bytes long and includes User Priority (three bits), Canonical Format Indicator "CFI" (one bit), and VLAN ID "VID" (12 bits)

The value in the Priority field defines the class of service, as shown in Table 3.1.

Table 3.1 QoS priority levels

Priority	Traffic Characteristic
0 (Lowest)	Background
1	Best effort
2	Excellent effort
3	Critical application
4	Video, < 100 ms latency
5	Voice, < 10 ms latency
6	Internetwork control
7 (Highest)	Network control

Hardware FCoE Adapters

Hardware (HW) FCoE adapters are CNAs that are capable of fully offloading FCoE processing and network connectivity. Although physically we see a CNA as one card, to the ESXi environment, CNAs show up in the UI as two separate adapters: a network adapter and an FC adapter. You can identify them by finding *FCoE* listed in the physical CNA's name. Figure 3.9 shows an example of how HW FCoE adapters are listed in the user interface (UI).

Figure 3.9 shows a dual-port 10GigE CNA based on an ISP81XX adapter. Its FCoE part shows up as Fibre Channel type and named vmhba4 and vmhba5.

If you look closely at the attached LUNs, you'll notice that the transport used is also Fibre Channel. However, the Details section shows the model as ISP81xx-based 10GigE FCoE to PCI Express CNA.

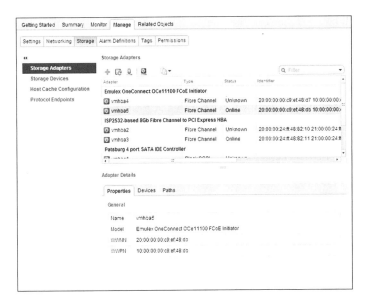

Figure 3.9   UI listing of HW FCoE adapters (CNA)

Configuring HW FCoE Adapters

Converged network adapters can be configured in one or more personalities supported by the adapter (for example, FCoE or iSCSI). To select the FCoE personality, you need to first access the adapter's BIOS by selecting a hotkey at boot time, selecting the mode, and configuring the relevant fields. Once the FCoE personality is selected, no further configuration is required because the FCF reports the port's configuration to the adapter. However, for the sake of exploring the various options in the adapter's BIOS, I will walk through the common options in this section.

The following steps walk through this process for an Emulex OCe11102-FM CNA:

> **NOTE**
>
> My configuration was on an HP ProLiant DL380 G8. Other vendors' screenshots may vary slightly.

1. At boot time watch for the prompt to press **Ctrl+P** to enter the Emulex PXE BIOS configuration (see Figure 3.10).

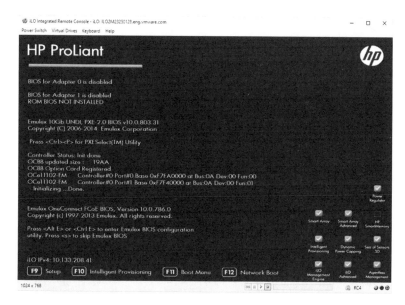

Figure 3.10   Accessing Emulex BIOS configuration

2. Tab into the **Personality** field, select **FCoE**, and press **Enter** (see Figure 3.11).

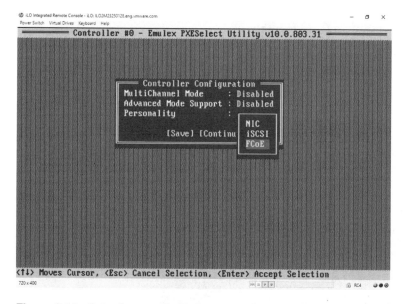

Figure 3.11   Selecting an adapter's personality

3. Tab into the **Save** option and press **Enter**.

4. Tab into the **Continue** option and press **Enter** (see Figure 3.12).

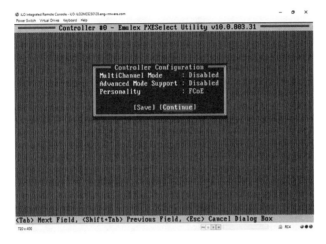

Figure 3.12   Continuing with the configuration

5. Press **Esc** until prompted to exit and reboot.

6. While rebooting, when prompted, press **Alt+E** or **Ctrl+E** to access the FCoE configuration BIOS (refer to Figure 3.10).

7. Select the FCoE port to configure and press **Enter** (see Figure 3.13). In this example, I will select port 2.

Figure 3.13   Selecting the port to configure

The configuration options are displayed, as shown in Figure 3.14. In this example, the BIOS screen shows the current port configuration at the top and lists the available configuration options at the bottom.

Figure 3.14   Available Port Configuration

8. If you need to change the configuration, select **Configure FCF CEE Parameters**, as shown in Figure 3.14. Figure 3.15 shows the available options that appear.

Figure 3.15   Modifying the configuration

9. To modify the adapter configuration, select **A**, **B**, or **D** in the first field to select the configuration record to modify (Active, Boot, or Delete). Then tab into each subsequent field and use **Page Up** or **Page Down** to change the field value.

10. Press **Page Down** to highlight the discovered FCF and then press **Enter** to select it. You now see a dialog similar to the one shown in Figure 3.16.

NOTE

In step 9 and step 10, you need to use **Page Up** or **Page Down** to place the cursor in the upper section of the display, and then you can press **Enter** to save the changes.

Figure 3.16   Saving configuration changes

11. Press **Y** to save the changes. If you do not wish to save them, press **N** and then confirm by pressing **Y**.

12. To verify connectivity after applying the changes, select **Scan for Target Devices** (refer to Figure 3.14). If successful, you should see the target devices listed. This assumes that this initiator has already been zoned to access the storage targets (see Figure 3.17).

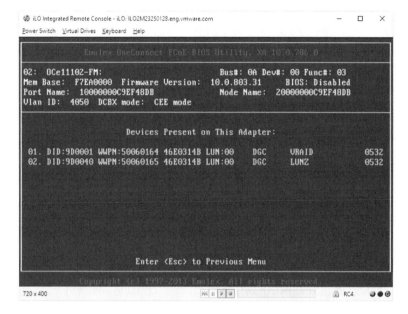

Figure 3.17   Result of scanning for target devices

13. Press **Esc** to return to the main menu and then press **Esc** again to return to the port selection menu.

14. Repeat steps 7 through 13 for the remaining ports, if desired.

15. When you are done, press **Esc** to exit the FCoE BIOS configuration screen. When prompted, press **Y** to exit and reboot the system.

Implementing SW FCoE in ESXi 6

A software FCoE adapter is a VMware-provided component on vSphere 6 that performs some FCoE processing. You can use it with a number of network cards (NICs) that support partial FCoE offload. The vSphere administrator needs to manually enable this adapter before it can be configured and used. Software FCoE is based on the Open-FCoE stack, which was created by Intel and is licensed under GPL. It is loaded as a VMkernel module that you can list by using the command shown in Listing 3.1.

Listing 3.1   Listing FCoE-related vmkernel modules

```
vmkload_mod -l |grep 'Name\|fc'
Name                    Used Size (kb)
qlnativefc               4    1648
lpfc                     4    1192
libfc_92                 2    112
libfcoe_92               1    40
libfc_9_2_0_0            0    8
libfcoe_9_2_0_0          0    8
vfc                      0    152
```

Notice that there are three modules: `libfc`, `libfcoe`, and `fcoe`. `fcoe` is the FCoE stack kernel module, and the other two are VMware common libraries that provide APIs used by the FCoE driver as well as third-party drivers.

The mechanism through which FCoE works on ESXi 6 is as follows:

- The NICs that support partial FCoE offloading create a pseudo-netdev interface for use by vmklinux. The pseudo-netdev interface is a Linux network device interface, and vmklinux is the ESXi facility that allows drivers ported from Linux to run on ESXi.

- The FCoE transport module is registered with vmklinux.

- Each NIC (or CNA capable of FCoE) is made visible to the user via vSphere Client. From there, the user can enable and configure software FCoE. Once it is configured, vmklinux performs the discovery.

- DCBD, which is located in /sbin/dcbd, with its `init` script in /etc/init.d/dcbd, is then started on the ESXi host.

- The FCoE module registers one adapter with the ESXi storage stack (refer to Chapter 5, "vSphere Pluggable Storage Architecture").

- FCoE adapter information is stored in the /etc/vmware/esx.conf file to ensure that the configuration and information persist across host reboots. Do not change any of the content of the esx.conf file directly. You should use `esxcli` command-line options to make FCoE changes. I cover the `esxcli` options where relevant throughout this chapter.

NOTE

FIP, jumbo frame (actually baby jumbo frames, which are configured on the physical switch and are used to accommodate the FC frame payload, which is 2112 bytes long), FCoE, and DCBX modules are enabled in ESXi 6 software FCoE initiators by default.

Configuring SW FCoE Network Connections

NIC ports, used with SW FCoE adapters, should be connected to switch ports and configured as follows:

- **Spanning Tree Protocol (STP)**—Set this to **Disabled**. If this is not done, FIP (see the "FCoE Initialization Protocol" section earlier in this chapter) response at the switch can experience excessive delays which, in turn, result in an All Paths Down (APD) state. (See Chapter 7, "Multipathing and Failover," for more information about APD.)

- **LLDP**—Set this to **Enabled**.

- **PFC**—Set this to **AUTO**.

- **VLAN ID**—Specify a VLAN dedicated to FCoE traffic. Do not mix FCoE traffic with other storage or data traffic because you need to take advantage of PFC.

> **NOTE**
>
> As of vSphere 5.0, VMware recommended the following minimum firmware versions for switches:
>
> Cisco Nexus 5000: version 4.1(3)N2
>
> Brocade FCoE switch: version 6.3.1
>
> Check with your switch vendor for the version of firmware that is compatible with FCoE.

In contrast to HW FCoE adapters, which do not require special ESXi network configuration, the NIC on which you configure a SW FCoE adapter must be bound to a VMkernel network adapter on a standard virtual switch. Follow this procedure:

1. Connect to the vCenter server that manages the ESXi 6 host, using the vSphere 6.0 Web Client as a user with Administrator privileges.

2. Navigate to the **Inventory—Hosts and Clusters** view.

3. Locate the vSphere 6.0 host in the inventory tree and select it.

4. Select the **Manage** tab. On vSphere 6.5, select the **Configure** tab.

5. Click the **Networking** button.

6. Select the **Virtual switches** section.

7. Select the **Add host networking** icon (see Figure 3.18).

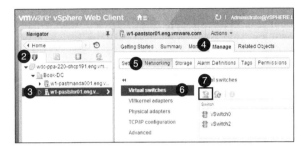

Figure 3.18   Network configuration tab—vSphere 6.0 Client

8. Select the **VMkernel Network Adapter** radio button.

9. Click **Next** (see Figure 3.19).

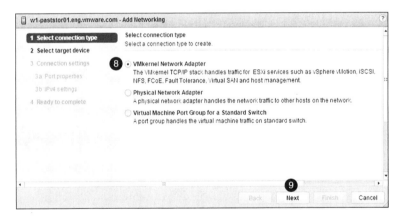

Figure 3.19   Creating a VMkernel port group—connection type—vSphere 6.0 Client

10. Select **the New standard switch** radio button.

11. Click the **Add adapters** icon (the green plus sign).

12. Make sure the **Active adapters** option is selected in the Failover order group field and then select a vmnic that supports FCoE. In this example, I am using **vmnic5**, which is an Intel 8259EB 10Gb SFI/SFP+ NIC.

13. Click **OK.**

14. Click **Next** (see Figure 3.20).

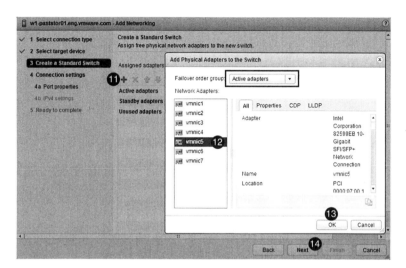

Figure 3.20   Creating a VMkernel port group—and creating a vSwitch—vSphere 6.0 Client

You might be tempted to add all ports that support FCoE to the newly created vSwitch. However, it is not recommended that you do so because any changes you make to the vSwitch in the future can be disruptive and would affect all FCoE traffic. This might result in an APD state. It would be a better design to create a separate vSwitch for each SW FCoE adapter. In addition, creating separate SW FCoE adapters provides multipathing on the initiator end.

NOTE

You can configure up to four SW FCoE adapters on a single vSphere 6 host.

15. Enter the port group name (for example, FCoE1, FCoE2).

16. Enter the VLAN ID configured on the physical switch for FCoE traffic.

17. If the target storage array is on a separate network, you would have created a separate TCP/IP stack configuration ahead of time. If so, select that TCP/IP stack. Otherwise, leave **Default** selected.

18. Leave all check boxes unchecked and then click **Next** (see Figure 3.21).

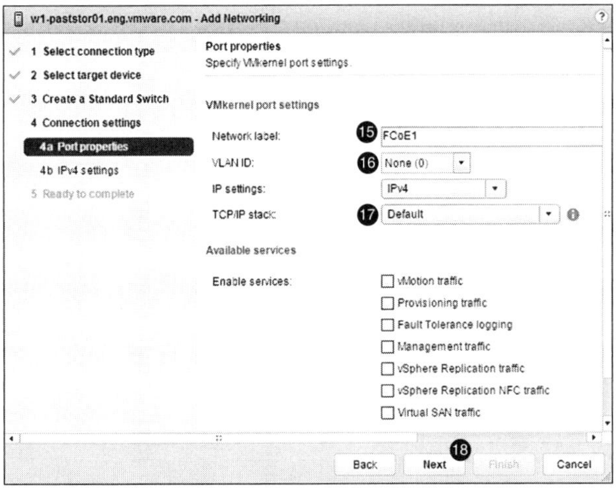

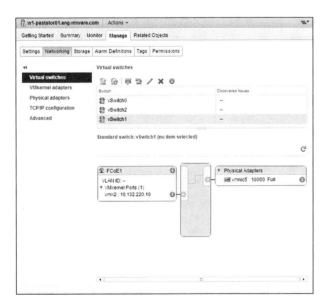

Figure 3.21   Configuring port group properties

19. Enter the IP configuration and then click **Next**.

20. Review your settings and then click **Finish**.

Figure 3.22 shows the host's network configuration after you add the FCoE port group and its standard virtual switch.

Figure 3.22   ESXi host networking with port group and standard virtual switch added

---

TIP

To perform all steps in this section via the CLI, you can run these commands while connected to the ESXi host directly or via SSH:

```
esxcli network vswitch standard add -v vSwitch1
esxcli network vswitch standard portgroup add -p FCoE1 -v vSwitch1
esxcli network vswitch standard uplink add -v vSwitch1 -u vmnic5
esxcfg-vmknic -a -i 10.132.220.10 -n 255.255.240.0 FCoE1
esxcli network vswitch standard portgroup set -p FCoE1 -v 4050
```

The first command creates the standard switch vSwitch1.

The second command creates the FCoE1 port group.

The third command adds vmnic5 as the uplink to vSwitch1.

The fourth command sets IPv4 configuration for the FCoE1 port group.

The last command, which is optional, sets the VLAN ID to 4050 for the FCoE1 port group.

Now all you have left to do is to enable the SW FCoE adapter, as described in the next section.

Enabling a Software FCoE Adapter

To enable a software FCoE adapter after completing the steps in the previous section, continue with the following steps:

1. While still in the Hosts and Clusters view, and with the ESXi host and the **Manage** tab selected, click the **Storage** button. (on vSphere 6.5, select the **Configure** tab instead of the **Manage** tab.)

2. Select the **Storage Adapters** section.

3. Click the **Add new storage adapter** icon.

4. Select the **Software FCoE adapter** option (see Figure 3.23).

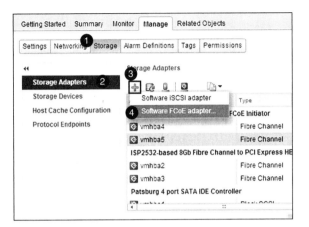

Figure 3.23   Adding a software FCoE initiator—vSphere 6.0 Web Client

5. In the dialog that appears (see Figure 3.24), select the vmnic that you bound to the vSwitch in step 12 in the previous section.

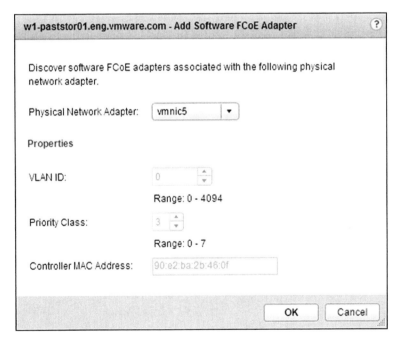

Figure 3.24   Selecting the vmnic to bind to a software FCoE adapter—vSphere 6.0 Web Client

NOTE

The VLAN ID is not selectable in the dialog shown in Figure 3.24. However, it was discovered automatically via the FIP VLAN discovery process.

Notice that the priority class, which is set to 3 in Figure 3.24, is also not selectable. Based on Table 3.1, this means that the priority is set to Critical Application.

6. Click **OK.**

The SW FCoE adapter should appear in the UI now as a vmhba; in this example, it is vmhba33. Figure 3.25 shows the FCoE adapter identified by arrows.

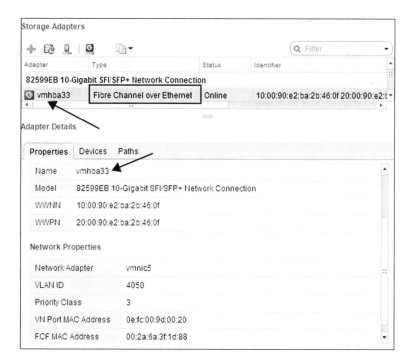

Figure 3.25   Software FCoE adapter added

> **TIP**
>
> To enable the SW FCoE adapter with a single command, run the following at the ESXi console directly or via SSH:
>
> ```
> esxcli fcoe nic discover -n vmnic5
> ```
>
> If the operation is successful, you should get a message like this one:
>
> ```
> Discovery enabled on device 'vmnic5'
> ```
>
> To verify that the outcome is similar to what is shown in Figure 3.25, run the following:
>
> ```
> esxcli fcoe adapter list
> ```
>
> The output should be similar to this:
>
> ```
> vmhba33
>     Source MAC: 90:e2:ba:2b:43:a3
>     FCF MAC: 00:2a:6a:3f:1d:8d
>     VNPort MAC: 0e:fc:00:02:00:40
>     Physical NIC: vmnic5
>     User Priority: 3
>     VLAN id: 4051
>     VN2VN Mode Enabled: false
> ```
>
> This means that vmnic5 has been successfully enabled for FCoE discovery and that you are ready to proceed.

> **TIP**
>
> The number assigned to the vmhba is a hint about whether it is a hardware or software FCoE adapter. vmhba numbers lower than 32 are assigned to hardware (SCSI-related) adapters, such as SCSI HBA, RAID Controller, FC HBA, HW FCoE, and HW iSCSI HBAs. vmhba numbers 32 and higher are assigned to software adapters and non-SCSI adapters, such as SW FCoE, SW iSCSI adapters, IDE, SATA, and USB storage controllers.

Notice that the new vmhba has been assigned an FC WWNN and WWPN. Also, when you select the **Devices** tab, you can see that the targets and LUNs have been discovered without the need to rescan.

At this point, let's compare Figure 3.25 to Figure 3.9. The HBA type in Figure 3.25 (the top red arrow) is **Fibre Channel over Ethernet** because this is a software FCoE adapter. In contrast, Figure 3.9 shows the type **Fibre Channel** because it is a hardware FCoE adapter.

NOTE

LUNs presented via SW FCoE are not supported for hosting core dump partitions. If you plan to boot an ESXi host from FCoE, you need to host the core dump partition on either a local device or another SAN-based block device not presented via SW FCoE.

Removing or Disabling a Software FCoE Adapter

You can remove a software FCoE adapter via the UI or the CLI.

Using the UI to Remove a Software FCoE Adapter

To remove a software FCoE adapter via the UI, follow this procedure:

1. While logged into vCenter Server and after selecting the ESXi 6 host that you want to modify, select the **Manage** tab. On vSphere 6.5, select the **Configure** tab.

2. Click the **Storage** button.

3. Select the **Storage Adapters** section.

4. Click the vmhba representing the SW FCoE adapter you want to remove.

5. Click the **Disable** button.

6. Confirm the removal by clicking **Yes** when prompted (see Figure 3.26). The adapter is now disabled in the ESXi host configuration, and it is removed when the host is rebooted.

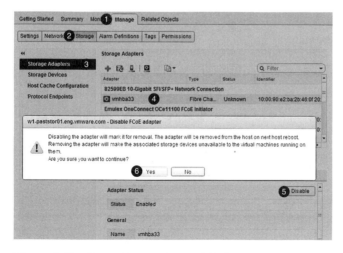

Figure 3.26   Removing a software FCoE adapter

Using the CLI to Remove a Software FCoE Adapter

To remove a software FCoE adapter via the CLI, follow this procedure:

1. Access vMA, vCLI, or SSH or directly access the ESXi host's CLI. (See the "Locating an HBA's WWPN and WWNN in ESXi 6 Hosts" section in Chapter 2 for details.)

2. Run the following command to identify which vmnic is used by the FCoE adapter:

```
esxcli fcoe adapter list
vmhba33
    Source MAC: 90:e2:ba:2b:46:0f
    FCF MAC: 00:2a:6a:3f:1d:88
    VNPort MAC: 0e:fc:00:9d:00:20
    Physical NIC: vmnic5
    User Priority: 3
    VLAN id: 4050
    VN2VN Mode Enabled: false
```

The field named `Physical NIC` lists the vmnic you use in the next step. In this example, it is `vmnic5`.

3. To remove the SW FCoE adapter, disable discovery on the vmnic it is using by running this command:

```
esxcli fcoe nic disable --nic-name=vmnic5
```

If the operation is successful, you should get the following message:

```
Discovery on device 'vmnic5' will be disabled on the next reboot
```

4. To complete the procedure, reboot the ESXi host.

Troubleshooting FCoE

Troubleshooting HW FCoE is similar to troubleshooting FC. Refer to Chapter 2 for details.

To troubleshoot and manage SW FCoE, you can use ESXCLI commands and DCBD messages in syslog.log.

ESXCLI

ESXCLI provides a dedicated software FCoE namespace, which you can list using the following command (see Figure 3.27):

```
esxcli fcoe
```

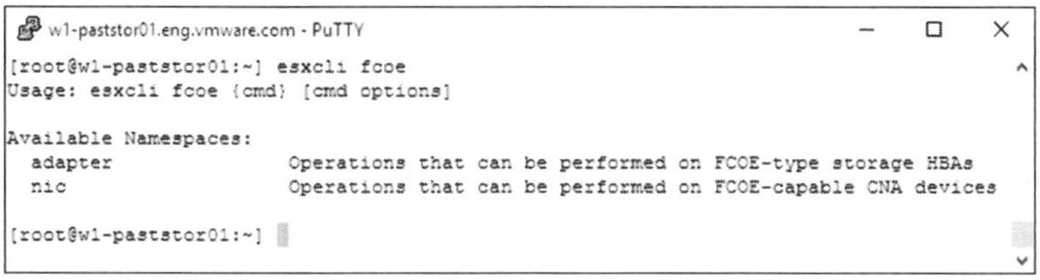

Figure 3.27 ESXCLI FCoE namespace

The next level is `adapter`, or `nic`. Running the following command returns the output shown in Figure 3.28:

```
esxcli fcoe adapter
```

Figure 3.28 ESXCLI FCoE adapter namespace

You can run the `list` command to get a list of the SW FCoE adapters and their configurations:

```
~ # esxcli fcoe adapter list
    vmhba33
        Source MAC: 90:e2:ba:2b:46:0f
        FCF MAC: 00:2a:6a:3f:1d:88
        VNPort MAC: 0e:fc:00:9d:00:20
        Physical NIC: vmnic5
        User Priority: 3
        VLAN id: 4050
        VN2VN Mode Enabled: false
```

NOTE

This output shows FCF MAC, which is the physical switch port MAC (FCF stands for FCoE Forwarder). This field is also displayed in the UI as shown in Figure 3.25 earlier in this chapter.

See the "FCoE Initialization Protocol" section, earlier in this chapter, for more information.

On the other hand, the `nic` namespace works directly on the physical NIC (vmnic) and provides `disable`, `discover`, and `list` options.

The `disable` option is used to disable rediscovery of FCoE storage on behalf of a specific vmnic, which is FCoE-capable, upon the next boot:

```
esxcli fcoe nic disable --nic-name=vmnic2
```

The `discover` option is used to initiate FCoE adapter discovery on behalf of an FCoE-capable vmnic. The command-line syntax is similar to that of the `disable` option (this time I am using the `-n` option, which is shorthand for the `--nic-name` option):

```
esxcli fcoe nic discover -n vmnic2
```

Let's look at some examples of output from this command in various configurations.

In this example, vmnic2 is successfully enabled for discovery:

```
~ # esxcli fcoe nic discover -n vmnic2
Discovery enabled on device 'vmnic2'
```

In the following example, vmnic0 is bound to a VMkernel port group on a standard vSwitch, but the NIC is not DCB capable, which means it is not FCoE-capable:

```
~ # esxcli fcoe nic discover -n vmnic0
PNIC "vmnic0" is not FCoE-capable
```

In the following example, the vmnic is not bound to a vmkernel port on a standard vSwitch. You cannot enable the vmnic for discovery until it is bound as such:

```
~ # esxcli fcoe nic discover --nic-name=vmnic4
Error: Failed to obtain the port for vmnic4. This adapter must be bound to
  a switch uplink port for activation.
```

In this example I used the expanded version of the `-n` option, `--nic-name`. Note that when expanded options are used, an equal sign is used before the option value. This is the same convention with any ESXCLI syntax.

Figure 3.29 shows a similar message when using the vSphere Client to add a software FCoE adapter for a vmnic that is not bound to a vSwitch uplink port.

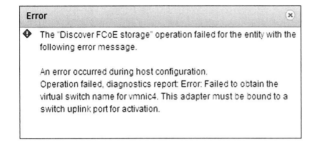

Figure 3.29 Error when adding a software FCoE adapter to an unbound vmnic

Finally, the `list` option is used to list all FCoE-capable vmnics:

```
~ # esxcli fcoe nic list
vmnic4
    User Priority: 3
    Source MAC: 90:e2:ba:2b:46:0e
    Active: false
    Priority Settable: false
    Source MAC Settable: false
    VLAN Range Settable: false
    VN2VN Mode Enabled: false

vmnic5
    User Priority: 3
    Source MAC: 90:e2:ba:2b:46:0f
    Active: true
    Priority Settable: false
    Source MAC Settable: false
    VLAN Range Settable: true
    VN2VN Mode Enabled: false
```

In this example, vmnic5 was already configured with FCoE, whereas vmnic4 was not but is FCoE-capable. You can tell that vmnic5 is configured because you see `Active: true`.

FCoE-Related Logs

FCoE discovery- and communication-related events generated by DCBD are logged to /var/log/syslog.log, and the events are prefixed with `dcbd`. If you don't see enough details in the log, you can run the DCB daemon with the verbose option:

```
/bin/dcbd -v
```

When you're done troubleshooting, you can revert to daemon mode (nonverbose) by running this command:

```
/usr/bin/dcbd -d
```

Listing 3.2 shows a sample log entry from /var/log/syslog.log (with the date and timestamps removed for readability):

Listing 3.2   FCoE-related events in the syslog.log file on an ESXi host

```
root: init Running dcbd start
watchdog-dcbd: [511440] Begin '/usr/sbin/dcbd ++group=net-daemons',
  min-uptime = 60, max-quick-failures = 1, max-total-failures = 5, bg_pid_
  file = '', reboot-flag = '0'
watchdog-dcbd: Executing '/usr/sbin/dcbd ++group=net-daemons'
dcbd: [info]    add_dcbx_ieee: device = default_cfg_attribs stype = 2
dcbd: [info]    add_ets_ieee: device = default_cfg_attribs
dcbd: [info]    add_pfc_ieee: device = default_cfg_attribs
dcbd: [info]    add_app_ieee: device = default_cfg_attribs subtype = 0
dcbd: [info]    Not adding inactive FCOE adapter: "vmnic4"
dcbd: [info]    Main loop running.
```

The first line shows starting the dcbd daemon.

The second line shows the watchdog for the dcbd daemon startup parameters. They are as follows:

- group is net-daemons, which means the watchdog monitors the status of this daemon in the group with that name.

- min-uptime is 60 seconds. It is the minimum time the daemon should be up. If it runs for less than that time, the watchdog considers it a *quick-failure* (described next).

- max-quick-failures is 1, which means the watchdog gives up on restarting the daemon if it runs for less than 60 seconds five times in a row. If the daemon stays up for 60 seconds or more, the watchdog reloads it. If this value is 2, the daemon has to die quickly two times in a row before the watchdog gives up.

  Consider the following sequence of events: The daemon could stay up for 40 seconds, get restarted, stay up for 70 seconds (not a quick failure), get restarted, stay up for 30 seconds, get restarted, stay up for 55 seconds, and then crash. In this sequence of events, the daemon stays down because there are two quick failures in a row.

- max-total-failures is 5, which is the total number of times the daemon fails to run over any length of time before the watchdog gives up on reloading the daemon.

For example, when the dcbd daemon has failed five times since the ESXi host booted, the watchdog no longer restarts it.

■ `bg_pid_file` is set to `null`, which means no background process ID file is created.

> **NOTE**
>
> The watchdog is a script that manages VMware services and is located in /usr/sbin/watchdog.sh. It launches the specified process and respawns it after it exits. It gives up after recording the specified number of quick failures in succession or after recording a specified total number of failures over any length of time.
>
> Note that /usr/bin and /usr/sbin are symbolically linked to the /bin directory.

The third line is the execution of loading the watchdog.

The fourth through seventh lines add DCBX, ETS, FPC, and APP devices with default configuration attributes.

The eighth line indicates that vmnic4 is not activated as an FCoE adapter.

The last line shows that the daemon is now running.

The log snippet in Listing 3.3 shows events related to adding vmnic5 as an FCoE adapter.

Listing 3.3   /var/log/syslog.log listing of adding vmnic5 as an FCoE adapter

```
dcbd: [info]     add_adapter (vmnic5)
dcbd: [info]       dcbx subtype = 2
dcbd: [info]     get_dcb_capabilities for "vmnic5"
dcbd: [info]     get_dcb_numtcs for "vmnic5"
dcbd: [info]     Reconciled device numTCs (PG 4, PFC 4)
dcbd: [info]     get mac addr for "vmnic5"
dcbd: [info]     is 90:e2:ba:2b:46:0d
dcbd: [info]     add_dcbx_ieee: device = vmnic5 stype = 2
dcbd: [info]     add_ets_ieee: device = vmnic5
dcbd: [info]     add_pfc_ieee: device = vmnic5
dcbd: [info]     add_app_ieee: device = vmnic5 subtype = 0
```

After the adapter vmnic5 is added, it is identified as a dcbx subtype 2. This means that it is a Converged Enhanced Ethernet (CEE) port that supports FCoE. In other words, the I/O card represented by vmnic5 is FCoE-capable.

Listing 3.4 shows that the log entries continue with negotiating the FCoE adapter's DCB features.

Listing 3.4   /var/log/syslog.log listing of negotiating FCoE adapter DCB features

```
dcbd: [info]     Set Syncd to 0 [4148]
dcbd: [info]     Feature state machine (flags 1)
dcbd: [info]       Local change: PG
dcbd: [info]     Set Syncd to 0 [4148]
dcbd: [info]     Feature state machine (flags 4)
dcbd: [info]       Local change:  PFC
dcbd: [info]       CopyConfigToOper vmnic5
dcbd: [info]     set_pfc_cfg for "vmnic5", operMode: 0
dcbd: [info]     set_pfc_state for "vmnic5", pfc_state: FALSE
dcbd: [info]     Set Syncd to 0 [4148]
dcbd: [info]     Feature state machine (flags 100)
dcbd: [info]       Local change:
dcbd: [info]     APP0
dcbd: [info]     DCB Ctrl in LISTEN
dcbd: [info]       Local change detected: PG PFC
dcbd: [info]     APP0
dcbd: [info]       Local SeqNo == Local AckNo
dcbd: [info]       *** Sending packet -- SeqNo = 1          AckNo =   0
dcbd: [info]     Set portset name for "vmnic5" : "vSwitch_FCoE_82599"
dcbd: [info]     Main loop running.
```

Log entries continue from the syslog.log file, which shows the negotiation of the FCoE adapter's DCB features and attributes:

> **NOTE**
>
> To interpret these entries, see the DCB reference document at www.ieee802.org/1/files/public/docs2008/az-wadekar-dcbx-capability-exchange-discovery-protocol-1108-v1.01.pdf.

- `Set Syncd to 0 (4148)`, `Feature state machine`, and `Local change: PG` mean that the priority group configuration has not been received by the peer.

- `Set Syncd to 0 Feature state machine`, `Local change`, and `PFC CopyConfigToOper vmnic5` mean that the priority-based flow control configuration has not been received by the peer. The configuration was going to be copied to vmnic5.

- `Set_pfc_cfg for "vmnic5"`, `operMode: 0` means that the PFC configuration was not set for vmnic5.

- Set_pfc_state for "vmnic5", pfc_state: FALSE means that the PFC state for vmnic5 was set to FALSE. This is due to the fact that the configuration has not been received by the peer. Note that the previous two sets of lines are associated with the Set Syncd: 0 listed just before them.

- Set Syncd to 0 Feature state machine (flags 100) and Local Change: App0 indicate that the adapter sent its first packet sequence number 1, including ack number 0.

Listing 3.5 shows DCBX packet content logged to the syslog.log file.

Listing 3.5   /var/log/syslog.log listing of DCBX packet content

```
dcbd: [info]        *** Received a DCB_CONTROL_TLV: -- SeqNo=1, AckNo=1
dcbd: [info]        *** Received CEE DCBX Packet on port: vmnic5
dcbd: [info]
dcbd: [info]        Src
dcbd: [info]        00
dcbd: [info]        2a
dcbd: [info]        6a
dcbd: [info]        3f
dcbd: [info]        1d
dcbd: [info]        88
dcbd: [info]
dcbd: [info]
dcbd: [info]        Dest
dcbd: [info]        90
dcbd: [info]        e2
dcbd: [info]        ba
dcbd: [info]        2b
dcbd: [info]        46
dcbd: [info]        0d
dcbd: [info]
dcbd: [info]        Port ID TLV:
dcbd: [info]
dcbd: [info]        E
dcbd: [info]        t
dcbd: [info]        h
dcbd: [info]        1
dcbd: [info]        /
dcbd: [info]        1
```

```
dcbd: [info]
dcbd: [info]      Chassis ID TLV:
dcbd: [info]
dcbd: [info]      MAC:
dcbd: [info]      00
dcbd: [info]      2a
dcbd: [info]      6a
dcbd: [info]      3f
dcbd: [info]      1d
dcbd: [info]      88
dcbd: [info]
dcbd: [info]      TTL TLV:
dcbd: [info]
dcbd: [info]      120 sec
dcbd: [info]
dcbd: [info]      Port Description TLV:
dcbd: [info]      E
dcbd: [info]      t
dcbd: [info]      h
dcbd: [info]      e
dcbd: [info]      r
dcbd: [info]      n
dcbd: [info]      e
dcbd: [info]      t
dcbd: [info]      1
dcbd: [info]      /
dcbd: [info]      1
dcbd: [info]
dcbd: [info]      System Name TLV:
dcbd: [info]
dcbd: [info]      w
dcbd: [info]      1
dcbd: [info]      j
dcbd: [info]      2
dcbd: [info]      1
dcbd: [info]      -
dcbd: [info]      p
dcbd: [info]      a
dcbd: [info]      s
dcbd: [info]      t
dcbd: [info]      s
dcbd: [info]      t
```

```
dcbd: [info]     o
dcbd: [info]     r
dcbd: [info]     -
dcbd: [info]     n
dcbd: [info]     e
dcbd: [info]     x
dcbd: [info]     u
dcbd: [info]     s
dcbd: [info]     5
dcbd: [info]     5
dcbd: [info]     4
dcbd: [info]     8
dcbd: [info]     -
dcbd: [info]     1
dcbd: [info]
dcbd: [info]     System Description TLV:
dcbd: [info]
dcbd: [info]     C
dcbd: [info]     i
dcbd: [info]     s
dcbd: [info]     c
dcbd: [info]     o
dcbd: [info]
dcbd: [info]     N
dcbd: [info]     e
dcbd: [info]     x
dcbd: [info]     u
dcbd: [info]     s
dcbd: [info]
dcbd: [info]     O
dcbd: [info]     p
dcbd: [info]     e
dcbd: [info]     r
dcbd: [info]     a
dcbd: [info]     t
dcbd: [info]     i
dcbd: [info]     n
dcbd: [info]     g
dcbd: [info]
dcbd: [info]     S
dcbd: [info]     y
dcbd: [info]     s
```

```
dcbd: [info]     t
dcbd: [info]     e
dcbd: [info]     m
dcbd: [info]
dcbd: [info]     (
dcbd: [info]     N
dcbd: [info]     X
dcbd: [info]     -
dcbd: [info]     O
dcbd: [info]     S
dcbd: [info]     )
dcbd: [info]
dcbd: [info]     S
dcbd: [info]     o
dcbd: [info]     f
dcbd: [info]     t
dcbd: [info]     w
dcbd: [info]     a
dcbd: [info]     r
dcbd: [info]     e
dcbd: [info]
dcbd: [info]     T
dcbd: [info]     A
dcbd: [info]     C
dcbd: [info]
dcbd: [info]     s
dcbd: [info]     u
dcbd: [info]     p
dcbd: [info]     p
dcbd: [info]     o
dcbd: [info]     r
dcbd: [info]     t
dcbd: [info]     :
dcbd: [info]
dcbd: [info]     h
dcbd: [info]     t
dcbd: [info]     t
dcbd: [info]     p
dcbd: [info]     :
dcbd: [info]     /
dcbd: [info]     /
```

```
dcbd:  [info]     w
dcbd:  [info]     w
dcbd:  [info]     w
dcbd:  [info]     .
dcbd:  [info]     c
dcbd:  [info]     i
dcbd:  [info]     s
dcbd:  [info]     c
dcbd:  [info]     o
dcbd:  [info]     .
dcbd:  [info]     c
dcbd:  [info]     o
dcbd:  [info]     m
dcbd:  [info]     /
dcbd:  [info]     t
dcbd:  [info]     a
dcbd:  [info]     c
dcbd:  [info]
dcbd:  [info]     C
dcbd:  [info]     o
dcbd:  [info]     p
dcbd:  [info]     y
dcbd:  [info]     r
dcbd:  [info]     i
dcbd:  [info]     g
dcbd:  [info]     h
dcbd:  [info]     t
dcbd:  [info]
dcbd:  [info]     (
dcbd:  [info]     c
dcbd:  [info]     )
dcbd:  [info]
dcbd:  [info]     2
dcbd:  [info]     0
dcbd:  [info]     0
dcbd:  [info]     2
dcbd:  [info]     -
dcbd:  [info]     2
dcbd:  [info]     0
dcbd:  [info]     1
dcbd:  [info]     2
```

```
dcbd: [info]       ,
dcbd: [info]
dcbd: [info]       C
dcbd: [info]       i
dcbd: [info]       s
dcbd: [info]       c
dcbd: [info]       o
dcbd: [info]
dcbd: [info]       S
dcbd: [info]       y
dcbd: [info]       s
dcbd: [info]       t
dcbd: [info]       e
dcbd: [info]       m
dcbd: [info]       s
dcbd: [info]       ,
dcbd: [info]
dcbd: [info]       I
dcbd: [info]       n
dcbd: [info]       c
dcbd: [info]       .
dcbd: [info]
dcbd: [info]       A
dcbd: [info]       l
dcbd: [info]       l
dcbd: [info]
dcbd: [info]       r
dcbd: [info]       i
dcbd: [info]       g
dcbd: [info]       h
dcbd: [info]       t
dcbd: [info]       s
dcbd: [info]
dcbd: [info]       r
dcbd: [info]       e
dcbd: [info]       s
dcbd: [info]       e
dcbd: [info]       r
dcbd: [info]       v
dcbd: [info]       e
dcbd: [info]       d
dcbd: [info]       .
```

```
dcbd: [info]
dcbd: [info]      System Capabilities TLV:
dcbd: [info]
dcbd: [info]      Supported:
dcbd: [info]      Bridge
dcbd: [info]
dcbd: [info]
dcbd: [info]      Enabled:
dcbd: [info]      Bridge
dcbd: [info]
dcbd: [info]      Management Address TLV:
dcbd: [info]
dcbd: [info]      IPv4 Addr:
dcbd: [info]      10.
dcbd: [info]      132.
dcbd: [info]      86.
dcbd: [info]      178
dcbd: [info]
dcbd: [info]
dcbd: [info]      ifIndex:
dcbd: [info]      83886080
dcbd: [info]      running DCB protocol for vmnic5, flags:1000a
```

The FCF responds with sequence number 1 with ack number 1 and includes the following information:

- Source: 00 2a 6a 3f 1d 88, which is the FCF MAC address (see Figure 3.30 later in this chapter)

- Destination: 90 e2 ba 2b 46 0d, which is the FCoE adapter's MAC address for vmnic5

- Port ID TLV: Eth1/1, which is the port ID on the FCF whose MAC address was listed as the source earlier and is reported via the MAC field listed the line after the next

- Chassis ID TLV, which is blank in this example

- MAC: 00 2a 6a 3f 1d 88, which is the MAC address of port Eth1/1 and is the same as the source MAC

- TTL TLV: 120 seconds

- Port Description TLV: Ethernet1/1

- System Name TLV: W1j21-paststor-nexus5548-1

- System Description TLV: Cisco Nexus Operating System (NX-OS)

- Software TAC support: http://www.cisco.com/tac

- Copyright 2002–2012, Cisco Systems, Inc. All rights reserved.

- System Capabilities TLV:Supported: Bridge Enabled: Bridge

- Management Address TLV: IPv4 Addr: 10.132.86.178 ifIndex: 83886080

Listing 3.6 shows the sync operation to get the FCoE adapter DCB features

Listing 3.6   /var/log/syslog.log listing of negotiating FCoE adapter DCB features

```
dcbd: [info]     Feature state machine (flags 2)
dcbd: [info]       Remote change: PG
dcbd: [info]       Set Syncd to 1 [4525]
dcbd: [info]       F18 - local willing,  peer NOT willing
dcbd: [info]       CopyConfigToOper vmnic5
dcbd: [info]     set_hw_pg for "vmnic5" operMode: 1
dcbd: [info]     Feature state machine (flags 8)
dcbd: [info]       Remote change:  PFC
dcbd: [info]       Set Syncd to 1 [4525]
dcbd: [info]       F18 - local willing,  peer NOT willing
dcbd: [info]       CopyConfigToOper vmnic5
dcbd: [info]     set_pfc_cfg for "vmnic5", operMode: 1
dcbd: [info]     set_pfc_state for "vmnic5", pfc_state: TRUE
dcbd: [info]     Feature state machine (flags 10000)
dcbd: [info]       Remote change:
dcbd: [info]      APP0
dcbd: [info]       Set Syncd to 1 [4525]
dcbd: [info]       F18 - local willing,  peer NOT willing
dcbd: [info]       CopyConfigToOper vmnic5
dcbd: [info]       Changing app data from 08 to 08
dcbd: [info]     set_hw_app for "vmnic5"
dcbd: [info]     wakeup_fcoe_from_dormant: vmnic5
dcbd: [info]     DCBX settings are valid on vmnic5
dcbd: [info]     set_hw_all for "vmnic5"
dcbd: [info]     set_hw_all: no hardware configuration change
dcbd: [info]     Check dormant mode and wakeup vmnic5
dcbd: [info]     DCB Ctrl in LISTEN
```

```
dcbd: [info]        Remote change detected: PG PFC
dcbd: [info]        APP0
dcbd: [info]        Current -- SeqNo = 2      MyAckNo =  2
```

Here the `syncd` is set to `1`, which triggers the negotiation for PG (priority group). However, the peer is not willing to sync. HW PG configuration is set for vmnic5, and the operational mode is set to `1` (which means enabled).

The same is repeated for PFC, where PFC configuration is set to `Operational Mode 1`, and PFC state is set to `TRUE`.

Again, the same is repeated for APP0, where the app data is changed from `08` to `08` (which means it remains the same value). The result is that no hardware configuration change occurs.

Now DCB control is in LISTEN mode, which detects remote change in PG and PFC.

Sequence number 2 is sent, containing Ack number 2.

This is the end of the sequence.

FCoE device and path claiming events are logged to the ESXi syslog.log file, which is located in the /var/log directory. A sample syslog.log file, taken from a different system, is shown in Listing 3.7.

Listing 3.7   /var/log/syslog.log snippet showing device and path claiming events

```
dcbd: [info] Connect event for vmnic2, portset name: "vSwitch1"

storageDeviceInfo.plugStoreTopology.adapter["key-vim.host.PlugStore
   Topology.Adapter-vmhba33"].path["key-vim.host.PlugStoreTopology.Path-fcoe.
   1000001b215cfee6:2000001b215cfee6-fcoe.500601609020fd54:500601611020fd54-
   naa.60060160d1911400a3878ec1656edf11"]

storageDeviceInfo.plugStoreTopology.path["key-vim.host.PlugStoreTopology.
   Path-fcoe.1000001b215cfee6:2000001b215cfee6-fcoe.500601609020fd54:5006016
   11020fd54-naa.60060160d1911400a3878ec1656edf11"],

storageDeviceInfo.plugStoreTopology.target["key-vim.host.PlugStoreTopology.
   Target-fcoe.500601609020fd54:500601611020fd54"],

storageDeviceInfo.plugStoreTopology.device["key-vim.host.PlugStoreTopology.
   Device-020008000060060160d1911400a3878ec1656edf11524149442030"],

storageDeviceInfo.plugStoreTopology.plugin["key-vim.host.PlugStoreTopology.
   Plugin-NMP"].device["key-vim.host.PlugStoreTopology.Device-0200080000
   60060160d1911400a3878ec1656edf11524149442030"],
```

```
storageDeviceInfo.plugStoreTopology.plugin["key-vim.host.PlugStoreTopology.
    Plugin-NMP"].claimedPath["key-vim.host.PlugStoreTopology.Path-fcoe.1000
    90e2ba2b460f:200090e2ba2b460f-fcoe.500601609020fd54:500601611020fd54-"],
```

In the log snippet shown in Listing 3.7, I removed the timestamp and added a blank line between log entries for readability.

The first line shows a connect event for the FCoE port that is on vmnic2 (what was bound on vSwitch1).

The second line shows the connection topology, which is as follows:

- The FCoE adapter name (as seen in the UI) is `vmhba33`.

- The adapter's WWNN:WWPN combination is `100090e2ba2b460f:200090e2ba2b460f`.

- The storage processor port WWNN:WWPN combination is `500601609020fd54:500601611020fd54`. Based on Table 2.1 in Chapter 2, the SP WWPN translates to SPA-Port 1 of a CLARiiON CX storage array.

- The LUN visible on this path has NAA ID `60060160d1911400a3878ec1656edf11`.

The third line identifies the path details—the adapter's WWNN:WWPN combination and the storage processor port WWNN:WWPN combination.

The fourth line identifies the target, which is the adapter's WWNN:WWPN combination.

The fifth line shows the device ID. This is similar to the vml device ID seen in /vmfs/devices/disks but without the prefix vml.

NOTE

vml is a *vmkernel list link* that points to the corresponding device ID (for example, NAA ID). This is for backward compatibility with earlier releases, prior to the introduction of device IDs. I provide more details on this in Chapter 13, "Virtual Disks and RDMs."

The following command lists the vml IDs and the device IDs to which they link:

```
ls -al /vmfs/devices/disks/

733909245952 Jan 22 06:05 naa.600508b10010373839414243444450400

36 Jan 22 06:05 vml.0200000000600508b100103738394142434445040004c4f4749
    4341 -> naa.600508b10010373839414243444450400
```

I truncated the permissions and owners from the output and added a blank line between outputs for readability.

The sixth line shows that the Native Multipathing Plugin (NMP) has claimed the device identified in the previous line. I discuss NMP in Chapter 5.

The last line shows that NMP has claimed the path that begins with the FCoE adapter's WWNN:WWPN combination, going through the SPA-Port1, as explained previously.

> **NOTE**
>
> The reference to `plugStoreTopology` refers to Pluggable Storage Architecture (PSA), which I discuss in Chapter 5. I also discuss the definition of path and multipathing in Chapter 7.

The log snippet shown in Listing 3.8 is a continuation of the previous log sample.

Listing 3.8   Continuation of /var/log/syslog.log

```
storageDeviceInfo.hostBusAdapter["key-vim.host.FibreChannelOverEthernet
  Hba-vmhba33"].status,

storageDeviceInfo.hostBusAdapter["key-vim.host.FibreChannelOverEthernet
  Hba-vmhba33"].linkInfo.vnportMac,

storageDeviceInfo.hostBusAdapter["key-vim.host.FibreChannelOverEthernet
  Hba-vmhba33"].linkInfo.fcfMac,

storageDeviceInfo.hostBusAdapter["key-vim.host.FibreChannelOverEthernet
  Hba-vmhba33"].linkInfo.vlanId]

storageDeviceInfo.scsiTopology.adapter["key-vim.host.ScsiTopology.
  Interface-vmhba33"].target["key-vim.host.ScsiTopology.Target-
  vmhba33:0:0"].lun["key-vim.host.ScsiTopology.Lun-020001000060060160d19114
  008de22dbb5e5edf11524149442035"],
```

This log snippet continues on to request the (vmhba33) HBA status on line 1.

On lines 2, 3, and 4, it requests the link information of the following entities:

- `linkInfo.vnportMac`—indicates the VN_Port, the FCoE equivalent of the FC's N_Port, which is the type of port for the FCoE adapters.

- `linkInfo.fcfMac`—indicates FCF, the FCoE Forwarder, which is the switch port's MAC.

- `linkInfo.vlanId` is the VLAN ID.

These three entities make up the FCoE link.

The last line shows the canonical name of the path (see Chapter 7) with the exception that the LUN is identified by its "vml" name, as mentioned previously. This is composed of the combination of the `Adapter:Channel:Target:LUN`. The channel number is always 0 except for direct attached storage via a dual-channel HBA (for example, a RAID adapter with an internal channel and an external one), where you use 0 for the internal channel and 1 for the external one—for example, `vmhba2:0:0` and `vmhba2:1:0`. However, because this does not apply to FCoE adapters, the channel number is always 0. So the canonical name here is `vmhba33:0:0:<LUN>`.

These connection properties are also displayed in the FCoE adapter's properties via the UI. Figure 3.30 shows these properties in addition to the physical NIC's vmnic name as well as the priority class, which is discussed in Table 3.1.

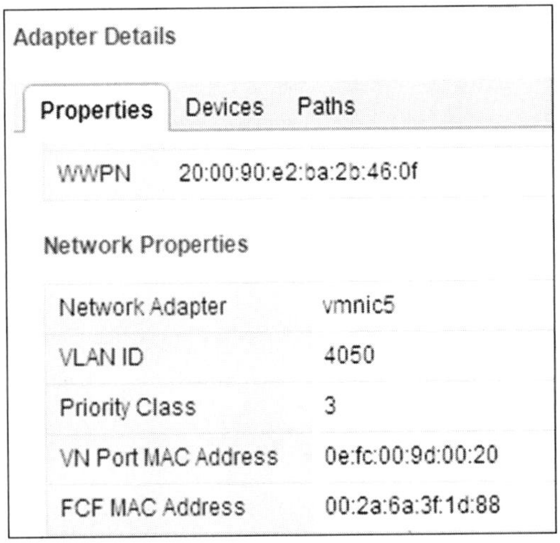

Adapter Details

Properties	Devices	Paths

WWPN   20:00:90:e2:ba:2b:46:0f

Network Properties

Network Adapter	vmnic5
VLAN ID	4050
Priority Class	3
VN Port MAC Address	0e:fc:00:9d:00:20
FCF MAC Address	00:2a:6a:3f:1d:88

Figure 3.30   FCoE adapter network properties

How to Verify SW FCoE Connectivity

To verify SW FCoE connectivity, you can use the `esxcfg-scsidevs` command on the ESXi host CLI directly or via SSH session to list the SW FCoE adapter. Figure 3.31 shows the command and its output.

```
w1-paststor01.eng.vmware.com - PuTTY                    —   □   ✕
[root@w1-paststor01:~] esxcfg-scsidevs -a |grep fcoe |less -S
vmhba33 fcoe              link-up   fcoe.100090e2ba2b460f:200090e2ba2b460f
```

Figure 3.31   Listing SW FCoE connectivity status

In this example, the command line is as follows:

```
esxcfg-scsidevs -a |grep fcoe |less -S
```

The output shows that the SW FCoE adapter vmhba33 link is up.

To list the vSwitch uplink for the FCoE port group, you use the `esxcfg-vswitch -l` command, as shown in Figure 3.32.

```
w1-paststor01.eng.vmware.com - PuTTY                    —   □   ✕
[root@w1-paststor01:~] esxcfg-vswitch -l
Switch Name      Num Ports   Used Ports   Configured Ports   MTU    Uplinks
vSwitch0         3072        4            128                1500   vmnic0

   PortGroup Name        VLAN ID   Used Ports   Uplinks
   VM Network            0         0            vmnic0
   Management Network    0         1            vmnic0

Switch Name      Num Ports   Used Ports   Configured Ports   MTU    Uplinks
vSwitch2         3072        2            128                1500

   PortGroup Name        VLAN ID   Used Ports   Uplinks
   Guest Network         0         0
   Host Network          0         1

Switch Name      Num Ports   Used Ports   Configured Ports   MTU    Uplinks
vSwitch1         3072        4            128                1500   vmnic5

   PortGroup Name        VLAN ID   Used Ports   Uplinks
   FCoE1                 0         1            vmnic5
```

Figure 3.32   Listing SW FCoE uplink

In this example, the port group is called `FCoE1` and is on `vSwitch1`. `vSwitch1` is uplinked to `vmnic5`. While the output shows that the VLAN ID is 0, the actual VLAN used is what is reported by the FCF. The best way to identify the VLAN ID in use is by using the `esxcli fcoe adapter list` command, as shown in Figure 3.28, earlier in this chapter.

Proc Nodes Can Be Useful, Too

You can also use the FCoE proc node at /proc/scsi/fcoe/[node-file] to obtain information similar to that listed in the previous sections. An example of the content of this node is presented in Listings 3.8 through 3.11.

Listing 3.9 shows the SW FCoE adapter information.

Listing 3.9   FCoE proc node: SW FCoE adapter information

```
ls /proc/scsi/fcoe/
7
cat /proc/scsi/fcoe/7
Driver Name            Open-FCoE.org FCoE Driver
Driver Version         1.0.29.9.3-0vmw
Uplink Name            vmnic5
Link State             LINK_UP
Physical Port WWNN     100090e2ba2b460f
Physical Port WWPN     200090e2ba2b460f
PortID                 0x9d0020
```

Listing 3.10 shows the FCoE Forwarder (FCF) information.

Listing 3.10   FCoE proc node: FCF information

```
FCFs List :
  FCF1
    Switch Name          2fd2002a6a3f1d81
    Fabric Name          2fd2002a6a3f1d81
    FC Map               efc00
    VFID                 4050
    Priority             80
    Flags                8007
    Keep Alive Period    320
    MAC Address          00:2a:6a:3f:1d:88
    Type                 Selected
```

Listing 3.11 shows the remote port information.

Listing 3.11   FCoE proc node: Remote port information

```
Remote Ports List :
  Port1
    WWNN       50060160c6e0314b
    WWPN       5006016546e0314b
    PortID     0x9d0040
  Port2
    WWNN       50060160c6e0314b
```

```
WWPN       5006016446e0314b
PortID     0x9d0001
Port3
WWNN       20000000c9ef48db
WWPN       10000000c9ef48db
PortID     0x9d0000
```

Listing 3.12 shows the FCoE adapter statistics.

Listing 3.12   FCoE proc node: Adapter statistics

```
FCoE Statistics :
    TX Frames                  69277708
    TX Words                   115835334618
    RX Frames                  120436209
    RX Words                   27152261343
    Error Frames               1
    Dumped Frames              0
    Link Failure Count         0
    Loss Signal Count          0
    Invalid TX Word Count      0
    Invalid CRC Count          0
    Input Reqs                 25161723
    Output Reqs                22057889
    Ctrl Reqs                  104
    Input Megabytes            431524814454
    Output Megabytes           460444749824
    Vlink Fail Count           0
    Misc Disc Adv Count        0
```

If the link failure count is high, you may have a network connectivity problem. Check the Ethernet cable as well as errors on the switch port.

If the invalid CRC count is high, you may have a problem with the network card.

Parting Tips

Consider the following scenario: A vSphere administrator configures FCoE on an ESXi 6 host. The linked vmnic is connected to a 10GigE network and, from there, to an FCoE switch, which in turn connects to the storage array via a 4Gig FC fabric. Because the FCoE traffic would not benefit from more than the bandwidth provided by the FC SAN, the administrator attempts to guarantee 4Gbps bandwidth by configuring network I/O control and assigns the FCoE 40% of the total bandwidth. So, effectively, the FCoE traffic gets assigned a priority on the networking stream after it has already assigned that priority via the protocol itself. However, the administrator notices that FCoE is not getting the bandwidth dedicated to it.

As a famous TV detective says, "I solved the case! Here is what happened": FCoE uses 802.1p user priority for dedicated bandwidth (Enhanced Transmission Selection —ETS]). The network I/O control feature of vSphere 6 also uses 802.1p user priority for quality of service (QoS). The bandwidth split happens at a priority group (PG) level between the NIC/CNA and the switch. Each PG consists of multiple priorities, and most administrators typically configure FCoE in a separate PG.

The switch sees multiple streams of data: FCoE and L2 network (which happen to be both for the same FCoE traffic). If the combined capacity exceeds the 40% allocated to FCoE traffic, the switch tries to throttle the rate by sending a PFC on the FCoE priority. This effectively stops the FCoE traffic.

The moral of the story: Don't get overzealous and attempt to guarantee FCoE bandwidth by using network I/O control because it is already assigned the appropriate priority via the FCoE protocol. Using network I/O control results in a negative effect, stopping the FCoE traffic instead.

Summary

This chapter covers the details of the FCoE protocol and its architecture and how it is implemented in vSphere 6. It also provides details of configuring SW FCoE adapters on vSphere 6. I shared some sample logs and familiarized you with how to interpret them. Finally, I discussed a potential gotcha that occurs when you use network I/O control and FCoE.

iSCSI Storage Connectivity

iSCSI Protocol

The Internet Engineering Task Force (IETF) is responsible for the iSCSI protocol. (See RFC 3720, at http://tools.ietf.org/html/rfc3720.)

Internet Small Computer System Interface (iSCSI) is an Internet Protocol (IP)–based storage standard that connects iSCSI initiators to iSCSI targets over IP networks. To put it simply, the SCSI packets are encapsulated in IP packets and sent over a standard IP network, where the initiators and targets reassemble the packets and interpret the commands carried by these packets.

iSCSI takes advantage of existing IP infrastructure, unlike Fibre Channel (FC), which requires special cables and switches.

Overview of iSCSI Connectivity

The main elements of iSCSI connectivity are initiators, targets, portals, sessions, and connections. I start with iSCSI sessions to provide a high-level connectivity overview, and then I cover the remaining elements in later sections of this chapter.

iSCSI Sessions

Each iSCSI initiator establishes a single session with each iSCSI target server via Transmission Control Protocol (TCP). Within that session, there can be one or more connections between initiators and portals on the target server (see Figure 4.1).

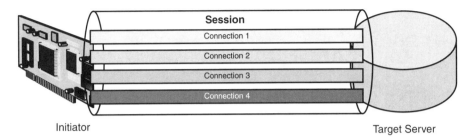

Figure 4.1   iSCSI sessions

A portal is an IP address and TCP port combination. (Find out more about portals in the next section, "iSCSI Portals.") The default TCP port is 3260.

Figure 4.2 shows an example of an ESXi 6.0 host with two iSCSI initiators (vmhba2 and vmhba3) connected to an iSCSI storage array.

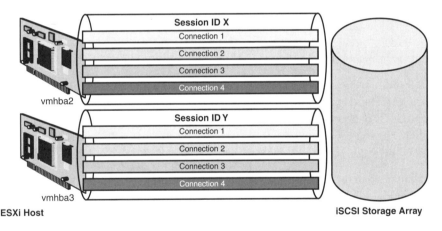

Figure 4.2   iSCSI sessions from multiple initiators

vmhba2 established session X with the storage array and has four connections within that session.

In the same fashion, vmhba3 established session Y with the same iSCSI storage array and also has four connections within that session.

To understand this better, examine Listing 4.1, with output collected from the ESXi host used in this example. I truncated some of the lines in the output and kept the lines that are relevant to this section.

Listing 4.1   Listing iSCSI Sessions

```
~ # esxcli iscsi session list

vmhba2,iqn.1992-04.com.emc:cx.apm00064000064.a0,00c0dd09b6c3
    Adapter: vmhba2
    Target: iqn.1992-04.com.emc:cx.apm00064000064.a0
    ISID: 00c0dd09b6c3
    TargetPortalGroupTag: 1


vmhba2,iqn.1992-04.com.emc:cx.apm00064000064.a1,00c0dd09b6c3
    Adapter: vmhba2
    Target: iqn.1992-04.com.emc:cx.apm00064000064.a1
    ISID: 00c0dd09b6c3
    TargetPortalGroupTag: 2


vmhba2,iqn.1992-04.com.emc:cx.apm00064000064.b0,00c0dd09b6c3
    Adapter: vmhba2
    Target: iqn.1992-04.com.emc:cx.apm00064000064.b0
    ISID: 00c0dd09b6c3
    TargetPortalGroupTag: 3


vmhba2,iqn.1992-04.com.emc:cx.apm00064000064.b1,00c0dd09b6c3
    Adapter: vmhba2
    Target: iqn.1992-04.com.emc:cx.apm00064000064.b1
    ISID: 00c0dd09b6c3
    TargetPortalGroupTag: 4


vmhba3,iqn.1992-04.com.emc:cx.apm00064000064.a0,00c0dd09b6c5
    Adapter: vmhba3
    Target: iqn.1992-04.com.emc:cx.apm00064000064.a0
    ISID: 00c0dd09b6c5
    TargetPortalGroupTag: 1


vmhba3,iqn.1992-04.com.emc:cx.apm00064000064.a1,00c0dd09b6c5
    Adapter: vmhba3
    Target: iqn.1992-04.com.emc:cx.apm00064000064.a1
    ISID: 00c0dd09b6c5
    TargetPortalGroupTag: 2
```

```
vmhba3,iqn.1992-04.com.emc:cx.apm00064000064.b0,00c0dd09b6c5
    Adapter: vmhba3
    Target: iqn.1992-04.com.emc:cx.apm00064000064.b0
    ISID: 00c0dd09b6c5
    TargetPortalGroupTag: 3


vmhba3,iqn.1992-04.com.emc:cx.apm00064000064.b1,00c0dd09b6c5
    Adapter: vmhba3
    Target: iqn.1992-04.com.emc:cx.apm00064000064.b1
    ISID: 00c0dd09b6c5
    TargetPortalGroupTag: 4
```

In Listing 4.1, notice the ISID value, which is the iSCSI session ID. Each HBA is associated with one session ID to four targets.

Table 4.1 shows the correlation between initiators, targets, sessions, and connections in this example.

Table 4.1 Correlating initiators, targets, sessions, and connections

Target IQN	Session ID	Target Portal Group Tag	Notes
vmhba2			
iqn.1992-04.com.emc:cx. apm00064000064.a0	00c0dd09b6c3	1	SPA Port 0
iqn.1992-04.com.emc:cx. apm00064000064.a1	00c0dd09b6c3	2	SPA Port 1
iqn.1992-04.com.emc:cx. apm00064000064.b0	00c0dd09b6c3	3	SPB Port 0
iqn.1992-04.com.emc:cx. apm00064000064.b1	00c0dd09b6c3	4	SPB Port 1
Target IQN	Session ID	Target Portal Group Tag	Notes
vmhba3			
iqn.1992-04.com.emc:cx. apm00064000064.a0	00c0dd09b6c5	1	SPA Port 0
iqn.1992-04.com.emc:cx. apm00064000064.a1	00c0dd09b6c5	2	SPA Port 1
iqn.1992-04.com.emc:cx. apm00064000064.b0	00c0dd09b6c5	3	SPB Port 0
iqn.1992-04.com.emc:cx. apm00064000064.b1	00c0dd09b6c5	4	SPB Port 1

Table 4.1 shows that vmhba2 and vmhba3 are connected to the same targets, which are ports on each storage processor (SP). Notice that the SP-Port combination is part of the target's IQN (which is explained further later in this chapter, in the "iSCSI Targets" section).

You can list active target sessions information for a given HBA by using the following command:

```
vmkiscsi-tool --connection <hba-name>
```

Or you can use this shortened version of the command:

```
vmkiscsi-tool -C <hba-name>
```

> **NOTE**
>
> vmkiscsi-tool is deprecated in ESXi 6 and may not be available in future releases. I use this tool here for completeness and as a transition from older releases.
>
> As a result of this deprecation, the verbose option --connection does not work and will not be fixed. Instead, use the -C option, which still works in the 6.x release.

Or you can use esxcli:

```
esxcli iscsi session list --adapter=<hba-name>
```

The following is the shorthand version of this command:

```
esxcli iscsi session list -A <hba-name>
```

The following is an example using vmkiscsi-tool:

```
vmkiscsi-tool -C vmhba2
```

The following is an example using esxcli:

```
esxcli iscsi session list -A vmhba2
```

To list the same information for one target, you can instead use the following command:

```
vmkiscsi-tool -C -t <target iqn> <hba-name>
```

Or you can use this:

```
esxcli iscsi session list --name <iSCSI Target Name>
```

Or you can use the shorthand version of this command:

```
esxcli iscsi session list -n <iSCSI Target Name>
```

Here is an example using `vmkiscsi-tool`:

```
vmkiscsi-tool -C -t iqn.1992-04.com.emc:cx.apm00064000064.a0 vmhba2
```

Here is an example using `esxcli`:

```
esxcli iscsi session list --name iqn.1992-04.com.emc:cx.apm00064000064.a0
```

Listing 4.2 shows sample output of the first command, `vmkiscsi-tool`.

Listing 4.2   Listing iSCSI sessions with a specific target using `vmkiscsi-tool`

```
vmkiscsi-tool -C -t iqn.1992-04.com.emc:cx.apm00064000064.a0 vmhba3
------ Target [iqn.1992-04.com.emc:cx.apm00064000064.a0] info ------
NAME                            : iqn.1992-04.com.emc:cx.apm00064000064.a0
ALIAS                           : 0064.a0
DISCOVERY METHOD FLAGS          : 8
SEND TARGETS DISCOVERY SETTABLE : 0
SEND TARGETS DISCOVERY ENABLED  : 1
Portal 0                        : 10.23.1.30:3260


-------------------------------------------
   Session info [isid:00:c0:dd:09:b6:c5]:
      - authMethod:            NONE
      - dataPduInOrder:        YES
      - dataSequenceInOrder:   YES
      - defaultTime2Retain:    0
      - errorRecoveryLevel:    0
      - firstBurstLength:      128
      - immediateData:         NO
      - initialR2T:            YES
      - isid:                  00:c0:dd:09:b6:c5
      - maxBurstLength:        512
      - maxConnections:        1
      - maxOutstandingR2T:     1
      - targetPortalGroupTag:  1
      Connection info [id:0]:
         - connectionId:             0
         - dataDigest:               NONE
```

```
        - headerDigest:                 NONE
        - ifMarker:                     NO
        - ifMarkInt:                    0
        - maxRecvDataSegmentLength:     128
        - maxTransmitDataSegmentLength: 128
        - ofMarker:                     NO
        - ofMarkInt:                    0
        - Initial Remote Address:       10.23.1.30
        - Current Remote Address:       10.23.1.30
        - Current Local Address:        10.23.1.215
        - Session Created at:           Not Available
        - Connection Created at:        Not Available
        - Connection Started at:        Not Available
        - State:                        LOGGED_IN
```

In Listing 4.2, the iSCSI session ID (ISID) is listed with colons separating the bytes. Listing 4.3 shows sample output from the second command, using `esxcli`.

Listing 4.3 Listing active iSCSI sessions with a specific target using `esxcli`

```
esxcli iscsi session list -n iqn.1992-04.com.emc:cx.apm00064000064.a0

vmhba3,iqn.1992-04.com.emc:cx.apm00064000064.a0,00c0dd09b6c5
    Adapter: vmhba3
    Target: iqn.1992-04.com.emc:cx.apm00064000064.a0
    ISID: 00c0dd09b6c5
    TargetPortalGroupTag: 1
    AuthenticationMethod: none
    DataPduInOrder: true
    DataSequenceInOrder: true
    DefaultTime2Retain: 0
    DefaultTime2Wait: 2
    ErrorRecoveryLevel: 0
    FirstBurstLength: Irrelevant
    ImmediateData: false
    InitialR2T: true
    MaxBurstLength: 512
    MaxConnections: 1
    MaxOutstandingR2T: 1
    TSIH: 0
```

Notice that the `esxcli` output does not include connection information. You can obtain a list of connections from the same iSCSI session by using the following `esxcli` command:

```
esxcli iscsi session connection list --isid=<session-id>
```

This is the shorthand version for this command:

```
esxcli iscsi session connection list -s <session-id>
```

Here is an example:

```
esxcli iscsi session connection list -s 00c0dd09b6c5
```

Listing 4.4 shows the output.

Listing 4.4 Listing iSCSI session's connection information

```
vmhba3,iqn.1992-04.com.emc:cx.apm00064000064.a0,00c0dd09b6c5,0
    Adapter: vmhba3
    Target: iqn.1992-04.com.emc:cx.apm00064000064.a0
    ISID: 00c0dd09b6c5
    CID: 0
    DataDigest: NONE
    HeaderDigest: NONE
    IFMarker: false
    IFMarkerInterval: 0
    MaxRecvDataSegmentLength: 128
    MaxTransmitDataSegmentLength: 128
    OFMarker: false
    OFMarkerInterval: 0
    ConnectionAddress: 10.23.1.30
    RemoteAddress: 10.23.1.30
    LocalAddress: 10.23.1.215
    SessionCreateTime: Not Available
    ConnectionCreateTime: Not Available
    ConnectionStartTime: Not Available
    State: logged_in

vmhba3,iqn.1992-04.com.emc:cx.apm00064000064.b0,00c0dd09b6c5,0
    Adapter: vmhba3    Target: iqn.1992-04.com.emc:cx.apm00064000064.b0
    ISID: 00c0dd09b6c5
    CID: 0
    DataDigest: NONE
    HeaderDigest: NONE
    IFMarker: false
```

```
IFMarkerInterval: 0
MaxRecvDataSegmentLength: 128
MaxTransmitDataSegmentLength: 16
OFMarker: false
OFMarkerInterval: 0
ConnectionAddress: 10.23.2.30
RemoteAddress: 10.23.2.30
LocalAddress: 10.23.1.215
SessionCreateTime: Not Available
ConnectionCreateTime: Not Available
ConnectionStartTime: Not Available
State: free
```

I truncated the output in Listing 4.4 to show two connections. Note in the listing that the two connections are between the same HBA, vmhba3, and the same remote address, 10.23.1.30. This is an example of multiple connections in the same session. Also note that the first connection shows that the state is `logged_in`, whereas the second one shows the state is `free`. This means that the first one is an active connection, and the second one is not.

iSCSI Portals

A *portal* is a component of a network entity that has a TCP/IP network address and may be used by an iSCSI node within that network entity for the connection within one of its iSCSI sessions.

A portal in an initiator is identified by its IP address. A portal in a target is identified by its IP address and its listening TCP port. The default port is 3260. Figure 4.3 shows network portals on an iSCSI server listening on port 3260. On the host's side, two iSCSI initiators also have network portals associated with the initiators' IP addresses.

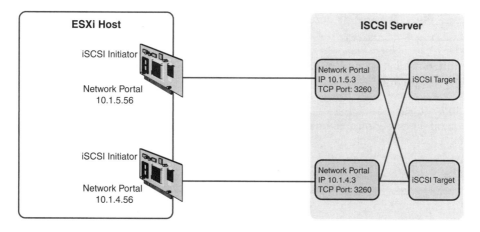

Figure 4.3 iSCSI portals

Using SSH, vMA, or ESXCLI (as discussed later in this chapter), you can list the iSCSI target portals with `esxcli` commands. The commands shown in Listings 4.5 and 4.6 return the target portals for HW initiators and SW initiators, respectively.

Listing 4.5   Listing iSCSI target portals—HW initiators

```
~ # esxcli iscsi adapter target portal list
Adapter Target                                        IP          Port  Tpgt
------- ------------------------------------------    ----------  ----  ----
vmhba2  iqn.1992-04.com.emc:cx.apm00064000064.a0      10.23.1.30  3260  1
vmhba2  iqn.1992-04.com.emc:cx.apm00064000064.a1      10.23.1.31  3260  2
vmhba2  iqn.1992-04.com.emc:cx.apm00064000064.b0      10.23.2.30  3260  3
vmhba2  iqn.1992-04.com.emc:cx.apm00064000064.b1      10.23.2.31  3260  4

vmhba3  iqn.1992-04.com.emc:cx.apm00064000064.a0      10.23.1.30  3260  1
vmhba3  iqn.1992-04.com.emc:cx.apm00064000064.a1      10.23.1.31  3260  2
vmhba3  iqn.1992-04.com.emc:cx.apm00064000064.b0      10.23.2.30  3260  3
vmhba3  iqn.1992-04.com.emc:cx.apm00064000064.b1      10.23.2.31  3260  4
```

NOTE

In Listing 4.5 I added a blank line between HBAs for readability.

Listing 4.6   Listing iSCSI target portals—SW initiators

```
~ # esxcli iscsi adapter target portal list

Adapter Target                                       IP           Port  Tpgt
------- ------------------------------------------   -----------  ----  ----
vmhba34 iqn.1992-04.com.emc:cx.apm00071501971.a0 10.131.7.179 3260  1
vmhba34 iqn.1992-04.com.emc:cx.apm00071501971.b0 10.131.7.180 3260  2
```

The main difference between HW and SW initiator output is the vmhba enumeration. (See the "iSCSI Initiators" section, later in this chapter.)

As shown in Listings 4.7 and 4.8, you can use an alternative command with `vmkiscsi-tool`, which might be deprecated in a future release. It is also not available remotely via vMA or vCLI.

Listing 4.7   Alternative method for listing iSCSI target portals—HW initiators

```
~ # vmkiscsi-tool -T -l vmhba3 |awk '/iqn/||/Portal/{print}'


------ Target [iqn.1992-04.com.emc:cx.apm00064000064.a0] info ------
NAME          : iqn.1992-04.com.emc:cx.apm00064000064.a0
Portal 0      : 10.23.1.30:3260
------ Target [iqn.1992-04.com.emc:cx.apm00064000064.a1] info ------
NAME          : iqn.1992-04.com.emc:cx.apm00064000064.a1
Portal 0      : 10.23.1.31:3260
```

Listing 4.8   Alternative method for listing iSCSI target portals—SW initiators

```
~ # vmkiscsi-tool -T -l vmhba34 |awk '/iqn/||/Portal/{print}'


------ Target [iqn.1992-04.com.emc:cx.apm00071501971.a0] info ------
NAME          : iqn.1992-04.com.emc:cx.apm00071501971.a0
Portal 0      : 10.131.7.179:3260
------ Target [iqn.1992-04.com.emc:cx.apm00071501971.b0] info ------
NAME          : iqn.1992-04.com.emc:cx.apm00071501971.b0
Portal 0      : 10.131.7.180:3260
```

The main difference between the output from HW and SW initiators is the vmhba number used. The next section, "iSCSI Initiators," provides details about the differences between these initiators.

iSCSI Initiators

iSCSI initiators are used to connect hosts to iSCSI storage arrays over an Ethernet network. vSphere 6 supports two types of iSCSI initiators:

- **Hardware initiators**—Hardware initiators are physical adapters that are available in two classes:

  - **Dependent**—These are physical adapters that depend on ESXi for network stack, initiator configuration, and management. The adapter offloads iSCSI processing from the host using TOE or TCP Offload Engine. It requires a VMkernel port group configured and linked to the adapter.

  - **Independent**—These are physical adapters that offload iSCSI and network processing from the host. They provide their own management capabilities via their firmware. However, you can still configure them via vSphere Client.

- **Software initiators**—This is a software implementation of the iSCSI initiator. ESXi includes this software as a VMkernel component. It requires a VMkernel port group configured and linked to physical network interface cards (NICs) in the ESXi host.

iSCSI Names and Addresses

According to RFC 3721 (http://tools.ietf.org/html/rfc3721):

> The main addressable, discoverable entity in iSCSI is an iSCSI node. An iSCSI node can be an initiator, a target, or both. The rules for constructing an iSCSI name are specified in RFC3720.

iSCSI nodes, initiators, and targets require special names for the purpose of identification. These names can be in one of the following formats:

- IQN (iSCSI qualified name)
- EUI (extended unique identifier)
- NAA (T11 Network Address Authority)
- Alias

IQN

IQN is an iSCSI naming scheme constructed to give an organizational naming authority the flexibility to further subdivide the responsibility for name creation to subordinate naming authorities.

This is the commonly used identifier among HBA and array vendors. The IQN format is defined in RFC 3721. The example in Figure 4.4 shows a hardware initiator's IQN.

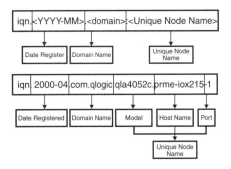

Figure 4.4   HW initiators—Anatomy of IQN

The IQN includes the following items:

- The string `iqn`

- `<YYYY-MM>`, which is a date code specifying the year and month in which the organization registered the domain or subdomain name used as the naming authority string

- `<domain>`, which is the organizational naming authority string and consists of a valid, reversed DNS domain or subdomain name

- `<Node Identifier>`, which is a unique identifier for each node and is assigned by the organizational naming authority stated in `<domain>` (for example, qlogic.com) or can be manually assigned during configuration

In Figure 4.4, the node name is based on the HBA's model (for example,qla4052c) in addition to other strings assigned during the HBA configuration. In this case, it is the ESXi relative DNS host name (that is, the FQDN without the domain name). The `-1` at the end of the name in this case is a port identifier of a dual-port HBA. The second port of this HBA would be named as follows:

```
iqn.2000-04.com.qlogic:qla4052c.prme-iox215-2
```

A similar approach is used for software initiators, as illustrated in Figure 4.5, with the difference that the naming authority in this example is com.vmware. The unique node name is a combination of the host name and a unique string.

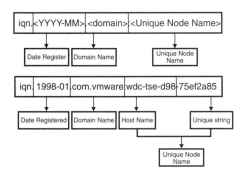

Figure 4.5   SW initiators—Anatomy of IQN

iSCSI EUI

The iSCSI EUI naming format allows a naming authority to use IEEE EUI-64 identifiers in constructing iSCSI names. The details of constructing EUI-64 identifiers are specified by the IEEE Registration Authority (see http://standards.ieee.org/develop/regauth/tut/eui64.pdf). I discuss this further in Chapter 5, "vSphere Pluggable Storage Architecture (PSA)."

EUI is not commonly used by HBA vendors. However, you might see some LUNs using this ID format, regardless of whether they are iSCSI-based, but the ID is usually longer than the following example:

```
eui.02004567A425678D
```

NAA ID

I discuss NAA IDs in Chapter 5, in the context of identifying LUNs.

Alias

iSCSI alias is used to simplify identification of initiators or targets. The alias is not used as part of the authentication credentials. It is ignored by arrays that do not use it.

Here is an example from a storage array configuration's alias table:

```
+--Connected-To-These-Targets----------------------
|
|  Alias            Target Name
|
|  ESXi1 HBA1       iqn.1995-04.com.example:sn.5551212.target.450
|  ESXi1 HBA2       iqn.1995-04.com.example:sn.5551212.target.489
|  Exchange 2       iqn.1995-04.com.example:sn.8675309
|
+--------------------------------------------------
```

Locating an iSCSI Initiator's IQN in vSphere 6 Hosts

In the process of troubleshooting iSCSI connectivity or mapping out an existing vSphere 6 host's iSCSI connectivity, you need to identify the installed initiators' IQNs. In this section I show you how to do that via the user interface (UI) as well as the command-line interface (CLI).

Locating an iSCSI Initiator's IQN Using the UI

To locate an iSCSI initiator's IQN using the UI, you follow this procedure (see Figure 4.6):

1. Log on to the vCenter server that manages the ESXi 6 host, using the vSphere 6.0 Web Client as a user with Administrator privileges.

2. Navigate to the Hosts and Clusters view.

3. Select the ESXi host you are examining.

4. Select the **Manage** tab.

5. Click the **Storage** button.

6. Select the **Storage Adapters** section.

7. Select the iSCSI vmhba. (In this example, it is vmhba33.) Note that the IQN is listed in the **Identifier** column.

8. In the Adapter Details section, select the **Properties** tab. In the General section, the IQN is listed in the **iSCSI Name** field. There, you also see the IQN.

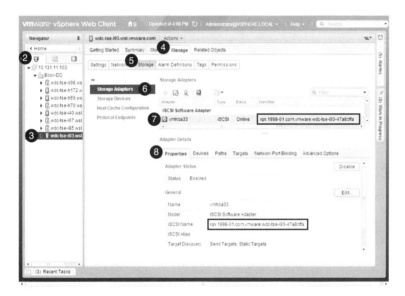

Figure 4.6   Example of a SW initiator—vSphere 6 Web Client UI

Observe that, in the Storage Adapters pane, the HBAs are grouped under the heading iSCSI Software Adapter, which is the HBA's type. You can also see this listed in the Details pane in the Model field.

The WWN column value here is as follows:

```
iqn.1998-01.com.vmware:wdc-tse-i93-47a8bffa
```

Based on the discussion from the previous sections, you can identify this IQN as follows:

1. The naming authority is registered as vmware.com.

2. The initiator's name is wdc-tse-i93.

3. The port ID/unique string is 47a8bffa.

HW initiators are listed in a similar fashion in the Storage Adapters pane. However, the HBAs are grouped under the heading of the adapter's model or model family (for example, QLA405Xc iSCSI host bus adapter, which is the HBA's model). You can see this model also listed in the Details pane in the field Model.

The following are examples of WWN column values:

```
iqn.2000-04.com.qlogic:qla4052c.prme-iox215-1
iqn.2000-04.com.qlogic:qla4052c.prme-iox215-2
```

These are the IQNs used as examples earlier in this chapter.

> **NOTE**
>
> An ESXi host can have only one SW initiator, which can be connected to more than one vmnic (uplink). (See more about port binding later in this chapter.)
>
> In contrast, the ESXi host can have more than one HW initiator, and they can be dedicated to one physical port each. More on that later in this chapter.

Locating an iSCSI Initiator's IQN Using SSH

To list the iSCSI initiators using the CLI, follow these steps:

1. Connect to the ESXi 6 host by using an SSH client as a user with root privileges.

2. Use the following command to list all iSCSI initiators in the ESXi host:

   ```
   esxcli iscsi adapter list
   ```

   Figure 4.7 shows an example of output from this command.

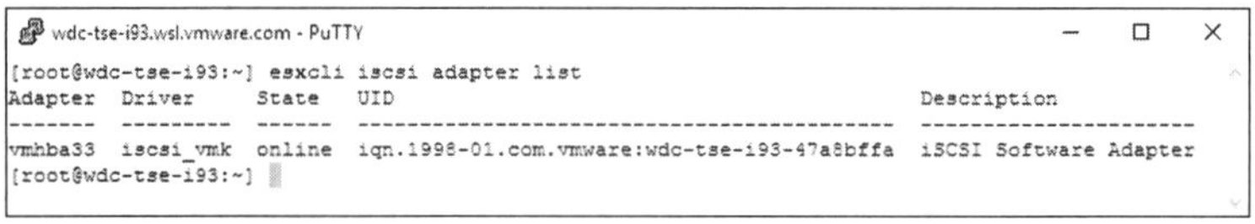

Figure 4.7   Listing SW initiators—SSH

In this example, the initiator has the attributes listed in Table 4.2. Also in this example, the initiator type is clearly stated in the Description column of the output.

Table 4.2 Attributes of an iSCSI initiator

Attribute	Value
Adapter (name)	vmhba33
Driver	iscsi_vmk
State	Online
UID	iqn.1998-01.com.vmware:wdc-tse-i93-47a8bffa
Description	iSCSI software adapter

Similar output for a HW initiator (for example, vmhba2) might have the attributes listed in Table 4.3.

Table 4.3 Attributes of an iSCSI HW initiator

Attribute	Value
Adapter (name)	vmhba2
Driver	qla4xxx
State	Online
UID	iqn.2000-04.com.qlogic:qla4052c.prme-iox215-1
Description	4022 Family iSCSI controller

An Alternative Approach to Listing iSCSI Initiators Using the CLI

For an alternative approach to listing the iSCSI initiators using the CLI, you can follow this procedure:

1. Connect to the ESXi 6 host by using an SSH client as a user with root privileges.

2. Use the following command to list all iSCSI initiators in the ESXi host:

    ```
    esxcli iscsi adapter list
    ```

3. Run the following command to list any iSCSI initiators:

    ```
    esxcli storage core adapter list |grep "Name\| ---\| iqn" |less -S
    ```

    Figure 4.8 shows an example of output from a host with a software initiator.

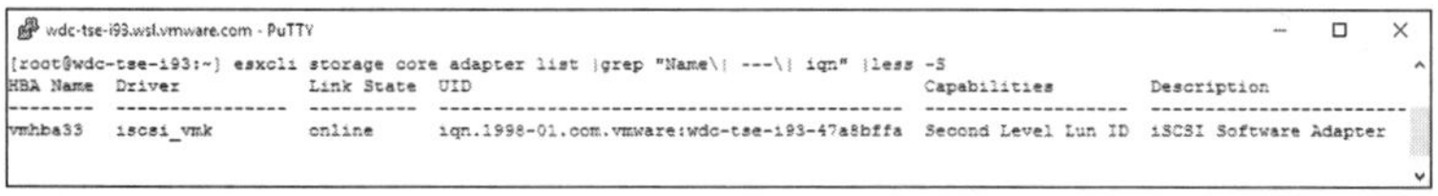

Figure 4.8 Alternative method for listing HW initiators—SSH

Hardware initiators have similar output, where the Driver column lists the actual adapter's driver (for example, qla4xxx for QLogic adapters).

You can verify the number of adapters by checking the PCI hardware information, using the following command:

```
lspci | grep -i qle
```

This command returns output similar to that shown in Figure 4.9.

```
10.112.9.10 - PuTTY                                                    —   □   ×
[root@blr-colo-eeqa-03:~] lspci |grep -i qle
0000:0b:01.1 Network controller: QLogic Corp QLE406Xc iSCSI Host Bus Adapter [vmhba4]
0000:0b:01.3 Network controller: QLogic Corp QLE406Xc iSCSI Host Bus Adapter [vmhba5]
[root@blr-colo-eeqa-03:~]
```

Figure 4.9   Finding PCI locations of iSCSI HW initiators—SSH

In this example, the ESXi host has two QLogic HW iSCSI initiators. Observe that both adapters share the same name but have two different port IDs, –1 and –3, which might indicate that this is a dual-port HBA.

In Figure 4.9, the first column shows the location of the adapter on the PCI bus, in this format:

```
ddd:BBB:DD:F
```

where:

```
ddd: PCI Domain number (this is usually 000)
BBB: PCI Bus number
DD: PCI Device number
F: PCI Function number
```

In this example, the adapters are at the following PCI location:

```
Bus 0b: Device 1: Function 1
Bus 0b: Device 1: Function 3
```

This means that it is a single adapter with two physical functions (PF—that is, ports). This is due to the adapter not having a PCI-to-PCI bridge; if it did, each adapter would have a different device number and a single PCI function.

Notice that the output also lists the assigned vmhba numbers: vmhba4 and vmhba5. You can match this with what you see in the UI.

3. Run the following command if you have a SW initiator presenting LUN1 and you
    want to list the initiator's IQN:

```
esxcfg-mpath --list-paths |grep -i iqn |grep L1 |sed 's/Target.*$//'
```

You can also run the shorthand version of the command:

```
esxcfg-mpath -b |grep -i iqn |grep L1 |sed 's/Target.*$//'
```

The output of the shorthand version looks as shown in Figure 4.10.

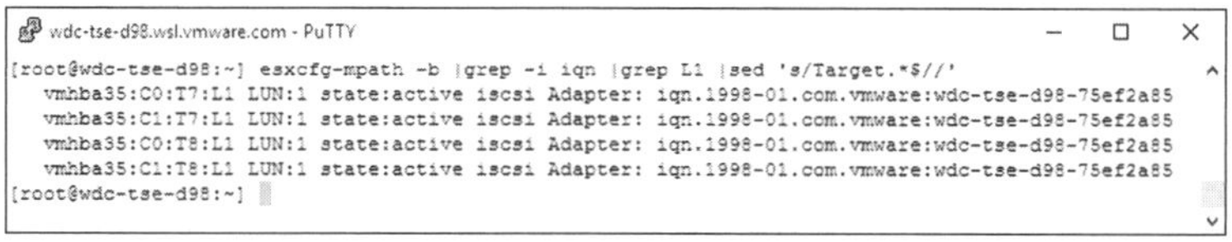

Figure 4.10 Alternative method for listing iSCSI SW initiators

In this example, the SW initiator is vmhba35, with WWN:

```
iqn.1998-01.com.vmware:wdc-tse-d98-75ef2a85
```

NOTE

The same procedure can be used for HW initiators. You can tell the difference from the
IQN; if it has com.vmware as the naming authority, it is a SW initiator. Otherwise, it is a
HW initiator.

Locating an iSCSI Initiator's IQN Using vMA 6.0

The following procedure assumes that you have already installed and configured vMA 6.0,
as outlined in the VMA guide available at www.vmware.com/go/vma, which is also where
you can download the appliance:

1. Log on to vMA as vi-admin or a user who can use sudo (which is added to the
    sudoers file using the visudo editor).

2. Add each ESXi host you plan to manage via this appliance:

```
vifp addserver <ESXi host name> --username root --password <root's
password>
```

3. Verify that the host has been successfully added:

```
vifp listservers
```

NOTE

If you omit the `-password` parameter, you are prompted to enter it.

---

4. Repeat steps 2 and 3 for each host you want to manage via this vMA.

5. Set the ESXi server as the target for subsequent commands:

```
vifptarget --set <ESXi host name>
```

You may also use the shorthand version of the command:

```
vifptarget -s <ESXi host name>
```

The output of the shorthand version of the command is shown in Figure 4.11.

Figure 4.11   Setting the target managed host—vMA 6.0

Notice that the prompt changes to include the ESXi host name.

6. Run the following command to list iSCSI initiators:

```
esxcli iscsi adapter list
```

If your environment does not use a Certificate Authority (CA), you may get an error that the server SHA-1 thumbprint is not trusted, as shown in Figure 4.12.

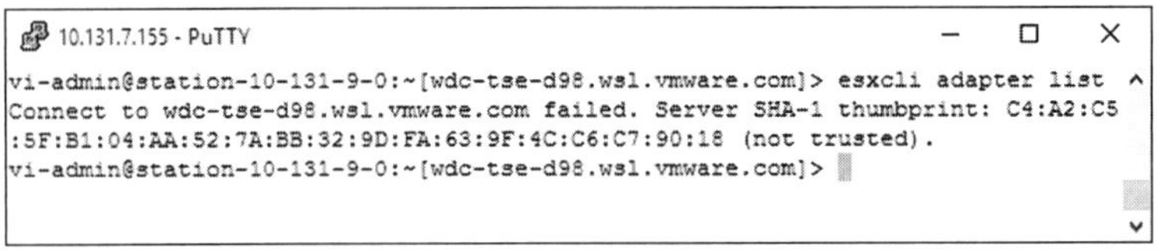

Figure 4.12   Host SHA-1 thumbprint not trusted error—vMA 6.0

To work around this, add the thumbprint to the credstore by using this command:

```
/usr/lib/vmware-vcli/apps/general/credstore_admin.pl add -s [server-name]
-t [thumbprint]
```

The following is an example:

```
/usr/lib/vmware-vcli/apps/general/credstore_admin.pl add -s wdc-tse-
  d98.wsl.vmware.com -t C4:A2:C5:5F:B1:04:AA:52:7A:BB:32:9D:FA:63:9F:4C:C6:
  C7:90:18
```

Now you can rerun the command without getting the error. The command and output are shown in Figure 4.13

Figure 4.13   Listing iSCSI SW initiators—vMA 6.0

In this example, the initiator has the attributes listed in Table 4.4.

Table 4.4 Attributes of an iSCSI initiator

Attribute	Value
Adapter (name)	vmhba35
Driver	lscsi_vmk
State	Online
UID	iqn.1998-01.com.vmware:wdc-tse-d98-75ef2a85
Description	iSCSI software adapter

Locating an iSCSI Initiator's IQN Using the Linux vCLI

Using vCLI is similar to using vMA but without the fast-pass (FP) facility, which provides `vifp` and `vifptarget` commands. This means you have to provide the host's credentials with each command, including `--server`, `--username`, and `--password`, in addition to the rest of the command options used in the preceding section. For example, you could use this command:

```
esxcli --server <host name> --username root --password <password> iscsi
adapter list
```

and this command:

```
esxcfg-mpath --list-paths --server <host name> --username root --password
<password> |grep iqn |sed 's/Target.*$//'
```

Or you could use this shorthand version:

```
esxcfg-mpath -b --server <host name> --username root --password <password>
|grep iqn |sed 's/Target.*$//'
```

TIP

You can use the `--credstore` option (variable `VI_CREDSTORE`) to avoid providing the cre-. dentials details with every command you run against the ESXi hosts.

The name of the credential store file defaults to `<HOME>/.vmware/credstore/` `vicredentials.xml` on Linux and `<APPDATA>/VMware/credstore/` `vicredentials.xml` on Windows.

If you receive the `SHA-1 thumbprint host not trusted` error, use `credstore_admin.pl`, as shown earlier under Figure 4.14. The path to the script on the Linux CLI is the same as for vMA. However, the path on the Windows CLI is C:\Program Files\VMware\ VMware vSphere CLI\perl\apps\general\credstore_admin.pl instead.

See the vMA 6.0 user guide for additional details.

NOTE

The syntax for using the Windows version of vCLI is the same as that for the Linux version. Keep in mind that additional OS-specific commands/tools available on Linux might not be available on Windows. I covered the Linux version only, and you may apply the same procedure on Windows, substituting non-ESXCLI commands with relevant commands that are available on Windows. For example, on Linux I infrequently use `sed` and `awk`, which are not available on Windows by default. You can get a Windows version of `sed` from http:// gnuwin32.sourceforge.net/packages/sed.htm and `awk` from http://gnuwin32.sourceforge.net/ packages/gawk.htm.

Configuring iSCSI Initiators

Configuring HW iSCSI initiators is somewhat different from configuring SW initiators. Before diving into the details of each, make sure to review the "Overview of iSCSI Connectivity" section at the beginning of this chapter.

Configuring an Independent HW Initiator

You can configure hardware initiators via their own firmware, and you can modify them by using vSphere Client.

Configuring a HW iSCSI Initiator via the HBA's BIOS

Using a QLA405x dual-port HBA as an example, here are the steps to configure the HBA using its BIOS:

1. Boot the host and, when prompted, press the key combination to access the HBA's BIOS. In this example, the hotkey for the QLogic HBA is **Ctrl+Q**.

2. If you have more than one HBA installed, select the HBA you want to configure and then press **Enter**.

3. In the QLogic Fast!UTIL Options menu that appears, select the **Configuration Settings** option and then press **Enter** (see Figure 4.14).

4. Select the **Host Adapter Settings** option and press **Enter** (see Figure 4.15).

5. Select **Initiator IP Settings** and press **Enter**. In the resulting menu, enter the HBA's IP settings by selecting each field and then pressing **Enter**. Fill in the corresponding address/subnet mask (see Figure 4.16). When you're done entering each field's value, press **Enter** to go back to the Initiator IP Settings menu.

6. Press **Esc** *three times*.

7. When prompted, select **Save Changes** and then press **Enter** (see Figure 4.17).

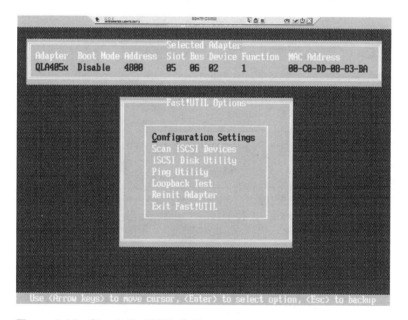

Figure 4.14   QLogic Fast!UTIL Options menu

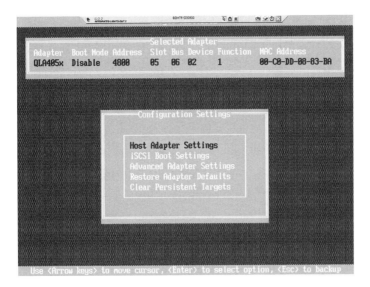

Figure 4.15   Accessing the Host Adapter Settings menu

Figure 4.16   Host Adapter Settings menu

8. To configure a second port on the HBA or on another QLogic iSCSI HBA, at the Fast!UTIL Options menu, scroll down to **Select Host Adapter** and then press **Enter**.

9. Select the adapter from the displayed list and then press **Enter**.

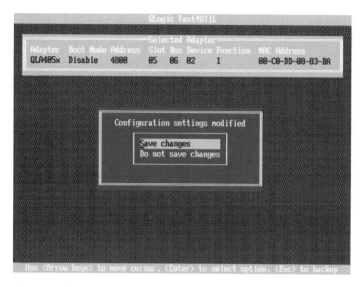

Figure 4.17 Saving adapter configuration changes

10. Repeat steps 2 through 7.

11. When you are done configuring all of the HBA's ports, press **Esc** *twice* at the Fast!UTIL Options menu.

12. When prompted, select **Reboot System** (see Figure 4.18).

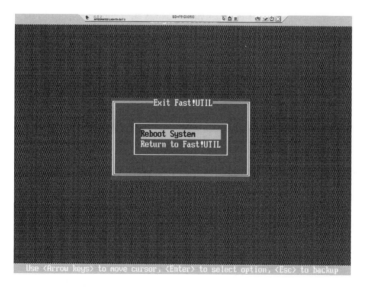

Figure 4.18 Exiting Fast!UTIL and rebooting the system

Modifying an Independent HW iSCSI Initiator's Configuration via vSphere 6 Web Client

There is no virtual network configuration required for this class of initiators. The following steps cover using vSphere Client to configure or make configuration changes to independent HW initiators:

1. Install the HBA into an available PCI slot, matching the adapter's PCI standard and clock speed.

2. Connect the HBA to the iSCSI network and configure the VLAN if the design calls for it.

3. Power on the ESXi host.

4. Connect to the vCenter server that manages the ESXi 6 host, using the vSphere 6.0 Web Client as a user with Administrator privileges.

5. Navigate to the **Hosts and Clusters** view, if you're not already there, then click the **Hosts and Clusters** tab.

6. Locate the ESXi 6 host in the inventory tree and select it.

7. Select the **Manage** tab.

8. Click the **Storage** button.

9. Select **Storage Adapters**.

10. Locate the HBA with the model name or HBA family name that matches the HBA you are configuring and select it. In this example, it is a QLA406xc family HBA, and the HBA name is vmhba3 (see Figure 4.19).

11. In the Adapter Details section, click the **Properties** tab. The display should look similar to Figure 4.19.

12. To modify the IQN, click the **Edit** button.

13. In the dialog that appears (see Figure 4.20), modify the vendor's name authority and the device name that are prepopulated in the iSCSI Name field, if the design calls for it.

14. Type an alias, if you want to assign one to this HBA.

15. Click **OK** to apply the changes and close the dialog.

16. Select the **Network Settings** tab.

17. Click the **Edit** button.

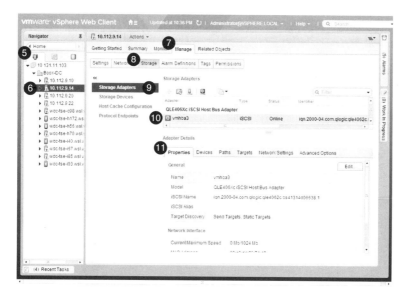

Figure 4.19   Displaying the iSCSI HW initiator properties—vSphere 6 Web Client

Figure 4.20   Modifying IQN and alias—vSphere 6 Web Client

18. Select **IPv4 Settings** or **IPv6 Settings** to fill in the IP settings with the IP address you want to assign to this HBA. (DNS settings are optional.)

19. Click **OK** to apply the changes and close the dialog (see Figure 4.21). (This figure was actually collected from an HBA that was already configured.)

If your storage array requires the CHAP (Challenge-Handshake Authentication Protocol) authentication method, proceed to the next step. Otherwise, proceed to the "Configuring Target Discovery" section, later in this chapter.

20. Select the **Properties** tab.

21. Scroll down to the **Authentication** section.

22. Click the **Edit** button. The Edit Authentication dialog shown in Figure 4.22 appears.

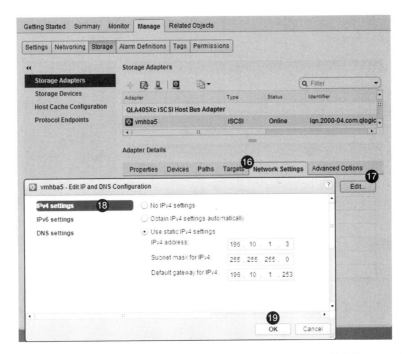

Figure 4.21   Configuring or modifying an iSCSI HW initiator's iSCSI properties and IP settings

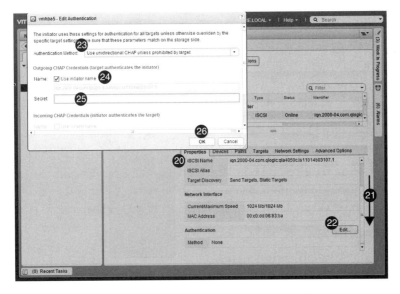

Figure 4.22   Configuring CHAP credentials—vSphere 6 Web Client

23. Select the **Use unidirectional CHAP unless prohibited by target** option from the pull-down menu.

24. Check the **Use initiator name** box unless you want to manually enter the IQN here. (But note that it is a good idea to use the check box to avoid making typographical errors.)

25. In the Secret field, enter the password assigned to this initiator by the storage array.

26. Click **OK**.

HW initiators provide static discovery as well as dynamic discovery of iSCSI targets. However, with certain iSCSI storage arrays that present each LUN on its own separate target, using static discovery can be impractical for a large number of LUNs.

To configure target discovery, proceed to the "Configuring Target Discovery" section, later in this chapter.

Configuring Dependent HW Initiators

You configure dependent HW initiators exactly the same way you configure independent HW initiators, as described earlier in this chapter. The only difference is that you can only configure dependent HW initiators via the vSphere UI, whereas you can configure independent HW initiators via the HBA's firmware as well. You also must create a VMkernel port group and then bind it to the dependent HW initiator's HBA.

Creating a VMkernel Port Group (vmknic) on a Distributed Switch (vDS)

Follow these steps to create a VMkernel Port group (vmknic) on a distributed switch (vDS):

1. Navigate to the **Network** tab in vSphere Web Client and locate the vDS.

2. Right-click the vDS and select **Distributed Port Group** and then select **New Distributed Port Group** (see Figure 4.23).

3. Assign a name to the port group (for example, **iSCSI Network**) and then click **Next**.

4. Select **Ephemeral - no binding** in the Port binding field.

5. Specify a value for Network resource pool or leave it as **(default)**, depending on your network design.

6. If your iSCSI targets are in a VLAN, select **VLAN** as the VLAN type. Otherwise, leave the selection as **None**. Generally, it is recommended to isolate your storage traffic on a dedicated physical network or VLAN.

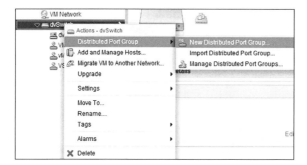

Figure 4.23   Creating a distributed port group

7. Click **Next**, and review the changes listed, and then click **Finish**.

8. Right-click the vDS and select **Add and Manage Hosts** (see Figure 4.24).

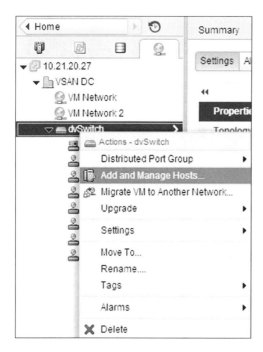

Figure 4.24   Managing vDS hosts

9. Select **Manage host networking** and then click **Next**.

10. Click **Attached hosts**.

11. Select all hosts assigned to the distributed switch from the list.

12. Click **OK**.

13. Click **Next** (see Figure 4.25).

TIP

You can select all hosts by clicking the check box to the left side of the Host column label.

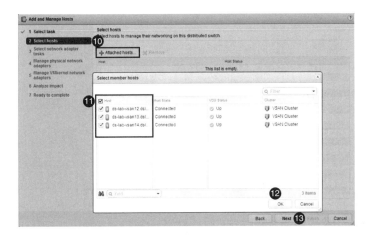

Figure 4.25   Selecting hosts to manage vDS

14. Select only the **Manage VMkernel adapters** box and then click **Next** (see Figure 4.26).

Figure 4.26   Selecting Manage VMkernel adapters

15. Select a host from the list then click **New adapter** (see Figure 4.27). For the new adapter, do the following:

Figure 4.27   Adding a new adapter

a. From Select an existing network, click **Browse**.

b. Select the port group you created in steps 2 through 7. In this example, the port group is **iSCSI Network**.

c. Click **OK**.

d. Click **Next** (see Figure 4.28).

Figure 4.28   Selecting a port group

16. In the Port properties dialog, select the IP setting according to your network design (for example, IPv4, IPv6, or IPv4 and IPv6) and then click **Next** (see Figure 4.29). vSphere 6 supports IPv6 for iSCSI network. Dependent iSCSI initiators offload the iSCSI workload to the physical adapter.

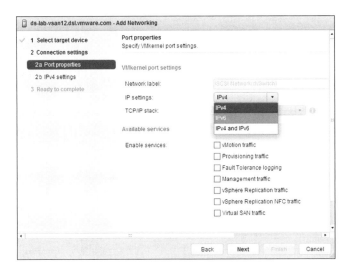

Figure 4.29   Configuring port group properties

17. Configure the port group IP settings by using DHCP or static setting and then click **Next**.

18. Review the settings and then click **Finish**.

19. Repeat steps 15 through 18 for the remaining hosts in the list. The added vmknics are listed in the dialog as **vmk(*n*) (new)**, where *n* is the vmknic number. In this example, it is **vmk3**.

20. Click **Next** (see Figure 4.30).

21. Click **Next** to see the impact analysis of this operation on the virtual network. If all hosts show No Impact status, you are clear to proceed by clicking **Next** (see Figure 4.31).

22. Review the settings selection dialog and then click **Finish**.

23. To verify that all vmknics were added to the hosts, repeat steps 8 through 14. The vmknics (in this case **vmk3**) show Source Port Group set to **iSCSI Network** (or whatever port group name you defined), and Destination Port Group set to **Do not migrate** (see Figure 4.32).

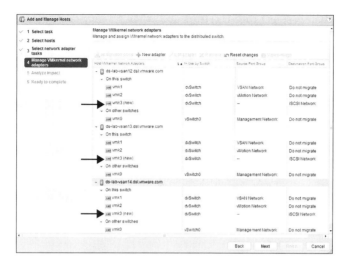

Figure 4.30   vmknic added

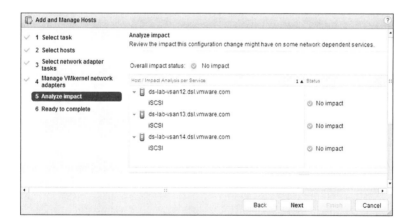

Figure 4.31   Impact analysis

The procedure so far has shown how to create the iSCSI port group and its associated vmknics. However, the configuration is not complete, and you can't yet utilize the dependent HW iSCSI adapter. Before finishing the configuration, let's inspect the adapter's status on one of the hosts first. I will show you how to do that using the vSphere Web Client and also using the CLI.

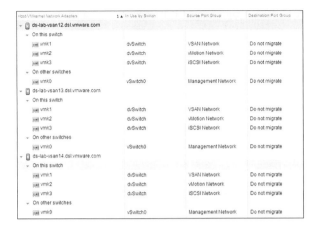

Figure 4.32   Verifying the vmknics added

Inspecting Dependent HW iSCSI HBA Status by Using vSphere Web Client

Follow these steps to inspect dependent HW iSCSI HBA status by using vSphere Web Client:

1. Using the vSphere Web Client, navigate to the **Hosts and Clusters** tab and then select one of the ESXi hosts in the inventory.

2. Select the **Manage** tab.

3. Select the **Storage** section on the top.

4. Select the **Storage Adapters** section.

5. Select the independent iSCSI HW adapter (in this example, it is **vmhba32**).

6. Inspect the **Status** column. Notice that the status is **unbound** (see Figure 4.33).

7. Select the **Targets** tab, and you should receive the error **The host bus adapter is not associated with a vmknic** (see Figure 4.33).

Figure 4.33   Unbound HBA error

Inspecting Dependent HW iSCSI HBA Status by Using the CLI:

Follow these steps to inspect dependent HW iSCSI HBA status by using the CLI:

1. Connect to the ESXi 6 host by using an SSH client as a user with root privileges.

2. Run this command:

   ```
   esxcli iscsi adapter list
   ```

   The output should look as shown in Figure 4.34.

Figure 4.34   Inspecting dependent iSCSI HBA status using the CLI

In this output, the State column for vmhba32 and vmhba33 shows the status as **unbound** for both HBAs.

Binding an Adapter to vmknic

Before you can bind a dependent HW iSCSI HBA to the vmknic assigned to the iSCSI port group, the port group must be configured with a single active uplink, without a standby one.

Binding an Adapter to vmknic with the vSphere Web Client

Follow these steps to bind an adapter to vmknic by using vSphere Web Client:

1. Connect to the vCenter server that manages the ESXi 6 host, using the vSphere 6.0 Web Client as a user with Administrator privileges.

2. Navigate to the **Network** tab and expand the distributed switch object in the inventory.

3. Select the **iSCSI Network** port group.

4. Select the **Manage** tab and then the **Policies** section.

5. Click **Edit** (see Figure 4.35).

6. Select the **Teaming and failover** section.

Figure 4.35   Editing the port group policy

7. Select **Uplink 2**.

8. Click the down arrow twice to move Uplink 2 to the **Unused uplinks** section.

9. Click **OK** (see Figure 4.36).

Figure 4.36   Moving uplink 2

10. Navigate to the **Hosts and Clusters** tab.

11. Select the ESXi host you are configuring.

12. Select **Manage**.

13. Select the **Storage** tab.

14. Select **Storage Adapters**.

15. Select the vmhba you want to bind. In this example, it is **vmhba32**.

16. Select the **Network Port Binding** tab.

17. Click the **Add** icon (the green plus icon) (see Figure 4.37).

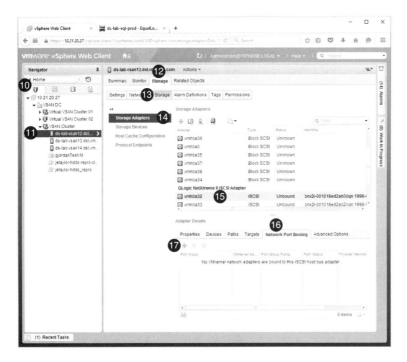

Figure 4.37   Adding port binding

18. In the Bind vmhba32 with VMkernel Adapter dialog, check the box next to **iSCSI Network (dvSwtich)**.

19. Click **OK** (see Figure 4.38).

20. Dismiss the message about rescanning. You will rescan after configuring all dependent HW iSCSI initiators on this host (see Figure 4.39).

Figure 4.38   Selecting a port to bind

Figure 4.39   End result of adding port binding

To configure additional dependent HW iSCSI initiators, repeat all the procedures listed in this section using another port group.

In this example, I use these values:

- Port group: **iSCSI Network 2**
- vmknic: **vmk4**
- Uplink: **uplink 2**
- Physical network adapter: **vmnic3**

Figures 4.40 through 4.43 show relevant screenshots.

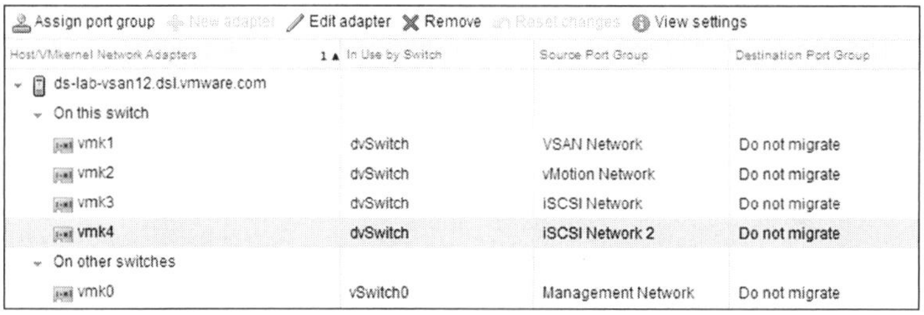

Figure 4.40 vmk4 vmknic added

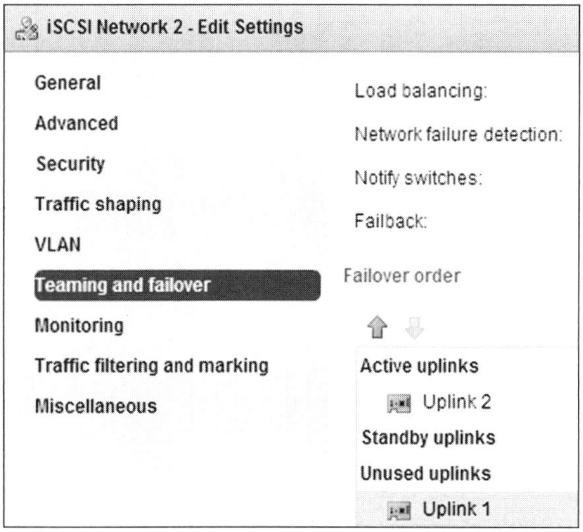

Figure 4.41 Selecting uplink 2

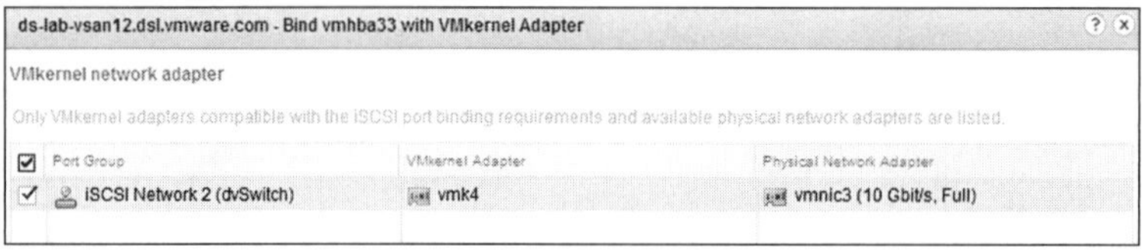

Figure 4.42 Selecting a port to bind to vmhba33

Figure 4.43 vmhba33 configuration final state

The final state of both dependent HW iSCSI initiators (vmhba32 and vmhba33) is now online. To list this state using the CLI, run the following command:

```
esxcli iscsi adapter list
```

The output should look similar to the output in Figure 4.44.

```
[root@ds-lab-vsan12:~] esxcli iscsi adapter list
Adapter  Driver     State   UID                                Description
-------  ---------  ------  --------------------------------  -----------------------------------
vmhba39  iscsi_vmk  online  iqn.1995-05.com.broadcom.vsan12   iSCSI Software Adapter
vmhba32  bnx2i      online  iscsi.vmhba32                     QLogic NetXtreme II iSCSI Adapter
vmhba33  bnx2i      online  iscsi.vmhba33                     QLogic NetXtreme II iSCSI Adapter
[root@ds-lab-vsan12:~]
```

Figure 4.44 Inspecting the final state of iSCSI initiators via the CLI

The next step is to configure iSCSI targets. For a detailed procedure, see the "Configuring Target Discovery" section, later in this chapter.

Configuring a SW iSCSI Initiator

Configuring a software initiator is identical to configuring an independent HW initiator, described earlier in this chapter. The only differences are that you can only configure it via the vSphere UI, and you cannot configure static discovery of iSCSI targets. You also must create a VMkernel port group to assign to the SW initiator.

To configure a software initiator, you need to first create a VMkernel port group and then create the SW iSCSI initiator.

Creating the Port Group

To create a VMkernel port group for use with a SW initiator, use the following steps:

1. Install one or more Ethernet NICs (1Gbps or, preferably, 10Gbps or faster) into an available PCI slot matching the adapter's PCI standard and clock speed.

2. Connect the NIC to the iSCSI network and configure the VLAN if the design calls for it. (Read more about design decisions later in this chapter.)

3. Connect to the vCenter server that manages the ESXi 6 host, using the vSphere 6.0 Web Client as a user with Administrator privileges.

4. If the VC view is at the Home screen, click the **Hosts and Cluster** icon under the Inventories section.

5. If the VC view is not at the Home screen, select the **Hosts and Clusters** tab.

6. Select the ESXi host in the inventory.

7. Click the **Manage** tab.

8. Select the **Networking** section.

9. Select **VMkernel Adapters**.

10. Select the **Add Host Networking** icon (see Figure 4.45).

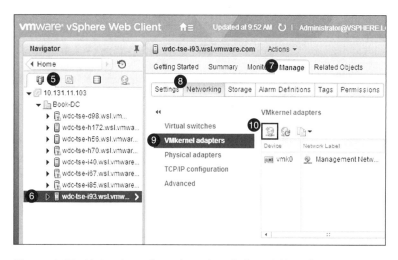

Figure 4.45   Network configuration tab — vSphere 6 Web Client

11. Select **VMkernel Network** as the connection type and then click **Next** (see Figure 4.46).

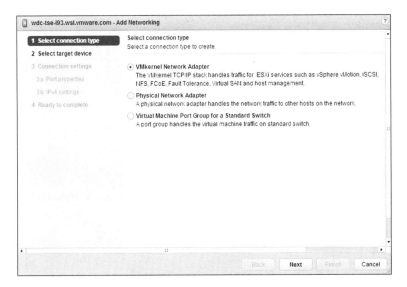

Figure 4.46 Creating a VMkernel port group—Connection type—vSphere 6 Web Client

12. This step depends on the choice of virtual switch you plan to use:

   a. **Exiting a standard switch**: Click Browse and then select the vSwitch from the list (in this example, it is vSwitch0) and then click **OK** and **Next**. Skip to step 19.

   b. **New standard switch:** Select the radio button **New standard switch** and then click **Next**.

   c. **Distributed switch (vDS):** Follow the steps in the section "Creating a VMkernel Port Group (vmknic) on a Distributed Switch (vDS)," earlier in this chapter.

   I cover the detailed network design choices later in this chapter.

13. Click **Add** icon (the green plus sign) to add physical adapters to the switch.

14. In the dialog that appears, select **Active adapter**s in the Failover order group section.

15. Select the vmnic you connected to the storage network. In this example, it is **vmnic3**.

16. To verify that it is connected to the correct network, select the **Properties** tab and then scroll down to the **Networks** row. There, you should see the range of networks listed.

17. Click **OK** (see Figure 4.47).

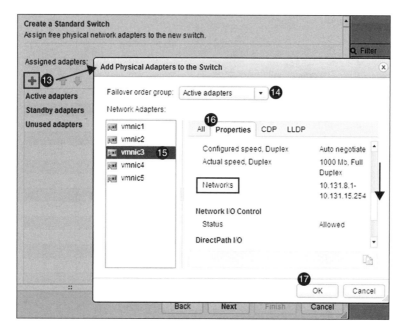

Figure 4.47   Creating a VMkernel port group—Selecting vSwitch—vSphere 6 Web Client

18. Because a software iSCSI initiator does not support NIC teaming, there is no need for additional adapters, so click **Next**.

19. Type the name you selected for the port group network label. In this example, I am using **iSCSI Network**.

20. Select the **VLAN ID** if your design calls for it. Make sure to match the VLAN to which the iSCSI storage array is connected.

21. If your storage network is not on the default TCP/IP stack, select the network from the dropdown list. vSphere 6 introduced support for multiple VMkernel TCP/IP stacks. This allows for connecting VMkernel ports to different networks with separate default gateway addresses. In the past, VMkernel allowed a single default gateway. I cover how to create a custom TCP/IP stack later in this chapter.

22. Leave all check boxes unchecked, as shown in Figure 4.48, and click **Next**.

23. Select the **Use static IPv4 settings** radio button and then enter the IP settings you allocated for this port group. The default gateway and DNS addresses are prefilled and cannot be edited here. If the iSCSI network has a default gateway that is different from the displayed addresses, go back to step 20 and select the corresponding TCP/IP stack.

Figure 4.48   Creating a VMkernel port group—Entering port group properties—vSphere 6 Web Client

24. Click **Next**.

25. Review the information in the preview screen and, if you have no corrections to make, click the **Finish** button.

Figure 4.49 shows the network configuration after the previous changes if you created a new vSwitch.

Figure 4.49   Networking configuration tab after adding a port group to a new vSwitch—vSphere 6 Web Client

I also added an additional VMkernel adapter to an existing vSwitch0. The network configuration (which I named iSCSI Network2) is shown in Figure 4.50.

Notice that both **Management Network** and **iSCSI Network2** are using **vmnic0** as the active uplink (vmnic2 shows as standby).

The software initiator does not support active/active or active/standby NIC teaming on vSphere 6. So, if you have no NIC teaming configured, your network properties should look as shown in Figure 4.52, and you can stop here. If your current configuration looks as shown in Figure 4.51, you need to change the NIC teaming configuration so that the iSCSI port group uses vmnic2 as the active uplink and vmnic0 as unused. In that case, proceed to step 26. I discuss NIC teaming design choices later in this chapter.

26. Select the **iSCSI Network2** port group.

27. Click the **Edit** button (see Figure 4.50).

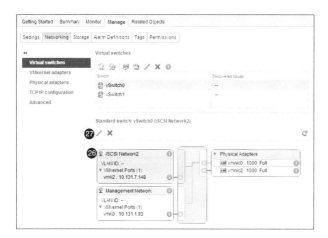

Figure 4.50   Networking configuration tab after adding a port group to an existing vSwitch—vSphere 6 Web Client

28. Select the **Teaming and failover** section.

29. Select the **Override** check box.

30. Select **vmnic0**.

31. Click the down arrow until vmnic0 is listed in the **Unused adapters** section.

32. Select **vmnic2**.

33. Click the up arrow until vmnic2 is listed in the **Active adapters** section (see Figure 4.51).

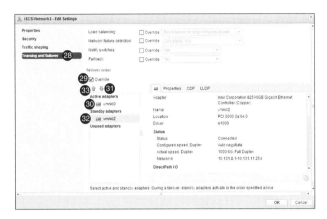

Figure 4.51   Editing iSCSI Port Group—vSphere 6 Web Client

34. The configuration should look similar to Figure 4.52. Click **OK**.

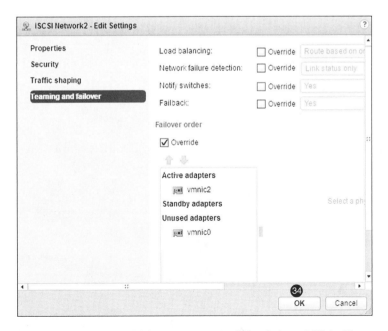

Figure 4.52   Editing iSCSI port group results—vSphere 6 Web Client

The final configuration should be similar to Figure 4.53.

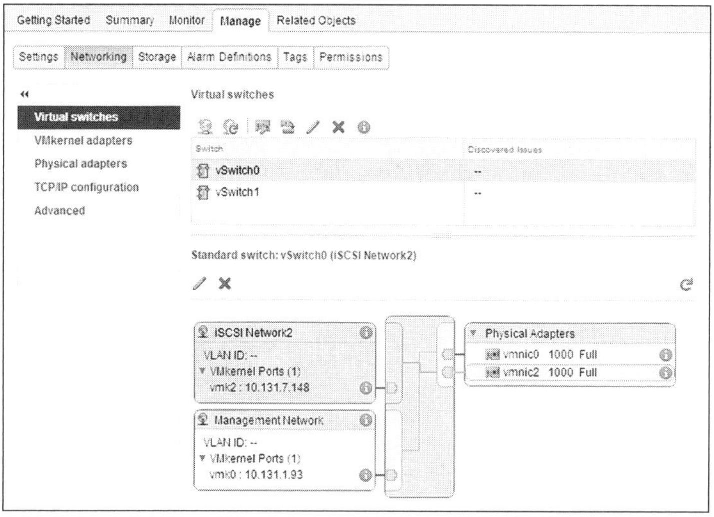

Figure 4.53   Displaying the iSCSI network port group failover order—vSphere 6 Web Client

Creating a SW iSCSI Initiator

Now that all the plumbing is done, you are ready to create the SW iSCSI initiator. Follow these steps:

1. Connect to the vCenter server that manages the ESXi 6 host, using the vSphere 6.0 Web Client as a user with Administrator privileges.

2. If the VC view is at the Home screen, click the **Hosts and Cluster** icon under the Inventories section.

3. If the VC view is not at the Home screen, select the **Hosts and Clusters** tab.

4. Select the ESXi host in the inventory.

5. Click the **Manage** tab.

6. Click the **Storage** button.

7. Select the **Storage Adapters** section (see Figure 4.54).

8. Under Storage Adapters, select the **Add new storage adapter** icon, which is a green plus sign, and then click the **Software iSCSI adapter** option (see Figure 4.55).

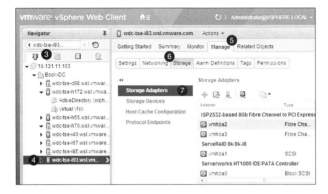

Figure 4.54   Adding an iSCSI SW initiator—Step 1—vSphere 6 Web Client

Figure 4.55   Adding an iSCSI SW initiator—vSphere 6.0 Client

9. Acknowledge the displayed message by clicking **OK**.

10. Ensure that you can see the SW initiator listed in the **Storage Adapters** section, under the **iSCSI Software Adapter** group, as shown in Figure 4.56.

NOTE

The number assigned to the SW initiator name (for example, vmhba34 or vmhba35) is based on the next available vmhba number. In this example, the next number is vmhba34 since the IDE adapter was assigned vmhba33. The reason for the high vmhba number is that the numbers lower than 32 are reserved for physical SCSI, FC, and independent FCoE/iSCSI HBAs.

---

11. In the Details section, select the **Properties** tab (see Figure 4.56).

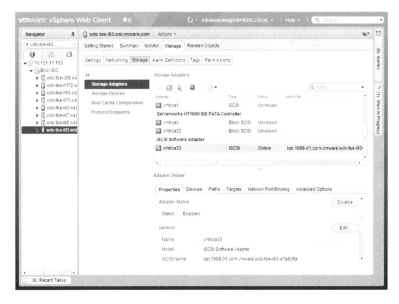

Figure 4.56 Viewing storage adapters after adding an iSCSI SW initiator

If you do not wish to configure a SW iSCSI initiator with multipathing, proceed to the "Configuring Target Discovery" section, later in this chapter. Otherwise, proceed to the next step to add network port binding.

12. Select the **Network Port Binding** tab and then click the **Add** icon (the green plus sign) (see Figure 4.57).

Figure 4.57 iSCSI initiator properties—Displaying the Network Port Binding tab—vSphere 6 web Client

13. Select the **iSCSI Network** port group (vmk1 VMkernel adapter) (see Figure 4.58). To configure multipathing and availability for the SW iSCSI initiator, you may also select iSCSI Network 2 port group (vmk3 VMkernel adapter) and then click OK.

Note that in this example, the second port group uses the management network port group's passive NIC because I don't have enough NICs in this host.

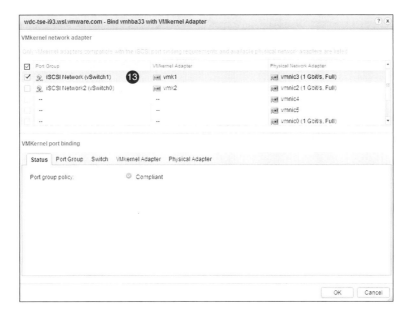

Figure 4.58   Selecting a VMkernel port group to bind with an iSCSI SW initiator—vSphere 6 Web Client

NOTE

If you do not change the NIC teaming failover order so that the iSCSI Network 2 port group has one active NIC and no standby NICs, you do not see the port group name displayed in the **VMkernel network adapter** list. If you select it, the status tab shows that the port group policy is **Not compliant**, much as in Figure 4.59, which also states the following:

The selected physical network adapter is not associated with VMkernel adapter with compliant teaming and failover policy. VMkernel network adapter must have exactly one active uplink and no standby uplinks to be eligible for binding to the iSCSI HBA.

All bound ports must be connected to the same network as the targets because software iSCSI initiator traffic is not routable in this release. This may change in a future release, though.

Figure 4.59   What you see if the failover order is not set correctly—vSphere 6 Web Client

A successful addition should look as shown in Figure 4.60.

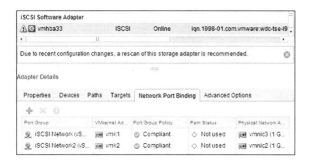

Figure 4.60   iSCSI SW initiator after port group binding—vSphere 6 Web Client

---

NOTE

Because the target discovery has not yet been configured, you can ignore the rescan message that appears.

Also note that the path status shows as Not Used. This will change later, after targets are discovered and paths are enumerated.

---

14. Proceed to the "Configuring Target Discovery" section, later in this chapter.

> **TIP**
>
> The iSCSI initiator configuration is facilitated by the iSCSI plug-ins installed on the ESXi host. To identify these plug-ins, run the following command:
>
> ```
> esxcli iscsi plugin list
> ```
>
> You should get output similar to that shown in Figure 4.61.
>
> In this example, there are two plug-ins: VMware and QLogic. For more information on the IMA iSCSI Management API, see the "vSphere 6 iSCSI Architecture" section, later in this chapter. Also, see the SNIA white paper at www.snia.org/sites/default/files/iSCSI_Management_API_SNIA_White_Paper.pdf.

```
wdc-tse-i93.wsl.vmware.com - PuTTY                                    —   □   ×
[root@wdc-tse-i93:~] esxcli iscsi plugin list
File Name       Vendor        Supported Ima Version  Implementation Version  Build Time
--------------  ------------  ---------------------  ----------------------  ----------
libisoft3.so    vmware                            2  5.0.2.0                 na
libQIMA4xxx.so  QLogic Corp.                      2  2.02.18                 na
[root@wdc-tse-i93:~]
```

Figure 4.61 Listing iSCSI plug-ins installed on an ESXi host—SSH

Configuring Target Discovery

In vSphere 6, target discovery configuration is the same regardless of the type of iSCSI initiators.

The following sections describe the procedures for dynamic discovery and for static discovery.

> **NOTE**
>
> Before proceeding with these procedures, make sure the iSCSI storage array has presented one or more LUNs by adding the initiators' IQN to a LUN's access list. This varies from one storage vendor to another.

Configuring Dynamic Discovery

This procedure assumes that you are already logged in to a vCenter server, using vSphere 6 Web Client:

1. Navigate to the **Hosts and Clusters** tab.
2. Select the ESXi host in the inventory tree.
3. Select the **Manage** tab.

4. Select **Storage**.

5. Select **Storage Adapters**.

6. Select the iSCSI initiator's vmhba.

7. Select **Targets**.

8. Select **Dynamic Discovery**.

9. Click **Add** (see Figure 4.62).

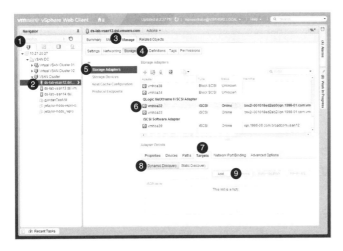

Figure 4.62   Adding dynamic discovery

10. Enter the iSCSI server's IP address or host name. Change the default port ID from 3260 if the iSCSI server is configured with a different one (which is very unlikely).

11. If the ISCSI array requires authentication, override the inherited settings by unchecking the **Inherit settings from parent** box.

12. Click **OK** (see Figure 4.63).

13. Repeat steps 1 through 12 for each storage array IP address on the same initiator or on another initiator. After each addition, you see the message **Due to recent configuration changes, a rescan of this adapter is recommended**.

14. When you are done adding iSCSI servers' IP addresses, proceed to the next step.

15. Click the **Rescan all storage adapters** icon (see Figure 4.64).

16. While still on the Targets tab, click the **Static discovery** button.

17. Sort by the iSCSI server column by clicking the column label. The discovered targets are listed under the Target Name column. In Figure 4.65, I selected, for visibility, all targets discovered on the iSCSI server address added in step 10.

Figure 4.63   Dynamic discovery parameters

Figure 4.64   Rescanning all adapters

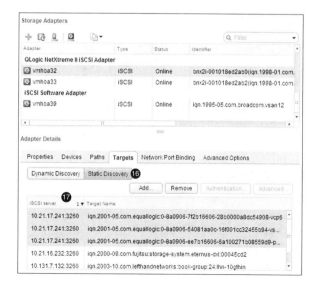

Figure 4.65   Listing dynamically discovered targets

Configuring Static Discovery

Using static discovery can be cumbersome and results in higher administrative efforts because it requires adding the IQN for each target. This is exaggerated with iSCSI storage servers, which present each LUN on its own target. However, I provide the procedure here for completeness.

This procedure assumes that you are already logged into a vCenter server, using vSphere 6 Web Client:

1. Navigate to the **Hosts and Clusters** tab.

2. Select the ESXi host in the inventory tree.

3. Select the **Manage** tab.

4. Select **Storage**.

5. Select **Storage Adapters**.

6. Select the iSCSI initiator's vmhba.

7. Select **Targets**.

8. Select **Static Discovery**.

9. Click the **Add** button. You should see the dialog shown in Figure 4.66.

Figure 4.66   Adding an iSCSI HW initiator's static discovery address

10. In the Add Static Target Server dialog, enter the following:

    a. iSCSI server IP address

    b. iSCSI port (default is 3260)

c. iSCSI target name, which is the IQN of one of the iSCSI ports on the storage array (You can obtain this name from the array management utility.)

In this example, I am using a specific LUN's IQN on a Dell EqualLogic iSCSI storage array. The IQN is `iqn.2003.com.lefthandnetwork:book-group:24:lhn-10gthin`.

Another example from an EMC VNX storage array would be an IQN for a storage processor (SP) port, like `iqn.1992-04.com.emc:cx.ckm00102400485.a2`, which is for SPA.

d. If the array requires authentication, uncheck **Inherit settings from parent** under the Authentication settings and provide the CHAP authentication information.

11. Click **OK**.

Customizing Storage Network Configuration

Storage network design may call for certain configurations other than the defaults. In this section, I cover some of the common features applicable to iSCSI storage design.

Configuring an Independent HW iSCSI Initiator with Jumbo Frames

To configure jumbo frames on independent HW iSCSI initiators, you can use the HBA's BIOS directly. The following is the procedure for doing that:

1. Boot the host and, when prompted, press the key combination to access the HBA's BIOS. In this example, the hotkey for the QLogic HBA is **Ctrl+Q**.

2. If you have more than one HBA installed, select the HBA you want to configure and then press **Enter**.

3. From the **QLogic Fast!UTIL** menu that appears, select the **Configuration Settings** option and then press **Enter**. (Refer to Figure 4.14 earlier in this chapter.)

4. Scroll down to **Advanced Adapter Settings** and then press **Enter** (see Figure 4.67).

5. Select the MTU field and press **Enter**— and then select the value **9000** (see Figure 4.68). Press **Enter**.

6. Press **Esc** to return to the previous menu. When prompted, select **Save changes**, as shown in Figure 4.69, and press **Enter**.

7. To configure a second port on the HBA or on another QLogic iSCSI HBA, at the Fast!UTIL Options menu, scroll down to **Select Host Adapter** and press **Enter** (see Figure 4.70).

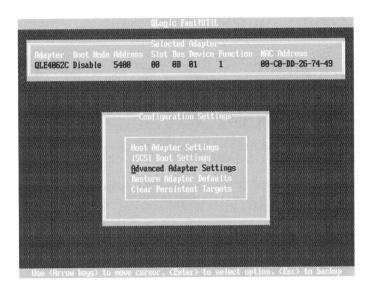

Figure 4.67   Selecting Advanced Adapter Settings

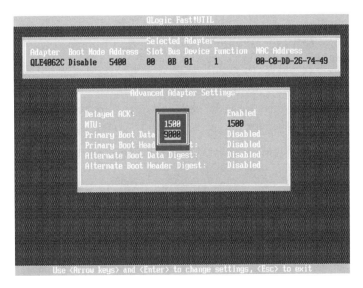

Figure 4.68   Modifying the MTU size

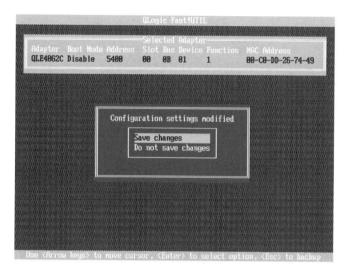

Figure 4.69   Saving MTU changes

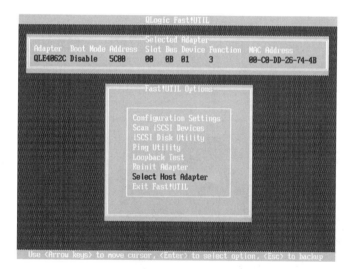

Figure 4.70   Preparing to select the host adapter

8. Select the adapter from the displayed list and press **Enter** (see Figure 4.71).

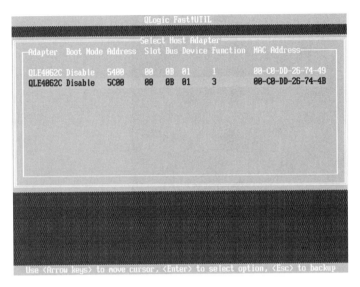

Figure 4.71   Selecting the host adapter

9. Repeat steps 1 through 3 in this procedure.

10. At the Fast!UTIL Options menu, press **Esc** again.

11. Select **Reboot System** (see Figure 4.72).

Figure 4.72   Exiting the Fast!UTIL menu and rebooting the system

Configuring a SW Initiator with Jumbo Frames

To compensate for lack of hardware offloading capabilities of the iSCSI SW initiator, enabling jumbo frames can significantly improve I/O throughput.

If your design meets the hardware configuration requirements, you can follow these steps to enable jumbo frames:

1. Connect to the vCenter server that manages the ESXi 6 host, using the vSphere 6.0 Web Client as a user with Administrator privileges.

2. Navigate to the **Inventory—Hosts and Clusters** view.

3. Locate the ESXi 6 host in the inventory tree and select it.

4. Select the **Manage** tab.

5. Click the **Networking** button.

6. Select the **Virtual switches** section.

7. Select the standard vSwitch to which the iSCSI port group is attached. In this example, it is **vSwitch2**.

8. Click the **Edit** button.

9. In the properties section of the resulting dialog, enter the value **9000** in the MTU field.

10. Click **OK** (see Figure 4.73).

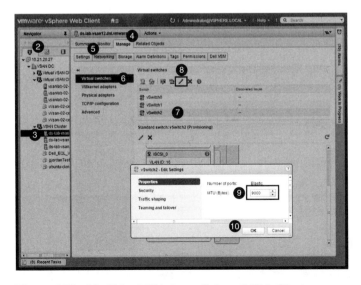

Figure 4.73 Modifying MTU size—vSphere 6 Web Client

11. Select the **VMkernel adapters** section.

12. Select the port group you bound to the iSCSI SW initiator (in this example, it is **iSCSI_0**).

13. Click the **Edit** button.

14. In the NIC settings section of the resulting dialog, enter the value **9000** in the MTU field

15. Click **OK** (see Figure 4.74).

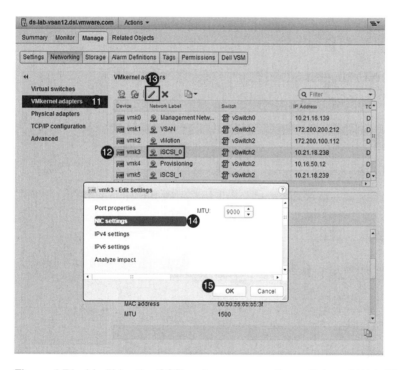

Figure 4.74   Modifying the iSCSI port group properties—vSphere 6 Web Client

16. Repeat steps 11 through 15 for each port group you bound to the iSCSI SW initiator.

iSCSI Targets

On most iSCSI storage arrays, targets are represented by storage processor ports. However, there are some exceptions, such as Dell EqualLogic, where each iSCSI LUN has a unique target. For the former type of iSCSI array, you can use the following procedure to identify iSCSI targets from ESXi 6 hosts. You can run this command to check for iSCSI targets for both HW and SW initiators:

```
esxcli iscsi adapter target list
```

Figure 4.75 shows the output of this command for SW initiators, and Figure 4.76 shows the output of this command for HW initiators.

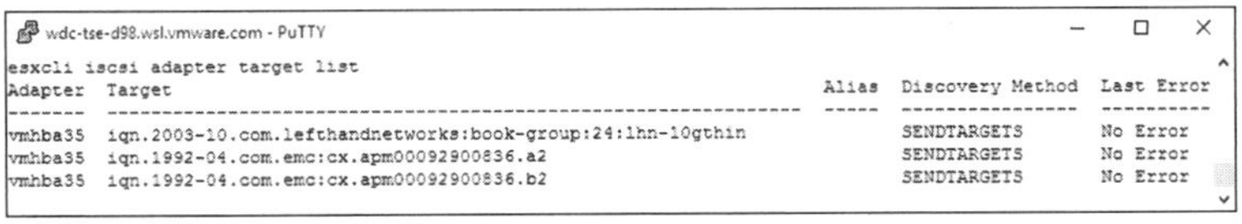

Figure 4.75   SW initiators—listing iSCSI targets—SSH

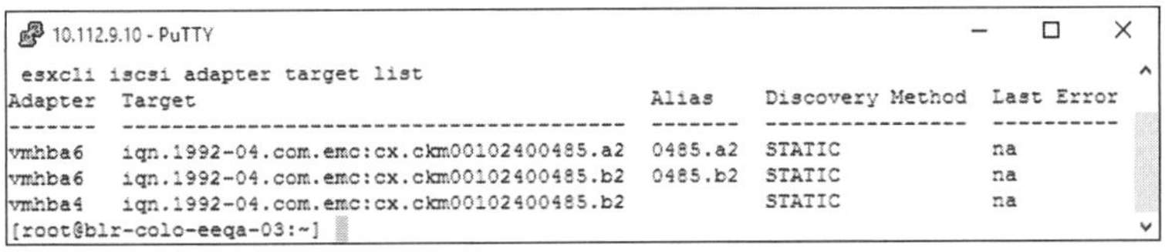

Figure 4.76   HW initiators—listing iSCSI targets—SSH

NOTE

In these two examples, the initiators' IQNs do not show in the output of this command. However, you might recognize a SW initiator from its adapter name, which by default has a high adapter number (for example, vmhba35), whereas the HW initiator has a lower number as it is assigned the next available adapter number after the local SCSI and other HBAs (for example, vmhba4 or vmhba6).

Also note that Figure 4.76 shows an example of using iSCSI aliases (discussed earlier in this chapter). In this case, the aliases are as shown in Table 4.5.

Table 4.5 iSCSI alias examples

Target IQN	Alias	Comment
iqn.1992-04.com.emc:cx.ckm00102400485.a2	0485.a2	SPA Port 2
iqn.1992-04.com.emc:cx.ckm00102400485.b2	0485.b2	SPB Port 2

Dissecting a SW Initiator's Configuration

If you have access to the ESXi host via the CLI, you can identify a SW initiator's various configurations and obtain enough information to create a logical diagram of the virtual network configuration. The following is a step-by-step process and gradual build-up of that logical diagram:

1. Identify the virtual adapter name (for example, vmhbaX) assigned to the SW initiator:

```
esxcli iscsi adapter list |less -S
```

The command output in Figure 4.77 shows that the iSCSI adapter is vmhba34, and the initiator type is iSCSI software adapter.

```
wdc-tse-h56.wsl.vmware.com - PuTTY                                    —   □   ×
~ # esxcli iscsi adapter list |less -S
Adapter  Driver     State   UID                                        Description
-------  ---------  ------  ----------------------------------------   ----------------------
vmhba34  iscsi_vmk  online  iqn.1998-01.com.vmware:wdc-tse-h56-3893cb7c  iSCSI Software Adapter
```

Figure 4.77   Identifying the SW initiator's adapter name

2. Identify the vmknic (also known as the VMkernel port) connected to the virtual adapter identified in step 1:

```
esxcli iscsi logicalnetworkportal list
```

The command output in Figure 4.78 shows that vmhba34 connects to two VMkernel ports (vmknics), named vmk0 and vmk1.

```
wdc-tse-h56.wsl.vmware.com - PuTTY                    —   □   ×
~ # esxcli iscsi logicalnetworkportal list
Adapter  Vmknic  MAC Address        MAC Address Valid  Compliant
-------  ------  -----------------  -----------------  ---------
vmhba34  vmk0    00:1f:29:e0:4d:52             true        true
vmhba34  vmk1    00:50:56:71:e4:94             true        true
~ #
```

Figure 4.78   Identifying SW initiator's VMkernel ports

Figure 4.79 depicts the details from steps 1 and 2 (apart from the MAC addresses).

3. Identify the name of the port group to which the VMkernel ports are attached:

```
# esxcfg-vmknic --list |less -S
```

You can also use the shorthand version of this command:

```
# esxcfg-vmknic -l |less -S
```

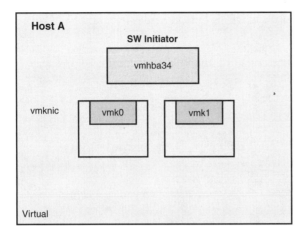

Figure 4.79 SW initiator virtual network build-up, steps 1 and 2

Figure 4.80 shows the output of the shorthand version of the command. It lists the VMkernel port names and associated port groups in addition to these ports' IP configurations.

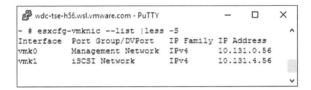

Figure 4.80 Listing port groups associated with VMkernel ports

The logical diagram now appears as shown in Figure 4.81.

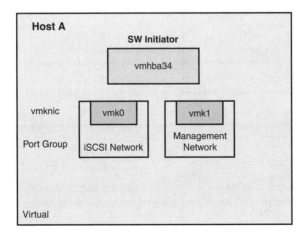

Figure 4.81 SW initiator virtual network build-up, step 3

Figure 4.81 shows the logical relationships between adapter name, VMkernel ports, and vSwitch port groups.

4. Find the name of the virtual switch by using the following command:

```
# esxcli network vswitch standard portgroup list
```

Figure 4.82 shows the output.

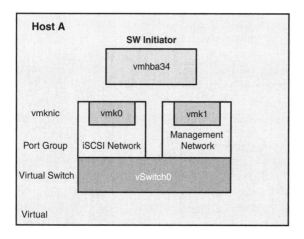

```
 wdc-tse-h56.wsl.vmware.com - PuTTY            —    □    ×
~ # esxcli network vswitch standard portgroup list
Name                    Virtual Switch  Active Clients  VLAN ID
------------------      --------------  --------------  -------
Cluster Network         vSwitch2                     0        0
Management Network      vSwitch0                     1        0
SVA-Network             vSwitch0                     3        0
VM Network              vSwitch1                     3        0
iSCSI Network           vSwitch0                     1        0
~ #
```

Figure 4.82   Identifying the vSwitch name

From the output in Figure 4.82, we can see that both port groups connect to vSwitch0. Adding this to the logical network diagram yields the build-up shown in Figure 4.83.

Figure 4.83   SW initiator virtual network build-up, step 4

5. Find out the uplinks:

```
# esxcfg-vswitch --list |less -S
```

You can also use the shorthand version of the command:

```
# esxcfg-vswitch -l |less -S
```

The output of this command lists the virtual switch's properties, as shown in Figure 4.84.

```
wdc-tse-h56.wsl.vmware.com - PuTTY                                        —    □    ×
~ # esxcfg-vswitch --list |less -S
Switch Name        Num Ports   Used Ports   Configured Ports   MTU    Uplinks
vSwitch0           1536        8            128                1500   vmnic0,vmnic1

    PortGroup Name          VLAN ID   Used Ports   Uplinks
    SVA-Network             0         3            vmnic0
    iSCSI Network           0         1            vmnic1
    Management Network      0         1            vmnic0
:
```

Figure 4.84   Listing vSwitch uplinks

Figure 4.84 shows that vSwitch0 has two uplinks: vmnic0 and vmnic1. It also shows that the iSCSI Network port group is connected to vmnic1, and Management Network is connected to vmnic0.

Based on steps 1 through 5, Figure 4.85 shows the final logical network diagram.

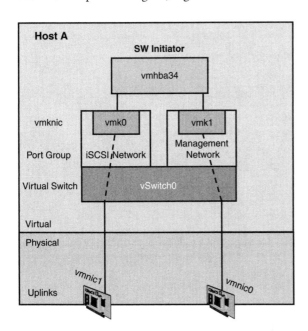

Figure 4.85   SW initiator final logical network diagram

You can list all these parameters—excluding vmnics—by using a single command:

```
# esxcli iscsi networkportal list
```

Listing 4.9 shows the output from this command, with the relevant parameters highlighted.

Listing 4.9   iSCSI portal parameters to identify the iSCSI logical network

```
vmhba34
    Adapter: vmhba34
    Vmknic: vmk0
    MAC Address: 00:1f:29:e0:4d:50
    MAC Address Valid: true
    IPv4: 10.131.4.56
    IPv4 Subnet Mask: 255.255.248.0
    IPv6:
    MTU: 1500
    Vlan Supported: true
    Vlan ID: 0
    Reserved Ports: 63488~65536
    TOE: false
    TSO: true
    TCP Checksum: false
    Link Up: true
    Current Speed: 1000
    Rx Packets: 25341947
    Tx Packets: 134
    NIC Driver: bnx2
    NIC Driver Version: 2.2.4f.v60.10
    NIC Firmware Version: bc 3.5.12 UMP 1.1.8
    Compliant Status: compliant
    NonCompliant Message:
    NonCompliant Remedy:
    Vswitch: vSwitch0
    PortGroup: iSCSI Network
    VswitchUuid:
    PortGroupKey:
    PortKey:
    Duplex:
    Path Status: active

vmhba34
    Adapter: vmhba34
    Vmknic: vmk1
```

```
MAC Address: 00:1f:29:e0:4d:52
MAC Address Valid: true
IPv4: 10.131.0.56
IPv4 Subnet Mask: 255.255.248.0
IPv6:
MTU: 1500
Vlan Supported: true
Vlan ID: 0
Reserved Ports: 63488~65536
TOE: false
TSO: true
TCP Checksum: false
Link Up: true
Current Speed: 1000
Rx Packets: 8451953
Tx Packets: 1399744
NIC Driver: bnx2
NIC Driver Version: 2.2.4f.v60.10
NIC Firmware Version: bc 3.5.12 UMP 1.1.8
Compliant Status: compliant
NonCompliant Message:
NonCompliant Remedy:
Vswitch: vSwitch0
PortGroup: Management Network
VswitchUuid:
PortGroupKey:
PortKey:
Duplex:
Path Status: last path
```

NOTE

The command that produced the output in Listing 4.9 works for SW initiators only. Running it with HW initiators just returns blank output. In the same output, you can also check the MTU size to verify whether jumbo frames (discussed in the previous section) are enabled. In Listing 4.9, the MTU value is 1500, which indicates no jumbo frames.

Dissecting a HW Initiator's Configuration

Compared to a SW initiator's configuration, the configuration of a HW initiator, either dependent or independent, is fairly simple.

The following command identifies the configured HW initiators on this host:

```
# esxcli iscsi adapter list
```

Figure 4.86 shows the output.

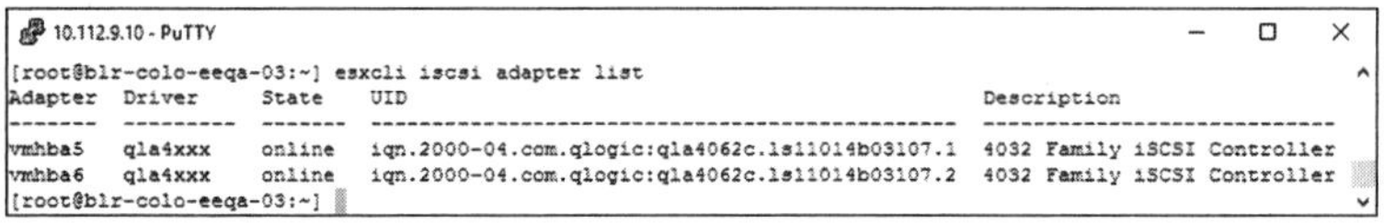

```
10.112.9.10 - PuTTY
[root@blr-colo-eeqa-03:~] esxcli iscsi adapter list
Adapter  Driver     State    UID                                           Description
-------  ---------  -------  --------------------------------------------  ----------------------------
vmhba5   qla4xxx    online   iqn.2000-04.com.qlogic:qla4062c.ls11014b03107.1  4032 Family iSCSI Controller
vmhba6   qla4xxx    online   iqn.2000-04.com.qlogic:qla4062c.ls11014b03107.2  4032 Family iSCSI Controller
[root@blr-colo-eeqa-03:~]
```

Figure 4.86 Listing configured HW initiators

Figure 4.86 shows that this host is configured with two QLogic 4032 family HW initiators. They have been assigned vmhba5 and vmhba6 adapter names.

You can list the network portals for these HW initiators by listing the physical network portals only. This is in contrast to the SW initiators, which have both logical and physical network portals.

The following command lists the HW initiators' physical network portals:

```
# esxcli iscsi physicalnetworkportal list
```

Figure 4.87 shows the output.

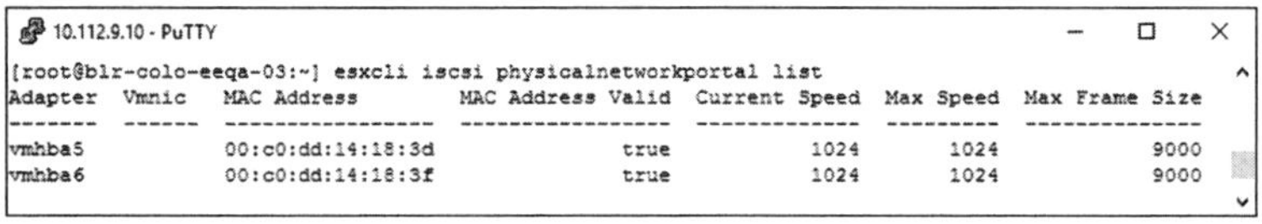

```
10.112.9.10 - PuTTY
[root@blr-colo-eeqa-03:~] esxcli iscsi physicalnetworkportal list
Adapter  Vmnic   MAC Address        MAC Address Valid  Current Speed  Max Speed  Max Frame Size
-------  ------  -----------------  -----------------  -------------  ---------  --------------
vmhba5           00:c0:dd:14:18:3d               true           1024       1024            9000
vmhba6           00:c0:dd:14:18:3f               true           1024       1024            9000
```

Figure 4.87 Listing HW initiators' physical network portals

You can conclude from Figure 4.87 that the HW initiators named vmhba5 and vmhba6 have QLogic assigned MAC addresses (OUI 00:c0:dd). This output also shows that jumbo frames are configured because the MTU size is 9000.

iSCSI Adapter Parameters

Occasionally you might need to identify the current iSCSI adapter's parameters for the purpose of troubleshooting or managing vSphere 6 storage. You can accomplish that via the UI or the CLI.

Using the UI to List and Modify iSCSI Adapter Parameters

The iSCSI adapter parameters are available via the advanced options of an iSCSI initiator's properties. Use the following steps to access these properties:

1. Connect to the vCenter server that manages the ESXi 6 host, using the vSphere 6.0 Web Client as a user with Administrator privileges.

2. Navigate to the **Hosts and Clusters** view.

3. Locate the ESXi 6 host in the inventory tree and select it.

4. Select the **Manage** tab.

5. Click the **Storage** button.

6. Select the **Storage Adapters** section.

7. Locate the HBAs with model names or HBA family names matching the dependent HW iSCSI HBA or iSCSI software adapter you are configuring and select it.

8. Select the **Properties** tab in the Adapter Details section (see Figure 4.88).

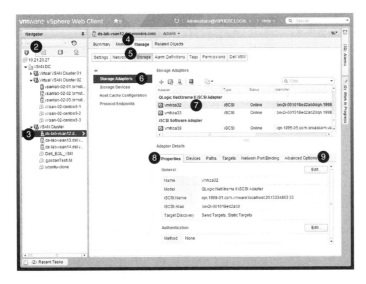

Figure 4.88   iSCSI initiator properties

9. Click the **Advanced** tab.

10. Click the **Edit** button. You see a dialog similar to the one in Figure 4.89.

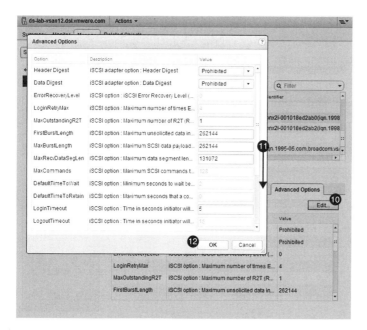

Figure 4.89   iSCSI adapter parameter list

11. Scroll down to locate the parameter you would like the list to modify. If the parameter's value is grayed out, then it is not settable. The parameter's descriptions as well as the minimum and maximum values are listed below each parameter.

12. Make the changes you want and then click **OK**.

Using the CLI to List and Modify iSCSI Adapter Parameters

In releases prior to vSphere 5, you could list the iSCSI adapter parameters via `vmkiscsi-tool`. This tool is still available in vSphere 5 and 6. However, because `vmkiscsi-tool` is not available remotely via vMA or vCLI, vSphere 5 and 6 provide the same capability via an `esxcli` namespace that is available locally or remotely:

```
esxcli iscsi adapter param get --adapter=<iSCSi-Adapter-Name>
```

Here is an example:

```
esxcli iscsi adapter param get --adapter=vmhba34
```

You can also use the shorthand version of this command, using `-A` instead of `--Adapter=`:

```
esxcli iscsi adapter param get -A vmhba34
```

Figure 4.90 shows the output of the shorthand version of this command.

wdc-tse-h56.wsl.vmware.com - PuTTY

```
~ # esxcli iscsi adapter param get --adapter=vmhba34
Name                  Current     Default     Min  Max       Settable  Inherit
--------------------  ----------  ----------  ---  --------  --------  -------
ErrorRecoveryLevel    0           0           0    2            false    false
InitialLoginRetryMax  4           4           0    64           false    false
InitialR2T            false       false       na   na           false    false
FirstBurstLength      262144      262144      512  16777215      true    false
MaxBurstLength        262144      262144      512  16777215      true    false
MaxRecvDataSegment    131072      131072      512  16777215      true    false
MaxOutstandingR2T     1           1           1    8             true    false
MaxCmds               128         128         2    2048         false    false
ImmediateData         true        true        na   na           false    false
DefaultTime2Retain    0           0           0    60           false    false
DefaultTime2Wait      2           2           0    60           false    false
LoginTimeout          60          5           1    60            true    false
LogoutTimeout         15          15          0    60           false    false
NoopOutInterval       15          15          1    60            true    false
NoopOutTimeout        10          10          10   30            true    false
RecoveryTimeout       10          10          1    120           true    false
DelayedAck            true        true        na   na            true    false
HeaderDigest          prohibited  prohibited  na   na            true    false
DataDigest            prohibited  prohibited  na   na            true    false
~ #
```

Figure 4.90 Listing iSCSI adapter parameters—SW or dependent HW initiator

This command applies to both software and dependent HW initiators. The output values from independent HW initiators might be different (see Figure 4.91). The main difference is that these values are not settable, while some of the SW and dependent HW initiators' parameters are. The only exception is the `LoginTimeout` value, which is settable on all iSCSI initiator types.

10.112.9.10 - PuTTY

```
[root@blr-colo-eeqa-03:~] esxcli iscsi adapter param get --adapter=vmhba6
Name                  Current     Default     Min  Max    Settable  Inherit
--------------------  ----------  ----------  ---  -----  --------  -------
ErrorRecoveryLevel    na          na          na   na        false    false
InitialLoginRetryMax  na          na          na   na        false    false
InitialR2T            false       false       na   na        false    false
FirstBurstLength      256         0           1    65535     false    false
MaxBurstLength        512         0           1    65535     false    false
MaxRecvDataSegment    128         0           1    65535     false    false
MaxOutstandingR2T     1           0           1    65535     false    false
MaxCmds               64          0           0    65535     false    false
ImmediateData         false       false       na   na        false    false
DefaultTime2Retain    20          0           0    65535     false    false
DefaultTime2Wait      2           0           0    0         false    false
LoginTimeout          10          10          3    30         true    false
LogoutTimeout         na          na          na   na        false    false
NoopOutInterval       14          0           0    65535     false    false
NoopOutTimeout        14          0           0    65535     false    false
RecoveryTimeout       na          na          na   na        false    false
DelayedAck            true        false       na   na        false    false
HeaderDigest          prohibited  prohibited  na   na        false    false
DataDigest            prohibited  prohibited  na   na        false    false
[root@blr-colo-eeqa-03:~]
```

Figure 4.91 Listing iSCSI adapter parameters—Independent HW initiator

Options with the value `true` in the `Settable` column can be modified using the `set` option. For example, to set the `NoopOutTimeout` value to `15`, use the following:

```
esxcli iscsi adapter param set --adapter vmhba34 --key [ic:ccc]
NoopOutTimeout --value 15
```

You can also use the shorthand version:

```
esxcli iscsi adapter param set -A vmhba34 -k NoopOutTimeout -v 15
```

This command does not provide any feedback if successful. It returns an error if it is unsuccessful. To verify the outcome, you can run the `get` command and then compare the output to that in Figure 4.91. The value in the Current column should reflect the changed value.

To reset the value back to the default, which is the value listed in the Default column, run this command:

```
esxcli iscsi adapter param set --adapter vmhba34 --default --key
NoopOutTimeout
```

You can also use the shorthand version:

```
esxcli iscsi adapter param set -A vmhba34 -D -k NoopOutTimeout
```

Should You Change iSCSI Adapter Parameters?

Keeping the default settings of the iSCSI adapter parameters is the best practice, and you should not change them. There is one exception, however: The `LoginTimeout` was not settable in vSphere 5, but now vSphere 6 allows it. If you observe in your environment that the target's response to login takes longer than the default value, 5 seconds, you might want to increase this option to 15 or 30 seconds to prevent the storage array from experiencing login storms (repeated attempts to login).

vSphere 6 iSCSI Architecture

Figure 4.92 shows the iSCSI architecture, which spans VMkernel modules, user-level daemons, and software components.

vSphere 6 iSCSI architecture includes the following components, which I discuss in subsequent sections:

- iSCSI database
- iSCSI daemon
- IMA (iSCSI management API)
- iSCSI transport module

- iSCSI protocol module

- Dependent iSCSI initiator modules

- Independent iSCSI HBA modules

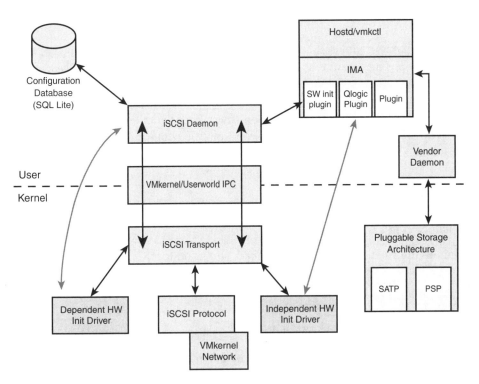

Figure 4.92   vSphere 6 iSCSI architecture

iSCSI Database

iSCSI configuration and the iSCSI runtime environment are stored in an SQL Lite database. Changes to the database persist between ESXi host reboots. The configuration is restored whenever the host is rebooted or the iSCSI daemon (vmkiscsid) is restarted. You can dump the database by using the following:

```
vmkiscsid --dump-db=<file-name>
```

From the database dump, you can easily locate various iSCSI configuration properties details. For example, the dump includes the following sections:

- `ISID`—iSCSI session ID information

- `InitiatorNodes`—iSCSI initiators information

- `Targets`—iSCSI targets information

- `discovery`—Target discovery information

- `ifaces`—The iSCSI network configuration, including the vmnic and vmknic names

iSCSI Daemon

The ESXi iSCSI daemon, vmkiscsid, runs on any vSphere host with iSCSI enabled as a User World process. This means that it is not a VMkernel module, and it runs like other applications and daemons, on top of VMkernel. vmkiscsid is started at boot time; if it finds a valid configuration or if iSCSI Boot Firmware Table (iBFT) is enabled in the NIC's BIOS, it continues to run. (iBFT is used for boot-from-iSCSI configurations.) It is also run whenever an iSCSI management command is run from the command line or via hostd. If it finds no valid iSCSI configuration, it stops.

The iSCSI daemon does the following tasks:

- Conducts dynamic and static iSCSI target discovery

- Authenticates iSCSI targets

- Maintains information about vmknics, ports, and so on for iSCSI use

- Establishes connections to iSCSI targets

- Reconnects to iSCSI targets if sessions get disconnected

- Updates the iSCSI configuration database based on sessions establishment or teardown

- Updates the iSCSI configuration database based on administrative input

- Listens for connections from IMA plug-ins (discussed in more detail in the next section)

- Communicates with iSCSI kernel components on connection events and session establishment

IMA (iSCSI Management API)

IMA is used to manage and configure iSCSI on the host. It is standardized by the Storage Networking Industry Association (SNIA; see the white paper at www.snia.org/sites/default/files/iSCSI_Management_API_SNIA_White_Paper.pdf).

IMA provides interfaces to do the following:

- Configure the iSCSI adapter, including network and iSCSI parameters

- Enter and examine iSCSI discovery information

- Enter and examine authentication types and credentials

- View target, LU (logical unit), session, and connection information

- Allocate and free lists for IMA consumers

The implementation on ESXi 6 includes four components: the IMA common library, the ESX IMA plug-in, third-party vendors' IMA plug-ins, and storage vendor daemons.

IMA Common Library

The IMA common library is mostly a shim interface to the IMA plug-ins. It is also responsible for serializing the commands to the IMA plug-ins, among other programmatic functions.

ESX IMA Plug-in

The ESXi IMA plug-in is called by the IMA common library and used to configure and manage the ESXi software iSCSI initiator and any dependent HW iSCSI initiators.

If vmkiscsid is not running when the ESX IMA plug-in is called, the plug-in starts vmkiscsid. This ensures that any iSCSI configuration on the system is returned any time an IMA call is made.

Vendor IMA Plug-ins

Third-party independent HW iSCSI initiator vendors are required to deliver IMA plug-ins to manage their adapters and drivers. These plug-ins present the standard IMA interfaces to the IMA common library and use vendor-specific methods to communicate with the associated driver and hardware. For example, the QLogic plug-in communicates with the qla4xxx driver to accomplish management functions.

Storage Vendor Daemons

Storage vendors may deliver session management daemons that make IMA library calls. The daemons are delivered as Common Information Model (CIM) providers, running in an unmanaged daemon mode, and they are used to manage sessions for a storage vendor's multipath software, delivered via Pluggable Storage Architecture (PSA). (For more information about PSA, see Chapter 5.) The CIM provider uses vendor-specific communication methods to coordinate and interact with PSA components. CIM is an industry standard management API that is used by VMware partners to monitor and manage systems' health as well as communicate with and manage software components on ESXi.

iSCSI Transport Module

The iSCSI transport module, iscsi_trans, is a VMware-provided module that facilitates communications between the iSCSI daemon (vmkiscsid) and any iSCSI media modules, such as the ESX SW iSCSI initiator or HW iSCSI initiator drivers.

iscsi_trans presents a set VMkernel API that facilitates the following:

- Gathering and setting configuration parameters in the ESX iSCSI module and any other VMkernel modules that might later consume these interfaces

- Passing network configuration information to dependent HW iSCSI initiators because they depend on VMkernel for networking

iSCSI Protocol Module

The iSCSI protocol (or media) module, iscsi_vmk, is the VMware-provided module that implements the iSCSI protocol for the ESX software iSCSI initiator. This module packages SCSI commands in iSCSI protocol data units (PDUs) and passes them to the VMkernel networking stack through a socket interface. iscsi_vmk accepts management calls from iscsi_trans, SCSI commands and data from the SCSI midlayer, and network transition information via its socket connections.

Dependent iSCSI Initiator Modules

Dependent iSCSI initiator modules are vmklinux drivers delivered by third-party vendors. (vmklinux is the ESXi facility that enables drivers ported from Linux to run on ESXi.) These modules utilize vmklinux driver interfaces and several VMkernel API interfaces to get the network configuration. Dependent iSCSI HBA drivers get their network configuration from a vmknic, including IP address information, MTU, and VLAN. (I covered these details in the "Configuring Dependent HW Initiators" section, earlier in this chapter.) Configuration management is handled by the ESX IMA plug-in.

The ESX IMA plug-in sends configuration information to the iSCSI daemon, which uses this information to discover and authenticate targets and then establish and tear down sessions.

Independent iSCSI HBA Modules

Independent iSCSI HBA modules are vmklinux modules delivered by third-party vendors. They utilize vmklinux driver interfaces for storage and iSCSI path information. They also rely on communication with IMA plug-ins supplied by the vendor for configuration and management. IMA plug-ins are used to provide discovery and authentication information and session management.

TIP

To list the VMkernel modules mentioned in the previous sections, you can run these commands from the ESXi shell:

```
~# vmkload_mod --list |grep iscsi
iscsi_trans              8    52
iscsi_linux              1    16
iscsi_vmk                4    204

~ # ps |grep iscsi
2670        iscsi_trans_vmklink
2693        iscsivmk-log
5891 5891 vmkiscsid              /usr/sbin/vmkiscsid
5892 5891 vmkiscsid              /usr/sbin/vmkiscsid
```

You can also run the shorthand version of the first command by using -1 instead of --list. These commands apply to both SW and HW iSCSI initiators, with slight differences in the outputs.

The first command lists the loaded VMkernel modules, which shows iscsi_trans and iscsi_vmk. The middle module, iscsi_linux, allows third-party vendors to port Linux iSCSI drivers with minimal changes.

The second command shows the running processes, which include two vmkiscsid processes, iscsi_trans_vmklink (see step 6 under "Software iSCSI Initiators"). The process called iscsivmk-log is the process used by the iSCSI stack to log events into the VMkernel logs.

Flow of Communication Through the iSCSI Architecture

To put things in perspective, let me share with you the logical flow of communication through the vSphere iSCSI architecture for the purpose of target discovery.

Understanding Communication Flow with Software iSCSI Initiators

The flow of communication with SW iSCSI Initiators is as follows:

1. A socket is open on a port or set of ports, connecting to an iSCSI target.

2. The iSCSI target returns a list of targets via a Send Target payload.

3. The iSCSI configuration database is populated with the returned target list.

4. vmkiscsid (the iSCSI daemon) logs into the iSCSI target.

5. vmkiscsid exchanges authentication parameters with the target and, if configured, performs CHAP authentication.

6. vmkiscsid, which is on the user side, communicates with iscsi_trans (the iSCSI transport module) on the kernel side, via a Userworld-VMkernel IPC socket. (IPC stands for interprocess communication.) This link is also known as vmklink.

7. After the session with the target is established, an open socket descriptor is passed on to the SW iSCSI initiator module. The SW iSCSI initiator module builds iSCSI PDUs to transport SCSI commands and data to the iSCSI target.

8. vmkiscsid updates the iSCSI configuration database with the following:

   - Target information

   - ESX port information

   - Session parameters

Unserstanding Communication Flow with Dependent HW iSCSI Initiators

Dependent HW iSCSI initiators are driven by vmkscsid. So, a similar flow would be the following:

1. vmkscsid passes the connection establishment commands to the dependent HW iSCSI initiator via the iSCSI transport module (iscsi_trans).

2. After the connection with the target is established, vmkscsid constructs PDUs to discover, authenticate, and establish sessions with the iSCSI target (as in steps 2 through 6 in the previous section).

3. The dependent HW iSCSI initiator builds iSCSI PDUs to transport SCSI commands and data to the iSCSI target (hardware offloading).

4. If the connection is lost, the dependent HW initiator driver informs vmkscsid via iscsi_trans. vmkscsid directs session reestablishment.

5. vmkiscsid updates the iSCSI configuration database with the following:

   - Target information

   - ESX port information

   - Session parameters

Unserstanding Communication Flow with Independent HW iSCSI Initiators

Independent HW iSCSI initiators communicate directly with iSCSI transport and handle their own connections and sessions establishment as well as constructing their own iSCSI PDUs to transport SCSI commands and data to iSCSI target.

Troubleshooting iSCSI Connectivity

iSCSI connectivity issues are mostly related to basic TCP/IP connectivity. The trouble-shooting process is simple:

1. Check the host port's IP configuration.

2. Ping the iSCSI server's IP address.

3. Check connectivity to the iSCSI server IP port (the default is 3260).

Checking Host Port IP Configuration

The easiest approach to listing the vmhba and its IP address is to use this command:

```
esxcli iscsi networkportal list |grep "Adapter\|IPv4\|Vmknic"
```

The following is an example of the output from this command:

```
Adapter: vmhba40
Vmknic: vmk3
IPv4: 10.21.18.238
IPv4 Subnet Mask: 255.255.252.0
Adapter: vmhba40
Vmknic: vmk4
IPv4: 10.21.18.239
IPv4 Subnet Mask: 255.255.252.0
Adapter: vmhba33
Vmknic: vmk3
IPv4: 10.21.18.238
IPv4 Subnet Mask: 255.255.252.0
Adapter: vmhba34
Vmknic: vmk4
IPv4: 10.21.18.239    IPv4 Subnet Mask: 255.255.252.0
```

This means that this host has three iSCSI vmhbas: vmhba40 with two ports bound (vmk3 and vmk4) and vmhba33 and vmhba34 with one port each (vmk3 and vmk4, respectively).

Pinging the iSCSI Server's IP Address

You can use this command to identify the iSCSI server's IP address, which is what you set as the dynamic target discovery address:

```
esxcli iscsi adapter target portal list
```

Figure 4.93 shows the output from this command.

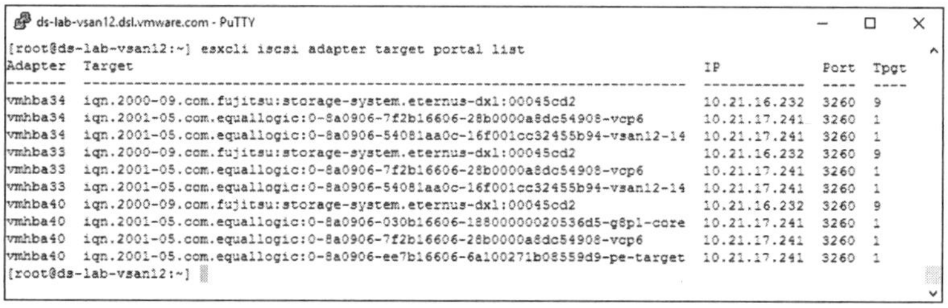

Figure 4.93 Listing iSCSI Servers' IP addresses

In this example, one of the iSCSI servers' IP address is 10.21.17.241, and the port ID is 3260. To ping that IP address, you can run the following command:

```
vmkping -I [vmknic] [iSCSI Server IP address]
```

Here is an example:

```
vmkping -I vmk3 10.21.17.241
```

This command sends the ping packets via interface vmk3 to server IP address 10.21.17.241. If the address is reachable, the output looks like this:

```
PING 10.21.17.241 (10.21.17.241): 56 data bytes
64 bytes from 10.21.17.241: icmp_seq=0 ttl=255 time=0.228 ms
64 bytes from 10.21.17.241: icmp_seq=1 ttl=255 time=0.147 ms
64 bytes from 10.21.17.241: icmp_seq=2 ttl=255 time=0.117 ms

--- 10.21.17.241 ping statistics ---
3 packets transmitted, 3 packets received, 0% packet loss
round-trip min/avg/max = 0.117/0.164/0.228 ms
```

You can repeat this command, using vmk4 with the -I option.

Checking Connectivity to the iSCSI Server IP Port

Using the output from vmkping with the port ID 3260, you can use this command to check connectivity to it:

```
nc -z -s [host's port IP address] [iSCSI server's IP address] [Port ID]
```

Here is an example:

```
nc -z -s 10.21.18.238 10.21.17.241 3260
Connection to 10.21.17.241 3260 port [tcp/*] succeeded!
```

The output indicates that TCP port ID 3260 on IP address 10.21.17.241 is accessible via the host's port that has the IP address 10.21.18.238.

You can repeat the same command, using vmk4's IP address with the -s parameter.

The nc command provides only abbreviated options. It does not provide verbose options.

If any of these troubleshooting commands fail, check the corresponding network configuration and correct as needed. Then repeat the commands to verify the outcome.

Summary

In this chapter I provided details of the iSCSI protocol, connectivity, and iSCSI implementation on vSphere 6. I also covered iSCSI initiators (both HW and SW) as well as iSCSI targets and how to identify them. I walked you through gradually building up a logical iSCSI network diagram, based on commands available on ESXi 6. Finally, I provided details of iSCSI architecture and the flow of communication between its components.

vSphere Pluggable Storage Architecture

vSphere 6 continues to utilize the Pluggable Storage Architecture (PSA), which was introduced with ESX 3.5. This architecture modularizes the storage stack, which makes it easier to maintain and enables storage partners to develop their own proprietary components that plug into this architecture.

Availability is critical, and redundant paths to storage are essential. One of the key functions of the storage component in vSphere is to provide multipathing (that is, which path a given I/O should use if there are multiple paths) and failover (that is, I/O switching to using another path when a path goes down).

VMware, by default, provides a generic multipathing plug-in (MPP) called the Native Multipathing Plug-in (NMP).

Native Multipathing

To understand how the pieces of PSA fit together, Figures 5.1, 5.2, 5.4, and 5.6 build up the PSA gradually.

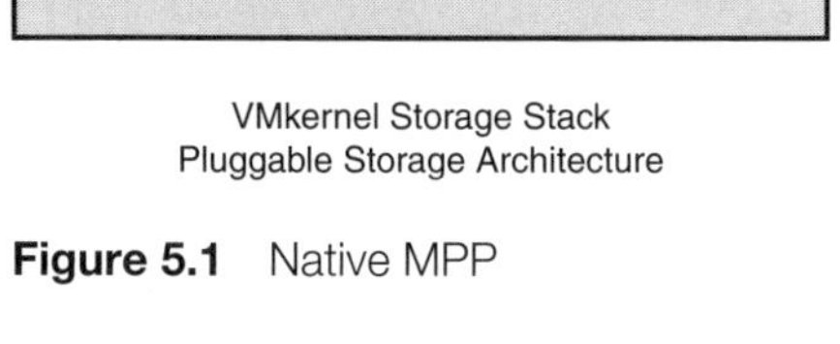

Native Multipathing (NMP)

VMkernel Storage Stack
Pluggable Storage Architecture

Figure 5.1   Native MPP

NMP is the component of vSphere 6 VMkernel that handles multipathing and failover. It exports two APIs, Storage Array Type Plug-in (SATP) and Path Selection Plug-in (PSP), which are implemented as plug-ins.

NMP performs the following functions (some done with help from SATPs and PSPs):

- Registers logical devices with the PSA framework
- Receives input/output (I/O) requests for logical devices it registered with the PSA framework
- Completes the I/Os and posts completion of the SCSI command block with the PSA framework, which includes the following operations:
  - Selecting the physical path to which it sends the I/O requests
  - Handling failure conditions encountered by the I/O requests
- Handles task management operations, such as aborts/resets

PSA communicates with NMP for the following operations:

- Opening/closing logical devices
- Starting I/O to logical devices
- Aborting an I/O to logical devices
- Getting the name of the physical paths to logical devices
- Getting the SCSI inquiry information for logical devices

Storage Array Type Plug-in (SATP)

Figure 5.2 shows the relationship between SATP and NMP.

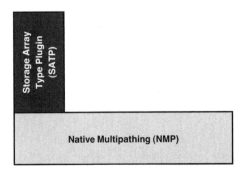

VMkernel Storage Stack
Pluggable Storage Architecture

Figure 5.2   SATP

SATPs are PSA plug-ins specific to certain storage arrays or storage array families. Some are generic for certain array classes—for example, active/passive, active/active, or ALUA-capable arrays.

SATPs handle the following operations:

- Monitoring the hardware state of the physical paths to the storage array
- Determining when a hardware component of a physical path has failed
- Switching physical paths to the array when a path has failed

NMP communicates with SATPs for the following operations:

- Setting up a new logical device—claiming a physical path
- Updating the hardware states of the physical paths (for example, active, standby, dead)
- Activating the standby physical paths of an active/passive array (when the active path's state is dead or unavailable)
- Notifying the plug-in that an I/O is about to be issued on a given path
- Analyzing the cause of an I/O failure on a given path (based on errors returned by the array)

Table 5.1 lists examples of SATPs.

Table 5.1 Examples of SATPs

SATP	Description
VMW_SATP_CX	Supports EMC CX that do not use the ALUA protocol
VMW_SATP_ALUA_CX	Supports EMC CX that use the ALUA protocol
VMW_SATP_SYMM	Supports EMC Symmetrix array family
VMW_SATP_INV	Supports EMC Invista array family
VMW_SATP_EVA	Supports HP EVA arrays
VMW_SATP_MSA	Supports HP MSA arrays
VMW_SATP_EQL	Supports Dell EquaLogic arrays
VMW_SATP_SVC	Supports IBM SVC arrays
VMW_SATP_LSI	Supports LSI arrays and others originally manufactured from it (for example, DS4000 family)
VMW_SATP_ALUA	Supports nonspecific arrays that support ALUA
VMW_SATP_DEFAULT_AA	Supports nonspecific active/active arrays
VMW_SATP_DEFAULT_AP	Supports nonspecific active/passive arrays
VMW_SATP_LOCAL	Supports direct attached devices

Listing SATPs on an ESXi 6 Host

To obtain a list of SATPs on a given ESXi 5 host, you can run the following command directly on the host or remotely via an SSH session, a vMA appliance, or ESXCLI:

```
# esxcli storage nmp satp list
```

Figure 5.3 provides an example of output from this command.

```
[root@wdc-tse-i67:~] esxcli storage nmp satp list
Name                    Default PSP     Description
--------------------    -------------   ----------------------------------------------------
VMW_SATP_CX             VMW_PSP_MRU     Supports EMC CX that do not use the ALUA protocol
VMW_SATP_ALUA_CX        VMW_PSP_RR      Supports EMC CX that use the ALUA protocol
VMW_SATP_ALUA           VMW_PSP_MRU     Supports non-specific arrays that use the ALUA protocol
VMW_SATP_MSA            VMW_PSP_MRU     Placeholder (plugin not loaded)
VMW_SATP_DEFAULT_AP     VMW_PSP_MRU     Placeholder (plugin not loaded)
VMW_SATP_SVC            VMW_PSP_FIXED   Placeholder (plugin not loaded)
VMW_SATP_EQL            VMW_PSP_FIXED   Placeholder (plugin not loaded)
VMW_SATP_INV            VMW_PSP_FIXED   Placeholder (plugin not loaded)
VMW_SATP_EVA            VMW_PSP_FIXED   Placeholder (plugin not loaded)
VMW_SATP_SYMM           VMW_PSP_RR      Placeholder (plugin not loaded)
VMW_SATP_LSI            VMW_PSP_MRU     Placeholder (plugin not loaded)
VMW_SATP_DEFAULT_AA     VMW_PSP_FIXED   Supports non-specific active/active arrays
VMW_SATP_LOCAL          VMW_PSP_FIXED   Supports direct attached devices
[root@wdc-tse-i67:~]
```

Figure 5.3   Listing SATPs

Notice that each SATP is listed in association with a specific PSP. The output shows the default configuration of a freshly installed ESXi 6 host. To modify these associations, refer to the "Modifying PSA Plug-in Configurations Using the UI" section, later in this chapter.

If you have installed third-party SATPs, they are listed along with the SATPs shown in Table 5.1.

> **NOTE**
>
> ESXi 6 loads only the SATPs that match detected storage arrays based on the corresponding claim rules. (See the "Claim Rules" section, later in this chapter, for more about claim rules.) Otherwise, you see them listed as (plugin not loaded), as in the output shown in Figure 5.3.

Path Selection Plug-in (PSP)

Figure 5.4 shows the relationship between SATP, PSP, and NMP.

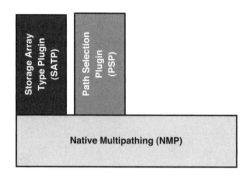

VMkernel Storage Stack
Pluggable Storage Architecture

Figure 5.4   PSP

PSPs are PSA plug-ins that handle path selection policies and are replacements for failover policies used by Legacy Multipathing (Legacy-MP), used in releases prior to vSphere 4.x.

PSPs handle the following operations:

- They determine on which physical path to issue I/O requests being sent to a given storage device. Each PSP has access to a group of paths to the given storage device and has knowledge of the paths' states—for example, active, standby, dead—as well as Asymmetric Logical Unit Access's (ALUA's) asymmetric access state (AAS), such as active optimized, active non-optimized, and so on. This knowledge is obtained from what SATPs report to NMP. (See Chapter 6, "ALUA," for additional details about ALUA.)

- They determine which path to activate next if the currently working physical path to the storage device fails.

NOTE

PSPs do not need to know the actual storage array type; this function is provided by SATPs. However, a storage vendor developing a PSP may choose to have the PSP be aware of the storage type. (See Chapter 8, "Third-Party Multipathing Plug-ins.")

NMP communicates with PSPs for the following operations:

- Setting up a new logical storage device and claiming the physical paths to that device
- Getting the set of active physical paths currently used for path selection
- Selecting a physical path on which to issue I/O requests for a given device
- Selecting a physical path to activate when a path failure condition exists

Listing PSPs on an ESXi 6 Host

To obtain a list of PSPs on a given ESXi 6 host, you can run the following command directly on the host or remotely via an SSH session, a vMA appliance, or ESXCLI:

```
# esxcli storage nmp psp list
```

Figure 5.5 shows an example of output from this command.

Figure 5.5   Listing PSPs

The output shows the default configuration of a freshly installed ESXi 6 host. If you have installed third-party PSPs, they are also listed.

Third-Party Plug-ins

Figure 5.6 shows the relationship between third-party plug-ins, NMP, and PSA.

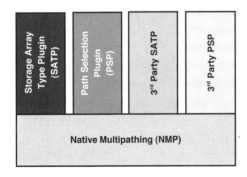

Figure 5.6   Third-party plug-ins

Because PSA is a modular architecture, VMware has provided APIs to its storage partners to develop their own plug-ins. These plug-ins can be SATPs, PSPs, or MPPs.

Third-party SATPs and PSPs can run side-by-side with VMware-provided SATPs and PSPs.

Third-party SATP and PSP providers can implement their own proprietary functions relevant to each plug-in that are specific to their storage arrays. Some partners implement only multipathing and failover algorithms, whereas others implement load balancing and I/O optimization as well.

The following are examples of such plug-ins in vSphere 4.x that are also certified for vSphere 5 and 6:

- **DELL_PSP_EQL_ROUTED**—This is a Dell EqualLogic PSP that provides the following enhancements:
    - Automatic connection management
    - Automatic load balancing across multiple active paths
    - Increased bandwidth
    - Reduced network latency

- **HTI_SATP_HDLM**—Hitachi ported its HDLM MPIO (multipathing I/O) management software to an SATP. It is currently certified for vSphere releases as early as 4.1, with most of the USP family of arrays from Hitachi and HDS. Versions 8.1.4-00 and 8.2.0-00 are certified with vSphere 6. Check the VMware HCL for a current list of certified arrays for vSphere 6 with this plug-in.

See Chapter 8 for further details.

Multipathing Plug-ins (MPPs)

Figure 5.7 shows the relationship between MPPs, NMP, and PSA.

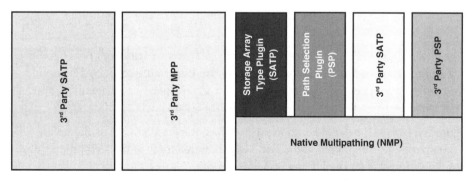

VMkernel Storage Stack
Pluggable Storage Architecture

Figure 5.7   MPPs, including third-party plug-ins

MPPs that are not implemented as SATPs or PSPs can be implemented as MPPs instead. MPPs run side-by-side with NMP. An example of this is EMC PowerPath/VE, which is certified with vSphere releases as early as 4.x. PowerPath/VE version 6 has been certified with vSphere 6. Check the VMware HCL for the current list of storage arrays certified with PowerPath/VE.

See Chapter 8 for further details.

Anatomy of PSA Components

Figure 5.8 is a block diagram that shows the components of the PSA framework.

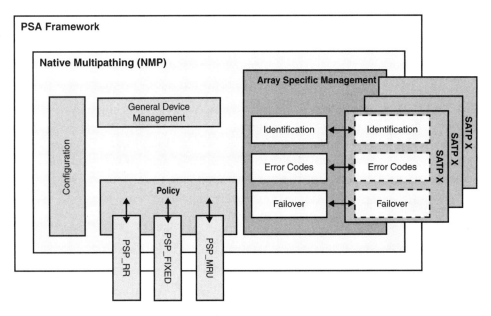

Figure 5.8   NMP components of the PSA framework

Now that we covered the individual components of the PSA framework, let's put together the pieces. Figure 5.8 shows the NMP components of the PSA framework. NMP provides facilities for configuration, general device management, array-specific management, and path selection policies.

The configuration of NMP-related components can be done via ESXCLI or the user interface (UI) provided by vSphere Client. Read more on this topic in the "Modifying PSA Plug-in Configurations Using the UI" section, later in this chapter.

NMP sets multipathing and failover policy with the aid of PSPs. For details on how to configure a PSP for a given array, see the "Modifying PSA Plug-in Configurations Using the UI" section, later in this chapter.

NMP handles array-specific functions via the following functions:

- **Identification**—This is done by interpreting the response data to various inquiry commands—Standard Inquiry and Vital Product Data (VPD) received from the array/storage. It provides details of device identification, including the following:

  - Vendor

  - Model

  - Logical unit number (LUN)

  - Device ID—for example, NAA ID, serial number

  - Supported mode pages—for example, page 80 or 83

  (I cover more details and examples of inquiry strings in Chapter 7, "Multipathing and Failover.")

- **Error codes**—NMP interprets error codes received from the storage arrays with help from the corresponding SATPs and acts on these errors. For example, an SATP can identify a path as dead.

- **Failover**—After NMP interprets the error codes, it reacts in response to them. Continuing with the example, after a path is identified as dead, NMP instructs the relevant SATP to activate standby paths and then instructs the relevant PSP to issue the I/O on one of the activated paths. In this example, there are no active paths remaining, so standby paths are activated (which is the case for active/passive arrays).

I/O Flow Through PSA and NMP

In order to understand how I/O sent to storage devices flows through the ESXi storage stack, you first need to understand some of the terminology relevant to this chapter.

Classification of Arrays Based on How They Handle I/O

Arrays can be one of the following types:

- **Active/active**—This type of array has more than one storage processor (SP) (also known as a storage controller) that can process I/O concurrently on all SPs (and SP ports) with similar performance metrics. This type of array has no concept of LUN ownership because I/O can be done on any LUN via any SP port from initiators given access to such LUNs.

- **Active/passive**—This type of array has two SPs. LUNs are distributed across both SPs in a fashion referred to as *LUN ownership*, in which one of the SPs owns some of the LUNs and the other SP owns the remaining LUNs. The array accepts I/O to a given LUN via ports on that SP that "owns" it. I/O sent to the non-owner SPs (also known as passive SP) is rejected with a SCSI check condition and a sense code that translates to ILLEGAL REQUEST. Think of this as a "No Entry" sign at the entrance of a one-way street in the direction opposite to the traffic. (For more details on sense codes, see Chapter 7.)

NOTE

Some older firmware versions of certain arrays, such as HP MSA, are a variety of the active/passive in which one SP is active and the other is standby. The difference is that all LUNs are owned by the active SP, and the standby SP is used only when the active SP fails. The standby SP still responds with a similar sense code to the code returned from the passive SP described earlier.

- **Asymmetric active/active (AAA; also known as pseudo active/active)**—LUNs on this type of array are owned by either SP, much as in the active/passive arrays concept of LUN ownership. However, the array allows concurrent I/O on a given LUN via ports on both SPs but with different I/O performance metrics, as I/O is sent via proxy from the non-owner SP to the owner SP. In this case, the SP providing the lower performance metric accepts I/O to that LUN without returning a check condition. You might think of this as a hybrid between active/passive and active/active types. The AAA type can result in poor I/O performance of all paths to the owner SP that are dead, either due to poor design or LUN owner SP hardware failure.

- **Asymmetric Logical Unit Access (ALUA)**—This type of array is an enhanced version of the asymmetric active/active arrays and also the newer generation of some of the active/passive arrays. This technology allows initiators to identify the ports on the owner SP as one group and the ports on the non-owner SP as a different group. This is referred to as Target Port Group Support (TPGS). The port group on the owner SP is identified as an active optimized port group, and the other group is identified as an active/non-optimized port group. NMP sends the I/O to a given LUN via a port in the ALUA optimized port group only as long as the ports in that group are available. If all ports in that group are identified as dead, I/O is sent to a port on the ALUA non-optimized port group. When sustained I/O is sent to the ALUA non-optimized port group, the array can transfer the LUN ownership to the non-owner SP and then transition the ports on that SP to the ALUA optimized state. (For more details on ALUA, see Chapter 6.)

Paths and Path States

From a storage perspective, the possible routes to a given LUN through which the I/O may travel are referred to as paths. A path consists of multiple points that start from the initiator port and end at the LUN. A path can be in one of the states listed in Table 5.2.

Table 5.2 Path states

Path State	Description
Active	A path via an active SP. I/O can be sent to any path in this state.
Standby	A path via a passive or standby SP. I/O is not sent via such a path.
Disabled	A path that is disabled, usually by the vSphere administrator.
Dead	A path that lost connectivity to the storage network. This can be due to host bus adapter (HBA), fabric or Ethernet switch, or SP port connectivity loss. It can also be due to HBA or SP hardware failure.
Unknown	The state could not be determined by the relevant SATP.

Preferred Path Setting

A *preferred path* is a setting that NMP honors for devices claimed by the VMW_PSP_ FIXED PSP only. All I/O to a given device is sent over the path configured as the preferred path for that device. When the preferred path is unavailable, I/O is sent via one of the surviving paths. When the preferred path becomes available, I/O fails back to that path. By default, the first path discovered and claimed by the PSP is set as the preferred path. (To change the preferred path setting, refer to the "Modifying PSA Plug-in Configurations Using the UI" section, later in this chapter.)

Figure 5.9 shows an example of a path to LUN 1 from Host A (interrupted line) and Host B (interrupted line with dots and dashes). This path goes through HBA0 to target 1 on SPA.

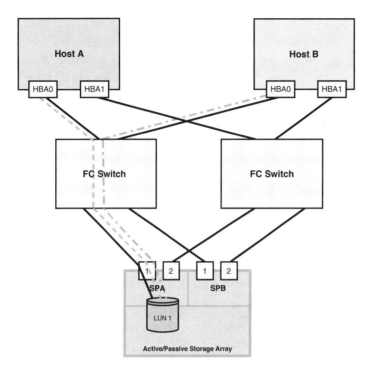

Figure 5.9 Paths to LUN 1 from two hosts

Such a path is represented by the following runtime name (formerly canonical name) naming convention: HBAx:Cn:Ty:Lz. An example is vmhba0:C0:T0:L1, which reads as follows: vmhba0, Channel 0, Target 0, LUN1. It represents the path to LUN 0, which can be broken down as follows:

- **HBA0**—This is the first HBA in this host. The vmhba number may vary based on the number of storage adapters installed in the host. For example, if the host has two RAID controllers installed, and they assume vmhba0 and vmhba1 names, the first FC HBA is named vmhba2.

- **Channel 0**—The channel number is mostly zero for FC- and iSCSI-attached devices to target 0, which is the first target. If the HBA were a SCSI adapter with two channels (for example, internal connections and an external port for direct attached devices), the channel numbers would be 0 and 1.

- **Target 0**—The target number is based on the order in which the SP ports are discovered by PSA. In this case, SPA-Port1 was discovered before SPA-Port2 and the other ports on SPB. Therefore, that port was given "target 0" as part of the runtime name. (The target definition was covered in Chapters 3, "FCoE Storage Connectivity," and 4, "iSCSI Storage Connectivity.")

NOTE

The runtime name, as the name indicates, does not persist between host reboots. This is because it is possible that any of the components that make up that name may change due to hardware or connectivity changes. For example, a host might have an additional HBA added or another HBA removed, which would change the number assumed by the HBA.

Flow of I/O Through NMP

Figure 5.10 shows the flow of I/O through NMP.

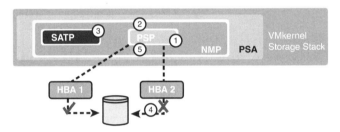

Figure 5.10   I/O flow through NMP

Figure 5.10 illustrates the following steps:

1. NMP calls the PSP assigned to the given logical device.

2. The PSP selects an appropriate physical path on which to send the I/O. If the PSP is VMW_PSP_RR, it load balances the I/O over paths whose states are active or, for ALUA devices, paths via a target port group whose AAS is active/optimized.

3. If the array returns an I/O error, NMP calls the relevant SATP.

4. The SATP interprets the error codes, activates inactive paths, and then fails over to the new active path.

5. The PSP selects a new active path to which it sends the I/O.

Listing Multipath Details

There are two ways you can display the list of paths to a given LUN:

- Listing paths to a LUN by using the user interface (UI)
- Listing paths to a LUN by using the command-line interface (CLI)

Listing Paths to a LUN by Using the UI

To list all paths to a given LUN in the ESXi 6 host, you may follow this procedure, which is similar to the procedure for listing all targets discussed in Chapter 2, "Fibre Channel Storage Connectivity," and Chapters 3 and 4:

1. Connect to the vCenter server that manages the ESXi 6 host, using the vSphere 6.0 Web Client as a user with Administrator privileges.

2. Navigate to the **Inventory—Hosts and Clusters** view and locate the ESXi 6.0 host in the inventory tree and select it.

3. Navigate to the **Manage** tab.

4. Click the **Storage** button.

5. Select **Storage Devices** section.

6. In the **Storage Devices** pane, select one of the SAN LUNs (see Figure 2.11). In this example, its name starts with **DGC Fibre Channel Disk**.

7. In the **Device Details** pane, select the **Properties** tab.

8. Scroll down and click the **Edit Multipathing** button (see Figure 5.11).

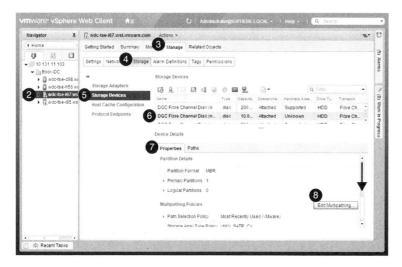

Figure 5.11   Listing LUN paths

Figure 5.12 shows the LUN multipathing details. Note that when the PSP is set to anything other than **Fixed**, the path listing is grayed out. So, for visibility in this example, I temporarily changed it from **MRU** to **Fixed**. (I will discuss PSP choices later in this chapter.)

In this example, I sorted on the Runtime Name field, in ascending order.
Figure 5.12 shows the following:

a. Runtime Name—vmhbaX:C0:Ty:Lz, where X is the HBA number, y is the
target number, and z is the LUN. (More on this later in the chapter.)

b. Status—The path state for each listed path.

c. Target—The WWNN followed by the WWPN of the target, separated by a
space.

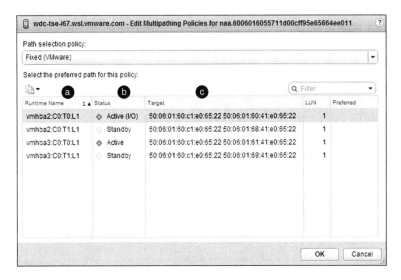

Figure 5.12   Listing paths to the SAN LUN

Figure 5.13 shows similar information for paths to a LUN on iSCSI-based
targets. Here the target iSCSI qualified name (IQN) is too long to fit in the
Target column. To view the full IQN, hover over the target field on the given
path, and you should see the full name in a yellow box. (The IQN was discussed
in Chapter 4.)

The **Target Name** is made up of the target's IQN, the LUN's volume
name, and the dynamic discovery address. In this example, I am using a Dell
EqualLogic PS series iSCSI storage array. Other vendors may compose the
target name slightly differently.

Figure 5.14 shows an example of a target on an EMC VNX. The target IQN
ends with the port number; in this example, it is a2, which is SPA port 2, or b2,
which is SPB port 2, followed by a colon and then the target dynamic discovery
address.

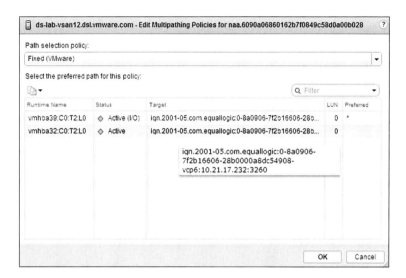

Figure 5.13   Listing paths to an iSCSI-attached LUN

Figure 5.14   Listing paths to an iSCSI-attached LUN

NOTE

Fibre Channel over Ethernet (FCoE)–based path listings are identical to FC-based path listings.

Listing Paths to a LUN by Using the CLI

ESXCLI provides similar details to the UI, discussed in the preceding section. (For details about the various facilities that provide access to ESXCLI, refer to Chapter 2.)

The namespace of ESXCLI in ESXi 6 is fairly intuitive. Simply start with `esxcli` followed by the area of vSphere you want to manage—for example, `esxcli network`, `esxcli` software, `esxcli storage`—to manage ESXi Network, ESXi Software, and ESXi Storage, respectively. For more available options, just run `esxcli -help`.

Figure 5.15 shows the `esxcli storage nmp` namespace.

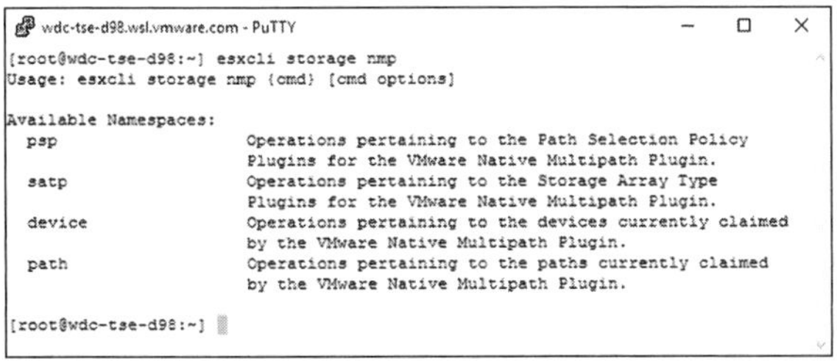

Figure 5.15 `esxcli storage nmp` namespace

The `esxcli storage nmp` namespace is for all operations pertaining to native multipathing, including `psp`, `satp`, `device`, and `path`.

I cover all these namespaces in detail later in this chapter, in the "Modifying PSA Plug-in Configurations Using the UI" section. These are the relevant operations for this section:

- `esxcli storage nmp path list`
- `esxcli storage nmp path list -d <device ID, e.g., NAA ID>`

The first command provides a list of paths to all devices, regardless of how they are attached to the host or which protocol is used.

The second command, which includes the `-d` option, lists the paths to the device specified by the device ID (for example, NAA ID).

Consider this example:

```
esxcli storage nmp path list -d naa.6006016055711d00cff95e65664ee011
```

You can also use the verbose command option, `--device`, instead of `-d`.

You can identify the NAA ID of the device you want to list by running a command like this:

```
esxcfg-mpath -b |grep -B1 "fc Adapter"| grep -v -e "--" |sed 's/Adapter.*//'
```

You can also use the verbose command option, `--list-paths`, instead of `-b`. Figure 5.16 shows the output of this command.

```
wdc-tse-d98.wsl.vmware.com - PuTTY                                    —  □  ×
[root@wdc-tse-d98:~] esxcfg-mpath -b |grep -B1 "fc Adapter"| grep -v -e "--" |sed 's/Adapter.*//'
naa.6006016055711d00cff95e65664ee011 : DGC Fibre Channel Disk (naa.6006016055711d00cff95e65664ee011)
   vmhba2:C0:T0:L1 LUN:1 state:active fc
   vmhba2:C0:T1:L1 LUN:1 state:standby fc
   vmhba3:C0:T0:L1 LUN:1 state:active fc
   vmhba3:C0:T1:L1 LUN:1 state:standby fc
```

Figure 5.16   Listing paths to an FC-attached LUN—CLI

This output shows all FC-attached devices. The device display name of each device is listed, followed immediately by the runtime name (for example, vmhba3:C0:T0:L1) of all paths to that device. This output is somewhat similar to the Legacy-MP output you may have seen with ESX Server release 3.5 and older.

The device display name is actually listed after the device NAA ID and a colon.

From the runtime name, you can identify the LUN and the HBA through which the device can be accessed. The HBA number is the first part of the runtime name, and the LUN is the last part of that name.

Every block device conforming to the SCSI-3 standard has an NAA device ID assigned, which is listed at the beginning and the end of the Device Display Name line in the preceding output. In this example, FC-attached LUN 1 has NAA ID `naa.6006016055711 d00cff95e65664ee011`, which I used in the output shown in Figure 5.17.

The following command is used in Figure 5.17:

```
esxcli storage nmp path list -d naa.6006016055711d00cff95e65664ee011
```

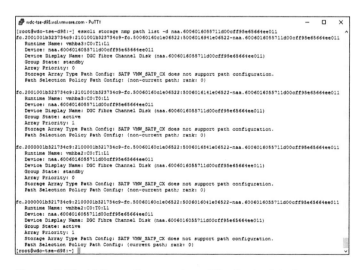

Figure 5.17   Listing pathnames to an FC-attached device

You can use the verbose version of the command shown in Figure 5.17 by using `--device` instead of `-d`.

From the output in Figure 5.16 and 5.17, you can see that LUN 1 has four paths.

Using the runtime name, you can see that the following paths lead to LUN 1:

- `vmhba3:C0:T1:L1`
- `vmhba3:C0:T0:L1`
- `vmhba2:C0:T1:L1`
- `vmhba2:C0:T0:L1`

This translates to the list shown in Figure 5.18, based on the physical pathnames. This output was collected using the following command:

```
esxcli storage nmp path list -d naa.6006016055711d00cff95e65664ee011
 |grep fc
```

The verbose option is as follows:

```
esxcli storage nmp path list --device naa.6006016055711d00cff95e65664ee011
 |grep fc
```

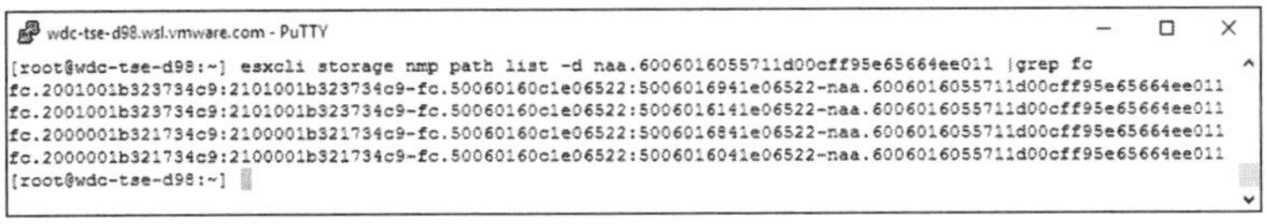

Figure 5.18 Listing physical pathnames of an FC-attached LUN

This output is similar to the aggregate of all paths that would have been identified using the corresponding UI procedure earlier in this section.

Using Table 2.1 from Chapter 2, we can translate the targets listed in the four paths as shown in Table 5.3:

Table 5.3 Identifying SP ports for LUN paths

Runtime Name	Target WWPN	SP Port Association
vmhba3:C0:T1:L1	5006016941e06522	SPB1
vmhba3:C0:T0:L1	5006016141e06522	SPA1
vmhba2:C0:T1:L1	5006016841e06522	SPB0
vmhba2:C0:T0:L1	5006016041e06522	SPA0

Identifying Path States and on Which Path the I/O Is Sent—FC

In the FC example (refer to Figure 5.17), two fields are relevant to the task of identifying the path states and the I/O path: `Group State` and `Path Selection Policy Path Config`. Table 5.4 shows the values of these fields and their meanings.

Table 5.4 Path state–related fields

Runtime Name	`Group State`	`PSP Path Config`	Meaning
vmhba3:C0:T1:L1	Standby	non-current path; rank: 0	Passive SP—no I/O
vmhba3:C0:T0:L1	Active	non-current path; rank: 0	Active-SP—no I/O
vmhba2:C0:T1:L1	Standby	non-current path; rank: 0	Passive SP—no I/O
vmhba2:C0:T0:L1	Active	current path; rank: 0	Active SP—I/O

Combining the last two tables, we can extrapolate the following:

- The LUN is currently owned by SPA (therefore, the state is active).
- The I/O to the LUN is sent via the path to SPA port 0.

> **NOTE**
>
> This information is provided by the PSP path configuration because its function is to determine on which physical path to issue I/O requests being sent to a given storage device.
>
> The rank configuration listed here shows the value of 0. I discuss ranked I/O in Chapter 7.

Example of Listing Paths to an iSCSI-Attached Device

To list paths to a specific iSCSI-attached LUN, try a different approach for locating the device ID:

```
esxcfg-mpath -m |grep iqn
```

You can also use the verbose command option:

```
esxcfg-mpath --list-map |grep iqn
```

Figure 5.19 shows the output from this command.

Figure 5.19   Listing paths to an iSCSI-attached LUN—CLI

Figure 5.19 shows the output lines wrapped. Each line actually begins with vmhba35 for readability. This output provides the information listed in Table 5.5.

Table 5.5 Matching runtime names with their NAA IDs

Runtime Name	NAA ID
vmhba35:C0:T13:L0	naa.6006016092c01c00947f91cc7181e411
vmhba35:C0:T9:L0	naa.6006016092c01c00947f91cc7181e411

This means that these two paths are to the same LUN, LUN 0, and the NAA ID is naa.6006016092c01c00947f91cc7181e411.

Now you can get the pathnames for this LUN. You use the same command that you used for listing the FC device:

```
esxcli storage nmp path list -d naa.6006016092c01c00947f91cc7181e411
```

You can also use the verbose version of this command:

```
esxcli storage nmp path list --device naa.6006016092c01c00947f91cc7181e411
```

Figure 5.20 shows the output from this command. Note that the pathname here are wrapped for readability.

Figure 5.20   Listing paths to an iSCSI-attached LUN—CLI

The output here is identical to what you observed with FC-attached devices except for the actual pathname. Here, it starts with `iqn` instead of `fc`.

The `Group State` and `Path Selection Policy Path Config` fields shows similar content as well. Based on that, I built Table 5.6.

Table 5.6 Matching runtime names with their target IDs and SP ports

Runtime Name	Target IQN	SP Port Association
vmhba35:C0:T13:L0	iqn.1992-04.com.emc:cx.apm00071501970.b0	SPB0
vmhba35:C0:T9:L0	iqn.1992-04.com.emc:cx.apm00071501970.a0	SPA0

To list only the pathnames in the output shown in Figure 5.20, you can append `|grep iqn` to the command.

The output of the command is listed in Figure 5.21. Note that it was wrapped for readability. Each pathname starts with `iqn`:

```
esxcli storage nmp path list --device naa.6006016092c01c00947f91cc7181e411
 |grep iqn
```

```
wdc-tse-d98.wsl.vmware.com - PuTTY                          —    □    ×
[root@wdc-tse-d98:~] esxcli storage nmp path list --device naa.6006016092
c01c00947f91cc7181e411 |grep iqn
iqn.1998-01.com.vmware:wdc-tse-d98-75ef2a85-00023d000001,iqn.1992-04.com.
emc:cx.apm00071501970.b0,t,5-naa.6006016092c01c00947f91cc7181e411
iqn.1998-01.com.vmware:wdc-tse-d98-75ef2a85-00023d000001,iqn.1992-04.com.
emc:cx.apm00071501970.a0,t,1-naa.6006016092c01c00947f91cc7181e411
[root@wdc-tse-d98:~]
```

Figure 5.21   Listing pathnames of iSCSI-attached LUNs

Identifying Path States and on Which Path the I/O Is Sent—iSCSI

The process of identifying path states and I/O paths for iSCSI is identical to the process used for FC, described in the preceding section.

Example of Listing Paths to an FCoE-Attached Device

The process of listing paths to HW FCoE-attached devices is identical to the process for FC except that the string you use is `fcoe Adapter` instead of `fc Adapter`.

Figure 5.22 provides sample output from an SW FCoE configuration.

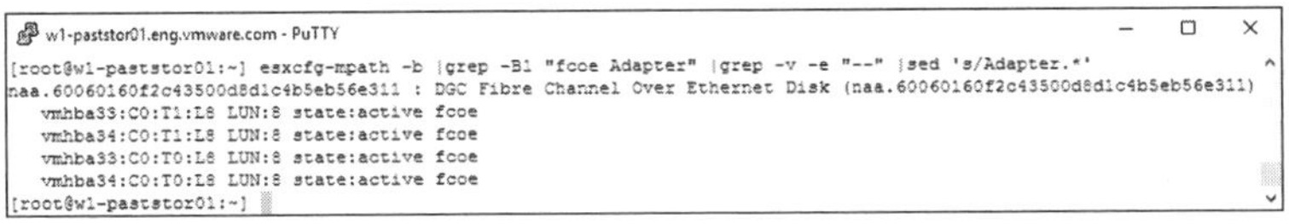

Figure 5.22 List of runtime paths of FCoE-attached LUNs—CLI

The command used in Figure 5.22 is as follows:

```
esxcfg-mpath -b |grep -B1 "fcoe Adapter" |sed 's/Adapter.*//'
```

You can also use the verbose command:

```
esxcfg-mpath --list-paths |grep -B1 "fcoe Adapter" |sed 's/Adapter.*//'
```

If you see more than one LUN, the output shows them separated by a dashed line. To remove these line, you can add `|grep -v -e "--"`, as shown here:

```
esxcfg-mpath --list-paths |grep -B1 "fcoe Adapter" |grep -v -e "--" |sed
's/Adapter.*//'
```

To list individual path details of a given LUN, use this command instead:

```
esxcli storage nmp path list -d naa.60060160f2c43500d8d1c4b5eb56e311
```

Using the NAA ID for LUN 8, Figure 5.23 shows the list of pathnames .

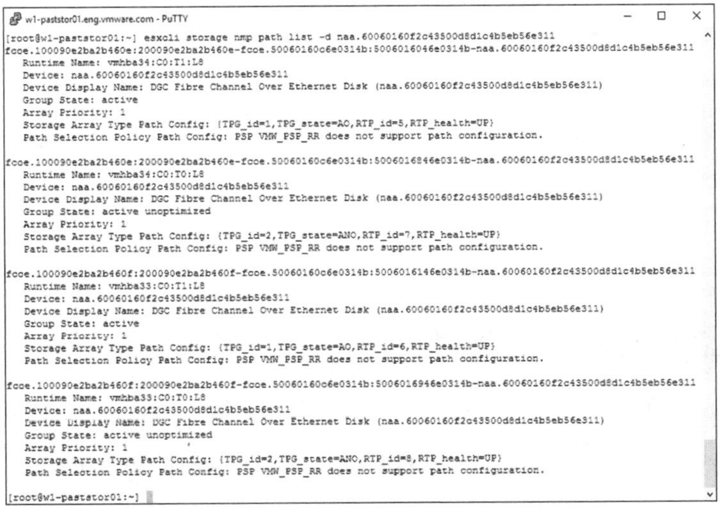

Figure 5.23 List of pathnames of an FCoE-attached LUN

You can also use the verbose version of the command shown in Figure 5.23 by using `--device` instead of `-d`. This translates to the physical pathnames shown in Figure 5.24.

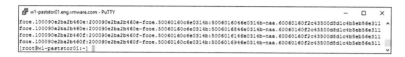

Figure 5.24 List of pathnames of an FCoE LUN

The following command is used to generate the output shown in Figure 5.24:

```
esxcli storage nmp path list -d naa.60060160f2c43500d8d1c4b5eb56e311
 |grep fcoe
```

By using Table 2.1 in Chapter 2, we can translate the targets listed in the four returned paths as shown in Table 5.7.

Table 5.7 Translation of FCoE targets

Runtime Name	Target WWPN	SP Port Association
vmhba34:C0:T1:L8	5006016046e0314b	SPA0
vmhba34:C0:T0:L8	5006016846e0314b	SPB0
vmhba33:C0:T1:L8	5006016146e0314b	SPA1
vmhba33:C0:T0:L8	5006016946e0314b	SPB1

Identifying Path States and on Which Path the I/O Is Sent—FC

Following the same process as in the FC example (refer to Figure 5.17), two fields are relevant to the task of identifying the path states and the I/O path: `Group State` and `Path Selection Policy Path Config`. Table 5.8 shows the values of these fields and their meanings.

Table 5.8 Interpreting path states—FCoE

Runtime Name	Group State	PSP Path Config	Meaning
vmhba34:C0:T1:L1	Standby	non-current path; rank: 0	Passive SP — no I/O
vmhba34:C0:T0:L1	Active	current path; rank: 0	Active-SP — I/O
vmhba33:C0:T1:L1	Standby	non-current path; rank: 0	Passive SP — no I/O
vmhba33:C0:T0:L1	Active	non-current path; rank: 0	Active SP — no I/O

Combining the last two tables, we can extrapolate the following:

- The LUN is currently "owned" by SPB (hence the state is active).
- The I/O to the LUN is sent via the path to SPB port 1.

Claim Rules

Each storage device is managed by one of the PSA plug-ins at any given time. In other words, a device cannot be managed by more than one PSA plug-in.

For example, if a host has a third-party MPP installed along with NMP, devices managed by the third-party MPP cannot be managed by NMP unless the configuration is changed to assign those devices to NMP. The process of associating certain devices with certain PSA plug-ins is referred to as *claiming*, and the process is defined by *claim rules*. These rules define the correlation between a device and NMP or MPP. NMP has additional association between the claimed device and a specific SATP and PSP.

This section shows how to list the various claim rules. The next section discusses how to change these rules.

Claim rules can be defined based on one or a combination of the following:

- **Vendor string**—In response to the standard inquiry command, the arrays return the standard inquiry response, which includes the vendor string. This can be used in the definition of a claim rule based on an exact match. A partial match or a string with padded spaces does not work.

- **Model string**—Similarly to the vendor string, the model string is returned as part of the standard inquiry response. As with the vendor string, a claim rule can be defined using the exact match of the model string, and padded spaces are not supported here.

- **Transport**—You can define a claim rule based on the transport type to claim all devices that use that transport. Valid transport types are `block`, `fc`, `iscsi`, `iscsivendor`, `ide`, `sas`, `sata`, `usb`, `parallel`, and `unknown`.

- **Driver**—You can specify a driver name as one of the criteria for a claim rule definition to allow all devices accessible via such a driver to be claimed. An example is a claim rule to mask all paths to devices attached to an HBA that uses the mptscsi driver.

MP Claim Rules

The first set of claim rules we look at in this section defines which MPP claims which devices. Figure 5.25 shows the default MP claim rules.

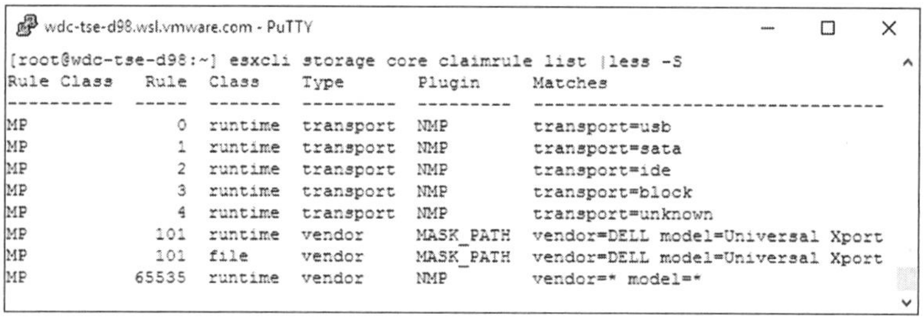

```
[root@wdc-tse-d98:~] esxcli storage core claimrule list |less -S
Rule Class  Rule  Class    Type       Plugin     Matches
----------  ----- -------  ---------  ---------  ------------------------------
MP              0  runtime  transport  NMP        transport=usb
MP              1  runtime  transport  NMP        transport=sata
MP              2  runtime  transport  NMP        transport=ide
MP              3  runtime  transport  NMP        transport=block
MP              4  runtime  transport  NMP        transport=unknown
MP            101  runtime  vendor     MASK_PATH  vendor=DELL model=Universal Xport
MP            101  file     vendor     MASK_PATH  vendor=DELL model=Universal Xport
MP          65535  runtime  vendor     NMP        vendor=* model=*
```

Figure 5.25 Listing MP claim rules

In Figure 5.25, the screenshot window was not wide enough to show the full width of the output. You can press the right-arrow key to see the rest of the output, as shown in Figure 5.26.

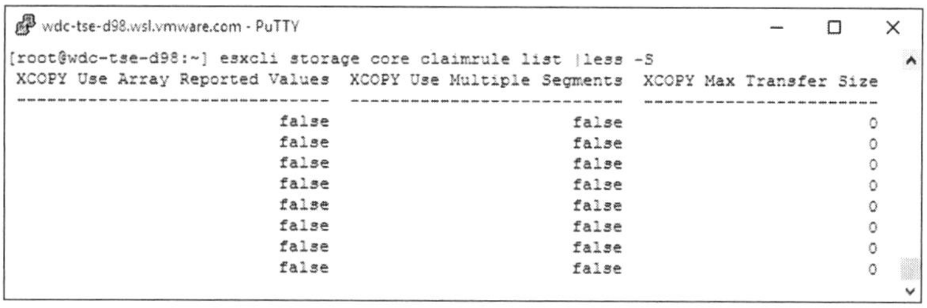

```
[root@wdc-tse-d98:~] esxcli storage core claimrule list |less -S
XCOPY Use Array Reported Values  XCOPY Use Multiple Segments  XCOPY Max Transfer Size
-------------------------------  ---------------------------  -----------------------
                         false                        false                        0
                         false                        false                        0
                         false                        false                        0
                         false                        false                        0
                         false                        false                        0
                         false                        false                        0
                         false                        false                        0
                         false                        false                        0
```

Figure 5.26 Listing MP claim rules—remaining output

You use the following command to list these rules:

```
esxcli storage core claimrule list |less -S
```

TIP

To preserve tab formatting of the output in Figures 5.25 and 5.26 so that columns are displayed aligned correctly, I piped the output to the command less -S.

The namespace here is for the core storage because the MPP definition is done on the PSA level. The output shows that this rule class is MP, which indicates that these rules define the devices' association to a specific multipathing plug-in.

Two plug-ins are specified here: NMP and MASK_PATH. I have already discussed NMP in the previous sections. The MASK_PATH plug-in is used for masking paths to specific devices and is a replacement for the deprecated Legacy Multipathing LUN masking vmkernel parameter. I provide some examples later in this chapter, in the section "Modifying PSA Plug-in Configurations Using the UI."

Table 5.9 lists each column name in the output in Figures 5.25 and 5.26, along with an explanation of each column.

Table 5.9 Explanation of claim rules fields

Column Name	Explanation
Rule Class	This is the plug-in class for which this claim rule set is defined. This can be MP, Filter, or VAAI.
Rule	This is the rule number. This defines the order in which the rules are loaded. As in firewall rules, the first match is used and supersedes conflicting rules with larger numbers.
Class	The value can be `runtime` or `file`. The value `file` means that the rule definitions were stored to the configuration files. (You'll learn more on this later in this section.) The value `runtime` means that the rule was read from the configuration files and loaded into memory. In other words, it means that the rule is active. If a rule is listed as `file` only and not `runtime`, the rule was just created but has not been loaded yet. (Find out more about loading rules in the next section.) Note that the default NMP rules 0 through 4 and 65545 have a `runtime` class only.
Type	The type can be `vendor`, `model`, `transport`, or `driver`. See the explanation earlier in this section.
Plugin	This is the name of the plug-in for which this rule was defined.
Matches	This is the most important field in the rule definition. This column shows the type specified for the rule and its value. When the specified type is `vendor`, an additional parameter, `model`, must be used. The `model` string must be an exact string match or must include an * as a wildcard. You can use a ^ as "begins with" and then the string, followed by an *— (for example, `^OPEN-*`).
XCOPY Use Array Reported Values	When this is enabled, XCOPY uses the storage array's reported parameters to size the XCOPY segment. (You'll learn more on this in Chapter 17, "VAAI.")
XCOPY Use Multiple Segments	When this is enabled, XCOPY uses multiple data segments in a single command (see Chapter 17)
XCOPY Max Transfer Size	Specifies the hardware max segment length. Requires the Use Array Reported Values option to be enabled (see Chapter 17).

The highest rule number in any claim rules set is 65535. It is assigned here to a catch-all rule that claims devices from "any" vendor with "any" model string. It is placed as the last rule in the set to allow lower-numbered rules to claim their specified devices. If the attached devices have no specific rules defined, they get claimed by NMP.

Figure 5.27 shows an example of third-party MP plug-in claim rules.

```
wdc-tse-d98.wsl.vmware.com - PuTTY                                    —    □    ×
Rule Class    Rule   Class     Type        Plugin      Matches
----------    ----   -------   ---------   ---------   -------------------------------------
MP               0   runtime   transport   NMP         transport=usb
MP               1   runtime   transport   NMP         transport=sata
MP               2   runtime   transport   NMP         transport=ide
MP               3   runtime   transport   NMP         transport=block
MP               4   runtime   transport   NMP         transport=unknown
MP             101   runtime   vendor      MASK_PATH   vendor=DELL model=Universal Xport
MP             101   file      vendor      MASK_PATH   vendor=DELL model=Universal Xport
MP             250   runtime   vendor      PowerPath   vendor=DGC model=*
MP             250   file      vendor      PowerPath   vendor=DGC model=*
MP             260   runtime   vendor      PowerPath   vendor=EMC model=SYMMETRIX
MP             260   file      vendor      PowerPath   vendor=EMC model=SYMMETRIX
MP             270   runtime   vendor      PowerPath   vendor=EMC model=Invista
MP             270   file      vendor      PowerPath   vendor=EMC model=Invista
MP             280   runtime   vendor      PowerPath   vendor=HITACHI model=*
MP             280   file      vendor      PowerPath   vendor=HITACHI model=*
MP             290   runtime   vendor      PowerPath   vendor=HP model=*
MP             290   file      vendor      PowerPath   vendor=HP model=*
MP             300   runtime   vendor      PowerPath   vendor=COMPAQ model=HSV111 (C)COMPAQ
MP             300   file      vendor      PowerPath   vendor=COMPAQ model=HSV111 (C)COMPAQ
MP             310   runtime   vendor      PowerPath   vendor=EMC model=Celerra
MP             310   file      vendor      PowerPath   vendor=EMC model=Celerra
MP             320   runtime   vendor      PowerPath   vendor=IBM model=2107900
MP             320   file      vendor      PowerPath   vendor=IBM model=2107900
MP             330   runtime   vendor      PowerPath   vendor=IBM model=2810XIV
MP             330   file      vendor      PowerPath   vendor=IBM model=2810XIV
MP             340   runtime   vendor      PowerPath   vendor=XtremIO model=XtremApp
MP             340   file      vendor      PowerPath   vendor=XtremIO model=XtremApp
MP             350   runtime   vendor      PowerPath   vendor=NETAPP model=*
MP             350   file      vendor      PowerPath   vendor=NETAPP model=*
MP           65535   runtime   vendor      NMP         vendor=* model=*

(END)
```

Figure 5.27   Listing EMC PowerPath/VE claim rules

Here you see that rules 250 through 320 were added by PowerPath/VE, which allows the PowerPath plug-in to claim all the devices listed in Table 5.10.

Table 5.10   Arrays claimed by PowerPath

Storage Array	Vendor	Model
EMC CLARiiON Family	DGC	Any (* is a wildcard)
EMC Symmetrix Family	EMC	Symmetrix
EMC Invista	EMC	Invista
HITACHI	Hitachi	Any
HP	HP	Any
HP EVA HSV111 family (Compaq Branded)	HP	HSV111 (C) COMPAQ
EMC Celerra	EMC	Celerra

Storage Array	Vendor	Model
IBM DS8000 family	IBM	2107900
IBM XIV	IBM	2810XIV
EMC XtremIO	XtremIO	XtremApp
NetApp	NETAPP	Any (* is a wildcard)

NOTE

There is currently a known limitation with claim rules that use a partial match on the model string. Versions of PowerPath/VE older than 5.7, which used to have rules stating `model=OPEN`, may not claim the devices whose model string is something such as `OPEN-V`, `OPEN-10`, and so on. As is evident in Figure 5.27, PowerPath/VE version 6 no longer uses partial matches. Instead, partial matches have been replaced with an `*`.

Plug-in Registration

The concept of plug-in registration was introduced in vSphere 5 and continues in vSphere 6. Actually, it existed in 4.x but was not exposed to the end user. When a PSA plug-in is installed, it gets registered with the PSA framework, along with dependencies, if any, as shown in the output in Figure 5.28.

The following command is used here:

```
esxcli storage core plugin registration list
```

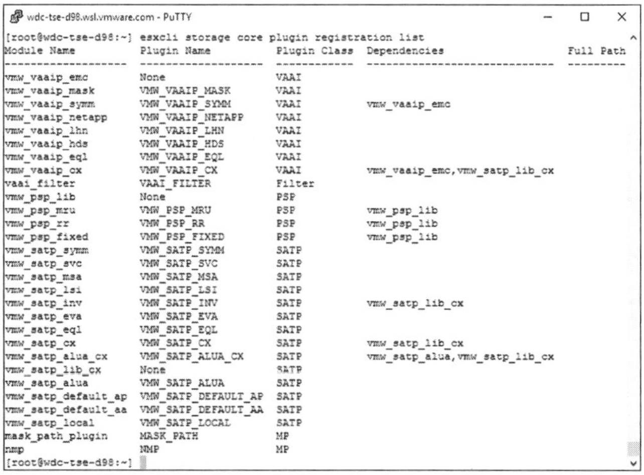

```
wdc-tse-d98.wsl.vmware.com - PuTTY
[root@wdc-tse-d98:~] esxcli storage core plugin registration list
Module Name          Plugin Name          Plugin Class  Dependencies                   Full Path
-------------------  -------------------  ------------  -----------------------------  ---------
vmw_vaaip_emc        None                 VAAI
vmw_vaaip_mask       VMW_VAAIP_MASK       VAAI
vmw_vaaip_symm       VMW_VAAIP_SYMM       VAAI          vmw_vaaip_emc
vmw_vaaip_netapp     VMW_VAAIP_NETAPP     VAAI
vmw_vaaip_lhn        VMW_VAAIP_LHN        VAAI
vmw_vaaip_hds        VMW_VAAIP_HDS        VAAI
vmw_vaaip_eql        VMW_VAAIP_EQL        VAAI
vmw_vaaip_cx         VMW_VAAIP_CX         VAAI          vmw_vaaip_emc,vmw_satp_lib_cx
vaai_filter          VAAI_FILTER          Filter
vmw_psp_lib          None                 PSP
vmw_psp_mru          VMW_PSP_MRU          PSP           vmw_psp_lib
vmw_psp_rr           VMW_PSP_RR           PSP           vmw_psp_lib
vmw_psp_fixed        VMW_PSP_FIXED        PSP           vmw_psp_lib
vmw_satp_symm        VMW_SATP_SYMM        SATP
vmw_satp_svc         VMW_SATP_SVC         SATP
vmw_satp_msa         VMW_SATP_MSA         SATP
vmw_satp_lsi         VMW_SATP_LSI         SATP
vmw_satp_inv         VMW_SATP_INV         SATP          vmw_satp_lib_cx
vmw_satp_eva         VMW_SATP_EVA         SATP
vmw_satp_eql         VMW_SATP_EQL         SATP
vmw_satp_cx          VMW_SATP_CX          SATP          vmw_satp_lib_cx
vmw_satp_alua_cx     VMW_SATP_ALUA_CX     SATP          vmw_satp_alua,vmw_satp_lib_cx
vmw_satp_lib_cx      None                 SATP
vmw_satp_alua        VMW_SATP_ALUA        SATP
vmw_satp_default_ap  VMW_SATP_DEFAULT_AP  SATP
vmw_satp_default_aa  VMW_SATP_DEFAULT_AA  SATP
vmw_satp_local       VMW_SATP_LOCAL       SATP
mask_path_plugin     MASK_PATH            MP
nmp                  NMP                  MP
[root@wdc-tse-d98:~]
```

Figure 5.28 Listing PSA plug-in registration

This output in Figure 5.28 includes the following columns:

- **Module Name**—This column shows the name of the plug-in kernel module; it is the actual plug-in software binary as well as required libraries, if any, that get plugged into vmkernel.
- **Plugin Name**—This column shows the name by which the plug-in is identified. It is exactly the name to use when creating or modifying claim rules.
- **Plugin Class**—This column shows the name of the class to which the plug-in belongs. For example, the previous section covered the MP class of plug-ins. The next sections discuss SATP and PSP plug-ins, and later chapters cover VAAI and VAAI_Filter classes.
- **Dependencies**—This column shows the libraries and other plug-ins that the registered plug-ins require to operate.
- **Full Path**—This column shows the full path to the files, libraries, or binaries that are specific to the registered plug-in. This is mostly blank in the default registration.

SATP Claim Rules

Now that you understand how NMP plugs into PSA, it's time to examine how SATP plugs into NMP.

Each SATP is associated with a default PSP. The defaults can be overridden using SATP claim rules. Before I show you how to list these rules, let's first review the default settings.

The following command is used to list the default PSP assignment to each SATP:

```
esxcli storage nmp satp list
```

Figure 5.29 shows the output from this command.

```
wdc-tse-d98.wsl.vmware.com - PuTTY
[root@wdc-tse-d98:~] esxcli storage nmp satp list
Name                 Default PSP    Description
-------------------  -------------  -------------------------------------------------------
VMW_SATP_CX          VMW_PSP_MRU    Supports EMC CX that do not use the ALUA protocol
VMW_SATP_ALUA_CX     VMW_PSP_RR     Supports EMC CX that use the ALUA protocol
VMW_SATP_ALUA        VMW_PSP_MRU    Supports non-specific arrays that use the ALUA protocol
VMW_SATP_MSA         VMW_PSP_MRU    Placeholder (plugin not loaded)
VMW_SATP_DEFAULT_AP  VMW_PSP_MRU    Placeholder (plugin not loaded)
VMW_SATP_SVC         VMW_PSP_FIXED  Placeholder (plugin not loaded)
VMW_SATP_EQL         VMW_PSP_FIXED  Placeholder (plugin not loaded)
VMW_SATP_INV         VMW_PSP_FIXED  Placeholder (plugin not loaded)
VMW_SATP_EVA         VMW_PSP_FIXED  Placeholder (plugin not loaded)
VMW_SATP_SYMM        VMW_PSP_RR     Placeholder (plugin not loaded)
VMW_SATP_LSI         VMW_PSP_MRU    Placeholder (plugin not loaded)
VMW_SATP_DEFAULT_AA  VMW_PSP_FIXED  Supports non-specific active/active arrays
VMW_SATP_LOCAL       VMW_PSP_FIXED  Supports direct attached devices
[root@wdc-tse-d98:~]
```

Figure 5.29 Listing SATPs and their default PSPs

The `esxcli` namespace used here is `storage`, `nmp`, and `satp`.

> **NOTE**
>
> In vSphere 5.5, the VMW_SATP_ALUA_CX plug-in was associated with VMW_PSP_FIXED since the functionality of VMW_PSP_FIXED_AP was rolled into VMW_PSP_FIXED in that release. This facilitated the use of the Preferred Path option with ALUA arrays while still handling failover-triggering events in a similar fashion to active/passive arrays. However, in vSphere 6, this plug-in is now associated with VMW_PSP_RR. Read more on this in Chapter 6.

Knowing which PSP is the default policy for which SATP is half the story. NMP needs to know which SATP it will use with which storage device. This is done via SATP claim rules that associate a given SATP with a storage device, based on matches to vendor, model, driver, and/or transport.

To list the SATP rule, run the following command:

```
esxcli storage nmp satp rule list
```

The output of this command is too long and too wide to capture in one screenshot. I have divided the output into a set of figures that each list partial output. Figures 5.30, 5.31, 5.32, and 5.33 show the four quadrants of the output.

> **TIP**
>
> To format the output of this command so that the text is arranged better for readability, you can pipe the output to `less -S`. This truncates the long lines and aligns the text under the appropriate columns. The command then looks like this:
>
> ```
> esxcli storage nmp satp rule list | less -S
> ```

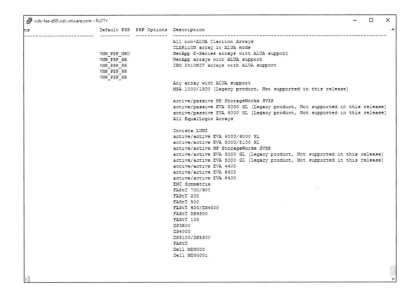

```
wdc-tse-d98.wsl.vmware.com - PuTTY                                                      —  □  X
Name                   Device  Vendor   Model            Driver  Transport  Options                      Rule Group  Claim Option ^
-----------------      ------  ------   --------------   ------  ---------  --------------------------   ----------  ------------
VMW_SATP_CX                    DGC                                                                       system      tpgs_off
VMW_SATP_ALUA_CX               DGC                                                                       system      tpgs_on
VMW_SATP_ALUA                  LSI      INF-01-00                            reset_on_attempted_reserve   system      tpgs_on
VMW_SATP_ALUA                  NETAPP                                        reset_on_attempted_reserve   system      tpgs_on
VMW_SATP_ALUA                  IBM      2810XIV                                                           system      tpgs_on
VMW_SATP_ALUA                  IBM      2107900                              reset_on_attempted_reserve   system
VMW_SATP_ALUA                  IBM      2145                                                              system
VMW_SATP_ALUA                                                                                            system      tpgs_on
VMW_SATP_MSA                            MSA1000 VOLUME                                                    system
VMW_SATP_DEFAULT_AP            DEC      HSG80                                                             system
VMW_SATP_DEFAULT_AP                     HSVX700                                                           system      tpgs_off
VMW_SATP_DEFAULT_AP                     HSV100                                                            system
VMW_SATP_DEFAULT_AP                     HSV110                                                            system
VMW_SATP_EQL                   EQLOGIC                                                                   system
VMW_SATP_INV                   EMC      Invista                                                           system
VMW_SATP_INV                   EMC      LUNZ                                                              system
VMW_SATP_EVA                            HSV200                                                            system      tpgs_off
VMW_SATP_EVA                            HSV210                                                            system      tpgs_off
VMW_SATP_EVA                            HSVX740                                                           system      tpgs_off
VMW_SATP_EVA                            HSV101                                                            system      tpgs_off
VMW_SATP_EVA                            HSV111                                                            system      tpgs_off
VMW_SATP_EVA                            HSV300                                                            system      tpgs_off
VMW_SATP_EVA                            HSV400                                                            system      tpgs_off
VMW_SATP_EVA                            HSV450                                                            system      tpgs_off
VMW_SATP_SYMM                  EMC      SYMMETRIX                                                         system
VMW_SATP_LSI                   IBM      ^1742^                                                            system      tpgs_off
VMW_SATP_LSI                   IBM      ^3542^                                                            system      tpgs_off
VMW_SATP_LSI                   IBM      ^3552^                                                            system      tpgs_off
VMW_SATP_LSI                   IBM      ^1722^                                                            system      tpgs_off
VMW_SATP_LSI                   IBM      ^1815^                                                            system      tpgs_off
VMW_SATP_LSI                   IBM      ^1724^                                                            system      tpgs_off
VMW_SATP_LSI                   IBM      ^1726-^                                                           system      tpgs_off
VMW_SATP_LSI                   IBM      ^1814^                                                            system      tpgs_off
VMW_SATP_LSI                   IBM      ^1818^                                                            system      tpgs_off
VMW_SATP_LSI                            Universal Xport                                                  system      tpgs_off
VMW_SATP_LSI                   DELL     MD3000                                                            system      tpgs_off
VMW_SATP_LSI                   DELL     MD3000i                                                           system      tpgs_off
VMW_SATP_LSI                   STK      OPENstorage 9176                                                  system      tpgs_off
VMW_SATP_LSI                   STK      OPENstorage D173                                                  system      tpgs_off
VMW_SATP_LSI                   STK      OPENstorage D178                                                  system      tpgs_off
```

Figure 5.30 Listing SATP claim rules—Top-left quadrant of output

```
wdc-tse-d98.wsl.vmware.com - PuTTY                                                      —  □  X
ns                     Default PSP  PSP Options  Description                                              ^
-------------------    -----------  -----------  ---------------------------------------------------------
                                                 All non-ALUA Clariion Arrays
                                                 CLARiiON array in ALUA mode
                       VMW_PSP_MRU               NetApp E-Series arrays with ALUA support
                       VMW_PSP_RR                NetApp arrays with ALUA support
                       VMW_PSP_RR                IBM 2810XIV arrays with ALUA support
                       VMW_PSP_RR
                       VMW_PSP_RR
                                                 Any array with ALUA support
                                                 MSA 1000/1500 [Legacy product, Not supported in this release]

                                                 active/passive HP StorageWorks SVSP
                                                 active/passive EVA 3000 GL [Legacy product, Not supported in this release]
                                                 active/passive EVA 5000 GL [Legacy product, Not supported in this release]
                                                 All EqualLogic Arrays

                                                 Invista LUNZ
                                                 active/active EVA 4000/6000 XL
                                                 active/active EVA 8000/8100 XL
                                                 active/active HP StorageWorks SVSP
                                                 active/active EVA 3000 GL [Legacy product, Not supported in this release]
                                                 active/active EVA 5000 GL [Legacy product, Not supported in this release]
                                                 active/active EVA 4400
                                                 active/active EVA 6400
                                                 active/active EVA 8400
                                                 EMC Symmetrix
                                                 FAStT 700/900
                                                 FAStT 200
                                                 FAStT 500
                                                 FAStT 600/DS4300
                                                 FAStT DS4800
                                                 FAStT 100
                                                 DS3X00
                                                 DS4000
                                                 DS5100/DS5300
                                                 FAStT
                                                 Dell MD3000
                                                 Dell MD3000i
```

Figure 5.31 Listing SATP claim rules—Top-right quadrant of output

```
wdc-tse-d98.wsl.vmware.com - PuTTY                                              —   □   ×
VMW_SATP_LSI       LSI       OPENstorage D210                    system    tpgs_off
VMW_SATP_LSI       LSI       OPENstorage D220                    system    tpgs_off
VMW_SATP_LSI       LSI       OPENstorage D240                    system    tpgs_off
VMW_SATP_LSI       LSI       OPENstorage D280                    system    tpgs_off
VMW_SATP_LSI       LSI       BladeCtlr BC82                      system    tpgs_off
VMW_SATP_LSI       LSI       BladeCtlr BC84                      system    tpgs_off
VMW_SATP_LSI       LSI       BladeCtlr BC88                      system    tpgs_off
VMW_SATP_LSI       LSI       BladeCtlr B210                      system    tpgs_off
VMW_SATP_LSI       LSI       BladeCtlr B220                      system    tpgs_off
VMW_SATP_LSI       LSI       BladeCtlr B240                      system    tpgs_off
VMW_SATP_LSI       LSI       BladeCtlr B280                      system    tpgs_off
VMW_SATP_LSI       LSI       INF-01-00                           system    tpgs_off
VMW_SATP_LSI       LSI       FLEXLINE 380                        system    tpgs_off
VMW_SATP_LSI       SUN       CSM100_R_FC                         system    tpgs_off
VMW_SATP_LSI       SUN       FLEXLINE 380                        system    tpgs_off
VMW_SATP_LSI       SUN       CSM200_R                            system    tpgs_off
VMW_SATP_LSI       SUN       LCSM100_F                           system    tpgs_off
VMW_SATP_LSI       SUN       LCSM100_I                           system    tpgs_off
VMW_SATP_LSI       SUN       LCSM100_S                           system    tpgs_off
VMW_SATP_LSI       SUN       STK6580_6780                        system    tpgs_off
VMW_SATP_LSI       ENGENIO   INF-01-00                           system    tpgs_off
VMW_SATP_LSI       IBM       ^1746*                              system    tpgs_off
VMW_SATP_LSI       DELL      MD32xx                              system    tpgs_off
VMW_SATP_LSI       DELL      MD32xxi                             system    tpgs_off
VMW_SATP_LSI       SGI       IS500                               system    tpgs_off
VMW_SATP_LSI       SGI       IS600                               system    tpgs_off
VMW_SATP_LSI       SUN       SUN_6180                            system    tpgs_off
VMW_SATP_LSI       DELL      MD36xxi                             system    tpgs_off
VMW_SATP_LSI       DELL      MD36xxf                             system    tpgs_off
VMW_SATP_DEFAULT_AA   HITACHI                                    system    inq_data[128
VMW_SATP_DEFAULT_AA   IBM     2810XIV                            system    tpgs_off
VMW_SATP_DEFAULT_AA                              fc              system
VMW_SATP_DEFAULT_AA                              fcoe            system
VMW_SATP_DEFAULT_AA                              iscsi           system
VMW_SATP_DEFAULT_AA   IBM     SAS SES-2 DEVICE                   system
VMW_SATP_DEFAULT_AA   IBM     1820N00                            system    tpgs_off
VMW_SATP_DEFAULT_AA   HITACHI                                    system
VMW_SATP_LOCAL                                   usb             system
VMW_SATP_LOCAL                                   ide             system
(END)
```

Figure 5.32   Listing SATP claim rules—Bottom-left quadrant of output

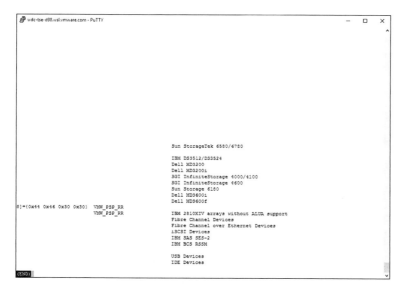

Figure 5.33   Listing SATP claim rules—Bottom-right quadrant of output

To make things a bit clearer, let's take a couple of lines from the output and examine what they mean.

Figure 5.34 shows the relevant rules for CLARiiON arrays, both non-ALUA and ALUA capable. For this figure, I removed three blank columns (Driver, Transport, and Options) to make room for the important content.

Figure 5.34 CLARiiON non-ALUA and ALUA Rules

The two lines in Figure 5.34 show the claim rules for the EMC CLARiiON CX/VNX family. Using these rules, NMP identifies the array as CLARiiON CX when the vendor string is DGC. If NMP had stopped at this, it would have used VMW_SATP_CX as the SATP for this array. However, this family of arrays can support more than one configuration. This shows where the value Claim Options column comes in handy. So, if that option is `tpgs_off`, NMP uses the VMW_SATP_CX plug-in, and if the option is `tpgs_on`, NMP uses VMW_SATP_ALUA_CX. (I explain what these options mean in Chapter 6.)

Figure 5.35 shows another example that utilizes additional options. I removed the Device column to fit the content to the display.

Figure 5.35 Claim rule that uses claim options

In this example, NMP uses VMW_SATP_DEFAULT_AA SATP with all arrays returning `HITACHI` as a vendor string. However, the default PSP is selected based on the values listed in the Claim Options column:

- If the Claim Options column is blank, the default PSP (which is VMW_PSP_FIXED and is based on the list shown earlier in this section, in Figure 5.29) is used. In Figure 5.29, you see that VMW_SATP_DEFAULT_AA is assigned the default PSP, named VMW_PSP_FIXED.

- If the Claim Options column shows `inq_data[128]={0x44 0x46 0x30 0x30}`, which is part of the data reported from the array via the inquiry response string, NMP overrides the default PSP configuration and uses VMW_PSP_RR instead.

Modifying PSA Plug-in Configurations Using the UI

You can modify the configuration of PSA plug-ins by using the CLI and, to a limited extent, the UI. The UI provides far fewer options for modification, as discussed in the following sections.

Which PSA Configurations Can Be Modified Using the UI?

You can change the PSP for a given device. However, this is done on a LUN level rather than at the array level. Are you wondering why you would want to do that? Think of the following scenario: Say that you have a virtual machine (VM) in your environment that uses physical mode raw device mappings (RDMs), which are also referred to as *passthrough RDMs*. Your storage vendor recommends using FIXED path selection policy (VMW_PSP_FIXED). However, you observe I/O errors on that RDM, and you were instructed to change the policy to MRU (VMW_PSP_MRU).

Changing the PSP Using the UI

The following procedure walks you through changing just the RDM LUN's PSP to the desired one:

1. In the vSphere 6 Web Client, select the VM in the Inventory pane. Right-click the VM and select **Edit Settings** (see Figure 5.36). You can do the same via the **Actions** pull-down menu or by clicking the **Edit virtual machine settings** link on the **Getting Started** tab.

Figure 5.36 Editing a VM's settings—UI

2. In the dialog that appears, click the **Manage other disks** button if available. Otherwise, skip to step 3.

3. Expand the **Hard disk** properties.

4. Click the **Manage Paths** link (see Figure 5.37).

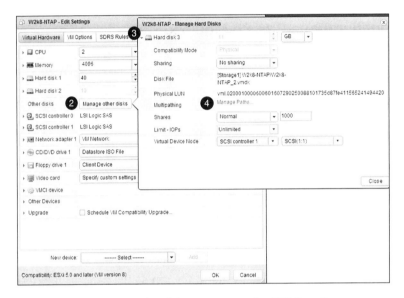

Figure 5.37   Accessing the dialog to manage the RDM's paths

Figure 5.38 shows the dialog that appears for managing the paths.

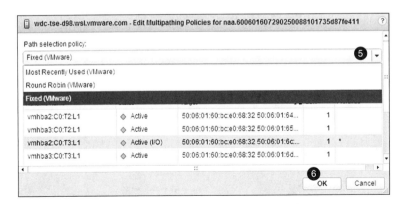

Figure 5.38   Modifying PSP selection—UI

5. Click the **Path selection policy** pull-down and change it from the current setting to **Round Robin (VMware)**.

6. Click **OK**.

7. Click **Close** to close the **Manage Hard Disks** dialog.

8. Click **OK** to close the **Edit Settings** dialog.

Modifying PSA Plug-ins Using the CLI

The CLI provides a range of options for configuring, customizing, and modifying PSA plug-in settings. I provide the various configurable options and their use cases in the following sections.

Available CLI Tools and Their Options

Starting with vSphere 5.0, ESXCLI functionality was expanded as the main CLI utility for managing ESXi 5.0. It has been expanded even further in vSphere 6. The same binary is used whether you log on to the host locally or remotely via SSH. It is also used by vMA and vCLI. This simplifies administrative tasks and improves portability of scripts written to use ESXCLI.

TIP

The only difference between the tools used locally or via SSH compared to those used in vMA and Remote CLI is that the latter two require providing the server name and the user's credentials on the command line. Refer to Chapter 4, in which I covered using the fast-pass (FP) facility of vMA and how to add users' credentials to the CREDSTORE environment variable on vCLI.

Assuming that the server name and user credentials are set in the environment, the command-line syntax in all the examples in this book is identical, regardless of where you use it.

The `esxcli` Namespace

Figure 5.39 shows the command-line help for `esxcli`.

```
wdc-tse-d98.wsl.vmware.com - PuTTY                                    —    □    ×
[root@wdc-tse-d98:~] esxcli
Usage: esxcli [options] {namespace}+ {cmd} [cmd options]

Options:
  --formatter=FORMATTER
                        Override the formatter to use for a given command. Available
                        formatter: xml, csv, keyvalue
  --debug               Enable debug or internal use options
  --version             Display version information for the script
  -?, --help            Display usage information for the script

Available Namespaces:
  device                Device manager commands
  elxnet                elxnet esxcli functionality
  esxcli                Commands that operate on the esxcli system itself allowing users
                        to get additional information.
  fcoe                  VMware FCOE commands.
  graphics              VMware graphics commands.
  hardware              VMKernel hardware properties and commands for configuring
                        hardware.
  iscsi                 VMware iSCSI commands.
  network               Operations that pertain to the maintenance of networking on an
                        ESX host. This includes a wide variety of commands to manipulate
                        virtual networking components (vswitch, portgroup, etc) as well
                        as local host IP, DNS and general host networking settings.
  rdma                  Operations that pertain to remote direct memory access (RDMA)
                        protocol stack on an ESX host.
  sched                 VMKernel system properties and commands for configuring
                        scheduling related functionality.
  software              Manage the ESXi software image and packages
  storage               VMware storage commands.
  system                VMKernel system properties and commands for configuring
                        properties of the kernel core system and related system
                        services.
  vm                    A small number of operations that allow a user to Control
                        Virtual Machine operations.
  vsan                  VMware VSAN commands.
[root@wdc-tse-d98:~] ▋
```

Figure 5.39 Listing the `esxcli` namespace

New to vSphere 6 are the following namespaces:

- `device`
- `elxnet`
- `graphics`
- `rdma`
- `sched`
- `vsan`

The relevant namespace for this chapter is `storage`. This is what most of the examples use. Figure 5.40 shows the command-line help for the `storage` namespace.

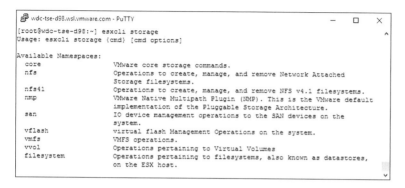

Figure 5.40   Listing the `esxcli storage` namespaces

Table 5.11 lists `esxcli` namespaces and their usage.

Table 5.11 Available namespaces in the `storage` namespace

Namespace	Usage
core	Use this for anything on the PSA level, such as other MPPs, PSA claim rules, and so on.
nmp	Use this for NMP and its "children," such as SATP and PSP.
vmfs	Use this for handling VMFS volumes on snapshot LUNs, managing extents, and upgrading VMFS manually.
filesystem	Use this to list, mount, and unmount supported datastores.
nfs	Use this to mount, unmount, and list NFS datastores.
nfs41	Use this as you would the `nfs` namespace with NFS v4.1.
san	Use this with `fc`, `Iscsi`, `fcoe`, and `sas` options to list related adapters information and stats.
vflash	Use this to list vFlash devices and module and cache information and stats.
vvol	Use this for operations pertaining to virtual volumes. (I will cover this in detail in Chapter 23, "Virtual Volumes (VVols).")

Adding a PSA Claim Rule

PSA claim rules can be for MP, Filter, and VAAI classes. I cover the latter two in Chapter 6, "ALUA." The sections that follow provide a few examples of claim rules for the MP class.

Adding a Rule to Change Certain LUNs to Be Claimed by a Different MPP

In general, most arrays function properly using the default PSA claim rules. In certain configurations, you might need to specify a different PSA MPP. A good example is the following scenario: Say that you installed PowerPath/VE on your ESXi 6.0 host but then later you experience repeated errors with a set of LUNs that are used with physical mode raw device mappings (RDMs). VMware Support informs you that you need to rule out PowerPath/VE as the root cause and suggests that you exclude the LUNs from being managed by PowerPath/VE. You need to identify the device ID (NAA ID) of each of the RDM LUNs and then identify the paths to each LUN. You use these paths to create the claim rule. To do this, you need to use the CLI because paths to LUNs claimed by PowerPath cannot be viewed by the Manage Paths UI. If you are using a different MPP, and you prefer to use the UI, skip to step 5.

Follow these steps to add a rule to change certain LUNs to be claimed by a different MPP:

1. Identify the VM ID. Assuming that the cluster node is named `node1`, the command and its output would look as shown in Listing 5.1.

Listing 5.1   Locating the VM ID

```
# vim-cmd vmsvc/getallvms |grep node1

Output:
26 node1 [Clusters_Datastore] node1/node1.vmx
```

The output in Listing 5.1 lists the VM ID in the first column. In this example, it is 26. Note that I truncated the output to show one VM only. In your environment, you will get several VMs. Just locate the name of the VM that you know is configured with RDM and identify the VM ID.

2. Using the VM ID, identify the logical device name to which each RDM maps, as shown in Listing 5.2.

Listing 5.2   Identifying an RDM LUN's logical device name by using the VM ID

```
# vim-cmd vmsvc/device.getdevices 26 | grep -B6 Raw |grep deviceName
Output:
 deviceName = "vml.02000100006006016072902500881017335d87fe411565241494420",
```

3. Identify the NAA ID by using the vml ID, as shown in Listing 5.3. Here I used the verbose version of the command options, but you can use the abbreviated version by using `-l` and `-d` instead of `--list` and `--device`.

Listing 5.3   Identifying the NAA ID by using the device vml ID

```
esxcfg-scsidevs --list --device vml.020001000060060160729025008810l735
d87fe411565241494420 |grep Display
Display Name: DGC Fibre Channel Disk (naa.6006016072902500888l0l735d87
fe411)
```

4. Now, use the NAA ID (highlighted in Listing 5.3) to identify the paths to the RDM LUN. Figure 5.41 shows the output of this command:

   ```
   'esxcfg-mpath -m |grep naa.6006016072902500888l0l735d87fe411 | sed 's/
   fc.*//'
   ```

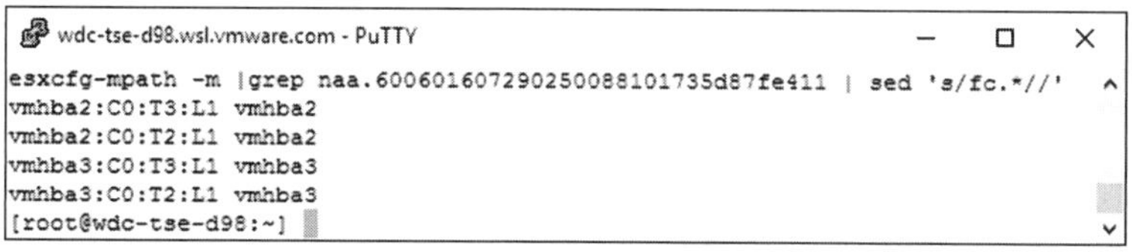

Figure 5.41   Listing runtime pathnames to an RDM LUN

You can also use the verbose version of the command:

```
esxcfg-mpath --list-map |grep naa.6006016072902500888l0l735d87fe411 |
  sed 's/fc.*//'
```

This truncates the output beginning with `fc` to the end of the line on each line. If the protocol in use is not FC, replace `fc` with `iqn` for iSCSI or `fcoe` for FCoE.

The output in Listing 5.4 shows that the LUN with the identified NAA ID is LUN 1, and it has four paths.

Listing 5.4   RDM LUN's paths

```
vmhba2:C0:T3:L1  vmhba2
vmhba2:C0:T2:L1  vmhba2
vmhba3:C0:T3:L1  vmhba3
vmhba3:C0:T2:L1  vmhba3
```

To identify the LUN runtime names via the UI, proceed to step 5. Otherwise, skip to step 10.

5. Using the vSphere 6 Web Client, select the VM in the Inventory pane. Right-click the VM and select **Edit Settings** (see Figure 5.42). You can do the same thing via the

Actions pull-down menu or by clicking the **Edit virtual machine settings** link on the Getting Started tab.

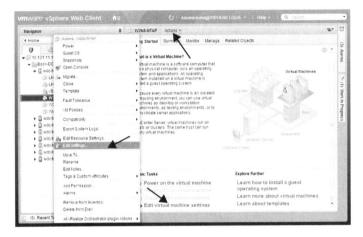

Figure 5.42   Editing the VM's settings—UI

6. In the resulting dialog, click the **Manage other disks** button, if it is available. Otherwise, skip to step 7.

7. Expand the **Hard disk** properties.

8. Click the **Manage Paths** link (see Figure 5.43).

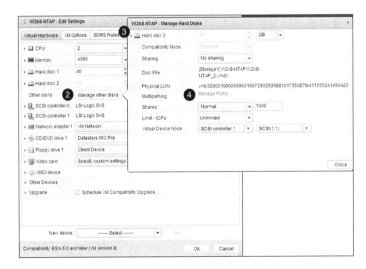

Figure 5.43   Accessing the dialog to manage the RDM's paths—UI

The resulting dialog is shown in Figure 5.44. If your environment is configured to use PowerPath/VE MPP, the Path selection policy dropdown in the dialog is blank because no PSP is used by that MPP.

9. Write down the list of paths shown in the **Runtime Name** column. Figure 5.44 shows the following paths:

```
vmhba2:C0:T2:L1
vmhba3:C0:T2:L1
vmhba2:C0:T3:L1
vmhba3:C0:T3:L1
```

Figure 5.44   Listing the runtime pathnames—UI

NOTE

The list of runtime pathnames in the UI may differ between hosts if they are not configured identically. If your servers are configured identically, the path list should be identical as well.

However, this is not critical because a LUN's NAA ID is the same regardless of the paths used to access it. This is what makes NAA ID the most unique element of any LUN, and it is the reason ESXi uses it for uniquely identifying the LUNs. (I cover this topic in more detail in Chapter 7.)

---

10. Create the claim rule.

We use the list of paths obtained in step 5 for creating the rule from the ESXi host from which it was obtained. The number of rules to create is four—one rule per path to the LUN, as identified in step 9.

The Ground Rules for Creating a Rule

Consider the following best practices for creating a claim rule:

- The rule number must be lower than the numbers of any of the rules created by PowerPath/VE installation. By default, they are assigned rules 250–320. (Refer to Figure 5.26 for the list of PowerPath claim rules.)

- The rule number must be higher than 101, which is used by the Dell Mask Path rule. This prevents claiming devices masked by that rule.

- If you have created other claim rules on this host in the past, use a rule number that is different from what you created before so that the new rules you are creating now do not conflict with the earlier rules.

- If you must place a new rule earlier than an existing rule but there are no rule numbers available, you may have to move one of the lower-numbered rules higher, based on the number of rules you plan on creating. For example, say that you have previously created rules numbered 102–110, and rule 109 cannot be listed prior to the new rules you are creating. If you have four new rules and need to assign them rule numbers 109–112, you need to move existing rules 109 and 110 to numbers 113 and 114. To avoid having to do such renumbering in the future, consider leaving gaps in the rule numbers among sections.

Here is an example of moving a rule:

```
esxcli storage core claimrule move --rule 109 --new-rule 113
esxcli storage core claimrule move --rule 110 --new-rule 114
```

You can also use this shorthand version:

```
esxcli storage core claimrule move -r 109 -n 113
esxcli storage core claimrule move -r 110 -n 114
```

Now, let's proceed with adding the new claim rules:

1. The set of four commands shown in Figure 5.45 create rules numbered 102–105. These are the criteria for the new rules:

    - The claim rule type is "location" (`-t location`).

    - The location is specified using each path to the same LUN, in this format:

        - `-A` or `--adapter vmhba(X)`, where `X` is the vmhba number associated with the path.

        - `-C` or `--channel (Y)`, where `Y` is the channel number associated with the path.

- ■ -T or --target (Z), where Z is the target number associated with the path.

- ■ -L or --lun (n), where n is the LUN.

- ■ The plug-in name is NMP, which means that this claim rule is for NMP, to claim the paths listed in each rule created.

NOTE

It would be easier to create a single rule using the LUN's NAA ID by using the --type device option and then using --device <NAA ID>. However, the use of device as a rule type is not supported with MP-class plug-ins.

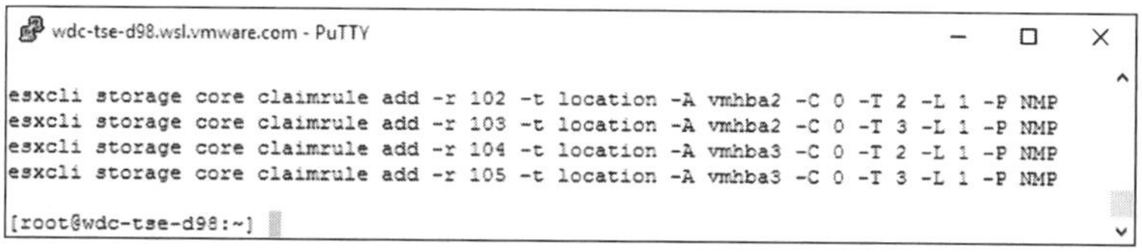

```
wdc-tse-d98.wsl.vmware.com - PuTTY                                    —    □    ×

esxcli storage core claimrule add -r 102 -t location -A vmhba2 -C 0 -T 2 -L 1 -P NMP
esxcli storage core claimrule add -r 103 -t location -A vmhba2 -C 0 -T 3 -L 1 -P NMP
esxcli storage core claimrule add -r 104 -t location -A vmhba3 -C 0 -T 2 -L 1 -P NMP
esxcli storage core claimrule add -r 105 -t location -A vmhba3 -C 0 -T 3 -L 1 -P NMP

[root@wdc-tse-d98:~]
```

Figure 5.45 Adding new MP claim rules

The commands from Figure 5.45 are listed here for readability:

```
esxcli storage core claimrule add -r 102 -t location -A vmhba2 -C 0 -T
2 -L 1 -P NMP
esxcli storage core claimrule add -r 103 -t location -A vmhba2 -C 0 -T
3 -L 1 -P NMP
esxcli storage core claimrule add -r 104 -t location -A vmhba3 -C 0 -T
2 -L 1 -P NMP
esxcli storage core claimrule add -r 105 -t location -A vmhba3 -C 0 -T
3 -L 1 -P NMP
```

2. Repeat step 1 for each LUN you want to reconfigure.

3. Verify that the rules are added successfully. To list the current set of claim rules, run the esxcli storage core claimrule list |less -S command, as shown in Figure 5.46.

```
wdc-tse-d98.wsl.vmware.com - PuTTY                                    —    □    ×
[root@wdc-tse-d98:~] esxcli storage core claimrule list |less -S
Rule Class    Rule   Class    Type        Plugin      Matches
----------    ----   -------  ---------   ---------   ----------
MP               0   runtime  transport   NMP         transport=usb
MP               1   runtime  transport   NMP         transport=sata
MP               2   runtime  transport   NMP         transport=ide
MP               3   runtime  transport   NMP         transport=block
MP               4   runtime  transport   NMP         transport=unknown
MP             101   runtime  vendor      MASK_PATH   vendor=DELL model=Universal Xport
MP             101   file     vendor      MASK_PATH   vendor=DELL model=Universal Xport
MP             102   file     location    NMP         adapter=vmhba2 channel=0 target=2 lun=1
MP             103   file     location    NMP         adapter=vmhba2 channel=0 target=3 lun=1
MP             104   file     location    NMP         adapter=vmhba3 channel=0 target=2 lun=1
MP             105   file     location    NMP         adapter=vmhba3 channel=0 target=3 lun=1
MP             250   runtime  vendor      PowerPath   vendor=DGC model=*
MP             250   file     vendor      PowerPath   vendor=DGC model=*
MP             260   runtime  vendor      PowerPath   vendor=EMC model=SYMMETRIX
```

Figure 5.46 Listing added claim rules

Notice that the four new rules are now listed, but the Class column shows them as `file`. This means that the configuration files were updated successfully, but the rules were not loaded into memory yet.

NOTE

I truncated the rest of PowerPath rules in Figure 5.47 for readability. Also note that using the Location type utilizes the current runtime names of the devices, and they may change in the future. If your configuration changes—for example, if new HBAs are added or existing ones are removed—the runtime names change, too. This results in these claim rules claiming the wrong devices. However, in a static environment, this should not be an issue.

TIP

To reduce the number of commands used and the number of rules created, you can omit the `-T` or `--target` option, which assumes a wildcard. You may also use the `-u` or `--autoas-sign` option to auto-assign the rule number. However, the latter assigns rule numbers starting with 5001, which may be higher than the existing claim rules for the device hosting the LUN you are planning to claim.

For example, the command line would look like this:

```
esxcli storage core claimrule add -r 104 -t location -A vmhba2 -C 0 -L
1 -P NMP
esxcli storage core claimrule add -r 105 -t location -A vmhba3 -C 0 -L
1 -P NMP
```

CAUTION

The convenience of using fewer claim rules utilizing wildcards comes with some risks. I deliberately used wildcards here to introduce such risks so that I can share the outcome. I will discuss this risk later in this section right after Listing 5.5.

Figure 5.47 shows a sample command line that implements a wildcard for the target. Notice that this results in creating two rules instead of four, and the "target" match is *.

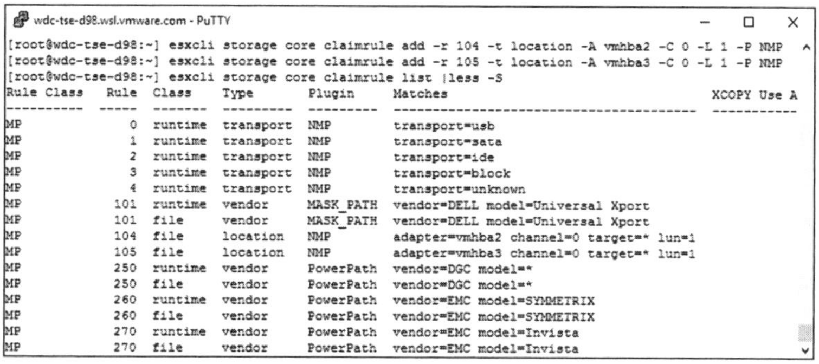

Figure 5.47 Adding MP claim rules using a wildcard

NOTE

Before proceeding with the remaining steps, ensure that the VM on this host using the RDM mapped to this LUN is powered off.

4. Check which MPP currently owns the LUN, using its NAA ID:

```
esxcli storage core device list -d naa. 60060160729025008810173 5d87fe4
11 | grep Plug
```

You get the following output:

```
Multipath Plugin: PowerPath
```

This means that PowerPath MPP still has the LUN claimed. So, before loading the new rules, you must first unclaim the paths to the LUN specified in that rule set. You use the NAA ID as the device ID:

```
esxcli storage core claiming unclaim --type device --device naa.600601
6072902500088101735d87fe411
```

You can also use the shorthand version:

```
esxcli storage core claiming unclaim -t device -d naa.6006016072902500
88101735d87fe411
```

5. Load the new claim rules so that the paths to the LUN get claimed by NMP:

```
esxcli storage core claimrule load
```

6. Use the following command to list the claim rules to verify that they are successfully loaded:

```
esxcli storage core claimrule list
```

Now you see that each of the new rules is listed twice—once with the file class and once with the runtime class. Figure 5.48 shows the output in a configuration resulting from using a wildcard for the -T option. If a wildcard was not used and four claim rules were created instead, the output would be similar but with claim rules 102–104 listed with the target field showing the target number in each of the four rules.

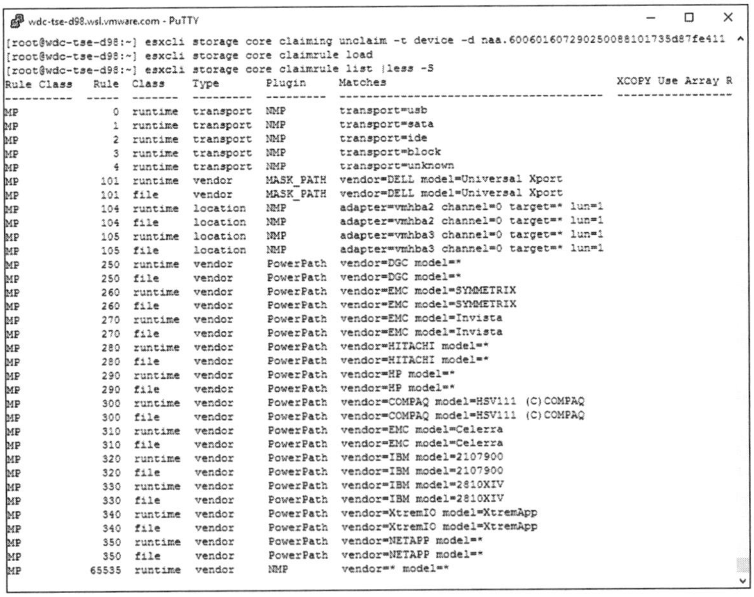

Figure 5.48   Listing MP claim rules

7. Finally, run the claim rules so that NMP can claim the LUN that was unclaimed in step 4:

```
esxcli storage core claimrule run
```

If you don't unclaim the LUN before using the `claimrule run` command, you get messages like the ones in Listing 5.5.

Listing 5.5   vmkernel.log events if LUN was not unclaimed before running the modified claim rules

ScsiClaimrule: 1165: The current claimrules indicate that path vmhba2:C0:T3:L1 should be claimed by plugin NMP.

ScsiClaimrule: 1169: Path vmhba35:C1:T8:L1 which appears to refer to the same physical media as path vmhba2:C0:T3:L1 is already claimed by plugin PowerPath.

ScsiClaimrule: 1171: If neither of these paths is being masked by ESX, this condition indicates a problem with the claimrules.

PowerPath:Path Claim: Successfully claimed path vmhba2:C0:T3:L1

ScsiPath: 5531: Plugin 'PowerPath' claimed path 'vmhba2:C0:T3:L1'

ScsiClaimrule: 1165: The current claimrules indicate that path vmhba2:C0:T2:L1 should be claimed by plugin NMP.

ScsiClaimrule: 1169: Path vmhba2:C0:T3:L1 which appears to refer to the same physical media as path vmhba2:C0:T2:L1 is already claimed by plugin PowerPath.

ScsiClaimrule: 1171: If neither of these paths is being masked by ESX, this condition indicates a problem with the claimrules.

PowerPath:Path Claim: Successfully claimed path vmhba2:C0:T2:L1

ScsiPath: 5531: Plugin 'PowerPath' claimed path 'vmhba2:C0:T2:L1'

WARNING: ScsiClaimrule: 1326: Path vmhba2:C0:T1:L1 is claimed by plugin PowerPath, but current claimrule number 104 indicates that it should be claimed by plugin NMP.

ScsiClaimrule: 1665: Error claiming path vmhba2:C0:T1:L1. Failure.

WARNING: ScsiClaimrule: 1326: Path vmhba2:C0:T0:L1 is claimed by plugin PowerPath, but current claimrule number 104 indicates that it should be claimed by plugin NMP.

ScsiClaimrule: 1665: Error claiming path vmhba2:C0:T0:L1. Failure.

WARNING: ScsiClaimrule: 1326: Path vmhba3:C0:T1:L1 is claimed by plugin PowerPath, but current claimrule number 105 indicates that it should be claimed by plugin NMP.

ScsiClaimrule: 1665: Error claiming path vmhba3:C0:T1:L1. Failure.

WARNING: ScsiClaimrule: 1326: Path vmhba3:C0:T0:L1 is claimed by plugin PowerPath, but current claimrule number 105 indicates that it should be claimed by plugin NMP.

ScsiClaimrule: 1665: Error claiming path vmhba3:C0:T0:L1. Failure.

ScsiClaimrule: 1165: The current claimrules indicate that path vmhba3:C0:T3:L1 should be claimed by plugin NMP.

ScsiClaimrule: 1169: Path vmhba2:C0:T3:L1 which appears to refer to the same physical media as path vmhba3:C0:T3:L1 is already claimed by plugin PowerPath.

```
ScsiClaimrule: 1171: If neither of these paths is being masked by ESX, this
condition indicates a problem with the claimrules.
PowerPath:Path Claim: Successfully claimed path vmhba3:C0:T3:L1
ScsiPath: 5531: Plugin 'PowerPath' claimed path 'vmhba3:C0:T3:L1'
ScsiClaimrule: 1165: The current claimrules indicate that path
vmhba3:C0:T2:L1 should be claimed by plugin NMP.
ScsiClaimrule: 1169: Path vmhba2:C0:T3:L1 which appears to refer to the
same physical media as path vmhba3:C0:T2:L1 is already claimed by plugin
PowerPath.
ScsiClaimrule: 1171: If neither of these paths is being masked by ESX, this
condition indicates a problem with the claimrules.
PowerPath:Path Claim: Successfully claimed path vmhba3:C0:T2:L1
ScsiPath: 5531: Plugin 'PowerPath' claimed path 'vmhba3:C0:T2:L1'
```

Listing 5.5 lists four sets of five-line events, one set for each path to LUN 1:

- vmhba2:C0:T3:L1

- vmhba2:C0:T2:L1

- vmhba3:C0:T3:L1

- vmhba3:C0:T2:L1

The five lines pertaining to each path are as follows:

- The current claim rule, which is what I just loaded, indicates that this path should be claimed by NMP.

- The LUN on the two different paths stated in the message is actually the same LUN and is still claimed by PowerPath. Notice that the first listing of this message indicates that the first path is on vmhba35. This is actually an iSCSI software initiator to which I accidentally presented the LUN, along with the FC HBAs vmhba2 and vmhba3. This is not recommended, and you should un-present the LUN to the iSCSI initiator or mask it on the host's end. (See the section "Masking Paths to a Certain LUN," later in this chapter.)

- If the neither of the two paths is masked by ESX (see the section "Masking Paths to a Certain LUN," later in this chapter), this means that there is a problem with the current claim rules. This is the effect of activating the new claim rules that I just added so that NMP claims the LUN. However, the LUN is still claimed by PowerPath MPP.

- PowerPath successfully claimed the stated path (which is not what I intended to do).

- The claim rule successfully allowed the PowerPath plug-in (MPP) to claim the stated path.

The eight events highlighted in Listing 5.5 indicate that when I used the wildcard for the -T option, there was a LUN 1 presented on targets other than targets 2 and 3. In this listing, the messages refer to LUN 1 on targets 1 and 0 on both vmhba2 and vmhba3. The claim rule numbers are 104 and 105.

I went back and reviewed the list of LUNs I have in my lab and realized that I have other storage arrays from which I had presented LUN 1 to vmhba2 and vmhba3 on targets 0 and 1. Because this LUN is not on the same storage array where the RDM LUN resides, it should not have been included in the claim rule.

The moral of the story is that if you use wildcards in your claim rules, make sure that LUNs with the same LUN number presented on all targets zoned to the HBAs are on the same physical device. Otherwise, a claim rule will claim LUNs from other storage arrays, which will result in unexpected consequences.

I deleted claim rules 104 and 105 that I created according to the tip under step 3. I then created four separate claim rules, numbered 102–104, as listed in step 1. (To delete claim rules, see the next section, "Deleting a Claim Rule")

8. To verify that NMP successfully claimed the device, run the following command:

```
esxcli storage core device list -d naa.6006016072902500088101735d87
 fe411 |grep Plugin
```

Listing 5.6 shows the commands used in steps 4, 5, and 7 and their outputs.

Listing 5.6   List of commands to unclaim a device and then claim it with an added rule

```
esxcli storage core device list -d naa.6006016072902500088101735d87fe411
 |grep Plug
Multipath Plugin: PowerPath
[root@wdc-tse-d98:~] esxcli storage core claiming unclaim -t device -d
 naa.6006016072902500088101735d87fe411
[root@wdc-tse-d98:~] esxcli storage core device list -d naa.600601607290250
 088101735d87fe411 |grep Plug
[root@wdc-tse-d98:~] esxcli storage core claimrule load
[root@wdc-tse-d98:~] esxcli storage core device list -d naa.600601607290250
 088101735d87fe411 |grep Plug
[root@wdc-tse-d98:~] esxcli storage core claimrule run
[root@wdc-tse-d98:~] esxcli storage core device list -d naa.600601607290250
 088101735d87fe411 |grep Plug
 Multipath Plugin: NMP
```

Notice that the `device list` command on the third line in Listing 5.6 does not return any output. This is because the LUN was just unclaimed, and no MPP has claimed it yet. In other words, no output is an indication of a successful `unclaim` command. Listing 5.7 lists the events related to a successful process.

Listing 5.7 List of log events related to unclaiming a device and then claiming it with an added rule

```
PowerPath:Successfully unclaimed path vmhba3:C0:T2:L1.
PowerPath:Successfully unclaimed path vmhba3:C0:T3:L1.
PowerPath:Successfully unclaimed path vmhba2:C0:T2:L1.
PowerPath:Successfully unclaimed path vmhba2:C0:T3:L1.
ScsiEvents: 545: Event Subsystem: Device Events, Destroyed!
StorageApdHandler: 1066: Freeing APD handle 0x43016ce65360 [naa.60060160729
 0250088101735d87fe411]
StorageApdHandler: 1150: APD Handle freed!
ScsiPath: 5531: Plugin 'NMP' claimed path 'vmhba2:C0:T3:L1'
ScsiPath: 5531: Plugin 'NMP' claimed path 'vmhba2:C0:T2:L1'
ScsiPath: 5531: Plugin 'NMP' claimed path 'vmhba3:C0:T3:L1'
ScsiPath: 5531: Plugin 'NMP' claimed path 'vmhba3:C0:T2:L1'

StorageApdHandler: 982: APD Handle Created with lock
[StorageApd-0x43016ce4f3e0]
ScsiEvents: 501: Event Subsystem: Device Events, Created!
VMWARE SCSI Id: Id for vmhba3:C0:T2:L1 0x60 0x06 0x01 0x60 0x72 0x90 0x25
 0x00 0x88 0x10 0x17 0x35 0xd8 0x7f 0xe4 0x11 0x56 0x52 0x41 0x49 0x44
 0x20
VMWARE SCSI Id: Id for vmhba3:C0:T3:L1 0x60 0x06 0x01 0x60 0x72 0x90 0x25
 0x00 0x88 0x10 0x17 0x35 0xd8 0x7f 0xe4 0x11 0x56 0x52 0x41 0x49 0x44
 0x20
VMWARE SCSI Id: Id for vmhba2:C0:T2:L1 0x60 0x06 0x01 0x60 0x72 0x90 0x25
 0x00 0x88 0x10 0x17 0x35 0xd8 0x7f 0xe4 0x11 0x56 0x52 0x41 0x49
 0x44 0x20
VMWARE SCSI Id: Id for vmhba2:C0:T3:L1 0x60 0x06 0x01 0x60 0x72 0x90 0x25
 0x00 0x88 0x10 0x17 0x35 0xd8 0x7f 0xe4 0x11 0x56 0x52 0x41 0x49 0x44
 0x20
ScsiDevice: 3830: Successfully registered device "naa.600601607290250088101
 735d87fe411" from plugin "NMP" of type 0
```

The first four lines of Listing 5.7 show that the PowerPath plug-in unclaimed the four paths successfully.

The fifth line shows that the device has been removed from the host, followed by two messages that the APD handle has been freed. I will cover APD (all paths down) in Chapter 7, "Multipathing and Failover."

This is followed by four events stating that NMP claimed each of the four paths to the LUN.

After the blank line that I added for readability is the event for creating an APD handle with lock.

Then, the device gets created, and finally the LUN ID is reported on each path. (There are more related events, which I will cover in Chapter 7.)

Deleting a Claim Rule

You must delete a claim rule with extreme caution. Make sure that you are deleting the rule you intend to delete. Prior to doing so, make sure to collect a VM support dump by running vm-support from a command line at the host or via SSH. Alternatively, you can select the menu option **Collect Diagnostics Data** via the vSphere Client.

To delete a claim rule, follow this procedure using the CLI (locally or via SSH, vCLI, or vMA):

1. List the current claim rules set and identify the claim rule or rules you want to delete. The command to list the claim rules is similar to what you ran in step 6 in the preceding section (refer to Figure 5.48).

2. For this procedure, use the previous example and delete the four claim rules added earlier: rules 102–105. The commands for doing this are listed in Listing 5.8.

Listing 5.8   Deleting claim rules

```
esxcli storage core claimrule remove -r 102
esxcli storage core claimrule remove -r 103
esxcli storage core claimrule remove -r 104
esxcli storage core claimrule remove -r 105
```

You can also run the verbose command:

```
esxcli storage core claimrule remove --rule <rule-number>
```

Running the claimrule list command results in output similar to what is shown in Figure 5.49.

3. Observe that even you delete the claim rules, they still show up in the list in Figure 5.49. This happens because you have not yet loaded the modified claim rules—and this is why the deleted rules show `runtime` in the Class column.

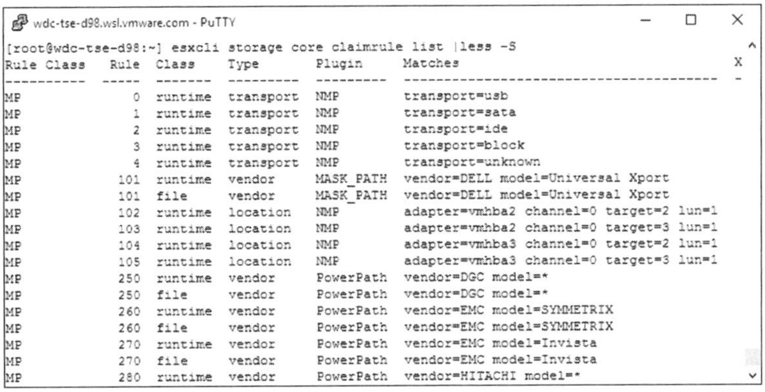

Figure 5.49 Listing MP claim rules

4. Because you know from the previous procedure the device ID (NAA ID) of the LUN whose claim rules you deleted, run the `unclaim` command using the `-t device` or `--type=device` option and then specify the `-d` or `--device` option with the NAA ID. You can then load the claim rules by using the `load` option. Instead of using the `unclaim`/`claim` sequence, you can use `reclaim`. (I will cover `reclaim` in the next section, "Masking Paths to a Certain LUN.") Listing 5.9 shows the commands used in this step and their outputs.

Listing 5.9 Listing commands to unclaim a device and then claim it after deleting a rule

```
esxcli storage core device list -d naa.6006016072902500088101735d87fe411
|grep Plug
 Multipath Plugin: NMP
esxcli storage core claiming unclaim -t device -d naa.60060160729025008810l
735d87fe411
esxcli storage core device list -d naa.6006016072902500088101735d87fe411
|grep Plug
esxcli storage core claimrule load
esxcli storage core claimrule run
esxcli storage core device list -d naa.6006016072902500088101735d87fe411
|grep Plug
 Multipath Plugin: PowerPath
```

The result of loading the claim rules is that the deleted claim rules are no longer listed (see Figure 5.50).

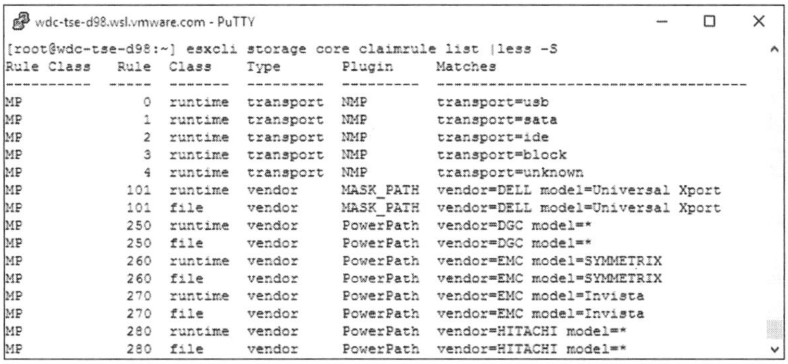

Figure 5.50   Results of loading the claim rules after deleting rules

You can also use the verbose command options:

```
esxcli storage core claiming unclaim --type device --device
<Device-ID>
```

The relevant events posted to /var/log/vmkernel.log are shown in Listing 5.10

Listing 5.10   Listing commands to unclaim a device and then claim it after deleting a rule

```
PowerPath:Path Claim: Successfully claimed path vmhba2:C0:T3:L1
ScsiPath: 5531: Plugin 'PowerPath' claimed path 'vmhba2:C0:T3:L1'
PowerPath:Path Claim: Successfully claimed path vmhba2:C0:T2:L1
ScsiPath: 5531: Plugin 'PowerPath' claimed path 'vmhba2:C0:T2:L1'
PowerPath:Path Claim: Successfully claimed path vmhba3:C0:T3:L1
ScsiPath: 5531: Plugin 'PowerPath' claimed path 'vmhba3:C0:T3:L1'
PowerPath:Path Claim: Successfully claimed path vmhba3:C0:T2:L1
ScsiPath: 5531: Plugin 'PowerPath' claimed path 'vmhba3:C0:T2:L1'
```

Masking Paths to a Certain LUN

Masking a LUN is a similar to the process of adding claim rules to claim certain paths to a LUN. The main difference is that the plug-in name is MASK_PATH instead of NMP, as used in the previous example. The end result is that the masked LUNs are no longer visible to the host.

> **NOTE**
>
> The claim rule numbers must be lower than the numbers of any claim rules that claim the LUN. For example, if a LUN is claimed by PowerPath, make sure that the Mask_PATH claim rule numbers are lower than the first PowerPath claim rule, which is 250. If you added claim rules to have the LUN claimed by NMP on a host with PowerPath installed and configured, as in the earlier example in this chapter, the NMP claim rule numbers need to be moved to numbers higher than 102. Then the MASK_PATH claim rules are numbered 102 and higher.

Follow these steps to mask paths to a certain LUN:

1. Assume that you want to mask LUN 1 from the previous example, and it still has the same NAA ID. You first run the command shown in Listing 5.11 to list the LUN visible to the ESXi host in the before state.

Listing 5.11   Listing LUN properties using NAA ID via the CLI

```
esxcli storage nmp device list -d naa.6006016072902500088101735d87fe411
 |grep naa
naa.6006016072902500088101735d87fe411
 Device Display Name: DGC Fibre Channel Disk (naa.600601607290250088
 101735d87fe411)
```

You can also use the verbose command option `--device` instead of `-d`.

2. Add the MASK_LUN claim rules and then list the rules, as shown in Listing 5.12.

Listing 5.12   Adding path-masking claim rules

```
esxcli storage core claimrule add -r 102 -t location -A vmhba2 -C 0
 -T 2 -L 1 -P MASK_PATH
esxcli storage core claimrule add -r 103 -t location -A vmhba2 -C 0
 -T 3 -L 1 -P MASK_PATH
esxcli storage core claimrule add -r 104 -t location -A vmhba3 -C 0
 -T 2 -L 1 -P MASK_PATH
esxcli storage core claimrule add -r 105 -t location -A vmhba3 -C 0
 -T 3 -L 1 -P MASK_PATH
esxcli storage core claimrule list |less -S
```

Figure 5.51 shows these commands and their output.

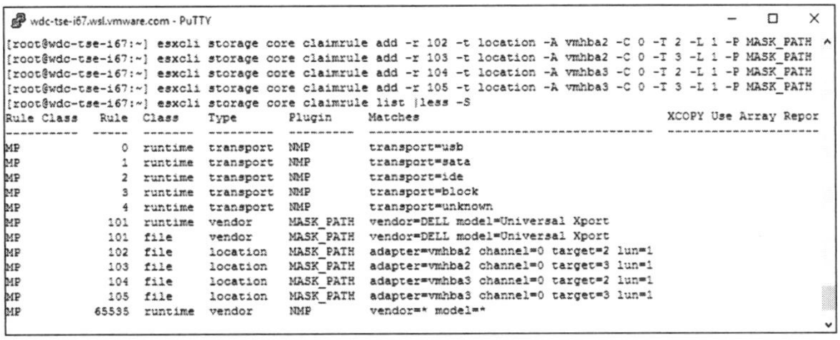

```
wdc-tse-i67.wsl.vmware.com - PuTTY
[root@wdc-tse-i67:~] esxcli storage core claimrule add -r 102 -t location -A vmhba2 -C 0 -T 2 -L 1 -P MASK_PATH
[root@wdc-tse-i67:~] esxcli storage core claimrule add -r 103 -t location -A vmhba2 -C 0 -T 3 -L 1 -P MASK_PATH
[root@wdc-tse-i67:~] esxcli storage core claimrule add -r 104 -t location -A vmhba3 -C 0 -T 2 -L 1 -P MASK_PATH
[root@wdc-tse-i67:~] esxcli storage core claimrule add -r 105 -t location -A vmhba3 -C 0 -T 3 -L 1 -P MASK_PATH
[root@wdc-tse-i67:~] esxcli storage core claimrule list |less -S
Rule Class   Rule  Class    Type       Plugin     Matches                                   XCOPY Use Array Repor
----------  -----  -------  ---------  ---------  ----------------------------------------  --------------------
MP              0  runtime  transport  NMP        transport=usb
MP              1  runtime  transport  NMP        transport=sata
MP              2  runtime  transport  NMP        transport=ide
MP              3  runtime  transport  NMP        transport=block
MP              4  runtime  transport  NMP        transport=unknown
MP            101  runtime  vendor     MASK_PATH  vendor=DELL model=Universal Xport
MP            101  file     vendor     MASK_PATH  vendor=DELL model=Universal Xport
MP            102  file     location   MASK_PATH  adapter=vmhba2 channel=0 target=2 lun=1
MP            103  file     location   MASK_PATH  adapter=vmhba2 channel=0 target=3 lun=1
MP            104  file     location   MASK_PATH  adapter=vmhba3 channel=0 target=2 lun=1
MP            105  file     location   MASK_PATH  adapter=vmhba3 channel=0 target=3 lun=1
MP          65535  runtime  vendor     NMP        vendor=* model=*
```

Figure 5.51 Adding path-masking claim rules

As you see in Figure 5.51, I added rule numbers 102 through 105 to have the MASK_PATH plug-in claim relevant targets to LUN 1 via vmhba2 and vmhba3. The claim rules are not yet loaded—hence the file class listing and no runtime class listings.

3. Load and then list the claim rules by using the following commands (see Figure 5.52):

```
esxcli storage core claimrule load
esxcli storage core claimrule list | less -S
```

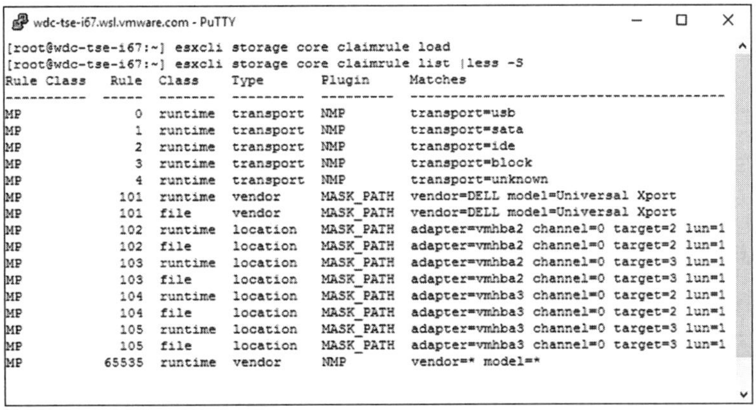

```
wdc-tse-i67.wsl.vmware.com - PuTTY
[root@wdc-tse-i67:~] esxcli storage core claimrule load
[root@wdc-tse-i67:~] esxcli storage core claimrule list |less -S
Rule Class   Rule  Class    Type       Plugin     Matches
----------  -----  -------  ---------  ---------  ----------------------------------------
MP              0  runtime  transport  NMP        transport=usb
MP              1  runtime  transport  NMP        transport=sata
MP              2  runtime  transport  NMP        transport=ide
MP              3  runtime  transport  NMP        transport=block
MP              4  runtime  transport  NMP        transport=unknown
MP            101  runtime  vendor     MASK_PATH  vendor=DELL model=Universal Xport
MP            101  file     vendor     MASK_PATH  vendor=DELL model=Universal Xport
MP            102  runtime  location   MASK_PATH  adapter=vmhba2 channel=0 target=2 lun=1
MP            102  file     location   MASK_PATH  adapter=vmhba2 channel=0 target=2 lun=1
MP            103  runtime  location   MASK_PATH  adapter=vmhba2 channel=0 target=3 lun=1
MP            103  file     location   MASK_PATH  adapter=vmhba2 channel=0 target=3 lun=1
MP            104  runtime  location   MASK_PATH  adapter=vmhba3 channel=0 target=2 lun=1
MP            104  file     location   MASK_PATH  adapter=vmhba3 channel=0 target=2 lun=1
MP            105  runtime  location   MASK_PATH  adapter=vmhba3 channel=0 target=3 lun=1
MP            105  file     location   MASK_PATH  adapter=vmhba3 channel=0 target=3 lun=1
MP          65535  runtime  vendor     NMP        vendor=* model=*
```

Figure 5.52 Loading and listing claim rules after adding path-masking rules

Now you can see the claim rules listed with both `file` and `runtime` classes.

4. Use the `reclaim` option to unclaim and then claim the LUN, using its NAA ID. Check if it is still visible by running the `device list` command (see Listing 5.13).

Listing 5.13   Reclaiming the paths after loading the path-masking rules

```
esxcli storage core claiming reclaim -d naa.60060160729025008810l735d8
 7fe411
esxcli storage nmp device list -d naa.6006016072902500888101735d87fe411
Unknown device naa.60060160729025008810l735d87fe411
```

You can also use the verbose command option `--device` instead of `-d`.

Notice that after you reclaim the LUN, it is an unknown device. Listing 5.14 shows the relevant vmkernel.log messages.

Listing 5.14   Adding path-masking claim rules

```
ScsiEvents: 545: Event Subsystem: Device Events, Destroyed!
StorageApdHandler: 1066: Freeing APD handle 0x43019fe5f520 [naa.600601
 607290250088101735d87fe411]
StorageApdHandler: 1150: APD Handle freed!
WARNING: NMP: nmpUnclaimPath:1586: Physical path "vmhba2:C0:T3:L1"
 is the last path to NMP device "Unregistered Device". The device has
 been unregistered.
ScsiPath: 5531: Plugin 'MASK_PATH' claimed path 'vmhba3:C0:T2:L1'
ScsiPath: 5531: Plugin 'MASK_PATH' claimed path 'vmhba3:C0:T3:L1'
ScsiPath: 5531: Plugin 'MASK_PATH' claimed path 'vmhba2:C0:T2:L1'
ScsiPath: 5531: Plugin 'MASK_PATH' claimed path 'vmhba2:C0:T3:L1'
```

The first line of Listing 5.14 indicates that the device reference has been destroyed.

The following two lines say that the APD handle was freed.

The fourth line shows that after the last path to the LUN has been claimed, the LUN gets unregistered.

The remaining four lines show that the MASK _PATH plug-in claimed all four paths to the LUN.

Unmasking a LUN

To unmask a LUN, you basically reverse the preceding steps and then reclaim the LUN, as follows:

1. Remove the MASK_PATH claim rules (numbers 102–105) and load the changes, as shown in Listing 5.15.

Listing 5.15   Deleting path-masking claim rules

```
esxcli storage core claimrule remove -r 102
esxcli storage core claimrule remove -r 103
esxcli storage core claimrule remove -r 104
esxcli storage core claimrule remove -r 105
esxcli storage core claimrule load
```

You can also use the verbose command options:

```
esxcli storage core claimrule remove --rule <rule-number>
```

2. Unclaim the paths to the LUN in the same fashion you used to add the MASK_
   PATH claim rules—that is, by using the -t location and providing the path
   parameters.

3. Rescan using both HBA names.

4. Verify that the LUN is now visible by running the list command. Listing 5.16
   shows the output from steps 2–4.

Listing 5.16   Adding path-masking claim rules

```
esxcli storage core claiming unclaim -t location -A vmhba2 -C 0 -T 2
 -L 1 -P MASK_PATH
esxcli storage core claiming unclaim -t location -A vmhba2 -C 0 -T 3
 -L 1 -P MASK_PATH
esxcli storage core claiming unclaim -t location -A vmhba3 -C 0 -T 2
 -L 1 -P MASK_PATH
esxcli storage core claiming unclaim -t location -A vmhba3 -C 0 -T 3
 -L 1 -P MASK_PATH
esxcli storage core adapter rescan --adapter vmhba2
esxcli storage core adapter rescan --adapter vmhba3
esxcli storage nmp device list -d naa.6006016072902500881017 35d87fe411
 |grep naa
naa.6006016072902500881017 35d87fe411
 Device Display Name: DGC Fibre Channel Disk (naa.600601607290250088
  101735d87fe411)
```

You can also use the verbose command options, as in this example:

```
esxcli storage core claiming unclaim --type location --adapter
  vmhba2 --channel 0 --target 2 --lun 1 --plugin MASK_PATH
```

If you are certain that all targets zoned to the HBAs are on the same storage
array, you can omit the -T (or --target) parameter, which will assume a
wildcard as the value.

Changing PSP Assignment via the CLI

The CLI enables you to modify the PSP assignment per device. It also enables you to change the default PSP for a specific storage array or family of arrays. I cover the former use case first because it is similar to what you did via the UI in the previous section. I then cover the latter use case.

Changing PSP Assignment for a Device

To change the PSP assignment for a given device, follow this procedure:

1. Log on to the ESXi 6 host locally or via SSH as root or using vMA 6.0 as vi-admin.

2. Identify the device ID for each LUN you want to reconfigure:

   ```
   esxcfg-mpath -b |grep -B1 "fc Adapter"| grep -v -e "--" |sed 's/
   Adapter.*// '
   ```

   You can also use the verbose version of this command:

   ```
   esxcfg-mpath --list-paths grep -B1 "fc Adapter"| grep -v -e "--" | sed
   's/Adapter.*//'
   ```

   Listing 5.17 shows the output from this command.

Listing 5.17   Listing a device's ID and paths

```
naa.60060e8005275100000027510000011a : HITACHI Fibre Channel Disk
 (naa.60060e8005275100000027510000011a)
 vmhba2:C0:T0:L1 LUN:1 state:active fc
 vmhba2:C0:T1:L1 LUN:1 state:active fc
 vmhba3:C0:T0:L1 LUN:1 state:active fc
 vmhba3:C0:T1:L1 LUN:1 state:active fc
```

   From this output, you can identify the device ID (in this case, it is the NAA ID). Note that this output was collected using a Universal Storage Platform V (USP V), USP VM, or Virtual Storage Platform (VSP). This output means that LUN 1 has device ID naa.60060e8005275100000027510000011a.

3. Using the device ID you identified in step 2, run this command:

   ```
   esxcli storage nmp device set -d <device-id> --psp=<psp-name>
   ```

   You can also use the verbose version of this command:

   ```
   esxcli storage nmp device set --device <device-id> --psp=<psp-name>
   ```

   Here is an example:

```
esxcli storage nmp device set -d naa.60060e8005275100000027510000011a
--psp=VMW_PSP_FIXED
```

This command sets the device with ID `naa.60060e8005275100000027510000`
`0011a` to be claimed by the PSP named **VMW_PSP_FIXED**.

Changing the Default PSP for a Storage Array

There is no simple way to change the default PSP for a specific storage array unless that array is claimed by an SATP that is specific for it. In other words, if it is claimed by an SATP that also claims other brands of storage arrays, changing the default PSP affects all storage arrays claimed by the SATP. However, you can add an SATP claim rule that uses a specific PSP, based on your storage array's vendor and model strings:

1. Identify the array's vendor and model strings by running the following command:

   ```
   esxcli storage core device list -d <device ID> |grep 'Vendor\|Model'
   ```

   Listing 5.18 shows an example for a device on an HP 3PAR storage array.

Listing 5.18 Listing a device's vendor and model strings

```
esxcli storage core device list -d naa.60002ac0000000000000003c0007e0b2
|grep 'Vendor\|Model'
 Vendor: 3PARdata
 Model: VV
```

In this example, the vendor string is `3PARdata`, and the model is `VV`.

2. Use the same device ID to identify the default SATP and PSP by running the following command:

   ```
   esxcli storage nmp device list -d <device ID> |grep 'Type:\|Policy:'
   ```

   Listing 5.19 shows an example for a device on an HP 3PAR storage array.

Listing 5.19 Listing a device's default SATP and PSP

```
esxcli storage nmp device list -d naa.60002ac0000000000000003c0007e0b2
|grep 'Type:\|Policy:'
 Storage Array Type: VMW_SATP_ALUA
 Path Selection Policy: VMW_PSP_MRU
```

The output in Listing 5.19 shows that the device was claimed by VMW_SATP_ALUA, and the PSP is VMW_PSP_MRU. If you refer to Figure 5.29 earlier in this chapter, you should conclude that this is the default PSP for VMW_SATP_ALUA. (See Chapter 6, for more details on ALUA.)

3. To rotate I/O over all active-optimized paths every I/O, use the identified values in the following command to change the PSP to MW_PSP_RR and set the number of IOPs to `1`:

```
esxcli storage nmp satp rule add --satp <current-SATP-USED> --vendor
<Vendor string> --model <Model string> --psp <PSP-name> --psp-option
<option> --claim-option <option> --description <Description>
```

> **TIP**
>
> It is always a good practice to document changes manually made to the ESXi host configuration. That is why I used the `--description` option to add a description of the rules I add. This way, other admins would know what I did if they forgot to read the change control record that I added using the company's change control software.

In this example, the command would be as follows (with the whole command on one line):

```
esxcli storage nmp satp rule add --satp VMW_SATP_ALUA --vendor "3PARdata"
 --model "VV" --psp VMW_PSP_RR --psp-option "iops=1" -- claim-option
 "tpgs_on" --description "HP 3PAR Custom iSCSI/FC/FCoE ALUA Rule"
```

It runs silently and returns an error if it fails. The following is an example of an error:

```
"Error adding SATP user rule: Duplicate user rule found for SATP VMW_SATP_
EVA matching vendor HP model HSV340 claim Options PSP VMW_PSP_FIXED and PSP
 Options"
```

This error means that a rule with these options already exists. I simulated this by first adding the rule and then rerunning the same command. To view the existing SATP claim rules list for all storage arrays that are claimed by VMW_SATP_ALUA, you can run the following command:

```
esxcli storage nmp satp rule list --satp VMW_SATP_ALUA |less -S
```

Figure 5.53 shows the output of this command. (In this figure, I deleted some blank columns, including Device, for readability.)

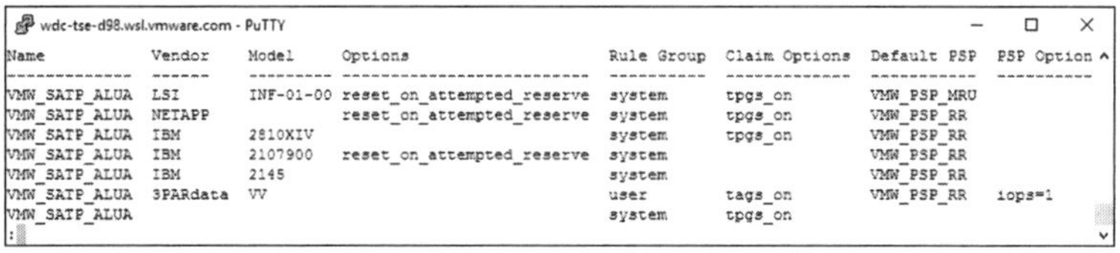
wdc-tse-d98.wsl.vmware.com - PuTTY

Name	Vendor	Model	Options	Rule Group	Claim Options	Default PSP	PSP Option
VMW_SATP_ALUA	LSI	INF-01-00	reset_on_attempted_reserve	system	tpgs_on	VMW_PSP_MRU	
VMW_SATP_ALUA	NETAPP		reset_on_attempted_reserve	system	tpgs_on	VMW_PSP_RR	
VMW_SATP_ALUA	IBM	2810XIV		system	tpgs_on	VMW_PSP_RR	
VMW_SATP_ALUA	IBM	2107900	reset_on_attempted_reserve	system		VMW_PSP_RR	
VMW_SATP_ALUA	IBM	2145		system		VMW_PSP_RR	
VMW_SATP_ALUA	3PARdata	VV		user	tags_on	VMW_PSP_RR	iops=1
VMW_SATP_ALUA				system	tpgs_on		

Figure 5.53 Listing SATP rule list for ALUA devices

You can easily identify non-system rules because the Rule Group column value is user. Such rules were added by a third-party MPIO installer or manually added by an ESXi 6 administrator. The rule in this example shows that I had already added VMW_PSP_RR as the default PSP for VMW_SATP_ALUA when the matching vendor is 3PARdata and the model is VV, as long as the value of tpgs is on. (I will cover this in more details in Chapter 6.)

I created this rule following HP's recommendation to use round-robin with 3PAR storage arrays, as stated on VMware HCL portal. When you use other storage arrays, you *must* verify from the array vendor which PSP is supported by, and certified for, your specific storage array.

In Figure 5.53, you can see that there is a claim rule with a blank vendor and the Claim Options setting is tpgs_on. This claim rule claims *any* device with *any* vendor string, as long as its Claim Options setting is tpgs_on.

Based on this rule, VMW_SATP_ALUA claims *all* ALUA-capable arrays, including HP storage arrays, based on a match on the Claim Options value tpgs_on. But what does this mean? It means that the claim rule I added for the 3PAR array is very specific because I matched on multiple values: --vendor 3PARdata, --model VV, and --claim-option tpgs_on. If I had not specified the vendor and model, the claim rule would have applied to *all* ALUA-capable arrays that have no explicit SATP rules. This would have resulted in all ALUA-capable storage arrays using VMW_SATP_RR. (I will cover this in more depth in Chapter 7.)

If you make any errors creating a rule or if you run into problems after adding a rule, you can remove the rule as follows:

1. To remove the SATP claim rule, use the same command you use to add but substitute remove for add:

```
esxcli storage nmp satp rule remove --satp VMW_SATP_ALUA --vendor
"3PARData --model VV --psp VMW_PSP_RR --psp-option "iops=1" --claim-
option "tpgs_on" --description "HP 3PAR Custom iSCSI/FC/FCoE ALUA
Rule"
```

2. Verify that the rule was removed correctly by running the same command used in the last procedure:

```
esxcli storage nmp satp rule list --satp VMW_SATP_ALUA |less -S
```

Figure 5.54 shows the output.

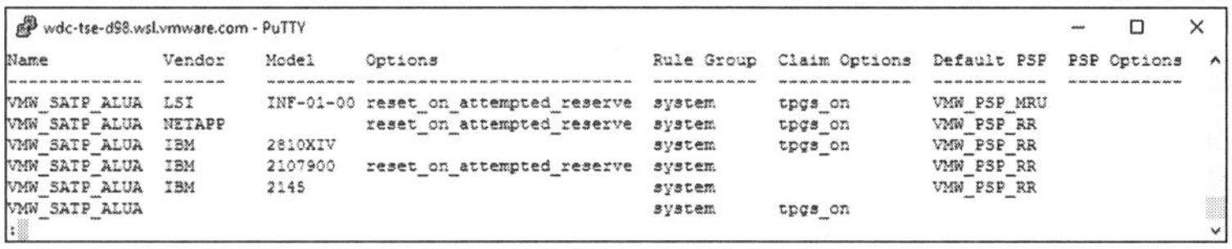

wdc-tse-d98.wsl.vmware.com - PuTTY

Name	Vendor	Model	Options	Rule Group	Claim Options	Default PSP	PSP Options
VMW_SATP_ALUA	LSI	INF-01-00	reset_on_attempted_reserve	system	tpgs_on	VMW_PSP_MRU	
VMW_SATP_ALUA	NETAPP		reset_on_attempted_reserve	system	tpgs_on	VMW_PSP_RR	
VMW_SATP_ALUA	IBM	2810XIV		system	tpgs_on	VMW_PSP_RR	
VMW_SATP_ALUA	IBM	2107900	reset_on_attempted_reserve	system		VMW_PSP_RR	
VMW_SATP_ALUA	IBM	2145		system		VMW_PSP_RR	
VMW_SATP_ALUA				system	tpgs_on		

Figure 5.54 SATP rule list after removing a rule

Notice that the last claim rule in this output is the "catch-all rule" described earlier. This means that this HP 3PAR array will be claimed by VMW_SATP_ALUA when the Claim Options value is `tpgs_on`, even if there is no specific SATP rule created for it.

NOTE

If you had manually set certain LUNs to a specific PSP previously, the preceding command will not affect that setting.

To reset such a LUN to use the current default PSP, use the following command:

```
esxcli storage nmp device set --device <device-ID> --default
```

Here is an example:

```
esxcli storage nmp device set --device naa.60002ac0000000000000003c0
 007e0b2 --default
```

Summary

This chapter has covered VMware Pluggable Storage Architecture (PSA) components. I showed you how to list PSA plug-ins and how they interact with vSphere ESXi 6. I also showed you how to list, modify, and customize PSA claim rules and how to work around some common issues.It also covered how ALUA-capable devices interact with SATP claim rules for the purpose of using a specific PSP.

## Chapter 6

ALUA

Storage arrays provide various configurations and features, depending on their class and design. Depending on how the arrays handle I/O to devices presented to hosts, they can be classified as follows:

- **Active/Active**—I/O (input/output) can be sent to logical unit numbers (LUNs) via any storage processor (SP) and port. Most of these arrays have large caches in place, and the I/O is done on the LUN representation in cache, and then the writes are flushed to the physical disks asynchronously from the I/O.

- **Active/Passive**—I/O can be sent only to any port on the storage processor that "owns" the LUN (also known as the *active SP*). If the I/O is attempted on the LUN via ports on the "non-owner" processor (also known as a *passive SP*), an error is returned to the initiator that means, simply, "No entry," or "No, you can't do that." (I provide the actual sense codes in Chapter 7, "Multipathing and Failover.")

- **Pseudo-active/Active (also known as *asymmetric active-active*)**—I/O can be sent to ports on either storage processor. However, I/O sent to the owner processor is faster than that sent to the non-owner processor because of the path the I/O takes to get to the devices from each SP. Going through the non-owner SP involves sending the I/O via some back-end channels, whereas there is a direct path via the owner SP.

The latter two types of arrays have recently started implementing a SCSI-3 specification referred to as *Asymmetric Logical Unit Access (ALUA)*. It allows access to the array devices via both SPs but clearly identifies to the initiators which targets are on the owner SP and which are on the non-owner SP. ALUA support was first introduced in vSphere 4.0.

ALUA Definition

ALUA is described in the T10 SCSI-3 specification SPC-3, section 5.8 (see www.t10.org/cgi-bin/ac.pl?t=f&f=spc3r23.pdf; access to this URL requires T10 membership or other organizational access). The official description from this standard is as follows:

> Asymmetric logical unit access occurs when the access characteristics of one port may differ from those of another port.

In simpler terms, ALUA specifies a type of storage device that is capable of servicing I/O to a given LUN on two different storage processors but in an uneven manner.

As I mentioned briefly earlier, using ALUA, I/O to a given LUN can be sent to available ports on any of the SPs in the storage array. This is closer to the behavior of asymmetric active/active arrays than to that of active/passive arrays. The I/O is allowed to the LUN, but the performance of the owner SP is better than that of the non-owner SP. To allow the initiators to identify which targets would provide the best I/O, the ports on each SP are grouped together into target port groups. Each target port group is given a distinctive "state" (asymmetric access state [AAS]) that denotes the optimization of ports on one SP compared to ports on the other SP (for example, active-optimized versus active-non-optimized).

ALUA Target Port Groups

According to SPC-3, a target port group (TPG) is described as follows:

> A target port group is defined as a set of target ports that are in the same target port asymmetric access state at all times. A target port group asymmetric access state is defined as the target port asymmetric access state common to the set of target ports in a target port group. The grouping of target ports is vendor specific.

This simply means that in a given storage array that has, say, two SPs—SPA and SPB—ports on SPA are grouped together, and ports on SPB are grouped in a separate group. Assume that this storage array presents two LUNs—LUN 1 and LUN 2—to initiators in E hosts and that LUN 1 is owned by SPA, whereas LUN 2 is owned by SPB. For the hosts, it is better to access LUN 1 via SPA and to access LUN 2 via SPB. Relative to LUN 1, ports on SPA are in the active-optimized (AO) TPGs, and ports on SPB are in the active-non-optimized (ANO) TPGs. The reverse is true for LUN 2 in this example, where TPGs on SPA are ANO, and TPGs on SPB are AO.

Figure 6.1 shows this example on an asymmetric active/active array. TPG with ID=1 (the left-hand rectangle on SPA) is AO (represented by the solid line connecting it to LUN 1). This same TPG is ANO for LUN2 (represented by the interrupted line connecting TPG 1 to LUN 2).

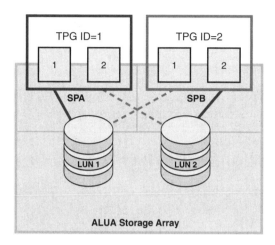

Figure 6.1 Illustration of TPGs

The reverse is true for TPG with ID=2. That is, it is AO for LUN 2 and ANO for LUN 1.

On some active/passive ALUA-capable arrays, you may see port groups with "Standby" AAS instead of "ANO" on the non-owner SP.

Asymmetric Access State

Ports in an ALUA TPG can be in the same AAS at all times with respect to a given LUN. The TPG's AAS are reported to the initiators in response to the REPORT TPGS command. The TPG descriptor is reported in byte 1 of that response.

The possible states are as follows:

1. **Active-optimized (AO)**—Ports are on the owner SP and provided the best I/O to the LUN.

   - **Active-non-optimized (ANO)**—Ports are on the non-owner SP. I/O to the LUN is less optimal compared to AO AAS.

   - **Transitioning**—The TPG AAS is in the process of switching from one state to another. For example, if the SP of an AO TPG is being rebooted or is taken offline, or if the SAN (storage area network) admin manually transfers LUN ownership (on EMC CLARiiON, this is known as *trespass*), the AAS of the TPG on the alternate SP changes to AO. While this process is ongoing, the TPG AAS is *transitioning*.

While the TPG is in this state, receiving requests from the initiators return BUSY or a CHECK CONDITION with sense key NOT READY and ASC (additional sense code) LOGICAL UNIT NOT ACCESSIBLE or ASYMMETRIC ACCESS STATE TRANSITION.

- **Standby**—This state is similar to a passive SP in a non-ALUA configuration and on certain ALUA-capable arrays. It returns a CHECK CONDITION with sense key NOT READY.

  When the TPG is in this AAS, it supports a subset of commands that it accepts when it is in AO AAS:

  ```
  INQUIRY
  LOG SELECT
  LOG SENSE
  MODE SELECT
  MODE SENSE
  REPORT LUNS (for LUN 0)
  RECEIVE DIAGNOSTIC RESULTS
  SEND DIAGNOSTIC
  REPORT TARGET PORT GROUPS
  SET TARGET PORT GROUPS
  REQUEST SENSE
  PERSISTENT RESERVE IN
  PERSISTENT RESERVE OUT
  Echo buffer modes of READ BUFFER
  Echo buffer modes of WRITE BUFFER
  ```

- **Unavailable**—This AAS is usually seen when the TPG's access to the LUN is restricted as a result of hardware errors or other SCSI device limitations. A TPG in this state is unable to transition to AO or ANO until the error subsides.

Some ALUA storage arrays certified with vSphere 6 might not support some of the latter three states.

ESXi 6 sends the I/O to TPGs that are in AO AAS, but if they are not available, I/O is sent to TPGs that are in ANO AAS. If the storage array receives sustained I/O on TPGs that are in ANO AAS, the array transitions the TPG's state to AO AAS. Who makes that change depends on the ALUA management mode of the storage array (see the next section).

ALUA Management Modes

The dynamic nature of multipathing and failover requires the flexibility of managing and controlling an ALUA TPG's AAS. This is done via a set of commands and responses to and from the storage arrays. These commands are as follows:

- **INQUIRY**—According to SPC-3, section 6.4.2, in response to this command, an array returns certain pages of the VPD (vital product data) or EVPD (extended vital product data). The inquiry data returned in response to this command includes the TPGS field. If the returned value in that field is nonzero, that device (LUN) supports ALUA. (See Table 6.3, later in this chapter, for the correlation between the value of the TPGS field and AAS management modes.)

- **REPORT TARGET PORT GROUPS (REPORT TPGs)**—This command requests that the storage array send the TPG information to the initiator.

- **SET TARGET PORT GROUPS (SET TPGs)**—This command requests that the storage array set the AAS of all ports in specified TPGs. For example, a TPG's AAS can transition from ANO to AO via the SET TPGs command.

The control or management of ALUA AAS can operate in one of four modes (see Table 6.1):

Table 6.1 ALUA AAS management modes

Mode	Managed By	REPORTPGs	SET TPGs
Not Supported	N/A	Invalid	Invalid
Implicit	Array	Yes	No
Explicit	Host	Yes	Yes
Both	Array/host	Yes	Yes

- **Not Supported**—The response to the REPORT TPGs and SET TPGs commands is invalid. This means that the storage array does not support ALUA or, in the case of EMC CLARiiON, the initiator records are not configured in a mode that supports ALUA.

- **Implicit**—The array responds to REPORT TPGs but not SET TPGs commands. In this case, setting the TPG's AAS is done only by the storage array.

- **Explicit**—The array responds to both REPORT TPGs and SET TPGs commands. In this case, setting the TPG's AAS can be done only by the initiator.

- **Both**—Same as Explicit, but both the array and the initiator can set the TPG's AAS.

ALUA Common Implementations

The combination of ALUA AAS and management modes varies by vendor. Table 6.2 shows a matrix of common combinations.

Table 6.2 Common ALUA implementations

Mode	AO	ANO	Standby	Array Vendor Example
Implicit	Yes	Yes	No	NetApp
Explicit and Implicit	Yes	Yes	No	HP EVA
				EMC VNX or CLARiiON CX
Explicit	Yes	No	Yes	IBM DS4000

ALUA Followover

To better explain what ALUA followover does, let me first describe what happens without it. Storage design that uses active/passive arrays must consider configurations that prevent a condition referred to as *path thrashing*, which is the case when, due to poor design or physical failure, some hosts have access to only one SP, whereas other hosts have access to the other SP and/or the incorrect Path Selection Plug-in (PSP) is selected for the array. I have seen this happen in two scenarios, which are described in the following sections.

Path Thrashing Scenario 1

Figure 6.2 shows a Fibre Channel SAN design for a non-ALUA active/passive array. Here Host A has access to SPA only, and Host B has access to SPB only. LUN 1 is owned by SPA. However, because Host B cannot access that SP, it requests from the array to transfer the LUN ownership to SPB. When the array complies, the result is that Host A loses access to the LUN because it is no longer owned by SPA. Host A attempts to recover from this state by requesting that the array to transfer the LUN ownership back to SPA. When the array complies, Host B starts this cycle again. This tug-of-war continues on and on, and neither host can issue any I/O on the LUN.

The only solution for this problem is to correct the design so that each host has access to both SPs and use the VMW_PSP_MRU Pluggable Storage Architecture (PSA) plug-in. Note that enabling ALUA without correcting the design may not prevent this problem.

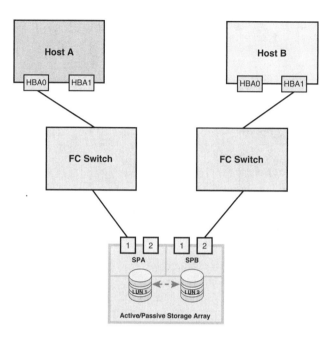

Figure 6.2   Scenario 1: Path thrashing due to a poor cabling design choice

Path Thrashing Scenario 2

Figure 6.3 shows a variation on Scenario 1 in which the Fibre Channel fabric was designed according to VMware best practices. However, both hosts were configured with VMW_PSP_FIXED instead of VMW_PSP_MRU. This by itself wouldn't result in path thrashing. However, the designer decided to customize each host so that they have different preferred paths to LUN 1. These preferred path settings are represented by the interrupted lines (a path from Host A and another path from Host B). The expected behavior in this configuration is that as long as the defined preferred path to LUN 1 is available, the host insists on sending I/O via that path. As a result, Host A attempts to send its I/O to LUN 1 via SPA, and Host B sends it I/O via SPB. However, LUN 1 is owned by SPA and attempts to send I/O via SPB, resulting in a check condition with the sense key `ILLEGAL_REQUEST` (more on this in Chapter 7). Host B insists on sending the I/O via its preferred path. So, it sends a `START_UNIT` or a `TRESPASS` command to the array. As a result, the array transfers LUN 1 ownership to SPB. Now Host A gets really upset and tells the array to transfer the LUN back to SPA, using the `START_UNIT` or `TRESPASS` commands. The array complies, and the tug-of-war begins!

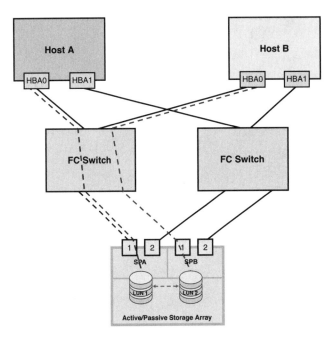

Figure 6.3   Scenario 2: Path thrashing due to a poor PSP design choice

Preventing Path Thrashing

These two examples prompted VMware to create the VMW_PSP_MRU plug-in for use with active/passive arrays. In older releases, prior to ESX 4.0, this used to be a policy setting for each LUN. In 4.0 and later, including 6.0 and 6.5, MRU is a PSA plug-in. (I the PSP design choices in Chapter 7.) With MRU, the host sends the I/O to the most recently used path. If the LUN moves to another SP, the I/O is sent on the new path to that SP instead of being sent to SP that was the previous owner. Note that MRU ignores the preferred path setting.

ALUA-capable arrays that provide AO AAS for TPGs on the owner SP and ANO AAS for TPGs on the non-owner SP allow I/O to the given LUN with high priority via the AO TPGs and, conversely, lower priority via the ANO TPGs. This means that the latter does not return a check condition with sense key `ILLEGAL_REQUEST` if I/O to the LUN is sent through it. This means that using VMW_PSP_FIXED with these arrays can result in a lighter version of path thrashing. In this case, I/O does not fail to be sent to the ANO TPGs if that is the preferred path. However, the I/O performance is much lower compared to using the AO TPGs. If more hosts are using the AO TPGs as the preferred path, the LUN ownership stays on the original SP that owns it. As a result, the ANO TPGs are not transitioned to AO for the offending host.

To accommodate this situation, VMware introduced a new feature for use with ALUA devices; however, it is not defined in the ALUA spec. This feature is referred to as *ALUA followover*.

ALUA followover simply means that when the host detects a TPG AAS change that it did not cause by itself, it does not try to revert the change even if it only has access to TPGs that are ANO. Effectively, this prevents the hosts from fighting for TPG AAS and, instead, they follow the TPG AAS of the array. Figures 6.4 and 6.5 illustrate ALUA followover interaction with TPG AAS.

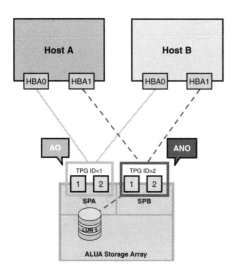

Figure 6.4   ALUA followover before failure

Figure 6.4 shows a logical storage diagram in which the switch fabrics have been removed to simplify the diagram . Here, TPG ID 1 is the AO on SPA, and both hosts send the I/O to that TPG. TPG ID 2 is ANO, and I/O is not sent to it. These TPGs are configured with ALUA Explicit mode.

Figure 6.5 shows what happens after a path to the AO TPG fails.

Figure 6.5 shows that Host A lost its path to the AO TPG (based on Figure 6.4). As a result, this host takes advantage of the ALUA Explicit mode on the array and sends a SET_TPGS command to the array so that TPG ID 2 is changed to AO and TPG ID 1 is changed to ANO. Host B recognizes that it did not make this change. But because ALUA followover is enabled, Host B just accepts this change and does not attempt to reverse it. Consequently, the I/O is sent to TPG ID 2 because it is now the AO TPG. (Notice that the array moved the LUN ownership to SPB because this is where the AO TPG is located.)

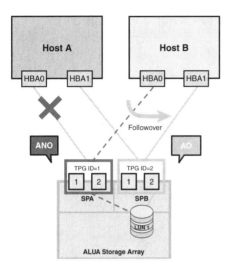

Figure 6.5   ALUA followover after failure

Some storage arrays implement the PREF (preference) bit, which enables an array to specify which SP is the preferred owner of a given LUN. This allows the storage administrator to spread the LUNs over both SPs (for example, even LUNs on one SP and odd LUNs on the other SP). Whenever the need arises to shut down one of the SPs, the LUNs owned by that SP (say SPA) get transferred to the surviving nonpreferred SP (SPB). As a result, the AAS of the port group on SPB is changed to AO. ALUA followover honors this change and sends the next I/O intended for the transferred LUNs to the port group on SPB. When SPA is brought back online, the LUNs it used to own get transferred back to it. This reverses the changes done earlier, and the AAS of the port group on SPA is set to AO for the transferred LUNs. Conversely, the AAS of the port group on SPB, which no longer owns the LUNs, is changed to ANO. Again, ALUA followover honors this change and switches the I/O back to the port group on SPA. This is the default behavior of ALUA-capable HP EVA storage arrays.

Identifying Device ALUA Configuration

ESXi 6 host configuration that enables use of ALUA devices is a PSA component in the form of a SATP (see Chapter 5, "vSphere Pluggable Storage Architecture [PSA]"). PSA claim rules determine which SATP to use, based on array information returned in response to an INQUIRY command. As mentioned earlier, part of the inquiry string is the TPGS field. The claim rules are configured such that if a field's value is nonzero, the device is claimed by the defined ALUA SATP. In the following sections, I show how to list these claim rules and how to identify ALUA configurations from the device properties.

Identifying ALUA Claim Rule

In Chapter 5, I showed you how to list all the SATP rules. I had to split the screenshots into four quadrants so that I could show all the content of the output. Here, I've tried to trim it down and list only the lines I need to show. To do so, I used the following command:

```
esxcli storage nmp satp rule list |grep -i 'model\|satp_alua\|---' |less -S
```

This command lists all SATP rules and then uses grep for the string's model, satp_alua, and ---. This causes the output to have column headers and separator lines, which are the first two lines in the output. The rest of the output shows only the lines with satp_alua in them. Notice that the -i argument causes grep to ignore the case.

Figure 6.6 shows the output from this command.

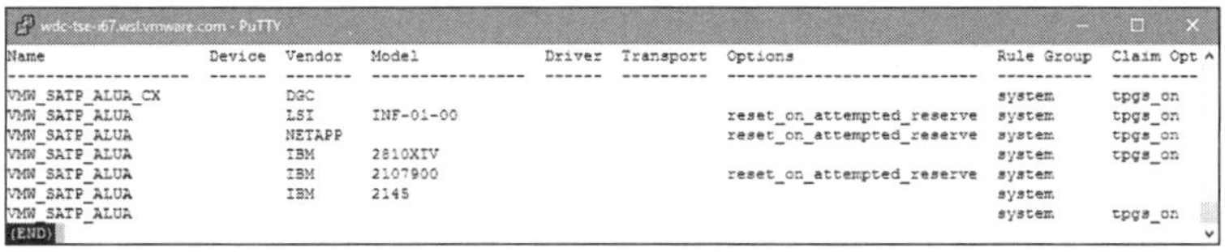

Figure 6.6   ALUA claim rules

The following is the text of the output with blank columns removed for readability:

Name	Vendor	Model	Options	Rule Group	Claim Options
VMW_SATP_ALUA_CX	DGC			system	tpgs_on
VMW_SATP_ALUA	LSI	INF-01-00	reset_on_attempted_reserve	system	tpgs_on
VMW_SATP_ALUA	NETAPP		reset_on_attempted_reserve	system	tpgs_on
VMW_SATP_ALUA	IBM	2810XIV		system	tpgs_on
VMW_SATP_ALUA	IBM	2107900	reset_on_attempted_reserve	system	
VMW_SATP_ALUA	IBM	2145		system	
VMW_SATP_ALUA				system	tpgs_on

In this output, notice that the EMC CLARiiON CX family is claimed by the VMW_SATP_ALUA_CX plug-in, based on matches on the Model column setting being DGC and the Claim Options setting being tpgs_on.

On the other hand, both LSI and IBM 2810-XIV are claimed by the VMW_SATP_ALUA plug-in, based on matches on the Vendor column, the Model column, and the value of `tpgs_on` in the Claim Options column.

NetApp is also claimed by the VMW_SATP_ALUA plug-in, based on matches on the Vendor column and the value of `tpgs_on` in the Claim Options column only. In this case, the Model column was not used.

IBM DS8000, which is model 2107-900 (listed in the output without the dash), and IBM SVC (listed here as model 2145) are claimed by the VMW_SATP_ALUA plug-in, based on the Vendor and Model columns only, even though the Claim Options column setting is not `tpgs_on`.

The remaining rule allows VMW_SATP_ALUA to claim devices with any Vendor or Model column value, as long as the Claim Options column value is `tpgs_on`. This means that any array not listed in the preceding rules that returns a nonzero value for the TPGS field in the inquiry response string gets claimed by VMW_SATP_ALUA. You might think of this as a catch-all ALUA claim rule that claims devices on all ALUA arrays that are not explicitly listed by vendor or model in the SATP claim rules.

Identifying Devices' ALUA Configurations

ALUA configurations are associated with LUNs in combination with TPGs. To list these configurations, you can run the following command:

```
esxcli storage nmp device list --device [device-ID]
```

Or you can use the abbreviated option `-d` instead of `--device`.

Here is an example:

```
esxcli storage nmp device list --device naa.60060160f2c43500bc280391f65
6e311
```

The output of this command is listed in the following sections, which show examples from various storage arrays.

An Example from an EMC VNX or CLARiiON CX Array

Figure 6.7 shows an example of an EMC VNX or CLARiiON CX LUN configured for ALUA.

Figure 6.7 ALUA Configuration of a VNX or CLARiiON CX family device

This output shows the `Storage Array Type` field set to `VMW_SATP_ALUA_CX`, which is the same as the VMW_SATP_ALUA plug-in with additional code to handle certain commands specific to CLARiiON CX ALUA arrays.

- The output also shows the `Storage Array Type Device Config` line, wrapped for readability, which includes a number of parts: The first set of curly brackets, {}, includes initiator registration–specific configuration. This is specific to EMC VNX and the CLARiiON family of arrays. Within this set, two options are listed:

  - **navireg=on**—This means that NaviAgent Registration option is enabled on this host. It registers the initiator with the VNX or CX array if it is not already registered. Note that you need to check the initiator record on the array to make sure that `Failover Mode` is set to `4`, which enables ALUA for this initiator. (You can find more details on this in Chapter 7.)

  - **ipfilter=on**—This option filters the host's IP address so that it is not visible to the storage array. (You'll learn more about this in Chapter 7.)

- The ALUA AAS management mode options are enclosed in a second set of curly brackets, within which is another nested pair of curly brackets for the TPG's AAS configuration. These are the ALUA AAS management mode options:

  - `Implicit_support=on`—This means that the array supports the Implicit mode of AAS management (refer to Table 6.1).

  - `Explicit_support=on`—This means that the array supports the Explicit mode of AAS management (refer to Table 6.1).

  - `Explicit_allow=on`—This means that the host is configured to allow the SATP to exercise its explicit ALUA capability if the need arises (for example, in the event of a failed controller).

  - `ALUA_followover=on`—This enables the ALUA followover option on the host. (See the "ALUA Followover" section, earlier in this chapter.)

  - `action_OnRetryErrors=off`—This option is set to `off` by default. This means that when and I/O on that path returns an error indicating the I/O can be retried, the path remains in an on state even after the I/O is retried indefinitely. When this option is set to on, the path eventually, after a certain timeout, is marked dead if the I/O retries still result in an error. (You'll learn more about this in Chapter 7.)

- The next set of options appear within the nested pair of curly brackets for the TPG IDs and AAS:

  - TPG_id—This field shows the target port group ID. If the LUN is accessible via more than one target port group (typically two groups), both IDs are listed here. This example has TPG_id 1 and 2. Each TPG is listed within its own pair of curly brackets.

  - TPG_state—This field shows the AAS of the TPG. Notice that TPG_id 1 is in AO AAS, whereas TPG_id 2 is in ANO AAS. Based on this configuration, I/O is sent to TPG_id 1.

I cover the path-related options in Chapter 7.

More Examples from an EMC VNX/CLARiiON CX Array

The example in Figure 6.8 shows similar output but from an EMC VNX array.

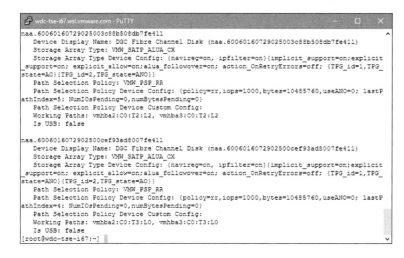

Figure 6.8   ALUA configuration of EMC VNX/CLARiiON CX FC devices

Figure 6.8 shows two devices on the same array. Both devices have identical information. Note the following observations:

- The first device in this example shows TPG_id 1 being in AO AAS, and on the second device, TPG_id 2 is also in the same state (AO AAS). This means that the devices are spread evenly over the array's SPs. For example, TPG 1 on SPA services I/O to LUN 2, whereas TPG 2 on SPB services I/O to LUN 0. You should also notice from the `Working Paths` field that for LUN 2, the target portion of the pathname is T2, via vmhba2 and vmhba3, whereas it is T3 for LUN 0. (I explain in Chapter 2, "Fibre Channel Storage Connectivity," Chapter 3, "FCoE Storage Connectivity," and Chapter 7, "Multipathing and Failover," how to identify which target belongs to which SP.)

- Both devices are claimed by `VMW_PSP_RR` (round-robin). This means that the I/Os rotate on SPA ports via vmhba2 and vmhba3 for LUN 2, whereas for LUN 0, the I/Os rotate on SPB ports via the same HBAs. This design balances the load on the storage array SPs as well as the host's initiators. (I explain this in Chapter 7.)

An Example from an IBM DS8000 Array

Figure 6.9 shows similar output from an IBM DS8000 array-based device.

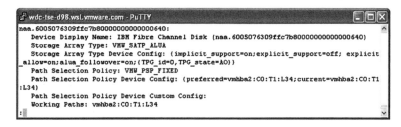

Figure 6.9 ALUA configuration of an IBM DS8000 device

The output is similar to the output in the preceding sections in many aspects, but note the following differences:

- The device is claimed by VMW_SATP_ALUA instead of VMW_SATP_ALUA_CX.
- `explicit_support=off` means that the array does not support the Explicit mode of AAS management.
- There is only one `TPG_id`, which is 0, and it is in an AO AAS.

NOTE

Even though `explicit_allow` is set to `on`, this does not take effect because the array does not support Explicit mode.

An Example from an IBM XIV Array

Figure 6.10 shows output from an IBM XIV array-based device.

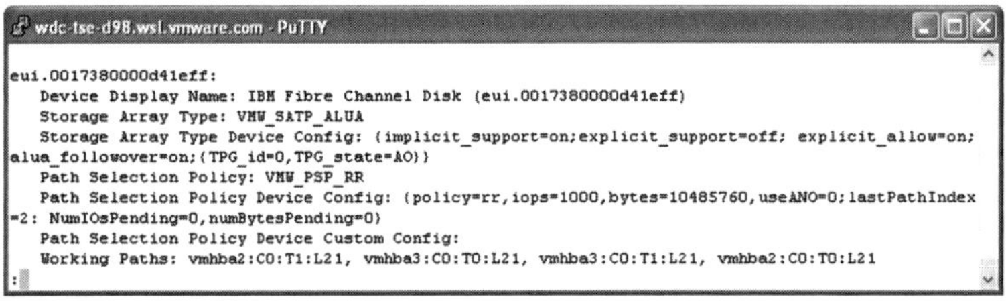

```
wdc-tse-d98.wsl.vmware.com - PuTTY
eui.0017380000d41eff:
    Device Display Name: IBM Fibre Channel Disk (eui.0017380000d41eff)
    Storage Array Type: VMW_SATP_ALUA
    Storage Array Type Device Config: {implicit_support=on;explicit_support=off; explicit_allow=on;
alua_followover=on;(TPG_id=0,TPG_state=AO)}
    Path Selection Policy: VMW_PSP_RR
    Path Selection Policy Device Config: {policy=rr,iops=1000,bytes=10485760,useANO=0;lastPathIndex
=2: NumIOsPending=0,numBytesPending=0}
    Path Selection Policy Device Custom Config:
    Working Paths: vmhba2:C0:T1:L21, vmhba3:C0:T0:L21, vmhba3:C0:T1:L21, vmhba2:C0:T0:L21
```

Figure 6.10   ALUA configuration of an IBM XIV device

The output is similar to that from the IBM DS8000 array (refer to Figure 6.9), with the following differences:

- The device ID uses the `eui` format instead of `naa`. This is usually the result of the array supporting an ANSI revision lower than 3. (See Chapter 1, "Storage Types," for details.)

- The PSP in use is VMW_PSP_RR (round-robin) rather than FIXED. (I discuss PSP choices and configuration in Chapter 7.)

An Example from a NetApp Array

Figure 6.11 shows an example from a NetApp array.

```
wdc-tse-d98.wsl.vmware.com - PuTTY
naa.60a98000572d4c6e434a637362413355:
    Device Display Name: NETAPP Fibre Channel Disk (naa.60a98000572d4c6e434a637362413355)
    Storage Array Type: VMW_SATP_ALUA
    Storage Array Type Device Config: {implicit_support=on;explicit_support=off; explicit_all
ow=on;alua_followover=on;(TPG_id=0,TPG_state=AO)(TPG_id=1,TPG_state=ANO)}
    Path Selection Policy: VMW_PSP_RR
    Path Selection Policy Device Config: {policy=rr,iops=1000,bytes=10485760,useANO=0;lastPat
hIndex=1: NumIOsPending=0,numBytesPending=0}
    Path Selection Policy Device Custom Config:
    Working Paths: vmhba2:C0:T0:L3, vmhba1:C0:T0:L3
```

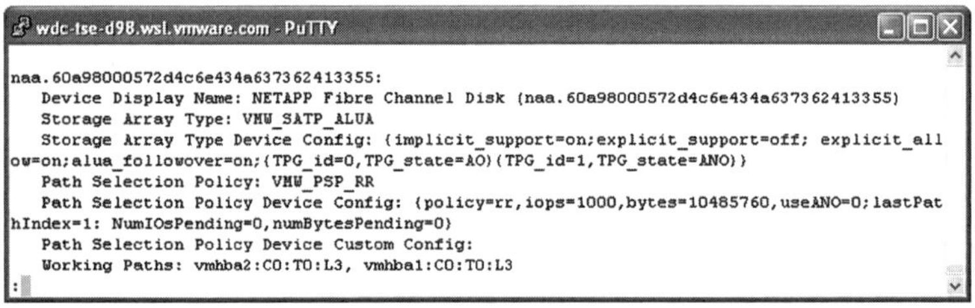

Figure 6.11   ALUA configuration of a NetApp FC device

This example is similar to the two-TPG EMC CX example in Figure 6.7, with the following differences:

- The device is claimed by VMW_SATP_ALUA instead of VMW_SATP_ALUA_CX.

- `explicit_support=off` means that the array does not support the Explicit mode of AAS management.

- Device is claimed by VMW_PSP_RR instead of VMW_PSP_FIXED.

An Example from an HP MSA Array

Figure 6.12 shows an example from an HP MSA array.

```
naa.600c0ff000dae2e74261b04d07000000:
   Device Display Name: HP Serial Attached SCSI Disk (naa.600c0ff000dae2e74261b04d07000000)
   Storage Array Type: VMW_SATP_ALUA
   Storage Array Type Device Config: {implicit_support=on;explicit_support=off; explicit_allow=on;
alua_followover=on;{TPG_id=0,TPG_state=AO}{TPG_id=1,TPG_state=ANO}}
   Path Selection Policy: VMW_PSP_MRU
   Path Selection Policy Device Config: Current Path=vmhba3:C0:T1:L11
   Path Selection Policy Device Custom Config:
   Working Paths: vmhba3:C0:T1:L11
```

Figure 6.12 ALUA configuration of an HP MSA FC device

This example is similar to the NetApp array output (refer to Figure 6.11), with the difference that the PSP is VMW_PSP_MRU.

Troubleshooting ALUA

In this section, I give some troubleshooting foundation that will hopefully help you learn how to fish (also known as TIY—troubleshoot it yourself)!

First, let me familiarize you with the normal log entries. When a device is discovered by vmkernel (logged to /var/log/vmkernel.log or /var/log/boot.gz files), as I mentioned earlier, the TPGS field is included with the inquiry string. The value of that field helps vmkernel identify the AAS management mode (that is, Explicit, Implicit, or Both).

Following are examples from the storage arrays I used in the previous sections. Figure 6.13 shows vmkernel.log entries from an ESXi 6 host connected to an EMC VNX storage array.

```
csiScan: 836: Path vmhba2:C0:T2:L0 supports REPORT LUNS 0x11
csiScan: 1173: Path 'vmhba2:C0:T2:L0': Vendor: 'DGC    ' Model: 'VRAID            ' Rev: '0532'
csiScan: 1176: Path 'vmhba2:C0:T2:L0': Type: 0x0, ANSI rev: 4, TPGS: 3 (implicit and explicit)
csiScan: 836: Path vmhba3:C0:T2:L0 supports REPORT LUNS 0x11
csiScan: 1173: Path 'vmhba3:C0:T2:L0': Vendor: 'DGC    ' Model: 'VRAID            ' Rev: '0532'
csiScan: 1176: Path 'vmhba3:C0:T2:L0': Type: 0x0, ANSI rev: 4, TPGS: 3 (implicit and explicit)
csiScan: 1738: Add path: vmhba2:C0:T2:L0
csiScan: 1738: Add path: vmhba3:C0:T2:L0
csiScan: 1173: Path 'vmhba2:C0:T2:L2': Vendor: 'DGC    ' Model: 'VRAID            ' Rev: '0532'
csiScan: 1176: Path 'vmhba2:C0:T2:L2': Type: 0x0, ANSI rev: 4, TPGS: 3 (implicit and explicit)
csiScan: 1173: Path 'vmhba3:C0:T2:L2': Vendor: 'DGC    ' Model: 'VRAID            ' Rev: '0532'
csiScan: 1176: Path 'vmhba3:C0:T2:L2': Type: 0x0, ANSI rev: 4, TPGS: 3 (implicit and explicit)
csiScan: 1738: Add path: vmhba2:C0:T2:L2
[root@wdc-tse-d98:~]
```

Figure 6.13 VMkernel.log entries of an EMC CLARiiON ALUA device

In this example, I truncated the first part of each line, which shows the data, timestamp, and host name. Notice that the ScsiScan lines show the TPGS field with a value of 3. This means that the array supports both Implicit and Explicit ALUA modes. This is printed in English at the end of each line as well.

Figure 6.14 shows log entries from an ESXi 6 host connected to a NetApp storage array.

```
wdc-tse-h56.wsl.vmware.com - PuTTY
ScsiScan: 1106: Path 'vmhba1:C0:T0:L0': Vendor: 'NETAPP  ' Model: 'LUN           ' Rev: '7350'
ScsiScan: 1109: Path 'vmhba1:C0:T0:L0': Type: 0x0, ANSI rev: 4, TPGS: 1 (implicit only)
ScsiScan: 1590: Add path: vmhba1:C0:T0:L0
ScsiScan: 1106: Path 'vmhba1:C0:T0:L1': Vendor: 'NETAPP  ' Model: 'LUN           ' Rev: '7350'
ScsiScan: 1109: Path 'vmhba1:C0:T0:L1': Type: 0x0, ANSI rev: 4, TPGS: 1 (implicit only)
ScsiScan: 1106: Path 'vmhba1:C0:T0:L2': Vendor: 'NETAPP  ' Model: 'LUN           ' Rev: '7350'
ScsiScan: 1109: Path 'vmhba1:C0:T0:L2': Type: 0x0, ANSI rev: 4, TPGS: 1 (implicit only)
ScsiScan: 1106: Path 'vmhba1:C0:T0:L4': Vendor: 'NETAPP  ' Model: 'LUN           ' Rev: '7350'
ScsiScan: 1109: Path 'vmhba1:C0:T0:L4': Type: 0x0, ANSI rev: 4, TPGS: 1 (implicit only)
ScsiScan: 1106: Path 'vmhba1:C0:T0:L3': Vendor: 'NETAPP  ' Model: 'LUN           ' Rev: '7350'
ScsiScan: 1109: Path 'vmhba1:C0:T0:L3': Type: 0x0, ANSI rev: 4, TPGS: 1 (implicit only)
ScsiScan: 1106: Path 'vmhba1:C0:T0:L5': Vendor: 'NETAPP  ' Model: 'LUN           ' Rev: '7350'
ScsiScan: 1109: Path 'vmhba1:C0:T0:L5': Type: 0x0, ANSI rev: 4, TPGS: 1 (implicit only)
:
```

Figure 6.14   VMkernel.log entries of a NetApp ALUA device

Notice that the ScsiScan lines show the TPGS field with a value of 1. This means that the array supports implicit ALUA mode only. This is printed in English as well at the end of each line.

Figure 6.15 shows log entries from an ESXi 6 host connected to an IBM DS8000 storage array.

```
wdc-tse-d98.wsl.vmware.com - PuTTY
ScsiScan: 1106: Path 'vmhba1:C0:T0:L0': Vendor: 'IBM     ' Model: '2107900       ' Rev: '.335'
ScsiScan: 1109: Path 'vmhba1:C0:T0:L0': Type: 0x0, ANSI rev: 5, TPGS: 1 (implicit only)
ScsiScan: 1590: Add path: vmhba1:C0:T0:L0
)ScsiScan: 1106: Path 'vmhba1:C0:T0:L1': Vendor: 'IBM     ' Model: '2107900       ' Rev: '.335'
)ScsiScan: 1109: Path 'vmhba1:C0:T0:L1': Type: 0x0, ANSI rev: 5, TPGS: 1 (implicit only)
ScsiScan: 1106: Path 'vmhba1:C0:T0:L2': Vendor: 'IBM     ' Model: '2107900       ' Rev: '.335'
ScsiScan: 1109: Path 'vmhba1:C0:T0:L2': Type: 0x0, ANSI rev: 5, TPGS: 1 (implicit only)
ScsiScan: 1106: Path 'vmhba1:C0:T0:L5': Vendor: 'IBM     ' Model: '2107900       ' Rev: '.335'
)ScsiScan: 1106: Path 'vmhba1:C0:T0:L3': Vendor: 'IBM     ' Model: '2107900       ' Rev: '.335'
)ScsiScan: 1106: Path 'vmhba1:C0:T0:L4': Vendor: 'IBM     ' Model: '2107900       ' Rev: '.335'
ScsiScan: 1109: Path 'vmhba1:C0:T0:L5': Type: 0x0, ANSI rev: 5, TPGS: 1 (implicit only)
)ScsiScan: 1109: Path 'vmhba1:C0:T0:L3': Type: 0x0, ANSI rev: 5, TPGS: 1 (implicit only)
ScsiScan: 1109: Path 'vmhba1:C0:T0:L4': Type: 0x0, ANSI rev: 5, TPGS: 1 (implicit only)
)ScsiScan: 1590: Add path: vmhba1:C0:T0:L1
)ScsiScan: 1106: Path 'vmhba1:C0:T0:L6': Vendor: 'IBM     ' Model: '2107900       ' Rev: '.335'
)ScsiScan: 1109: Path 'vmhba1:C0:T0:L6': Type: 0x0, ANSI rev: 5, TPGS: 1 (implicit only)
:
```

Figure 6.15   VMkernel.log entries of an IBM DS8000 ALUA device

This log shows the array as Model: '2107900'. Notice that the ScsiScan lines show the TPGS field with a value of 1. This means that the array supports Implicit ALUA mode only. This is printed in English as well at the end of each line.

Figure 6.16 shows log entries from an ESXi 6 host connected to an IBM XIV storage array.

This log shows the array as Model: '2810XIV'. Notice that the ScsiScan lines show the TPGS field with a value of 1. This means that the array supports Implicit ALUA mode only. This is printed in English as well at the end of each line.

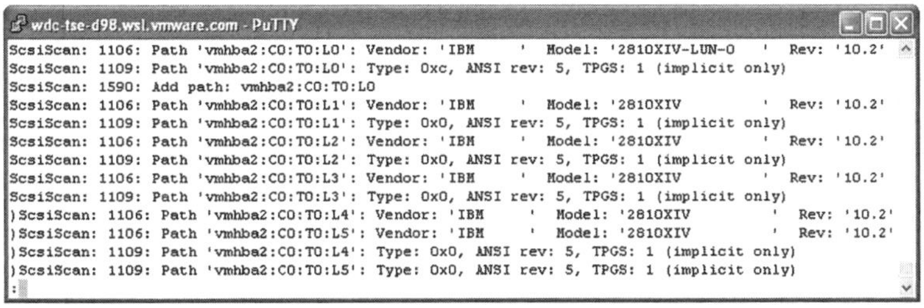

Figure 6.16   VMkernel.log entries of an IBM XIV ALUA device

At this time, I don't have access to an array that supports an explicit ALUA-only mode. However, the log from such an array would show the value of the TPGS field as 2.

Table 6.3 summarizes the different values of TPGS field and their meaning.

Table 6.3 TPGS field value meanings

TPGS Field Value	ALUA Mode
0	Not Supported
1	Implicit only
2	Explicit only
3	Both Implicit and Explicit

Identifying ALUA Devices' Path State

The next step in troubleshooting is to identify the state of the path or paths to the ALUA device. (I cover the details of multipathing in Chapter 7.) In this section, I show you how to identify the path states. Figure 6.17 shows output from the following command:

```
esxcli storage nmp path list
```

Figure 6.17 shows four paths to LUN 2, which is on an EMC VNX array configured for ALUA.

Figure 6.17 Listing of paths to an EMC VNX ALUA device

The following are the troubleshooting-related fields in this output:

- `Group State`—Shows the target port group AAS; `Active` means AO, and `Active unoptimized` means ANO.

- `Storage Array Type Path Config`—This field can be set to `TPG_id`, `TPG_state`, `RTP_id`, or `RTP_health`:

  - `TPG_id`—As in the output of the device list, this is the target port group ID.

  - `TPG_state`—As in the output of the device list, this matches the value equivalent to the previous field, `Group State` (for example, AO or ANO).

  - `RTP_id`—This is the relative target port ID, the port ID from which the inquiry response was sent to the initiator. The vital product data (VPD) included in this string includes the relative target port ID. So, with two paths per HBA in this example, two inquiry strings were received by each HBA. The first, on vmhba2, came from RTP ID 13, and the second came from RTP ID 5. In contrast, on vmhba3, the first inquiry string was received from RTP ID 14, and the second was received from RTP ID 6.

- RTP_health—This is the health status of the RTP. It can be either UP or DOWN. In the output shown in Figure 6.17, it is UP. If it were DOWN, the Group State value would be Dead instead of Active or Active Unoptimized.

> **NOTE**
>
> Because each HBA sees different RTP IDs, you know that each HBA is connected to a separate fabric. This is the recommended configuration to avoid a single point of failure, as shown in the examples in Chapter 2. (I provide further details in Chapter 7.)

Summary

In this chapter I covered ALUA, including how it is implemented in vSphere 6, how to identify various ALUA configurations, and how different configurations affect the hosts. Detailed interactions between ALUA and multipathing and failover are covered in Chapter 7.

Multipathing and Failover

One of the most critical elements of storage availability in the enterprise is multipathing and failover. ESXi has included native multipathing (NMP) right out of the box since ESX 1.5. Although it does not provide the complex level of input/output (I/O) load balancing that storage vendors' proprietary Multipathing I/O (MPIO) software provides, NMP does an excellent job maintaining access to the shared storage that the infrastructure uses.

In ESX versions prior to 4.0, the portion of the VMkernel responsible for multipathing and failover was referred to as *Legacy Multipathing* (*Legacy-MP*). It was monolithic code built into the VMkernel. Any changes or updates to this code required installing a new version of the VMkernel, which made it less practical for availability as it required rebooting the host after updates were installed. As the expression goes, "Necessity is the mother of invention." The need for better availability and more flexibility in the virtual environment led to the birth of Pluggable Storage Architecture (PSA), which is covered in Chapter 5, "vSphere Pluggable Storage Architecture (PSA)." In that chapter, I provided the detailed under-the-hood architecture and configurations. In this chapter, I get into more details about how multipathing and failover work and how to identify various conditions leading to and resulting from failover events.

What Is a Path?

The I/O sent from vSphere 6 hosts to their assigned logical unit numbers (LUNs) travels through a specific route that starts with an HBA and ends at a LUN. This route is referred to as a *path*. Each host in a properly designed infrastructure should have more than one path to each LUN.

Figure 7.1 shows a highly available design with no single points of failure (refer to Chapter 5).

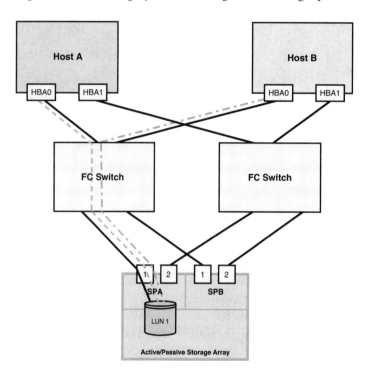

Figure 7.1   Illustration of a path to a LUN

In this example, a path to LUN 1 from Host A is represented by an interrupted line, and a path from Host B is shown with an interrupted line with dots and dashes. This path goes through HBA0 to port 1 on SPA. Such a path is represented by the following runtime name (formerly canonical name) naming convention: HBAx:Cn:Ty:Lz. An example is vmhba0:C0:T0:L1, which reads as follows:

vmhba0, Channel 0, Target 0, LUN1. It represents the path to LUN 0, which can be broken down as follows:

- **HBA0**—This is the first HBA in this host. The vmhba number may vary based on the number of storage adapters installed in the host. For example, if the host has two RAID controllers installed, and they assume vmhba0 and vmhba1 names, the first FC HBA is named vmhba2.

- **Channel 0**—The channel number is mostly zero for FC- and iSCSI-attached devices to target 0, which is the first target. If the HBA were a SCSI adapter with two channels (for example, internal connections and an external port for direct attached devices), the channel numbers would be 0 and 1.

- **Target 0**—The target number is based on the order in which the SP ports are discovered by PSA. In this case, SPA-Port1 was discovered before SPA-Port2 and the other ports on SPB. Therefore, that port was given "target 0" as part of the runtime name. (The target definition was covered in Chapters 2, "Fibre Channel Storage Connectivity," and 4, "iSCSI Storage Connectivity.")

> **NOTE**
>
> Runtime naming, as the name indicates, does not persist between host reboots, nor is it identical across hosts sharing the same LUN. This is because it is possible that any of the components that make up that name may change due to hardware or connectivity changes. For example, a host may have an additional HBA added or another HBA removed, which would change the number assumed by the HBA.

Let's expand on this example and enumerate the remaining paths to LUN 1 from Host A, which also applies to Host B.

Host A has two HBAs, vmhba0 and vmhba1, which are represented in Figure 7.1 by HBA0 and HBA1, respectively. HBA0 is connected to a fabric switch that is, in turn, connected to port 1 on SPA and port 1 on SPB. HBA1 is connected to a separate fabric switch (on a separate fabric), which is, in turn, connected to port 2 on SPA and port 2 on SPB.

This provides two paths to the LUN from each HBA, for a total of four paths. To list these four paths via the CLI, run the following command:

```
esxcli storage nmp path list --device <LUN's NAA ID>
```

You can also use the shorthand option -d instead of --device:

```
esxcli storage nmp path list -d <LUN's NAA ID>
```

The output in Figure 7.2 was collected from a host equipped with two FC HBAs named vmhba2 and vmhba3.

vmhba2 has two paths to LUN 1:

```
vmhba3:C0:T3:L1
vmhba3:C0:T2:L1
```

vmhba3 has two paths to LUN 1:

```
vmhba2:C0:T3:L1
vmhba2:C0:T2:L1
```

```
wdc-tse-h56.wsl.vmware.com - PuTTY                                          □  ×
~ # esxcli storage nmp path list -d naa.6006016072902500881017358d87fe411
fc.2000001b321314a7:2100001b321314a7-fc.50060160bce06832:5006016c3ce06832-naa.6006016072902500881017358d87fe411
   Runtime Name: vmhba2:C0:T3:L1
   Device: naa.6006016072902500881017358d87fe411
   Device Display Name: DGC Fibre Channel Disk (naa.6006016072902500881017358d87fe411)
   Group State: active
   Array Priority: 1
   Storage Array Type Path Config: {TPG_id=2,TPG_state=AO,RTP_id=13,RTP_health=UP}
   Path Selection Policy Path Config: PSP VMW_PSP_RR does not support path configuration.

fc.2000001b321314a7:2100001b321314a7-fc.50060160bce06832:500601643ce06832-naa.6006016072902500881017358d87fe411
   Runtime Name: vmhba2:C0:T2:L1
   Device: naa.6006016072902500881017358d87fe411
   Device Display Name: DGC Fibre Channel Disk (naa.6006016072902500881017358d87fe411)
   Group State: active unoptimized
   Array Priority: 0
   Storage Array Type Path Config: {TPG_id=1,TPG_state=ANO,RTP_id=5,RTP_health=UP}
   Path Selection Policy Path Config: PSP VMW_PSP_RR does not support path configuration.

fc.2001001b323314a7:2101001b323314a7-fc.50060160bce06832:5006016d3ce06832-naa.6006016072902500881017358d87fe411
   Runtime Name: vmhba3:C0:T3:L1
   Device: naa.6006016072902500881017358d87fe411
   Device Display Name: DGC Fibre Channel Disk (naa.6006016072902500881017358d87fe411)
   Group State: active
   Array Priority: 1
   Storage Array Type Path Config: {TPG_id=2,TPG_state=AO,RTP_id=14,RTP_health=UP}
   Path Selection Policy Path Config: PSP VMW_PSP_RR does not support path configuration.

fc.2001001b323314a7:2101001b323314a7-fc.50060160bce06832:500601653ce06832-naa.6006016072902500881017358d87fe411
   Runtime Name: vmhba3:C0:T2:L1
   Device: naa.6006016072902500881017358d87fe411
   Device Display Name: DGC Fibre Channel Disk (naa.6006016072902500881017358d87fe411)
   Group State: active unoptimized
   Array Priority: 0
   Storage Array Type Path Config: {TPG_id=1,TPG_state=ANO,RTP_id=6,RTP_health=UP}
   Path Selection Policy Path Config: PSP VMW_PSP_RR does not support path configuration.
~ #
```

Figure 7.2 Listing paths to a LUN using its NAA ID

These paths read as vmhba2, Channel 0, Target 3, LUN 1, and so on.

Even though each HBA uses the same target numbers, these targets are actually different. This is because there are two separate fabrics to which each HBA is connected. As illustrated in Figure 7.1, each fabric connects to different ports on SPA and SPB.

How can you tell that these targets are actually different? Recall from Chapters 2, 4, and 5 the target IDs using worldwide port name (WWPN) for FC and iSCSI qualified name (IQN) for iSCSI. This example is from an FC configuration, so we can walk through the output to identify these targets. Table 7.1 shows the correlation between runtime names (refer to Chapter 2) and targets' WWPNs.

Table 7.1 Identifying targets

Runtime Name	Target WWPN	SP/Port
vmhba2:C0:T3:L1	5006016c3ce06832	SPB/Port 4
vmhba2:C0:T2:L1	500601643ce06832	SPA/Port 4
vmhba3:C0:T3:L1	5006016d3ce06832	SPB/Port 5
vmhba3:C0:T2:L1	500601653ce06832	SPA/Port 5

The highlighted bytes are the unique portion of the WWPNs that help identify the EMC CLARiiON and VNX SP ports. (See Chapter 2 for details and identifiers of other known arrays ports.)

Figure 7.3 shows a similar example from an iSCSI configuration with two paths instead of four.

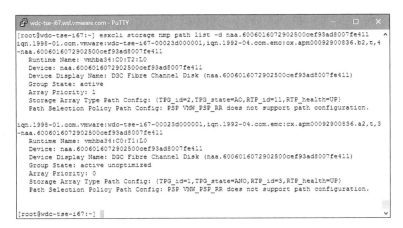

```
wdc-tse-i67.wsl.vmware.com - PuTTY                                        —  □  X
[root@wdc-tse-i67:~] esxcli storage nmp path list -d naa.6006016072902500cef93ad8007fe411
iqn.1998-01.com.vmware:wdc-tse-i67-00023d000001,iqn.1992-04.com.emc:cx.apm00092900836.b2,t,4
-naa.6006016072902500cef93ad8007fe411
   Runtime Name: vmhba34:C0:T2:L0
   Device: naa.6006016072902500cef93ad8007fe411
   Device Display Name: DGC Fibre Channel Disk (naa.6006016072902500cef93ad8007fe411)
   Group State: active
   Array Priority: 1
   Storage Array Type Path Config: {TPG_id=2,TPG_state=AO,RTP_id=11,RTP_health=UP}
   Path Selection Policy Path Config: PSP VMW_PSP_RR does not support path configuration.

iqn.1998-01.com.vmware:wdc-tse-i67-00023d000001,iqn.1992-04.com.emc:cx.apm00092900836.a2,t,3
-naa.6006016072902500cef93ad8007fe411
   Runtime Name: vmhba34:C0:T1:L0
   Device: naa.6006016072902500cef93ad8007fe411
   Device Display Name: DGC Fibre Channel Disk (naa.6006016072902500cef93ad8007fe411)
   Group State: active unoptimized
   Array Priority: 0
   Storage Array Type Path Config: {TPG_id=1,TPG_state=ANO,RTP_id=3,RTP_health=UP}
   Path Selection Policy Path Config: PSP VMW_PSP_RR does not support path configuration.

[root@wdc-tse-i67:~]
```

Figure 7.3   Listing paths to an iSCSI LUN using its NAA ID

Figure 7.3 shows two paths to a LUN with NAA ID `naa.6006016072902500cef93` `ad8007fe411`. This configuration has a single software iSCSI initiator vmhba35 that is connected to two iSCSI targets: `iqn.1992-04.com.emc:cx.apm00092900836.` `b2,t,4` and `iqn.1992-04.com.emc:cx.apm00092900836.a2,t,3`.

Based on the device display name and the Storage Array Type Plug-in (SATP) that claimed this LUN (VMW_SATP_CX), the LUN is on an EMC CLARiiON CX or VNX family array. Based on the iSCSI aliases of these two targets, the LUN is accessible via SPB2 and SPA2, which were assigned target numbers 4 and 3, respectively.

Figure 7.4 shows a Serial Attached SCSI (SAS)–attached LUN that is accessible on two targets via vmhba3 and has the NAA ID `naa.600c0ff000dae2e73763b04d02000000`. Based on the device display name, the LUN is on an HP storage array.

To identify which array model it is, use this command:

```
esxcli storage core device list --device naa.600c0ff000dae2e73763b0
 4d02000000 |grep "Vendor\|Model"
```

You can also use the shorthand option `-d` instead of `--device`:

```
esxcli storage core device list -d naa.600c0ff000dae2e73763b04d02000000
 |grep "Vendor\|Model"
```

The output of this command would be something similar to this:

```
Vendor: HP
Model: P2000 G3 SAS www
```

This means that the LUN is on an HP MSA P2000 G3 SAS array.

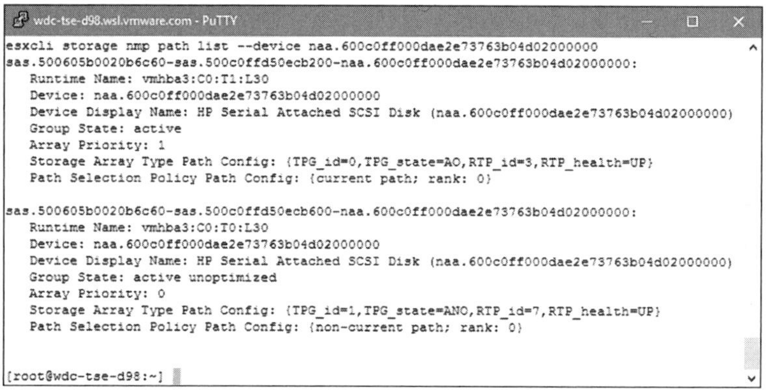

Figure 7.4   Listing paths to a SAS LUN using its NAA ID

Where Is the Active Path?

In ESX releases earlier than ESX/ESXi 4.0, there used to be an active path listed in the CLI output as well as in the UI. This was the path through which the ESX host sent the I/O to the LUN. Starting with ESX/ESXi 4.0, the reference to active has shifted to refer to the path to the SP that owns the LUN in the active/passive array configuration. It also refers to all paths to a LUN on an active/active array. This path is listed in command output as `working path`, as I show you later in this section. This continues to be the case in ESXi 6.

In the following sections, I show how to identify the path formerly known as the active path by using the CLI as well as the UI. In short, this path is listed in the CLI as `current path`. In the UI, the path is indicated by I/O.

Identifying the Current Path Using the CLI

Check the examples I used in Figures 7.2, 7.3 and 7.4, for FC-, iSCSI-, and SAS-based LUNs, respectively. The `Path Selection Policy Path Config` field shows one of the paths as `current path`, whereas the remaining paths show as `non-current path`. The former is the path through which the host sends the I/O to the LUN, while the latter are not used until the current path becomes unavailable or, when using Round Robin PSP, the I/O rotates on each of these active paths.

Identifying the I/O (Current) Path Using the UI

To identify the current path through which the I/O is sent, follow this procedure:

1. Connect to the vCenter server that manages the ESXi 6 host, using the vSphere 6.0 Web Client as a user with Administrator privileges.

2. Navigate to the **Inventory—Hosts and Clusters** view and locate the ESXi 6.0 host in the inventory tree and select it.—

3. Navigate to the **Manage** tab.

4. Click the **Storage** button.

5. Select the **Storage Devices** section.

6. In the Storage Devices pane, select one of the SAN LUNs (see Figure 7.5). In this example, its name starts with **DGC Fibre Channel Disk**.

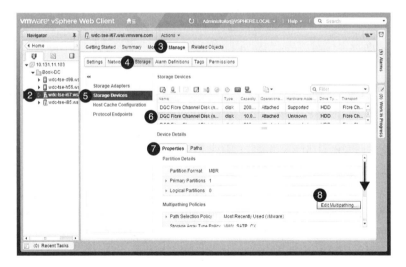

Figure 7.5   Listing devices

7. In the Device Details pane, select the **Properties** tab.

8. Scroll down and click the **Edit Multipathing** button (see Figure 7.5).

9. Figure 7.6 shows the LUN multipathing details. Note that when the PSP is set to anything other than **Fixed**, the path listing is grayed out. So, for visibility in this

example, I temporarily changed it from **MRU** to **Fixed**. (I discussed PSP choices in Chapter 5.)

Figure 7.6   Listing paths to the SAN LUN

In this example, I sorted on the Runtime Name field, in ascending order. Figure 7.6 shows the following:

    a. Runtime Name—vmhbaX:C0:Ty:Lz, where X is the HBA number, y is the target number, and z is the LUN (You'll learn more about this later in this chapter.)

    b. Target—The WWNN followed by the WWPN of the target, separated by a space.

10. Notice **(I/O)** listed in the Status column; this indicates the current path. In this example, only one path is listed with this indicator. This is true for fixed and MRU PSPs. However, when RR is in use, you may see more than one path marked with **(I/O)** as it rotates over the paths to the SP ports in **Active** state.

NOTE

The `Preferred` column is blank in Figure 7.6 because the PSP was **MRU**, which ignores the preferred path option. The preferred path option is valid only with "FIXED" PSP. Figure 7.7 shows an example in which the preferred path is marked with an asterisk (*). Note that the current path is also the preferred one, which is the expected behavior.

Listing the paths to an iSCSI LUN is similar to the procedure I just discussed. However, the UI looks as shown in Figure 7.7.

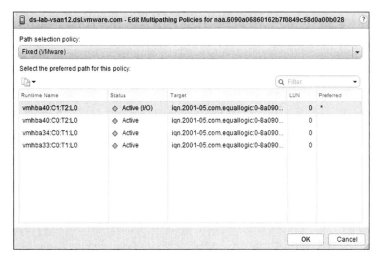

Figure 7.7   Listing paths of an iSCSI LUN—UI

LUN Discovery and Path Enumeration

Understanding how LUNs are discovered helps you identify any problems that arise. In this section, I go over some SCSI commands and log entries that explain this process and how paths to LUNs are enumerated.

The process of LUN discovery and path enumeration is done via a sequence of SCSI commands and interpreting responses to these commands (that is, SCSI sense codes). Table 7.2 lists common SCSI commands that you may encounter on ESXi 6 hosts. (Most of these commands apply to earlier releases as well.)

Table 7.2 Common SCSI commands

Command	Operation Code	Service Action
ACCESS CONTROL IN	0x86	
ACCESS CONTROL OUT	0x87	
CHANGE ALIASES	0xA4	0x0B
EXTENDED COPY	0x83	
INQUIRY	0x12	
LOG SELECT	0x4C	

Command	Operation Code	Service Action
LOG SENSE	0x4D	
MODE SELECT(6)	0x15	
MODE SELECT(10)	0x55	
MODE SENSE(6)	0x1A	
MODE SENSE(10)	0x5A	
PERSISTENT RESERVE IN 5	0xE	
PERSISTENT RESERVE OUT	0x5F	
PREVENT ALLOW MEDIUM REMOVAL	0x1E	
READ ATTRIBUTE	0x8C	
READ BUFFER	0x3C	
READ MEDIA SERIAL NUMBER	0xAB	0x01
RECEIVE COPY RESULTS	0x84	
RECEIVE DIAGNOSTIC RESULTS	0x1C	
REPORT ALIASES	0xA3	0x0B
REPORT DEVICE IDENTIFIER	0xA3	0x05
REPORT LUNS	0xA0	
REPORT PRIORITY	0xA3	0x0E
REPORT SUPPORTED OPERATION CODES	0xA3	0x0C
REPORT SUPPORTED TASK MANAGEMENT FUNCTIONS	0xA3	0x0D
REPORT TARGET PORT GROUPS	0xA3	0x0A
REPORT TIMESTAMP	0xA3	0x0F
REQUEST SENSE	0x03	
SEND DIAGNOSTIC	0x1D	
SET DEVICE IDENTIFIER	0xA4	0x06
SET PRIORITY	0xA4	0x0E
SET TARGET PORT GROUPS	0xA4	0x0A
SET TIMESTAMP	0xA4	0x0F

In Table 7.2, note that some commands require a combination of operation code and service action.

SCSI sense codes are returned in response to the SCSI commands listed in Table 7.2. For information on common sense codes, see Tables 7.4, 7.5, 7.6, and 7.7 later in this chapter.

LUN discovery is done in the following order:

1. The host sends the REPORT LUNS command (0xA0) to the storage array.

2. The array responds with the LUNs that are masked (presented) to the initiators on this host.

3. The host sends the INQUIRY command (0x12) on page 0 to each of the reported LUNs. This should return the list of supported VPD (vital product data) pages. VPD provides specific information about the device, depending on which VPD page the device supports.

4. If the device supports VPD page 83, an INQUIRY command is issued on that page. This returns the device unique ID (NAA ID).

5. If the device does not support page 83, the host sends an INQUIRY command for VPD page 80. This provides the device serial number instead because the NAA ID is not supported.

The VPD page provides one or more of the following identification descriptors:

- Logical unit names

- SCSI target port identifiers

- SCSI target port names

- SCSI target device names

- Relative target port identifiers

- SCSI target port group number

- Logical unit group number

Sample LUN Discovery and Path Enumeration Log Entries

The main log in ESXi 6 is the /var/log/vmkernel.log file. However, some events that occur during system boot are logged to /var/log/boot.gz. This file is a compressed boot log that you can read by using the zcat /var/log/boot.gz |less -S command. This is because the file is compressed to save on visorFS space. (visorFS, which I discuss in Chapter 19, is a memory-based file system in which the ESXi compressed boot image is loaded.) If you want to expand it by using the `gunzip` command, don't do that in the /var/log directory. Instead, copy the file to a Virtual Machine File System (VMFS) volume or transfer it to your management workstation using `scp` or a similar tool, and expand it there.

Figure 7.8 shows a snippet from /var/log/boot.gz after expansion. I cropped the output for readability.

```
🖳 wdc-tse-d98.wsl.vmware.com - PuTTY                                    —    □    ×
ScsiScan: 1173: Path 'vmhba2:C0:T2:L1': Vendor: 'DGC      ' Model: 'VRAID           ' Rev: '0430' ∧
ScsiScan: 1176: Path 'vmhba2:C0:T2:L1': Type: 0x0, ANSI rev: 4, TPGS: 3 (implicit and explicit)
ScsiScan: 1173: Path 'vmhba3:C0:T2:L1': Vendor: 'DGC      ' Model: 'VRAID           ' Rev: '0430'
Path 'vmhba3:C0:T2:L1': Type: 0x0, ANSI rev: 4, TPGS: 3 (implicit and explicit)
ScsiScan: 1738: Add path: vmhba2:C0:T2:L1
ScsiScan: 1738: Add path: vmhba3:C0:T2:L1                                                        ∨
```

Figure 7.8   Log entries showing new paths added

Here you see vmhba2:C0:T2:L1, which is LUN 1, via vmhba2 on target 2, with discovery via the `ScsiScan` function of VMkernel. The LUN properties show the `Vendor`, `Model`, and `Rev` fields in the first line of the output. In this example, the vendor is `DGC` (Data General Corporation), which represents the EMC CLARiiON CX and VNX families of arrays. The model in this case is `VRAID`, which means the array is a VNX. If the model is the RAID type backing the LUN—for example, `RAID5`—the array family is CLARiiON instead. Finally, the `Rev` field shows the storage array's firmware revisions. In this case, it is `0430`, which, for the CX family, means FLARE code 30.

Then, in the second line of the log output, the device type is identified as `Type: 0x0`, which indicates a direct access block device. Table 7.3 lists the common device types you might encounter in the vSphere 6 environment.

Table 7.3   Common device types

Device Type	Description
0x0	Direct access block device
0x1	Sequential access device (for example, tape drive)
0x3	Processor device
0x4	Write-once device
0x5	CD/DVD device
0x8	Tape library

The next field listed is `ANSI rev`, which is the SCSI standard supported by the device. In this case, the value is 4, which means a later revision of SCSI-3 (for example, SAM-2; see Chapter 2 for more details). The last field is TPGS, which is 3 in this example, meaning that the device supports Asymmetric Logical Unit Access (ALUA; see Chapter 6, "ALUA"). These two lines repeat for the second path to LUN 1 on target 2 via vmhba3.

These are follow by two lines in the log that shows Add path: vmhba2:C0:T2:L1 and vmhba3:C0:T2:L1. This means that a path to LUN 1 on target 2 has been added on vmhba2 and also on vmhba3.

The log entry for additional paths to the same LUN via both HBAs in this host (shown in Figure 7.9) is similar to that in Figure 7.8, with the difference being that the target is T3.

```
wdc-tse-d98.wsl.vmware.com - PuTTY                                          —  □  ×
ScsiScan: 1173: Path 'vmhba3:C0:T3:L1': Vendor: 'DGC     ' Model: 'VRAID        ' Rev: '0430' ^
ScsiScan: 1176: Path 'vmhba3:C0:T3:L1': Type: 0x0, ANSI rev: 4, TPGS: 3 (implicit and explicit)
ScsiScan: 1173: Path 'vmhba2:C0:T3:L1': Vendor: 'DGC     ' Model: 'VRAID        ' Rev: '0430'
ScsiScan: 1176: Path 'vmhba2:C0:T3:L1': Type: 0x0, ANSI rev: 4, TPGS: 3 (implicit and explicit)
ScsiScan: 1738: Add path: vmhba3:C0:T3:L1
ScsiScan: 1738: Add path: vmhba2:C0:T3:L1                                               v
```

Figure 7.9   Log entries showing continuation of new paths and additional events

Finally, all discovered paths are claimed by NMP, as shown in Listing 7.1.

Listing 7.1   Log entries showing paths claimed by NMP

```
ScsiPath: 5531: Plugin 'NMP' claimed path 'vmhba3:C0:T2:L1'
ScsiPath: 5531: Plugin 'NMP' claimed path 'vmhba3:C0:T3:L1'
ScsiPath: 5531: Plugin 'NMP' claimed path 'vmhba2:C0:T2:L1'
ScsiPath: 5531: Plugin 'NMP' claimed path 'vmhba2:C0:T3:L1'
```

After all paths to a given device have been enumerated, PSA collapses all paths to that device so that the host identifies it as a single device with multiple paths. For this to be done successfully, the device must meet the following criteria:

- The device ID (for example, NAA ID, EUI) must be identical on all paths.
- The LUN must be identical on all paths.

Several factors contribute to the required uniqueness of the device ID and the LUN, such as Symmetrix FA director bits configuration and choice of host type in several storage arrays on VMware's HCL.

A sample log entry for enumerating a device ID is shown in Figure 7.10.

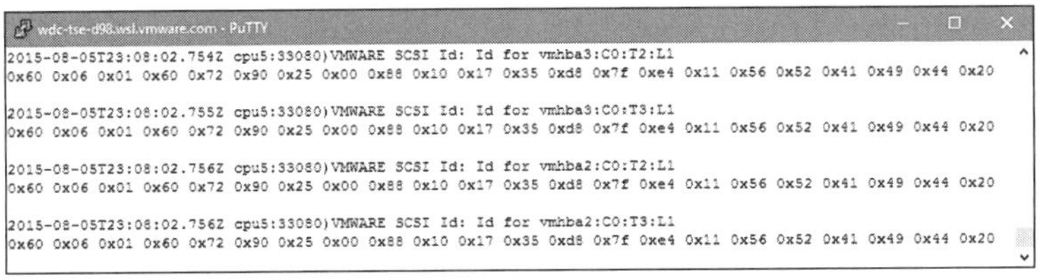

Figure 7.10   Enumerating device ID log entries

The log entries are for all four paths to the device listing the device ID (`Id for vmhba...`). The bytes of the ID are listed in hexadecimal values. In this example, the ID is the first 16 bytes (the first 16 hex values in Listing 7.2 that are highlighted). This translates to NAA ID `naa.6006016072902500088101735d87fe411`. The remaining 6 bytes map to ACSII characters VRAID followed by a white space (0x20).

Listing 7.2   Locating NAA ID in Inquiry Response

```
0x60  0x06  0x01  0x60  0x72  0x90  0x25  0x00  0x88  0x10  0x17  0x35  0xd8  0x7f  0xe4
0x11  0x56  0x52  0x41  0x49  0x44  0x20
```

To list all paths to a given device, you can run the following command:

```
esxcfg-mpath --list-paths --device naa.6006016072902500088101735d87fe411
```

You can also use the shorthand options `-b` and `-d` instead of `--list-paths` and `--device`:

```
esxcfg-mpath -b -d naa.6006016072902500088101735d87fe411
```

Figure 7.11 shows an example of the output.

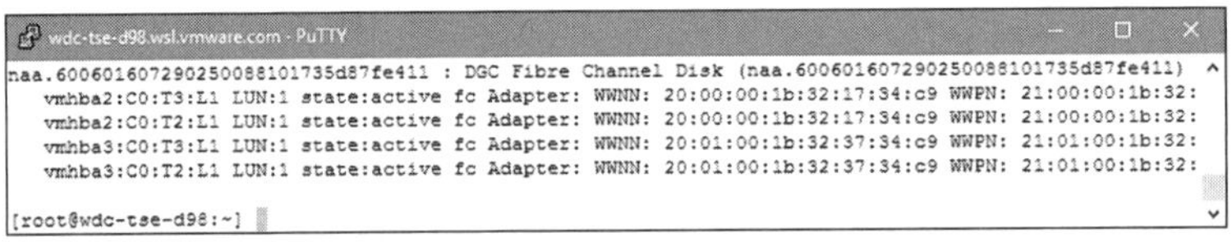

Figure 7.11   Listing paths to a LUN

The output in Figure 7.11 shows all four paths to LUN 1 that I listed in Figure 7.10. Here you see the discovered paths grouped under the LUN's device ID, which is the NAA ID in this case. Because that LUN has the same number (LUN 1) and the same NAA ID on all four paths, they are collapsed to a single LUN with four paths. If there were a misconfiguration on the array, with the device having a different LUN, even though the device may have the same device ID, the paths would not be collapsed in this fashion. The same is true if the device is assigned a different device ID on different targets, which would result in identifying it as a different device based on the device ID. In other words, we can assume that the NAA ID on target 0 on vmhba2 and vmhba3 is different from that assigned on target 1 on vmhba2 and vmhba3; the result identifies the LUN as two different LUNs with two paths each.

Factors Affecting Multipathing

Several factors play important roles in the functionality of multipathing. Among these factors are the following VMkernel advanced settings:

- `Disk.MaxLUN`—The default is 1024, and the value cannot be larger than this. When a rescan is issued, this is the maximum LUN that is scanned on each target. So, counting from LUN 0, the maximum LUN is LUN 1023. As a result, LUNs presented with numbers higher than 1023 are not discovered by vSphere 6 hosts.

NOTE

The maximum number of paths usable by any vSphere 6 host is 1024. (This applies to earlier releases as well.) So, if the host is equipped with two HBAs, and each of them is zoned to two targets on a storage array, the total number of paths per LUN presented from that array is four. If the array presents 256 LUNs to this host, the total number of paths is 1024 (4 paths × 256 LUNs). vSphere 6.5 doubled the maximum number of LUNs to 512 and the maximum number of paths to 2048.

Virtual volume (VVol) protocol endpoints (PE) are treated as LUNs from the perspective of multipathing and failover. The default LUNs assigned to VVol PEs are higher than 255. (You'll learn more about this in Chapter 23, "Virtual Volumes.")

Depending on your design requirements, you must consider this fact when deciding on the number of LUNs presented to vSphere 6 hosts. In other words, if you plan to use more initiators or more targets per host, the maximum number of LUNs decreases. Also consider the paths to local devices on the host. Even though multipathing is not supported with these devices, paths to them reduce the number of paths available for SAN-attached devices.

- `Disk.SupportSparseLUN`—This is a legacy setting carried over from releases as old as ESX 1.5. The parameter listed next, `Disk.UseReportLUN`, when enabled, negates the need for using this one, regardless of its value. Sparse LUN is the case where there is a gap in the sequence of discovered LUNs. For example, say that you have an array that presents to your host LUNs 0–10 and then skips the next nine LUNs so that the next group of LUNs is LUN 20–255. When this option is set to 0, the host stops scanning for LUNs beyond LUN 10 because LUN 11 is missing. It does not continue to scan for higher LUNs. When this option is enabled (set to 1), which is the default setting, the host continues to scan for the next LUN until it is done with all 256 LUNs or the value of `Disk.MaxLUN`, whichever is larger. Imagine what this does to the host's boot time if it has to wait until each LUN is scanned, compounded by the number of HBAs. That is why VMware introduced the next parameter, `Disk.UseReportLUN`.

- `Disk.UseReportLUN`—This parameter is enabled by default (set to 1). It enables the use of the command `ReportLUN`, which is sent to all targets, and the storage array should respond with the list of LUNs presented to the initiators in this host. This means that the host no longer needs to scan for each LUN individually. This improves both boot time and scan time. This is the only command filtered when the SCSI commands are passed through from a guest operating system to a mapped LUN. (For more on this, see Chapter 13, "Virtual Disks and RDMs.")

Accessing Advanced Options

To access VMkernel advanced options, follow this procedure:

1. Connect to the vCenter server that manages the ESXi 6 host, using the vSphere 6.0 Web Client as a user with Administrator privileges and navigate to the Inventory - Hosts and Clusters view.

2. Locate the vSphere 6.0 host in the inventory tree and select it.

3. Select the **Manage** tab.

4. Click the **Settings** button.

5. Expand the **System** section and select **Advanced System Settings**.

6. In the search field, type the advanced option you want to modify, such as **Disk. MaxLUN**, and press **Enter**. (The search string is not case sensitive.)

7. Click the **Disk.MaxLUN** option row.

8. Click the **Edit** icon, which looks like a pencil (see Figure 7.12).

Figure 7.12   Accessing advanced settings

9. In the dialog that appears, modify the value and click **OK** (see Figure 7.13).

Figure 7.13   Advanced settings

10. To modify additional advanced options, repeat steps 6 through 9.

NOTE

When you change options as just described, you do not need to reboot for the changes to take effect.

Failover Triggers

Under normal conditions, I/O is sent on the current path until certain SCSI events occur that trigger path failover. These triggers differ, depending on whether the storage array is active/active or active/passive. Before I go into the actual list of triggers, though, I want to give you a quick primer on SCSI sense codes.

SCSI Sense Codes

Devices communicate with nodes on a SAN by sending specific hexadecimal strings that are in response to either a command or a hardware event.

The structure of the sense codes (as seen in vmkernel logs entries) is as follows:

```
H:<value> D:<value> P:<value> Valid sense data <a set of 3 hexadecimal
values>
```

You can interpret this structure as follows:

- H—Comes from the host (initiator) and provides the host status. Table 7.4 lists sense codes that you might encounter while sifting through the vSphere host logs.

Table 7.4 Host status codes

Code	Meaning
0x0	SCSI_HOST_OK
0x1	SCSI_HOST_NO_CONNECT
0x2	SCSI_HOST_BUS_BUSY
0x3	SCSI_HOST_TIMEOUT
0x4	SCSI_HOST_BAD_TARGET
0x5	SCSI_HOST_ABORT
0x6	SCSI_HOST_PARITY
0x7	SCSI_HOST_ERROR
0x8	SCSI_HOST_RESET
0x9	SCSI_HOST_BAD_INTR
0xA	SCSI_HOST_PASSTHROUGH
0xB	SCSI_HOST_SOFT_ERROR
0xC	SCSI_HOST_RETRY

- D—Comes from the device and provides the device status (see Table 7.5).

Table 7.5 Device status codes

Code	Meaning
0x0	No errors
0x2	Check condition
0x8	Device busy
0x18	Device reserved by another host

- P—Comes from the PSA plug-in and provides the plug-in status.

- Valid sense data—A set of three hexadecimal values, broken into the following:

  - SCSI sense key (see Table 7.6)

Table 7.6 SCSI sense key

Code	Meaning
0x0	There is no sense information.
0x1	Last command completed successfully but used error correction in the process.
0x2	The addressed LUN is not ready to be accessed.
0x3	The target detected a data error on the medium.
0x4	The target detected a hardware error during a command or self-tests.
0x5	ILLEGAL_REQUEST. Either the command or the parameter list contains an error.
0x6	The LUN has been reset (bus reset of medium change).
0x7	Access to the data is blocked.
0x8	Reached an unexpected written or unwritten region of the medium.
0xA	COPY, COMPARE, or COPY AND VERIFY was aborted.
0xB	The target aborted the command.
0xC	Comparison for SEARCH DATA was unsuccessful.
0xD	The medium is full.
0xE	Source and data on the medium do not agree.

  - Additional sense code (ASC) and Additional sense code qualifier (ASCQ), which are always reported in pairs (Sometimes these codes and the sense key are preceded by "Possible sense data" instead of "Valid sense data"; see Table 7.7.)

Table 7.7 Additional sense code (ASC)/Additional sense code qualifier (ASCQ) combinations

ASC	ASCQ	Meaning
0x4	0x2	LOGICAL Unit NOT READY—INITIALIZING COMMAND REQUIRED
0x5	0x3	LOGICAL Unit NOT READY—MANUAL INTERVENTION REQUIRED
0x29	0x0	POWER ON, RESET, OR BUS DEVICE RESET OCCURRED
0x29	0x2	BUS RESET OCCURRED
0x29	0x3	DEVICE RESET OCCURRED
Vendor-Specific Codes (IBM FAStT/DS4000 example)		
0x8B	0x2	QUIESCENCE HAS BEEN ACHIEVED
0x94	0x1	INVALID REQ DUE TO CURRENT LU OWNERSHIP

The combination of sense key, ASC, and ASCQ, along with the host, device, and/or plug-in status can be translated to a specific SCSI event code. These codes are mostly standard across vendors, although you might see some vendor-specific codes along the way.

Here is an example of a sense code:

```
H:0x0 D:0x2 P:0x0 Valid sense data: 0x5 0x20 0x0
```

These codes are listed at T10.org, in the document "SCSI Primary Commands—3 (SPC-3)" (see www.t10.org/members/w_spc3.htm). Vendor-specific codes are available from the corresponding vendors.

> **NOTE**
>
> ASC and ASCQ values 0x80–0xFF are vendor-specific.

Now you are ready to see the actual failover triggers!

Path Failover Triggers

Table 7.8 lists the SCSI sense codes of events that trigger the I/O path to fail over to an alternate path. The columns A/P and A/A denote whether the code is relevant to active/active arrays or active/passive arrays. The rows are sorted by sense codes.

Table 7.8 Path failover triggers

Host	Device	Key	ASC	ASCQ	A/P	A/A	Meaning
0x1	0x0	0x0	0x0	0x0	YES	YES	DID_NO_CONNECT
0x0	0x2	0x2	0x4	0x1	Yes	No	LOGICAL UNIT NOT READY - LOGICAL UNIT IN THE PROCESS OF BECOMING READY
0x0	0x2	0x2	0x4	0xA	YES	NO	LOGICAL UNIT NOT READY— - AAS TRANSITION
0x0	0x2	0x2	0x4	0xB	YES	NO	LOGICAL UNIT NOT READY— - TARGET IN STANDBY STATE
0x0	0x2	0x3	0x4	0x3	YES	NO	LOGICAL UNIT NOT READY - MEDIUM ERROR
0x0	0x2	0x5	0x4	0x3	YES	NO	ILLEGAL REQUEST - LOGICAL UNIT NOT READY
0x0	0x2	0x5	0x94	0x1	YES	NO	ILLEGAL REQUEST— - DUE TO CURRENT LU OWNERSHIP
0x0	0x2	0x6	0x2A	0x6	YES	NO	UNIT ATTENTION - AAS CHANGED
0x7	0x0	0x0	0x0	0x0	YES	NO	DID_ERROR (CLARiiON SP hang)

Table 7.8 shows all the SCSI events that would trigger a path failover. Here are more details about these events:

> **NOTE**
>
> Table 7.8 does not list the plug-in status because it is 0x0 in all combinations listed.

- **DID_NO_CONNECT**—When the initiator loses connectivity to the SAN (for example, cable disconnected, switch port disabled, bad cable, bad GBIC), the HBA driver reports this error. It looks like as follows in the /var/log/vmkernel.log file:

  ```
  vmhba2:C0:T1:L0" H:0x1 D:0x0 P:0x0 Possible sense data 0x0 0x0 0x0
  ```

  This means that the host status is 0x1, which matches the first row in Table 7.8.

- **LOGICAL UNIT NOT READY**—The SATP claiming the device monitors the hardware state of the physical paths to the device. Part of that process, for active/passive arrays, is that it sends the SCSI command `Check_Unit_Ready` to the device on all paths. Under normal conditions, the array would respond with READY for the device on all targets on the active SP. The passive SP would respond with LOGICAL_UNIT_NOTREADY. The SATP interprets these responses to mean that the LUN is accessible from the targets that responded with READY. If, for some reason, the LUN used to be READY on a certain target but now it returns NOTREADY, the I/O cannot be sent there, and a path failover must be done to a target that returns UNIT_READY in response to the `Check_Unit_Ready` command (CUR for short).

Four sense codes fall under this category:

- **LOGICAL UNIT IN THE PROCESS OF BECOMING READY**—This means the LUN is in the final stage of becoming ready on the target. The sense code looks like this:

  ```
  vmhba2:C0:T1:L0" H:0x0 D:0x2 P:0x0 Valid sense data 0x2 0x4 0x1
  ```

  This matches the second row in Table 7.8.

- **AAS TRANSITION**—As discussed in Chapter 6, asymmetric access state (AAS) transition occurs when a target port group is transitioning from active/optimized (AO) to active/non-optimized (ANO) or vice versa. The sense code looks like this:

  ```
  vmhba2:C0:T1:L0" H:0x0 D:0x2 P:0x0 Valid sense data 0x2 0x4 0xA
  ```

  This matches the third row in Table 7.8.

- **TARGET IN STANDBY STATE**—This means the target is on a storage processor that is not in an active state and cannot service I/O to the LUN. The sense code looks like this:

  ```
  vmhba2:C0:T1:L0" H:0x0 D:0x2 P:0x0 Valid sense data 0x2 0x4 0xB
  ```

  This matches the fourth row in Table 7.8

- **MEDIUM_ERROR**—This means that the LUN needs manual intervention. The sense code looks like this:

  ```
  vmhba2:C0:T1:L0" H:0x0 D:0x2 P:0x0 Valid Sense Data 0x3 0x4 0x3
  ```

  This matches the fifth row in Table 7.8.

  the SATP interprets these four sense codes to mean that I/O cannot be sent there, and a path failover must be done.

- **ILLEGAL REQUEST - LOGICAL UNIT NOT READY**—This looks like MEDIUM_ERROR, listed earlier, with the difference that the sense key is 0x5 instead of 0x2. It means that the LUN is not ready, and a manual intervention is required. Until this is done, the path should be failed over to another target that returns UNIT_READY in response to the CUR command. The sense code looks like this:

```
vmhba2:C0:T1:L0" H:0x0 D:0x2 P:0x0 Valid Sense Data 0x5 0x4 0x3
```

  This matches the sixth row in Table 7.8.

- **ILLEGAL REQUEST - DUE TO CURRENT LU OWNERSHIP**—This is different from the illegal request in the previous sense code. It means that a command or an I/O was sent to a LUN via a target that does not own the LUN (that is, via the passive SP). The sense code looks like this:

```
vmhba2:C0:T1:L0" H:0x0 D:0x2 P:0x0 Valid Sense Data 0x5 0x94 0x1
```

  This is specific to arrays made by LSI (now owned by NetApp) that are originally manufactured by IBM as FAStT and DS4000 series as well as by Oracle (formerly Sun) as StorageTek series. These arrays have a feature referred to as auto volume transfer (AVT). This feature, when enabled, enables LUNs owned by one of the storage processors to be automatically transferred to the passive SP to allow I/O processed through it. This simulates active/active configuration. However, this is not the recommended configuration for use with vSphere as it may result in a path thrashing condition (see Chapter 6). So, with AVT disabled as recommended, I/O can be processed only via the active SP. When I/O is sent to the passive SP, this sense code is returned to the initiator.

TIP

An easy way to identify which arrays belong to this group (originally manufactured by LSI) is to check the SATP claim rules for devices claimed by VMW_SATP_LSI. You can check for these claim rules by using the following command:

```
esxcli storage nmp satp rule list --satp VMW_SATP_LSI
```

You can also use the shorthand option -s instead of --satp:

```
esxcli storage nmp satp rule list -s VMW_SATP_LSI
```

- **UNIT ATTENTION - AAS CHANGED**—This sense code means the AAS of the TPG has changed for the given LUN to a different state than it was in before. Refer to Chapter 6. The sense code looks like this:

```
vmhba2:C0:T1:L0" H:0x0 D:0x2 P:0x0 Valid Sense Data 0x6 0x2a 0x6
```

- **DID_ERROR**—This sense code was added to handle a special case where an EMC CLARiiON array exhibits a storage processor hang. When this sense code is reported, the SATP issues additional commands to the peer SP to check with it about the status of the problematic SP. If the peer SP fails in getting a response from the problematic one, the SATP marks the latter as hung/dead and proceeds with the path failover process. The sense code looks like this in the logs:

```
vmhba2:C0:T1:L0" H:0x7 D:0x0 P:0x0 Possible Sense Data 0x0 0x0 0x0
```

> **NOTE**
>
> It is possible to see the **DID_ERROR** sense code in configurations with storage arrays other than the CLARiiON series. However, if you do, it may have a different meaning than described here. You should investigate it further with the storage vendor.

Path States

Paths to storage devices are constantly monitored by the SATP plug-ins that claimed them. SATP plug-ins report to NMP these changes, and NMP acts accordingly.

A path can be in one of the following states:

- **Active (also known as "On")**—The path is connected to the storage network and is functional. This is the normal state for all paths to targets on an active SP. For active/active array configuration, all paths to the array should be in this state. With active/passive array configuration, half of the paths are in this state if configured according to VMware's best practices.

- **Standby (formerly known as "On" in ESX versions prior to 3.5)**—The path is connected to the storage network and is functional. This is the normal state for all paths to targets on a passive SP. These are the remaining half of the paths to an active/passive array just mentioned.

- **Dead**—The HBA lost connectivity to the storage network, or the target to which it is zoned is unreachable. This can be due to several factors, including the following:

  - **Cable unplugged from the HBA port**—This would show in the logs as a "loop down" error with sense code **DID_NO_CONNECT**.

  - **Cable unplugged from the SP port**—In this case, you would not see the "loop down" error because the HBA still has a valid connection to the storage network.

  - **Bad connection**—The connection is lost due to a defective GBIC, fibre cable, or Ethernet cable. This is similar to "Cable unplugged from the HBA port."

- **Defective switch port**—The connection is lost. This is similar to "Cable unplugged from the HBA port."

- **Device returns a retry-able error and SATP**—In this case, the `action_OnRetryErrors` option is ON. See more about this option in the next section.

Factors Affecting Paths States

Several factors affect paths states, as discussed in the following sections.

Disk.PathEvalTime

The Fibre Channel path state is evaluated at a fixed interval by sending Test_Unit_Ready (TUR) to the device or when there is an I/O error. The path evaluation interval is defined via the advanced configuration option `Disk.PathEvalTime` in seconds. The default value is 300 seconds. This means that the path state is evaluated every 5 minutes, unless an error is reported sooner on that path, in which case the path state might change, depending on the interpretation of the reported error.

Figure 7.14 shows the Advanced Settings dialog that appears when you follow the procedure in the section "Accessing Advanced Options," earlier in this chapter and search for the **Disk.PathEvalTime** option.

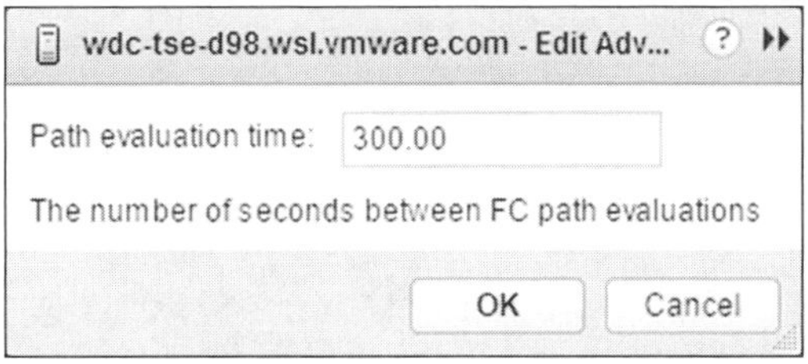

Figure 7.14   Disk.PathEvalTime advanced settings

To see this advanced setting by using the CLI, run the following command:

```
esxcli system settings advanced list --option /Disk/PathEvalTime
```

You can also use `-o` abbreviated option instead of `--option`

The output looks like this:

```
Path: /Disk/PathEvalTime
Type: integer
Int Value: 300
Default Int Value: 300
Min Value: 0
```

```
Max Value: 31536000
String Value:
Default String Value:
Valid Characters:
Description: The number of seconds between FC path evaluations
```

Alternatively, you can use the `vsish` command:

```
vsish -e get /config/Disk/intOpts/PathEvalTime
```

Notice that using `vsish` requires a slightly longer node name compared to using `esxcli`. The latter does not require `intOpts`.

The output looks like this:

```
Vmkernel Config Option {
   Default value:300
   Min value:0
   Max value:31536000
   Current value:300
   hidden config option:0
   Description:The number of seconds between FC path evaluations
```

Notice that this output includes the `hidden config` option field. In this case, the value 0 means that the option is *not* hidden in the UI.

To modify the value, use the following command:

```
esxcli system settings advanced set --option /Disk/PathEvalTime --int-value
[value in seconds]
```

You can also use the abbreviated options `-o` and `-i` for `--option` and `--int-value`.

This command requires specifying the value type as **Integer** via `--int-value` or **String** via `--string-value`. The corresponding abbreviated options are be `-i` and `-s`, respectively.

This is the `vsish` command to make the same change:

```
vsish -e set /config/Disk/intOpts/PathEvalTime [value in seconds]
```

Here is an example:

```
vsish -e set /config/Disk/intOpts/PathEvalTime 200
```

Reducing this value might result in faster path state detection. However, this is not advisable on a storage area network (SAN) that is changing frequently. You need to give the fabric enough time to converge to avoid unnecessary path failover due to transient events.

action_OnRetryErrors

When TUR or an I/O on a given path returns one of the host status errors listed in Table 7.9, the I/O is retried indefinitely, and the path remains in an On state.

Table 7.9 Common retry-able errors

Host Status Code	Host Status
0x2	SCSI_HOST_BUS_BUSY
0xB	SCSI_HOST_SOFT_ERROR
0xC	SCSI_HOST_RETRY

This behavior results in situations in which the I/O does not fail over to an alternate path. vSphere 6 introduced a new SATP option, action_OnRetryErrors. When this option is turned on, the path will eventually, after a certain timeout or retry count, be marked Dead if the I/O retries or TUR still results in an error. Table 7.10 shows timeout and retry count values for SATP.

Table 7.10 SATP I/O retry count/timeout

SATP	Retry Count	Timeout (Seconds)
VMW_SATP_ALUA_CX	40	N/A
VMW_SATP_ALUA	40	N/A
VMW_SATP_CX	20	N/A
VMW_SATP_INV	20	N/A
VMW_SATP_LOCAL	N/A	N/A
All other SATPs	N/A	60

Once a path is set to Dead state, the I/O fails over to an alternate path that is in an On state. The next time the Disk.PathEvalTime interval is reached, a TUR is sent to the device, and if the response is UNIT_READY, the path state is changed back to the On state.

> **NOTE**
>
> This option is not available with VMW_SATP_LOCAL because it typically provides a single path to each attached device. Setting the state of such a single path to Dead would result in an APD state. (See the "PDL and APD" section, later in this chapter.)

Enabling the `action_OnRetryErrors` Setting for Individual Devices

If you observe that I/O on some devices does not fail over to available alternate paths after the initiator reports any of the host status codes listed in Table 7.9, you may need to enable this option per device. Here's how you do it:

1. Log in to the affected ESXi host's console directly or via SSH as a user with root privileges.

2. From the vmkernel.log entries, locate the device ID with a host status code 0x2, 0xB, or 0xC.

3. Run this command to enable the option:

```
esxcli storage nmp satp generic deviceconfig set -c enable_action_
OnRetryErrors -d [device-ID]
```

   Here is an example:

```
esxcli storage nmp satp generic deviceconfig set -c enable_action_
OnRetryErrors -d naa.6000eb39a16fb1100000000000000204
```

4. To verify that the setting has been enabled successfully, run the following command:

```
esxcli storage nmp satp generic deviceconfig get -d [device ID]
```

   Here is an example:

```
esxcli storage nmp satp generic deviceconfig get -d naa.6000eb39a16
fb1100000000000000204
```

   The output looks like this for VMW_SATP_EQL:

```
{action_OnRetryErrors=on}
```

   The output looks like this for VMW_SATP_ALUA_CX:

```
{navireg=on, ipfilter=on}{implicit_support=on;explicit_support=on;
explicit_allow=on;alua_followover=on; action_OnRetryErrors=on;
{TPG_id=1,TPG_state=ANO}{TPG_id=2,TPG_state=AO}}
```

   To reduce the output length, you can exclude the TPG info by adding `-e` or `--exclude-tpg-Info`, in which case the command and output look like this:

```
esxcli storage nmp satp generic deviceconfig get -e -d naa.60060160729
0250088101735d87fe411
{navireg=on, ipfilter=on}{implicit_support=on;explicit_support=on;
explicit_allow=on;alua_followover=on; action_OnRetryErrors=off; }
```

   The output looks like this for VMW_SATP_CX:

```
{navireg ipfilter    action_OnRetryErrors}
```

From these examples, you should notice that some SATPs show the config option with a value of On, while others just show the option itself, without any setting listed. In the latter case, the option is returned only when it is enabled, and it is absent from the output when it is disabled.

TIP

Changes made in this section persist when the host is rebooted because the option is stored in the /etc/vmware/esx.conf file, much as in the following line:

```
/storage/plugin/NMP/device[naa.6006016055711d00cff95e65664ee011]/
 satpConfig = "enable_action_OnRetryErrors"
```

Enabling the `action_OnRetryErrors` Option for a Given Storage Array Vendor

While it has not been officially tested by VMware, I have successfully set up a SATP claim rule to enable the `action_OnRetryError` option based on specific field matches for a specific SATP. This rule takes effect after you reboot the host. It applies to all devices presented by any storage array that match the specified field values and the SATP name.

In this case, the claim rule applies to all non-ALUA EMC CLARiiON CX arrays that are claimed by VMW_SATP_CX, based on matches for the fields listed in Table 7.11.

Table 7.11 SATP claim rule fields

Field	Value
SATP Name	VMW_SATP_CX
Vendor	DGC
Claim Option	tpgs_off

You can use this command to add the SATP claim rule:

```
esxcli storage nmp satp rule add -V DGC -s VMW_SATP_CX -o enable_action_
 OnRetryErrors -c tpgs_off -e "All non-ALUA Clariion Arrays modified"
```

You can also use the expanded options, as follows:

```
esxcli storage nmp satp rule add --vendor DGC --satp VMW_SATP_CX --option
 enable_action_OnRetryErrors --claim-option tpgs_off --description "All
 non-ALUA Clariion Arrays modified"
```

Because there is already an existing system SATP claim rule with the same matching fields, the added user SATP claim rule gets listed right below the system claim rule. A good sign that the claim rule took effect is the following message being listed in /var/log/vmkernel. log file during host boot:

```
WARNING: VMW_SATP_CX: satp_cx_setDeviceConfig:857: Turning on action on
probe retry errors on dev Unregistered Device.
```

If the rule takes effect for some devices but not others from the same storage array, check the content of /etc/vmware/esx.conf for the option listed in the Tip at the end of the previous section. If the option exists with `disable_action_OnRetryErrors`, it may have been a remnant of your previous attempt to enable and then disable the option using the CLI.

Evidence of such a setting interfering with the global claim rule option is a message like this in the /var/log/vmkernel.log or /var/run/log/vmkernel.0.gz files:

```
WARNING: VMW_SATP_CX: satp_cx_setDeviceConfig:866: Turning off action on
 probe retry errors on devnaa.6006016055711d00cff95e65664ee011.
```

In this case, just delete the corresponding option line from the /etc/vmware/esx.conf file and reboot the host.

Disabling the `action_OnRetryErrors` Setting

If you need to reverse the changes done in the previous section, you can simply repeat the command you ran in step 3 by using `disable_action_OnRetryErrors` instead of `enable_action_OnRetryErrors`. Here is an example:

```
esxcli storage nmp satp generic deviceconfig set -c disable_action_
 OnRetryErrors -d naa.6000eb39a16fb1100000000000000204
```

QLogic HBA Driver Options

The QLogic FC HBA driver in ESXi 6 is a native driver called `qlnativefc`. It also existed in ESXi 5.5 but not earlier releases. A native driver does not require the vmklinux module because the driver is developed for VMkernel directly. Earlier drivers were ported from Linux, which is why they require the vmklinux module.

Listing the QLogic Native Driver Parameters

You can list the driver runtime details and options by using `vmkmgmt_keyval`, which is located in the /usr/lib/vmware/vmkmgmt_keyval directory on ESXi.

You can use this command to list all ESXi native drivers' runtime options:

```
/usr/lib/vmware/vmkmgmt_keyval/vmkmgmt_keyval --allKeys
```

You can also use the abbreviated command `-a`.

This command lists the key/value pairs of all options for all adapters driven by native drivers. The output is very long and includes all native drivers on the given ESXi host. You need to filter on what you need to list. To do so, you can use these options:

- `--instance` or `-i`—Lists all key/value pairs of a specific driver instance. This cannot be combined with the `--allKeys` option.

- `--dumpInstances` or `-d`—Lists all instances in the system. This cannot be combined with the `--allKeys` option. If the ESXi 6 host has multiple native drivers installed, this command makes it easy to identify the exact instance name to use with the previous command option, `--instance`.

For example, on a host with the QLogic native driver installed, the `--dumpInstances` option returns the following:

```
Dumping all key-value instance names:
Key Value Instance:  QLNATIVEFC/qlogic
```

In this case, there is a single instance, regardless of how many QLogic adapters are in the ESXi host.

In contrast, this would be the corresponding output on an ESXi 6 host with an Emulex native driver installed:

```
Dumping all key-value instance names:
Key Value Instance:  vmhba64/Emulex
Key Value Instance:  vmhba1/Emulex
```

In this case, the Emulex instance is named after the vmhba name assigned to the HBA on this host. The value may differ on other hosts.

You can correlate this output with that of this command:

```
esxcli storage core adapter list
```

The following is the output, which I truncated to show only the columns relevant to this discussion:

```
HBA Name  Driver
--------  -------
vmhba1    lpfc
vmhba64   lpfc
```

A QLogic native driver provides two settings that control how soon the driver reports a DID_NO_CONNECT to VMkernel. To list these options and their current values, run the following command:

```
/usr/lib/vmware/vmkmgmt_keyval/vmkmgmt_keyval -i "QLNATIVEFC/qlogic"
-l |grep 'vmhba\|down'
Host Device Name vmhba2
Link down Timeout =   030
Port down retry =   010
Host Device Name vmhba3
Link down Timeout =   030
Port down retry =   010
```

The output shows two HBAs—vmhba2 and vmhba3—and the options are as follows:

- **Link down timeout**—Default value is 30 seconds. This setting specifies the number of seconds vmkernel waits for a link that is down to come up. This does not affect the failover time in vSphere 6.

- **Port-down retry**—Default value is 10 seconds. This setting specifies the number of seconds vmkernel waits to retry a command to a port returning port-down status.

In ESXi 6, and as early as ESXi 5, the time it takes for VMkernel to fail over to an alternate path after receiving DID_NO_CONNECT is calculated by the following formula: Port-down retry value + 5. Based on the default values, the failover time is 15 seconds. In vSphere releases older than 5.0, the formula was different, and the default value was 30, with failover time of 60 seconds.

> **NOTE**
>
> There is no need to modify this setting or the QLogic driver's setting as 15 seconds of failover time is sufficient in most cases.

Modifying the QLogic Native FC Driver Parameters

If you must change the QLogic Native FC driver's options, you can do it by using the following `esxcli` command:

```
esxcli system module parameters set -p "[parameter=value]" -m qlnativefc
```

Here is an example:

```
esxcli system module parameters set -p "qlport_down_retry=15" -m qlnativefc
```

This command sets the port-down retry to 15 seconds, and the change will take effect after you reboot the ESXi host.

Emulex HBA Driver Options

The Emulex FC HBA driver in ESXi 6 is a native driver called `lpfc`. Much as with the QLogic adapter, the Emulex HBA native driver was shipped as early as ESXi 5.5.

The equivalent option for Emulex drivers is `devloss_tmo`, with a default value of 10 seconds. The total failover time is 10 seconds as well.

As with the QLogic driver, listing the current option's value for an Emulex native driver is done using `mkmgmt_keyval`. To obtain the values for `devloss-tmo` only, you can run this command while in the /usr/lib/vmware/vmkmgmt_keyval directory:

```
./vmkmgmt_keyval --instance "[Instance]" --key param --get |grep
"Name\|devloss"
```

Here is an example:

```
./vmkmgmt_keyval --instance "vmhba1/Emulex" --key param --get |grep
"Name\|devloss"
```

Or you can use the abbreviated option:

```
./vmkmgmt_keyval -i "vmhba1/Emulex" -k param -g |grep "Name\|devloss"
```

The output looks like this:

```
Name            Low   High    Dflt Current     Description
devloss-tmo      1     ff       a      a       Seconds driver hold I/O
waiting for a loss device to return
```

To list the same parameter for additional adapters in this system, you can repeat the command, using the adapter's corresponding instance, such as vmhba64/Emulex. To identify the instance name, run the command `vmkmgmt_keyval` with the `-d` or `--dumpInstances` argument.

The output means that the default value is 10 (Hex a), and the current value is the same. This also means that the parameter's value has not been modified from the default.

Modifying the Emulex Native FC Driver Parameters

If you must change the Emulex Native FC driver's options, you can do it by using the following `esxcli` command:

```
esxcli system module parameters set --parameter "[parameter=value]"
 --module lpfc
```

Here is an example:

```
esxcli system module parameters set --parameter "lpfc_devloss_tmo=11"
 --module lpfc
```

Or you can use the abbreviated option:

```
esxcli system module parameters set -p "lpfc_devloss_tmo=11" -m lpfc
```

This command sets `devloss-tmo` to 11 seconds, and the change will take effect after you reboot the ESXi host.

After rebooting, you can use `vmkmgmt_keyval --get` or `-g` to list the updated value.

> **NOTE**
>
> Even though `vmkmgmt_keyval` output displays the parameter value in hex, the value to use with the `esxcli` command to change it must be in decimal.

If the driver fails to load after you change the option value, check the content of the /etc/vmware/esx.conf file for a line similar to this:

```
/vmkernel/module/lpfc/options = "lpfc_devloss_tmo=11"
```

If the value was not entered in decimal, or if there is a typographical error in the parameter, delete that line from the esx.conf file and reboot. The system then loads the driver using the defaults. Repeat the procedure to modify the option value with the correct syntax and decimal value.

Path Selection Plug-ins

Path Selection Plug-ins (PSPs) play a major role in failover as their main job is to select which path is used for sending I/O to the device. Failover activities vary depending on the PSP.

VMW_PSP_FIXED

The VMW_PSP_FIXED PSP honors the preferred path setting. I/O is sent to paths marked as preferred until they become unavailable. At that time, the PSP selects another path. When the preferred path becomes available, I/O fails back to it. vSphere 4.1 provided an additional plug-in, VMW_PSP_FIXED_AP, that allowed active/passive arrays to be configured with the preferred path option without the risk of path thrashing when used with ALUA storage arrays. The functionality of that plug-in was merged into the VMW_PSP_FIXED plug-in starting with vSphere 5. This explains why several ALUA arrays now default to VMW_PSP_FIXED on vSphere 6.

VMW_PSP_MRU

The VMW_PSP_MRU PSP ignores the preferred path setting. I/O is sent to the most recently used path that is known to work. If that path becomes unavailable, the PSP selects another path to the active SP. The I/O continues to the newly selected path until it becomes unavailable.

VMW_PSP_RR

The VMW_PSP_RR round-robin PSP rotates I/O to all paths to the active SP or SP port groups that are in AO (active/optimized) state. The rotation depends on two configurations that control the number and the size of I/O sent to the device before switching to another path.

When and How to Change the Default PSP

In Chapter 5, I showed how to list the default PSP for each SATP. (Refer to Figure 5.29 in Chapter 5.)

To recap, each SATP is configured with a default PSP, as identified by the output of the following command:

```
esxcli storage nmp satp list
```

In most cases, the default configuration is sufficient. However, some storage vendors develop their own SATPs and PSPs, which require you to modify the default rules for the ESXi host to take advantage of what these plug-ins have to offer. The corresponding partner provides its own documentation on how to configure the environment for its plug-ins. In the following sections, I show you how to make such changes and when.

When Should You Change the Default PSP?

The most common use case for changing the default PSP is when you want to utilize Round Robin failover policy (VMW_PSP_RR). Although VMware supports this policy with all arrays listed on its HCL, you must check with the storage vendor before making such a change. Storage vendors also have documentation about specific configurations that I highlight next.

> **NOTE**
>
> The Round Robin PSP is now supported by VMware on vSphere 6 with virtual machines (VMs) configured with MSCS (Microsoft Clustering Services, also known as Microsoft Windows Failover Clustering).

How to Change the Default PSP

In Chapter 5, I showed how to change the PSP for a given LUN via the UI. Here, I show you how to change the default PSP for a family of arrays. As I explained in Chapter 5, the default PSPs are associated with specific SATPs. The SATP claim rules decide which array is claimed by which SATP and, in turn, which default PSP is used. So the premise of changing the default PSP is to create a PSA claim rule that associates a specific PSP with a SATP.

The following example changes the default PSP to VMW_PSP_RR for storage arrays claimed by SATP VMW_SATP_CX:

```
esxcli storage nmp satp set --default-psp VMW_PSP_RR --satp VMW_SATP_CX

Default PSP for VMW_SATP_CX is now VMW_SATP_RR
```

You can run the following command to list the default PSPs and verify that the previous command has done its job:

```
esxcli storage nmp satp list
```

The output of this command is shown in Figure 7.15.

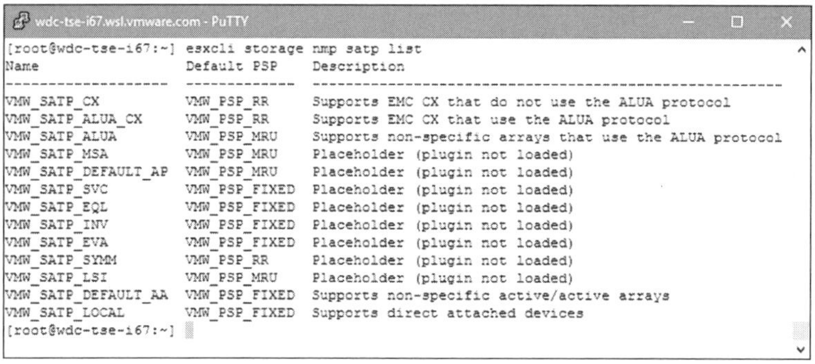

Figure 7.15 Listing default PSPs

Changing the default PSP does not apply to LUNs already discovered and claimed by other PSPs until you reboot the host.

To verify that the change took effect for a certain device, run this command:

```
esxcli storage nmp device list --device <device-ID>
```

You can also use the shorthand option -d instead of --device:

```
esxcli storage nmp device list -d <device-ID>
```

Figure 7.16 shows an example of the command and its output.

When and How to Change the Default PSP

```
wdc-tse-i67.wsl.vmware.com - PuTTY                              —    □    X
[root@wdc-tse-i67:~] esxcli storage nmp device list -d naa.6006016055711d00cff95e65664ee011
naa.6006016055711d00cff95e65664ee011
   Device Display Name: DGC Fibre Channel Disk (naa.6006016055711d00cff95e65664ee011)
   Storage Array Type: VMW_SATP_CX
   Storage Array Type Device Config: {navireg ipfilter   }
   Path Selection Policy: VMW_PSP_RR
   Path Selection Policy Device Config: {policy=rr,iops=1000,bytes=10485760,useANO=0; lastPath
Index=2; NumIOsPending=0,numBytesPending=0}
   Path Selection Policy Device Custom Config:
   Working Paths: vmhba3:C0:T1:L1, vmhba2:C0:T1:L1
   Is USB: false
[root@wdc-tse-i67:~]
```

Figure 7.16   Checking whether RR PSP changes took effect after reboot

Part of the output in Figure 7.16 shows the `Path Selection Policy Device Config` options. Table 7.12 lists these options and their corresponding values.

Table 7.12 `Path Selection Policy Device Config` options

Option	Value	Comments
Policy	rr	The current policy is `rr` because VMW_PSP_RR is in use.
Iops	1000	This is the default setting. I/O stays on one of the working paths (see the section "Where Is the Active Path?" earlier in this chapter) until 1,000 IOPS are sent, and then it switches the I/O to the next working path.
Bytes	10485760	This is the default setting. I/O stays on one of the working paths until 10,485,760 bytes, which is 10MB, are sent and switch the I/O to the next working path.
useANO	0	This is the default. With ALUA configuration, I/O is *not* sent to target port group in an active/non-optimized state.
lastPathIndex	Varies	The value listed here is the path number through which the I/O was last sent. So, if there are two active paths (1 and 2) that are based on the output in Figure 7.17, the current path in use is path 2; the next path to be used is path 1.
NumIOsPending	Varies	This value lists the number of I/Os pending at the time the output was collected.
numBytesPending	Varies	This value lists the number of bytes pending at the time the output was collected.

In this example, LUN 1 actually has four paths. However, because two of these paths are active and the other two are Standby, only the two active paths are used by the round-robin policy (see Figure 7.17).

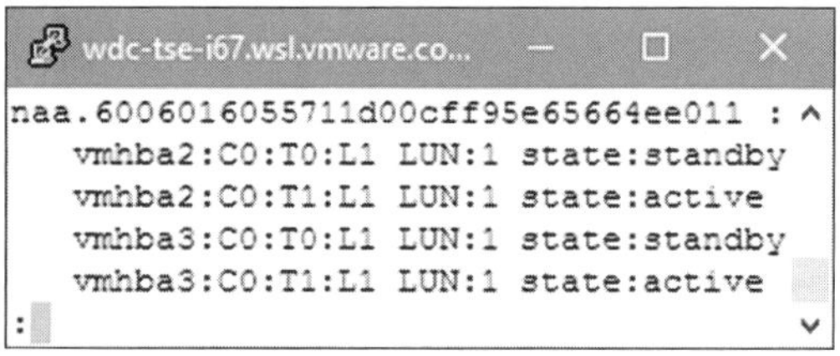

```
naa.6006016055711d00cff95e65664ee011 : ^
   vmhba2:C0:T0:L1 LUN:1 state:standby
   vmhba2:C0:T1:L1 LUN:1 state:active
   vmhba3:C0:T0:L1 LUN:1 state:standby
   vmhba3:C0:T1:L1 LUN:1 state:active
:                                        ∨
```

Figure 7.17   Listing paths to LUN 1

If this LUN were configured on an ALUA array, the two active paths would be to a target port group in the AO state, and the two Standby paths would be to a target port group in the ANO state. The end result would be the same because the option `useANO` is set to `0`.

PDL and APD

Careful designs that provide storage availability components (see Chapters 2 and 4) should prevent complete loss of connectivity to the shared storage. However, in some uncommon situations loss of connectivity might occur (for example, accidental zoning changes resulting in loss of access to the originally available storage targets, storage array processors being rebooted simultaneously). Upon rescanning, these situations result in a state referred to as all paths down (APD). As a result, access to the affected LUNs is lost and, as a side effect, other LUNs might become unresponsive for a limited period of time or permanently. vSphere 5 and earlier do not support this state. However, beginning with vSphere 4.0 Update 3 and 4.1 Update 1, VMware introduced some changes aimed at helping handle such a state gracefully. vSphere 5 improved on these changes, and vSphere 6 improved them even further.

In most cases, the events leading to the APD state are transient. However, if they are not, they result in a state referred to as permanent device loss (PDL). The most common examples of such events are LUN removal by either deleting the LUN on the storage array or unmapping it (unmasking). When this happens, the storage array returns to the ESXi host a specific PDL error for each path to the removed LUN. Such an error is reported as a SCSI sense code (see the "SCSI Sense Codes" section, earlier in this chapter).

An example of a PDL sense code is 0x5 0x25 0x00, LOGICAL UNIT NOT SUPPORTED, or sense code 0x00 0x68 0x00, LOGICAL UNIT NOT CONFIGURED.

Table 7.13 lists possible SCSI sense codes for the PDL state.

Table 7.13 Possible SCSI sense codes for the PDL state

SCSI Sense Code	Description
H:0x0 D:0x2 P:0x0 Valid sense data: 0x__ /0x25/0x0	LOGICAL UNIT NOT SUPPORTED
H:0x0 D:0x2 P:0x0 Valid sense data: 0x__/0x68/0x0	LOGICAL UNIT NOT CONFIGURED
H:0x0 D:0x2 P:0x0 Valid sense data: 0x4/0x4c/0x0	HARDWARE ERROR/LOGICAL UNIT FAILED SELF-CONFIGURATION
H:0x0 D:0x2 P:0x0 Valid sense data: 0x4/0x3e/0x3	HARDWARE ERROR/LOGICAL UNIT FAILED SELF-TEST
H:0x0 D:0x2 P:0x0 Valid sense data: 0x4/0x3e/0x1	HARDWARE ERROR/LOGICAL UNIT FAILURE
H:0x0 D:0x2 P:0x0 Valid sense data: 0x2/0x4c/0x0	NOT READY/LOGICAL UNIT FAILED SELF-CONFIGURATION
H:0x0 D:0x2 P:0x0 Valid sense data: 0x2/0x3e/0x3	NOT READY/LOGICAL UNIT FAILED SELF-TEST
H:0x0 D:0x2 P:0x0 Valid sense data: 0x2/0x3e/0x1	NOT READY/LOGICAL UNIT FAILURE

For the sense codes in the first two rows in Table 7.13, ESXi identifies PDL state from the ASC/ASCQ combination only (0x25 0x00 or 0x68 0x00), regardless of the rest of the sense code values.

In an ideal situation, vSphere administrators would get advance warning from the storage administrators that a device (LUN) is being removed permanently from the set of LUNs presented to a given ESXi 6 host. This is referred to as *planned PDL*. You should follow these steps to prepare for a planned PDL:

1. Power off all VMs running on the VMFS volume on the LUN.

2. Unmount the VMFS volume.

3. Detach the device (LUN).

Unmounting a VMFS Volume

When you have moved the files on the VMFS datastore to be unmounted to their new VMFS datastore(s) either with Storage VMotion or manually, you are ready to unmount the datastore on the device that is planned to be decommissioned.

You can complete the unmount operation via the UI or the CLI, as described in the following sections.

Unmounting a VMFS Datastore via the UI

You need to verify that the datastore you plan to unmount is on the LUN that is planned to be removed and then do the actual unmounting. Follow these steps:

1. Connect to the vCenter server that manages the ESXi 6 host, using the vSphere 6.0 Web Client as a user with Administrator privileges.

2. Click the **Storage** view tab if you started from the Hosts and Clusters view, or click the **Storage** icon if you started from the Home view.

3. Click the datastore.

4. Select the **Manage** Tab.

5. Click the **Settings** button.

6. Select the **Connectivity and Multipathing** section.

7. Select one of the hosts that shows the datastore as mounted.

8. Verify the device ID, which is enclosed in a rectangle in Figure 7.18.

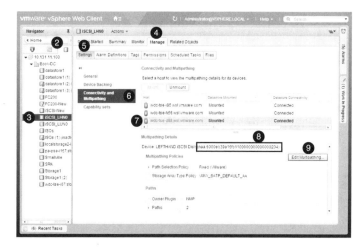

Figure 7.18 Listing the datastore to be unmounted

9. Click the **Edit Multipathing** button. Figure 7.19 shows the dialog that appears.

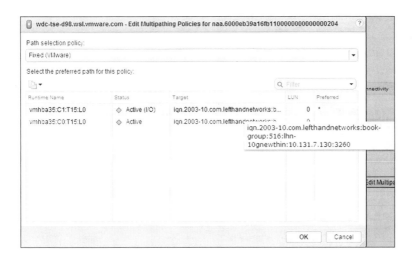

Figure 7.19 Listing paths to the backing LUN

The LUN is listed under the LUN column. In this example, it is LUN 0. However, because this is an iSCSI LUN on a storage array that presents each LUN on a unique target ID and all LUNs have 0 as the LUN, you need to pay close attention to the target IDs and each target's IQN. Because the Target column is not wide enough to display the full IQN, you need to hover over the LUN's IQN on one of the listed paths to see the full IQN in a rectangular bubble. In this case, the IQN is iqn.2003-1.com.lefthandnetworks: book-group:516:lhn-10gnewthin:10.131.7.130:3260. This translates to the following in this example, which is for an HP P4000 family of arrays (LeftHand Network iSCSI storage):

- **Target Port IQN**—iqn.2003-1.com.lefthandnetworks
- **Management Group Name**—book-group
- **Volume Name**—lhn-10gnewthin
- **iSCSI Portal Address**—10.131.7.130:3260

This matches the configuration on the array in Figure 7.20, which shows the relevant part of the HP StoreVirtual Centralized Management Console.

Now that you have verified that you are dealing with the correct datastore, you can proceed with unmounting it.

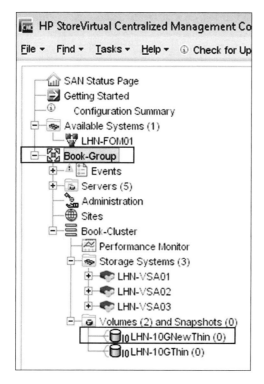

Figure 7.20   Identifying an iSCSI LUN on the storage array

10. Click **Cancel** on the previous dialogs. While the ESXi host is still selected in the hosts' list, click the **Unmount** button (refer to Figure 7.18 earlier).

11. Select each of the remaining hosts on the list and then click the **Unmount** button until the datastore shows as unmounted on all hosts.

12. If you get the error shown in Figure 7.21, it means that VM files are still on the datastore, so dismiss the message and move the files to another datastore or unregister the related VM and then retry the unmount operation.

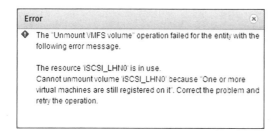

Figure 7.21   Datastore still has VM files on it, so you cannot proceed

Figure 7.22 shows a successful unmount operation result.

Figure 7.22 Datastore unmounted

TIP

To remount a datastore, select each host and then click the **Mount** button.

Unmounting a VMFS Datastore via the CLI

To unmount a VMFS datastore with the CLI, follow this procedure:

1. Connect to the ESXi 6 host via SSH as a root user or to vMA 6 as vi-admin. (See Chapter 4 for details.)

2. Run the following command to verify the LUN of the datastore you plan to unmount:

```
vmkfstools  --queryfs  /vmfs/volumes/[Volume  Name]  |grep  naa  |sed
's/:.*$//'
```

In this example, you would use this command:

```
vmkfstools --queryfs /vmfs/volumes/ISCSI_LUN0 |grep naa |sed 's/:.*$//'
```

You can also use the shorthand version of the command:

```
vmkfstools -P /vmfs/volumes/ISCSI_LUN0 |grep naa |sed 's/:.*$//'
```

This command returns the datastore's NAA ID and truncates the partition number from the output.

Then you can use that ID to find the LUN by using the following command:

```
esxcli storage nmp device list --device [Device ID] |grep Working
```

In this example, you would use this command:

```
esxcli   storage   nmp   device   list   --device   naa.6000eb39a16
fb1100000000000000204 |grep Working
```

You may also use the shorthand version of the command:

```
esxcli storage nmp device list -d naa.6000eb39a16fb1100000000000000204
|grep Working
```

The output of these two commands is shown in Figure 7.23.

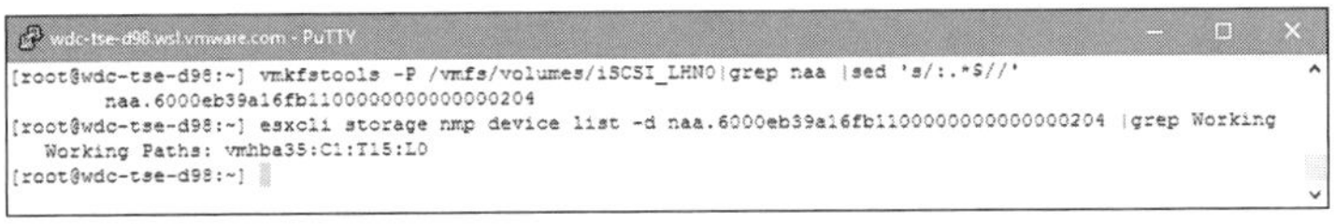

Figure 7.23 Listing a datastore's LUN

In this example, the LUN is 0 on target 15.

NOTE

Before proceeding with the next command, make sure that no VMs' files are still on the datastore. Using the CLI does not return any warnings if VMs on the datastore are still registered on this host.

---

3. Proceed with unmounting the datastore by using this command:

```
esxcli storage filesystem unmount --volume-label <datastore-name>
```

You can also use the shorthand option -l instead of --volume-label:

```
esxcli storage filesystem unmount -l <datastore-name>
```

Notice that if the command is successful, no status or feedback is returned.

4. To verify that the datastore has been unmounted, run the following:

```
esxcli storage filesystem list |less -S
```

Figure 7.24 shows the output of both of these commands.

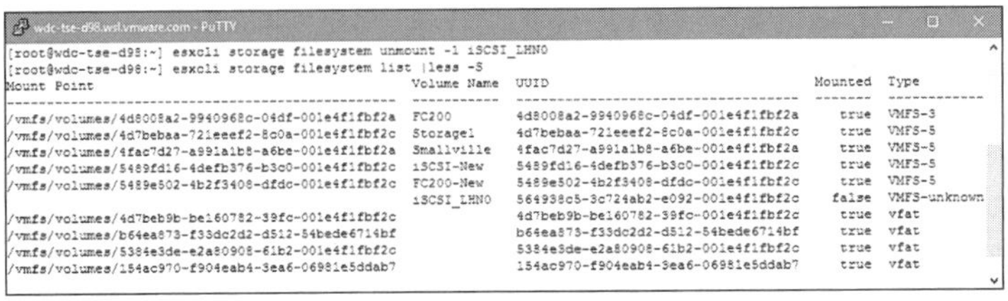

Figure 7.24 Unmounting a datastore—CLI

The output shows that the `Mounted` column status is `false`, and that the `Mount Point` column is blank. Notice that the `Type` column shows `VMFS-unknown` because the volume is not mounted.

5. If you plan on detaching the device, repeat steps 1 through 4 on each host on which the datastore is mounted before moving on to the next procedure.

TIP

To remount a datastore, repeat the command in step 3, using `mount` instead of `unmount`.

The following are sample /var/log/vmkernel.log events:

```
2015-11-21T17:27:11.984Z cpu2:34778 opID=7480d037)World: 15447: VC opID
817a94cb maps to vmkernel opID 7480d037
2015-11-21T17:27:11.984Z cpu2:34778 opID=7480d037)LVM: 15158: File system
'[iSCSI_LHN0, 564938c5-3c724ab2-e092-001e4f1fbf2c]' (LV 564938be-21f2588a-
21a2-001e4f1fbf2c) un-mounted.
```

Detaching a Device Whose Datastore Was Unmounted

In the previous sections, you saw how to unmount the datastore via the UI and the CLI. Once you have unmounted the datastore, you are ready to detach the device in preparation for removing it from the storage array. You can accomplish this task via the vSphere 6 Web Client or the CLI.

Detaching a Device Using the vSphere 6 Client

Continuing with the example used for unmounting the datastore, you can now detach LUN 0 on vmhba35 target 15 as follows:

1. Connect to the vCenter server that manages the ESXi 6 host, using the vSphere 6.0 Web Client as a user with Administrator privileges.

2. Navigate to the **Inventory—Hosts and Clusters** view and locate the ESXi 6.0 host in the inventory tree and select it.

3. Navigate to the **Manage** tab.

4. Click the **Storage** button.

5. Select the **Storage Devices** section.

6. Locate the device identified in the previous procedure and select it.

7. To verify that you selected the correct device, select the **Properties** tab in the Device Details pane and match the device ID to that listed in the **Identifier** field in the General section (see Figure 7.25).

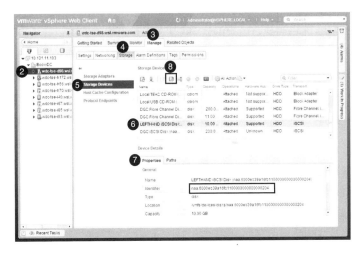

Figure 7.25   Locating a LUN to detach—UI

8. Click the **Detach** button, as highlighted in Figure 7.25. You see the dialog shown in Figure 7.26. Click **Yes** to continue.

Figure 7.26   Confirming detaching a device

If you have not unmounted the datastore, you get the dialog shown in Figure 7.27 instead, and you cannot proceed until you unmount the datastore.

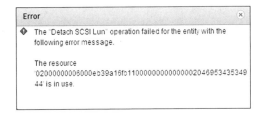

Figure 7.27   Device still has datastore mounted and cannot proceed with detach

The host continues to "have knowledge" about the detached device until it is actually removed from the SAN and a rescan is done. In technical terms, the PSA does not "unclaim" the device, but the device state is off. The device continues to be listed in the UI as an italicized item in the **Storage Devices** list, as shown in Figure 7.28.

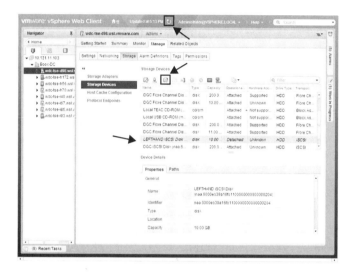

Figure 7.28   Device detached

If you need to reattach a device, simply select the device in the list and click the **Attach** button, as highlighted in Figure 7.28. You may need to refresh the view by clicking the refresh icon at the top of the UI.

> **NOTE**
>
> Reattaching a device does not automatically mount the datastore on that device. You must mount it manually, as described in the tip at the end of the "Unmounting a VMFS Datastore via the UI" section.

Detaching a Device Using the CLI

To detach a device using the CLI, you need to know the device ID (for example, NAA ID). Continuing with the example from the previous section, you get the device ID as described in step 2 of the "Unmounting a Datastore Using the UI" section. Then follow these steps:

1. Run the following command to detach the device:

```
esxcli storage core device set --state off --device naa. 6000eb39a16
fb1100000000000000204
```

Or use the shorthand version of this command:

```
esxcli storage core device set --state off -d naa. 6000eb39a16fb1100
  000000000000204
```

2. To verify that the operation was successful, run the following command.

```
esxcli storage core device detached list
```

Figure 7.29 shows the output from these commands.

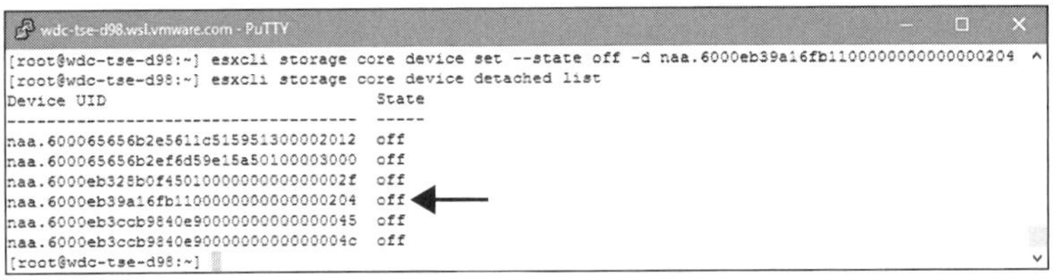

Figure 7.29 Detaching a device—CLI

To reattach the device via the command line, repeat step 1, using --state=on, as follows:

```
esxcli storage core device set --state=on --device naa.6000eb39a16
  fb1100000000000000204
```

Or you can use the shorthand version of this command:

```
esxcli storage core device set --state=on -d naa.6000eb39a16fb110000
  0000000000204
```

NOTE

If the datastore has not been unmounted before you run the commands in steps 1 and 2, you get no warning or errors via the command line, and the datastore is unmounted automatically. If you reattach the device after doing so, the datastore is mounted automatically.

However, if the datastore was unmounted prior to detaching the device, reattaching it does not mount the datastore automatically.

Relevant events posted to vmkernel.log file would be similar to these:

```
cpu5:34144 opID=b31e902c)World: 15447: VC opID cca3a8bd-4a39-40ef-945a-
c8d3f3294db7-2013-ngc-4-e4-7909 maps to vmkernel opID b31e902c
cpu5:34144 opID=b31e902c)ScsiDevice: 1738: Device naa.6000eb39a16
fb1100000000000000204  has been turned off administratively.
```

Path Ranking

vSphere 4.1 through 6.5 provide a feature that enables you to rank the order in which the I/O is sent to a device over available paths when path failover is required. This feature is referred to as *path ranking*. It is implemented differently in 5.0 than in 4.1. It also works with ALUA arrays differently from how it works with non-ALUA arrays.

Path Ranking for ALUA and Non-ALUA Storage

In storage configurations using ALUA storage arrays (see Chapter 6), path selection is based on the target port group AAS, which can be in one of the following states:

- AO
- ANO
- Transitioning
- Standby

To recap from Chapter 6, I/O can be sent to ports in the AO state, and if no such ports are available, I/O is sent to ports in the ANO state. If neither port group AAS is available, the last resort is to send the I/O to the ports in Standby AAS. So, as long as there are ports in AO AAS, I/O is sent only to these ports. However, when there is more than one port in an AO port group, there is no preference in terms of to which port the I/O will be sent. If VMW_PSP_FIXED policy is used and a preferred path is set, the I/O will be sent to the preferred path. If the PREF bit is supported by and enabled on the ALUA array *and* a preferred LUN owner is set in the array configuration, the I/O will be sent to a target on the SP that is set as the preferred owner.

On the other hand, with non-ALUA active/passive storage arrays, when used by hosts configured with the VMW_PSP_MRU policy, the ports are in one of two modes: active or standby. With this policy, you cannot configure a "preferred path," and it is not recommended to use the VMW_PSP_FIXED policy because the arrays do not support ALUA. As an alternative and to facilitate ranking of these paths, VMware introduced a new PSP in vSphere 4.1, VMW_PSP_MRU_RANKED, which later got merged into VMW_PSP_MRU in vSphere 5 and newer.

How Does Path Ranking Work for ALUA Arrays?

Path ranking allows vSphere administrators to assign ranks to individual paths. The VMW_PSP_MRU plug-in goes through the active path group state in the order mentioned in the previous section (AO to ANO) and then to standby and chooses a path that has the highest rank for I/O.

It is important to note that as long as there are paths to ports in the AO state, I/O is sent through them, even when paths to ports in ANO or Standby AAS states are ranked higher. In other words, the path selection occurs in this order:

1. Paths to ports in AO AAS, based on the rank of each path.

2. If there are no ports in AO state, the paths to ports in ANO AAS are used, based on the rank of each path.

3. Finally, if neither AO nor ANO is available, the paths to ports in Standby AAS state are used, based on the rank of each path.

In the output shown in Figure 7.30, notice the field named `Group State` in the properties of each path. Because the attached array is configured to support ALUA, one of the path group states is active, and the other is active/non-optimized.

This is in contrast with the AAS, which is listed in the field named `Storage Array Type Path Config`. In Figure 7.30, AAS are `TPG_state=AO` and `TPG_state=ANO`, respectively, which also match their corresponding group state.

The command used in Figure 7.30 is as follows:

```
esxcli storage nmp path list -d naa.6006016072902500881101735d87fe411
```

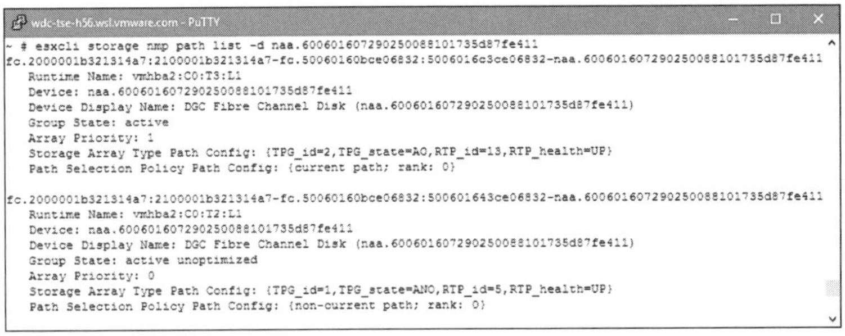

Figure 7.30 Listing paths to an ALUA LUN

Path Failover to a Ranked Path in ALUA Configuration

When an AO path with the highest rank becomes unavailable, the I/O fails over to the next-highest-ranked path to ports in the AO state. If none is available, the I/O fails over to the next-highest-ranked path to a port in ANO state. If neither an AO path nor an ANO path is available, the I/O fails over to the next-highest-ranked path to a port in the Standby state.

If all paths are ranked the same, VMW_PSP_MRU behaves as if ranking is not configured and fails over to the next available path to a port in AO state, and, if none is available, it fails over to a path to a port in ANO state and then a Standby state, as detailed earlier in this chapter and in Chapters 5 and 6.

Path Failback to a Ranked Path in ALUA Configuration

VMW_PSP_MRU fails back to a better-ranked path or a path with a better state when such a path becomes available.

> **NOTE**
>
> This does not result in path thrashing because VMW_PSP_MRU never fails back to a path that requires activation (for example, AO to Standby or AO to ANO).

How Does Path Ranking Work for Non-ALUA Arrays?

The VMW_PSP_MRU plug-in goes through the path group states that are active, and if none are available, it goes through the path group states that are standby. By default, all paths are ranked 0, which results in I/O going through the normal MRU algorithm of path selection. When path rank values are set higher, only paths in an active group state are used, based on the rank order. The only time path ranks are used on Standby path group state is when paths on the active group state are not available. See Figure 7.31 for an example of various paths' group states.

The command used in Figure 7.31 is as follows:

```
esxcli storage nmp path list -d naa.6006016055711d00cff95e65664ee011
```

You can also use the expanded command with `--device` instead of `-d`, as follows:

```
esxcli storage nmp path list --device naa.6006016055711d00cff95e65664ee011
```

In Figure 7.31, notice the field named `Group State` in the properties of each path. Because the attached array is active/passive and not configured to support ALUA, all path group states are either `active` or `standby`.

Notice that there are no values in the field `Storage Array Type Path Config` because the SATP is not an ALUA type, which is why the message `SATP VMW_SATP_CX does not support path configuration` is displayed.

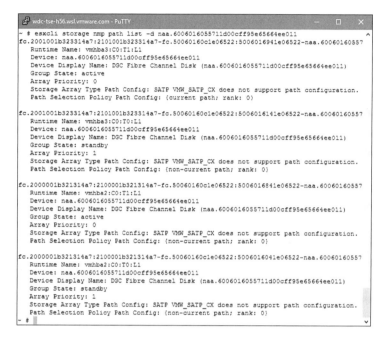

Figure 7.31   Listing paths to a non-ALUA LUN

Path Failover to a Ranked Path in Non-ALUA Configuration

When a path in an active path group state with the highest rank becomes unavailable, the I/O fails over to the next-highest-ranked path in an active path group state. If none is available, it fails over to the next-highest-ranked path in a standby path group state. This triggers a trespass on CLARiiON or START_UNIT on other active/passive arrays, which effectively transfers the LUN ownership to the formerly passive SP, which changes the path group state to active.

Path Failback to a Ranked Path in Non-ALUA Configuration

VMW_PSP_MRU fails back to a better-ranked path or a path with a better state when such a path becomes available. This means that if the failover was to a path on an active path group state, the failback is to the highest-ranked path in an active path group state.

Configuring Ranked Paths

Path ranking can be set via the CLI only. There is no UI available in vSphere 6 for this configuration.

Getting Path Rank

To get the path rank, run the following command:

```
esxcli storage nmp psp generic pathconfig get --path <pathname>
```

You can also use the shorthand version of the command, using -p in place of --path:

```
esxcli storage nmp psp generic pathconfig get -p <pathname>
```

Here is an example:

```
esxcli storage nmp psp generic pathconfig get -p fc.200000e08b9aeba6:210000
 e08b9aeba6-fc.50060160c1e06522:5006016041e06522-naa.6006016055711d00cff
 95e65664ee011
```

Or you can use the runtime pathname:

```
esxcli storage nmp psp generic pathconfig get -p vmhba2:C0:T0:L1
```

You get output similar to this:

```
{non-current path; rank: 0}
```

Setting Path Rank

To set the rank of a given path, use the following command:

```
esxcli storage nmp psp generic pathconfig set --config "rank=<value>"
--path <pathname>
```

You can also use the shorthand version of the command, using -c and -p in place of --config and --path, respectively:

```
esxcli storage nmp psp generic pathconfig set -c "rank=<value>" -p
<pathname>
```

Here is an example using the physical pathname:

```
esxcli storage nmp psp generic pathconfig set -c "rank=1" -p fc.200000e0
 8b9aeba6:210000e08b9aeba6-fc.50060160bce06832:500601643ce06832-naa.600601
 607290250088101735d87fe411
```

Here is an example using the runtime pathname:

```
esxcli storage nmp psp generic pathconfig set -c "rank=1" -p
vmhba2:C0:T0:L1
```

This sets the rank to 1 for the path listed. The higher the value, the higher the rank. After setting the rank, you can run the get command, as described in the preceding section, to verify that it has been successfully set.

> **TIP**
>
> Using VMW_PSP_MRU with ALUA arrays or non-ALUA active/passive arrays with ranked paths enables you to set something similar to a preferred path without having to use the VMW_PSP_FIXED plug-in. You can think of this as having multiple preferred paths but with different weights.

Summary

This chapter has covered multipathing and failover algorithms and has provided details about failover triggers as well as factors affecting multipathing and failover. I have also covered improvements introduced in vSphere 6 to better handle the APD state. Finally, this chapter has covered the little-known path ranking feature, including how it works and how to configure it.

## Chapter 8

Third-Party Multipathing I/O Plug-ins

VMware Pluggable Storage Architecture (PSA) is designed to be modular and act as a foundation for VMware storage partners to port their Multipath I/O (MPIO) software to run on ESXi. This chapter covers in some detail the MPIO plug-ins that are currently certified with vSphere 6. This chapter provides an overview of each package supported by vSphere 6 and some insights into what goes on behind the scenes in ESXi after each is installed and configured. This chapter is not intended to replace or be a substitute for the documentation you can get from each package's vendor.

MPIO Implementations on vSphere 6

VMware storage partners have the choice of delivering their MPIO software in one of the following formats:

- **MPP (Multipathing Plug-in)**—This type of plug-in runs on top of the PSA framework, side-by-side with NMP (VMware's Native Multipathing Plug-in). It may include other components that vary from partner to partner. An example of an MPP is EMC PowerPath/VE.

- **PSP (Path Selection Plug-in)**—This type of plug-in runs on top of NMP, side-by-side with other PSPs already included with vSphere 6. This type of plug-in, too, may include other components that vary from partner to partner. (See Chapter 7, "Multipathing and Failover," for details on SATP and PSP.) An example of a PSP MPIO is the Dell EqualLogic DELL_EQL_PSP_ROUTED plug-in.

- **A combination of both PSP and SATP (Storage Array Type Plug-in)**—An example is the combination of the Hitachi HTI_PSP_HDLM_EXLBK, HTI_PSP_HDLM_EXLIO, HTI_PSP_HDLM_EXRR, and HTI_SATP_HDLM plug-ins.

EMC PowerPath/VE 6

PowerPath/VE has been updated to run on ESXi 6 as well as ESXi version 5.5. The certified version as of this writing is 6.0.0.00.00-b329.

As mentioned previously, PowerPath/VE is implemented on ESXi as an MPP (also referred to as MEM [Multipathing Extension Module]). For details on PSA, NMP, and MPP and how the pieces fit together, refer to Chapter 5, "vSphere Pluggable Storage Architecture (PSA)."

Downloading PowerPath/VE

PowerPath/VE is available for download from EMC's support site (https://support.emc.com/downloads/). Follow these steps to locate the files:

1. Log on to the EMC support download page and search for **PowerPath/VE for VMware**, as shown in Figure 8.1.

Figure 8.1   EMC support download page

2. In the Browse Products section, select version **6.1** on the left-hand side bar.

3. In the middle section, find these three items:

   - PowerPath/VE 6.1 for VMware vSphere

   - PowerPath/VE 6.1 Stand-Alone Tools Bundle

   - PowerPath Virtual Appliance 2.1 SP1

4. Click on each item you want to download (see Figure 8.2).

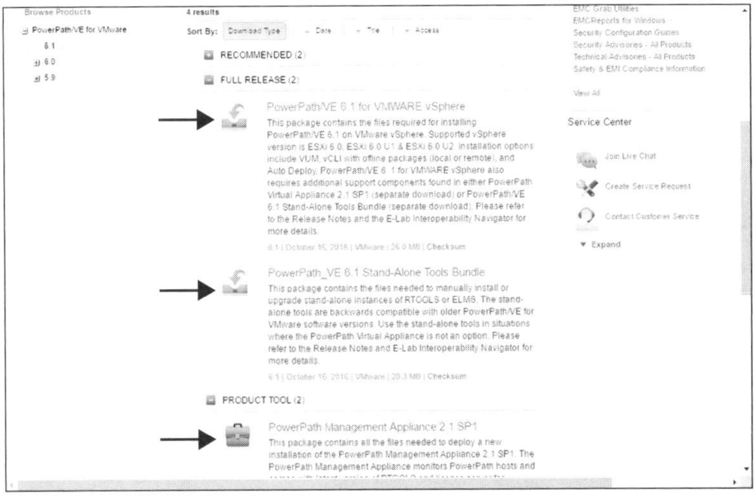

Figure 8.2 Accessing the PowerPath for VMware download page

5. Download and read **PowerPath/VE Software Download FAQ**, which answers many of the questions you are likely to have.

6. All you need to install PowerPath/VE is available on the download page including the following:

  a. Three PowerPath/VE vSphere installation bundles (VIBs): LIB (Library), CIM (Common Information Model), and PLUGIN (See the section "PowerPath/VE Installation Overview," later in this chapter.

  b. The PowerPath/VE offline bundle, which is what you use to install PowerPath/VE via vSphere Update Manager (VUM).

  c. The Read Me file.

7. Download the Tools bundle named PowerPath_VE_6.1_Stand-Alone_Tools_Bundle. zip, which includes the following:

  a. Both Windows and RedHat Enterprise Linux versions of the license server, which may or may not be included in future revisions of downloaded zip file.

  b. Both Windows and RedHat Enterprise Linux versions of RTOOLs.

8. If you prefer, download Tools Virtual Appliance, which delivers the RTOOLS and license servers in a convenient virtual appliance, in OVA format.

9. Alternatively, if you have already deployed an earlier version of Virtual Appliance, you can download the smaller upgrade bundle only.

10. Read the FAQ document by clicking the **Documentation** link at the top of the page and then selecting **Frequently Asked Questions: EMC PowerPath/VE for VMware vSphere Software Download** link.

NOTE

PowerPath/VE requires that each host be licensed using one of two available licensing modes: unserved or served.

You need one unserved license for each ESXi 6.x host, and it must be locked to the system UUID of each host. This is a manual process, and it's difficult to keep track of how many licenses are used. Also, when a host is out of order or decommissioned, you might be able to request to rehost the license to a new host, but this is possible for only a limited number of rehosting requests.

On the other hand, the served license mode uses a centralized electronic license management (ELM) server, which makes it easier to count the licensed hosts and also reassign the licenses to other hosts, as needed. (This is why it is referred to as *Floating* or *Counted mode*.) This is flexible and more practical.

PowerPath/VE Installation Overview

The following is a high-level overview of PowerPath/VE installation:

1. Obtain the license file(s) from EMC. If you are using unserved licenses, you need to get the system UUID from each ESXi host that you are licensing. To do so, run the following:

```
esxcli system uuid get
```

2. Install PowerPath Management Appliance, which includes RTOOLS.

3. If you are using served licenses, the license server is included with PowerPath Management Appliance.

4. Install PowerPath/VE 6.1. It can be installed via one of three facilities:

   a. **VUM (vSphere Update Manager)**—This is the preferred method if you have VUM in your environment. This chapter doesn't cover installing VUM because it is identical to installing any other offline bundle.

  b. **Auto-Deploy**—This facility allows for booting ESXi from a shared image via Preboot Execution Environment (PXE). It is available with vSphere 6.

  c. **vCLI (VMware vSphere CLI)**—You can install via the local CLI or via SSH if you have them enabled.

vSphere 6.5 and newer include VUM preinstalled in the environment. Using VUM is the recommended method of installing PowerPath/VE, and using it is similar to installing any other VIBs. Because the command line is less obvious, this chapter shows you the procedures for using the local CLI only.

5. Use the `rpowermt` utility, installed by RTOOLS, to check the license registration and device status.

What Gets Installed?

Regardless of the PowerPath/VE installation facility, the following VIBs are installed, in the order shown here:

1. EMC_bootbank_powerpath.lib.esx_6.1.0.00.00-b56.vib

2. EMC_bootbank_powerpath.cim.esx_6.1.0.00.00-b56.vib

 This is the PowerPath CIM provider that is used to manage PowerPath/VE remotely via `rpowermt`.

3. EMC_bootbank_powerpath.plugin.esx_6.1.0.00.00-b56.vib

 This is the MPP plug-in itself, which gets plugged into the PSA framework.

Before you install the VIBs, the ESXi host must be placed in maintenance mode, and it requires a reboot at the end of the installation. If you have a downtime window to reboot all hosts, you need to power off or suspend all running VMs. Otherwise, you can use a rolling outage and install on one host at a time. This is when your brilliant design comes in handy if you planned your HA/DRS cluster as N+1 or N+2 capacity. This means you have a cluster configured for one or two host failures. It also means that the surviving hosts have enough reserve capacity to run all VMs that were running on the one or two hosts you place in maintenance mode.

NOTE

Although VMware and EMC support a rolling upgrade approach, in which you install PowerPath/VE on one host at a time while the remaining hosts in the cluster still run NMP, this mixed-mode configuration should be used on a temporary basis only. You should plan on installing PowerPath/VE on *all* hosts in the cluster as soon as it is reasonably possible to do so.

If your storage is a Symmetrix or newer family of arrays, make sure the SPC-2 FA Director Bit is enabled. If it was not enabled and you apply this required change, be aware of a very important fact: *All* your VMFS volumes might have to be resignatured as a result of this change because the device IDs change from mpx.<ID> to NAA.<ID>, where the <ID> value is longer and partially different. This is discussed further in Chapter 15, "Snapshot Handling."

Installing PowerPath/VE by Using the Local CLI

To install PowerPath/VE using the local CLI, do the following:

1. Copy the offline installation bundle (named EMCPower.VMWARE.6.1.b56.zip at this writing) to the shared VMFS volume. You can use the vSphere Web Client **Browse Datastore** feature or a tool such as **WinSCP** on Windows or **SCP** on Linux to securely transfer the file to an ESXi host that has access to that VMFS volume.

2. Log on to the ESXi host locally or via an SSH client (for example, **Putty** on Windows or **ssh** on Linux) as root or as a user with root privileges.

3. Place the host in maintenance mode if you have not already done so. You can do that via the vSphere Client. You can also do it by using the CLI:

   ```
   esxcli system maintenanceMode set --enable=1 --timeout=60
   ```

4. Verify the software acceptance level setting on the host:

   ```
   [root@esx1:~] esxcli software acceptance get
   PartnerSupported
   ```

   This output means that the software acceptance level is set to `PartnerSupported`.

   If the returned value is `VMwareCertified` or `VMwareAccepted`, you must change it to `PartnerSupported`. Here's how you do that:

   ```
   [root@esx1:~] esxcli software acceptance set --level=PartnerSupported
   Host acceptance level changed to 'PartnerSupported'.
   ```

This is required because the PowerPath/VE VIBs were digitally signed by EMC as PartnerCertified acceptance level. The way acceptance level enforcement works is that you cannot install any VIBs that are lower than the current acceptance level of the host. This is the order of these levels:

a. `VMwareCertified`—Highest level

b. `VMwareAccepted`—Second-highest level

c. `PartnerSupported`—Third-highest level

d. `CommunitySupported`—Lowest level

So, if a host is set at a given level, you can install bundles of that level or higher, which means that with a host set to `PartnerSupported` acceptance level, you can install VIBs that are signed as `PartnerSupported`, `VMwareAccepted`, or `VMwareCertified`.

5. Perform a dry run of the installation to make sure you don't get any errors:

```
esxcli  software  vib  install  --depot=/<Path-to-offline-bundle>/
EMCPower.VMWARE.6.1.b56.zip --dry-run
```

Listing 8.1 shows an example.

Listing 8.1 Dry run of installing a PowerPath/VE offline bundle

```
esxcli software vib install --depot=/vmfs/volumes/FC200-2
/EMCPower.VMWARE.6.1.b56.zip --dry-run
Installation Result
   Message: Dryrun only, host not changed. The following installers will be
applied: [BootBankInstaller]
   Reboot Required: true
   VIBs Installed: EMC_bootbank_powerpath.cim.esx_6.1.0.00.00-b56, EMC_
bootbank_powerpath.lib.esx_6.1.0.00.00-b56, EMC_bootbank_powerpath.plugin.
esx_6.1.0.00.00-b56
   VIBs Removed:
   VIBs Skipped:
```

In Listing 8.1, notice that no errors result from the installation, three VIBs are installed, and a reboot is required.

6. Repeat the command shown in Listing 8.1 without the `--dry-run` option. Listing 8.2 shows the output.

Listing 8.2   Installing a PowerPath/VE offline bundle

```
esxcli software vib install --depot=/vmfs/volumes/FC200/EMCPower.
VMWARE.6.1.b56.zip
Installation Result
   Message: The update completed successfully, but the system needs to be
rebooted for the changes to be effective.
   Reboot Required: true
   VIBs Installed: EMC_bootbank_powerpath.cim.esx_6.1.0.00.00-b56, EMC_
bootbank_powerpath.lib.esx_6.1.0.00.00-b56, EMC_bootbank_powerpath.plugin.
esx_6.1.0.00.00-b56
   VIBs Removed:
   VIBs Skipped:
```

7. Reboot the host. Don't take the host out of maintenance mode yet. You will do that after verifying the installation. (See the next section, "Verifying the PowerPath/VE Installation.") When you are done with that, you can exit the host from maintenance mode via the UI. To do that via the CLI, run this command:

```
esxcli system maintenanceMode set --enable=0 --timeout=60
```

Verifying the PowerPath/VE Installation

To verify the PowerPath/VE installation, make the changes outlined in the following steps:

1. Install the three VIBs listed earlier. To list the installed VIBs, you can run the following:

```
esxcli software vib list |grep EMC
```

Figure 8.3 shows the output.

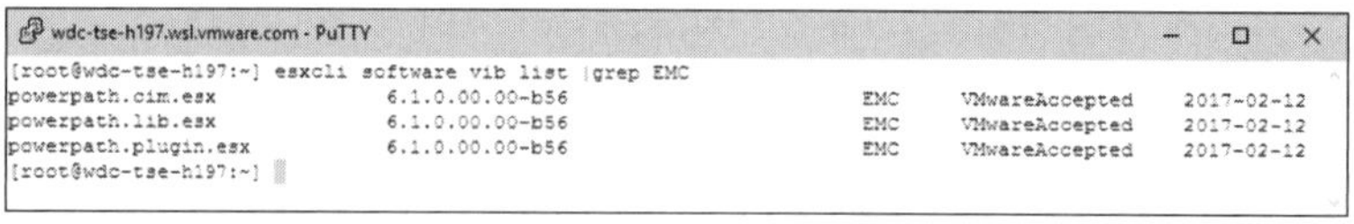

Figure 8.3   Listing installed PowerPath VIBs

You can also check the software profile for the three VIBs by using the following (see Figure 8.4):

```
esxcli software profile get
```

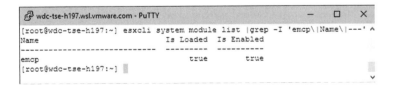

```
wdc-tse-h197.wsl.vmware.com - PuTTY                    —  □  ✕
[root@wdc-tse-h197:~] esxcli software profile get       ^
(Updated) ESXi-6.0.0-2809209-standard
   Name: (Updated) ESXi-6.0.0-2809209-standard
   Vendor: wdc-tse-h197
   Creation Time: 2017-02-12T04:37:15
   Modification Time: 2017-02-12T04:37:15
   Stateless Ready: True
   Description:

      (Original Vendor):VMware, Inc.
      2017-02-12T04:37:15.075209+00:00: The following VIBs are
      installed:
        powerpath.cim.esx      6.1.0.00.00-b56
        powerpath.lib.esx      6.1.0.00.00-b56
        powerpath.plugin.esx   6.1.0.00.00-b56
      ----------                                          v
```

Figure 8.4   Listing the PowerPath software profile

Note that the installed VIBs' names do not include the `EMC_Bootbank_` prefix.

2. Register the PowerPath plug-in with PSAs by using the JumpStart script
    `register-emc-powerpath.json`. List the registered plug-in by running the
    following (see Figure 8.5):

```
esxcli storage core plugin registration list |grep "PowerPath \|
Module \|---"
```

```
wdc-tse-h197.wsl.vmware.com - PuTTY                                        —   □  ✕
[root@wdc-tse-h197:~] esxcli storage core plugin registration list |grep "PowerPath \|Module \|---" ^
Module Name        Plugin Name         Plugin Class  Dependencies                Full Path
-----------------  ------------------  ------------  --------------------------  ---------
emcp               PowerPath           MP
[root@wdc-tse-h197:~]                                                                        v
```

Figure 8.5   Listing the PowerPath PSA module registration

You can verify that the PowerPath vmkernel module (`emcp`) was successfully
loaded by running the following (see Figure 8.6):

```
esxcli system module list |grep -I 'emcp\|Name\|---'
```

```
wdc-tse-h197.wsl.vmware.com - PuTTY                    —   □  ✕
[root@wdc-tse-h197:~] esxcli system module list |grep -I 'emcp\|Name\|---' ^
Name                               Is Loaded  Is Enabled
-----------------------------      ---------  ----------
emcp                                  true       true
[root@wdc-tse-h197:~]                                      v
```

Figure 8.6   Listing the PowerPath vmKernel module

The output in Figure 8.6 shows that the `emcp` kernel module was loaded and
enabled.

You can also check that the PowerPath MPP (Multipathing Plug-in) was successfully added by running the following (see Figure 8.7):

```
esxcli storage core plugin list
```

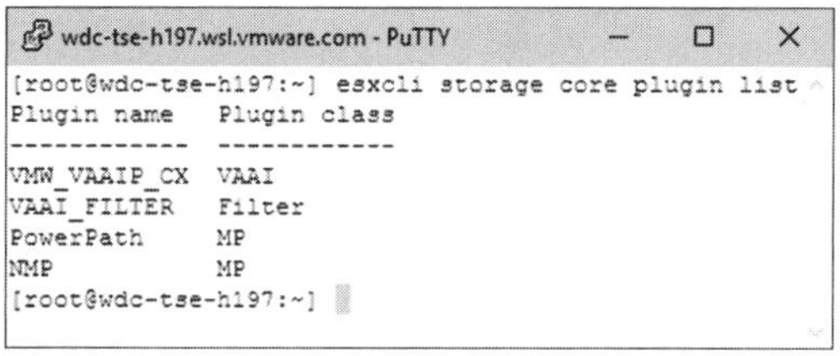

Figure 8.7 Listing the PowerPath MP plug-in

In Figure 8.7, you can see that there is an MP class plug-in named PowerPath along with NMP.

3. Add PowerPath PSA claim rules by using the JumpStart script **psa-powerpath-pre-claim-config.json**. List the added claim rules by running the following (see Figure 8.8):

```
esxcli storage core claimrule list
```

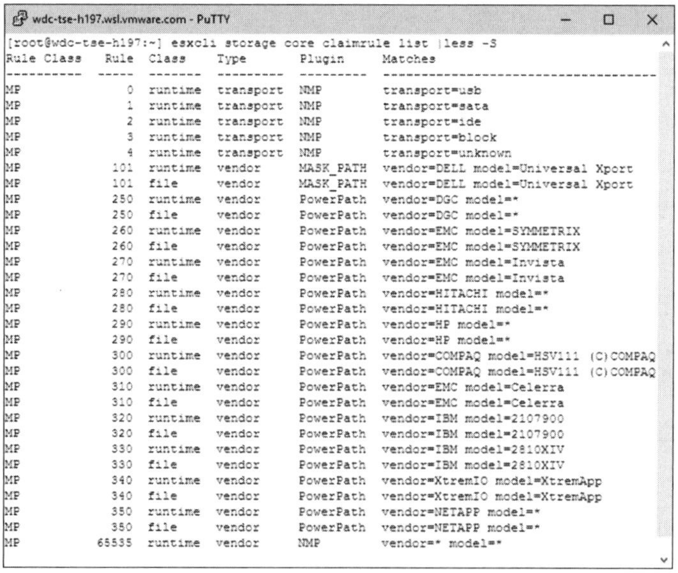

Figure 8.8 Listing PowerPath PSA claim rules

The output in Figure 8.8 shows that rules 250 through 350 have been added. Each rule is listed with runtime and file classes. This means that the rules that were written to the configuration files (file class) have also been loaded (runtime class).

4. Add the following JumpStart scripts to the /usr/libexec/jumpstart/plugins directory:

   a. register-emc-powerpath.json

   b. psa-powerpath-pre-claim-config.json

The first script (a) runs a command equivalent to this:

```
esxcli storage core plugin registration add -m emcp -N MP -P PowerPath
```

This is the verbose version of the command:

```
esxcli storage core plugin registration add --module-name=emcp
--plugin-class=MP --plugin-name=PowerPath
```

This command registers with PSA a vmkernel module named emcp as an MP class plug-in named PowerPath.

The second script (b) loads the emcp vmkernel module and then adds the PSA claim rules for storage array families supported by PowerPath/VE. It runs commands equivalent to those shown in Listing 8.3.

Listing 8.3 Commands run by the psa-powerpath-pre-claim-config.json script

```
esxcli system module load --module emcp


esxcli storage core claimrule add --claimrule-class MP --rule 250 --plugin
PowerPath --type vendor --vendor DGC --model *
esxcli storage core claimrule add --claimrule-class MP --rule 260 --plugin
PowerPath --type vendor --vendor EMC --model SYMMETRIX
esxcli storage core claimrule add --claimrule-class MP --rule 270 --plugin
PowerPath --type vendor --vendor EMC --model Invista
esxcli storage core claimrule add --claimrule-class MP --rule 280 --plugin
PowerPath --type vendor --vendor HITACHI --model *
esxcli storage core claimrule add --claimrule-class MP --rule 290 --plugin
PowerPath --type vendor --vendor HP --model *
esxcli storage core claimrule add --claimrule-class MP --rule 300 --plugin
PowerPath --type vendor --vendor COMPAQ --model \"HSV111 (C)COMPAQ\"
esxcli storage core claimrule add --claimrule-class MP --rule 310 --plugin
PowerPath --type vendor --vendor EMC --model Celerra
esxcli storage core claimrule add --claimrule-class MP --rule 320 --plugin
PowerPath --type vendor --vendor IBM --model 2107900
```

```
esxcli storage core claimrule add --claimrule-class MP --rule 330 --plugin
PowerPath --type vendor --vendor IBM --model 2810XIV
```

```
esxcli storage core claimrule add --claimrule-class MP --rule 340 --plugin
PowerPath --type vendor --vendor XtremIO --model XtremApp
```

```
esxcli storage core claimrule add --claimrule-class MP --rule 350 --plugin
PowerPath --type vendor --vendor NETAPP --model *
```

Listing Devices Claimed by PowerPath/VE

To verify that supported devices have been claimed by PowerPath MPP, you can run the following (see Figure 8.9):

```
esxcli storage core device list |grep -B6 Power
```

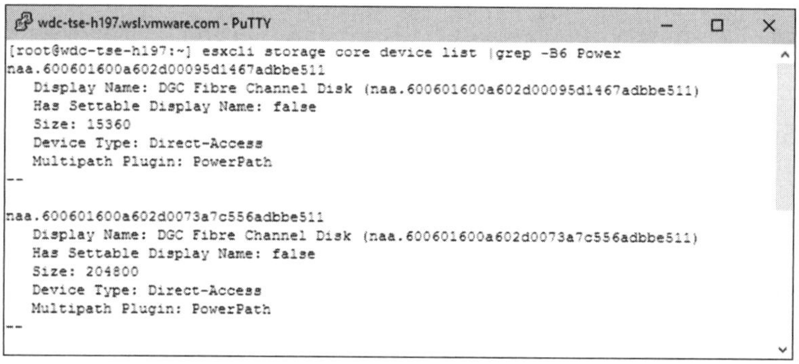

Figure 8.9   Listing PowerPath managed FC device properties

The output shown in Figure 8.9 is an example from Fibre Channel LUNs on a CLARiiON storage array. Notice that the MPP is PowerPath.

Figure 8.10 shows another example of a device claimed by PowerPath, which is an iSCSI device on a CLARiiON or VNX storage array.

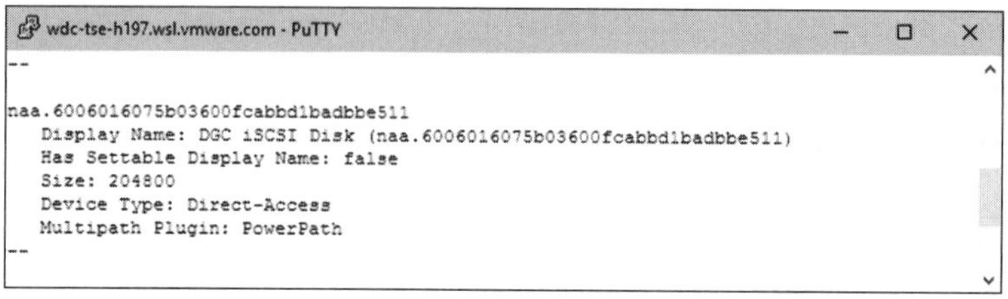

Figure 8.10   Listing PowerPath managed iSCSI device properties

Managing PowerPath/VE

You can manage PowerPath/VE remotely by using `rpowermt` on Windows or Red Hat Linux if you have installed the RTOOLS package. For details on using `rpowermt`, refer to the PowerPath maintenance/configuration document described in the "What Gets Installed?" section, earlier in this chapter.

You can also use the local `powermt` utility that is installed on each ESXi server when you install PowerPath/VE. This tool, located in /opt/emc/powerpath/bin, enables you to run a subset of commands that are available with `rpowermt`.

Uninstalling PowerPath/VE

If you are going to experiment with PowerPath/VE, you might need to uninstall it when you are done playing. You can do so by following the same steps you used for the installation except substituting the installation step with this command:

```
esxcli software vib remove -n <bundle1>  -n <bundle2> -n <bundle3>
```

This is the verbose version of this command:

```
esxcli software vib remove --vibname=<bundle1>  --vibname=<bundle2>
--vibname=<bundle3>
```

Listings 8.4, 8.5, 8.6, and 8.7 show the commands you use for everything from beginning to rebooting the host. This is all done within vMA 6.5.

Listing 8.4   Entering maintenance mode

```
vi-admin@station-1:~[wdc-tse-h197]> esxcfg-hostops --operation enter

Host wdc-tse-h197.wsl.vmware.com entered into maintenance mode successfully.
```

Listing 8.5   Listing a PowerPath VIB profile

```
vi-admin@station-1:~[wdc-tse-h5197]> esxcli software vib list |grep
powerpath

powerpath.cim.esx     6.1.0.00.00-b56   EMC PartnerSupported 2017-02-12

powerpath.lib.esx     6.1.0.00.00-b56   EMC PartnerSupported 2017-02-12

powerpath.plugin.esx  6.1.0.00.00-b56   EMC PartnerSupported 2017-02-12
```

Listing 8.6 Uninstalling PowerPath

```
vi-admin@station-1:~[wdc-tse-h197]> esxcli software vib remove --vibname
powerpath.cim.esx --vibname powerpath.lib.esx --vibname powerpath.plugin.esx

Removal Result
   Message: The update completed successfully, but the system needs to be
rebooted for the changes to be effective.
   Reboot Required: true
   VIBs Installed:
   VIBs Removed: EMC_bootbank_powerpath.cim.esx_6.1.0.00.00-b56, EMC_
bootbank_powerpath.lib.esx_6.1.0.00.00-b56, EMC_bootbank_powerpath.plugin.
esx_6.1.0.00.00-b56
   VIBs Skipped:
```

Listing 8.7 Rebooting a host

```
vi-admin@station-1:~[wdc-tse-h197]> esxcfg-hostops --operation reboot

Host wdc-tse-h197.wsl.vmware.com rebooted successfully.
```

After the host is rebooted, while you're still in vMA 6.5, run the following command to verify that the VIBs were removed successfully:

> **NOTE**
>
> The beauty of vMA is that you don't have to log on to the host after it boots back up. Because it was the last managed target, vMA uses the cached credentials in the FastPass configuration files to reconnect at the first command you run after the host is booted.

```
esxcli software vib list |grep powerpath
```

You should not get any VIBs returned, which confirms that they are no longer installed.

Use the following command to list the claim rules and verify that all claim rules that were added by the installer—claim rules 250 through 350, as shown previously in Figure 8.8—have been removed:

```
esxcli storage core claimrule list
```

Figure 8.11 shows the output of these two commands.

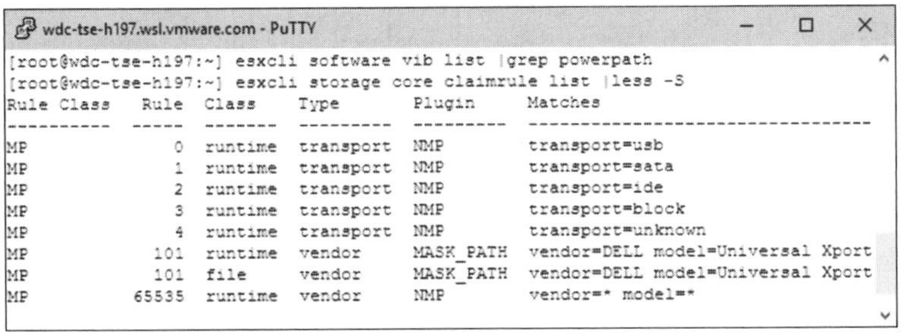

Figure 8.11 Verifying uninstalling PowerPath

After you have confirmed that PowerPath/VE has been uninstalled, you can take the host out of maintenance mode by using the following command:

```
vi-admin@station-1:~[wdc-tse-h197]> esxcfg-hostops --operation exit
Host wdc-tse-h5197.wsl.vmware.com exited from maintenance mode
successfully.
```

Hitachi Dynamic Link Manager (HDLM)

The Hitachi Dynamic Link Manager (HDLM) MPIO solution is available on several operating systems. It also developed for vSphere 6 in the form of one SATP, three PSPs, and one ESXCLI extension module, as follows:

- `hti_satp_hdlm`
- `hti_psp_hdlm_exlio` (extended least I/Os)
- `hti_psp_hdlm_ex rr` (extended round-robin)
- `hti_psp_hdlm_exlbk` (extended least blocks)
- `hex-hdlm-dlnkmgr`

> **NOTE**
>
> The product information in this section is based on the latest information as of press time.

Obtaining Installation Files

To obtain HDLM for VMware installation files, contact Hitachi Data Systems or Hitachi. You will receive a set of CDs/DVDs with the software and related files and documentation. The installation files are on the DVD labeled Hitachi Dynamic Link Manager Software v8 Advanced (with Hitachi Global Link Manager Software).

Follow these steps on a system or a VM (running Windows version supported by HDLM) that will assist you in extracting the required installation files:

1. Install vCLI. You can download the installation file for vSphere 6.5 from https://code.vmware.com/web/dp/tool/vsphere-powercli/6.5 and then click the **Download** button under VMware vSphere CLI. You can also get older versions from the same URL by selecting the desired version listed next to the Support Versions section. You are redirected to the VMware download site for the selected version. Run the downloaded file and follow the prompts to install it.

2. Insert the HDLM installation DVD into your DVD drive. (If you are installing to a VM, connect the DVD drive to the VM.)

3. If AutoRun is disabled on your system/VM, browse the DVD drive for the **index. html** file and run it.

4. Your browser should show a screen similar to the one in Figure 8.12. Click the **Install** button for VMware in the Hitachi Dynamic Link Manager Software section to copy the setup.exe file to a local disk.

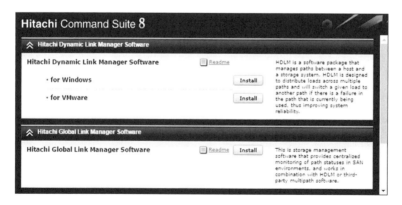

Figure 8.12   Accessing HDLM installation files

5. Run the setup.exe file to start the installation wizard and follow the installation prompts. See the Hitachi Command Suite Dynamic Link Manager User Guide (for VMware) on the documentation list in the index.html file of the Hitachi Command Suite v8 Software Documentation Library DVD that you received from Hitachi.

6. The HDLM remote management client is installed, and the HDLM for VMware offline bundle file is placed in <HDLM-Installation-Folder>\plugin—for example, c:\Program files(x86)\HITACHI\DynamicLinkManagerForVMware\plugin.

The filename as of the time of this writing is hdlm-0850000101-0600.zip, which is for vSphere 6. A file for vSphere 5, named hdlm-0850000101.zip, is also included.

Installing HDLM

You install HDLM via the single offline bundle file identified in the "Obtaining Installation Files" section: hdlm-0850000101-0600.zip. This file includes the five plug-ins listed earlier— four PSA plug-ins and an esxcli extension for HDLM.

Follow these steps:

1. Transfer the offline bundle zip file to a VMFS volume shared by all hosts on which you plan to install HDLM.

   You can transfer the files by using the vSphere 6.x Web Client or a file transfer tool such as WinSCP. To transfer the files using the vSphere 6.x Web Client, perform the following tasks:

   a. Log on to vSphere 6.x Web Client with Administrator privileges or equivalent. (This example uses vSphere 6.5.)

   b. Navigate to the **Storage inventory** view.

   c. Right-click the datastore to which you want to transfer the files.

   d. Select the **Browse Files** menu option. Alternatively, click the **Navigate to the datastore file browser** icon, which looks like a magnifying glass on a yellow folder.

   On vSphere 6.5 Client, you can select the **Files** tab instead (see Figure 8.13).

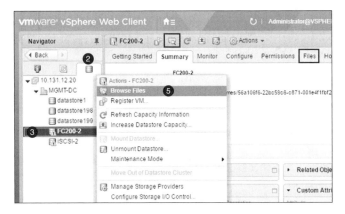

Figure 8.13   Browsing the datastore—vSphere Web Client

e. Navigate to the folder to which to transfer the file and click the **Upload a file to the Datastore** icon, which looks like a cylinder with a green up arrow (see Figure 8.14).

Figure 8.14   Uploading files to a datastore—vSphere Client

f. Locate the zip file on your desktop, right-click it, and click **Open**. A progress status is displayed at the bottom of the datastore browser. When the upload is completed, proceed to step 2 of this procedure.

2. Log on to the host locally via SSH as root or use vMA 6.x. You can also use vCLI on the system on which you installed the HDLM remote management client if you already installed vCLI on it earlier. When you use the HDLM remote management client, the commands are identical to what is listed here, but you need to add vCLI connection options, such as `--server`, `--username`, and `--password`, with each command you run. If your host does not have a trusted certificate (for example, self-signed), you get an error similar to this:

```
Connect    to    wdc-tse-h197.wsl.vmware.com    failed.    Server    SHA-1
thumbprint: CF:86:C8:C9:FC:F0:7A:F5:D8:5D:42:E8:FA:1C:46:77:BA:46:75:
D1 (not trusted).
```

To work around this, add `--thumbprint` or the `-d` option and use the thumbprint shown in the error.

3. Go through an installation dry run to verify if there are any problems that would result in failure to install the output, which is shown in Listing 8.8:

```
esxcli software vib install -d /vmfs/volumes/FC200/mpio/hdlm/
hdlm-0850000101-0600.zip --dry-run
```

Using the vCLI, this is the command to use:

```
esxcli -s wdc-tse-h197.wsl.vmware.com -d CF:86:C8:C9:FC:F0:7A:F5:D8:5D
:42:E8:FA:1C:46:77:BA:46:75:D1 -u root software vib install -d /vmfs/
volumes/FC200-2/plugins/hdlm/hdlm-0850000101-0600.zip --dry-run
```

You are prompted for the root user password.

This is the verbose version of this command:

```
esxcli software vib install --depot /vmfs/volumes/FC200-2/plugins/
hdlm/hdlm-0850000101-0600.zip --dry-run
```

This is the vCLI verbose option:

```
esxcli --server wdc-tse-h197.wsl.vmware.com --thumbprint CF:86:C8:C9:
FC:F0:7A:F5:D8:5D:42:E8:FA:1C:46:77:BA:46:75:D1 --user root software
vib install --depot /vmfs/volumes/FC200-2/plugins/hdlm/hdlm-
0850000101-0600.zip --dry-run
```

Listing 8.8 shows the abbreviated command and its output using the vCLI.

Listing 8.8   Dry run of installing HDLM on an ESXi host remotely by using vCLI

```
C:\>esxcli -s wdc-tse-h197.wsl.vmware.com -d CF:86:C8:C9:FC:F0:7A:F5:D8:
5D:42:E8:FA:1C:46:77:BA:46:75:D1 -u root software vib install -d /vmfs/
volumes/FC200-2/plugins/hdlm/hdlm-0850000101-0600.zip --dry-run
Enter password:
Installation Result
   Message: Dryrun only, host not changed. The following installers will be
applied: [LiveImageInstaller, BootBankInstaller]
   Reboot Required: false
   VIBs Installed: Hitachi_bootbank_hex-hdlm-dlnkmgr_08.5.0-01,
Hitachi_bootbank_psp-hdlm-exlbk_08.2.0-00, Hitachi_bootbank_psp-hdlm-
exlio_08.2.0-00, Hitachi_bootbank_psp-hdlm-exrr_08.2.0-00, Hitachi_
bootbank_satp-hdlm_08.5.0-01
   VIBs Removed:
   VIBs Skipped:

C:\>
```

Notice that the `Installation Result` section shows that Live Image Installer and Boot Bank Installer will be applied.

NOTE

Even though the dry run output shows `Reboot Required: false`, which means that rebooting the ESXi host after the installation is not required, you might actually need to reboot the host in order to have certain services be restarted. Otherwise, you can run `/sbin/services.sh restart` (only from the ESXi Shell via SSH or locally on the ESXi host), which restarts these services.

4. Repeat the command without the `--dry-run` option to install the offline bundle. Listing 8.9 shows the installation command and its output.

Listing 8.9 Installing HDLM on an ESXi host remotely by using vCLI

```
C:\>esxcli -s wdc-tse-h197.wsl.vmware.com -d CF:86:C8:C9:FC:F0:7A:F5:D8:
5D:42:E8:FA:1C:46:77:BA:46:75:D1 -u root software vib install -d /vmfs/
volumes/FC200-2/plugins/hdlm/hdlm-0850000101-0600.zip
Enter password:
Installation Result
   Message: Operation finished successfully.
   Reboot Required: false
   VIBs Installed: Hitachi_bootbank_hex-hdlm-dlnkmgr_08.5.0-01,
Hitachi_bootbank_psp-hdlm-exlbk_08.2.0-00, Hitachi_bootbank_psp-hdlm-
exlio_08.2.0-00, Hitachi_bootbank_psp-hdlm-exrr_08.2.0-00, Hitachi_
bootbank_satp-hdlm_08.5.0-01
   VIBs Removed:
   VIBs Skipped:

C:\>
```

5. Reboot the host. The installation configures the default PSP for HTI_SATP_HDLM as HTI_PSP_HDLM_EXLIO. However, the other two PSPs are available by changing the default PSP or by changing it per device.

Changes Made to the ESXi Host Configuration by the HDLM Installation

The installation makes a number of changes. First, it adds the following JumpStart scripts to the /usr/libexec/jumpstart/plugins directory:

- nmp-hti_psp_hdlm_exlbk-rules.json
- nmp-hti_psp_hdlm_exlbk.json
- nmp-hti_psp_hdlm_exlio-rules.json
- nmp-hti_psp_hdlm_exlio.json
- nmp-hti_psp_hdlm_exrr-rules.json
- nmp-hti_psp_hdlm_exrr.json
- nmp-hti_satp_hdlm-rules.json
- nmp-hti_satp_hdlm.json

These JumpStart scripts do the following:

- Scripts with the `-rules` suffix load the kernel module of the PSP/SATP at boot time.
- Scripts without the `-rules` suffix register the plug-in with the PSA framework.

The installation process registers the modules listed in Table 8.1 as plug-ins.

Table 8.1 HDLM plug-ins list

Module	Plug-in	Plug-in Class
`hti_satp_hdlm`	HTI_SATP_HDLM	SATP
`hti_psp_hdlm_exlbk`	HTI_PSP_HDLM_EXLBK	PSP
`hti_psp_hdlm_exlio`	HTI_PSP_HDLM_EXLIO	PSP
`hti_psp_hdlm_exrr`	HTI_PSP_HDLM_EXRR	PSP

Figure 8.15 shows the `esxcli storage core plugin registration list` command that is used to list the registered plug-ins. In addition, upon reboot, JumpStart scripts without the `-rules` suffix run the equivalents to the commands shown in Listing 8.10.

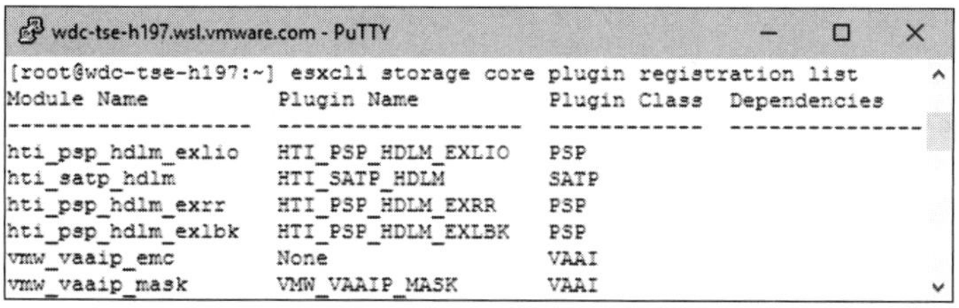

Figure 8.15 Listing HDLM PSA plug-ins registration

Listing 8.10 Commands run by PowerPath JumpStart scripts

```
esxcli storage core plugin registration add --module-name=hti_satp_hdlm
--plugin-class=SATP - --plugin-name=HTI_SATP_HDLM

esxcli storage core plugin registration add --module-name=hti_psp_hdlm_
exlbk --plugin-class=PSP --plugin-name=HTI_PSP_HDLM_EXLBK

esxcli storage core plugin registration add --module-name=hti_psp_hdlm_
exlio --plugin-class=PSP --plugin-name=HTI_PSP_HDLM_EXLIO

esxcli storage core plugin registration add --module-name=hti_psp_hdlm_exrr
--plugin-class=PSP --plugin-name=HTI_PSP_HDLM_EXRR
```

The s configures HTI_PSP_HDLM_EXLIO as the default PSP for SATP HTI_SATP_HDLM. Figure 8.16 shows how to verify the default PSP by using this command:

```
esxcli storage nmp satp list
```

```
[root@wdc-tse-h197:~] esxcli storage nmp satp list
Name                    Default PSP          Description
--------------------    -------------------  ------------------------------
HTI_SATP_HDLM           HTI_PSP_HDLM_EXLIO   Supports Hitachi arrays.
VMW_SATP_ALUA_CX        VMW_PSP_RR           Supports EMC CX that use the
VMW_SATP_ALUA           VMW_PSP_MRU          Supports non-specific arrays
VMW_SATP_MSA            VMW_PSP_MRU          Placeholder (plugin not loade
```

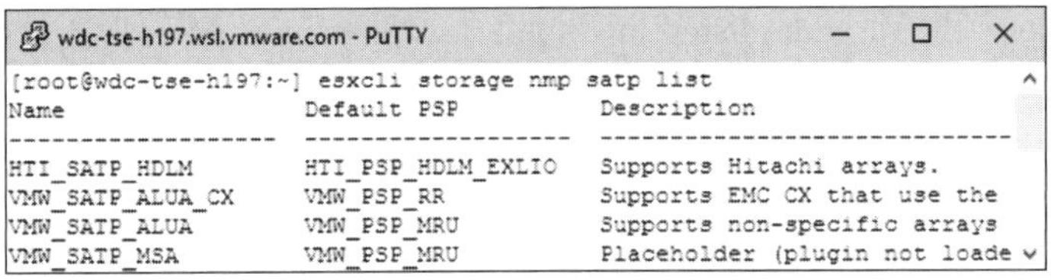

Figure 8.16   HDLM SATP default configuration

The default PSP configuration is also done upon reboot by the JumpStart script `nmp-hti_satp_hdlm-rules.json`, which runs the equivalent to the following command:

```
esxcli storage nmp satp set --satp HTI_SATP_HDLM --default-psp HTI_PSP_HDLM_EXLIO
```

The installation adds three SATP rules, which associate HTI_SATP_HDLM with the vendors and model strings listed in Table 8.2 and verified in Figure 8.17.

Table 8.2 Vendor and model strings used by HDLM claim rules

Vendor String	Model String
HITACHI	DF600F
HITACHI	^OPEN-*
HP	^OPEN-*

The model strings in Table 8.2 represent Hitachi AMS, VSP, and HP P9000 families, respectively. For the list of the supported array makes and models, check the VMware HCL.

Figure 8.17 shows a list of SATP claim rules for HTI_SATP_HDLM, using this command:

```
esxcli storage nmp satp rule list --satp HTI_SATP_HDLM| less -S
```

```
[root@wdc-tse-h197:~] esxcli storage nmp satp rule list --satp HTI_SATP_HDLM |less -S
Name            Device  Vendor   Model      Driver  Transport  Options  Rule Group  Clai
-------------   ------  -------  ---------  ------  ---------  -------  ----------  ----
HTI_SATP_HDLM           HITACHI  ^DF600F*                               user
HTI_SATP_HDLM           HITACHI  ^OPEN-*                                user
HTI_SATP_HDLM           HP       ^OPEN-*                                user
```

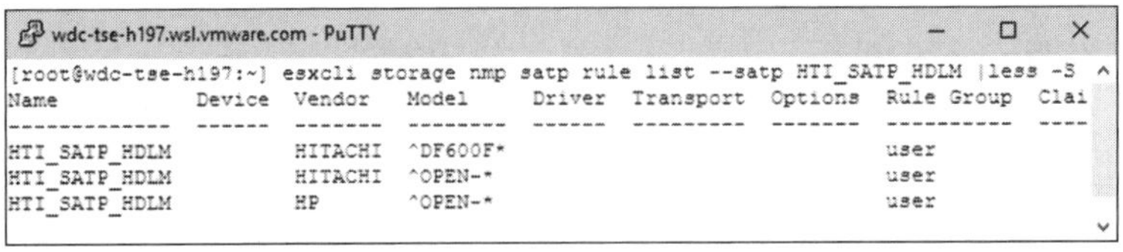

Figure 8.17   HDLM SATP rules

This means that storage arrays that return the vendor string `HITACHI` and the model string `DF600F` or `^OPEN-*` are claimed by the HTI_SATP_HDLM plug-in. The third row in the table and output means that storage arrays that return the vendor string `HP` and return the model string `^OPEN-*` are also claimed by the same SATP.

The wildcards used in the model string `^OPEN-*` cover all model strings that end with `OPEN` and a hyphen followed by any value (for example, `OPEN-V`).

Adding the same three rules is also done upon reboot by the JumpStart script `nmp-hti_satp_hdlm-rules.json`, which runs the equivalent to the commands in Listing 8.11.

Listing 8.11   Commands run by the `nmp_hti_satp_hdlm-rules.json` JumpStart script

```
esxcli storage nmp satp rule add --satp HTI_SATP_HDLM --vendor HITACHI
--model DF600F

esxcli storage nmp satp rule add --satp HTI_SATP_HDLM --vendor HITACHI
--model ^OPEN-*

esxcli storage nmp satp rule add --satp HTI_SATP_HDLM --vendor HP --model
^OPEN-*
```

Modifying HDLM PSP Assignments

Because you can have only one default PSP per SATP, you can assign different PSPs on a per-device basis. For example, say that you have three different LUNs on a Hitachi Adaptable Modular Storage (AMS) array that are presented to a set of ESXi 6.x hosts. These hosts have been configured with the HDLM plug-ins. Each of the three LUNs has different I/O requirements that match one of the three installed HDLM PSPs. You can configure each LUN to be claimed by the PSP that matches the desired I/O criteria. This can be done via the vSphere Client, the CLI, or the HDLM remote management client (see the section "Obtaining Installation Files," earlier in this chapter). The HDLM remote management client has its own CLI and is used to manage HDLM for VMware remotely. Using it is sort of like using vMA or vCLI to manage ESXi 6.x remotely.

Changing PSP Assignment by Using the UI

To change the PSP assignment by using the UI, follow this procedure:

1. Follow steps 1 through 8 in the section "Listing Paths to a LUN by Using the UI" in Chapter 5.

2. Select the desired PSP from the **Path Selection** pull-down menu (see Figure 8.18).

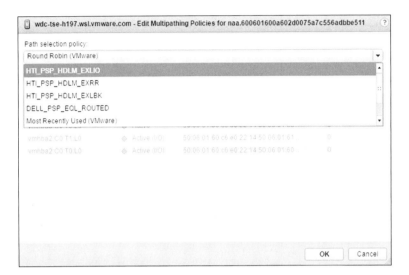

Figure 8.18 Modifying the HDLM PSP assignment—vSphere Client

3. Click **OK** to apply the changes and close the dialog.

4. Repeat steps 1 through 3 for each LUN, using the PSP that matches its I/O characteristics.

5. Repeat steps 1 through 3 for the same set of LUNs on all ESXi 6.x hosts sharing them. Make sure to use the same PSP for a given LUN on all hosts.

Changing PSP Assignment by Using the CLI

To change the PSP assignment by using the CLI, follow this procedure:

1. Log on to the ESXi 6.x host locally or via SSH as root or using vMA 6.x as vi-admin. You can also use vCLI on Windows or Linux.

2. Identify the device ID for each LUN you want to reconfigure:

```
esxcfg-mpath -b |grep -B1 "fc Adapter"| grep -v -e "--" |sed 's/
Adapter.*//'
```

This is the verbose version of the command:

```
esxcfg-mpath --list-paths |grep -B1 "fc Adapter"| grep -v -e "--" |sed
's/Adapter.*//'
```

Figure 8.19 displays the output of this command.

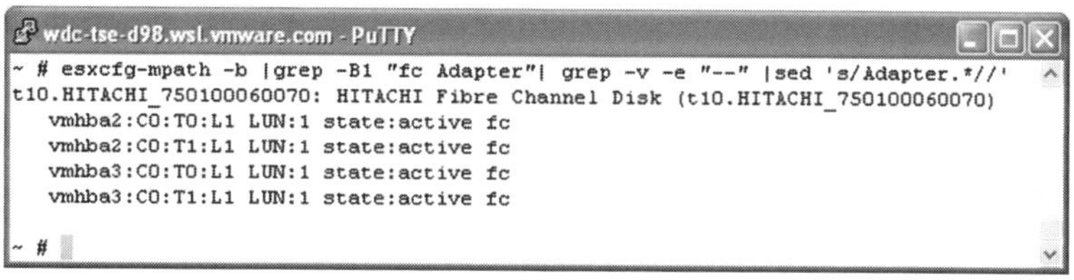

Figure 8.19 Listing a device ID on an AMS array

In this output, you can identify the device ID (in this case, it is the `t10`). Note that this output was collected using an AMS array. Universal Storage Platform V (USP V), USP VM, or Virtual Storage Platform (VSP) would show `naa` as the ID instead, as shown in Figure 8.20.

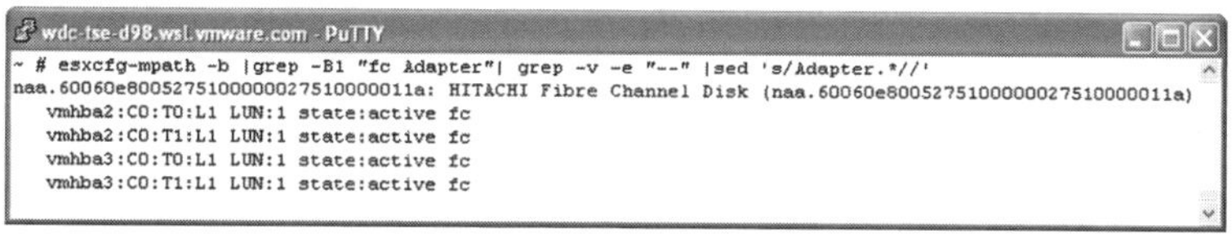

Figure 8.20 Listing a device ID on a USP array

3. Using the device ID you identified in step 2, run this command:

```
esxcli storage nmp device set --device=<device-id> --psp=<psp-name>
```

Here is an example for an AMS LUN:

```
esxcli storage nmp device set --device=t10.HITACHI_750100060070
--psp=HTI_PSP_HDLM_EXLIO
```

Here is an example for a VSP LUN:

```
esxcli storage nmp device set --device=naa.60060e8005275100000027510000
0011a --psp=HTI_PSP_HDLM_EXLIO
```

4. Repeat steps 2 and 3 for each device.

NOTE

HTI_SATP_HDLM has been tested, certified, and supported for use with VMW_PSP_MRU. See the section "Locating Certified Storage on the VMware HCL," later in this chapter.

Changing the Default PSP

If the I/O on most of your HDLM-managed LUNs is characterized such that they would benefit from using one of the HDLM PSPs other than the default one, it is advisable to change the default PSP and then modify the exception LUNs to use a suitable one.

For example, if you have 100 LUNs whose I/O would benefit from using HTI_PSP_ HDLM_EXLBK and 5 LUNs that would be more suited to use HTI_PSP_HDLM_ EXLIO (which is the current default), you might opt to change the default PSP to the former and then change the five LUNs to use the latter.

To change the default PSP, you can use the following command:

```
esxcli storage nmp satp set --satp HTI_SATP_HDLM --default-psp HTI_PSP_
HDLM_EXLBK
```

If you want to set the default PSP to be HTI_PSP_HDLM_EXRR instead, simply replace the last parameter in the command with that PSP name.

> **NOTE**
>
> If you had manually set certain LUNs to a specific PSP previously, the `esxcli storage nmp satp set` command does not affect that setting.
>
> To reset such a LUN to use the current default PSP, use the following command:
>
> ```
> esxcli storage nmp device set --device=<device-ID> --default
> ```
>
> Here is an example:
>
> ```
> esxcli storage nmp device set --device=naa.6006016055711d00cef95e65664
> ee011 --default
> ```

Locating Certified Storage on the VMware HCL

To locate arrays certified with HDLM on the VMware HCL, follow this procedure:

1. Go to **www.vmware.com/go/hcl** (see Figure 8.21).

2. Select **Storage/SAN** from the What Are You Looking For pull-down menu.

3. In the Product Release Version field, select **ESXi 6.5** or earlier 6.0 versions.

4. In the Partner Name field, select the storage vendor's name, such as **Hitachi** or **Hitachi Data Systems (HDS)**.

5. In the SATP Plugin field, select **HTI_SATP_HDLM v08.5.0-00** or the version you are installing.

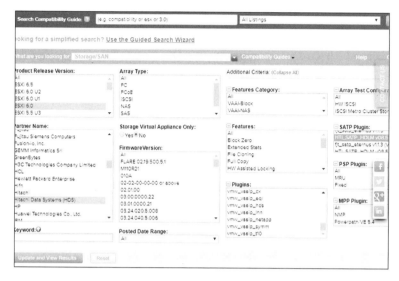

Figure 8.21 HCL search criteria for HDLM

6. Click the **Update and View Results** button.

7. Scroll down to see the list of certified arrays, as shown in Figure 8.22.

Figure 8.22 HCL search results for HDLM

8. Click the hyperlink of the storage array model (for example, **Hitachi Virtual Storage Platform**) listed in the Model column to see the details.

9. Locate the row where the SATP Plugin column lists the version you are installing— for example, **HTI_SATP_HDLM v08.2.0-00**.

10. Look in the PSP Plugin column for the certified PSP plug-ins. In this example (see Figure 8.23), all three HDLM PSP plug-ins are listed, along with VMW_PSP_MRU. This means that you are free to use any combination of HTI_SATP_HDLM and any of the listed PSPs.

```
HTI_SATP_HDLM v08.2.0-00  HTI_PSP_HDLM_EXLBK
                          v08.2.0-00,
                          HTI_PSP_HDLM_EXLIO
                          v08.2.0-00,
                          HTI_PSP_HDLM_EXRR
                          v08.2.0-00
```

Figure 8.23   HCL product details of HDLM listing

Dell EqualLogic PSP Routed

Dell's EqualLogic MPIO is implemented as a PSP. It also includes an additional component that runs in the user world: the EqualLogic Host Connection Manager (EHCM). It is actually designed as a CIM provider. Its main function is to manage iSCSI (Internet Small Computer System Interface) sessions to the EqualLogic array.

Downloading Documentation

You can download the reference document "Dell EqualLogic Multipathing Extension Module Installation and User's Guide Version 1.4" from `https://eqlsupport.dell.com/support/download_file.aspx?id=3236`. On that page, click the **Download** button to obtain the file 110-6267-EN_MEM_Users_Guide_web.pdf.

NOTE

Dell Support account access credentials are required to access the Dell EqualLogic URLs listed in this chapter.

NOTE

Most of the content presented in the following sections is based on the linked Dell document and my own hands-on experience.

Downloading the Installation File and the Setup Script

To download the installation file and the setup script in one zip file, you need to have a valid login account at EQL support site. The download area is at https://support.equallogic.com/support/download.aspx?id=1484.

At that URL, select the link under the Recommended Multipathing Extension Module for VMware vSphere section. At this writing, the available version is 1.4.

How Does EQL MEM Work?

The PSP has knowledge of how the PS series volumes are distributed over the PS group members. It has a map of the physical location of data on the volumes and utilizes that map to provide I/O load balancing.

The EHCM creates sessions to the EqualLogic volumes based on the SAN topology and the PSP settings (on each ESXi host). It creates two sessions per volume slice (the portion of the volume residing on a single member of the PS series group). The maximum number of sessions per volume (the combination of sessions for all volume slices) is six. This is configurable via the EqualLogic Host Connection Manager (EHCM) configuration file.

Figure 8.24 shows the Dell EqualLogic PSP architecture.

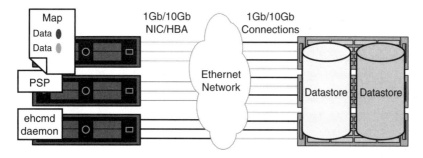

Figure 8.24 Dell EqualLogic PSP architecture

Installing EQL MEM on vSphere 6

The zip file you downloaded from the EqualLogic download site includes the following:

- **setup.pl**—You use this PERL script on vMA to install EQL MEM on ESXi hosts and to configure the iSCSI network on the ESXi 6 host, including configuring jumbo frames.

- **dell-eql-mem-<ESX version>-<version>.zip**—You use this for installing via VUM or the local CLI.

348

Installing EQL MEM by Using the CLI

The following steps show the installation process using the local CLI, which is identical to using vMA 6.x after you set the managed target host to the ESXi 6.x host on which you will install the VIB:

1. Copy the downloaded zip file to a VMFS volume shared by all hosts on which you plan to install this VIB. You can use a tool like WinSCP to transfer the file.

2. Log on to the ESXi 6.x host directly or via SSH as root.

3. Expand the zip file to obtain the setup.pl script as well as the offline bundle:

```
cd /vmfs/volume/<datastore-name>
unzip <downloaded-file>.zip
```

4. Run the installation command, as shown in see Figure 8.25 is:

```
esxcli software vib install --depo /[path to zip file]
```

```
[root@wdc-tse-h197:~] esxcli software vib install --depot /vmfs/volumes/FC200-2/EQL/EqualLogic
-ESX-Multipathing-Module/dell-eql-mem-esx6-1.4.0.426823.zip
Installation Result
   Message: Operation finished successfully.
   Reboot Required: false
   VIBs Installed: Dell_bootbank_dell-eql-host-connection-mgr_1.4.0-426823, Dell_bootbank_dell
-eql-hostprofile_1.4.0-426823, Dell_bootbank_dell-eql-routed-psp_1.4.0-426823
   VIBs Removed:
   VIBs Skipped:
[root@wdc-tse-h197:~]
```

Figure 8.25 Installing the Dell EQL PSP

Notice that the output states that `Reboot Required` is `false`. However, hosts should still be rebooted after installation is done.

Installing EQL MEM by Using vMA

The downloaded zip file includes the setup.pl script, which can be used to install EQL MEM on one or more ESXi hosts managed by vMA. The following process assumes that you had already added ESXi hosts as managed targets on the vMA appliance. Follow these steps to install EQL MEM:

1. Transfer the zip file to vMA (for example, on vi-admin's home directory).

2. Log on to vMA 6.x as vi-admin.

3. Expand the zip file by using the following:

```
unzip <downloaded-file>.zip
```

4. Navigate to the extracted directory, which includes setup.pl and two installation zip files.

5. Add the executable bit to the script file:

```
chmod +x setup.pl
```

6. Run the installation command:

```
./setup.pl --install --server=<hostname> [--bundle=<filename>]
```

Here is an example:

```
./setup.pl --install --server=wdc-tse-h197.wsl.vmware.com --bundle=
dell-eql-mem-esx6-1.4.0.426823.zip
```

Figure 8.26 shows this command and its output.

```
10.131.10.43 - PuTTY                                                    —    □    ×
vi-admin@vma65:~/EqualLogic-ESX-Multipathing-Module> ./setup.pl --install --server=wdc-tse-h197.ws
1-mem-esx6-1.4.0.426823.zip
Clean install of Dell EqualLogic Multipathing Extension Module.
        Bundle being installed dell-eql-mem-esx6-1.4.0.426823.zip
Copying dell-eql-mem-esx6-1.4.0.426823.zip to [datastore1]/dell-eql-mem-esx6-1.4.0.426823.zip
The install operation may take several minutes.  Please do not interrupt it.
        Check to see if the install succeeded
Found Dell EqualLogic Multipathing Extension bundle installed: 1.4.0-426823
        Install succeeded
Clean install was successful.
vi-admin@vma65:~/EqualLogic-ESX-Multipathing-Module>
```

Figure 8.26   Installing EQL MEM—vMA

7. Reboot the host:

```
vifptarget set <host-name>
esxcfg-hostops --operation reboot
```

A successful result returns the following:

```
Host <host-name> rebooted successfully.
```

Changes Made to the ESXi Host Configuration by the MEM Installation

The MEM installation makes a number of changes. First, it installs three VIBs:

- `dell-eql-routed-psp`
- `dell-eql-host-connection-mgr`
- `dell-eql-hostprofile`

The installation also registers the module `dell-psp-eql-routed` as the plug-in DELL_PSP_EQL_ROUTED (see Figure 8.27).

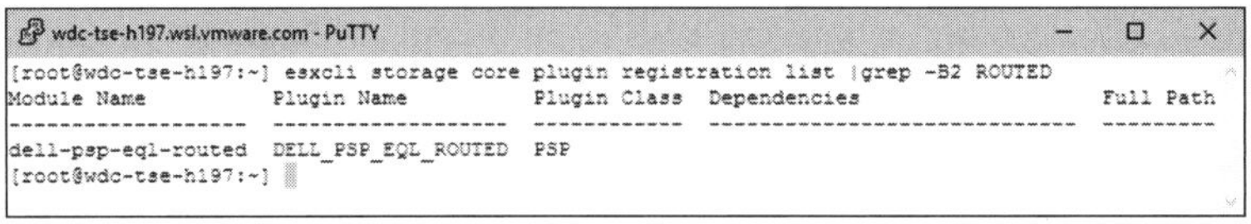

```
[root@wdc-tse-h197:~] esxcli storage core plugin registration list |grep -B2 ROUTED
Module Name          Plugin Name          Plugin Class  Dependencies                    Full Path
-------------------  -------------------  ------------  ------------------------------  ---------
dell-psp-eql-routed  DELL_PSP_EQL_ROUTED  PSP
[root@wdc-tse-h197:~]
```

Figure 8.27 Dell EQL PSP registration

The PSP registration is also done upon host reboot by the JumpStart script `psp-eql.json`, which runs the equivalent to this command:

```
esxcli storage core plugin registration add --module-name=dell-psp-eql-
routed --plugin-class=PSP --plugin-name=DELL_PSP_EQL_ROUTED
```

The installation configures DELL_PSP_EQL_ROUTED as the default PSP for SATP VMW_SATP_EQL (see Figure 8.28).

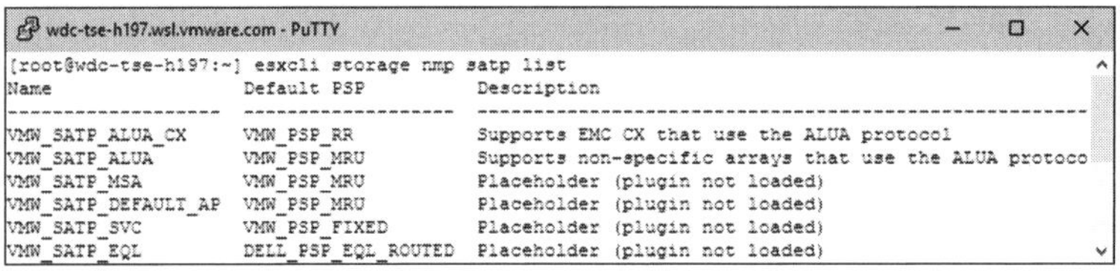

```
[root@wdc-tse-h197:~] esxcli storage nmp satp list
Name                 Default PSP          Description
-------------------  -------------------  -------------------------------------------------------
VMW_SATP_ALUA_CX     VMW_PSP_RR           Supports EMC CX that use the ALUA protocol
VMW_SATP_ALUA        VMW_PSP_MRU          Supports non-specific arrays that use the ALUA protoco
VMW_SATP_MSA         VMW_PSP_MRU          Placeholder (plugin not loaded)
VMW_SATP_DEFAULT_AP  VMW_PSP_MRU          Placeholder (plugin not loaded)
VMW_SATP_SVC         VMW_PSP_FIXED        Placeholder (plugin not loaded)
VMW_SATP_EQL         DELL_PSP_EQL_ROUTED  Placeholder (plugin not loaded)
```

Figure 8.28 Default Dell EQL PSP for EQL SATP

The default PSP is also set upon reboot by the JumpStart script `psp-eql-load.json`, which runs the equivalent to this command:

```
esxcli storage nmp satp set --satp=VMW_SATP_EQL --default-psp=DELL_PSP_EQL_
ROUTED
```

The installation adds the `equallogic` namespace to `esxcli`. Figure 8.29 shows that namespace's command-line help.

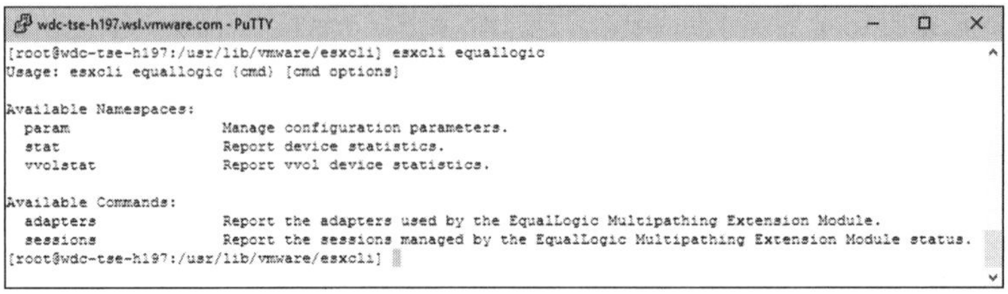

```
[root@wdc-tse-h197:/usr/lib/vmware/esxcli] esxcli equallogic
Usage: esxcli equallogic {cmd} [cmd options]

Available Namespaces:
  param                 Manage configuration parameters.
  stat                  Report device statistics.
  vvolstat              Report vvol device statistics.

Available Commands:
  adapters              Report the adapters used by the EqualLogic Multipathing Extension Module.
  sessions              Report the sessions managed by the EqualLogic Multipathing Extension Module status.
[root@wdc-tse-h197:/usr/lib/vmware/esxcli]
```

Figure 8.29 Listing `esxcli equallogic` namespace options

Uninstalling the Dell PSP EQL Routed MEM

To uninstall the VIBs by using local CLI, follow these steps:

1. Get the VIB name from the installed VIBs list (see Figure 8.30):

```
esxcli software vib list |grep eql
```

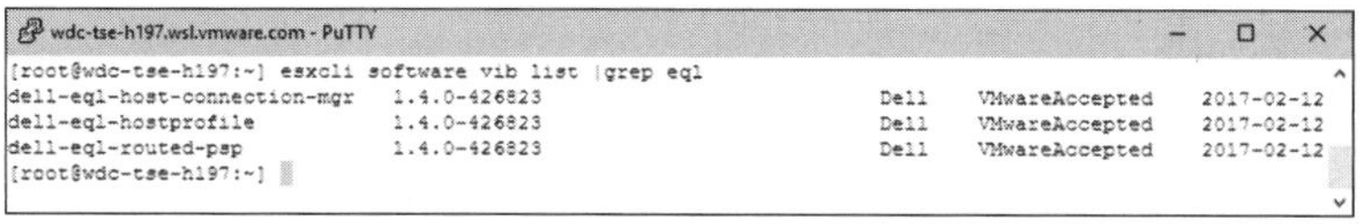

Figure 8.30   Listing installed Dell EQL PSP VIB

2. Remove the VIB by using the following command:

```
esxcli software vib remove --vibname=dell-eql-routed-psp --vibname=
dell-eql-hostprofile --vibname=dell-eql-host-connection-mgr
```

Listing 8.12 shows the outcome of this command.

Listing 8.12   Removing EQL VIBs—local CLI

```
Removal Result
    Message: The update completed successfully, but the system needs to be
rebooted for the changes to be effective.
    Reboot Required: true
    VIBs Installed:
    VIBs Removed: Dell_bootbank_dell-eql-host-connection-mgr_1.4.0-426823,
Dell_bootbank_dell-eql-hostprofile_1.4.0-426823, Dell_bootbank_dell-eql-
routed-psp_1.4.0-426823
    VIBs Skipped:
```

3. Reboot the host.

4. Verify that the host was removed by using the following command:

```
esxcli software vib list |grep eql
```

This command should return a blank output.

To uninstall the VIBs by using vMA with the sctup.pl script, follow this procedure:

1. Log on to vMA as vi-admin.

2. Navigate to the directory where seup.pl was extracted.

3. Run the following command:

```
./setup.pl --remove --server=<host-name>
```

Listing 8.13 shows this command and its output

Listing 8.13   Removing EQL VIBs using setup.pl—vMA

```
./setup.pl --remove --server=wdc-tse-h197.wsl.vmware.com
Uninstalling existing Dell EqualLogic Multipathing Extension Module: 1.4.0-
426823.
Package removed successfully.
You must reboot the host to complete the operation.
```

4. Reboot the host:

```
vifptarget set <host-name>
esxcfg-hostops --operation reboot
```

A successful result returns the following:

```
Host <host-name> rebooted successfully.
```

Summary

VMware partners have developed MPIO software for use on ESXi 6.x. This chapter covers three of these products, from Dell EMC, Hitachi Data Systems, and Dell EqualLogic. It provides details about installing these MPIO software packages and the changes they make to the ESXi host.

## Chapter 9

Using Heterogeneous Storage Configurations

People often ask me, "Can I mix different storage arrays in my vSphere environment?"

The short answer is "yes!" This chapter explains why and how.

vSphere 6, as well as earlier releases, support a maximum of 1,024 paths to storage while vSphere 6.5 doubled that to 2048 paths (refer to Chapter 7, "Multipathing and Failover"). This maximum number of paths is the combined paths to all devices presented to the ESXi 6 host from all storage arrays, including local storage and direct attached storage.

What Is a "Heterogeneous" Storage Environment?

As the word *heterogeneous* indicates, a heterogeneous storage environment is an environment that uses different arrays–different vendors, models, and protocols. You can use a mix of storage array models from the same vendor or from multiple vendors. You can also mix Internet Small Computer System Interface (iSCSI) and Fibre Channel (FC)–but not for the same device from the same array via the same host. In other words, you must not access a given device (logical unit number [LUN]) via different protocols on the same array from the same host.

> **NOTE**
>
> Network-attached storage (NAS) is one of the classes of storage you can use in a heterogeneous storage environment. However, its effect on resources needed by existing block devices is minimal. This chapter deals with block devices only.

Heterogeneous Storage Scenarios

The most common scenario for using heterogeneous storage is simply *storage sprawl*. Say that you start with a storage array from a given vendor and later outgrow it. You then add more storage from whatever is available at the time. You might get a deal you cannot refuse from another storage vendor that would provide faster, larger, and more modern storage. You have four choices:

- Install the new storage array and migrate your data from the old array. This is a waste of resources if your old array still has enough juice in it and you still have a valid maintenance agreement with the old array's vendor.

- Keep your old data in place and just add the new array. This sounds like getting the best of both worlds! Well, maybe. It depends on the class of storage of your old array, its age, and the type and speed of storage connectivity compared to the new array. Does your old array still perform and meet your current applications' service level agreements (SLAs)?

- If the array provides a *storage virtualization* feature, present your old array's LUNs to the ESXi hosts as virtual LUNs on the new array and add new physical LUNs on the new array for the additional storage your hosts need. I cover this topic in Chapter 11, "Storage Virtualization Devices (SVDs)," but to give you a basic idea, this feature allows the new array to act as an initiator to the old arrays to which you present the LUNs from the old arrays. The SVD then presents the physical LUNs from the old array as virtual LUNs to your ESXi hosts. This configuration takes advantage of the features available from the new array as if the virtual LUNs were actually located physically on the SVD.

- Some storage vendors might not provide the ability to directly import the data from the virtualized LUNs. This is the case, for example, with SVDs presenting back-end block devices as the Network File System (NFS). In such a case, you need to create NFS shares on the virtualized LUNs. The hosts do not see these LUN but see only the NFS datastores created on them by the SVD.

Another scenario for using heterogeneous storage is designing a storage environment to serve as *tiered* storage. vSphere 6 provides Storage DRS, which automates migration of virtual machine files from one datastore to another within a group of datastores that share similar capabilities.

In this scenario, you integrate either a mix of storage arrays of varying storage classes or storage arrays of the same model with varying storage classes. vSphere 6 provides a storage API referred to as *VASA*, which stands for vSphere APIs for Storage Awareness. This API enables storage array vendors to report certain physical device capabilities–including RAID type and types of disks backing LUNs presented to ESXi hosts–to vCenter. This scenario may include storage arrays from the same vendor or multiple vendors of varying classes and storage capabilities. For example, you might mix EMC VMAX/Symmetrix arrays with EMC CLARiiON/VNX arrays and IBM DS4000 arrays. These arrays might utilize physical disks of the following types:

- SSD
- FC SCSI
- FC SAS
- Copper SCSI
- Copper SAS
- Copper SATA

Each type is categorized in a storage tier, and you present LUNs backed by each tier to ESXi hosts within their relevant applications' SLAs.

NOTE

Newer models of most storage arrays provide automatic tiering features that would be a good substitute for this design if you no longer need your old storage arrays.

ESXi 6 View of Heterogeneous Storage

In Chapter 7, I explained multipathing, and in Chapters 2, "Fibre Channel Storage Connectivity," 3, "FCoE Storage Connectivity," and 4, "iSCSI Storage Connectivity," I explained initiators and targets. The following sections show you how to apply these concepts to help identify how ESXi 6 hosts *see* the various storage arrays in a heterogeneous environment.

Basic Rules of Using Heterogeneous Storage

There is a set of basic rules to observe when designing a heterogeneous storage environment. These rules can be organized in three groups: common rules, FC/FCoE rules, and iSCSI rules.

These are the common rules:

- Each storage array may have more than one storage processor.
- Each storage processor may have more than one port.

- Each LUN has a unique device ID.

- The total number of paths is limited to 1,024 per host, which includes paths to locally attached devices.

These are the FC/FCoE rules:

- Each initiator (HBA port on the ESXi host) is zoned to certain SP ports on *all* relevant storage arrays in the environment.

- VMkernel assigns a target number to each SP port *seen* by each initiator as a unique target number.

These are the iSCSI rules:

- Some iSCSI storage arrays present each LUN on a unique target, which means the number of targets on the array is equal to the number of LUNs presented from that array. An example of this is the Dell EqualLogic PS series.

- iSCSI software initiators can be bound to physical uplink ports (vmnics) on vSphere 6 virtual switches. This was possible with vSphere 4.x but was done manually. vSphere 5 and 6 have a UI to configure port binding. A given ESXi 6 host may have multiple hardware iSCSI initiators or a single software iSCSI initiator. The latter can be bound to certain uplink ports.

Naming Conventions

As I mentioned in Chapter 7, each path to a given LUN is identified by its runtime name or by its full pathname. The *runtime name* is the combination of vmhba number, channel number, target number, and LUN–for example, vmhba0:C0:T1:L5. The *full pathname* is the combination of the same elements, using their physical IDs (and not including the channel number). For example, here is how you translate fc.20000000c971bc62:10000000c971bc62-fc.50060160 c6e00304:5006016046e00304-naa.60060160403029005a59381bc161e011:

- **fc.20000000c971bc62:10000000c971bc62**–This is the HBA's WWNN:WWPN. It is represented in the runtime name by vmhba0.

- **fc.50060160c6e00304:5006016046e00304**–This is the Target WWNN:WWPN. It is the SP port represented in the runtime name by target number T1.

- **naa.60060160403029005a59381bc161e011**–This is the LUN's device ID. It is represented in the runtime name by LUN 5.

iSCSI devices are addressed in a similar manner but using the iSCSI qualified names (IQNs) instead of FC worldwide node names (WWNNs) and worldwide port names (WWPNs). LUN (device) IDs of iSCSI LUNs are similar to those of FC LUNs.

How Does All This Fit Together?

All physical identifiers in the same storage area network (SAN) are unique. When each of two different storage arrays presents one LUN to an ESXi host, using the same LUN number, each LUN has a unique device ID. As a result, ESXi 6 does not confuse the two LUNs as being the same LUN. The same is true for target port IDs.

Let's make the trip from a given initiator to LUN 5 on each array, using the runtime name elements first and then the physical pathname elements.

Here is an example of an FC LUN's runtime name: vmhba2:C0:T1:L5. In this example, the first hop is the HBA on the host, which is named vmhba2.

The next hop is the switch. The final hope is the target. (The channel can be ignored for now because it is always zero for HBAs other than internal RAID controllers.) In this case, the target is assigned number 1. This value does not persist between reboots because it is assigned based on the order in which the targets are enumerated by the host. That order is based on the order of discovering these targets at boot time and during rescanning. The switch port ID to which the target is connected into the FC fabric affects that order of discovery.

To better illustrate that concept, let me take you through a set of FC cabling diagrams, starting with a simple one (see Figure 9.1) and then gradually building up to a more complex environment.

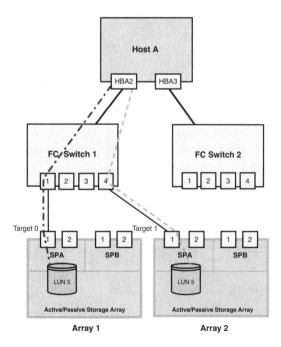

Figure 9.1   Target numbers in a simple configuration

Figure 9.1 shows the connections between HBA2 on Host A and LUN 5 on Array 1 and LUN 5 on Array 2 via FC Switch 1. Array 1 connects to port 1 on Switch 1, and Array 2 connects to Switch 1 on port 4. As a result, because these are the only targets discovered by Host A, the port on Array 1 is assigned target 0, whereas the port on Array 2 is assigned target 1.

> **NOTE**
>
> Figure 9.1 is oversimplified to illustrate the point. In this case, Switch 2 is not connected to either storage array.

When you realize that the SAN connectivity is vulnerable to storage processors' port failure, you ask the SAN administrator to add redundant connections to the second SP on each storage array. Figure 9.2 shows the result of this change.

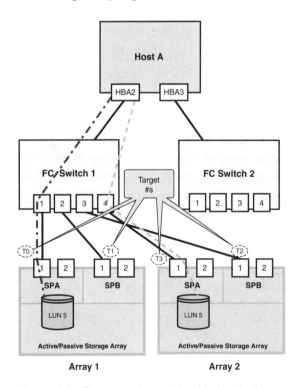

Figure 9.2   Target numbers with added paths from one switch

What the SAN administrator did here is connect ports 2 and 3 on Switch 1 to Array 1 SPB port 1 and Array 2 SPB port 1.

Now the order of target discovery upon booting Host A causes what was previously known as target 1 to change to target 3 because the targets connected to ports 2 and 3 of Switch 1 are assigned target numbers 1 and 2, respectively. (Target numbers are listed in dotted black rectangles in Figure 9.2.)

While checking Host A configurations, you notice that HBA3 is connected to the fabric but does not see any targets. You check with the SAN administrator, who tells you that this switch was added recently and connected to the hosts, but no connections to the storage array have been made yet. You request that FC Switch 2 be connected to both storage arrays, with redundant connections to both SP on each array. Figure 9.3 shows the result of these changes.

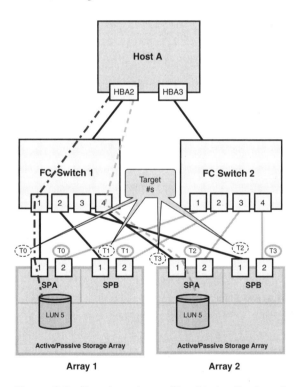

Figure 9.3   Target numbers with added paths from the second switch

How would the host see the newly added targets?

From the perspective of HBA3, they are actually numbered in a similar order, starting with target 0 through target 3. (To differentiate from HBA2's targets, the target numbers are shown in solid ovals in Figure 9.3.)

Table 9.1 summarizes the target enumeration order.

Table 9.1 Order of target enumeration

HBA Number	Switch Number	Switch Port	Storage Array	Target Port	Active SP?	Target Number
2	1	1	1	SPA-1	Yes	0
		2	1	SPB-1	No	1
		3	2	SPB-1	No	2
		4	2	SPA-1	Yes	3
3	2	1	1	SPA-2	Yes	0
		2	1	SPB-2	No	1
		3	2	SPA-2	Yes	2
		4	2	SPB-2	No	3

The best practice is symbolized as A-B/A-B. This means that the order of connection is to a port on SPA and then a port on SPB on each storage array.

With that in mind, it should be obvious from Table 9.1 that connections from FC Switch 1 ports 3 and 4 to Storage Array 2 are reversed compared to the rest of the connections.

How would the target order affect the runtime names of LUN 5 on each storage array? Note that I did not include the LUNs in the table because this applies to all LUNs presented from each array. You just add the LUN at the end of each path, as I show you next.

Let's use Table 9.1 to walk the first path discovered to LUN 5 on Array 1 active SP:

HBA2 → target 0 → LUN 5

Here's how you do the same for LUN 5 on Array 2 active SP:

HBA2 → target 3 → LUN 5

Based on this, the runtime names for LUN 5 on each array (after rebooting Host A) would be as follows:

vmhba2:C0:T0:L5 for LUN 5 on array 1

vmhba2:C0:T3:L5 for LUN 5 on array 2

> **NOTE**
>
> The runtime name is based on the first target on which the LUN returns a READY state, which is the first path available from the initiators to the active SP.

Why doesn't the runtime name use paths on HBA3 in this example?

The reason is that at boot time, the LUNs are discovered on HBA2 first because it was the first HBA to be initialized by the HBA's driver.

Here is the full list paths to LUN 5 on Array 1:

> vmhba2:C0:T0:L5 active (the current path)
>
> vmhba2:C0:T1:L5 standby
>
> vmhba3:C0:T0:L5 active
>
> vmhba3:C0:T1:L5 standby

And here is the list of paths to LUN 5 on Array 2:

> vmhba2:C0:T2:L5 standby
>
> vmhba2:C0:T3:L5 active (the current path)
>
> vmhba3:C0:T2:L5 active
>
> vmhba3:C0:T3:L5 standby

Observe that the path to the active SP for the current path is the second path in the ordered list for LUN 5 on Array 2. This matches the observations from Table 9.1.

Let's get back to our scenario. Based on your observations, you ask the SAN administrator to swap ports 3 and 4 on FC Switch 1 to meet best practices. The next time you reboot this host, the targets are renumbered as shown in Figure 9.4.

Why Do We Care? Should We Care at All?

In releases earlier than vSphere 4.x, target numbers were critical to certain functions because the only canonical (currently known as runtime) naming of LUNs and paths to them was done via the combination of HBAs, targets, and LUNs. vSphere 4.x introduced a new naming convention using physical IDs of the same three components (HBA, target, and LUN). This continues to be the case in vSphere 5 and 6.

So, to illustrate the naming in vSphere 4.x and later, let's take a look at LUN 5 from Array 1 (on an EMC CLARiiON): fc.20000000c971bc62:10000000c971bc62-fc.50060160 c6e00304:5006016046e00304-naa.60060160403029005959381bc161e011.

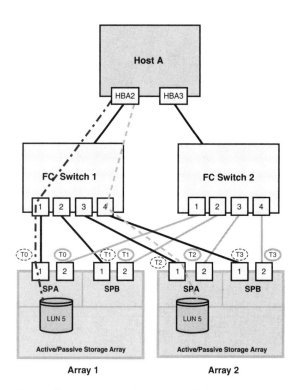

Figure 9.4   Best-practices connectivity

Table 9.2 shows how to substitute the element names.

Table 9.2 Naming convention comparison

Element	Old Name	New Name
HBA number	vmhba2	fc.20000000c971bc62:10000000c971bc62
Target number	T0	fc.50060160c6e00304:5006016046e00304
LUN	L5	naa.600601604030290059593381bc161e011

See the "Naming Conventions" section, earlier in this chapter, for further explanation.

Now that you understand the naming convention, it should be clear that the order of target discovery does not affect the target numbers or, therefore, the pathnames. This is not true for the display names.

Summary

VMware supports heterogeneous storage environments, which aid in expanding your storage environment while preserving your existing investment. You can also use a heterogeneous storage environment for establishing tiered storage for various applications' SLAs when your existing storage array does not provide tiered storage.

Using runtime names, targets are numbered in the order in which they are discovered. When you add targets, they are enumerated in the order in which they are added as well as by their connections to the switches. At boot time, they are re-enumerated in the order in which they are connected to the switches.

LUNs with the same LUN number on different storage arrays are identified by their device IDs and association with the target port IDs.

## Chapter 10

Using VMDirectPath I/O

One of the least-known features introduced in vSphere 4.x that continues to be available in vSphere 5 and 6 is VMDirectPath I/O. This chapter explains what it is, shows how it works, and provides some practical design implementations. vSphere 6 also supports Single Root I/O Virtualization (SR-IOV), which offers performance benefits similar to those of VMDirectPath I/O.

What Is VMDirectPath?

Have you ever wanted to access a certain storage device directly from within a virtual machine (VM) but found that the devices was not raw device mapping (RDM) capable? Do you have a Fibre-attached tape library that you want to use within a VM and provide multipathing to it? Do you have an application that requires a specific peripheral component interconnect (PCI) device accessed directly from within the VM? If you answer yes to any of these questions, VMDirectPath is for you.

VMDirectPath on vSphere 4.x, 5.x, and 6 uses a hardware implementation of an IOMMU (I/O memory management unit). This implementation is referred to as VT-d (Virtual Technology for Directed I/O) on an Intel platform and AMD IOMMU on an AMD platform. (AMD IOMMU was experimental in vSphere 4.x and vSphere 5 but is supported on vSphere 5.5 and later, including 6.0 and 6.5.) This technology allows for passing through input/output (I/O) directly to a VM, to which you dedicate a supported PCI I/O device, such as a 10Gbps Ethernet NIC or an 8Gbps FC HBA.

Which I/O Devices Are Supported?

Currently the list of supported I/O devices is limited, and there is no official HCL (hardware compatibility list) listing them. The current support model for these devices is the PVSP (Partner Verified and Supported Products) program. This support model means that VMware partners test and verify the implementation and interoperability of a specific I/O device within a specific configuration. Such configuration is documented in a VMware Knowledge Base (KB) article. The partner qualifying the configuration is the first line of support for such a configuration. Check with the IO device vendors for their current support status.

> **TIP**
>
> The I/O device assigned to a VM is dedicated to that VM and cannot be shared with the ESXi host. Certain devices with multiple PCI physical functions may be shared with other VMs on the same host (one function per VM).
>
> To identify which devices are known to be shareable, check the /etc/vmware/passthru.map file. See Table 10.1 for a tabulation of the current version content on ESXi 6.

Table 10.1 Passthru.map file listing

Vendor ID	Device ID	Reset Method	fptShareable
Intel 82598 (Oplin) 10Gig cards can be reset with d3d0			
8086	10b6	d3d0	default
8086	10c6	d3d0	default
8086	10c7	d3d0	default
8086	10c8	d3d0	default
8086	10dd	d3d0	default
Broadcom 57710/57711/57712 10Gig cards are not shareable			
14e4	164e	default	false
14e4	164f	default	false
14e4	1650	default	false
14e4	1662	1077	false
QLogic 8Gb FC card cannot be shared			
1077	2532	default	false
QLogic QL45604 cards need to be reset with "link" and cannot be shared			
1077	1634	1077	false
1077	1629	1077	false

Vendor ID	Device ID	Reset Method	fptShareable
QLogic QL45604 cards need to be reset with "link" and cannot be shared			
1077	1636	1077	false
1077	1656	1077	false
1077	1644	1077	false
1077	1654	1077	false
LSILogic 1068–based SAS controllers			
1000	0056	d3d0	default
1000	0058	d3d0	default
NVIDIA			
10de	ffff	bridge	false

The basic rule is that if the device can be reset via the d3d0 reset method, it can be shareable between VMs on the same ESXi host. The possible values for the Reset Method column are flr, d3d0, link, bridge, and default.

The default method is flr (function level reset) if the device supports it. Otherwise, ESXi defaults next to link reset and then bus reset. The latter two methods can prevent the device from being shareable. The reset methods are summarized in Table 10.2.

Table 10.2 Reset methods comparison

Reset Method	Explanation	Device Shareable?
Function level reset	When the VM using the pass-through device requests a PCI reset, only the PCI function on the device is reset. For example, if there are two Ethernet ports on the NIC, only the port used by the VM is reset.	Yes
Link reset	When a reset is required, the physical function (PF) link is reset instead of the PCI function itself being reset.	No
Bus reset	When a reset is required, the PCI bus is reset instead of the PCI function itself. This affects all functions on the PCI device.	No

The last column in Table 10.1, fptShareable, means full passthrough shareable. The possible values are default, true, and false. The default value is true.

Locating Hosts Supporting VMDirectPath I/O on the HCL

The list of devices verified with vSphere 4.x should still be usable on vSphere 5 and 6. Although there is no dedicated HCL for the I/O devices, systems supporting IOMMU and certified with vSphere 6 are listed on the VMware HCL. You can search for certified systems by following this procedure:

1. Go to www.vmware.com/go/hcl.

2. Select **Systems/Servers** from the What Are You Looking For dropdown list (see Figure 10.1).

3. Select **ESXi 6.0** as the product release version.

4. Select **VM Direct Path IO** in the Features field.

5. Click the **Update and View Results** button.

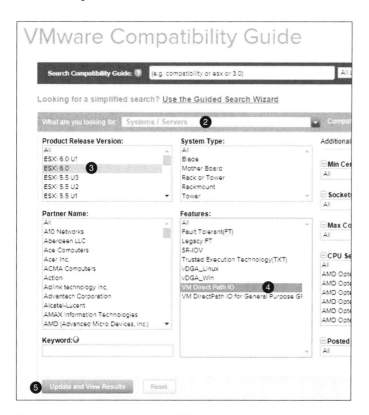

Figure 10.1   Preparing to view HCL search results

6. Scroll down to view the search results (see Figure 10.2).

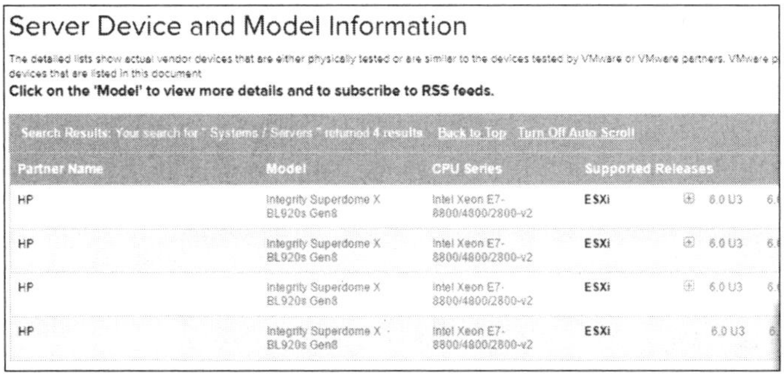

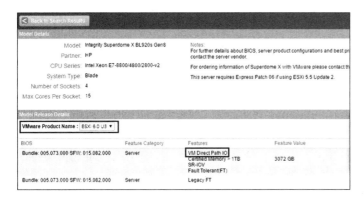

Figure 10.2 Viewing HCL search results

Although the list shows ESXi 6.0U3 under Supported Releases, when you select one of the systems in the list, other versions are listed there as supported (see Figure 10.3).

Other systems not on the list may work, but if issues with VMDirectPath are reported on such systems, you will probably not get support from VMware or the I/O device partner.

Figure 10.3 Viewing HCL search results

Configuring VMDirectPath I/O on vSphere 6.0

After you have verified that your system is on the HCL supporting the VMDirectPath I/O feature or if you are adventurous and use a system based on the Intel XEON 55xx family of central processing units (CPUs) in a non-production environment, you are now ready to configure VMDirectPath I/O. Follow these steps:

1. Connect to the vCenter server that manages the ESXi 6 host, using the vSphere Client as a user with Administrator privileges. Note that the vSphere Web Client does not provide this feature's UI at this time.

2. Locate the host in the inventory tree and select it.

3. Select the **Configuration** tab.

4. Select the **Advanced Settings** link in the Hardware section (see Figure 10.4).

Figure 10.4 Accessing the passthrough configuration menu

If the system is not capable of this feature, you see a `Host does not support passthrough configuration` message, as shown in Figure 10.5. Notice that the **Configure Passthrough** link is not enabled because the feature is not supported.

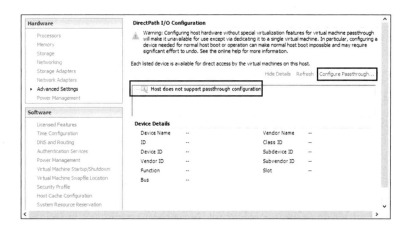

Figure 10.5 Host does not support passthrough configuration

If your system is capable of passthrough configuration, you see the message No devices currently enabled for Passthrough.

To start the configuration process, you can follow this procedure, starting from the view in Figure 10.4:

1. Click the **Configure Passthrough** link. You see the dialog shown in Figure 10.6. If you highlight a device, you see its PCI information in the lower part of the dialog.

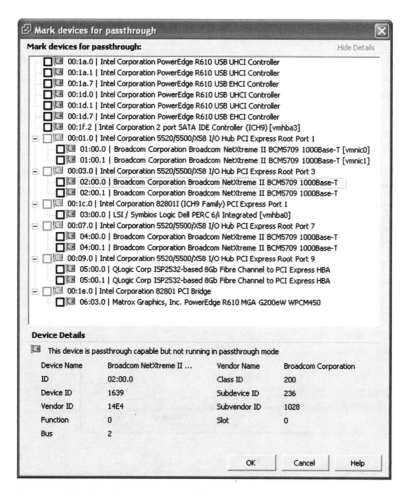

Figure 10.6   Passthrough device list

2. To enable a device, select the check box next to it.

3. If a device you selected has a dependent device, you see the message shown in Figure 10.7. An example of this is a dual-port network interface card (NIC) where

each port shows as a separate PCI function of the device. This is due to the lack of PCI-to-PCI bridge on the dual-port NIC. In this example, you see the PCI ID 2.00.0 and 2.00.1. If the NIC had a PCI-to-PCI bridge, it would have a separate device or slot number for each port—for example, 2.00.0 and 2.01.0. Clicking **OK** enables both ports. Also see the tip in the "Which I/O Devices Are Supported" section, earlier in this chapter.

Figure 10.7   Dependent device message

4. To complete the configuration, click the **OK** button (see Figure 10.8).

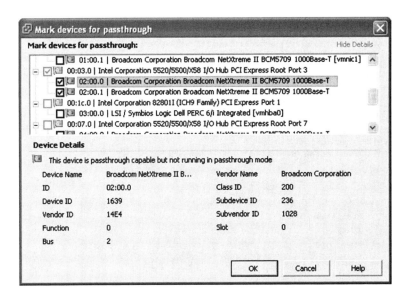

Figure 10.8   Dependent devices selection

5. You must click the **Refresh** link for the selected devices to show up in the list (see Figure 10.9). In the future, if you need to select more devices, you can select the **Edit** link, which takes you to a device selection dialog similar to the dialog in Figure 10.6.

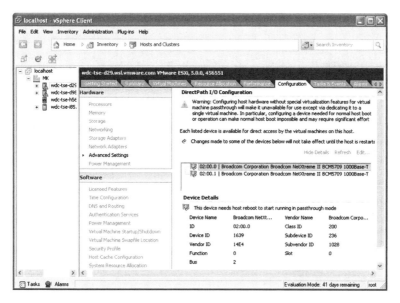

Figure 10.9   Configured devices require reboot

6. Notice that selecting one of the configured devices in Figure 10.9 shows a `This device needs host reboot to start running in passthrough mode` message in the Device Details section. This is due to the fact that the device was controlled by vmkernel, and now you need to reboot so that it can be passed through directly to the virtual machine that you configure in the next steps.

7. After the host is rebooted, the devices should show up on the list with a green icon (see Figure 10.10).

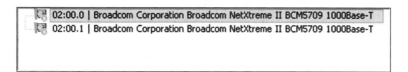

Figure 10.10   Passthrough devices ready

8. Locate the VM to which you plan to add the passthrough PCI device, power it off, right-click it, and then select the **Edit Settings** option (see Figure 10.11).

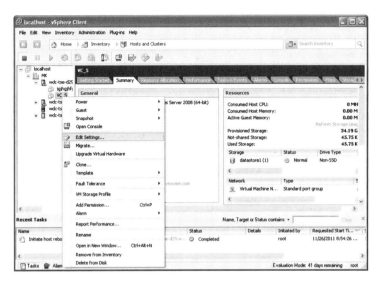

Figure 10.11 Editing a VM

9. On the Hardware tab, click the **Add** button (see Figure 10.12).

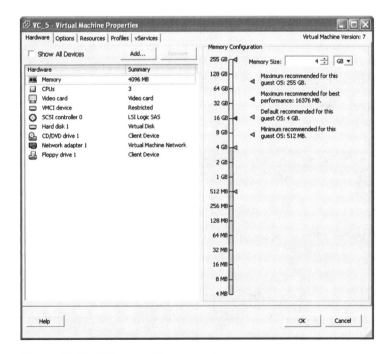

Figure 10.12 Virtual machine properties

10. Select the **PCI Device** type and then click **Next** (see Figure 10.13).

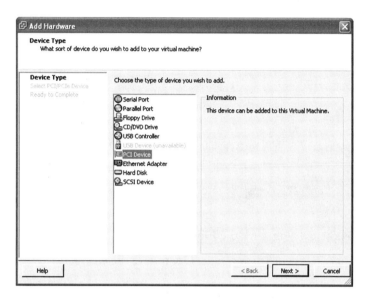

Figure 10.13 The Add Hardware dialog

11. Select the device from the pull-down list in the **Connection** section and then click **Next**, as shown in Figure 10.14.

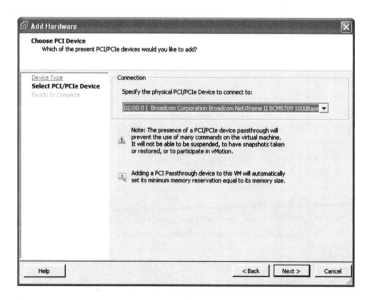

Figure 10.14 Adding a PCI device

NOTE

As the dialog in Figure 10.14 indicates, there are limitations imposed on the virtual machine design:

- The VM cannot be suspended.
- The VM cannot have a snapshot taken or restored.
- The VM cannot be vMotioned, which means limited availability when it is part of a DRS cluster.
- The VM cannot be protected by HA (high availability).
- The VM cannot be protected by FT (fault tolerance).
- The VM's minimum memory reservation is automatically set to its memory size.

12. In the Ready to Complete dialog, click the **Finish** button.

13. In the Virtual Machine Properties dialog, click **OK** to save the changes (see Figure 10.15).

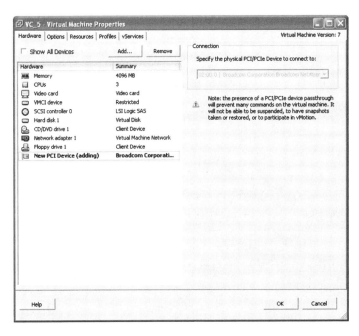

Figure 10.15   Saving VM configuration changes

14. Power on the VM. The guest OS detects the newly added device and prompts you to install its driver (see Figure 10.16). Select the relevant option to proceed with the driver installation.

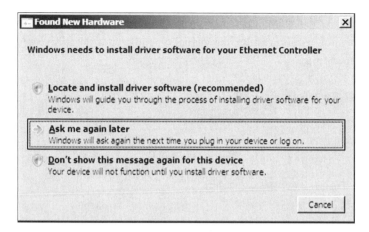

Figure 10.16 Guest detects new device

15. Figure 10.17 shows the device manager in the guest OS after the NIC driver is installed. Notice that it is listed under Network Adapters as well as System Devices. If the device is a SCSI, SAS, or FC HBA, it appears under the Storage Controllers node.

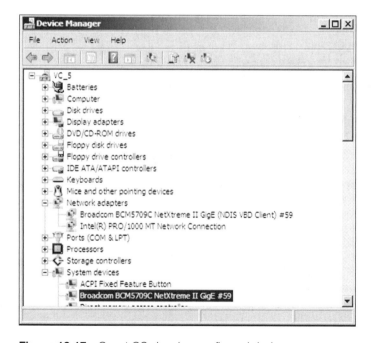

Figure 10.17 Guest OS showing configured device

What Gets Added to the VM's Configuration File?

The procedure in the previous section results in a virtual machine configuration (.vmx) file with the entries shown in Listing 10.1.

Listing 10.1   PCI passthrough entries in a .vmx file

```
pciPassthru0.present = "TRUE"
pciPassthru0.deviceId = "1639"
pciPassthru0.vendorId = "14e4"
pciPassthru0.systemId = "4ea55642-5e38-0525-7664-00219b99ddd8"
pciPassthru0.id = "02:00.0"
sched.mem.min = "1072"
```

The first entry enables PCI passthrough device number 0.

The second entry sets the passthrough device ID based on the physical device PCI properties. If you look at Figure 10.9, you see that value listed as `1639`.

The third entry sets the vendor ID from the same information in Figure 10.9.

The fourth entry sets the system ID, which is the ESXi host's UUID. You can obtain this ID by using the following command:

```
esxcli system uuid get
4ea55642-5e38-0525-7664-00219b99ddd8
```

The fifth entry sets the PCI ID (in *slot:device.function* format).

The last entry sets the VM's minimum memory to match the limit that was specified when this VM was created.

Toggling an I/O Adapter as Passthrough on vSphere 6.5

vSphere 6.5 does not support vSphere Client. To enable an I/O adapter for passthrough configuration (VMDirectPath I/O), use the vSphere Host Client, which is a browser-based client, as follows:

NOTE

This example used vSphere 6.5, Patch 02.

1. Log on to the ESXi host client as root via https://<host-name>/ui.

2. Navigate to the **Manage** section in the Navigator pane.

3. Select the **Hardware** tab.

4. Select **PCI Devices**.

5. Select the I/O adapter to toggle for passthrough. You may need to scroll down the device list to locate it.

6. Click the **Toggle passthrough** icon at the top of the manage pane (see Figure 10.18).

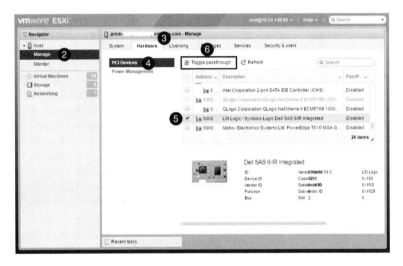

Figure 10.18   Toggling an I/O adapter for passthrough on vSphere 6.5

Figure 10.18 shows four adapters that are VMDirectPath I/O capable and disabled:

- Intel Corporation 2 port SATA-IDE Controller (ICH9)

- QLogic Corporation QLogic NetXtreme III BCM5709 1000Base-T

- LSI Logic/Symbios Logic Dell SAS 6/iR Integrated

- Matrox Electronics Systems Ltd. PowerEdge T610 MGA G200eW WPCM450

These adapters represent the classes of I/O adapters that you can enable for VMDirectPath I/O: network, storage, and display adapters.

> **TIP**
>
> I/O adapters that you enable for VMDirectPath I/O must be dedicated to that purpose. Do not share a storage adapter's storage with the host and VMDirectPath if the host will have VMFS datastores on that storage.

7. Select **Host** in the Navigator pane. Notice the message in the Details pane which: `This host needs to be rebooted to complete configuration.` Before proceeding, make sure that all VMs on the ESXi host have either been migrated to other hosts using vMotion or powered off.

8. Click the **Actions** icon next to the message or at the top right.

9. Select the **Enter Maintenance Mode** menu option (see Figure 10.19).

10. In the confirmation dialog that appears, click **Yes** to proceed.

Figure 10.19   Putting an ESXi host into Maintenance Mode

11. Click the **Reboot** icon at the top. Alternatively, you can click the **Actions** icon to the right of the message and then select **Reboot** menu option (refer to Figure 10.19).

12. In the confirmation dialog that appears, click **Reboot**.

13. After the host is rebooted, exit Maintenance Mode.

Adding a Passthrough PCI Device to a VM by Using vSphere Web Client

When you are done enabling PCI devices for VMDirectPath I/O, you can add them to virtual machines by following this procedure:

1. Connect to the vCenter server that manages the ESXi 6 host, using the vSphere 6.0 Web Client as a user with Administrator privileges.

2. Navigate to **Virtual Machines** in the Navigator pane.

3. If you are adding the passthrough device to an existing VM, power off the VM first, right-click its inventory object, and then click **Edit Settings**. Skip to step 6.

4. If you are creating a new VM, right-click the data center and then click **New Virtual Machine** menu option.

5. Go through the steps of creating the VM until you get to the **Customize Hardware** step.

6. Select **PCI Device** from the **New Device** menu.

7. Click **Add** (see Figure 10.20).

Figure 10.20 Accessing the New Device menu by using vSphere Web Client

8. Select the passthrough PCI device from the pull-down list.

9. Observe the warning displayed under the newly selected PCI device: The VM will not power on until its memory reservation equals its memory size. To resolve this issue, click the **Reserve all memory** button (see Figure 10.21).

Figure 10.21   Selecting the passthrough PCI device

10. Click **OK** if you are editing an existing VM or **Next** and then **Finish** if this is a new VM.

Adding a Passthrough PCI Device to a VM by Using the HTML5 ESXi Host Client

If you are using vSphere 6.0, Update 1 or later, including vSphere 6.5, an HTML5 host client is installed on each ESXi host out of the box. You can access it at https://[host-name_or_IP_address]/ui.

If the host is managed by vCenter, it is not advisable to modify the host or its VMs directly on the host. However, for demonstration purposes and in the rare configuration where you do not use vCenter, follow this procedure to add a device to a VM:

1. Connect directly to the ESXi host by using the HTML5 host client as root user.

2. Select the **Host** inventory object in the Navigator pane.

3. Right-click the **Host** object and then select the **Create/Register VM** menu option. Alternatively, you can click the **Create/Register VM** icon in the Details pane (see Figure 10.22).

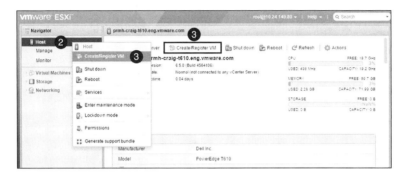

Figure 10.22   Accessing the Create/Register VM menu by using HTML5 host client

4. Go through the steps of creating the VM until you reach the Customize Settings step.

5. Click the **Add other device** icon (see Figure 10.23).

Figure 10.23   Accessing the Add other device menu by using the HTML5 host client

6. Select the **PCI device** menu option.

7. Scroll to the bottom of the dialog until you see the **New PCI device** section and expand it.

8. Select the passthrough device from the pull-down list in.

9. Observe the warning displayed under the newly select PCI device: The VM will not power on until its memory reservation equals its memory size. To resolve this issue, click the **Reserve all memory** button.

10. Click **Next** (see Figure 10.24).

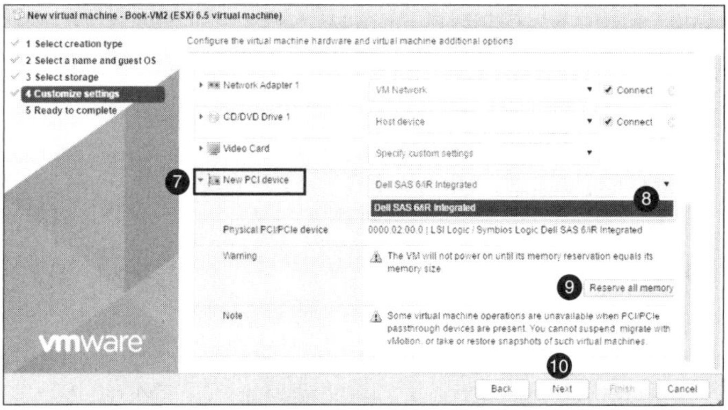

Figure 10.24   Selecting the passthrough PCI device

11. Review your setting and then click **Finish**.

Practical Examples of VM Design Scenarios Using VMDirectPath I/O

Some configurations were qualified by VMware partners under vSphere 4.1. As of this writing, they have not been updated for vSphere 5. However, because this feature was not changed between 4.1 and 6, you can safely assume that what was qualified on vSphere 4.1 ends up being qualified on vSphere 5 and 6.

Hyperconverged Infrastructure

A good example of using VMDirectPath I/O is the Cisco HyperFlex System (www.cisco.com/c/en/us/td/docs/unified_computing/ucs/UCS_CVDs/HX171_VSI_ESXi6U2.html), which is a partnership between Cisco and a storage startup company called Springpath.

The solution uses VMDirectPath to pass through storage devices, attached to Cisco 12Gbps SAS HBA cards on ESX 6.x hosts, to storage platform controller VMs running their firmware. The storage platform controllers VMs aggregate the raw storage passed through and present it as NFS shares to NFS clients, which are in this case ESXi hosts.

Passing Through Physical Tape Devices

Configuring a VM with a passthrough HBA enables the guest OS to drive tape devices attached to the HBA. So, if the HBA is an FC initiator, the VM can gain direct access to

FC-attached tape libraries and drives that are zoned to the HBA. This is different from NPIV (N_Port ID virtualization), in which the VMkernel creates virtual N-Ports assigned to the VM, and the devices are accessed as RDMs.

This also works with SAS and SCSI HBAs for direct-attached tape drives and media libraries, even if they did not work on the ESXi host directly or with generic passthrough configuration.

If you configure more than one FC HBA, you can use multipathing, with guest OS–based multipathing software.

Using VMDirectPath I/O does not require N-Port virtualization, nor does it need RDMs configured. The host has no access to the attached devices because it does not have access to the HBA assigned to the VM.

CAUTION

This configuration is not supported by VMware. If your storage partner is willing to support it, make sure that the partner qualifies it and submits the results to VMware under the PVSP or Request for Product Qualification (RPQ) program.

A few issues have been reported to VMware regarding some I/O devices failing to work or the VMs failing to use the assigned device. I strongly recommend that you check the VMware Knowledge Base for reported issues. I would love to hear from you about your experience via my blog at http://vSphereStorage.com or on Twitter, @mostafavmw.

Supported VMDirectPath I/O Devices

There is no HCL for VMDirectPath I/O devices per se. Rather, devices as well as qualified configurations are planned to be listed on the PVSP page, at www.vmware.com/resources/compatibility/vcl/partnersupport.php.

This page will list both generations of devices. As of this writing, there were no qualified devices or configurations listed yet. However, some solutions that use partner qualified devices are listed on the VMware Solutions Exchange such as Springpath Data Platform at https://solutionexchange.vmware.com/store/products/springpath-data-platform.

DirectPath I/O Example

Consider an example of a VM running on an ESXi 6 host on a Cisco Unified Computing System (UCS) that is equipped with Cisco Virtual Machine Fabric Extender (VM-FEX) distributed switches. The following features are available with VMDirectPath I/O configuration (and VM-FEX must be in high-performance mode):

- The VM can be suspended and resumed.

- The VM can have a snapshot taken or restored.

- The VM can be vMotioned, which means it can be part of a DRS cluster.

- The VM can be protected by HA (high availability).

The trick for supporting vMotion is that the vmkernel quiesces and checkpoints the Cisco Dynamic Ethernet interface presented by the Cisco virtual interface card (VIC).

The state created by the checkpoint process is transferred to the destination host in a similar fashion to how the memory checkpoint used to be done for vMotion.

Troubleshooting VMDirectPath I/O

Possible issues you may encounter fall into three groups: interrupt handling, device sharing, and IRQ (interrupt request) sharing—both virtual and physical IRQ.

Interrupt Handling and IRQ Sharing

The default interrupt handling for PCI passthrough on vSphere 5 and 6 is MSI/MSI-x (Message Signaled Interrupts). This works with most devices by default. If you come across a device that fails to be configured with VMDirectPath, you may need to disable MSI for the VM that uses that device. Effectively, this allows the VM to use IO-APIC (Advanced Programmable Interrupt Controller) instead of MSI. Common examples of such devices are Broadcom 57710 and 57711 when assigned to a Windows 2003 or 2008 VM.

To disable MSI for the given device in the VM, edit the VM's .vmx file by adding the following line:

```
pciPassthru0.msiEnabled = "FALSE"
```

If the virtual device number is higher than 0 (that is, you have more than one passthrough device), substitute the relevant value for 0 in this line.

Some devices are known to work with the MSI-enabled option set to TRUE:

- QLogic 2500 FC HBA

- LSI SAS 1068E HBA

- Intel 82598 10Gbps NIC

Device Sharing

When an I/O device has more than one PCI function (for example, a dual- or quad-port NIC) and there is no PCI-to-PCI bridge on the card, it is probably not fptShareable (full passthrough shareable). Refer to Table 10.1, earlier in this chapter, for details. If you are using a device that is not listed in that table and you know it is capable of resetting itself properly using D3 to D0 power transition (d3d0 value in Table 10.1), you might need to add an entry to the /etc/vmware/pcipassthru.map file. The following is an example of the format:

```
<Vendor ID>  <Device ID>  d3d0  default
```

To identify the device's PCI ID info, you can run the following command on the ESXi Shell locally, via SSH:

```
esxcli hardware pci list
```

Listing 10.2 shows sample output for a device.

Listing 10.2   Sample listing of PCI device ID info

```
000:001:00.1
   Address: 000:001:00.1
   Segment: 0x0000
   Bus: 0x01
   Slot: 0x00
   Function: 0x01
   VMkernel Name: vmnic1
   Vendor Name: Broadcom Corporation
   Device Name: Broadcom NetXtreme II BCM5709 1000Base-T
   Configured Owner: Unknown
   Current Owner: VMkernel
   Vendor ID: 0x14e4
   Device ID: 0x1639
   SubVendor ID: 0x1028
   SubDevice ID: 0x0236
   Device Class: 0x0200
   Device Class Name: Host bridge
   Programming Interface: 0x00
   Revision ID: 0x20
   Interrupt Line: 0x0e
   IRQ: 14
   Interrupt Vector: 0x88
```

```
PCI Pin: 0x66
Spawned Bus: 0x00
Flags: 0x0201
Module ID: 27
Module Name: bnx2
Chassis: 0
Physical Slot: 0
Slot Description: Embedded NIC 2
Passthru Capable: true
Parent Device: PCI 0:0:1:0
Dependent Device: PCI 0:0:1:0
Reset Method: Link reset
FPT Sharable: true
```

The values you need are highlighted in this listing for easier identification.

So, the sample line looks like this for the device in this example:

```
14e4    1639    d3d0    default
```

> **NOTE**
>
> Based on the sample device in Listing 10.2, the reset method is link reset. This output also shows that `Passthru Capable` and `FPT Shareable` are both set to `true`.
>
> This means that without adding the entry in the `pcipassthru.map` file, the default values are what are reported by the PCI info shown in Listing 10.2 and that the device is shareable and supports full passthrough sharing. Adding the entries in the file overrides the reset method only because you are leaving fptShareable set to the default.

Summary

VMDirectPath I/O has been available since vSphere 4.x and continues to exist in vSphere 5 and 6. You can use it to pass through physical storage or network devices, exposing the physical I/O card to the guest OS, which installed the physical card's driver. Design scenarios include FC-attached and direct-attached tape drives and media libraries and other devices that otherwise are not available via vmkernel.

## Chapter 11

Storage Virtualization Devices (SVDs)

Storage vendors competing in the enterprise had to come up with ways to first coexist with and then migrate from their competitors' storage. This need begat a storage feature that is the topic of this chapter: storage virtualization devices (SVDs). As simple as it may sound, it is a complex concept and varies from one vendor to another. This chapter deals with this topic from a vSphere 6 perspective. It is not intended to be an in-depth discussion of SVD configuration details.

The SVD Concept

The SVD concept basically involves presenting existing third-party block storage to initiators as if it is the SVD's own storage. The SVD then presents virtualized storage as block devices or network file systems.

How Does It Work?

Virtualizing storage can be done via any—or a mix—of the following approaches:

- **Address space remapping**—The SVD can abstract the physical location of the data and provide a logical representation of that data to the initiators. For example, more than one logical unit number (LUN) on the back-end array (the one being virtualized) can be pooled together as one large LUN. The front-end array (the SVD itself) keeps a mapping table showing which blocks of the virtual LUN (the one it presents to the initiators) are mapped to which blocks on the back-end LUNs.

- **Metadata**—This is "data about data" that presents the big picture to the initiators. In simple words, the metadata holds the structure of the data presented to the initiators and might include the mapping table mentioned in the previous point. The device details—LUN size, boundaries, RAID type, and so on—are presented by the metadata of the SVD. This is somewhat like Virtual Machine File System (VMFS) presenting a physical device to a VM as a raw device mapping (RDM). The properties of the device are stored in the VMFS metadata, but the physical block locations are obtained from the storage array hosting the physical LUN.

- **I/O redirection**—When I/O is sent from an initiator to a specific block on a virtualized device, it gets redirected to the mapped physical block on the back-end device. This is somewhat like how VMkernel redirects the I/O sent from a VM to an RDM. This function is based on one or more of the three mechanisms just described (see Figure 11.1).

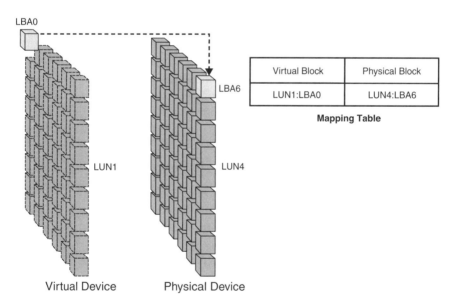

Figure 11.1   I/O redirection and address space mapping

For example, when I/O is sent to a block on the virtual device—such as Logical Block Address 0 (LBA0) on LUN1—it gets redirected to the logical block address of the block on the physical device—such as LBA6 on LUN4—based on the mapping table defined by the address space remapping. The metadata would have pointers to the data on the virtual LUN so that the initiator would know where the data is located.

SVD Architecture

SVDs are available mostly in hardware configurations with specialized firmware. Some varieties are available in software form. However, the latter are certified with vSphere in association with certain hardware configurations or as software-only configurations. For example, IBM SVC, HDS USPv, and NetApp V-series are certified as hardware solutions, whereas Falcon Store NSS Gateway is certified as a storage virtual appliance.

Figure 11.2 shows a diagram depicting the SVD architecture.

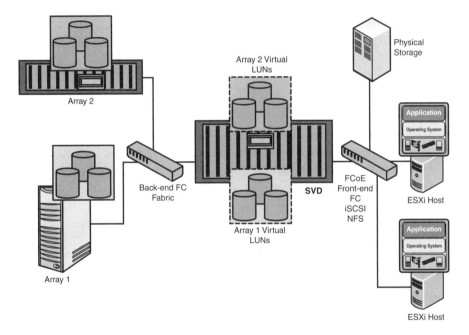

Figure 11.2 SVD architecture

SVD storage connects to two different sets of fabrics: the front-end and back-end fabrics. The front-end fabric connects the hosts to the SVD, and the back-end fabric connects the SVD to the back-end storage arrays. The front-end FC fabric may be substituted with iSCSI, FCoE, or NFS protocols in the few configurations certified with iSCSI, FCoE, or NFS front-end connectivity. Regardless of the front-end protocol, the back-end fabric is supported only with Fibre Channel (FC) connectivity between the SVD and the back-end storage.

In this configuration, the SVD acts as an initiator to the back-end storage arrays, while it acts as a target for the ESXi hosts.

NOTE

In the case of FC front and back ends, the fabric separation can be physical or logical. For example, zoning can be used so that the hosts and the front-end array's ports are in one set of zones, and the front-end array's ports and back-end array's ports are in a separate set of zones.

Constraints

The SVD configuration certified for vSphere 6 restricts the back-end storage arrays' connectivity to FC only. Other protocols are not supported for back-end storage. The ESXi hosts must never be given access to the back-end arrays while zoned to the SVD to prevent data corruption because the hosts may treat the physical LUNs and the virtual LUNs as different devices. Back-end LUNs must never be presented to hosts.

If the physical LUNs on the back-end storage have VMFS3 or VMFS5 volumes on them, the virtual LUNs representing them are seen by the ESXi hosts as snapshot LUNs, and the VMFS volumes are not mounted automatically. (I discuss the behavior of snapshot technologies with VMFS datastores, or volumes, in Chapter 15, "Snapshot Handling.")

The ESXi hosts can access the VMFS volumes via the virtual LUNs by one of two methods:

- **Resignaturing the VMFS volumes**—This is the process of regenerating a new VMFS volume signature and writing it to the metadata. This result is a renamed volume with the prefix *snap*.

- **Force mounting the VMFS volumes**—This is a new feature in vSphere 6 that allows the vSphere administrator to mount a VMFS volume that resides on a snapshot LUN without having to resignature the VMFS volume.

I discuss these methods in Chapter 15 as well.

Migrating Back-end Storage to the SVD

If your final goal of using an SVD is to migrate your data to the new storage array and then decommission the old storage, you can proceed further beyond the configuration discussed in this chapter by using features provided by the SVD to migrate the data from the back-end physical LUNs to physical storage on the SVD to back the virtual LUNs. This process is transparent to the front-end initiators (ESXi hosts) and does not usually impose a negative effect on I/O performance. When the data is completely migrated, a virtual LUN is switched to being a physical LUN internally by the SVD. At this point, the SVD acts as a physical storage array, like any others, connected to the initiators via the front-end fabric.

SVD Design Decisions

There are several choices to consider in SVD design. Here, I group them into two major groups: front-end and back-end choices.

Front-End Design Choices

There are several front-end design choices, which I cover in the following sections.

Choosing an SVD

You should choose an SVD based on the features available, supported storage tiers, supported protocols, capacity, and so on.

The front-end array must be on the VMware Hardware Compatibility List (HCL) as an SVD certified with ESXi 6. The back-end array must also be certified with ESXi 6 (with FC connectivity). To verify this, you can follow these steps:

1. Go to www.vmware.com/go/hcl.

2. Select **Storage/SAN** from the pull-down menu, as shown in Figure 11.3.

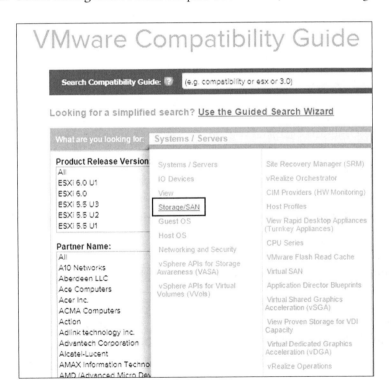

Figure 11.3 Accessing storage/SAN HCL page

3. Select **ESXi 6.0** in the **Product Release Version** box (see Figure 11.4).

4. Select **SVD** in the **Array Type** box.

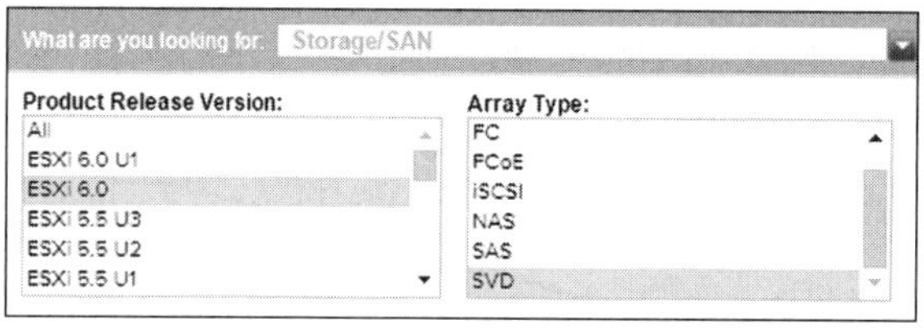

Figure 11.4   Selecting release version and array type

5. Click the storage vendor's name from the **Partner Name** box. You can select more than one by pressing **Ctrl** and clicking on each partner's name.

6. Click the **Update and View Results** button.

7. Scroll down to see the results.

Choosing a Protocol

The next design choice for the front end is the supported protocols. As I mentioned earlier, SVDs are supported with the FC protocol as well as Fibre Channel over Ethernet (FCoE), Internet Small Computer System Interface (iSCSI), and Network File System (NFS). If you plan to use an SVD as a migration tool to the SVD's physical storage, you might want to consider the additional storage capacity that you plan to use after the migration is complete. For example, you might want to add more disks on the array to accommodate the data to be migrated from the back-end storage.

Determining the Bandwidth

As for the connection speed, your choice is limited by what is listed on the HCL for the SVD. To identify which speeds are supported, follow these steps as a continuation of the HCL search described earlier:

1. In the search results, locate the storage array you plan to use and select the hyperlink under the **Model** column for the array, as shown in Figure 11.5.

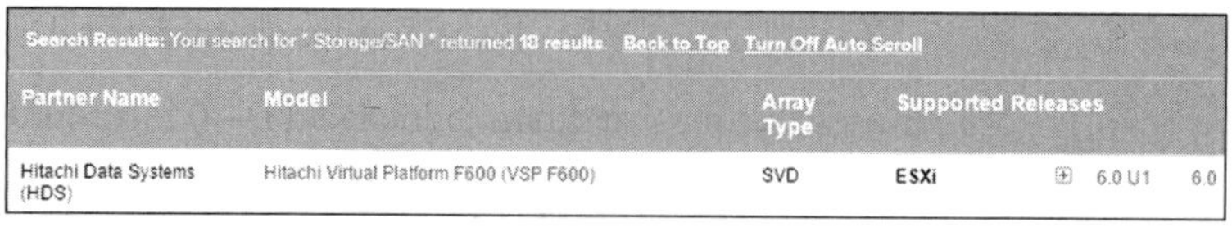

Figure 11.5   Search results

2. Read over the array details that are displayed (see Figure 11.6).

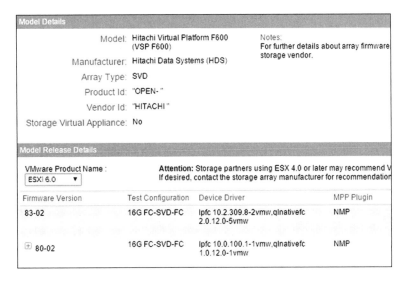

Figure 11.6 Array details

The connection speed is based on the **Test Configuration** column's value, as shown in Table 11.1.

Table 11.1 Test configuration and connection speeds

Test Configuration	Front-end Connection Speed	Back-end Minimum Connection Speed
FC-SVD-FC	FC 4Gbps or 2Gbps	FC 4Gbps or 2Gbps
8G FC-SVD-FC	FC 8Gbps	FC 4Gbps or 2Gbps
16G FC-SVD-FC	FC 16Gbps	FC 4Gbps or 2GBps
iSCSI-SVD-FC	iSCSI 1Gbps or 10Gbps	FC 4Gbps or 2Gbps
FCoE-SVD-FC	FCoE 10Gbps or faster	FC 4Gbps or 2Gbps
NAS-SVD-FC	Ethernet 1Gbps or 10Gbps	FC 4Gbps or 2Gbps

To narrow your search result to one of these test configurations, simply select the desired test configuration from the **Array Test Configuration** field (see Figure 11.7).

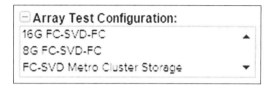

Figure 11.7 Selecting the test configuration

How About Initiator Records on the Front-End Array?

The front-end array must be configured with initiator records, FA director bits, host records, and so on, based on the storage vendor's recommendations, which are similar to those provided for configuring an array with physical LUNs.

Back-end Design Choices

The back-end array choices are actually constraints imposed on your design because they are existing configurations, and you have to consider the risks resulting from these constraints and mitigate them.

Determining the Bandwidth

The common scenario is that the back-end connection speed may be equal to or slower than the front-end connection speed because the back-end devices are older generation with slower ports. Your configuration's effective speed is the least common denominator of the front-end and the back-end connection speeds. In most cases when using an SVD for the purpose of migrating storage from the back end to the SVD, the existing hosts may be equipped with FC HBAs with speeds matching the back-end connection speed. This is another constraint imposed on your design. You can mitigate this by later adding faster FC HBAs to the ESXi hosts after the storage migration is complete and the back end is disconnected.

Choosing a Protocol

If the front-end array supports additional protocols—for example, FCoE or iSCSI— you may plan on adding matching initiators in the ESXi hosts. For example, say that your choice of storage arrays provides 10Gbps iSCSI SP ports and your network design provides this bandwidth. You can migrate one host at a time (using vMotion to vacate the host) and then replace the FC HBAs with 10Gbps iSCSI initiators. You then present the same LUNs on the SVD to the host via iSCSI protocol. You need to ensure that the LUN and UUID are not changed. After booting, the upgraded ESXi host should start enjoying the added bandwidth.

Configuring Initiator Records

Because the front-end arrays pose as initiators to the back-end arrays, you need to check with the corresponding front-end array's configuration requirements.

LUN Presentation Considerations

As briefly mentioned earlier in this chapter, depending on the storage array vendor and model, the back-end LUNs' properties might not be preserved when presenting their equivalent SVD virtual LUNs. These properties are as follows:

- LUN
- Device ID (for example, NAA ID)

I discuss this in further detail in Chapter 15, but the basic idea is that the VMFS datastore's signature is partly based on the LUN as well as the device ID. If either of these values changes (especially the device ID), the ESXi hosts treat the datastore as if it is on a snapshot LUN. This is a major constraint that can be addressed in this environment by VMFS datastore resignature. (I discuss other alternatives in Chapter 15.)

RDM Considerations

If ESXi hosts use LUNs on back-end arrays as RDMs, you need to re-create the RDM entries on the "resignatured" VMFS volumes because the original entries were created using the original LUN properties (LUN and device ID). (I provide further details in Chapter 13, "Virtual Disks and RDMs.")

TIP

If the main business requirement for a design is to migrate the data from the old arrays to the new arrays, I strongly recommend using a phased approach in which you begin with a heterogeneous storage configuration and add the new array to the SAN as an additional physical storage. You can then use Storage vMotion to move the VMs from the old datastores to the new ones. This has an effect on your design because you need to consider the target LUN sizing, I/O SLAs, and availability.

Storage vMotion moves the RDM entries to the target datastore. However, you need to plan for downtime to migrate the mapped physical LUNs to the new storage array and re-create the RDM entries.

After the data migration is complete, you can move on to the next phase, in which you disconnect and decommission the old storage arrays.

Pros and Cons of Using SVDs

SVDs offer many advantages that you can leverage compared to the older storage arrays that hide behind them:

- You can migrate your old data with less downtime. (I can't say "no downtime" because you need to resignature the VMFS datastores.) (Hmm…Storage vMotion does data migration, too, and with no downtime—unless you have RDMs. See Chapter 13.)

- You can migrate your current data from overutilized storage arrays. (I've heard of that before! Oh yeah! vSphere 6 does it automatically, using Storage DRS.)

- You can handle data replication, mirroring, snapshots, and so on if your old array does not provide it and the SVD does.

- SVD might have larger cache, faster processors, faster ports, and larger command queue. You need to consider the costs associated with adding an SVD compared to upgrading the storage array.

On the other hand, there are a few disadvantages to using SVDs:

- VMFS datastores typically need to be resignatured. This involves reregistering all VMs residing on these datastores. You can avoid this by using Storage vMotion because you are moving the VMs to a new datastore instead of using a virtualized LUN on an SVD.

- To migrate RDMs, you must re-create their VMFS entries.

- You cannot use rotating outages of the ESXi hosts to migrate the data because you should never present the back-end LUNs to some hosts while other hosts access them via the SVD's virtual LUNs. This means that all hosts in the cluster must be down while the switchover is done. Alternatively, you can follow the approach outlined in the following section.

Migration Process

Let me take you through the journey from the old array to the new one with a stop in the twilight zone—the SVD:

1. Connect the SVD to the fabric that will serve as the front-end fabric.

2. Connect the SVD to the fabric that will serve as the back-end fabric.

3. Zone the SVD SP ports designated to the connectivity with the back-end storage to the SP ports on the back-end storage.

4. Shut down all VMs running on the back-end storage.

5. For all ESXi hosts, follow the procedure described in the section "Unmounting a VMFS Volume" in Chapter 7, "Multipathing and Failover," to unmount the back-end–based VMFS volumes.

6. For all ESXi hosts, follow the procedure described in the section "Detaching a Device Whose Datastore Was Unmounted" in Chapter 7 to detach the LUNs associated with the VMFS volumes you unmounted in step 5.

7. Remove all hosts from the zones with the old storage array on the back-end fabric.

8. Add all hosts to the zones with the SVD on the front-end fabric.

9. Create the virtual LUNs on the SVD mapping to the physical LUNs on the old storage array.

10. Present the virtual LUNs to one ESXi host, using the same LUN numbers as the old ones (for ease of management rather than functionality).

11. Using the ESXi host mentioned in step 10 (via vCenter Server), mount the VMFS datastores presented by the virtual LUNs. This gives you the choice to resignature the datastores. See the detailed procedure described in the section "Resignaturing Datastores" in Chapter 15.

12. Present the virtual LUNs to the remaining ESXi hosts and rescan to discover the virtual LUNs and mount the VMFS datastores.

13. Using vCenter, remove the orphaned virtual machines from the inventory and browse the datastores to register the VMs on their corresponding ESXi hosts.

14. Make sure to place the VMs in the resource pools to which they belonged prior to this procedure.

15. Power on the VMs. Everything should be back to normal (though a better normal, I hope).

If your goal is to decommission an old storage array, start the data migration process to the SVD. It is best to plan this for off-peak hours. After this process is complete, switch the virtual LUNs to physical mode, depending on the SVD's specific procedures. (See the SVD's documentation for details.) Finally, disconnect the SVD from the back-end fabric when all the back-end data has been migrated to the SVD.

Summary

SVDs present older back-end arrays' LUNs to initiators as if they are physically located within the SVDs themselves. Back-end connectivity is limited to the FC Protocol, whereas the front-end varies by SVD and spans FC, FCoE, iSCSI, and NFS. Data migration is one of the main features of most SVDs. After the data is migrated, you can decommission the back-end arrays as needed. VMFS volumes on the back-end arrays are detected as being on snapshot LUNs when presented to the host via the SVD. RDM entries need to be re-created, regardless of whether you keep the RAW LUNs on the back-end arrays or migrate them to the SVDs.

## Chapter 12

VMFS Architecture

vSphere 6 and its near predecessors are inherently highly scalable clustered environments. From the very beginning of the life of ESX, VMware Virtual Machine File System (VMFS) has been the core element that holds the environment together.

VMFS is the core component of vSphere's storage virtualization, as it abstracts the underlying storage and presents it to virtual machines (VMs) in various formats: virtual disks, passthrough RDMs, non-passthrough RDMs, snapshots, and so on.

History of VMFS

VMFS evolved from a flat file system to a highly specialized clustered file system over four generations.

VMFS1

The first version of VMFS, which shipped with ESX 1.x, was a flat file system (that is, it did not provide directories) and provided three modes:

- **Private**—Private mode VMFS was used for storing virtual disks of VMs that were not shared between hosts. This resided mostly on local storage internal to the host or directly attached to it.

- **Public**—Public mode VMFS was used on shared storage for storing virtual disks of VMs that could run on more than one ESX host and used a file-locking mechanism to prevent the same virtual disks from being opened by multiple hosts concurrently.

- **Shared**—Shared mode VMFS was used exclusively for MSCS-clustered VMs. This mode did not enforce file-level locking and left that function to the clustering software in the guest OS. Shared mode VMFS was created on local or shared storage to support cluster-in-a-box (CIB) and cluster-across-boxes (CAB).

Due to the fact that the file system was flat, VM configuration files had to be stored in a hierarchy of directories on a local EXT2 file system. (In the early days, the VM configuration file extension was .cfg, and it was changed to .vmx in later releases.) The directory structure used to be located within the user's home directory, which provided some level of ACL (access control list) based on local users' Linux-style accounts.

NOTE

I had an ESX 1.5.2 host running in my home office closet for more than five years, and its uptime was most of these five years (apart from a couple of prolonged power outages that depleted my UPS battery). I had so many panics on my physical Linux hosts and BSODs (blue screen of death) on my physical Windows desktop, I almost forgot that I was still running the ESX 1.5.2 host.

TIP

You may see a Private mode file system on ESXi 6 but not on VMFS. Rather, it is a property of the ESXi 6 bootbanks, which are VFAT file systems.

VMFS2

With the release of ESX 2, VMware upgraded the file system to version 2, which was also a flat file system. However, Private mode was deprecated.

VMFS2 added multi-extent capability to extend the datastore onto additional logical unit numbers (LUNs) up to 32 extents.

ESX 2.5 introduced vMotion, which requires the use of Public mode VMFS2 datastores shared between hosts in a data center.

VMFS3

Virtual Infrastructure 3 (VI3) introduced the first hierarchical version of VMFS and added file system journaling for enhanced resiliency and recoverability. Also, with this release, the Shared mode was deprecated, leaving Public as the sole mode available from VMFS. Now you know the origin of that mode you may have observed in the properties of VMFS3 and 5 file systems (see Figure 12.1).

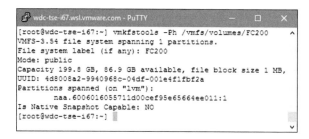

Figure 12.1   VMFS3 properties

VI3 also introduced Logical Volume Manager (LVM) for VMFS3, which enhanced the ability to span a VMFS datastore onto multiple LUNs to form a larger datastore beyond 2TB. LVM simply concatenates multiple smaller LUNs into a larger VMFS3 volume, up to 32 extents. The main difference between VMFS3 and VMFS2 is that loss of any of the extents (other than the head extent) does not invalidate the rest of the VMFS3 datastore. (You'll learn more about this later in this chapter, in the "Span or Grow?" section.)

LVM also handles resignature of VMFS3 or VMFS5 datastores that are detected to be on snapshot LUNs. (For more details, see Chapter 15, "Snapshot Handling.")

VI3 supported VMFS2 but in Read-Only mode for the sole purpose of live migration of VMs from the old VMFS2 datastores to VMFS3 datastores. This was done using the early version of Storage vMotion, which was command-line based in the first release of VI3 via remote command-line interface (RCLI) or VIMA (Virtual Infrastructure Management Assistant).

The Storage vMotion process organized the VMs in directories on the target VMFS3 datastore.

vSphere 6 does not support the creation of new VMFS3 datastores; however, it supports existing VMFS3 datastores for read/write. Future releases of vSphere will no longer support VMFS3 datastores. This is why you may see the following warning displayed in vSphere 6 web client's Summary tab of any ESXi host with VMFS3 datastores: `Depre-cated VMFS volume(s) found on the host. Please consider upgrading volume(s) to the latest version.`

VMFS5

What about VMFS4? VMware decided to skip version number 4 to sync up the numbering with the vSphere 5 release version. vSphere 5 introduced VMFS5, and vSphere 6 continues to support it as well as added enhancements. (vSphere 6.5 introduced VMFS6, which I cover briefly near the end of this chapter.) VMFS5 provides improved scalability and architectural changes to enable scalability, including the following:

- GUID Partition Table (GPT) supports a larger datastore extent size (greater than 2TB).

- A single block size (1MB) supports all file sizes. With VMFS3, the maximum file size was tied to various block sizes ranging from 1 to 8MB.

- The sub-block size, 8KB, is smaller than the 64KB size in VMFS3.

- Datastores can be tagged as ATS-only volumes after the storage arrays hosting the LUNs backing them are detected as supporting the ATS (atomic test and set) VAAI primitive. (See Chapter 17, "VAAI.")

VMFS3 on-Disk Layout

I cannot share with you the exact VMFS layout because it is proprietary VMware IP. However, I am allowed to share with you some publicly available diagrams that I used in some of VMworld and Partner Exchange presentations.

Figure 12.2 shows the VMFS3 layout.

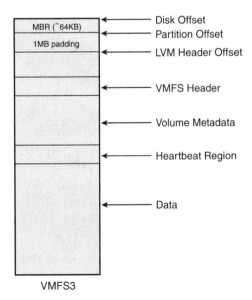

Figure 12.2 VMFS3 on-disk layout

The regions illustrated in Figure 12.2 are as follows:

- **VMFS3 partition offset**—This is at a certain location relative to the disk offset. I show you how to identify this location later in this chapter, in the section "Re-creating a Lost Partition Table for VMFS3 Datastores."

- **LVM**—The Logical Volume Manager (LVM) header starts 1MB from the partition offset. (Remember this fact later, when I show you how to restore the partition table.) It exists on all devices on which the volume is spanned and holds the following:

  - The number of extents that are logical building blocks of the file system.

  - The number of devices on which the volume is spanned. These are commonly referred to as *extents* or *physical extents* and should not be confused with the number of extents that are logical building blocks of the file system.

  - Volume size.

  - Whether this is a snapshot. This attribute is turned on by VMFS when it identifies that the LUN housing the datastore has a different device ID from that stored in the metadata. I explain snapshot volumes in Chapter 15.

- **VMFS header**—I am not authorized to share the details of VMFS header.

- **Volume metadata**—The volume metadata exists on all devices on which the volume is spanned. The following regions make up the metadata and are represented by five system files—the volume header and four resource system files (see Figure 12.3). These files are hidden (with a leading period and .sf suffix). On VMFS3 volumes with extents, the system files exist on the head extent only.

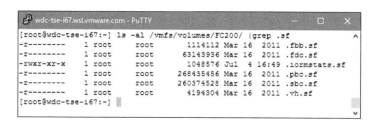

Figure 12.3 VMFS3 system files

This command is used in Figure 12.3:

```
ls -al /vmfs/volumes/FC200/ |grep .sf
```

The system files are the following:

- The volume header (.vh.sf) defines the volume structure, including the following:

  - **Volume name**—There is a misconception that the "volume name" is located in the LVM header, but it is actually in the volume header, in the datastore's metadata.

  - **VMFS3 UUID**—This is the volume's unique identifier, which is partially composed of the MAC address of the uplink used by the management port on the ESXi host that was used to first create or resignature the volume. This is also referred to as the volume "signature." (See Chapter 15.)

    Accessing the datastore via the ESXi Shell or via SSH is done via the following directory structure:

    ```
    /vmfs/volumes/<volume-UUID>
    ```

    or

    ```
    /vmfs/volumes/<volume-label>
    ```

  - **Volume label**—The volume label is a symbolic link to the volume UUID. Such links are automatically created by vmkernel at the time it mounts the datastore based on the volume name. To see the link, use the ls -al command, as shown
    in Figure 12.4.

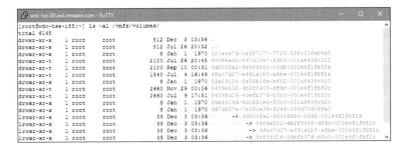

Figure 12.4   VMFS labels are symbolic links

The first column of the output shows the file system modes, which are UNIX/Linux-style modes that can be modified using chmod. The first mode in this example is either d or l. The former means that this is a directory, and the latter means that this is a link. The remaining modes are the permissions for the group, user, and others, in the form rwx, which means read, write, and execute. The last mode, for the others, is sometimes t, which means sticky. The sticky bit means that the directory or link can only be modified by root or the owner.

The second column shows the number of inodes—also known as file descriptors—used by this directory entry.

The third and fourth columns show the group names and usernames of the file owner, which is the account used to create the entry.

The fifth column shows the size in bytes. This is the size of the file or the directory (not the directory's content size).

The sixth column is the date and timestamp of the last time the file or the directory was modified.

The last column shows the file or directory name and, if the entry is a symbolic link, to which entry it is linked.

> **NOTE**
>
> The output in Figure 12.4 shows some UUIDs that have no symbolic links. These are related to VisorFS.

- **Extent ID**—This is the ID that the LVM header uses to identify which physical extent of the datastore this device holds.

- **Disk block size**—Do not confuse this with the file block size.

The file system resources are organized in clusters. Each resource in the cluster has associated metadata and locks (see Figure 12.5).

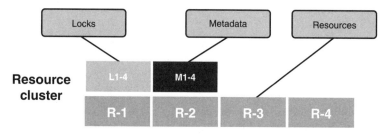

Figure 12.5   VMFS3 resource cluster

The clusters are grouped into cluster groups, which repeat to make the file system (see Figure 12.6):

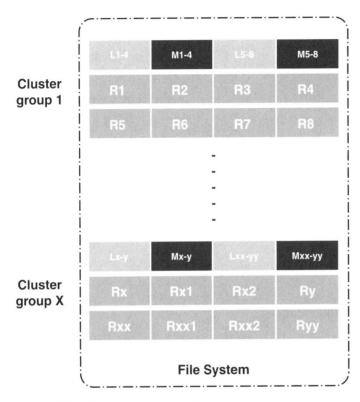

Figure 12.6 Cluster groups form file system

- **File Descriptor Cluster (fdc)**—File descriptors (inodes) keep track of the location of file data, using a fixed number of addresses (256) stored within each inode. These addresses may be sub-blocks, file blocks (see Figure 12.7), or pointer blocks (see Figure 12.8). They are for sub-blocks when the file is 64KB or smaller in size. They are for file blocks when the file is more than 1MB but not larger than 256 × file block size. They are for pointer blocks when the file is larger than 256 × file block size.

- **Sub-Block Cluster (sbc)**—Files that are equal to or smaller than VMFS3 sub-block size occupy a sub-block each (64KB). If a file grows beyond a VMFS3 sub-block size, it is no longer suballocated. This helps reduce wasting space occupied by smaller files. VMFS5 provides smaller sub-blocks (8KB), as discussed later in this chapter, in the "File Allocation Improvements" section.

Figure 12.7 shows an example of file block direct addressing.

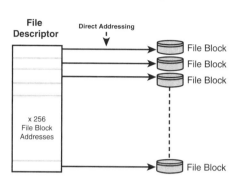

Figure 12.7   VMFS3 direct block addressing

Figure 12.8 shows an example of indirect block addressing using pointer blocks.

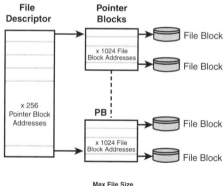

Figure 12.8   VMFS3 indirect block addressing

- **Pointer Block Cluster (pbc)**—When a file is larger than the direct block addressing limit (refer to Figure 12.7), where each file descriptor holds 256 block addresses × file block size, indirect block addressing is used. In indirect block addressing, the file descriptors hold pointer block addresses instead of file block addresses. Each pointer block holds up to 1024 file block addresses. Pointer blocks are used for indirect addressing. Figure 12.8 shows an indirect addressing block diagram. Each file descriptor holds 256 pointer block addresses. Each pointer block in turn holds (or references) 1024 file block addresses. Pointer blocks are assigned to hosts in cluster groups for better efficiency.

To better understand the correlation between the file size and VMFS3 resources, see Table 12.1.

Table 12.1 File size correlation with VMFS3 resources

File Size	Type of Addresses Stored in File Descriptor	Type of Resources Files That the Data Is Stored In
<= 64KB	Sub-block	Sub-blocks
> 64KB, <= 256 × XMB	File block	File blocks
> 256 ts] XMB	Pointer block	File blocks

- **File Block Bitmap (fbb)**—These are the bitmaps of the file blocks' data on-disk. File blocks themselves are fixed-size basic units of storage on VMFS. VMFS3 provided four different file block sizes that support different max file sizes (see Table 12.2).

Table 12.2 VMFS3 file block sizes

File Block Size	Max File Size
1MB	256GB
2MB	512GB
4MB	1TB
8MB	2TB (minus 512 bytes)

The formula for these max file sizes is (256 pointer block addresses per file descriptor × 1024 file block addresses per pointer block × file block size)

For example, the max file size for a 1MB file block is: 256 × 1024 × 1MB = 256GB.

NOTE

Max file size for 8MB block size–based VMFS3 datastores is short by 512 bytes. In other words, the size is 2TB minus 512B.

TIP

You can list the pointer block and sub-block counts on VMFS3 using the following command:

```
vmkfstools -Ph -v10 /vmfs/volumes/FC200/
```

```
VMFS-3.54 file system spanning 1 partitions.
File system label (if any): FC200
```

```
Mode: public
Capacity 199.8 GB, 86.9 GB available, file block size 1 MB, max supported
file size 256 GB
Volume Creation Time: Wed Mar 16 00:47:30 2011
Files (max/free): 30720/4926
Ptr Blocks (max/free): 64512/64409
Sub Blocks (max/free): 3968/0
Volume Metadata size: 597262336
UUID: 4d8008a2-9940968c-04df-001e4f1fbf2a
Logical device: 4d8008a2-5dadcc3a-9587-001e4f1fbf2a
Partitions spanned (on "lvm"):
        naa.6006016055711d00cef95e65664ee011:1
Is Native Snapshot Capable: NO
OBJLIB-LIB: ObjLib cleanup done.
WORKER: asyncOps=0 maxActiveOps=0 maxPending=0 maxCompleted=0
```

- **Heartbeat region**—Chapter 14, "Distributed Locks," explains the function of this region as well as locking mechanisms and concurrent access to the shared VMFS datastores.

VMFS5 Layout

Figure 12.9 shows VMFS5 on-disk layout.

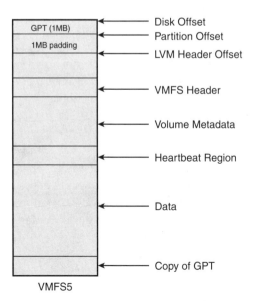

Figure 12.9 VMFS5 on-disk layout

VMFS5 layout is somewhat similar to VMFS3 layout, but it has some major differences, including the following:

- The partition is GPT based (see the section "GPT on-Disk Layout," later in this chapter). The move to adopt this format was intended to break loose from the limitations of the MBR's (master boot record's) 32-bit address space:

  - GPT address space allows vSphere to utilize LUNs larger than 2TB as VMFS5 extents as well as passthrough RDMs (see the section "Double Indirect Addressing," later in the chapter). For more information about GPT, see the Wikipedia page http://en.wikipedia.org/wiki/GUID_Partition_Table.

  - GPT allows for a theoretical maximum disk and partition size of 8 zettabytes (1024 exabytes)! However, vSphere 5 limits this to 64TB, which is the largest LUN size it supports.

  - GPT supports more than four primary partitions compared to MBR, which is limited to four primary partitions.

> **NOTE**
>
> When VMFS3 is upgraded to VMFS5, it retains its MBR partition table. After the datastore grows beyond 2TB, the MBR partition table is switched to GPT.

- At the end of the device is a secondary GPT. However, vSphere 5 does not provide tools for utilizing this for partition table recovery (at least not yet!)

- In between the two regions just discussed lies the VMFS5 partition layout. The VMFS5 partition layout appears similar to that of VMFS3, but I am over simplifying this because I am not authorized disclose the actual details. However, what I can share with you are some architectural changes that aim at improving VMFS scalability and performance. These changes are listed in the following sections.

Spanned Device Table

VMFS3 and VMFS5 are capable of spanning a volume onto multiple LUNs (see the "Span or Grow?" section, later in this chapter). VMFS5 introduced a new property, Spanned Device Table, which stores the device IDs (for example, NAA IDs) for easier identification of extents. This table is stored in the Spanned Device Descriptor on the first device of the spanned VMFS datastore (also referred to as device 0, or the head extent).

To list the content of this table, you can do the following:

1. Identify the device ID of the head extent by using the following:

```
vmkfstools -Ph /vmfs/volumes/<datastore-name>
```

For example, if the volume name is Datastore1, this is the command:

```
vmkfstools -Ph /vmfs/volumes/Storage1
```

The output would be something like Listing 12.1.

Listing 12.1   Listing extents' device IDs

```
VMFS-5.61 file system spanning 2 partitions.
File system label (if any): Storage1
Mode: public
Capacity 19.5 GB, 18.6 GB available, file block size 1 MB, max supported
file size 62.9 TB
UUID: 566e4cba-5cb58738-b6b0-001e4f1fbf2c
Partitions spanned (on "lvm"):
        naa.6000eb39a16fb1100000000000000204:1
        naa.6000eb39a16fb110000000000000020a:1
Is Native Snapshot Capable: YES
```

This means that the datastore is spanned on two devices. The first one is the head extent.

2. Use the head extent device ID you located (including the partition number) to list the Spanned Device Table property, as shown in Figure 12.10. This is the command to use:

```
hexdump -C -n 512 -s 1565184 /vmfs/devices/disks/[head extent device
ID]:[partition number]
```

This is an example:

```
hexdump -C -n 512 -s 1565184 /vmfs/devices/disks/naa.6006016012d021002
a49e23fa349e011:1
```

The displayed text in the right column of the output in Figure 12.10 is the list of devices matching the earlier output of vmkfstools.

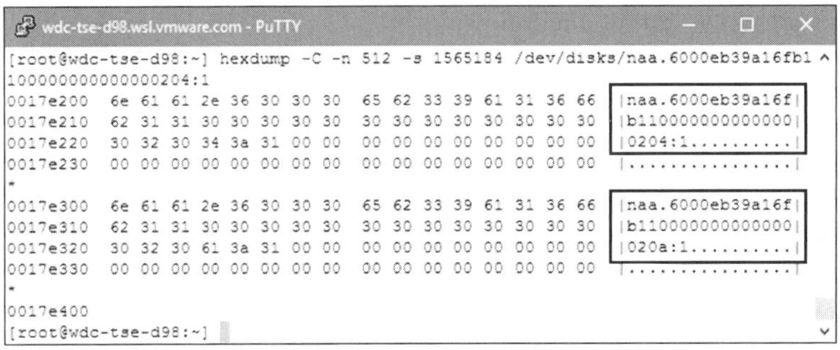

```
wdc-tse-d98.wsl.vmware.com - PuTTY                              —   □   ✕
[root@wdc-tse-d98:~] hexdump -C -n 512 -s 1565184 /dev/disks/naa.6000eb39a16fb1 ^
10000000000000000204:1
0017e200  6e 61 61 2e 36 30 30 30  65 62 33 39 61 31 36 66  |naa.6000eb39a16f|
0017e210  62 31 31 30 30 30 30 30  30 30 30 30 30 30 30 30  |b110000000000000|
0017e220  30 32 30 34 3a 31 00 00  00 00 00 00 00 00 00 00  |0204:1..........|
0017e230  00 00 00 00 00 00 00 00  00 00 00 00 00 00 00 00  |................|
*
0017e300  6e 61 61 2e 36 30 30 30  65 62 33 39 61 31 36 66  |naa.6000eb39a16f|
0017e310  62 31 31 30 30 30 30 30  30 30 30 30 30 30 30 30  |b110000000000000|
0017e320  30 32 30 61 3a 31 00 00  00 00 00 00 00 00 00 00  |020a:1..........|
0017e330  00 00 00 00 00 00 00 00  00 00 00 00 00 00 00 00  |................|
*
0017e400
[root@wdc-tse-d98:~]
```

Figure 12.10 Listing the Spanned Device Table property

> **NOTE**
>
> As long as the head extent remains accessible, you can get the information listed in steps 1 and 2. The spanned datastore can survive any of its extents—except the head extent—going offline. If the head extent goes offline and the datastore is missing one of these extents, any input/output (I/O) destined for blocks on the missing extent results in an I/O error, while I/O to the rest of the datastore is successful.

To identify the missing device, you can run the vmkfstools -Ph command; the output shown in Listing 12.2 clearly states which device is offline.

Listing 12.2 Listing the volume extent's device ID

```
VMFS-5.54 file system spanning 2 partitions.
File system label (if any): Storage1
Mode: public
Capacity 19.5 GB, 18.6 GB available, file block size 1 MB, max supported
file size 62.9 TB
UUID: 566e4cba-5cb58738-b6b0-001e4f1fbf2c
Partitions spanned (on "lvm"):
    naa.6000eb39a16fb1100000000000000204:1
    (Device naa.6000eb39a16fb110000000000000020a:1 might be offline)
    (One or more partitions spanned by this volume may be offline)
```

File Allocation Improvements

To illustrate the following points, let's first get some verbose VMFS5 properties by running the command shown in Listing 12.3.

Listing 12.3 Listing VMFS5 properties

```
vmkfstools -Ph -v10 /vmfs/volumes/FC200-New/
VMFS-5.60 file system spanning 1 partitions.
File system label (if any): FC200-New
Mode: public ATS-only
Capacity 199.8 GB, 134.5 GB available, file block size 1 MB, max supported
file size 62.9 TB
Volume Creation Time: Thu Dec 11 18:40:02 2014
Files (max/free): 130000/125798
Ptr Blocks (max/free): 64512/64386
Sub Blocks (max/free): 32000/31032
Secondary Ptr Blocks (max/free): 256/256
File Blocks (overcommit/used/overcommit %): 0/66853/0
Ptr Blocks  (overcommit/used/overcommit %): 0/126/0
Sub Blocks  (overcommit/used/overcommit %): 0/968/0
Volume Metadata size: 804683776
UUID: 5489e502-4b2f3408-dfdc-001e4f1fbf2c
Logical device: 5489e501-e93a5baa-665a-001e4f1fbf2c
Partitions spanned (on "lvm"):
        naa.6006016072902500cef93ad8007fe411:1
Is Native Snapshot Capable: YES
OBJLIB-LIB: ObjLib cleanup done.
WORKER: asyncOps=0 maxActiveOps=0 maxPending=0 maxCompleted=0
```

The following are VMFS5 improvements to file allocation:

- Block size is now 1MB only, which supports all file sizes. There is no longer a need to specify larger block sizes to be able to support larger file sizes.

  Listing 12.3 shows output taken from a freshly created VMFS5 datastore. The block size is listed as 1 MB; in contrast, VMFS3 provided block sizes 1, 2, 4, and 8MB, which supported max file sizes.

- The maximum number of files has increased to 130,000, compared to 30,720 on VMFS3.

- The maximum file size has increased to 62TB, which includes Virtual mode RDMs. For Physical mode RDMs, the limit is 64TB.

- The maximum datastore size remains at 64TB. However, the extent size can be more than 2TB, with the max being 64TB.

- Sub-block allocation is now 8KB block size, compared to 64KB on VMFS3, effectively increasing the number of sub-blocks.

- Small file packing (also known as zero-level address [ZLA])—is used to store a file within its own file descriptor (inode) when the file size is smaller than 1KB. When the file grows beyond that size, its data is copied out to a sub-block if it has not reached 8KB in size. When it grows beyond that, it is stored in file blocks.
- The efficiency of handling Pointer Block Cluster (pbc) caching has been improved.
- .sdd.sf, which is a system data directory, has been added. It extends the file system resources for features planned for a future release.
- The .pb2.sf system file has been added to support pbc growth when upgrading from vSphere 5.x to 6. In vSphere 5, the max limit for pbc was 64,512, and the max limit in vSphere 6 is much larger. Figure 12.11 shows VMFS5 system files. They are the same system files as in VMFS3 (refer to Figure 12.3), with the addition of .pb2.sf and .sdd.sf.

```
wdc-tse-i67.wsl.vmware.com - PuTTY
[root@wdc-tse-i67:~] ls -al /vmfs/volumes/FC200-New/ |grep .sf
-r--------    1 root     root       1114112 Dec 11  2014 .fbb.sf
-r--------    1 root     root     267026432 Dec 11  2014 .fdc.sf
-rwxr-xr-x    1 root     root       1048576 Jul  4 16:49 .iormstats.sf
-r--------    1 root     root       1179648 Dec 11  2014 .pb2.sf
-r--------    1 root     root     268435456 Dec 11  2014 .pbc.sf
-r--------    1 root     root     262733824 Dec 11  2014 .sbc.sf
drwx------    1 root     root           280 Dec 11  2014 .sdd.sf
-r--------    1 root     root       4194304 Dec 11  2014 .vh.sf
[root@wdc-tse-i67:~]
```

Figure 12.11 VMFS5 system files

Double Indirect Addressing

A freshly created VMFS5 datastore provides 1MB file blocks only. To support varying file sizes beyond 256GB, VMFS5 resorts to using double indirect addressing. If you look at VMFS3's implementation of indirect addressing, you notice that the maximum number of file blocks is fixed and the max file size depends on the file block size. On the other hand, VMFS5 has a fixed file block size (1MB), and to be able to address file sizes beyond 256GB, each secondary pointer block points to the 1024 primary pointer block. Because the primary pointer block can store up to 1024 file block addresses, it effectively increases the addressable file blocks 1024-fold (see Figure 12.12).

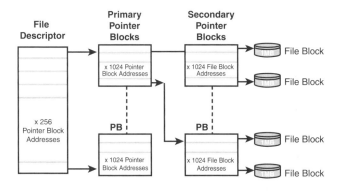

Figure 12.12   VMFS5 double indirect block addressing

This architecture would provide a theoretical max file size of 256TB, based on the following formula:

256 block addresses per file descriptor × 1024 addresses per secondary pointer block × 1024 file block addresses per primary pointer block × 1MB per file block

That is:

$256 \times 1024 \times 1024 \times 1MB = 256TB$

However, vSphere 6 increased the max virtual disk size from 2TB to 62TB, which is the same for non-passthrough RDM, while the max size of passthrough RDM as well as the LVM (max datastore size) are limited to 64TB.

The secondary pointer blocks resources are partially used in vSphere 6. They are limited to 256 addresses, which explains the 64TB limit, which, based on the formula, is the result of $256 \times 256 \times 1024 \times 1MB = 64TB$.

Table 12.3 shows Table 12.1 revised for VMFS5.

Table 12.3 File size correlation with VMFS5 resources

File Size	Type of Addresses Stored in File Descriptor	Secondary Pointer Blocks Used?	Type of Resources File That the Data Is Stored In
<= 8KB	Sub-block	No	Sub-blocks
> 8KB, <= 256 × 1MB	File block	No	File blocks
> 256MB, <= 256 × 1024 × 1MB	Pointer block	No	File blocks
> 256GB,<= 256 × 256*1024 × 1MB (that is, 64TB)	Pointer block	Yes	File Blocks

Common Causes of Partition Table Problems

I have seen several cases where a VMFS3 partition table has been corrupt or lost. The most common cause is presenting the VMFS3 LUN to non-ESXi hosts, especially those running Windows. You are probably familiar with the dialog you get when you first run the Disk Management tool on a Windows OS that prompts you to "initialize the disk." Even if you do not partition it or format it using this tool, initializing the disk results in overwriting the partition table. Positive proof of that was evident from the dump of the first few sectors of the LUN housing the VMFS volume where I frequently found the Windows signature.

The same can happen, although by a different mechanism, with Linux or Solaris hosts given access to the VMFS3 LUN.

The next most common cause is user error. VMware has introduced some mechanisms to prevent such corruption, except for hardware/firmware issues, to prevent the partition table that is in use from being clobbered or deleted.

I have not seen this as much recently. However, older logs often showed the following messages:

```
in-use partition modification is not supported
Can't clobber active ptable for LUN <Device ID>
```

It is strongly recommended that you utilize a logical grouping of initiator records on storage arrays—for example, host groups—and assign the LUNs to that group only. This prevents accidental presentation of ESXi hosts' LUNs to non-ESXi hosts.

Another less common cause is a storage array rebuilding the RAID set after losing one of the backing disks. Sometimes with a faulty cache or firmware, some blocks fail to be written to the disk, and all you see on these blocks are some fixed pattern similar to that used by the disk manufacturer to test the media. This has been fixed by the storage vendors with which VMware has collaborated on identifying this mode of corruption. Depending on which blocks were affected, the partition table could get corrupt.

Re-creating a Lost Partition Table for VMFS3 Datastores

For the increasingly rare situation of the partition table being missing or corrupt, let me share with you a process you can use to re-create it. This process works most of the time, as long as the corruption does not extend into the metadata.

Understanding the Normal Partition Table

Before we begin with the re-creation process, let's first review how the normal partition table looks.

To list the partition table, you use `fdisk`. This tool is based on Linux and was modified to support VMFS3 file system. This is the command to use on ESXi 6:

```
fdisk -lu /vmfs/devices/disks/<device ID>
```

or this:

```
fdisk -lu /dev/disks/<device ID>
```

> **NOTE**
>
> /vmfs/devices is a symbolic link to /dev on ESXi 6.

The output of a healthy partition table looks as shown in Figure 12.13.

Figure 12.13 Listing a healthy VMFS3 partition table

In this example, I used the `-lu` option to get the units in sectors that are physical disk blocks of 512 bytes each. You see why it's important to use this unit when going through the process of rebuilding the partition table. If you use `-l` instead, you get something like this:

```
fdisk -l /dev/disks/naa.6006016055711d00cef95e65664ee011

Disk /dev/disks/naa.6006016055711d00cef95e65664ee011: 214.7 GB, 214748364800
bytes
255 heads, 63 sectors/track, 26108 cylinders
Units = cylinders of 16065 * 512 = 8225280 bytes

                        Device Boot  Start End    Blocks     Id System
/dev/disks/naa.6006016055711d00cef95e65664ee011p1  1  26108  209711486 fb VMFS
```

Notice that the output here uses cylinders as units, with size 16,065 × 512, which makes it difficult to count blocks in the procedure.

Now let's continue with the output shown in Figure 12.13. It shows that the VMFS partition with ID `fb` starts at sector 2048, which means it starts 1MB from the disk offset. The partition ends at sector 419425019. Note that `fb` is the system ID for VMFS. This was an available ID at the time VMware first extended `fdisk` for use with ESX. Another ID VMware uses is `fc`, which is for a vmkcore or vmkernel core dump partition. You typically encounter the latter type on ESXi boot devices.

Repairing a Corrupt or Lost Partition Table

Now, on to the important part of this section—the actual process of repairing the partition table. These are the basic steps, and they're explained in more detail in the following sections:

1. Identify the device name that represents the affected LUN.
2. Locate the LVM header offset.
3. Calculate the partition offset.
4. Use `fdisk` to re-create the partition table.
5. Mount the datastore.

Identifying Device Name

Follow these steps to identify the device name that represents the affected LUN:

1. List the VMFS datastores and their associated device names by using `esxcli`. Figure 12.14 show the output of this command:

   ```
   esxcli storage vmfs extent list
   ```

   This command lists all VMFS datastore extents and their associated device names and partition numbers.

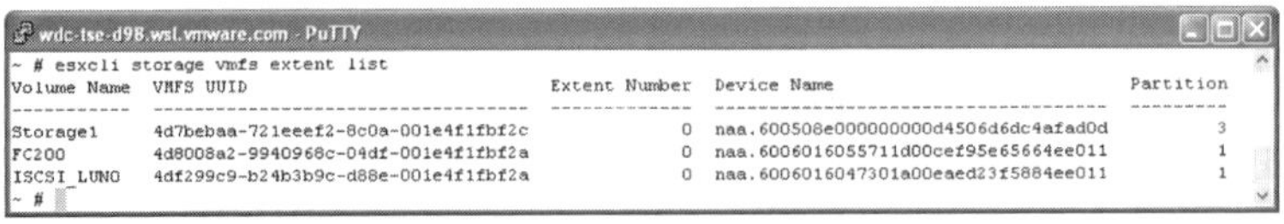

Figure 12.14   Listing VMFS extents (devices)

2. List all devices on this host by using the `esxcfg-scsidevs` command. In the example shown in Figure 12.15, I used the `-c` option to get a compact list of devices and their associated console device names. (Figure 12.15 is cropped to show only the relevant columns.)

```
wdc-tse-d98.wsl.vmware.com - PuTTY
~ # esxcfg-scsidevs -c |less -S
Device UID                             Device Type    Console Device
mpx.vmhba0:C0:T0:L0                    CD-ROM         /vmfs/devices/cdrom/mpx.vmhba0:C0:T0:L0
mpx.vmhba32:C0:T0:L0                   CD-ROM         /vmfs/devices/cdrom/mpx.vmhba32:C0:T0:L0
naa.600508e000000000d4506d6dc4afad0d   Direct-Access  /vmfs/devices/disks/naa.600508e000000000d4506d6dc4afad0d
naa.6006016047301a00eaed23f5884ee011   Direct-Access  /vmfs/devices/disks/naa.6006016047301a00eaed23f5884ee011
naa.6006016055711d00cef95e65664ee011   Direct-Access  /vmfs/devices/disks/naa.6006016055711d00cef95e65664ee011
naa.6006016055711d00cff95e65664ee011   Direct-Access  /vmfs/devices/disks/naa.6006016055711d00cff95e65664ee011
```

Figure 12.15   Listing all storage devices

3. Notice in Figure 12.15 that I have four `Direct-Access` devices, but Figure 12.14 shows three VMFS datastores. Comparing both outputs, I can identify the device ID and console device name of the potentially affected LUN, which is `naa.6006016055 711d00cff95e65664ee011`.

From steps 1 and 2, I know that this is the device name I need to use with this procedure:

`/dev/disks/naa.6006016055711d00cff95e65664ee011`

Notice that I changed /vmfs/devices to /dev because the former is linked to the latter, and it makes the command line shorter.

To verify that you have located the affected device, you can run `fdisk -lu` to list its partition table:

```
fdisk -lu /dev/disks/naa.6006016055711d00cff95e65664ee011

Disk /dev/disks/naa.6006016055711d00cff95e65664ee011: 10.7 GB, 10737418240
bytes
255 heads, 63 sectors/track, 1305 cylinders, total 20971520 sectors
Units = sectors of 1 * 512 = 512 bytes

Disk /dev/disks/naa.6006016055711d00cff95e65664ee011 doesn't contain a
valid partition table
```

What if the Datastore Has Extents?

If you have a datastore with extents and one or more of these extents suffers from a damaged or lost partition table *and* the head extent is intact, the best way to identify the affected devices is by running the following:

`vmkfstools -P /vmfs/volumes/<volume-name>`

This should list the extents and their device names. Use the device name whose status is offline. The rest of the procedure stays the same.

If the head extent is also affected, attempt to rebuild the partition tables on all affected devices and, if it's successful, it all comes together, and the volume is mounted.

Locating the LVM Header Offset

To locate the LVM header offset, you can use `hexdump`, as shown in Listing 12.4.

Listing 12.4   Locating the LVM header offset by using `hexdump`

```
hexdump /dev/disks/naa.6006016055711d00cff95e65664ee011|grep -m 1 "d00d c001"
0200000 d00d c001 0003 0000 0015 0000 1602 0000
```

By using the `hexdump` utility included with ESXi 6, you can list the hex content of the device.

The LVM header offset would show `d00d c001` as the first 4 bytes. The following 2 bytes show the major VMFS version. In this example, it is `0003`, which means this volume was VMFS3. If it were VMFS5, the value would be `0005`.

TIP

Do not use the `-C` option with `hexdump` because it lists the output in reverse byte order. For example, `d00d c001` would be listed as `0d d0 01 c0`, which can get you confused.

Based on the dump shown in Listing 12.4, the LVM header offset is at 0200000.

Calculating the Partition Offset

Now you can use the LVM header offset to count backward 1MB, which is how far it lies from the partition offset:

1. Convert the LVM header offset value from hex to decimal:

   0200000 Hex = 2097152 Decimal

2. Convert the byte count to sectors (divide by 512, which is the sector size):

   2097152 / 512 = 4096 sectors

3. Subtract the number of sectors that add up to 1MB (2048 sectors of 512 bytes each):

   4096 − 2048 = 2048

   This means the partition starts at sector 2048.

Using `fdisk` to Re-create the Partition Table

The process of re-creating the partition table is fairly straightforward. First, use the following command to specify sectors instead of cylinders:

```
fdisk -u /dev/disks/naa.6006016055711d00cff95e65664ee011
```

You use the following options and values:

- n to create a new partition

- p to specify that this is a primary partition

- 1 to specify that this is the first partition

- 2048 to set the partition offset

- Enter to accept the default value for the last sector

- t to change the system type

- fb to specify VMFS as the system type

- w to write the changes and exit `fdisk`

Mounting the Recovered Datastore

To mount the VMFS datastore, rescan the device for VMFS datastore by running the following:

```
vmkfstools -V
```

This hidden option probes the file system and mounts the datastore found on the re-created partition table. To verify whether the datastore was mounted successfully, check the content of the /vmfs/volumes directory by using the following:

```
ls /vmfs/volumes
```

Re-creating a Lost Partition Table for VMFS5 Datastores

VMFS5 datastores have a relatively similar partition table geometry to VMFS3 datastores but use GPT instead of MBR.

The process of identifying the partition offset is identical to that in VMFS3, as discussed in the previous section. The only difference is that the major version of VMFS is 5 instead of 3 in the hexdump.

In addition, the command used for re-creating the partition table is `partedUtil` instead of `fdisk`.

GPT on-Disk Layout

Let's review the GPT on-disk layout. Figure 12.16 shows the GUID partition table scheme.

GUID Partition Table Scheme

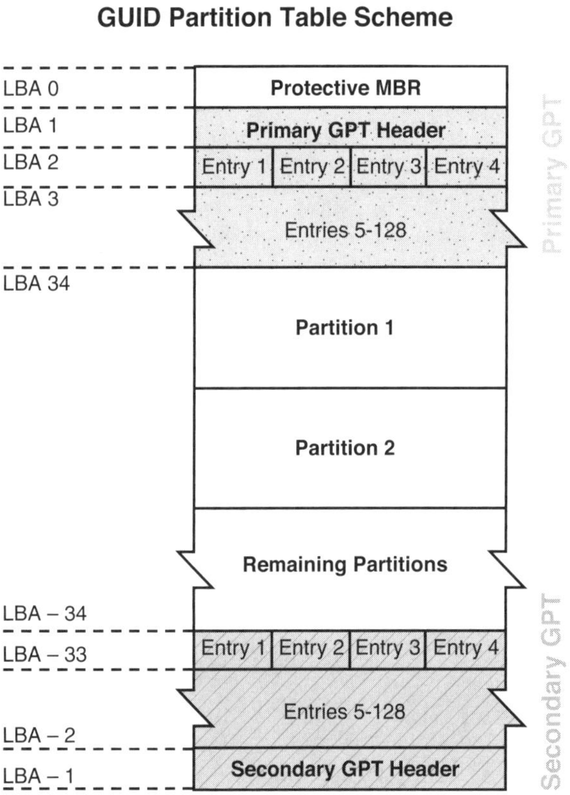

Figure 12.16   GPT layout [Image courtesy CC-By-SA-2.5 from Wikipedia]

Note the following in Figure 12.16:

- The first LBA (sector), which is LBA0, is occupied by a protective MBR.

- The primary GPT header is on LBA1 (second disk sector).

- LBA2 has the first four entries, followed by entries 5 through 128, which end on LBA33. VMFS partition can be anywhere beginning from LBA34 (the 35th disk sector).

- The secondary GPT header is on the last LBA on the disk. So, it starts at LBA –1, which means that if the device has 1024000 sectors, the last LBA would be number 1024000 minus 1, or 1023999.

- The backup entries 5 through 128 are on the previous 31 sectors (LBA –2 through LBA –32).

- The remaining entries, 1 through 4, are on the previous sector (LBA –33).

This means that the usable sectors on the device begin on LBA 34 and end on LBA —34.

To illustrate this, examine the following output:

```
partedUtil getptbl /dev/disks/naa.6000eb39a16fb1100000000000000204

gpt
1305 255 63 20971520
1 2048 20971486 AA31E02A400F11DB9590000C2911D1B8 vmfs 0
```

This command lists the healthy GPT partition table from the device I used as a recovery example. This output was produced before the partition table was removed. The output shows the following:

- It shows the partition type, which in this example is gpt. Another value you might see is msdos, which is what you see when you use partedUtil with a VMFS3 partition created by pre-ESXi 5 hosts.

- The second line shows the disk geometry in the format C, H, S, Sectors—or cylinders, heads, sectors per track, and total sector count.

- The last line shows the VMFS partition details in the format Partition Number, Offset (first sector), Last Sector, GUID, Partition type, and finally the attribute.

The GUID is specific to VMFS. You can get this value from the following output:

```
partedUtil showGuids

Partition Type         GUID
vmfs                   AA31E02A400F11DB9590000C2911D1B8
vmkDiagnostic          9D27538040AD11DBBF97000C2911D1B8
vsan                   381CFCCC728811E092EE000C2911D0B2
virsto                 77719A0CA4A011E3A47E000C29745A24
VMware Reserved        9198EFFC31C011DB8F78000C2911D1B8
Basic Data             EBD0A0A2B9E5443387C068B6B72699C7
Linux Swap             0657FD6DA4AB43C484E50933C84B4F4F
Linux Lvm              E6D6D379F50744C2A23C238F2A3DF928
```

```
Linux Raid            A19D880F05FC4D3BA006743F0F84911E
Efi System            C12A7328F81F11D2BA4B00A0C93EC93B
Microsoft Reserved    E3C9E3160B5C4DB8817DF92DF00215AE
Unused Entry          00000000000000000000000000000000
```

The partition type is `vmfs`, and the attribute is always `0` for VMFS partitions.

This command lists the first and last usable sector on the device:

```
partedUtil getUsableSectors /dev/disks/naa.6000eb39a16fb1100000000000000204
```

```
34 20971486
```

Based on the GPT on-disk layout details provided in the `getptbl` command, the last usable sector is LBA –34. This example shows that the total number of sectors on this device is 20971520. If you subtract 34 to get the last usable sector, that would be (20971520 – 34 = 20971486), which matches the `getptbl` command output.

Using VOMA to List a Partition Table

VOMA (vSphere On-disk Metadata Analyzer) is a new VMFS analysis tool. It was introduced In ESXi 5.5 with read-only capabilities and has been enhanced in ESXi 6 to include some repair capability.

One of the options available is `ptbl`, which means *partition table*. The following is the syntax to use for listing a VMFS partition table:

```
voma --module ptbl --func check --device /dev/disks/[device ID]
```

The following example uses the same device ID used earlier in this chapter with `partedUtil`:

```
voma -m ptbl -f check -d /dev/disks/naa.6000eb39a16fb1100000000000000204
Running Partition table checker version 0.1 in check mode
Phase 1: Checking device for valid primary GPT
   Detected valid GPT signatures
   Number    Start       End           Type
   1         2048        20971486      vmfs


Found a valid partition table on the device


Total Errors Found:       0
```

This output provides the following:

- **Partition table type**—GPT

- **Partition offset**—2048

- **Partition end (which is the same as `lastUsableSector` listed by `partedUtil`)**—20971486

- **Partition type (which is similar to using `showGuids` option used by `partedUtil`)**—vmfs

As you see here, VOMA provides several details in a single step that combines equivalent information obtained using three separate `partedUtil` commands. Moreover, VOMA check the health of the partition table.

> **NOTE**
>
> When you use the `ptbl` module, you must use the `--device` argument with the device name and without any partition number. All other VOMA modules either require the partition number or can tolerate not using it, as shown in the next section, "**More About VOMA.**"

If there is a problem with the partition table, you may get an error like this in phase 4:

```
Disk should have a GPT partition table with VMFS partition, start sector:
2048, end sector: 20971486
```

Take note of the reported start and end sectors, which you'll learn more about in the section "Re-creating the Partition Table," later in this chapter.

More About VOMA

VOMA can be used for more than just displaying a partition table. It has the potential to repair a few issues with a partition table, as well as VMFS resources such as heartbeat records. (See Chapter 14.)

The available command-line options can be listed by running:

```
voma --help
```

The output is shown in Figure 12.17.

```
 [root@localhost:~] voma --help
Usage:
voma [OPTIONS] -m module -d device
 -m, --module      Name of the module to run.
                   Available Modules are
                      1. lvm
                      2. vmfs
                      3. vmfsl
                      4. ptbl
 -f, --func        Function(s) to be done by the module.
                   Options are
                      query  - list functions supported by module
                      check  - check for Errors
                      fix    - check & fix
 -d, --device      Device/Disk to be inspected
 -s, --logfile     Path to file, redirects the output to given file
 -v, --version     Prints voma version and exit.
 -h, --help        Print this help message.
Example:
voma -m vmfs -f check -d /vmfs/devices/disks/naa.xxxx:x

[root@localhost:~]
```

Figure 12.17   VOMA command-line help

The minimum required option is `--device`:

This is the syntax:

```
voma -d /vmfs/devices/disks/[device ID]
```

Here is an example:

```
voma --device /vmfs/devices/disks/naa.6006016072902500cef93ad8007fe411
```

This is the first part of the output of this command:

```
Module name is missing. Using "vmfs" as default
Checking if device is actively used by other hosts
Running VMFS Checker version 1.2 in default mode
Initializing LVM metadata, Basic Checks will be done
```

This means that the default options are `--module vmfs` and `--func check`.

Note that the path to the device can be shortened by using `/dev` instead of `/vmfs/devices` because the latter is a symbolic link to the former. So, this would be the command:

```
voma --device /dev/disks/naa.6006016072902500cef93ad8007fe411
```

By using this command along with the partition table, you can check only for hosts actively using the device. The command identifies the hosts' management port MAC addresses from their corresponding heartbeat records.

Here is an example:

```
voma -d /dev/disks/naa.6006016055711d00cef95e65664ee011:1
Module name is missing. Using "vmfs" as default
Checking if device is actively used by other hosts
Found 4 actively heartbeating hosts on device '/dev/disks/naa.6006016055711
d00cef95e65664ee011:1'
1): MAC address 00:1e:4f:1f:bf:2c
2): MAC address 00:1a:64:36:c3:20
3): MAC address 00:1f:29:e0:4d:52
4): MAC address 00:14:5e:da:a8:0a
```

VOMA Modules

VOMA provides four modules, and except for `lvm`, each of them has a fix function:

- `lvm`—This module checks the validity of the datastore's logical device header, logical volume header, and physical extent mappings.

- `vmfs`—This module checks the VMFS datastore in five phases:

  Phase 1: VMFS header and resource files

  Phase 2: VMFS heartbeat region

  Phase 3: File descriptors

  Phase 4: Pathname and connectivity

  Phase 5: Resource reference counts

- `vmfsl`—This module checks the vSAN datastore's file system validity. This was design for vSAN 1.0 (on vSphere 5.5 Update 1 and newer).

- `ptbl`—This module checks the partition table and provided table structure. If it detects problems, it reports the relevant VMFS partition table type as well as partition start and end sectors.

Re-creating the Partition Table

The following is the syntax to re-create the partition table:

```
partedUtil setptbl "/dev/disks/<DeviceName>" DiskLabel "partNum startSector
endSector type/guid attribute"
```

These are the required parameters:

- `DeviceName`—This is the NAA ID of the affected device, including the path— (for example, `/dev/disks/naa. 6000eb39a16fb1100000000000000204`).

- `DiskLabel`—This is the partition type, which for our purpose can be either `msdos` or `gpt`. The former creates a partition `fdisk` style, (MBR) whereas the latter creates a partition for use with ESXi 6 datastores. To rebuild a VMFS5 partition table, this must be `gpt`.

- `partNum`—This is the partition number. Because any VMFS5 datastores are stored on a single partition (other than local storage used for booting ESXi or boot-from-SAN LUNs), the partition number is always 1.

- `startSector`—This is the partition offset that you calculated from the hexdump analysis in the "Locating the LVM Header Offset" section. In this example, it is 2048.

- `endSector`—This is the last usable sector, discussed in the "GPT on-Disk Layout" section. So, to get the last usable sector number, you subtract 34 from the total number of sectors of the affected device.

To refresh your memory, earlier you identified the size of the device in sectors, by running the following:

```
partedUtil get /dev/disks/<device-ID>
```

Here is an example:

```
partedUtil get /dev/disks/naa.6000eb39a16fb1100000000000000204
1305 255 63 20971520
```

In this example, the total number of sectors on this device is 20971520. To get the last usable sector, subtract 34 from that, and you get 20971486.

If this does not work, possibly because the primary GPT was also damaged or deleted, you can use VOMA instead:

```
voma --module ptbl -d /dev/disks/<device-id>
```

Here is an example:

```
voma --module ptbl --device /dev/disks/naa.6000eb39a16fb1100000000000000204

Running Partition table checker version 0.1 in check mode
Phase 1: Checking device for valid primary GPT
Phase 2: Checking device for a valid backup GPT
Phase 3: Checking device for valid MBR table
Phase 4: Searching for valid file system headers
```

```
Detected valid LVM headers at offset 2097152
Detected VMFS file system (labeled:'iSCSI_LHN1') with UUID: 566e4cba-
5cb58738-b6b0-001e4f1fbf2c, Version 5:60
Newly formatted VMFS5 file system detected
Disk should have a GPT partition table with VMFS partition, start sector:
2048, end sector: 20971486
```

In this example, the start sector is 2047, and the end sector is 20971486.

- The GUID is AA31E02A400F11DB9590000C2911D1B8, which I listed earlier in the output of `partedUtil showGuids`. The Partition attribute is always 0 for VMFS partitions.

Using these guidelines, the following is the command to re-create the partition table for this example:

```
partedUtil setptbl "/dev/disks/naa.6000eb39a16fb1100000000000000204" gpt "1
2048 20971486 AA31E02A400F11DB9590000C2911D1B8 0"
```

After the partition table has been re-created, you can mount the datastore automatically by running the following:

```
vmkfstools -V
```

If the operation is successful, you should see the datastore listed in the /vmfs/volumes directory.

TIP

Check /var/log/vmkernel.log for the following error:

```
LVM: 2907: [naa. 6000eb39a16fb1100000000000000204:1] Device expanded
(actual size 20969439 blocks, stored size 20964092 blocks)
```

This message means that the last sector used in re-creating the partition table did not match the original value. You can simply calculate the difference and add it to the `partedUtil` command's last sector value that you used to re-create the table. (In the example that generated this message, I had deliberately used a last sector value that was 5347 sectors short of the correct last usable sector.)

You do not need to delete the table you created. Just rerunning the command with the new values overwrites the current table.

ONE MORE TIP

If you see the following message in /var/log/vmkernel.log, it means that the "protective MBR" on the first sector was deleted or corrupt:

```
WARNING: Partition: 434: No Prot MBR for "naa. 6000eb39a1
6fb1100000000000000204". GPT entries will be skipped
```

Re-creating the table as outlined in this section should help you recover from this situation as long as the corruption was limited to the first 34 sectors of the device.

YET ANOTHER TIP

In the very rare situation where the primary GPT is corrupt and the protective MBR is still intact, you get the following output when you run the `partedUtil getptbl` command:

```
partedUtil getptbl /dev/disks/naa. 6000eb39a16fb1100000000000000204

Error: The primary GPT table is corrupt, but the backup appears OK,
so that will be used.

gpt

1305 255 63 20971520
```

If this is the case, you might be able to recover the primary GPT by using `partedtUtil fix <device-name>`, which copies the secondary GPT and places it in the primary GPT blocks.

Preparing for the Worst: Recovering from a File System Corruption

The procedures previously discussed assume that the extent of corruption was limited to certain sectors, whose structure is repairable using generally available tools such as `fdisk` and `partedUtil`. However, damage beyond the VMFS partition offset that involves the metadata is much harder to repair without enlisting the services of a data recovery service such as Kroll-Ontrack or Seagate and others (see VMware KB 1015413, at http://kb.vmware.com/kb/1015413).

To improve your chances of recovering VMFS, you should have a BC/DR (business continuity/disaster recovery) plan that provides backup of your data, storage replication/mirroring/snapshots/and so on, recovery site(s), and infrastructure/fabric redundancy. The following sections provide a few tips that can improve your chances, using simple tasks that do not take much of your time.

Maintaining a List of Your VMFS Partition Tables

The easiest way to gather a partition table is to collect vm-support dumps either locally on the host or preferably via vSphere 6 Web Client.

Collecting Diagnostic Data

To collect vm-support dumps, follow this procedure:

1. Log on to vCenter Server using the vSphere 6 Web Client.

2. Navigate to the **Hosts and Clusters** section.

3. Right-click the vCenter Server from the Inventory list and then click the **Export System Logs** menu option (see Figure 12.18). If you want to collect logs from a single ESXi host, right-click the host in the inventory tree instead and skip to step 5.

Figure 12.18   Accessing the Export System Logs menu

4. In the Source dialog (see Figure 12.19), select the list of ESXi hosts from which you want to collect the dumps. If you want to include vCenter Server and vSphere Web Client logs, select the check box at the bottom of the dialog and then click **Next**.

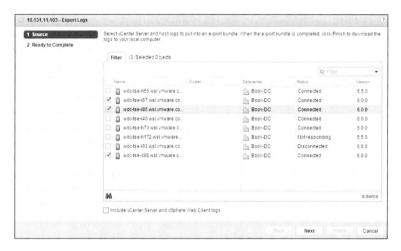

Figure 12.19   Selecting hosts for exporting system logs

5. In the Ready to Complete dialog, you can accept the defaults and click the **Generate Log Bundle** button to start the log collection process. This may take some time, depending on the logs and core dump sizes. If you want to reduce the dump size, you can uncheck everything except the log types you want to collect. You may need to expand each grouping to show the subselections. I recommend including the vmfsheader suboption of the FileSystem option to collect the .vh.sf system files from all VMFS datastores on the ESXi host (see Figure 12.20). To understand what gets collected by each selection, read the corresponding manifests located in the /etc/vmware/vm-support directory on one of the ESXi 6 hosts.

Figure 12.20   Selecting the option to collect the VMFS header

6. Once the bundles are generated and the button name changes to **Download Log Bundle**, click this button and, in the Save As dialog, specify a folder that is accessible to your vSphere 6 Web Client desktop and then click **Save**.

7. A download progress bar appears below the download button. When it is complete, click **Finish** to exit the completed collection process. The logs are located in the folder you specified in step 6, in a zip file named using following pattern:

```
VMware-vCenter-support-YYYY-MM-DD@HH-MM-SS.zip
```

The `vm-support` dumps included in the zip file are named using the following pattern:

```
ESXiHostName-vmYYYY-MM-DD@HH-MM-SS.tgz
```

8. When the need arises to use the collected data, you can do the following:

   - Transfer the dump to an ESXi host or a Linux host.
   - Extract the dump by using the following:
     - `tar zxvf <dump-file-name>`
   - The extracted files are in a directory named using the following pattern:
     - `esx-ESXiHostname-YYYY-MM-DD--HH.MM`
   - Before proceeding with utilizing the content of the extract dump, you must first reconstruct some output that was collected in chunks. You do so by running the following:

     ```
     cd <path-to-extracted-dump>
     ./reconstruct.sh
     ```

Which Parts of the Dump Provide Partition Table Details?

After expanding the `vm-support` dump as outlined in step 8, you can locate the output of `esxcfg-info -a` in the /commands directory, in a file named esxcfg-info_-a.txt. In this output are all the publicly available ESXi host properties and configuration as of the time the dump was collected. This output is organized in a text-based tree structure. Branches are known as VSI nodes, and they include objects that hold certain properties.

Each VMFS volume's info, including its extents and partition table, is located in nodes like those shown in Figure 12.21.

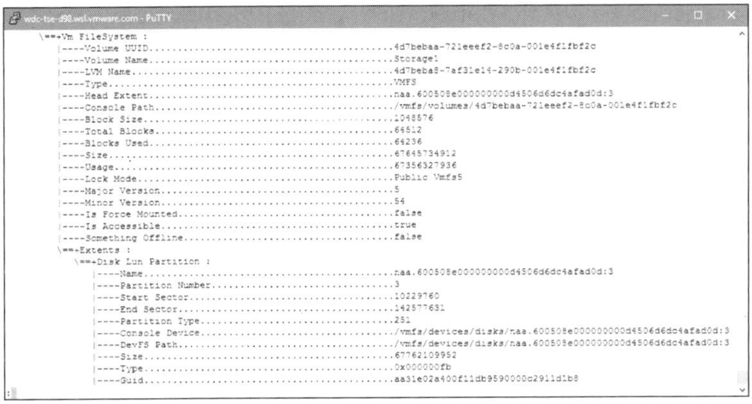

Figure 12.21   VMFS5 VSI nodes

Here you see all properties of the VMFS volume, which helps you identify the following:

- The volume's UUID (signature)

- The VMFS version (in this example, the major version is 5, and the minor one is 54)

- The device ID (NAA ID), which is the Name field listed under Extents, which also includes the partition number after a colon (:)

- The start sector (in this example, 2048)

- The end sector (in this example, 20971487) (Notice that this value is always one sector larger than in the partedUtil output. I am investigating this discrepancy as of the time of this writing.)

Manually Collecting Partition Info Summary

If you have a small number of hosts, or otherwise have the time, you can collect a list of partitions from each host by using the following:

```
esxcli storage core device partition list
```

This gives you output similar to the output shown in Figure 12.22.

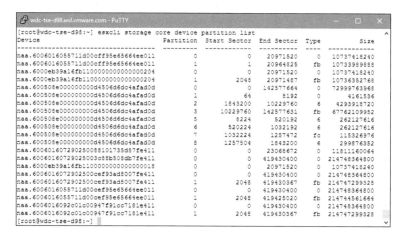

```
wdc-tse-d98.wsl.vmware.com - PuTTY                                              —   □   X

[root@wdc-tse-d98:~] esxcli storage core device partition list
Device                                       Partition  Start Sector  End Sector  Type       Size
-------------------------------------------  ---------  ------------  ----------  ----  ------------
naa.6006016055711d00cff95e65664ee011                 0             0    20971520     0   10737418240
naa.6006016055711d00cff95e65664ee011                 1             1    20964825    fb   10733989888
naa.6000eb39a16fb1100000000000000204                 0             0    20971520     0   10737418240
naa.6000eb39a16fb1100000000000000204                 1          2048    20971487    fb   10736352768
naa.600508e000000000d4506d6dc4afad0d                 0             0   142577664     0   72999763968
naa.600508e000000000d4506d6dc4afad0d                 1            64        8192     0       4161536
naa.600508e000000000d4506d6dc4afad0d                 2       1843200    10229760     6    4293918720
naa.600508e000000000d4506d6dc4afad0d                 3      10229760   142577631    fb   67762109952
naa.600508e000000000d4506d6dc4afad0d                 5          8224      520192     6     262127616
naa.600508e000000000d4506d6dc4afad0d                 6        520224     1032192     6     262127616
naa.600508e000000000d4506d6dc4afad0d                 7       1032224     1257472    fc     115326976
naa.600508e000000000d4506d6dc4afad0d                 8       1257504     1843200     6     299876352
naa.6006016072902500881017 35d87fe411               0             0    23068672     0   11811160064
naa.6006016072902500 3c88b508db7fe411               0             0   419430400     0  214748364800
naa.6000eb39a16fb1100000000000000018                 0             0    20971520     0   10737418240
naa.6006016072902500cef93ad8007fe411                 0             0   419430400     0  214748364800
naa.6006016072902500cef93ad8007fe411                 1          2048   419430367    fb  214747299328
naa.6006016055711d00cef95e65664ee011                 0             0   419430400     0  214748364800
naa.6006016055711d00cef95e65664ee011                 1          2048   419425020    fb  214744561664
naa.6006016092c01c00947f91cc7181e411                 0             0   419430400     0  214748364800
naa.6006016092c01c00947f91cc7181e411                 1          2048   419430367    fb  214747299328
[root@wdc-tse-d98:~]
```

Figure 12.22 Listing partitions on all devices

The output includes the following columns:

- **Device ID**—This is the NAA ID of the LUN on which the VMFS datastore resides.

- **Partition**—When the partition number listed is 0, this means that the listing represents the whole LUN, which is why the start sector is 0. Conversely, the end sector in this case refers to the last LBA (logical block address) on the LUN.

  The output shown in Figure 12.22 was collected from an ESXi 6 host with typical configuration, which boots from a local disk because one of the devices has eight partitions (1 through 8).

- **Start Sector**—This is the first LBA in the partition. If the value is 0, the partition number is also 0 because the listing is for the whole device. A value higher than 0 means the actual LBA numbers on which the partition offset is located.

- **End Sector**—This is the last LBA in the partition. For devices with a single partition, this value should match the last usable sector obtained by the partedUtil getUsableSectors command listed earlier in this chapter, in the section "GPT on-Disk Layout."

  For listings representing the whole device, this value represents the last LBA on the LUN.

NOTE

This output is derived from the VSI nodes I mentioned in relation to Figure 12.21. As such, I want to draw your attention to the fact that the end sector from this output is always one sector more than what you get from `partedUtil` output. Keep this in mind when you calculate the partition's last sector for the purpose of rebuilding the partition table.

For example, if you get the partition table listing of the boot device that has eight partitions (device ID `naa.600508e000000000d4506d6dc4afad0d`), you observe this as well. See the values in the third column in the following output for comparison:

```
partedUtil getptbl /dev/disks/naa.600508e000000000d4506d6dc4afad0d
gpt
8875 255 63 142577664
1 64        8191     C12A7328F81F11D2BA4B00A0C93EC93B systemPartition 128
5 8224      520191   EBD0A0A2B9E5443387C068B6B72699C7 linuxNative      0
6 520224    1032191  EBD0A0A2B9E5443387C068B6B72699C7 linuxNative      0
7 1032224   1257471  9D27538040AD11DBBF97000C2911D1B8 vmkDiagnostic     0
8 1257504   1843199  EBD0A0A2B9E5443387C068B6B72699C7 linuxNative      0
2 1843200   10229759 EBD0A0A2B9E5443387C068B6B72699C7 linuxNative      0
3 10229760 142577630 AA31E02A400F11DB9590000C2911D1B8 vmfs             0
```

(I have arranged this output for readability.) If you collect this output, you will have a more reliable calculation.

- **Partition Type**—For VMFS partitions, the type is always `fb` in this output, even though it is a GUID partition table, which means that the type should have been VMFS. This output uses the partition type similar to that used by `fdisk`, regardless of the partition table format.

- **Partition Size**—The size is in sectors. Notice that for listings whose partition number is 0, the size represents the total number of sectors in the LUN.

Maintaining a Set of Metadata Binary Dumps

One more step you can take to improve your chances of data recovery is to regularly collect metadata binary dumps of the first 32MB of the devices on which VMFS3 or VMFS5 datastores reside, as well as their extents, if any, using `dd`.

This is the syntax for collecting the dumps:

```
dd if=/dev/disks/<device-name> of=/<path-to-enough-space>/<Vol-x>-dump.bin
count=32 bs=1M
```

Just fill in the path to the place where you want to store the dumps and give each a name denoting the VMFS volume name from which it is collected.

This command collects 32MB from the device offset, which includes the protective MBR/primary GPT and VMFS metadata binary dump. This is sufficient for most file system and partition table recovery.

To collect backup of other resources that may also be affected by corruption, it is a good idea to increase the size of the dump to the first 1200MB of each device. This is what VMware support would ask you to collect if you were to report VMFS corruption.

The syntax for this is the same as for the `dd` command, but the count is 1200 instead of 32:

```
dd if=/dev/disks/<device-name> of=/<path-to-enough-space>/<Vol-x>-dump.bin
count=1200 bs=1M
```

TIP

Save the collected dumps in a safe place! It would be a good idea to get their md5sum as well and store them with the dumps.

Span or Grow?

Careful design that accounts for expected workloads and capacity requirements usually provisions storage that satisfies these requirements. However, there is always a possibility that new business requirements will justify a design change.

A VMFS3 or VMFS5 datastore can be spanned onto additional LUNs or grown onto additional free space added to the existing device. However, before making this decision, you should also consider using Storage DRS (Distributed Resource Scheduler), which can effectively provide additional space that meets both I/O and availability SLAs (service level agreements).

For the sake of completeness, I discuss both extending and expanding VMFS5. Similar operations for VMFS3 are possible, but because it has been deprecated, I do not cover it here.

Spanning VMFS Datastores

Adding physical LUNs to an existing VMFS3 or VMFS5 datastore spans the file system over these LUNs. The first LUN used to create the datastore is referred to as the head LUN because it includes part of the metadata without which the VMFS datastore cannot be mounted. The added LUNs are referred to as *extents*. VMFS3 and later can tolerate loss of any of the extents except for the head extent. If a non-head extent is unavailable, the VMFS3 or VMFS5 datastores remain accessible. Any I/O destined to blocks on the missing extent result in I/O errors.

Spanning a VMFS Datastore onto a New Extent

To span a VMFS datastore onto a new extent, follow this procedure:

1. Connect to the vCenter server that manages the ESXi 6 host, using the vSphere 6.0 Web Client as a user with Administrator privileges.

2. Navigate to the **Storage inventory** view.

3. Select the datastore you want to span.

4. Right-click and select **Increase Datastore Capacity** (see Figure 12.23).

Figure 12.23   Selecting a datastore to span

5. In the Increase Datastore Capacity dialog, you see all devices that are not part of a VMFS volume or mapped via an RDM (see Figure 12.24). vCenter Server hides such devices to protect them from being used. Otherwise, it results in corrupting the file system already on these devices. Select a device to add and then click **Next**.

Figure 12.24   Selecting a device to add to a VMFS5

6. The Specify Configuration step (see Figure 12.25) shows that the new extent is blank. From the Partition Configuration pull-down menu, select **Use all available partitions** option.

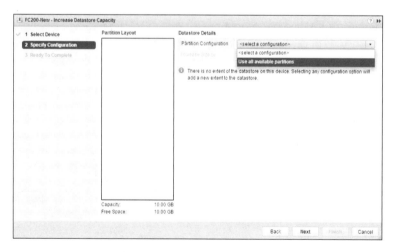

Figure 12.25   Spanning a VMFS volume—Selecting the extent's partition configuration

7. The dialog now (see Figure 12.26) enables you to use the maximum available space on the device or use less by moving the slider bar next to the **Increase Size by** field or typing the capacity to use, in GB. For this example, I'm using the whole device.

Notice that the Partition Layout diagram now shows the datastore name occupying the whole device. Click **Next** to continue.

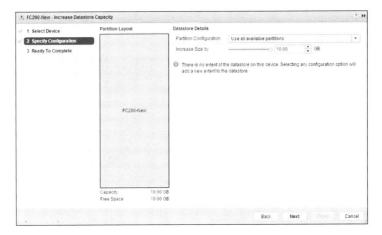

Figure 12.26   Spanning a VMFS volume—Extent size

8. The Ready to Complete step shows the new spanned volume size as well as the extent's size (see Figure 12.27). Notice that the partition format is GPT because this is VMFS5. If this were a VMFS5 datastore upgraded from VMFS3, the partition format would be GPT instead of the original MBR format. Click **Finish** when complete.

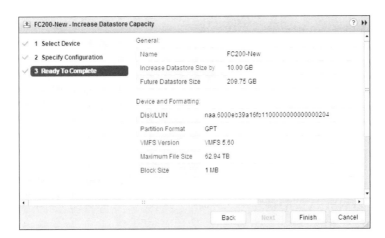

Figure 12.27   Spanning VMFS3 datastore—Ready to complete

9. vCenter Server triggers a rescan operation on all hosts sharing this volume so that they all can recognize the newly added capacity.

> **TIP**
>
> Although this is not enforced by vCenter Server, it is not advisable to span VMFS datastores onto extents of differing properties (RAID type, Physical Disk type, Disk Interface type, Disk RPM rating, Storage Processor Port Speed, and Protocol).
>
> The LUNs should practically be identical in all properties except for the capacity, which can vary according to need and availability. Using vStorage APIs for Storage Awareness (VASA) can help you identify these properties from within vCenter Server.
>
> If you plan to enable Storage I/O Control (SIOC), do not use VMFS extents because that feature is not supported.

How Does LVM Know the Members of the Datastore?

The VMFS5 LVM header has the Spanned Device Table property, which lists the device IDs of all the volume's extents. This makes it easier to identify the members of the spanned volume.

How Is Data Spread over Extents?

When a datastore has extents, data is written to them such that all extents are used concurrently, not sequentially. There is a misconception that data is written sequentially on the first extent and then when it is full, the next extent gets used. This is not true. VMFS Resource Manager, which is built into the file system kernel modules, uses all extents that make up the spanned VMFS volume when hosts require that new space be allocated on that volume. The Resource Manager bases its block allocation decisions on a variety of factors that I cannot publically disclose. The net effect is that blocks from any LUN in a spanned VMFS volume may be allocated at any time. The exact sequence varies by volume, connectivity, and sequence of events, among other factors. The VMFS resources are assigned to each host in resource groups across all available extents. Hosts distance the physical locations of the files they create from those written by other hosts. However, they try to keep the objects they manage within close proximity.

Spanning VMFS Pros and Cons

In medicine, each drug has several effects. For treating some diseases, one or more of these effects are therapeutic, and the rest are side effects. Depending on the desired outcome from taking a drug, the classification of the effects changes.

This concept lends itself to the computer industry, which usually refers to pros and cons. (I am tempted to use the joke about the Congress and Progress, but I will restrain myself.)

Pros of Spanning a VMFS Volume

Spanning a VMFS volume can provide the following benefits:

- Obviously, it adds more space to a space-constrained VMFS datastore.

- Because SCSI reservations are done on the head extent only, spanning a VMFS volume reduces the SCSI reservations overall. However, this can be achieved better by using VMFS5 with a VAAI-enabled array that supports the ATS primitive. VMFS5 has the property ATS Only, which improves on using ATS without the need to check whether the array supports it. (See Chapter 17.)

- It can possibly reduce "hot spots" on the array because the data is spread over multiple extents on different disk groups.

- If the extents are on devices on different storage arrays or on the same or different controllers on the same array, this may help reduce the device queue exhaustion under high I/O utilization. This benefit is on the array's end only. The initiator is still limited to the max queue depth provided by the HBA's driver.

- Using spanned datastores with VMFS5 no longer imposes the limitation of the file block size. So, you can span the datastore to use fewer larger files. However, if these files belong to fewer VMs, then the benefit of using VMFS5—which also adds the use of ATS-Only mode and effectively eliminates SCSI-2 reservations as long as the array supports that primitive—ends up diminishing the need to use the lower number of files. On the other hand, you must pay attention to your defined RTO; will you be able to restore such a large file fast enough to meet that SLA?

Cons of Spanning a VMFS Volume

Spanning a VMFS volume has the following side effects, drawbacks, or disadvantages:

- There is no easy way to identify which files live on which extent. So, if you happen to lose an extent, you only lose the data on that extent, while the surviving ones keep chugging along. (You may say that this is a benefit by itself.) The only way you can tell what was affected is by observing which VMs get I/O errors writing to the missing blocks. How would you mitigate this risk? Backups! Do backups on the hardware level and the file level. Taking hardware snapshots or making a replica of the business-critical VMs/datastores/extents should help you recover more quickly than if you have one large single extent-based datastore of the same size as the spanned one. The time it takes you to restore the humongous datastore may go way beyond your RTO (recovery time objective). Another way to mitigate this is to use datastore clusters with Storage DRS.

- Losing the head extent can result in losing the whole datastore. However, this is the same outcome if you are using a large LUN equal in size to the total size of extents making up the spanned datastore.

Growing VMFS Datastores

Many storage arrays provide the capability of growing LUNs. In the past, utilizing this space required manual changes to the partition table: You needed to add a new partition in the added space and then create a VMFS extent on it in the same fashion you usually do with spanning VMFS volumes. Beginning with vSphere 4.0, VMware introduced a new feature of growing a VMFS datastore onto free space available on the physical LUN on which it resides. This effectively resizes the partition and modifies the metadata to add the new space as available resources.

Architecturally speaking, the end result is similar to freshly creating the VMFS volume on the device. The main difference between using this feature with VMFS3 and VMFS5 is that the latter can be grown onto LUNs larger than 2TB in size.

How to Grow a VMFS Volume

You can grow a VMFS volume by using the vSphere 6 Web Client or `vmkfstools` via the CLI.

Growing a VMFS Volume by Using the vSphere 6 Web Client

To grow a VMFS datastore by using the vSphere 6 Web Client, follow this procedure:

1. Connect to the vCenter server that manages the ESXi 6 host, using the vSphere 6.0 Web Client as a user with Administrator privileges.
2. Navigate to the **Storage inventory** view.
3. Select from the inventory list the datastore you want to grow.
4. Select the **Manage** tab. On vSphere 6.5 the tab name is **Configure**.
5. Click the **Settings** button.
6. Select the **Device Backing** section and take note of the device ID.
7. Select the **General** section.
8. Click the **Increase** button in the Capacity section (see Figure 12.28).

Figure 12.28   Selecting a datastore to grow

9. In the Select Device step of the resulting dialog (see Figure 12.29), select the device with the same device ID you noted in step 6. Notice that the Expandable column shows **Yes**. This means you can proceed.

10. Click **Next**.

Figure 12.29   Selecting a device

11. You are almost there! The Specify Configuration dialog shows that there is one primary partition and lists the free space available that can be used to expand the VMFS volume. This dialog allows you to use the maximum available space or use a custom space setting, which allows you to use part of the available space. In this example, you want to use all available space, so in the Partition configuration pull-down menu, select the **Use 'Free space [size] GB' to expand the datastore** option (see Figure 12.30).

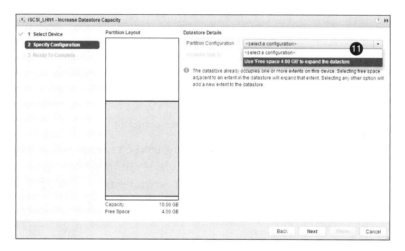

Figure 12.30   Current disk layout

12. The top part of the partition layout now shows the space being added, with the datastore volume name listed in it. Click **Next** to proceed (see Figure 12.31).

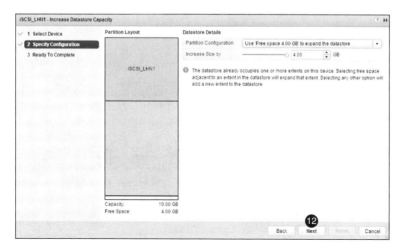

Figure 12.31   Modified disk layout

13. The Ready to Complete dialog shows the final settings that will be applied to the volume. The primary partition will be resized to utilize full device capacity instead of requiring a second primary partition utilizing the free capacity you specified in the previous step. The partition format will be GPT. If the original datastore was upgraded from VMFS3, the MBR partition format would have been retained until now. However, this process of growing the datastore switches this to GPT. Click **Finish** to complete the operation.

14. In the Recent Tasks pane, you should notice that the following actions took place, in this order:

   a. Compute the disk partition information.

   b. Expand the VMFS datastore.

   c. Rescan the VMFS on all ESXi hosts in the data center.

Step c ensures that all hosts in the data center can see the capacity added to the VMFS volume. This prevents other hosts in the cluster or data center from accidentally repeating this process because they have not seen the added capacity.

> **NOTE**
>
> If you compare this process to the process of adding a new device as an extent on which to span the VMFS volume, you see that the only difference is that in step 7 you would select a different device from that used by the datastore already.
>
> In this case, instead of modifying the partition table on the head extent, the VMFS metadata is modified to reflect the added extent and its resources. See the previous section for details about spanning a VMFS volume.

Growing a VMFS Volume by Using `vmkfstools`

Growing a datastore onto newly added device capacity by using `vmkfstools` is not as straightforward as using the vSphere 6 Web Client and is error prone since it requires the following high-level steps:

1. Use `partedUtil` to resize the partition. This process effectively overwrites the GPT partition table and relocates the secondary GPT to the last sectors on the device. The VMFS partition is also resized. To find out the last sector that will be used by the resized partition, you use `partedUtil getUsableSectors`.

2. Use `vmkfstools -G` to grow the volume.

As you see, using `partedUtil` can introduce errors because of typographical errors or miscalculations of the last sector number. It is a lot safer and faster to use the UI instead.

Upgrading to VMFS5

The upgrade process from VMFS3 to VMFS5 can be done live while VMs are actively running on the datastore. It is a very simple process that can be done via the UI or the CLI.

Before you upgrade, you must make sure that all hosts sharing the datastores you plan to upgrade have been themselves upgraded to ESXi 5 or 6. Once a datastore is upgraded, you cannot reverse the process, and all hosts running versions older than 5.0 will lose access to the upgraded datastores.

Upgrading to VMFS5 by Using the CLI

To upgrade VMFS3 to VMFS5 datastore using the CLI, follow this procedure:

1. Log in to the ESXi host directly, via SSH or vMA 6.0.

2. Run the `upgrade` command, using the following syntax:

   ```
   esxcli storage vmfs upgrade --volume-label [vmfs3-volume-name]
   ```

   Or you can use this `vmkfstools` command if using SSH to the ESXi host:

   ```
   vmkfstools -T /vmfs/volumes/<volume-name>
   ```

3. The `esxcli` command runs silently and returns no feedback unless there is an error. If you use `vmkfstools`, you are prompted with a reminder about the older ESX versions on hosts sharing the datastore. The prompt asks you to select 0 (Yes) or 1 (No) to continue or abort the process, respectively. Select 0 and press **Enter** to continue (see Figure 12.32).

```
 wdc-tse-i67.wsl.vmware.com - PuTTY                               —    □    ×

[root@wdc-tse-i67:~] vmkfstools -T /vmfs/volumes/smallville/

VMware ESX Question:
Please ensure that the VMFS-3 volume /vmfs/volumes/4f0a2605-2cdf65d1-f2b3-001f29
e04d52 is not in active use by any local or remote ESX 3.x/4.x server.

We recommend the following:
1. Back up data on your volume as a safety measure.
2. Take precautions to ensure no ESX 3.x/4.x servers are accessing this volume.

Continue converting VMFS-3 to VMFS-5?

0) _Yes
1) _No

Select a number from 0-1:
```

Figure 12.32 Upgrading VMFS—CLI

The upgrade process continues, showing the following text:

```
Checking if remote hosts are using this device as a valid file system.
This may take a few seconds...
Upgrading file system /vmfs/volumes/smallville...
done.
```

4. Rescan from all ESXi 6 hosts sharing the upgraded datastore. This is the main drawback of using the CLI to upgrade the datastore. In comparison, the UI process described next triggers a rescan automatically after the upgrade is complete.

To verify the outcome, run the following command:

```
vmkfstools -Ph /vmfs/volumes/Smallville/
VMFS-5.61 file system spanning 1 partitions.
File system label (if any): Smallville
Mode: public
Capacity 9.8 GB, 3.5 GB available, file block size 2 MB, max supported file
size 62.9 TB
UUID: 4f0a2605-2cdf65d1-f2b3-001f29e04d52
Partitions spanned (on "lvm"):
        naa.6006016055711d00cff95e65664ee011:1
Is Native Snapshot Capable: NO
```

The new version is now listed in the output as VMFS-5.61. I highlighted the relevant text. Notice that the file block size is still 2MB because the VMFS3 datastore was originally formatted with that block size. The VMFS5 minor version (after the hyphen) depends on the ESXi 6 update release version. GA release (without any updates) would be 5.60 and that with Update 1 is 5.61. Newer update releases may create higher minor versions, if needed.

Table 12.4 compares upgraded VMFS5 datastores to those that are freshly created.

Table 12.4 Comparing upgraded VMFS5 datastores to freshly created datastores

Features	Upgraded VMFS5	Formatted VMFS5
File-block size	1, 2, 4, and 8MB	1MB
Sub-block size	64KB	8KB
Partition type	MBR (GPT when grown)	GPT
Number of sub-blocks, file descriptors, and pointer blocks	Inherited from VMFS3	Limits proportionate to file system size
ATS only support (see Chapter 17)	No	Yes

Upgrade-Related Log Entries

Events related to the upgrade process are posted to /var/log/vmkernel.log. The following output shows entries from the previous example:

```
cpu0:6155853)FS3: 199: <START pb2>
cpu0:6155853)256 resources, each of size 4096
cpu0:6155853)Organized as 1 CGs, 64 C/CG and 16 R/C
cpu0:6155853)CGsize 4259840. 0th CG at 65536
cpu0:6155853)FS3: 201: <END pb2>
cpu0:6155853)Vol3: 3347: Successfully upgraded file system 4f0a28e3-
4ea353b6-08b6-001e4f1fbf2a to 5.561 from 3.54
```

In this output, I cropped the date and timestamps for readability.

Do you recall the pb2 discussed earlier in this chapter, in the section "VMFS5 Layout"? The first five lines of this log show the creation of this new system file. They also show the following properties:

- **Resources**—256

- **Resource size**—4096

- **Number of resource clusters (R/C)**—16

- **Number of clusters per cluster group (C/CG)**—64

- **Number of cluster groups (CGs)**—1

- **Cluster group size (**CGsize**)**—4259840

- **Offset of cluster group number 0 (0th CG)**—65536

NOTE

You need to run the following command on each host that accesses the upgraded datastore:

```
vmkfstools -V
```

This refreshes the metadata into the hosts' memory and reflects the version upgrade.

The following are examples of vmkernel.log messages you might get after you run vmkfstools -V:

```
Vol3: 2298: FS 4d8008a2-9940968c-04df-001e4f1fbf2a (FC200) version change
(3.54 -> 5.61) detected!
```

```
Vol3: 2335: vol 'FC200': PB2 found at FD address 494927876, vol address
4534272
Vol3: 2342: vol 'FC200': SDD found at FD address 490733572, vol address
4532224
```

Note that the new metadata properties PB2 and SDD are unique to VMFS5 and were added as a result of the upgrade.

Upgrading to VMFS5 by Using the vSphere 6 Web Client

To upgrade VMFS3 to VMFS5 using the UI, follow this procedure:

1. Connect to the vCenter server that manages the ESXi 6 host, using the vSphere 6.0 Web Client as a user with Administrator privileges.

2. Navigate to the **Storage inventory** view.

3. Select from the inventory list the datastore you want to upgrade. Note that the current version is 3.x (in this example, it is 3.31).

4. Select the **Manage** tab. On vSphere 6.5 the tab name is **Configure**.

5. Click the **Settings** button.

6. Select the **General** section.

7. Click the **Upgrade to VMFS-5** button (see Figure 12.33).

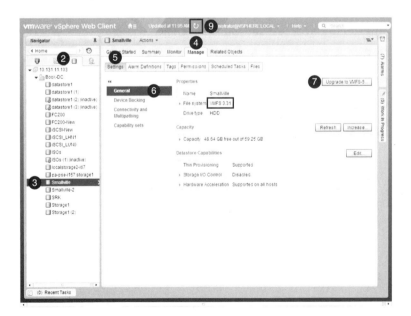

Figure 12.33 Upgrade to VMFS-5 option—UI

> **TIP**
>
> You can combine steps 4 through 6 in one by right-clicking the datastore and selecting the **Upgrade to VMFS-5** menu option. You can also choose this option from the **Actions** pull-down menu.

8. If you still have ESXi hosts older than 5.0, you see an error stating that there are hosts accessing this datastore that don't support VMFS5. To remedy this, click the **View Incompatible Hosts** link to display a list of hosts that you must upgrade before proceeding.

9. If, after upgrading the identified hosts, you no longer see the Upgrade to VMFS-5 button, click the **Refresh** icon at the top of the vSphere Web Client UI. Now you should be able to click the **Upgrade to VMFS-5** button.

10. In the **Upgrade to VMFS-5** dialog shown in Figure 12.34, select the check box next to the datastore listing.

11. Click **OK** to proceed with the upgrade.

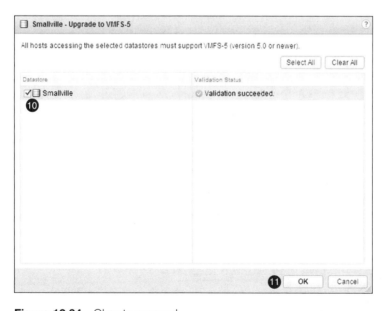

Figure 12.34   Okay to proceed

12. When the upgrade process is complete, vCenter triggers a rescan on all ESXi 6 hosts sharing the datastore.

13. To verify the outcome, check the value displayed in the **File System** field in the Datastore Properties section (see Figure 12.35). You may need to expand the File System field to display the details. In this example, the version is 5.61. Also notice the block size, 1MB, which was the original volume's file block size. If the original block size were larger, it would have retained the original block size.

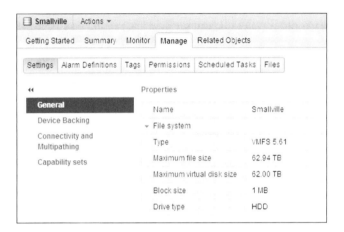

Figure 12.35   Locating the upgraded volume's version in the UI

If you check the /var/log/vmkernel.log file for the upgrade events, notice that they match those that I listed earlier, when I ran the upgrade via the CLI. However, this time around, I had originally formatted the VMFS3 datastore using ESXi 4.1. This explains the last line in the set of log entries shown in the next line:

```
Successfully upgraded file system 4f0a521b-94ef49da-7f00-001a64664b44 to
5.61 from 3.31
```

Notice that the previous version is 3.31, compared to the 3.54 listed earlier under the CLI procedure. The reason is that the higher "minor" version of the file system was created using ESXi 5.x. The difference in minor versions has no effect on features available for VMFS3 on ESXi 5.x or 6.

What if the VMFS5 Datastore Is Presented to ESXi 4.x?

Assume that your SAN administrator accidentally presented a device, on which a VMFS5 volume resides, to an ESXi host older than 5.0. What would happen?

The answer is nothing. The reason is that the older version of the vmkernel has a module for VMFS3 only. VMFS3 identifies the major version as 5 and gracefully fails to mount the VMFS5 datastore.

How about another variation on this scenario? In the procedure for upgrading using the CLI, the process depends on *you* verifying that all hosts accessing this datastore have been upgraded to ESXi 5 or 6. Let's say you overlooked one or two hosts. The process still continues, and the datastore is upgraded to version 5.54.

What actually happens with the older hosts? You should see something like the following messages in /var/log/vmkernel on the 4.x hosts:

```
WARNING: LVM: 2265: [naa.6006016047301a00eaed23f5884ee011:1] LVM
major version mismatch (device 5, current 3)

FSS: 3647: No FS driver claimed device
'naa.6006016047301a00eaed23f5884ee011:1': Not supported

FSS: 3647: No FS driver claimed device
'48866acd-d8ef78ec-5942-001a6436c322': Not supported
```

(I added blank lines between these messages for readability.) The first message states that the LVM version on the datastore is newer. What is on the disk is version 5; what the host has in memory is version 3. This means that the host has not rescanned the storage area network (SAN) since the datastore was upgraded.

The second and third lines are the same, but one references the device ID (NAA ID) and the other references the volume signature (UUID). They indicate that this host has a VMFS kernel module that does not support this version. As a result, none of the file system drivers claimed the device(s).

VMFS6

vSphere 6.5 introduced a new VMFS6 file system. These are the main improvements in this version:

- It supports 512e drives, which use 4KB sectors but emulate 512-byte sectors. These drives are still not supported with earlier versions of VMFS. Metadata is aligned at the disk sector size. If the sector size is less than 4KB, the metadata is still aligned at 4KB.

- Deleted space is automatically reclaimed using the UNMAP VAAI primitive, which is covered in Chapter 17. This helps reduce thin provisioned LUNs' space consumption on the storage arrays.

- SE sparse file is the default format for snapshots and linked clones on LUNs larger than 2TB.

NOTE

Versions prior to VMFS6 cannot be upgrade in-place to VMFS6. You must freshly create a VMFS6 datastore on a new device and then migrate the data from older datastores, one at a time, using Storage vMotion. Then you delete the older datastore and format it with the VMFS6 version. You can then use that newly formatted datastore as a target for Storage vMotion to vacate additional pre-VMFS6 datastores.

Creating a VMFS6 Datastore by Using the UI

To create a VMFS datastore, follow this procedure:

1. Connect to the vCenter server that manages the ESXi 6 host, using the vSphere 6.0 Web Client as a user with Administrator privileges.

2. Navigate to the **Storage inventory** view.

3. Select the data center to which to add the new datastore.

4. Select the **Getting Started** tab.

5. Click the **Add a datastore** link in the Basic Tasks section (see Figure 12.36).

Figure 12.36   Creating a new VMFS6 datastore

6. In the Location step, click **Next** to select the listed data center.

7. Select **VMFS** as the datastore type and then click **Next**.

8. Enter the datastore name.

9. From the pull-down menu select a host to which a new LUN was presented.

10. Select the LUN on which to create the datastore.

11. Click **Next** (see Figure 12.37).

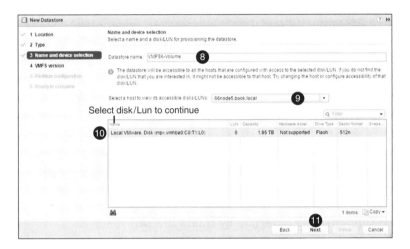

Figure 12.37   Selecting the host and LUN

12. Select the **VMFS 6** radio button and click **Next**.

13. In the partition configuration step, select the following:

   a. **Partition Configuration**—Use all available partitions.

   b. **Datastore Size**—Select the maximum size by sliding the slider to the far right-hand side.

   c. **Block Size**—Only 1MB block size is available with VMFS6.

   d. **Space Reclamation Granularity**—Only 1MB is available with VMFS6.

   e. **Space Reclamation Priority**—The slider's choice are **None** or **Low**. The choice of **None** disables the feature, while the choice of **Low** enables it with low priority. This works only on thin provisioned LUNs on VAAI-capable storage arrays that support the UNMAP primitive.

14. Click **Next** (see Figure 12.38).

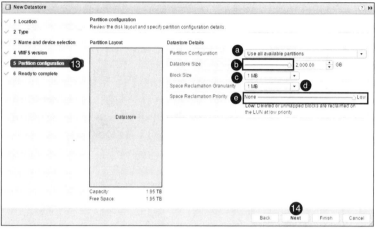

Figure 12.38   VMFS6 partition configuration

15. Review your selections in the Ready to complete step and then click **Finish**.

Listing the VMFS Datastore's Properties by Using the UI

To list the VMFS6 datastore's properties using the UI, follow this procedure:

1. Connect to the vCenter server that manages the ESXi 6 host, using the vSphere 6.0 Web Client as a user with Administrator privileges. If you are using vSphere 6.5, you can also use vSphere HTML5 Client, as I do in this example.

2. Navigate to the **Storage inventory** view.

3. Select the datastore from the inventory tree.

4. Click the **Configure** tab.

5. Select **General**.

In this view, you see the following:

- **Properties**—The properties section includes the following:
  - **Name**—This is the datastore volume label.
  - **File system**—The file system field is collapsed, by default showing the VMFS version. In this example, the version is 6.81. Expanding this section shows the file system version in the Type field, followed by the following fields:

- **Maximum File Size**, which is 64TB

- **Maximum Virtual Disk Size**, which is 62TB

- **Block Size**, which is 1MB

- **Space Reclamation Granularity**, which is 1MB

- **Drive Type**—This is the drive type on which the datastore was created. In this example, the drive type is Flash.

- **Capacity**—The Capacity section lists the Total Capacity, Provisioned Space, and Free Space fields.

The rest of the configurations are similar to those for a VMFS5 datastore (see Figure 12.39).

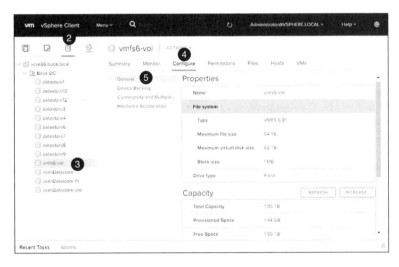

Figure 12.39   Displaying the VMFS6 datastore's properties

Listing a VMFS6 Datastore's Properties by Using the CLI

Listing a new datastore's properties via the CLI is identical to listing VMFS5 datastore. You use this command:

```
vmkfstools -Ph /vmfs/volumes/<volume-name>
```

Here is an example of the command and its output:

```
vmkfstools -Ph /vmfs/volumes/VMFS6-Volume
VMFS-6.81 (Raw Major Version: 24) file system spanning 1 partitions.
File system label (if any): VMFS6-Volume
Mode: public
Capacity 2.0 TB, 2.0 TB available, file block size 1 MB, max supported file
size 64 TB
UUID: 58cf4390-8e923788-be15-000c299e6b3f
Partitions spanned (on "lvm"):
        mpx.vmhba0:C0:T1:L0:1
Is Native Snapshot Capable: NO
```

In this example, notice that the max supported file size is 64TB. In similar output from a VMFS5 datastore, the size is 62.9TB.

Summary

VMFS5 is the version of a VMware clustered file system that introduced several scalability and performance enhancements. VMFS6, which was introduced in vSphere 6.5, adds support for 512e devices and automatic deleted space reclamation. In this chapter I shared with you the file system history, architecture, and recovery tips.

Chapter 13

Virtual Disks and RDMs

VMware vSphere 6 and earlier releases abstract storage and present it to virtual machines in various forms, including virtual disks, raw device mappings (RDMs), and generic passthrough SCSI devices. This chapter deals with virtual disks and RDMs.

The Big Picture

To help you better understand how virtual disks and RDMs are abstracted, Figure 13.1 provides a high-level diagram.

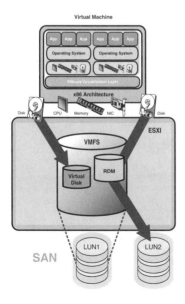

Figure 13.1   Virtual disks and RDMs

In Figure 13.1, the Virtual Machine File System (VMFS) datastore was created on LUN1 on the storage area network (SAN). A virtual disk is a file on the VMFS datastore. When the virtual disk is attached to the virtual machine, it sees it as a VMware SCSI disk. In contrast, an RDM is created on the VMFS datastore that is simply a file that acts as a pointer to LUN2. When the RDM is attached to the virtual machine, it sees it as one of two possible modes: a VMware SCSI disk or a native physical LUN (for example, VNC VRAID LUN). I explain the differences in the section "Raw Device Mappings," later in this chapter.

Virtual Disks

Virtual disks are files created on VMFS or Network File System (NFS) datastores. These files have a .vmdk extension, and each is made up of more than one file, with the number of files depending on the type of virtual disk represented.

The main file, referred to as the virtual disk descriptor file, is an ASCII (actually, UTF-8 encoded) text file that defines the structure of the virtual disk. Listing 13.1 shows an example of such a file.

Listing 13.1   Sample virtual disk descriptor file

```
# Disk DescriptorFile
version=1
encoding="UTF-8"
CID=fffffffe
parentCID=ffffffff
isNativeSnapshot="no"
createType="vmfs"

# Extent description
RW 33554432 VMFS "vSphere Management Assistant 5.0_1-flat.vmdk"

# The Disk Data Base
#DDB

ddb.virtualHWVersion = "4"
ddb.longContentID = "0481be4e314537249f0f1ca6fffffffe"
ddb.uuid = "60 00 C2 93 7f fb 16 2a-1a 66 1f 50 ed 10 51 ee"
ddb.geometry.cylinders = "2088"
ddb.geometry.heads = "255"
ddb.geometry.sectors = "63"
ddb.adapterType = "lsilogic"
```

The virtual disk descriptor file has the following sections:

- `Disk DescriptorFile`—The fields in this section are listed in Table 13.1.

Table 13.1 `Disk DescriptorFile` section fields

Field	Possible Values	Notes
CID	fffffffe or a lower hexadecimal value	Content ID, which is unique per disk hierarchy. Read more details in the "Linked Clones" section, later in this chapter.
ParentCID	ffffffff for the top-level virtual disk and lower for children in a snapshot or linked clone	Snapshot files or linked clone files identify their parent virtual disk by its parent virtual disk's content ID (CID). Read more details in the "Linked Clones" section, later in this chapter.
isNativeSnapshot	No or Yes	For use by a future vSphere release.
createType	Vmfs	Virtual disk.
	vmfsRawDeviceMap	Virtual mode RDM.
	vmfsPassthroughRaw DeviceMap	Physical mode RDM.
	twoGbMaxExtentSparse	2GB sparse disk.
	vmfsSparse	Virtual disk snapshot.

- `Extent description`—This section lists the virtual disk extent files and is made up of four fields, listed in Table 13.2. The actual field names are not stated in the VMDK file. All values are listed on one line under the `Extent Description` section in the VMDK file.

Table 13.2 `Extent Description` section fields

Field	Possible Values	Notes
Access	RW	Inherited from older releases. On ESXi 5, it is always RW (read-write).
Size	<device block count>	Size of the extent file, in 512-byte disk blocks.
Type	VMFS	Virtual disk extent. One extent per virtual disk.
	VMFSRDM	RDM extent (both virtual and physical). One extent per RDM.

Field	Possible Values	Notes
	`SPARSE`	Extents of virtual disk created via `vmkfstools`, using `2gbsparse` option. (Read more details in the "Creating Virtual Disks Using `vmkfstools`" section.)
	`VMFSSPARSE`	Extents of virtual disks of a VM snapshot.
	`VSANSPARSE`	vSAN 6.2 and later sparse file format (see Chapter 22).
Extent Files	`*-flat.vmdk`	This is where the virtual disk data gets written.
	`*-rdm.vmdk`	This is the VMFS pointer to the raw device (virtual mode).
	`*-rdmp.vmdk`	This is the VMFS pointer to the raw device (physical mode).
	`*.s00(n).vmdk`	These represent the 2GB segments of the sparse virtual disk. The size can be smaller than 2GB. The `(n)` represents the extent number, counting from 1.
	`vsan://<ObjectID>`	Virtual SAN–based virtual disks are VSAN objects rather than VMFS files. More on that in Chapter 21, "vSAN Core Features."
	`vvol://<vvol-ID>`	Virtual volumes based virtual disks are referenced by the VVol ID representing the virtual disk. More on that in Chapter 23, "Virtual Volumes (VVols)."

- `Disk Database`—This section lists the virtual disk properties as seen by the VM. It includes the seven fields listed in Table 13.3 (and one additional field for thin provisioned virtual disks).

Table 13.3 `Disk Database` section fields

Field	Possible Values	Notes
`ddb.virtualHWVersion`	`4` or `8`	Virtual hardware version.
`ddb.longContentID`	Hexadecimal value	The long content ID is used to resolve conflicts in CID. For example, if there are multiple descriptor files with the same CID, the long CID is used as a unique ID instead.

Field	Possible Values	Notes
`ddb.uuid`	Hexadecimal value	Random text. Unique to the virtual disk. Generated from the SHA1 hash of the host ID, timestamp, and a random number.
`ddb.geometry.cylinders`	Decimal value	The number of cylinders of the disk presented to the guest OS.
`ddb.geometry.heads`	Decimal value	The number of heads of the disk presented to the guest OS.
`ddb.geometry.sectors`	Decimal value	The number of sectors of the disk presented to the guest OS.
`ddb.adapterType`	`lsilogic,` `buslogic,` or `ide`	Matches the virtual storage adapter used by the VM.
`ddb.thinProvisioned`	`1`	Denotes that the virtual disk was created as thin provisioned. This field will not have a value other than `1`. If the virtual disk is not thin provisioned, this property does not exist in the descriptor file.

Virtual Disk Types

Virtual disks on ESXi 6–based VMFS3 or VMFS5 datastores are categorized according to their disk provisioning, as follows:

- **Zeroed thick**—In the UI, this is referred to as a *flat disk*. Disk blocks are pre-allocated at creation time, but the blocks are zeroed out (that is, zeros are written to the blocks) upon first write. The file is created faster because all that is done is to create the metadata file entry and specify the file blocks it occupies that are not zeroed out.

- **Eager zeroed thick**—Disk blocks are pre-allocated and zeroed out at creation time. This is the most secure type of virtual disk because any previous data that might have been on the allocated disk blocks is overwritten with zeros. On VMFS3 or VMFS5, datastores that are on non-VAAI (vStorage APIs for Array Integration) storage arrays (see Chapter 17, "VAAI"), the creation process takes more time compared to the creation time for the zeroed thick type and is proportionate to the virtual disk size. If the storage array supports WRITE_SAME (also known as block zeroing) primitive, the block zeroing is offloaded to the storage array. This significantly reduces the file creation time.

- **Thin**—This type of virtual disk is analogous to thin provisioning physical LUNs. The virtual disk file size is predefined, but the disk blocks are not allocated at the time the file is created.

Table 13.4 compares all three types.

Table 13.4 Virtual disk types comparison

Characteristic	Zeroed Thick	Eager Zeroed Thick	Thin
Disk allocation	Fully pre-allocated.	Fully pre-allocated.	On demand.
Block placement on file system	Higher chance of using contiguous file blocks.	Same as zeroed thick.	Depending on how active the datastore is at the time the file is grown, the allocated blocks might not be contiguous.
Block zeroing	On demand upon first write.	At the time the file is created.	At the time the file is grown.
Reading previously unwritten blocks	Blocks are not read from disk. Rather, memory buffers are filled with zeros. This is very fast because zeroing memory is much faster than zeroing a disk.	Read request sent to disk. This might return stale data from disk. This is slower than zeroed thick because it reads from disk instead of memory.	Same as zeroed thick.
Writing previously unwritten blocks	Blocks are zeroed before sending the write to disk. This results in higher latency of the original write (from guest OS). This is much slower than eager zeroed thick.	Write requests are sent to disk because the blocks were zeroed at the time the file was created.	Block is allocated and zeroed on the disk first. Then the write is sent to disk. This is slightly slower than zeroed thick and has a higher latency of the original write (from the guest OS). Allocating blocks results in some distributed locking traffic unless the VAAI ATS and Write_Same primitives are supported.
Reading previously written blocks	Requests sent to disk. If this occurs while the first writes to the blocks are still in progress, the reads are queued until the writes are done.	Request is forwarded to disk. No other overhead.	Same as zeroed thick.

Characteristic	Zeroed Thick	Eager Zeroed Thick	Thin
Writing previously written blocks	Same as reading previously written blocks.	Same as reading previously written blocks.	Same as zeroed thick.
Physical disk space usage	Does not need more space while the VM is running because the file blocks were pre-allocated.	Same as zeroed thick.	Because the file blocks are allocated on demand, the guest may be paused if the VMFS volume runs out of space or, if on thin provisioned LUN, the LUN reaches its maximum capacity. See more details in the "Thin-on-Thin Configuration" section, later in this chapter.
Appearance in vSphere Web UI	Thick provision lazy zeroed.	Thick provision eager zeroed.	Thin provision.
Datastore compatibility	VMFS3	VMFS3	VMFS3
	VMFS5	VMFS5	VMFS5
	VMFS6	VMFS6	VMFS6
	NFS*	vSAN	vSAN (default type)
		NFS*	NFS (default type)

* NFS datastore on storage arrays must support VAAI NAS (network attached storage) primitives. See more details about VAAI in Chapter 17. For thin provisioned virtual disks, VAAI support is not required as this is the default format for NFS datastores.

Thin-on-Thin Configuration

Using thin provisioned virtual disks on thin provisioned LUNs poses the risk of LUNs running out of space before thin virtual disks reach their maximum provisioned capacity. To mitigate this risk, VMware introduced alarms and VOBs (vSphere observations) to alert the vSphere administrator of two possible states:

- **Out of Space Warning**—Storage array vendors can provide a Free Space Soft Threshold Limit setting on the array. When this is set, a warning is sent to the ESXi host that attempted to write blocks and resulted in reaching the threshold. The write operation would succeed, though. This warning can be sent in-band or out-of-band. This means it can be sent as a SCSI error directly to the host (as a check condition with sense key 0x6 ASC 0x38 ASCQ 0x7) or as a VASA (vStorage APIs for Storage Awareness) event polled by the VASA provider installed in the vSphere environment. Storage vendors opt to use one or the other but not both. The vSphere environment can be configured to move virtual disks to other datastores if using the Storage DRS feature.

- **Out of Space Error**—This is a similar setting to be configured on the storage array as a hard threshold that generates an out-of-space error (to the host directly as a check condition with sense key 0x6 ASC 0x27 ASCQ 0x7). This results in failing the I/O (input/output) that resulted in reaching the hard threshold of free space. Similar integration with Storage DRS is implemented in vSphere 5.

Virtual Disk Modes

Virtual disk modes dictate how the virtual disks are affected by VM snapshots (see the "Virtual Machine Snapshots" section, later in this chapter):

- **Dependent**—This is the default mode. It means that when a snapshot of the VM is taken, the virtual disk has a snapshot created.

- **Independent**—The virtual disk is independent from VM snapshot activities. So, when a VM snapshot is taken, the virtual disk does not have a snapshot created. In this mode, the virtual disk can be set as persistent or non-persistent:

  - **Persistent**—Data written to the virtual disk persists when the VM is powered off and then powered on.

  - **Non-persistent**—Data written to the virtual disk is redirected to a delta file (also known as a REDO file) that is discarded upon powering off the VM. Note that just rebooting the guest operating system (GOS) does not result in discarding the delta files. Only powering off the VM does.

Creating Virtual Disks Using the UI

You can create virtual disks during the process of creating a VM or during process of editing existing VMs to add new virtual disks.

Creating Virtual Disks During VM Creation

The custom VM creation path enables you to specify the type, mode, and location of the virtual disks that you define, as outlined in this procedure:

1. Connect to the vCenter server that manages the ESXi 6 host, using the vSphere 6.0 Web Client as a user with Administrator privileges.

2. Navigate to the **Hosts and Clusters** view.

3. Select the datacenter or cluster in which you want to create the new VM.

4. Right-click the datacenter or cluster object in the inventory tree and then select **New Virtual Machine** and then **New Virtual Machine** (see Figure 13.2).

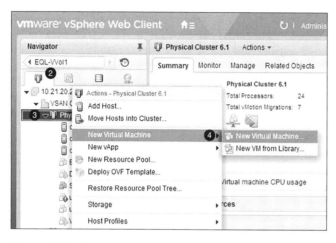

Figure 13.2   Selecting the New Virtual Machine Menu Option

5. In the Select a creation type section in the left pane, select the **Create a new virtual machine** option and then click **Next**.

6. Type the VM name.

7. Select in which inventory location you want to store the VM.

8. Click **Next**.

9. In the Select a compute resource section in the left pane, select the host or cluster on which you want to run the VM.

10. When the Compatibility section shows Compatibility checks succeeded, click **Next** (see Figure 13.3).

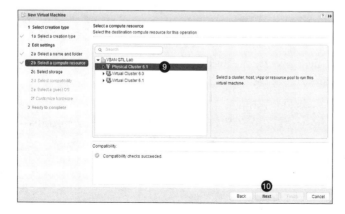

Figure 13.3   Selecting the VM Compute Resource

11. Select the VM storage policy relevant to where the VM files will be stored. This choice helps with selecting datastores that can provide the VM's I/O and availability design requirements, such as datastore type (VMFS, vSAN, VVol container, and so on), I/O profile (read intensive, write intensive, mixed I/O, and so on), and availability (mirrored LUN, native snapshots, and so on)

12. Select a datastore that is compliant with the selected policy.

13. Click **Next** (see Figure 13.4).

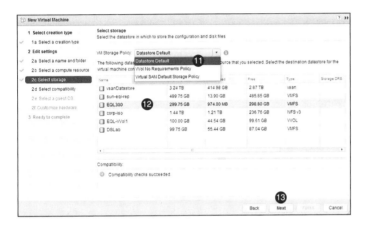

Figure 13.4   Selecting the VM's Datastore

14. In Select compatibility section in the left pane, select one of the ESXi versions listed. For this example, I select **ESXi 6.0 and later** option. This choice dictates the virtual hardware version used by the VM.

15. Select the guest OS family and type and then click **Next**.

16. Select the number of virtual sockets and cores per virtual socket and the VM memory size.

17. In the **New Hard disk** field, specify the disk size. Expand the section by clicking the arrow on the left side (see Figure 13.5) to edit the following disk details:

- **VM storage policy**—This can be the same policy or a different policy from that you selected in step 11. The selection here applies to the virtual disk you are currently defining. You can change the policy per disk so that the VM and each virtual disk have the same or different policies. This is practical when you need to provide a different I/O profile for each virtual disk. (For more on this, see Chapters 20–23).

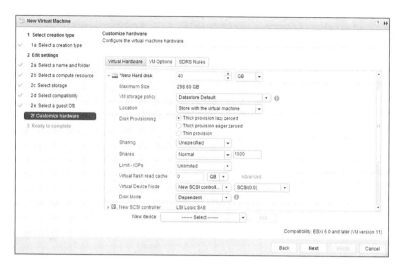

Figure 13.5   Selecting virtual disk capacity, disk provisioning, and VM location

- **Location**—This is the datastore on which the virtual disk is stored. The location can be different from where the VM is stored. When you select the **Browse** option from this field's pull-down menu, the list of datastores provided shows the storage policy compatible datastores on the top.

- **Disk Provisioning**—This choice depends on the application and VM design and the storage backing the datastore:

  - If the VM will be protected by VMware Fault Tolerance (FT), the choice should be **Thick provision eager zeroed** (eager zeroed thick [EZT]). Devices capable of WRITE_SAME (block zeroing) VAAI primitive will improve the provisioning time as the block zeroing operation gets offloaded to the storage array.

  - Some applications, such as Oracle RAC configuration and some Microsoft Windows Failover Cluster designs, require the VMDK to be EZT.

  - The previous two design choices are suitable for use with thick provisioned LUNs as all VMDK blocks are allocated at provisioning time.

- **Sharing**—This field is new in vSphere 6 Update 1 and newer. The default is **Unspecified**. Use the **Multi-writer** option if the virtual disk will be shared with other VMs in a specific clustering configuration, such as Oracle RAC. (I discuss this option further in Chapter 14, "Distributed Locks.")

- **Shares** and **Limit - IOPs**—These fields are for controlling I/O resource utilization by this virtual disk. These fields cannot be modified on VVols.

- **Virtual flash read cache**—This feature utilizes local flash storage for read cache.

- **Virtual Device Node**—For the VM's system disk, this node should remain SCSI(0:0). For additional disks, the selection depends on the application design. (I address relevant choices throughout the book, as the need arises.)

- **Virtual Disk Modes**—See the "Virtual Disk Modes" section, earlier in this chapter, for details.

18. Select the virtual SCSI controller. The default selection is based on your choice of guest OS in step 15. See the section "Virtual Storage Adapters," later in the chapter, for more details.

19. Select the virtual NIC type and the port group.

20. To add additional virtual disks to this VM at this time, select **New** and then **New Hard Disk** and then click **Add**. (This is similar to the procedure I cover in the following sections.)

21. Click **Next**.

22. Review your selections and click **Finish** to create the VM.

The virtual disk created using this procedure is stored in the location you selected in step 17 and is named using the virtual machine name you specified in step 6.

Creating a Virtual Disk After VM Creation

You can add virtual disks to existing VMs while they are powered on if the guest OS supports hot adds; otherwise, the VM must be powered off. The process is the same, regardless of the power state:

1. Connect to the vCenter server that manages the ESXi 6 host, using the vSphere 6.0 Web Client as a user with Administrator privileges.

2. Navigate to the **VMs and Templates** view.

3. Locate the VM to which you want to add a virtual disk. Right-click it and then select **Edit Settings** (see Figure 13.6).

4. In the dialog that appears, click the **New device** pull-down menu.

5. Click the **New Hard Disk** option (see Figure 13.7).

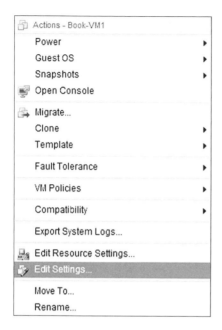

Figure 13.6 Editing VM settings

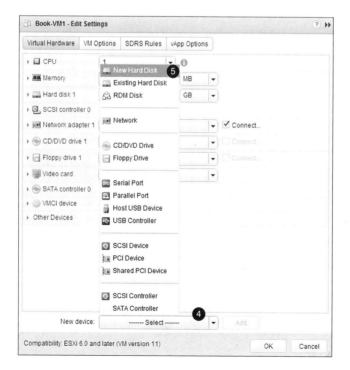

Figure 13.7 Adding a new hard disk

6. The New Device field now shows **New Hard Disk** as the current selection. Click the **Add** button.

7. Follow steps 17 and 18 in the previous section, "Creating Virtual Disks During VM Creation." The end result should look similar to Figure 13.8.

8. To add more virtual disks, click the **Add** button and repeat steps 6 and 7.

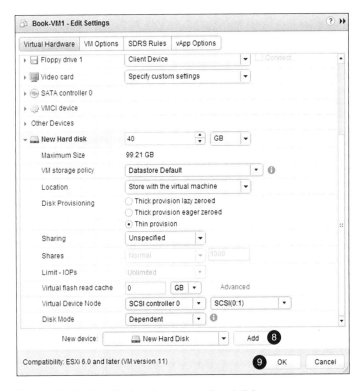

Figure 13.8   Result of adding a new virtual disk

9. Click **OK**.

NOTE

In step 7 of this procedure, you can change the virtual device node as well as the virtual disk mode if you forgot to select them during the earlier steps.

I discuss the design choices for the virtual device node in the "Virtual Storage Adapters" section, later in this chapter.

Creating Virtual Disks Using `vmkfstools`

`vmkfstools` is the ESXi tool to use for managing VMFS datastores and virtual disks. It is available on the ESXi 6 host as well as vMA 6.x and vCLI 6.x. If you run `vmkfstools` without any parameters, it displays the available options, as shown in Listing 13.2.

Listing 13.2   vmkfstools options

```
~# vmkfstools
vmkfstools: unrecognized option

OPTIONS FOR VIRTUAL DISKS:

vmkfstools -c --createvirtualdisk #[bBsSkKmMgGtT]
          -d --diskformat [zeroedthick
                          |thin
                          |eagerzeroedthick
                          ]
          -a --adaptertype [deprecated]
          -W --objecttype [file|vsan|vvol]
          --policyFile <fileName>
       -w --writezeros
       -j --inflatedisk
       -k --eagerzero
       -K --punchzero
       -U --deletevirtualdisk
       -E --renamevirtualdisk srcDisk
       -i --clonevirtualdisk srcDisk
          -d --diskformat [zeroedthick
                          |thin
                          |eagerzeroedthick
                          |rdm:<device>|rdmp:<device>
                          |2gbsparse]
          -W --object [file|vsan|vvol]
          --policyFile <fileName>
          -N --avoidnativeclone
       -X --extendvirtualdisk #[bBsSkKmMgGtT]
          [-d --diskformat eagerzeroedthick]
       -M --migratevirtualdisk
       -r --createrdm /vmfs/devices/disks/...
       -q --queryrdm
```

```
        -z --createrdmpassthru /vmfs/devices/disks/...
        -v --verbose #
        -g --geometry
        -x --fix [check|repair]
        -e --chainConsistent
        -Q --objecttype name/value pair
           --uniqueblocks childDisk
    vmfsPath
```

The relevant options for this chapter are the ones listed in the OPTIONS FOR VIRTUAL DISKS: section of Listing 13.2. I removed the other options from the output.

In the output shown in Listing 13.2, the reference to vmfsPath in the context of virtual disk options represents the virtual disk filename, including the path to the VMFS datastore. It is also worth noting that a subset of the virtual disk–related options apply to manipulating virtual disk files on NFS datastores as well as VSAN and VVol objects. I point these out where appropriate.

Creating a Zeroed Thick Virtual Disk Using vmkfstools

Zeroed thick virtual disks have pre-allocated blocks on the datastore (refer to Table 13.4), but the blocks are not zeroed out at creation time. This is the default type for virtual disks created on VMFS3, VMFS5, or VMFS6 datastores. You can create this type of virtual disk by using this command:

```
vmkfstools --createvirtualdisk <size> --diskformat zeroedthick /<vmfs-path
to VM directory>/<Virtual Disk filename>
```

This is the shorthand version of this command:

```
vmkfstools -c <size> -d zeroedthick /<vmfs-path to VM directory>/<Virtual
Disk filename>
```

Here is an example:

```
vmkfstools --createvirtualdisk 40G --diskformat zeroedthick /vmfs/volumes/
datastore1/Book-Demo/bookdemo-disk2.vmdk
```

This creates a 40GB zeroed thick virtual disk named bookdemo-disk2.vmdk in the datastore named datastore1 in a VM directory named Book-Demo.

The size option accepts a single letter, b, s, k, m, g, or t, in upper- or lowercase, representing bytes, sectors, KB, MB, GB, and TB units, respectively. The number preceding the letter is the virtual disk size in the specified unit.

> **NOTE**
>
> ESXi 6 introduced the new units bytes, sectors, and TB. The sector size in this release is 512 bytes.
>
> ESXi 6 also deprecated the `--adaptertype` parameter. The default type is `lsilogic`.
>
> ESXi 5.5 introduced the subparameters `--objecttype` or `-W` and `--createvirtualdisk` or `-c`. These subparameters specify the `file` or `vsan` argument. The latter is used to create or clone VSAN objects. This also applies as a subparameter of `--clonevirtualdisk` or `-i`.
>
> ESXi 6 added to the same `--objecttype` parameter a `vvol` argument, which you can use to create or clone VVol objects. This also applies as a subparameter of `--clonevirtualdisk` or `-i`.

Creating an Eager Zeroed Thick Virtual Disk Using `vmkfstools`

Eager zeroed thick virtual disks have pre-allocated blocks on the datastore, and all blocks have zeros written to them to ensure that any data from files previously occupying the allocated blocks gets overwritten with zero patterns.

To create such a file using `vmkfstools`, you use the same command from the previous section but substitute `zeroedthick` with `eagerzeroedtick`, as follows:

```
vmkfstools --createvirtualdisk <size> --diskformat eagerzeroedthick
/<vmfs-path to VM directory>/<Virtual Disk filename>
```

This is the shorthand version of this command:

```
vmkfstools -c <size> -d eagerzeroedthick /<vmfs-path to VM
directory>/<Virtual Disk filename>
```

Here is an example:

```
vmkfstools --createvirtualdisk 40G --diskformat eagerzeroedthick /vmfs/vol-
umes/datastore1/Book-Demo2/bookdemo-disk3.vmdk
```

Listing 13.3 shows sample output.

Listing 13.3   Output of creating an eager zeroed thick virtual disk

```
Creating disk '/vmfs/volumes/datastore1/Book-Demo2/bookdemo-disk3.vmdk' and
zeroing it out...
Create: 74% done.
```

As the file creation progresses, the percentage done is incremented in the `Create` line until it reaches 100%.

To measure how long it takes for the file creation to complete, you can run the command shown in Listing 13.4.

Listing 13.4   Measuring the time to create an eager zeroed thick virtual disk

```
time vmkfstools -c 40G --diskformat eagerzeroedthick
/vmfs/volumes/iSCSI_LUN0/Book-Demo2/bookdemo-disk4.vmdk
Creating disk '/vmfs/volumes/iSCSI_LUN0/Book-Demo2/bookdemo-disk4.vmdk'
and zeroing it out...
Create: 100% done.
real    3m 16.99s
user    0m 1.68s
sys     0m 0.00s
```

The command `time` tracks the time taken for the task to complete. The value you need to track is listed in the `real` field. In this example, it took 3 minutes, 16 seconds, and 99 milliseconds to create a 40GB eager zeroed thick virtual disk on the datastore named iSCSI_LUN0.

Running the same command to create the same virtual disk on a datastore located on a VAAI-capable storage array completes almost immediately because the process of writing zeroes is offloaded to the storage array. I discuss this further in Chapter 17.

Creating a Thin Virtual Disk Using `vmkfstools`

Thin virtual disk blocks are allocated as needed when data is written to the virtual disk and the file grows in size. This is the default type for virtual disks created on NFS datastores.

To create a thin virtual disk, use this command:

```
vmkfstools --createvirtualdisk <size> --diskformat thin /<vmfs-path to VM
directory>/<Virtual Disk filename>
```

This is the shorthand version of this command:

```
vmkfstools -c <size> -d thin /<vmfs-path to VM directory>/<Virtual Disk
filename>
```

Here is an example:

```
vmkfstools --createvirtualdisk 40G --diskformat thin /vmfs/volumes/datas-
tore1/Book-Demo2/bookdemo-disk5.vmdk
```

This creates a 40GB thin virtual disk file named book-demo-disk5.vmdk on a datastore named datastore1.

Listing File System Usage by Thin Virtual Disks

To VMs, thin virtual disks appear to be pre-allocated, but they actually occupy the blocks used by data written to the virtual disk only. To demonstrate that, I'll show you a couple commands.

> **NOTE**
>
> Most of the commands in this section do not apply to virtual disks located on VSAN datastores or VVol containers. This is due to the fact that *_flat.vmdk files are replaced with VSAN objects or virtual volumes. I will cover the relevant details in Chapters 21 through 23.

The following command lists a virtual disk file named book-demo-thin-flat.vmdk in the current directory:

```
ls -al book-demo-thin*
-rw------- 1 root root 4294967296 Mar 25 02:39 book-demo-thin-flat.vmdk
-rw------- 1 root root 499 Mar 25 02:39 book-demo-thin.vmdk
```

I named this file thin for demonstration purposes. Normally thin virtual disks are named whatever you name them, and the provisioning type is not included in the filename. This file is the extent of the virtual disk with a descriptor file named book-demo-thin.vmdk.

The size of the extent file is 4294967296 bytes, which is 4GB (4GB × 1024MB × 1024KB × 1024 bytes). This is the size the file system reports to the virtual machine that uses it as a virtual disk.

Listing 13.5 shows the actual number of disk blocks this file occupies on the file system.

Listing 13.5   Count of blocks used by the thin virtual disk

```
stat book-demo-thin-flat.vmdk
 File: "book-demo-thin-flat.vmdk"
 Size: 4294967296      Blocks: 0             IO Block: 131072 regular file
Device: d03aaeed4049851bh/15004497442547270939d Inode: 88096004 Links: 1
Access: (0600/-rw-------) Uid: ( 0/ root) Gid: ( 0/ root)
Access: 2012-03-25 02:39:10.000000000
Modify: 2012-03-25 02:39:10.000000000
Change: 2012-03-25 02:39:10.000000000
```

The command `stat` lists the filename, the file size, and how many disk blocks it occupies. In this example, the file size matches what we got from the directory listing. However, the block count is zero! Why is it zero? The answer is small file packing or zero-level addressing, which is discussed in Chapter 12, "VMFS Architecture."

Where is the file actually stored if it occupies zero blocks? It is stuffed into the VMFS file descriptor block (Inode). In this example, the Inode number is 88096004. When a VM writes data to this file and it grows beyond 1KB, it is placed in a VMFS sub-block (64KB for VMFS3 and 8KB for VMFS5) until it grows beyond the sub-block size, which is when it occupies whole file system block (1MB for newly created VMFS5 or whatever block size is used to format VMFS3). See Chapter 12.

In comparison, Listing 13.6 shows what a thick disk block allocation looks like.

Listing 13.6   Count of blocks used by a thick virtual disk

```
stat book-demo-thick-flat.vmdk
 File: "book-demo-thick-flat.vmdk"
 Size: 4294967296       Blocks: 8388608       IO Block: 131072 regular file
Device: d03aaeed4049851bh/15004497442547270939d Inode: 71318788 Links: 1
Access: (0600/-rw-------) Uid: ( 0/ root) Gid: ( 0/ root)
Access: 2012-03-25 02:36:33.000000000
Modify: 2012-03-25 02:36:33.000000000
Change: 2012-03-25 02:36:33.000000000
```

In Listing 13.6, I created a thick virtual disk with exactly the same size as the thin one from earlier, and I used the word *thick* in the filename for demonstration purposes. The output of stat shows that the size is 4294967296, which is 4GB, and the number of disk blocks is 8388608. If you multiply the number of blocks by the disk block size, which is 512 bytes, you get 4294967296, which is the total file size in bytes.

Cloning Virtual Disks Using vmkfstools

The process of creating a copy of a virtual disk via vmkfstools is referred to as *cloning*. It used to be known as *importing*, but because the output can be any supported virtual disk type, which can be different from the original virtual disk, the term *cloning* is more appropriate. Do not confuse this process with the cloning process in vCenter Server, which clones a whole VM. The latter clones the VM configuration along with the virtual disks. This process is also used by View Composer, which creates full clones or linked clones. I explain that further in Chapter 15, "Snapshot Handling."

To clone a virtual disk, you need to decide on the following items:

- Source virtual disk name
- Target virtual disk name
- Target virtual disk format

The first two items are self-explanatory. The third item can be any of the following disk formats:

- `zeroedthick` (zeroed thick)

- `thin` (thin)

- `eagerzeroedthick` (eager zeroed thick)

- `rdm` (virtual mode RDM)

- `rdmp` (physical mode RDM)

- `2gbsparse` (2GB sparse disk)

I already covered the first three types, and I discuss RDMs later in this chapter, in the "Raw Device Mappings" section.

2GB sparse disk format is the default VMware Workstation and VMware Fusion virtual disk format. To clone a virtual disk using this disk format, you can use this command:

```
vmkfstools --clonevirtualdisk <source-virtual-disk) --diskformat 2gbsparse
<target-virtual-disk>
```

This is the shorthand version of this command:

```
vmkfstools -i <source-virtual-disk) -d 2gbsparse <target-virtual-disk>
```

Here is an example:

```
vmkfstools -i book-demo-thin.vmdk -d 2gbsparse book-demo-thin-clone.vmdk
```

> **NOTE**
>
> On ESXi 6.0, running the `clonevirtualdisk` command results in the error "Failed to clone disk: The system cannot find the file specified (25)" because the `multiextent` vmkernel module is not loaded by default. To load it, run the following:
>
> ```
> esxcli system module load -m multiextent
> ```
>
> ESXi 6.5 and later are not subject to this error.

This cloning command results in the creation of the files shown in Listing 13.7.

Listing 13.7 Sparse files created by using the cloning option

```
ls -al book-demo-thin-clone*
-rw-------  1 root root 327680 Mar 25 20:40 book-demo-thin-clone-s001.vmdk
-rw-------  1 root root 327680 Mar 25 20:40 book-demo-thin-clone-s002.vmdk
-rw-------  1 root root  65536 Mar 25 20:40 book-demo-thin-clone-s003.vmdk
-rw-------  1 root root    619 Mar 25 20:40 book-demo-thin-clone.vmdk
```

The smallest file is the virtual disk descriptor file is book-demo-thin-clone.vmdk. The remaining files are the extents of the virtual disk with a suffix s00x, where x is a sequential numeric value starting from 1.

Listing 13.8 shows a sample of the relevant content from the descriptor file.

Listing 13.8 Content of a sparse disk descriptor file

```
# Disk DescriptorFile
version=1
encoding="UTF-8"
CID=fffffffe
parentCID=ffffffff
isNativeSnapshot="no"
createType="twoGbMaxExtentSparse"

# Extent description
RW 4192256 SPARSE "book-demo-thin-clone-s001.vmdk"
RW 4192256 SPARSE "book-demo-thin-clone-s002.vmdk"
RW 4096 SPARSE "book-demo-thin-clone-s003.vmdk"

# The Disk Data Base
#DDB

ddb.deletable = "true"
```

In this example, the `createType` property is `twoGbMaxExtentSparse`, which means that the virtual disk is divided into extents of 2GB or smaller. The extents are specified in the `Extent description` section of the descriptor file.

These are the extents in this example:

- book-demo-thin-clone-s001.vmdk
- book-demo-thin-clone-s002.vmdk
- book-demo-thin-clone-s003.vmdk

The first two extents are each less than 2GB in size (4192256 disk blocks of 512 bytes each). The last extent is the balance of the 4GB. All three extents are of the sparse type. It is evident from the directory listing shown in Listing 13.7 that the extents' size on disk is smaller than the provisioned size. Note the source virtual disk from which I cloned; it was freshly created and had no data written to it at the time I cloned it. If there had been data written to the source virtual disk, the target virtual disk extents would have been larger than this example. They would have been equivalent to the nonzero blocks cloned from the source virtual disk.

To identify the number of VMFS blocks these extents occupy on the datastore, run the `stat` command, as shown in Listing 13.9.

Listing 13.9   Count of blocks used by a sparse disk

```
stat book-demo-thin-clone* |grep 'vmdk\|Blocks'
  File: "book-demo-thin-clone-s001.vmdk"
  Size: 327680        Blocks: 2048         IO Block: 131072 regular file
  File: "book-demo-thin-clone-s002.vmdk"
  Size: 327680        Blocks: 2048         IO Block: 131072 regular file
  File: "book-demo-thin-clone-s003.vmdk"
  Size: 65536         Blocks: 2048         IO Block: 131072 regular file
  File: "book-demo-thin-clone.vmdk"
  Size: 619           Blocks: 0            IO Block: 131072 regular file
```

In this output, I used `grep` to search for text that includes `vmdk` and `Blocks` to filter out the rest of the output and list the filename and related size information. Here you should notice that the number of blocks used by each extent is 2048 disk blocks, which are equal to 1MB. The reason the disk blocks used only 1MB is that the file size is less than 1MB and more than 8KB. In other words, they are smaller than the VMFS5 file block size and larger than the VMFS5 sub-block size. If the datastore were a VMFS3 volume or upgraded from VMFS3, the last two files would have instead occupied a 64KB sub-block each. This is also why the descriptor file, which is the last one on the list, occupies zero blocks: It is smaller than 1KB in size.

> **NOTE**
>
> You cannot freshly create a virtual disk by using the `vmkfstools 2gbsparse` option. This option is only available when you use the `vmkfstools --clonevirtualdisk` option. Beginning with vSphere 6, this format is no longer supported due to negative performance impact. To convert it to other supported formats, use the same cloning command with a supported target `--diskformat` option.

Raw Device Mappings

Certain virtualized applications—for example, Microsoft Cluster Service (MSCS) or storage layered applications—require direct access to raw storage devices. A storage layered application interacts directly with a storage device by issuing native SCSI commands on the device. vSphere enables these applications via raw device mappings (RDMs), which are pointers to the physical LUN and stored on VMFS datastores. These RDMs can be attached to virtual machines in the same fashion as virtual disks. The VMFS metadata entry representing the RDM pointer on the file system occupies no data blocks. (I show how that works later in this chapter.)

RDMs are available in two modes:

- **Virtual mode RDMs** (also known as *non-passthrough RDMs*)—These RDMs hide the physical properties of the mapped device, and VMs using them see these RDMs as VMware SCSI disks, similarly to how they see the virtual disks.

- **Physical mode RDMs** (also known as *passthrough RDMs*)—These RDMs expose the physical properties of the mapped LUNs and the virtual machines using them to see these RDMs as physical LUNs directly presented from the storage array. All SCSI commands issued by the guest OS to the mapped LUNs are passed through to the storage array unmodified. The only SCSI command that is not passed through is REPORT_LUN because the VM cannot discover targets not presented to it via RDMs.

Creating Virtual Mode RDMs Using the UI

The process of creating virtual mode RDMs is relatively similar to that of creating virtual disks:

1. Connect to the vCenter server that manages the ESXi 6 host, using the vSphere 6.0 Web Client as a user with Administrator privileges.

2. Navigate to the **VMs and Templates** view.

3. Locate the VM to which you want to add a virtual disk. Right-click it and then select **Edit Settings**.

4. In the dialog that appears, click the **New device** pull-down menu.

5. Click **RDM Disk** option.

6. Click **Add** (see Figure 13.9).

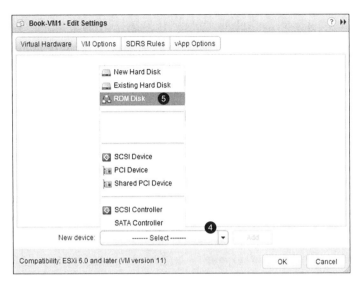

Figure 13.9 Adding an RDM

7. In the Select Target LUN dialog, select the LUN you want to map and then click **OK**.

8. Expand the **New Hard disk** section.

9. In the **Location** field, select where you want to store the LUN mapping. You can either store it with the VM or specify a datastore. If the VM is stored on an NFS datastore, VSAN datastore, or VVol container, you need to have a VMFS datastore available on which to store the RDM-related files. In this example, the VM is stored on a VVol container, which is why there is a red error icon next to the **New Hard disk** field label as well as a red rectangle around the **Store with virtual machine** option. However, if you hover over the latter, an error bubble says "Mapping for LUNs cannot be stored on NFS datastore. Select VMFS datastore." This may be a bit misleading, but the recommendation to select the VMFS datastore is the same regardless of the underlying incompatible datastore or container (see Figure 13.10). If the VM is stored on a VMFS datastore and you want to store the RDM with the VM files, skip to step 13.

Figure 13.10 RDM not on a VMFS datastore

10. Select the **Browse** option from the Location pull-down menu.

11. Select a VMFS datastore. If this RDM will be shared by VMs on other hosts, make sure the datastore shows **Multiple hosts** in the Access column (see Figure 13.11). You may need to scroll to the right to see that column.

12. Click **OK**.

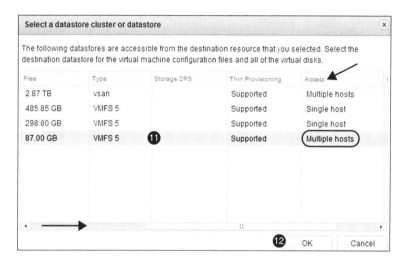

Figure 13.11 Selecting the datastore for RDM entry

NOTE

The basic rule for shared virtual mode RDMs is that they are used for cluster-in-a-box (CIB) configurations, where all nodes in the cluster reside on the same ESXi host. One exception to this rule is Oracle RAC configuration, in which the virtual mode RDM can be shared by nodes in the cluster located on up to eight ESXi hosts utilizing multi-writer locks. In this case, the shared disk can be a virtual mode RDM or VMDK. Physical mode RDMs are not supported for multi-writer locks. See step 13.

The added RDM shows up in the listed VM devices as **New Hard Disk**, as shown in Figure 13.12. You should also see, in the Physical LUN field, the mapped device, which is the LUN's NAA ID in the /vmfs/devices/disks/ directory.

13. Select the **Virtual** option from the Compatibility Mode pull-down list.

14. If this RDM will be shared by Oracle RAC nodes, select the **Multi-writer** option from the Sharing pull-down list. Notice that both the **New Hard disk** and **Sharing** fields now show an asterisk (*), denoting a changed configuration (see Figure 13.12).

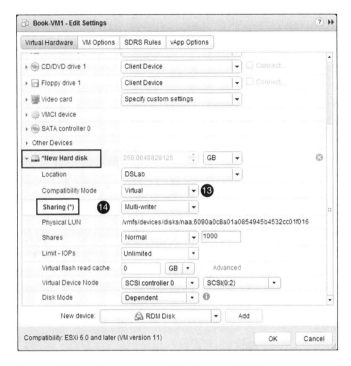

Figure 13.12   Selecting the datastore for RDM entry

NOTE

The Sharing pull-down list was introduced in vSphere 6 Update 1. It does not exist prior to that update release.

15. As I will discuss later in this chapter, a separate SCSI controller may be recommended for certain shared disk configurations. In such a case, you may add a SCSI controller from the New device pull-down menu and then click **Add** (see Figure 13.13).

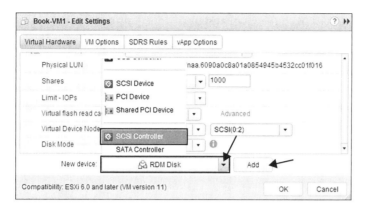

Figure 13.13   Adding a SCSI controller

16. Select **New SCSI Controller** in the Virtual Device Node row. Notice that the second field now shows SCSI(1:0). It is a common practice to select a different virtual SCSI adapter number from that assigned to the guest OS's system disk. In this example, it is **SCSI(1:0)**, which means the RDM will be attached as the first device on the second virtual SCSI adapter, which is SCSI1 (see Figure 13.14). I will discuss more design options later in this chapter, in the section, "Virtual Storage Adapters."

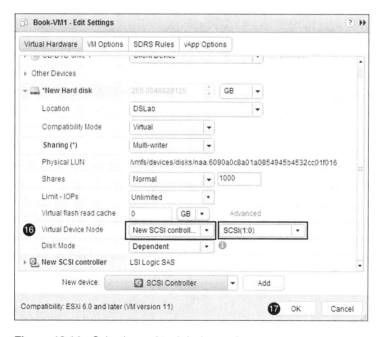

Figure 13.14   Selecting a virtual device node

17. Review your selections and then click **OK** to create the RDM and save the changes to the VM configuration (see Figure 13.14).

NOTE

Because the RDM you created in this procedure is a virtual mode, the row labeled Disk Mode shows that the Independent mode option is available. This is because the virtual mode RDM is treated like a virtual disk from the VM's point of view. This option is not available for physical mode RDMs.

18. At this point, to see the actual datastore mapping file representing the RDM, edit the virtual machine settings again and expand the hard disk representing the RDM—in this example, **Hard disk 2**. The mapping file descriptor is Book-VM1.vmdk in the Book-VM1 directory on the DSLab datastore (see Figure 13.15). Note that the physical LUN now shows as the VML file instead of the NAA ID. This is simply a symbolic link to the device, as described in the "Listing RDM Properties Using `vmkfstools`" section, later in this chapter. Click **Cancel** when done.

Figure 13.15   Viewing RDM properties

Creating Physical Mode RDMs Using the UI

To create a physical mode RDM, follow the procedure in the "Creating Virtual Mode RDMs Using the UI" section, earlier in the chapter, with the following exceptions:

- In step 13, select the **Physical** option instead of **Virtual**.

- In step 16, even though the **Independent** mode option is available, any choices made at this point will be ignored, and the Disk Mode field will not be displayed when you edit the VM settings later (see Figure 13.18).

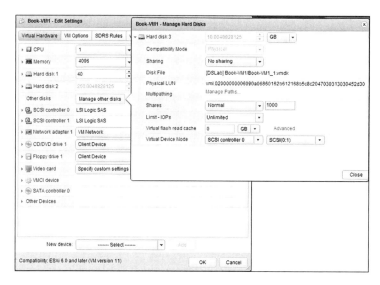

Figure 13.16   No Disk Modes Available for Physical Mode RDM

Creating RDMs Using the Command-Line Interface

You can create RDMs, both virtual and physical, using the `vmkfstools -r` and `-z` commands, respectively. See Listing 13.10 and Listing 13.11 for command-line examples.

Listing 13.10   `vmkfstools` command to create a virtual mode RDM

```
vmkfstools --createrdm /vmfs/devices/disks/<naa ID> /vmfs/
volumes/<Datastore>/<vm-directory>/<rdm-file-name>.vmdk
```

This is the shorthand version of this command:

```
vmkfstools -r /vmfs/devices/disks/<naa ID>
/vmfs/volumes/<Datastore>/<vm-directory>/<rdm-file-name>.vmdk
```

Here is an example:

```
vmkfstools -r /vmfs/devices/disks/naa.6006016055711d00cff95e65664ee011/
vmfs/volumes/iSCSI_LUN0/Book-Demo/Book-Demo_2.vmdk
```

Listing 13.11   `vmkfstools` command to create physical mode RDM

```
vmkfstools --createrdmpassthru /vmfs/devices/disks/<naa ID> /vmfs/
volumes/<Datastore>/<vm-directory>/<rdm-file-name>.vmdk
```

This is the shorthand version of this command:

```
vmkfstools -z /vmfs/devices/disks/<naa ID> /vmfs/volumes/<Datastore>/<vm-
directory>/<rdm-file-name>.vmdk
```

Here is an example:

```
vmkfstools -z /vmfs/devices/disks/naa.6006016055711d00cff95e65664ee011 /
vmfs/volumes/iSCSI_LUN0/Book-Demo/Book-Demo_3.vmdk
```

Listing RDM Properties

After an RDM is created, you might need to identify its properties. The user interface (UI), as shown in Figure 13.16 earlier in this chapter, only shows the VML name of the mapped device. The VMFS entries of a given RDM appear to be similar to those of virtual disks. Each RDM has two VMDK files on the datastore on which you created the RDM. These files are the virtual machine descriptor file and the RDM pointer file.

To list the files in the VM directory, you can run the following command:

```
ls -al /vmfs/volumes/<datastore>/<vm-directory> |sed 's/.*root //'
```

This assumes that the file owner is root. This command truncates the output to remove the word root and all text before it, leaving only the size, date, and timestamp as well as the filenames. Sample output is shown in Listing 13.12.

Listing 13.12 Listing VM files

```
ls -al /vmfs/volumes/iSCSI/Book-Demo/ |sed 's/.*root //'
        4294967296 Feb 14 04:44 Book-Demo-flat.vmdk
               468 Feb 14 04:44 Book-Demo.vmdk
                 0 Feb 14 04:44 Book-Demo.vmsd
              1844 Apr 9 19:47 Book-Demo.vmx
               264 Apr 9 19:47 Book-Demo.vmxf
        10737418240 Apr 9 17:51 Book-Demo_1-rdm.vmdk
               486 Apr 9 17:51 Book-Demo_1.vmdk
        10737418240 Apr 9 19:01 Book-Demo_2-rdm.vmdk  ← Pointer
               486 Apr 9 19:01 Book-Demo_2.vmdk  ← Descriptor
        10737418240 Apr 9 19:14 Book-Demo_3-rdmp.vmdk
               498 Apr 9 19:14 Book-Demo_3.vmdk
```

In this example, there are three RDM descriptor files, named Book-Demo_1.vmdk through Book_Demo_3.vmdk. The RDM pointer files (one of them indicated with a comment), which are equivalent to the virtual disk extent files, have the suffix .rdm or .rdmp. Files with the .rdm suffix are pointers to a virtual mode RDM. Conversely, files with the .rdmp suffix are pointers to physical mode RDMs, which are also known as passthrough RDMs.

Each RDM pointer file appears to be 10GB in size. These match the mapped LUNs' sizes. However, because these are not actual file blocks on the datastore, they should be zero bytes in size. To find out the actual size of these files, you can run this command:

```
cd /vmfs/volumes/<datastore>/<vm-directory>
stat *-rdm* |awk '/File/||/Block/{print}'
```

Sample output is shown in Listing 13.13.

Listing 13.13   Output of commands listing an RDM pointer block count

```
stat *-rdm* |awk '/File/||/Block/{print}'
  File: "Book-Demo_1-rdm.vmdk"
  Size: 10737418240     Blocks: 0         IO Block: 131072 regular file
  File: "Book-Demo_2-rdm.vmdk"
  Size: 10737418240     Blocks: 0         IO Block: 131072 regular file
  File: "Book-Demo_3-rdmp.vmdk"
  Size: 10737418240     Blocks: 0         IO Block: 131072 regular file
```

This output clearly shows that, although the size is 10GB (listed here in bytes), the actual number of blocks is zero for all three files. This is easily explained by the fact that the actual file blocks are mapped to blocks on the physical LUN that each RDM represents.

Listing 13.14 shows the content of a virtual mode RDM descriptor file.

Listing 13.14   Content of a virtual mode RDM descriptor file

```
# Disk DescriptorFile
version=1
encoding="UTF-8"
CID=fffffffe
parentCID=ffffffff
isNativeSnapshot="no"
createType="vmfsRawDeviceMap"

# Extent description
RW 20971520 VMFSRDM "Book-Demo_1-rdm.vmdk"

# The Disk Data Base
#DDB
```

```
ddb.adapterType = "lsilogic"

ddb.geometry.cylinders = "1305"
ddb.geometry.heads = "255"
ddb.geometry.sectors = "63"
ddb.longContentID = "2d86dba01ca8954da334a0e4ffffffffe"
ddb.uuid = "60 00 C2 9c 0e da f3 3f-60 7a f7 fe bc 34 7d 0f"
ddb.virtualHWVersion = "11"
```

The highlighted lines in the output are unique to virtual mode RDMs:

- The `createType` field value is `vmfsRawDeviceMap`, which indicates a virtual mode RDM.

- The `Extent description` section shows the RDM sectors count, which is in 512-byte disk blocks. It also shows the extent type, which is `VMFSRDM`. This type is also used by physical mode RDMs as well, which I show you in Listing 13.15.

Listing 13.15 shows the content of a physical mode RDM descriptor file.

Listing 13.15   Content of a physical mode RDM descriptor file

```
# Disk DescriptorFile
version=1
encoding="UTF-8"
CID=fffffffe
parentCID=ffffffff
isNativeSnapshot="no"
createType="vmfsPassthroughRawDeviceMap"

# Extent description
RW 20971520 VMFSRDM "Book-Demo_3-rdmp.vmdk"

# The Disk Data Base
#DDB

ddb.adapterType = "lsilogic"
ddb.geometry.cylinders = "1305"
ddb.geometry.heads = "255"
ddb.geometry.sectors = "63"
ddb.longContentID = "307b5c6b4c696020ffb7a8c7ffffffffe"
ddb.uuid = "60 00 C2 93 34 90 2c ca-c9 96 f2 a6 7f a6 65 e1"
ddb.virtualHWVersion = "11"
```

Again, I highlighted the lines in the output that are unique to physical mode RDMs:

- The `createType` field value is `vmfsPassthroughRawDeviceMap`, which indicates a physical mode RDM (also known as a passthrough RDM).

- The `Extent description` section shows the RDM sectors count, which is in 512-byte disk blocks. It also shows the extent type, which is `VMFSRDM`. As I mentioned in the explanation of the virtual mode RDM, this extent type is common for both types of RDMs.

Now that I have shown you the file structure of RDMs, it's time to identify the RDM properties to locate the device it maps. You can do this by using `vmkfstools` at the CLI or by using the UI.

Listing RDM Properties Using `vmkfstools`

To list RDM properties by using `vmkfstools`, follow these steps:

1. Use `vmkfstools --queryrdm` or the shorthand version, `vmkfstools -q`, to identify the VML ID of the mapped LUN (see Listing 13.16). This option lists the RDM properties, including the RDM type—for example, passthrough RDM or non-passthrough RDM.

Listing 13.16   Using `vmkfstools` to list RDM properties

```
vmkfstools -q /vmfs/volumes/FC200/win2K3Enterprise/win2K3Enterprise.vmdk

Disk /vmfs/volumes/FC200/win2K3Enterprise/win2K3Enterprise.vmdk is a
Passthrough Raw Device Mapping
Maps to: vml.02000100006006016055711d00cff95e65664ee011524149442035
```

2. Use the VML ID (highlighted in Listing 13.16) with the `esxcli storage core device` command to find the device ID of the mapped LUN (see Listing 13.17). This is the syntax:

```
esxcli storage core device list --device <vml ID>
```

This is the shorthand version of this command:

```
esxcli storage core device list -d <vml ID>
```

Listing 13.17   Identifying device ID by using VML ID

```
esxcli storage core device list --device vml.02000100006006016055711d00cff9
5e65664ee011524149442035 |grep naa
naa.6006016055711d00cff95e65664ee011
    Display Name: DGC Fibre Channel Disk
(naa.6006016055711d00cff95e65664ee011)
    Devfs Path: /vmfs/devices/disks/naa.6006016055711d00cff95e65664ee011
```

I highlighted the device ID in the output. The NAA ID is usually sufficient to identify the LUN. However, if you need to identify the LUN number as well, you can run this command using the NAA ID you just identified:

```
esxcli storage nmp device list --device=<NAA ID> |grep Current
```

This is the shorthand version of this command:

```
esxcli storage nmp device list -d <NAA ID> |grep Current
```

Listing 13.18 shows the output of this command.

Listing 13.18   Identifying the LUN, based on the device ID

```
esxcli storage nmp device list --device=naa.6006016055711d00cff95e65664
ee011 |grep Working
Working Path: vmhba3:C0:T1:L1
```

The output shows that this LUN's runtime name is `vmhba3:C0:T1:L1`, which means the LUN is LUN 1 on the storage array port on target 1. (See the "FC Targets" section in Chapter 2, "Fibre Channel Storage Connectivity," for details.)

Listing RDM Properties Using the UI

To list RDM properties using the UI, follow these steps:

1. Connect to the vCenter server that manages the ESXi 6 host, using the vSphere 6.0 Web Client as a user with Administrator privileges.

2. Navigate to the **VMs and Templates** view.

3. Locate the VM to which you want to add a virtual disk. Right-click it and then select **Edit Settings**. You should see a dialog similar to the one shown in Figure 13.17.

4. Expand one **Hard disk** section at a time. If there is a field named Other disks, click the **Manage other disks** button to list the additional disks. There, you can further expand one **Hard disk** section at a time.

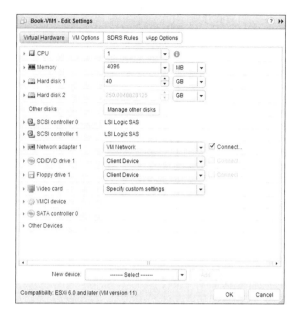

Figure 13.17   Listing VM properties using the UI

Look for fields named Compatibility Mode and Physical LUN. If the section has such fields, the hard disk represents an RDM. The value of the **Compatibility Mode** field reflects the RDM type—virtual or physical. The **Physical LUN** field shows the device's VML ID, which is this in the example vml.02000000006090a 06860162b612168b5c8c2047030313030452d30.

5. Click the **Manage Paths** link in the Multipathing field (see Figure 13.18).

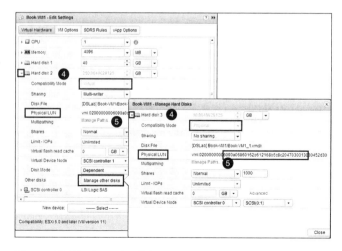

Figure 13.18   Locating RDMs using the UI

If this does not show the **Edit Multipathing Policies** dialog at this point, you may need to close the Edit Settings dialog, which will cause the Edit Multipathing Policies dialog to open (see Figure 13.19).

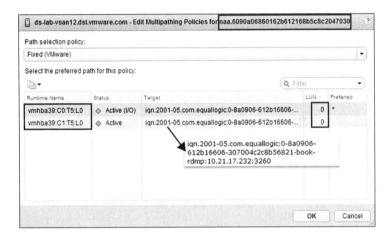

Figure 13.19   Listing an RDM's NAA ID

6. The device ID is listed in the status bar at the top of the resulting dialog. The LUN and paths to it are listed under the LUN and Runtime Name columns, respectively. To list the target ID, simply hover over the target field for a given path. In this example, the target is on a Dell EqualLogic iSCSI storage array. Click **Cancel** when done.

In this example, the device ID is as follows:

```
naa.6090a06860162b612168b5c8c2047030
```

The LUN is 0. Note that some iSCSI storage arrays, like EqualLogic, use LUN 0 for all LUNs but assign unique target IDs. So, you must pay close attention to the target ID to avoid any mix-up.

TIP

If you look closely at the VML and NAA ID in this example, you will notice that the NAA ID is actually part of the VML ID or, if you look at it the other way, the VML ID is based on the NAA ID of the device:

```
vml.02000000006090a06860162b612168b5c8c2047030313030452d30
naa.6090a06860162b612168b5c8c2047030
```

For example, the matching bytes are highlighted here as well as in Figure 13.18.

Virtual Storage Adapters

VMs use virtual disks and RDMs as SCSI disks attached to a virtual SCSI HBA. Some virtual disks may also be connected to an IDE or a SATA adapter.

Virtual machine configuration files (*.vmx) show the type of virtual storage adapter. For example, running the following command while in a virtual machine directory returns its list of virtual SCSI HBAs:

```
fgrep -i virtualdev *.vmx |grep scsi

scsi0.virtualDev = "lsisas1068"
scsi1.virtualDev = "lsilogic"
scsi3.virtualDev = "buslogic"
```

This example shows that the VM has three different virtual SCSI HBAs:

- Virtual SCSI HBA number 0 is `lsisas1068`, which is LSI Logic SAS type

- Virtual SCSI HBA number 1 is `lsilogic`, which is LSI Logic Parallel type

- Virtual SCSI HBA number 2 is `buslogic`, which is BusLogic Parallel type

Selecting the Type of Virtual Storage Adapter

One of the most critical VM design decisions is the number and type of virtual storage adapters. The default first storage adapter is based on the guest OS type selected at the time you create the VM. It is a good practice to separate application-specific disks from the system disk as they require different I/O profiles. You can then place the corresponding virtual disks on datastores or RDMs backed by LUNs that meet the expected workload and I/O profile. Similarly, the choice of virtual adapter type and which virtual disks distribution among them is a decision better made prior to installing the guest OS and applications.

Whatever you do, unless you are following this procedure before installing the guest OS, *do not* change the type of the storage adapter to which the VM's boot disk is connected. Doing so will render most guest operating systems unbootable. Commonly, the boot disk is attached to SCSI controller 0.

This procedure covers changing SCSI controller 1. You can follow the same procedure to modify additional SCSI controllers.

To select the type of virtual storage adapter, follow this procedure using vSphere 6 Web Client while logged in as a user with Administrator privileges:

1. Locate the VM in the inventory tree, right-click it, and select **Edit Settings**.

2. Expand the SCSI controller you want to modify in the list of devices.

3. Select the SCSI controller type from the Change Type pull-down (see Figure 13.20).

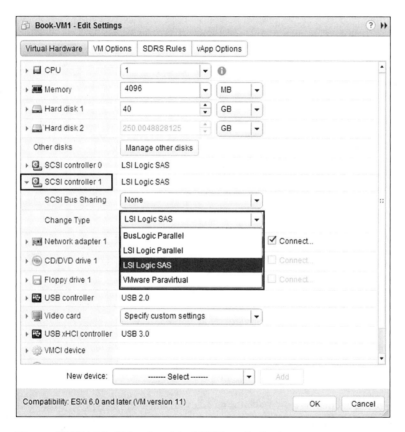

Figure 13.20   Modifying the virtual SCSI controller type

Figure 13.21 shows the device list after you modify SCSI controller 1. The dialog shows what will be done, along with a warning about the effect of modifying the adapter to which the boot disk is attached. Below the warning, two buttons are present: Change Type and Don't change.

4. To apply the change, click **Change Type** and then click **OK.** Otherwise click **Don't change**.

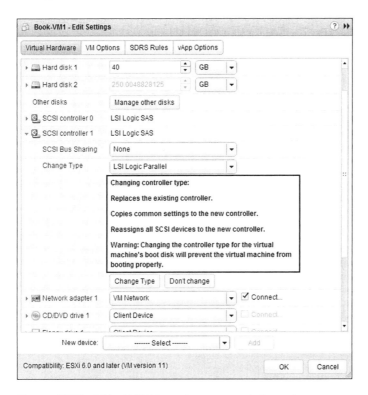

Figure 13.21   Virtual HBA type changes, ready to apply

TIP

When a virtual disk is attached to a virtual storage adapter, the adapter type is listed in the descriptor file as a value of the `ddb.adapterType` field. The adapters LSI_Logic Parallel and LSI Logic SAS are represented with a value **lsilogic** in that field. Buslogic Parallel is represented by the value **buslogic**.

VMware Paravirtual SCSI Controller

Paravirtualization is a technique that allows ESXi to present to the GOS a high-performance virtual SCSI controller that is almost identical to the underlying physical SCSI controller.

This high-performance virtual SCSI controller is referred to as VMware Paravirtual SCSI Controller (PVSCSI). It utilizes specialized GOS kernels that support paravirtualization. Such a combination provides better I/O throughput and reduces CPU utilization. As a general rule, if the VMware Tools for your GOS provide a PVSCSI driver, it should work. However, the VMware HCL, after ESXi 5.1, appears to have stopped listing guest operating systems that are supported with PVSCSI.

Explicit support for PVCSI with Windows Server Failover Clustering (WSFC) is stated in the "What's New in VMware vSphere 6.0 Platform" document at www.vmware.com/files/pdf/vsphere/VMW-WP-vSPHR-Whats-New-6-0-PLTFRM.pdf. This implies support for PVSCSI on Windows Server 2008 through 2012-R2.

Configuring a VM to Use PVSCSI

To configure a VM to use PVSCSI, follow steps 1 through 4 in the earlier section "Selecting the Type of Virtual Storage Adapter." However, in step 3, you need to select **VMware Paravirtual** as the adapter type.

CAUTION

Do not change the type of virtual SCSI controller to which the GOS system disk is attached. Doing so may render the GOS unbootable.

PVSCSI Limitations

The following limitations are imposed on the PVSCSI controllers:

- If you hot add or hot remove a virtual disk to the VM attached to the PVSCSI controller, you must rescan the SCSI BUS from within the GOS.

- If the virtual disks attached to the PVSCSI controller have snapshots, they will not benefit from the performance improvements.

- If the ESXi host memory is overcommitted, the VM does not benefit from the PVSCSI performance improvement.

- PVSCSI controllers are not supported for GOS boot devices (see the earlier warning).

- WSFC is now supported with PVSCSI on vSphere 6 and later. It was not supported on any earlier releases.

SCSI Bus Sharing

You might have noticed in Figure 13.21 that there is a field named SCSI Bus Sharing. This field is designed mainly to support WSFC clustered VMs.

There are two bus sharing policies: virtual and physical. Do not confuse them with RDM compatibility modes bearing the same names. SCSI bus sharing allows multiple VMs to open the same shared virtual disks or RDMs concurrently. You accomplish this by turning off file locking for virtual disks attached to virtual SCSI controllers with bus sharing enabled. To prevent concurrent writes to the shared virtual disks, the GOS must provide the functionality that elects which node in the cluster is allowed to write to the shared disks. This is provided by WSFC and the use of quorum disks. This is in contrast to utilizing multi-writer locking, which allows up to eight hosts to concurrently lock a virtual disk or virtual mode RDM. This is handled by VMFS metadata and requires no SCSI bus sharing. Actually, multi-writer locks do not function if SCSI bus sharing is enabled.

Table 13.5 compares virtual and physical bus sharing policies.

Table 13.5 Virtual and physical bus sharing comparison

Feature	Virtual	Physical	None
Concurrent access for virtual disks	Yes	No	No
Concurrent access for virtual mode RDMs	Yes	Yes	No
Concurrent access for physical mode RDMs	No	Yes	No
Supported with VM snapshots (see next section)	No	No	Yes
Supported with multi-writer locking*	No	No	Yes

* Multi-writer locking is discussed in Chapter 14.

Virtual Machine Snapshots

Have you ever installed an OS patch or update that rendered a virtual machine unbootable or made it crash repeatedly? You probably wished you could turn back the time to right before you installed the problematic patches.

I once got a VMware t-shirt that had an "Undo Your Whole Day" slogan on the back. This was the slogan we used when VMware first introduced the concept —of going back in time with a VM. This feature was referred to as REDO logs. The logs enabled you to discard changes made to the VM after the REDO logs were created.

Now the VM is all grown up, and so are its features. The concept of REDO logs has evolved into virtual machine snapshots. You can take a point-in-time snapshot of the virtual machine state, which includes the virtual disks and, optionally, if the VM was powered on at the time, the VM memory. These states are saved to a set of files stored in the VM directory.

Before I show you how to take a snapshot, look at the baseline set of files in the VM directory, shown in Listing 13.19.

Listing 13.19 Virtual machine files before taking a snapshot

```
ls -Al |sed 's/.*root//'
        8589934592 Jan 3 21:17 Book-Demo3-flat.vmdk
               497 Jan 3 21:17 Book-Demo3.vmdk
                 0 Jan 3 21:17 Book-Demo3.vmsd
              1506 Jan 3 21:17 Book-Demo3.vmx
```

Table 13.6 lists the extensions of these files and their functions.

Table 13.6 VM file extensions

File Extension	Function	Comments
.vmdk	Virtual disk	There are two files with this extension for each virtual disk. The file without the `-flat` suffix is the descriptor file, and the file with the `-flat` suffix is the extent file; I covered these files in the "Virtual Disks" section, earlier in this chapter.
.vmsd	Virtual machine snapshot dictionary	Defines the snapshot hierarchy. More about that in the following section. The file is blank before any snapshots are taken.
.vmx	Virtual machine configuration file	Defines the virtual machine structure and virtual hardware.

Creating the VM's First Snapshot While the VM Is Powered Off

To create a snapshot, follow this procedure, using vSphere 6 Web Client:

1. Connect to the vCenter server that manages the ESXi 6 host, using the vSphere 6.0 Web Client as a user with Administrator privileges.

2. Locate the VM in the inventory tree and right-click it, select the **Snapshots** menu, and then select **Take Snapshot** (see Figure 13.22).

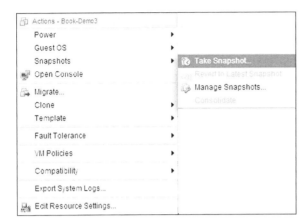

Figure 13.22   Creating a VM snapshot

3. When prompted, fill in the Name and Description fields with the snapshot display name and its description, respectively, and then click **OK** (see Figure 13.23). Note the two check boxes in this figure; they are grayed out because the VM is not powered on at this time. (I discuss these checkboxes later in this chapter.)

Figure 13.23   Entering the snapshot name and description

You should see a task created in the Recent Tasks pane, indicating that the **Create virtual machine snapshot** status is **in progress**. The status changes to **completed** when it's done.

> **NOTE**
>
> Attempting the same procedure on a VM with shared disks configuration (using multi-writer locking or SCSI bus sharing) results in the error "An error occurred while taking a snapshot: Cannot snapshot shared disk." This is the expected behavior as snapshots are not supported with this configuration.

Let's see now which files were added or modified when the snapshot was created. Listing 13.20 shows three new files created and two files modified.

Listing 13.20   VM directory listing after the first snapshot is created

```
ls -Al |sed 's/.*root//'
        20480 Jan 3 21:27 Book-Demo3-000001-delta.vmdk
          323 Jan 3 21:27 Book-Demo3-000001.vmdk
        10214 Jan 3 21:27 Book-Demo3-Snapshot1.vmsn
   8589934592 Jan 3 20:17 Book-Demo3-flat.vmdk
          498 Jan 3 20:17 Book-Demo3.vmdk
          465 Jan 3 21:27 Book-Demo3.vmsd
         2729 Jan 4 00:02 Book-Demo3.vmx
```

Table 13.7 lists and explains the added and modified files.

Table 13.7 Files added or modified by snapshot creation

Filename	Description	Comments
Book-Demo3-000001-delta.vmdk	Delta disk extent	New data written after the snapshot is taken gets redirected to this extent file. Its type is vmfsSparse. This file does not get created if the VM is stored on a VVol container or VSAN datastore.
Book-Demo3-000001.vmdk	Delta disk descriptor file	Descriptor file defining the snapshot virtual disk. See Listing 13.20 for content.

Filename	Description	Comments
Book-Demo3- Snapshot1. vmsn	VM snapshot file	This is the actual snapshot file, which is the state of the VM configuration. It combines the original unmodified content of VMX file. If the VM is powered on at the time you take the snapshot and you choose to take a snapshot of the VM's memory, this file includes that as well as the CPU state.
Book-Demo3.vmsd	VM snapshot dictionary	This file used to be blank before the snapshot was taken. Now it includes the snapshot hierarchy. See Listing 13.21 for the content.
Book-Demo3.vmx	VM configuration file	The value of scsi0:0.fileName is changed to be the delta disk descriptor filename.

To better understand the relationships between these files, let me walk you through the relevant content of each file. Note that all added files are named based on the VM name, which is also the default system disk virtual disk name. In this example, it is `Book-Demo3`:

1. The VM configuration file (VMX) is modified as follows:

Before snapshot:

```
scsi0:0.fileName = "Book-Demo3.vmdk"
```

After snapshot:

```
scsi0:0.fileName = "Book-Demo3-000001.vmdk"
```

This means that the virtual disk attached to scsi0:0 is now the delta disk file descriptor.

2. The delta disk descriptor file content is shown in Listing 13.21. It shows that the delta disk is a sparse file with `vmfsSparse` type.

Listing 13.21   Delta disk descriptor file content

```
# Disk DescriptorFile
version=1
encoding="UTF-8"
CID=fffffffe
parentCID=fffffffe
```

```
isNativeSnapshot="no"
createType="vmfsSparse"
parentFileNameHint="Book-Demo3.vmdk"
# Extent description
RW 16777216 VMFSSPARSE "Book-Demo3-000001-delta.vmdk"

# The Disk Data Base
#DDB

ddb.longContentID = "a051b9fb9b43b7ae0b351f1dffffffe"
```

The highlighted lines from Listing 13.21 are explained in Table 13.8.

Table 13.8 Delta disk descriptor properties

Property	Value	Comments
parentCID	ffffffe	The parent disk's content ID.
isNativeSnapshot	no	For snapshots on VVol containers, with the value yes.
createType	vmfsSparse vmfs	All delta disks are sparse files, regardless of their parent disks type. The only exception is VVols, where this value is vmfs.
parentFileNameHint	Book-Demo3.vmdk	The name of the parent disk. This disk stays unmodified.
Extent Description	Multivalues	The relevant values are the type, again, is vmfsSparse, and the extent filename which has the -delta suffix. If the virtual disk is located on a VVol container or VSAN datastore, the value of this field starts with vvol:// or vsan:// respectively.

The parent disk remains unmodified. When the VM is powered on, that file is opened with read-only locks. This is the same function done by the VADP (vStorage APIs for Data Protection) API when it backs up a virtual disk while the VM is running. This allows the backup software to copy the parent disk since the read-only lock allows multiple readers to access and open the parent virtual disk for reads.

NOTE

Many types of storage arrays implement snapshot backup capabilities. These technologies are often implemented in one of two fashions: copy-on-write (EMC) or pointer-based (NetApp and ZFS-based arrays). These technologies provide a means for arrays to provide LUN and file system snapshots. With VMware, storage partners, such as NetApp, are able to provide file-based snapshots on NFS datastores. Because VMDKs are files that can take advantage of such technology, this capability provides a more granular level of functionality.

vSphere 6 enables the same functionality on VVols, where taking a VM snapshot results in creating VVol-based snapshot. For example, looking at a VM from the perspective of a Dell PS series iSCSI storage array based VVol, you would see only the VM `Config` object and the parent virtual disk `Data` object. However, when you scroll to the right, you see the snapshot count value under the Snapshots column for the `Data` object representing the virtual disk (see Figure 13.24). In this view, I moved the Snapshots column to the left for visibility.

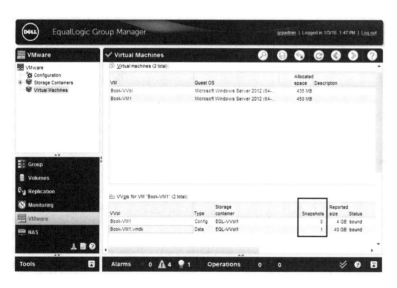

Figure 13.24   View of VVol-based snapshot on a Dell EqualLogic iSCSI storage array

3. The virtual machine snapshot dictionary file (VMSD) stores the properties that define the snapshot hierarchy, which is the relationship between snapshot files and the snapshot to which they belong. Listing 13.22 shows the content of this file.

Listing 13.22 Virtual machine snapshot dictionary file content

```
.encoding = "UTF-8"
snapshot.lastUID = "1"
snapshot.current = "1"
snapshot0.uid = "1"
snapshot0.filename = "Book-Demo3-Snapshot1.vmsn"
snapshot0.displayName = "Before installing patch xyz"
snapshot0.description = "Snapshot taken before installing patch xyz"
snapshot0.createTimeHigh = "310664"
snapshot0.createTimeLow = "1673441029"
snapshot0.numDisks = "1"
snapshot0.disk0.fileName = "Book-Demo3.vmdk"
snapshot0.disk0.node = "scsi0:0"
snapshot.numSnapshots = "1"
```

Because this is the first snapshot taken for the VM, there is only one snapshot definition listed, and its ID is 1. All properties in that file have the prefix snapshot0. Table 13.9 explains the properties without the prefix.

Table 13.9 Properties in the virtual machine snapshot dictionary file

Property	Value	Comments
lastUID	1	ID of the most recently created snapshot.
current	1	ID of the snapshot currently in use.
uid	1	Snapshot ID.
filename	"Book-Demo3-Snapshot1. vmsn"	Name of the snapshot file.
displayName	"Before installing patch xyz"	Snapshot name entered in the dialog shown in Figure 13.26.
description	"Snapshot taken before installing patch xyz"	Description of snapshot entered in the dialog shown in Figure 13.26.
numDisks	1	Number of virtual disks that are *not* configured as independent. This is the number of virtual disks that will have delta files.
disk0.filename	"Book-Demo3.vmdk"	Name of the first parent virtual disk.
disk0.node	scsi0:0	Parent virtual disk node.
numSnapshots	1	Total number of snapshots taken for this VM.

These properties dictate how the Snapshot Manager displays the current hierarchy of the snapshots in the UI. Figure 13.26 shows the hierarchy of the first snapshot of this VM. To display the Snapshot Manager, right-click the VM in the inventory tree and then select **Snapshot menu** followed by **Manage Snapshot**. This opens the dialog shown in Figure 13.25.

Figure 13.25   Displaying Snapshot Manager

In this figure, you can easily identify the parent disk, the snapshot display name, and the description. The **You are here** marker is the current state that points to the snapshot. (I explain the **Revert to** and **Delete** buttons in the "Snapshot Operations" section, later in this chapter.) Click the **Close** button (not shown here) to close dialog.

Creating a VM Second Snapshot While Powered On

Now take a second snapshot, this time with the VM powered on. Follow the same steps you used to create the first snapshot:

1. Connect to the vCenter server that manages the ESXi 6 host, using the vSphere 6.0 Web Client as a user with Administrator privileges or as a virtual machine power user.

2. Locate the VM in the inventory tree, right-click it, and then select the **Snapshot** menu and then **Take Snapshot**.

3. When prompted, fill in the Name and Description fields with the snapshot display name and its description, respectively, and then click **OK** (see Figure 13.26). Note the two check boxes at the bottom of the dialog. The first one, **Snapshot the virtual machine's memory**, is selected by default and is selectable because the VM is powered on. The second check box uses the same function that the VADP uses to take a snapshot before backing up the parent virtual disk. As the option indicates, VMware Tools must be installed in the VM for this to work. The reason is that the Tools installation includes a set of scripts that are run when this function is used. In this example, I have not installed VMware Tools yet, so the option is unavailable.

Figure 13.26   Entering the snapshot name and description of a powered-on VM

Let's see which files were added or modified in the VM directory. Listing 13.23 shows the VM directory after the second snapshot is created.

Listing 13.23   VM directory content after the second snapshot is created (with the VM powered on)

```
ls -Al |sed 's/.*root//'
       20480 Jan 3 21:27 Book-Demo3-000001-delta.vmdk
         323 Jan 3 21:27 Book-Demo3-000001.vmdk
       20480 Jan 4 00:28 Book-Demo3-000002-delta.vmdk
         330 Jan 4 00:28 Book-Demo3-000002.vmdk
       10214 Jan 3 21:27 Book-Demo3-Snapshot1.vmsn
  4294967296 Jan 4 00:29 Book-Demo3-Snapshot2.vmem
     1260293 Jan 4 00:29 Book-Demo3-Snapshot2.vmsn
  4294967296 Jan 4 00:02 Book-Demo3-d22852c7.vswp
  8589934592 Jan 3 20:17 Book-Demo3-flat.vmdk
         498 Jan 3 20:17 Book-Demo3.vmdk
         890 Jan 4 00:28 Book-Demo3.vmsd
        2729 Jan 4 00:28 Book-Demo3.vmx
```

The highlighted files in Listing 13.23 were added or modified. Notice that the Book-Demo3-Snapshot2.vmsn file is much larger than the snapshot1 one. This is because the VM is powered on, and I have chosen to snapshot the VM's memory. The CPU state and the memory state are both kept in the corresponding snapshot file.

Book-Demo3-000002.vmdk and Book-Demo3-000002-delta.vmdk are the virtual disk snapshot for this new snapshot. However, its parent disk is not the same as the first snapshot's parent. How did we know that? Listing 13.24 shows the descriptor file.

Listing 13.24   Content of the second snapshot's delta disk descriptor file

```
# Disk DescriptorFile
version=1
encoding="UTF-8"
CID=fffffffe
parentCID=fffffffe
isNativeSnapshot="no"
createType="vmfsSparse"
parentFileNameHint="Book-Demo3-000001.vmdk"
# Extent description
RW 16777216 VMFSSPARSE "Book-Demo3-000002-delta.vmdk"

# The Disk Data Base
#DDB

ddb.longContentID = "a051b9fb9b43b7ae0b351f1dfffffffe"
```

I highlighted the relevant properties in Listing 13.24. The `parentFileNameHint` clearly shows that the parent disk is Book-Demo3-000001.vmdk, which is the first snapshot's delta disk. This means that all new data gets redirected to the Book-Demo3-000002-delta.vmdk file.

Also note that the VMX file has been changed to reflect that the new delta file is the current virtual disk attached to scsi0:0.

This is the device property in the VMX file after the first snapshot:

```
scsi0:0.fileName = "Book-Demo3-000001.vmdk"
```

This is the device property in the VMX file after the second snapshot:

```
scsi0:0.fileName = "Book-Demo3-000002.vmdk"
```

In addition, the VMSD file now shows an additional snapshot, whose properties are prefixed with `snapshot1` (see Listing 13.25).

Listing 13.25   VMSD file content

```
.encoding = "UTF-8"
snapshot.lastUID = "2"
snapshot.current = "2"
snapshot0.uid = "1"
snapshot0.filename = "Book-Demo3-Snapshot1.vmsn"
snapshot0.displayName = "Before installing patch xyz"
snapshot0.description = "Snapshot taken before installing patch xyz"
snapshot0.createTimeHigh = "310664"
snapshot0.createTimeLow = "1673441029"
snapshot0.numDisks = "1"
snapshot0.disk0.fileName = "Book-Demo3.vmdk"
snapshot0.disk0.node = "scsi0:0"
snapshot.numSnapshots = "2"
snapshot1.uid = "2"
snapshot1.filename = "Book-Demo3-Snapshot2.vmsn"
snapshot1.parent = "1"
snapshot1.displayName = "After Installing App X"
snapshot1.description = "Second snapshot taken after installing
Application X"
snapshot1.type = "1"
snapshot1.createTimeHigh = "310667"
snapshot1.createTimeLow = "1030355829"
snapshot1.numDisks = "1"
snapshot1.disk0.fileName = "Book-Demo3-000001.vmdk"
snapshot1.disk0.node = "scsi0:0"
```

In Listing 13.25 I highlighted the lines that were added or changed.

All lines prefixed with `snapshot1` are the properties of the newly added snapshot. They look identical to those of the first snapshot file but with different values. A new property was added: `snapshot1.parent`. It simply states that this snapshot's parent is another snapshot, whose ID is `1`, which is the first snapshot we covered earlier. Also note that the `numSnapshots` value is now `2`. This means that the total count of snapshots for the VM is currently `2`.

The `snapshot1.uid` is `2`. Why wasn't it given a higher number? The reason is that this number is the next number in sequence after the value of the field named `snapshot.` `lastUID` in the previous version of the VMSD file. If you look at Table 13.9, you see notice that the value was `1`. If it were higher, the second snapshot's UID would have been higher than `2`.

Figure 13.27 shows how these properties look in the Snapshot Manager's UI.

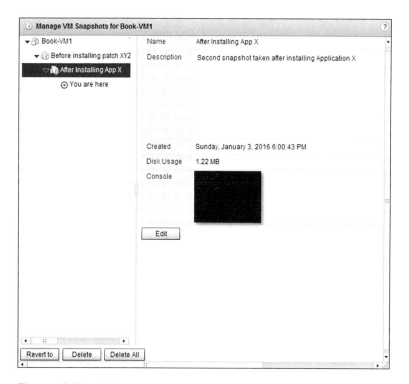

Figure 13.27   Listing the second snapshot

Note that now the **You are here** marker points to the second snapshot.

Snapshot Operations

Several snapshot operations are available:

- Revert to a snapshot
- Delete a snapshot
- Consolidate a snapshot (a new feature introduced earlier in vSphere 5)

NOTE

Go To a snapshot option is no longer available in vSphere 6 Web Client. All operations formerly done by that option are now done by the **Revert To** option.

The sections that follow examine these snapshot options in detail.

Reverting to a Snapshot

Imagine that I am testing an application that is still in beta, and I am not comfortable with what damage it might do to my VM. So, I take a snapshot before installing the application. In Figure 13.28, the snapshot is labeled **Before installing App X** (because it was taken before instead of after installing the app, as in the previous section). Then what I expected happens: The VM crashes. I'm not certain I can reproduce the crash. So, I take a snapshot to save the state of the VM, showing the problem. I name this snapshot **Crashed App X**. Because the application is a beta quality, there is no live support for it. I decide that I need to rule out patch xyz, which I installed before the application, as the root cause of the problem. So, the plan is to go to the VM state before I installed patch xyz and then take another snapshot. Then I can install the application. Figure 13.28 displays the Snapshot Manager (cropped) showing the current state.

To revert to a snapshot, follow these steps:

1. Click the snapshot labeled **Before installing patch xyz** and then click the **Revert to** button.

   The dialog in Figure 13.29 opens. Note that the icon for the **Before installing patch XYZ** does not have the power-on symbol (the right-pointing triangle) as do the other two below it. This means that when it was taken, the VM was powered off. So, when you click the **Revert to** button, the VM is powered off because it was in that state at the time that snapshot was taken.

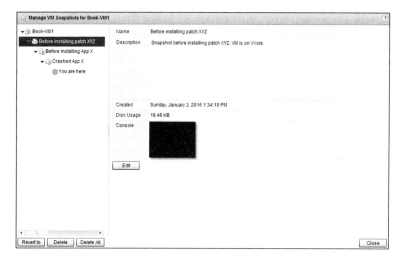

Figure 13.28   Snapshot Manager, showing a crashed VM snapshot

2. Click **Yes** in the dialog shown in Figure 13.29.

Figure 13.29   Confirming the Revert To operation

3. After the process is done, the Snapshot Manager should look as shown in Figure 13.30, and the VM is powered off.

Figure 13.30   The completed Revert To operation

4. Now take another snapshot before installing App X. If the Snapshot Manager is still open, click **Close**. Then do the following:

   a. Make sure the VM is still selected in the inventory tree.

   b. Click the **Actions** pull-down menu.

   c. Click the **Snapshots** menu.

   d. Click **Take Snapshot** (see Figure 13.31).

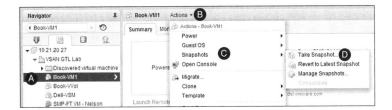

Figure 13.31   Taking a new snapshot to create a new branch

5. Enter the snapshot name and description (for example, **Side Branch Before Installing App X**), and then click **OK**.

6. Power on the VM and install App X. So far, so good! The application seems stable.

7. To be on the safe side, take a snapshot in this state. Follow steps 4a through 4d, enter the snapshot name and description (for example, **After Installing App X**), and click **OK**.

8. Click the Manage Snapshots dialog to display the current snapshot hierarchy (see Figure 13.32).

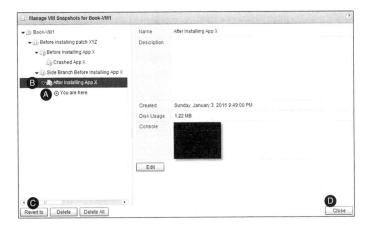

Figure 13.32   Listing the second snapshot branch in Snapshot Manager

> **TIP**
>
> Keep an eye on the target—that is, the **You are here** marker. This represents the current state of the VM since you took the last snapshot. Assume that the VM is powered off at this time. If you want to discard what you have done since you took the snapshot, select the snapshot to which the target is pointing and then click the **Revert to** button. Click **OK** to proceed. You should observe that the VM is now powered on and is in the state taken by that snapshot. Click **Close** (D) to dismiss the dialog.

Deleting a Snapshot

After taking a VM snapshot, the original VM CPU and, optionally, memory states are kept in the VM snapshot file (VMSN), and the original unmodified data is kept in the parent virtual disk file. All changes to the CPU and memory state are kept in the running VM memory and don't get written to a snapshot file until you take another snapshot. Continuing with the example from the previous section, assume that App X, installed on the OS without a patch, is proven to be stable. You can safely delete the snapshot because you no longer need to restore the VM to its pre-App X state. Say that you want to delete the Side Branch Before Installing App X snapshot and keep the most recent one. The following procedure continues from the end of the procedure from the "Reverting to a Snapshot" section. The VM is now running in the state after installing App X:

1. Still referring to Figure 13.32 at the end of the previous section, click the **Side Branch Before Installing App X** snapshot and then click the **Revert to** button. Click **Yes** to continue. Snapshot Manager should look as shown in Figure 13.33 now, and the VM is powered off.

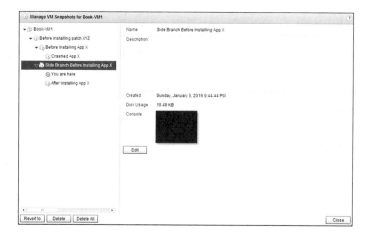

Figure 13.33   Reverting to the parent snapshot before deleting it

2. Click the **Delete** button. In the Confirm Delete dialog that appears, click **Yes** to proceed with deleting the snapshot. The Snapshot Manager should look as shown in Figure 13.34, and the VM is still powered off.

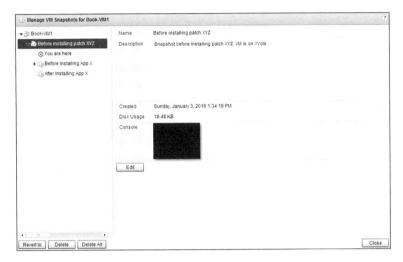

Figure 13.34 Side branch snapshot deleted

What actually happened here is that all the changes that were written to the delta file—in this example, to the VVol snapshot—of the side branch **Before Installing App X** snapshot got written to its parent virtual disk. This means that these changes can no longer be discarded.

3. To switch to the state with the installed App X, select the **After Installing App X** snapshot and then click the **Revert To** button.

4. Click **Yes** to confirm the operation. The Snapshot Manager should look as shown in Figure 13.35.

5. Click **Close**.

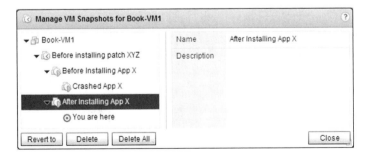

Figure 13.35 Reverting to a child snapshot

Consolidating Snapshots

Snapshot consolidation involves searching for snapshot hierarchies, or delta disks, to combine without violating data dependency. The outcome of consolidation is the removal of redundant disks. This improves virtual machine performance and saves storage space.

Identifying Consolidation Candidates

To identify which VMs require snapshot consolidation, follow this procedure:

1. Connect to the vCenter server that manages the ESXi 6 host, using the vSphere 6.0 Web Client as a user with Administrator privileges.

2. Navigating from the home screen, click **VMs and Templates** in one of the following three locations:

   A. The Navigator pane

   B. The Inventories section on the Home tab

   C. The Home pull-down menu (see Figure 13.36)

   Otherwise, if you are already in the **Hosts and Clusters** view, click the **VMs and Templates** tab at the top of the Navigation pane.

3. The view changes to the VM and Templates view (see Figure 13.37). Select the cluster or datacenter object in the Navigator pane.

4. Select the **Related Objects** tab.

5. Click the **Virtual Machines** button.

6. Right-click on any of the column headers and select **Show/Hide Columns** (see Figure 13.37).

Figure 13.36   Switching to the VMs and Templates view

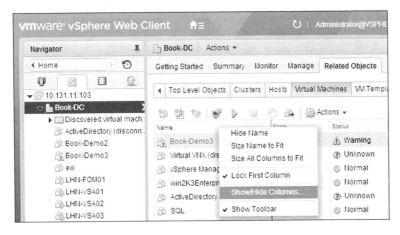

Figure 13.37   Adding a new column

7. Scroll down the list of options and select the **Needs Consolidation** check ox. The column is added to the far-right side of the view.

8. Reposition the column that was just added by clicking and dragging the column header to the desired location in the view. You can click the column header twice to sort it in descending order. If a VM needs consolidation, the value of this column is **Required**. Otherwise, it is **Not Required** (see Figure 13.38).

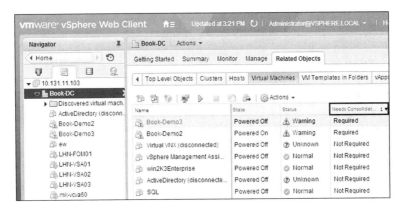

Figure 13.38   Result of adding a Needs Consolidation column

9. Right-click a VM that needs consolidation and then click **Snapshots** followed by **Consolidate** (see Figure 13.39).

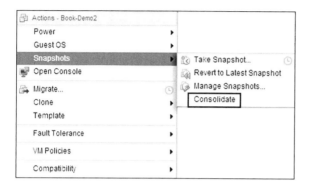

Figure 13.39   The Consolidate command

10. Confirm the operation when prompted by clicking **Yes**.

TIP

The VM that needs consolidation would have this line in the VMSD file:

```
snapshot.need Consolidate = "1"
```

This line gets removed when the consolidation process is complete.

What Actually Happens When Snapshots Are Consolidated?

The deletion in the "Deleting a Snapshot" section left behind a delta disk. To find out which one, I collected some output before and after the consolidation process. Listing 13.26 through 13.29 show this output.

Listing 13.26   Virtual disk descriptors before consolidation

```
323 Apr 14 20:26 Book-Demo3-000001.vmdk
330 Apr 14 20:29 Book-Demo3-000002.vmdk
330 Apr 15 00:57 Book-Demo3-000003.vmdk
346 Apr 15 03:27 Book-Demo3-000004.vmdk
330 Apr 15 04:10 Book-Demo3-000005.vmdk
520 Apr 15 03:27 Book-Demo3.vmdk
```

Listing 13.27   Virtual disk descriptors after consolidation

```
323 Apr 14 20:26 Book-Demo3-000001.vmdk
330 Apr 14 20:29 Book-Demo3-000002.vmdk
346 Apr 15 04:47 Book-Demo3-000004.vmdk
330 Apr 15 04:47 Book-Demo3-000005.vmdk
520 Apr 15 03:27 Book-Demo3.vmdk
```

Comparing Listings 13.26 and 13.27, it is obvious that one delta disk was removed (which I highlighted in Listing 13.26). This is the virtual disk descriptor for the delta file used by the snapshot I deleted earlier. Because its blocks have been converged with its parent disk, it is no longer needed. To find out which was its parent disk, I ran the following command:

```
fgrep vmdk Book-Demo3-00000?.vmdk |grep parent
```

Listing 13.28 and Listing 13.29 show the output before and after the consolidation process.

Listing 13.28   Snapshot of parent disks before consolidation

```
fgrep vmdk Book-Demo3-00000?.vmdk |grep parent
Book-Demo3-000001.vmdk:parentFileNameHint="Book-Demo3.vmdk"
Book-Demo3-000002.vmdk:parentFileNameHint="Book-Demo3-000001.vmdk"
Book-Demo3-000003.vmdk:parentFileNameHint="Book-Demo3-000004.vmdk"
Book-Demo3-000004.vmdk:parentFileNameHint="Book-Demo3.vmdk"
Book-Demo3-000005.vmdk:parentFileNameHint="Book-Demo3-000003.vmdk"
```

Listing 13.29   Snapshot of parent disks after consolidation

```
fgrep vmdk Book-Demo3-00000?.vmdk |grep parent
Book-Demo3-000001.vmdk:parentFileNameHint="Book-Demo3.vmdk"
Book-Demo3-000002.vmdk:parentFileNameHint="Book-Demo3-000001.vmdk"
Book-Demo3-000004.vmdk:parentFileNameHint="Book-Demo3.vmdk"
Book-Demo3-000005.vmdk:parentFileNameHint="Book-Demo3-000004.vmdk"
```

Listing 13.28 shows, from the bottom up, that delta disk Book-Demo3-000005.vmdk had a parent disk Book-Demo3-000003.vmdk. It also shows that delta disk Book-Demo3-000003.vmdk had a parent disk, Book-Demo3-000004.vmdk. So, when the snapshot that used Book-Demo3-000003.vmdk as the delta disk was deleted, the content of that disk was combined with its parent, Book-Demo3-000004.vmdk. This left the snapshot using the Book-Demo3-00005.vmdk delta disk still pointing to the deprecated delta disk, Book-Demo3-000003.vmdk.

The consolidation process corrected this discrepancy by modifying Book-Demo3-000005.vmdk to point to its new parent, Book-Demo3-000004.vmdk, which was evident in Listing 13.29.

How about the VM snapshot dictionary? It, too, should be corrected. Listings 13.30 and 13.31 show before and after consolidation for the output of the following command:

```
fgrep vmdk Book-Demo3.vmdk
```

This command lists all references to virtual disks in the dictionary file, which shows their associations with their corresponding snapshots.

Listing 13.30   Virtual disks association with snapshots before consolidation

```
fgrep vmdk Book-Demo3.vmsd
snapshot0.disk0.fileName = "Book-Demo3.vmdk"
snapshot1.disk0.fileName = "Book-Demo3-000001.vmdk"
snapshot2.disk0.fileName = "Book-Demo3-000003.vmdk"
snapshot3.disk0.fileName = "Book-Demo3-000002.vmdk"
```

Listing 13.31   Virtual disks association with snapshots after consolidation

```
fgrep vmdk Book-Demo3.vmsd
snapshot0.disk0.fileName = "Book-Demo3.vmdk"
snapshot1.disk0.fileName = "Book-Demo3-000001.vmdk"
snapshot2.disk0.fileName = "Book-Demo3-000004.vmdk"
snapshot3.disk0.fileName = "Book-Demo3-000002.vmdk"
```

The highlighted lines in Listing 13.30 and Listing 13.31 show that snapshot2 was changed from using Book-Demo3-000003.vmdk to Book-Demo3-000004.vmdk, which is consistent with the changes demonstrated in Listing 13.28 and Listing 13.29.

Figure 13.40 shows the combined relations from the previous six output examples before and after consolidation.

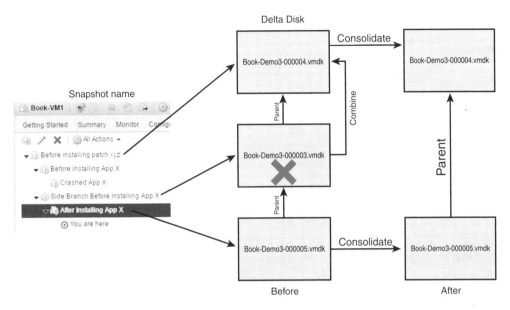

Figure 13.40   Snapshot consolidation process flow

Reverting to the Latest Snapshot

Continuing with the example from the previous few sections, I now have an application that is stable, but somehow the VM got infected by a virus that I am unable to clean without reinstalling the GOS. I had to power off the VM to prevent it from spreading to other VMs. All changes done to the VM after taking the After Installing App X snapshot got written to what is represented by the **You are here** state. Now all I need to do is discard the current state and return to the snapshot itself (see Figure 13.41). The process of discarding the current state is referred to as reverting to a current snapshot.

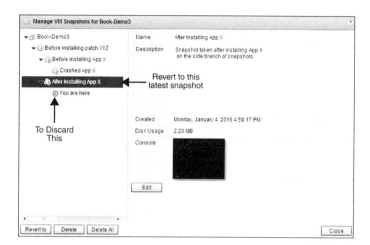

Figure 13.41 Snapshot hierarchy of the current snapshot state

To revert to the latest snapshot, follow this procedure:

1. Right-click the VM in the inventory tree.

2. Select **Snapshots**.

3. Click the **Revert to Latest Snapshot** menu option (see Figure 13.42).

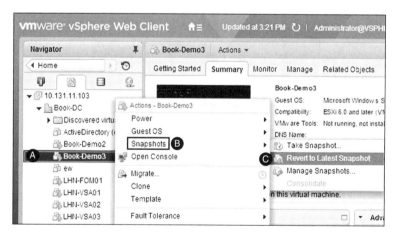

Figure 13.42 Reverting to the latest snapshot

4. Click **Yes** to confirm the operation. A new feature in the confirmation dialog is the
   check box **Suspend this virtual machine when reverting to selected snapshot**,
   which is not selected by default. If the snapshot was taken while the VM was in a

powered-off state, the check box is not displayed in the confirmation dialog. (This is not dependent on the current power state.)

Notice that the VM is now powered on, even though it was off before I reverted to the current snapshot. This is because of how I took the snapshot originally: The VM was powered on when I took a memory snapshot.

Linked Clones

Looking back at the setup of the example used so far, I wonder whether I should use the two branches of snapshots concurrently.

For example, say that App X tech has support finally gotten back to me on the beta support call I submitted when the app crashed on the OS with patch xyz. However, I can't stop what I am doing with the stable branch of snapshots. I step back from my whiteboard, covered in scribbles depicting my snapshot hierarchy, and take a look at the bigger picture. It looks like what I saw with a VMware Virtual Desktop Infrastructure (VDI) setup I did a while back, in which multiple VMs share a parent disk and get deployed in seconds, with minor customization efforts. I think I can get away with this for a short period. But what I have in mind is to create a temporary linked clone of my VM, using the crashed state snapshot, if I connect the temporary VM to an isolated network. So, I go for it, and it saves me a ton of time that I might have wasted trying to re-create the crash state. In the following pages, I walk you through how I handle this.

To identify the virtual disk used by the snapshot called Crashed App X, you use using the following procedure:

1. Search the VM snapshot dictionary file (VMSD) for the word `Crashed` to identify the snapshot prefix in that file (see Listing 13.32).

Listing 13.32   Locating the snapshot prefix of the crashed the App X snapshot

```
fgrep Crash Book-Demo3.vmsd
snapshot3.displayName = "Crashed App X"
```

In Listing 13.32, I highlighted the snapshot prefix, which is snapshot3.

2. Search the VMSD for the virtual disk name associated with the snapshot prefix (see Listing 13.33).

Listing 13.33   Locating the delta virtual disk used by a snapshot

```
fgrep snapshot3.disk Book-Demo3.vmsd
snapshot3.disk0.fileName = "Book-Demo3-000002.vmdk"
snapshot3.disk0.node = "scsi0:0"
```

In Listing 13.33, I highlighted the virtual disk name. Also note the node name, which is scsi0:0.

3. Create a new VM with custom options to use an existing disk. Browse for the filename identified in step 2 and select it. Make sure to change the virtual network to use a port group on a virtual switch connected to a different network from that of the original VM.

4. To be able to preserve the crashed state, set the virtual disk as independent, nonpersistent. This creates a REDO log to store all changes done while the VM is powered on. The REDO log gets discarded when the VM is powered off.

5. Go through the debugging needed for the crashed VM. If you need to start over again, just power off the VM and then power it on.

6. Delete the VM but make sure not to delete the virtual disk.

> **NOTE**
>
> Using linked clones is supported by VMware in VDI and VMware vCloud Director environments only. If you decide to play with linked clones in a vSphere environment, do not use a production environment and be sure not to do this playing on a permanent basis. When linked clones are created by a tool or product supported by VMware for creating linked clones, the result takes advantage of the underlying datastore. For example, if the datastore is a VVol container or an NFS share, linked clones will be native in nature. This means the storage array will create pointers to the parent disk's physical blocks and all changes.

Summary

In this chapter, I have introduced the basics of virtual disks and the structure, layout, and types of RDMs, which are eager zeroed thick, zeroed thick, and thin. I also explained the various virtual disks types from the file system's perspective: SPARSE, VMFSSPARSE, and VMFSRDM. In this chapter I have also discussed RDMs (both virtual and physical modes) in detail. I will cover VSANSPARSE format in Chapter 22.

I have explained virtual machine snapshots and how they affect virtual disks. In addition, I have covered deleting, going to, reverting to, and consolidating snapshots. I have given you a quick glance at linked clones and how they correlate to certain snapshot hierarchies.

## Chapter 14

Distributed Locks

By default, a logical unit number (LUN) is not designed to be accessed concurrently by multiple hosts. VMware developed Virtual Machine File System (VMFS), its clustered file system, to allow ESXi hosts concurrent access to shared datastores. To prevent corruption resulting from more than one host writing to the same file or metadata area, an on-disk distributed locking mechanism is used. To put it simply, VMFS "tells" each host which areas in the metadata and disk it can update. It tracks this via on-disk lock records in the metadata. At the time each ESXi host is first installed and configured, it is assigned a unique ID, referred to as host UUID (universally unique identifier). You can locate this ID on each host by running the following:

```
esxcli system uuid get
4d7ab650-e269-3374-ef05-001e4f1fbf2c
```

When an ESXi host first mounts a VMFS3 or VMFS5 volume, it is assigned a slot within the VMFS heartbeat region, where the host writes its own heartbeat record. This record is associated with the host UUID. All subsequent operations done by this host on the file system that require metadata updates are associated with this heartbeat record. However, for the host to create its heartbeat record, it must first get a lock on its slot in the heartbeat region to which it will write that record. This, like any other updates to the metadata, requires SCSI-2 reservation on the VMFS LUN or head extent (if it is a spanned volume) if the array does not support vStorage APIs for Array Integration (VAAI) atomic test and set (ATS) primitive. (I discuss ATS in detail in Chapter 17, "VAAI.")

NOTE

SCSI-2 reservations are nonpersistent and are acquired by one host at a time.

Basic Locking

The typical sequence of distributed locking operations before ESXi 3.5 is reserve–read–modify–write–release. This translates to the following:

1. The ESXi host requests a SCSI-2 reservation from the storage array on the LUN.

2. The ESXi host reads the on-disk lock records into memory. On-disk locks are kept close to the metadata records they protect.

   Figure 14.1 shows a block diagram representing the VMFS resource cluster (see Chapter 12, "VMFS Architecture").

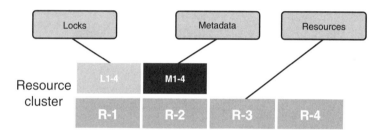

Figure 14.1   VMFS3 resource cluster

3. The ESXi host acquires a free on-disk lock, writes it to disk, and then releases the SCSI-2 reservation.

4. The ESXi host modifies, in memory, the metadata protected by the lock(s) but does not write it to disk yet.

5. If the host ID is not set in the heartbeat region, the host also updates the following in an available heartbeat slot:

   - **Host ID**—This is the system UUID, which you can list by using the `esxcli system uuid get` command.

   - **Generation number**—This number is set when the host first creates its heartbeat record. From that point on, it updates the live-ness (see the next bullet). If the host loses access to the datastore or otherwise crashes, leaving a stale heartbeat record, it breaks the lock on its own heartbeat, and a new generation number is set.

   - **Live-ness**—This is also referred to as the timestamp. It is changed by the host at a regular interval. If it fails to update the timestamp, other hosts interpret that as the host being dead or having lost access to the datastore.

- **Journal offset**—This is where the heartbeat's journal is located on disk. It is used by other hosts that need to break a dead host's lock by replaying the heartbeat's journal. (See the section "What Happens When a Host Crashes?" later in this chapter.)

6. If the host needs additional on-disk locks, it repeats steps 1–4 but does not write the changes to disk yet. Each of these cycles requires a separate SCSI-2 reservation.

7. The host writes the updated metadata to the journal.

8. The journal is committed to the file system.

9. The host releases the on-disk locks.

If the requested lock modifies certain VMFS resources or the metadata—creating a file or growing it—the relevant file descriptor clusters (FDCs) are assigned to this host in the form of a cluster group. If the files require *pointer blocks* (ptrs) and/or *secondary pointer blocks* (secondary ptrs) in addition to the range of file blocks, the host updates these resources and associates them with its own heartbeat record. ESXi 4 and later increased the size of the VMFS resource clusters, which makes them easier to cache.

> **NOTE**
>
> The VMFS resources are kept close to their metadata on disk to provide better performance.

Using ATS for the Heartbeat

ESXi 6 and 5.5 Update 2 introduced a new feature to enable using ATS for the following VMFS heartbeat operations:

- Acquiring a heartbeat
- Clearing a heartbeat
- Reclaiming a heartbeat
- Replaying a heartbeat journal

This feature was inspired by the fact that this record must be updated on the VMFS metadata very frequently, and the updates may result in a performance hit, especially when using a SCSI-2 reservation, regardless of ATS support. The basic premise of this feature is that if a datastore supports ATS primitive, the VMFS vmkernel module takes advantage of that and always uses ATS for heartbeat record operations for the given ESXi 6 host instead of using SCSI-2 reservations. However, several customers reported to VMware that they lost access to VMFS5 datastores shortly after upgrading to ESXi 5.5 Update 2 or 6.0. The problem was attributed to the increase in the number of ATS commands sent to the storage array, which increased the load significantly and may have resulted in false ATS miscompare errors.

When the ATS command writes to the metadata record, the normal sequence of events is that it reads what was written and compares it to what is in memory. This is done by using COMPARE AND WRITE command 0x89. If both copies match, the ATS command is successful. However, due to the excessive load on the array, some of the responses to the 0x89 command fail. As a result, the host assumes that the heartbeat record update/create operation failed, and the datastore becomes inaccessible. This is an ATS miscompare.

An example of a /var/log/vmkernel.log message would look like this:

```
ScsiDeviceIO: 2645: Cmd(0x439dd0d7c400) 0x89, CmdSN 0x2f3dd6 from world
3937465 to dev naa.6006016055711d00cff95e65664ee011; failed H:0x0 D:0x2
P:0x0 Valid sense data: 0xe 0x1d 0x0.
```

or like this:

```
ATS Miscompare detected between test and set HB images at offset XXX on vol
YYY
```

This is a multivendor issue that could be related to a problem with the QLogic FC adapter's native vmkernel driver or the adapter's firmware. This has not been confirmed at the time of this writing, though.

Meanwhile, if you run into this problem, it is recommended that you revert the ESXi host's configuration to pre-6.0/5.5 Update2 state. You can do this by disabling the new advanced vmkernel option /VMFS3/UseATSForHBOnVMFS5.

Listing 14.1 shows the command for checking the current value of this option, modifying the setting, and verifying the change.

Listing 14.1 Modifying UseATSForHBOnVMFS5 option

```
esxcli system settings advanced list -o /VMFS3/UseATSForHBOnVMFS5
    Path: /VMFS3/UseATSForHBOnVMFS5
    Type: integer
    Int Value: 1
    Default Int Value: 1
    Min Value: 0
    Max Value: 1
```

```
    String Value:
    Default String Value:
    Valid Characters:
    Description: Use ATS for HB on ATS supported VMFS5 volumes

esxcli system settings advanced set -i 0 -o /VMFS3/UseATSForHBOnVMFS5

esxcli system settings advanced list -o /VMFS3/UseATSForHBOnVMFS5
    Path: /VMFS3/UseATSForHBOnVMFS5
    Type: integer
    Int Value: 0
    Default Int Value: 1
    Min Value: 0
    Max Value: 1
    String Value:
    Default String Value:
    Valid Characters:
    Description: Use ATS for HB on ATS supported VMFS5 volumes
```

The highlighted line shows the original value and the modified one.

This is the command you use to change this option:

```
esxcli system settings advanced set -i 0 -o /VMFS3/UseATSForHBOnVMFS5
```

You can also use this verbose version:

```
esxcli system settings advanced set --int-value 0 --option /VMFS3/
UseATSForHBOnVMFS5
```

When this issue is finally resolved by VMware or its partners, you can reverse the change by using the value 1 instead of 0 in this command.

NOTE

The root node of this option is /VMFS3, even though the option is for VMFS5. This is due to the fact that all VMFS advanced options for both VMFS3 and VMFS5 are part of the same VMware code stream, and /VMFS3 was kept for an easier upgrade experience. Don't let this confuse you.

If you still have VMFS3 datastores around, this issue should not affect them because the option is disabled by default for VMFS3. If you want to see for yourself, just run the list command, using the /VMFS3/UseATSForHBOnVMFS3 option instead.

What Happens When a Host Crashes?

When a host suffers from a crash, it might leave behind stale locks on the VMFS datastore. If you have configured the HA (High Availability) feature, it attempts to power on the protected VMs on one of the surviving hosts in the cluster. However, due to the stale locks, this might not be possible. For this operation to succeed, the host attempting to power on the VM does the following:

1. It checks the heartbeat region of the datastore for the lock owner's ID.

2. A few seconds later, it checks to see if this host's heartbeat record was updated. Because the lock owner crashed, it is not able to update its heartbeat record.

3. The recovery host ages the locks left by this host. After this is done, other hosts in the cluster do not attempt to break the same stale locks.

4. The recovery host replays the heartbeat's VMFS journal to clear and then acquire the locks.

5. When the crashed host is rebooted, it clears its own heartbeat record and acquires a new one (with a new generation number). As a result, it does not attempt to lock its original files because it is no longer the lock owner.

Optimistic Locking

Optimistic locking, introduced in ESX 3.5, enabled the host to modify all metadata protected by free locks and then request a single SCSI-2 reservation when it was ready to write these changes to disk.

The revised process follows:

1. The ESXi host reads on-disk locks into memory.

2. The host modifies all metadata that is protected by free locks in memory (in other words, those that were not locked by other hosts at that time) instead of doing this one record at a time.

3. Before the host can write these metadata updates to the journal, it acquires all the necessary disk locks with one SCSI-2 reservation.

4. All metadata updates are written to the journal.

5. The journal is committed to disk.

6. The host releases all on-disk locks.

Optimistic locking requires a lot fewer SCSI-2 reservations and reduces the chances of SCSI (Small Computer System Interface) reservation conflicts.

If, at the time the host attempts to acquire the on-disk locks (step 3), another host has stolen the locks, this ESXi host falls back to the standard locking mechanism for the whole batch of locks it tried to acquire optimistically.

Dynamic Resource Allocation

As the contention for and/or occupancy of on-disk locks increases, the optimistic locks are decreased. So, in an extremely busy environment, this mechanism might still run into reservation conflicts. To reduce the number of locks required for these operations, the number of resources per cluster (for example, FDC and pointer block cluster [PBC]) were increased, which may increase chances of cross-host contention. To work around that, the number of clusters per resource group was also increased, but this might increase contention and distance between the data and its metadata.

The combination of optimistic locking and dynamic resource sizing helps with operations such as these:

- File creation
- File deletion
- File extension

However, they do not help with file open operations such as the following:

- Powering on VMs
- Resuming VMs
- Migrating VMs with vMotion

These operations require a SCSI reservation to lock the files for exclusive access by the VMs.

SAN Aware Retries

As you have read in this chapter, SCSI reservation conflicts are prone to happen in a busy environment that is overutilized or undersized (for example, too few datastores for the number of running VMs across multiple ESXi hosts, which results in contention for SCSI reservations). To help reduce the effect on the running VMs, VMware introduced the SAN Aware Retries mechanism in vSphere 4.

To see what it does, take a look at the block diagram in Figure 14.2.

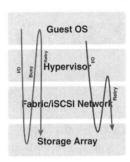

Figure 14.2   SAN Aware Retries

Figure 14.2 shows the path of I/O and its related error when there are SCSI reservation conflicts. The arrow on the left side shows that I/O traversing the hypervisor and the SAN from the VM on its way to the storage array.

Without SAN Aware Retries, the I/O makes the following journey:

1. The VM sends the I/O.

2. If the hypervisor encounters SCSI reservation conflicts, a "device busy" error is returned to the guest OS.

3. The guest OS retries the I/O until the host runs out of conflict retries, at which point the I/O fails, and the failure is reported to the guest OS.

With SAN Aware Retries, the I/O makes the following journey, represented in Figure 14.2 by the shorter arrow on the right side:

1. The VM sends the I/O.

2. If the hypervisor encounters SCSI reservation conflicts, it retries the I/O (not the reservation).

3. The guest OS does not receive a "device busy" error as frequently as without SAN Aware Retries. If the hypervisor exhausts the conflict retries, the guest receives an I/O failure error.

4. The guest OS retries the I/O.

As a result, the guest OS receives significantly fewer "device busy" errors.

Optimistic I/O

Optimistic locking and dynamic resource allocation do not address SCSI reservations resulting from a file open operation at VM power-on time. These are characterized by the following:

- Most of the file open operations are to read and reread VM files such as *.vmx (virtual machine configuration files) or *.vmdk (virtual disks). See Chapter 13, "Virtual Disks and RDMs," for further detail about VM files.

- Most of these files are closed almost immediately after being read.

- As application complexity increases, the number of file open operations increase as well.

vSphere 4.x introduced optimistic I/O to address this issue. It leverages optimistic locking for reading, rereading, validating, and invalidating file contents without using SCSI reservations.

The way this works is by requesting the optimistic locks and proceeding with the read I/O, assuming that the locks will succeed. This approach results in significant reductions in SCSI reservations during VM boot time (also known as boot storm).

Operations That Require SCSI Reservations

Two groups of operations require SCSI-2 reservations: VMFS datastore–specific operations and on-disk lock–related operations.

VMFS Datastore–Specific Operations

VMFS datastore–specific operations result in metadata modifications such as these:

- Creating a datastore

- Spanning or growing a datastore

- Resignaturing a datastore

On-Disk Locks–Related Operations

In the previous sections I discussed the distributed locking mechanism and how it requires on-disk lock acquisition. It should be clear from that discussion that SCSI reservations are required to complete such operations in the absence of ATS. The following are examples of on-disk lock–related operations:

- Powering on a VM (Optimistic I/O alleviates the need for the reservation.)

- Acquiring a lock on a file

- Creating or deleting a file

- Creating a virtual machine template (The previous two bullets apply here.)

- Deploying a VM from a template

- Creating a new VM

- Migrating a VM with vMotion (This involves both the source and target hosts on the shared datastore.)

- Growing a file—for example, a snapshot file or a thin provisioned virtual disk (see Chapters 13)

MSCS/WSFC-Related SCSI Reservations

One of the most common questions I receive is related to Microsoft Windows Failover Clustering (WSFC) on Windows Server 2008 and later (also known as MSCS or Microsoft Clustering Services on Windows Server 2003 R2 and earlier). Many people want to know how WSFC interacts with storage shared between cluster nodes. I am not going to discuss MSCS itself here. However, the following sections discuss its effect on shared storage and the types of SCSI reservations used.

MSCS SCSI-2 Reservations

Windows 2003 and earlier implemented MSCS to utilize SCSI-2–style reservations on the quorum and shared data disks. The latter are mostly raw device mappings (RDMs), which I cover in Chapter 13. They can also be virtual disks if both cluster nodes reside on the same ESXi host and will not be migrated onto separate hosts in the future (also known as cluster-in-a-box [CIB]). The active node of the MSCS cluster acquires a reservation on the shared storage and does not release this reservation. The reservation is reset by one of the passive nodes if the active node fails to send its heartbeat over the network as well as onto the quorum disk. The process of releasing the reservation is done by the passive node, by sending a `Device Reset` SCSI command to the shared storage. This results in the storage array releasing the reservation. The passive node then sends a SCSI reservation request that gets granted because the active node is either offline or has received a "poison pill" from the passive node if it is reachable over the network.

The activities are handled differently by the ESXi host, depending on how the MSCS-clustered VMs are configured—that is, whether they are configured as CIB or as cluster-across-boxes (CAB).

NOTE

The virtual SCSI HBA (host bus adapter) used by the cluster nodes for the shared storage must be LSI logic parallel, which is a parallel SCSI HBA supporting SCSI-2 standard.

Cluster-in-a-Box Shared Storage

In the CIB configuration, both nodes reside on the same ESXi host. This provides the vmkernel visibility into what each node is doing to the shared storage. As a result, there is no need to communicate via the shared storage in the form of SCSI reservation events. This means the shared storage can be in the form of either virtual disks or virtual mode RDMs (non-passthrough RDMs). Concurrent access to such shared storage configurations is arbitrated via file-level locks. In other words, the active node is granted a read-write lock on the file until the passive node takes over the active role, at which time it sends a `Device Reset` command to the shared storage. VMkernel translates this command to releasing the lock acquired by the active node. When this is done, the lock on the file is granted to the new active node. Note that I am referring to the shared storage "file," regardless of whether it is a virtual disk or a virtual mode RDM, because the latter is treated like a virtual disk from the lock-handling perspective. If a VM on another host attempts to access the LUN mapped by this RDM, it fails because the other host (with the CIB nodes) has a SCSI reservation on it, based on the lock granted to the active MSCS node.

Cluster-Across-Boxes Shared Storage

In the CAB configuration, each node in the cluster resides on a separate host. This means that each host has no knowledge of what the VM on the alternate host is doing to the shared storage, and the only way for them to have such knowledge is via SCSI reservations. For this to work correctly, the shared storage must be physical mode RDM (also known as passthrough RDM). In this RDM mode, SCSI reservation requests are passed through to the storage array. In other words, the active node of the MSCS cluster acquires SCSI-2 reservations on the shared storage (both quorum and data disks). If the passive node attempts to write to the shared storage, it receives an error because it is reserved by the active node.

When the active node fails to communicate its heartbeat, the passive node sends a `Device Reset` command to the storage array. This results in releasing the reservation, and the passive node sends a reservation request that is granted by the array.

WSFC SCSI-3 Reservations

WSFC on Windows 2008 and later uses Persistent Group Reservation (PGR), which is a SCSI-3 reservation. This is the main reason Windows Server 2008 and later VMs must be configured with LSI Logic SAS (Serial Attached SCSI) virtual SCSI HBA for the shared storage—because that virtual adapter supports the SCSI-3 standard required for supporting PGR.

> **NOTE**
>
> Regardless of which version of Windows you use for MSCS/WSFC, virtual disks and virtual mode RDMs are supported *only* with CIB configurations. Physical mode RDMs are the only supported shared store for CAB configurations.
>
> If your cluster nodes do not use shared storage—for example, Exchange CCR (Cluster Continuous Replication) or DAG (Database Availability Group)—there is no effect on SCSI reservations beyond what is used by non-clustered VMs.

Perennial Reservations

Having MSCS/WSFC cluster nodes spread over several ESXi hosts necessitates the use of passthrough RDMs, which are shared among all hosts on which a relevant cluster node will run. As a result, each of these hosts has some RDMs reserved, whereas the remaining RDMs are reserved by the other hosts. At boot time, LUN discovery and device claiming processes require a response from each LUN. Such a response takes much longer for LUNs reserved by other hosts. This results in an excessively prolonged boot time for all hosts with that configuration. The same issue might also affect the time it takes for a rescan operation to complete.

vSphere 5 introduced the concept of perennial reservations, which is a device property that makes it easier for an ESXi 5 host to recognize if a given LUN is reserved by another host perennially. At boot time or upon rescanning, the host does not wait for a response from a LUN in that state. This improves boot and rescan times on ESXi 5 hosts sharing MSCS shared LUNs.

To identify whether a LUN is perennially reserved, run this command:

```
esxcli storage core device list -d <device-ID>
```

You can also use the verbose version of this command:

```
esxcli storage core device list --device <device-ID>
```

Listing 14.2 shows sample output of a LUN that is *not* marked as reserved. (The property is highlighted in the listing.)

Listing 14.2   Sample output of a LUN that is not reserved

```
esxcli storage core device list -d naa.6006016055711d00cff95e65664ee011

naa.6006016055711d00cff95e65664ee011
    Display Name: DGC Fibre Channel Disk
      (naa.6006016055711d00cff95e65664ee011)
    Has Settable Display Name: true
    Size: 10240
    Device Type: Direct-Access
    Multipath Plugin: NMP
    Devfs Path: /vmfs/devices/disks/naa.6006016055711d00cff95e65664ee011
    Vendor: DGC
    Model: RAID 5
    Revision: 0326
    SCSI Level: 4
    Is Pseudo: false
    Status: on
    Is RDM Capable: true
    Is Local: false
    Is Removable: false
    Is SSD: false
    Is Offline: false
    Is Perennially Reserved: false
    Thin Provisioning Status: unknown
    Attached Filters:
    VAAI Status: unknown
    Other UIDs: vml.02000100006006016055711d00cff95e65664ee011524149442035
```

You need to set this option manually for all LUNs mapped as RDMs for MSCS shared storage on all ESXi 5 hosts sharing them. This setting is stored in the host's configuration file (that is, /etc/vmware/esx.conf). You enable this option by using the following `esxcli` command:

```
esxcli storage core device setconfig --device <ID> --perennially-
reserved=true
```

Listing 14.3 shows an example of setting the perennially reserved option.

Listing 14.3   Setting the perennially reserved option

```
esxcli storage core device setconfig --device naa.6006016055711d00cff95e656
64ee011 --perennially-reserved=true

esxcli storage core device list -d naa.6006016055711d00cff95e65664ee011
naa.6006016055711d00cff95e65664ee011
   Display Name: DGC Fibre Channel Disk
     (naa.6006016055711d00cff95e65664ee011)
   Has Settable Display Name: true
   Size: 10240
   Device Type: Direct-Access
   Multipath Plugin: NMP
   Devfs Path: /vmfs/devices/disks/naa.6006016055711d00cff95e65664ee011
   Vendor: DGC
   Model: RAID 5
   Revision: 0326
   SCSI Level: 4
   Is Pseudo: false
   Status: on
   Is RDM Capable: true
   Is Local: false
   Is Removable: false
   Is SSD: false
   Is Offline: false
   Is Perennially Reserved: true
   Thin Provisioning Status: unknown
   Attached Filters:
   VAAI Status: unknown
   Other UIDs: vml.02000100006006016055711d00cff95e65664ee011524149442035
```

The first command in Listing 14.3 sets the option to `true`, and the second command lists the device properties of the LUN you just configured. Notice that the `Is Perennially Reserved` value is now `true`.

> **NOTE**
>
> The perennially reserved property cannot be set via a host profile in this release. As a result, this configuration cannot persist between reboots of Auto Deploy ESXi hosts.

Locating the Device ID for a Mapped LUN

This topic is discussed in greater detail in Chapter 13, but I touch on it here for convenience.

Locating the Device ID for a Mapped LUN Using the CLI

You can use the following procedure to locate the device ID for a mapped LUN by using the CLI while logged on to the ESXi Shell either directly, via SSH, or via vMA 5.0:

1. Use `vmkfstools -q` to identify the VML ID of the mapped LUN. The output of this command is shown in Listing 14.4, with the VML ID highlighted in the output.

Listing 14.4   Identifying the VML ID of a mapped LUN

```
vmkfstools -q /vmfs/volumes/FC200/win2K3Enterprise/win2K3Enterprise.vmdk

Disk /vmfs/volumes/FC200/win2K3Enterprise/win2K3Enterprise.vmdk is a
Passthrough Raw Device Mapping
Maps to: vml.02000100006006016055711d00cff95e65664ee011524149442035
```

2. Use the VML ID with the `esxcfg-scsidevs` command to find the device ID of the mapped LUN. Listing 14.5 shows the output from this command, with the device ID highlighted.

Listing 14.5   Identifying an RDM device ID by using its VML ID

```
esxcfg-scsidevs -l -d vml.02000100006006016055711d00cff95e65664
 ee011524149442035

naa.6006016055711d00cff95e65664ee011
   Device Type: Direct-Access
   Size: 10240 MB
   Display Name: DGC Fibre Channel Disk (naa.6006016055711d00cff95e
65664ee011)
   Multipath Plugin: NMP
   Console Device: /vmfs/devices/disks/naa.6006016055711d00cff95e65
664ee011
   Devfs Path: /vmfs/devices/disks/naa.6006016055711d00cff95e65664
ee011
   Vendor: DGC        Model: RAID 5              Revis: 0326
   SCSI Level: 4  Is Pseudo: false Status: on
   Is RDM Capable: true  Is Removable: false
```

```
Is Local: false Is SSD: false
Other Names:
    vml.02000100006006016055711d00cff95e65664ee011524149442035
VAAI Status: unknown
```

Locating the Device ID for a Mapped LUN Using the UI

To locate the device ID for a mapped LUN by using the UI, follow this procedure:

1. Connect to the vCenter server that manages the ESXi 6 host, using the vSphere 6.0 Web Client as a user with Administrator privileges.

2. Navigate to the **VMs and Templates** view.

3. Locate the VM to which you want to add a virtual disk. Right-click it and then select **Edit Settings**. You should see a dialog similar to the one shown in Figure 14.3.

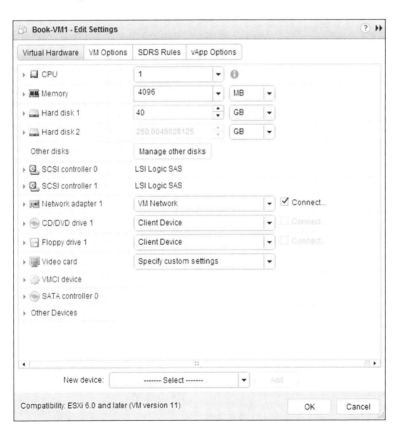

Figure 14.3 Listing VM properties—UI

4. Expand one **Hard disk** section at a time. If there is a field named Other disks, click the **Manage other disks** button to list the additional disks. Then you can further expand one **Hard disk** section at a time.

   Look for fields named Compatibility Mode and Physical LUN. If the section has such fields, the hard disk represents an RDM. The value of the **Compatibility Mode** field reflects the RDM type—virtual or physical. The **Physical LUN** field shows the device's VML ID, which is this in the example

   `vml.02000000006090a06860162b612168b5c8c2047030313030452d30`

5. Click the **Manage Paths** link in the Multipathing field (see Figure 14.4).

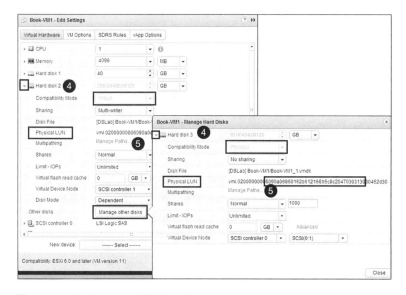

Figure 14.4   Locating RDMs—UI

TIP

If you look closely at the VML and NAA ID in this example, you will notice that the NAA ID is actually part of the VML ID or, if you look at it the other way, the VML ID is based on the NAA ID of the device:

vml.02000000006090a06860162b612168b5c8c2047030313030452d30
naa. 6090a06860162b612168b5c8c2047030

For example, the matching bytes are highlighted here as well as in Figure 14.4.

If this does not show the **Edit Multipathing Policies** dialog at this point, you may need to close the Edit Settings dialog, which will cause the Edit Multipathing Policies dialog to open (see Figure 14.5).

Figure 14.5   Listing an RDM's NAA ID

6. The device ID is listed in the status bar at the top of the resulting dialog. The LUN and paths to it are listed under the LUN and Runtime Name columns, respectively. To list the target ID, simply hover over the target field for a given path. In this example, the target is on a Dell EqualLogic iSCSI storage array. Click **Cancel** when done.

In this example, the device ID is as follows:

```
naa.6090a06860162b612168b5c8c2047030
```

The LUN is 0. Note that some iSCSI storage arrays, like EqualLogic, use LUN 0 for all LUNs but assign unique target IDs. So, you must pay close attention to the target ID to avoid any mix-up.

Under the Hood of Distributed Locks

Most of the issues related to distributed locks can be identified by reading the vmkernel logs. In the following sections, I share with you some normal and problematic logs, along with explanations.

> **NOTE**
>
> In the following sections, I have cropped or wrapped log entries for readability.

Heartbeat Corruption

In some reported cases the heartbeat record of a host got corrupted. As a result, it could neither clear its heartbeat record nor acquire any of the locks required for normal operation. In such a case, the vmkernel logs show an error like the one in Listing 14.6.

Listing 14.6   Sample log entries of a corrupt heartbeat

```
vmkernel: 25:21:39:57.861 cpu15:1047)FS3: 130: <START [file-name].vswp>
vmkernel: 25:21:39:57.861 cpu15:1047)Lock [type 10c00001 offset 52076544 v
69, hb offset 4017152
vmkernel: gen 109, mode 1, owner 4a15b3a2-fd2f4020-3625-001a64353e5c mtime
3420]
vmkernel: 25:21:39:57.861 cpu15:1047)Addr <4, 1011, 10>, gen 36, links 1,
type reg, flags 0x0, uid 0, gid 0, mode 600
vmkernel: 25:21:39:57.861 cpu15:1047)len 3221225472, nb 3072 tbz 0, zla 3,
bs 1048576
vmkernel: 25:21:39:57.861 cpu15:1047)FS3: 132: <END [file-name].vswp>
```

Listing 14.7 shows another example of a corrupt heartbeat.

Listing 14.7   Another sample log of a corrupt heartbeat

```
vmkernel: 0:00:20:51.964 cpu3:1085)WARNING: Swap: vm 1086: 2268: Failed
to open swap file '/volumes/<vol-UUID>/<vm-directory>/<file-name.vswp>':
Invalid metadata

vmkernel: 0:00:20:51.964 cpu3:1085)WARNING: Swap: vm 1086: 3586: Failed to
initialize swap file '/volumes/4730e995-faa64138-6e6f-001a640a8998/mule/
mule-560e1410.vswp': Invalid metadata
```

You may be able to fix the corrupt heartbeat by using the following command:

```
voma -m vmfs -f fix -d /dev/disks/naa.6000eb39a16fb1100000000000000204:1
```

Or you can use the verbose version:

```
voma --module vmfs --func fix --device /dev/disks/naa.6000eb39a16
fb1100000000000000204:1
```

If this fails to fix the error, you might need to contact VMware technical support for assistance. Be prepared with a binary dump of the first 30MB or 1200MB of the device on which the VMFS volume resides. Technical support will attempt to repair the heartbeat records for the affected host.

File System Corruption

During the beta of ESXi 5, a file system corruption was reported by an internal user. During the process of resignaturing a VMFS datastore, another host attempted the same process. Listing 14.8 shows the relevant log messages from this case.

Listing 14.8   Sample log entries of corrupt VMFs

```
cpu7:2128)FS3: ReportCorruption:379: VMFS volume snap-6787757b-datastore-
X/4cfed840-657ae77f-9555-0026b95121da on naa.600601601932280083528fe3c40
2e011:1 has been detected corrupted

cpu7:2128)FS3: ReportCorruption:381: While filing a PR, please report the
names of all hosts that attach to this LUN, tests that were running on
them,

cpu7:2128)FS3: ReportCorruption:383: and upload the dump by 'dd if=/vmfs/
devices/disks/naa.600601601932280083528fe3c402e011:1 of=X bs=1M count=1200
conv=notrunc',

cpu7:2128)FS3: ReportCorruption:384: where X is the dump file name on a
different volume

cpu15:2128)FS3: DescriptorVerify:323: Volume Descriptor mismatch

cpu15:2128)FS3: DescriptorVerify:325: (Check if volume is involved in a
Format/Upgrade/dd from other hosts)

cpu15:2128)FS3: DescriptorVerify:326: In Memory Descriptor:magic
0x2fabf15e, majorVer 12, minorVer 51 uuid 4cfed840-657ae77f-
9555-0026b95121da, label <snap-6787757b-datastore-X>creationTime
1291049806config 6, diskBlockSize 512, fileBlockSize 1048576

cpu15:2128)FS3: DescriptorVerify:328: On Disk Descriptor:magic 0x2fabf15e,
majorVer 12, minorVer 51 uuid 4cfed79c-94250e53-64b8-0026b9511d8d, label
<snap-2042dfa8-datastore-X>creationTime 1291049806config 6, diskBlockSize
512, fileBlockSize 1048576
```

The last two lines in this example show that the file system's UUID in memory is different from that on disk. To identify which host is the offending one, the last segment of the on-disk UUID is the MAC address of that host's management port. In this case, it is 00:26:b9:51:1d:8d. This was fixed in the final release build, and we have not seen this issue reported outside the beta. Notice that the file system version is identified as `majorVer 12` and `minorVer 51`. This was a prerelease version. The released version is `majorVer 14` and `minorVer 54`, which translates to version 5.54.

Notice the new enhancement in the log message, where it identifies the corruption and provides the command line you need to use to collect the file system binary dumps needed for repairing the corruption.

Marking the Heartbeat and Replaying the Journal

Sometimes, an ESXi host may attempt to clear or mark the heartbeat and replay the journal. Listing 14.9 shows an example of replaying the heartbeat journal.

Listing 14.9 Replaying the heartbeat journal

```
HBX: FS3_MarkOrClearHB:4752: Marking HB [HB state abcdef02 offset 3158016
gen 5 stampUS 3345493920478 uuid 4cc0d786-d2f90077-9479-0026b9516a0d jrnl
<FB 1800> drv 12.51] on vol 'snap-6787757b-datastore-X'

HBX: FS3_MarkOrClearHB:4829: Marked HB [HB state abcdef04 offset 3158016
gen 5 stampUS 4064734308197 uuid 4cc0d786-d2f90077-9479-0026b9516a0d jrnl
<FB 1800> drv 12.51] on vol 'snap-6787757b-datastore-X'

J3: ReplayJournal:2970: Replaying journal at <FB 1800>, gen 5

HBX: FS3PostReplayClearHB:3985: Cleared pulse on vol 'snap-6787757b-datas-
tore-X' for [HB state abcdef01 offset 3158016 gen 6 stampUS 4064734365500
uuid 00000000-00000000-0000-000000000000 jrnl <FB 0> drv 12.51]
```

The message prefix is HBX (for heartbeat). The first two messages are attempting to mark the heartbeat first with HB state abcdef02 and then with HB state abcdef04. After this, it replays the journal, which in this case is at file block 1800. This message prefix is J3 (for journal).

The last message in the example is prefixed with HBX, and the code is FS3PostReplay-ClearHB, which is the code that clears the heartbeat after journal has been replayed. Notice that the heartbeat UUID is all zeros.

Checking Whether a Lock Is Free

The messages in Listing 14.10 demonstrate the activities a host does to check whether a given lock is free.

Listing 14.10   Checking whether a lock is free

```
cpu2:176604)DLX: FS3RecheckLock:3349: vol 'datastore-X', lock at 4327424:
Lock changed from:

cpu2:176604)[type 10c00001 offset 4327424 v 20, hb offset 3407872gen 29,
mode 1, owner 4e693687-57255600-7546-001ec933841c mtime 2568963num 0 gblnum
0 gblgen 0 gblbrk 0]

cpu2:176604)DLX: FS3RecheckLock:3350: vol 'datastore-X', lock at 4327424:
To:

cpu2:176604)[type 10c00001 offset 4327424 v 22, hb offset 3407872gen 29,
mode 1, owner 4e693687-57255600-7546-001ec933841c mtime 2662975num 0
gblnum 0 gblgen 0 gblbrk 0]

cpu2:176604)DLX: FS3LeaseWaitAndLock:4109: vol 'datastore-X': [Retry 0]
Lock at 4327424 is not free after change

cpu2:176604)DLX: FS3LeaseWaitOnLock:3565: vol 'datastore-X', lock at
4327424: [Req mode 1] Checking liveness:

cpu2:176604)[type 10c00001 offset 4327424 v 22, hb offset 3407872gen 29,
mode 1, owner 4e693687-57255600-7546-001ec933841c mtime 2662975num 0
gblnum 0 gblgen 0 gblbrk 0]

cpu2:176604)DLX: FS3CheckForDeadOwners:3279: HB on vol 'datastore-X'
changed from [HB state abcdef02 offset 3407872 gen 29 stampUS 337574575701
uuid 4e693687-57255600-7546-001ec933841c jrnl <FB 22186800> drv 14.56]

cpu2:176604)DLX: FS3CheckForDeadOwners:3280: To [HB state abcdef02
offset 3407872 gen 29 stampUS 337580579826 uuid 4e693687-57255600-7546-
001ec933841c jrnl <FB 22186800> drv 14.56]

cpu2:176604)DLX: FS3LeaseWaitAndLock:4089: vol 'datastore-X', lock at
4327424: [Req mode: 1] Not free:
```

The first line in Listing 14.10 shows that the disk-lock code (DLX) is checking a lock for the file system on a datastore named datastore-X. The lock location is at 4327424 offset. It reports that the lock has changed.

The second line shows the lock info before it was changed:

- Lock type
- Lock offset
- Lock version
- Heartbeat offset
- Heartbeat generation
- Lock mode, which can be a value between 0 and 3

Table 14.1 lists the meaning of each of these lock modes.

Table 14.1 VMFS lock modes

Lock Mode	Meaning	Comments
0	Unlocked	This indicates that there is no lock.
1	Exclusive lock	This is the mode commonly used to lock files frequently modified by one host—for example, virtual disks and VM swap files.
2	Read-only lock	This is used mostly at VM power-on to allow the host to read the virtual machine configuration files (*.vmx) and virtual disk files (*.vmdk) in a linked clone configuration. This is the type of lock used with optimistic I/O, which uses optimistic locking. Using ATS facilitates acquiring these locks without reservations.
3	Multi-writer lock	This allows multiple hosts to write to shared virtual disks concurrently. The arbitration of who should write to these files is done by the clustering software running in the guest OS.

The following are some practical examples of lock mode uses.

Multi-writer locks are the most dangerous type of locks, and unless they're used with a qualified clustering solution—for example, Oracle RAC—they can lead to corruption of files locked by this mode. This log entry shows the UUIDs of the multiple lock owners. These owners arc hosts sharing this file using this mode. If you are familiar with VMware

Workstation, you might notice that this lock mode is similar to what you achieve by using the VMX option `Disk.Locking = FALSE`:

- **Lock owner UUID**—The last segment of this ID is the MAC address of the management port on the host that owns this lock.

- **Num**—This is the number of hosts holding the lock. For read-only and multi-writer locks, this value can be more than 1.

The third and fourth lines show the lock record after it is changed. I highlighted the changed values.

The fifth line was generated by the VMFS `wait on lock` code because it identified that the lock is not free.

The sixth line is the beginning of the process of checking for the live-ness of the lock owner. It does this by checking the heartbeat slot of the lock owner for a change of the heartbeat region. If it is changed, it means the lock owner is alive and was able to write to its heartbeat. This is done by the `check for dead owners` code.

Taking Over a Lock

The messages in Listing 14.11 are related to breaking a lock.

Listing 14.11   Breaking a lock

```
cpu3:228427)DLX: FS3CheckForWrongOwners:3302: Clearing wrong owner for
lock at 184719360 with [HB state abcdef01 offset 3313664 gen 1076 stampUS
938008735 uuid 00000000-00000000-0000-000000000000 jrnl <FB 0> drv 14.58]

cpu2:228427)Resv: UndoRefCount:1386: Long reservation time on naa.60060160
55711d00cff95e65664ee011 for 1 reserve/release pairs (reservation held for
3965 msecs, total time from issue to release 4256 msecs).

cpu2:228427)Resv: UndoRefCount:1396: Performed 5 I/Os / 7 sectors in (8t 0q
01 8i) msecs while under reservation

cpu2:228427)Resv: UndoRefCount:1404: (4 RSIOs/ 7 sectors),(0 FailedIOs / 0
sectors)

cpu2:228427)FS3Misc: FS3_ReleaseDevice:1465: Long VMFS rsv time on
'datastore-X' (held for 4297 msecs). # R: 3, # W: 1 bytesXfer: 7 sectors

cpu3:228427)DLX: FS3LeaseWaitOnLock:3686: vol 'datastore-X', lock at
66318336: [Req mode 1] Checking liveness:
```

```
cpu3:228427)[type 10c00001 offset 66318336 v 2887, hb offset 3469312 gen
2763, mode 1, owner 4efb041c-235d1b95-f0cb-001e4f43718e mtime 27954 num 0
gblnum 0 gblgen 0 gblbrk 0]
```

The first line has the following elements:

- DLX—This refers to the vmkernel code that handles disk locks.

- FS3CheckForWrongOwners—This is the part of the disk lock code that checks for wrong owners of on-disk locks. It starts the process of clearing the lock by first listing the current lock information, including the following:

  - Lock location

  - Heartbeat state

  - Heartbeat offset

  - Heartbeat generation

  - Timestamp, listed here as stampUS

  - UUID of the host that owns the lock, listed here as all zeros

  - Journal location

The second line is a SCSI reservation and release pair showing the time that elapsed between these events. In this case, it is a long reservation time as it held the reservation for more than three seconds when normally it should not take more than a few milliseconds. Notice that the message begins with Resv, which is the code that handles SCSI reservations. This reservation was held on the device whose ID is the NAA ID I highlighted.

The third line shows how many I/Os are done on how many sectors with the device under reservation.

The fourth line shows the count of reservation I/Os on how many sectors (four I/Os on seven sectors) and that there were no failed I/Os.

The fifth line shows the device release action.

The sixth line shows that the host has requested a lock at sector 66318336 on the volume named datastore-X.

The final line shows that an exclusive lock (mode 1) at sector 66318336 is now owned by host UUID 4efb041c-235d1b95-f0cb-001e4f43718e. This exclusive lock is on that sector only. What this log does not show is that this lock protects a certain file descriptor cluster that occupies a specific resource. The log entry would have looked like <FD c1 r21>, which translates to file descriptor cluster 1 resource 21.

Summary

vSphere releases prior to 6.0 introduced enhancements in distributed lock handling. In the absence of VAAI-capable storage arrays, these mechanisms are still used by vSphere 6. A new device property in vSphere 5 and newer is perennial device reservation, which helps improve boot and rescan time for hosts with RDMs reserved by MSCS/WSFC nodes on other ESXi hosts. I discuss VAAI in Chapter 17.

## Chapter 15

Snapshot Handling

Data is written to storage devices frequently in the dynamic environment of vSphere 6. Losing a few hours' worth of data, for whatever reason, could mean a large amount of data loss. Storage arrays provide various forms of business continuity/disaster recovery (BC/DR) capability to help mitigate this risk, including the following:

- Snapshots
- Replicas
- Mirrors

In this chapter, I cover details of these features in relationship to Virtual Machine File System (VMFS) datastores.

What Is a Snapshot?

A *storage snapshot* is a static view of data at a certain point in time. Snapshots are commonly implemented as pointers to unmodified blocks on the primary logical unit number (LUN) at the time the snapshot is taken. If and when any of the blocks are modified, an unmodified block is copied to a snapshot LUN, and then the modification is written to the block on the primary LUN. The end result is two LUNs: the primary LUN, with the current state of data, and the snapshot LUN, with a combination of blocks copied before being modified and pointers to unmodified blocks on the primary LUN. The snapshot LUN coexists with the primary LUN on the same storage array. It is read-only but can be configured for read-write operations and presented as a separate LUN.

What Is a Replica?

As the name indicates, a *replica* is a block-for-block copy of a storage device (LUN). Depending on the frequency and type of replication—that is, synchronous (sync) or asynchronous (async)—the replica (copy) LUN (R2) has identical content to the primary LUN (R1) at any point in time (sync) or is missing the modified blocks of the R1 LUN since the last replication took place (async).

The distance and latency of the connection between storage arrays hosting a pair of replicas (R1 and R2) influences the design choice between sync and async replication. For the topic at hand, I am only highlighting the details relevant to the effects of replication on VMFS datastores. So, for now, you just need to know that a synchronous replica has identical content, while an asynchronous one (R2) lags behind the R1 content by the replication period at the most. VMFS datastore signature is identical on R1 and R2 LUNs.

What Is a Mirror?

One of the types of RAID is RAID1, in which two devices are attached to the same storage adapter and all write input/output (I/O) is sent to both devices concurrently, which results in identical content. This is referred to as *mirroring*. RAID adapters have cache memory that can be read, write, or both read and write. Depending on the presence of battery backup on the RAID adapter, the write cache can be write-back (with battery backup) or write-through (without battery backup). This cache is ECC RAM type or better to prevent bit-level corruption which, in turn, prevents possible on disk data corruption.

A similar concept applies to most storage arrays, which use a much larger cache and use various caching algorithms, depending on the vendor. The bottom line is that storage arrays can do more types of RAID. However, in the case of a storage array, RAID is done at a lower level, with a set of disks grouped together as disk pools. One or more RAID types can be created on each pool. For example, one disk pool can host RAID1 and RAID5 concurrently or just RAID1 on one pool and RAID5 on another. The RAID set can then be carved up into multiple LUNs protected by the underlying RAID set.

LUNs can be mirrored so that any write operation done on one gets done on the mirror at the same time. Say that the primary LUN is M1, and the mirror is M2. Both M1 and M2 can be on the same storage array or on separate ones within synchronous distance or closer— for example, two buildings in the same campus or across the river between Manhattan and Brooklyn. The latter scenario is commonly referred to as a metro area network (MAN).

A mirror pair can have M1 read-write and M2 read-only or write-protected. When the need arises to use M2 in the absence of M1, you can break the mirror and change M2 writable. When M1 becomes available, you can change the mirroring roles so that M2 syncs up with M1 and then write-protect M2 after M1 is back online. The VMFS datastore is identical between M1 and M2. Furthermore, for some arrays, both LUNs may have the same device ID if the storage array firmware provides the option.

VMFS Signature

When a new VMFS3 or VMFS5 datastore is created, it is assigned a unique identifier, referred to as the volume universally unique identifier (UUID). The volume UUID is stored in the Logical Volume Manager (LVM) header, along with the device ID, such as the NAA ID.

Here is an example of a volume UUID:

```
4d7bebaa-721eeef2-8c0a-001e4f1fbf2c
```

The volume UUID is composed of four portions:

- **System time**—System time at volume creation
- **TSC time**—Internal timestamp counter kept by the CPU
- **Random**—A random number
- **MAC**—Management port uplink (VMNIC) MAC address of the host used to create or resignature the datastore

If the VMFS5 datastore spans multiple LUNs, the LVM header also holds the spanned device table (see Chapter 12, "VMFS Architecture"), which lists the device IDs of all volume extents.

Listing Datastores' UUIDs via the CLI

To list a datastore's UUID via the CLI, you can run this command:

```
esxcli storage filesystem list
```

The output looks as shown in Figure 15.1.

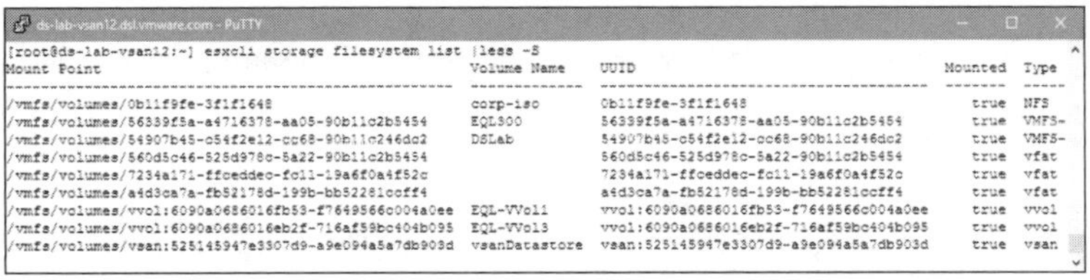

Figure 15.1 Listing datastores' UUIDs

In Figure 15.1, I cropped the output to fit this page. I truncated the Size column and the Free column. The Volume Name column shows the list of datastores, and the rest of the output is self-explanatory.

Effects of Snapshots on VMFS Signatures

If the device ID of a LUN on which there is a VMFS3 or VMFS5 volume is changed, the following takes place:

1. When the host rescans for new devices, it discovers the presented LUN.

2. When the host rescans for datastores, the VMkernel compares the physical device ID to that stored in the VMFS datastore LVM. It identifies a mismatch and does not automatically mount the discovered datastore.

3. If the snapshot LUN is an extent of a spanned VMFS datastore and the remaining extents were not snapshot LUNs and presented to the host, the ESXi host refuses to resignature or force-mount the volume. You can check for this condition by using this command:

   ```
   esxcli storage vmfs snapshot list
   ```

   Listing 15.1 shows the output of this command.

Listing 15.1   Listing VMFS snapshot of a spanned datastore

```
esxcli storage vmfs snapshot list
4faeba13-6bf41bdd-6dd0-001f29e04d52
   Volume Name: LHN-LUN
   VMFS UUID: 4faeba13-6bf41bdd-6dd0-001f29e04d52
   Can mount: false
   Reason for un-mountability: some extents missing
   Can resignature: false
   Reason for non-resignaturability: some extents missing
   Unresolved Extent Count: 1
```

Notice in Listing 15.1 that the reasons for un-mountability and for non-resignaturability are both some extents missing. This protects against accidental resignaturing of any of the extents of a spanned VMFS volume.

How to Handle VMFS Datastores on Snapshot LUNs

For a snapshot LUN–based VMFS datastore to be mounted on an ESXi 6 host, it needs a new volume UUID written to it (resignatured) or it needs to be force-mounted with its signature unmodified. The choice between these options depends on whether the primary LUN from which the snapshot LUN was taken is presented to the same host. If the primary and snapshot LUNs are not presented to the same host and will not be presented to it at any time in the future, it would be safe to force-mount the datastore. Otherwise, you must resignature the snapshot datastore before you mount it alongside its primary LUN. If you do not resignature the snapshot datastore, you are guaranteed to corrupt the datastore on both primary and snapshot LUNs accessed concurrently by the same host.

If you have multiple ESXi 6 hosts sharing a set of datastores, they all must access these datastores uniformly; that is, you should not force-mount a snapshot on one host in the cluster while other hosts access the datastore on the primary LUN. vCenter Server has some validation checks in place to prevent this from happening as long as you do not manage any host in the cluster by logging in to it directly (if you still use vSphere 6 Client instead of vSphere 6 Web Client).

ESX version 3.5 and older offered LVM advanced VMkernel options to resignature snapshot datastores in bulk (`LVM.EnableResignature`) or to allow them to be mounted unmodified (`LVM.DisallowSnapshotLun`). The `LVM.EnableResignature` option enables automatic resignaturing of the snapshot datastores. The `LVM.DisallowSnapshotLun` option allows snapshot datastores to be mounted without resignaturing. These options are hidden from the UI as well as ESXCLI in vSphere 6, 5, and 4.x, and they have been replaced with per-datastore operations to provide better control and reduce accidental operations that might result in data corruption.

Resignaturing Datastores

The process of resignaturing a VMFS datastore is the same for both VMFS3 and VMFS5. It can be done via the user interface (UI) or ESXCLI.

Resignaturing a VMFS Datastore Using vSphere 6 Web Client

To resignature a VMFS datastore using vSphere 6 Web Client, you can follow this procedure:

1. Connect to the vCenter server that manages the ESXi 6 host, using the vSphere 6.0 Web Client as a user with Administrator privileges.

2. Navigate to the **Hosts and Clusters** view.

3. In the inventory tree, right-click the ESXi host on which you will mount the datastore and then select **Storage** and then **New Datastore** (see Figure 15.2).

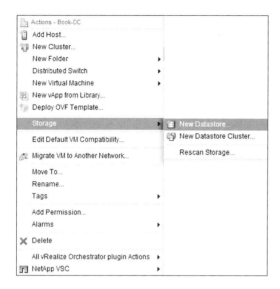

Figure 15.2   Selecting the New Datastore menu option

4. Select the **VMFS** radio button when prompted for the datastore type and then click **Next**.

5. Select the LUN representing the snapshot. In the example shown in Figure 15.3, the LUN shows a value under the Snapshot Volume column.

Figure 15.3   Selecting a snapshot LUN

6. Click **Next**.

7. Select the **Assign a new signature** radio button in the Mount option section of the dialog (see Figure 15.4).

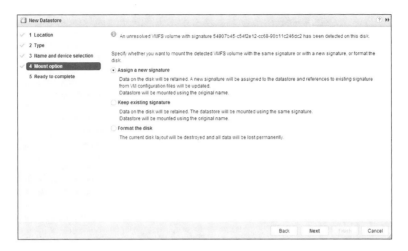

Figure 15.4 Selecting the resignaturing option

8. Click **Next**.

9. Review the summary and click **Finish** (see Figure 15.5).

Figure 15.5 Reviewing selections

The VMFS datastore is now mounted and renamed following the syntax `snap-<random-number>-<original-volume-name>`—in this case, `snap-10a5d283-DSLab`, as shown in Figure 15.6.

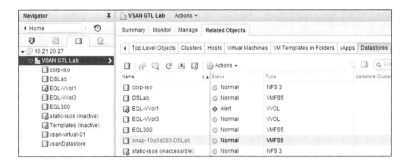

Figure 15.6   Mounted snapshot datastore

To use the VMs on this datastore, you can right-click a datastore, select the **Browse Files** menu, navigate to each VM directory, right-click its VMX file, and select the **Add to Inventory** option.

Resignaturing a VMFS Datastore Using ESXCLI

Using ESXCLI to resignature VMFS datastores is a process you can do on all snapshot LUN–based datastores that are accessible by the host. It involves using a hidden option that will be deprecated in future releases. This process is time-consuming and takes longer, per datastore, than it takes to resignature and then mount the same datastore via the UI. Although this is a VMware-supported operation, it is not recommended for a large number of datastores if your recovery time objective (RTO) is shorter than the time it takes for this operation to complete.

> **NOTE**
>
> VMware Site Recovery Manager does this process programmatically on the recovery site in a much shorter time than it takes by using ESXCLI. The reason the ESXCLI takes longer is that some of the APIs used by ESXCLI serialize certain operations and wait for acknowledgement of each operation to guarantee data integrity and prevent race conditions.

If your environment does not involve a large number of VMFS datatores, you can use the following steps to resignature and mount a datastore via ESXCLI:

1. Log on to ESXi locally via SSH or use the vMA 6.0 appliance. If you have multiple hosts on which to mount the resignatured VMFS datastores, it would be more practical to use vMA 6.0, as I will show you in this example.

2. Continuing with the example of using vMA, while logged in as vi-admin user, run the `vifp listservers` command to verify that the ESXi host was previously added to the managed targets list (see Listing 15.2).

Listing 15.2 Listing vMA 6 managed targets

```
vifp listservers

wdc-tse-d98.wsl.vmware.com        ESXi
prme-iox215.eng.vmware.com        ESXi
wdc-tse-h56.wsl.vmware.com        ESXi
wdc-tse-i83.wsl.vmware.com        ESX
10.131.11.215                     vCenter
```

This example shows four ESXi hosts and one vCenter server registered on this vMA 5 appliance.

3. If the host you want to manage is not on the return list, you can add it by using the `vifp addserver` option:

```
vifp addserver wdc-tse-i85.wsl.vmware.com --username root
```

You can also add a `--password` parameter. Otherwise, you are prompted for the password. If the operation is successful, no message is provided.

4. Use `vifptarget` to set which target server to manage:

```
vi-admin@vma5:~> vifptarget --set wdc-tse-h56.wsl.vmware.com
vi-admin@vma5:~[wdc-tse-h56.wsl.vmware.com]>
```

Notice that the prompt now shows the name of the managed target host.

From this point on, the process is similar to the process using SSH or when logged in to the host locally.

5. List the current setting of the `/LVM/EnableResignature` VSI node (see Listing 15.3).

Listing 15.3 Listing the current `EnableResignature` advanced system setting

```
esxcli system settings advanced list --option /LVM/EnableResignature
   Path: /LVM/EnableResignature
   Type: integer
   Int Value: 0
   Default Int Value: 0
   Min Value: 0
   Max Value: 1
   String Value:
   Default String Value:
   Valid Characters:
   Description: Enable Volume Resignaturing. This option will be deprecated
in future releases.
```

In Listing 15.3 I highlighted the current value, which is 0. This means that the default ESXi host's behavior is to not automatically resignature snapshot volumes.

Note that this parameter type is an integer. If you are logged in via SSH or locally on the ESXi host and you want to see the corresponding VSI node, you can run the command shown in Listing 15.4.

Listing 15.4   Listing `EnableResignature` VSI node content

```
vsish -e get /config/LVM/intOpts/EnableResignature
Vmkernel Config Option {
   Default value:0
   Min value:0
   Max value:1
   Current value:0
   hidden config option:1
   Description:Enable Volume Resignaturing. This option will be deprecated
in future releases.
}
```

Note that because this is a configuration parameter, the root of its node is `/config`. Similarly, because the parameter type is integer, the VSI node is `/config/LVM/intOpts/EnableResignature`. The highlighted text here means `Integer Options`. If this node type were `string`, the node would be `/config/LVM/strOpts/<parameter>` instead. LVM has no string type parameters. Also note from Listing 15.3 that the fields `String Value` and `Default String Value` are blank because the parameter type is `Integer`.

6. Change the value of the parameter from 0 to 1 to enable the host to automatically resignature snapshot datastores. To turn on the advanced setting /LVM/EnableResignature, you can run the following command:

   ```
   esxcli system settings advanced set -o /LVM/EnableResignature -i 1
   ```

   Or you can use the verbose option:

   ```
   esxcli system settings advanced set --option /LVM/EnableResignature
   --int-value 1
   ```

7. The command returns no messages if successful, so to verify that the change took place, run the following command:

   ```
   esxcli system settings advanced list -o /LVM/EnableResignature
   ```

   Listing 15.5 shows the output from this command.

Listing 15.5   Verifying the outcome of changing the `EnableResignature` setting

```
esxcli system settings advanced list -o /LVM/EnableResignature
    Path: /LVM/EnableResignature
    Type: integer
    Int Value: 1
    Default Int Value: 0
    Min Value: 0
    Max Value: 1
    String Value:
    Default String Value:
    Valid Characters:
    Description: Enable Volume Resignaturing. This option will be deprecated
in future releases.
```

8. Rescan the host for the datastore. When you do, LVM automatically resignatures the discovered snapshot datastores (see Listing 15.6).

Listing 15.6   Rescanning for datastores

```
vmkfstools -V

Rescanning for new Vmfs on host

Successfully Rescanned for new Vmfs on host
```

9. To verify that the resignatured datastore are mounted now, run the following command:

```
esxcli storage filesystem list |grep 'UUID\|---\|snap' |less -S
```

Figure 15.7 shows the output from this command.

Figure 15.7   Listing mounted snapshots

In Figure 15.7 I truncated the output—eliminating the columns, Size, and Free—for readability. If you compare the UUID here to the UUID in the original VMFS volume, you should notice the new one listed here.

If the other hosts share the same datastores you just resignatured, you can mount the snapshot LUNs on the other hosts by repeating only steps 4 and 8.

Force-Mounting

Force-mounting a snapshot datastore simply means mounting it without modifying its signature. I reiterate that you must never do this on the same host that has the original datastore mounted.

Force-Mounting a VMFS Snapshot Using vSphere 6 Web Client

The process for force-mounting a datastore snapshot is similar to the earlier procedure "Resignaturing a VMFS Datastore Using vSphere 6 Web Client," except that in step 7, select the **Keep existing signature** radio button (see Figure 15.8). The VMFS datastore signature and name are retained.

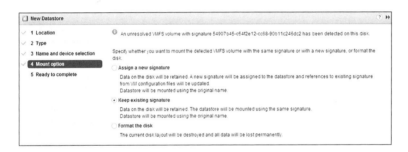

Figure 15.8   Force-mounting a snapshot

Force-Mounting a VMFS Snapshot Using ESXCLI

The process of force-mounting a VMFS snapshot using ESXCLI can be summarized as follows: Obtain a list of datastores identified as snapshots (also referred to as *unresolved volumes*) and then mount each one, using the datastore name.

The following procedure shows the details involved in force-mounting a VMFS snapshot using ESXCLI:

> **NOTE**
>
> You can adapt the sample script listed in the next section, "Sample Script to Force-Mount All Snapshots on Hosts in a Cluster," to automate this process.

1. Follow steps 1– through 4 in the "Resignaturing a VMFS Datastore Using ESXCLI" section, earlier in this chapter, or connect to the host by using SSH.

2. To get a list of snapshot datastores, run the following command:

```
esxcli storage vmfs snapshot list
```

This returns a list of snapshot datastores, as shown in Listing 15.7.

Listing 15.7 Listing snapshot datastores using `esxcli`

```
esxcli storage vmfs snapshot list
4faeba13-6bf41bdd-6dd0-001f29e04d52
   Volume Name: LHN-LUN
   VMFS UUID: 4faeba13-6bf41bdd-6dd0-001f29e04d52
   Can mount: true
   Reason for un-mountability:
   Can resignature: true
   Reason for non-resignaturability:
   Unresolved Extent Count: 1
```

The output in Listing 15.7 shows the original VMFS volume name and its original UUID (signature). It also shows that the volume can be mounted because there is no reason for un-mountability listed. In the same fashion, it shows that it can be resignatured because there is no reason for non-resignaturability. The last line in the output is the number of extents of this volume that will be resignatured.

If the original volume is still online, the volume will not be mounted until it is resignatured. Again, this safeguards the mounted datastore from corruption if the snapshot and the original datastore are both mounted.

To identify whether snapshots exist, you can run again this command:

```
esxcli storage vmfs snapshot list
```

Listing 15.8 shows the output of the command in this case.

Listing 15.8 Listing reasons for un-mountability

```
esxcli storage vmfs snapshot list
4faeba13-6bf41bdd-6dd0-001f29e04d52
   Volume Name: LHN-LUN
   VMFS UUID: 4faeba13-6bf41bdd-6dd0-001f29e04d52
   Can mount: false
   Reason for un-mountability: the original volume is still online
   Can resignature: true
   Reason for non-resignaturability:
   Unresolved Extent Count: 1
```

In Listing 15.8, there is no reason for non-resignaturability but there is a reason for un-mountability: The original volume is still online.

It is possible for more than one snapshot of the original LUN extent or extents to be presented to the same host. In this case, you get the output shown in Listing 15.9.

Listing 15.9   Listing duplicate extent cases

```
4faeba13-6bf41bdd-6dd0-001f29e04d52
   Volume Name: LHN-LUN
   VMFS UUID: 4faeba13-6bf41bdd-6dd0-001f29e04d52
   Can mount: false
   Reason for un-mountability: duplicate extents found
   Can resignature: false
   Reason for non-resignaturability: duplicate extents found
   Unresolved Extent Count: 2
```

3. Mount each datastore identified in step 2 by using the following command:

   ```
   esxcli storage vmfs snapshot mount --volume-label=<volume-label>
   ```

   Or you can use the shorthand version:

   ```
   esxcli storage vmfs snapshot mount -l <volume-label>
   ```

   You can also use the datastore's UUID:

   ```
   esxcli storage vmfs snapshot mount --volume-uuid=<volume-UUID>
   ```

   Or you can use the shorthand version:

   ```
   esxcli storage vmfs snapshot mount -u <volume-UUID>
   ```

4. Verify that the datastores have been mounted by running the following command:

   ```
   esxcli storage filesystem list |less -S
   ```

Sample Script to Force-Mount All Snapshots on Hosts in a Cluster

Listing 15.10 shows a sample PERL script that you can adapt to your environment to force-mount all snapshots on hosts that are members of a specific cluster. It was built based on examples shipped with the vMA 5 appliance and is located in the /opt/vmware/vma/samples/perl directory. This script is usable on vMA 5.0 only. It has not been tested on vMA 6 but is expected to work there as well. You must change the managed host to be the vCenter Server before running this script.

This script does the following:

1. It takes in the cluster name as an argument.

2. It obtains the list of hosts in this cluster from vCenter Server.

3. On each host on the list from step 2, it runs `vmkfstools -V` to scan for VMFS datastores.

4. On each host on the list from step 2, it gets a list of snapshot of volumes by using the following command:

   `esxcli storage vmfs snapshot list`

5. On each host on the list from step 2, it persistently mounts the datastores from the list in step 4.

This is the syntax for this script:

`mountAllsnapshots.pl --cluster <cluster-name>`

Here is an example:

`mountAllsnapshots.pl --cluster BookCluster`

Listing 15.10   Sample PERL script that mounts all snapshot volumes on a list of hosts in a cluster

```
#!/usr/bin/perl -w

# mountAllsnapshots script
# Copyright VMware, Inc. All rights reserved.
# You may modify this script as long as you maintain this
# copyright notice.
# This sample demonstrates how to get a list of all VMFS
# snapshots # on a set of hosts that are members of a vCenter
# cluster using "esxcli storage vmfs snapshot -l" command then
# mount them using "esxcli storage vmfs snapshot mount -l"
# command.
# Use at your own risk! Test it first and often.
# Make sure to not mount any VMFS volume and its snapshot on
# the same host.

use strict;
use warnings;
use VMware::VIRuntime;
use VMware::VILib;
```

```perl
my %opts = (
   cluster => {
      type => "=s",
      help => "Cluster name (case sensitive)",
      required => 1,
   },
);
Opts::add_options(%opts);

Opts::parse();
Opts::validate();
Util::connect();

# Obtain all inventory objects of the specified type
my @lines;
my $cluster = Opts::get_option('cluster');
my $clusters_view = Vim::find_entity_views(view_type => "ComputeResource");
my $found = 0;

foreach my $cluster_view (@$clusters_view) {
   # Process the findings and output to the console
   if ($cluster_view->name eq $cluster) {
      print "Cluster $cluster found!\n";
      my $hosts = Vim::find_entity_views(view_type => "HostSystem",
                                         begin_entity => $cluster_view);

      foreach my $host_view  (@$hosts) {
         my $host_name = $host_view->name;
         push(@lines, $host_name);
      }
      $found = 1;
   }
}

if ($found eq 0) {
   print STDERR "Cluster $cluster not found!\n";
   exit 1;
}

# Disconnect from the server
Util::disconnect();
```

```perl
if ((!defined $ENV{'LD_PRELOAD'}) ||
    ($ENV{'LD_PRELOAD'} !~ /\/opt\/vmware\/vma\/lib64\/libvircli.so/ )) {
   print STDERR "Error: Required libraries not loaded. \n";
   print STDERR "        Try mountAllsnapshots command after running ";
   print STDERR "\"vifptarget -s | --set <server>\"  command.\n";

   exit 1;
}

my $command;
my $err_out = "";
my @out;
my $TERM_MSG = "\nERROR:   Terminating\n\n";
foreach my $line (@lines){
   if($err_out eq $TERM_MSG) {
      print STDERR $err_out;
      last;
   }

   if($line) {
      print "Mounting all snapshot volumes on ". $line ."\n";

      #step1:  perform rescan
      $command = "vmkfstools";
      $command = $command . " --server " . $line . " " . "-V";
      $err_out = '$command 2>&1';

      #step2:  list all snapshots
      $command = "esxcli";
      $command = $command . " --server " . $line . " " . "storage vmfs
snapshot -l";
      @out = '$command';

      #step3: mount all listed snapshots.
      foreach my $ol (@out) {
         if ($ol =~ /([0-9a-f]{8}-[0-9a-f]{8}-[0-9a-f]{4}-[0-9a-f]{12})/) {
            $command = "esxcli";
            $command = $command . " --server " . $line . " " . "storage
vmfs snapshot mount -l $1";
            $err_out = '$command 2>&1';
         }
      }
```

```perl
        if ($?) {
            if ( $! ) {
                print STDERR ": ".$!;
                $err_out = $TERM_MSG;
            } else {
                print STDERR $err_out."\n";
                if ($err_out =~ /Common VI options:/) {
                    $err_out = $TERM_MSG;
                }
            }
        } else {
            print STDOUT $err_out."\n";
        }
        print "\n";
    }
}

exit 0;
```

Summary

This chapter has provided an overview of storage snapshots, replication, and mirroring. I have explained the effects of these storage features on VMFS datastore signatures and how vSphere handles them. I have also included a sample PERL script to force-mount all snapshot datastores on hosts that are members of the same cluster.

## Chapter 16

NFS

Along with the dawn of personal computing and its increased adoption by businesses and universities came the need for file sharing. This need prompted several computer industry giants, including Sun Microsystems, IBM, Digital, HP, AT&T, and Apollo, to invest time and resources in defining a file system protocol to serve this purpose.

Sun Microsystems developed the Network File System (NFS) protocol, which uses Remote Procedure Calls (RPC); it was initially named SUN-RPC and later converged with Open Network Computing RPC (ONC RPC). The protocol eventually became an open standard defined in Requests for Comments (RFCs). Since version 4, the protocol has been overseen, developed, and managed by the Internet Engineering Task Force (IETF).

History of NFS

Sun Microsystems developed NFSv1 for in-house use, and it released NFSv2 (defined in RFC 1094) for external use in 1989. NFSv2 initially used User Datagram Protocol (UDP) as a transport protocol but was later revised to use Transmission Control Protocol (TCP) for better reliability and to enable use over WANs. This switch also broke the limit on the 8KB transfer size imposed by UDP limitations.

NFSv3, defined in RFC 1813, was released in 1995, and it provided these enhancements:

- Support for 64-bit file sizes and offsets, making possible files larger than 2GB (which was important on 64-bit-based computers)

- Improved performance via support for asynchronous writes on the server

- Improved process for getting file handles, attributes, and filenames during directory scanning

NFSv4, defined in RFC 3010, was released in 2000, and it was later revised in 2003 in RFC 3530. Then, in 2015, it was further revised in RFC 7530. NFSv4, which is the first version developed by the IETF, adds the following enhancements to NFSv3:

- Further performance improvements
- Strong security
- Introduction of a stateful protocol

NFSv4.1, defined in RFC 5661, was released in 2010. It takes advantage of clustered server deployments (for example, VMware vSphere 6) and makes it possible to provide scalable parallel access to files distributed over multiple servers (pNFS extension). vSphere does not support the pNFS extension, but it provides session trunking to support multipathing.

NFS on vSphere 6

VMware supported NFSv3 as early as ESX 3.x, and with the introduction of vSphere 6, it added support for NFSv4.1, which removed many of the limitations of NFSv3. Table 16.1 compares the two protocol versions from vSphere's perspective.

Table 16.1 NFSv3 and NFSv4.1 comparison

Feature	NFSv3	NFSv4.1
Multipathing	Managed by ESXi	Native multipathing and session trunking
Authentication	AUTH_SYS (root)	Optional Kerberos authentication
File locking	VMware proprietary	Built in
Error tracking	Client side	Sever side

I/O Flow to NFS Datastores

The flow of I/O from the virtual machines through the various layers of ESXi starts with the virtual SCSI (VSCSI) adapter layer and then moves on through the file system switch (FSS). These two steps are identical for all I/Os leaving a VM. Depending on the datastore type, FSS sends the I/O to the corresponding file system type. In this case, the next stop is either NFSv3 or NFSv4.1 file system logic. For NFSv3, the I/O is sent via SunRPC to the NFS share via TCPIP. This is done via a character device created on the host representing the NFS share.

On the other hand, the NFSv4.1 system logic sends the I/O to path handling layer, which includes cluster, server, session, and connection functions. From there, the I/O is sent to the NFS share via SunRPC over TCP/IP. Figure 16.1 shows a block diagram of the NFSv4.1 case.

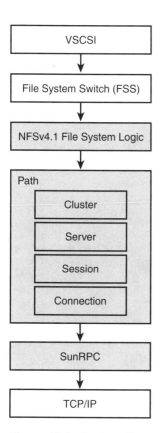

Figure 16.1 Logical I/O path to datastore (The blocks with the dark background are within the vmkernel.)

NOTE

vSphere uses TCP only for NFSv3 and NFSv4.1. UDP is not used.

NFS Clients on vSphere 6

vSphere 6 includes two NFS clients, 3.0 and 4.1, as vmkernel modules. While they can be used with the same NFS servers, they should not concurrently access the same NFS shares. I first focus on the NFSv3 client in this section and then cover NFSv4.1 in sections that follow.

The NFSv3 client accesses NFS shares as root, using AUTH_SYS. Most Linux NFS servers default to disabling root access to NFS shares, which is referred to as root_squash. For this client to have read/write access to the NFS shares, the NFS server must disable the `root_squash` option. This is done by enabling an option called `no_root_squash` on the NFS server.

However, the NFSv4.1 client no longer requires this setting because it can use Kerberos to authenticate as a non-root user on the network attached storage (NAS) server. If the server does not require authentication, depending on the NFS share's configuration, the client falls back to NFSv3 authentication (`AUTH_SYS`) as root user. If you use Kerberos authentication, make sure to use the same Kerberos user account with the NFSv4.1 client on all hosts in the cluster to facilitate access to the NFS datastore by these hosts during and after VMotion.

> **NOTE**
>
> The Active Directory domain name used as the Kerberos server must be different from the domain name used with the single sign-on (SSO) server configured for the vSphere environment.

Host Networking for NFS Storage

Access to NFS storage via ESXi hosts requires an open NFS client's port in the ESXi firewall as well as a VMkernel port group defined in the virtual network.

The ESXi host's firewall disables both NFS3 and NFS4 clients by default. To verify that this is the case, run this command:

```
esxcli network firewall ruleset list |grep 'Name\|---\|nfs'
```

Listing 16.1 shows this command and its output.

Listing 16.1   Listing an NFS client's firewall status

```
esxcli network firewall ruleset list |grep 'Name\|---\|nfs'
Name                          Enabled
----------------------        -------
nfsClient                     false
nfs41Client                   false
```

These settings automatically change to `enabled` when you mount your first NFS datastore of the corresponding NFS version. (I revisit this subject after I go through the procedure to mount NFSv3 and NFSv4.1 datastores later in this chapter.)

Each host in the cluster needs to be configured with a vmkernel port for IP storage access. It is recommended to configure a dedicated storage network for better security and bandwidth requirements. Because NFSv3 does not offer encryption, it is safer to isolate the storage network from other user networks. This isolation can be physical (for example, dedicated network) or logical (for example, VLANs).

NFS traffic in general can benefit greatly from faster NICs. NFSv4.1 is capable of session trunking, which gives it even greater bandwidth as well as native multipathing. Standard vSwitch or Distributed Switch can be used, depending on the network design and the type of license available. I use a standard vSwitch example here.

TIP

Chapter 2, "Fibre Channel Storage Connectivity," discusses the concept of points of failure for FC SANs. The same concept applies to network attached storage (NAS). The basic concept is to provide redundant connections to the storage device so that any component failure does not result in loss of connectivity to the storage. Generally speaking, you need to have at least two network adapters per host connected to two switches, which in turn connect to two ports on the NAS server. Figure 16.2 shows a simplified logical design of such a network.

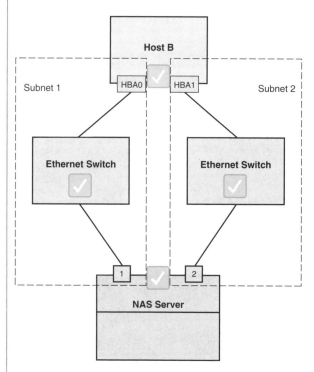

Figure 16.2 NAS logical network design without single points of failure

---

In this example, each host has two network ports on two separate NICs. Each port is connected to a separate Ethernet switch. The NAS server has two ports, which are connected to two separate switches. These ports are in separate subnets that each include one port per host and a corresponding NAS server port. This means you have dual exports for each datastore. The reason for this is NFSv3 does not provide multipathing support, whereas NFSv4.1 provides session trunking support, as discussed later in this chapter.

The previous example requires active/standby NIC teaming configuration on the host's port group used for NAS connectivity. If you need active/active configuration, follow the next example instead (see Figure 16.3).

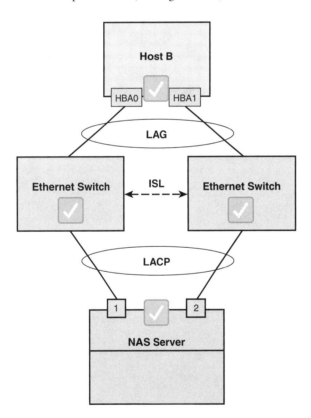

Figure 16.3 NAS logical network design with fewer single points of failure, with Link Aggregation Control Protocol (LACP)

In this example, link aggregation groups (LAGs) and EtherChannel (trunking) are added, which requires stacking the switches with Inter-Switch Link (ISL). You would use this configuration with LAGs configured on vDS and active/active NIC teaming with IP hash load balancing on the host's end and EtherChannel (or equivalent) on the NAS server's side. (See the section "Creating an Interface Group and Assigning Ports," later in this chapter.) Additional considerations must be noted as outlined in the following tip.

TIP

When using IP hash load balancing, consider the following:

- You cannot use it with beacon probing.
- You cannot configure standby or unused uplinks.
- You must configure 802.3ad aggregation (or equivalent) on the switch port.

To add another level of redundancy, use the storage server's clustering capabilities, if available (for example, use Clustered Data ONTAP with two nodes or use EMC Unity with two SPAs). Figure 16.4 shows the additional storage server in the design.

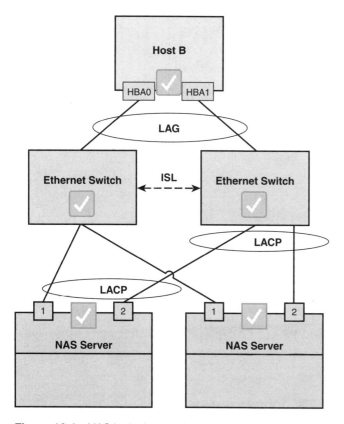

Figure 16.4   NAS logical network design without single points of failure, with LACP

Configuring a Host Network for NAS

To configure a simplified ESXi host virtual network to prepare for access to NAS-based datastores for both NFSv3 and NFSv4.1 (refer to Figures 16.3 and16.4), follow this procedure for standard vSwitch:

1. Log on to VC 6 with Administrator privileges, using vSphere 6 Web Client.

2. Navigate to the **Hosts and Clusters** view (see Figure 16.5).

3. Select the ESXi host in the inventory tree.

4. Select the **Manage** tab.

5. Select the **Networking** button.

6. Select the **VMkernel adapters** section.

7. Click the **Add Host Networking** icon, which looks like a globe with a green plus sign.

Figure 16.5 Accessing the **Add Host Networking** icon

8. In the dialog that appears, select the **VMkernel Network Adapter** radio button.

9. In the same dialog, select the **New standard switch** radio button and then click **Next**.

10. In the same dialog click the **Add Physical Adapter** icon, which is a green plus sign (see Figure 16.6).

11. Select **Active Adapters** from the Failover order group pull-down menu.

12. Select one of the vmnics from the **Network Adapters** column. This is the NIC that will be assigned to the NAS storage network port group to be created later.

13. Click **OK**.

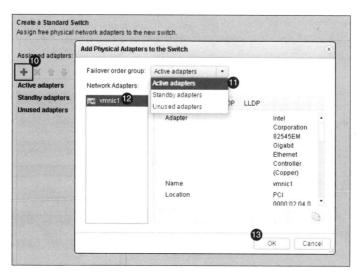

Figure 16.6   Adding a physical NIC to new standard switch

14. Ensure that the list of assigned adapters shows the newly added NIC in the Active adapters section. Click **Next**.

15. In the Port Properties step, enter the VMkernel port's network label (see Figure 16.7).

Figure 16.7   Defining the storage port group

16. Select the VLAN ID if your design calls for it.

17. Select the IP version from the IP settings pull-down menu. The design decision for using IPv6 should involve a dependency on the vSphere version. Table 16.2 lists possible design choices.

Table 16.2 IP version design decision

NFS Version	vSphere 6.0	vSphere 6.5
NFSv3	Either IPv4 or IPv6	Either IPv4 or IPv6
NFSv4.1	IPv4 only	Either IPv4 or IPv6
Both NFSv3 and NFSv4.1	IPv4 and IPv6 option	Either IPv4 or IPv6

18. Select the TCP/IP stack from the pull-down menu. If your design does not require a separate TCP/IP stack, leave the selection set to **Default**.

19. Leave all the Available services options unchecked and then click **Next**.

20. In the IPv4 (or IPv6, depending on your previous selections), enter static or dynamic options. If you selected both IPv4 and IPv6, you first get the IPv4 settings step, followed by the IPv6 setting step separately. When you're done, click **Next**.

21. The final step is the Ready to complete step. Review your selections and then click **Finish**.

The new vmknic should be now listed as `vmk1` (or whatever the next available vmk number is). If you select the **Virtual switches** section, the newly added vSwitch is now listed. Selecting it shows you the new Storage Network port group (see Figure 16.8).

Figure 16.8   A new vSwitch with a storage port group

TIP

The decision of whether to create a new standard vSwitch instead of use the existing vSwitch depends on how many NICs and their speed ratings as well as requirement to use physical versus logical network separation. If a distributed vSwitch (vDS) license is available, I prefer to use it for networks other than the management network. An important benefit of using vDS is the ability to configure jumbo frame granularly on the port group level as well as its support for LAGs. If you configure jumbo frames, make sure to set the largest MTU supported by the switch (higher than 9000) and configure it end-to-end to avoid fragmentation.

Otherwise, you should create a standard vSwitch for each set of port groups with similar functions. However, if you have a limited number of network ports per host, a single vSwitch would suffice, and you can assign one or more vmnics to each port group as active, standby, or both, depending on your network design. If you have only a dual-port 10GigE NIC and your network switches are VLAN capable, I would assign both NICs to a single standard vSwitch, and the configuration would look as shown in Figure 16.9.

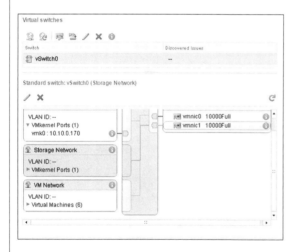

Figure 16.9   Existing vSwitch with storage port group active/passive NIC teaming

If your network is routed, ensure that you use redundant routers for better availability and enable the following:

- **For Cisco routers**—Hot Standby Router Protocol (HSRP)
- **For other vendors' routers**—Virtual Router Redundancy Protocol (VRRP)

Do not enable Ethernet flow control on the host or NetApp filer ports' ends.

If you were to use NFSv4.1 only on vSphere 6.5, I would you should configure active/active NIC teaming (IP hash) on vDS and trunk both ports (in a LAG) for higher bandwidth if the switch supports LACP.

Now that the network configuration is done, let's consider what needs to be done on the NAS server.

Configuring an NFS Volume on NAS Servers

Among the most popular NAS servers for vSphere environments are NetApp and EMC VNX and its successor EMC Unity. In this section, I cover examples from NetApp C-Mode and EMC Unity Appliances. Both are also available for you to practice and learn in the form of virtual appliances.

NFS Exports on EMC Unity

EMC Unity is the latest EMC unified storage offering. It offers support for both NFSv3 and NFSv4.1, as well as iSCSI protocols and both NAS and SCSI VMware Virtual Volumes (VVols). Before creating an NFS volume, you need to first create a NAS server with the corresponding NFS protocol version. If you have already created a NAS server, skip to the section "Creating an NFSv3 Share on EMC Unity."

Creating an NFSv3 NAS Server on EMC Unity

To create an NFSv3 NAS server on EMC Unity, follow these steps:

1. Log on to EMC Unity via the EMC Unisphere management UI.

2. Navigate to the **File** option in the STORAGE section.

3. Select the **NAS Servers** link.

4. Click the **Create a NAS Server** icon, which is a plus sign that changes to green when you hover over it (see Figure 16.10). (In the example shown in Figure 16.10, I already have a NAS server configured; however, I will go over the steps for demonstration.)

Figure 16.10   Launching the **Create a NAS Server** option

5. Enter the server name.

6. Select a storage pool from the Pool field's pop-up list.

TIP

The pool design depends on the planned workload I/O profile. I cover more details on EMC Unity pool creation and types later in this chapter and in Chapter 23, "Virtual Volumes (VVols)."

---

7. Select the storage processor on which to run this NAS server. In the example shown in Figure 16.11, I have only a single choice; SP A, because I am using the virtual appliance. The physical appliance, however, provides two SPs.

8. Click **Next**.

Figure 16.11   Configuring a NAS server's general settings

9. In the Interface section, enter the following:

   a. Select which Ethernet port on the SP to use for this server. Best practice is to separate SCSI traffic from NAS as well as replication traffic. I prefer to reserve the highest port number for replication traffic. The first two ports, 0 and 1, are for iSCSI traffic, and port 2 is for NAS traffic.

   b. Enter the interface's IP address.

c. Enter the subnet mask or subnet prefix (that is, the number of bits in the mask). In this example, I use the class C subnet prefix 24. This is equivalent to using the 255.255.255.0 subnet mask.

d. Enter the gateway's IP address (optional).

e. If you set up a VLAN for NAS traffic, click the Edit link and then enter the VLAN ID. Otherwise, click **Next** (see Figure 16.12).

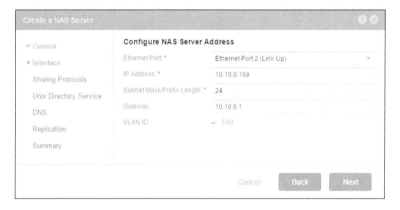

Figure 16.12   Configuring a NAS server's interface

10. In the Sharing Protocols step, select **Linux/Unix shares (NFS)**.

11. To configure NFSv3, leave the remaining options unchecked (see Figure 16.13). These options are for enabling VVols (see Chapter 23) or enabling NFSv4. The default NFS protocol version is NFSv3.

12. Click **Next**.

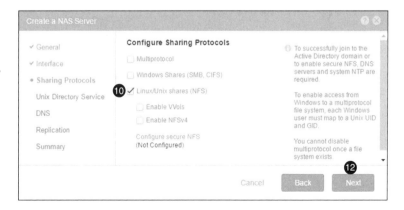

Figure 16.13   Configuring a NAS server's sharing protocols

13. Skip the Unix Directory Service step by clicking **Next** again.

14. If you plan on using ESXi host names in NFS volumes' ACLs, enable the DNS option in the DNS step. (Another reason to enable it is if you plan on joining Active Directory. However, this is not required for NFSv3 shares.)

TIP

If your design does not call for a specific recovery point objective (RPO) for the NFS shares, skip to step 19. Otherwise, continue with step 15.

---

15. If you have already set up a replication peer with this appliance and your design calls for replicating the NFS shares, select the **Enable Replication** option (see Figure 16.14).

16. Select **Replication mode**.

TIP

With NFS on EMC Unity, only asynchronous replication is available.

---

17. Enter your RPO value, in minutes. The shorter the time, the more replication traffic will be on the replication ports.

18. Select the replication peer from the **Replicate To** pull-down list.

TIP

The choice of local destination does not protect from storage array failure or site disaster. In this example, I selected a peer EMC Unity appliance in a different site.

If you have no peer defined, follow the procedures in the section "Configuring Replication on EMC Unity," later in this chapter. When you're done, return to this procedure.

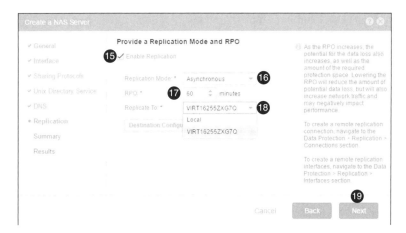

Figure 16.14   Configuring a NAS server's replication

19. Click **Next**.

20. Review the summary of choices and then click **Finish**.

The newly added NAS server should now be listed in the NAS Servers list.

Creating an NFSv4.1 NAS Server on EMC Unity (Without Kerberos)

To create an NFSv4.1 NAS server on EMC Unity, follow steps 1 through 10 from the previous section, "Creating an NFSv3 NAS Server on EMC Unity," and continue with the following steps:

11. Select the **Enable NFSv4** check box.

12. Click **Next**.

13. Skip the Configure Unix Directory Service step by clicking **Next**.

14. If you plan on later modifying this NAS server to use Kerberos, or if the shares' ACL will use hosts' FQDNs, enable DNS in this step and enter the domain name and one or more DNS servers' IP addresses.

15. Click **Next**.

16. Enable replication if your design calls for it and click **Next**.

17. Review the summary of choices and click **Finish**.

18. Either wait until the overall status indicator reaches 100% or let it run in the background and click Close to dismiss the Create a NAS Server dialog.

Creating an NFSv4.1 NAS Server on EMC Unity (with Kerberos)

At press time, EMC Unity did not support Kerberos authentication; however, I cover the process of configuring it just in case it becomes supported soon.

The easiest approach to configuring Kerberos authentication with NFSv4.1 on EMC Unity is to configure the NAS server with multiprotocol file sharing, which combines CIFS and NFSv4.1 protocols. EMC Unity has the following high-level prerequisites for EMC Unity:

- Configure an EMC Unity appliance to use NTP.

- Configure DNS on the NAS server.

- Have the NAS server join Active Directory (AD). The easiest approach for doing this is to configure the NAS server for CIFS protocol. Secure NFS configuration can utilize the Kerberos realm, which is automatically configured when CIFS is enabled.

- After the NAS server joins the AD domain, create a DNS host record (A record) and Reverse Lookup (PTR) record for it in the AD domain zone.

- Configure UNIX Directory Services (UDS). The preferred method for Unity is LDAP.

To configure NFSv4.1 with Kerberos authentication, you can follow steps 1 through 11 in the previous section and then continue with the following steps:

12. Select the **Windows Shares (SMB, CIFS)** option and make sure the **Join to the Active Directory domain** radio button is selected (see Figure 16.15).

13. Enter a computer name to represent this NAS server in AD.

14. Enter Windows AD domain name (for example, **book.local**).

15. Enter an AD user name with Administrator privileges. This enables the wizard to join the NAS server to the AD domain.

16. Enter the user's password.

17. To enable use of Kerberos authentication with NFSv4.1, click the **Configure secure NFS** link.

18. Select the **Enable Secure NFS (with Kerberos)** check box.

19. Select the **Use SMB server account** radio button. Both the Realm and SPN fields are automatically populated with the required values, based on the AD computer name assigned in step 13. SPN (Service Principal Name) is an AD property associated with the computer's AD account object. It is in the format `nfs/<computer-name>.AD-domain` (for example, `nfs/UnityMP.book.local`).

Figure 16.15   Configuring an NFSv4.1 NAS server's sharing protocols

20. Click **OK** to save the **Secure NFS Settings** and return to the wizard (see Figure 16.16).

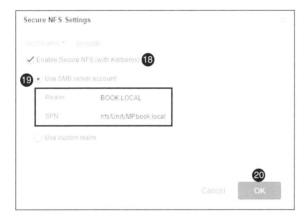

Figure 16.16   Configuring an NFSv4.1 NAS server's NFS settings

21. Click **Next** to go to the Configure Unix Directory Service step. The **Enable Unix Directory Service** check box is selected by default and cannot be changed.

22. Select LDAP from the **Unix Directory Service** pull-down list if it is not already selected (see Figure 16.17).

23. In the **Servers** field, click **Add**. The **Add New IP Address** dialog appears.

24. Enter the AD server's IP address and then click **Add** to close the dialog.

25. Leave the **Port** field with the default value, 389. This is the LDAP service's port address.

26. Ensure that the Authentication pull-down list is set to Kerberos.

27. Select the **Use configured SMB domain** radio button if it is not already selected. The **Base DN** field is prepopulated, based on the AD domain name. In this example, it is dc=book,dc=local.

28. Click **Next**.

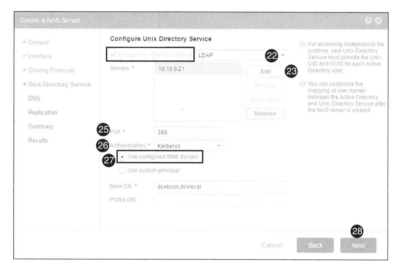

Figure 16.17   Configuring an NFSv4.1 NAS server's UNIX directory services

This next step is Configure NAS Server DNS. The **Enable DNS** check box is already selected and cannot be modified. The AD domain is prepopulated in the Domain field.

29. Click the **Add** button (see Figure 16.18). The **New IP Address for DNS Server** dialog appears.

30. Enter the IP address of the DNS server used by AD and then click **Add** to close the dialog.

31. Click **Next**.

Figure 16.18   Configuring an NFSv4.1 NAS server's DNS

TIP

The next step is to configure replication if your design calls for it. This is a design decision similar to that made while creating an NFSv3 NAS server, as discussed earlier in this chapter. EMC Unity provides only asynchronous replication option with NFS protocols. It is advisable to place the replication target in a separate building or site, depending on the bandwidth and latency of the link between storage servers. Asynchronous replication is generally supported with distances longer than 10 kilometers and latency above 5 milliseconds.

---

32. If desired, select the **Enable Replication** check box and make the relevant choices for the Replication Mode, RPO and Replicate To fields. Otherwise, leave the option unselected and click **Next**.

33. Review the summary screen. If no changes are required, click **Finish**.

The Results screen is displayed, showing the progress of the steps defined in this procedure. If all steps complete successfully, a green checkmark is displayed next to the Completed status. Click **Close** to dismiss the Results screen.

NOTE

As this writing, and as mentioned earlier, NFSv4.1 Kerberos authentication is not yet supported by EMC Unity 4.0.x. This could explain why these configuration steps result in an error on the NAS server, indicating failure to contact the LDAP server. Hopefully, by the time EMC supports Kerberos authentication, this error would be resolved.

Creating an NFSv3 Share on EMC Unity

With the required storage server configuration out of the way, now you are ready to create NFS shares to export to the vSphere 6 environment.

To create an NFSv3 share, follow this procedure:

1. Log on to the EMC Unity Unisphere management UI with Administrator privileges or equivalent.

2. Navigate to the **VMware** section, under STORAGE.

3. Select the **Datastores** link.

4. Launch the **Create Datastore Wizard** by clicking the plus sign icon (see Figure 16.19).

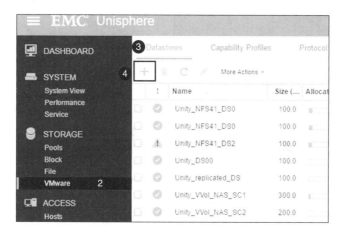

Figure 16.19   Launching the Create Datastore Wizard

5. Select **File** as the VMware Datastore Type.

6. If you have a single NAS server on this storage server, it will already be selected in the field NAS Server. Otherwise, click in that field and select a server that you created for NFSv3, from the pop-up list and then click the **Select NAS Server** button.

7. Click **Next**.

8. Enter the datastore name and optionally a description and then click **Next**.

9. Select a storage pool on which to create this datastore. When you click in the **Storage Pool** field, a pop-up list with the available storage pools is displayed. Select the pool that has the tier suitable to the I/O profile for the VMs planned to reside on this datastore (see Figure 16.20).

> **TIP**
>
> If you installed and configured multiple tiers of storage in your storage server and it supports dynamic or automatic tiering, select a pool composed of the storage tiers within the range of tiers the VMs' I/O will utilize. Dynamic tiering takes care of placing the blocks backing the datastore on which the VMs' virtual disks reside according to the I/O profile.

The next step explains the various tiering policies that EMC Unity offers.

10. Select the tiering policy by choosing one of the following:

   - **Start High Then Auto-Tier**—Data is placed first on the highest tier available, and then parts of it are moved to lower tiers, depending on the I/O activities.

   - **Auto-Tier**—Data is placed on the tier that the storage server deems optimal but gets relocate to higher or lower tiers, based on the I/O activities.

   - **Highest Available Tier**—Data is placed on the highest available tier. It may get relocated to higher tiers when space becomes available and the I/O activities justify it.

   - **Lowest Available Tier**—The initial data placement is on the lowest available tier. If space becomes available on lower tiers, data may be relocated there, as needed. This is the opposite of the **Highest Available Tier** setting.

11. Specify the datastore size. EMC Unity's NFS shares are thin provisioned by default and cannot be changed via this UI.

12. Select the host I/O size. This option defines the expected I/O size issued by the host using this datastore. The default is 8KB, which is optimal for general-purpose vSphere NFS I/O types.

> **TIP**
>
> If this datastore will house VMs with specific I/O size requirements, select the best size for the I/O profile. This storage server offers various sizes, ranging from 8K to 64K. It also offers predefined I/O sizes for business-critical applications such as Exchange 2007, 2010, and 2013, as well as Oracle, SQL, VMware Horizon VDI, SharePoint, and SAP servers.

13. Click **Next**.

Figure 16.20   Configuring storage for an NFSv3 datastore

14. Select the default access to this datastore.

TIP

Best practice for NFSv3 is to set the default access to No Access to prevent unauthorized access to the datastore. This effectively enables the `root_squash` option. You can then specify the access type per host that you will add to the access control list (ACL) in the next step.

---

15. To add hosts to the ACL, click the plus sign icon. The Select Host Access dialog pops up.

16. Select the access type that will be granted to the list of hosts you will choose in the next step. The available access types are **No Access, Read-Only** and **Read/Write, allow root** (see Figure 16.21). The first one is already the default. Read-only access is typically used for storing installation images and other static content. If you use that, you need to initially grant read/write access to one host, such as a management host, from which you can copy the planned content. For datastores that will host VMs, select **Read/Write, allow root**, which allows root access that effectively disables the `root_squash` option for NFSv3.

17. Select vSphere cluster or data center host members that will share access to the datastore.

> **TIP**
>
> If you want to provide access to a whole subnet or a specific ESXi host that's not on the list, select the **More Actions** pull-down menu and then select the appropriate option. For example, if you want to add an ESXi host, select the **Add ESXi Host** option, and the Discover ESXi Host wizard appears. There you can enter a host name (FQDN) or IP address and root user name and password and then click **Find**. You can do this for one host at a time. To configure multiple hosts or discover VC servers and the hosts it manages, you should do that before creating the datastore by using the **Access**, **VMware** menu options.

18. Click **OK**.

Figure 16.21   Adding hosts to a datastore's ACL

19. The ACL is now populated with the list of hosts, along with their access type.

> **NOTE**
>
> The dialog displays the warning `Granting write access to multiple hosts can cause data corruption unless hosts are part of a supported cluster configuration`. This warning does not apply here because vSphere 6 handles file locking on its end, using hidden .lck files. I will show you how they look and related configuration later in this chapter.

20. Click **Next** (see Figure 16.22).

Figure 16.22   Hosts added to the ACL

21. If your design calls for creating snapshots for this datastore, enable the option in this step and specify a schedule. In this example, I am not configuring a snapshots schedule. Click **Next**.

22. If your BC/DR design calls for replicating the datastore, enable the replication in this step. This creates a replication session with the same attributes as the NAS server replication session. However, if you did not configure replication on the NAS server created earlier in this chapter, the option is grayed out here, and you see the information message `Replication session must be created on the associated NAS Server before the NFS Datastore replication session can be configured`. Click **Next**.

23. Review the summary screen, and if no changes are needed, click **Finish**.

EMC Unity automatically mounts the NFSv3 datastore on all hosts listed in the ACL. This operation posts messages to /var/run/log/vmkernel.log, and these messages are shown in Listing 16.2

Listing 16.2   Mounting NFSv3 datastore–related vmkernel messages

```
opID=71a18ae1)World: 15514: VC opID 159ae6c2-bd-e15f maps to vmkernel opID
71a18ae1

opID=71a18ae1)NFS: 157: Command: (mount) Server: (10.10.0.55) IP:
(10.10.0.55) Path: (/Unity_NFS3_DS0) Label: (Unity_NFS3_DS0) Options:
(None)
```

```
opID=71a18ae1)StorageApdHandler: 982: APD Handle 8b78b99c-a3638457 Created
with lock[StorageApd-0x43065405afc0]
opID=71a18ae1)NFS: 347: Restored connection to the server 10.10.0.55 mount
point /Unity_NFS3_DS0, mounted as 8b78b99c-a3638457-0000-000000000000
("Unity_NFS3_DS0")
opID=71a18ae1)NFS: 218: NFS mount 10.10.0.55:/Unity_NFS3_DS0 status:
Success
```

The first message shows vCenter's (VC's) operation ID and its equivalent ID on vmkernel. This is due to the fact that EMC Unity utilizes VMware APIs to pass the relevant commands to the ESXi hosts via VC.

The second message lists the `mount` command issued by EMC Unity to the hosts on the ACL. This is equivalent to the following command, which you can use to mount the datastore manually from other NFS servers that do not offer this type of automation:

```
esxcli storage nfs add --host 10.10.0.55 --share /Unity_NFS3_DS0 --
volume-name Unity_NFS3_DS0
```

Or you can use the abbreviated version:

```
esxcli storage nfs add -H 10.10.0.55 -s /Unity_NFS3_DS0 -v Unity_NFS3_DS0
```

The `nfs` parameter represents NFSv3. If the datastore were NFSv4.1 based, the parameter would be `nfs41`. (I show the NFSv4.1 command in the **"Mounting an NFSv4.1 Datastore"** section, later in this chapter.)

The third message shows that an All-Paths-Down (APD) handle has been created from this datastore, along with a lock ID. VMkernel uses this handle to track that datastore's access state. If it gets disconnected, the APD handling mechanism kicks in and tracks the connectivity state of this datastore. (I cover APD in Chapter 7, **"Multipathing and Failover."**) However, in this case, it is an NFS datastore, and the APD handle is created using the datastore's mount point on the host. To list this mount point, run the following command:

```
esxcli storage filesystem list |grep "Type\|---\|NFS"
```

Listing 16.3 shows the output of this command.

Listing 16.3   Listing an NFSv3 datastore's mount point

Mount Point	Volume Name	UUID	Mounted	Type
/vmfs/volumes/8b78b99c-a3638457	Unity_NFS3_DS0	8b78b99c-a3638457	true	NFS

I truncated the last two columns in Listing 16.3, Size and Free, for readability.

Observe that the volume UUID is the same as the APD handle. This UUID is also listed in the fourth vmkernel log message, padded with zeros to make up the datastore's standards UUID length. In this example, it is 8b78b99c-a3638457-0000-000000000000. The same ID can be listed using the vmkfstools command:

```
vmkfstools --queryfs --humanreadable /vmfs/volumes/Unity_NFS3_DS0
```

Or you can use the abbreviated version:

```
vmkfstools -Ph /vmfs/volumes/Unity_NFS3_DS0
```

Listing 16.4 shows the output of this command.

Listing 16.4   Using vmkfstools to list an NFSv3 datastore's properties

```
NFS-1.00 file system spanning 1 partitions.
File system label (if any): Unity_NFS3_DS0
Mode: public
Capacity 98.5 GB, 98.5 GB available, file block size 4 KB, max supported
file size 131072 TB
UUID: 8b78b99c-a3638457-0000-000000000000
Partitions spanned (on "notDCS"):
        nfs:Unity_NFS3_DS0
NAS VAAI Supported: NO
Is Native Snapshot Capable: NO
```

The output shows that the file system version is NFS-1.00 and that the datastore's partitions span notDCS, which means "not direct-connect storage." It also lists the device name as nfs:Unity_NFS3_DS0, which is the datastore type followed by the datastore's name. There is no partition number because this is not a block device.

Back in the vmkernel.log messages, the final line shows a successful operation.

Recall that earlier I checked on the status of the NFS client's firewall ports, which showed up as being disabled. Running this command lists the current status:

```
esxcli network firewall ruleset list |grep 'Name\|---\|nfs'
```

Listing 16.5 shows the command and its output.

Listing 16.5   Listing an NFS client's firewall status

```
esxcli network firewall ruleset list |grep 'Name\|---\|nfs'
Name                              Enabled
----------------------------      -------
nfsClient                            true
nfs41Client                          false
```

This means the NFSv3 client is now enabled in the host's firewall, while NFSv4.1 is still disabled.

Configuring Replication on EMC Unity

EMC Unity replication requires configuring a replication network interface on at least one port per SP on each node that will be the source or destination of replication traffic. Then replication connections need to be created.

Creating Replication Network Interfaces on EMC Unity

To create replication interfaces, follow this procedure:

1. Log on to EMC Unisphere with Administrator privileges or equivalent.

2. Select the **Replication** option in the Data Protection section (see Figure 16.23).

3. Select the **Interfaces** link at the top of the screen.

4. Click the **Create Replication Interface** icon, which is a plus sign that turns green when the mouse hovers over it.

5. Select an available Ethernet port. In this example, I selected Ethernet port 3.

TIP

Because replication traffic can saturate the bandwidth of the SP port selected in this step, if the data change rate is high, it is a good idea to dedicate one port for replication traffic and not share it with data interfaces. I usually pick the highest port number on each SP of source and target storage servers.

---

6. Enter an IP address and subnet mask to assign to this interface. The gateway address setting is optional.

7. If your design calls for logical separation of replication traffic from user networks, set the VLAN ID by clicking the **Set** link at the bottom of the Create Network Interface dialog. (This assumes that your switches were configured accordingly.)

8. Click **OK** to create the interface and close the dialog.

Figure 16.23   Creating a replication interface on EMC Unity

9. Repeat steps 1 through 6 on each EMC Unity appliance that will participate in data replication.

Creating Replication Connections on EMC Unity

Next, you create replication connections between each pair of EMC Unity appliances. You need to follow this procedure on only one appliance, and the corresponding connections will be automatically created on the destination appliance. Before you can complete this procedure, you need to create replication interfaces, as described in the preceding section. Follow these steps:

1. Log on to EMC Unisphere with Administrator privileges.

2. Click **Replication** in the Data Protection section (see Figure 16.24).

3. Select the **Connections** link at the top of the screen.

4. Click the **Create Replication Connection** icon, which is a plus sign that turns green when the mouse hovers over it.

5. In the Remote System section, enter the management IP address of the remote appliance as well as user name and password. This user must have Administrator privileges or equivalent.

6. In the Local System section, enter the local user's password. The user name is already populated with the currently logged in user.

7. Click **OK**.

Figure 16.24 Creating a replication connection on EMC Unity

8. While the job is being processed, you can click the progress status percentage link to open the list of tasks currently being processed for this job and their status. When the job is completed successfully, the remote server's ID will be available as a replication connection.

TIP

Depending on your disaster recovery (DR) design, data can be replicated to one or more remote sites. If you have several production sites to protect and a single recovery site, you can configure a hub-and-spoke replication topology, where all production sites replicate to the same DR site. Alternatively, you can configure each site as a DR site for one production site in a circular topology. For example, site A replicates to site B, and site B replicates to site C, which replicates to site A (see Figure 16.25). There are many topologies to use other than these two, and they can be as simple or as complex as you design them to be. Your choices here depend on available capacity on the storage appliances in each site and whether all sites provide production data (that is, active/active or active/standby configurations). Replicas are write-protected until a failover is done.

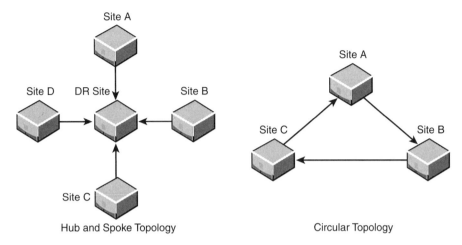

Figure 16.25   Replication topologies

Creating an NFSv3 Storage VM (SVM) on a NetApp Filer

NetApp has been one of the pioneers in NFS storage, and it keeps on innovating in how it integrates management and provisioning tools into vSphere environments. Here is a brief overview of how I configured NetApp in my lab:

1. I deployed the NetApp simulator VSIM Data ONTAP (DOT) versions 9 virtual appliance (OVF) on an ESXi 6.x host. The OVF is also available for VMware Workstation or Fusion. At this writing, VSIM version 9 release candidate (RC) has just been released. For the purpose of this chapter, I configured a single appliance as a single-node cluster.

2. I created a root aggregate and named it Data.

3. I created a storage virtual machine (SVM) for NFSv3. Here are the steps to follow to create an SVM:

    a. Click the **SVMs** tab.

    b. Click **Create** (see Figure 16.26).

Figure 16.26   Creating a NetApp SVM

c. Enter the SVM name (see Figure 16.27).

d. I am using the default **IPspace**. If you created a custom IPspace, select it. Otherwise, leave the default selected.

e. Select the **NFS** check box.

f. Select **UNIX** as the Security Style.

g. Select the root aggregate if you have more than one. If there is only a single root aggregate, it is selected by default. DNS configuration is optional because it is only required for CIFS protocol, which is not used in the vSphere environment.

h. Click the **Submit & Continue** button.

Figure 16.27 Entering NFS SVM properties

The Configure NFS Protocol dialog is displayed. In the Data LIF Configuration section, enter the following:

i. If you already defined a subnet, select it in the Assign IP Address field. Otherwise, select **Without a subnet** (see Figure 16.28). This opens a dialog where you enter the IP address, subnet mask, and, optionally, gateway address.

j. Click the **Browse** button and select the port to assign to this SVM. (NIS configuration is optional for an NFSv3 implementation with vSphere 6.x.)

k. Click the **Submit & Continue** button.

Figure 16.28   Configuring the NFS protocol

The SVM Administration dialog is displayed. While this step is labeled optional, you must enter a password in the Administrator Details section. This password is for a user named vsadmin. This user can create NFS volumes on this SVM because I assigned it a root aggregate earlier. This also enables applications like SnapManager and SnapDrive, which use this account for their interactions with the filer.

l. Click the **Submit & Continue** button.

m. In the summary screen, review your selections and click **OK** to proceed with creating the SVM.

4. Install NetApp Virtual Storage Console (VSM) version 6.2 or later on a 64-bit Windows Server machine.

5. Register the VSM with VMware Virtual Center 6.x (see Figure 16.29). This is done on the Windows Server machine on which VSM is installed. At the end of the

installation process, a link to the registration UI is provided. The default URL is https://localhost:8143/Register.html.

6. Log out of vSphere 6.x Web Client and then log back in. The VSM icon appears in VC's home screen, in the Inventories pane. Selecting that icon opens the VSM user interface (UI).

7. Navigate to the **Storage Systems** section.

8. Select the **Add** icon.

9. In the **Add Storage System** dialog, enter the NetApp Appliance management port's IP address or host name.

10. Enter a user name for a user with Administrator privileges on the file.

11. Enter the user's password.

12. Click **OK**.

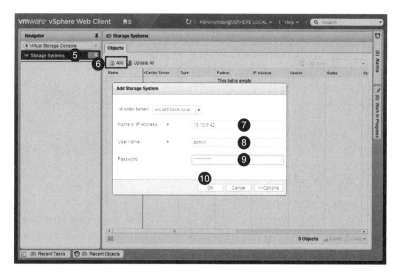

Figure 16.29   Adding a storage system to VSC

Creating an NFSv3 Datastore on a NetApp Filer

The process of creating an NFSv3 datastore on NetApp 8.2.x, 8.3.x, or 9.0 and mounting it on one or more ESXi 6.x hosts is a very simple procedure. Follow these steps:

1. Log on to VC with Administrator privileges.

2. Navigate to the **Hosts and Clusters** view.

3. Right-click the host or cluster on which you want to mount the datastore being provisioned and then click **NetApp VSC** and finally click the **Provision Datastore** menu option (see Figure 16.30).

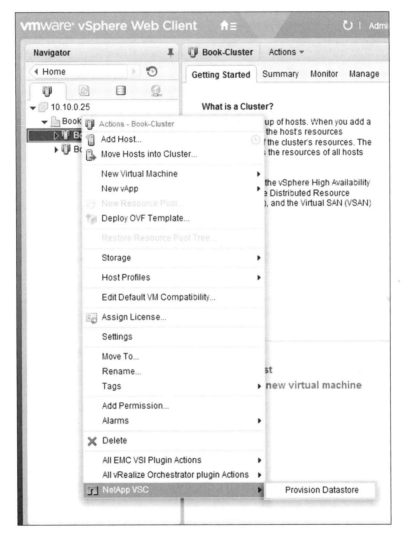

Figure 16.30 Launching the VSC Provision Datastore Wizard

4. In the Name and type step, enter the datastore name and select **NFS** as the datastore type and then click **Next**.

5. In the Storage system step, select the NetApp filer and the SVM you created earlier from the corresponding pull-down lists and then click **Next** (see Figure 16.31).

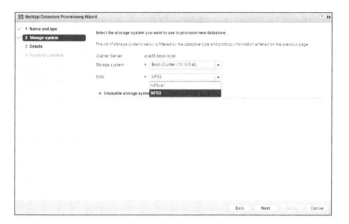

Figure 16.31   Selecting the storage system and SVM

6. If your design calls for thin provisioned NFS datastores, select the **Thin Provision** check box (see Figure 16.32).

7. Specify the datastore size, in gigabytes.

8. Select the aggregate on which to create the datastore.

NOTE

If the Thin Provision option is not selected, the list of aggregates automatically excludes those with free space smaller than the specified datastore size.

---

9. If your design calls for automatically growing the datastore size, select the **Auto grow** check box and enter the maximum datastore size, in gigabytes, and the increment in which it will grow, in gigabytes.

10. If you enabled Storage DRS in the cluster and this datastore will be part of an existing datastore cluster, select that cluster from the corresponding pull-down list.

11. Click **Next**.

12. Review your selections, and if no changes are required, click **Finish** to proceed with provisioning this datastore.

The datastore is provisioned on the storage server and then mounted on all hosts in the cluster. If you selected a single host in step 3, the datastore is mounted on that host only. You can track the progress of this operation via the Recent Tasks pane in the vSphere 6 Web Client. Figure 16.33 shows the tasks relevant to this section. The newest tasks are listed at the top.

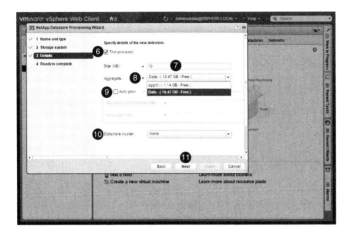

Figure 16.32   Setting the details of a new datastore

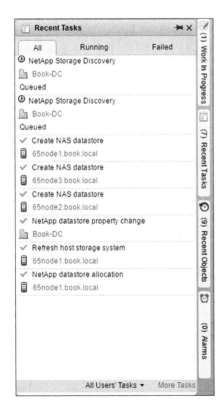

Figure 16.33   Selecting the storage system and SVM

Figure 16.33 was taken using vSphere 6.5 HTML5 Web Client.

Listing NFSv3 Datastores via vSphere 6 Web Client

To explore the NFSv3 datastores via the UI, follow this procedure:

1. Log on to VC with Administrator privileges, using vSphere 6 Web Client.

2. Navigate to the **Storage** inventory tab (see Figure 16.34).

3. Select the datacenter object in the inventory tree.

4. Select the **Related Objects** tab.

5. Select the **Datastores** tab. (In vSphere 6.5 Web Client, steps 4 and 5 are combined: You just click the **Datastores** tab.)

6. Click the **Type** column header to sort on it in ascending order. In vSphere 6.5 Web Client, sorting is available only in the Name column.

Figure 16.34   Listing an NFSv3 datastore in the UI

In this example, the NFSv3 datastore I mounted in the previous sections is shown at the top of the list, with NFS 3 type.

7. Click the datastore name in the list, which takes you to the datastore properties.

8. Select the **Summary** tab.

9. Expand the **Details** pane (see Figure 16.35).

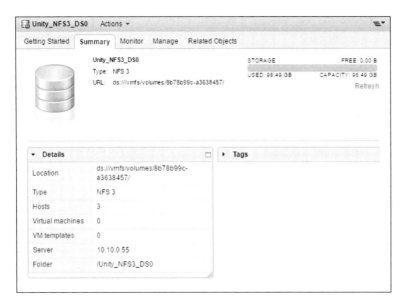

Figure 16.35   Listing NFSv3 datastore details in the UI

This example shows the following details:

- **Location**—This is the URI, in the format ds:///vmfs/volumes/<volume-UUID>, which is the path to the mount point on the host.

- **Type**—The NFS 3 setting is a clear indicator that this datastore is NFSv3.

- **Hosts**—This is the number of hosts on which this datastore is mounted.

- **Virtual machines**—This is the count of VMs residing on this datastore. Because this is a freshly created VM, the count is zero.

- **VM templates**—This is similar to the previous field but is for templates.

- **Server**—This is the IP address of the NAS server's port.

- **Folder**—This is the name of the export associated with this datastore.

In the top pane, a subset of these details are listed, along with the space consumption on the datastore.

Using Kerberos Authentication with NFSv4.1 Datastores

vSphere 6.0 introduced support for Kerberos 5 authentication for NFSv4.1 datastores. Table 16.3 lists the supported Kerberos encryption types.

Table 16.3 Supported Kerberos encryption types

Encryption Type	vSphere 6.0	vSphere 6.0, Update 1 and Update 2	vSphere 6.5
3DES	Yes	No	No
AES128	No	Yes	Yes
AES256	No	Yes	Yes

The following sections go over how to configure NFSv4.1 for NetApp filers. Data ONTAP version 8.2.x and earlier supported DES and 3DES encryption types only. Later versions added support for AES128 and AES256.

As for Kerberos security modes supported by Data ONTAP, version 8.2.x and earlier supported krb5, version 8.3.x supported both krb5 and krb5i (which provides support for data integrity), and version 9 supports krb5, krb5i, and krb5p. However, vSphere 6.0 supports only krb5, and vSphere 6.5 adds support for krb5i. vSphere 6.x does not support krb5p because it does not support pNFS.

At this writing, EMC Unity 4.0.x does not support Kerberos authentication with NFSv4.1. However, you can still mount NFSv4.1 volumes with AUTH_SYS security.

ESXi Kerberos 5 Components

Authentication via Kerberos 5 goes through several ESX components that communicate with AD, VC, the ESXi host, and the NFS server. Figure 16.36 shows all the involved components and entities, as well as the logical path in establishing a security context per RPC operations. In this diagram, numbers in dark circles on dotted arrows are for security context establishment. Numbers in white circles on continuous arrows are for specific RPC operations.

The numbers in Figure 16.36 indicate the following:

1. The user name (U) and password are set via vSphere Web Client per host. The API call to set them is sent from VC to hostd, which forwards it to the NFSv4.1 vmkernel module, where it is saved to the corresponding configuration files.

2. When a VM issues I/O on a VMDK residing on an NFSv4.1 datastore, the host needs to authenticate with the NFS server. The request is eventually sent to the NFSv4.1 vmkernel module.

3. To initiate the process of establishing the security context, NFSv4.1 sends the stored user name (U) and password to the RPCSEC vmkernel module.

4. The RPCSEC module sends the call to KGSSAPI, which is the Generic Security Service API vmkernel module.

5. KGSSAPI sends a call to GSSD, which is a user space daemon.

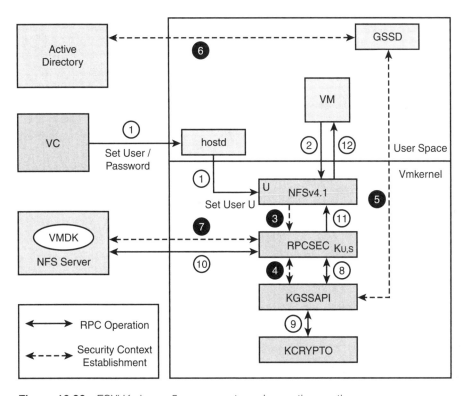

Figure 16.36 ESXi Kerberos 5 components and operations path

6. GSSD sends the request for a Ticket-Granting-Ticket (TGT) to the KDC on AD. The KDC looks up the user's credentials and returns a TGT to the host for the user. The TGT is returned from GSSD to KGSSAPI, which forwards the credentials back to RPCSEC. RPCSEC then decrypts the TGT, using the user's password, and sends it back to AD via GSSD. AD responds with the service ticket.

7. RPCSEC sends the access request along with the service ticket to the NFS server, and the NFS server does Kerberos-to-UNIX name mapping to identify the UNIX user name configured on the NFS server. After successfully authenticating the user's SPN, the NFS server allows access for the user. A successful operation results in the establishment of the security context by RPCSEC. From this point on, future RPC operations use the established security context, which is also used by shared sessions between the host and the NFS server.

8. The security context is sent back to KGSSAPI via an RPC operation.

9. The RPC operation that was sent by the VM earlier is now ready to proceed on to the KCRYPTO module to encrypt the RPC header with the configured Kerberos encryption type (etype).

10. The NFS server responds to RPCSEC with the requested RPC operation.

11. RPCSEC sends the response to NFSv4.1.

12. NFSv4.1sends the response to the calling VM, which completes the RPC operation.

Configuring a NetApp Filer for NFSv4.1

The following sections describe almost end-to-end configuration via the Clustered Data ONTAP CLI as well as the UI. (See NetApp KB 1015522, at https://kb.netapp.com/support/index?page=content&id=1015522 and TR4073 www.netapp.com/us/media/tr-4073.pdf.)

Creating an NFSv4.1 Storage VM (SVM) on a NetApp Filer by Using the CLI

This section assumes that you have already created the root aggregate that you will use with the SVM. This example uses the following parameters:

- **SVM Name**—NFSv41
- **Root Volume Name**—NFSv41_root
- **Root Aggregate**—Data
- **AD Domain**—book.local
- **AD Domain Controller Name**—win2008
- **Cluster Name**—Book-Cluster
- **Cluster Node 1 name**—Book-Cluster-01
- **Cluster Node 2 name**—Book-Cluster-02

You can substitute your own values for these.

To create NFSv4.1 SVM on a NetApp filer using the CLI, follow this procedure.

1. Log on with Administrator privileges or equivalent to a NetApp filer by using SSH to the management IP address.

2. Create an SVM and a root volume:

```
vserver create -vserver NFSv41 -rootvolume NFSv41_root -aggregate Data
-rootvolume-security-style unix -language C.UTF-8 -snapshot-policy
default -is-repository false -ipspace Default
```

3. Modify the NFS protocol to enable NFSv4.1:

```
vserver nfs create -vserver NFSv41 -access true -v4.1 enabled
```

4. If you will use LACP, create an interface group (otherwise, it's optional):

```
ifgrp create -node Book-Cluster-01 -ifgrp a0a -distr-func ip -mode
multimode_lacp
```

5. Assign ports to the group (which is optional unless the group was created):

```
ifgrp add-port -node Book-Cluster-01 -ifgrp a0a -port e0g
ifgrp add-port -node Book-Cluster-01 -ifgrp a0a -port e0h
```

Chaining the port names in one command does not seem to work on Data ONTAP 9RC. So you may need to repeat the command for each port to add, as shown here.

6. Create a broadcast domain if you created the interface group and you will enable jumbo frames. Otherwise, you may substitute the interface port name with an available port name (for example, instead of a0a, use e0c or e0d) on each cluster node:

```
broadcast-domain create -broadcast-domain <broadcast domain name> -mtu
<integer> -ipspace <IPspace> -ports <<node>:<port>>, ...]
broadcast-domain create -broadcast-domain 10.10.0.0/24 -mtu 9000
-ipspace Default -ports Book-Cluster-01:a0a,Book-Cluster-02:a0a
```

7. Create the data logical interface (LIF):

```
network interface create -vserver NFSv41 -lif NFSv41_nfs_lif1
-role data -home-node Book-Cluster-01 -home-port e0b -address
10.10.0.49 -netmask 255.255.255.0
```

In this example, I am not using interface groups. If you do, use the group name, such as a0a, with the -home-port parameter.

8. Create an export policy for the SVM root vol:

```
vserver export-policy create -vserver NFSv41 -policyname NFSv41_root_
policy
```

9. Create a rule for the root export policy:

```
export-policy rule create -vserver NFSv41 -policyname NFSv41_root_
policy -protocol nfs4 -clientmatch 0.0.0.0/0 -rorule krb5 -rwrule
never -anon 0 -superuser krb5 -ruleindex 1
```

10. Assign the root policy to the root volume:

```
vol modify -vserver NFSv41 -volume NFSv41_root -policy NFSv41_root_
policy
```

This is the output of this command:

```
Volume modify successful on volume NFSv41_root of Vserver NFSv41.
```

11. If you're using vSphere 6.0 without any updates, which supports DES/3DES encryption type only, modify encryption:

```
nfs modify -vserver NFSv41 -permitted-enc-types des,des3
nfs show -vserver NFSv41 -fields permitted-enc-types
vserver permitted-enc-types
------- ------------------
NFSv41 des,des3
```

vSphere 6.0 Update 2 and vSphere 6.5 do not support DES/3DES encryption types.

12. Enable and configure DNS on the SVM:

```
dns create -vserver NFSv41 -domains BOOK.LOCAL -name-servers
10.10.0.21 -state enabled
```

13. Create the Kerberos realm:

```
vserver nfs kerberos realm create -realm BOOK.LOCAL -kdc-vendor
Microsoft -kdc-ip 10.10.0.21 -kdc-port 88 -clock-skew 5 -adminserver-
ip 10.10.0.21 -adminserver-port 749 -passwordserver-ip 10.10.0.21
-passwordserver-port 464 -vserver NFSv41 -adserver-name WIN2008
-adserver-ip 10.10.0.21
```

14. Enable Kerberos on the data LIF:

```
vserver nfs kerberos interface enable -vserver NFSv41 -lif NFSv41_
nfs_lif1 -spn nfs/ntap9.book.local@BOOK.LOCAL -admin-username
administrator
```

When you are prompted for the AD admin password, if you enter it on the command line, it will fail, and you will get a message to remove the password from the command.

The command in step 14 registers the array in AD as NFS-NTAP9-BOOK.

Proceed to the section **"Preparing ESXi Hosts for Kerberos Authentication,"** later in this chapter.

Creating an NFSv4.1 Storage VM (SVM) on a NetApp Filer by Using the UI

To create the same SVM used in the previous section via the UI, you can use the NetApp OnCommand System Manager UI for Data ONTAP 9, as described in the following sections. For Data ONTAP 8.2.3, the steps are similar, with minor UI differences (for example, in version 9, there is no tree structure on the left-hand side of the UI).

The order of the steps is a bit different when using the UI than when using the CLI. If you plan on creating the network interface group and broadcast domain, do that before creating the SVM. If do not plan on creating them, skip to the "Creating an NFS4.1 SVM and Its Root Volume" section, later in this chapter.

Creating an Interface Group and Assigning Ports

To provide NFS4.1 multipathing, vSphere 6 uses session trunking; however, configuring an Interface port group on the NetApp server would also add high availability on the filer's end, utilizing LACP. To create an interface group you can follow this procedure, assuming that you have already logged on to NetApp OnCommand System Manager with Administrator privileges:

1. Select the **Network** tab (see Figure 16.37).

2. Select the **Ethernet Ports** tab.

3. Click **Create Interface Group**.

4. Select the node on which to create this group.

5. Enter the Interface Group Name. The default for the first group is **a0a**.

6. Select two or more ports from the listed ports (for example, **e0g** and **e0h**).

7. Select **LACP** in the Mode section.

8. Select **IP based** in the Load Distribution section.

9. Do not select the broadcast domain at this time. Click the **Create** button.

Figure 16.37   Creating an interface group

Repeat steps 1 through 9 for each node in the cluster.

Creating a Broadcast Domain

This section shows how to create a broadcast domain and assign the interface group on each node to it. After you have logged on to NetApp OnCommand System Manager with Administrator privileges, follow these steps:

1. Select the **Network** tab (see Figure 16.38).

2. Select the **Broadcast Domains** tab.

3. Click **Create**.

4. Enter the broadcast domain name.

5. Enter the MTU size. It is recommended to use jumbo frames if your network supports them. If so, enter **9000**. Otherwise, enter **1500**.

6. Select an IPspace setting. In this example, I selected **Default**.

7. Select the interface group created in the previous section. In this example, it is **a0a**. Once it is selected, all nodes in the cluster configured with this interface group name get selected automatically. If you do not plan on using interface groups, select one or more available ports on each cluster node.

8. Click the **Create** button.

Figure 16.38   Creating a broadcast domain

Creating an NFS4.1 SVM and Its Root Volume

Next, you create the SVM for NFSv4.1 protocol:

1. Log on to the NetApp OnCommand System Manager with Administrator privileges.

2. Navigate to the **SVM** section of the UI.

3. Click the **Create New Storage Virtual Machine** button (labeled **Create**).

   The first step in the wizard that appears is a dialog where you enter the SVM basic details. (See Figure 16.39 for steps 4 through 12.)

4. Enter **NFSv41** as the SVM name (see Figure 16.39).

5. Because I did not create a custom IPspace, the default is selected and grayed out in this example. Otherwise, the option would be available to select from a pull-down list.

6. Select the **FlexVol volumes** volume type. The FlexVol volumes choice enables the SVM to contain multiple volumes, whereas Infinite Volume allows only a single one.

7. Select **NFS** as the data protocol.

8. Select **C.UTF-8** as the default language.

9. Select **UNIX** as the security style.

10. If you have created more than one root aggregate, select one. If you have a single root aggregate, it will be selected by default.

11. Enter the DNS configuration at this step because it is required for Kerberos support.

12. Click the **Submit & Continue** button.

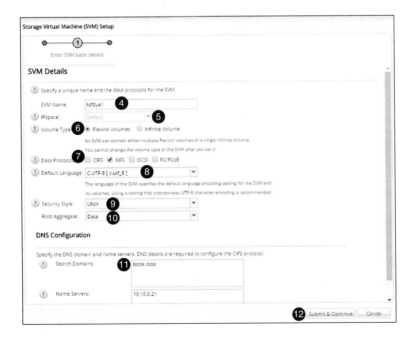

Figure 16.39   The Create SVM Wizard, step 1

In the second step of the wizard, Configure NFS protocol, enter the Data LIF Configuration.

13. If you created subnet configurations earlier, select the subnet for this configuration and skip to step 15. Otherwise, select the **Without a subnet** option from the Assign IP Address pull-down menu.

14. In the Add Details dialog that pops up, enter the IP address, subnet mask, and, optionally, gateway address, and then click **OK** (see Figure 16.40).

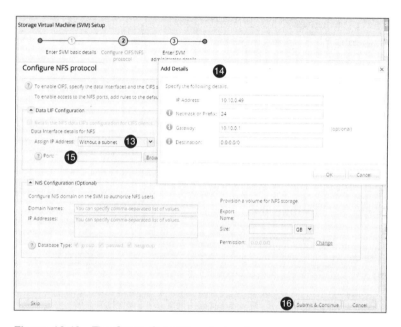

Figure 16.40   The Create SVM Wizard, step 2

15. Select a port by clicking **Browse** and picking a port from one of the cluster nodes if you have a cluster configured or from the single node, such as **e0c**. Alternatively, if you configured interface groups, select one, such as **a0a**. Click **OK** (see Figure 16.41).

16. Click the **Submit & Continue** button.

17. In the final step of the wizard, enter a password for the SVM admin and click the **Submit & Close** button. There is no need to create a new LIF for NFS SVM management because the data LIF already has management enabled by default.

Figure 16.41 Selecting an SVM's ports

TIP

If your design calls for separating the management network from the storage network or if you plan to delegate NFS volume creation, it is advisable to configure a management LIF separate from the data LIF and enable management on the former.

---

18. Review the summary screen, which shows the SVM and NFS configuration details. It also shows that the SVM administrator password was modified. Click **Close**.

In these 18 steps, you did the following:

- Created an SVM named NFSv41.

- Configured DNS properties.

- Created a data logical interface (LIF) named after the SVM, which in this example is NFSv41_lif_1. This LIF port is an interface group named a0a on cluster node 1 or, if you do not use interface groups, one of the node's ports, such as **e0c**.

- Created a SVM root volume, which in this example is called NFS41_root.

The only remaining step for configuring the SVM is to enable NFSv4.1 on it.

19. Navigate to the SVMs list by clicking the **SVMs** tab.

20. Select the SVM from the list.

21. Click the **NFS** hyperlink in the Details pane. This is a shortcut to the SVM Settings menu (see Figure 16.42).

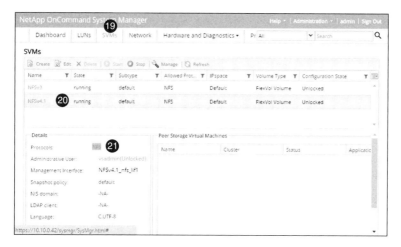

Figure 16.42   Accessing SVM settings

Make sure the SVM name is selected on the top-left corner and that **NFS** is highlighted in the Protocols section. In this example, because the SVM has only one protocol defined, NFS is the only protocol listed.

22. Click **Edit**. The NFS Settings dialog opens.

23. Deselect the **Support version 3** check box.

24. Select the **Support version 4.1** check box.

25. Enter the default Windows user account. This is the Active Directory user account that you will create later in this chapter, in the section "Preparing AD for NFSv4.1 Kerberos Authentication." In this example, the default Windows user is `nfsclient`.

26. Click the **Save and Close** button (see Figure 16.43).

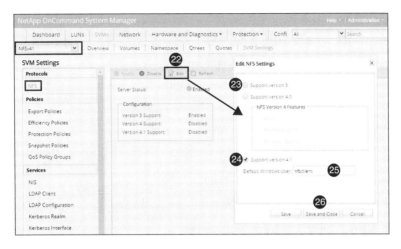

Figure 16.43   Selecting an SVM's ports

TIP

Your design must prevent concurrent access to an NFSv4.1 datastore by NFSv3 clients. To ensure this, you must configure a single NFS version in the SVM created to host NFSv4.1 volumes. This is done in steps 23 and 24 of this procedure. In other words, you need to create a separate SVM for each NFS version you want to support.

To prevent unauthorized access to NFSv4.1 volumes, you must create a default root volume policy with read-only privileges for any IP address. This privilege allows listing the NFSv4.1 shares' names but does not allow mounting or writing to them. I cover this in the next two sections.

Creating an Export Policy

The next step is to create an export policy. This procedure assumes that you have completed the previous procedures. Follow these steps:

1. Click the **SVMs** tab.

2. Click the name of the SVM under the name column in the SVMs view.

3. Click the **NFS** link in the Protocols section.

4. Click **Export Policies** link in the Policies section.

5. Click **Create**.

6. Enter a policy name.

7. In the **Export Rules** section, click **Add**. This opens the Create Export Rule dialog.

8. Enter the client specification. This is the default access policy, to which you can later add exceptions at the datastore level. In this example, the value is `0.0.0.0/0`, which means any IP address.

9. Select **NFSv4** in as the access protocol.

10. Deselect the **Read-Only** check box, which unchecks all check boxes in that column.

11. Select **Kerberos 5** in the Read-Only column.

12. Deselect the **Read/Write** check box, which unchecks all check boxes in that column.

13. Deselect the **Allow Superuser access** check box.

    The net result of these settings is that the root volume's default access is read-only to all users from any IP address using Kerberos 5. This enables all clients to list the export names that you will create later on this SVM.

14. Click **OK**.

15. Click **Create** to complete the policy creation procedure (see Figure 16.44).

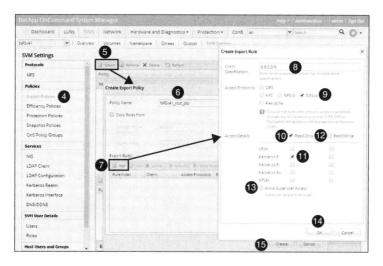

Figure 16.44   Creating an NFSv4.1 Kerberos export policy

Now you should have the new policy listed right before the default policy. Selecting the new policy displays its associated rule in the Export Rules pane. At this point, no rules are associated with it yet. See the section **"Creating a Default Export Rule,"** later in this chapter.

Assigning an Export Policy to a SVM Root Volume

The SVM root volume was assigned the default export policy when the SVM was created. To assign the new export policy to the SVM root volume, follow this procedure:

1. Continuing from the previous procedure, click the **Namespace** tab.

2. Select the root volume.

3. Click **Change Export Policy**.

4. Select the export policy from the pull-down menu.

5. Click **Change** (see Figure 16.45).

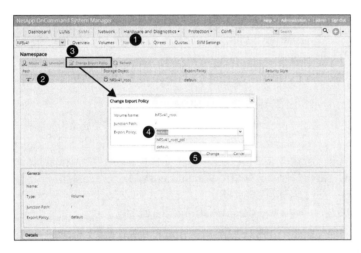

Figure 16.45   Creating an NFSv4.1 Kerberos export policy

Now the Export Policy column should list the new policy assignment.

Creating a Default Export Rule

Now that you have protected the root volume, you need to provide a default export rule associated with the default export policy to allow only hosts in your vSphere cluster read/write access to specific NFSv4.1 shares.

Follow this procedure to create the rule:

1. Navigate to the **SVMs** tab or section.

2. Click the name of the SVM under the name column in the SVMs view.

3. Click **SVM Settings**.

4. Click the **Export Policies** link in the Policies section.

5. Select a default policy.

6. In the rules pane (at the bottom), click **Add**. This opens the Create Export Rule dialog.

7. Enter the hosts' IP addresses assigned to their corresponding vmkernel port (vmknic) dedicated to the NFS storage network. Separate the addresses with commas. If you configured a subnet, you can specify it by using its network address and the subnet length (for example, 10.10.0.40/27), which is also referred to as Classless Inter-Domain Routing (CIDR) addressing. In this example, I have a few hosts, which is why I am using the actual IP addresses instead.

8. Select the **NFSv4** check box.

9. Uncheck **UNIX**, **Kerberos 5p**, and **NTLM** in both the Read-Only and Read/Write columns. If your hosts are ESXi 6.5, you can also select the **Kerberos 5i** check boxes. Otherwise, uncheck them.

Modifying Permitted Encryption Types for an SVM

For the NFSv4.1 SVM to use Kerberos 5 authentication, it needs to be configured with the highest encryption types supported by the KDC server. If the ESXi hosts are version 6.0 without any updates, they use DES and 3DES only. ESXi 6.0 Update 1 and later as well as 6.5 no longer use DES or 3DES. When the SVM is created, the default permitted encryption types are DES, DES3, AES-128, and AES-256. In this example, I use ESXi 6.5, which should be okay with the default settings here.

For an SVM named NFSv41, to enable DES and 3DES only, you can modify the SVM by using this command:

```
nfs modify -vserver NFSv41 -permitted-enc-types des,des3
```

To verify the changes, run the following command:

```
nfs show -vserver NFSv41 -fields permitted-enc-types
```

Listing 16.6 shows the output from this command.

Listing 16.6 Listing permitted encryption types after changing the default values

```
nfs show -vserver NFSv41 -fields permitted-enc-types
vserver permitted-enc-types
------- -------------------
NFSv41  des,des3
```

Listng 16.7 shows the default output for NetApp Clustered Data ONTAP 8.3.x and later

Listing 16.7   Listing permitted encryption types (unmodified default values)

```
nfs show -vserver NFSv41 -fields permitted-enc-types
vserver permitted-enc-types
------- -------------------
NFSv41  des,des3,aes-128,aes-256
```

Creating a Kerberos Realm for Windows KDC Server

An SVM needs to have a computer account created in AD to enable Kerberos 5 authentication. You therefore need to create a Kerberos 5 realm in AD.

Continuing from the previous procedure, follow these steps to create the realm by using the UI:

1. Navigate to **SVM settings** (see Figure 16.46).

2. Select the **Kerberos Realm** option in the **Services** section.

3. Click **Create**.

4. On the wizard's welcome screen, click **Next**. The basic details step is displayed.

5. Enter the Kerberos realm, which is the AD domain, in uppercase letters.

6. Enter the KDC IP address. This is usually the same as the AD domain controller (DC) IP address. Leave the KDC port set to its default value, **88**.

7. Select **Microsoft** as the KDC vendor.

8. Click **Next**.

9. The Password Server IP setting defaults to the KDC server's IP address. If it is different, enter it here.

10. Enter an AD server name. This is the DC server's name—in this example, **WIN2008**.

11. Enter the AD server IP address.

12. Click **Next**.

13. Review the Kerberos realm configuration summary. If no changes are required, click **Next**.

14. If no errors are found, a success message is displayed in the final wizard screen. Click **Finish** to exit the wizard.

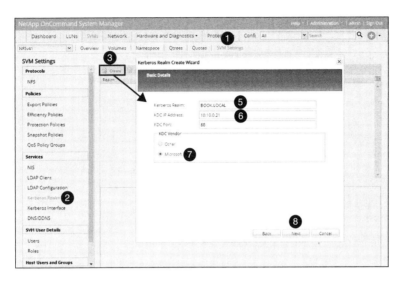

Figure 16.46   Creating an NFSv4.1 Kerberos realm

Configuring a Kerberos Interface

The previous procedure shows how to create a Kerberos realm and assign the SVM's LIF as the Kerberos interface. However, Kerberos needs be enabled on the interface for the SVM computer account to be created in AD. Follow these steps:

1. While still in the SVM settings, select the **Kerberos Interface** option in the Services section (see Figure 16.47).

2. Select the listed interface.

3. Click **Edit**.

4. Select the **Enable Kerberos** check box.

5. Select the Kerberos realm from the pull-down list.

6. In the Service Principal Name (SPN) field, enter the fully qualified domain name that matches the DNS host record (A record) that you will create later in the AD DNS server. In this example, it is in this format:

   nfs/ntap9.book.local@BOOK.LOCAL

   The prefix nfs/ and the realm are already populated in the field. All you need to do is insert the SVM server's FQDN between the slash and the @ sign, as I highlighted here.

7. Skip the Keytab URI field as it is optional for AD configuration. Enter the admin user name. This is an AD account with domain admin privileges that is capable of joining computers to the domain. In this example, it is **administrator**.

8. Enter the admin password.

9. Click **OK**.

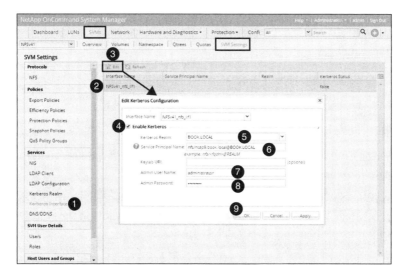

Figure 16.47   Enabling NFSv4.1 Kerberos on the interface

The end result of this procedure is that Kerberos gets enabled on the interface, and a computer account is created on AD for this interface, which represents the SVM (see the section "Creating Required DNS Records and Modifying AD Properties," later in this chapter).

Creating Additional LIFs for the NFSv4.1 SVM

To take advantage of NFSv4.1 session trunking, create additional LIFs for the SVM and repeat the last procedure for each LIF. In vSphere 6.x, the NFSv4.1 client rotates I/O on the interfaces in the trunk in a round-robin fashion, so there is no need to use DNS round-robin configuration. This means that each LIF will have a unique IP address and its corresponding AD computer account.

Creating LIFs by Using the UI

To create additional LIFs for the SVM using the UI, follow this procedure:

1. Log on to NetApp OnCommand System Manager with Administrator privileges or equivalent.

2. Select the **Network** tab (see Figure 16.48).

3. Select the **Network Interfaces** tab.

4. Click **Create** to open the Create Network Interface dialog.

5. Enter the LIF name, such as **NFSv41_nfs_lif3**.

6. Select **Serves Data** as the interface role.

7. Select the SVM from the dropdown list—for example, **NFSv41**.

8. Select the **NFS** check box as the protocol access.

9. (Optional) Select **Enable Management Access** if your design requires that. In this example, I leave it unchecked.

10. In the Assign IP Address field, select **Using a subnet** if you have already created one. Otherwise, select **Without a subnet** and enter the IP details in the Add Details dialog that appears and then click **OK** to close this dialog.

11. Select a port. In this example, I use port **e0d** on the second node in the cluster.

12. Uncheck the **Enable Dynamic DNS** option because it is disabled on the SVM.

13. Click **Create** to complete the procedure and close the Create Network Interface dialog.

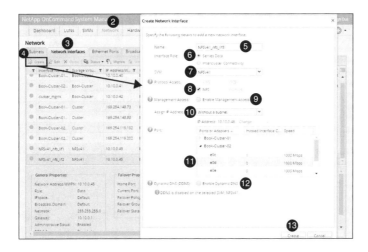

Figure 16.48   Creating an additional data interface on an SVM

14. Follow the procedure in the section "Configuring a Kerberos Interface," earlier in this chapter, to enable Kerberos on the interface and register it with the AD domain.

15. Follow the procedure in the section "Creating Required DNS Records and Modifying AD Properties," later in this chapter, for this and other LIFs of the SVM.

Creating LIFs by Using the CLI

To create LIFs using the command line, follow this procedure:

1. Log on to the NetApp server's console directly or via SSH, with Administrator privileges or equivalent.

2. Run the following:

```
network interface create -vserver <vserer-name> -lif <LIF name>
-address <IP-Address> -netmask-length <netmask-length-in-bits> -home-
port <port> -role data -data-protocol nfs -home-node <cluster-node>
-is-dns-update-enabled false
```

For example, to create a data LIF named NFSv41_nfs_lif2 on an SVM named NFSv41 using NFS protocol with IP address 10.10.0.45 and a class C IP address (24 bits), you would run this command:

```
network interface create -vserver NFSv41 -lif NFSv41_nfs_lif2 -address
10.10.0.45 -netmask-length 24 -home-port e0d -role data -data-protocol
nfs -home-node Book-Cluster-01 -is-dns-update-enabled false
```

In this example I include -is-dns-update-enabled option because I am not using dynamic DNS (DDNS).

3. Enable Kerberos on the LIF:

```
kerberos interface enable -lif <LIF-Name< -spn nfs/<LIF-
FQDN>@<Kerberos-REALM> -admin-username <AD-admin-username>
```

For example, to enable Kerberos on a LIF named NFSv4_nfs_lif2 and join the book.local AD domain with the ntap92.book.local host name, you would use this command:

```
kerberos interface enable -lif NFSv41_nfs_lif2 -spn nfs/ntap92.book.
local@BOOK.LOCAL -admin-username administrator
```

Observe that even though I do not use the -vserver option here, the command works because the LIF name is associated with the SVM I am modifying. You are prompted for the AD domain admin's password. As mentioned earlier, if you use the -admin-password option, the command refuses to work because the password is in clear text, which can pose a security risk.

4. Follow the procedure in the section "Creating Required DNS Records and Modifying AD Properties," later in this chapter, for this and other LIFs of the SVM.

Preparing ESXi Hosts for Kerberos Authentication

Before you can configure ESXi hosts for Kerberos authentication, you must first configure them with DNS and NTP to meet AD requirements.

Configuring DNS for ESXi Hosts

1. Log on to VC with Administrator privileges via vSphere 6 or 6.5 Web Client.

2. Navigate to the **Hosts and Clusters** view (see Figure 16.49).

3. Select the ESXi host in the inventory tree.

4. Select the **Manage** (or, on vSphere 6.5 Web Client, **Configure**).

5. Click the **Networking** button (or, on vSphere 6.5 Web Client, expand the **Networking** section on the left-hand side of the details pane).

6. Select the **TCP/IP configuration** section.

7. Select **Default** in the System stacks column.

8. Select the **edit** icon, which looks like a yellow penci).

9. Select the **DNS configuration** section.

10. Select the **Enter settings manually** radio button and enter DNS information in the corresponding fields.

11. Click **OK**.

Figure 16.49   Configuring a host's DNS

Configuring NTP for ESXi Hosts

Configuring ESXi hosts with NTP is identical on vSphere 6.0 and 6.5. Follow these steps:

1. Follow steps 1 through 5 in the previous section, "Configuring DNS for ESXi Hosts"

2. Select the **Time Configuration** option (see Figure 16.50).

3. Click the **Edit** button.

4. Select the **Use Network Time Protocol (Enable NTP client)** radio button.

5. Select the **Start and stop with host** option from the NTP Service Startup Policy pull-down menu.

6. Enter IP addresses or host names for one or more NTP servers, separated by commas (for example, **0.pool.ntp.org,1.pool.ntp.org**).

7. Click the **Start** button.

8. After the NTP service status changes to Running, click **OK** to close the dialog.

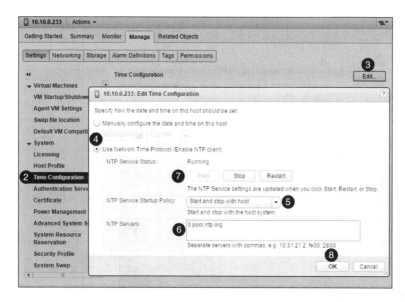

Figure 16.50   Configuring NTP on an ESXi host

9. Verify that the correct date and time are displayed in the UI. If not, verify the NTP servers' addresses.

Configuring ESXi Hosts for Kerberos Authentication

For ESXi hosts to utilize an NFSv4.1 client, they must be added to an AD domain and use Kerberos for authentication. The procedure for is identical on ESXi versions 6.0 and 6.5, where hosts can join AD via vSphere 6 Web Client using Authentication Services in the System section of the ESXi 6.0 host Manage tab or the ESXi 6.5 host Configure tab.

Configuring ESXi Hosts for Kerberos Authentication by Using vSphere 6.0 or 6.5 Web Client

To configure an ESXi host for Kerberos authentication using the UI, do the following:

1. Log on to VC 6.0 via vSphere 6 Web Client with Administrator privileges.

2. Navigate to the **Hosts and Clusters** view. (Figure 16.51 shows vSphere Web Client 6.0.)

3. Select the ESXi host from the inventory tree.

4. Select the **Manage** tab (or, on vSphere 6.5 Web Client, select the **Configure** tab). (Figure 16.52 shows vSphere Web Client 6.5.)

5. Click the **Settings** button. (On vSphere 6.5 Web Client, the Settings button does not exist. Just skip to the next step)

6. In the System section, select the **Authentication Services** option.

7. Click the **Join Domain** button.

8. Enter the domain name and a user with Administrator privileges on the AD and then click **OK**.

Figure 16.51   Joining an ESXi host to an AD domain on vSphere 6

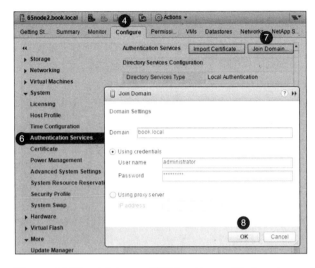

Figure 16.52   Joining an ESXi host to an AD domain on vSphere 6.5

9. Scroll to the bottom of the screen, to the **NFS Kerberos Credentials** section. (Figure 16.53 shows vSphere 6.5 Client.)

10. Click the **Edit** button.

11. Enter the user name and password for an account you will create later in this chapter, in the section "Preparing AD for NFSv4.1 Kerberos Authentication." This account will be used by `nfs4client`. It will be validated when you mount the Kerberos-authenticated NFSv4.1 datastore.

12. Click **OK**.

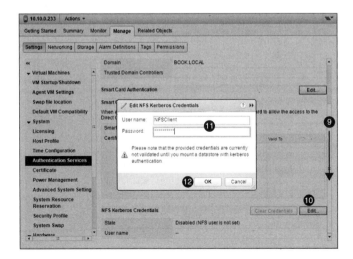

Figure 16.53   Configuring NFS Kerberos credentials

13. Repeat this procedure for each host in the cluster. Make sure to use the same NFS client's user account on all hosts.

Preparing AD for NFSv4.1 Kerberos Authentication

The other side of the coin for NFSv4.1 Kerberos authentication is the KDC server. vSphere 6.x supports only KDC provided by Microsoft Active Directory. Here is what happens when the procedures in the previous sections are done:

1. When the NetApp filer's SVM Kerberos realm is created and Kerberos is enabled on the LIF for the SVM, the SVM gets registered in AD in the Computers container. In this example, the service principal name (SPN) `nfs/ntap9.book.local@BOOK.LOCAL` and a computer named `NFS-NTAP9-BOOK` are created. This includes the SPN and related aliases. To list them, run the following in a command prompt on an AD domain controller:

```
setspn -L [Host Name as listed in AD]
```

Here is an example:

```
setspn -L NFS-NTAP9-BOOK
```

Listing 16.8 shows the command and its output.

Listing 16.8 Listing a storage server's SPN in AD

```
setspn -L NFS-NTAP9-BOOK
Registered ServicePrincipalNames for CN=NFS-NTAP9-BOOK,CN=Computers,
DC=book,DC=local:
        nfs/ntap9.book.local
        nfs/nfs-ntap9-book.book.local
        nfs/NFS-NTAP9-BOOK
        HOST/nfs-ntap9-book.book.local
        HOST/NFS-NTAP9-BOOK
```

2. When an ESXi host joins the AD domain, a computer account is created in the Computers container as well. However, its SPN is a bit different from that of the storage server. Listing 16.9 shows the SPN's details.

Listing 16.9 Listing an ESXi host's SPN in AD

```
setspn -L 65Node1
Registered ServicePrincipalNames for
CN=65NODE1,CN=Computers,DC=book,DC=local:
        HOST/65node1
        HOST/65node1.book.local
```

Observe that the `nfs` prefix is not included because this is not an NFS server.

Now that you understand what was added to the AD domain, you can proceed with making the necessary configuration changes to the corresponding AD objects.

Configuring AD for UNIX Identity Management

Before you proceed to creating an AD user that will be used for Kerberos authentication, you need to configure UNIX Identity Management on AD. Follow these steps:

> **NOTE**
>
> This example was created on Windows Server 2008 R2. Windows 2012/2012R2 has a different UI but has roughly the same high-level steps.

1. Log on to AD with Administrator privileges or equivalent.

2. Launch **Server Manager**.

3. Select **Roles** (see Figure 16.54).

4. Scroll down to display the **Roles Services** section.

5. Select the **Identity Management for UNIX** role service.

6. Click **Add Role Services**.

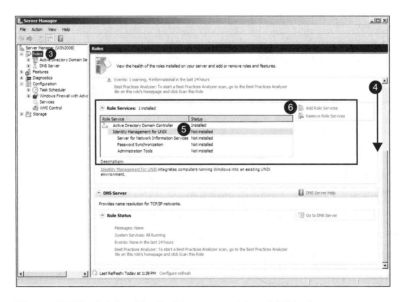

Figure 16.54   Adding Identity Management for a UNIX role

7. Select the **Identity Management for UNIX** check box. The options **Server for Network Information Services**, **Password Synchronization** and **Administrative Tools** are automatically selected.

8. Click **Next**.

9. At the confirmation step, click **Install**.

10. The progress step displays the progress of the installation process. When it is done, the Results step shows that the Windows server needs to be restarted. Click **Close**.

11. Reboot the server when you can schedule a downtime.

12. After rebooting, the installation results should show that the installation succeeded (see Figure 16.55). Click **Close**.

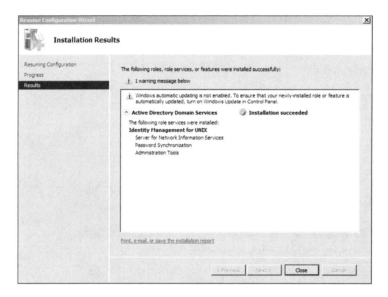

Figure 16.55   Adding Identity Management for a UNIX role — conclusion

Creating Required DNS Records and Modifying AD Properties

The next task is to create DNS records for the NFS server and all ESXi hosts that joined the AD domain. Both forward and reverse lookup records must be created because Kerberos requires them. Follow these steps:

NOTE

vSphere 6.x NFS4 Client does not require Kerberos Master SRV records.

1. In the DNS server used by AD, create DNS A (host) and PTR (Pointer or Reverse Lookup) records for each ESXi host and storage server added to the domain. The DNS A record must match that of the host name, as listed in the `setspn -L` command output. For example, if the SPN is called `HOST/65node.book.local`, create the A record in the `book.local` DNS forward lookup zone.

   For the NFS server's host name, use the first line in `setspn -L`, which, in this example, is `nfs/ntap9.book.local`, without the service prefix `nfs/`. In this example, the host name would be `ntap9.book.local`.

   You can automatically create the PTR record during the creation of the A record by selecting the **Create associated pointer (PTR) record** check box (see Figure 16.56).

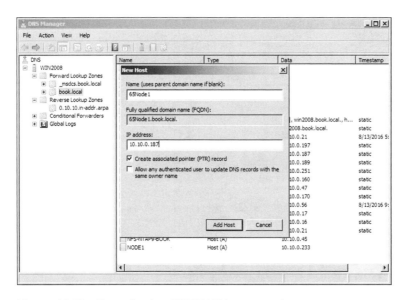

Figure 16.56   Example of an ESXi DNS host record

2. Modify the NetApp storage server's AD account to specify the supported encryption type supported by the NetApp Clustered Data ONTAP firmware version. To do that, follow these steps:

   a. Launch the **Active Directory Users and Computers** management snap-in for the AD domain.

   b. Click **View** and then select the **Advanced Features** menu option to enable the Attribute Editor tab.

c. Navigate to the **Computers** container.

d. Double-click the storage server's account.

e. Select the **Attribute Editor** tab.

f. Scroll down until you locate the `msDS-SupportedEncryptionTypes` atribute and double-click it.

g. For Data ONTAP version 8.2.x or earlier, enter **0x3** in the Value field. This is the hex value representing the required encryption types, `DES_CBC_CRC| DES_CBC_MD5` (see Figure 16.57).

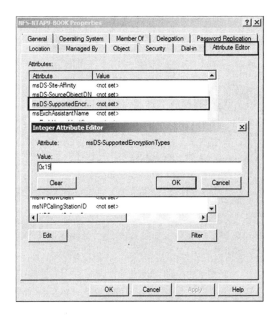

Figure 16.57   Modifying supported encryption types in an AD account (3DES)

h. For Data ONTAP version 8.3 or later (including 9.0), enter **0x1F**. This is the hex value representing the required encryption types, `DES_CBC_CRC| DES_CBC_MD5|RC4_HMAC_MD5|AES128_CTS_HMAC_SHA1_96|AES256_CTS_HMAC_SHA1_96`.

i. Click **OK** and then click **OK** again (see Figure 16.58).

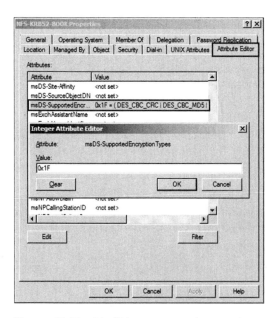

Figure 16.58   Modifying supported encryption types in an AD account (AES)

For other vendors' NFS servers, check with the corresponding vendor for the required encryption types. Some vendors, such as EMC Unity, create the required type automatically.

NOTE

EMC Unity, when configured with LDAP, creates the computer account in the EMC NAS Servers\Computers container.

Repeat steps d through i for each ESXi host's record, matching the encryption types to the ESXi version on each host. For example, use the value **0x3** for ESXi 6.0 and the value **0x1F** for ESXi 6.0 Update 1 and later, including ESXi 6.5.

3. Verify that the storage server as well as all ESXi hosts are configured with the same DNS server's IP address as the AD domain's DNS server.

4. Verify that the NFS storage server as well as all ESXi hosts and VC server are configured with the same NTP servers' IP addresses.

> **TIP**
>
> Use the AD domain controller's host name or IP address as the NTP server's address to guarantee that VC, ESXi, and the storage server are in sync with the KDC server.

Creating an AD User Account for Kerberos Authentication

The next task is to create the AD user account that will be used by ESXi hosts and NFS storage servers to authenticate to AD with Kerberos 5 authentication. This procedure continues from the previous procedure (steps 1 through 4).

5. Navigate to the **Users** container or wherever container your design calls for using to store the service account. This is the account you specified on ESXi as well as the storage server's NFSv4.1-related configurations.

6. Click the **Create New User** icon.

7. Enter the user's first, last, and login names in the corresponding fields.

8. Click **Next**.

9. Enter the user's password in both the **Password** and **Confirm password** fields.

10. Deselect the **User must change password at next logon** check box.

11. Select the **Password never expires** check box.

12. Click **Next**.

13. Click **Finish**.

14. Locate the newly created user in the list of users and double-click it.

15. Click the **Account** tab.

16. For NetApp Data ONTAP 8.2.x and earlier, scroll down the Account options pane until you see **Use Kerberos DES encryption types for this account** check box and select it (see Figure 16.59).

> **NOTE**
>
> Because vSphere 6.0 without Update 1 does not support Kerberos encryption types higher than 3DES, the only possible option is the one shown in step 16. If your host has vSphere 6.0 Update 1 or later, including 6.5, installed, skip to step 17 instead and make sure the NetApp Clustered Data ONTAP firmware version is 8.3.x or higher.

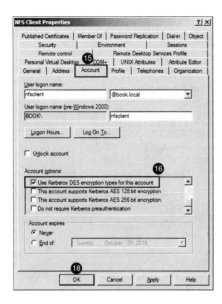

Figure 16.59 Creating a new AD user account

17. For NetApp Clustered Data ONTAP 8.3.x and later, including 9.0, select the **This account supports Kerberos AES 128 bit encryption** and/or **This account support Kerberos AES 256 bit encryption** options instead.

18. Click **OK** to save the changes and close the dialog (see Figure 16.60).

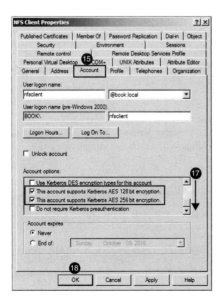

Figure 16.60 Configuring AD user account for Kerberos AES encryption.

19. Create an AD security group named ESX Admins and add the user to it. This will prevent a common error message from being posted to ESXi hosts' syslog files.

Creating Kerberos-to-UNIX User Name Mapping

NetApp Clustered Data ONTAP firmware includes an implicit user named nfs that is used for NFSv4.1 Kerberos authentication. This user has a default name mapping to the NFSv4.1 SVM LIF. To list this mapping, follow these steps:

1. Log on to the NetApp Clustered Data ONTAP console directly or via SSH with Administrator privileges or equivalent.

2. Identify the LIF's SPN by using the following:

```
kerberos interface show -fields spn -vserver <SVM>
```

Here is an example:

```
kerberos interface show -fields spn -vserver NFSv41
```

3. Enable diagnostic commands by using the following:

```
set diagnostic
```

or this:

```
set diag
```

Then confirm that you want to continue. The prompt shows an asterisk (*) after the cluster name prompt (for example, Book-cluster::*>).

4. Run this command:

```
diag secd name-mapping show -node <cluster-node-name> -vserver <SVM>
-direction krb-unix -name <SPN obtained from step 2>
```

Here is an example:

```
Book-Cluster::*> diag secd name-mapping show -node Book-Cluster-01
-vserver NFSv41 -direction krb-unix -name nfs/ntap9.book.local@BOOK.
LOCAL
```

Omitting the Kerberos realm from the SPN should also work.

Listing 16.10 shows the commands from this procedure and their output.

Listing 16.10   Listing a storage server LIF's SPN in a NetApp Clustered Data ONTAP console

```
login as: admin
Using keyboard-interactive authentication.
Password:
```

```
Book-Cluster::> kerberos interface show -fields spn -vserver NFSv41
  (vserver nfs kerberos interface show)
vserver lif             spn
------- --------------- -------------------------------
NFSv41  NFSv41_nfs_lif1 nfs/ntap9.book.local@BOOK.LOCAL
NFSv41  NFSv41_nfs_lif2 nfs/ntap92.book.local@BOOK.LOCAL
NFSv41  NFSv41_nfs_lif3 nfs/ntap93.book.local@BOOK.LOCAL
3 entries were displayed.


Book-Cluster::> set diag

Warning: These diagnostic commands are for use by NetApp personnel only.
Do you want to continue? {y|n}: y


Book-Cluster::*> diag secd name-mapping show -node Book-Cluster-01 -vserver
NFSv41 -direction krb-unix -name nfs/ntap9.book.local@BOOK.LOCAL

'nfs/ntap9.book.local@BOOK.LOCAL' maps to 'nfs'
```

TIP

The user name nfs is derived from the SPN's service prefix nfs/. If you experiment with
typing any random SPN with any other prefix, such as host/, the user name mapping returned is host. In other words, as long as the service prefix for the SPN is nfs/, the implied
user name mapping will always be nfs.

If your design calls for using a specific account, you can create an AD user account and
map it to the corresponding a UNIX account that you create on the storage server. In this
example, I use nfsclient as the user name.

Identity Management for UNIX, installed in the **"Configuring AD for UNIX Identity
Management"** section, earlier in this chapter, adds the UNIX Attributes tab to the AD
object properties. For Kerberos authentication to succeed, the designated AD user account,
created in the previous section, needs to be known to the NFS server. You can ensure that
by using Kerberos-to-UNIX user mapping, which needs to be done in two places:

- AD, where you configure the UNIX attributes of the user account
- NetApp OnCommand System Manager, where you define the user mapping

Configuring the UNIX Attributes of the AD User Account

To configure the UNIX attributes of the AD user account (named `nfsclient` in this example), follow this procedure:

1. Log on to the AD domain controller with Administrator privileges or equivalent and launch the **Active Directory Users and Computers** tool.

2. Navigate to the **Users** container or the corresponding container in which you created the user.

3. Locate the user account and double-click it.

4. Select the **UNIX Attributes** tab (see Figure 16.61).

5. Select the Active Directory domain from the NIS Domain dropdown list.

6. Select **ESX Admins** as the primary group name. This is the same group to which the AD user was added earlier. (NetApp Clustered Data ONTAP does not provide a facility for mapping groups from AD to UNIX.)

7. Take note of the value in the UID field, which you will need in the next section, "Configuring Kerberos-to-UNIX Name Mapping on an NFS Server."

8. Click **OK** to save the changes and exit the dialog.

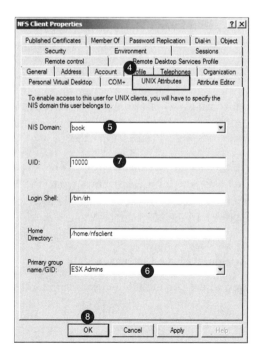

Figure 16.61   Configuring AD user account's Unix Attributes

Configuring Kerberos-to-UNIX Name Mapping on an NFS Server

Next you need to move on to the NFS server to configure a mapping for the AD user account. Follow these steps:

1. Log on to NetApp OnCommand System Manager with Administrator privileges or equivalent.

2. Navigate to the list of SVMs.

3. Select the SVM you created for the NFSv4.1 protocol. In this example, the SVM name is `NFSv41`.

4. Select the **SVM Settings** option (see Figure 16.62).

5. Select the **UNIX** option in the Host Users and Groups section.

6. Select the **Users** tab.

7. Click **Add User**.

8. In the dialog that appears, enter the user name (for example, `nfsclient`).

9. Enter the user ID which you obtained in step 7 of the preceding section, " Configuring the UNIX Attributes of the AD User Account." In this example, it is 10000.

10. Select **nobody** from the Group Name pull-down list.

11. Click **Add** to finish creating the user account.

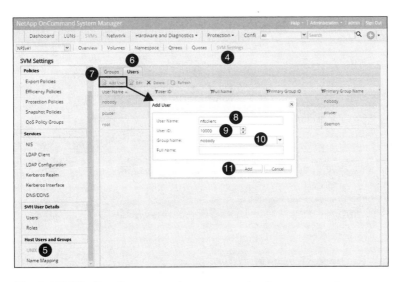

Figure 16.62   Creating a new storage server host user account

12. Select **Name Mapping** option in the Host Users and Groups section (see Figure 16.63).

13. Click **Add**. The Add Name Mapping Entry dialog appears.

14. Select **Kerberos to UNIX** from the Direction pull-down list.

15. Leave the Position field's value as **1**.

16. In the Pattern field enter the NFS Server's SPN, obtained earlier under Listing 16.10, suffixed with the Kerberos realm. In this example, the server's SPN is `nfs/ntap9.book.local@BOOK.LOCAL`, which also matches the DNS record for this host (without the service prefix nfs/). The value entered in this field can be without the realm suffix (for example, `nfs/ntap9.book.local`).

17. In the Replacement field, enter the user name created earlier in this procedure. In this example, the user name is `nfsclient`.

18. Click **Add** to finish creating the name mapping entry.

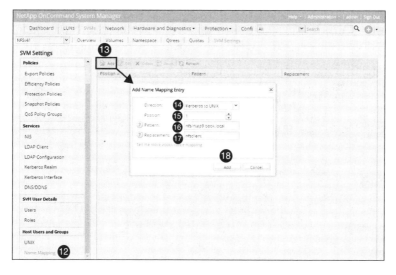

Figure 16.63   Creating a Kerberos-to-UNIX name mapping entry

19. Repeat steps 12 through 18 for each LIF's SPN of this SVM.

Enabling Relevant Kerberos Encryption Types

The next task is to ensure that AD supports Kerberos encryption types matching those supported by the ESXi host and NFS server combination. The relevant Kerberos encryption types will vary based on the vSphere version and the storage server's firmware version.

If the KDC server is provided by Windows Server 2008 R2 or later, Kerberos authentication does not support DES encryption types by default. To use it with NFSv4.1 Kerberos authentication, you need to manually enable DES and 3DES. Follow this procedure to accomplish this task:

1. Log on to the AD DC with Administrator privileges or equivalent.

2. Launch the Group Policy Editor (gpedit.msc).

3. Navigate to **Forest**, **Domains**, **<domain FQDN>**, **Default Domain Policy** and right-click. Then select the **Edit** option.

3. Navigate to **Computer Configuration**, **Policies**, **Windows Settings**, **Security Settings**, **Local Policies**, **Security Options**.

4. Locate the policy named **Network security: Configure encryption types allowed for Kerberos** and double-click it (see Figure 16.64).

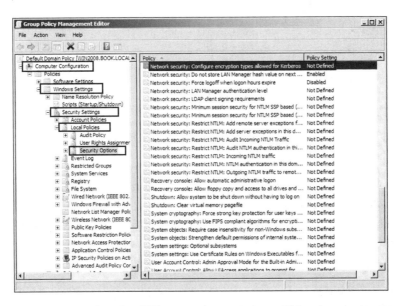

Figure 16.64   Enabling DES encryption types in an AD local computer account

> **NOTE**
>
> You need to enable only the highest encryption type required by both the vSphere and NFS server's configurations.

5. Select the **DES_CBC_CRC** and **DES_CBC_MD5** check boxes or, if your environment requires higher encryption types, select **AES128_HMAC_SHA1** and **AES256_HMAC_SHA1** instead.

6. Click **OK** (see Figure 16.65).

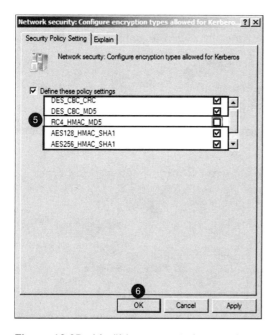

Figure 16.65   Modifying supported encryption types in an AD account

Verifying Client Authentication with Kerberos Encryption

Before attempting to mount NFSv4.1 datastores using the Kerberos authentication method, here is a quick method for verifying whether the client will log on successfully to the AD and obtain the relevant ticket from the KDC:

1. Log on to the ESXi host's shell via SSH or directly on the host's console.

2. Run the `klist -e` command, which should return blank output because the client has not attempted to log on to the AD yet.

3. To manually log on, run `kinit <username>` (for example, `kinit nfsclient`).

4. Enter the user's password. If logon is successful, no feedback is provided. If logon fails, an error message is displayed.

5. Run `klist -e` again. This time, you should see output similar to that shown in Listing 16.11

Listing 16.11 Verifying authentication with Kerberos encryption

```
[root@65Node1:~] klist -e
[root@65Node1:~] kinit nfsclient
Password for nfsclient@BOOK.LOCAL:

[root@65Node2:~] kinit -V
Using principal: nfsclient@BOOK.LOCAL
Password for nfsclient@BOOK.LOCAL:
Authenticated to Kerberos v5

[root@65Node1:~] klist -e
Ticket cache: FILE:/tmp/krb5cc_0
Default principal: nfsclient@BOOK.LOCAL
Valid starting Expires Service principal
09/02/2016 04:25:22 09/02/2016 14:25:22 krbtgt/BOOK.LOCAL@BOOK.LOCAL
renew until 09/03/2016 04:25:21, Etype (skey, tkt): arcfour-hmac,
arcfour-hmac
```

If any of these commands return errors, double-check the AD configurations and try again.

Now that you are done with the required configurations, you can proceed to creating NFSv4.1 datastores.

Creating an NFSv4.1 Datastore on a NetApp Filer

To create an NFSv4.1 datastore on a NetApp filer, do the following:

1. Log on to NetApp OnCommand System Manager with Administrator privileges.

2. Navigate to the **SVMs** section. On version 9, the various sections are tabs at the top of the page.

3. Click the SVM's link in the Name column (see Figure 16.66). (On 8.x, the SVMs are listed on the left-hand side, in a tree structure.)

Figure 16.66 Accessing the NFSv4.1 SVM properties

4. Select the **Volumes** section (see Figure 16.67).

5. Click **Create** to launch the Create Volume wizard.

6. Enter the volume's name.

7. Click the **Choose** button to select the aggregate for this volume.

8. Leave the **NAS** storage type radio button selected.

9. Specify the total size and the size unit.

10. If you plan on taking snapshots of this volume, specify a value for the Snapshot Reserve (%)option.

11. If your design calls for utilizing thin provisioning for this volume, select the **Thin Provisioned** check box.

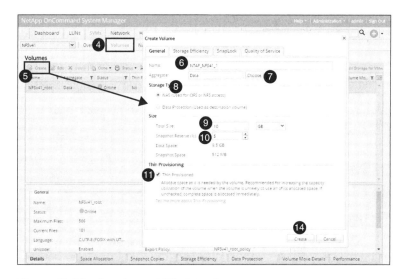

Figure 16.67   Creating an NFSv4.1 volume

12. If your design calls for utilizing data deduplication, select the **Storage Efficiency** tab. Otherwise, skip to step 14.

13. Select the **Background Deduplication** check box.

14. Click **Create** to complete the operation.

Assigning an Export Policy to a New Volume

All newly created volumes are assigned the default export policy. If your design requires using custom export policies, follow the procedure in the section "Assigning an Export Policy to a SVM Root Volume," earlier in this chapter, but with a few minor differences:

1. Select the newly created volume instead of the root volume.

2. Select the custom export policy you created for the corresponding share or shares.

Mounting an NFSv4.1 Datastore

Mounting an NFSv4.1 datastore is similar to manually mounting an NFSv3 datastore with the difference that the choice of NFS 4.1 client as well as Kerberos are available as options. The datastore can be mounted via the ESX host's CLI or via vSphere 6 or 6.5 Web Client.

You need to know the following properties before you can manually mount an NFSv4.1 datastore:

- The volume nam,e as defined on the storage server

- One or more of the SVM's port IP addresses

- The authentication method configured for the volume

Using vSphere 6 or 6.5 Web Client to Mount an NFSv4.1 Datastore

The process of mounting an NFSv4.1 datastore via vSphere 6 or 6.5 Web Client is almost identical to the process used to mount an NFSv3 datastore, with a few differences.

By using the following procedure, you can mount the datastore on a vSphere 6.x cluster instead of a single ESXi 6.x host. The procedure for mounting it on a cluster is similar, with the difference that the starting point is the cluster object instead of the host object. Also, it mounts the datastore on all hosts or selected hosts in the cluster. Follow these steps:

1. Log on to vSphere 6 or 6.5 Web Client with Administrator privileges or equivalent.

2. Navigate to the **Hosts and Clusters** view.

3. Right-click the cluster on which to mount the datastore and then select **Storage**, **New Datastore**.

4. At step 1, Location, the cluster is already selected, so click **Next**.

5. Select **NFS** as the datastore type and then click **Next**.

6. Select **NFS 4.1** as the NFS version.

7. Enter the datastore name (see Figure 16.68).

8. Enter the NFS 4.1 share name in the Folder field. This is the NFS volume's mount point on the storage server.

9. Enter the port IP addresses or host names of one or more NAS servers. If you make multiple entries, separate them with commas. Alternatively, enter one address at a time and then click the plus icon on the right end of the Server(s) field. This adds the server addresses to the list. Figure 16.68 shows two addresses already in the list and a third one in the Server(s) field.

10. If you need to mount the datastore for read-only access, check the **Mount NFS as read-only** check box.

11. Click **Next**.

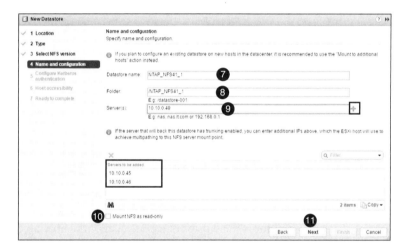

Figure 16.68   Mounting an NFSv4.1 volume: Entering the name and configuration

12. To use Kerberos authentication, select the **Enable Kerberos-based authentication** check box (see Figure 16.69).

13. Select the **Use Kerberos for authentication only (krb5)** radio button. In vSphere 6.0, this is the only option displayed. However, vSphere 6.5 introduces a new feature of using Kerberos for data integrity as well. If you are using vSphere 6.5 and your design calls for using this new feature and the storage server supports it, along

with Kerberos authentication, select **Use Kerberos for authentication and data integrity (krb5)** radio button instead. If the host is ESXi 6.0 and managed by VC 6.5, this option is shown but grayed out.

14. Click **Next**.

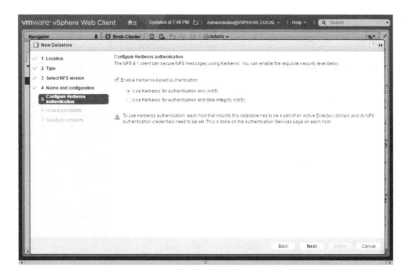

Figure 16.69   Mounting an NFSv4.1 volume: Selecting authentication

15. In the Host accessibility step, select hosts in the cluster on which to mount the datastore and then click **Next**.

16. In the Ready to complete step, review your selections and then click **Finish**. If the operation is successful, you see this indicated in the recent tasks pane.

17. To explore the datastore properties, navigate to the **Storage** view (see Figure 16.70).

18. Select the datastore in the inventory tree.

19. Select the **Summary** tab. Here you see in the details section the IP addresses of the storage server ports.

20. For another view of these addresses, select the **Configure** tab. On vSphere 6.0 Web Client, select the **Manage** tab instead.

21. Select **Device Backing**. Here you should see the IP addresses of the storage server ports and the NFS volume's folder name.

Figure 16.70   Viewing the device backing of an NFSv4.1 datastore

Using `esxcli` to Mount an NFSv4.1 Datastore

You need to complete this procedure on each host in the cluster that will share the datastore:

1. Log on to the ESXi host's console directly or via SSH as a root user.

2. Run this command:

```
esxcli storage nfs41 add --hosts=[host1,host2 or IP-Address1,IP-
Address2] --sec= [AUTH_SYS or SEC_KRB5] --share=[share name] --volume-
name=DatastoreName
```

   Or you can use the abbreviated parameters, as follows:

```
esxcli storage nfs41 add -H [host1,host2 or IP1,IP2] -a [AUTH_SYS or
SEC_KRB5] -s [share name] -v [DatastoreName]
```

   Here is an example:

```
esxcli storage nfs41 add -H 10.10.0.53.10.10.0.54 -a AUTH_SYS -s /
Unity_NFS41_1 -v Unity)NFS41_1
```

   A successful operation returns no message.

   The following is a similar operation using SCE_KRB5 authentication:

```
esxcli storage nfs41 add -H 10.10.0.45 -a SEC_KRB5 -s /NTAP_NFS41_1 -v
NTAP_NfS41_1
```

After the first NFSv4.1 datastore is mounted successfully on the host, check the firewall rule set again. Listing 16.12 shows the command and its output.

Listing 16.12   Listing NFS clients firewall status after mounting an NFSv4.1 datastore

```
esxcli network firewall ruleset list |grep 'Name\|---\|nfs'
Name                   Enabled
---------------------- -------
nfsClient              true
nfs41Client            true
```

This means that NFSv4.1 client is now enabled as well in the host's firewall.

Listing 16.13 shows vmkerenel.log events corresponding with the mount operation, using AUTH_SYS authentication.

> **NOTE**
>
> EMC Unity 4.0 (including 4.0.1) does not support Kerberos encryption at the time of this writing. However, NFSv4.1 can be mounted with AUTH_SYS instead, as shown in the previous example.

Listing 16.13   vmkernel.log NFSv4.1 mounting events

```
NFS41: NFS41_VSIMountSet:402: Mount server: 10.10.0.54,10.10.0.55, port:
2049, path: /Unity_NFS41_1, label: Unity_NFS41_2, security: 1 user: ,
options: <none>
StorageApdHandler: 982: APD Handle Created with lock[StorageApd-
0x430648c9fda0]
NFS41: NFS41FSCompleteMount:3582: Lease time: 18
NFS41: NFS41FSCompleteMount:3583: Max read xfer size: 0x10000
NFS41: NFS41FSCompleteMount:3584: Max write xfer size: 0x10000
NFS41FSCompleteMount:3585: Max file size: 0x1fffffffffffffff
NFS41FSCompleteMount:3586: Max file name: 255
WARNING: NFS41: NFS41FSCompleteMount:3591: The max file name size (255) of
file system is larger than that of FSS (128)
NFS41: NFS41FSAPDNotify:5651: Restored connection to the server
10.10.0.54,10.10.0.55 mount point Unity_NFS41_2, mounted as bd3825b5-
c59af9d9-0000-000000000000 ("/Unity_NFS41_1")
NFS41: NFS41_VSIMountSet:414: Unity_NFS41_2 mounted successfully
```

In this example, the NFSv4.1 share named /Unity_NFS41_1 was mounted as a datastore named Unity_NFS41_1 via storage server ports with IP addresses 10.10.0.54 and 10.10.0.55. This datastore was assigned the UUID bd3825b5-c59af9d9-0000-000000000000.

The lock lease time is 18 seconds. (I discuss this in the section "NFS Locking Mechanism," later in this chapter.)

The maximum file size is 0x1fffffffffffff Hex or 127 PiB (binary petabytes).

Listing 16.14 shows similar events for mounting a datastore using SEC_KRB5.

Listing 16.14   vmkernel.log NFSv4.1 mounting events using SEC_KRB5

```
World: 12232: VC opID esxcli-43-387d maps to vmkernel opID 13fce974
NFS41: NFS41_VSIMountSet:423: Mount server: 10.10.0.45,10.10.0.46,10.10.0.4
9, port: 2049, path: /NTAP_NFS41_1, label: NTAP_NfS41_1, security: 2 user:
nfsclient, options: <none>
StorageApdHandler: 977: APD Handle Created with lock[StorageApd-
0x43056a720d70]
NFS41: NFS41FSCompleteMount:3774: Lease time: 30
NFS41: NFS41FSCompleteMount:3775: Max read xfer size: 0x10000
NFS41: NFS41FSCompleteMount:3776: Max write xfer size: 0x10000
NFS41: NFS41FSCompleteMount:3777: Max file size: 0xff7f3eda000
NFS41: NFS41FSCompleteMount:3778: Max file name: 255
WARNING: NFS41: NFS41FSCompleteMount:3783: The max file name size (255) of
file system is larger than that of FSS (128)
NFS41: NFS41FSAPDNotify:5943: Restored connection to the server 10.10.0.
45,10.10.0.46,10.10.0.49 mount point NTAP_NfS41_1, mounted as c81a1594-
b92c8f20-0000-000000000000 ("/NTAP_NFS41_1")
NFS41: NFS41_VSIMountSet:435: NTAP_NfS41_1 mounted successfully
```

In this example, the NFSv4.1 share named /NTAP_NFS41_1 was mounted as a datastore named NTAP_NFS41_1 via storage server ports with IP addresses 10.10.0.45, 10.10.0.46, and 10.10.0.49. This datastore was assigned the UUID c81a1594-b92c8f20-0000-000000000000.

The lock lease time is 30 seconds.

The maximum file size is 0xff7f3eda000 hex or 15 PiB (binary petabytes).

If the datastore fails to mount, you can check the file system status by using the following command:

```
esxcli storage filesystem list
```

Listing 16.15 shows this command and its output.

Listing 16.15 Listing file system status after failure to mount the datastore

```
esxcli storage filesystem list
Mount Point     Volume Name     UUID      Mounted Type     Size     Free
-----------     -----------     ----      ------- ----     -----    ----
                Unity_NFS41_1             false   NFS41    0        0
```

In this example, the datastore was registered with the host but not mounted. To mount the datastore in a situation like this, you can use the following:

```
esxcli storage filesystem mount [volume name]
```

Here is an example:

```
esxcli storage filesystem mount Unity_NFS41_1
```

Repeat the command in Listing 16.15, and it should now show that the datastore is mounted. If it is not, check the events in /var/run/log/vmkernel.log.

To list NFSv4.1 datastores only, run this command:

```
esxcli storage nfs41 list
```

Listing 16.16 shows this command and its output.

Listing 16.16 Listing NFSv4.1 file system status (with AUTH_SYS authentication)

```
esxcli storage nfs41 list
Volume Name   Host(s)     Share   Accessible  Mounted  Read-Only  Security
------------------------------------------------------------------------------
NFS41_3       10.10.0.46  /vol3   true        true     false      AUTH_SYS
```

In this example, the datastore is mounted with NFSv4.1 for read/write, using AUTH_SYS authentication. I truncated the last two columns in the output, which are isPE and Hardware Acceleration (with the value `false`).

Listing 16.17 shows similar output from the host that mounted another NFSv4.1 datastore, using SEC_KRB5.

Listing 16.17 Listing NFSv4.1 file system status (with Kerberos authentication)

```
esxcli storage nfs41 list
Volume Name   Host(s)       Share          Accessible  Mounted  Read-Only  Security
------------------------------------------------------------------------------------
NTAP_NFS41_1  10.10.0.45,   /NTAP_NFS41_1  true        true     false      SEC_KRB5
              10.10.0.46,
              10.10.0.49
```

In this output, I manually wrapped the IP addresses in the Host(s) column for readability. In the actual output, they are on the same line. I also truncated the last two columns in the output, which are isPE and Hardware Acceleration (with the value `false`).

Using the ESX CLI to List an NFSv4.1 Datastore's Information

In the process of analyzing or troubleshooting NFSv4.1 datastores on vSphere 6.x, it is a good idea to be familiar with relevant utilities available at the ESXi host's console. A few tools that the VMware support team commonly uses are `esxcli`, `vsish`, and `esxcfg-nas`.

Using `esxcli`

I have been using various `esxcli` commands throughout this chapter. If you run `esxcli storage nfs41` without any other options, you get output like that shown in Listing 16.18

Listing 16.18 Listing `esxcli storage nfs41` options

```
esxcli storage nfs41
Usage: esxcli storage nfs41 {cmd} [cmd options]

Available Namespaces:
  param            Operations on volume parameters of NFS v4.1 filesystems.

Available Commands:
  add              Add a new NFS v4.1 volume to the ESX Host and mount it
with the given volume name.
  list             List the NFS v4.1 volumes currently known to the ESX host.
  remove           Remove an existing NFS v4.1 volume from the ESX host.
```

The output shows three options:

- `add`—Use this to mount an NFSv4.1 datastore. I used this earlier in the chapter to mount a datastore.

- `list`—Use this to list NFSv4.1 datastores. I also used this earlier in the chapter to list mounted datastores.

- `remove`—Use this to unmount NFSv4.1 datastores. I use this in the next section, "Using the ESX CLI to Unmount an NFSv4.1 Datastore."

Using `vsish`

The `vsish` tool provides access to vmkernel's VSI nodes. Other than non-interactive mode's `get` and `set` commands, this tool offers abbreviated command options only.

NOTE

VSI nodes are to vmkernel what proc nodes are to Linux kernel. They are memory-based hierarchical structures of the various vmkernel components' runtime settings. To access these nodes, use the ESXi utility `vsish` (VSI Shell). VSI nodes can change between releases and even with update releases. Therefore, you should not depend on the current naming and location of any nodes to remain unchanged if you plan to automate or script any functionalities using these nodes.

Listing 16.19 shows the command-line options.

Listing 16.19 Listing vsish command-line options

```
vsish --help
vsish: <options> <commands>
        -e: non-interactive mode. Executes commands specified on the cmdline.
            All text following this flag is assumed to be part of a command.
        -E <status>: checks for status, currently requires -e.
            see vmkapi_status.h for error code strings.
        -b: batch mode. doesn't print prompt
        -f: ignore vsi version check
        -l <level>: set loglevel
        -r: raw output mode.
        -p: python output mode.
        -d: drsa output mode.
        -c <file>: use <file> instead of live kernel
        -m: print the VSI MD5 checksum corresponding to the running vmkernel
        -R <new root>: use <new root> as the root node instead of '/'
        -h: print friendly help message
```

To obtain VSI nodes values, you need to know the path to each node and use the `-e` option for non-interactive mode.

For example, the NFSv4.1 client's node is /vmkModules/nfs41client, and under it, all NFSv4.1-related information is stored. All mounted NFSv4.1 datastores reside in the /vol node, within subnodes named after their UUIDs.

To list a datastore's VSI node, run the following command:

```
vsish -e get /vmkModules/nfs41client/vol/<volume-UUID>
```

Identify the volume UUID, by running this command:

```
vmkfstools --queryfs --humanreadable --verbose 10 /vmfs/volumes/ <volume>
|grep UUID
```

Or you can run the abbreviated options:

```
vmkfstools -Ph -v10 /vmfs/volumes/<volume> |grep UUID
```

Here is an example:

```
vmkfstools -Ph -v10 /vmfs/volumes/NFS41_3 |grep UUID
```

The output looks something like this:

```
UUID: 1ef31ad0-0c34cd1d-0000-000000000000
```

Listing 16.20 shows the output of using the returned UUID with the `vsish` command.

Listing 16.20   Listing an NFSv4.1 datastore's VSI node (AUTH_SYS authentication)

```
vsish -e get /vmkModules/nfs41client/vol/1ef31ad0-0c34cd1d-0000-
000000000000
file system properties {
   volume name:NFS41_3
   name(s) for server:10.10.0.46
   server IP address(es):10.10.0.46
   server path:/vol3
   UUID:1ef31ad0-0c34cd1d-0000-000000000000
   busy:0
   max read:65536
   max write:65536
   read-only:0
   hidden:0
   security:Security Type: 1 -> AUTH_SYS
   user name:
   NFSv4.1 operational state:NFS41 Operational State: 0 -> Up
```

The datastore in Listing 16.20 was mounted using AUTH_SYS encryption. For a datastore mounted using SEC_KRB5 encryption, the two highlighted fields would have different values, as shown in Listing 16.21.

Listing 16.21   Listing an NFSv4.1 datastore's VSI node (SEC_KRB5 authentication)

```
vmkfstools -Ph -v10 /vmfs/volumes/NTAP_NFS41_1 |grep UUID
UUID: c81a1594-b92c8f20-0000-000000000000
vsish -e get /vmkModules/nfs41client/vol/c81a1594-b92c8f20-0000-
000000000000
```

```
file system properties {
   volume name:NTAP_NFS41_1
   name(s) for server:10.10.0.45,10.10.0.46,10.10.0.49
   server IP address(es):10.10.0.45,10.10.0.46,10.10.0.49
   server path:/NTAP_NFS41_1
   UUID:c81a1594-b92c8f20-0000-000000000000
   busy:0
   max read:65536
   max write:65536
   read-only:0
   hidden:0
   security:Security Type: 2 -> Kerberos authentication
   user name:nfsclient
   NFSv4.1 operational state:NFS41 Operational State: 0 -> Up
```

In this example, the datastore's VSI node shows that the Security Type is 2, which indicates Kerberos authentication. It also shows that the user name authenticated with Kerberos is nfsclient.

To browse the VSI nodes in interactive mode, just run vsish without any options. This opens the VSI Shell's prompt, which looks like a Linux prompt.

The following are some VSI Shell commands for navigation and other common operations:

- cd—Move down the nodes tree.

- cd . .—Move up to the previous level.

- ls—List the content of the current node.

- ls <path>—List the content of the node at the end of the specified path.

- get—List the content of a leaf object in the node. This is the command option used earlier in this section, with the non-interactive mode -e parameter.

- cat—Do the same thing as the get command but in interactive mode.

- set—Modify the value of the key/value pair of a leaf object. You can use this option with non-interactive mode to modify vmkernel VSI nodes. For example, to set a value in a VSI node via the command line, run the following command:vsish -e set <value> <path/node>

> **TIP**
>
> If you modify VSI nodes, the changes are made in memory. Until the host's state is saved in
> a periodic save or by an orderly shutdown/reboot of the host, the changes will be lost if the
> host loses power or crashes. To save the state manually, run the following command: /bin/
> backup.sh 0

A word of advice: If you don't know what you are doing, do not make any changes to the
VSI nodes without directions from VMware support engineers or a documented procedure
published by VMware, such as this book.

Using esxcfg-nas

The `esxcfg-nas` tool offers a wide variety of options related to network attached storage
(NAS), which is a synonym for NFS in general. To list available commands, you can run it
at the ESXi host's console without any options. Listing 16.22 shows the output.

Listing 16.22   Listing `esxcf-nas` command-line options

```
esxcfg-nas
esxcfg-nas <options> [<label>]
-a|--add                    Add a new NAS filesystem to /vmfs volumes.
                            Requires --host and --share options.
                            Use --readonly option only for readonly access.
-o|--host <host>            Set the host name or ip address for a NAS mount.
                            For version 4.1, can be a comma-separated list.
-s|--share <share>          Set the name of the NAS share on the remote system.
-y|--readonly               Add the new NAS filesystem with readonly access.
-d|--delete                 Unmount and delete a filesystem.
-l|--list                   List the currently mounted NAS file systems.
-v|--version <version>      Specify NFS version (3 or 4.1)
                            Required for add; optional for list.
-U|--user <user>            Set per host NFS user and password
                            Requires --version 4.1 option
-C|--user-clear             Clear per host NFS user and password
                            Requires --version 4.1 option
-L|--user-list              List per host NFS user and number of passwords
                            Requires --version 4.1 option
-r|--restore                Restore all NFS version 3 mounts from the
configuration file.
                            (FOR INTERNAL USE ONLY).
-h|--help                   Show this message.
```

To list mounted NFSv4.1 datastores using `esxcfg-nas`, run the following command:

```
esxcfg-nas --list --version 4.1
```

Or you can use the abbreviated version:

```
esxcfg-nas -l -v 4.1
```

Listing 16.23 shows the abbreviated command and its output.

Listing 16.23   Using `esxcf-nas` to list mounted NFSv4.1 datastores

```
esxcfg-nas -l -v4.1
Unity_NFS41_1 is /Unity_NFS41_1 from 10.10.0.54,10.10.0.55 mounted
available
NTAP_NFS41_1 is /NTAP_NFS41_1 from 10.10.0.45,10.10.0.46,10.10.0.49 mounted
available
```

The output in Listing 16.23 indicates that two NFSv4.1 datastore were mounted on this host, along with their datastore names, NFSv4.1 folder name (namespace or export), the NFS servers' ports IP addresses, mount status, and availability.

If you make a mistake and use `-L` instead of `-l`, the output lists the NFS user name and the number of passwords for it on this host. It is a handy command to use if you don't have access to VC when you are troubleshooting Kerberos 5 authentication issues. Listing 16.24 shows this command and its output.

Listing 16.24   Using `esxcf-nas` to list the NFSv4.1 user name

```
esxcfg-nas -L -v4.1
File System User: "nfsclient", Number of Passwords: 1
```

This tool can be used to correct the NFS user name with the option `--user` or `-U` to overwrite the current user name. To clear it altogether, use the `--user-clear` or `-C` option.

TIP

Using `esxcfg-nas` to modify username or password or to mount or unmount datastores, you must specify the NFS version by using the `--version` or `-v` option because this tool works for both NFSv3 and NFSv4.1. If you don't specify the version, you get an error for an option that is NFSv4.1 specific. For example, to change the user name with the `-U` option without using the `-v` option, you get an error that NFS v3 supports only AUTH_SYS with the root user. This implies that the tool defaults to NFS v3 if no version is specified. The moral of the story is to always state the version with any `esxcfg-nas` options. Using the ESX CLI to Unmount an NFSv4.1 Datastore

Unmounting an NFSv4.1 datastore via the ESX CLI is a simple operation, using this command:

```
esxcli storage nfs41 remove --volume-name [Datastore name]
```

Or you can use the abbreviated version:

```
esxcli storage nfs41 remove -v [Datastore name]
```

Here is an example:

```
esxcli storage nfs41 remove -v NTAP_NFS41_1
```

A successful operation returns no messages.

Listing 16.25 shows vmkernel log events related to unmounting the datastore.

Listing 16.25   vmkernel log events for unmounting an NFSv4.1 datastore

```
cpu0:67453 opID=1d9f2956)World: 12232: VC opID esxcli-9a-331b maps to
vmkernel opID 1d9f2956
cpu0:67453 opID=1d9f2956)NFS41: NFS41_VSIUnmountSet:482: Unmount label:
NTAP_NFS41_1
cpu0:67453 opID=1d9f2956)StorageApdHandler: 1062: Freeing APD handle
0x43056a720d70 [c81a1594-b92c8f20-0000-000000000000]
cpu0:67453 opID=1d9f2956)StorageApdHandler: 1147: APD Handle freed!
cpu0:67453 opID=1d9f2956)NFS41: NFS41_VSIUnmountSet:490: NTAP_NFS41_1
unmounted successfully
```

In Listing 16.25 I removed the date and timestamp for readability.

The first message in Listing 16.25 shows the VC operation ID assigned to this operation. If I had used `localcli` instead of `esxcli`, this message would not be posted because `localcli` does not communicate with VC and runs locally only. Otherwise, such an operation ID assigned by VC indicates that the outcome of the operation on this host will be reflected in the host's information in VC's inventory.

The value prefixed with `cpu0:` is the vmkernel thread on that CPU, which runs a kernel process, also referred to as a world, number `12232`.

The VC `opID` in this example is `esxcli-9a-331b`, which maps to the kernel `opID` `1d9f2956`.

The second message in Listing 16.25 shows the unmount operation. The third and fourth messages show the process of freeing the All Paths Down (APD) handle and its UUID. The final message shows that the unmount operation completed successfully.

NFS Locking Mechanism

vSphere 6.x, like earlier releases, requires access to shared storage by all hosts in the cluster for certain features to function. To prevent concurrent writes to files accessible by hosts in the cluster, arbitration between hosts' write operations is done via file locking mechanisms. VMFS has its native lock handling, as discussed in Chapter 12, "VMFS Architecture." The NFS locking mechanism depends on which NFS protocol version is used to access the datastore.

NFSv3 Locking

NFSv3, supported on vSphere 6.x and earlier, leaves file locking to be done out-of-band by the clients. ESXi `nfsclient` handles this operation via lock files it creates on the datastore within the directory where the file resides. Listing 16.26 shows an example of a VM that is in a powered-on state on an NFSv3 datastore.

Listing 16.26   Listing NFSv3 file locks

```
ls -Al /vmfs/volumes/NTAP_NFS3_1/NFS-VM2/
total 592
-rwxrwxr-x 1 root root 84 Aug 22 02:35 .lck-2847896500000000
-rwxrwxr-x 1 root root 84 Aug 22 02:35 .lck-2e47896500000000
-rwxrwxr-x 1 root root 84 Aug 22 02:35 .lck-7a32896500000000
-rwxrwxr-x 1 root root 84 Aug 22 02:35 .lck-8532896500000000
-rw-r--r-- 1 root root 90 Aug 20 06:43 NFS-VM2-161cb30a.hlog
-rw------- 1 root root 536870912 Aug 20 06:36 NFS-VM2-354390b8.vswp
-rw------- 1 root root 5368709120 Aug 20 06:20 NFS-VM2-flat.vmdk
-rw------- 1 root root 8684 Aug 20 06:43 NFS-VM2.nvram
-rw------- 1 root root 494 Aug 20 06:20 NFS-VM2.vmdk
-rw-r--r-- 1 root root 0 Aug 20 06:20 NFS-VM2.vmsd
-rwxr-xr-x 1 root root 2702 Aug 20 06:43 NFS-VM2.vmx
-rw------- 1 root root 0 Aug 20 06:43 NFS-VM2.vmx.lck
-rw-r--r-- 1 root root 182307 Aug 20 06:32 vmware-1.log
-rw-r--r-- 1 root root 187943 Aug 20 06:43 vmware-2.log
-rw-r--r-- 1 root root 177999 Aug 20 23:28 vmware.log
-rw------- 1 root root 115343360 Aug 20 06:43 vmx-NFS-VM2-893620408- 2.vswp
```

The files with the .lck prefix are hidden files representing the lock records on this datastore for files in this directory. The lock file suffix is the file ID returned from a GETATTR request from the filer for the file being locked. The lock files contain the lock counter, hostname, and UUID of the locker.

The host updates the lock every 10 seconds. If the lock is not updated after three lock update intervals (that is, 30 seconds), another host can take over the lock, such as with an HA event.

NFSv4.1 Locking

NFSv4.1, supported on vSphere 6.x, implements locking in-band on the storage server's end. This is done via lock lease (a share reservation) that is established by the OPEN operation. Five different types of NFSv4.1 locks are implemented by vSphere 6.x, according to RFC 5661 (see https://tools.ietf.org/html/rfc5661#page-184). Table 16.4 lists these lock types and their corresponding storage server share reservation types.

Table 16.4 NFSv4.1 lock types

ESXi Lock Type	NFSv4.1 Share Reservation	
	Access	**Deny**
Exclusive	Both read and write for this host	Both read and write to other hosts
Read-only	Read for this host	Write for this host
Read	Read for this host	None
Write	Write for this host	None
Multi-writer	Both read and write for this host	None

Here is a typical sequence of events for an exclusive lock:

1. Host A issues an I/O on a file located on an NFSv4.1 datastore. This is done through a session between the host and the storage server.

2. If the file lock is free, the storage server offers the NFSv4.1 client (the ESXi host) a lease on the lock for a certain time. This lease time varies by vendor between 18 and 90 seconds.

TIP

To obtain the current lease time on the datastore, run this command at the ESXi shell:

```
vsish -e get /vmkModules/nfs41client/clusters/1/info |grep lease
```

The output would be something like lease Time:18.

---

3. Host A's I/O succeeds on the file. If the host needs to maintain the lock lease on the file, it interacts with the storage server before the current lease expires. This is done over any of the existing sessions between the host and the storage server.

NOTE

`nfs4client` does not use the `RENEW` command for lease renewal. It also does not support byte range locking. Instead, it uses `ACCESS` and `DENY` share reservation bits at file open time to obtain the locks (refer to Table 16.4). These locks persist over the entire time the file remains open on the client. This way, if the client loses access to the datastore because the host crashes or network connectivity is lost, when the lease expires, HA operations can obtain new locks leases via one of the other hosts in the cluster.

4. If Host B issues an I/O on the same file while it is currently locked by Host A, the storage server denies the lock to Host B because the lock lease has not expired for Host A. If the lease time expires for Host A, the next time Host B retries the I/O on the file, the server grants it a file lock lease.

Lock Recovery

The following are the possible scenarios in which a host might need to recover a lock lease:

- **Host crashes**—When the host is back online, it reestablishes its previous sessions with the server by sending an `EXCHANGE_ID` request. If the lease has not expired yet, it reclaims the lock lease and continues as if nothing happened. If the lease has expired, and has not been granted to another host, the host attempts the lock, and the server grants it to the host.

- **Network partition**—A host might lose network connection to the server, or the server might lose connectivity to the network. While this is considered a network partition, however, the server has no way of knowing that the host is partitioned until the lock lease expires. If the network partition heals before the lease expires, the host can reestablish the session or sessions with the server by using the existing `EXCHANGE_ID` requests and reclaim the lock within a grace period set by the server. Otherwise, the server clears all locks, and the host clears all the stale `EXCHANGE_ID` requests before attempting the lock again.

- **Server restart**—The client can resume its sessions with the server by using the existing `EXCHANGE_ID`. Then the server checks the lease expiration. If the lease expired, the host requests the lock leases from the server as if it is the first time it is acquiring the lock lease.

NFS Client Advanced Configurations

The ESXi 6.x default configuration is sufficient for the majority of use cases. However, there may be a need to modify the default configuration. The following sections cover a set of advanced configurations and when to modify them.

Maximum NFS Volumes

By default, each host can mount no more than eight NFSv3 and NFSv4.1 volumes—that is, eight for each version. If you need to mount more than that, you need to increase the value of the following advanced options:

/NFS/MaxVolumes
/NFS41/MaxVolumes

To list the current settings, you can use this command:

```
esxcli system settings advanced list |grep -A9 MaxVolumes
```

Listing 16.27 shows this command and its output.

Listing 16.27 Listing NFS and NFSv4.1 MaxVolumes options

```
esxcli system settings advanced list |grep -A9 MaxVolumes
 Path: /NFS/MaxVolumes
 Type: integer
 Int Value: 8
 Default Int Value: 8
 Min Value: 8
 Max Value: 256
 String Value:
 Default String Value:
 Valid Characters:
 Description: Maximum number of mounted NFS v3 volumes. TCP/IP heap must be
increased accordingly (Requires reboot)
 --
 Path: /NFS41/MaxVolumes
 Type: integer
 Int Value: 8
 Default Int Value: 8
 Min Value: 8
 Max Value: 256
 String Value:
 Default String Value:
 Valid Characters:
 Description: Maximum number of mounted NFS v4.1 volumes. TCP/IP heap must
be increased accordingly (Requires reboot)
```

In Listing 16.27 I highlighted the current value for each version. Note that the maximum value is 256 volumes for each client version.

To change this value, run this command for NFSv3:

```
esxcli system settings advanced set -i <value> -o /NFS/MaxVolumes
```

Run this command for NFSv4.1:

```
esxcli system settings advanced set -i <value> -o /NFS41/MaxVolumes
```

Changing this setting does not require a host reboot.

This configuration change must be paired with another setting to increase the heap memory to accommodate the increased number of mounted volumes. There are two settings involved:

- /Net/TcpipHeapSize—This is the initial size of TCP/IP module heap (in megabytes). It can grow up to the value set in the next option, TCP/IP Heap Max. In other words, this is the minimum value of the heap size. Setting it to a nonzero value reserves this space for the heap.

- /Net/TcpipHeapMax—This is the maximum size up to which the heap can grow.

To list the current settings of these two options, run the following command:

```
esxcli system settings advanced list | grep /Net/TcpipHeap -A9
```

Listing 16.28 shows this command and its output.

Listing 16.28 Listing TCP/IP heap options

```
esxcli system settings advanced list | grep /Net/TcpipHeap -A9
 Path: /Net/TcpipHeapSize
 Type: integer
 Int Value: 0
 Default Int Value: 0
 Min Value: 0
 Max Value: 32
 String Value:
 Default String Value:
 Valid Characters:
 Description: Initial size of the tcpip module heap in megabytes. (REQUIRES
REBOOT!)
 --
 Path: /Net/TcpipHeapMax
 Type: integer
 Int Value: 512
```

```
Default Int Value: 512
Min Value: 32
Max Value: 1536
String Value:
Default String Value:
Valid Characters:
Description: Max megabytes the tcpip module heap can grow to. (REQUIRES
REBOOT!)
```

The output in Listing 16.28 was collected from a host with unmodified default values. This means that the heap size starts at zero and grows up to 512MB, which is sufficient for eight NFSv3 or eight NFSv4.1 volumes.

> **TIP**
>
> After you change the heap options values, you need to reboot the server. Plan ahead, based on your target number of NFSv3 and/or NFSv4.1 volumes to mount. If you configure them liberally and do not mount all volumes, the heap space is wasted.
>
> Because this heap is shared by other consumers of the TCP/IP stack, you need to be careful when calculating the new values to set here. The best approach is to scale the values linearly, in proportion to the MaxVolumes value.
>
> For example, say that you increase the MaxVolumes value in increments of 8. Each 8 mounts would need 6MB minimum and 30MB maximum. Divide the total number of volumes into 8 and round up the result. If you plan to mount 36 volumes, the result would be 5 (36 / 8 = 4.5). Then multiply the result by 6 and 30. This would mean 33 to 40 volumes would need 30MB minimum and 150MB maximum. In the same fashion, 41 to 48 volumes would need 36MB minimum and 180MB maximum, and so on. Note that the default TcpipHeapMax value is 512, which should be sufficient for up to 120 mounts total. However, other consumers of the TCP/IP stack may erode into that, so your mileage will vary!

To apply the changes by using the CLI, use these commands:

```
esxcli system settings advanced set -i <value> -o /Net/TcpipHeapSize
esxcli system settings advanced set -i <value> -o /Net/TcpipHeapMax
```

A successful update returns no messages. However, /var/log/vmkernel.log shows messages like those in Listing 16.29.

Listing 16.29 Successful option change messages in vmkernel.log

```
2016-09-22T20:34:35.502Z cpu1:67482 opID=f5621564)World: 12232: VC opID
esxcli-15-ed90 maps to vmkernel opID f5621564
2016-09-22T20:34:35.502Z cpu1:67482 opID=f5621564)Config: 706:
"TcpipHeapSize" = 30, Old Value: 0, (Status: 0x0)
```

To apply the changes by using the UI, there are two approaches:

- In NetApp configurations, use VSC
- In other configurations, use vSphere Web Client

Using VSC to Apply Configuration Changes

NetApp simplified the process of updating ESXi host configurations to meet best practices by using the VSC UI within vSphere 6.x Web Client. You can accomplish this by following this procedure.

1. Log on to VC with Administrator privileges or equivalent.

2. Navigate to the **Host and Clusters** view.

3. Right-click one of the hosts in the cluster and select **NetApp VSC** and then select the **Show Details** menu option (see Figure 16.71).

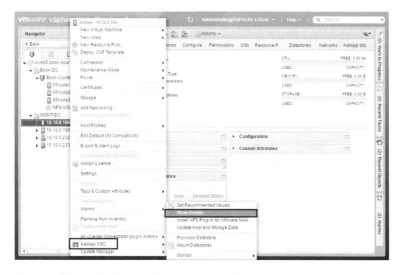

Figure 16.71 Viewing NetApp recommended host settings

4. In the ESXi Host Details window that appears, scroll down to the **nfssettingsmap** section, which lists the following options:

- Net.TcpipHeapSize—The recommended value is 30.

- Net.TcpipHeapMax—The recommended value is 120.

- NFS.MaxVolumes—The recommended value is 64.

- NFS.HeartbeatFrequency—The recommended value is 12.

- NFS.HeartbeatTimeout—The recommended value is 5.

- NFS.HeartbeatMaxFalures—The recommended value is 10.

Close the Details windows.

> **NOTE**
>
> The current version of VSC, 6.2, does not show or set the recommended settings for NFSv4.1. You need to use the CLI or vSphere 6.x Web Client Advanced Settings UI (see the next section). VSC version 6.2 is not compatible with vSphere 6.5, and trying to use them together leads to the creation of incorrect VC MOREF (Management Object Reference) IDs that result in errors accessing the Add Storage option in the UI. I assume that this will be fixed in the version certified with vSphere 6.5 by the time this book is in print.

5. If any of the settings do not match the recommended value, right-click the host and select **NetApp VSC** and then select the **Set Recommended Values** menu option.

6. Repeat steps 3 through 5 for each host in the cluster.

If any of the TcpipHeap settings were modified, schedule downtime to reboot the modified hosts.

Using vSphere 6.x Web Client to Apply Configuration Changes

To change the settings covered in the preceding two sections, you can use the vSphere 6.x Web Client. Follow these steps:

1. Log on to VC with Administrator privileges or equivalent.

2. Navigate to the **Hosts and Clusters** view.

3. Select the ESXi host in the inventory tree.

4. If using vSphere 6.0 Web Client, select the **Manage** tab. For vSphere 6.5 Web Client, select the **Configure** tab.

5. In the System section, select the **Advanced System Settings** option.

6. Click the **Edit** button (see Figure 16.72).

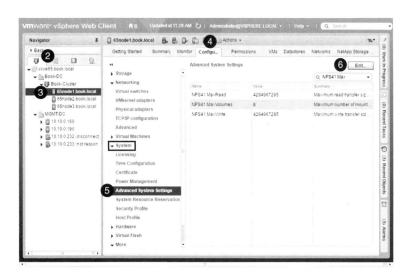

Figure 16.72 Accessing advanced system settings

7. In the Edit Advanced System Settings dialog that appears, in the Filter field, enter the first part of the option you want to change—for example, **NFS.Max** or **NFS41. Max**—and press **Enter**.

8. Locate the option in the resulting list and modify the value.

9. Click **OK** to save the changes (see Figure 16.73).

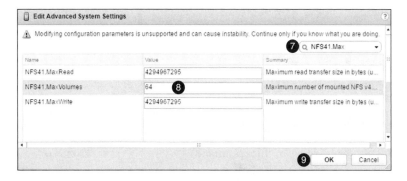

Figure 16.73 Modifying advanced system settings

Repeat steps 6 through 9 for each setting or group of settings. If you modify Net. TcpipHeap values, you need to reboot the hosts in order for the changes to take effect.

Useful Authentication-Related Commands

Authentication failures can have several root causes. Because AD authentication is done by the lLikewise tool included with the host, most of the relevant binaries are in the /usr/lib/vmware/likewise/bin directory.

To get domain information, run the following command on the affected ESXi host:

```
/usr/lib/vmware/likewise/bin/lw-get-dc-name <AD DC Name>
```

Here is an example:

```
/usr/lib/vmware/likewise/bin/lw-get-dc-name book.local
```

Listing 16.30 shows this command and its output.

Listing 16.30   Listing the Active Directory domain

```
/usr/lib/vmware/likewise/bin/lw-get-dc-name book.local
Printing LWNET_DC_INFO fields:
==============================
dwDomainControllerAddressType = 23
dwFlags = 13309
dwVersion = 5
wLMToken = 65535
wNTToken = 65535
pszDomainControllerName = WIN2008.book.local
pszDomainControllerAddress = 10.10.0.21
pucDomainGUID(hex) = B2 F1 5F FD BE 9A 4E 48 96 31 DF E1 9C C4 B5 FE
pszNetBIOSDomainName = BOOK
pszFullyQualifiedDomainName = book.local
pszDnsForestName = book.local
pszDCSiteName = Default-First-Site-Name
pszClientSiteName = Default-First-Site-Name
pszNetBIOSHostName = WIN2008
pszUserName = <EMPTY>
```

In the example shown in Listing 16.30, the returned values are for a working configuration.

To get user information from AD, run this command:

```
/usr/lib/vmware/likewise/bin/lw-lsa find-user-by-name <user-name>
```

Here is an example:

```
/usr/lib/vmware/likewise/bin/lw-lsa find-user-by-name nfsclient@book.local
```

Listing 16.31 shows this command and its output.

Listing 16.31   Listing the Active Directory user account

```
/usr/lib/vmware/likewise/bin/lw-lsa find-user-by-name nfsclient@book.local
User info (Level-0):
====================
Name:                BOOK\nfsclient
SID:                 S-1-5-21-1688003860-815373413-57943987-1127
Uid:                 1018692711
Gid:                 1018692097
Gecos:               NFS Client
Shell:               /bin/sh
Home dir:            /home/local/BOOK/nfsclient
Log on restriction:  NO
```

Listing 16.31 shows an example of a working configuration. The user name is preceded with the AD domain name. The default detail level is 0. If you add `--level 1` or `--level 2`, you get more details. Listing 16.32 shows an example of using each of these options.

Listing 16.32   Listing a detailed Active Directory user account

```
/usr/lib/vmware/likewise/bin/lw-lsa find-user-by-name --level 1 nfsclient@
book.local
User info (Level-1):
====================
Name:                BOOK\nfsclient
SID:                 S-1-5-21-1688003860-815373413-57943987-1127
UPN:                 nfsclient@BOOK.LOCAL
Generated UPN:       NO
Uid:                 1018692711
Gid:                 1018692097
Gecos:               NFS Client
Shell:               /bin/sh
Home dir:            /home/local/BOOK/nfsclient
LMHash length:       0
NTHash length:       0
Local User:          NO
Log on restriction:  NO

/usr/lib/vmware/likewise/bin/lw-lsa find-user-by-name --level 2 nfsclient@
book.local
```

```
User info (Level-2):
====================
Name:                            BOOK\nfsclient
SID:                             S-1-5-21-1688003860-815373413-57943987-1127
UPN:                             nfsclient@BOOK.LOCAL
Generated UPN:                   NO
DN:                              CN=NFS Client,CN=Users,DC=book,DC=local
Uid:                             1018692711
Gid:                             1018692097
Gecos:                           NFS Client
Shell:                           /bin/sh
Home dir:                        /home/local/BOOK/nfsclient
LMHash length:                   0
NTHash length:                   0
Local User:                      NO
Account disabled (or locked):    FALSE
Account expired:                 FALSE
Password never expires:          TRUE
Password expired:                FALSE
Prompt for password change:      NO
User can change password:        YES
Days till password expires:      0
Log on restriction:              NO
```

The `--level 2` option shows information such as the Distinguished Name (DN) and password expiration.

Troubleshooting NFS Connectivity

If a host loses network connection with a storage server, without a proper design, the datastores on that storage server enter an APD state, and the /var/run/log/vmkernel.log file shows messages like those in Listing 16.33.

Listing 16.33 vmkernel.log events when host loses network connection to a storage server (example 1)

```
2016-09-13T02:10:17.905Z cpu0:66295)WARNING: SunRPC: 3948: fail all pending
calls for client 0x43032b6c06d0 IP 10.10.0.49.8.1 (socket half closed)
2016-09-13T02:10:17.906Z cpu0:66281)WARNING: NFS41: NFS41FSAPDNotify:5891:
Lost connection to the server 10.10.0.49 mount point vol1, mounted as
b7c75721-2810dd94-0000-000000000000 ("/vol1")
2016-09-13T02:10:17.906Z cpu0:66281)StorageApdHandler: 1205: APD start for
0x4305a83dfd70 [b7c75721-2810dd94-0000-000000000000]
```

```
2016-09-13T02:10:17.906Z cpu1:65696)StorageApdHandler: 419: APD start event
for 0x4305a83dfd70 [b7c75721-2810dd94-0000-000000000000]
2016-09-13T02:10:17.906Z cpu1:65696)StorageApdHandlerEv: 110: Device or
filesystem with identifier [b7c75721-2810dd94-0000-000000000000] has
entered the All Paths Down state.
2016-09-13T02:10:32.909Z cpu0:66295)WARNING: SunRPC: 3948: fail all pending
calls for client 0x43032b6c06d0 IP 10.10.0.49.8.1 (socket disconnected)
2016-09-13T02:10:47.913Z cpu0:66295)WARNING: SunRPC: 3948: fail all pending
calls for client 0x43032b6c06d0 IP 10.10.0.49.8.1 (socket disconnected)
2016-09-13T02:10:49.828Z cpu0:68673)WARNING: NFS41:
NFS41FSOpGetObject:2147: Failed to get object 0x43912209b386 [40 b7c75721
2810dd94 101 0 0 40 57d626fc 80fe8666 0 0 0 0]: IO was aborted
```

In the example shown in Listing 16.33, I artificially introduced a failure by disconnecting all data LIFs on both nodes of the NFS cluster. In real life, this should not happen.

Another example is the host losing connectivity to the storage network. Relevant vmkernel log message are shown in Listing 16.34.

Listing 16.34   vmkernel.log events when host loses network connection to a storage server (example 2)

```
2016-09-13T03:34:41.767Z cpu0:65921)<6>e1000: vmnic0: e1000_watchdog_task:
NIC Link is Down
2016-09-13T03:34:51.785Z cpu1:66301)WARNING: SunRPC: 3948: fail all pending
calls for client 0x43032b6c0e00 IP 10.10.0.54.8.1 (socket half closed)
2016-09-13T03:34:54.405Z cpu1:66295)WARNING: SunRPC: 3948: fail all pending
calls for client 0x43032b6c06d0 IP 10.10.0.49.8.1 (socket half closed)
2016-09-13T03:34:54.405Z cpu1:66281)WARNING: NFS41: NFS41FSAPDNotify:5891:
Lost connection to the server 10.10.0.49 mount point vol1, mounted as
b7c75721-2810dd94-0000-000000000000 ("/vol1")
2016-09-13T03:34:54.405Z cpu1:66281)StorageApdHandler: 1205: APD start for
0x4305a83dfd70 [b7c75721-2810dd94-0000-000000000000]
2016-09-13T03:34:54.405Z cpu0:65696)StorageApdHandler: 419: APD start event
for 0x4305a83dfd70 [b7c75721-2810dd94-0000-000000000000]
2016-09-13T03:34:54.405Z cpu0:65696)StorageApdHandlerEv: 110: Device or
filesystem with identifier [b7c75721-2810dd94-0000-000000000000] has
entered the All Paths Down state.
2016-09-13T03:34:56.155Z cpu1:66281)WARNING: NFS41: NFS41FSAPDNotify:5891:
Lost connection to the server 10.10.0.54,10.10.0.55 mount point Unity_
NFS41_1, mounted as 4a6d4cdf-b977c954-0000-000000000000 ("/Unity_NFS41_1")
2016-09-13T03:34:56.155Z cpu1:66281)StorageApdHandler: 1205: APD start for
0x4305a83e2640 [4a6d4cdf-b977c954-0000-000000000000]
2016-09-13T03:34:56.155Z cpu1:65696)StorageApdHandler: 419: APD start event
for 0x4305a83e2640 [4a6d4cdf-b977c954-0000-000000000000]
2016-09-13T03:34:56.155Z cpu1:65696)StorageApdHandlerEv: 110: Device or
filesystem with identifier [4a6d4cdf-b977c954-0000-000000000000] has
entered the All Paths Down state.
```

```
2016-09-13T03:35:12.584Z cpu1:66087)StorageApdHandler: 1205: APD start for
0x4305733f0e80 [0422aa85-3127778c]

2016-09-13T03:35:12.584Z cpu1:65696)StorageApdHandler: 419: APD start event
for 0x4305733f0e80 [0422aa85-3127778c]

2016-09-13T03:35:12.585Z cpu1:65696)StorageApdHandlerEv: 110: Device or
filesystem with identifier [0422aa85-3127778c] has entered the All Paths
Down state.

2016-09-13T03:35:21.791Z cpu1:66301)WARNING: SunRPC: 3948: fail all pending
calls for client 0x43032b6c0e00 IP 10.10.0.54.8.1 (socket disconnected)

2016-09-13T03:35:24.411Z cpu0:66295)WARNING: SunRPC: 3948: fail all pending
calls for client 0x43032b6c06d0 IP 10.10.0.49.8.1 (socket disconnected)

2016-09-13T03:35:26.162Z cpu1:66302)WARNING: SunRPC: 3948: fail all pending
calls for client 0x43032b6c1420 IP 10.10.0.55.8.1 (socket disconnected)

2016-09-13T03:36:36.586Z cpu1:66087)WARNING: NFS: 337: Lost connection to
the server 10.10.0.53 mount point /Unity_NFS3_DS0, mounted as 0422aa85-
3127778c-0000-000000000000 ("Unity_NFS3_DS0")

2016-09-13T03:37:14.410Z cpu1:65696)StorageApdHandler: 609: APD timeout
event for 0x4305a83dfd70 [b7c75721-2810dd94-0000-000000000000]

2016-09-13T03:37:14.410Z cpu1:65696)StorageApdHandlerEv: 126: Device or
filesystem with identifier [b7c75721-2810dd94-0000-000000000000] has
entered the All Paths Down Timeout state after being in the All Paths Down
state for 140 seconds. I/Os will now $

2016-09-13T03:37:16.159Z cpu1:65696)StorageApdHandler: 609: APD timeout
event for 0x4305a83e2640 [4a6d4cdf-b977c954-0000-000000000000]

2016-09-13T03:37:16.159Z cpu1:65696)StorageApdHandlerEv: 126: Device or
filesystem with identifier [4a6d4cdf-b977c954-0000-000000000000] has
entered the All Paths Down Timeout state after being in the All Paths Down
state for 140 seconds. I/Os will now $

2016-09-13T03:37:21.818Z cpu1:66301)WARNING: SunRPC: 3948: fail all pending
calls for client 0x43032b6c0e00 IP 10.10.0.54.8.1 (socket disconnected)

2016-09-13T03:37:24.436Z cpu0:66295)WARNING: SunRPC: 3948: fail all pending
calls for client 0x43032b6c06d0 IP 10.10.0.49.8.1 (socket disconnected)

2016-09-13T03:37:26.187Z cpu1:66302)WARNING: SunRPC: 3948: fail all pending
calls for client 0x43032b6c1420 IP 10.10.0.55.8.1 (socket disconnected)

2016-09-13T03:37:32.589Z cpu1:65696)StorageApdHandler: 609: APD timeout
event for 0x4305733f0e80 [0422aa85-3127778c]

2016-09-13T03:37:32.589Z cpu1:65696)StorageApdHandlerEv: 126: Device or
filesystem with identifier [0422aa85-3127778c] has entered the All Paths
Down Timeout state after being in the All Paths Down state for 140 seconds.
I/Os will now be fast failed.
```

In this example, the first message indicates that vmnic0's link is down. This is a dead giveaway about the root cause. Then messages from SunRPC are about failing all pending calls for client <ID> IP <server's port IP>.8.1. If you have not seen this message and want to verify network connectivity to the NFS server's IP address, simply use the vmkping command as follows:

```
vmkping <ip-address>
```

Here is an example:

```
vmkping 10.10.0.49
```

The output remains blank until the request times out. If the network connection is still up, you see reply packages.

```
 esxcfg-nics -l
```

Listing 16.35 shows this command and its output.

Listing 16.35 Listing NICs and their connection status

```
Name    PCI          Driver    Link    Speed    Duplex  MAC Address       MTU    Description
vmnic0 0000:02:01.0 e1000      Down    0Mbps    Full    00:0c:29:2c:b9:74 1500   Intel
Corporation 82545EM Gigabit Ethernet Controller (Copper)
```

The Link column shows the state as Down. The Description column wraps to the next line in this output.

Now let's go back to the rest of log messages in Listings 16.33 and 1634.

The NFS41 module sends a notification about the lost connection to one of the servers and states its IP address. It also references the mount point and the UUID, followed by the share name (for example, /vol1).

Then StorageApdHandler reports the start of the APD event for that datastore.

Next, StorageApdHandlerEv reports that the device also entered the APD state.

The same set of events repeat for another datastore on a different server IP address. In this case, it is a dual-pathed datastore on an EMC Unity NFS server. It had session trunked connectivity with two paths, one on 10.0.0.54 and the other on 10.10.0.55. This is why the datastore is mentioned as once having been associated with server 10.10.0.52,10.10.0.55.

The rest of the messages are about failing pending calls for each client and finally the remaining datastores on the failed connections entering the APD state.

You can avoid this state by having more than one storage vmkernel port group on one more virtual switches uplinked to separate NICs on the same storage network. I discuss this configuration in the section "Configuring a Host Network for NAS," near the beginning of this chapter.

If the output of esxcfg-nics -l shows that the link is up and you get replies from the NFS server's IP address, you can test whether the NFS service is running on the server by running this command on the ESXi host:

`nc -z <Server IP Address> 2049` (which is the TCP port for the NFS service on the server)

Here is an example:

`nc -z 10.10.0.49 2049`

The output looks like this:

`Connection to 10.10.0.49 2049 port [tcp/nfs] succeeded!`

Summary

This chapter provides details about Network File System (NFS) architecture, implementation, and design. It provides examples from NetApp Clustered Data ONTAP and EMC Unity 4.0.x. NFSv3.0 and NFSv4.1 are covered in detail, along with detailed configurations on vSphere 6.x and NFS servers. This chapter also provides details on configuring and implementing Kerberos authentication, where supported.

Chapter 17

VAAI

As vSphere 6 environments get larger and larger, the amount of data vSphere handles gets even larger. This can have a negative effect on input/output (I/O) throughput and bandwidth as several operations done frequently by ESXi servers demand processing cycles and erode valuable bandwidth. VMware designed a set of application programming interfaces (APIs) to offload most of the storage processing and bandwidth to the storage arrays, which frees up precious central processing unit (CPU) cycles and storage area network (SAN)/data local area network (LAN) bandwidth and allocates it to where it is needed.

This set of APIs is referred to as vStorage APIs for Array Integration (VAAI). VAAI uses the T10 standard set of commands defined in SCSI Block Commands-3 (SBC-3).

What Is VAAI?

VAAI is a set of VMware vStorage APIs and new Small Computer System Interface (SCSI) commands designed to provide an efficient protocol between ESXi hosts and storage arrays that implement specific T10 standard commands. This is in addition to a set of fundamental storage operations (also known as *primitives*) that ESXi uses to speed up I/O operations that are more efficiently accomplished by the storage hardware. The ESXi host uses these primitives to improve performance of data transfer (via DataMover) via standard T10 VAAI functions built in to the VMkernel and, for some primitives, via VAAI plug-ins installed on the ESXi host. The storage array must implement the VAAI T10 standard commands in its firmware in order to support some or all of the VAAI primitives.

In comparison, VAAI was implemented on ESX and ESXi 4.1 mainly via VAAI plug-ins built by VMware as well as some of the storage vendors that certified their arrays with that release for VAAI. Those that did not develop a plug-in were able to use the VMware-provided standard T10 plug-in named VMW_VAAIP_T10, which supported only the block zeroing primitive.

VAAI Primitives

vSphere 6 supports two groups of APIs: hardware acceleration APIs and thin provisioning APIs.

Hardware Acceleration APIs

Hardware acceleration APIs enable ESXi 6 hosts to offload the following primitives to the storage hardware:

- Block storage devices that support the following primitives:

  - Full copy (also known as XCOPY)

  - Block zeroing (also known as WRITE_SAME)

  - Hardware-assisted locking using atomic test and set (ATS)

- NAS devices that support the following primitives:

  - Full file clone

  - Lazy file clone

  - Reserve space

  - Extended file statistics

You'll learn more details later in this chapter.

Thin Provisioning APIs

Block devices have no visibility into the Virtual Machine File System (VMFS) structure or file allocation. For a VMFS volume that resides on a thin provisioned logical unit number (LUN), ESXi 6 has no way of identifying when the LUN is unable to grow on the storage array due to lack of disk space. In the reverse direction, the ESXi host has no way of informing the storage array of deleted blocks on the VMFS volume. This means that because the storage array is unaware of freed blocks on the thin LUN, it cannot reclaim them to make room for the growth of this LUN or other ones.

vSphere 5 introduced thin provisioning APIs to bridge the gap between the ESXi host and block device–based storage arrays. This API continues to be available in vSphere 6.

Thin provisioning APIs provide the following primitives:

- Dead space reclamation (also known as UNMAP)
- Used space monitoring to avoid running out of space (OOS) for LUN growth

You'll learn more details later in this chapter.

Full Copy Primitive (XCOPY)

One of the most taxing operations on VMFS datastores is cloning or copying virtual disks. This is also known as *full clone*. It involves reading the virtual disks' blocks and then sending the copied blocks over the network—whether Fibre Channel (FC) fabric, an Internet SCSI (iSCSI) network, or a Fibre Channel over Ethernet (FCoE) network. Then the array allocates the needed blocks and writes to them. This process, which uses the software DataMover, requires compute resources on the host, network bandwidth, and storage array port and LUN queues. DataMover is the VMkernel component that handles the block copy process in the absence of VAAI hardware acceleration.

The full copy primitive eliminates most of these operations by doing the following:

1. The host identifies the range of blocks to be copied and sends the block addresses to the array as part of the XCOPY command.
2. The array starts the copy process on its end.
3. When the process is done, the array informs the host that the operation is done.

The full copy primitive offloads the processing to the storage array, which reduces the host's overhead as well as network traffic.

Figure 17.1 shows a storage array processor and total bandwidth utilization from an EMC CLARiiON without VAAI and with VAAI.

It is clear from Figure 17.1 that the total bandwidth is significantly lower (close to zero) when VAAI is used. The storage processor utilization is slightly lower. The host CPU utilization overhead, which is not shown in this diagram, is almost zero when VAAI is used.

ESXi 6 introduced custom options for this primitive; see the section "XCOPY Custom Options," later in this chapter.

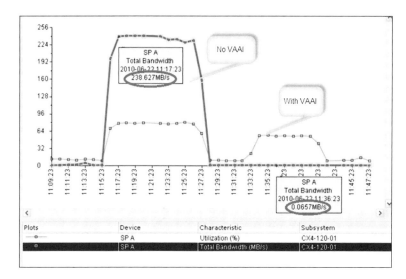

Figure 17.1   Comparing storage array performance with and without VAAI

Block Zeroing Primitive (`WRITE_SAME`)

Zeroed thick is the default virtual disk format, which means that all the virtual disk blocks are preallocated but are not zeroed out at creation time. As the virtual machine (VM) writes to these blocks, a zeros pattern is written to them before the data is written. In the absence of VAAI, this process utilizes the host CPU, the storage processor, and bandwidth.

When you create an EagerZeroedThick virtual disk to avoid this, without VAAI, it takes a long time for the file creation to complete because the host is writing zeros to all blocks. The larger the file, the longer it takes to complete the creation process. (For additional details about virtual disk types, refer to Chapter 13, "Virtual Disks and RDMs.")

Another example is the process of cloning a virtual disk and opting to use Eager-ZeroedThick as the target format. This operation is a combination of full clone and block zeroing. Without VAAI, the overhead is the combination of both operations.

With VAAI, the host sends the `WRITE_SAME` SCSI command to the array along with the range of blocks to be zeroed, and the array writes the same pattern (zeros) to all specified blocks. Some storage arrays have native features to accelerate this operation even more. In any case, offloading the block zeroing operation to the storage array significantly reduces the host's CPU, memory, and network load from such operation.

Hardware Accelerated Locking Primitive (ATS)

The ATS primitive eliminates the need for SCSI-2 reservations during on-disk lock acquisition (see Chapter 14, "Distributed Locks"). ATS works as follows:

1. The ESXi host acquires an on-disk lock for a specific VMFS resource or resources.

2. It reads the block address on which it needs to write the lock record on the array.

3. If the lock is free, it atomically writes the lock record.

4. If the host receives an error—because another host may have beaten it to the lock—it retries the operation.

5. If the array returns an error, the host falls back to using a standard VMFS locking mechanism, using SCSI-2 reservations.

ATS Enhancements on VMFS5

When a VMFS5 volume is created on a LUN located on a storage array that supports ATS primitive, after an ATS operation is attempted successfully, the ATS Only attribute is written to the volume. From that point on, any host sharing the volume always uses ATS.

If, for whatever reason, the storage array no longer supports ATS—for example, in the case of a firmware downgrade—all VMFS5 volumes configured with ATS Only are not mounted and cannot be mounted. The only way to mount such volumes is to either upgrade the storage array firmware to a version that supports VAAI or disable the ATS Only attribute on the volume. To do the latter, you may use the vmkfstools hidden option --configATSOnly, like this:

```
vmkfstools --configATSOnly 0 /vmfs/devices/disks/<device-ID>:<Partition>
```

Here is an example:

```
vmkfstools --configATSOnly 0 /vmfs/devices/disks/naa.6006016055711d00cff95e
65664ee011:1
```

Running the command results in the following prompt:

```
VMware ESX Question:
VMFS on device /dev/disks/naa.600601607ae02600e85affc3f022e411:1 will be
upgraded to or downgraded from ATS capability. Please ensure that the
VMFS-5 volume is not in active use by any local or remote ESX 4.x servers.
```

```
Continue with configuration of ATS capability?

0) _Yes
1) _No

Select a number from 0-1:
```

To proceed, enter 0 at the prompt. A successful outcome returns the following:

```
Attempt to configure non-ATS locking mode on '/vmfs/volumes/FC200':
succeeded.
```

You can reenable the option by repeating this command using 1 instead of 0. If you attempt to enable this on an upgraded VMFS5 volume, it fails with an error:

```
Only newly formatted VMFS-5 can be configured as ATS only
Error: Operation not supported
```

Thin Provisioned APIs

To better utilize thin provisioned block devices, vSphere 5 introduced vStorage APIs specific to such devices. These APIs are the UNMAP and Used Space Monitoring primitives:

- **UNMAP**—This deleted block reclamation primitive enables ESXi 6 hosts to report the list of deleted blocks on a VMFS datastore to the storage array. The storage arrays can then reclaim these blocks from the thin provisioned LUN, which effectively reduces the thin LUN's used size to the actual used blocks. On vSphere 6.5, the VMFS6 datastore supports automatic deleted space reclamation. VMFS5 requires manual reclamation, discussed later in this chapter, in the section "Troubleshooting VAAI Primitives."

- **Used Space Monitoring**—This primitive implements SCSI additional sense codes (ASCs) and additional sense code qualifiers (ASCQs) on the storage array's firmware; the ASCs and ASCQs are sent to the hosts when a soft threshold and a hard threshold are reached. For example, the storage array is configured with a soft threshold of 20% of free space available for growing thin provisioned LUNs and a hard threshold of 10% of free space available. When the soft threshold is reached, the host receives a check condition with the sense key 0x6, the ASC 0x38, and the ASCQ 0x7. The host can then move the virtual disks to another datastore with sufficient space by using Storage DRS (Distributed Resource Scheduler). Otherwise, the host is allowed to continue to write to the LUN until the hard threshold is reached. This is reported to the host as a check condition with sense key `0x7`, ASC `0x27`, and ASCQ `0x7`. When that happens, the offending VM that wrote the last block that triggered the alarm is paused until free space is added or files are moved out of the datastore.

Used Space Monitoring enables the ESXi host to monitor the available space on which the thin provisioned LUN can grow. This is done in-band by receiving the status via the VAAI primitive. The host can then alert the administrator to request to add space to the LUN or move files to another datastore before the LUN runs out of blocks on which the storage array can grow the thin provisioned LUN. Most storage vendors have opted not to use this primitive and instead use VASA-based reporting. Chapter 20, "VASA," covers vStorage APIs for Storage Awareness (VASA) in more detail. Basically, VASA is a set of APIs that enable a storage vendor to expose device capabilities to the initiators. This is done via an out-of-band proxy referred to as a VASA provider.

NAS VAAI Primitives

Another set of VAAI enhancements introduced in vSphere 5 is the network-attached storage (NAS) VAAI primitives. These primitives attempt to bring parity between NFS datastores and VMFS on block devices' VAAI capability.

The NAS VAAI primitives are Full File Clone, Reserve Space, and Extended File Stats:

- **Full File Clone**—This primitive, which is equivalent to `XCOPY`, allows offline virtual disks to be cloned by the NFS server.

- **Reserve Space**—Using this primitive is equivalent to creating a thick virtual disk (preallocated) on an NFS datastore. Typically, when you create a virtual disk on an NFS datastore, the NAS server determines the allocation policy. The default allocation policy on most NAS servers does not guarantee backing storage to the file. However, the reserve space operation can instruct the NAS device to use vendor-specific mechanisms to reserve space for a virtual disk of nonzero logical size.

  If either of these two primitives fails, the host falls back to using the software DataMover as if VAAI is not supported. There is no ATS equivalent for NFS datastores.

- **Extended File Stats**—This primitive allows the NAS filer to report accurate file stats to the host. This helps in accurately reporting the size of thin provisioned virtual disks as they grow.

Table 17.1 provides a comparison between NAS and block device primitives.

Table 17.1 Comparing NAS and block device primitives

Use Case	NAS Primitive	Block Device Primitives
Creating thick (pre-allocated) virtual disks	Reserve Space	No primitive required; native to the file system
Hardware-assisted cloning (offline for NAS) of virtual disks (for example, cold migration, clone from a template)	Full File Clone	XCOPY and WRITE_SAME (full copy and block zeroing)
Hardware-accelerated locking	N/A	ATS

Enabling and Disabling VAAI Primitives

Block VAAI primitives are enabled by default. However, you may need to disable one or more of the supported primitives, as is the case with the UNMAP primitive. UNMAP was reported to have performance issues with implementation on some if not most of the supported storage arrays. As a result, VMware resorted to automatically disabling the UNMAP primitive upon installing ESXi 5 Patch 1 as well as Update 1 and later releases, including ESXi 6.

You install NAS VAAI primitives by installing the vendor-specific NAS plug-ins. They are available as vSphere installation bundles (VIBs), which you can install using Update Manager or the following command on the ESXi host directly:

> **NOTE**
>
> To obtain a VIB, check the VMware HCL listing for the device, which includes a link to the storage vendor's download and installation instructions. (See the "Locating Supported VAAI-Capable NAS Devices" section, later in this chapter, for HCL details.)

```
esxcli software vib install -d /<path-vib-file>/<VIB-file-name> --dry-run
```

Here is an example:

```
esxcli software vib install -d /vmfs/volumes/FC200/NetAppNasPlugin.v22.zip
--dry-run
```

You can also use the verbose option, --depot, instead of --d.

The command just shown does a dry run, going through the process of installing the VIB without actually installing it. It's a good idea to do a dry run to see if you run into any errors and to determine whether the host needs to be rebooted. Listing 17.1 shows the output of this dry run command.

Listing 17.1   VIB installation dry run

```
esxcli software vib install -d /vmfs/volumes/FC200/NetAppNasPlugin.v22.zip
--dry-run
Installation Result
   Message: Dryrun only, host not changed. The following installers will be
applied: [BootBankInstaller]
   Reboot Required: true
   VIBs Installed: NetApp_bootbank_NetAppNasPlugin_1.1.0-0
   VIBs Removed: NetApp_bootbank_NetAppNasPlugin_1.0-21
   VIBs Skipped:
```

From this output, you can conclude that there are no errors and that the host needs to be rebooted. Therefore, you have to plan for downtime for the installation. The output also shows that you currently have version 1.0-21 of the plug-in, which will be removed and replaced with the new one.

When you are ready to actually install the VIB, run the same command without the --dry-run option, as shown in Listing 17.2.

Listing 17.2   Installing the NAS VAAI plug-in VIB

```
esxcli software vib install -d /vmfs/volumes/FC200/NetAppNasPlugin.v22.zip
Installation Result
   Message: The update completed successfully, but the system needs to be
rebooted for the changes to be effective.
   Reboot Required: true
   VIBs Installed: NetApp_bootbank_NetAppNasPlugin_1.1.0-0
   VIBs Removed: NetApp_bootbank_NetAppNasPlugin_1.0-21
   VIBs Skipped:
```

You can disable the block device primitives by using the user interface (UI) or the command-line interface (CLI).

Disabling Block Device Primitives by Using the UI

You can configure the settings of VAAI block device primitives via the Advanced VMkernel Configuration option, as follows:

1. Connect to the vCenter server that manages the ESXi 6 host, using the vSphere 6.0 Web Client as a user with Administrator privileges.

2. In the inventory tree, select the ESXi host on which you will mount the datastore.

3. Click the **Manage** tab.

4. Click the **Settings** button.

5. Select **Advanced System Settings** in the System section.

6. Search for **VMFS3** in the filter field.

7. Select the **VMFS3.HardwareAcceleratedLocking** option.

8. Click the **Edit** button. Your display should be similar to Figure 17.2.

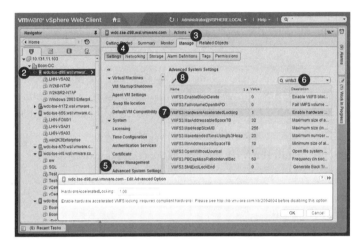

Figure 17.2 Modifying ATS VAAI primitives

9. Change the value of VMFS3.HardwareAcceleratedLocking to **0** and click **OK**.

10. Repeat steps 6 through 9, searching on **DataMover**, and then change the value of DataMover.HardwareAcceleratedinit to **0** and the value of DataMover.Hardware-AcceleratedMove to **0** (see Figure 17.3).

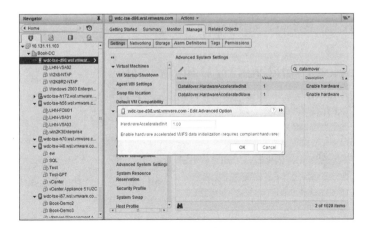

Figure 17.3 Modifying the `XCOPY` and `WRITE_SAME` block device VAAI primitives

Disabling Block Device VAAI Primitives by Using the CLI

If you want to reconfigure a large number of hosts to disable one or more of the VAAI block device primitives, you can use the following steps:

1. Log on to a vMA 6 appliance as vi-admin.

2. Run the `vifp listservers` command to verify that the ESXi hosts you want to modify were previously added to the managed targets list (see Listing 17.3).

Listing 17.3 Listing vMA 6 managed targets

```
vifp listservers

wdc-tse-d98.wsl.vmware.com        ESXi
prme-iox215.wsl.vmware.com        ESXi
wdc-tse-h56.wsl.vmware.com        ESXi
wdc-tse-i83.wsl.vmware.com        ESX
10.131.11.215                     vCenter
```

This example shows four ESXi hosts and one vCenter server registered on this vMA 6 appliance.

3. If the host you want to manage is not on the returned list, you can add it by using the `vifp addserver` option:

```
vifp addserver wdc-tse-i85.wsl.vmware.com --username root
```

You can also add the `--password` parameter. Otherwise, you are prompted for the password. If the operation is successful, no message is provided.

4. Set the target server to manage by using `vifptarget`:

```
vi-admin@vma6:~> vifptarget --set wdc-tse-h56.wsl.vmware.com
vi-admin@vma6:~[wdc-tse-h56.wsl.vmware.com]>
```

Notice that the prompt now shows the name of the managed target host.

From this point on, the process is similar to what you would do via SSH or when logged in locally to the host.

5. List the current settings in the VAAI primitives' configuration (see Listing 17.4).

Listing 17.4 Listing current VAAI primitive settings

```
esxcli system settings advanced list -o /DataMover/HardwareAcceleratedMove
   Path: /DataMover/HardwareAcceleratedMove
   Type: integer
```

```
Int Value: 1
Default Int Value: 1
Min Value: 0
Max Value: 1
String Value:
Default String Value:
Valid Characters:
Description: Enable hardware accelerated VMFS data movement (requires
compliant hardware)


esxcli system settings advanced list -o /DataMover/HardwareAcceleratedInit
    Path: /DataMover/HardwareAcceleratedInit
    Type: integer
Int Value: 1
Default Int Value: 1
Min Value: 0
Max Value: 1
String Value:
Default String Value:
Valid Characters:
Description: Enable hardware accelerated VMFS data initialization
(requires compliant hardware)
esxcli system settings advanced list -o /VMFS3/HardwareAcceleratedLocking
    Path: /VMFS3/HardwareAcceleratedLocking
    Type: integer
Int Value: 1
Default Int Value: 1
Min Value: 0
Max Value: 1
String Value:
Default String Value:
Valid Characters:
Description: Enable hardware accelerated VMFS locking (requires
compliant hardware)
```

Listing 17.4 shows the current value for each of the three primitives, which
is 1, highlighted. Note that this parameter type is an integer (this is what int
means).

6. Change the value of each of the parameters to 0 by using the following command:

```
esxcli system settings advanced set -o /<node>/<parameter> -i 0
```

Here is an example:

```
esxcli system settings advanced set -o/DataMover/
HardwareAcceleratedMove -i 0
```

```
esxcli system settings advanced set -o/DataMover/
HardwareAcceleratedinit -i 0
```

```
esxcli system settings advanced set -o/VMFS3/
HardwareAcceleratedLocking -i 0
```

You can also use the verbose version of this command to disable the corresponding primitive:

```
esxcli system settings advanced set --option /VMFS3/
HardwareAcceleratedLocking --int-value 0
```

7. The command does not return any messages if it is successful. To verify that the change took place, repeat step 5, and you should get the value 0 returned for each primitive.

8. Repeat steps 4 through 7 for each ESXi host.

Disabling the UNMAP Primitive by Using the CLI

To disable the UNMAP primitive using the CLI, you can follow the procedure just shown but using the following command in step 6:

```
esxcli system settings advanced set -o /VMFS3/EnableBlockDelete -i 0
```

You can also use the verbose version of this command, as follows:

```
esxcli system settings advanced set --option /VMFS3/EnableBlockDelete
--int-value 0
```

Then you can verify that the setting has been changed by using this command:

```
esxcli system settings advanced list -o /VMFS3/EnableBlockDelete
```

Listing 17.5 shows the output.

Listing 17.5   Disabling and verifying the change of the `EnableBlockDelete` setting

```
esxcli system settings advanced set -o /VMFS3/EnableBlockDelete -i 0
esxcli system settings advanced list -o /VMFS3/EnableBlockDelete
   Path: /VMFS3/EnableBlockDelete
   Type: integer
   Int Value: 1
   Default Int Value: 1
   Min Value: 0
   Max Value: 1
   String Value:
   Default String Value:
   Valid Characters:
   Description: Enable VMFS block delete
```

Disabling NAS VAAI Primitives

You cannot disable NAS VAAI primitives by using specific configuration parameters as you can with block device primitives. The only way to disable them is by uninstalling the storage array vendor provided VIB for the support of the NAS primitives. You need to reboot the host to complete the removal process, so plan some downtime for that.

To uninstall a VIB, follow this procedure:

1. List the installed VIBs whose acceptance level is VMwareAccepted by using this command:

   ```
   esxcli software vib list |grep 'Name\|---\|Accepted'
   ```

   Figure 17.4 shows sample output.

Figure 17.4   Listing installed partners' VIBs

2. If more than one VIB is listed in the output, identify which one is related to the NAS device (in this example, it is `NetAppNasPlugin`) and remove it by using this command:

   ```
   esxcli software vib remove -n <VIB Name>
   ```

   Here is an example:

   ```
   esxcli software vib remove -n NetAppNasPlugin
   ```

You can also use the verbose version of the command:

```
esxcli software vib remove --vibname <VIB Name>
```

It is a good idea to try it first by using the `--dry-run` option to determine what the removal results will be.

Listing 17.6 shows the output of these commands.

Listing 17.6   Removing the NAS VAAI plug-in VIB

```
esxcli software vib remove -n NetAppNasPlugin --dry-run
Removal Result
   Message: Dryrun only, host not changed. The following installers will be
applied: [BootBankInstaller]
   Reboot Required: true
   VIBs Installed:
   VIBs Removed: NetApp_bootbank_NetAppNasPlugin_1.1.0-0
   VIBs Skipped:


~ # esxcli software vib remove -n NetAppNasPlugin
Removal Result
   Message: The update completed successfully, but the system needs to be
rebooted for the changes to be effective.
   Reboot Required: true
   VIBs Installed:
   VIBs Removed: NetApp_bootbank_NetAppNasPlugin _1.1.0-0
   VIBs Skipped:
```

   3. Reboot the host when you're done.

VAAI Filter and VAAI Plug-in

VAAI is handled on the host's end by PSA core plug-ins, which are as follows:

- **VAAI Filter**—VAAI Filter is a single plug-in installed by default on ESXi 6 hosts. It plugs into the Pluggable Storage Architecture (PSA) framework side-by-side with Native Multipathing Plug-in (NMP) and Multipathing Plug-in (MPP) (see Figure 17.5). All devices supporting VAAI are claimed first by VAAI Filter followed by VMkernel T10.

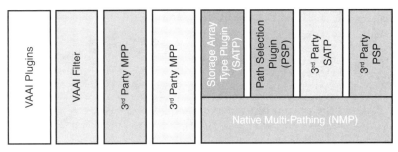

VMkernel Storage Stack
Pluggable Storage Architecture

Figure 17.5   PSA showing VAAI Filter and other plug-ins

- **VAAI plug-ins**—Storage arrays that do not fully implement the T10 standard commands can be supported with VAAI when the storage vendor creates and certifies a VAAI plug-in specific to its storage. Other storage arrays that support T10 do not require this plug-in because VMkernel in ESXi 6 integrates what used to be the T10 plug-in in ESXi 4.1.

  These VAAI plug-ins sit alongside the VAAI filter on top of a PSA framework (see Figure 17.5).

How do you know if a storage array requires a VAAI plug-in? This is easily answered by looking up the storage array on the VMware HCL (also known as the VMware Compatibility Guide [VCG]). The device details include the VAAI support status and whether plug-ins are required.

Locating Supported VAAI-Capable Block Devices

You can follow this procedure to look up the HCL:

1. Go to **www.vmware.com/go/hcl**.

2. Select **Storage/SAN** from the What Are You Looking For pull-down list.

3. Select **ESXi 6.0** and/or **ESXi 6.0 U1** in the Product Release Version field.

4. Select **VAAI-Block** in the Features Category field.

5. Select the partner's name in the Partner Name field.

6. Click the **Update and View Results** button (see Figure 17.6).

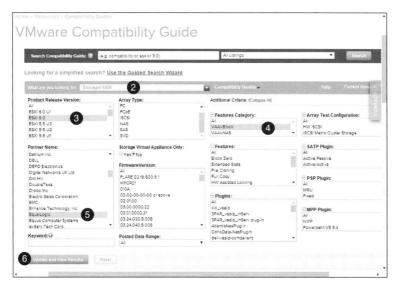

Figure 17.6   VAAI block device HCL search criteria

7. Scroll down to view the search results. Locate your storage array in the results and click the link with your ESXi release—for example, 6.0 or 6.0 U1 (see Figure 17.7).

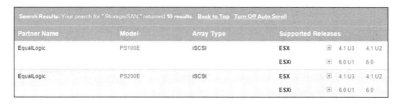

Figure 17.7   Locating a certified VAAI-capable device on the HCL

8. In the array details that are displayed, click View in the Features column to expand the array details and see the list of features, including VAAI. Figure 17.8 shows a sample device that supports block zero, full copy, and HW-assisted locking. The Plugin column shows `vmw_vaaip_eql`, which means the listed version of firmware requires the plug-in to support VAAI. In this case, the plug-in has a VMW prefix, which means it is preinstalled on the ESXi 6 host, and no further configuration is required. Otherwise, you can obtain the plug-in from the storage vendor and install it by following the storage vendor's directions.

Figure 17.8   Displaying device details to locate VAAI plug-ins

In another example (see Figure 17.9), 3PAR (now HP) storage arrays with 2.3.1 MU2 or higher firmware are certified for VAAI on vSphere 5.0 using the 3PAR_vaaip_inServ VAAI plug-in. The link to the HP download portal is listed in the footnote. However, with vSphere 6, the same array with firmware version 3.1.2 does not require a specialized plug-in. This means it supports T10 standard commands.

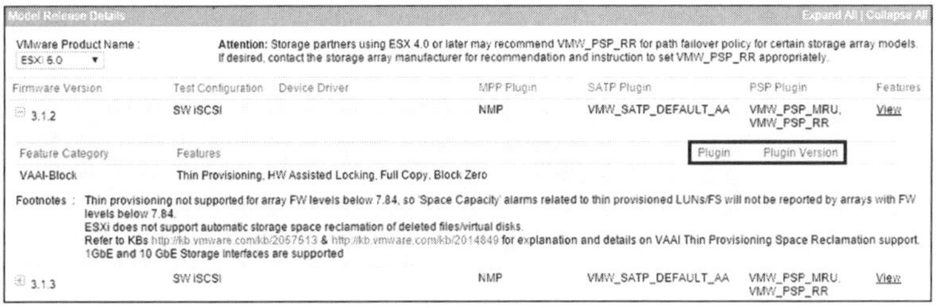

Figure 17.9   Listing device details showing that no plug-in is required

Locating Supported VAAI-Capable NAS Devices

To locate a list of NAS devices that support NAS VAAI primitives, you can follow this procedure:

1. Go to **www.vmware.com/go/hcl**.

2. Select **Storage/SAN** from the What Are You Looking For pull-down list.

3. Select **ESXi 6.0** and/or **ESXi 6.0 U1** in the Product Release Version field.

4. Select **VAAI-NAS** in the Feature Category field.

5. Select the partner's name in the Partner Name field.

6. Click the **Update and View Results** button (see Figure 17.10).

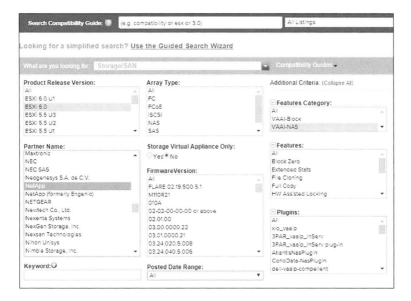

Figure 17.10   NAS VAAI HCL search criteria

7. Scroll down to view the search results. Locate your storage array in the results and click the link with your ESXi release (for example, 6.0 or 6.0 U1).

8. In the array details that are displayed, click **View** in the Features column to expand the array details and display the list of features, including VAAI (see Figure 17.11). You need to contact the storage vendor for instructions on how to obtain the plug-in VIB.

Clustered Data ONTAP 8.2.3	NFS		
Feature Category	Features	Plugin	Plugin Version
VAAI-NAS	Space Reserve, Native SS for LC, File Cloning	NetAppNASPlugin	1.0-21

Footnotes : 1GbE and 10 GbE Storage Interfaces are supported
NetApp Clustered Data ONTAP 8.2.3 doesn't support Extended Stats features.

Figure 17.11   Device details, showing the NAS plug-in in the HCL

9. After obtaining the plug-in VIB, follow the vendor's directions for installing it. This may require a host reboot, so plan some downtime for doing that. See the "Enabling and Disabling VAAI Primitives" section, earlier in this chapter, for an example.

Listing Registered Filter and VAAI Plug-ins

Preinstalled and newly installed VAAI Filter and VAAI plug-ins are actually VMkernel modules that are registered with the PSA framework. You can list the registered plug-ins by using the following:

```
esxcli storage core plugin registration list |grep 'Module\|---\|VAAI'
```

Figure 17.12 shows the output.

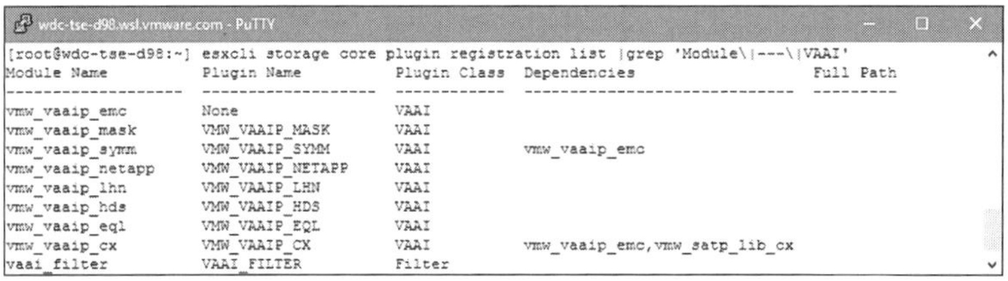
```
[root@wdc-tse-d98:~] esxcli storage core plugin registration list |grep 'Module\|---\|VAAI'
Module Name          Plugin Name          Plugin Class  Dependencies                    Full Path
-------------------  -------------------  ------------  ------------------------------  ---------
vmw_vaaip_emc        None                 VAAI
vmw_vaaip_mask       VMW_VAAIP_MASK       VAAI
vmw_vaaip_symm       VMW_VAAIP_SYMM       VAAI          vmw_vaaip_emc
vmw_vaaip_netapp     VMW_VAAIP_NETAPP     VAAI
vmw_vaaip_lhn        VMW_VAAIP_LHN        VAAI
vmw_vaaip_hds        VMW_VAAIP_HDS        VAAI
vmw_vaaip_eql        VMW_VAAIP_EQL        VAAI
vmw_vaaip_cx         VMW_VAAIP_CX         VAAI          vmw_vaaip_emc,vmw_satp_lib_cx
vaai_filter          VAAI_FILTER          Filter
```

Figure 17.12 Listing VAAI plug-in registration

In this example, VAAI Filter is registered, along with the VAAI plug-ins `symm`, `netapp`, `lhn`, `hds`, `eql`, and `cx`, which are the plug-ins for EMC Symmetrix, NetApp, LeftHand Network (now HP), HDS, EQL (now Dell), and the CLARiiON CX family, respectively. There is also a VMW_VAAIP_MASK plug-in, which is used for masking devices from being claimed by VAAI. (The next section discusses all these plug-ins.)

> **NOTE**
>
> Look at the Plugin Name column and should notice that it is blank for the `vmw_vaaip_emc` module. The values in the Dependencies column show that the `vmw_vaaip_symm` module has a dependency on `vmw_vaaip_emc`. The same is true for `vmw_vaaip_cx`, which is also dependent on the `vmw_satp_lib_cx` library module.
>
> In this example, the dependency is on a common library used by EMC storage–specific VAAI plug-ins. These types of libraries are installed by the VAAI plug-in installer or are already installed for VAAI plug-ins included with the ESXi standard image.

Listing the Configurations of VAAI Filters and Plug-ins

For a device to be claimed by a VAAI plug-in, it must first be claimed by the VAAI Filter plug-in, as shown in the output of the following command:

```
esxcli storage core claimrule list --claimrule-class=Filter
```

Or you can use shorthand version:

```
esxcli storage core claimrule list -c Filter
```

Note that the parameter `Filter` must use an uppercase `F`. Figure 17.13 shows the output of this command.

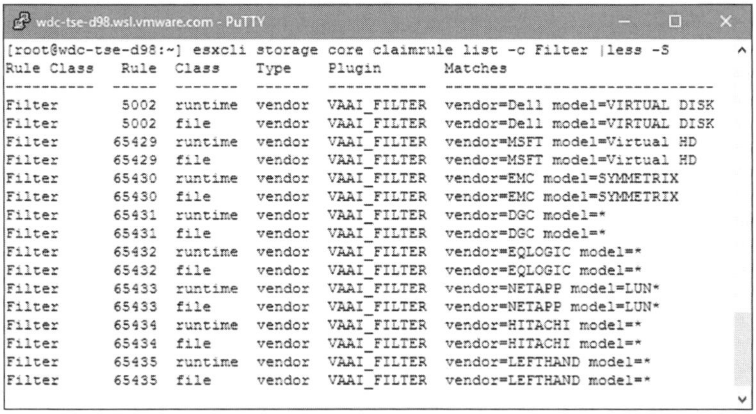

Figure 17.13   Listing VAAI filter claim rules

For an explanation of the columns in this output, see the section "XCOPY Custom Options," later in this chapter.

To verify whether a VAAI plug-in has been installed, you can list the VAAI claim rules by using this command:

```
esxcli storage core claimrule list --claimrule-class=VAAI
```

Or you can use the shorthand version:

```
esxcli storage core claimrule list -c VAAI
```

Note that the parameter `VAAI` must be all uppercase. Also, both the longhand and shorthand versions of the command can be used with or without the equal sign. vSphere 4.1 required the equal sign. The shorthand version is documented without the equal sign, but it accepts the equal sign if it's used.

Figure 17.14 shows the output of this command.

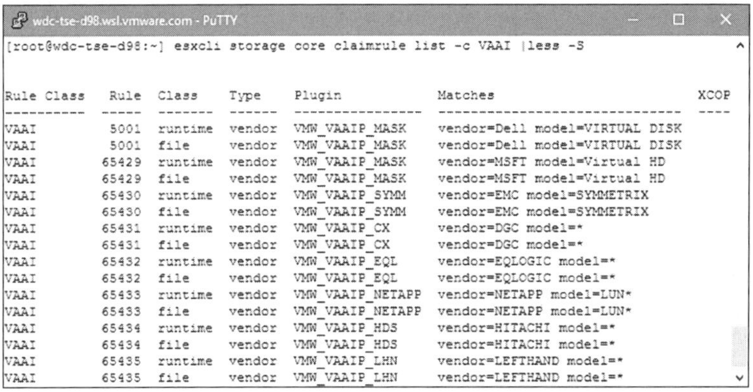

```
wdc-tse-d98.wsl.vmware.com - PuTTY
[root@wdc-tse-d98:~] esxcli storage core claimrule list -c VAAI |less -S

Rule Class   Rule  Class    Type    Plugin            Matches                         XCOP
----------  -----  -------  ------  ----------------  ------------------------------  ----
VAAI         5001  runtime  vendor  VMW_VAAIP_MASK    vendor=Dell model=VIRTUAL DISK
VAAI         5001  file     vendor  VMW_VAAIP_MASK    vendor=Dell model=VIRTUAL DISK
VAAI        65429  runtime  vendor  VMW_VAAIP_MASK    vendor=MSFT model=Virtual HD
VAAI        65429  file     vendor  VMW_VAAIP_MASK    vendor=MSFT model=Virtual HD
VAAI        65430  runtime  vendor  VMW_VAAIP_SYMM    vendor=EMC model=SYMMETRIX
VAAI        65430  file     vendor  VMW_VAAIP_SYMM    vendor=EMC model=SYMMETRIX
VAAI        65431  runtime  vendor  VMW_VAAIP_CX      vendor=DGC model=*
VAAI        65431  file     vendor  VMW_VAAIP_CX      vendor=DGC model=*
VAAI        65432  runtime  vendor  VMW_VAAIP_EQL     vendor=EQLOGIC model=*
VAAI        65432  file     vendor  VMW_VAAIP_EQL     vendor=EQLOGIC model=*
VAAI        65433  runtime  vendor  VMW_VAAIP_NETAPP  vendor=NETAPP model=LUN*
VAAI        65433  file     vendor  VMW_VAAIP_NETAPP  vendor=NETAPP model=LUN*
VAAI        65434  runtime  vendor  VMW_VAAIP_HDS     vendor=HITACHI model=*
VAAI        65434  file     vendor  VMW_VAAIP_HDS     vendor=HITACHI model=*
VAAI        65435  runtime  vendor  VMW_VAAIP_LHN     vendor=LEFTHAND model=*
VAAI        65435  file     vendor  VMW_VAAIP_LHN     vendor=LEFTHAND model=*
```

Figure 17.14 Listing VAAI plug-in claim rules

Scroll the output to the right, and you will see more columns that are new to ESXi 6, as shown in Figure 17.15.

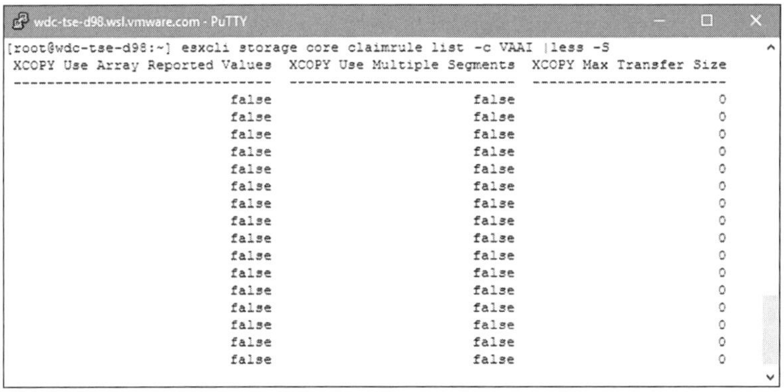

```
wdc-tse-d98.wsl.vmware.com - PuTTY
[root@wdc-tse-d98:~] esxcli storage core claimrule list -c VAAI |less -S
 XCOPY Use Array Reported Values  XCOPY Use Multiple Segments  XCOPY Max Transfer Size
 -------------------------------  ---------------------------  -----------------------
                           false                        false                        0
                           false                        false                        0
                           false                        false                        0
                           false                        false                        0
                           false                        false                        0
                           false                        false                        0
                           false                        false                        0
                           false                        false                        0
                           false                        false                        0
                           false                        false                        0
                           false                        false                        0
                           false                        false                        0
                           false                        false                        0
                           false                        false                        0
                           false                        false                        0
                           false                        false                        0
```

Figure 17.15 Listing VAAI Filter claim rules

In this example, only in-box plug-ins have been preinstalled on this host. The claim rules have a similar structure to the NMP claim rules discussed in Chapter 5, "vSphere Pluggable Storage Architecture (PSA)." To recap, when a device is discovered by the PSA framework, the rule is matched to its corresponding VAAI plug-in by the `Vendor` and `Model` strings identified from the response to the `INQUIRY` command. For example, in the output shown in Figure 17.14, an HP P4000 is a LeftHand Network storage array that returns a `Vendor` string `LEFTHAND`, and any model will be claimed by the VMW_VAAIP_LHN plug-in.

> **TIP**
>
> One of the plug-ins listed in Figure 17.14 is `VMW_VAAIP_MASK`. If you have a family of storage arrays that share the same `Vendor` and `Model` strings and you want to prevent the ESXi 6 host from using VAAI with it, you can add a claim rule for `VMW_VAAIP_MASK` with a number smaller than 65429.

The following is an example of adding a VMW_VAAIP_MASK claim rule:

```
esxcli storage core claimrule add --rule=65428 --type=vendor --plugin
VMW_VAAIP_MASK --vendor=EMC --claimrule-class=VAAI
```

This is the shorthand version:

```
esxcli storage core claimrule add -r 65428 -t vendor -P VMW_VAAIP_MASK -V
EMC -c VAAI
```

Either version of this command adds a VAAI claim rule for the VMW_VAAIP_MASK plug-in to claim all devices whose `Vendor` string is `EMC`. Because that device already has a filter claim rule in place, you only need to add the VAAI claim rule.

The command does not return any feedback unless there is an error. To verify that the rule was added successfully, run this command:

```
esxcli storage core claimrule list -c VAAI
```

Figure 17.16 shows the output of this command.

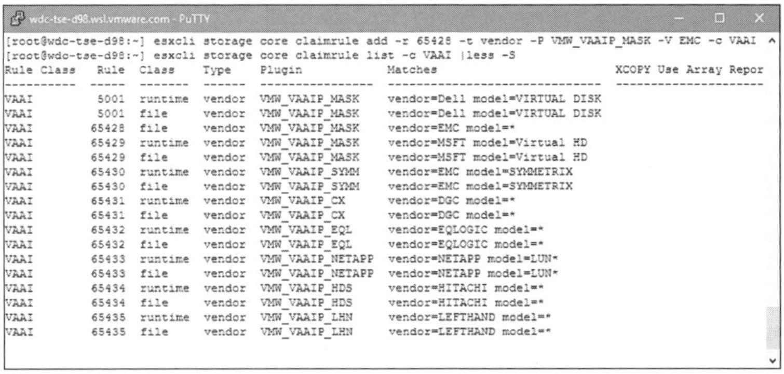
```
[root@wdc-tse-d98:~] esxcli storage core claimrule add -r 65428 -t vendor -P VMW_VAAIP_MASK -V EMC -c VAAI
[root@wdc-tse-d98:~] esxcli storage core claimrule list -c VAAI |less -S
Rule Class   Rule  Class    Type    Plugin            Matches                           XCOPY Use Array Repor
----------  -----  -------  ------  ----------------  --------------------------------  --------------------
VAAI         5001  runtime  vendor  VMW_VAAIP_MASK    vendor=Dell model=VIRTUAL DISK
VAAI         5001  file     vendor  VMW_VAAIP_MASK    vendor=Dell model=VIRTUAL DISK
VAAI        65428  file     vendor  VMW_VAAIP_MASK    vendor=EMC model=*
VAAI        65429  runtime  vendor  VMW_VAAIP_MASK    vendor=MSFT model=Virtual HD
VAAI        65429  file     vendor  VMW_VAAIP_MASK    vendor=MSFT model=Virtual HD
VAAI        65430  runtime  vendor  VMW_VAAIP_SYMM    vendor=EMC model=SYMMETRIX
VAAI        65430  file     vendor  VMW_VAAIP_SYMM    vendor=EMC model=SYMMETRIX
VAAI        65431  runtime  vendor  VMW_VAAIP_CX      vendor=DGC model=*
VAAI        65431  file     vendor  VMW_VAAIP_CX      vendor=DGC model=*
VAAI        65432  runtime  vendor  VMW_VAAIP_EQL     vendor=EQLOGIC model=*
VAAI        65432  file     vendor  VMW_VAAIP_EQL     vendor=EQLOGIC model=*
VAAI        65433  runtime  vendor  VMW_VAAIP_NETAPP  vendor=NETAPP model=LUN*
VAAI        65433  file     vendor  VMW_VAAIP_NETAPP  vendor=NETAPP model=LUN*
VAAI        65434  runtime  vendor  VMW_VAAIP_HDS     vendor=HITACHI model=*
VAAI        65434  file     vendor  VMW_VAAIP_HDS     vendor=HITACHI model=*
VAAI        65435  runtime  vendor  VMW_VAAIP_LHN     vendor=LEFTHAND model=*
VAAI        65435  file     vendor  VMW_VAAIP_LHN     vendor=LEFTHAND model=*
```

Figure 17.16 Result of adding a `VMW_VAAIP_MASK` claim rule

Because rule number 65428 is lower than the existing VAAI claim rule number 65430 for the EMC devices, the VMW_VAAIP_MASK claim rule claims all EMC devices, so they are not claimed by VMW_VAAIP_SYMM.

The only remaining step is to load the claim rule for it to take effect. To do that, run this command:

```
esxcli storage core claimrule load --claimrule-class=VAAI
```

Or you can use the shorthand version:

```
esxcli storage core claimrule load -c VAAI
```

The command does not return any feedback unless there is an error. To verify the outcome, run the following:

```
esxcli storage core claimrule list -c VAAI
```

Figure 17.17 shows the output of this command.

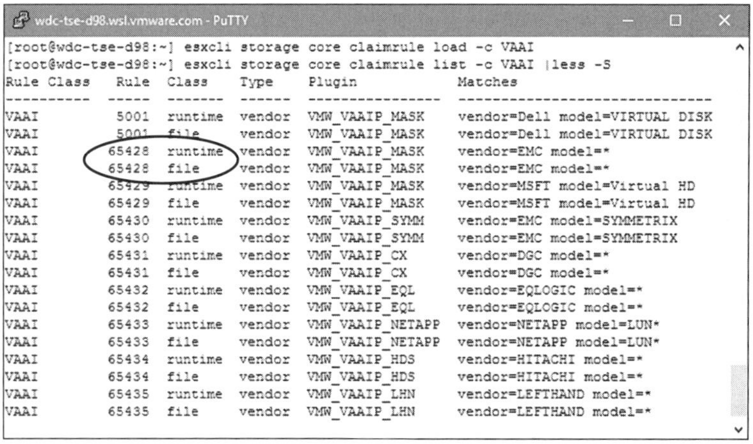

Figure 17.17   VMW_VAAIP_MASK claim rule loaded

As with MP claim rules, the Class column of the output of loaded VAAI claim rules shows `runtime` as well as `file`.

To reverse the effects of adding the VMW_VAAIP_MASK claim rule, you simply delete the rule you created, as shown in this example:

```
esxcli storage core claimrule remove --rule=65428 --claimrule-class=VAAI
```

This example deletes VAAI class rule number 65428.

Next, you need to load the claim rules so that the deleted rule is no longer running:

```
esxcli storage core claimrule load --claimrule-class=VAAI
```

XCOPY **Custom Options**

Prior to ESXi 6, the XCOPY command was configurable using a hidden advanced system setting that is still available with ESXi 6; however, the setting is global and applies to the command on all storage arrays accessible by the ESXi host.

The setting is /DataMover/MaxHWTransferSize. Its default value is 4MB, and its max value is 16MB. You can display the current configuration by using this command:

```
esxcli system settings advanced list -o /DataMover/MaxHWTransferSize
```

Listing 17.7 shows output for the unmodified configuration.

Listing 17.7 Listing the MaxHWTransferSize option

```
esxcli system settings advanced list -o /DataMover/MaxHWTransferSize
   Path: /DataMover/MaxHWTransferSize
   Type: integer
   Int Value: 4096
   Default Int Value: 4096
   Min Value: 1
   Max Value: 16384
   String Value:
   Default String Value:
   Valid Characters:
   Description: Maximum transfer size in KB per hardware DM I/O
```

Because this option is global, ESXi 6 introduced a more granular approach in the form of new claim rule options (shown earlier, in Figure 17.14). You will learn how to create such rules later in this section.

At the time of this writing, the following options are supported with EMC VMAX storage arrays, and you can check with your storage vendor for support status:

- XCOPY Use Array Reported Values—With this option, **the** XCOPY command uses the values reported by the storage array. If this option is not set (the default is FALSE), the global setting value /DataMover/MaxHWTransferSize is used instead. In other words, to utilize custom values for the next two options, the XCOPY Use Array Report Values option must bet set to TRUE. The idea is to override the array reported values of the next two options. This means that if you enable XCOPY Use Array Reported Values without configuring the next two options, the array reported values will be used, and they could be much too large for vmkernel to handle.

- XCOPY Max Transfer Size—With this option, the XCOPY command instructs the storage array to copy data in 4MB chunks by default. Note that the value listed in Figure 17.15 is zero. It does not actually mean that the option is set to zero. Rather, it means that the option is not set, and the default global setting `XCOPY Use Multiple Segments` is used. When `XCOPY MAX Transfer Size` is set to a value larger than 30MB, which is the max segment size, you must enable `XCOPY Use Multiple Segments`; otherwise, VMkernel falls back to using the value of the global setting `/DataMover/MaxHWTransferSize`. EMC recommends setting `XCOPY Max Transfer Size` to 240MB for VMAX storage arrays. Because this value is larger than the max segment size, which is 30MB, the next option must be set.

- `XCOPY Use Multiple Segments`—When the `XCOPY MAX Transfer Size` option is set to a value larger than 30MB, which is the max segment size, you must enable `XCOPY Use Multiple Segments`; otherwise, VMkernel falls back to using the value of the global setting `/DataMover/MaxHWTransferSize`.

If you follow EMC's recommendation, setting `XCOPY Max Transfer Size` to 240MB means that `XCOPY` will use eight segments of 30MB each.

Configuring `XCOPY` Custom Options

To configure `XCOPY` custom options, you can create a custom claim rule in the same way you created the VMW_VAAIP_MASK claim rule earlier but using the specific storage array's VAAI plug-in name instead. To learn the available options, run the `esxcli storage core claimrule add` command. Listing 17.8 lists the relevant outputs.

Listing 17.8 Listing `claimrule` add command options

```
esxcli storage core claimrule add
Error: Missing required parameter -t|--type
      Missing required parameter -P|--plugin


Usage: esxcli storage core claimrule add [cmd options]


Description:
  add       Add a claimrule to the set of claimrules on the system.
[output snipped]
  -c|--claimrule-class=<str>
            Indicate the claim rule class to use in this operation [MP,
Filter, VAAI].
[output snipped]
  -M|--model=<str>    Indicate the model of the paths to use in this
operation.
  -P|--plugin=<str>   Indicate which PSA plugin to use for this operation.
(required)
```

```
    -r|--rule=<long>     Indicate the rule ID to use for this operation.
[output snipped]
    -m|--xcopy-max-transfer-size=<long>
                          Maximum transfer size in MB to use for
                          XCOPY commands if admin wants to use a
                          transfer size different than array reported.
                          This option only takes effect when
                          --xcopy-use-array-values is specified.
    -a|--xcopy-use-array-values
                          Use array reported values for XCOPY ommands.

    -s|--xcopy-use-multi-segs
                          Use multiple segments for XCOPY commands.
                          This option only takes effect when
                          --xcopy-use-array-values is specified.
[output snipped]
Examples:


[output snipped]
    Add a VAAI rule enabling using array reported values & multiple segments
while issuing XCOPY Commands.
# esxcli storage core claimrule add -r 65430 -t vendor -V EMC -M SYMMETRIX
-P VMW_VAAIP_SYMM -c VAAI -a -s -m 200
```

The example listed at the end of Listing 17.8 sets XCOPY Max Transfer Size to 200MB and uses multiple segments with the XCOPY command.

You might have noticed earlier, in Figure 17.14, that there is a VAAI claim rule number 65430 for EMC Symmetrix. This rule matches on EMC as the vendor ID and SYMMETRIX as the model. There is a matching VAAI Filter rule number 65430. This meets the requirement for the VAAIP_SYMM plug-in to claim all devices presented by EMC Symmetrix and its newer sibling, VMAX. To configure XCOPY custom options for the VMAX storage array, you have two choices: create a new VAAI rule with a number lower than 65430 or delete VAAI rule number 65430 and re-create it with the custom options added.

EMC recommends deleting the VAAI claim rule and then re-creating it. To delete the VAAI claim rule, you can run the following:

```
esxcli storage core claimrule remove --rule=65428 --claimrule-class=VAAI
```

To re-create the deleted rule along with added custom options, you can run the following:

```
esxcli storage core claimrule add --rule 65430 --type vendor --vendor
EMC --model SYMMETRIX --plugin VMW_VAAIP_SYMM --claimrule-class VAAI
--xcopy-use-array-values --xcopy-use-multi-segs --xcopy-max-transfer-
size 240
```

Or you can use the abbreviated version:

```
esxcli storage core claimrule add -r 65430 -t vendor -V EMC -M SYMMETRIX -P
VMW_VAAIP_SYMM -c VAAI -a -s -m 240
```

To confirm the added claim rule configuration, run the `claimrule list` command:

```
esxcli storage core claimrule list --claimrule-class VAAI |less -S
```

Or you can use the abbreviated version:

```
esxcli storage core claimrule list -c VAAI |less -S
```

Then you can scroll to the right to display the modified options, as shown in Figure 17.18.

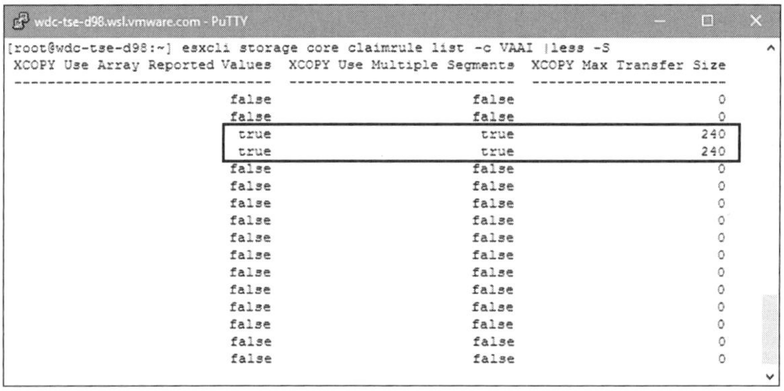

Figure 17.18   VAAI MASK claim rule loaded

The re-created claim rule takes effect after you reboot the ESXi host.

Listing VAAI VMkernel Modules

As mentioned earlier, VAAI plug-ins and the VAAI Filter plug-in are vmkernel modules. To list these modules, you can run the following command:

```
esxcli system module list |grep 'Name\|---\|vaai'
```

Listing 17.9 shows the output.

Listing 17.9   Listing VAAI VMkernel modules

```
esxcli system module list |grep 'Name\|---\|vaai'
Name                Is Loaded  Is Enabled
------------------  ---------  ----------
vaai_filter                    true        true
```

```
vmw_vaaip_mask          true        true
vmw_vaaip_emc           true        true
vmw_vaaip_cx            true        true
vmw_vaaip_netapp        true        true
vmw_vaaip_lhn           true        true
```

NOTE

The output in Listing 17.9 shows only the modules related to devices connected to this ESXi host as well as the MASK and Filter plug-ins. In other words, the VAAI plug-in modules are loaded on demand.

Identifying VAAI Primitives Supported by a Device

When a device is first discovered, its support for VAAI primitives is *unknown*. Periodically, the ESXi host checks the device for support of each VAAI primitive. If the device supports a given primitive, it is identified as *supported*. Otherwise, it is identified as *not supported*.

You can list the current VAAI support status of one or more devices by using either the CLI or the UI.

Listing Block Device VAAI Support Status by Using the CLI

VAAI is one of the namespaces of ESXCLI:

```
esxcli storage core device vaai
```

The only available option for this command is `status`, with the suboption `get`. So this is the complete command:

```
esxcli storage core device vaai status get
```

Listing 17.10 shows the output of this command.

Listing 17.10   Listing VAAI support status

```
esxcli storage core device vaai status get

naa.60a98000572d54724a346a643979466f
   VAAI Plugin Name: VMW_VAAIP_NETAPP
   ATS Status: supported
   Clone Status: supported
```

```
    Zero Status: supported
    Delete Status: supported


mpx.vmhba1:C0:T0:L0
    VAAI Plugin Name:
    ATS Status: unsupported
    Clone Status: unsupported
    Zero Status: unsupported
    Delete Status: unsupported


naa.6001405497cd5c9b43f416e93da4a632
    VAAI Plugin Name:
    ATS Status: unsupported
    Clone Status: unsupported
    Zero Status: supported
    Delete Status: unsupported
```

If you want to limit the output to a single device, you can use the `--device` or `-d` option along with the device ID, as shown in Listing 17.11.

Listing 17.11   Listing a single-device VAAI support

```
esxcli storage core device vaai status get -d naa.60a98000572d5472
4a34695755335033
naa.60a98000572d54724a34695755335033
    VAAI Plugin Name: VMW_VAAIP_NETAPP
    ATS Status: supported
    Clone Status: supported
    Zero Status: supported
    Delete Status: supported
```

Listing 17.10 shows three devices:

- Device ID naa.60a98000572d54724a346a643979466f was claimed by the VMW_
  VAAIP_NETAPP plug-in and shows that four VAAI primitives are supported: ATS,
  Clone, Zero, and Delete. These correspond to hardware-assisted locking, full copy,
  block zeroing, and dead space reclamation, respectively.

- Device ID mpx.vmhba1:C0:T0:L0 was not claimed by a specific VAAI plug-in and
  shows none of the VAAI primitives as supported. This device is locally attached
  to the host, which is why its ID is prefixed with mpx (which indicates generic [x]
  multipathing [mp]).

- Device ID `naa.6001405497cd5c9b43f416e93da4a632` was not claimed by a specific VAAI plug-in. However, it shows that it supports only the ATS primitive. This simply means that the device supports hardware-assisted locking, but it does not have a specific VAAI plug-in installed on the host. How did the ATS support show up then? The reason is that on ESXi 6, VMkernel already includes support for T10 VAAI standard commands. This used to be provided via the VMW_VAAIP_T10 plug-in on ESXi 4.1. When it attempted all primitives, only ATS was successful.

You can list individual device properties, which include VAAI-related information. Listing 17.12 shows an example.

Listing 17.12   Listing device properties

```
esxcli storage core device list -d naa.60a9800042574b6a372441582d6b5937

naa.60a9800042574b6a372441582d6b5937
    Display Name: NETAPP iSCSI Disk (naa.60a9800042574b6a372441582d6b5937)
    Has Settable Display Name: true
    Size: 10240
    Device Type: Direct-Access
    Multipath Plugin: NMP
    Devfs Path: /vmfs/devices/disks/naa.60a9800042574b6a372441582d6b5937
    Vendor: NETAPP
    Model: LUN
    Revision: 810a
    SCSI Level: 4
    Is Pseudo: false
    Status: degraded
    Is RDM Capable: true
    Is Local: false
    Is Removable: false
    Is SSD: false
    Is Offline: false
    Is Perennially Reserved: false
    Thin Provisioning Status: yes
    Attached Filters: VAAI_FILTER
    VAAI Status: supported
    Other UIDs: vml.020001000060a9800042574b6a372441582d6b59374c554e202020
```

The three highlighted lines in Listing 17.12 show that the LUN is thin provisioned, VAAI Filter has claimed it, and it supports VAAI. However, this listing does not show which primitives are supported.

Listing NAS Device VAAI Support Status

With NAS devices, you can list support for VAAI by using this command:

```
esxcli storage nfs list
```

Figure 17.19 shows sample output from this command.

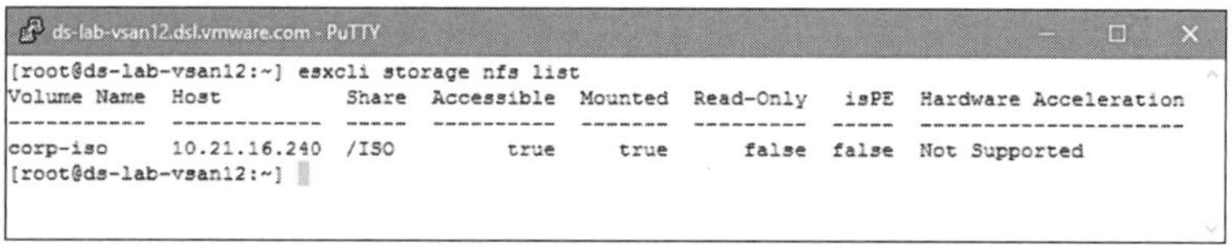

Figure 17.19   Listing NAS device VAAI support

In this output, the support status is listed in the Hardware Acceleration column.

Listing VAAI Support Status by Using the UI

To list devices' support status via the UI, use this procedure:

1. Connect to the vCenter server that manages the ESXi 6 host, using the vSphere 6.0 Web Client as a user with Administrator privileges.

2. Navigate to the **Datastores** view and select the data center in the inventory tree.

3. Select the **Related Objects** tab and then click the **Datastores** button.

4. Right-click any of the columns and select **Show/Hide Columns options**.

5. Select the **Hardware Acceleration** check box and then click **OK** (see Figure 17.20).

Figure 17.21 shows a combined list of NFS and VMFS datastores.

The VAAI support status is listed in the Hardware Acceleration column. In this example, some devices show the status as Unknown and others show Not Supported or Supported. If the block device on which the VMFS datastore reside supports all three of the block device VAAI primitives, the status is listed as Supported. If it supports fewer than the three block device primitives, it is listed as Unknown. If it supports none, it is listed as Not Supported. Table 17.2 shows a grid of support decisions.

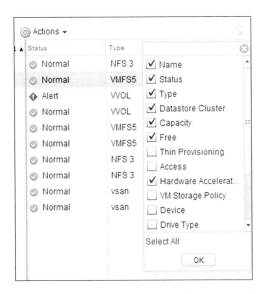

Figure 17.20   Customizing the UI to display VAAI support

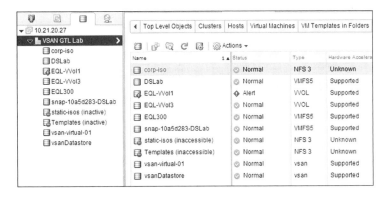

Figure 17.21   Listing block and NAS devices, VAAI support

If the NAS device exporting the NFS datastore supports VAAI and its corresponding plug-in is installed on the ESXi host, the Hardware Acceleration column shows `Supported` status. Otherwise, it shows `Not Supported`.

NOTE

The Hardware Acceleration column is the last one in the list and would be outside the viewing pane in the resolution used to take the screenshot of Figure 17.21. You can move it to the left by clicking the column header and dragging it to the desired position.

Table 17.2 VAAI support status decisions

Support Status	ATS	Clone	Zero
Supported	Supported	Supported	Supported
Unknown	Not Supported	Supported	Supported
Unknown	Not Supported	Not Supported	Supported
Unknown	Supported	Not Supported	Supported
Not Supported	Not Supported	Not Supported	Not Supported

NOTE

There are no arrays that support ATS and/or Clone that do not support block zeroing. This is why Table 17.2 does not list the case where Zero is Not Supported other than in the last row, where all three are Not Supported.

Displaying Block Device VAAI I/O Stats Using `esxtop`

To display I/O statistics, you can use `esxtop` directly on the ESXi host, via SSH, or using `resxtop` on vMA 6.0.

To display these stats, follow this procedure:

1. At the command prompt, type `esxtop`.

2. Type the letter `u` to switch the view to Device Stats.

3. Type the letter `f` to display the list of column headers.

4. To toggle a column selection, type its corresponding letter (upper- or lowercase). When a column is selected, an asterisk (*) is displayed next to the column's letter. By default, A, B, F, G, and I are selected (see Listing 17.13).

Listing 17.13 Selecting device I/O stats columns to display in `esxtop`

```
Current Field order: ABcdeFGhIjklmnop

* A:   DEVICE = Device Name
* B:   ID = Path/World/Partition Id
  C:   NUM = Num of Objects
  D:   SHARES = Shares
  E:   BLKSZ = Block Size (bytes)
* F:   QSTATS = Queue Stats
```

```
*  G:   IOSTATS = I/O Stats
   H:   RESVSTATS = Reserve Stats
*  I:   LATSTATS/cmd = Overall Latency Stats (ms)
   J:   LATSTATS/rd = Read Latency Stats (ms)
   K:   LATSTATS/wr = Write Latency Stats (ms)
   L:   ERRSTATS/s = Error Stats
   M:   PAESTATS/s = PAE Stats
   N:   SPLTSTATS/s = SPLIT Stats
   O:   VAAISTATS= VAAI Stats
   P:   VAAILATSTATS/cmd = VAAI Latency Stats (ms)
```

```
Toggle fields with a-p, any other key to return:
```

5. Type the letters **B**, **F**, **G**, and **I** to deselect their corresponding columns (to save on display space).

6. Type the letter **O** to select the VAAI Stats column. If you want to display the latency stats, type **P** as well. However, if your display is not wide enough to display all columns related to these two selections, you can select one at a time. So, for now, select **O** only.

7. Press **Enter** to return to the stats display. Figure 17.22 shows the outcome.

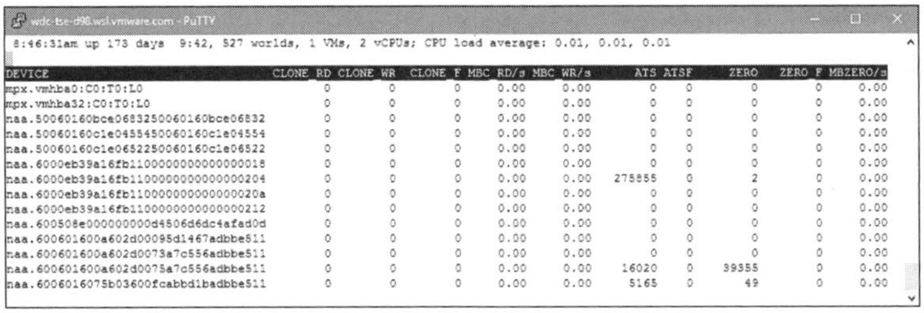

Figure 17.22   Listing VAAI block device primitive stats in `esxtop`

NOTE

To reduce the Device column width to be able to display all the stats in the Figure 17.22, type L and then the size of the field. To reset it, repeat the same process using the size 0.

The columns listed in this view are as follows:

- **CLONE_RD**—Block clone (XCOPY) reads
- **CLONE_WR**—Block clone writes

- **CLONE_F**—Number of failed `XCOPY` commands
- **MBC_RD/s**—Megabytes of cloned data read per second
- **MBC_WR/s**—Megabytes of cloned data written per second
- **ATS**—Number of ATS successful commands
- **ATSF**—Number of failed ATS commands
- **ZERO**—Number of successful block zeroing (**WRITE_SAME**) commands
- **ZERO_F**—Number of failed block zeroing commands
- **MBZERO/s**—Megabytes zeroed per second
- **DELETE**—Number of successful deleted block reclamation commands
- **DELETE_F**—Number of failed deleted block reclamation commands
- **MBDEL/S**—Megabytes of deleted blocks reclaimed per second

If you typed `P` in step 6 to display the VAAI latency stats, the result would look similar to that in Figure 17.23.

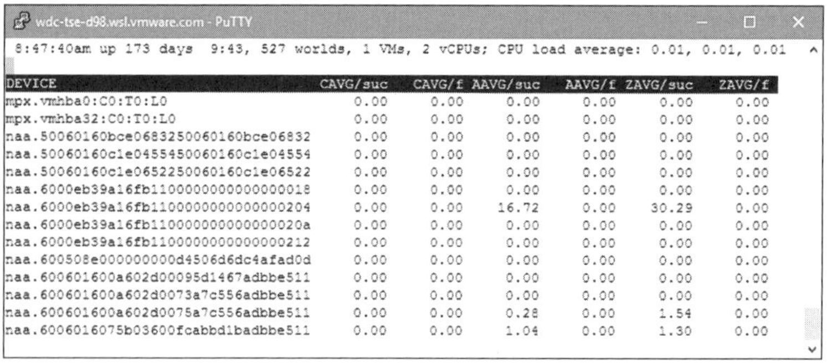
wdc-tse-d98.wsl.vmware.com - PuTTY

8:47:40am up 173 days 9:43, 527 worlds, 1 VMs, 2 vCPUs; CPU load average: 0.01, 0.01, 0.01

DEVICE	CAVG/suc	CAVG/f	AAVG/suc	AAVG/f	ZAVG/suc	ZAVG/f
mpx.vmhba0:C0:T0:L0	0.00	0.00	0.00	0.00	0.00	0.00
mpx.vmhba32:C0:T0:L0	0.00	0.00	0.00	0.00	0.00	0.00
naa.50060160bce0683250060160bce06832	0.00	0.00	0.00	0.00	0.00	0.00
naa.50060160c1e0455450060160c1e04554	0.00	0.00	0.00	0.00	0.00	0.00
naa.50060160c1e0652250060160c1e06522	0.00	0.00	0.00	0.00	0.00	0.00
naa.6000eb39a16fb1100000000000000018	0.00	0.00	0.00	0.00	0.00	0.00
naa.6000eb39a16fb1100000000000000204	0.00	0.00	16.72	0.00	30.29	0.00
naa.6000eb39a16fb110000000000000020a	0.00	0.00	0.00	0.00	0.00	0.00
naa.6000eb39a16fb1100000000000000212	0.00	0.00	0.00	0.00	0.00	0.00
naa.600508e000000000d4506d6dc4afad0d	0.00	0.00	0.00	0.00	0.00	0.00
naa.600601600a602d00095d1467adbbe511	0.00	0.00	0.00	0.00	0.00	0.00
naa.600601600a602d0073a7c556adbbe511	0.00	0.00	0.00	0.00	0.00	0.00
naa.600601600a602d0075a7c556adbbe511	0.00	0.00	0.28	0.00	1.54	0.00
naa.6006016075b03600fcabbd1badbbe511	0.00	0.00	1.04	0.00	1.30	0.00

Figure 17.23 Listing block device VAAI latency in `esxtop`

The latency stats are self-explanatory. The following columns list the average times to complete a command, measured in milliseconds:

- **CAVG/suc**—Successful clone average
- **CAVG/f**—Failed clone average
- **AAVG/suc**—Successful ATS average
- **AAVG/f**—Failed ATS average

- **AVG/suc**—This is actually ZAVG/suc, which is the latency of successful zero commands

- **ZAVG/f**—Failed zero command average

In general, you want a lower average for the successful commands (lower latency) and a higher number of successful commands. Ideally, there should be no failed commands unless there is contention with a large number of hosts that can result in falling back to using DataMover. If you see this scenario, you need to optimize your environment by spreading the load over more datastores—for example, using Storage DRS with datastore clusters.

The VAAI T10 Standard Commands

This chapter has mentioned VAAI T10 standard SCSI commands several times. To examine the T10 documentation, visit www.t10.org/cgi-bin/ac.pl?t=d&f=09-100r5.pdf.

Table 17.3 provides a list of ATS op-codes used by VAAI plug-ins in vSphere 6.

Table 17.3 ATS op-codes

VAAI Plugin Name	Supported Storage Arrays	Op-code
vaaip_cx	CLARiiON arrays	0xf1
vaaip_emc	Generic Library for EMC arrays (Symmetrix/CLARiiON)	0xf1
vaaip_eql	Dell EqualLogic arrays	(Service action out 0x9f/action 0x12)
vaaip_hds	Hitachi arrays	0xc0
vaaip_lhn	HP LeftHand arrays	0xc1
vaaip_netapp	NetApp arrays	0x89
vaaip_symm	Symmetrix arrays	0xf1
No plugin	T10 standard compliant arrays	0x89

The standard VAAI commands are specified in the SCSI Primary Commands-4 (SPC-4) document on T10 site, at www.t10.org/cgi-bin/ac.pl?t=f&f=spc4r35c.pdf.

The remaining commands are op-codes (SCSI operations codes), which are in Table E.2 under Section E.3.1 of the same SPC-4 document.

The WRITE_SAME op-code is 41h (0x41).

The UNMAP op-code is 42h (0x42).

The following is a sample vmkernel.log showing one of these commands:

```
cpu40:8232)ScsiDeviceIO: 2305: Cmd(0x41248092e240) 0x42, CmdSN 0x13bb23 to
dev "naa.60000970000292602427533030304536" failed H:0x0 D:0x2
```

The highlighted value is the op-code, which indicates that the failed command was UNMAP.

Thin provision sense codes appear in Table 56 in the SPC-4 document. These sense codes are for the following: and

- **Out-of-space (OOS) warning**—ASC 38h ASCQ 07h

- **OOS error**—ASC 27h ASCQ 07h

See the next section, "Troubleshooting VAAI Primitives," for some examples.

OOS warning means the thin provisioning soft threshold has been reached. This is the condition in which a thin provisioned LUN on which a VMFS datastore resides reaches the preset soft threshold of available LUN expansion space on the array. The LUN may run out of space soon, and the vSphere administrator needs to take action to either free some space on the datastore and reclaim the deleted blocks or move some files to another datastore. This can be accomplished via Storage DRS or manually via Storage vMotion.

Troubleshooting VAAI Primitives

One of the issues the VMware support team has seen is slow UNMAP performance, such as when using the UNMAP primitive to reclaim deleted blocks. VMware identified that some implementation changes need to be made on most storage array vendors' firmware, along with some changes on the ESXi side. Meanwhile, VMware released ESXi 5 Update 1 as well as Patch 1, which upon installation disables the UNMAP primitive. This continues to be the case with ESXi 6 for VMFS5. However, ESXi 6.5 now supports automated deleted space reclamation on VMFS6 only. To reclaim the deleted blocks manually, run the esxcli storage vmfs unmap command. With this command, there is no need to schedule downtime or to place the host in maintenance mode.

If you run this command without any options, you get the following message:

```
A target VMFS volume must be specified either by label or uuid.
```

Running the command with --help returns the following:

```
Usage: esxcli storage vmfs unmap [cmd options]

Description:
  unmap  Reclaim the space by unmapping free blocks from VMFS Volume
```

```
Cmd options:
  -n|--reclaim-unit=<long>
        Number of VMFS blocks that should be unmapped per iteration.
  -l|--volume-label=<str>
        The label of the VMFS volume to unmap the free blocks.
  -u|--volume-uuid=<str>
        The uuid of the VMFS volume to unmap the free blocks.
```

Example Using the VMFS Volume Label

To reclaim deleted space on a VMFS datastore using the volume label, use this command:

```
esxcli storage vmfs unmap --volume-label iSCSI-2
```

Or you can use the abbreviated version:

```
Esxcli storage vmfs unmap -l iSCSI-2
```

Example Using VMFS Volume UUID

To reclaim deleted space on a VMFS datastore using the volume UUID, use this command:

```
esxcli storage vmfs unmap --volume-uuid 56a10867-5c9b30e8-fc27-001e4f1fbf2c
```

Or you can use the abbreviated version:

```
Esxcli storage vmfs unmap -u 56a10867-5c9b30e8-fc27-001e4f1fbf2c
```

The default `--reclaim-unit` or `-n` value is `200`. This indicates the number of VMFS blocks to reclaim. In other words, with the default 1MB block size of VMFS5 datastores, the reclaimed space would be up to 200MB. For VMFS3 or VMFS5 datastores upgraded from VMFS3, you should factor in the actual datastore block size. Check with your storage vendor for the recommended value.

The `esxcli storage vmfs unmap` command creates temporary files named `.asyncUnmapFile` on the datastore and signals the storage array to reclaim the blocks. This file does not grow beyond the reclaim unit size. It gets deleted after the operation is completed. If the reclaim operation is aborted or fails, the file may be left behind at the root level of the datastore. However, it will be deleted when the command is run again to completion.

Sample Log Entries Related to VAAI

Remember the OOS warning mentioned earlier in this chapter, in the "Thin Provisioned APIs" section? Listing 17.14 shows an example of a /var/log/vmkernel.log message with an OOS warning.

Listing 17.14   A sample log entry message with an out-of-space warning

```
cpu4:2052)NMP: nmp_ThrottleLogForDevice:2318: Cmd 0x2a (0x41240079e0c0)
to dev "naa.6006016055711d00cff95e65664ee011" on path "vmhba35:C0:T24:L0"
Failed: H:0x0 D:0x2 P:0x0 Valid sense data: 0x6 0x38 0x7.Act:NONE
cpu4:2052)WARNING: ScsiDeviceIO: 2114: Space utilization on thin-
provisioned device naa.6006016055711d00cff95e65664ee011 exceeded configured
threshold
cpu4:2052)ScsiDeviceIO: 2304: Cmd(0x41240079e0c0) 0x2a, CmdSN 0x3724 to dev
"naa.6006016055711d00cff95e65664ee011" failed H:0x0 D:0x2 P:0x7 Possible
sense data: 0x6 0x38 0x7.
```

In Listing 17.14, the highlighted entries are the relevant entries, which are as follows:

- **First line reported by NMP**—A SCSI `WRITE` command (`0x2a`) failed with a check condition (`D:0x2`) and a sense key and ASC/ASCQ combination that means OOS warning.

- **Second line reported by SCSI device I/O VMkernel component**—This line provides an explanation of the event, which is that space utilization on the device exceeded the configured threshold.

- **Third line also reported by SCSI device I/O**—The `WRITE` command (`0x2a`) failed for the same reason reported by NMP on the first line.

Listing 17.15 provides an example of a /var/log/vmkernel.log with an OOS error.

Listing 17.15   Out-of-space error sample log entries

```
cpu1:2049)NMP: nmp_ThrottleLogForDevice:2318: Cmd 0x2a (0x412400726c40)
to dev "naa.6006016055711d00cff95e65664ee011" on path "vmhba35:C0:T24:L0"
Failed: H:0x0 D:0x2 P:0x0 Valid sense data: 0x7 0x27 0x7.Act:NONE

cpu1:2049)ScsiDeviceIO: 2315: Cmd(0x412400726c40) 0x2a, CmdSN 0x8f6d to dev
"naa.6006016055711d00cff95e65664ee011" failed H:0x0 D:0x2 P:0x8 Possible
sense data: 0x7 0x27 0x7.

cpu7:37308)FS3DM: 1787: status No space left on device copying 1 extents
between two files, bytesTransferred = 0 extentsTransferred: 0
```

The messages in this log are related to an OOS error (rather than warning). This type of error is reported when a VM using thin provisioned virtual disks attempts to write to a thin provisioned LUN that exceeds the hard threshold set by the array.

In Listing 17.15, the highlighted entries are the relevant entries, which are as follows:

- **First line reported by NMP**—The WRITE command (0x2a) failed with a sense key and ASC/ASCQ combination that means out-of-space error.

- **Second line reported by SCSI device I/O**—The WRITE command (0x2a) failed with the same sense key and ASC/ASCQ combination.

- **Third line reported by VMFS3 DataMover (FS3DM)**—A copy operation failed between the two files.

Summary

This chapter discusses VAAI, which provides block device primitives, thin provision primitives, and NAS primitives (which are supported in vSphere 6). It also covers the details of how to enable and disable VAAI primitives as well as how to identify support for each primitive on various devices.

## Chapter 18

Storage vMotion

One of the wonders of vSphere is live migration of virtual machines (VMs) from one ESXi host to another without detectable disruption. The feature that enables this is called vMotion. vMotion was created to help with vacating hosts for maintenance or decommissioning without the need for scheduling downtime. However, there was no facility to move VM files between datastores without disruption or service outage—well, not until ESXi 3.5 introduced Storage vMotion (SvMotion)

Storage vMotion History

The first release of VMware Virtual Infrastructure (VI) that introduced Storage vMotion was VI 3.5, which was also the first release of the ESXi embedded form factor. The official feature name is Migration with Storage vMotion, but it is commonly referred to as Storage vMotion.

The feature was limited to Fibre Channel (FC)–based datastores and required cumbersome CLI-based commands which had to be run on VMware Virtual Infrastructure Management Assistant (VIMA) virtual appliance or Remote CLI (RCLI). This hindered the adoption of the feature and prompted one of VMware's savvy users to develop a Virtual Center 2.5 (VC) plug-in after reverse-engineering VC plug-ins code. While it had its limitations, the plug-in was a big hit, and VMware ended up hiring the developer of that plug-in.

With release 4.0, VMware rebranded the VI as vSphere, synced up VC version to 4.0, and added a user interface (UI) for Storage vMotion, with full functionality that far exceeded that of the user-developed plug-in.

Storage Distributed Resources Scheduler (SDRS) was introduced in vSphere 5.0. It provides a facility to group datastores in a cluster and balances I/O on the member datastores, leveraging Storage vMotion to move VMs around the cluster. This release also added support for migrating VMs with snapshots, using Storage vMotion. A mirror driver is used to synchronize the source disk to the destination disk, which improved migration time.

vSphere 5.1 added a new feature that migrates VMs' compute and storage resources between hosts and datastores. This feature is referred to as XvMotion, Cross-host Storage vMotion, or Enhanced Storage vMotion.

vSphere 6.0 and 6.5 did not introduce tangible enhancements to Storage vMotion.

Storage vMotion Requirements

Storage vMotion on vSphere 6.x has the following requirements:

- Source and destination datastores must support the file size if it exceeds 2 TiB. This can be VMFS, vSAN, NFSv3, or NFSv4.1.

- If migrating storage only within the same host, the host must have access to both source and destination datastores.

- If migrating running VM and storage between hosts using XvMotion, the source and destination hosts must meet standard vMotion CPU compatibility requirements. This also requires that the vMotion network be configured. The vMotion network is a VMkernel network (vmknic) with vMotion service enabled.

Storage vMotion Within the Same Host

Storage vMotion has many use cases for migrating VMs and their files between datastores on the same host. The following are some examples:

- Freeing up disk space on the source datastore

- Vacating a source datastore planned for decommissioning

- Redistributing VMDKs of a VM from a single datastore to multiple ones to support various I/O profiles (for example, moving the VMDK housing the guest OS memory page file to a datastore on a fast SSD device or a database VMDK to a RAID 10–based datastore)

- Helping with the Storage DRS load balancing process

- Converting VMDKs to different types from the source format (for example, from Lazy Zeroed Thick to Eager Zeroed Thick)

- Migrating a running VM from a datastore that lost its partition table but for which the layout is still in the host's memory to another healthy datastore (This may help rescue the data if the partition table is not repairable.)

- Migrating VMs and their VMDKs to datastores on VAAI-capable storage arrays or NFS servers to take advantage of hardware acceleration

- Migrating VMs and their VMDKs to Virtual Volume (VVol)–capable storage arrays or NFS servers

- Migrating VMs and their VMDKs from multiple storage arrays to a single storage array to consolidate storage and take advantage of newer storage capabilities (for example, VASA, VAAI, VVols)

Follow this procedure to migrate a VM and its VMDKs from one datastore to another:

1. Connect to the vCenter server that manages the ESXi 6 host, using the vSphere Client as a user with Administrator privileges.

2. Navigate to the **Hosts and Clusters** section.

3. Locate the VM in the inventory tree and select it.

4. Click the **Actions** pull-down menu.

5. Select the **Migrate** option (see Figure 18.1).

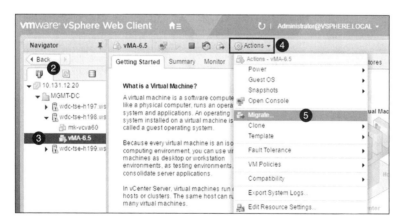

Figure 18.1   Accessing the Migrate menu

6. Select the **Change storage only** radio button and then click **Next**.

7. Select the destination datastore from the presented list. Observe the compatibility pane for status. In this example, it shows `Compatibility checks succeeded.`

8. From the Select Virtual Disk Format dropdown, select one of the following:

   ▪ Select **Same format as source** to keep the current format. Use this with RDMs virtual or physical modes to keep their format. This moves an RDM file and related pointer. If the VM you are moving is part of a Microsoft Windows Server failover cluster, you cannot migrate the cluster nodes that share the RDMs, whether they are virtual or physical modes.

   ▪ Select a format different from the current format. If the source includes RDMs, the destination will be virtual disks.

9. If the source and destination datastores support storage policy–based management (SPBM), do one of the following:

   ▪ Leave the selection as **Keep existing VM storage policies** if the source and destination support the same type of policies.

   ▪ Select a storage policy from the list that matches the destination datastore's. Do this to migrate from standard datastores to VVol- or vSAN-based datastores. This choice will dictate the object's placements on the destination.

10. Click **Next** (see Figure 18.2).

Figure 18.2   Selecting the destination storage policy

11. At the Ready to Complete step of the wizard, review the information, and if no changes are needed, click **Finish** to start the migration process.

Storage vMotion Within the Same Host Using the Advanced Option

If you need to move a VM's virtual disks to more than one destination datastore, follow the previous procedure's steps 1–6 and then continue with these steps:

7. Click the **Advanced** button at the bottom of the datastores list. The list is changed to display the VM's files, including the configuration file and all its virtual disks, in separate rows. For each row you can select the storage and disk format.

8. To select a datastore for a given row, select **Browse** from the Storage pull-down menu (see Figure 18.3). The Select a datastore cluster or datastore list is displayed.

Figure 18.3   Selecting the destination storage

9. Select a datastore from the list and then click **OK**.

10. If the selected datastore supports SPBM, the compatibility check succeeded message is displayed in the bottom of the dialog.

11. When you are done with all the selections, click **Next** (see Figure 18.4).

12. In the Ready to complete step, review the configuration, and if no changes are needed, click **Finish**.

You can monitor the task progress in the Recent Tasks pane.

Figure 18.4   Completing the Selection of the destination storage

Storage vMotion Between Hosts' Local Datastores

A VM that resides on a local datastore on an ESXi 6 host can be migrated to another ESXi host without sharing any storage. This process is referred to as *Cross-Host Storage vMotion*, or *XvMotion*.

To use XvMotion, follow this procedure:

1. Connect to the vCenter server that manages the ESXi 6 host, using the vSphere Client as a user with Administrator privileges.

2. Navigate to **Hosts and Clusters** section.

3. Right-click the VM in the inventory tree and select **Migrate**.

4. Select the **Change both compute resource and storage** radio button.

5. Select either of the following radio buttons:

    a. **Select compute resource first:** Select this to list available hosts to which to migrate the VM.

    b. **Select storage first:** Select this to list available datastores, both local and shared, to which you can migrate the VM's files.

6. Depending on the choice selected in step 5, either select the target host or datastore and then click **Next**. For this example, select the compute resource first and select the destination host.

7. Select the local datastore on the destination host and then click **Next**.

8. Select the network mapping on the destination host and then click **Next**.

9. If prompted to select vMotion priority, select high or low priority.

10. Review the listed information, and if no changes are required, click **Finish**.

You can monitor the task progress in the Recent Tasks pane.

How Does SvMotion Actually Work?

The magic behind the scenes with Storage vMotion (SvMotion) is really amazing. Some magicians use mirrors to perform their illusions. —SvMotion also uses a mirror—a mirror driver—to do its trick, which is definitely not an illusion!

The process of using SvMotion between datastores that are accessible by the same host is analogous to the vMotion process but involves migrating the virtual machine's data instead of its state. With vMotion, the VM's state is copied between hosts over the vMotion network, and when that is complete, the VM is "stunned" on the source host and then resumed on the target host. The process of resuming the VM is somewhat analogous to resuming a suspended VM, which is referred to as Fast Suspend and Resume (FSR). SvMotion does not change hosts; rather, it changes datastores.

SvMotion on the Same Host

The overall process of using SvMotion without changing hosts is as follows:

1. The VM is stunned briefly while the mirror driver is inserted between the virtual SCSI (vSCSI) layer and the file system. Then the VM is un-stunned (that is, resumed).

2. The VM's files are copied from the source to the destination datastore.

3. While the copy process is in progress, the mirror driver does the following for new I/Os in the virtual disks' regions:

   a. If the region has not been copied, I/O is written to the source.

   b. If the regions has been copied, the I/O is written to both the source and the target.

   c. If the region is currently being copied, vSCSI defers writes by retuning BUSY to the guest.

4. When the copy operation is complete, the VM is stunned again, and the mirror driver is removed. If both the source and destination datastores are on the same

storage array that supports the VAAI XCOPY primitive, the copy operations are offloaded to the storage array. Otherwise, a data mover handles the copy operations. The data mover is a VMkernel module named dm.

5. The VM is un-stunned, and subsequent I/Os go directly to the virtual disks on the target datastore.

6. The original files are removed from the source datastore.

These operations log events to the vmware.log file in the VM directory as well as to the vmkernel.log, vpxa.log, and *.hlog files in the /var/run/log directory.

To locate relevant events in vmkernel.log, including rotated logs named vmkernel.<n>.gz files, search for MigrationWizard, which should be near the beginning of an SvMotion event. Listing 18.1 shows sample entries in the host log, or hlog, file. I added some comments with arrows pointing to relevant parts of the log content.

Listing 18.1   Sample migration events in the hlog file

```
33 39 39 35 32 34 55 53-45 38 34 32 4e 42 58 37 ← Helper World UUID
1844006956906266117 ← Migration ID
Success ←Host Log state
From ← Direction of SvMotion (To/From)
fsr ← Migration Type is Fast Suspend and Resume
vmotion ← Operation Type
2240499 ← World ID
Dir F "/vmfs/volumes/56a10867-5c9b30e8-fc27-001e4f1fbf2c/Book-VM1"
Previous line is the path to the VM's directory
File F "/vmfs/volumes/56a10867-5c9b30e8-fc27-001e4f1fbf2c/Book-VM1/
Book-VM1.nvram"
File F "/vmfs/volumes/56a10867-5c9b30e8-fc27-001e4f1fbf2c/Book-VM1/
vmware-0.log"
File F "/vmfs/volumes/56a10867-5c9b30e8-fc27-001e4f1fbf2c/Book-VM1/
vmware.log"
Disk F "/vmfs/volumes/56a10867-5c9b30e8-fc27-001e4f1fbf2c/Book-VM1/
Book-VM1.vmdk"
Disk F "/vmfs/volumes/56a10867-5c9b30e8-fc27-001e4f1fbf2c/Book-VM1/
Book-VM1_1.vmdk"
Disk F "/vmfs/volumes/56a10867-5c9b30e8-fc27-001e4f1fbf2c/Book-VM1/
Book-VM1_2.vmdk"
Previous lines are the list of files to migrate
Vm F "/vmfs/volumes/56a10867-5c9b30e8-fc27-001e4f1fbf2c/Book-VM1/
Book-VM1.vmx"
The last line is the VM's configuration file (vmx)
```

In Listing 18.2, the helper world ID is that of a shadow VM that is spawned and to which the mirror driver is attached. The type of migration is FSR.

The hlog file has matching entries in the hostd.log file, as shown in Listing 18.2

Listing 18.2 Host log dump in hostd.log

```
CopyFromDisk: Hostlog_Dump: Hostlog /vmfs/volumes/56a10867-5c9b30e8-fc27-
001e4f1fbf2c/Book-VM1/Book-VM1-7a58f92c.hlog
    UUID: 33 39 39 35 32 34 55 53-45 38 34 32 4e 42 58 37
    MigID: 1844006956906266117
    HLState: success
    ToFrom: from
    MigType: fsr
    OpType: vmotion
    WorldID: 2240499
    Item Dir F "/vmfs/volumes/56a10867-5c9b30e8-fc27-001e4f1fbf2c/Book-VM1"
    Item File F "/vmfs/volumes/56a10867-5c9b30e8-fc27-001e4f1fbf2c/Book-VM1/
Book-VM1.nvram"
    Item File F "/vmfs/volumes/56a10867-5c9b30e8-fc27-001e4f1fbf2c/Book-VM1/
vmware-0.log"
    Item File F "/vmfs/volumes/56a10867-5c9b30e8-fc27-001e4f1fbf2c/Book-VM1/
vmware.log"
    Item Disk F "/vmfs/volumes/56a10867-5c9b30e8-fc27-001e4f1fbf2c/Book-VM1/
Book-VM1.vmdk"
    Item Disk F "/vmfs/volumes/56a10867-5c9b30e8-fc27-001e4f1fbf2c/Book-VM1/
Book-VM1_1.vmdk"
    Item Disk F "/vmfs/volumes/56a10867-5c9b30e8-fc27-001e4f1fbf2c/Book-VM1/
Book-VM1_2.vmdk"
    Item Vm F "/vmfs/volumes/56a10867-5c9b30e8-fc27-001e4f1fbf2c/Book-VM1/
Book-VM1.vmx"
```

In Listing 18.2, I truncated the content for readability. All lines except the first and last ones were originally prefixed with the following text:

```
ub=Libs opID=MigrationWizard-applyOnMultiEntity-164979-ngc-ee-01-80-6360
user=vpxuser:VSPHERE.LOCAL\Administrator]
```

Listing 18.3 shows examples of SvMotion events from the vmkernel.log file.

Listing 18.3 Examples of migration events in the vmkernel.log file

```
VC opID MigrationWizard-applyOnMultiEntity-164979-ngc-ee-01-60-631a maps to
vmkernel opID c8d5f01d
opID=c8d5f01d)Config: 679: "SIOControlFlag2" = 1, Old Value: 0, (Status: 0x0)
opID=770cbb31)World: 15447: VC opID MigrationWizard-applyOnMultiEntity-
164979-ngc-ee-01-29-6327 maps to vmkernel opID 770cbb31
```

```
opID=770cbb31)Config: 679: "SIOControlFlag2" = 2, Old Value: 1, (Status: 0x0)
World: vm 2240499: 1646: Starting world vmm0:Book-VM1 of type 8
Sched: vm 2240499: 6485: Adding world 'vmm0:Book-VM1', group 'host/user',
cpu: shares=-3 min=0 minLimit=-1 max=-1, mem: shares=-3 min=0 minLimit=-1
max=-1
Sched: vm 2240499: 6500: renamed group 16521273 to vm.2240498
Sched: vm 2240499: 6517: group 16521273 is located under group 4
MemSched: vm 2240498: 8109: extended swap to 48460 pgs
```
Previous lines prepared the VM for migration

```
Migrate: vm 2240499: 3382: Setting FSR info: Dest ts = 1844006956906266117,
src ip = <127.0.0.1> dest ip = <127.0.0.1> Dest wid = 0 using UNSHARED swap
```
Previous line defines the migration source and target which is localhost.
No swap file will be shared

```
WARNING: Migrate: 3451: 1844006956906266117 D: Unable to set NUMA affinity
mask for world 2240499
Hbr: 3394: Migration start received (worldID=2240499) (migrate Type=2)
(event=0) (isSource=0) (sharedConfig=0)
```
Target world ID defined. This is the ID stated in the hlog file under
listing 18.2 earlier. mgrateType=2 means FSR

```
Migrate: vm 2240342: 3382: Setting FSR info: Source ts = 1844006956906266117,
src ip = <127.0.0.1> dest ip = <127.0.0.1> Dest wid = 2240499 using UNSHARED
swap
Migration start received (worldID=2240342) (migrateType=2) (event=0)
(isSource=1) (sharedConfig=0)
```
Source world ID defined. This is the original VM.

```
Swap: vm 2240499: 1419: Successfully initialized normal swapfile.
```
Target VM swap file created

```
FSR: 1500: 1844006956906266117 S: Swap copy helper world starting swap
copy.
```
Fast Suspend and Resume (FSR) started swap copy

```
SVM: 5041: SkipZero 0, dstFsBlockSize 0, preallocateBlocks 0,
vmfsOptimizations 1, useBitmapCopy 0, skipPlugGrain 0
SVM: 5139: SVM_MakeDev.5139: Creating device 19beed6-1f7f097-svmmirror:
Success
```
Storage vMotion inserted the mirror driver

SVM: 5188: Created device 19beed6-1f7f097-svmmirror, primary 19beed6, secondary 1f7f097

Storage vMotion created primary and secondary mirrors

SVM: 2858: scsi255:255 Completed copy in 4 ms. vmmLeaderID = 2240342.

FSR: 1186: 1844006956906266117 S: Swap copy complete successfully.

FSR: 1534: 1844006956906266117 S: Swap copy complete.

Swap file copy completed

VSCSI: 6726: handle 8245(vscsi0:0):Destroying Device for world 2240342 (pendCom 0)

VSCSI: 6726: handle 8246(vscsi0:1):Destroying Device for world 2240342 (pendCom 0)

VSCSI: 6726: handle 8247(vscsi0:2):Destroying Device for world 2240342 (pendCom 0)

Virtual SCSI destroyed 3 virtual devices on source VM.

SVM: 5041: SkipZero 0, dstFsBlockSize 0, preallocateBlocks 0, vmfsOptimizations 1, useBitmapCopy 0, skipPlugGrain 0

SVM: 5139: SVM_MakeDev.5139: Creating device 17deedb-185f09b-svmmirror: Success

SVM: 5188: Created device 17deedb-185f09b-svmmirror, primary 17deedb, secondary 185f09b

SVM: 5041: SkipZero 1, dstFsBlockSize 1048576, preallocateBlocks 1, vmfsOptimizations 1, useBitmapCopy 0, skipPlugGrain 0

SVM: 5139: SVM_MakeDev.5139: Creating device 1a0eede-189f096-svmmirror: Success

SVM: 5188: Created device 1a0eede-189f096-svmmirror, primary 1a0eede, secondary 189f096

VSCSI: 4038: handle 8248(vscsi0:0):Creating Virtual Device for world 2240342 (FSS handle 24768223) numBlocks=104857600 (bs=512)

Target vmdk for vscsi0:0 is created

VSCSI: 273: handle 8248(vscsi0:0):Input values: res=0 limit=-2 bw=-1 Shares=1000

SVM: 5041: SkipZero 1, dstFsBlockSize 1048576, preallocateBlocks 1, vmfsOptimizations 1, useBitmapCopy 0, skipPlugGrain 0

SVM: 5139: SVM_MakeDev.5139: Creating device 18beee0-1c9f099-svmmirror: Success

SVM: 5188: Created device 18beee0-1c9f099-svmmirror, primary 18beee0, secondary 1c9f099

```
VSCSI: 4038: handle 8249(vscsi0:1):Creating Virtual Device for world
2240342 (FSS handle 23457505) numBlocks=209715200 (bs=512)
Target vmdk for vscsi0:1 is created


VSCSI: 273: handle 8249(vscsi0:1):Input values: res=0 limit=-2 bw=-1
Shares=1000
SVM: 5041: SkipZero 1, dstFsBlockSize 1048576, preallocateBlocks 1,
vmfsOptimizations 1, useBitmapCopy 0, skipPlugGrain 0


SVM: 5139: SVM_MakeDev.5139: Creating device 1a3eee2-1d1f09a-svmmirror:
Success
SVM: 5188: Created device 1a3eee2-1d1f09a-svmmirror, primary 1a3eee2,
secondary 1d1f09a
VSCSI: 4038: handle 8250(vscsi0:2):Creating Virtual Device for world
2240342 (FSS handle 30011107) numBlocks=314572800 (bs=512)
Target vmdk for vscsi0:2 is created


VSCSI: 273: handle 8250(vscsi0:2):Input values: res=0 limit=-2 bw=-1
Shares=1000
SVM: 2858: scsi0:0 Completed copy in 19 ms. vmmLeaderID = 2240342.
SVM: 2858: scsi0:1 Completed copy in 36 ms. vmmLeaderID = 2240342.
SVM: 2858: scsi0:2 Completed copy in 54 ms. vmmLeaderID = 2240342.
SVM: 2851: file# 0: Completed copy in 13 ms. vmmLeaderID = 2240342.
3 virtual disks and 1 file (swap) copied


VSCSI: 6726: handle 8248(vscsi0:0):Destroying Device for world 2240342
(pendCom 0)
VSCSI: 6726: handle 8249(vscsi0:1):Destroying Device for world 2240342
(pendCom 0)
VSCSI: 6726: handle 8250(vscsi0:2):Destroying Device for world 2240342
(pendCom 0)
Connections of 3 disks to mirror driver removed


SVM: 2428: SVM Mirrored mode IO stats for device: 1a3eee2-1d1f09a-svmmirror
SVM: 2432: Total # IOs mirrored: 0, Total # IOs sent only to source: 0,
Total # IO deferred by lock: 0
SVM: 2436: Deferred IO stats - Max: 0, Total: 0, Avg: 1 (msec)
SVM: 2450: Destroyed device 1a3eee2-1d1f09a-svmmirror
SVM: 2428: SVM Mirrored mode IO stats for device: 18beee0-1c9f099-svmmirror
SVM: 2432: Total # IOs mirrored: 0, Total # IOs sent only to source: 0,
Total # IO deferred by lock: 0
SVM: 2436: Deferred IO stats - Max: 0, Total: 0, Avg: 1 (msec)
```

SVM: 2450: Destroyed device 18beee0-1c9f099-svmmirror

SVM: 2428: SVM Mirrored mode IO stats for device: 1a0eede-189f096-svmmirror

SVM: 2432: Total # IOs mirrored: 0, Total # IOs sent only to source: 0, Total # IO deferred by lock: 0

SVM: 2436: Deferred IO stats - Max: 0, Total: 0, Avg: 1 (msec)

SVM: 2450: Destroyed device 1a0eede-189f096-svmmirror

SVM: 2428: SVM Mirrored mode IO stats for device: 17deedb-185f09b-svmmirror

SVM: 2432: Total # IOs mirrored: 0, Total # IOs sent only to source: 0, Total # IO deferred by lock: 0

SVM: 2436: Deferred IO stats - Max: 0, Total: 0, Avg: 1 (msec)

Stats of mirror copy operations stated

SVM: 2450: Destroyed device 17deedb-185f09b-svmmirror

Mirror driver removed

Swap: vm 2240499: 1289: Swapfile already initialized. No work to do.

VSCSI: 4038: handle 8251(vscsi0:0):Creating Virtual Device for world 2240499 (FSS handle 25817243) numBlocks=104857600 (bs=512)

VSCSI: 273: handle 8251(vscsi0:0):Input values: res=0 limit=-2 bw=-1 Shares=1000

VSCSI: 4038: handle 8252(vscsi0:1):Creating Virtual Device for world 2240499 (FSS handle 22409373) numBlocks=209715200 (bs=512)

VSCSI: 273: handle 8252(vscsi0:1):Input values: res=0 limit=-2 bw=-1 Shares=1000

VSCSI: 4038: handle 8253(vscsi0:2):Creating Virtual Device for world 2240499 (FSS handle 23982236) numBlocks=314572800 (bs=512)

VSCSI: 273: handle 8253(vscsi0:2):Input values: res=0 limit=-2 bw=-1 Shares=1000

Swap file initialized and 3 virtual devices created and attached to original VM world ID

VMMVMKCall: 235: Received INIT from world 2240499

PVSCSI: 3330: scsi0: wdt=1 intrCoalescingMode=2 flags=0x1f

WARNING: NetDVS: 658: portAlias is NULL

Net: 2441: connected Book-VM1 eth0 to VM Network, portID 0x300000e

SVM Mirrored mode IO stats for device: 19beed6-1f7f097-svmmirror

SVM: 2432: Total # IOs mirrored: 0, Total # IOs sent only to source: 0, Total # IO deferred by lock: 0

SVM: 2436: Deferred IO stats - Max: 0, Total: 0, Avg: 1 (msec)

SVM: 2450: Destroyed device 19beed6-1f7f097-svmmirror

Hbr: 3488: Migration end received (worldID=2240499) (migrateType=2) (event=1) (isSource=0) (sharedConfig=0)

Migration process ended for source world ID

```
Swap: vm 2240499: 3781: Migration swap file is empty.
Config: 679: "SIOControlFlag2" = 1, Old Value: 2, (Status: 0x0)


Swap: vm 2240499: 4106: Finish swapping in migration swap file. (faulted 0
pages, pshared 0 pages). Success.
Swap migration completed


Hbr: 3488: Migration end received (worldID=2240342) (migrateType=2)
(event=1) (isSource=1) (sharedConfig=0)
Migration process ended for target world ID


Net: 3646: disconnected client from port 0x300000d
Config: 679: "SIOControlFlag2" = 0, Old Value: 1, (Status: 0x0)
```

The events from the VMX process are written to the vmware.log file in the VM directory. There should be two files: vmware.log and vmware-0.log. The latter is the events before the VM was stunned by FSR, and the former is after the VM is resumed by FSR.

SvMotion Between Hosts (XvMotion)

The process of moving a VM's files between hosts depends on whether shared storage is available between the source and destination hosts. If shared storage is available, the process is similar to the process of SvMotion on the same host followed by the vMotion process. In other words, the VM's files are copied, the VM is registered on the target host, and FSR is used to stun the VM on the source, removes the mirror driver, and then resumes the VM on the target.

On the other hand, if no shared storage is available, XvMotion (also referred to as Cross-SvMotion) is used. vCenter plays a major role in the XvMotion process as follows:

1. vCenter computes the migration configuration specifications for XvMotion.

2. vCenter prepares the destination VM on the destination host.

3. The VM is registered on the destination host.

4. vCenter uses Network File Copy (NFC) to copy the files from the source to the destination hosts/datastores combinations. If the VM is not running, there is no need to use FSR.

5. The VM's state is also copied to the destination.

6. The VM is stunned on the source and resumed on the destination host using FSR.

7. The VM is unregistered and cleaned up on the source host and datastore.

Listing 18.4 shows XvMotion's hlog file contents.

Listing 18.4   Example of migration events in the hlog file

```
33 39 39 35 32 34 55 53-45 38 33 37 4e 34 42 31 ← Helper World UUID
1844007132194203820 ← Migration ID
Success ←Host Log state
From ← Direction of SvMotion (To/From)
vmotion← Migration Type is vmotion which uses NFC
vmotion ← Operation Type
1130013 ← World ID
Dir F "/vmfs/volumes/58867afb-8f028810-9568-0022640548aa/vMA-6.5"
Previous line is the path to the VM's directory
File F "/vmfs/volumes/58867afb-8f028810-9568-0022640548aa/vMA-6.5/
vMA-6.5.nvram"
File F "/vmfs/volumes/58867afb-8f028810-9568-0022640548aa/vMA-6.5/
vmware-1.log"
File F "/vmfs/volumes/58867afb-8f028810-9568-0022640548aa/vMA-6.5/
vmware-0.log"
File F "/vmfs/volumes/58867afb-8f028810-9568-0022640548aa/vMA-6.5/
vmware.log"
Disk F "/vmfs/volumes/58867afb-8f028810-9568-0022640548aa/vMA-6.5/
vMA-6.5.vmdk"
Previous lines are the list of files to migrate. The last line is Disk
which means VMDK
Vm F "/vmfs/volumes/58867afb-8f028810-9568-0022640548aa/vMA-6.5/
vMA-6.5.vmx"
The last line is the VM's configuration file (vmx)
```

Listing 18.5 shows the hlog-relevant events on the destination host.

Listing 18.5   Initial host log dump, as shown in hostd.log on the destination host

```
Task Created : haTask--vim.host.OperationCleanupManager.createEntry-187904
CopyFromEntry: Hostlog_Dump: Hostlog /vmfs/volumes/<destination-DS>/vMA-
6.5/vMA-6.5-0fed5ac0.hlog
    UUID: 33393935-3234-5553-4538-34324e425837
    MigID: 1844007132194203820
    HLState: none
    ToFrom: none
    MigType: invalid
    OpType: nfc
    WorldID: 0
```

```
Item Dir F "/vmfs/volumes/<destination-DS>/vMA-6.5"

Item File F "/vmfs/volumes/<destination-DS>/vMA-6.5/vMA-6.5.nvram"

Item File F "/vmfs/volumes/<destination-DS>/vMA-6.5/vmware-1.log"

Item File F "/vmfs/volumes/<destination-DS>/vMA-6.5/vmware-0.log"

Item File F "/vmfs/volumes/<destination-DS>/vMA-6.5/vmware.log"

Item Disk F "/vmfs/volumes/<destination-DS>/vMA-6.5/vMA-6.5.vmdk"

Item Vm F "/vmfs/volumes/<destination-DS>/vMA-6.5/vMA-6.5.vmx"
```

In Listing 18.5, I truncated the content for readability. All lines except the first and last ones were originally prefixed with the following text:

```
sub=Libs opID=MigrationWizard-applyOnMultiEntity-209812-ngc-b7-01-e-06ba
user=vpxuser:VSPHERE.LOCAL\Administrator]
```

Observe that the migration type is invalid and the world ID is 0. This means the migration ID and the operation type only are set. Subsequent hostd.log events show the rest of the story. Listing 18.6 lists events related to destination preparation.

Listing 18.6 Host preparation events, as shown in hostd.log on the destination host

```
Task Completed : haTask--vim.host.OperationCleanupManager.
createEntry-187904 Status success

Task Created : haTask--vim.host.LowLevelProvisioningManager.createVm-187905

CreateVm: Path is not on object datastore ([]/vmfs/volumes/<Destination-
DS>/vMA-6.5/vMA-6.5.vmx) ←previous 3 messages are related to creating the
destination VM.

SetVmxVersion: switching environment browser to vmx version 'vmx-07'

ValidateAddDisk: diskProperties are not loaded, using size from passed disk
spec. ←Disk added using size of the source VMDK

Event 306 : Assigned new BIOS UUID (423587e3-220b-8f6f-4020-e76c616c467e)
to vMA-6.5 on wdc-tse-h197.wsl.vmware.com in ha-datacenter ←Destination VM
is assigned a new BIOS UUID

Event 307 : Assign a new instance UUID (5035fdbd-6ae1-3dfa-53ab-
81bbcebcce41) to vMA-6.5

UpdatePortOnVmReconfigure: _vmInstanceUuidAfter is set to inSpec [5035fdbd-
6ae1-3dfa-53ab-81bbcebcce41] ←Destination VM is assigned and instance UUID

Snapshot tree refresh ignored because the disk access is not enabled.

PopulateCache failed: _diskAccess : false, _storageAccessible : true

CannotRetrieveCorefiles: VM disk access is turned off

State Transition (VM_STATE_INITIALIZING -> VM_STATE_OFF) ←Destination VM
state is changed from initializing to off

Initialized virtual machine. ←VM is initialized

State Transition (VM_STATE_OFF -> VM_STATE_UNREGISTERING) ←VM state is
unregistered

State Transition (VM_STATE_UNREGISTERING -> VM_STATE_GONE)← VM state is
gone
```

```
Task Completed : haTask--vim.host.LowLevelProvisioningManager.
createVm-187905 Status success ← Destination VM creation is successful
Virtual machine object cleanup
PrepareDestinationEx [1844007132194203820] ←Preparing vMotion destination
VMotionEntry: migrateType = 1 ← Migration type is vMotion
Completed PrepareDestinationEx [1844007132194203820] ←vMotion destination
is completed.
```

The destination VM is then started on the destination host. Listing 18.7 shows relevant events from hostd.log on the destination host.

Listing 18.7   Events of starting the VM, as shown in hostd.log on the destination host

```
InitiateDestination [1844007132194203820], VM = '/vmfs/
volumes/<Destination-DS>/vMA-6.5/vMA-6.5.vmx' ← Initiating destination VM
Task Created : haTask-ha-folder-vm-vim.Folder.registerVm-187918
Register called: []/vmfs/volumes/<Destination-DS>/vMA-6.5/vMA-6.5.vmx
Registering destination VM
SetVmxVersion: switching environment browser to vmx version 'vmx-07'
Snapshot tree refresh ignored because the disk access is not enabled.
PopulateCache failed: _diskAccess : false, _storageAccessible : true
Replicator: ReconfigListener failed to look up VM (id=7)
CannotRetrieveCorefiles: VM disk access is turned off
State Transition (VM_STATE_INITIALIZING -> VM_STATE_OFF) ←Destination VM
state changed to off
Initialized virtual machine. ←VM initialized
Skip a duplicate transition to: VM_STATE_OFF
Send config update invoked
PopulateCache failed: _diskAccess : false, _storageAccessible : true
Replicator: ReconfigListener failed to look up VM (id=7)
FetchUpdatedLayout: No cached layout files available. Doing a full fetch
CannotRetrieveCorefiles: VM disk access is turned off
Event 308 : Registered vMA-6.5 on wdc-tse-h197.wsl.vmware.com in
ha-datacenter ← Destination VM registered in datacenter
Complete Task: task haTask-ha-folder-vm-vim.Folder.registerVm-187918 not
registered as started
Task Completed : haTask-ha-folder-vm-vim.Folder.registerVm-187918 Status
success ← VM registration succeeded
sub=Libs] SNAPSHOT: SnapshotConfigInfoReadEx: Creating new snapshot
dictionary, '/vmfs/volumes/<Destination-DS>/vMA-6.5/vMA-6.5.vmsd'.
←Snapshot registry .vmsd file created on destination VM
State Transition (VM_STATE_OFF -> VM_STATE_IMMIGRATING) ←VM state is
immigrating
```

```
VMotionPrepare: srcLoggingIp=
VMotionPrepare: dstLoggingIp=
VMotionPrepare: srcMgmtIp=10.131.0.198 ← source host IP
VMotionPrepare: dstMgmtIp=10.131.0.197 ← Destination Host IP
VMotionPrepare: dstVmDirPath=/vmfs/volumes/<Destination-DS>/vMA-6.5/
VMotionPrepare: dstVmFileName=vMA-6.5.vmx ← Destination VM's config
VMotionPrepare: set disk spec (scsi:0:0) -> /vmfs/volumes/<Destination-DS>/
vMA-6.5/vMA-6.5.vmdk, transform: 2, parent disk: , policy: '(null)'
←Virtual SCSI device mapped to vmdk on destination VM preserving source
format and has no storage policy
SetVirtualDeviceChange: deviceChange # 0
VMotionPrepare (1844007132194203820): Sending 'from' srcIp=10.131.0.198
dstIp=10.131.0.197, type=1, encrypted=false, remoteThumbprint=CE:0A:41:D3:
22:9C:D6:2B:96:C5:07:F1:58:5B:15:EB:89:90:80:A1
←vMotion source, target IPs set. Migration type is vMotion (type=1) over
unencrypted connection.
SIOC: SIOC is notified not to start injector
Starting vmx as /bin/vmx
Starting vmx as /bin/vmx ← Starting destination VMX binary
sub=vm:VigorExecVMXExCommon: VM /vmfs/volumes/<Destination-DS>/vMA-6.5/
vMA-6.5.vmx in directory /vmfs/volumes/<Destination-DS>/vMA-6.5
sub=vm:VigorExecVMXExCommon: Exec()'ing /bin/vmx /vmfs/
volumes/<Destination-DS>/vMA-6.5/vMA-6.5.vmx ← Executing the VM i.e.
starting it
sub=Libs Vigor: VMKernel_ForkExec(/bin/vmx, detached=1): status=0
pid=1130012
sub=Vcsvc.VMotionDst (1844007132194203820) Initiate: Waiting for WID
← Waiting for VM's world ID
sub=Vigor.Vmsvc.vm:/vmfs/volumes/<Destination-DS>/vMA-6.5/vMA-6.5.vmx]
Could not retrieve Bootstrap state: N3Vim5Fault12InvalidState9ExceptionE
(vim.fault.InvalidState)
sub=Vmsvc.vm:/vmfs/volumes/<Destination-DS>/vMA-6.5/vMA-6.5.vmx GetWid: got
1130013 ← World ID received
sub=Vcsvc.VMotionDst (1844007132194203820) Initiate: Got WID 1130013
sub=Vmsvc.vm:/vmfs/volumes/<Destination-DS>/vMA-6.5/vMA-6.5.vmx]
VigorMigrateNotifyCb:: hostlog state changed from none to immigrating
← Destination VM state changed to immigrating
VMX reports needsUnregister = false for migrateType MIGRATE_TYPE_VMOTION
← Migration type is vMotion
Succeeded ← Registration succeeded
```

At this stage, the VM has been created and registered on the destination host. It has already been started and is in immigrating state. Next, the destination VM enters a listening state for the vMotion process, and the copy operation is started. Listing 18.8 shows the relevant events in hostd.log on the destination host.

Listing 18.8   The destination VM is in listening mode, and migration starts

```
State Transition (VM_STATE_IMMIGRATING -> VM_STATE_ON)
Entered VmPowerStateListener
VmPowerStateListener succeeded ← VM in listening state
Replicator: powerstate change VM: 7 Old: 0 New: 1 ← VM power is on
Decremented SIOC Injector Flag2
Upgrade is required for virtual machine, version: 7
Send config update invoked
FetchUpdatedLayout: No cached layout files available. Doing a full fetch
Initial tools version: 8:guestToolsUnmanaged
VMotion cleanup completed
Vmotion task succeeded with result: (vim.host.VMotionManager.VMotionResult)
{
-->    dstVmId = <unset>,
-->    vmDowntime = 1406787,
-->    vmStunTime = 0,
-->    vmPagesSrcTime = 0,
-->    vmNumRemotePageFaults = 0
--> }
VigorMigrateNotifyCb:: hostlog state changed from immigrating to success
← Host log migration state record is update to success
Upgrade is required for virtual machine, version: 7
Send config update invoked
Skip a duplicate transition to: VM_STATE_ON
Setting the tools properties cache.
```

Next, events happen on the source host where migration configuration is defined. Listing 18.9 shows the initial host log dump-related events.

Listing 18.9   Initial host log dump, as shown in hostd.log on the source host

```
CopyFromEntry: Hostlog_Dump: Hostlog /vmfs/volumes/58868d88-6cb3103b-1907-
0022649fd19e/vMA-6.5/vMA-6.5-4f464993.hlog
    UUID: 33393935-3234-5553-4538-34324e425837
    MigID: 1844007132194203820
    HLState: none
    ToFrom: none
    MigType: invalid
```

```
OpType: nfc
WorldID: 0
Item File S "/vmfs/volumes/58868d88-6cb3103b-1907-0022649fd19e/vMA-6.5/
vMA-6.5.nvram"
Item File S "/vmfs/volumes/58868d88-6cb3103b-1907-0022649fd19e/vMA-6.5/
vmware-1.log"
Item File S "/vmfs/volumes/58868d88-6cb3103b-1907-0022649fd19e/vMA-6.5/
vmware-0.log"
Item File S "/vmfs/volumes/58868d88-6cb3103b-1907-0022649fd19e/vMA-6.5/
vmware.log"
Item Vm S "/vmfs/volumes/58868d88-6cb3103b-1907-0022649fd19e/vMA-6.5/
vMA-6.5.vmx
```

In Listing 18.9, I truncated the content for readability. All lines except the first and last ones were originally prefixed with the following text:

```
sub=Libs opID=MigrationWizard-applyOnMultiEntity-209812-ngc-b7-01-e3-eaa7
user=vpxuser:VSPHERE.LOCAL\Administrator]
```

These events show that the migration ID was assigned as 1844007132194203820, and the operation type is nfc. This matches what was done on the listening destination VM.

Observe that the migration type is invalid and the world ID is 0. This means the migration ID and the operation type only are set. Subsequent hostd.log events show the rest of the story. Listing 18.10 lists events related to source preparation.

Listing 18.10 Host preparation events, as shown in hostd.log on the source host

```
PrepareSourceEx [1844007132194203820], VM = '13'
Previous line shows Migration ID and the VM ID (you can get the latter
using vim-cmd vmsvc/getallvms command
VMotionEntry: migrateType = 1 ← Migration type is vMotion which used NFC
Operation type
State Transition (VM_STATE_ON -> VM_STATE_EMIGRATING) ←VM state changed
from ON to EMIGRATING
VMotionPrepare: srcLoggingIp=
dstLoggingIp=
VMotionPrepare: srcMgmtIp=10.131.0.198 ← Source host's IP
VMotionPrepare: dstMgmtIp=10.131.0.197 ← Destination host's IP
VMotionPrepare: dstVmDirPath=/vmfs/volumes/58867afb-8f028810-9568-
0022640548aa/vMA-6.5/ ← Destination datastore/VM directory
VMotionPrepare: dstVmFileName=vMA-6.5.vmx ← VM's file name remains
unmodified (default)
VMotionPrepare: set disk spec (scsi:0:0) -> /vmfs/volumes/58867afb-
8f028810-9568-0022640548aa/vMA-6.5/vMA-6.5.vmdk, transform: 2, parent disk:
, policy: '(null)' ← VSCSI 0:0 VMDK format unmodified
SetVirtualDeviceChange: deviceChange # 0
```

```
VMotionPrepare (1844007132194203820): Sending 'to' srcIp=10.131.0.198
dstIp=10.131.0.197, type=1, encrypted=false, remoteThumbprint=CF:86:C8:
C9:FC:F0:7A:F5:D8:5D:42:E8:FA:1C:46:77:BA:46:75:D1 ← States Migration ID,
Source and destination IPs, unencrypted connection and the destination
host's thumbprint.
SIOC: SIOC is notified not to start injector
Completed scheduling PrepareSourceEx [1844007132194203820].
Previous message states the preparation is scheduled
VigorMigrateNotifyCb:: hostlog state changed from none to emigrating
Previous message shows that host log now shows VM as emigrating
VMotionStatusCb [1844007132194203820] : Prepare task completed successfully
Last message shows that preparation task is completed.
```

Shortly after the preparation is completed, the pre-copy process begins. It involves copying the VM's state, configuration, and VMDK files to the destination datastore.

Next, the source host unregisters the source VM from the data center. Relevant events are displayed in Listing 18.11.

Listing 18.11   Events of unregistering the source VM, as shown in hostd.log on the source host

```
Event 605 : Renamed vMA-6.5 from vMA-6.5 to /vmfs/volumes/<Source-DS>/
vMA-6.5/vMA-6.5.vmx in ha-datacenter ← source VM renamed in datacenter
VMX reports needsUnregister = true for migrateType MIGRATE_TYPE_VMOTION
← Source VM needs to be unregistered
Succeeded
State Transition (VM_STATE_EMIGRATING -> VM_STATE_OFF) ← Source VM
transitioned to off state
Entered VmPowerStateListener
VmPowerStateListener succeeded
Replicator: powerstate change VM: 13 Old: 1 New: 0
Replicator: Poweroff for VM: (id=13) ←VM is now powered off
Decremented SIOC Injector Flag2
State Transition (VM_STATE_OFF -> VM_STATE_UNREGISTERING) ←VM transitioned
to unregistered state
VmOperationListener: unregister notification received for VM: 13
Failed to find activation record, event user unknown.
VmOperationListener succeeded
Replicator: UnregisterListener triggered for config VM 13
Event 606 : Removed /vmfs/volumes/<Source-DS>/vMA-6.5/vMA-6.5.vmx on
wdc-tse-h198.wsl.vmware.com from ha-datacenter ← VM removed from inventory
on source host
State Transition (VM_STATE_UNREGISTERING -> VM_STATE_GONE) ←VM is now gone
VMotion cleanup and unregistration completed ← vMotion cleanup done and
source VM is unregistered
```

```
CompleteOp: Vmotion task succeeded with result: (vim.host.VMotionManager.
SrcVMotionResult) {
-->    vmDowntime = 21943,
-->    vmPrecopyStunTime = 51494,
-->    vmPrecopyBandwidth = 117068401
--> }
Virtual machine object cleanup
```

The end result is that the VM is now running on the destination host and destination datastore. The source VM has been removed from the inventory, and vMotion-related content is cleaned up.

The final stage is to update the hlog file on the destination host with the end result. Listing 18.12 shows these events in the hostd.log file.

Listing 18.12   Events related to updating the host log, as shown in hostd.log on the destination host

```
CopyFromEntry: Hostlog_Dump: Hostlog /vmfs/volumes/<Destination-DS>/
vMA-6.5/vMA-6.5-0fed5ac0.hlog
   UUID: 33 39 39 35 32 34 55 53-45 38 33 37 4e 34 42 31
   MigID: 1844007132194203820
   HLState: success
   ToFrom: from
   MigType: vmotion
   OpType: vmotion
   WorldID: 1130013
   Item Dir F "/vmfs/volumes/<Destination-DS>/vMA-6.5"
   Item File F "/vmfs/volumes/<Destination-DS>/vMA-6.5/vMA-6.5.nvram"
   Item File F "/vmfs/volumes/<Destination-DS>/vMA-6.5/vmware-1.log"
   Item File F "/vmfs/volumes/<Destination-DS>/vMA-6.5/vmware-0.log"
   Item File F "/vmfs/volumes/<Destination-DS>/vMA-6.5/vmware.log"
   Item Disk F "/vmfs/volumes/<Destination-DS>/vMA-6.5/vMA-6.5.vmdk"
   Item Vm F "/vmfs/volumes/<Destination-DS>/vMA-6.5/vMA-6.5.vmx"
The remaining event report XvMotion was successful
Task Completed : haTask--vim.host.OperationCleanupManager.
updateEntry-187955 Status success
CompleteDestination [1844007132194203820]
haTask--vim.OverheadService.downloadVMXConfig-187961
haTask--vim.OverheadService.downloadVMXConfig-187961 Status success
```

SvMotion of VMs with Snapshots

The process of using SvMotion with VMs that have snapshot files preserves them on the target. If the target storage is a datastore or VVol container that supports native snapshots capability, the resulting VMs will use native snapshots. See Chapter 23, "Virtual Volumes (VVols)," for more details.

Summary

This chapter provides details about the Storage vMotion feature, which facilitates migration of VMs and their files between datastores on the same hosts or across different hosts, with and without shared storage.

## Chapter 19

VisorFS

VMware ESXi Server has evolved quite a bit over the past 16 years. Originally called ESX Server, it required a Linux bootstrap to load its own kernel (VMkernel). Today, its name is ESXi Server, and it has its own bootstrap based on VMkernel. VMware shipped both flavors until version 4.0, and then since ESXi 4.1, it has shipped the ESXi format only.

In the process of this transition, ESXi Server was referred to as Embedded ESX Server and was designed to boot from embedded flash storage or a USB stick. This meant the size of the server's boot image was reduced to fit on the 2GB flash storage available at that time. The vision was to have system vendors embed ESXi boot images on all servers they shipped and allow customers to enable it with a small BIOS configuration change. This is almost how it works today, but the system vendors now ship their systems preinstalled with their custom images of ESXi Server that include their own hardware administration utilities and drivers for their own I/O cards. How did VMware pull this trick and shrink the huge ESX Server footprint to fit on such a small storage device? The secret was VisorFS.

What Is VisorFS?

ESX classic (the name fondly given to the pre-ESXi Server code) booted from a Linux-based service console, using a boot loader from the pre-ESXi Server code, which then loaded the VMkernel. The service console provided a user-level environment for the purpose of running the virtual machine executable (VMX) as well as other user-level needs, such as local and remote console (SSH) and various command-line tools. To remove the large footprint, VMware added a thin layer to the VMkernel to render it multi-boot compliant. A bootloader that understands multi-boot standard was added, and the VMkernel is loaded through it.

The excision of the Linux-based service console removed the POSIX environment that facilitated running the standard Linux commands and the ESX CLI-related commands. VMware integrated a set of tools (referred to as *busybox*) to provide a management shell called *ESXi Shell*. This is what you see when you use the Alt+F1 key combination. It also provides the environment that enables SSH access to the host remotely. The commands you run in ESXi Shell—common Linux commands, such as `ls`, `cp`, `cd`, and `mv`—are provided by the busybox environment. The original plan was to make ESXi a blackbox with a web-based UI, without any locally or remotely accessible shell. The VMware technical support team lobbied to add a shell to facilitate troubleshooting, which is especially handy if network connectivity is unavailable. This resulted in the adoption of the busybox environment approach.

Now you know how the boot process made its way into the VMkernel. How about the reduction of the size of the VMkernel, drivers, and other binaries needed by ESXi Server?

VMware modularized the various sets of binaries and compressed them as tar archives (.gz and .tgz files). This allows for a smaller footprint at rest on the physical boot device that is limited on disk space (which, on average, has 4GB capacity). The boot process creates a RAM disk in which the tar archives are expanded. VMware killed two birds with one stone using this technique because it also facilitates the option of using Preboot Execution Environment (PXE) booting via network cards that support this feature. Such a boot environment is referred to as a stateless environment and is the foundation for the Auto-Deploy feature of ESXi. Having a small stateless boot image makes it easy to transfer over the network from a TFTP server and load onto a RAM disk. ESXi therefore follows the principle of no installation and statelessness and does not assume any storage. (This has been slightly modified in vSphere 6 to enable persistent state configuration while still using PXE booting, which is beyond the scope of this chapter.)

The ESXi booting sequence is as simple as this:

1. The bootloader creates a RAM disk and expands the tar archives into it.

2. The bootloader loads VMkernel from the boot image that has been expanded in the RAM disk.

3. The bootloader hands off control to VMkernel.

4. VMkernel loads the required drivers and other binaries. As mentioned in earlier chapters, drivers come in two flavors: native and vmklinux drivers. The former runs directly on top of VMkernel, and the latter requires a shim, `vmklinux`, to enable drivers ported from Linux to be loaded on top of VMkernel.

The process of expanding the tar archives into a RAM disk needs some sort of a file system to provide directory structure and file pointers. This is the job of VisorFS, which is a nonpersistent memory-based file system.

This is the process:

1. When VisorFS is initialized, it starts with an empty array of descriptors (inodes), which is a small fixed array that can handle 256 files.

2. VisorFS mounts the tar archives in a certain order. Why mount them instead of expand them? VisorFS does this to maintain the integrity of the tar archives. This also enables the tar archives to be overlaid or unmounted.

NOTE

The processes of mounting and unmounting a tar archive are somewhat similar to mounting an ISO file on your desktop using a loopback mount with integration into the file system's namespace. Unmounting the tar archive makes all of its content disappear from the namespace at once.

3. VisorFS parses the contents of each archive.

4. When files in a tar archive are initially parsed, VisorFS creates an inode (pointer) for each file. These inodes point to the parent inode of the directory in which they reside, based on their pathnames, which were defined before the files were added to the tar archive. Directory inodes are just names and do not contain lists of their members. In other words, the members know their parents but not vice versa. It is somewhat like with virtual machine snapshot files: The delta disks know their parent's content ID (CID), but the parent has no knowledge of the children's existence. This means that listing the contents of a directory requires checking the entire list of inodes for their pathnames to find the inodes pointing to the directory. This does not have much of an impact on performance because the number of inodes is small.

5. If VisorFS encounters a duplicate file in other tar archives, it simply assigns it the inode of the inode already in place. The file parsed earlier becomes inaccessible but remains in memory as part of the tar archive to which it belongs. This is why there is a strict order of loading the .tar archives: The last one parsed takes precedence.

6. If a file needs to be created, VisorFS treats it as a temporary file; it is on a RAM disk, which is not persistent. It does that by creating an inode for the file and pointing it to the parent directory's inode. This file entry starts first as *void*, indicating and empty file. When a write operation is done, a sufficient amount of memory is allocated from a VisorFS RAM disk to hold the file's content and its inode.

7. On subsequent modifications to the file, the memory allocated to it is reused if there is sufficient allocated memory. If there is not enough, the file is reallocated with a larger block size. This ensures that the file content does not get fragmented.

VisorFS implements a POSIX file system, which provides all expected operations on top of the tar disks and RAM disks—for example, directory and file creation, deletion, attribute management, and symbolic links.

RAM Disks

Some vSphere administrators have been under the impression that there is a single RAM disk (ramdisk) used by a given ESXi host. To see that this is not the case, you can run this command on any ESXi 6 host:

```
localcli system visorfs ramdisk list
```

The output is too wide to list in one screenshot. Thanks to some graphics magic, Figures 19.1 and 19.2 show the output, with the first two columns repeated in each half.

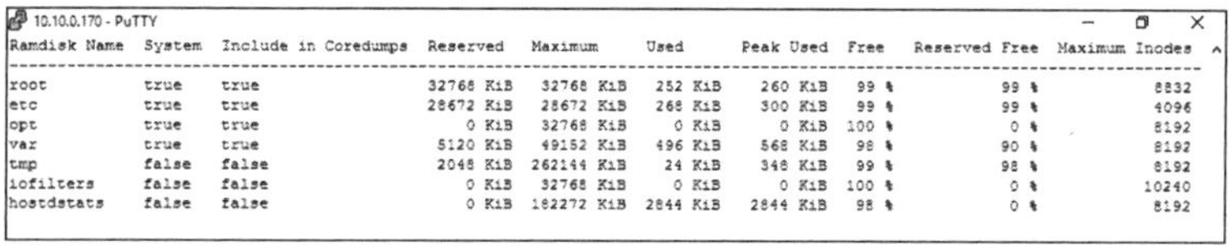

Ramdisk Name	System	Include in Coredumps	Reserved	Maximum	Used	Peak Used	Free	Reserved Free	Maximum Inodes
root	true	true	32768 KiB	32768 KiB	252 KiB	260 KiB	99 %	99 %	8832
etc	true	true	28672 KiB	28672 KiB	268 KiB	300 KiB	99 %	99 %	4096
opt	true	true	0 KiB	32768 KiB	0 KiB	0 KiB	100 %	0 %	8192
var	true	true	5120 KiB	49152 KiB	496 KiB	568 KiB	98 %	90 %	8192
tmp	false	false	2048 KiB	262144 KiB	24 KiB	348 KiB	99 %	98 %	8192
iofilters	false	false	0 KiB	32768 KiB	0 KiB	0 KiB	100 %	0 %	10240
hostdstats	false	false	0 KiB	182272 KiB	2844 KiB	2844 KiB	98 %	0 %	8192

Figure 19.1   Listing VisorFS ramdisks, part 1

Figure 19.1 shows seven ramdisks: root, etc, opt, var, tmp, iofilters, and hostdstats. It also shows whether each ramdisk is a system disk. A ramdisk that is a system disk is part of the ESXi system.

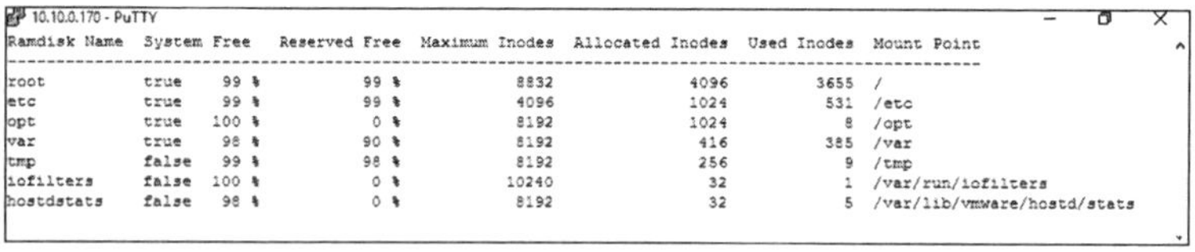

Ramdisk Name	System	Free	Reserved Free	Maximum Inodes	Allocated Inodes	Used Inodes	Mount Point
root	true	99 %	99 %	8832	4096	3655	/
etc	true	99 %	99 %	4096	1024	531	/etc
opt	true	100 %	0 %	8192	1024	8	/opt
var	true	98 %	90 %	8192	416	385	/var
tmp	false	99 %	98 %	8192	256	9	/tmp
iofilters	false	100 %	0 %	10240	32	1	/var/run/iofilters
hostdstats	false	98 %	0 %	8192	32	5	/var/lib/vmware/hostd/stats

Figure 19.2   Listing VisorFS ramdisks, part 2

Figure 19.2 shows the remaining columns for these ramdisks. The last column is the mount point.

Stateful or Stateless?

What happens to changes made to the configurations? ESXi was designed to be stateless, but that does not mean that the state cannot be changed.

This is what stateless means:

- The master state is inherited on boot from an authoritative entity (for example, the local boot image or, for PXE boot, the TFTP server.

- State changes get recorded by the authority. In the case of ESXi, they are written to a file named local.tgz at the root RAM disk. A script named /bin/backup.sh runs hourly and upon shutdown. It saves local.tgz by archiving it into file called state.tgz on the /bootbank partition.

The /bootbank partition is a physical disk partition on which the ESXi image is installed. It is a physical VFAT partition on the boot device. The same boot device also has an /altbootbank partition.

A file named boot.cfg exists in each /bootbank partition. When a new VIB is installed or when the ESXi image is updated live, the new bundles get installed onto the /altbootbank partition, and then boot.cfg on that /altbootbank partition is updated so that the field named *updated* has a value larger than its peer on /bootbank.

Another field in the boot.cfg to be modified on /altbootbank is *bootstate*. Table 19.1 lists the possible values of this field and their meaning.

Table 19.1 ESXi boot.cfg bootstate field values

Value	Meaning for Bootbank
0	Bootbank booted successfully
1	Updated but not booted yet
2	Being booted but not finished yet
3	Empty
4	New Image profile has been staged. Update not finished yet.

The bootstate in both /bootbank and /altbootbank partitions is 0 upon completing a successful boot. The value of the current /bootbank partition does not change during runtime. All boot image changes are done to the /altbootbank partition.

During the host's shutdown process, the /bin/backup.sh script checks the value of the *updated* field of the boot.cfg file in both /bootbank and /altbootbank partitions, and for the one with the higher value, the boot option is updated to use that partition's UUID as the BootUUID.

To identify the current boot options, run this command:

```
bootOption -o
```

This returns a string like this:

```
Options : vmbTrustedBoot=false tboot=0x0x101b000
installerDiskDumpSlotSize=2560 no-auto-partition
bootUUID=79383cb125ec8a951b0a7c24fd6c110b
```

The last field in the output is updated by the boot loader to reflect the UUID of the boot partition that corresponds to the /bootbank partition whose boot.cfg file had a larger value for the *updated* field during the last boot.

This is the sequence of events for updating and saving the host's state:

1. Configuration changes are made to the relevant configuration files in the /etc ramdisk and its children.

2. ESXi advanced system configurations are stored in VSI nodes (which are VMkernel equivalents to proc nodes).

3. When the host shutdown process starts, the /bin/shutdown.sh script is called.

4. This script calls the /bin/backup.sh script (which is also run hourly), which does the following:

   a. Saves any modified files located in the /etc ramdisk and its children to the / bootbank/local.tgz file.

   b. Creates, or if it already exists, updates the /bootbank/state.tgz file and inserts in it the local.tgz file.

   c. Checks the /bootbank partition for the presence of the state.tgz file, and if it exists, updates the boot.cfg file to include it in the list of the tar disk's load order.

   d. Updates the /bootbank/useropts.gz file with the output of esxcfg-info.

   e. Checks the /altbootbank/boot.cfg *bootstate* field. If the value is 1 (which means updated; refer to Table 19.1), it copies the current state.tgz file to / altbootbank. If /bootbank/useropts.gz exists, it copies it to /altbootbank.

The result is two partitions, where the current state (state.tgz and useropts.gz) is saved to /bootbank, and if /altbootbank is to be used for the next boot, the state is saved to it as well. Upon booting, the local.tgz file is extracted from the /bootbank/state.tgz file and mounted on the root ramdisk.

Boot Device Partitions

If an ESXi host boots from a USB flash or SD card, it is partitioned into the system partition on which the bootloader resides and four VFAT partitions. The ESXi installation process detects these types of devices and switches to embedded installation mode, which does not include coredump or log partitions. In addition, if the boot device is a SATADOM (newer SLC-based models) or a larger device (for example, a Magnetic Disk or SSD), the installer creates a vmkernel coredump partition and, in the leftover space, a VMFS5 partition.

To list the current partition table of the boot device, first identify the device name by its prefix using `vmkfstools`:

```
vmkfstools --queryfs --humanreadable /bootbank |grep naa
```

Or you can use the abbreviated option:

```
vmkfstools -Ph /bootbank |grep naa
```

If you are running a nested ESXi environment (for example, test lab where ESXi hosts run in VMs), the device prefix may be `mpx`. Some physical or virtual devices may also have a `t10` prefix.

The output looks something like this:

```
naa.600508e000000000d4506d6dc4afad0d:6
```

This means that the boot device is `naa.600508e000000000d4506d6dc4afad0d` (omitting the partition number that appears at the end of the output).

Now, list the partition table of that device:

```
partedUtil getptbl /dev/disks/naa.600508e000000000d4506d6dc4afad0d
```

Listing 19.1 shows this command and its output.

Listing 19.1 Listing a boot device partition table by using `partedUtil`

```
partedUtil getptbl /dev/disks/naa.600508e000000000d4506d6dc4afad0d
gpt
8875 255 63 142577664
1 64 8191 C12A7328F81F11D2BA4B00A0C93EC93B systemPartition 128
5 8224 520191 EBD0A0A2B9E5443387C068B6B72699C7 linuxNative 0
6 520224 1032191 EBD0A0A2B9E5443387C068B6B72699C7 linuxNative 0
7 1032224 1257471 9D27538040AD11DBBF97000C2911D1B8 vmkDiagnostic 0
8 1257504 1843199 EBD0A0A2B9E5443387C068B6B72699C7 linuxNative 0
2 1843200 10229759 EBD0A0A2B9E5443387C068B6B72699C7 linuxNative 0
3 10229760 142577630 AA31E02A400F11DB9590000C2911D1B8 vmfs 0
```

The two highlighted partitions may not exist on USB flash or similar small flash-based boot devices.

The four partitions with LinuxNative as the partition type are actually VFAT partitions. To list these partitions, simply run this command at the root level:

```
ls -Al |grep /vmfs
```

Listing 19.2 shows this command and its output, with the leading columns truncated for readability.

Listing 19.2 Listing directories representing VFAT partitions

```
ls -Al |grep /vmfs
altbootbank -> /vmfs/volumes/154ac970-f904eab4-3ea6-06981e5ddab7
bootbank -> /vmfs/volumes/b64ea873-f33dc2d2-d512-54bede6714bf
scratch -> /vmfs/volumes/5384e3de-e2a80908-61b2-001e4f1fbf2c
store -> /vmfs/volumes/4d7beb9b-be160782-39fc-001e4f1fbf2c
```

The output in Listing 19.2 shows four directories symbolically linked to four datastores. These directories are:

- **altbootbank**—The ESXi image is installed here. This is the alternate bootbank.

- **bootbank**—The ESXi image is installed here as well. However, this is the current bootbank.

- **scratch**—This is where temporary nonsystem files are stored. It has five subdirectories:

  - **Core**—This is where vmkernel and other related core dumps are copied from the vmkDiagnostic partition (refer to Listing 19.1).

  - **Downloads**—This is for storing downloaded files that are not related to patches or updates.

  - **log**—This is a persistent log storage location for an ESXi host. The /var/run/log directory is symbolically linked to this one. Also, many log files in the /var/log directory are symbolically linked to corresponding files in the /scratch/log directory if the boot device is a USB flash or SD card since their endurance is not usually very high. This results in the device failing due to the amount of data written to it daily. It is recommended to redirect the scratch partition to a more durable flash storage, hard disk, SAN device, or NFS datastore. See Chapter 21, "vSAN Core Features," for more information about flash storage durability.

- **var**—Currently, this directory hosts the tmp/sfcb_cache.txt file, which is the small-footprint CIM broker–related cache file. This cache file includes the system's vendor and model names.

- **vsantraces**—This is where vSAN keeps its trace files, which are critical for diagnosing certain types of vSAN issue. This, too, writes to the partition frequently, which is another justification for redirecting the /scratch partition to a more durable device.

- **store**—This is a root-level directory. The locker is symbolically linked to this partition, which includes two subdirectories:

  - **packages**—This includes two directories: 6.0.0 and var. A root-level directory, productLocker, is symbolically linked to 6.0.0. It houses certain guest OS drivers' floppy images and VM tools ISOs. The var directory houses metadata about some of the product packages.

  - **var**—This includes a core directory.

How do you know that these partitions are VFAT partitions, even though the partedUtil output states they are LinuxNative type? To find out, run this command:

```
localcli storage filesystem list |grep 'Mount\|---\|vfat' |less -S
```

Figure 19.3 shows the command and its output.

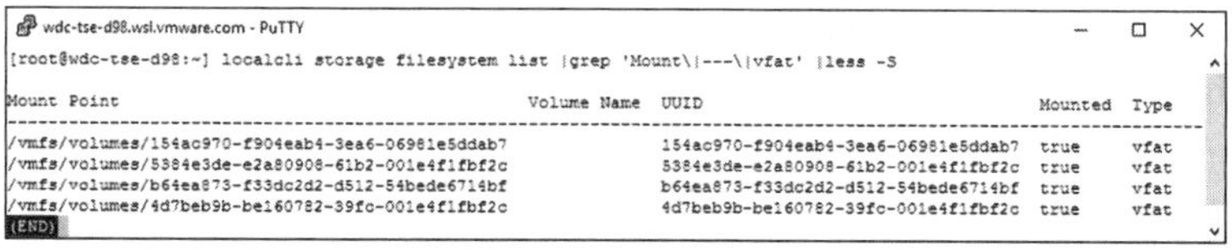

Figure 19.3 Listing VFAT partitions

Figure 19.3 shows the mount points and the UUIDs of the partitions, and the Type column shows that the partition type is vfat.

Many other files and directories are symbolically linked to maintain backward compatibility with earlier releases and older versions of certain utilities. Some of the links are for the purpose of storing the linked files and directories on persistent storage.

Rolling Back to a Previous Version

The ESXi host boot loader offers an option to roll back to the previous installation, thanks to the dual-/bootbank configuration. As mentioned earlier, when an update or upgrade is installed on ESXi hosts, it is written to the /altbootbank partition, and then, upon next boot, that bank becomes the /bootbank partition, and the older one becomes /altbootbank. If the host fails to boot into the newly installed update or upgrade, you can reboot the host and press the **Shift+r** keyboard combination when the prompt appears on the boot screen. This option is referred to as recovery mode (see Figure 19.4).

Figure 19.4   ESXi recovery mode

This triggers the process of swapping bootbank roles by changing the value of the *updated* field in /altbootbank/boot.cfg to a value higher than that in the current /bootbank/boot.cfg file. Rebooting after that boots into the version prior to the latest update or upgrade.

Summary

VisorFS is a memory-based file system. Seven ramdisks are created by default. System tar files are mounted on five of them. An ESXi host boot image is installed on two partitions: /bootbank and /altbootbank. Which partition is used upon boot depends on the highest value of a field named *updated* in the boot.cfg file in that bootbank directory. The name /bootbank is given to the directory from which the host boots, and the other bank is named /altbootbank. This is done dynamically at boot time. System state is saved to local. tgz and then the latter added to state.tgz hourly and upon shutdown. The state gets loaded from the /bootbank partition upon booting the host.

## Chapter 20

VASA

Have you ever wanted to create a datastore for a specific I/O profile or on a device with a specific RAID type? To do that in the past, you had to ask the storage administrator to either tell you the capabilities of a device or create one with the required capabilities. Those days are long gone, now that VMware has defined APIs that enable storage arrays to expose their capabilities to vCenter Server (VC) and, in turn, to the ESXi hosts. This set of APIs is referred to as vStorage APIs for Storage Awareness (VASA).

What Is VASA?

The VASA APIs are a building block of VMware's software-defined storage. VASA enables storage partners to create VMware vCenter storage providers that allow an administrator to monitor physical storage topology, capabilities, and state. This makes storage usage for daily operation more transparent for vSphere administrators.

VASA is an integral part of VMware storage policy–based management (SPBM), which is covered in Chapters 21, "vSAN Core Features," 22, "vSAN Advanced Features," and 23, "Virtual Volumes (VVols)."

VASA Architecture

Communications between VC and the storage arrays are facilitated by VASA providers (also referred to as vendor providers). The storage vendors create these providers by using the APIs that are defined by VASA and that are available as virtual appliances or integrated into the storage arrays' firmware. These providers are certified by VMware and listed in the VMware Compatibility Guide (vCG).

VASA Versions

VASA was first introduced in vSphere 5.0 as VASA version 1.0, which was revised to VASA 1.5 in vSphere 5.5 to enable the first release of VMware's vSAN. vSphere 6 further updated the APIs to version 2 to enable version 6 of vSAN as well as VMware Virtual Volumes (VVols). (Chapter 21 discussed vSAN, and Chapter 22 covers VVols.).

Figure 20.1 shows a high-level VASA architecture.

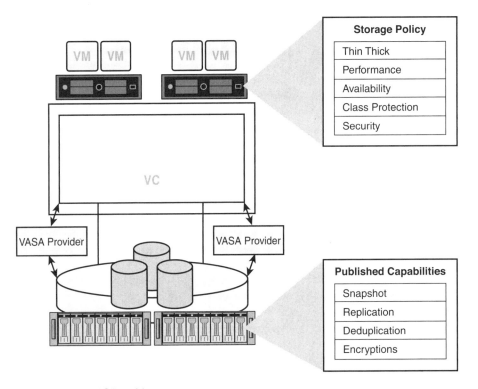

Figure 20.1   VASA architecture

Effectively, VASA providers (VPs) act as proxies between VC and the storage arrays. One provider per storage vendor is sufficient for communicating with all storage arrays supported by that provider. In other words, it is one-to-many relationship. However, for high availability, it is recommended that you use a pair of VASA providers per storage vendor if that vendor implements High Availability (HA) functions. If such functions are not supported, you might want to protect the VP virtual machines (VMs) by using the VMware HA feature of VC cluster objects.

Configuring the vSphere Environment to Use VASA

The following are the high-level steps involved in using VASA 1.0 in the vSphere 6 environment:

1. Verify that the storage array you plan to use is certified for VASA.

2. Obtain and install the VASA provider specific to the storage array.

3. Register the VASA provider in vCenter Server.

4. Create storage devices on the array and present them to your ESXi hosts.

5. Create virtual machine storage policies.

6. As you deploy new VMs, specify the storage policies relevant to the design requirements. The use of a policy would limit the VM components' deployment to datastores that are compliant with the corresponding policies.

The following sections provide detailed procedures for these steps.

Locating VASA-Certified Storage Arrays on vCG

The VMware Hardware Compatibility List (HCL) has recently been renamed the VMware Compatibility Guide (vCG) because it includes non-hardware as well as hardware listings. Go to www.vmware.com/go/vcg and follow these steps:

1. In the field What are you looking for, select **vSphere APIs for Storage Awareness (VASA)**.

2. Select the product release version, array type, and partner name.

3. Optionally, select the VASA provider name to narrow down the results.

4. Click the **Update and View Results** button.

5. Scroll down to see the results, which include VASA provider download links where you can obtain the installation packages and documentation. You can click the link in the VASA Provider Name column to open a detailed page with a list of storage arrays certified with this provider.

Common VASA Providers

Various vendors offer their VASA providers as part of specific software or solutions. Following the procedure in the preceding section will take you as far as the landing page of a VASA provider's deliverables. However, it may be a bit confusing because some vendors do not clearly state what to download. Table 20.1 lists some VASA providers and deliverables. This is not intended as an exhaustive list. Rather, it should give you an idea of the variety of deliverables that include VASA providers.

Table 20.1 Common VASA providers

Vendor	Array Family	Deliverable	Notes
Dell	EqualLogic	Virtual Storage Manager (VSM)	Part of VMware Host Integration Tools (HIT)
	Compellent	CIT	Part of Compellent Integration Tools for VMware (CIT
EMC	Unity	Unity VASA provider	Integrated in 4.0 firmware
	VPLEX	VPLEX VASA provider	Not certified with vSphere 6 at the time of this writing
	VNX	EMC VASA provider	Not certified with vSphere 6 at the time of this writing
	ViPER	ViPER VASA provider	Not certified with vSphere 6 at the time of this writing
			Includes support for VNX and VMAX Arrays
HP	3PAR	3PARVASAPROVIDER HPICSM	Some array firmware/models were not certified with vSphere 6 at the time of this writing
			Both delivered in Open Virtual Appliance (OVA) format
	LHN	HPICSM	Includes support for HP StoreVirtual VSA
NetApp	FAS	NetApp VASA provider for Clustered Data ONTAP	VASA provider delivered in OVA format
			Requires use of NetApp Virtual Storage Console (VSC), which is downloaded and installed separately and requires a Windows Server
			Minimum Firmware Version 8.3
			VP version 6.x is required for VVol support

Vendor	Array Family	Deliverable	Notes
IBM	XIV Flashsystem A9000 SVC	IBM Storage Provider for VMware VASA	IBM Spectrum Control Base Edition v3.0.0 Not available as an OVA and requires Red Hat Enterprise Linux (RHEL) 7 or 8 (this applies to the other two IBM array families as well)
	DS8000	IBM Storage Provider for VMware VASA Version 2.2.1	IBM Spectrum Control Base Edition v2.2.1 Requires DS8000 Management GUI/CLI Minimum firmware version 7.5
	XIV	IBM Storage Provider for VMware VASA Version 2.2.0, 2.1.1	IBM Spectrum Control Base Edition v2.2.0 and 2.1.1
HDS	VSP Hitachi Unified Storage	Hitachi Storage Provider for VMware vCenter	Versions 2.5 and 2.5.1 certified for VASA 1.0 Version 3.x certified for VVols Delivered as an OVA

Installing VASA Providers

As you may have noticed in the previous section, most storage vendors deliver VASA providers as a virtual appliance, and a few vendors integrate their providers into their firmware (for example, EMC VNX). Installable VASA providers are usually delivered as an OVA bundle. The method of installing the OVA bundle depends on which client you use: vSphere 6 Web Client, vSphere 6.5 Host Client (which is HTML5 based), or vSphere Client (also known as a C# client or thick client).

Installing a VASA Provider by Using vSphere Web Client

vSphere 6 Web Client requires the Client Integration browser plug-in in order for the OVA deployment process to work. vSphere 6.5 Web Client does not require this plug-in to be installed. To deploy the OVA using the vSphere 6 Web Client, follow this procedure (for vSphere 6.5, skip steps 4-7):

1. Log in to VC with Administrator privileges, using a supported web browser.

2. Navigate to the **Host and Clusters** view.

3. Right-click the host on which to install the OVA and then select **Deploy OVF Template** (see Figure 20.2).

Figure 20.2   Accessing the **Deploy OVF Template** option

4. If the Client Integration plug-in was not already installed on your desktop, you should see a message similar to the one in Figure 20.3, with the link **Download the Client Integration Plug-in**. Click that link and save the file; otherwise, skip to step 8. If you are using vSphere 6.5, Client Integration Plug-in is not required. Skip to step 8.

Figure 20.3   Link to download the Client Integration plug-in

5. Close all browser sessions before proceeding.

6. Locate the installation file and launch it to begin the installation process.

7. Repeat steps 1 through 3 of this procedure. This time the dialog should look similar to the one in Figure 20.4.

Figure 20.4 Selecting the OVA bundle to deploy

8. Either enter a URL where the OVA bundle is located or click the **Browse** button and navigate to the local or network folder where you saved the OVA bundle. Click **Next** (see Figure 20.5).

9. For most vendors, at this stage, you should be prompted to accept an end user license agreement (EULA). Click **Accept** and then click **Next**.

10. Type the VM name and select the inventory folder where you want to install the VM. Click **Next**.

Figure 20.5 Entering a VM name and location

11. Select the datastore on which to install the VM.

12. Select the virtual disk format (for example, **Thin Provision**).

13. Select **VM Storage Policy** (discussed later in this chapter).

14. Select the virtual network mapping. Here you should select a port group that you have already created for virtual machine traffic. This network should have access to VC and storage array management port networks. (see Figure 20.6).

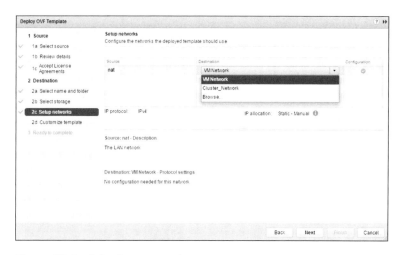

Figure 20.6   Selecting a network

15. Enter host name, IP address, and DNS information. Or you can ignore these and use DHCP-assigned properties. Click **Next**.

16. Review your selections. If you want to power on the VM after deployment is done, select the **Power on after deployment** check box and then click **Finish**.

17. Check the inventory tree for the newly deployed VM.

Installing a VASA Provider by Using the vSphere Host Client

vSphere Host Client is preinstalled on vSphere 6.5. Alternatively, if you have 6.0 installed, you can install the Host Client fling from https://labs.vmware.com/flings/esxi-embedded-host-client, provided that you have ESXi 6.0 Update 2 (U2) installed. Earlier versions of 6.0 had a licensing problem. Download either the VIB or the offline bundle.

To install the Host Client VIB from the web directly, use this command on ESXi host using SSH as a root user:

```
esxcli software vib install --viburl http://download3.vmware.com/software/
vmw-tools/esxui/esxui-signed-3843236.vib
```

If a later version is available at the time you want to install it, substitute the newer VIB name for the one shown here.

To install the Host Client using an offline bundle, you first place the zip file in a datastore accessible by this ESXi 6.0 U2 host by using this command:

```
esxcli software vib Install --depot /vmfs/volumes/<datastore-name> /
esxui-offline-bundle-6.x-3843236.zip
```

Once the host client is installed, the procedure to deploy the OVA is similar to the procedure outlined in the previous section.

Installing a VASA Provider by Using the vSphere Client

Using vSphere Client has been de-emphasized in vSphere 6 and has been deprecated in vSphere 6.5 and later. However, for those who are using pre vSphere 6.5 version, the procedure is similar to the procedure for using the vSphere 6 Web Client.

Registering VASA Providers

Once a VP has been installed, it needs to authenticate with both VC and the storage arrays for which it was certified. Authenticating with VC requires registering the provider with VC. How this is done varies by storage vendor. For example, EMC Unity 4.0 has an embedded VP listening on TCP port 8443, whose URL is https://<Storage Array Management IP address>:8443/vasa/version.xml.

To register a VP, follow this procedure:

1. Log in to VC using vSphere 6 Web Client.

2. Navigate to the **Hosts and Clusters** inventory object.

3. Locate the VC inventory object and select it.

4. Select the **Manage** tab and then click the **Storage Providers** button. In vSphere 6.5, select the **Configure** tab then select **Storage Providers** from the More section.

5. Click the **Register new storage provider** button, which is a green plus sign.

6. Enter these values:

   - **Name**—This is a friendly name that identifies this VP.

   - **URL**—This value varies by vendor.

   - **User name**—This is a user on the storage array with Administrator privileges. For the EMC Unity example, you can use local/<user-name>, or if it is an LDAP account, use <domain>/<user-name> format.

- **Password**—This is the storage array admin user's password.

- **Use storage provider certificate**—(Optional) Some storage providers require a vendor signed certificate. It you need to use one, select this check box, click **Browse**, locate the provider certificate file, and select it.

The provider list should now show the newly added VP. Some of the fields may remain blank until you click the **Rescan the storage provider for new storage systems and storage capabilities** button, which is a cylinder with a green underline. The view should look similar to Figure 20.7.

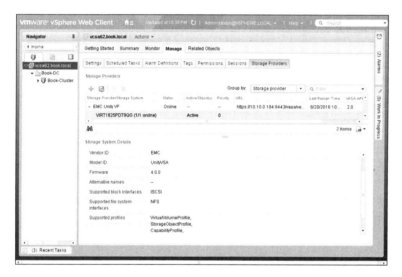

Figure 20.7   Results of adding a VASA provider

In this example, the VP shows one storage system that has these properties:

- **Name**—This is the storage array's name, which is, in this example, VIRT1625PDT9QG. That is the name automatically assigned to the Unity virtual storage appliance (VSA) that I am using to simulate the EMC Unity storage array.

- **UUID**—In this example, the UUID is the vendor's ID and the storage system's name, separated by a colon. (The UUID column is not shown in Figure 20.7.)

- **Vendor ID**—This is similar to the vendor string discussed in Chapter 5, " VMware Pluggable Storage Architecture (PSA)."

- **Model ID**—This is similar to the model string discussed earlier in Chapter 5.

- **Firmware**—This is the firmware running on the storage array controller.

- **Alternative names**—In this example, it is blank.

- **Supported block interfaces**—This could be FC, iSCSI, or FCoE. In this example, it is iSCSI.

- **Supported file system interfaces**—This is the NFS in this example.

- **Supported profiles**—These are the classes of profiles supported by this storage array. In this example, they are as follows:

  - **VirtualVolumeProfile**—This means that this storage array supports VVols.

  - **StorageObjectProfile**—This, too, is used by VVols configurations.

  - **FileSystemProfile**—This means that this storage array supports NFS VASA capabilities.

  - **BlockDeviceProfile**—This means that this storage array supports block devices' VASA capabilities.

> **NOTE**
>
> The highest VASA API version supported by this VP is listed in the VASA API Version column, which in this example is version 2.0. If you scroll the UI to the right, you should see a Priority column. When VPs are configured as a highly available pair, the VP with the highest priority value is used first. However, when that VP is not available, the VP with the next highest priority gets used next.

Creating Virtual Machine Storage Policies

Now that you have configured the storage and vSphere environment to communicate with each other, the next step in utilizing the storage capabilities is to create one or more virtual machine storage policies. This assumes that you already have at least one LUN presented to the ESXi hosts and that it has been formatted with a VMFS5 datastore.

The following procedure uses a Dell EqualLogic storage array, but it is similar to other block storage arrays. The only differences would be the name of the VASA provider and exposed capabilities. Follow these steps:

1. Log in to VC with Administrator privileges.

2. Navigate to the **Home** page.

3. Click the **VM Storage Policies** icon in the Monitoring section (see Figure 20.8).

Figure 20.8   Accessing the **VM Storage Policies** icon

4. Click the **Create New Storage Policy** icon (see Figure 20.9).

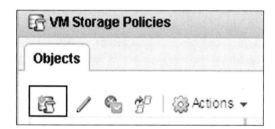

Figure 20.9   Locating the **Create New Storage Policy** icon

5. If you have multiple vCenter servers, select the relevant one.

6. Enter a name for the policy.

7. Enter a description (optional).

8. In the Rule Sets Overview screen, click **Next**.

9. In the Rules based on data services field, select the VASA 1.0 specific provider. In this example, it is **com.dell.storageprofile.equallogic.std.VASA10**, which is the VP for Dell EqualLogic storage arrays (see Figure 20.10).

Figure 20.10   Selecting the storage policy's VASA provider

NOTE

Figure 20.10 shows additional VPs in the pull-down list. The last one in the list, com.dell.storageprofile.equallogic.std, is used for VVol-related policies. See Chapter 23 for more details. vSAN VP is used with vSAN, which is covered in Chapters 21 and 22.

10. Select the VP, and a new <Add rule> dropdown list appears in the dialog. Select the relevant rule from the list. In this example, it is **SystemLabel.label**. Other VPs will have different choices. The rule in this example may have a more descriptive value in a future release of the VP (see Figure 20.11).

Figure 20.11   Selecting the storage policy's rule

11. Now you should have a pull-down list of capabilities exposed by the selected rule. Select the desired capability from the list. (Table 20.2 lists capabilities from Dell EqualLogic to illustrate the available capabilities.) Other storage vendors have many other capabilities. This example shows the **RAID, SNAP** capability selected (see Figure 20.12).

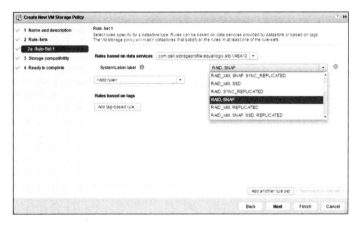

Figure 20.12   Selecting the storage capability

12. You can add more rules to Rule-Set 1, depending on the combination of capabilities your design requires. If the storage array supports creating tags, click the **Add tag-based-rule** button and select a tag from the list. Otherwise, click **Next**.

13. The storage compatibility list is displayed. On the top you see two groups: compatible and incompatible sets of datastores. If you select the **Compatible** row, the bottom half of the dialog lists the datastores in this group (see Figure 20.13). In this example, two datastore meet the requirements of this policy: DSLab and EQL300. This means they are compliant with the policy. Click **Next**.

Figure 20.13   Listing compatible storage

14. Review the choices listed in the Ready to complete screen and then click **Finish**. Now the newly created policy is listed in the VM Storage Policies list.

Table 20.2 lists the various storage capabilities exposed by the Dell EqualLogic VASA provider. The capabilities are a combination of four LUN properties:

- **RAID**—Whether the storage pool includes a single RAID type or a mix of RAID types.

- **SSD**—Whether the disk group is made up of SSDs only.

- **Snapshots**—Whether the LUN is protected with snapshots.

- **Replication**—Whether the LUN is replicated. If so, is it synchronously replicated or asynchronously replicated?

Table 20.2 Explanation of storage capabilities

Storage Capability	RAID	SSD	Snapshot	Replicated
RAID, SSD, REPLICATED	Yes	Yes	No	Async
RAID, SNAP, SSD, REPLICATED	Yes	Yes	Yes	Async
RAID, SNAP, SSD, SYNC_REPLICATED	Yes	Yes	Yes	Sync
RAID_MIX, SNAP, SYNC_REPLICATED	Mixed	No	Yes	Sync
RAID_MIX, SSD	Mixed	Yes	No	No
RAID, SYNC_REPLICATED	Yes	No	No	Sync
RAID, SNAP	Yes	No	Yes	No
RAID_MIX, REPLICATED	Mixed	No	No	Async
RAID_MIX, SNAP, SSD, REPLICATED	Mixed	Yes	Yes	Async
RAID_MIX, SNAP, REPLICATED	Mixed	No	Yes	Async
RAID, SSD, SYNC_REPLICATED	Yes	Yes	No	Sync
RAID_MIX, SYNC_REPLICATED	Mixed	No	No	Sync
RAID_MIX, SSD, REPLICATED	Mixed	Yes	No	Async
RAID	Yes	No	No	No
RAID, REPLICATED	Yes	No	No	Async
RAID_MIX, SNAP	Mixed	No	Yes	No
RAID, SSD	Yes	Yes	No	No
RAID_MIX, SNAP, SSD	Mixed	Yes	Yes	No
RAID_MIX, SSD, SYNC_REPLICATED	Mixed	Yes	No	Sync
RAID_MIX	Mixed	No	No	No

Storage Capability	RAID	SSD	Snapshot	Replicated
RAID, SNAP, SSD	Yes	Yes	Yes	No
RAID_MIX, SNAP, SSD, SYNC_ REPLICATED	Mixed	Yes	Yes	Sync
RAID, SNAP, SYNC_REPLICATED	Yes	No	Yes	Sync
RAID, SNAP, REPLICATED	Yes	No	Yes	Async

As you can see from Table 20.2, the combinations of up to 4 different properties where 2 of the properties have 2 values (which makes 6 different properties altogether) results in 24 combinations. Create a number of policies that combine the various capabilities you want to use with your VMs.

Deploying New VMs Using Storage Policies

The final step in using VASA exposed storage capabilities is to create a VM and select a storage policy for the VMFS datastore selections. A good storage design should meet certain application I/O requirements. It should take advantage of the exposed storage capabilities to better place each virtual disk on the datastore to meet such I/O requirements. For example, a VM storage design for a Microsoft SQL Server would be divided into four type of virtual disks: System disk, Data disk, TempDB disk, and Transaction Logs disks. If you want to be even more granular, you can add a fifth virtual disk for the guest OS swap/page file. Such a design also allows for providing data protection service level agreements (SLAs) for only the subset of virtual disks that need such protection. In other words, virtual disk placement on VMFS datastores would be dictated by the data protection services provided by the LUNs backing these datastores. Because VASA exposes these services as storage capabilities, it is easy to apply a separate storage policy to each virtual disk so that they get placed on datastores that provide the required I/O profile as well as data protection services. Table 20.3 shows the I/O profiles and data protection services required for the virtual disks that comprise a Microsoft SQL Server VM. You will use the contents of this table later on for disk placement design decisions and decisions about corresponding storage policies.

Table 20.3 SQL VM's virtual disk I/O profiles and data protection services requirements

Virtual Disk Class	I/O Profile		RAID Type	Backing Disk Type	Data Protection Services	
	Random/ Sequential	Read/ Write			Snapshot	Replication
Guest OS system disk	Random	Read	RAID 5 or 10	HDD	Yes	Async; for DR only
Swap/page file disk	Random	Read/ write	RAID 10	HDD	No	No

Virtual Disk Class	I/O Profile		RAID Type	Backing Disk Type	Data Protection Services	
	Random/ Sequential	Read/ Write			Snapshot	Replication
Data disk	Random	Read/ write	RAID 10	HDD/ SSD	Yes	Sync; for DR only
Transaction logs disk	Sequential	Write	RAID 10	HDD/ SSD	Yes	Sync; for DR only
TempDB disk	Random	Read/ write	RAID 10	HDD	No	No

The following sections show how to create a storage policy for each row except for the swap/page file and TempDB disks, which can use the same policy. This means you will have four storage policies to use with this VM. This environment is not planning for a DR site and therefore does not use replicated devices. The following sections show how to use the following storage policies:

- System disk policy

- SQL TempDB or swap disk policy

- SQL Data disk policy

- SQL Logs disk policy

Creating a New VM Using Storage Profiles

The following steps show how to apply policies for a Microsoft SQL Server VM, as described earlier. You can modify it for other applications according to the number of virtual disks and I/O profile for each disk. Follow these steps:

1. Log in to VC with Administrator privileges, using vSphere 6 Web Client.

2. Navigate to the **Hosts and Clusters** view.

3. Locate and select the data center on which the VM will reside.

4. Select the **Actions** pull-down menu then select the **New Virtual Machine** submenu.

5. In the Select a creation type step, select the **Create a new virtual machine** option and click **Next**.

6. Enter a name for the VM (for example, **SQL-Server01**).

7. Select the data center and then click **Next**.

8. Select the cluster or ESXi host and then click **Next**.

9. In the Select storage step, select the storage policy you created for the guest OS system disk placement.

10. Select one of compatible datastores listed at the bottom of the dialog. Observe the **Compatibility** section at the bottom of the dialog, which should state **Compatibility checks succeeded** (see Figure 20.14).

11. Click **Next**.

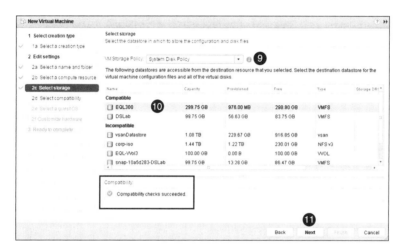

Figure 20.14   Creating a new VM and selecting the storage policy

12. Select the VM compatibility—in this example, **ESXi 6.0 and later**—and then click **Next**.

13. Select the guest OS family and version—in this example, **Windows - Microsoft Windows Server 2012 (64-bit)**—and then click **Next**.

Now comes the tricky part. In the Customize hardware step, the high-level customizations are as follows:

- Configure the CPU count (for example, the number of sockets and cores per socket) and any other VM options. You customize the CPU options by expanding the CPU section in the dialog (see Figure 20.15).

- Configure the System disk's size per your VM design. The default may not always be large enough for the applications to be installed in the guest OS.

- Add the remaining virtual disks per your VM design, using the storage policies created earlier.

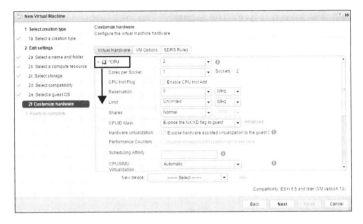

Figure 20.15   Creating a new VM and customizing the CPU

NOTE

The following steps cover the addition of only one of the virtual disks because the process is identical with the exception of selecting the corresponding storage policy for each disk.

14. Add a second SCSI controller to which you will attach the SQL data–related virtual disks. You add it by selecting **SCSI Controller** from the New Device field and then clicking **Add** (see Figure 20.16).

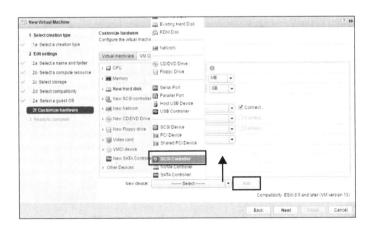

Figure 20.16   Creating a new VM and adding a SCSI controller

15. If your design calls for using the VMware Paravirtual adapter, scroll down and expand the **New SCSI controller** section of the window. Otherwise, skip to step 17.

16. Select **VMware Paravirtual** from the Change Type pull-down menu (see Figure 20.17).

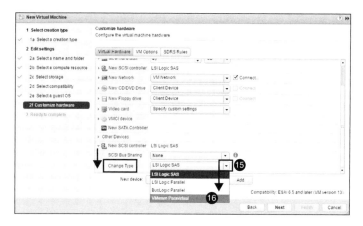

Figure 20.17   Creating a new VM and selecting the VMware Paravirtual adapter

17. Select **New Hard Disk** from the New device pull-up menu.

18. Click **Add**.

19. Scroll down and expand the newly added **New Hard disk** section.

20. Select the relevant disk size.

21. In the Virtual Device Node field, select the second instance of **New SCSI controller** (see Figure 20.18). This is the controller just added in step 14. Notice that the SCSI Device Node number has changed from SCSI(0:1) to SCSI(1:0). This means the new disk will be the first disk attached to the new SCSI controller.

Figure 20.18   Creating a new VM and customizing the added virtual disk

22. Click the Location field and select **Browse** which opens a dialog called **select a datastore cluster or datastore**.

23. Select the VM storage policy for that virtual disk (see Figure 20.19).

24. Select a datastore from the Compatible section.

25. Click **OK**.

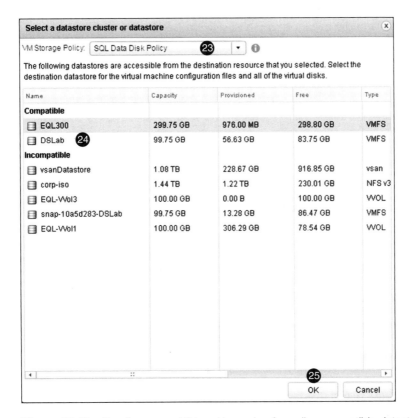

Figure 20.19   Creating a new VM and browsing for policy compatible datastores

26. Select the Disk Provisioning option per your VM design.

27. Repeat steps 17 through 26 for the remaining virtual disks. If you will use a separate virtual disk for the guest OS swap/page file, it may be advisable to leave it attached to the SCSI0 controller (that is, SCSI0:1 in step 21).

28. Click **Next**.

29. Review your selections and then click **Finish** to create the VM.

Listing a VM's Policies After Deployment

The example used here had five virtual disks with four storage policies. To verify that they were deployed correctly, check the virtual machine's policies and verify the compliance with these policies. To do that, follow these steps:

1. Log on to VC with Administrator privileges, using vSphere 6 Web Client.

2. Navigate to the **VMs and Templates** view.

3. Locate the VM in the inventory tree and select it (see Figure 20.20).

4. Select the **Manage** tab.

5. Click the **Policies** button.

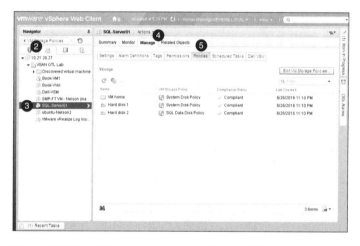

Figure 20.20   Listing the storage policies of a VM

The virtual machine's virtual disks are listed, along with their corresponding storage policies. Note that there is a non-virtual disk item listed here, which is the VM home. This is the virtual machine directory. It is on the same datastore as the system disk in this case because there was no change to the default location, which was **Store with the virtual machine**. Because the I/O profile and data protection service are required for both the VM home and the system disk, there is no need to apply a separate storage policy to each.

In this view, all items listed are compliant with their corresponding storage policies.

Demonstrating the Effects of Storage Policy on Storage vMotion

To experience the influence of storage policies on virtual disk placement, try to use Storage vMotion to migrate the SQL-Server01 VM's one or more virtual disks to a noncompliant datastore. Here are the steps to do so:

1. Log on to VC with Administrator privileges, using vSphere 6 Web Client.

2. Navigate to the **VMs and Templates** view.

3. Locate the VM in the inventory tree and select it.

4. Select the **Actions** pull-down menu.

5. Select the **Migrate** option (see Figure 20.21).

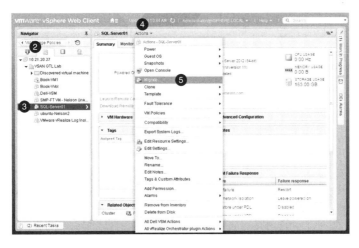

Figure 20.21   Accessing the option to migrate a VM

6. In the Select the migration type step, select the **Change storage only** radio button and click **Next**.

7. In the Select storage step, click the **Advanced >>** button (see Figure 20.22).

Figure 20.22   Selecting the advanced storage migration option

8. Select one of the virtual disks and click the **Storage** pull-down menu and select the **Browse** option (see Figure 20.23).

Figure 20.23   Browsing for the datastore advanced storage selection

9. In the Select a datastore cluster or datastore dialog, select a datastore listed in the Incompatible section and then click **OK**.

10. The selection is validated but results in a message displayed in the Compatibility section. In this example, it states `Datastore does not satisfy compatibility since it does not support one or more required properties."(RAID, SNAP)"` in VM profile (see Figure 20.24). This means the selected datastore does not meet the policy requirements.

Figure 20.24   Policy compliance validation after selecting the migration target datastore

If for whatever reason you must migrate that virtual disk to the incompatible datastore, you may do so by changing the storage policy for that virtual disk to **Datastore Default** policy prior to validation.

Summary

This chapter provides details about VASA, which provides APIs for storage vendors to expose the physical storage capabilities as well as to monitor certain storage events. Storage policy–based management (SPBM) is leveraged to create VM storage policies, which are used to simplify VMs' virtual disk placement on datastores that meet the virtual disks' I/O and availability requirement. This chapter also provides detailed procedures for creating and utilizing storage policies while deploying new virtual machines.

vSAN Core Features

Storage virtualization has evolved and continues to evolve. The latest trend in storage virtualization is the concept of combining compute, network, and storage resources into a logical entity referred to as *hyperconverged infrastructure (HCI)*. The storage part of HCI is done by pooling storage that is locally attached to multiple hypervisors and presented to storage clients as a unified storage resource. Most HCI vendors use NFS or iSCSI as the storage protocol through which they present the storage resources to the clients.

VMware created a tightly integrated HCI solution, called VMware Virtual SAN (vSAN), that is native to vSphere.

What Is vSAN?

In a nutshell, vSAN is an object-oriented, software-defined, distributed storage platform. It is a vSphere 6 cluster configuration that pools locally attached disks into disk groups on each host and creates a single datastore distributed across all nodes in the cluster. These nodes communicate with each other over a dedicated vSAN network. Data is placed on the disk groups in compliance with storage policies applied to each virtual machine and its objects.

Figure 21.1 shows the logical architecture of vSAN.

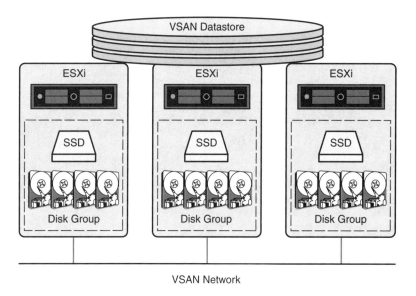

Figure 21.1   vSAN logical architecture

vSAN was first released with vSphere 5.5, Update 1 and was named vSAN 1.0 and then later renamed vSAN 5.5. A major update/redesign of vSAN was released with vSphere 6.0, referred to as vSAN 6.0. vSphere 6.0, Update 1 and Update 2 included vSAN 6.1 and 6.2, respectively. vSphere 6.5 includes the vSAN 6.5 release. vSphere 6.5, Express Patch 2 includes vSAN 6.6. This chapter and Chapter 22, **"vSAN Advanced Features,"** cover the vSAN 6.0 through 6.6 releases only.

vSAN Requirements

These are the basic requirements for configuring vSAN:

- **License**—A specific license is required to enable vSAN. Certain features of vSAN are enabled based on the license class. I cover license details where relevant in this chapter and Chapter 22.

- **Direct attached storage**—vSAN requires two tiers of storage: the cache tier and capacity tier. The cache tier must be SSD/flash enterprise-class devices. The capacity tier can be SSD or magnetic (spinning) disks. One cache tier disk per disk group is required. The maximum capacity tier disks is seven disks. The minimum capacity tier required is one device. All devices must be on the VMware Compatibility Guide (vCG).

- **I/O controller**—Storage adapters can be RAID controllers or passthrough SCSI host bus adapters (in JBOD [just a bunch of disks] mode). These, too, must be on the vSAN vCG to be supported.

- **Network**—vSAN requires a dedicated network for cluster communication and replication traffic. The minimum requirement is a 1Gbps Ethernet NIC, but a 10Gbps Ethernet NIC is recommended. I provide more details in the section "**vSAN Network**," later in this chapter.

The File System on the vSAN Datastore

vSAN 6.x implements VMware Virsto as the foundation for software-defined storage. Earlier versions of vSAN 5.5 used another VMware proprietary technology. This is how it works:

1. Writes are staged on the caching tier of the disk group, using a specialized logging mechanism.

2. With data that is less frequently read or when space is needed on the caching tier, the data gets destaged to the capacity tier disks.

3. For magnetic disks, if destaged data needs to be read, it is first copied to the cache tier and then the read I/O is done from there. However, for SSD capacity tier disks, reading from destaged data is done directly from the capacity tier disks. Because vSAN is a distributed file system, the cache tiers from all disk groups on all nodes in the cluster participate in the read and write operations, based on where the objects' components are placed.

vSAN uses object store file system (OSFS), which means that large files are stored as objects. Each object is assigned a universally unique identifier (UUID) within the vSAN cluster. A virtual disk is represented by a descriptor file with the vmdk extension, which is an ASCII file with sections and key/value pairs describing the properties of the virtual disk. One of the sections is `Extent description`, which looks like this:

```
# Extent description
RW 20480 VMFS "vsan://bd0f8c56-3610-a747-9a3b-90b11c2b5454"
```

In this example, the extent is read/write, and the size is 20,480 sectors (512 bytes per sector). The extent type is Virtual Machine File System (VMFS), and the extent file is `vsan://bd0f8c56-3610-a747-9a3b-90b11c2b5454`. This is actually not a file. Rather, it is a vSAN object whose UUID is listed after `vsan://`. If this is a vSAN datastore, why is the extent type VMFS?

The answer is that vSAN utilizes OSFS, which is a pseudo-file system, to map vSAN objects to their corresponding UUIDs. However, to provide backward compatibility with VMFS, each VM is assigned a `namespace` object, `VM Home`, that appears as a directory under the root level of the vSAN datastore. This namespace is formatted with VMFS. In other words, each `VM Home` directory plays the role of a VMFS volume, along with most VMFS-related features, such as file locking. When you read Chapter 23, "**Virtual Volumes (VVols)**," you will notice some similarities because VVols use OSFS as well.

vSAN Network

vSAN requires a low-latency, high-bandwidth network for cluster-specific traffic. Such traffic includes the following:

- **vSAN transport (data traffic)**—This type of traffic is used for component access, replication, and resynchronization. It occurs via Reliable Datagram Transport (RDT), which is a VMware proprietary protocol. It uses TCP port 2233 and occurs over a unicast network. You find RDT in the following UI locations:

    - **vSphere 6.0 hosts**—Under **Manage**, **Settings**, **Security Profile**, **Firewall**, in both incoming and outgoing connections

    - **vSphere 6.5 hosts**—Under **Configure**, **Security Profile**, **Firewall**, in both incoming and outgoing connections.

- **vSAN clustering service communications**—This type of traffic is used by vSAN for the process of nodes joining and leaving the cluster in addition to intra-cluster communications and occurs over Multicast or Unicast network depending on vSAN version in use.

vSAN version 6.6 uses a unicast network on the vSAN network. However, in earlier vSAN versions, this communication uses multicast groups, which have dependencies on Internet Group Management Protocol (IGMP) and Protocol-Independent Multicast (PIM). Default configuration uses UDP ports `12345`, `12321`, and `23451` for multicast groups (MGs). These ports are not open by default. They are automatically opened on the firewall once vSAN is configured. The default MG address is `224.1.2.3`, and the default MG agent address is `224.2.3.4`. The most common network-related issues in vSAN are related to multicast misconfigurations. Such misconfigurations can result in the following:

- vSAN node fails to join the cluster
- vSAN node is partitioned (loses communications with other nodes)

To list vSAN network configuration via the CLI, run the following:

```
esxcli vsan network list
```

Listing 21.1 shows this command and its output for vSAN 6.5.

Listing 21.1   Listing vSAN 6.5 network configuration via the CLI

```
esxcli vsan network list
Interface
   VmkNic Name: vmk2
   IP Protocol: IP
   Interface UUID: 86defd57-7eb1-3757-2534-000c29d918dd
   Agent Group Multicast Address: 224.2.3.4
   Agent Group IPv6 Multicast Address: ff19::2:3:4
   Agent Group Multicast Port: 23451
   Master Group Multicast Address: 224.1.2.3
   Master Group IPv6 Multicast Address: ff19::1:2:3
   Master Group Multicast Port: 12345
   Host Unicast Channel Bound Port: 12321
   Multicast TTL: 5
   Traffic Type: vsan
```

Listing 21.2 lists the output of the same command for vSAN 6.1, which is the same as the output in 6.0 and 6.2.

Listing 21.2   Listing vSAN 6.1 network configuration via the CLI

```
esxcli vsan network list
Interface
   VmkNic Name: vmk2
   IP Protocol: IPv4
   Interface UUID: 73482358-46f0-2500-5c54-90b11c2b5454
   Agent Group Multicast Address: 224.2.3.4
   Agent Group Multicast Port: 23451
   Master Group Multicast Address: 224.1.2.3
   Master Group Multicast Port: 12345
   Host Unicast Channel Bound Port: 12321
   Multicast TTL: 5
```

Based on the output in Listings 21.1 and 21.2, you should observe that vSAN 6.5 added support for IPv6 for vSAN traffic. In addition, vSAN 6.5 output shows a new field named `Traffic Type`, which is set to `vsan`.

> **TIP**
>
> vSAN clusters are commonly located within a single Layer 2 Ethernet segment, which is the recommended configuration. In this case, configure IGMP Snooping version 2 or 3 on the switches to which ESXi hosts' vSAN port group uplinks are connected and configure one of the switches on the Layer 2 segment as an IGMP snooping querier. This prevents IP multicast floods within the Layer 2 segment and limits them to switch ports where IGMP join requests are observed.
>
> Alternatively, vSAN stretched cluster and fault domains configurations may require placing some nodes on different Layer 3 segments (which means routing is required). In this case, if the network supports only IGMP version 2, VMware recommends using Protocol Independent Multicast Sparse Mode (PIM-SM). If the networks are configured with IGMP version 3, use Protocol Independent Multicast Source Specific Multicast (PIM-SSM) and make sure that the receivers support IGMP version 3. Using this configuration is similar to using PIM-SM, but it also carries information about the IP of the source. The receivers join multicast groups (MGs) based on the source of the MG. This is a more secure and scalable model for a limited number of applications. Make sure to configure an IGMP snooping querier on the default gateway of each L3 segment.
>
> If you will have multiple vSAN clusters on the same Layer 2 network segment, unless they are in separate VLANs, it is recommended to change the default master MG address as well as the agent MG address. If you do so, keep them within the MG address range 239.0.0.0/8. This prevents clusters from receiving multicast frames not intended for them. I cover the detailed procedure for making this change next.

Changing Default Master and Agent MG Addresses by Using the CLI

vSAN design guidelines recommend not having multiple vSAN clusters on the same Layer 2 network segment. However, if you must do that, each vSAN cluster should be in its own default and agent MGs. This procedure details how to make this change on each node in the cluster:

1. Log on to the ESXi host via SSH as root.

2. Run this command to configure the MG address for both master and agent groups on ESXi 6.0:

```
esxcli vsan network ipv4 set --interface-name <vmknic> --agent-mc-
addr <agent address> --master-mc-addr <master address> --agent-mc-port
<agent port number> --master-mc-port <master port number>
```

You can also use the abbreviated options:

```
esxcli vsan network ipv4 set -i <vmknic> -d <agent address> -u <master
address> -p <agent port number> -o <master port number>
```

Here is an example:

```
esxcli vsan network ipv4 set -i vmk2 -d 224.2.3.5 -u 224.1.2.4 -p
23452 -o 12346
```

The vmknic name is listed in the output shown earlier, in Listing 21.2, as the value of the VmkNic Name field.

The same command works on ESXi 6.5 because the IPv4 namespace is actually an alias for the IP namespace. In ESXi 6.5, ESXCLI has been revised with corresponding options for IPv6 because that release introduced support for that IP version.

To modify IPv6 MGs addresses for the agent's multicast address, use the same command with the following options:

```
--agent-v6-mc-addr
```

or the abbreviated version:

```
-D
```

For the master's multicast address, use the following command:

```
--master-v6-mc-addr
```

or the abbreviated version:

```
-U
```

NOTE

Changing the MGs' addresses from the default, on all nodes, results in vSAN Health Check reporting a network error; however, all nodes in the cluster remain connected to the cluster network and continue to function.

If the change is done on some but not all nodes in the cluster, it will result in network partitioning with all changed nodes being in one partition and the remaining unmodified nodes in another partition. If the cluster gets into this state, make sure all nodes are uniformly configured with the same multicast configurations.

Table 21.1 lists the design decisions involved in multicast configurations.

Table 21.1 Multicast design decisions

Network Topology	IGMP Version	IGMP Snooping	IGMP Snooping Querier	PIM Mode	MG and MG Agent addresses
Single cluster/ single L2 segment	3	Enabled on all switches	Enabled on a single switch	PIM-SSM	Default.
	2			PIM-SM	
Multiple clusters/ single L2 segment	3			PM-SSM	One cluster with default addresses.
	2			PM-SM	
					Remaining clusters with modified addresses. If the clusters are in separate VLANs, no change is required.
Multiple L3 segments	3		Enabled on a switch or default gateway on each L3 segment	PIM-SSM	Change addresses per cluster on each segment.
	2			PIM-SM	

TIP

The vSAN network should be a dedicated network with the highest available bandwidth. Depending on regulatory requirements to be met, it can be physically or logically separated from the VM and management network.

A vSAN license includes a vSphere Distributed Switch (vDS) license. It is recommended to use vDS for vSAN and VM networks because it provides the benefits of utilizing Link Aggregation Control Protocol (LACP), Load Based Teaming (LBT), Link Layer Discovery Protocol (LLDP), bidirectional Cisco Discovery Protocol (CDP), and Network I/O Control (NIOC). Once the vDS configuration is finalized, make sure to export it just in case you lose vCenter in the future and you have to rebuild it. Importing the vDS configuration is a much faster and simpler way of rebuilding the vDS network configuration.

Configuring vDS

As I mentioned earlier, a vSphere Distributed Switch (vDS) license is included with a vSAN license. To configure vDS, follow this procedure:

1. Connect to the vCenter server using the vSphere 6.x Web Client or vSphere 6.5 HTML5 client as a user with Administrator privileges.

2. Navigate to the **Networking** tab in the inventory tree (see Figure 21.2).

3. Select the data center object in the inventory tree.

4. If you are using vSphere 6.x, right-click your data center and select **Distributed Switch** and then click the **New Distributed Switch** submenu. Skip to step 8.

5. If you are using vSphere 6.5, select the **Networks** tab.

6. Click the **Distributed Switches** button.

7. Click the **New Distributed Switch** button (see Figure 21.2).

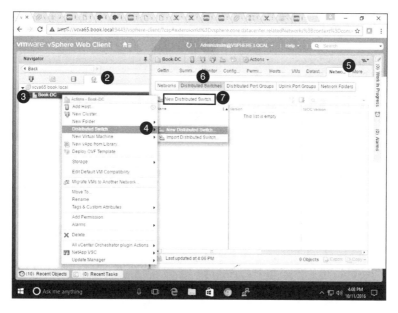

Figure 21.2 Accessing the vSphere Distributed Switch menu

8. Enter the switch name and then click **Next**.

9. Select the distributed switch version. You must select 6.0.0 or higher. This provides IGMP snooping and NIOC features on the switch, among other features (see Figure 21.3).

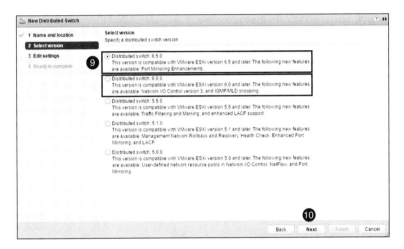

Figure 21.3   Selecting the vSphere distributed switch version

10. Click **Next**.

11. Enter the number of uplinks (see Figure 21.4). This value is per host. At this time, the number does not have to match the current number of physical NICs in each ESXi host. Rather, you can plan ahead and select the number of uplinks that you plan to use in the future. You can modify this number later to increase the uplinks count.

12. If you plan on using Network I/O Control (NOIC), select **Enabled** in the corresponding field's pull-down menu.

TIP

If you have a limited number of uplinks, such as two 10Gbps Ethernet ports that you will share for multiple types of traffic, it is recommended to enable NIOC so that you can assign relative shares to each traffic type.

---

13. Select the **Create a default port group** check box.

14. Enter the port group name. In this example, I am creating the vSAN port group named VSAN-DPG. You can later add port groups for vMotion and virtual machine traffic.

15. Click **Next**.

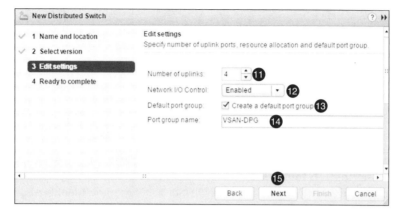

Figure 21.4   Entering vSphere distributed switch settings

16. Review the settings shown in the Ready to Complete screen and then click **Finish**. The vDS is created in the selected data center. Next, you need to select which hosts will participate in this switch and assign uplinks from each host.

17. Select the vDS in the list of distributed switches.

18. Click the **Add and Manage Hosts** button or right-click the switch and select the **Add and Manage Hosts** menu option. You can also access that menu option via the **Actions** pull-down menu (see Figure 21.5).

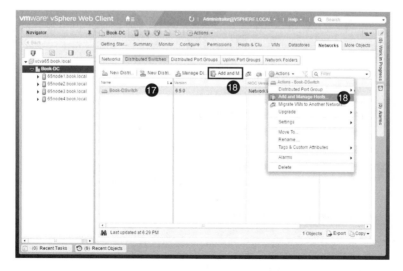

Figure 21.5   Accessing the Add Hosts menu for the vDS

19. In the Select Task step, select the **Add Hosts** radio button and then click **Next**.

20. In the Select Hosts step, click the **New hosts** button, which is a green plus sign.

21. Select one or more hosts from the list. These are the hosts that you will add to the cluster later.

22. Click **OK** to close the **Select New Hosts** dialog and see the hosts selected in the previous step.

TIP

If you have a large number of hosts to configure, you may take advantage of the **Configure identical network settings on multiple hosts (template mode)** check box. When this option is checked, you can select one host as a template, for which you then configure physical adapters (VMNICs) and vmkernel network adapters (VMK NICs). This configuration is then applied to the rest of the hosts selected in step 21.

I go through the process of using a template host here. For the manual procedure, see the section "**Adding Hosts to vDS Without Using a Template Host**," later in this chapter.

---

23. Select the **Configure identical settings on multiple hosts (template mode)** check box (see Figure 21.6).

24. Click **Next**.

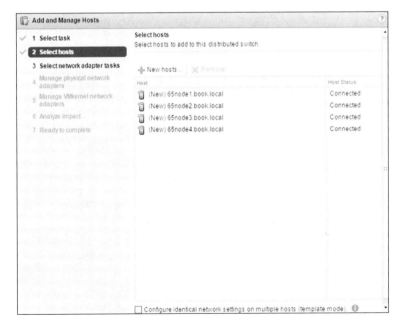

Figure 21.6   Selecting hosts to add to the vDS

25. Select one of the hosts to use as a template (see Figure 21.7).

26. Click **Next**.

Figure 21.7   Selecting the vDS host template

27. In the Select Network Adapter Tasks step, select both the **Manage physical adapters** and **Manage VMkernel adapters** check boxes (see Figure 21.8).

28. Click **Next**.

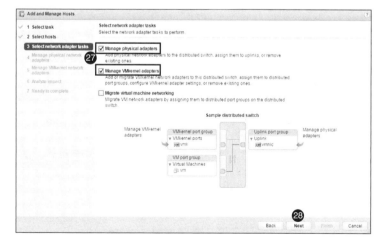

Figure 21.8   Selecting vDS network adapters tasks

29. In the Manage Physical Network Adapters step, select one of the VMNICs listed without an associated switch.

30. Click the **Assign uplink** button to open the **Select an Uplink for vmnic(n)** dialog, where (n) is the VMNIC number selected in the previous step (for example, vmnic1).

31. Select an uplink. The uplinks listed here are the ones you created in step 11, earlier in this procedure.

32. Click **OK**. The dialog closes, and you return to the Manage Physical Network Adapters step. The end result would look similar to Figure 21.9.

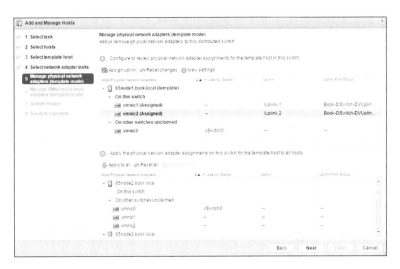

Figure 21.9 Assigning VMNICs to the template host

33. If you will set up NIC teaming, select a second VMNIC and repeat steps 29–32 to assign a second VMNIC to the vDS.

TIP

If you implement NIC teaming for a vSAN port group, VMware recommends using Load Based Teaming (LBT).

---

34. Click **Apply to all** icon. The result should look similar to Figure 21.10.

Figure 21.10   Assigning VMNICs from the template host

The difference between Figure 21.9 and Figure 21.10 is that the latter shows the assigned NICs in both the template (top pane) and target hosts (bottom pane), while the former shows them only in the template (top pane).

35. Click **Next** to go to the Manage VMkernel network adapters (template mode) step.

36. Click the **New Adapter** icon (the green plus sign). The **Add Networking** dialog box appears.

37. While the **Select an existing network** radio button is selected, click the **Browse** button.

38. Select the vSAN port group created in steps 13–15 earlier in this procedure.

39. Click **OK** to complete the selection and close the dialog.

40. Click **Next**. This takes you to the **Port properties** step.

41. Select the **Virtual SAN** check box in the Available Services section. You can later create an additional port group for vMotion traffic, in which case you select the **vMotion** check box (see Figure 21.11).

42. Click **Next**.

Figure 21.11   Selecting a service for a VMK NIC

43. In the IPv4 Settings step, enter the static IP settings for the vSAN VMKNIC and click **Next**.

44. Review the settings in the Ready to Complete step, and if no changes are needed, click **Finish**. This takes you back to the Manage VMkernel Network Adapters step of the Add and Manage Hosts wizard. There, you should see the newly created VMK NIC listed with (new) indicated next to it (for example, vmk2 (new)).

45. Click the **Apply to all** icon to open a dialog where you set the IP addresses for the remaining host's vSAN port group's VMK NICs. (If DHCP is selected, which is not recommended, steps 44 and 45 are not required.)

46. Enter the remaining IP addresses, separated by commas.

47. Click **OK** to close the Apply VMkernel Network Adapter Configuration to Other Hosts dialog (see Figure 21.12). The wizard should now show the newly created VMK NIC (for example, vmk2 (new)) reflected in all remaining hosts' listings.

Figure 21.12 Entering VMK NICs' IP addresses

48. Click **Next** to analyze the impact.

49. If no port groups will be impacted, click **Next**.

50. Click **Finish** to complete the procedure.

Adding Hosts to vDS Without Using a Template Host

If you have a small number of hosts to add to vDS, you can follow the process of adding them to vDS without using a template host. To do so, follow steps 1-22 of the previous procedure, "**Configuring vDS**," and then continue on with the following steps:

23. Deselect the **Configure identical network settings on multiple hosts (template mode)** check box if it is already selected and then click **Next**.

24. In the Select Network Adapter Tasks step, select both the **Manage physical adapters** and **Manage VMkernel adapters** check boxes.

25. Click **Next** (see Figure 21.13).

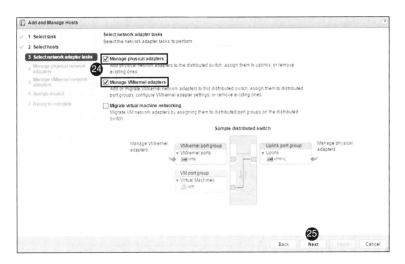

Figure 21.13   Selecting vDS network adapters tasks

26. In the Manage Physical Network Adapters step, select one of the VMNICs listed without an associated switch.

27. Click **Assign uplink** button. The **select an Uplink for vmnic(n)** dialog appears (where (n) is the VMNIC number selected in the previous step—for example, vmnic1).

28. Select an uplink. The uplinks listed here are those you created in step 11, earlier in this procedure.

29. Click **OK** to close the dialog and return to the Manage Physical Network Adapters step.

30. Scroll down to the next host and repeat steps 26–29 for the first VMNIC for each remaining host. The end result should look similar to Figure 21.14.

Figure 21.14 Assigning VMNICs to vDS

31. If you will set up NIC teaming, select a second VMNIC and repeat steps 26–30 to assign a second VMNIC to vDS.

TIP

If you implement NIC teaming for a vSAN port group, VMware recommends Load Based Teaming (LBT).

---

32. Click **Next**.

33. In the Manage VMkernel Network Adapters step, select a host from the list and then click **New Adapter** icon (the green plus sign). The Add Networking dialog box appears.

34. While the **Select an existing network** radio button is selected, click the **Browse** button.

35. Select the vSAN port group created in steps 13–15 earlier in this procedure and then click **OK** to complete the selection and close the dialog.

36. Click **Next** to go to the **Port properties** step.

37. Select the **Virtual SAN** check box in the Available Services section (see Figure 21.15). You can later create an additional port group for VMotion traffic, in which case you select the **vMotion** check box.

38. Click **Next**.

Figure 21.15 Selecting a service for the VMK NIC

39. In the **IPv4 settings** step, enter the static IP settings for the VMK NIC and click **Next**.

40. Review the settings in the Ready to Complete step, and if no changes are needed, click **Finish**. This takes you back to the Manage VMkernel Network Adapters step of the Add and Manage Hosts wizard. There, you should see the newly created VMK NIC listed with (new) indicated next to it (for example, vmk2 (new)).

41. Repeat steps 33–40 for each host in the list. When you're done, proceed to the next step.

42. Click **Next** to analyze the impact of this change. If **No impact** status is listed under the Status column, proceed to the next step.

43. Click **Next**.

44. Review the Ready to Complete screen and then click **Finish** to conclude the procedure.

Exporting vDS Configuration

When you have vDS configured and all the required distributed port groups created, you can export the vDS configuration by using this procedure:

1. Connect to the vCenter server using the vSphere 6.x Web Client as a user with Administrator privileges.

2. Navigate to the **Networking** view.

3. Select the vDS object in the inventory tree.

4. Right-click the vDS object and select **Settings**, **Export Configuration**. Or you can select the **Actions** pull-down menu and select **Settings**, **Export Configuration** (see Figure 21.16).

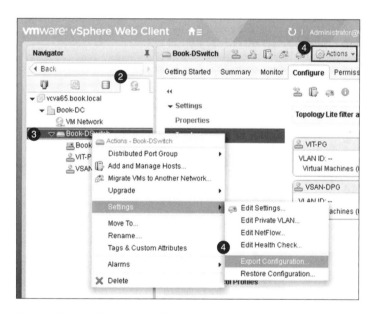

Figure 21.16 Exporting vDS configurations

5. Select the **Distributed switch and all port groups** radio button.

6. Optionally type a description.

7. Click **OK**.

8. When the export process is complete, the Confirm Configuration Export dialog asks if you want to save the exported file. Click **Yes** and navigate to where you want to save the export file on your desktop and specify the filename. The file is in zip format, and it includes `data` and `META-INF` folders.

Restoring vDS Configurations

I have seen situations in which vCenter had to be rebuilt due to catastrophic hardware failure or user error. With vCenter being a dependency for complex vDS configurations, the best approach for recovery is to rebuild vCenter and import the vDS configurations using the backup file created in the previous section. You can then create the data center, create the cluster, enable vSAN, and add the nodes to the cluster. This should restore the vSAN cluster to a manageable state. Note that the vSAN cluster data plane can operate without vCenter, but no further management is possible until vCenter is restored.

To restore vDS configurations from a backup file, follow this procedure:

1. Connect to the vCenter server using the vSphere 6.x Web Client as a user with Administrator privileges.

2. Navigate to the **Networking** view.

3. Select the data center object in the inventory tree.

4. Right-click the data center object and then select **Distributed Switch**, **Import Distributed Switch** (see Figure 21.17). The Import Distributed Switch Wizard appears.

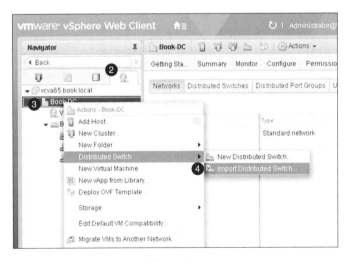

Figure 21.17   Importing vDS configurations

5. Click **Browse** in the Select a Distributed Switch Backup File field.

6. Navigate to where the backup file is located, select the file, and click **Open**.

7. Select the **Preserve original distributed switch and port group identifiers** check box and then click **Next**.

8. Review the import settings details in the Ready to Complete step of the wizard and click **Finish**.

Solid State Drives and Flash Storage

Demand for flash storage, including solid state drives (SSDs), has increased since the HCI (including vSAN) concept was introduced. The following sections cover the various types of flash drives and their suitability for vSAN use.

History of Flash Storage

My first transistor radio had a logo on it that stated "solid state." At that time, I had no idea what that meant except that the radio had no vacuum tubes, like those in my parents' vintage radio. In high school I learned about transistors, which were in my solid state radio, and how they revolutionized the electronics industry. What is the relevance of my radio to storage? It points to the evolution of transistors into flash storage, among many other computer industry applications.

A transistor is a semiconductor device used to amplify or switch electronic signals and electrical power. The name *transistor* is a contraction of *trans-resistance*. The idea of transistors, called field effect transistors (FET), was patented around 1926, long before it was possible to actually manufacture a transistor, which didn't happen until the late 1940s, after World War II had ended. The *field effect* part of the name refers to the fact that the transistor uses an electric field to control the electrical behavior of a device. For example, it can amplify a signal or an electrical current's voltage. A transistor has two terminals, which are commonly labeled *source* and *drain*, with a gate in between. The gate controls the current between the two terminals. This means that the transistor can amplify, reduce, or not pass the electrical current or signal (that is, switch it on or off). This capability lent itself to using transistors in switches and amplifiers. Such applications used a metal-oxide-semiconductor field-effect transistor (MOSFET).

MOSFET evolved into floating-gate MOSFET (FGMOS), where the gate is electrically isolated, creating a floating node in the direct current (DC) and a number of secondary gates or inputs are deposited above the floating gate (FG) and electrically isolated from it.

FGMOS is the technology used in electrically erasable programmable read-only memory (EEPROM), like the memory used by a computer's basic input/output system (BIOS). The process of erasing and reprogramming EEPROM takes such a very short time that it is as fast as a flash. This is probably the origin of the name the *EEPROM flash* memory.

EEPROM that is made up of transistors with two inputs (secondary gates) that utilize a derivative of Boolean logic is said to have *digital logic gates*. These gates, commonly named

A and B, implement Boolean algebra with 0 and 1, where 0 is represented by a voltage close to 0, or "ground," while 1 is represented by a voltage close to the supply voltage. The digital logic determines the output's value based on the combination of the two inputs' values, as shown in Table 21.2.

Table 21.2 Digital logic names

Logic	Name	Output
Exclusive A or B	Exclusive OR (XOR)	1 if the two gates are different values; otherwise, 0
Negative value of XOR	XNOR	Inverted XOR
A or B	OR	1 if either gate or both are 1; otherwise, 0
Negative value of OR	NOR	Inverted value of OR
A and B	AND	1 if both gates are 1; otherwise, 0
Negative value of AND	Negative-AND (NAND)	Inverted value of AND

To understand the output values of each logic, see Table 21.3.

Table 21.3 Digital logic output values

Two-Input Gates			Inverted Two-Input Gates		
Gate A	Gate B	Output	Gate A	Gate B	Output
XOR Logic			**XNOR Logic**		
0	0	0	0	0	1
0	1	1	0	1	0
1	0	1	1	0	0
1	1	0	1	1	1
OR Logic			**NOR Logic**		
0	0	0	0	0	1
0	1	1	0	1	0
1	0	1	1	0	0
1	1	1	1	1	0
AND Logic			**NAND Logic**		
0	0	0	0	0	1
0	1	0	0	1	1
1	0	0	1	0	1
1	1	1	1	1	0

Out of all the digital logics listed in Table 21.3, EEPROM eventually evolved into flash memory, using NAND gates. This type of flash memory is used in USB flash drives (thumb drives) and solid state drives (SSDs). It is also used in other storage applications, such as the internal storage of mobile devices like tablets and mobile phones.

SSD and Flash Memory Architecture

SSDs and flash storage devices are composed of many NAND gates arranged in cells. A cell is simply a MOSFET with two NAND gates, A and B, as explained earlier. Each cell can store 1, 2, or 3 bits, depending on how many levels the cell has. Single-level cell (SLC) SSDs stores a single bit per cell, multi-level cell (MLC) SSDs store 2 bits per cell, and triple-level cell (TLC) SSDs store 3 bits per cell. V-NAND is a denser architecture where the cells are arranged vertically instead of being at the same plane.

SLCs are the most expensive of all SSD types due to the lower density, but they offer lower latency and higher endurance (see the following section, "**SSD Endurance**").

MLC is less expensive and offers higher density at the expense of latency and endurance due to cell degradation. However, an enterprise version of MLC (eMLC) was developed to mitigate cell degradation and offers better endurance.

The cells are grouped to form an SSD chip. Several of these chip are soldered on a circuit board that functions as a controller. The type of controllers or connectivity currently available are Serial AT Attachment (SATA), SATA Express (commonly name U.2), Peripheral Component Interconnect Express (PCIe), and M.2. A newer storage that uses nonvolatile memory is referred to as nonvolatile memory express (NVMe), and it uses the PCIe interface.

SSD Endurance

A flash cell can only be erased and written a limited number of time before the metal oxide in its cell's gates begin to deteriorate. Most flash storage manufacturers use an endurance metric that is measured by drive writes per day (DWPD), which means how many times the drive is written to fully each day before it fails during the drive's warranty period. For example, with a drive rated 10 DWPD with a warranty of 5 years, you can fill the drive 10 times a day for 5 years before it is expected to fail.

Another endurance metric is terabytes written (TBW), which measures how many terabytes are written to the drive before it fails within the drive's warranty period.

SSD endurance is classified using the TBW metric as follows:

Class A: ≥ 365 TBW

Class B: ≥ 1825 TBW

Class C: ≥ 3650 TBW

Class D: ≥ 7300 TBW

VMware requires any of the following minimum endurances for SATA, SAS, and PCIe SSDs:

- 10 DWPD

- 3500 TBW of random writes on 8KB transfer size per NAND module

- 2500 TBW of random writes on 4KB transfer size per NAND module

SSD IOPS Classes

SSDs are classified by their write I/Os per second (IOPS), as follows:

> Class A: 2500–5000 write IOPS
>
> Class B: 5000–10,000 write IOPS
>
> Class C: 10,000–20,000 write IOPS
>
> Class D: 20,000–30,000 write IOPS
>
> Class E: 30,000–10,0000 write IOPS

I/O Adapters

I/O adapters to which SSD and magnetic disks are attached in a vSAN cluster node must pass VMware certification tests. It is crucial that the combination of adapter, firmware, and driver matches the certified configuration. Do not just use an adapter that is the same model as a certified one without scrutinizing the firmware version and driver to be used with it.

I/O adapters are identified by two classes: RAID controllers and host bus adapters (HBAs). HBAs are used to access raw capacity of attached disks. RAID controllers, on the other hand, can be used to configure the attached disks into RAID sets or in a passthrough configuration, in which case the controller behaves like an HBA. If you decide to use a controller that is certified with RAID mode, make sure to configure each disk attached to the controller in a single disk RAID0 configuration and configure the cache, if it exists, in write-through mode. When deciding which controller/HBA to use, look very closely at the VMware Compatibility Guide (vCG) to identify the type of controller/HBA and the certified configuration as well as firmware and driver versions. (I discuss this topic further in the next section.)

Some RAID controllers are equipped with battery-backed cache. vSAN does not require such cache. However, if you disable the cache or buy a version of the adapter without the cache, this may reduce the adapter's queue depth. Again, check the vCG closely for the certified configuration.

VMware Certification Guide (vCG)

The vSAN hardware certification program is one of the most stringent programs at VMware for ensuring that all certified components are up to the task of serving your data reliably and with the best performance. VMware worked closely with its partners to certify combinations of systems, I/O controllers/HBAs, cache and capacity tier disks, firmware, and drivers. This combination is referred to as vSAN Ready Nodes.

vSAN Ready Nodes are classified according to their capacity types and I/O profiles, as shown in Table 21.4.

Table 21.4 Ready Nodes profiles

Profile Name	Capacity Tier Disks		Cache Tier Disks		CPU Cores	Memory	Max IOPS
	Count/ Type	Minimum Endurance/ Performance Class	Count/ Type	Minimum Endurance/ Performance Class			
HY-2	2x1TB NL-SAS 7.2K RPM	N/A	1x200GB SSD	≥B ≥B	1x6 cores	32GB	Up to 4K
HY-4	4x1TB NL-SAS 7.2K RPM	N/A	1x200GB SSD	≥C ≥D	2x8 cores	128GB	Up to 10K
HY-6	8x1TB NL-SAS 7.2K RPM	N/A	2x200GB SSD	≥C ≥D	2x10 cores	256GB	Up to 20K
HY-8	12x1TB SAS 10K RPM	N/A	2x400GB SSD	≥D ≥E	2x12 cores	384GB	Up to 40K
AF-4	4x1TB SSD	≥A ≥C	1x200GB SSD	≥C ≥C	2x10 cores	128GB	Up to 25K
AF-6	8x1TB SSD	≥A ≥C	2x200GB SSD	≥C ≥D	2x12 cores	256GB	Up to 50K
AF-8	12x1TB SSD	≥A ≥C	2x400GB SSD	≥D ≥F	2x12 cores	384GB	Up to 80K

For the most up-to-date profile definitions, go to www.vmware.com/resources/compatibility/vsan_profile.html.

Looking Up vSAN Ready Nodes on the vCG

To locate certified vSAN Ready Nodes on the vCG, do the following:

1. Go to www.vmware.com/go/vcg.

2. Select **vSAN** from the What Are You Looking For pull-down list.

3. In the vSAN ReadyNode Types field, select **All**, **All Flash**, or **Hybrid**.

4. Select the vSAN or ESXi version from the vSAN ReadyNode Supported Releases field.

5. Select the **Pre-install** option.

6. Select the vendor.

7. Select **vSAN ReadyNode Profile**.

8. If you require a specific raw storage capacity, select one from the Raw Storage Capacity (TB) pull-down list. I prefer to leave the selection set to All.

9. Click the **Update and View Results** button. The search result is listed at the bottom of the screen as a collapsed section (see Figure 21.18).

Figure 21.18   Searching the vCG for vSAN Ready Nodes

10. Expand the search result.

11. Scroll down to display the expanded results.

12. To display the details of a listed Ready Node, click the link in the Model column (see Figure 21.19). In the expanded vSAN Ready Node model details, you get the build of material that makes up the Ready Node.

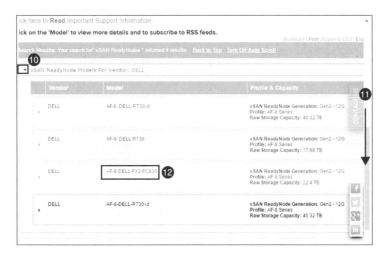

Figure 21.19 Listing the vCG search results

13. To list the details of a component in the list, click the link in the Details column. A new browser session with the content appears (see Figure 21.20).

Figure 21.20 Listing a Ready Node's details in the vCG

14. In the item's details (for example, for the cache SSD), pay close attention to the following properties (see Figure 21.21):

   ■ Endurance

   ■ Endurance Class

   ■ Performance Class

   ■ Flash Technology

   ■ Minimum Firmware Version

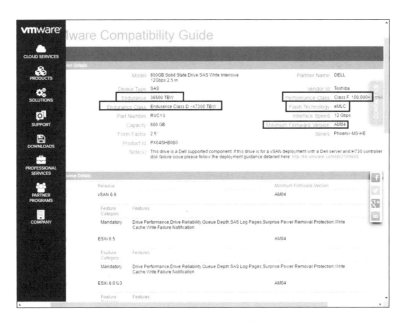

Figure 21.21   Listing an item's details in the vCG

You can also use the vSAN Ready Node Configurator tool, which is available at vsanreadynode.vmware.com. It is self-explanatory, and I do not cover it here due to space limitations.

The less preferred method is to build your own. This process is prone to errors and interoperability issues for the components and systems. If you must build your own, however, go to www.vmware.com/resources/compatibility/search. php?deviceCategory=vsan. Again, I do not cover the build-your-own lookup due to space limitations.

Ruby vSphere Console (RVC)

vCenter Server Virtual Appliance (vCSA) and vCenter Server for Windows include a vSAN management tool called the Ruby vSphere Console (RVC). It uses vSAN management APIs to communicate with vSAN cluster nodes. RVC has been deprecated as of vSAN 6.6; however, it will continue to be included with vCSA but not updated.

> **NOTE**
>
> I cover RVC this early in the chapter because I use it where relevant in subsequent sections.

To access the RVC, you need to log on to vCenter via the virtual appliance local login or via SSH.

Verifying VC Access Configuration

Before you can access vCenter via SSH or local login, you need to first verify whether either or both options are enabled. To do that, follow this procedure:

1. Connect to the vCenter server using the vSphere 6.x Web Client as a user with Administrator privileges.

2. Using the mouse, hover over the **Home** icon (see Figure 21.22).

3. Select the **Administration** menu option from the menu that appears.

   The **Navigator** pane should now show the **Administration** related options.

4. Select the **System Configuration** option in the Deployment section.

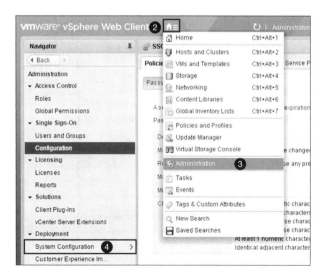

Figure 21.22   Accessing the VC Administration menu

5. In the resulting System Configuration view, select **Nodes**.

6. Select the VCSA in the Nodes pane.

7. Select the **Manage** tab.

8. Click the **Settings** button.

9. Select **Access** in the Common section. The Access pane shows three access facilities: local, SSH, and bash login. If the facility you plan to use is not enabled, proceed with the next step. Otherwise, if it is enabled, stop here. No change is required.

10. Click the **Edit** button (see Figure 21.23).

11. Select the check box next to the access facility you want to enable.

12. Bash shell is enabled by default for root user on vCenter 6.5. If you want to enable if for other users, you can select the **Enable bash shell** option and set the timeout value in minutes. The maximum is 1440 minutes (24 hours). This value counts down from the time the bash shell option is enabled. After the timeout is reached, the option goes back to being disabled. For pre-6.5 versions of vCenter, the shell can be enabled at logon time, as discussed later in this chapter, in the section "**Logging on to the vCenter Console**."

13. Click **OK** to apply the changes and close the Edit Settings dialog.

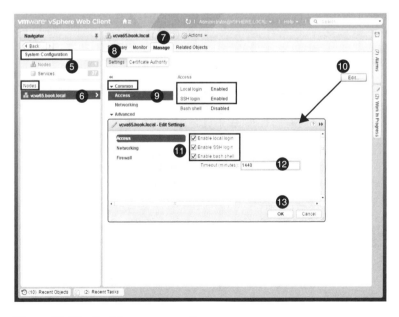

Figure 21.23 Enabling access options

Logging on to the vCenter Console

To access the vCenter console, follow this procedure:

1. To use the local login, open a remote console to the vCSA by using vSphere Web Client and then press **Alt+F1** to go to Virtual Terminal 1.

   Otherwise, use an SSH client like **PuTTY** and use vCenter's host name or IP address. If vCenter is using the default certificate or other self-signed certificate, you are prompted to verify the signature the first time you access the server. If you accept it, the key will be stored in the local key ring, and you will not be prompted to verify it again in the future.

2. Log on using vCenter's root or equivalent. This takes you to the command prompt (`Command>`).

3. For vCenter 6.0, enter the following to enable bash shell access:

   `shell.set --enabled True`

   For vCenter 6.5, the bash shell is enabled for the root user by default. For other users, I have already enabled it in the previous section, and this step is not required.

4. To launch the bash shell, type `shell` and press **Enter** (see Figure 21.24).

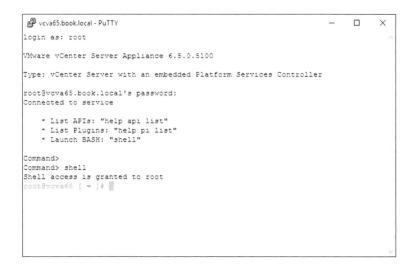

Figure 21.24 Enabling access options

TIP

If you do not run RVC after starting the SSH session and the session stays idle until it times out, you will be returned to the `Command>` prompt. To return to the bash shell, just type `shell` and press **Enter**.

Accessing the RVC Prompt

Once you are logged on to the vCenter console, you can start RVC in interactive mode or string an RVC command along with options and path.

Running the RVC in Interactive Mode

To run the RVC in interactive mode, follow this procedure:

1. Type `rvc` without any options or type the following:

   ```
   rvc <user@host>
   ```

   For example, if the user name is administrator@vsphere.local and the vCenter host name is vcva65, you would use this command:

   ```
   rvc administrator@vsphere.local@vcva65
   ```

   Observe the two @ signs in the login credentials. The first one is part of the user's name combined with the SSO domain or AD domain. The second one is for the VC server name on which to run the RVC commands. Alternatively, you can run `rvc <VC-host-name>`, which defaults to `administrator@vsphere.local` the user name.

   If this is the first time to run `rvc` against this server, the server's public key fingerprint is displayed, and you are prompted to confirm that you want to continue connecting.

   A warning is displayed, saying that the server name is permanently added to the list of known hosts, which is stored in the `.rvc/knownhosts` file.

2. Enter the user's password when prompted.

A welcome message is displayed, along with the suggestion `Try the 'help' command`.

The prompt places you at the top of the logical structure of the inventory tree.

Listing 21.3 shows what has happened in this procedure so far.

Listing 21.3 Starting the RVC in interactive mode

```
root@vcva65 [ ~ ]# rvc
Install the "ffi" gem for better tab completion.
Host to connect to (user@host): administrator@vsphere.local@vcva65
The authenticity of host 'vcva65' can't be established.
Public key fingerprint is
927107c6b68fee4924fb34f4307f334d51f49b09136ca17384ecc72d83d83353.
Are you sure you want to continue connecting (y/n)? y
Warning: Permanently added 'vcva65' (vim) to the list of known hosts
password:
Welcome to RVC. Try the 'help' command.
0 /
1 vcva65/
>
```

Listing 21.4 shows the hierarchy of the inventory tree with added comments after left pointing arrows.

Listing 21.4 RVC inventory tree hierarchy

```
/  ← Root level
vcva65/  ← VC Server
        Book-DC (datacenter)  ← Datacenter
            storage/
                vmprofiles/
            computers [host]/ ← Compute Resources
                    [cluster) ← vSAN Cluster
                        Hosts/ ← vSAN Nodes reside here
                            [list-of-hosts]
                                vms/ ← VMs Homes reside here
                                datastores/
                                networks/
                            resourcePool/
            networks [network]/
                    [Distributed Switch] (vds)
                    [Standard Switch Port Group]
            datastores [datastore]/
                    [list of datastores]
                    [vsanDatastore]
            vms [vm]/
                    [list of VMs]
```

In Listing 21.4, I inserted highlighted comments for the inventory nodes relevant to running vSAN-related RVC commands. The most important ones are `computers` and `cluster`.

To list the content of each level, run the `ls` command. The output lists child directories along with a numeric value. Here is an example:

```
> ls
0 /
1 vcva65/
```

To change into a child directory, you can either use `cd <number>` or `cd <name>`. Here is an example:

```
cd 1
```

Here is another example:

```
cd vcva65
```

With experience and practice, you will memorize the content of each level. However, changing into a child level directory using its number will fail unless you first list the content of the current directory. You must run the `ls` command at each level before you can use the number assigned to the next level with the `cd` command. In other words, you cannot just string the full path to a nested directory two or three levels deep from the root level by using the assigned numeric values (for example, `cd 1/0/0`). However, you can use the explicit path names (for example, `/vcva65/computers/Book-Cluster/`) while in RVC interactive mode.

Using the `ls` command populates the buffer with the directory content listing along with the corresponding numeric names.

For vSAN commands, the relevant levels are `/<VCServer>/<Datacenter>/computers` and the next level down into the vSAN cluster level, `/<VCServer>/<Datacenter>/computers/<cluster>`.

If you run commands at the `computers` level, you need to use the cluster name or its directory number. Here is an example:

```
vsan.check_state 0
```

Here is another example:

```
vsan.check_state Book-Cluster
```

However, if you move one level down into the `cluster` level, you need to use a period to denote the current directory as the parameter of the command. Here is an example:

```
vsan.check_state .
```

Running the RVC in Batch Mode

When troubleshooting vSAN issues using the RVC, it is a good idea to collect the output of certain commands and redirect it to text files. In this way, you can document what you experienced and share it with the VMware support team or other relevant parties.

Collecting such output is not practical using RVC interactive mode because it does not allow redirection of output to text files. I prefer running the following string of command options instead:

```
rvc --cmd "vsan.[command] [path-to-inventory-node]" --cmd "quit" "User-
name:password"@[VC-name-or-IP-address]
```

Or you can use abbreviated options, like this:

```
rvc -c "vsan.[command] [path-to-inventory-node]" -c "quit" "User-
name:password"@[VC-name-or-IP-address]
```

Observe the quotes around the `User-name:password` combination. If you do not format the command in this fashion, it will exit with errors. Single quotes work as well which are required if the password includes special characters like an exclamation mark "!".

The second `-c "quit"` command says to exit the RVC when done. If this is omitted, you end up in the `rvc` prompt while you are redirecting the output to a file, and the process does not complete until you type `quit` or `exit`. Otherwise, it appears to hang. If you get into this state, just type `exit`, and you are returned to the VC console prompt. Here is an example:

```
rvc -c "vsan.check_state /vcva65/Book-DC/computers/Book-Cluster" -c "quit"
"administrator@vsphere.local:VMware123!"@vcva65 >output.txt
```

TIP

A shortcut to collect vSAN configuration and health information is to run the Python script `vsan-vc-health-status.py` that is used by vSAN Health Check. However, this command is available only on the vCenter console and uses the default user account set in SSO, which in this example is administrator@vsphere.local. The output includes some JSON-formatted sections that are used by vSAN Health Check. You can skip them if they're not of interest to you. Alternatively, you can use the previous batch command example, using `vsn.support_information` instead of `vsan.check_state`, and you can name the output file something meaningful, like Book-Cluster-SupportInfo.txt.

To append the current date and time to the filename, run the following command once per SSH session prior to collecting the output:

```
today='date '+%Y-%m-%d_%H-%M-%S''
```

Then append the variable $today to the end of the output file name.

This is the command using the Python script:

```
python /usr/lib/vmware-vpx/vsan-health/vsan-vc-health-status.py
>vsan-health-$today.txt
```

This is the command using the RVC in batch mode:

```
rvc -c "vsan.support_information /vcva65/Book-DC/computers/Book-
Cluster" -c "quit" "administrator@vsphere.local:VMware123!"@vcva65
>Book-Cluster-SupportInfo-$today.txt
```

Continuing with the example, the latter part of the output collected in the previous tip can be collected by the RVC using this command:

```
rvc -c " vsan.support_information /vcva65/Book-DC/computers/Book-
Cluster" -c "quit" "administrator@vsphere.local:VMware123!"@vcva65
>vsanSupportInfo.txt
```

If you study the output collected by either of the last two commands, you will learn a lot about several RVC commands that you can run individually to get each subsection of the output. To list the set of commands used in the output, you can run this command against the output file:

```
grep command <output-file>
```

Listing 21.5 shows an example of this command and its output.

Listing 21.5   RVC commands run by the `vsan.support_information` command

```
root@vcva65 [ ~ ]# grep command vsanSupportInfo.txt
*** command> vsan.support_information Book-Cluster
*** command>vsan.cluster_info Book-Cluster
*** command>vsan.host_info 65node1.book.local
*** command>vsan.vm_object_info
*** command>vsan.host_info 65node2.book.local
*** command>vsan.vm_object_info
*** command>vsan.host_info 65node3.book.local
*** command>vsan.vm_object_info
*** command>vsan.host_info 65node4.book.local
*** command>vsan.vm_object_info
*** command>vsan.host_info 65node5.book.local
*** command>vsan.vm_object_info
*** command>vsan.host_info 65node6.book.local
```

```
*** command>vsan.vm_object_info
*** command>vsan.disks_info
*** command>vsan.disks_stats
*** command>vsan.check_limits Book-Cluster
*** command>vsan.check_state Book-Cluster
*** command>vsan.lldpnetmap Book-Cluster
*** command>vsan.obj_status_report Book-Cluster
*** command>vsan.resync_dashboard Book-Cluster
```

The commands listed after `*** command>` are what you can run at the `rvc` prompt while you're in the relevant directory level. For example, for commands that use the cluster name as a parameter, `/vcva65/Book-DC/computers/` would be the current directory level.

To get command-line help for a command, append `--help` to the command line, as in this example:

```
vsan.cluster_info --help
```

Table 21.5 lists relative paths used with each command while at the `/vcva65/Book-DC/computers/` level. This list is not exhaustive. I call out commands in relevant sections throughout this chapter and Chapter 22.

Table 21.5 Relative paths used with RVC `vsan.*` commands

Command	Relative path
vsan.support_information	0 or [cluster-name]
vsan.cluster_info	
vsan.check_limits	
vsan.check_state	
vsan.lldpnetmap	
vsan.obj_status_report	
vsan.resync_dashboard	
vsan.ondisk_upgrade	
vsan.proactive_rebalance	
vsan.proactive_rebalance_info	

Command	Relative path
`vsan.vm_object_info`	Uses a combination of two parameters:
`vsan.vmdk_stats`	`0` or `[cluster-name]`
	followed by:
	`[cluster-name]/hosts/[host-name]/vms/` `[vm-home]`
	You can also replace `[vm-home]` with `*` to get all VMs on the host.
`vsan.host_[*]`	`[cluster-name]/hosts/[host-name]`
which means all commands that begin with `vsan.host`	This parameter does not accept wildcards.
`vsan.vm_object_info`	To list all VMs objects on the given host:
	`[cluster-name]/hosts/[host-name]/vms/*`
	To list a single VM's objects: `[cluster-name]/` `hosts/[host-name]/vms/[vm-home]`

vSAN Software Components

vSAN provisions software-defined storage using several software components, or modules. Figure 21.25 shows these components and their intercommunication paths.

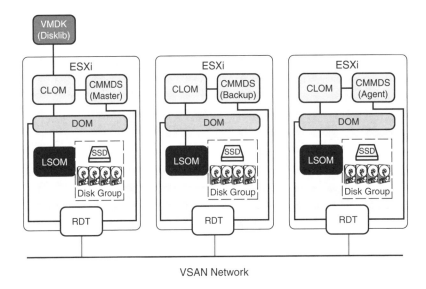

Figure 21.25   vSAN software components

Reliable Datagram Transport (RDT)

RDT is a vmkernel module that facilitates vSAN nodes' communication with each other over the vSAN network. RDT is optimized for very large files.

Cluster Monitoring, Membership, and Directory Services (CMMDS)

CMMDS is a vmkernel module with the same name, cmmds. Its main job is to discover and maintain the vSAN cluster membership. Upon discovery, it elects a master node and a backup node. The remaining nodes have an agent role. The master node has a read/write copy of the CMMDS data, and the backup has a read-only copy.

CMMDS stores metadata such as cluster nodes, disks, policies, and relationships between objects and their components. You can use the cmmds-tool tool on ESXi hosts to list the content of CMMDS metadata:

```
cmmds-tool find --format <format>
```

You can also use the abbreviated option -f with the command:

```
cmmds-tool find -f <format>
```

where format can be json, python, or simple. The default format is simple.

The option --type allows you to list specific vSAN object types, such as NODE, DISK, DOM_OBJECT, LSOM_OBJECT, POLICY, and HOSTNAME. I will point out relevant types as I use cmmds-tool throughout this chapter and Chapter 22.

TIP

To format JSON output for easier readability, add |python -m json.tool at the end of cmmds-tool command line.

Listing 21.6 shows the command using JSON format.

Listing 21.6 Listing CMMDS metadata via the CLI in JSON format

```
cmmds-tool find -t NODE -f json |python -m json.tool
{
 "entries":
[
 {
   "uuid": "57f93a38-27ed-3916-7d3a-000c29da46c3",
   "owner": "00000000-0000-0000-0000-000000000000",
```

```
   "health": "Healthy",
   "revision": "0",
   "type": "NODE",
   "flag": "2",
   "minHostVersion": "0",
   "md5sum": "c006eb36668b07b569eb7926b3812d65",
   "valueLen": "40",
   "content": {"majorVersionNum": 2, "minorVersionNum": 2, "flags": 0,
"requiredVsanMajorVersion": 2, "requiredVsanMinorVersion": 1},
   "errorStr": "(null)"
 }
,{
   "uuid": "57b67c43-71ef-7d94-52b0-000c29d918dd",
   "owner": "00000000-0000-0000-0000-000000000000",
   "health": "Healthy",
   "revision": "0",
   "type": "NODE",
   "flag": "2",
   "minHostVersion": "0",
   "md5sum": "c006eb36668b07b569eb7926b3812d65",
   "valueLen": "40",
   "content": {"majorVersionNum": 2, "minorVersionNum": 2, "flags": 0,
"requiredVsanMajorVersion": 2, "requiredVsanMinorVersion": 1},
   "errorStr": "(null)"
 }
,{
   "uuid": "57b67f25-0080-ca9d-77da-000c292cb974",
   "owner": "00000000-0000-0000-0000-000000000000",
   "health": "Healthy",
   "revision": "0",
   "type": "NODE",
   "flag": "2",
   "minHostVersion": "0",
   "md5sum": "c006eb36668b07b569eb7926b3812d65",
   "valueLen": "40",
   "content": {"majorVersionNum": 2, "minorVersionNum": 2, "flags": 0,
"requiredVsanMajorVersion": 2, "requiredVsanMinorVersion": 1},
   "errorStr": "(null)"
 }
,{
   "uuid": "57b68127-135e-e2a1-dd78-000c298ef254",
```

```
    "owner": "00000000-0000-0000-0000-000000000000",
    "health": "Healthy",
    "revision": "0",
    "type": "NODE",
    "flag": "2",
    "minHostVersion": "0",
    "md5sum": "c006eb36668b07b569eb7926b3812d65",
    "valueLen": "40",
    "content": {"majorVersionNum": 2, "minorVersionNum": 2, "flags": 0,
"requiredVsanMajorVersion": 2, "requiredVsanMinorVersion": 1},
    "errorStr": "(null)"
  }
]
}
```

Cluster Level Object Manager (CLOM)

CLOM calculates the number of components and witnesses needed for an object to meet the storage policy rules. It then checks whether there are enough disk groups with available space and determines the initial object placement to comply with the assigned storage policy.

Distributed Object Manager (DOM)

DOM is part of vsan kernel module. After CLOM identifies suitable disk groups, DOM creates the object's components and distributes them across the cluster nodes according to CLOM's specified placements. vSAN-based objects are referred to as *DOM objects*; examples include VMDKs, snapshots, and swap, mem, and namespace objects. Once an object is created, all subsequent reads and writes go directly through DOM. A DOM object is assigned an owner, which is one of the nodes in the vSAN cluster. There is a DOM client on each vSAN node, which the vSAN nodes use to read and write to the object via its current DOM owner. If the DOM owner goes offline or gets network partitioned (that is, loses connectivity to the vSAN network), a new DOM owner gets assigned, and clients communicate with it for I/O on the object.

DOM communicates with CLOM via a simple vmkernel character device, /dev/dom, which is a symbolic link to /dev/char/vmkdriver/dom.

Listing 21.7 shows an example of such communications, according to events posted to /var/log/clomd.log.

Listing 21.7   CLOM-DOM communications events in the clomd.log file

```
CLOMFetchDOMEvent: Read 1112 bytes of 1512 bytes from DOM


CLOMFetchDOMEvent: Read an additional 400 bytes from DOM


CLOMFetchDOMEvent: DOM requested policy:


Object size 273804165120 bytes with policy: (("stripeWidth"
i1) ("cacheReservation" i0) ("proportionalCapacity" (i0 i100))
("hostFailuresToTolerate" i1) ("forceProvisioning" i0) ("spbmProfileId"
"aa6d5a82-1c88-45da-85d3-3d74b91a5bad") ("spbmProfileGenerationNumber" l+0)
("spbmProfileName" "Virtual SAN Default Storage Policy"))


CLOM_PostWorkItem: Posted a work item for 2e373258-b77c-8509-4e5e-
000c292cb974 group: 2e373258-b77c-8509-4e5e-000c292cb974 Type: PLACEMENT
delay 0 (Success)
[snip]
CLOM_LogDomMessage: referent 2e373258-b77c-8509-4e5e-000c292cb974 length
1960 object size: 273804165120 type: 2
CLOM_LogDomMessage: expression ("Configuration" (("addressSpace"
142949672960) ("objectVersion" i4) ("groupUuid" 2e373258-b77c-8509-4e5e-
000c292cb974) ("compositeUuid" 56373258-4cf8-04bd-672c-000c292cb974))
("RAID_1" () ("Component" (("addressSpace" 142949672960) ("faultDomainId"
57b67c43-71ef-7d94-52b0-000c29d918dd)) UUID_NULL 52e11f22-4416-764d-d8d3-
42191b0e38a1) ("Component" (("addressSpace" 142949672960) ("faultDomainId"
57f93a38-27ed-3916-7d3a-000c29da46c3)) UUID_NULL 524c260c-3da8-7f41-dacc-
9ed3bcf447dc)) ("Witness" (("isWitness" i1) ("faultDomainId" 57b68127-135e-
e2a1-dd78-000c298ef254)) UUID_NULL 520ea260-e2ad-3ccb-24ec-7d116c8bd73f))
```

In Listing 21.7, I removed the date/timestamp and added a blank line between events for readability.

The first event is CLOMFetchDOMEvent, which is the function CLOM uses to read messages posted to the /dev/dom device by DOM. The message size is 1512 bytes, of which CLOM reads 1112 bytes.

The second event is CLOM reading the balance of the message, which is 400 bytes.

The third event shows that DOM's message was to request policy.

The fourth event shows the requested policy, which is Virtual SAN Default Storage Policy.

The fifth event is CLOM_PostWorkItem, which is when CLOM successfully posted the work item of the PLACEMENT type.

I snipped a couple of events at this point, and the next event shown here is CLOM_LogDomMessage, which is CLOM posting a message for DOM that is 1960 bytes long.

The message states the new object's reference:

```
UUID: 2e373258-b77c-8509-4e5e-000c292cb974
Size: 273804165120
Type: 2
```

The last related event is also CLOM_LogDomMessage, which lists the detailed object configuration. I reformatted the object configuration in Listing 21.8 for readability.

Listing 21.8   Breakdown of configuration messages listed in clomd.log

```
("Configuration"
        (("addressSpace" 1273804165120)
        ("objectVersion" i4)
        ("groupUuid" 2e373258-b77c-8509-4e5e-000c292cb974)
        ("compositeUuid" 2e373258-b77c-8509-4e5e-000c292cb974)
        ("objClass" i2)
)

("RAID_1" ()
        ("Component"
        (
        ("capacity" (l0 1273804165120))
        ("addressSpace" 1273804165120)
         ("faultDomainId" 57f93a38-27ed-3916-7d3a-000c29da46c3)
         )
         UUID_NULL 52fe3a3a-2609-d590-f178-911dba48357a)

        ("Component"
        (("capacity" (l0 1273804165120))
        ("addressSpace" 1273804165120)
        ("faultDomainId" 57b68127-135e-e2a1-dd78-000c298ef254))
        UUID_NULL 52433c34-7e6f-d24b-1a9b-1deed7ce980e)
)

  ("Witness"
   (("isWitness" i1)
    ("faultDomainId" 57b67c43-71ef-7d94-52b0-000c29d918dd)
   )
  UUID_NULL 5223142d-2e6f-1e33-3708-517a1782e93f)
)
```

These events were related to creating a new VM with two VMDKs with `RAID5` storage policy for the second VMDK and `Virtual SAN Default Policy` for the first VMDK, as well as the VM's home directory (`namespace`) DOM objects. I listed the events related to DOM requesting the storage policy for the namespace DOM object. You can easily locate similar events related to the remaining objects following the same patterns.

In Listing 21.8, the `groupUuid` and `compositeUuid` are the same, which is also the DOM object's UUID. As a rule of thumb, `groupUuid` always represents the VM's namespace (VM home), and `compositUuid` represents the DOM object's UUID of the given object. This means that the referenced object is the VM's namespace object. If they were different UUIDs, that would mean that it is an object whose descriptor file resides in the VM's namespace.

The `RAID_1` configuration includes two mirrored (replicas) components and a witness component. Each component references a `faultDomainId` and a `UUID_NULL`. The former is the vSAN UUID of the node on which the component will be created, and the latter is the capacity disk UUID in the vSAN node on which the component will be stored. The disk UUID is called `UUID_NULL` until the component is created, at which time `UUID_NULL` is replaced with that disk's UUID.

NOTE

For a vSAN cluster that is not configured with fault domains, each cluster node is in its own fault domain. This is why the `faultDomainId` is the same as the node's UUID. I cover more details in the section **"Fault Domains"** in Chapter 22.

We see here that the two replica components are on separate nodes (`faultDomainId`), and the witness component is on a third node.

In a cluster not configured with fault domains, to identify the host name given its UUID, use this `cmmds-tool` command:

```
cmmds-tool find --format json --type HOSTNAME --uuid <faultDomainId> |grep
hostname
```

You can also use these abbreviated options:

```
cmmds-tool find -f json -t HOSTNAME -u <faultDomainId> |grep hostname
```

Here is an example:

```
cmmds-tool find -f json -t HOSTNAME -u 57b67c43-71ef-7d94-52b0-000c29d918dd
|grep hostname
```

The output looks like this:

```
"content": {"hostname": "65Node1.book.local"},
```

Next, DOM passes on to each vSAN node's LSOM its corresponding component's properties.

Local Log-Structured Object Manager (LSOM)

LSOM is responsible for storing objects' components on local disks according to the decisions made by CLOM and as created by DOM. Components stored by LSOM are referred to as *LSOM components*. In other words, LSOM provides persistence for vSAN components, policies, configurations, and so on.

LSOM also enforces object policies and helps in the recovery of objects. If LSOM experiences transient device errors, it retries the I/O.

Listing 21.7, earlier in this chapter, lists each LSOM component's capacity, UUID, and node UUID on which the component is to be created. LSOM on the corresponding node gets informed, by DOM, of the component details. LSOM then stores the corresponding component on a disk of the specified capacity.

LSOM uses two structured logs:

- **LLOG**—The logical log (LLOG) stores log entries of data that has just arrived in the write buffer (WB) but has not yet been assigned capacity tier blocks.

- **PLOG**—The physical log (PLOG) sits below the file system and above capacity tier disks. If I/O is for metadata updates, it buffers LSOM components' metadata on the cache tier, along with log entries that map the cache to the capacity tier's LBA-to-physical blocks mapping to ensure their recovery after a crash. Otherwise, when the WB data is ready to be evicted (destaged), PLOG uses an elevator algorithm to evict the least-read data to capacity tier disks and then removes the data from the WB.

The capacity tier and cache tier disks have two partitions: a small `vsan` partition and a larger `virsto` partition. On capacity tier disks, the PLOG uses the `vsan` partition to store vSAN metadata and uses the `virsto` partition for storing components data. On vSAN 5.5, a `vmfs` partition was used instead of the `virsto` partition.

Creating and Configuring a vSAN Cluster

vSAN is a property of a vSphere cluster and can be configured on an existing Distributed Resource Scheduler (DRS) cluster or a freshly created one. If configured on an existing cluster, the vSphere High Availability (HA) feature must be disabled first if it is already enabled. If this is not done, HA will neither utilize vSAN-specific integrated features nor function as expected. You'll learn more details later in this chapter, in the section **"HA on vSAN."**

The process of creating or configuring a vSAN cluster depends on several design choices and the starting point. The following procedure starts with a freshly created data center with all hosts added to it. No cluster has been created yet:

1. Connect to the vCenter server using the vSphere 6.x Web Client as a user with Administrator privileges.

2. Navigate to the **Hosts and Clusters** view.

3. Right-click the data center inventory object and select the **New Cluster** menu option.

4. Enter the cluster name.

5. Do not turn on any features at this time. Click **OK**.

6. Right-click the newly created cluster object in the inventory tree and select the **Move Hosts into Cluster** menu option.

7. Select all hosts that will participate in the cluster and then click **OK**.

8. Right-click the cluster object again and select the **Settings** menu option. At this stage, the next step varies between vSphere 6.0 and 6.5:

   - For vSphere 6.0, you select the **Manage** tab, click the **Settings** button, and go to the **Virtual SAN General** section.

   - For vSphere 6.5, you select the **Configure** tab, click **Virtual SAN**, and go to the **General** section.

   For vSphere 6.0, Update 2 or 6.5 and later, continue with the next step. For 6.0, Update 1 or earlier, go to the next section, "**Configuring vSAN on vSphere 6.0 Update 1 and later.**"

9. Click the **Configure** button to open the Configure Virtual SAN Wizard (see Figure 21.26).

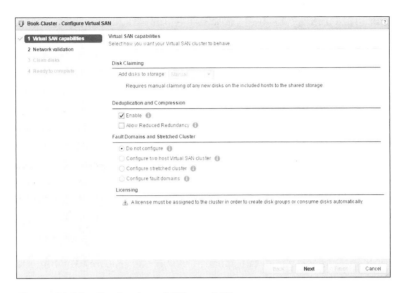

Figure 21.26 Configuring vSAN capabilities

Step 1 of the wizard, Virtual SAN Capabilities, has four sections:

- **Disk Claiming**—This setting determines how disks will be claimed by disk groups in each host. The Automatic setting adds all nonpartitioned direct attached disks (local disks) to the corresponding host's disk group. The Manual setting allows you to create the disk group(s) manually and select which disks and their corresponding roles to add to each group. The default setting is Automatic. For now, select **Manual**.

TIP

I prefer to use manual mode first until I create all disk groups to my liking, especially when multiple disk groups per host are to be configured. I can switch to automatic mode later, if the I/O controller is configured in passthrough mode (JBOD), which does not require creating any RAID 0 logical volumes. Assuming that passthrough is the vSAN-certified mode for the adapter, this makes adding disks to the disk groups easier when the need arises to scale up the storage capacity. See the section "**Disk Group Design Guidelines**," later in this chapter.

- **Deduplication and Compression**—These two features reduce the data stored on physical disks in the cluster in all-flash configurations. I cover these features in detail in the section "**Deduplication and Compression**" in Chapter 22. This section includes two options:
    - **Enable**—Enables the feature. When enabled, disk claiming mode is set to Manual, regardless of which choice you made earlier, and only all-flash disk groups can be added. You cannot create hybrid disk groups (SSD cache and MD capacity). When this option is selected, the Disk Claiming option is grayed out because you are not allowed to change it when Dedupe is enabled.
    - **Allow Reduced Redundancy**—This option helps when deduplication and compression are being enabled on an existing cluster with limited resources (for example, if some or all VMs were configured with the number of failures to tolerate [FTT] set to 1 [RAID 1] on a three-node cluster and there is insufficient space to convert the data format to enable the feature). Enabling the Allow Reduced Redundancy option allows the conversion process to use a single replica when two are required (RAID 1 configuration). This saves space momentarily until the conversion process is done. Then, all objects configured with RAID 1 are re-protected through the creation of the required replica components. It is highly recommended to have full backups of all VMs with FTT = 1 policy prior to enabling this feature because the VMs are not protected during the conversion process under limited resources.

TIP

Unless you are upgrading from an earlier version of vSAN, it is much cleaner and easier to enable deduplication and compression at cluster creation time to avoid resource pressure that occurs if they are enabled later.

If the configuration is an upgraded all-flash cluster from vSphere 6.0, Update 1 or older, it would be advisable to add resources, such as adding a temporary host with sufficient disks, to increase available resources and avoid allowing reduced redundancy.

- **Fault Domains and Stretched Cluster**—See the "**Fault Domains**" and "**Stretched Cluster**" sections in Chapter 22 for further details. These are the suboptions:
    - **Do not configure**—This is the default option, which configures each cluster node as its own fault domain.

- **Configure two hosts Virtual SAN cluster**—This option enables remote office/branch office (ROBO)configuration. See the section **"Remote Office/Branch Office (ROBO)"** in Chapter 22 for more details. This configuration includes two nodes in a single site and a witness-only host, or virtual appliance, in another site.

- **Configure stretched cluster**—This option is used to configure two active data sites with equal number of hosts and storage devices in each site. A witness-only host, or virtual appliance, is placed in a third site. See the section **"Stretched Cluster"** in Chapter 22 for more details.

- **Configure fault domains**—This option configures two or more groups of hosts to be in their own fault domain. This means that each group is treated as a single fault domain so that when any host in the group fails, the whole group is considered to have failed. vSAN does not place more than one replica of the same object within a fault domain. This configuration protects against rack failure. For more details, see the section **"Fault Domains"** in Chapter 22.

10. Select options matching your design requirements and then click **Next**. The Network Validation step of the wizard appears (see Figure 21.27).

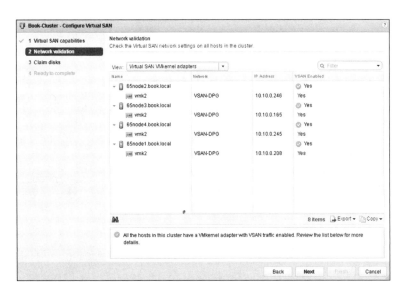

Figure 21.27   vSAN network validation

11. In the Network Validation step, the wizard verifies that each cluster node has a vmkernel adapter (VMNIC) with the vSAN traffic option enabled. If any of the nodes reports an error, cancel the wizard, correct the configuration, and then restart the wizard. Otherwise, click **Next**.

The Claim Disks step of the wizard appears. If Automatic mode was selected, this step would be skipped. The wizard does its best to claim the suitable disks for cache and capacity tiers. The logic is that for hybrid disk groups, all SSD disks qualify for cache tier, and magnetic disks (MDs) qualify for capacity tier. For all-flash disk groups, the smaller SSDs qualify for the cache tier, and the larger ones for capacity tier. The assumption is that the smaller SSDs are of a more durable enterprise class.

12. Review the wizard's selections. If a change is needed, click the **Claim For** field of the corresponding disk to change and select the correct tier (see Figure 21.28).

Figure 21.28   Claiming disks

The lower portion of the dialog shows the total capacity for the cache and capacity tiers. The bottom section shows configuration validation. If it shows anything other than Configuration Correct status, review the selections and correct accordingly. Each host needs at least one disk group with one cache tier and at least one capacity tier disk.

In this example, I expanded the cache tier selections and clicked the last row's **Claim For** field to show the available choices:

- **Cache tier**—Claim this disk for the cache tier

- **Capacity tier**—Claim this disk for the capacity tier

- **Do not claim**—Do not claim this disk for any tier.

TIP

If you have disks attached to multiple storage adapters, scroll to the right to see the Adapter column while the tiers are expanded to see the vmhba number to which each disk is attached. This is helpful when creating separate disk groups attached to separate storage adapters.

---

13. Click **Next**.

14. In the Ready to complete step, review the settings, and if no changes are required, click **Finish**.

In my configuration, I intentionally misconfigured the vSAN port group on one of the hosts. As a result, vSAN Health Check reported this issue. See more details about this in the "**vSAN Health Check UI**" section in Chapter 22.

Configuring vSAN on vSphere 6.0, Update 1 and later

To configure vSAN on vSphere 6.0, Update 1 and later, follow steps 1–8 of the previous procedure and then continue with these steps:

9. Click the **Edit** button next to Virtual SAN is Turned OFF (see Figure 21.29).

10. Select the **Turn ON Virtual SAN** check box. The default selection for Add Disks to Storage is **Automatic**. This enables automatic creation of a disk group per host and claims all locally attached disks that have no partition tables on them. For now, select **Manual** instead.

11. Click **OK** to enable the feature.

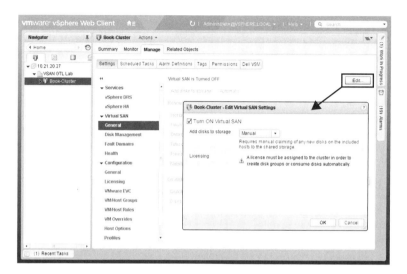

Figure 21.29   Creating a vSAN cluster

The end result is a vSAN cluster without disk groups. Next, you need to create the disk groups. For details on doing that, see the section "Disk Group Design Guidelines," later in this chapter.

Enabling Internet Connectivity of a vSAN Cluster

If vCenter can access the Internet, and you plan on using features that require access (for example, Health Check or Update Manager), you need to configure Internet connectivity for this cluster. You can do so by following this procedure:

1. Connect to the vCenter server using the vSphere 6.x Web Client as a user with Administrator privileges.

2. Navigate to the **Hosts and Cluster** view (see Figure 21.30).

3. Right-click the cluster inventory object and then select the **Settings** menu option.

4. Select **General** in the Virtual SAN section.

5. In the Internet Connectivity section, click the **Edit** button.

6. Select the **Enable Internet access for this cluster** check box. Enter the proxy configuration details, if required, for Internet access.

7. Click **OK**.

Figure 21.30 Enabling Internet access

vSAN Disk Groups

vSAN uses pools of locally attached disks that are grouped as disk groups which are, at least, one group per vSAN node. Some vSAN nodes may join the cluster as consumers without contributing any storage resources. However, vSAN licenses are consumed by all nodes in the cluster, regardless of their storage contribution roles.

Each disk group is limited to 1 cache tier disk and up to 7 capacity tier disks. Each host can have up to 5 disk groups with total capacity of 35 tier disks and 5 cache tier disks.

Disk Group Design Guidelines

vSAN Ready Nodes is a VMware reference architecture for certified combinations of systems, I/O adapters, and storage devices. Instead of using Ready Nodes, you can build your own combinations, but there is no guarantee of the validity of a combination even if every single component is certified on its own. This is due to the fact that interoperability of the various components is uncertain unless they were tested and certified together. However, depending on the node design, the backplane of the storage enclosure (where you plug the disks) may be connected to one or more I/O adapters. Some high-density enclosures use SAS expanders to overcome the limitations on the number of SAS ports per adapter. This could mean that one adapter can handle upward of 24 disks—or even more.

SAS expanders act like SAS switches. SAS expanders must be on the vCG to be supported. Several issues that have been reported with vSAN have been attributed to using unsupported SAS expanders or certain firmware versions of supported ones. Make sure to look up these details on the vCG before deploying vSAN.

Depending on the hardware design, each node in a vSAN cluster can be equipped with one or more storage adapters.

TIP

Do not mix all-flash disk groups and hybrid disk groups in the same vSAN cluster. Doing so will result in failure of features that require all-flash configuration (for example, RAID 5/6 or deduplication) when the need arises to place a host in maintenance mode with full data migration or an all-flash host gets network partitioned. Capacity provided by hybrid disk groups is not available for all-flash features.

In addition, vSAN caching is handled differently with all-flash than with hybrid disk groups. All-flash groups use the cache tier for the write buffer only and use the capacity tier for the read cache. In contrast, hybrid disk groups use the cache tier for both the write buffer and read cache.

I/O adapters can be certified with RAID 0 mode, passthrough mode (JBOD), or both. Passthrough mode (JBOD) enables an adapter to access each attached disks directly.

With RAID 0 mode, each disk attached to the adapter is configured as a RAID 0 logical volume with a single member. In this configuration, a RAID adapter's cache must be disabled or configured as write-through because vSAN has its own cache tier disks.

Passthrough mode adapters usually do not have a cache option.

TIP

An I/O adapter must never be used for vSAN and VMFS mixed load. If you must have VMFS datastores for any reasons, disks on which they are configured must be attached to a separate I/O adapter from that used by vSAN disk groups.

---

vSAN 6.5 introduced support for nonvolatile memory express (NVMe) devices. Each of these devices includes its own PCIe controller. NVMe devices are also available in a 2.5-inch form factor that provides a four-lane PCIe interface through U.2 connectors. Only use devices listed on the vCG.

> **TIP**
>
> While VMware suggests a rule of thumb of having a cache tier–to–capacity tier ratio of 10%, the actual size depends on storage policies that will be applied to DOM objects. At minimum, the default vSAN datastore policy FTT = 1 reduces size of the cached objects to half. This means you need 10% of half the total capacity tier disks, in the disk group. If you plan on using FTT = 2 on most objects, the cache size would be 10% of one-third the total capacity tier disks, in the disk group. For RAID5/6 configurations, since they require all-flash disk groups, consider write buffer only because all-flash capacity tier disks are used for read cache.

Marking a Drive Type as Flash

In some situations, vSphere fails to detect a flash device correctly and ends up identifying it as a hard disk drive (HDD). This is usually due to firmware or driver issues. After ruling out firmware and driver issues, you may have to manually mark the disk type as flash. A typical environment is when using a nested ESXi host's configuration in a home lab or training environment. A nested environment is where ESXi hosts are configured as virtual machines running on an ESXi host or VMware workstation.

To mark an HDD as flash, follow this procedure before adding the drive to a vSAN disk group:

1. Connect to the vCenter server using the vSphere 6.x Web Client as a user with Administrator privileges. This example uses vSphere 6.5; the 6.0 UI is slightly different.

2. Navigate to the **Hosts and Clusters** view (see Figure 21.31).

3. Select the ESXi host in the inventory tree. This is the host on which the disk was detected as an HDD.

4. Select the **Configure** tab or right-click the host and select the **Settings** menu option.

5. Select **Storage Devices** in the Storage section.

6. Select the disk you want to tag as flash. If you need to mark more than one disk, press **Ctrl** and click each disk.

7. Click the icon with an **F** in it (if you hover over it, it displays the caption `Marks the select disks as flash disks`).

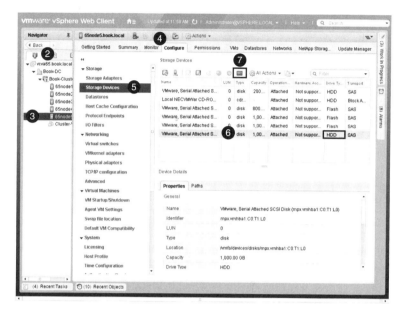

Figure 21.31   Marking an HDD as a flash disk

A successful operation results in the drive type changing from HDD to flash. If other HDDs need to be marked in the same fashion, repeat the procedure for each drive.

Manually Creating a Disk Group by Using the UI

To manually create a disk group by using the UI, do the following:

1. Connect to the vCenter server using the vSphere 6.x Web Client as a user with Administrator privileges.

2. Navigate to the **Hosts and Clusters** view (see Figure 21.32).

3. Select the cluster object in the inventory tree.

4. Right-click the cluster object and then select the **Settings** menu option.

5. Select **Disk Management** in the Virtual SAN section.

6. To use the Claim Disks wizard, click the **Claim Disks** icon. The remaining steps are identical to steps 12–14 in the section "**Creating and Configuring a vSAN Cluster**," earlier in this chapter.

   However, to manually create a disk group on each node in the cluster, proceed with step 7.

7. To manually create a disk group on a node in the cluster, select one of the hosts.

8. Click the **Create a new disk group** icon.

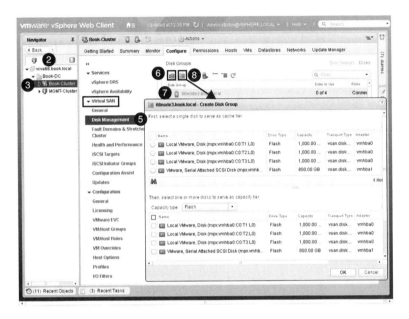

Figure 21.32   Manual disk group creation

9. Select one cache tier SSD from the top section's list. Only one cache tier is allowed to be selected, so the selection is done via a radio button. Initially, if SSDs are attached to multiple I/O adapters, all disks are listed in both the top and bottom sections. Once a cache tier SSD is selected, it gets removed from the bottom list, which shows the capacity tier candidates. Otherwise, if SSDs are attached to a single I/O adapter, the smaller SSDs are listed under the cache tier list, and the rest are listed under the capacity tier list.

   Similarly, in hybrid configurations, with a single SSD and multiple HDDs, the SSD is listed under the cache tier list and the HDDs under the capacity tier list.

10. Select one or more capacity tier disks from the bottom list by selecting the corresponding check box(es). Figure 21.33 shows cache and capacity tier disks attached to the same vmhba.

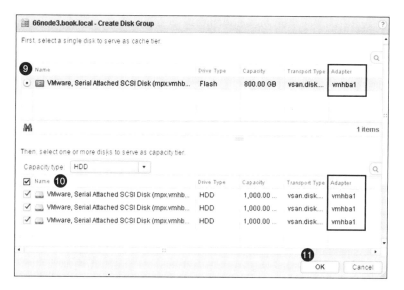

Figure 21.33   Selecting a cache tier disk—manual DG creation

---

TIP

If you have multiple I/O adapters to which multiple cache and capacity tier disks are attached, create a separate disk group for each adapter and its attached cache/capacity tier
disks combination. The adapter name is listed under the **Adapter** column as vmhba(x),
where x is the adapter number in this host (for example, vmhba2, vmhba3).

---

11. Click **OK** to conclude the disk group creation.

12. Repeat steps 7-11 for each node contributing storage to the cluster.

Listing Candidate Disks via the CLI

To list disks available for creation/addition to a disk group via the CLI, run this command
at the ESXi host console or via SSH:

```
vdq --query --human
```

Or use the abbreviated option:

```
vdq -q -H
```

Omitting the --human option returns the output in the default Python format.

Listing 21.9 shows the command and its output.

Listing 21.9 Listing disk group candidate disks via the CLI

```
[root@65Node2:~] vdq --query --human
DiskResults:
      DiskResult[0]:
             Name:  mpx.vmhba2:C0:T1:L0
          VSANUUID:
             State:  Eligible for use by VSAN
            Reason:  None
            IsSSD?:  1
  IsCapacityFlash?:  1
            IsPDL?:  0


      DiskResult[1]:
             Name:  mpx.vmhba2:C0:T0:L0
          VSANUUID:
             State:  Eligible for use by VSAN
            Reason:  None
            IsSSD?:  1
  IsCapacityFlash?:  0
            IsPDL?:  0


      DiskResult[2]:
             Name:  mpx.vmhba1:C0:T0:L0
          VSANUUID:
             State:  Ineligible for use by VSAN
            Reason:  Has partitions
            IsSSD?:  0
  IsCapacityFlash?:  0
            IsPDL?:  0


      DiskResult[3]:
             Name:  mpx.vmhba2:C0:T3:L0
          VSANUUID:
             State:  Eligible for use by VSAN
            Reason:  None
            IsSSD?:  1
  IsCapacityFlash?:  1
            IsPDL?:  0
```

```
    DiskResult[4]:
             Name:  mpx.vmhba2:C0:T2:L0
         VSANUUID:
            State:  Eligible for use by VSAN
           Reason:  None
           IsSSD?:  1
IsCapacityFlash?:  1
           IsPDL?:  0
```

NOTE

The sample output in Listing 21.9 was collected from a nested ESXi environment (where ESXi runs as a VM on another ESXi host or VMware workstation). This explains why all the device names in this output have the mpx prefix (which means *generic multipathing*). In physical environments, the device name would mostly have an naa or a t10 prefix.

The State field in the output indicates whether the disk is eligible for use by vSAN. DiskResult[2] is an example of an ineligible device because the Reason field states Has Partitions. If this device is one of the disks you are certain should be added to the disk group, you have to remove the partition table on it to make it eligible for use by vSAN. Otherwise, leaving existing partitions on the disk prevents it from being listed in the UI as a candidate device.

To list the partition table on that device, run this command:

```
partedUtil getptbl /dev/disks/<device-ID>
```

In this example, the device ID is mpx.vmhba1:C0:T0:L0, so this is what the command would be:

```
partedUtil getptbl /dev/disks/mpx.vmhba1:C0:T0:L0
```

Listing 21.10 shows the command and its output.

Listing 21.10 Listing a disk's partition table via the CLI

```
partedUtil getptbl /dev/disks/mpx.vmhba1:C0:T0:L0
gpt
26108 255 63 419430400
1 64 8191 C12A7328F81F11D2BA4B00A0C93EC93B systemPartition 128
5 8224 520191 EBD0A0A2B9E5443387C068B6B72699C7 linuxNative 0
6 520224 1032191 EBD0A0A2B9E5443387C068B6B72699C7 linuxNative 0
```

```
7 1032224 1257471 9D27538040AD11DBBF97000C2911D1B8 vmkDiagnostic 0
8 1257504 1843199 EBD0A0A2B9E5443387C068B6B72699C7 linuxNative 0
9 1843200 7086079 9D27538040AD11DBBF97000C2911D1B8 vmkDiagnostic 0
2 7086080 15472639 EBD0A0A2B9E5443387C068B6B72699C7 linuxNative 0
3 15472640 419430366 AA31E02A400F11DB9590000C2911D1B8 vmfs 0
```

This output means that the device is the ESXi host's boot device. In this case, stay away from it, or you will render the host unbootable.

Manually Creating a Disk Group via the CLI

While it is not recommended to create vSAN disk groups via the CLI, you may have to resort to this approach if vCenter is not accessible because creating a new disk group may help resolve the issue that made vCenter inaccessible. To do that, follow this procedure:

1. Logon to ESXi host console directly or via SSH as root.

2. Identify the list of SSD disks attached to the host by running this command:

   ```
   esxcli    storage    core    device    list|grep    SSD    -B    13    |grep
   "Devfs\|SSD\|Size"
   ```

   Listing 21.11 shows this command and its output.

Listing 21.11 Listing attached SSD disks via the CLI

```
esxcli storage core device list|grep SSD -B 13 |grep "Devfs\|SSD\|Size"
   Size: 1024000
   Devfs Path: /vmfs/devices/disks/mpx.vmhba2:C0:T1:L0
   Is SSD: true
   Size: 819200
   Devfs Path: /vmfs/devices/disks/mpx.vmhba2:C0:T0:L0
   Is SSD: true
   Size: 0
   Devfs Path: /vmfs/devices/cdrom/mpx.vmhba64:C0:T0:L0
   Is SSD: false
   Size: 204800
   Devfs Path: /vmfs/devices/disks/mpx.vmhba1:C0:T0:L0
   Is SSD: false
   Size: 1024000
   Devfs Path: /vmfs/devices/disks/mpx.vmhba2:C0:T3:L0
```

```
Is SSD: true
Size: 1024000
Devfs Path: /vmfs/devices/disks/mpx.vmhba2:C0:T2:L0
Is SSD: true
```

In this example, I have four SSD devices attached to vmhba2; three devices are 1TiB in size, and one is 800GiB. The rest of the devices are not SSD: The value of the Is SSD field is false.

Before proceeding, verify that all identified disks are eligible for use by vSAN by using vdq command as shown earlier, in Listing 21.9.

This is an example of an all-flash configuration. Typically, the cache tier devices are smaller than the capacity tier devices and are more durable. This is true in this case, where I use the 800GiB SSD device as the cache tier. Using the device ID associated with it in the next step.

3. Create the disk group by using this command:

```
esxcli vsan storage add --ssd <device ID> --disks <hdd1> --disks
<hdd2> --disks <hdd3>
```

where hdd(n) is the capacity tier disk repeated for the total number of disks to add.

Or you can use the abbreviated version:

```
esxcli vsan storage add -s <device ID> -d <hdd1> -d <hdd2> -d <hdd3>
```

In this example, this would be the command with abbreviated options:

```
esxcli vsan storage add -s mpx.vmhba2:C0:T0:L0 -d mpx.vmhba2:C0:T1:L0
-d mpx.vmhba2:C0:T2:L0 -d mpx.vmhba2:C0:T3:L0
```

Listing 21.12 shows the related events in /var/log/clomd.log.

Listing 21.12 Events related to creating a disk group in the clomd.log file

```
Added 5254ce21-703d-a906-a046-596dd712f170, owner 57b67f25-0080-ca9d-77da-
000c292cb974 of type CdbObjectDisk to CLOMDB, v4 health:0 allflash dg
Added 521c8169-7776-e878-d831-89cb1780e968, owner 57b67f25-0080-ca9d-77da-
000c292cb974 of type CdbObjectDisk to CLOMDB, v4 health:0
Added 5262b603-bcb0-210a-f18d-9a31a5d85acf, owner 57b67f25-0080-ca9d-77da-
000c292cb974 of type CdbObjectDisk to CLOMDB, v4 health:0
Added 5285b69b-a276-79f8-1808-8d9fb5f533db, owner 57b67f25-0080-ca9d-77da-
000c292cb974 of type CdbObjectDisk to CLOMDB, v4 health:0
```

The first message is from creating the disk group using the cache tier UUID. The remaining three message are from adding the three capacity tier disks to the disk group.

In addition to clomd.log messages, other messages are logged to /var/log/vmkernel.log file. Listing 21.13 lists a relevant message from that file.

Listing 21.13 Events related to creating a disk group in the vmkernel.log file

```
Added 5254ce21-703d-a906-a046-596dd712f170, owner 57b67f25-0080-
```

Removing a Disk from a Disk Group

If for some reason—most commonly because a disk has failed or is predicted to fail—you need to decommission and remove a disk from a disk group, you can do so for a capacity tier disk or a cache tier disk. However, removing a cache tier disk from the disk group results in removal of the whole group. The reason is that certain metadata logs and tables that hold the disk group structure reside on the cache tier. The capacity tier disks cannot stand on their own without it. The process of removing either type is identical. However, whereas data has to be evacuated from all the capacity tier disks in the disk group, when a single capacity tier disk is removed, only data on that disk is evacuated.

Using the UI to Remove a Disk

To decommission a disk from a disk group via the UI, follow steps 1–5 in the section "Manually Creating a Disk Group by Using the UI," earlier in this chapter, and continue with these steps:

6. Select the disk group from which to remove a disk (see Figure 21.34).

7. In the lower pane, select the disk to be removed. If more than one disk will be removed, hold down **Ctrl** as you click each disk.

TIP

If you do not know in which storage chassis slot the disk is plugged, you can ascertain that you select the correct disk by selecting the disk in the UI and then clicking the **Turn on the locator LED of the select disk(s)** icon, which is a green sphere.

When you do this, an indicator light flashes repeatedly on the disk in the storage chassis. If it is the correct disk to remove, you can proceed with the next step. Otherwise, repeat this process until you locate the correct disk. This will help you avoid decommissioning the wrong disk. To turn off the locator LED light, click the sphere next to the one clicked earlier.

---

8. Click the **Remove Disk** icon.

Figure 21.34   Removing a disk from a disk group

If the icon is grayed out or, in later versions (for example, 6.5), you get a dialog that states `Action not available when Auto claim mode is enabled on cluster`, this means the **Add disk to storage vSAN cluster** option was set to **Automatic**. Changing it to **Manual** enables the remove disk feature.

vSAN 6.6, shipped with vSphere 6.5, Patch 2, revised the UI to list migration modes as radio buttons and provides an evaluation of each mode's success potential (see Figure 21.35).

Remove Disk

Disk "VMware, Serial Attached SCSI Disk (mpx.vmhba1:C0:T3:L0)" is about to be removed from the disk group "Disk group (0000000000766d686261313a303a30)". Unless the data on the disk(s) is evacuated first, removing the disk(s) might disrupt working VMs.

Data on disk group: 0 B

Select data migration mode: ⓘ

● Full data migration
   ○ Can be completed successfully.

○ Ensure accessibility
   ○ Can be completed successfully.

○ No data migration
   ○ Can be completed successfully.

Remove disk?

        Yes   No

Figure 21.35   Removing a disk from disk group in vSAN 6.6

9. Select **Full data migration** from the **Migration mode** pull-down list (or radio button). If this disk is a failed disk whose data is not recoverable, select **No data migration** instead.

The choice of modes is a new feature in vSAN 6.5. In earlier 6.x versions of vSAN, a single check box is available to enable full data migration mode only. When not selected, the process is equivalent to selecting no data migration mode in vSAN 6.5. In other words, vSAN 6.0 through 6.2 versions do not offer ensure accessibility mode for the process of removing disks or disk groups. Figure 21.36 shows this dialog from vSAN 6.0 through 6.2.

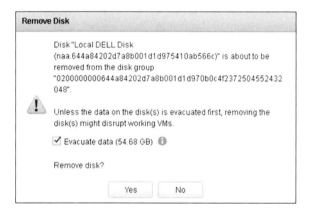

Figure 21.36   Data migration mode in vSAN 6.0–6.2

10. Click **Yes** to close the Remove Disk dialog and start the removal process.

The data evacuation process takes some time, depending on the amount of data on the disk(s) being removed. There should be enough space on capacity tier disks on this or other disk groups in the cluster to receive the evacuated data. If the **No data migration** option is selected, the process goes much faster. Only select that for failed disks, though. I explain the various modes further in the next section.

Using the CLI to Remove a Disk

If vCenter is unavailable and you have to replace a disk in a vSAN disk group, the only recourse is to use the CLI to remove the existing disk. This is the command to remove a disk from a disk group via the CLI:

```
esxcli vsan storage remove --disk <disk-ID> --evacuation-mode <mode>
```

where `mode` can be any of the following:

- `evacuateAllData`—Evacuate all data from the disk before removing it. This is the same as the **Full data migration** option in the UI. This evacuates all data from the disk, regardless of the current status of objects whose components reside on this disk. This is also referred to as **DECOM Mode 2**.

- `ensureObjectAccessibility`—Evacuate data from the disk to ensure object accessibility in the vSAN cluster before removing the disk. This is also referred to as DECOM Mode 1. This mode is the same as the **Ensure accessibility** option in the UI. This is sort of a what-if scenario. This mode checks the current status vSAN DOM objects that have LSOM components on the disk to be removed. If the status is active, it could be possible to not evacuate the LSOM components if the remaining disks in the disk group as well as other nodes' disk groups are sufficient to provide a majority quorum for the object. In other words, if the number of votes assigned to the LSOM components on this disk are less than the sum of votes on the remaining components for a given DOM object, the latter will still be available after the disk is removed, albeit in a degraded state. If you choose this option, there is a risk of losing access to the DOM object if a failure happens somewhere else in the cluster (for example, if a host fails or another disk fails).

  It is therefore safer to use `evacuateAllData` mode at all times. The only exception is if the disk you are removing has already failed and components on it are not recoverable or there is insufficient disk space for the data to be migrated. In such a case, you should use the next mode, `noAction`, instead.

- `noAction`—Do not move vSAN data out of the disk before removing it. This mode is the same as the **No data migration** option in the UI. As with `ensureObjectAccessibility`, you should use this mode exclusively when removing a failed disk from a disk group or when there is insufficient disk space for the data to be migrated. This is also referred to as DECOM Mode 0.

TIP

Before removing a disk that appears to have failed, try to mount it first. (See the section **"Mounting an Unmounted Disk in a Disk Group,"** later in this chapter.) Sometimes a faulty I/O adapter driver or faulty firmware results in unmounting a disk when the disk has not physically failed. If it mounts successfully and all objects become active again, unmount it again, using `evacuateAllData` mode, before the original problem ends up unmounting it again.

Otherwise, if the mount attempt still fails, try upgrading the adapter's driver and/or firmware to the latest certified version. If it still fails to mount the disk, you may then proceed with the removal process using `noAction` mode. Note that if the driver/firmware upgrade process is expected to take less than 60 minutes, you can place the host into maintenance mode by using `noAction` (which means no data migration). If the disk has been in an unmounted state already for more than 60 minutes, it is highly likely that the absent components that were on this disk have already been resynchronized to other disks, if possible. This tip applies only if the absent components are not otherwise recoverable.

Listing 21.14 shows the `remove` command for the same disk removed in the previous section, "**Using the UI to Remove a Disk**."

Listing 21.14 Removing a disk via the CLI

```
esxcli vsan storage remove --disk mpx.vmhba2:C0:T1:L0 --evacuation-mode
evacuateAllData
```

Successful operation returns no feedback on the command line; however, related messages are posted to the /var/log/clomd.log file, as shown in Listing 21.15.

Listing 21.15 clomd.log message from removing a disk via the CLI

```
CLOM_ProcessDecomUpdate: Disk 52610395-d7df-157e-0607-9dafa5f2400c
state change. Old:DECOM_STATE_NONE New:DECOM_STATE_ACTIVE Mode:2 JobUu
id:00000000-0000-0000-0000-000000000000

CLOMDecomCleanupInMemState: Cleaning in-memory state

CLOMDecomCleanupObjLists: Cleaning up decommissioning lists.

CLOMDecomPublishDecomStateEntryInt: Disk 52610395-d7df-157e-0607-
9dafa5f2400c: Publishing state DECOM_STATE_INITIALIZED

CLOMDecomPublishDecomStateEntryInt: Disk 52610395-d7df-157e-0607-
9dafa5f2400c: Published state DECOM_STATE_INITIALIZED. Affected objects: 0,
Progress: 0, Update: 0

CLOM_ProcessDecomUpdate: Disk 52610395-d7df-157e-0607-9dafa5f2400c
state change. Old:DECOM_STATE_ACTIVE New:DECOM_STATE_INITIALIZED Mode:2
JobUuid:5e15fd31-d551-1e0a-4e88-e08cc2548b9b

CLOMDecomCMMDSResponseCb: CMMDS update response received: Success

CLOM_ProcessDecomUpdate: Disk 52610395-d7df-157e-0607-9dafa5f2400c state
change. Old:DECOM_STATE_INITIALIZED New:DECOM_STATE_DOM_READY Mode:2
JobUuid:5e15fd31-d551-1e0a-4e88-e08cc2548b9b

CLOMDecomPublishDecomStateEntryInt: Disk 52610395-d7df-157e-0607-
9dafa5f2400c: Publishing state DECOM_STATE_COMPLETE

CLOMDecomPublishDecomStateEntryInt: Disk 52610395-d7df-157e-0607-
9dafa5f2400c: Published state DECOM_STATE_COMPLETE. Affected objects: 0,
Progress: 0, Update: 0
```

```
CLOM_ProcessDecomUpdate: Disk 52610395-d7df-157e-0607-9dafa5f2400c
state change. Old:DECOM_STATE_DOM_READY New:DECOM_STATE_COMPLETE Mode:2
JobUuid:5e15fd31-d551-1e0a-4e88-e08cc2548b9b
CLOMDecomCleanupInMemState: Cleaning in-memory state
CLOMDecomCleanupObjLists: Cleaning up decommissioning lists.
CLOMDecomCMMDSResponseCb: CMMDS update response received: Success
CLOM_CdbEventCallback: Disk:52610395-d7df-157e-0607-9dafa5f2400c health
state has changed from: 0 to: 64
Removing 52610395-d7df-157e-0607-9dafa5f2400c of type CdbObjectDisk from
CLOMDB
```

As you can see in Listing 21.15, the CLOM conducts the following sequence of events:

1. Starts the process of removal (that is, decommissioning, or DECOM) by changing the DECOM state from NONE to STATE_ACTIVE. The DECOM mode used here is 2, which means evacuateAllData mode. The job ID for this process is first set to all zeros.

2. Cleans up the in-memory state of the disk.

3. Cleans up the decommissioning list.

4. Publishes the DCOM state change as INITIALIZED.

5. States the number of objects affected. In this example, I used an empty disk group, which is why the object count is zero.

6. Changes the DECOM state from ACTIVE to INITIALIZED and assigns the job an actual UUID. The DECOM mode is still 2.

7. Receives a success response from CMMDS.

8. Changes the DECOM STATE to DOM_READY.

9. Publishes the change of DCOM STATE to COMPLETE.

10. Enumerates the count of affected objects. Again, in this example, the count is zero because I used an empty disk group.

11. Changes the DECOM STATE to COMPLETE.

12. Cleans up the in-memory state.

13. Cleans up DECOM list.

14. Receives a success response from CMMDS.

15. Changes the disk's health state from 0 to 64, which means unclaimed (or available to be claimed).

16. Removes the disk from the CLOM database.

Adding a Disk to an Existing Disk Group by Using the UI

When you remove a failed disk, as shown in the previous procedure, you can simply replace it with a new disk of the same type and size.

To add the new disk to the disk group, follow this procedure, continuing from the procedure in the section "**Removing a Disk from a Disk Group**," earlier in this chapter:

1. Select the disk group to which you will add the new disk (see Figure 21.37).

2. Click the **Add a disk to the selected disk group** icon.

3. In the dialog that appears, select the check box next to the new disk shown in the list.

4. Click **OK** to close the dialog, which begins the process of adding the selected disk to the disk group.

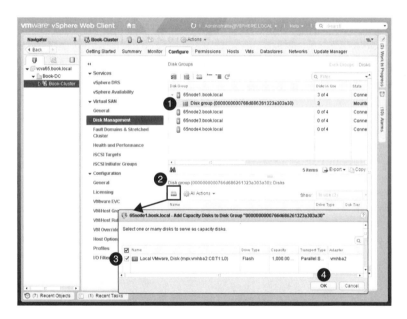

Figure 21.37 Adding a disk to a disk group

Adding a Disk to an Existing Disk Group via the CLI

To add a disk to an existing disk group via the CLI, run this command:

```
esxcli vsan storage add --disks <Disk ID> --ssd <SSD ID>
```

where `Disk ID` is the device ID of the disk being added (regardless of whether the disk type is MD or SSD) and `SSD ID` is the device ID of the cache tier SSD.

In this example, here is the command:

```
esxcli vsan storage add --disks mpx.vmhba2:C0:T1:L0 --ssd mpx.
vmhba2:C0:T0:L0
```

Again, a successful outcome returns no messages on the command line.

Listing 21.16 shows a /var/log/clomd.log-related message from this command.

Listing 21.16   clomd.log message from adding a disk

```
Added 52e11f22-4416-764d-d8d3-42191b0e38a1, owner 57b67c43-71ef-7d94-52b0-
000c29d918dd of type CdbObjectDisk to CLOMDB, v4 health:0
```

Mounting an Unmounted Disk in a Disk Group

In some situations, a disk in a disk group gets unmounted, most commonly due to adapter firmware or driver issues. After remediating the cause, you may need to manually mount the unmounted disk(s). To do so, first identify the device ID of the disk to be mounted, using either the CLI or the UI.

To identify unmounted disks via the CLI, run this command on the ESXi host:

```
esxcli vsan storage list |grep -B4 Used
```

Listing 21.17 shows this command and its output.

Listing 21.17   Listing unmounted vSAN disks via the CLI

```
esxcli vsan storage list |grep -B4 Used
   Device: mpx.vmhba2:C0:T3:L0
   Display Name: mpx.vmhba2:C0:T3:L0
   Is SSD: true
   VSAN UUID: 5223142d-2e6f-1e33-3708-517a1782e93f
   VSAN Disk Group UUID: 526c9371-f0c9-a7c4-5f6a-d5fd24671e36
   VSAN Disk Group Name: mpx.vmhba2:C0:T0:L0
   Used by this host: true
--
   Device: mpx.vmhba2:C0:T1:L0
   Display Name: mpx.vmhba2:C0:T1:L0
   Is SSD: true
```

```
VSAN UUID: 52610395-d7df-157e-0607-9dafa5f2400c
VSAN Disk Group UUID: 526c9371-f0c9-a7c4-5f6a-d5fd24671e36
VSAN Disk Group Name: mpx.vmhba2:C0:T0:L0
Used by this host: false
--

Device: mpx.vmhba2:C0:T0:L0
Display Name: mpx.vmhba2:C0:T0:L0
Is SSD: true
VSAN UUID: 526c9371-f0c9-a7c4-5f6a-d5fd24671e36
VSAN Disk Group UUID: 526c9371-f0c9-a7c4-5f6a-d5fd24671e36
VSAN Disk Group Name: mpx.vmhba2:C0:T0:L0
Used by this host: true
--

Device: mpx.vmhba2:C0:T2:L0
Display Name: mpx.vmhba2:C0:T2:L0
Is SSD: true
VSAN UUID: 52e4034a-9244-8ff0-ae73-86a0472f8aa2
VSAN Disk Group UUID: 526c9371-f0c9-a7c4-5f6a-d5fd24671e36
VSAN Disk Group Name: mpx.vmhba2:C0:T0:L0
Used by this host: true
```

In this example, the second device shows the value `false` in the `Used by this host` field. The device ID is the value of the `Device` field.

To list the unmounted device via the UI, do the following:

1. Navigate to the **Disk Management** section of the cluster settings, as described in earlier procedures in this chapter (see Figure 21.38).

2. Locate the disk group with an exclamation point in a red diamond and select it.

3. In the Disk Group Disks pane, locate the disk with a similar indicator. If you scroll to the right, the State column shows it as Unmounted, and the Healthy column shows two hyphens (--). The device ID is listed in the Name column.

In this example, the device ID is `mpx.vmhba2:C0:T1:L0`.

Figure 21.38 shows the UI with an unmounted disk.

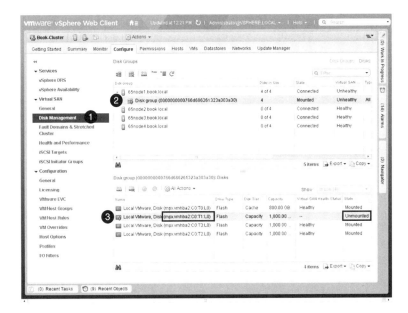

Figure 21.38   Unmounted disk status in the UI

If the unmounted device were the cache tier disk, the disk group and all its disks would be in an unmounted state.

To mount the disk, use this command:

```
esxcli vsan storage diskgroup mount --disk <device-ID>
```

Regardless of the disk's type, SSD or MD, `--disk` is the option to use for any capacity tier disks.

If the device is the cache tier disk, use `--ssd` instead:

```
esxcli vsan storage diskgroup mount --ssd <device-ID>
```

Here is an example:

```
esxcli vsan storage diskgroup mount --disk  mpx.vmhba2:C0:T1:L0
```

A successful outcome returns no messages. However, the /var/log/clomd.log file shows this message:

```
Added 52610395-d7df-157e-0607-9dafa5f2400c, owner 57b67c43-71ef-7d94-52b0-
000c29d918dd of type CdbObjectDisk to CLOMDB, v4 health:0
```

To verify the current status of the mounted disk via the CLI, run this command:

```
esxcli vsan storage list |grep -A5  <device-ID>
```

Here is an example:

```
esxcli vsan storage list |grep -A5  mpx.vmhba2:C0:T1:L0
```

Listing 21.18 shows this command and its output.

Listing 21.18   Listing a mounted vSAN disk via the CLI

```
esxcli vsan storage list |grep -A5 mpx.vmhba2:C0:T1:L0
mpx.vmhba2:C0:T1:L0
    Device: mpx.vmhba2:C0:T1:L0
    Display Name: mpx.vmhba2:C0:T1:L0
    Is SSD: true
    VSAN UUID: 52610395-d7df-157e-0607-9dafa5f2400c
    VSAN Disk Group UUID: 526c9371-f0c9-a7c4-5f6a-d5fd24671e36
    VSAN Disk Group Name: mpx.vmhba2:C0:T0:L0
    Used by this host: true
```

The value of Used by this host is now true. The UI should also show the disk as healthy and mounted.

If the unmounted disk was the cache tier disk, mounting it using the --ssd option results in mounting the disk group along with all the capacity tier disks.

/var/log/clomd.log shows the events in Listing 21.19 for successful mount events.

Listing 21.19   clomd.log events of successful disks mounting events

```
Added 526c9371-f0c9-a7c4-5f6a-d5fd24671e36, owner 57b67c43-71ef-7d94-52b0-
000c29d918dd of type CdbObjectDisk to CLOMDB, v4 health:0 allflash dg
Added 52610395-d7df-157e-0607-9dafa5f2400c, owner 57b67c43-71ef-7d94-52b0-
000c29d918dd of type CdbObjectDisk to CLOMDB, v4 health:0
Added 52e4034a-9244-8ff0-ae73-86a0472f8aa2, owner 57b67c43-71ef-7d94-52b0-
000c29d918dd of type CdbObjectDisk to CLOMDB, v4 health:0
Added 5223142d-2e6f-1e33-3708-517a1782e93f, owner 57b67c43-71ef-7d94-52b0-
000c29d918dd of type CdbObjectDisk to CLOMDB, v4 health:0
```

In Listing 21.19, I removed the date and timestamps for readability. Observe that the end of the first message states allflash dg, which means the mounted disk group is for an all flash configuration. If this were a hybrid disk group, the message would be hybrid dg instead.

The first message is for the cache tier, which is why `dg` is stated at the end of the message. The remaining messages are for the capacity tier disks.

The ID stated after the `Added` statement is the cache or capacity tier disk's UUID. The ID listed after `owner` is the UUID of the vSAN node that owns the disk. In this case, it is the UUID of the ESXi host on which I mounted the disk group.

The type of record added is `cdbObjectDisk`, which means that the object type being added is a disk.

To what are the disks being added? They are being added to CLOMDB. which is the CLOM database. See the **"vSAN Software Components"** section earlier in this chapter.

Each message also states v4, which means that the disk format is version 4; however, it is listed in the UI as version 3. Confusing, isn't it?

The reason for the version number difference between the UI and the CLI is that the UI uses version 2.5 as a transitional format during upgrading from version 2 to version 3. However, the engineering team that worked on the back end did not use 2.5. Rather, they used v3 as the transitional on-disk format version. This results in upgrading v2 to v4 from the CLI perspective, while the UI refers to v4 as v3. In other words, this is the upgrade path:

> CLI: v1 → v2 → v3 → v4
>
> UI: v1 → v2 → v2.5 → v3

NOTE

On-disk format CLI version 4, aka UI version 3, is the version used by vSAN 6.2 and 6.5. This version is required for new features such as deduplication, compression, and erasure coding (RAID 5/6).

vSphere 6.5, Patch 2 (which includes vSAN 6.6), introduced on-disk format v5, which adds support for nested fault domains and encryption for data at rest. In this release, both the UI and CLI show the same version. In other words, UI version 4 was skipped to bring it in sync with the version displayed in the CLI.

---

vSAN VASA Storage Provider

When an ESXi host joins a vSAN cluster, the host registers with vCenter as a VASA storage provider named vSAN provider [hostname] (for example, vSAN provider

`65node4.book.local`). Compared to block and file storage providers, which usually reside on the storage array controller or in a dedicated virtual appliance, vSAN's VASA providers reside on each ESXi host that is a node in the vSAN cluster. The purpose of registering vSAN VASA providers is that this information is used to create storage policy–based management (SPBM) rules, which play an important role in vSAN object placement. See the **"vSAN Storage Policies"** section later in this chapter.

In the storage providers' list, each node has a different priority, and all are in `standby` mode except for one, the vSAN master node, which is in `active` mode. The two nodes with highest priority are those assuming the master and backup roles. In this example, the priorities are 131 and 130. The remaining nodes have lower priorities, which are 128 and 4 in this example. Nodes assume different roles based on certain events that result in the master node being absent (for example, network partitioning or host reboot). This is reflected in the priority and active/standby state on this list (see Figure 21.39).

To list the vSAN VASA storage providers, follow this procedure:

1. Connect to the vCenter server using the vSphere 6.x Web Client or vSphere 6.5 HTML5 client as a user with Administrator privileges.

2. Navigate to the **Hosts and Clusters** view.

3. Right-click the vCenter server's inventory object and then click the **Settings** menu option.

4. If using vSphere 6.x, click the **Storage Providers** button. Otherwise, for vSphere 6.5, select **Storage Providers** in the **More** section, as shown in Figure 21.35.

5. The Storage Providers pane lists all nodes in the cluster, along with other non-vSAN VASA providers. Scroll down the list until you see the first vSAN provider.

6. Select one vsanDatastore for one of the nodes (the second line of the node's listing).

7. Scroll down in the Storage System Details pane until you see the Supported Profiles field. The value of that field is **Storage Object Profile**, which represents the object store file system (OSFS) capability of vSAN.

Figure 21.39 shows four nodes where the provider suffixed with `65node1` is in an active state and has the highest priority, 131. The next-highest-priority provider is `65node2` in a standby state, with priority 130.

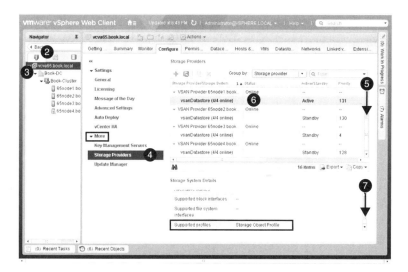

Figure 21.39   Listing vSAN VASA storage providers

To verify the cluster nodes' roles, log on to each node's console directly or via SSH and then run the following:

```
esxcli vsan cluster get
```

Listing 21.20 shows the command and its output from master and backup nodes.

Listing 21.20   Listing vSAN cluster nodes via the CLI

```
[root@65Node1:~] esxcli vsan cluster get
Cluster Information
   Enabled: true
   Current Local Time: 2016-10-17T01:47:44Z
   Local Node UUID: 57b67c43-71ef-7d94-52b0-000c29d918dd
   Local Node Type: NORMAL
   Local Node State: MASTER
   Local Node Health State: HEALTHY
   Sub-Cluster Master UUID: 57b67c43-71ef-7d94-52b0-000c29d918dd
   Sub-Cluster Backup UUID: 57b67f25-0080-ca9d-77da-000c292cb974
   Sub-Cluster UUID: 52d99970-8422-cf21-f4b4-b0f762946c2c
   Sub-Cluster Membership Entry Revision: 1
   Sub-Cluster Member Count: 4
   Sub-Cluster Member UUIDs:
```

```
57b67c43-71ef-7d94-52b0-000c29d918dd,
57b67f25-0080-ca9d-77da-000c292cb974,
57b68127-135e-e2a1-dd78-000c298ef254,
57f93a38-27ed-3916-7d3a-000c29da46c3
   Sub-Cluster Membership UUID: b3e90358-f9aa-dfea-33b4-000c29d918dd


[root@65Node2:~] esxcli vsan cluster get
Cluster Information
   Enabled: true
   Current Local Time: 2016-10-17T01:55:27Z
   Local Node UUID: 57b67f25-0080-ca9d-77da-000c292cb974
   Local Node Type: NORMAL
   Local Node State: BACKUP
   Local Node Health State: HEALTHY
   Sub-Cluster Master UUID: 57b67c43-71ef-7d94-52b0-000c29d918dd
   Sub-Cluster Backup UUID: 57b67f25-0080-ca9d-77da-000c292cb974
   Sub-Cluster UUID: 52d99970-8422-cf21-f4b4-b0f762946c2c
   Sub-Cluster Membership Entry Revision: 1
   Sub-Cluster Member Count: 4
   Sub-Cluster Member UUIDs:
57b67c43-71ef-7d94-52b0-000c29d918dd,
57b67f25-0080-ca9d-77da-000c292cb974,
57b68127-135e-e2a1-dd78-000c298ef254,
57f93a38-27ed-3916-7d3a-000c29da46c3
   Sub-Cluster Membership UUID: b3e90358-f9aa-dfea-33b4-000c29d918dd
```

In Listing 21.20, I listed the subcluster member UUID values on separate lines for readability. In the actual output, they all appear on the same line.

In this output, host `65node1` shows `Local Node State` as `MASTER`, while that of host `65node2` is `Backup`.

Observe that the outputs from both nodes show the following:

```
Sub-Cluster Master UUID: 57b67c43-71ef-7d94-52b0-000c29d918dd
Sub-Cluster Backup UUID: 57b67f25-0080-ca9d-77da-000c292cb974
```

These UUIDs match the master and backup nodes' `Local Node UUID` field values at the time these outputs were collected.

The remaining nodes in the cluster would have an agent role. The role of each node may change after events that result in the master or backup node going down or losing network connectivity to the vSAN network (resulting in a state commonly referred to as *network partitioned*).

vSAN Storage Policies

vSAN uses storage policy–based management (SPBM) to facilitate data placement on cluster nodes, disk groups, and disks. For details on storage policies, see Chapter 20, "**VASA**."

To create vSAN storage policies, follow this procedure:

1. Connect to the vCenter server using the vSphere 6.x Web Client as a user with Administrator privileges.

2. On the home page, click **VM Storage Policies** in the Operations and Policies section.

3. Click the **Create VM Storage Policy** button (see Figure 21.40).

Figure 21.40   Creating a new storage policy

The Create New VM Storage Policy wizard dialog pops up. It includes four major steps.

4. In step 1 of the wizard, Name and Description, enter a name for the policy (for example, **RAID1**) and an optional description. Then click **Next**.

5. In step 2 of the wizard, Policy Structure, click **Next**. This takes you to step 2a of the wizard, Common Rules. You use this step if you want to configure VM encryption or storage I/O control. I do not use these features with this policy.

6. Click **Next**. This takes you to step 2b of the wizard, Rule-set 1. This is where you find all the vSAN-specific storage policy options. The **Use rule-sets in this storage policy** check box is selected by default. Below it is the Placement section. Choices made here dictate how data is placed on the storage according to the capabilities or features exposed by the corresponding VASA provider. For vSAN, data is placed on capacity tier disks according to the defined placement rules.

7. Select **VSAN** from the Storage Type pull-down list (see Figure 21.41).

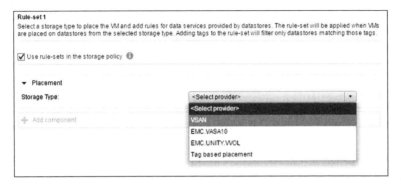

Figure 21.41   Selecting a VASA provider

A pull-down menu named <add rules> is added. I cover more details on each rule available from this menu in the **"vSAN Storage Policy Placement Rules"** section later in this chapter.

8. To configure RAID 1 policy, select the **Number of failures to tolerate** rule. The **Number of failures to tolerate** rule is added to the dialog where you can enter the rule's value.

NOTE

If this rule is not listed, you may be using vSphere 6.5, Express Patch 2 or newer with a vSAN stretched cluster configuration. In that case, for new FTT placement rules, refer to the **"Nested Fault Domains"** section in Chapter 22.

9. Set the value in the added rule to **1**. A section named Storage Consumption Model on the right-hand side of the Placement section explains the amount of storage space to be consumed by an objects to which this rule will be applied.

10. Click **Next** (see Figure 21.42).

Figure 21.42 Selecting a placement rule

Using vSAN 6.2 or 6.5, an alternate method for creating a RAID 1 policy is to select a rule named **Failure tolerance method** instead of **Number of failures to tolerate**. Then select **RAID-1 (mirroring) - Performance** from the pull-down menu, as shown in Figure 21.43.

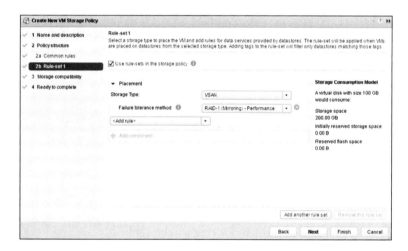

Figure 21.43 Alternate placement rule for creating a RAID 1 policy

This configuration is equivalent to using the FTT = 1 rule. However, if you need to tolerate more than one failure using mirroring, using FTT is the only approach.

11. Step 3 of the wizard displays the list of datastores available to this cluster and groups them by compatibility to the proposed policy. Selecting the **Compatible** row in

the Storage Compatibility section displays `vsanDatastore` in the Compatible Storage section.

12. Click **Next** (see Figure 21.44).

Figure 21.44   A new policy's storage compatibility

13. In the final step, step 4 of the wizard, Ready to Complete, review the settings and then click **Finish**.

The newly created policy is now listed on the VM Storage Policies tab. This policy is effectively identical to the vSAN default storage policy, which is FTT = 1, SW (Stripe Width) = 1, OSR (Object Space Reservation) = 0. The reason for this is that for any rules not specified by the storage policy, the policy inherits the default vSAN storage policy values.

I cover SW and OSR rules in the section "**vSAN Storage Policy Placement Rules**," later in this chapter.

To create other policies with different rules, repeat this procedure and use the following to create various RAID types:

- **RAID 10**—FTT = 1, SW = X, where X is the number of stripes suitable for the expected I/O profile. The SW value must not exceed the number of capacity tier disks per node.

- **RAID 0**—FTT = 0, SW = X (This is not a recommended configuration because it provides no data availability. Use it only for disposable data that benefits from striping at runtime.)

- **RAID 5 and RAID 6**—I cover these in section "**Erasure Coding (RAID 5 and RAID 6)**" later in this chapter.

If you are going to use the VMDKs with Oracle Real Application Cluster (RAC) as shared storage along with multi-writer locks, set OSR to 100%. The same rule of thumb applies to policies to be applied to vSAN iSCSI target (VIT) LUNs that will be used as shared storage for a guest OS or physical node–based software clusters. For more information about VITs, see the section "**vSAN iSCSI Targets (VITs),**" in Chapter 22.

Applying a vSAN Storage Policy at VM Creation Time

Now let's look at how a vSAN storage policy places data on capacity tier disks. The following steps apply to any vSAN storage policy:

1. Go through the process of creating a new VM on one of the cluster nodes until you reach the step where you select storage.

2. Select **Virtual SAN Default Policy** from the VM storage policy pull-down menu. The vSAN datastore is listed in the Compatible section of the list.

> **TIP**
>
> The vSAN default policy provides FTT = 1, SW = 1, OSR = 0, which are sufficient for the VM home (where the VM's metadata and logs are stored). I prefer to do this so that I can apply virtual disk–specific storage policies independently from the VM home (namespace).

3. Select the vSAN datastore and observe the green checkmark in the Compatibility section.

4. Click **Next** (see Figure 21.45).

Figure 21.45   Selecting the VM home's storage policy

5. Continue with the remaining steps of the New Virtual Machine Wizard until you reach step 2f, Customize Hardware.

6. Expand **New Hard disk** under Virtual Hardware.

7. Select the RAID 1 storage policy created in the previous section (see Figure 21.46).

Figure 21.46 Selecting a virtual disk's storage policy

Observe the values listed in the Virtual SAN Storage Consumption section and how they change with different policies. (I provide more figures about that later in this section.)

8. To add more virtual disks to the new VM, select the **New Hard Disk** option from the New Device pull-down menu and then click **Add**.

9. Repeat steps 6 and 7 for each new hard disk added and select the corresponding VM storage policy to apply to it.

10. Click **Next** to apply the policy to the virtual disks only and leave the VM home with the Virtual SAN **default** policy applied.

11. Review your selections listed in the Ready to Complete step of the wizard. If no changes are required, click **Finish**.

Applying a vSAN Storage Policy to an Existing VM

To apply a vSAN storage policy to an existing VM, follow the procedure in the section "**Reconfiguring Existing Virtual Disks' Storage Policies**," later in this chapter.

vSAN Storage Policy Placement Rules

Every vSAN object requires a storage policy to determine where to place its components. If none is specified, the vSAN default policy is used.

vSAN provides a default storage policy for each different policy class. To list these defaults, run the following command on the ESXi host console (directly or via SSH):

```
esxcli vsan policy getdefault
```

Listing 21.21 shows this command and its output.

Listing 21.21   Listing the default vSAN storage policy via the CLI

```
esxcli vsan policy getdefault
Policy Class   Policy Value
------------   ----------------------------------------------------------
cluster        (("hostFailuresToTolerate" i1))
vdisk          (("hostFailuresToTolerate" i1))
vmnamespace    (("hostFailuresToTolerate" i1))
vmswap         (("hostFailuresToTolerate" i1) ("forceProvisioning" i1))
vmem           (("hostFailuresToTolerate" i1) ("forceProvisioning" i1))
```

The output in Listing 21.21 shows the following:

- All object in the cluster default to FTT = 1
- Virtual disk objects default to FTT = 1
- Virtual machines' home directories (namespace) default to FTT = 1
- Virtual machines' swap file objects default to FTT = 1 and Force Provisioning = 1
- The virtual machine memory snapshot file (vmem) defaults to FTT = 1, Force Provisioning = 1

Many rules can be set in a vSAN storage policy, including the following:

- Number of failures to tolerate (FTT)
- Number of disk stripes per object (SW)
- Flash read cache reservation (%)
- Failover tolerance method (new in 6.2 and later)
- IOPS limit for object (new in 6.2 and later)
- Disable object checksum (new in 6.2 and later)

- Force provisioning

- Object space reservation (%) (OSR)

- Tag from category

Table 21.6 summarizes policy rules and their basic use cases. I further expand on details of these rules in the following sections.

Table 21.6 vSAN storage policy rules

Rule		Use Case	Value
FTT (RAID 1—mirroring)		Redundancy/availability (non-stretched cluster)	Default: 1 Max: 3
Nested fault domains FTT	PFTT (primary level of failures to tolerate)	Site redundancy with nested fault domains in stretched cluster configurations	Default: 1 Max: 3 (current implementation uses value of 1 only)
	SFTT (secondary level of failures to tolerate)	Availability. Treat this like FTT when used with nested fault domains in stretched cluster configurations.	Default: 1 Max: 3
SW (RAID 0—striping)		Performance	Default: 1 Max: 12
Failure tolerance method (erasure coding)	RAID-1	Redundancy Same as FTT=1	RAID-1 (default)
	RAID-5	Fault tolerance Combined with FTT = 1 Provides striping with single parity Requires all-flash configuration	RAID-5/6 (when combined with FTT = 1 or SFTT = 1 in nested fault domains)
	RAID-6	Fault tolerance Combined with FTT = 2 Provides striping with double parity Requires all-flash configuration	RAID-5/6 (when combined with FTT = 2 or SFTT = 2 in nested fault domains)

Rule	Use Case	Value
OSR	Percentage of VMDK file to be pre-allocated (thick)	Default: 0 Max: 100%
Flash read cache (RC) reservation	Percentage of VMDK file to be reserved in the read cache	Default 0 Max 100%
Force provisioning	Override policy	Default: Disabled
Disable object checksum	Double Negative setting! When set to no, checksum is calculated for the object. When set to yes, checksum is disabled for the object.	Default: No
IOPS limit for object	Defines IOPS limit for the object. 1 I/O = 32KiB	Default: 0
Tags from category	Custom tags	None

Number of Failures to Tolerate

This rule, abbreviated as FTT, dictates how many hosts may fail without resulting in loss of access to an object. However, other failures can be network or disk failures. This is why some documents, such as the `esxcli` command-line help, less commonly refer to it as hosts failure to tolerate (HFTT).

If using vSphere 6.5, Patch 2 with vSAN stretched clusters, SFTT is equivalent to FTT in single-site configurations. For more details, see the "**Stretched Clusters**" and "**Nested vSAN Fault Domains**" sections in Chapter 22.

Applying this rule to an object creates a mirror copy (or copies) of that object, referred to as a replica (or replicas). If you need to tolerate more host failures, you can set this value to no larger than 3. The following are the possible values of this rule and their corresponding required numbers of nodes:

- FTT = 1, three nodes
- FTT = 2, five nodes
- FTT = 3, seven nodes

I prefer to refer to the required number of nodes as the required number of fault domains instead because each fault domain is considered failed if any of its members fails or loses network connectivity to the cluster. You'll learn more details in the **"Fault Domains"** section in Chapter 22.

The total number of replica components required would be (n+1), where n is the value set in this rule. For example, if a policy with this rule that has a value of 1 is applied to a VMDK object that is 255MiB or smaller, a RAID 1 component gets placed on a capacity disk on two different nodes in the cluster with total of two components. The total number of hosts in the cluster required to support this configuration is based on the formula (n*2)+1, where n is the value set in this rule. This means that for FTT=1, the number of hosts required is three: (1*2)+1.

The reason for requiring more nodes than replicas has to do with placement of the witness component(s).

Figure 21.47 shows an example with the FTT = 1 rule applied to the VM home (namespace).

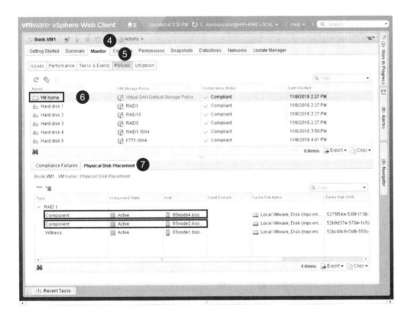

Figure 21.47   Listing component placement for FTT = 1

I arrived at this screen by using the following steps:

1. Connect to the vCenter server using the vSphere 6.x Web Client as a user with Administrator privileges.

2. Navigate to **VMs and Templates** view.

3. Select the VM in the inventory tree.

4. Navigate to the **Monitor** tab.

5. Click the **Policies** button.

6. Select **VM home** in the Name column.

7. If it's not already selected, click the **Physical Disk Placement** tab in the lower pane.

In this example, one RAID 1 component was placed on host 65node4, and the second component was place on host 65node2. The witness component was placed on host 65node1.

Listing DOM Object Properties

To list the DOM object's properties via the CLI, follow this procedure:

1. Log on to one of the cluster nodes via SSH as root.

2. Identify the VM home object UUID by using this command:

```
ls -al /vmfs/volumes/vsanDatastore/ |grep [vm name]
```

The following is an example for a VM named Book-VM1:

```
ls -al /vmfs/volumes/vsanDatastore/ |grep Book-VM1
```

The output would look like this (with permissions and date/timestamps removed for readability):

```
Book-VM1 -> 657d1d58-48ca-92db-5a64-000c29d918dd
```

The value listed after the arrow is the namespace object's UUID.

Using the UUID, run this command:

```
cmmds-tool find --uuid [UUID] --format json |python -m json.tool
```

Here is an example:

```
cmmds-tool find --uuid 657d1d58-48ca-92db-5a64-000c29d918dd --format json
|python -m json.tool
```

You can also use the abbreviated version:

```
cmmds-tool find -u 657d1d58-48ca-92db-5a64-000c29d918dd -f json
```

The output and its breakdown are similar to those provided in Listing 21.22 and Listing 21.23 later in this chapter.

Number of Disk Stripes per Object

The number of disk stripes per object rule is also referred to as stripe width (SW). This rule splits an object equally into a number of chunks (or *stripe components*) specified by the rule. They are placed on separate capacity tier disks within the same or different disk groups on one or more nodes in the cluster.

When combined with the FTT rule, the minimum requirement is to have a number of capacity disks equal to S×(n+1), where S is the number of disk stripes set by the rule.

For example, if SW = 3 and FTT = 1, the number of capacity disks would be 3×(1+1) = 6. If each host has at least three capacity disks, then two nodes will have one RAID 1 replica on each that is further split into three RAID 0 components. A single witness component is placed on a capacity disk on a third host. Figure 21.48 shows an example of such placement.

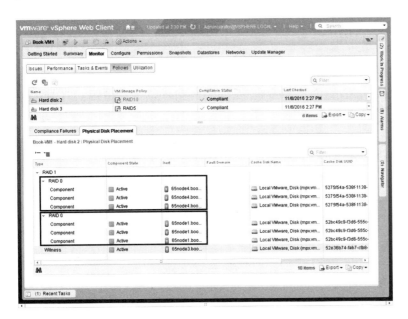

Figure 21.48 Listing component placement for FTT = 1,SW = 3

In this example, the first RAID 1 mirror component has three RAID 0 stripe components, placed on the 65node4 host.

The second RAID 1 mirror component has three RAID 0 stripe components, which were all placed on the 65node1 host. The witness component was placed on the 65node3 host.

Listing Object Properties of a VMDK with FTT = 1, SW = 3

To list the DOM object properties of a virtual disk with RAID 10 (made up of FTT = 1 and SW = 3) policy applied to it, run this command, as a root user, while connected to the host via SSH:

```
cmmds-tool find --uuid [UUID] --format json
```

To identify the VMDK's UUID, run this command, using the VMDK's descriptor file located within the VM home directory:

```
grep VMFS [VMDK descriptor file name]
```

Here is an example:

```
grep VMFS Book-VM1_1.vmdk
```

The output would look like this:

```
RW 209715200 VMFS "vsan://9f7d1d58-4e0d-86bf-631f-000c29d918dd"
```

The value listed after `vsan://` is the VMDK's UUID.

Listing 21.22 shows this command and its output, using the identified VMDK's UUID.

Listing 21.22   Listing the VMDK object's properties

```
cmmds-tool find -u 9f7d1d58-4e0d-86bf-631f-000c29d918dd -f json
{
 "entries":
[
 {
   "uuid": "9f7d1d58-4e0d-86bf-631f-000c29d918dd",
   "owner": "57f93a38-27ed-3916-7d3a-000c29da46c3",
   "health": "Healthy",
   "revision": "27",
   "type": "DOM_OBJECT",
   "flag": "2",
   "minHostVersion": "3",
   "md5sum": "97d4cd0c685c7f565f90f6eac89ae717",
   "valueLen": "2768",
   "content": {"type": "Configuration", "attributes": {"CSN":
13, "SCSN": 11, "addressSpace": 107374182400, "scrubStartTime":
1478327711925777, "objectVersion": 4, "highestDiskVersion": 4,
"muxGroup": 496184051960832, "groupUuid": "657d1d58-48ca-92db-5a64-
000c29d918dd", "compositeUuid": "9f7d1d58-4e0d-86bf-631f-000c29d918dd"},
"child-1": {"type": "RAID_1", "attributes": {}, "child-1": {"type":
```

"RAID_0", "attributes": {"stripeBlockSize": 1048576}, "child-1":
{"type": "Component", "attributes": {"aggregateCapacity": 34002173952,
"addressSpace": 35792093184, "componentState": 5, "componentStateTS":
1478327711, "faultDomainId": "57f93a38-27ed-3916-7d3a-000c29da46c3",
"lastScrubbedOffset": 34002173952}, "componentUuid": "9f7d1d58-7ce7-fbc0-
b8cf-000c29d918dd", "diskUuid": "52b9a046-b8bf-40d4-20b4-cfa28d6ce2a7"},
"child-2": {"type": "Component", "attributes": {"aggregateCapacity":
34002173952, "addressSpace": 35791044608, "componentState": 5,
"componentStateTS": 1478327711, "faultDomainId": "57f93a38-27ed-3916-
7d3a-000c29da46c3", "lastScrubbedOffset": 34002173952}, "componentUuid":
"9f7d1d58-009a-fdc0-803b-000c29d918dd", "diskUuid": "5296167d-ca4f-1112-
b32a-18efcdfd265f"}, "child-3": {"type": "Component", "attributes":
{"aggregateCapacity": 34001125376, "addressSpace": 35791044608,
"componentState": 5, "componentStateTS": 1478327711, "faultDomainId":
"57f93a38-27ed-3916-7d3a-000c29da46c3", "lastScrubbedOffset":
34001125376}, "componentUuid": "9f7d1d58-1823-fec0-2e87-000c29d918dd",
"diskUuid": "522109dd-8167-ffa7-c72b-073ad310f5da"}}, "child-2": {"type":
"RAID_0", "attributes": {"stripeBlockSize": 1048576}, "child-1":
{"type": "Component", "attributes": {"aggregateCapacity": 34002173952,
"addressSpace": 35792093184, "componentState": 5, "componentStateTS":
1478376646, "faultDomainId": "57b67c43-71ef-7d94-52b0-000c29d918dd"},
"componentUuid": "9f7d1d58-02b5-fec0-3bf9-000c29d918dd", "diskUuid":
"52e134bb-e6a6-ec63-2aff-84e5aaefd1c3"}, "child-2": {"type": "Component",
"attributes": {"aggregateCapacity": 34002173952, "addressSpace":
35791044608, "componentState": 5, "componentStateTS": 1478376648,
"faultDomainId": "57b67c43-71ef-7d94-52b0-000c29d918dd"}, "componentUuid":
"9f7d1d58-3742-ffc0-7497-000c29d918dd", "diskUuid": "5241c49f-007d-b349-
f73f-50c07c1dd693"}, "child-3": {"type": "Component", "attributes":
{"aggregateCapacity": 34001125376, "addressSpace": 35791044608,
"componentState": 5, "componentStateTS": 1478376642, "faultDomainId":
"57b67c43-71ef-7d94-52b0-000c29d918dd"}, "componentUuid": "9f7d1d58-
3bb5-ffc0-0459-000c29d918dd", "diskUuid": "5273aff0-4473-4adc-69dc-
e5cff8572295"}}}, "child-2": {"type": "Witness", "attributes":
{"componentState": 5, "componentStateTS": 1478474391, "isWitness": 1,
"faultDomainId": "57b68127-135e-e2a1-dd78-000c298ef254", "nVotes": 3},
"componentUuid": "97ba1f58-7ed4-fb74-3071-000c29da46c3", "diskUuid":
"5289fe6f-90e0-6dcb-54c2-cbd8c6f83b68"}},
    "errorStr": "(null)"
 }
,{
    "uuid": "9f7d1d58-4e0d-86bf-631f-000c29d918dd",
    "owner": "57f93a38-27ed-3916-7d3a-000c29da46c3",
    "health": "Healthy",
    "revision": "12",
    "type": "POLICY",
    "flag": "2",
    "minHostVersion": "3",
    "md5sum": "f687272422e11504cf4f8d5bb2c4d725",
    "valueLen": "312",

```
   "content": {"stripeWidth": 3, "hostFailuresToTolerate":
1, "spbmProfileId": "75d1a275-80e5-41a0-9738-1fec7d08d5a3",
"spbmProfileGenerationNumber": 0, "CSN": 13, "SCSN": 11, "spbmProfileName":
"RAID10"},
   "errorStr": "(null)"
 }
,{
   "uuid": "9f7d1d58-4e0d-86bf-631f-000c29d918dd",
   "owner": "57f93a38-27ed-3916-7d3a-000c29da46c3",
   "health": "Healthy",
   "revision": "25",
   "type": "CONFIG_STATUS",
   "flag": "2",
   "minHostVersion": "3",
   "md5sum": "53bf6bb4ea9305c574a4de919d2d319b",
   "valueLen": "96",
   "content": {"state": 7, "CSN": 13, "SCSN": 11},
   "errorStr": "(null)"
 }
]
}
```

The output includes three properties whose Type field values are DOM_OBJECT, POLICY, and CONFIG_STATUS. The DOM_OBJECT property is for the Distributed Object Manager (DOM) object. The content field includes several details that are highlight in Listing 21.23. I formatted the output with group indentations for readability, with each child indented below its corresponding parent. You can obtain similar formatting by adding |python -m json.tool at the end of cmmds-tool command line.

I inserted highlighted comments with left pointing arrows in the output.

Listing 21.23 Breakdown of the VMDK's DOM object properties

```
   "content":
   {"type": "Configuration",
   "attributes":
     {"CSN": 13,
     "SCSN": 11,
     "addressSpace": 107374182400,
     "scrubStartTime": 1478327711925777,
     "objectVersion": 4,
     "highestDiskVersion": 4,
     "muxGroup": 496184051960832,
     "groupUuid": "657d1d58-48ca-92db-5a64-000c29d918dd",
```

```
      "compositeUuid": "9f7d1d58-4e0d-86bf-631f-000c29d918dd"},
        "child-1": ← RAID 1 Object
        {"type": "RAID_1",
        "attributes": {},
            "child-1": ← First RAID 1 Replica
            {"type": "RAID_0", ← Replica is striped as RAID0
            "attributes":
              {"stripeBlockSize": 1048576},
                "child-1": ← 1st Stripe of 1st Replica's RAID 0
                {"type": "Component",
                "attributes":
                  {"aggregateCapacity": 34002173952,
                  "addressSpace": 35792093184,
                  "componentState": 5,
                  "componentStateTS": 1478327711,
                  "faultDomainId": "57f93a38-27ed-3916-7d3a-
000c29da46c3",
                  "lastScrubbedOffset": 34002173952},
                  "componentUuid": "9f7d1d58-7ce7-fbc0-b8cf-
000c29d918dd",
                  "diskUuid": "52b9a046-b8bf-40d4-20b4-cfa28d6ce2a7"},
                "child-2": ← 2nd Stripe of 1st Replica's RAID 0
                {"type": "Component",
                "attributes":
                  {"aggregateCapacity": 34002173952,
                  "addressSpace": 35791044608,
                  "componentState": 5,
                  "componentStateTS": 1478327711,
                  "faultDomainId": "57f93a38-27ed-3916-7d3a-
000c29da46c3",
                  "lastScrubbedOffset": 34002173952},
                  "componentUuid": "9f7d1d58-009a-fdc0-803b-
000c29d918dd",
                  "diskUuid": "5296167d-ca4f-1112-b32a-18efcdfd265f"},
                "child-3": ← 3rd Stripe of 1st Replica's RAID 0
                {"type": "Component",
                "attributes":
                  {"aggregateCapacity": 34001125376,
                  "addressSpace": 35791044608,
                  "componentState": 5,
                  "componentStateTS": 1478327711,
```

```
                   "faultDomainId": "57f93a38-27ed-3916-7d3a-
000c29da46c3",
                   "lastScrubbedOffset": 34001125376},
                   "componentUuid": "9f7d1d58-1823-fec0-2e87-
000c29d918dd",
                   "diskUuid": "522109dd-8167-ffa7-c72b-073ad310f5da"}},
         "child-2": ← Second RAID 1 Replica
         {"type": "RAID_0", ← SecondReplica's RAID 0 Definition
         "attributes":
          {"stripeBlockSize": 1048576},
            "child-1": ← 1st Stripe of 2nd Replica's RAID 0
            {"type": "Component",
            "attributes":
               {"aggregateCapacity": 34002173952,
               "addressSpace": 35792093184,
               "componentState": 5,
               "componentStateTS": 1478376646,
               "faultDomainId": "57b67c43-71ef-7d94-52b0-
000c29d918dd"},
               "componentUuid": "9f7d1d58-02b5-fec0-3bf9-000c29d918dd",
               "diskUuid": "52e134bb-e6a6-ec63-2aff-84e5aaefd1c3"},
            "child-2": ← 2nd Stripe of 2nd Replica's RAID 0
            {"type": "Component",
            "attributes":
              {"aggregateCapacity": 34002173952,
              "addressSpace": 35791044608,
              "componentState": 5,
              "componentStateTS": 1478376648,
              "faultDomainId": "57b67c43-71ef-7d94-52b0-000c29d918dd"},
              "componentUuid": "9f7d1d58-3742-ffc0-7497-000c29d918dd",
              "diskUuid": "5241c49f-007d-b349-f73f-50c07c1dd693"},
            "child-3": ← 3rd Stripe of 2nd Replica's RAID 0
            {"type": "Component",
            "attributes":
               {"aggregateCapacity": 34001125376,
               "addressSpace": 35791044608,
               "componentState": 5,
```

```
                   "componentStateTS": 1478376642,
                   "faultDomainId": "57b67c43-71ef-7d94-52b0-
    000c29d918dd"},
                   "componentUuid": "9f7d1d58-3bb5-ffc0-0459-000c29d918dd",
                   "diskUuid": "5273aff0-4473-4adc-69dc-e5cff8572295"}}},
          "child-2": ← Witness component of DOM Object
          {"type": "Witness",
          "attributes":
             {"componentState": 5,
             "componentStateTS": 1478474391,
             "isWitness": 1, ← This component is a witness
             "faultDomainId": "57b68127-135e-e2a1-dd78-000c298ef254",
             "nVotes": 3}, ← Witness has 3 votes
             "componentUuid": "97ba1f58-7ed4-fb74-3071-000c29da46c3",
          "diskUuid": "5289fe6f-90e0-6dcb-54c2-cbd8c6f83b68"}},
     "errorStr": "(null)"
    }
```

Listing 21.23 also shows that each on-disk component has the following fields:

- faultDomainId—In configurations without defined fault domains, each host is in its own fault domain. This means that this field lists the host's vSAN UUID as the fault domain's UUID.

- componentUuid—This is the corresponding component's vSAN UUID.

- diskUuid—This is the vSAN UUID of the disk on which the component was placed.

In this example, all components have a value of 5 for componentState, which indicates that all the object's components are healthy and are in an Active state.

Components can be in any of 12 states. These states are mainly visible via RVC. CMMDS outputs may not show all states. For example, healthy components show states as 5. However, while resyncing, state 6 is listed in output instead of state 8. Table 21.7 lists the 12 states and what they mean.

Table 21.7 DOM component states

State Value	State Name	Notes
0	Invalid	
1	None	
2	Needs config	Should not be seen in most cases
3	Initializing	
4	Initialized	
5	Active	Normal state—healthy
6	Absent	Network is partitioned or host is missing
7	Stale	Component is available but needs resyncing to change to state 5
8	Resyncing	Component is available but being reconciled from a healthy replica; it serves no data but accepts new ones while resynch is in progress
9	Degraded	Component is dead; it has to be fully rebuilt from a healthy component
10	Reconfiguring	Policy change being applied (for example, adding/removing stripes/mirrors)
11	Cleanup	DOM is cleaning up the component; applies mostly to transient and orphaned objects

The policy section defines the storage policy properties. Listing 21.24 lists the storage policy properties. I highlighted what each property means.

Listing 21.24   Object's storage policy properties

```
{
   "uuid": "9f7d1d58-4e0d-86bf-631f-000c29d918dd",
   "owner": "57f93a38-27ed-3916-7d3a-000c29da46c3",
   "health": "Healthy",
   "revision": "12",
   "type": "POLICY",
   "flag": "2",
   "minHostVersion": "3",
   "md5sum": "f687272422e11504cf4f8d5bb2c4d725",
   "valueLen": "312",
   "content":
```

```
{"stripeWidth": 3, ← SW=3
 "hostFailuresToTolerate": 1, ← FTT=1
 "spbmProfileId": "75d1a275-80e5-41a0-9738-1fec7d08d5a3",
"spbmProfileGenerationNumber": 0,
 "CSN": 13,
 "SCSN": 11,
"spbmProfileName": "RAID10"}, ← Policy name
   "errorStr": "(null)"
 }
```

Flash Read Cache Reservation (%)

This rule reserves space on the cache tier disk as read cache for the object to which the rule is applied. This option is for hybrid disk groups only because all-flash configurations use the cache tier for write buffer only, while all capacity tier flash disks are used for read cache. Reserve cache cannot be used by other objects. Remaining space on the cache tier is shared fairly among other objects. The default value is 0%, and the max is 100%.

Failure Tolerance Method

This rule defines the method used to tolerate failures. It provides three methods:

- **RAID 1**—Achieves failure tolerance using mirrors and provides better performance. The storage cost is 100% of the object size because it requires double the object size for the mirror copy (replica).

- **RAID 5**—Achieves failure tolerance using a single parity block (when combined with the default value of FTT = 1). The storage cost is 33% of the object size for space used by the parity block. For example, a 100GiB object would use 133GiB of capacity tier space. The data components are striped over three capacity tier disks on three separate hosts. This configuration requires a minimum of four vSAN nodes. However, I prefer to use five nodes to provide capacity for placing a host in maintenance mode with `Full Data Migration`. You'll learn more details in the section **"Erasure Coding (RAID 5 and RAID 6),"** later in this chapter.

- **RAID 6**—Same as RAID 5 with an additional parity block when combined with FTT = 2. Cost is 50% of the object size for space used by the double parity components. For example, a 100GiB object would use 150GiB of capacity tier space.

IOPS Limit for Object

This rule defines the IOPS limit for a virtual disk object. IOPS is calculated as the number of I/Os using a weighted size. The default base I/O size is 32KB. This means that a 64KB

I/O is calculated as 2 I/Os. For the purpose of calculating IOPS, reads and writes are treated as equivalent. Cache hit ratio or I/Os being sequential are not taken into account.

The default value of this rule is 0, which means unlimited IOPS. The value is set to nonzero; I/O is throttled when it exceeds the set value.

Force Provisioning

When this rule is set to 1, it allows the object to be provisioned even if other policy rules cannot be met. Such rules can be FTT, SW, or flash read cache reservations during initial object deployment. vSAN attempts to find a placement that meets all policy requirements. If it is unable to meet them, it attempts simpler requirements, such as FTT = 0 instead of FTT = 1.

For example, the VM swap file object (vswp) defaults to force provisioning set to 1. This means that when a VM is powered on and there is sufficient capacity for a single replica of the default FTT = 1 (RAID 1), the vswp object is created with one replica. The object is displayed in the monitoring status as noncompliant. vSAN does not want to hold these operations back due to noncompliance.

When the cause for noncompliance is alleviated in the future, the object is brought into compliance as needed as vSAN continues to reevaluate the object placement until it brings it to compliant state.

It is not recommended to enable this rule for VMDKs because they would run the risk of data loss if a failure occurred without meeting availability requirements.

> **NOTE**
>
> If an object has this rule enabled and is currently force provisioned (that is, is noncompliant), if you have to place the host in maintenance mode with full data migration mode, it will behave as if insure accessibility mode is used instead. This exposes the object to higher risk if a failure is experienced before the object is brought back into compliance. Use force provisioning only for objects you don't mind losing, such as vswp and nonpersistent linked clones in a virtual desktop infrastructure (VDI) environment.

Object Space Reservation (OSR)

This rule defines how much of the object will be reserved on the capacity tier disks so that as data is written to the components, it will not experience out-of-space (OOS) state. This is also referred to as proportional capacity (PC), as seen in CLI outputs. The default value is 0%, which means thin provisioned.

Compared to VMFS, provisioning a VMDK using lazy zeroed thick (LZT) versus eager zeroed thick (EZT) format, vSAN treats both as LZT since vSAN silently ignores eager zero request and creates the object with 100% OSR. The reason is that all writes in vSAN go first to the write buffer (WB) on the cache tier SSDs. The WB uses a logical log (LLOG), which stores the location of the data blocks that just arrived in the write buffer but has not been assigned to capacity tier blocks yet. By default, WB is 30% of the cache tier space. When that limit is reached, vSAN batches the process of destaging, moving blocks from WB to capacity tier disks. Before this can be done, the data blocks are removed from the LLOG and recorded in a physical log (PLOG) to list the logical block address (LBA) on the capacity tier disk's `virsto` partition, where the data will end up when it is time to evict (destage) it. With that in mind, the very low latency writing to WB negates the write penalty of block zeroing.

Why use OSR? It provides balance in addition to guaranteed space. When an object is provisioned with OSR, the proportional space is reserved for the object's components on the capacity tier disks.

Consider the use case of a large number of objects being deployed in batches. Knowing space is being set aside in advance for OSR allows vSAN to better estimate the remaining space available for component placement with new batches of objects. The new components will then be spread evenly on the remaining space on the capacity tier disks on all nodes in the cluster. If this is not done, vSAN will have to rebalance the components over the capacity tier disks, which requires additional resources, space, and compute to achieve a safe balance.

TIP

How much object space should be reserved? The answer depends on the anticipated data size to be written. For example, with a VDI configuration that expects the average user's data to be 30GiB while the parent image of the desktops' linked clones is 50GiB, the parent image is always read-only. This mean that the parent disk should be provisioned with OSR = 0%, and the delta disks of the linked clones should be provisioned with OSR = 60% (30 / 50 × 100). This reduces the chances of users running into the out-of-space (OOS) state.

TIP

To use a vSAN-based VMDK as a shared disk in Oracle RAC configuration along with multi-writer locks, the VMDK must be provisioned using OSR = 100%. This prevents the cluster from experiencing the OOS state.

> **NOTE**
>
> Using `vmkfstools` to create an EZT VMDK translates to using OSR = 100%.

To demonstrate the fact that using `vmkfstools` to create an EZT VMDK translates to using OSR = 100%, create a VMDK using `vmkfstools` and observe the related /var/log/clomd.log messages. The command to use is as follows:

```
vmkfstools --createvirtualdisk <size> --diskformat eagerzeroedthick
--objecttype vsan <path to VMDK>
```

You can also use the abbreviated version:

```
vmkfstools -c <size> -d eagerzeroedthick -W vsan <path to VMDK>
```

Here is an example:

```
vmkfstools -c 100G -d eagerzeroedthick -W vsan /vmfs/volumes/vsanDatastore/
Cluster-VM1/EZT.vmdk
```

Listing 21.25 lists the relevant messages in /var/log/clomd.log.

Listing 21.25   Breakdown of the VMDK's DOM object properties

```
CLOMFetchDOMEvent: Read 1112 bytes of 1192 bytes from DOM
CLOMFetchDOMEvent: Read an additional 80 bytes from DOM

CLOMFetchDOMEvent: DOM requested policy:
Object size 107374182400 bytes with policy: (("proportionalCapacity" i100)
("hostFailuresToTolerate" i1))

CLOM_PostWorkItem: Posted a work item for b47f4058-6931-e956-b0da-
000c29d918dd group: 2e373258-b77c-8509-4e5e-000c292cb974 Type: PLACEMENT
delay 0 (Success)
Object size 107374182400 bytes with policy: (("proportionalCapacity" i100)
("hostFailuresToTolerate" i1))

CLOMComputeVersionCompatMatrix: minVersion: 0 maxVersion: 4
Object size 107374182400 bytes with policy: (("readOPS" (i0 i200))
("stripeWidth" i1) ("capacity" l107374182400) ("proportionalCapacity"
i100) ("hostFailuresToTolerate" i1) ("availability" i99999992)
("reliabilityExponent" i30) ("reliabilityBase" i100) ("affinity"
[ 520ea260-e2ad-3ccb-24ec-7d116c8bd73f 5256ac61-b8a9-8f47-d54e-
8ddb6d080f63]) ("storageType" "AllFlash"))
```

```
CLOMChooseFromEnumeration: Cost 214748364802 sane compliant 1

CLOMMarshalConfiguration: Marshaling config for UUID b47f4058-6931-e956-
b0da-000c29d918dd

CLOM_LogDomMessage: referent b47f4058-6931-e956-b0da-000c29d918dd length
1896 object size: 107374182400 type: 2

CLOM_LogDomMessage: expression ("Configuration" (("addressSpace"
1107374182400) ("objectVersion" i4) ("groupUuid" 2e373258-b77c-8509-4e5e-
000c292cb974) ("compositeUuid" b47f4058-6931-e956-b0da-000c29d918dd))
("RAID_1" () ("Component" (("capacity" 1107374182400) ("addressSpace"
1107374182400) ("faultDomainId" 57b68127-135e-e2a1-dd78-000c298ef254))
UUID_NULL 520ea260-e2ad-3ccb-24ec-7d116c8bd73f) ("Component" (("capac-
ity" 1107374182400) ("addressSpace" 1107374182400) ("faultDomainId"
5816591a-e016-49bb-093b-000c294c357c)) UUID_NULL 5256ac61-b8a9-8f47-d54e-
8ddb6d080f63)) ("Witness" (("isWitness" i1) ("faultDomainId" 57b67c43-71ef-
7d94-52b0-000c29d918dd)) UUID_NULL 5223142d-2e6f-1e33-3708-517a1782e93f))
```

In Listing 21.25, I removed the date/timestamp and added blank lines between messages for readability. I also highlighted two items specific to proportionalCapacity (PC or OSR). Observe that 100% is specified, even though a policy file is not specified in the vmkfstools command line. Therefore, the default policy would have been used, which is ("proportionalCapacity" i0).

Disable Object Checksum

This rule enables or disables calculation of checksum information of the object. This can be a bit confusing because enabling the option, set to Yes, results in disabling the checksum. The default is No, which means the checksum is calculated—which is a double negative.

The objective of the checksum option is to calculate the data checksum as early as possible and to verify it as late as possible by the DOM client. The checksum is calculated and stored on the write path by the DOM owner. If the DOM owner and DOM client are on different nodes, the DOM client verifies the checksum before sending it to the DOM owner for write. The DOM owner compares the checksum of the received data before committing it to the write buffer. This prevents the possibility of writing corrupt data to all mirrors if the checksum changes in transit.

The performance cost of using the checksum is relatively small, between 1% and 3% of compute resources and uses special CPU instructions on Intel CPUs. It should be safe to leave this feature enabled (that is, leave the rule set to No). However, if the checksum is handled at a higher layer within the VM, you can disable it for this VM's VMDKs (that is, the rule is set to Yes).

Erasure Coding (RAID 5 and RAID 6)

Erasure coding (EC) is a method of data protection in which data is broken into fragments, expanded and encoded with redundant data pieces, and stored across a set of different locations or storage media.

vSAN 6.2 and later implements EC with RAID 5 and RAID 6 DOM objects.

RAID 5 EC requires a minimum of four hosts (using the 3 + 1 logic). It tolerates a single host failure without loss of access to data. When the lost host is replaced, the stripe is rebuilt from parity and/or the surviving components.

In contrast, RAID 6 EC requires a minimum of six hosts (using the 4 + 2 logic) and tolerates two hosts failure—hence the FTT = 2 rule in the storage policy.

> **NOTE**
>
> RAID 5 and RAID 6 (EC) are not supported with vSAN stretched clusters. The reason is that RAID 5 requires a minimum of four nodes, and RAID 6 requires at least six nodes. A stretched cluster is limited to two fault domains, which is analogous to two hosts from a component placement perspective. This restriction has been removed in vSAN 6.6 using nested fault domains.

RAID 5 components are placed on disk groups on four vSAN nodes.

To list the component placement for RAID 5, follow these steps:

1. Connect to the vCenter server using the vSphere 6.x Web Client as a user with Administrator privileges. In this example, I am using vSphere 6.5.

2. Navigate to the **VMs and Templates** view and select the VM whose configuration you want to inspect.

3. Select the **Monitor** tab.

4. Click the **Policies** button.

5. Select a virtual disk whose storage policy was configured for RAID 5.

6. In the lower pane, select the **Physical Disk Placement** tab.

The lower pane shows the type as RAID 5, composed of four components, each placed on a separate host. Figure 21.49 shows RAID 5 component placement.

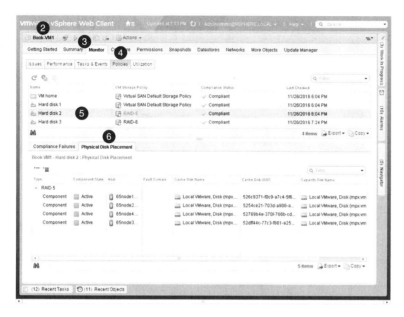

Figure 21.49   Component placement for RAID 5

The same approach can be followed to list RAID 6 components, where six components are each placed on a separate node in the cluster.

These components play the same role that disks play in physical RAID sets. For RAID 5 EC, vSAN writes each stripe across three components in 1MiB data blocks and places the corresponding parity block on a fourth component. The subsequent stripes are written such that the parity blocks are not on the same component as that of the previous stripe. For example, three data blocks written to segment A, B, and C components have their parity block written on the segment D component. RAID 5 EC uses XOR for calculating the single parity block.

Figure 21.50 shows a logical diagram that illustrates this arrangement.

In this figure, the long rectangle spanning three data blocks and a parity block shows one stripe. Each block is 1MiB in size. A vSAN RAID 5 DOM object is $255\text{GiB} \times 3 = 765\text{GiB}$. The reason is that the maximum LSOM component size is 255GiB. To create RAID 5 DOM objects larger than 765GiB, vSAN resorts to splitting each RAID 5 component (segment in the diagram) into RAID 0 vSAN stripes up to 255GiB each. This is the same approach vSAN uses to handle RAID 1 DOM objects larger than 255GiB. Each RAID 0 child component is placed on a separate capacity disk on the same host if space is available; otherwise, these child components are placed on other capacity disks on other hosts. Figure 21.51 illustrates this placement.

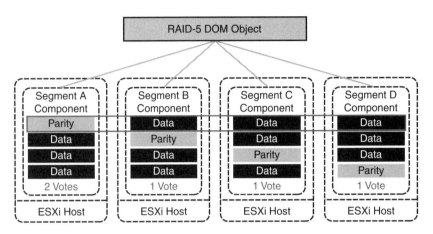

Figure 21.50   EC placement for RAID 5

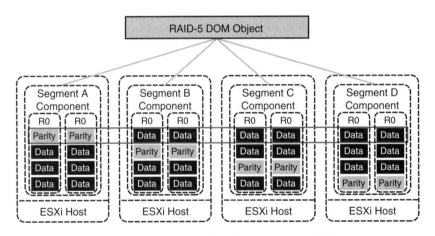

Figure 21.51   EC placement for a RAID 5 DOM object >765GiB

Each data or parity block is striped across the two child R0 LSOM components of the corresponding parent's RAID 5 LSOM component. Loss of a disk on which one of the two RAID 0 LSOM components resides results in recalculation of the whole parent LSOM component from parity once the lost disk is replaced. You can consider the RAID 0 child components of the RAID 5 parent component as a single entity for the purpose of availability and recovery. The same concept applies to RAID 1 components. However, with RAID 1, resynchronizing the surviving RAID 1 replica component is done to create the missing component, which is then split into RAID 0 child components.

Figure 21.52 shows the component placement in the UI.

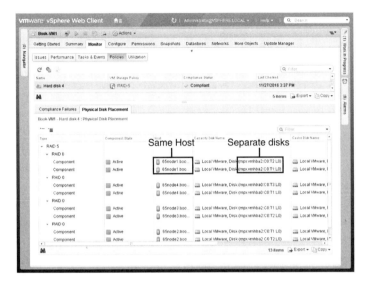

Figure 21.52   Component placement for RAID 5 >765GiB

The same applies to RAID 6, where four data blocks are written to four components, and their corresponding two parity blocks are written to two additional components.

RAID 6 uses XOR for calculating the first parity block and Multiply on XOR (MULXOR) for the second parity block.

Figure 21.53 shows the component placement in the UI.

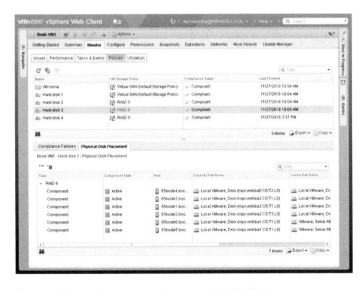

Figure 21.53   Component placement for RAID 6

To inspect CMMDS metadata of a RAID 6 VMDK using its UUID, follow this procedure:

1. Log on to one of the vSAN nodes as root via SSH or at the server's console.

2. Locate the VMDK's descriptor file in the VM's home directory. In this example, it is at `/vmfs/volumes/vsanDatastore/Book-VM1/Book-VM1_1.vmdk`

3. Identify the VMDK's UUID by using this command:

   ```
   grep vsan [path to descriptor file]
   ```

   Here is an example:

   ```
   grep vsan /vmfs/volumes/vsanDatastore/Book-VM1/Book-VM1.vmdk
   ```

   Here is the output:

   ```
   RW 209715200 VMFS "vsan://e8513a58-e6bc-4594-042b-000c292cb974"
   ```

   The UUID is the value listed after `vsan://` in the output.

4. Run this command to obtain the metadata:

   ```
   cmmds-tool find --format json --uuid <object UUID> --type DOM_OBJECT
   ```

   Here is an example:

   ```
   cmmds-tool  find  --format  json  --uuid  e8513a58-e6bc-4594-042b-
   000c292cb974 --type DOM_OBJECT
   ```

   You can also use the abbreviated version:

   ```
   cmmds-tool find -f json -u e8513a58-e6bc-4594-042b-000c292cb974 -t
   DOM_OBJECT
   ```

Listing 21.26 lists this command's output.

Listing 21.26   RAID 6 DOM object metadata

```
{
 "entries":
[
 {
   "uuid": "e8513a58-e6bc-4594-042b-000c292cb974",
   "owner": "57b68127-135e-e2a1-dd78-000c298ef254",
   "health": "Healthy",
   "revision": "9",
   "type": "DOM_OBJECT",
```

```
    "flag": "2",
    "minHostVersion": "3",
    "md5sum": "e519eef294c94422c3cc70553ed4c5eb",
    "valueLen": "2392",
    "content": {"type": "Configuration", "attributes": {"CSN": 6, "SCSN": 6,
"addressSpace": 107374182400, "scrubStartTime": 1480217064932254,
"objectVersion": 4, "highestDiskVersion": 4, "muxGroup": 374875720584192,
"groupUuid": "2e373258-b77c-8509-4e5e-000c292cb974", "compositeUuid":
"e8513a58-e6bc-4594-042b-000c292cb974"}, "child-1": {"type": "RAID_6",
"attributes": {"stripeBlockSize": 1048576}, "child-1": {"type":
"Component", "attributes": {"aggregateCapacity": 26843545600,
"addressSpace": 26843545600, "componentState": 5, "componentStateTS":
1480217064, "faultDomainId": "57f93a38-27ed-3916-7d3a-000c29da46c3",
"nVotes": 2, "lastScrubbedOffset": 26843545600}, "componentUuid":
"e8513a58-4f0f-df94-e545-000c292cb974", "diskUuid": "52d2c6e1-70fa-7e17-
263b-7e5705a41f11"}, "child-2": {"type": "Component", "attributes":
{"aggregateCapacity": 26843545600, "addressSpace": 26843545600,
"componentState": 5, "componentStateTS": 1480295987, "faultDomainId":
"57b67f25-0080-ca9d-77da-000c292cb974", "lastScrubbedOffset":
26843545600}, "componentUuid": "e8513a58-a11a-e194-2cf0-000c292cb974",
"diskUuid": "521c8169-7776-e878-d831-89cb1780e968"}, "child-3":
{"type": "Component", "attributes": {"aggregateCapacity": 26843545600,
"addressSpace": 26843545600, "componentState": 5, "componentStateTS":
1480295546, "faultDomainId": "57b67c43-71ef-7d94-52b0-000c29d918dd"},
"componentUuid": "e8513a58-fbdf-e194-bb11-000c292cb974", "diskUuid":
"52e11f22-4416-764d-d8d3-42191b0e38a1"}, "child-4": {"type": "Component",
"attributes": {"aggregateCapacity": 26843545600, "addressSpace":
26843545600, "componentState": 5, "componentStateTS": 1480217064,
"faultDomainId": "57b68127-135e-e2a1-dd78-000c298ef254"}, "componentUuid":
"e8513a58-fc86-e294-ca26-000c292cb974", "diskUuid": "520ea260-e2ad-3ccb-
24ec-7d116c8bd73f"}, "child-5": {"type": "Component", "attributes":
{"aggregateCapacity": 26843545600, "addressSpace": 26843545600,
"componentState": 5, "componentStateTS": 1480217064, "faultDomainId":
"5816591a-e016-49bb-093b-000c294c357c"}, "componentUuid": "e8513a58-
7c40-e394-1ba6-000c292cb974", "diskUuid": "52a6ffd1-ae62-2e46-4aee-
c9e24211ede5"}, "child-6": {"type": "Component", "attributes":
{"aggregateCapacity": 26843545600, "addressSpace": 26843545600,
"componentState": 5, "componentStateTS": 1480217064, "faultDomainId":
"58165b6e-6d3a-0342-8956-000c29f08be1"}, "componentUuid": "e8513a58-
81ff-e394-6674-000c292cb974", "diskUuid": "5292cf02-05a6-d3a3-6915-
6eb3eb533f50"}}},
    "errorStr": "(null)"
  }
]
}
```

Listing 21.27 lists the content field, reformatted manually for readability.

Listing 21.27   RAID 6 DOM object content field

```
"content":
 {"type": "Configuration",
         "attributes": {"CSN": 2,
         "addressSpace": 107374182400, ← Object Size in bytes =100GiB
         "scrubStartTime": 1480217064932254,
         "objectVersion": 4, ← Object version. It is 4 in 6.2 and 6.5
         "highestDiskVersion": 4, ← On-disk format version
         "muxGroup": 409813635369984,
         "groupUuid": "2e373258-b77c-8509-4e5e-000c292cb974", ← VM Home
UUID
         "compositeUuid": "e8513a58-e6bc-4594-042b-000c292cb974"}, ← Object
UUID
         "child-1":
             {"type": "RAID_6", ← Object RAID Type
             "attributes":
                  {"stripeBlockSize": 1048576}, ← RAID Stripe Block Size in
bytes
                  "child-1": ← First of 6 LSOM Components
                     {"type": "Component",
                         "attributes":
                         {"aggregateCapacity": 26843545600, ← 1/4 Object
size=25GiB
                         "addressSpace": 26843545600, ← same as component
size
                         "componentState": 5, ← Component state is Active
                         "componentStateTS": 1480217064,
                         "faultDomainId": "57f93a38-27ed-3916-7d3a-
000c29da46c3",
                         "nVotes": 2, ← This component's vote count
                         "lastScrubbedOffset": 26843545600},
                         "componentUuid": "e8513a58-4f0f-df94-e545-
000c292cb974",
                         "diskUuid": "52d2c6e1-70fa-7e17-263b-
7e5705a41f11"},
                  "child-2": ← 2nd of 6 LSOM components
                     {"type": "Component",
                         "attributes":
                         {"aggregateCapacity": 26843545600,
                         "addressSpace": 26843545600,
                         "componentState": 5,
                         "componentStateTS": 1480217064,
```

```
                            "faultDomainId": "57b67f25-0080-ca9d-77da-
000c292cb974"},

                            "componentUuid": "e8513a58-a11a-e194-2cf0-
000c292cb974",

                            "diskUuid": "521c8169-7776-e878-d831-
89cb1780e968"},
                "child-3":  ← 3rd of 6 LSOM components
                    {"type": "Component",
                        "attributes":
                        {"aggregateCapacity": 26843545600,
                        "addressSpace": 26843545600,
                        "componentState": 5,
                        "componentStateTS": 1480217064,
                        "faultDomainId": "57b67c43-71ef-7d94-52b0-
000c29d918dd"},

                        "componentUuid": "e8513a58-fbdf-e194-bb11-
000c292cb974",

                        "diskUuid": "52e11f22-4416-764d-d8d3-
42191b0e38a1"},
                "child-4":  ← 4th of 6 LSOM components
                    {"type": "Component",
                        "attributes":
                        {"aggregateCapacity": 26843545600,
                        "addressSpace": 26843545600,
                        "componentState": 5,
                        "componentStateTS": 1480217064,
                        "faultDomainId": "57b68127-135e-e2a1-dd78-
000c298ef254"},

                        "componentUuid": "e8513a58-fc86-e294-ca26-
000c292cb974",

                        "diskUuid": "520ea260-e2ad-3ccb-24ec-
7d116c8bd73f"},
                "child-5":  ← 5th of 6 LSOM components
                    {"type": "Component",
                        "attributes":
                        {"aggregateCapacity": 26843545600,
                        "addressSpace": 26843545600,
                        "componentState": 5,
                        "componentStateTS": 1480217064,
                        "faultDomainId": "5816591a-e016-49bb-093b-
000c294c357c"},

                        "componentUuid": "e8513a58-7c40-e394-1ba6-
000c292cb974",
```

```
                                "diskUuid": "52a6ffd1-ae62-2e46-4aee-
c9e24211ede5"},
                    "child-6":    ← 6th of 6 LSOM components
                       {"type": "Component",
                                "attributes":
                                {"aggregateCapacity": 26843545600,
                                "addressSpace": 26843545600,
                                "componentState": 5,
                                "componentStateTS": 1480217064,
                                "faultDomainId": "58165b6e-6d3a-0342-8956-
000c29f08be1"},
                                "componentUuid": "e8513a58-81ff-e394-6674-
000c292cb974",
                                "diskUuid": "5292cf02-05a6-d3a3-6915-
6eb3eb533f50"}
                    }
},
```

In Listing 21.27, I added highlighted comments about specific properties in the output.

The first attribute of the RAID 6 object is stripeBlockSize, which is 1,048,576 bytes (1MiB). This is the size of a block written to each LSOM component as RAID 6 EC stripes the data and parity across the LSOM components.

There are six LSOM components to accommodate the 4+2 logic for RAID 6 EC. The DOM object size is divided into four (the number of data components), which makes each LSOM component one-quarter of the DOM object's size. The size of the VMDK I created is 100GiB, which is why each LSOM component is 25GiB in size.

Each LSOM component has an associated componentUUID and diskUuid, which represent the LSOM component's UUID and the UUID of the disk on which the component is stored. The faultDomainId in this example is the same as the host UUID hosting the LSOM component. That is due to the fact that I have not defined fault domains in this cluster, which means that each node is in its own fault domain.

The attribute nVotes states the number of votes assigned to this component. The remaining components do not show this attribute, which implies the value of 1 vote each. The reason for using vote count in this case is the lack of witness components with RAID 5 and RAID 6 objects. This means that the total vote count for all six LSOM components is seven (the first one has two, and the remaining five have one each). This prevents a split-brain state if the six vSAN nodes are partitioned into two groups of three. The partition that has the component with two votes would have four of the seven votes, which gives it a majority quorum (>50% of total votes). In this state, components on that partition are used for reads and writes. You will learn more related details later in this chapter, in the section **"HA on vSAN."**

Based on the maximum LSOM component size of 255GiB, the vSAN RAID 6 DOM object maximum size is $255 \times 4 = 1020$GiB because the number of data blocks in a RAID 6 EC stripe is four plus two parity blocks. This means that for a given RAID 6 DOM object, capacity equivalent to four LSOM components is used for data, with two components used for double parity.

Figure 21.54 shows a logical diagram of EC placement of data and parity blocks in a RAID 6 DOM object.

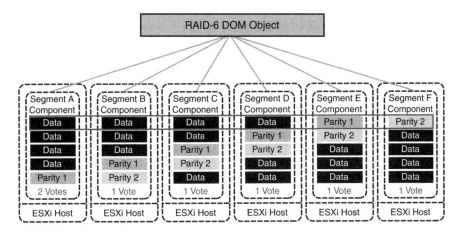

Figure 21.54   EC placement for RAID 6

The same concept I discussed for RAID 5 earlier applies here: When creating RAID 6 DOM objects larger than the maximum size of 1020GiB, a RAID 0 child LSOM component is created for each RAID 6 LSOM component.

Reconfiguring Existing Virtual Disks' Storage Policies

Careful design clearly defines storage policy association with each VM and its virtual disks. However, if the need arises to reconfigure the policy of some of the virtual disks after the fact, the possibilities are based on available placement rules. Prior to vSAN 6.2, only RAID 1 and RAID 0 were available options. With the introduction of erasure coding in vSAN 6.2 and later, RAID 5 and RAID 6 are available. The possible combinations are RAID 1 to RAID 5, RAID 1 to RAID 6, and RAID 5 to RAID 6. The basic approach of reconfiguring a DOM object is to create a transitional mirror copy of the existing configuration. However, the new copy is actually the destination EC placement. This means you need available raw capacity equal to the target RAID type configuration. For example, if the target is RAID 5, you need 133% of the current object size before proceeding with the reconfiguration. Eventually, the source configuration–related components will be deleted upon successful reconfiguration.

To reconfigure a virtual disk with a different policy, follow this procedure:

1. Connect to the vCenter server using the vSphere 6.x Web Client as a user with Administrator privileges.

2. Navigate to the **VMs and Templates** view (see Figure 21.55).

3. Select the VM whose virtual disk you want to reconfigure.

4. If you're using vSAN 6.5, click the **Configure** tab. If you're using vSAN 6.2, skip to step 10.

5. Select **Policies** in the More section.

6. Click the **Edit VM Storage Policies** button.

Figure 21.55   Editing VM storage policies

7. Select the virtual disk you want to reconfigure—in this example, **Hard disk 2** (see Figure 21.56).

8. Select the policy from the VM Storage Policy pull-down menu. In this example, I select a policy named **RAID-5**. The Predicted Impact section reflects the impact on storage space usage.

9. Click **OK**. To continue with the vSAN 6.5, directions, skip to step 15.

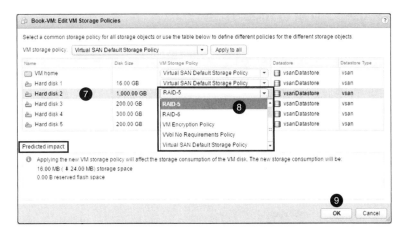

Figure 21.56 Selecting VM storage policies

10. Click the **Manage** tab.

11. Click the **Manage VM Storage Policies** button.

12. Select the virtual disk you want to reconfigure.

13. Select the policy from the VM Storage Policy pull-down menu.

14. Click **OK**.

15. You should see the reconfigured virtual disk with the reconfigured storage policy and the Compliance Status column showing **Compliant**.

The procedure is identical to the procedure for applying any storage policy on existing virtual disks.

TIP

Do not change the VM home object from the Virtual SAN default storage policy because it provides sufficient availability via RAID 1 mirrored replicas. There is no performance gain for using any other RAID types.

To see what happens under the hood during the reconfiguration process, I cover two scenarios in the next two sections, **"Reconfiguring a RAID 1 Object to RAID 5"** and **"Reconfiguring a RAID 5 Object to RAID 6."**

Reconfiguring a RAID 1 Object to RAID 5

The process of reconfiguring a RAID 1 object to RAID 5 starts with creating an extra replica of one of the exiting replica components of the RAID 1 set where the target replica is a RAID 5 EC.

Immediately after you click the OK button in the previous procedure, you can list the CMMDS metadata of the transient state of the DOM object collected by using the following command, which should be familiar to you by now:

```
cmmds-tool find --format json --uuid <Object UUID>
```

Or you can use the abbreviated version:

```
cmmds-tool find -f json -u <Object UUID>
```

Listing 21.28 shows the command and the DOM object's content field values from vSAN 6.5, reformatted for better readability.

Listing 21.28   RAID 1 to RAID 5 transient DOM object content field

```
cmmds-tool find -f json -u 56373258-4cf8-04bd-672c-000c292cb974
[Below is the content field of the DOM_OBJECT]
"content":
  {"type": "Configuration",
  "attributes":
    {"CSN": 19,
    "addressSpace": 42949672960,
    "scrubStartTime": 1480143381461729,
    "objectVersion": 4,
    "highestDiskVersion": 4,
    "muxGroup": 374875720584192,
    "groupUuid": "2e373258-b77c-8509-4e5e-000c292cb974",
    "compositeUuid": "56373258-4cf8-04bd-672c-000c292cb974"},
        "child-1":
          {"type": "RAID_1",  ← RAID 1 definition
          "attributes": {},
          "child-1":  ← RAID 1 First original component
            {"type": "Component",
            "attributes":
            {"addressSpace": 42949672960,
            "componentState": 5,
            "componentStateTS": 1479685974,
            "transient": 1,  ← Transient
            "faultDomainId": "57b67c43-71ef-7d94-52b0-000c29d918dd"},
```

```
        "componentUuid": "56373258-3a15-81be-ba29-000c292cb974",
        "diskUuid": "52e11f22-4416-764d-d8d3-42191b0e38a1"},
    "child-2": ← RAID 1 Second original component
      {"type": "Component",
      "attributes":
      {"addressSpace": 42949672960,
      "componentState": 5,
      "componentStateTS": 1479785441,
      "transient": 1, ← Transient
      "faultDomainId": "57b68127-135e-e2a1-dd78-000c298ef254"},
      "componentUuid": "e1bb3358-2bb9-ea05-dcf4-000c29da46c3",
      "diskUuid": "52433c34-7e6f-d24b-1a9b-1deed7ce980e"},
    "child-3": ← RAID 1 New transient component
      {"type": "RAID_5", ← RAID 5 definition
      "attributes":
      {"stripeBlockSize": 1048576},
          "child-1": ← RAID 5 First component
            {"type": "Component",
            "attributes":
            {"capacity": [143162082, 14316208128],
            "addressSpace": 14316208128,
            "componentState": 5,
            "componentStateTS": 1480376503,
            "faultDomainId": "57b67f25-0080-ca9d-77da-
000c292cb974",
            "nVotes": 3}, ← Component has 3 votes
            "componentUuid": "b7c03c58-4a99-625c-b569-
000c298ef254",
            "diskUuid": "5285b69b-a276-79f8-1808-8d9fb5f533db"},
          "child-2": ← RAID 5 Second component
            {"type": "Component",
            "attributes":
            {"capacity": [143162082, 14316208128],
            "addressSpace": 14316208128,
            "componentState": 5,
            "componentStateTS": 1480376503,
            "faultDomainId": "58165b6e-6d3a-0342-8956-
000c29f08be1",
            "nVotes": 2}, ← Component has 2 votes
            "componentUuid": "b7c03c58-2230-655c-8c01-
000c298ef254",
            "diskUuid": "5292cf02-05a6-d3a3-6915-6eb3eb533f50"},
          "child-3": ← RAID 5 Third component
```

```
                    {"type": "Component",
                    "attributes":
                    {"capacity": [143172568, 14317256704],
                    "addressSpace": 14317256704,
                    "componentState": 5,
                    "componentStateTS": 1480376503,
                    "faultDomainId": "57b68127-135e-e2a1-dd78-
  000c298ef254"},
                    "componentUuid": "b7c03c58-325c-665c-bccd-
  000c298ef254",
                    "diskUuid": "52433c34-7e6f-d24b-1a9b-1deed7ce980e"},
                "child-4": ← RAID 5 Fourth component
                    {"type": "Component",
                    "attributes":
                    {"capacity": [143172568, 14317256704],
                    "addressSpace": 14317256704,
                    "componentState": 5,
                    "componentStateTS": 1480376503,
                    "faultDomainId": "57b67c43-71ef-7d94-52b0-
  000c29d918dd"},
                    "componentUuid": "b7c03c58-c844-675c-c1f3-
  000c298ef254",
                    "diskUuid": "52e4034a-9244-8ff0-ae73-86a0472f8aa2"}
                                                                }
            }
    }
```

The output in Listing 21.28 shows the original two RAID 1 replica components as transient.

There is a third child of the RAID 1 configuration. This child is a RAID 5 configuration, under which there are four children, which are the RAID 5 components.

Let's inspect the content field of the POLICY object from the same command's output. Listing 21.29 lists the POLICY object.

Listing 21.29 RAID 1 to RAID 5 transient POLICY objects

```
{
    "uuid": "56373258-4cf8-04bd-672c-000c292cb974",
    "owner": "57b68127-135e-e2a1-dd78-000c298ef254",
    "health": "Healthy",
"revision": "20",
    "type": "POLICY",
```

```
"flag": "2",
"minHostVersion": "3",
"md5sum": "5a4f4ddf0c5b8c2ef2d073cd4b6cb132",
"valueLen": "304",
"content":
    {"hostFailuresToTolerate": 1,
    "spbmProfileId": "55516e2a-98ef-441d-9def-d1770763a757",
    "spbmProfileGenerationNumber": 0,
    "replicaPreference": "Capacity",
    "CSN": 63,
    "spbmProfileName": "RAID 5"}
```

In the output in Listing 21.29, I highlighted the two values relevant to this transitional state: HostFailureToTolerate: 1 and replicaPreference: Capacity. The latter means RAID 5/6 EC, and the former makes the combination a RAID 5. If the value were 2, the combination would have meant RAID 6. The reference to replica here is to the replica component created as the target of the reconfiguration.

If this reconfiguration is done in the reverse direction—that is, from RAID 5/6 to RAID 1—the replicaPreference value is Performance.

Figure 21.57 shows the transitional state's logical representation, based on Listing 21.28 and Listing 21.29.

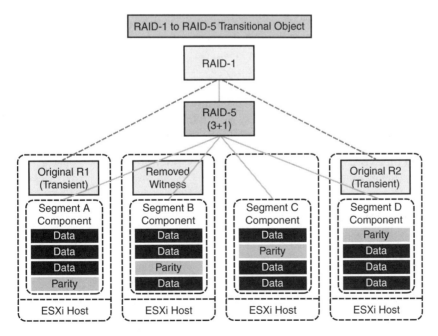

Figure 21.57 RAID 1 to RAID 5 transition logical diagram

As part of the transition, the witness component of the original RAID 1 configuration is removed. Once the reconfiguration is complete, both transient RAID 1 components (R1 and R2) are removed, leaving only the RAID 5 configuration.

Reconfiguring a RAID 5 Object to RAID 6

Reconfiguration of RAID 5 to RAID 6 is done using a similar approach, with a mirror replica of the RAID 5 configuration with RAID 6 for the target replica. After reconfiguration is complete, the original RAID 5 configuration and related components are removed, leaving only the RAID 6 configuration.

HA on vSAN

vSphere High Availability (also referred to as *vSphere HA*) has been around since before VMware began shipping vSAN. The main purpose of using HA is to provide an automated recovery of VMs if the host on which they run crashes or fails. It is commonly designed to protect against a certain number of hosts failures. This is usually referred to as N+(x), where x is the number of host failures that HA protects against.

HA is somewhat analogous to the vSAN FTT rule, which protects against host failures. HA monitors the HA cluster node's heartbeat via an HA network as well as via a shared datastores heartbeat. However, the latter is not supported on a vSAN datastore. When HA is used on vSAN clusters, HA must be enabled after vSAN is enabled—not before. In earlier vSAN releases, this was not enforced, which resulted in failure to use HA–vSAN interoperations. In later versions of vSAN, including 6.0 through 6.6, if vSAN is enabled on an existing HA cluster, this message is displayed: "`Turn off vSphere HA to turn on/off Virtual SAN`".

The reason for this order is that HA has to be aware that it runs on a vSAN cluster so that it can follow a specific logic when interacting with vSAN. In this section, I highlight these interoperability features and how they work.

Once HA is enabled on a vSAN cluster, the HA heartbeat is monitored over the vSAN network, along with the vSAN cluster nodes' heartbeat.

Configuring HA on vSAN

To configure HA on vSAN, follow this procedure:

1. Connect to the vCenter server using the vSphere 6.x Web Client as a user with Administrator privileges. This example uses vSphere 6.5, Patch 2 (vSAN 6.6).

2. Navigate to the **Hosts and Clusters** view (see Figure 21.58).

3. Right-click the cluster object in the inventory tree and select the **Settings** menu option.

4. Select the **vSphere DRS** section.

5. Click the **Edit** button. The Edit Cluster Settings dialog pops up.

6. If your design calls for using DRS, in the vSphere DRS section of the dialog, select the **Turn ON vSphere DRS** check box. Otherwise, skip to step 9.

7. Select the DRS Automation option that matches your design requirements. To configure advanced options, expand the **DRS Automation** section and select the relevant options. In this example, I am using partial automation.

8. To select specific DRS policies, expand the **DRS Policies** section.

9. Select the **vSphere Availability** section.

10. Select the **Turn on vSphere HA** check box.

11. Select the **Failures and Responses** section of the dialog.

12. The **Enable Host Monitoring** check box is already selected. To select additional conditions and their responses, select the corresponding response from the pull-down list next to each failure condition. For a vSAN cluster, configure only the following two options:

   ■ **Host Failure Response**—Leave the **Restart VMs** option selected.

   ■ **Response for Host Isolation**—Select **Power off and restart VMs**. Because the HA heartbeat is monitored over the vSAN network, if a host gets network partitioned on a vSAN cluster, it is also detected as isolated for the HA cluster. Powering off the VMs enables HA to restart them on hosts that have majority votes of the DOM object.

Leave the remaining options disabled.

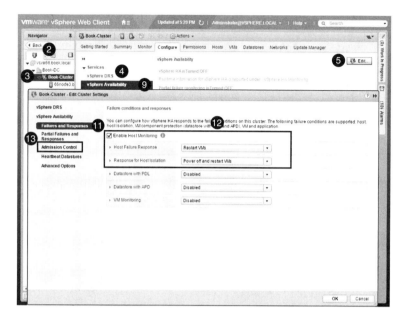

Figure 21.58   Configuring HA on vSAN

13. Select the **Admission Control** section (see Figure 21.59).

14. If the vSAN cluster is not stretched, for Host Failure Cluster Tolerates, select the number matching the highest FTT setting used with vSAN. For example, if you have storage policies configured with FTT = 1 or RAID 5 EC, select **1** here, and if you have FTT = 2 or RAID 6 EC, select **2** here. Otherwise, if you have FTT = 3, select **3** here and skip to step 18.

15. If vSAN is configured in a stretched cluster, with or without nested FDs (see Chapter 22), you need to reserve 50% of the resources on each site to accommodate a full site failure. To do that, select the **Cluster resource percentage** option from the Define Host Failover Capacity pull-down menu.

16. Select the **Override failover capacity by the number of host failures cluster tolerates** check box.

17. Enter 50% in both the CPU and Memory fields.

18. Leave the remaining options unmodified and select the **Advanced Options** section.

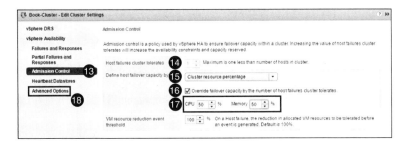

Figure 21.59   Configuring HA admission control on vSAN

19. Click the **Add** button.

20. In the Option field, enter `das.useDefaultIsolationAddress`.

21. In the Value field, enter `false`.

22. Repeat steps 19 and 20, using `das.isolationAddress0` in the Option field.

23. The content of the Value field depends on the vSAN cluster design:

    ■ **Single-site cluster**—Enter an IP address on the vSAN network.

    ■ **Stretched cluster**—Enter an IP address on the intersite vSAN network. If it is a Layer 3 network, enter that network's default gateway.

    Use of a witness node IP address would not be valid because a stretched cluster should continue to function in the absence of the witness node, albeit in a noncompliant state.

24. Click **OK** to conclude the procedure.

vSAN coverage is continued in Chapter 22.

vSAN Easy Installation

vSphere 6.5 Express Patch 2 includes a new approach to installing vCenter and configuring vSAN cluster using easy install feature of the **vCenter Server Appliance 6.5 Installer**. This process is commonly called *bootstrapping*. You must first install ESXi 6.5 with Patch 2 or later on all hosts that will be members of the vSAN cluster and leave all disks that will be claimed by the cluster unmodified.

The high level installation process is as follows:

1. vCenter Server Installer connects to one of the ESXi hosts that will be the first node in the vSAN cluster.

2. The installer configures a single node vSAN on the ESXi host and mounts the vSAN datastore with a special policy that allows for creating vSAN objects on the single node

3. The installer deploys vCenter Server Appliance (VCSA) on the vSAN datastore and configures the appliance.

4. The appliance is powered on.

5. You then access vCenter as a user with administrator privileges and add the remaining ESXi hosts to the cluster.

Detailed Easy Installation Steps

To deploy VCSA and configure vSAN cluster using the easy installation feature, do the following:

1. Install and configure ESX hosts on all servers that will be members of the vSAN cluster.

2. Mount the ISO image that includes VCSA 6.5 installer. It must be version 6.5 Patch 2 or later.

3. Launch the UI installer which is located under /vcsa-ui-installer directory. There is an installer for Linux, Mac and Windows located in lin64, mac and win32 directories respectively.

4. Click **Install**.

5. At the **Install - Stage 1** screen click **Next**.

6. Read and accept the end user license agreement and then click **Next**.

7. Select **vCenter Server with an Embedded Platform Controller** option. You cannot use the External Platform Services Controller option with the easy installation process. (See Figure 21.60)

8. Click Next.

Figure 21.60   Selecting Embedded Platform Services Controller option

9. Enter the IP address or host name of the ESXi host that will be the first node in the cluster.

10. Leave HTTPS port 443 unmodified.

11. In the **User name** field, enter root.

12. Enter the password of the root account.

13. Click Next.

14. Accept the **Certificate Warning** dialog.

15 .Enter the VCSA VM name, root password and confirm that password.

16. Click **Next**.

17. Select the deployment size and storage size of the VCSA and then click **Next**.

18. At the Select datastore step, select Install on a new Virtual SAN cluster containing the target host option. (See Figure 21.61)

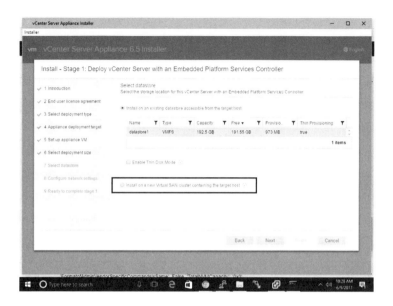

Figure 21.61   Selecting Install on a New vSAN cluster

19. An additional screen is opened with 2 choices:

    ■ Install on an existing datastore accessible from the target host

    ■ Install on a new Virtual SAN cluster containing the target host.

    Select the second choice. (See Figure 21.62)

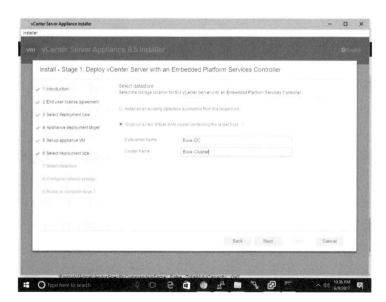

Figure 21.62   Selecting datastore

20. Enter the datacenter and cluster names.

21. Click **Next**.

22. For hybrid configuration, the flash disks are automatically claimed for cache tier and the magnetic disks for capacity tier.

    For all flash configuration, initially, all flash disks are claimed for cache tier. Select each disk that will be used for capacity and click **Claim for capacity tier** icon. (See Figure 21.63). You should end up with one disk claimed for cache tier and the rest claimed for capacity tier. If you plan on using multiple disk groups per host, select one cache disk per group.

TIP

Distribute capacity tier disks evenly between disk groups. Using easy installation wizard, select the number of cache tier disks equal to the number of disk groups and select the capacity tier disks in multiples of the number of disk groups. For example, for 2 disk groups, select 2 cache tier disks and an even number of capacity tier disks that is divisible by 2. Conversely, for 3 disk groups, select 3 cache tier disks and select an odd number of capacity tier disks divisible by 3 and so on.

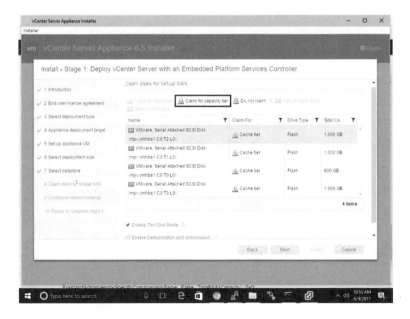

Figure 21.63 Claiming disks.

23. You can select **Enable Deduplication and compression** checkbox if you want to enable this option. In this example, I did not select it.

24. Click **Next**.

25. Enter the network configuration details in the Configure network settings step of the wizard and then click Next.

26. Review your settings and then click **Finish**.

27. A progress bar appears that shows the progress of creating vSAN and claiming disks for vSAN. Once the vSAN datastore is created, VCSA is deployed on it and is powered on. Follow the steps of stage 2, **Setup vCenter Server Appliance**, which are identical to VCVA deployment on other environments.

28. After VCVA is fully configured with SSO domain and is up and running, connect to vCenter server using vSphere 6.5 web client as a user with administrator privileges and add the remaining ESXi hosts to the datacenter.

29. Configure vSAN Network on each host and then move the hosts into to the cluster. You will need to create the disk groups on the added hosts to complete the installation. You can follow the steps outlined by the Configuration Assist menu to complete all needed configurations. For information about **Configuration Assist**, see Accessing the Configuration Assist Menu section in chapter 22.

Summary

This chapter provides details about vSAN basic features, software architecture, requirements, and file system details.

vSAN storage policies affect placement of vSAN objects' components on disks in vSAN disk groups.

RAID 5 and RAID 6 EC are new in vSAN 6.2 and later. In this chapter, I cover how to apply a new storage policy to a virtual disk and its effect on storage.

HA must be enabled after a vSAN cluster is created—not before—as it enables HA awareness of vSAN-related events.

vSAN Advanced Features

Chapter 21, "vSAN Core Features," introduces vSAN basic features and functionalities. This chapter covers advanced vSAN features, including fault domains, stretched clusters, nested fault domains, remote office branch office (ROBO) stretched clusters, vSAN Internet Small Computer Systems Interface (iSCSI) targets (VITs), deduplication, and compression. It provides extensive details about how to accomplish common and advanced tasks, as well as command-line exploration and troubleshooting of vSAN.

Fault Domains

One vSAN design consideration is host placement on racks within one or more data centers. If many cluster nodes are on the same rack, it is recommended to design the rack with redundant power sources to protect all components within that rack. However, human error can contribute to a rack failure, regardless of all precautions. To mitigate the risk of rack failure, VMware introduced the concept of vSAN fault domains (FDs) in version 6.0. The idea is to group vSAN cluster nodes in logical groupings that treat all members of each group as a single fault domain. This means that any fault experienced by the group is considered a failure for the whole group.

Recall from Chapter 21 that the `cmmds-tools` output shows that each vSAN node has its own fault domain UUID, which also matches the host's UUID. The process of adding hosts to a fault domain changes the corresponding fault domain UUID to match the UUID of that fault domain. This concept is also referred to as *rack awareness*.

A design where each rack, or fault domain, is placed in a separate building or data site would be more suited for stretched cluster design. I cover this in more detail in the **"Stretched Clusters"** section, later in this chapter.

Creating vSAN Fault Domains

To create vSAN fault domains, follow this procedure:

1. Connect to the vCenter server using the vSphere 6 Web Client as a user with Administrator privileges.

2. Navigate to the **Hosts and Clusters** view (see Figure 22.1).

3. Select the vSAN cluster inventory object.

4. Right-click the cluster object and select the **Settings** menu option.

5. Select **Fault Domains & Stretched Cluster** in the Virtual SAN section.

6. Click the **Create a new fault domain** icon (the green plus sign).

7. Enter the new fault domain name in the Name field (for example, Rack1).

8. Select the hosts to add to this fault domain from the Show pull-down menu. I prefer using the default view, **Hosts not in fault domains**. This prevents selecting hosts that are already in existing fault domains.

9. Click **OK**.

10. Repeat steps 6–9 to create additional fault domains.

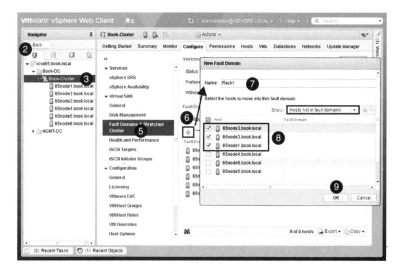

Figure 22.1   Creating a vSAN fault domain

In this example, I have six hosts split evenly on two racks. (This is done incorrectly, though! Later in this chapter you'll see why and how to resolve this.) I created the Rack1 and `Rack2` fault domains and placed hosts 1–3 in the first fault domain and hosts 4–6 in the second one. Figure 22.2 shows the result.

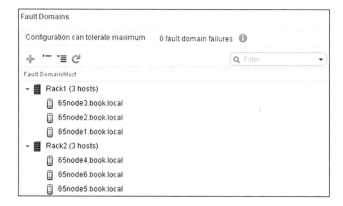

Figure 22.2   Fault domains created

Listing Fault Domains via the CLI

Another exercise in using `cmmds-tools` is to list all fault domains in a vSAN cluster. You can do so by using this command:

```
cmmds-tool find --format json --type NODE_FAULT_DOMAIN
```

You can also use the abbreviated version:

```
cmmds-tool find -f json -t NODE_FAULT_DOMAIN
```

Listing 22.1 shows the abbreviated command and its output.

Listing 22.1   Listing vSAN fault domains via the CLI

```
{
 "entries":
[
 {
   "uuid": "57f93a38-27ed-3916-7d3a-000c29da46c3",
   "owner": "57f93a38-27ed-3916-7d3a-000c29da46c3",
   "health": "Healthy",
   "revision": "1",
   "type": "NODE_FAULT_DOMAIN",
   "flag": "2",
   "minHostVersion": "0",
```

```
   "md5sum": "ab20f7e0a21c305c361b74ff1b06b012",
   "valueLen": "40",
   "content":
      {"faultDomainId": "f33b9cdb-9a77-eb94-7f45-f5990955687a",
      "faultDomainName": "Rack2"},
   "errorStr": "(null)"
 }
,{
   "uuid": "58165b6e-6d3a-0342-8956-000c29f08be1",
   "owner": "58165b6e-6d3a-0342-8956-000c29f08be1",
   "health": "Healthy",
   "revision": "1",
   "type": "NODE_FAULT_DOMAIN",
   "flag": "2",
   "minHostVersion": "0",
   "md5sum": "ab20f7e0a21c305c361b74ff1b06b012",
   "valueLen": "40",
   "content":
      {"faultDomainId": "f33b9cdb-9a77-eb94-7f45-f5990955687a",
      "faultDomainName": "Rack2"},
   "errorStr": "(null)"
 }
,{
   "uuid": "57b67c43-71ef-7d94-52b0-000c29d918dd",
   "owner": "57b67c43-71ef-7d94-52b0-000c29d918dd",
   "health": "Healthy",
   "revision": "1",
   "type": "NODE_FAULT_DOMAIN",
   "flag": "2",
   "minHostVersion": "0",
   "md5sum": "57bf15efeddc6e8421af75eaaaac0d3e",
   "valueLen": "40",
   "content":
      {"faultDomainId": "32138073-e900-d4d3-6910-ba18d6b16dd2",
      "faultDomainName": "Rack1"},
   "errorStr": "(null)"
 }
,{
   "uuid": "57b67f25-0080-ca9d-77da-000c292cb974",
   "owner": "57b67f25-0080-ca9d-77da-000c292cb974",
   "health": "Healthy",
   "revision": "1",
```

```
    "type": "NODE_FAULT_DOMAIN",
    "flag": "2",
    "minHostVersion": "0",
    "md5sum": "57bf15efeddc6e8421af75eaaaac0d3e",
    "valueLen": "40",
    "content":
      {"faultDomainId": "32138073-e900-d4d3-6910-ba18d6b16dd2",
      "faultDomainName": "Rack1"},
    "errorStr": "(null)"
  }
,{
    "uuid": "57b68127-135e-e2a1-dd78-000c298ef254",
    "owner": "57b68127-135e-e2a1-dd78-000c298ef254",
    "health": "Healthy",
    "revision": "1",
    "type": "NODE_FAULT_DOMAIN",
    "flag": "2",
    "minHostVersion": "0",
    "md5sum": "57bf15efeddc6e8421af75eaaaac0d3e",
    "valueLen": "40",
    "content":
      {"faultDomainId": "32138073-e900-d4d3-6910-ba18d6b16dd2",
      "faultDomainName": "Rack1"},
    "errorStr": "(null)"
  }
,{
    "uuid": "5816591a-e016-49bb-093b-000c294c357c",
    "owner": "5816591a-e016-49bb-093b-000c294c357c",
    "health": "Healthy",
    "revision": "1",
    "type": "NODE_FAULT_DOMAIN",
    "flag": "2",
    "minHostVersion": "0",
    "md5sum": "ab20f7e0a21c305c361b74ff1b06b012",
    "valueLen": "40",
    "content":
      {"faultDomainId": "f33b9cdb-9a77-eb94-7f45-f5990955687a",
      "faultDomainName": "Rack2"},
    "errorStr": "(null)"
  }
]
}
```

In the output in Listing 22.1, I wrapped the lines and indented the content field's values. In this example, the fault domains have the following properties (highlighted in the output):

- **faultDomainId**—32138073-e900-d4d3-6910-ba18d6b16dd2

- **faultDomainName**—Rack1

- **faultDomainId**—f33b9cdb-9a77-eb94-7f45-f5990955687a

- **faultDomainName**—Rack2

In this example, I had no VMs on the datastore. However, I had enabled vSAN Performance Service, which created a database on the .vsan.stats namespace. The virtual SAN default storage policy, which was FTT = 1, was applied to that namespace. Because I split the vSAN nodes into two FDs, the .vsan.stats namespace object shows as noncompliant (see Figure 22.3).

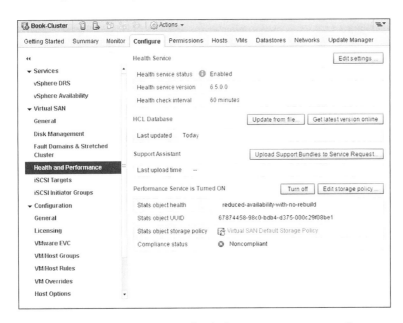

Figure 22.3 vSAN Performance Service's namespace noncompliance

Why would this happen even when there are three nodes in each FD?

The reason is that the three nodes in each FD are treated as a single entity for the purpose of fault tolerance, which is the purpose of using FDs.

Because the default policy is FTT = 1, the number of fault domains required is three. This means that what I did here was to artificially introduce one host failure for any object configured with FTT = 1. That is why the `Stats` object health field shows `reduced-availability-with-no-rebuild` state. I should remedy this situation before things get worse.

TIP

I prefer to equate each FD to a vSAN node for the purpose of calculating design minimum requirements. In other words, if a configuration requires three nodes minimum, I would have to design three FDs.

With this in mind, if I plan on using RAID 5 or RAID 6 erasure coding in my vSAN cluster design, I would require four FDs or six FDs, respectively.

The correct design is to split the cluster nodes over at least three racks and three corresponding FDs or to use a witness VM and configure a stretched cluster. vSAN 6.6 introduced the nested fault domain concept for stretched cluster configurations. That solution would avoid this constraint and mitigate the risk of a single node failure within a fault domain. For more details on this, see the "Nested vSAN Fault Domains" section, later in this chapter.

To rearrange the configuration to include a third FD, follow this procedure, continuing from the FD creation procedure:

1. While in the Fault Domains & Stretched Cluster menu option in the Virtual SAN section, click the **Create new fault domain** icon.

2. Enter the new FD name (for example, `Rack3`).

3. Select **All hosts** from the **Show** pull-down menu to see all hosts, including those that are part of a fault domain (see Figure 22.4).

4. Select the hosts to move to this new FD.

5. Click **OK**.

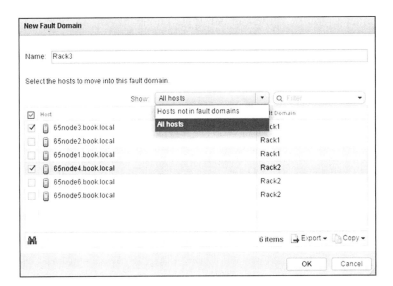

Figure 22.4   Selecting hosts to move to FD

Now I have three FDs with two hosts in each. Figure 22.5 shows the final state.

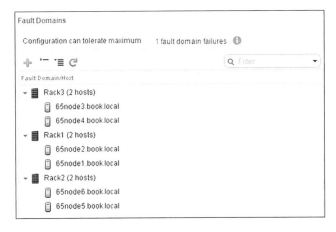

Figure 22.5   Hosts assigned to three FDs

Having the third FD should now resolve the storage policy noncompliance state of the
.vsan.stats namespace. However, the UI still shows that the state is noncompliant.
A simple refresh of the vSphere Web Client view is all I actually need to do because the

policy compliance is remediated automatically when the cause of noncompliance has been remediated. The best way to refresh the view is by clicking the refresh arrow (which looks like a circular arrow) located between the home icon and the current user name listed at the top of the vSphere 6.x Web Client UI (see Figure 22.6).

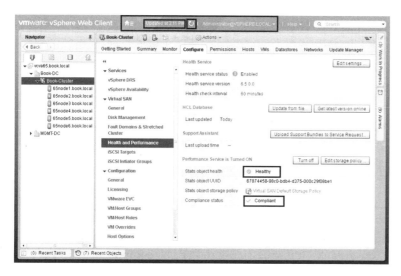

Figure 22.6   vSAN Performance Service's namespace compliance

After refreshing the view, observe that "updated at <time>" is displayed.

Component Placement on Fault Domains

Creating vSAN objects on a cluster with FDs results in placing components in the same fashion as without FDs. The only difference is that each FD is treated like a vSAN node for the purpose of component placement.

In this example, I created a VM with two virtual disks using the **virtual SAN default storage policy**. The first one is 100GiB, and the second is 300GiB.

To display component placement, you monitor the VM's policies.

Figure 22.7 shows the first virtual disk's component placement.

Observe that each replica is on a separate FD, and the witness is on the third FD.

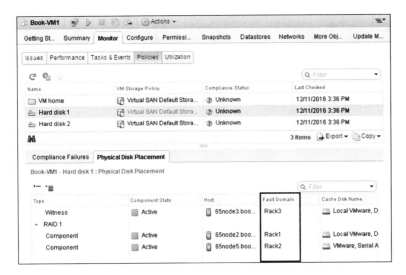

Figure 22.7   Small RAID 1 object's component placement on fault domains

Because the second virtual disk's size, 300GiB, is more than the maximum component size, 255GiB, the RAID 1 replicas have been further split into RAID 0 components, as shown in Figure 22.8.

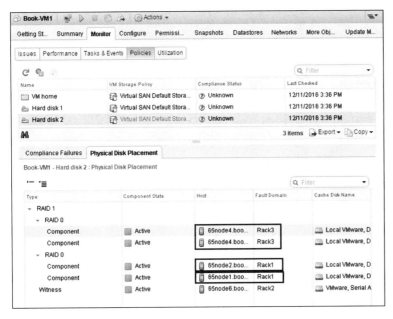

Figure 22.8   Large RAID 1 object's component placement on hosts within fault domains for objects >255GiB

Observe that while the replica on the `Rack3` FD was split into two RAID 0 components and placed on the same host, `65node4`, its mirror replica on the `Rack1` FD was also split into two RAID 0 components but was placed on separate hosts (`65node1` and `65node2`) in the `Rack1` FD. The witness component was placed on the `Rack2` FD. This is a good example of the variations in component placement depending on several factors that the Cluster Level Object Manager (CLOM) considers in making placement decisions.

The reason for the decision to split each RAID 1 replica into smaller RAID 0 components was that the object's size is larger than 255GiB. The rule here is to meet the component max size constraint (capacity) and not for performance. This means that when the RAID 0 components are placed on the same host, they can also be on the same capacity tier disk, if needed.

In contrast to the last use case, I created a similarly sized `vmdk` object (300GiB) and applied a RAID 10 policy to it. The outcome is to create the same number of components with one major difference: While the RAID 1 configurations were placed on separate FDs, the RAID 0 components of each RAID 1 configuration were placed on separate disks on a single host in each FD. The rationale for this is that CLOM attempts first to place RAID 0 stripes on different disks in one or more disk groups on one host. If insufficient space is available, the RAID 0 components may be placed on different hosts in the same FD. However, best effort is made for same host placement than placement on different hosts.

Figure 22.9 shows the resulting component placement.

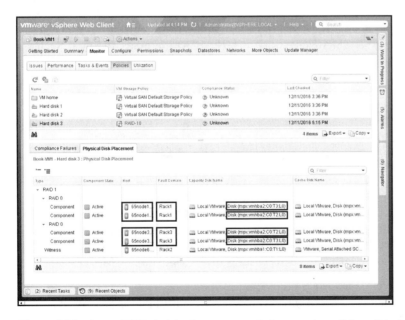

Figure 22.9   Large RAID 1 object's component placement on disks within fault domains

In this example, if Host 1 (65node1) or Host 2 (65node2) fails, the Rack1 FD is considered to have failed altogether. In this case, both RAID 0 components are in the absent state, and the object is in the degraded state.

As demonstrated in the last three use cases, replicas are guaranteed to be placed in separate FDs and the witness component on a third FD. If I had enough hosts to configure four or six FDs, RAID 5 or RAID 6 would be possible, and each component would be placed in a separate FD. With RAID 5 or RAID 6, there would be no witness components. However, with nested fault domains, RAID 5 and RAID 6 can be achieved with two top FDs that have enough hosts in each to meet the corresponding minimum host number requirements. The section "Nested vSAN Fault Domains," later in the chapter, covers this concept in more detail.

Stretched Clusters

Disaster avoidance and automated recovery are among the business requirements for organizations that stand to suffer significant financial losses if a datacenter or a site experiences a catastrophe. One of the design concepts used to avoid such disasters is referred to as *stretched clusters*.

Taking advantage of the fault domains feature in vSAN (see the previous section, "**Fault Domains**"), VMware introduced stretched clusters in vSAN 6.1 (vSphere 6.0, Update 1). The basic design elements for this feature are two fault domains (one in each data site) and a witness host, or virtual appliance, in a third site. In this configuration, vSAN cluster nodes are split evenly between the two data sites, which are within metro distance. Such configurations are commonly referred to as $N+N+1$, where N is the number of nodes in each data site, and 1 refers to the witness host, or virtual appliance.

> **NOTE**
>
> In this case, *metro* refers to a metropolitan area, which means an area within a city. A network backbone connecting data center networks within such an area is referred to as a metropolitan area network (MAN). Sometimes a MAN is also called a campus network because it connects buildings within the same campus.

vSAN node states are assigned such that the cluster master is in one data site, and the cluster backup is in the second data site. This ensures that a copy of the CMMDS database exists on each data site.

A vSAN stretched cluster requires a specific license. Table 22.1 lists these licenses.

Table 22.1 vSAN stretched cluster licensing

vSAN Version	Supported Licenses
6.1	Enterprise
6.2	Enterprise
6.5	Enterprise
6.6	Enterprise

> **NOTE**
>
> Before proceeding, create a vSphere cluster that will be used by vSAN and add it to it all ESXi hosts that will participate in the vSAN cluster. Apply to the cluster the corresponding vSAN license that includes the vSAN stretched cluster option.

A vSAN Stretched Cluster Inter-data Site Network

The distance between data sites can vary, as long as the network meets the following requirements:

- Latency cannot be greater than 5 milliseconds round-trip time (RTT).

- Bandwidth depends on the workload. However, VMware recommends 10Gbps or faster.

- A Layer 2 stretched network or Layer 3 network is required. A Layer 2 stretched network makes VMs' movements between sites easier as there is no need to reconfigure the IP addresses of the VMs' networks.

Calculating a vSAN Network's Minimum Bandwidth Requirement

While VMware recommends 10Gbps bandwidth for an intersite vSAN network, the actual requirement can be calculated based on anticipated workload.

The formula to calculate the minimum bandwidth is as follows:

$$B = WB \times MD \times MR$$

where:

- B is the bandwidth between data sites.

- WB (write bandwidth) is the required bandwidth for the basic write IOPS. Read bandwidth is not a factor here because read I/O is done from the cache local to the data site and does not cross the intersite network.

- MD (metadata multiplier) is the overhead of the vSAN metadata traffic and related operations. 1.4 is the VMware recommended multiplier.

- MR (resync multiplier) is the overhead of resync-related events in addition to actual resync needed bandwidth. The VMware recommended multiplier is 25% added to the base vSAN bandwidth—that is, 125% (1.25 including resync bandwidth).

For example, consider a vSAN stretched cluster with the following I/O profile:

- **Workload**—25,000 read IOPS and 10,000 write IOPS

- **Write I/O size**—4KB (not KiB)

To calculate the write bandwidth, multiply the write IOPS by the I/O size and divide by 1000 to convert the results into MB unites (1MB = 1000KB):

$10,000 \times 4 / 1000 = 40$MBps, or 320Mbps ($40$MB $\times 8$ bits to convert to Mbps)

Calculate the minimum vSAN network bandwidth:

320Mbps $\times 1.4 \times 1.25 = 560$Mbps

In light of these calculations, for a workload with 100,000 write IOPS (4KB size), the bandwidth would be 10 times the calculation—that is, 5,600Mbps (or 5.6Gbps).

Following this pattern, the maximum write IOPS count that would saturate a 10Gbps connection would be around 170,000 IOPS (4KB size I/O), which is calculated as follows:

Write bandwidth = $170,000 \times 4 / 1000 = 680$MBps, or 5440 Mbps

Minimum vSAN network bandwidth = $5440 \times 1.4 \times 1.25 = 9520$Mbps (or 9.52Gbps)

vSAN Stretched Cluster Witness

The vSAN stretched cluster architecture requires a separate vSAN node to host the witness components. Because there is very small workload on that node, to be more economical, VMware designed a specialized virtual appliance that runs a nested ESXi server to store the witness components. (*Nested* means running ESXi server within a virtual machine.) This ESXi server cannot run any virtual machines and uses a built-in license that does not count against the total CPU count of your existing vSphere and vSAN licenses. However, the host on which the witness virtual appliance runs must be licensed.

The virtual appliance is available for download at the same location where vSphere 6.x binaries are available.

Because the witness virtual appliance or host will be the tie-breaker in case of intersite network connectivity failure, it must run in a third site, outside the two data sites (which can also be in a cloud datacenter). It can be connected to both sites using a more relaxed network connectivity requirements than is used for a vSAN network between data sites.

vSAN Stretched Cluster Witness-to-Data-Sites Network

The network connection between the witness virtual appliance and each vSAN cluster data site must meet or exceed the following requirements:

- Latency cannot be greater than 200ms RTT.

- Bandwidth can be 100Mbps or greater.

- A Layer 3 network is required.

Deploying a Witness Virtual Appliance

Before configuring a vSAN stretched cluster, an external witness host or VM must be deployed. The witness VM is available in *Open Virtualization Appliance* (*OVA*) format. This format is a portable packaging of a VM template that includes all the required files and configurations in a single package.

> **NOTE**
>
> Make sure to download the most recently posted version of the OVA file for the corresponding vSAN version.
>
> For example, the OVA version 6.1 initial build does not include separate management and vSAN virtual networks. Instead, it offers a single virtual NIC for both types of traffic. Two additional builds have been posted at the time of this writing, and the newest build is named 6.1b. For OVA version 6.2, the newest build is named 6.2a, and for OVA version 6.5, the newest build is named 6.5d. The newest build has resolved a few other issues.

To deploy a witness VM from the OVA, follow this procedure:

> **NOTE**
>
> This example uses version 6.5d.

1. Download the witness OVA file from the VMware download site. You can store the file locally on your management desktop or on an internal website.

2. Connect to the vCenter server using the vSphere 6.x Web Client as a user with Administrator privileges. This example uses vSphere 6.5, Patch 2.

3. Navigate to the **Hosts and Clusters** view.

4. Right-click a host object located outside both data sites and then select the **Deploy OVF Template** menu option.

5. Enter the VM name, ensure that the correct external datacenter is selected, and then click **Next**.

6. If you placed the OVA file on a web server, select the **URL** radio button and enter the URL of the file location. Skip to step 9.

7. If you stored the OVA file locally, select the **Local file** radio button and then click the **Browse** button.

8. Navigate to the location where the file is stored locally. Select the file and then click **Open**.

9. Click **Next**.

10. Select the datacenter that is external to both stretched cluster data sites.

11. Click **Next**.

12. Select a host on which to run the witness VM. This host must be configured with a network that can reach the vSAN cluster network on both data sites.

13. Click **Next**.

14. Review the template details and then click **Next**.

15. Read and accept the VMware end user license agreement (EULA) and then click **Next**.

16. Select the Configuration size that meets the planned maximum number of VMs to be stored on the vSAN stretched cluster. These are the available sizes (see Figure 22.10):

    - **Tiny**—10 VMs or fewer

    - **Medium**—Up to 500 VMs

    - **Large**—More than 500 VMs

17. Click **Next**.

Figure 22.10   Selecting the witness VM configuration size

18. Select the virtual disk format and the datastore on which to store the VM and then click **Next**.

19. Select the destination network for the witness network and management network and then click **Next**.

> **NOTE**
>
> In the network selection step, there is an IP Allocation Settings section at the bottom of the dialog. While the IP allocation is set to Static, Manual, the wizard does not allow for specifying the static IP settings. This results in the appliance obtaining a DHCP IP address instead. See the "Customizing Nested ESXi Witness VM Network" section, later in this chapter, for how to configure static IP.

20. Enter the root account password for the nested ESXi host that will run in this VM. Confirm the password and then click **Next**.

21. Review the configuration data, and if no changes are required, click **Finish**.

22. Monitor the **Recent Tasks** pane in the vSphere Web Client for the progress of the VM deployment.

23. Once the VM is deployed successfully, power on the VM and launch the remote console to monitor its boot process.

Customizing the Nested ESXi Witness VM Network

Out of the box, the witness VM is configured with DHCP. It is recommended to use static IP and DNS configuration. To modify this configuration, follow this procedure continuing from the previous section, "Deploying a Witness Virtual Appliance." To customize the nested ESXi witness VM network, follow these steps:

1. In the VM remote console, press **F2** and log on to the Direct Connect UI (DCUI) as root.

2. Scroll to the **Configure Management Network** menu option and press **Enter**.

3. Scroll to the **IPv4 Configuration** menu option and press **Enter**.

4. Scroll to the **Set static IPv4 address and network configuration** menu option and press the spacebar to select it.

5. Enter the **IPv4 Address**, **Subnet Mask**, **Default Gateway** and press **Enter** (see Figure 22.11).

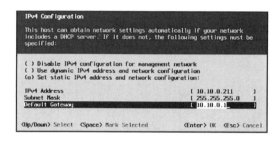

Figure 22.11   Configuring static IPv4 on a witness host or VM

6. Scroll to the **DNS Configuration** menu option and press **Enter**.

7. Scroll to the **Use the following DNS server addresses and hostname** menu option and press the spacebar to select it.

8. Enter the primary DNS server IP address and the host name.

9. Press **Enter** to save the changes (see Figure 22.12).

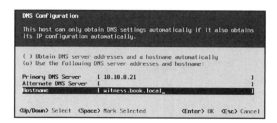

Figure 22.12   Configuring static DNS on a witness host or VM

10. Scroll to the **Custom DNS Suffixes** menu option and press **Enter**.

11. Enter the DNS domain suffix(s) and press **Enter**.

    If the vSAN version is 6.2 or newer, stop here and continue to the next section. For vSAN 6.1, continue with step 12 to remove IPv6 configuration because that version does not support it.

12. Scroll to the **IPv6 Configuration** menu option and press **Enter**.

13. Scroll to the **Disable IPv6 (restart required)** menu option and press the spacebar to select it.

14. Press **Enter** to save the changes and return to **Configure Management Network** menu.

15. Press **Esc**. The dialog shown in Figure 22.13 appears, asking you whether to apply the changes and reboot the host.

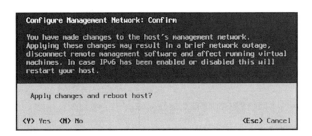

Figure 22.13   Confirming the management network

16. Press **Y** to confirm and reboot the appliance.

Next you need to add the nested ESXi witness node to a datacenter.

Adding a Nested ESXi Witness Node to a Datacenter

Now that the witness appliance is configured and booted, it needs to be added to a datacenter. It must not be added to a cluster because it will be used as the external witness node in the vSAN stretched cluster.

The procedure for adding the node to a datacenter is identical to the procedure for adding a physical ESXi host. During this process, ensure that the included witness vSphere license is applied.

Verifying Witness Network Configuration

A witness VM is preconfigured with two standard vSwitches: `vSwitch0` and `witnessS-switch`.

To verify the network configuration, follow this procedure:

1. Connect to the vCenter server using the vSphere 6 Web Client as a user with Administrator privileges. This example uses vSphere 6.5, Patch 2.

2. Navigate to the **Hosts and Clusters** view.

3. Select the witness host under its datacenter. In this example, the datacenter is called `Witness-DC`, and the host is `witness.book.local`.

4. Select the **Configure** tab or right-click the host object and then select the **Settings** menu option.

5. Select the **VMkernel adapters** menu option in the Networking section.

6. Select `vmk1` in the VMkernel Adapters pane and take note of the IP address assigned to it.

7. Select the **Properties** tab in the lower pane. Verify that **Enabled services** under Port properties says **Virtual SAN** (see Figure 22.14).

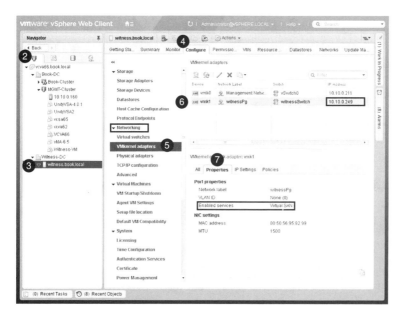

Figure 22.14   Verifying nested witness network configuration

8. Log on to the witness ESXi node as root via SSH. (You may need to enable SSH and ESXi Shell on it first)

9. Ping the IP address of the vSAN VMKNIC on each vSAN node candidate in both data sites. You can do so by using `vmkping`, as shown in Listing 22.2

Listing 22.2   Pinging the witness IP address from vSAN node candidates

```
[root@witness:~] vmkping -I vmk1 10.10.0.156
PING 10.10.0.156 (10.10.0.156): 56 data bytes
64 bytes from 10.10.0.156: icmp_seq=0 ttl=64 time=1.069 ms
64 bytes from 10.10.0.156: icmp_seq=1 ttl=64 time=1.745 ms
64 bytes from 10.10.0.156: icmp_seq=2 ttl=64 time=2.200 ms
--- 10.10.0.156 ping statistics ---
3 packets transmitted, 3 packets received, 0% packet loss
round-trip min/avg/max = 1.069/1.671/2.200 ms
```

The last line in the output shows the round-trip (latency) stats in milliseconds. The max should not exceed 200ms RTT.

Repeat this ping from a host in the first data site to a host in the second data site. The latency should not exceed 5ms RTT.

TIP

To test a jumbo frame, add `-s 9000` to the `vmkping` command.

NOTE

`vmkping` offers only abbreviated arguments/options.

Configuring a Stretched Cluster

Configuring a stretched cluster is a straightforward wizard-driven procedure. However, before starting it, you need to make sure that all items on this list have already been done:

- The vSAN network between sites has been configured and tested.

- The witness network between sites and the location where the witness host or VM is located is configured and tested.

■ Relevant valid licenses have been applied to vCenter, the cluster, and each vSAN node in both sites. See Table 22.1, earlier in this chapter, for license requirements for each vSAN version.

You can configure the stretched cluster at vSAN cluster configuration time or after a single cluster has been created. The latter is mostly the case when an existing cluster is being reconfigured to a stretched one.

Configuring a Newly Created Cluster

This procedure assumes that you have already created a cluster and added ESXi hosts to it but have not yet enabled any cluster features. Follow these steps to configure a newly created cluster:

1. Connect to the vCenter server using the vSphere 6, Update 1 or later Web Client as a user with Administrator privileges.

2. Navigate to the **Hosts and Clusters** view.

3. Right-click the cluster object in the inventory tree and then select **Settings**.

4. Select **General** in the Virtual SAN section.

5. Click the **Configure** button. The Configure vSAN Wizard appears.

6. In step 1 of the wizard, select the **Configure stretched cluster** option in the Fault Domains and Stretched Cluster section and then click **Next**.

7. Steps 2 and 3 of the wizard are similar to the steps involved in creating a new cluster, as explained in the section "Creating and Configuring a vSAN Cluster" in Chapter 21.

   Step 4 of the wizard is where you name both data sites and place each host in its corresponding data site. The default site names are Preferred and Secondary. By default, all hosts are in the Preferred FD.

8. Select one or more hosts from the list. (Hold down the **Ctrl** key and click to select multiple hosts.)

9. Click the button with two right arrows to move the selected hosts to the Secondary FD (see Figure 22.15).

10. Click **Next**.

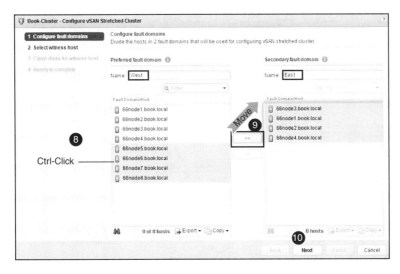

Figure 22.15 Assigning hosts to the stretched cluster data site at cluster creation

11. In step 5 of the wizard, select a witness host from the inventory tree. The wizard checks the selected host for the required configurations. If it passes, the `Compatibility checks succeeded` message is displayed in the Compatibility pane (see Figure 22.16).

12. Click **Next**.

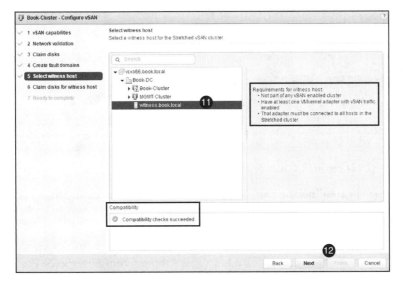

Figure 22.16 Configuring a stretched cluster at creation time

13. In step 6 of the wizard, select cache and capacity tier disks from the listed devices. In this example, I am using a witness virtual appliance that includes one cache and one capacity tier disks. Select each disk.

14. Click **Next** (see Figure 22.17).

Figure 22.17   Claiming disks for the witness host

15. In the final step of the wizard, review your settings, and if no changes are needed, click **Finish**.

Reconfiguring an Existing Cluster

To reconfigure an existing vSAN cluster as a stretched cluster, do the following:

1. Connect to the vCenter server using the vSphere 6.0 Update 1 or later Web Client as a user with Administrator privileges.

2. Navigate to the **Hosts and Clusters** view.

3. Right-click the cluster object in the inventory tree and then select **Settings**.

4. Select the **Fault Domains & Stretched Cluster** option in the Virtual SAN section.

5. Click the **Configure** button in the stretched clusters pane. The Configure vSAN Stretched Cluster Wizard appears. This is a subset of the Configure vSAN Wizard used in the previous procedure. It has four steps:

- Configure fault domains

- Select witness host

- Claim disks for witness host

- Ready to complete

6. In the Configure Fault Domains step, select the hosts to assign to each data site, click the right or left arrow button to move them to their corresponding fault domain, and then click **Next**.

7. Select the witness host from the inventory tree and then click **Next**.

8. Select the disks to claim for the witness host. In this example, I have one disk each.

Figure 22.18 shows the final results.

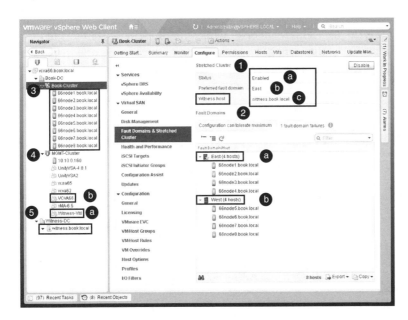

Figure 22.18   Stretched cluster configuration results

The final results of this example show the following:

1. Stretched Cluster pane:

   a. **Status**—Enabled

   b. **Preferred fault domain**—East

   c. **Witness host**—witness.book.local

2. Fault Domains pane:

   a. East fault domain has four hosts

   b. West fault domain has four hosts

3. Book-Cluster has eight nodes. Note that the witness node is not included in the vSAN cluster nodes because it is an external witness node. It is listed in the Stretched Cluster pane instead (see item 1-c in Figure 22.18).

4. MGMT-Cluster, which is located at a third site, shows the following:

   a. Witness-VM—This is the nested ESXi VM running the witness host.

   b. VCVA66—This is the vCenter server virtual appliance.

   In this example, the design calls for separating the management resources from the compute and storage resources, into two separate clusters.

5. Witness-DC—This is the datacenter where all witness nodes are registered. This DC physically resides within the management site because the witness nodes are actually nested ESXi hosts running as VMs in the MGMT-Cluster. Configuring HA in the MGMT-Cluster provides better availability for the witness VMs, which, in turn, translates to witness node availability.

Figure 22.19 shows the logical design of the three sites in this example.

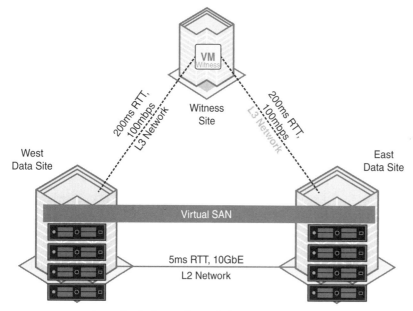

Figure 22.19 Stretched cluster logical design

This configuration is equivalent to a three-node cluster in which one node is the witness host or witness VM and each of the two data sites is in a separate fault domain. This means that the highest FTT setting can be 1 only. In other words, only RAID 1 or RAID 10 can be configured.

Figure 22.20 shows a VM with two virtual disks.

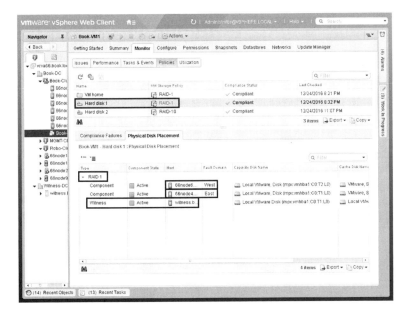

Figure 22.20 Effect of RAID 1 policy on a VM on a vSAN stretched cluster

The VM home (namespace) and `Hard disk 1` have RAID 1 policy applied to them (FTT = 1), while `Hard disk 2` has RAID 10 policy applied (FTT = 1, SW = 3). `Hard disk 1` was selected to show its component placement.

In this example, the RAID 1 object has two replicas, each on a host in separate fault domains, and the witness component is on the witness host.

So far, this looks similar to a single-site cluster with no fault domains configured. The main difference is the enforcement of placing a replica component in each site, regardless of which host is within each site. The other difference is that the witness component is strictly placed on the witness host. In vSAN 6.5 and earlier (6.2 and 6.1), you never see the witness component placed anywhere outside the witness host. However, this changed in vSAN 6.6, with the introduction of nested fault domains, as discussed in more detail in the section "Nested vSAN Fault Domains," later in the chapter.

In this example, the preferred domain is East, which means that if network connectivity between data sites fails while each site maintains network connectivity with the witness host, vSAN will count the witness's votes with the East FD's votes to gain a majority. This means that all I/Os to the DOM objects will be done only on components located in the East FD.

Continuing on with the comparison between vSAN stretched clusters and single-site vSAN clusters, let's take a closer look at Hard disk 2 in this VM with a RAID 10 policy applied (see Figure 22.21).

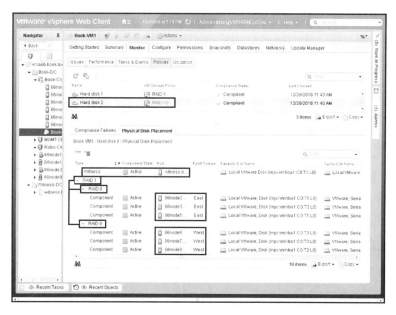

Figure 22.21   Effect of RAID 10 policy on a VM on a vSAN stretched cluster

In this example, the RAID 1 replicas are two RAID 0 configurations. Three stripes of one RAID 0 configuration are placed on three hosts in the West FD, and the other RAID 0 stripes are placed on two hosts in the East FD: one on Host 5 and two on Host 3 (on separate disks, though). The witness is, again, on the witness host.

The main difference between a single-site cluster without fault domains and this configuration is that each RAID 1 replica is guaranteed to be placed in a separate fault domain. The witness component is on the witness host, whereas a vSAN host is within the single site cluster.

Using RVC to List Stretched Cluster Witness Information

You can use RVC to list vSAN stretched cluster witness information with the `vsan.stretchedcluster.witness_info` command.

Listing 22.3 shows this command and its output.

Listing 22.3   Using RVC to list witness information

```
/vcva66/Book-DC/computers> vsan.stretchedcluster.witness_info Book-Cluster
Found witness host for Virtual SAN stretched cluster.
+-----------------------+---------------------------------------+
| Stretched Cluster     | Book-Cluster                          |
+-----------------------+---------------------------------------+
| Witness Host Name     | witness.book.local                    |
| Witness Host UUID     | 585ecbbe-506d-431c-30e1-005056b5b4b0  |
| Preferred Fault Domain| East                                  |
| Unicast Agent Address | 10.10.0.211                           |
+-----------------------+---------------------------------------+
```

This output was taken from a vSAN 6.6 environment and is self-explanatory. Observe the use of a unicast network by the stretched cluster—hence the `Unicast Agent Address` field.

vSAN Stretched Cluster I/O Path

In RAID 1 configurations, a VM's DOM objects each have one replica on each FD. To optimize read I/Os on vSAN stretched clusters, they are done from the cache and replica located within the FD where the VM runs. In other words, data proximity is leveraged for read I/O in this scenario.

If a storage component on the host that stores the local replica's component fails, the read I/O is done from the remote cache and replica until the absent component is recovered.

On the other hand, write I/O must be acknowledged by all replicas of the DOM object before returning acknowledgement to the VM that initiated the I/O. Thus, regardless of where the VM runs, the write I/O is mirrored on both FDs.

vSAN Stretched Cluster Failure Modes

The vSAN heartbeat is sent once a second. A failure is detected if a heartbeat is missing five consecutive times.

The possible failures in a vSAN stretched cluster, from the perspective of affected DOM objects' availability, can be any of the following:

- **Data site failure**—By design, a vSAN stretched cluster protects against site failure. If the whole site suffers a catastrophic failure, the surviving site that still maintains network connectivity to the witness host resumes I/O to the DOM objects via components on the surviving site—but in `Reduced Availability` state. This is due to the fact that the available vote count is more than 50% of total votes. This failure mode affects all DOM objects on the datastore. HA restarts the VMs that were running on the failed site so that they now run on the surviving site. Figure 22.22 depicts a site failure.

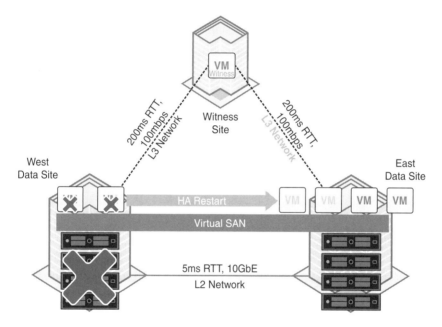

Figure 22.22   Example of failure mode: One site failure with RAID 1 objects

- **Network connectivity lost between data sites (intersite network partition):**

    - If both sites maintain network connectivity to the witness host or VM, the preferred site gets the majority of the votes with the aid of the witness components' votes.

    - HA restarts the VMs that were running on the non-preferred FD so that they now run on the preferred FD.

    - This failure mode affects all DOM objects on the datastore. They get into `Reduced Availability` state.

Figure 22.23 depicts an intersite network partition.

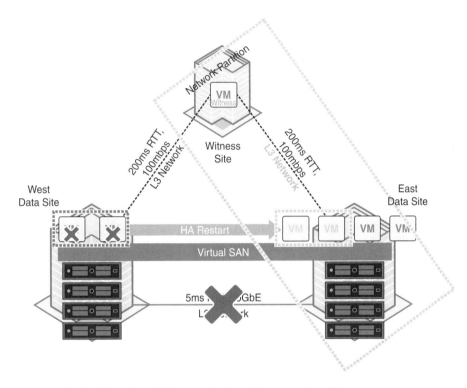

Figure 22.23 Example of failure mode: Intersite network partition

- **Network connectivity lost between witness node and both data sites (witness is isolated; see Figure 22.24):**
  - Failure is detected if both master and backup nodes do not receive a witness heartbeat five consecutive times.
  - Both data sites are in one network partition, and the witness is in a second network partition.
  - This is similar to no failures because the votes on both sites combined is still >50% of votes. However, objects are in `Non-compliant` state.
  - If any component fails while the DOM object is in this state, the object goes into `Inaccessible` state because <50% of votes are available.
  - No HA is triggered by this failure mode.
  - Resync with the witness begins when network connectivity is restored.

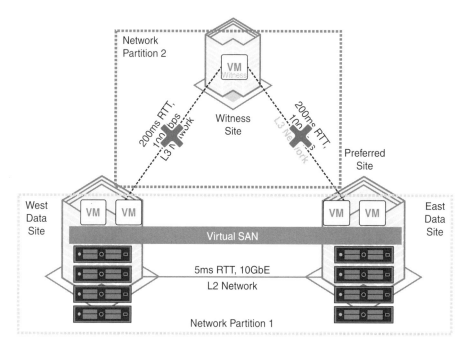

Figure 22.24   Example of failure mode: Witness network partition

- **Network connectivity lost between witness and nonpreferred FD**—The outcome depends on which version of vSAN is in use:

  - **vSAN versions 6.1 and 6.2**: Quorum (>50% of votes) remains with the witness and preferred FD. This is the same as a intersite network partition because the preferred FD is still connected even though both data sites are still connected.

  - **vSAN versions 6.5 and newer**: The witness must have access to both master and backup nodes (preferred and nonpreferred sites). If it loses access to one of them, the outcome is similar to the witness VM getting isolated from both FDs. In other words, the quorum is established between both data sites, and no HA is triggered.

- **Network connectivity lost between witness and preferred FD**: The outcome depends on which version of vSAN is in use:

  - **vSAN versions 6.1 and 6.2**: The witness forces quorum with the nonpreferred FD. HA restarts the VMs that were running on the preferred FD so that they now run on the nonpreferred FD.

- **vSAN version 6.5 and newer**: This is the same as the previous failure mode (witness partitioned) for versions 6.5 and newer (see Figure 22.25).

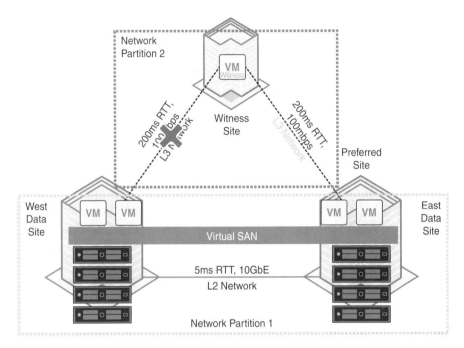

Figure 22.25   Example of failure mode: Witness to preferred FD network loss on vSAN 6.5 and newer

---

NOTE

The last two failure modes also apply to ROBO clusters (covered later in this chapter).

- **Single-host failure in one data site (see Figure 22.26):**
    - HA restarts VMs that were running on the failed host so that they now run on another node in the same site. If no resources are available, DRS may move the VM to the other data site.
    - The witness is notified of affected objects.
    - If the host does not recover in 60 minutes, components on that host are rebuilt on another node in the same site if there is no violation of storage policy.
    - The witness is notified when the components rebuild is complete.

■ The affected DOM objects are those with components on the failed host.

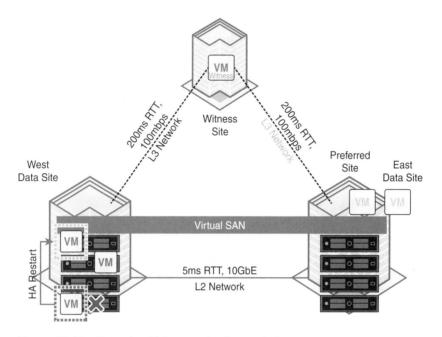

Figure 22.26   Example of failure mode: One node failure

■ **Single host decommissioned (maintenance mode with full data migration)—** Similar to host failure but resync starts as soon as possible.

■ **Single capacity disk failure in one data site—**The witness is notified of affected objects. Resync starts to rebuild missing components in the affected site in the case of sufficient capacity tier disks. The affected DOM objects are those with components on the failed capacity disk. No HA is triggered by this failure mode.

■ **Multiple capacity disk failures within one data site—**This is similar to single disk failure. The affected DOM objects are those with components on the failed disks.

■ **Single cache disk failure in one data site—**This results in disk group failure. The effect is similar to multiple disk failure on a single host. The affected DOM objects are those with components on the failed disk group.

■ **Multiple cache disks failures within the same data site—**This results in corresponding disk groups' failure. Recovery depends on the number of nodes with sufficient capacity tier disks, as long as no storage policy is violated. Affected DOM objects are those with components on the failed disk groups. No HA is triggered in this failure mode.

- **Single capacity disk failure in each data site**—DOM objects that have any components residing on *both* failed disks are in `Inaccessible` state. Otherwise, they would be in `Degraded` state.

- **Single host failure in each site**—DOM objects that have any components residing on *both* failed hosts are in `Inaccessible` state. Otherwise, they would be in `Degraded` state.

- **Single cache disk failure in each site**—This results in failure of the corresponding disk groups. DOM objects that have any components residing on *both* disk groups are in `Inaccessible` state; otherwise, they would be in `Degraded` state.

- **Witness node failure**—This is similar to the witness isolated failure mode discussed earlier. If the witness node is not recoverable, create a new node and add it to the stretched cluster. This can be done by disabling the stretched cluster and then enabling it and then selecting the new witness node.

- **Any disk failure in witness VM**—This is the same as witness node failure because the VM has one cache and one capacity tier disks. If a physical witness host is used, the outcome depends on the number of failed disk and in which tier:

  - If the cache tier fails, the effect is similar to a witness node failure.

  - If one of the capacity tier disks fails, the effect is similar to a witness node failure but is limited to the DOM objects whose witness components reside on the failed disk. If enough capacity tier space is available, the absent witness component is re-created.

> **NOTE**
>
> Depending on the failure mode, if a single failure of a RAID 1 object lasts more than 60 minutes, vSAN creates a new mirror replica from the surviving component. The new component is placed on another host or disk in the same data site as the failed component as long as this does not violate the object's storage policy. This does not apply to full site failure because no resources will be available on which to create the new replica.

Sample UI and `cmmds-tool` Output from vSAN Stretched Cluster Failures

To give you an idea about how DOM objects are impacted by some of the failure modes discussed in the previous section, I share some screenshots and outputs in this section. The screenshots are taken from the vSAN 6.6 UI while in the **Virtual Objects** tab. To reach that tab, follow this procedure:

1. Connect to the vCenter server using the vSphere 6 Web Client as a user with Administrator privileges.

2. Navigate to the **Hosts and Clusters** view.

3. Select the cluster object in the inventory tree. In this example, it is called `Book-Cluster`.

4. Select the **Monitor** tab.

5. Click the **vSAN** button (or the **Virtual SAN** button in versions earlier than vSAN 6.6).

6. Select the **Virtual Objects** section.

7. Locate the affected VM in the list and expand it to list its objects.

8. Select the object whose health status is anything other than `Healthy`.

Instead of using the UI, you can obtain DOM object's properties by using the `cmmds-tool`, as follows:

1. Identify the affected VMDK or namespace DOM object's UUID as explained in the section "Listing DOM Object Properties" in Chapter 21.

2. Run this command to obtain the DOM object's properties:

   ```
   cmmds-tool find --format json --type DOM_OBJECT --uuid [object UUID]
   ```

   You can also use the abbreviated version:cmmds-tool find -f json -t DOM_OBJECT -u [object UUID]

   To obtain the `content` field only, append `|grep content` to the end of the command line.

3. To obtain the DOM object owner's UUID, append `|grep owner` to the end of the command line instead.

4. To get the DOM object owner's host name using its UUID, run the following:

   ```
   cmmds-tool find --format json --type HOSTNAME --uuid [owner's UUID]|grep hostname
   ```

   Or you can use the abbreviated version:

   ```
   cmmds-tool find -f json -t HOSTNAME -u [owner's UUID]|grep hostname
   ```

RAID 1 Examples

Host failure of the following examples are for a RAID 1 DOM object after a single host failure in one FD. Figure 22.27 shows the UI.

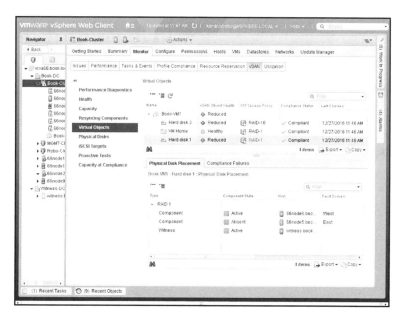

Figure 22.27 Example of a failure mode of one host with a RAID 1 object

Listing 22.4 shows the CLI from the same state. I inserted highlighted comments with left pointing arrows to point out relevant properties.

Listing 22.4 RAID 1 DOM object info after a single host failure in one FD

```
grep vsan /vmfs/volumes/vsanDatastore/Book-VM1/Book-VM1.vmdk
RW 209715200 VMFS "vsan://bc485f58-dd37-c2b0-9b6f-000c29870766"


cmmds-tool find -f json -t DOM_OBJECT -u bc485f58-dd37-c2b0-9b6f-
000c29870766
{
 "entries":
[
 {
    "uuid": "bc485f58-dd37-c2b0-9b6f-000c29870766",
    "owner": "585472f2-a2fe-b12a-9d88-000c29a9b9c2",  ← DOM Owner
    "health": "Healthy",
```

```
"revision": "74",
"type": "DOM_OBJECT",
"flag": "2",
"minHostVersion": "3",
"md5sum": "fba71e08f4d777146f61eaacc9c7db6e",
"valueLen": "1528",
"content": {"type": "Configuration",
    "attributes":
    {"CSN": 48, ← Config Sequence Number
    "SCSN": 48, ← Seal Config Sequence Number
    "addressSpace": 107374182400,
    "scrubStartTime": 1482868435466753,
    "objectVersion": 5,
    "highestDiskVersion": 5,
    "muxGroup": 495577639488512,
    "groupUuid": "9a485f58-7da8-14f3-5edc-000c29870766",
    "compositeUuid": "bc485f58-dd37-c2b0-9b6f-000c29870766"},
    "child-1": {"type": "RAID_1", ← RAID 1 Config
            "attributes":
            {"scope": 3},
            "child-1": {"type": "Component", ← RAID 1 1st Replica
Component
                    "attributes":
                    {"addressSpace": 107374182400,
                    "componentState": 5, ← Active State
                    "componentStateTS": 1482865601,
                    "faultDomainId": "bf495fc0-48d8-d44b-7f32-
536df5cf3930",
                                    Previous line is West FD UUID
                    "subFaultDomainId": "585472f2-a2fe-b12a-9d88-
000c29a9b9c2"},
                                    Previous line is Host 6 UUID
                    "componentUuid": "dfb86258-f1d8-7cc7-aa26-
000c29c1c241",
                    "diskUuid": "52c1ddff-031b-2e57-fd72-ef65e108a198"},
            "child-2": {"type": "Component", ← RAID 1 2nd Replica
Component
                    "attributes":
                    {"addressSpace": 107374182400,
                    "componentState": 6, ← Component state is Absent
                    "componentStateTS": 1482869869,
                    "staleLsn": 440, ← Stale Log Sequence Number
```

```
                    "staleCsn": 47,   ← Stale Config Sequence Number
                    "faultDomainId": "a99dc62d-017d-04cf-6726-
6593f9c3761e",

                               Previous line is East FD UUID
                    "flags": 1, ← Flagged for an error
                    "subFaultDomainId": "585472eb-9df5-502c-25f5-
000c299e6b3f",

                               Previous line is Host 5 UUID
                    "rLsn": 440},
                    "componentUuid": "c6c16258-9db9-d04a-f196-
000c29c1c241",

                    "diskUuid": "52768761-0138-5ab2-8151-be75dad6db8b"}},
        "child-2": {"type": "Witness", ← Witness Component
                "attributes":
                {"componentState": 5,  ← Active State
                "componentStateTS": 1482867658,
                "isWitness": 1,
                "faultDomainId": "585ecbbe-506d-431c-30e1-005056b5b4b0",
                        Previous line is witness Host UUID
                "isFastCCPEnabled": 1, ← Fast Config-Change Proposal enabled
                "subFaultDomainId": "585ecbbe-506d-431c-30e1-005056b5b4b0"},
                        Previous line is witness Host UUID
                "componentUuid": "c8c16258-032a-37a0-5626-000c29c1c241",
                "diskUuid": "5250f7cc-08a9-5b7f-6a68-6c5a434e1c11"}},
    "errorStr": "(null)"
}
[root@66node3:~] cmmds-tool find -f json -t HOSTNAME -u "585472f2-a2fe-
b12a-9d88-000c29a9b9c2"|grep hostname
    "content": {"hostname": "66node6.book.local"}, ← DOM Owner Host Name
```

In this example, RAID 1 object's `child-2` component is in an Absent state (`component-State` = 6). It resides on Host 5, which has failed. That host was in the East FD.

TIP

Witness components residing on a witness host will always have `isFastCCPEnabled` set to 1. This means that DOM can look up the config policy from a surviving replica instead of from the witness component. This is faster because it is done on the vSAN network between data sites, which is usually much faster than on the network to the witness host.

DOM ownership of objects with active I/O is automatically changed to the surviving host in RAID 1 configuration. The DOM owner in this example is a host on the data site where the component is in an `Active` state, which in this example is in the `West` FD. The witness component holds 1 vote, and the surviving RAID 1 component holds one vote. The absent RAID 1 component held one vote. This means that the `West` FD plus the witness hold two out of total three votes, which is >50% of the votes. The outcome is that the object is still accessible but in a `Reduced Availability` state.

RAID 10 Examples

The following examples are from a RAID 10 DOM object after a single host failure in one FD. Figure 22.28 shows the UI.

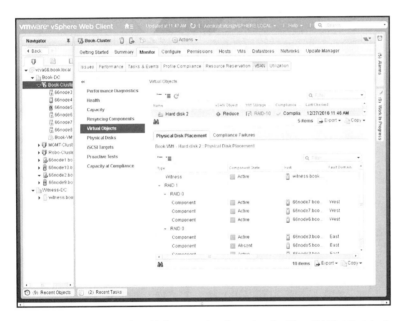

Figure 22.28   Example of failure mode of one host with a RAID 10 object

In this example, one of the stripes of RAID 10 in the `East` data site is in an `Absent` state due to Host 5 failure. This resulted in the DOM object (VMDK) being in a `Reduced availability` state. This means that the majority votes ae still available to maintain access to the object via the `West` data site. Because there are still two hosts left in the `East` data site, if Host 5 does not recover after 60 minutes, the `Absent` component will be repli-cated on one of the two surviving hosts—but striped on two different disk to meet the SW placement policy that is part of RAID 10.

Listing 22.5 shows the CLI for the same example. I inserted highlighted comments with left pointing arrows to point out relevant properties.

Listing 22.5   RAID 10 DOM object info after a single host failure in one FD

```
grep vsan /vmfs/volumes/vsanDatastore/Book-VM1/Book-VM1_1.vmdk
RW 209715200 VMFS "vsan://1f705f58-6ef6-d3a5-bd6f-000c29870766"

cmmds-tool find -f json -t DOM_OBJECT -u 1f705f58-6ef6-d3a5-bd6f-
000c29870766
{
 "entries":
[
 {
   "uuid": "1f705f58-6ef6-d3a5-bd6f-000c29870766", ← DOM Object UUID
   "owner": "5854511c-a92e-62f3-27af-000c29870766", ← DOM Owner
   "health": "Healthy",
   "revision": "52",
   "type": "DOM_OBJECT",
   "flag": "2",
   "minHostVersion": "3",
   "md5sum": "38532f54996de9367214442ddf5a252b",
   "valueLen": "3072",
   "content": {"type": "Configuration",
"attributes":
        {"CSN": 33,
        "SCSN": 33,
        "addressSpace": 107374182400,
        "scrubStartTime": 1482649631792441,
        "objectVersion": 5,
        "highestDiskVersion": 5,
        "muxGroup": 393657495129088,
        "groupUuid": "9a485f58-7da8-14f3-5edc-000c29870766",
        "compositeUuid": "1f705f58-6ef6-d3a5-bd6f-000c29870766"}, ← Same as
Object UUID
        "child-1": {"type": "RAID_1", ← RAID 1 Config
          "attributes":
          {"scope": 3},
            "child-1": {"type": "RAID_0", ← RAID 0 Config - 1st RAID 1 Mirror
            "attributes":
              {"stripeBlockSize": 1048576},
```

```
    "child-1": {"type": "Component",  ← 1st Stripe component of 1st RAID 0
            "attributes":
            {"addressSpace": 35792093184,
            "componentState": 5, ← Component state is Active
            "componentStateTS": 1482801548,
            "faultDomainId": "a99dc62d-017d-04cf-6726-6593f9c3761e",
                    Previous line is East FD UUID
            "lastScrubbedOffset": 35792093184,
            "subFaultDomainId": "5854511c-a92e-62f3-27af- 000c29870766"},
                    Previous line is Host 3 UUID
            "componentUuid": "1f705f58-5905-70a6-dac7-000c29870766",
            "diskUuid": "52246da9-7b49-f221-d94b-cf4acfbb7bb8"},
    "child-2": {"type": "Component",  ← 2nd Stripe component of 1st RAID 0
            "attributes":
            {"addressSpace": 35791044608,
            "componentState": 6, ← Component state is Absent
            "componentStateTS": 1482869869,
            "staleLsn": 342,
            "staleCsn": 32,
            "faultDomainId": "a99dc62d-017d-04cf-6726-6593f9c3761e",
                    Previous line is East FD UUID
            "flags": 1, ← Flagged for an error
            "lastScrubbedOffset": 35791044608,
            "subFaultDomainId": "585472eb-9df5-502c-25f5-000c299e6b3f",
                    Previous line is Host 5 UUID
            "rLsn": 342},
            "componentUuid": "1f705f58-602e-73a6-a4f1-000c29870766",
            "diskUuid": "529d41c4-a49d-4122-c337-0c18588f3191"},
    "child-3": {"type": "Component",  ← 3rd Stripe component of 1st RAID 0
            "attributes":
            {"addressSpace": 35791044608,
            "componentState": 5, ← Component state is Active
            "componentStateTS": 1482801548,
            "faultDomainId": "a99dc62d-017d-04cf-6726-6593f9c3761e",
                    Previous line is East FD UUID
            "lastScrubbedOffset": 35791044608,
            "subFaultDomainId": "5854511c-a92e-62f3-27af-000c29870766"},
                    Previous line is Host 3 UUID
            "componentUuid": "1f705f58-40c7-74a6-8965-000c29870766",
            "diskUuid": "527f8c83-430f-36b0-d7e2-1d62a3f9e3e5"}},
```

```
    "child-2": {"type": "RAID_0", ← RAID 0 Config - 2nd RAID 1 Mirror
          "attributes":
          {"stripeBlockSize": 1048576},
    "child-1": {"type": "Component", ← 1st Stripe component of 2nd RAID 0
              "attributes":
              {"addressSpace": 35792093184,
              "componentState": 5, ← Component state is Active
              "componentStateTS": 1482865606,
              "faultDomainId": "bf495fc0-48d8-d44b-7f32-536df5cf3930",
                       Previous line is West FD UUID
              "subFaultDomainId": "585472f2-a2fe-b12a-9d88-000c29a9b9c2"},
                       Previous line is Host 6 UUID
              "componentUuid": "a2236258-d0c5-c35f-385f-000c29870766",
              "diskUuid": "52d3f3a5-7f2a-dac4-57b3-7b59de7decbe"},
    "child-2": {"type": "Component", ← 2nd Stripe component of 2nd RAID 0
              "attributes":
              {"addressSpace": 35791044608,
              "componentState": 5, ← Component state is Active
              "componentStateTS": 1482864866,
              "faultDomainId": "bf495fc0-48d8-d44b-7f32-536df5cf3930",
                       Previous line is West FD UUID
              "subFaultDomainId": "585472ff-dd82-a3cc-42b7000c29f69b4e"},
                       Previous line is host 7 UUID
              "componentUuid": "e1b86258-5be1-c5a2-3b3c-000c29870766",
              "diskUuid": "52725df5-5f6d-74e7-f812-810960cd76d0"},
    "child-3": {"type": "Component", ← 3rd Stripe component of 2nd RAID 0
              "attributes":
              {"addressSpace": 35791044608,
              "componentState": 5, ← Component state is Active
               "componentStateTS": 1482864865,
              "faultDomainId": "bf495fc0-48d8-d44b-7f32-536df5cf3930",
                       Previous line is West FD UUID
              "subFaultDomainId": "585472ff-dd82-a3cc-42b7-000c29f69b4e"},
                       Previous line is host 7 UUID
              "componentUuid": "e1b86258-2a25-c9a2-995a-000c29870766",
              "diskUuid": "52a7bfee-770c-68eb-c2c9-06aff48bf915"}}},
  "child-2": {"type": "Witness", ← Witness Component of RAID 1 Config
          "attributes":
          {"componentState": 5, ← Component state is Active
          "componentStateTS": 1482867658,
```

```
        "isWitness": 1, ← This component is a witness
        "faultDomainId": "585ecbbe-506d-431c-30e1-005056b5b4b0",
                        Previous line is Witness Host UUID
        "nVotes": 3, ← This witness holds 3 votes
        "isFastCCPEnabled": 1, ← Fast Config-Change Proposal enabled
        "subFaultDomainId": "585ecbbe-506d-431c-30e1-005056b5b4b0"},
                        Previous line is Witness Host UUID
        "componentUuid": "e4b86258-4dc0-3ff7-e4d9-000c29870766",
        "diskUuid": "5250f7cc-08a9-5b7f-6a68-6c5a434e1c11"}},
    "errorStr": "(null)"
  }
]
}


[root@66node3:~] cmmds-tool find -f json -t DOM_OBJECT -u 1f705f58-6ef6-
d3a5-bd6f-000c29870766 |grep owner
    "owner": "5854511c-a92e-62f3-27af-000c29870766", ← DOM Owner UUID


[root@66node3:~] cmmds-tool find -f json -t HOSTNAME -u "5854511c-a92e-
62f3-27af-000c29870766"|grep hostname
    "content": {"hostname": "66node3.book.local"}, ← DOM Owner Host Name
```

In this example, Host 5 in the East FD failed. The RAID 0 stripe component on that host is now in an Absent state. The witness component has three votes. Each RAID 1 replica has three votes—one from each replica's RAID 0 stripe component.

This means that the West FD plus the witness have six of the total nine votes, which is >50%. The outcome is that the object is still accessible but in a Reduced Availability state.

Figure 22.29 shows another example of the same DOM object at a later time, with different component placement collected via the RVC command vsan.object_info.

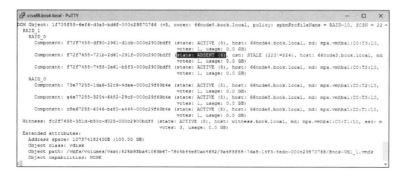

Figure 22.29 Example of failure mode of one host with a RAID 10 object via RVC

This is the command:

```
vsan.object_info /vcva66/Book-DC/computers/[cluster-name] [ObjectUUID]
```

Here is an example:

```
vsan.object_info /vcva66/Book-DC/computers/Book-Cluster 1f705f58-6ef6-d3a5-
bd6f-000c29870766
```

The highlighted text in Figure 2.29 shows that the component state is six, which means `Absent` on the `66node3` host. It also shows the vote count for each component is one, except for the witness, which is three. This matches the same vote assignment as in the previous example (refer to Listing 22.5).

Comparison Between Fault Domains and Stretched Clusters

Fault domain use cases differ from those of vSAN stretched clusters. Table 22.2 compares the features for easier differentiation.

Table 22.2 Comparing fault domains to stretched clusters

Topic	Fault Domains	Stretched Clusters
Main use case	Protect against rack failure	Protect against site failure
Supported FD count	Minimum: 3	Minimum: 3
	Maximum: 64	Maximum: 3
Node configuration	All FDs must be evenly configured (compute storage, node count)	Two data sites must be evenly configured (compute, storage, node count)
		Witness node is a special-purpose nested ESXi node that hosts no data—only witness components.
Storage and compute resources	All FDs contribute to storage and compute resources	Two data sites contribute to storage and compute resources.
		Witness does not contribute to any.

Topic	Fault Domains	Stretched Clusters
Network configuration	Latency: 5ms or less	Intersite: 5ms latency, 10Gbps bandwidth.*
	Bandwidth: 10Gbps	
	Layer 2 network only	Layer 2 stretched or Layer 3 network
		Site witness: 200ms latency, 100Mbps bandwidth
		Layer 3 network

* The actual intersite bandwidth requirement can be determined by the formula detailed earlier in this chapter, in the section "Calculating a vSAN Network's Minimum Bandwidth Requirement."

Nested vSAN Fault Domains

The introduction of the fault domains concept helped mitigate the risk of a single rack failure (rack awareness). However, it imposed a constraint of creating a number of FDs required to meet availability requirements. For example, configuring a RAID 1 (FTT = 1) object requires three FDs or a stretched cluster with a witness VM external to two FDs. The same applies to configuring a RAID 5 or RAID 6 object, which requires four or six FDs, respectively, and cannot be done on a stretched cluster.

This prompted VMware to introduce the concept of nested fault domains in vSAN 6.6. (It was originally planned for release with vSphere 6.5 but got deferred.) The nested FD concept means you can create FDs within the top-level (site) FDs of a vSAN stretched cluster. In other words, each of the two top-level FDs of the stretched cluster supports further grouping of its hosts into child FDs, which can support various RAID types that are, otherwise, supported only with single-site vSAN clusters.

Nested FDs tolerate host and disk failures in addition to site failure in vSAN stretched clusters. Creating nested FDs requires the new on-disk format version 5. (It was supposed to be on-disk format v4. However, due to the confusion that v3 generated, where the UI displayed the on-disk format as v3, while the vSAN metadata listed it as v4, VMware resorted to skipping UI v4 and synced up with the physical on-disk format v5.)

Nested FD Storage Policies

Nested FD are accomplished via new VM storage policy placement rules available in vSphere 6.5, Patch 2:

1. **Primary level of failures to tolerate (PFTT)**—This rule is at the top FD level, which means the replication scope is between sites. In other words, it defines the number of FD or site failures to tolerate. In this release, it is limited to the maximum

value 1, which tolerates a single site failure in a two-site stretched cluster configuration. The UI states that the maximum value is 3; however, the architecture limits it to 1 though. The higher values are reserved for possible future implementation of multisite configurations.

If the value is set to 0, the object is confined to one site and does not tolerate that site's failure. This is similar to a single-site vSAN cluster configuration.

2. **Secondary level of failures to tolerate (SFTT)**—This rule is on the nested FD level, which means the replication scope is between hosts within a site. You can consider this to be equivalent to the old FTT placement rule that is now expanded to each data site in the stretched cluster. I consider each nested FD as a single vSAN cluster that is protected by a mirror on a second site. Whatever applied to a single site cluster would apply to a nested FD and is duplicated in the nested FD's mirror site. In other words, you get the best of both worlds and mitigate risks of single points of failure introduced by vSAN stretched clusters.

The *replication scope* mentioned in the last two points defines the boundaries of replica placement and is one of the DOM object's child properties. Refer to Listings 22.4 and 22.5 earlier in this section.

Table 22.3 lists the various replication scope levels and what they mean.

Table 22.3 Nested fault domain replication scope

Scope Value	Scope Level	Meaning
0	None	Not defined
1	Local	Transient scope while fixing a problem
2	Lower-level FDs	Host-level replication
3	Upper-level FD	Site-level replication

Configuring a Nested FD Policy

To configure a nested FD policy, follow this procedure:

1. Follow steps 1–6 of the procedure in the "vSAN Storage Policies" section in Chapter 21.

2. From the <add rules> pull-down menu, select the **Primary level of failures to tolerate** option. This defines the number of sites failure to tolerate (see Figure 22.30).

Figure 22.30   Selecting primary level of failures to tolerate (PFTT)

3. Enter 1 in the resulting field. This defines a configuration that tolerates one site failure in a two-site vSAN stretched cluster.

4. Add another rule within the same rule set by selecting the **Secondary level of failure to tolerate** placement rule. Observe that the primary level option is no longer listed in the UI. This prevents accidental addition of the same rule twice within the same rule set (see Figure 22.31).

Figure 22.31   Selecting the secondary level of failures to tolerate (SFTT)

5. To define a RAID 1 nested policy, enter 1 in the resulting field and skip to step 8. To define policies other than RAID 1, proceed to the next step.

6. To define a RAID 10, 5, or 6 policy, follow the corresponding substep here:

   ▪ **RAID 10**—Add a **Number of disk stripes per object** placement rule and set the stripe width value.

   ▪ **RAID 5**—Add a **Failure tolerance method** placement rule and then select the **RAID-5/6 (Erasure Coding) - Capacity** option from the resulting pull-down menu.

   ▪ **RAID 6**—Add a **Failure tolerance method** placement rule and then select the **RAID-5/6 (Erasure Coding) - Capacity** option from the resulting pull-down menu. Then change the value for **Secondary level of failures to tolerate** to 2.

Figure 22.32 shows the option for configuring a nested RAID 5 configuration.

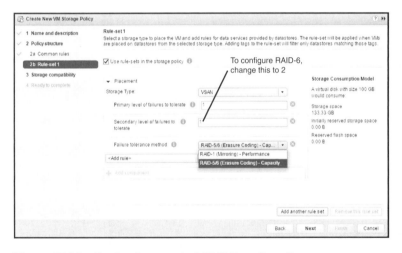

Figure 22.32   Configuring a nested RAID 5 configuration

7. Click **Next**.

8. Review the storage compatibility of the listed datastores. If the vSAN datastore is not listed on the **Compatible** row, the number of nodes per FD may be too small to support the defined policy. You need three nodes for RAID 1 and RAID 10, four nodes for RAID 5, and six nodes for RAID 6. You can continue with the wizard and correct the deficiency later, before you apply the policy to existing objects or while creating new objects. Click **Next**.

9. In the Ready to Complete step, click **Finish**.

Next, you can apply the policy to an object or to the whole VM and its objects.

Nested RAID 1 Configuration

In practice, a given design would choose the RAID level for specific VMDKs to meet their anticipated I/O profile. The default datastore policy can be changed to the most common policy for the design and apply the exceptions via specific policies on the corresponding VMDK objects.

To demonstrate the nested RAID 1 configuration, I applied the corresponding rule to one VMDK object (Hard disk 3). Figure 22.33 shows object placement for the nested RAID 1 FD.

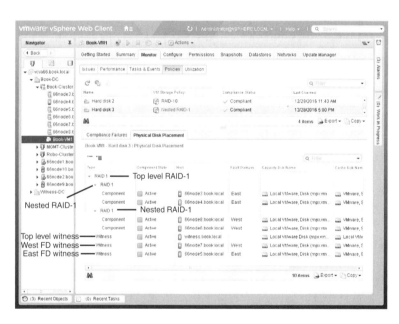

Figure 22.33   Example of nested RAID 1 FDs

In this example, the Nested RAID-1 policy was applied to Hard disk 3. By displaying the VM's policies in the Monitor tab, you can see the component placement on physical disks:

1. **Top level RAID 1 configuration**—This provides one-site (FD) failure tolerance as it creates mirror replicas of one site onto the other site. The children of this configuration are the two nested RAID 1 configurations.

2. **Nested RAID 1 configuration on the** `East` **FD**—The children of this configuration are two replicas, one placed on a capacity tier disk on the `66node3` host and the other on the `66node4` host.

3. **Nested RAID 1 on the** `West` **FD**—The mirror of `East` FD's Nested RAID 1 is placed on the `West` FD to provide site failure tolerance. This nested RAID 1 configuration has two children, which are two replicas—one on the `66node8` host and the other on the `66node6` host.

4. **Top-level witness**—The witness component of the top-level RAID 1 configuration is placed on the witness node. It is a witness for site failure tolerance. This is similar to the non-nested FD in a stretched cluster configuration.

5. **Nested FD witnesses**—Each FD has a separate witness component for each nested RAID 1 configuration. In this example, the `West` FD's witness is placed on the `66node7` host within that FD, and the `East` FD's witness is placed on the `66node5` host within that FD.

The benefit of this configuration is that failure of a single component in either or both FDs can be tolerated. For example, if a disk on which a replica component resides fails in one FD, the component is resynced, from the surviving component on the same FD, to another disk on the same host. With more than three hosts per FD, the resync can be done to a disk on the fourth host in the same FD if it results in a better balance.

Conversely, if the I/O controller in one of the hosts in an FD fails, the components located on the disks attached to the failed controller become `Absent`. With the current configuration, the VMDK object (DOM object) continues to be available because its witness component along with the surviving RAID 1 replica have >50% of the votes. However, the object state is `Reduced Availability`. If each FD had four nodes, the surviving components get resynced to disks on the fourth node if there is sufficient disk space. In this failure mode, VMs that were running on the affected host continue to run because the host is still serving compute resources and maintains network connectivity to the rest of the cluster.

A single host failure within one FD has the same effect as the I/O controller failure, but the resync starts 60 minutes after failure detection. However, HA restarts VMs that were running on that host so that they are now running on other hosts in the same data site.

Another failure mode is a whole site failing (for example, a disaster event). Assuming that the second data site and the witness site are still available and communicating, the surviving data site continues to serve I/O to the vSAN datastore. In this state, HA restarts the failed VMs on hosts within the surviving site.

Listing 22.6 shows the content section of the RAID 1 VMDK's DOM object, using `cmmds-tool`. It shows component placement matching the placement shown in Figure 22.33. I inserted highlighted comments with left-pointing arrows to point out relevant properties.

Listing 22.6   Nested RAID 1 DOM object configuration

```
"content": {"type": "Configuration",
 "attributes":
 {"CSN": 75,
 "SCSN": 101,
 "addressSpace": 107374182400,
 "scrubStartTime": 1483289798824038,
 "objectVersion": 5,
 "highestDiskVersion": 5,
 "muxGroup": 367906733493248,
 "groupUuid": "9a485f58-7da8-14f3-5edc-000c29870766",
 "compositeUuid": "37606458-255c-3f33-3c8a-000c29c1c241"},
 "child-1": {"type": "RAID_1", ← Top Level Site RAID 1 configuration
   "attributes":
   {"scope": 3}, ← Site Level Replication
   "child-1": {"type": "RAID_1", ← Nested East FD RAID 1 configuration
       "attributes":
       {"scope": 2}, ← Host Level Replication
       "child-1": {"type": "Component", ← First RAID 1 replica component
          "attributes":
          {"addressSpace": 107374182400,
          "componentState": 5,
          "componentStateTS": 1483387764,
          "faultDomainId": "a99dc62d-017d-04cf-6726-6593f9c3761e",
                      Previous line is East FD UUID
          "lastScrubbedOffset": 107374182400,
          "subFaultDomainId": "5854511c-a92e-62f3-27af-000c29870766"},
                      Previous line is host 66node3 UUID
          "componentUuid": "37606458-933e-2f34-e4ab-000c29c1c241",
          "diskUuid": "52d40db2-57c9-9faf-7e39-b14b8bdaa072"},
        "child-2": {"type": "Component", ← 2nd RAID 1 replica component
          "attributes":
          {"addressSpace": 107374182400,
          "componentState": 5,
          "componentStateTS": 1483387254,
```

```
               "faultDomainId": "a99dc62d-017d-04cf-6726-6593f9c3761e",
                      Previous line is East FD UUID
               "lastScrubbedOffset": 107374182400,
               "subFaultDomainId": "5854512b-fc8c-e32b-ea7b-000c29c1c241"},
                      Previous line is host 66node4 UUID
               "componentUuid": "37606458-1e1f-3134-f32e-000c29c1c241",
               "diskUuid": "52b98ab8-b006-cf0a-5a74-f99ad934ad1a"}},
       "child-2": {"type": "RAID_1", ← Nested West FD RAID 1 configuration
           "attributes":
           {"scope": 2}, ← Host Level Replication
           "child-1": {"type": "Component", ← First RAID 1 replica component
               "attributes":
               {"addressSpace": 107374182400,
               "componentState": 5,
               "componentStateTS": 1483337163,
               "faultDomainId": "bf495fc0-48d8-d44b-7f32-536df5cf3930",
                      Previous line is West FD UUID
               "lastScrubbedOffset": 107374182400,
               "subFaultDomainId": "5854730c-c07b-7191-662c-000c2900bdf8"},
                      Previous line is host 66node8 UUID
               "componentUuid": "37606458-1a09-3234-646d-000c29c1c241",
               "diskUuid": "52bd5dcd-8da8-e627-3284-7e995079ec9d"},
           "child-2": {"type": "Component", ← 2nd RAID 1 replica component
               "attributes":
               {"addressSpace": 107374182400,
               "componentState": 5,
               "componentStateTS": 1483387167,
               faultDomainId": "bf495fc0-48d8-d44b-7f32-536df5cf3930",
                      Previous line is West FD UUID
               "subFaultDomainId": "585472f2-a2fe-b12a-9d88-000c29a9b9c2"},
                      Previous line is host 66node6 UUID
               "componentUuid": "37606458-59c0-3234-c2f4-000c29c1c241",
               "diskUuid": "5218969d-c772-6e5d-619a-5b8e8f7074aa"}}},
    "child-2": {"type": "Witness", ← Top level (site) Witness component
       "attributes":
       {"componentState": 5,
       "componentStateTS": 1483387254,
       "isWitness": 1,
       "faultDomainId": "585ecbbe-506d-431c-30e1-005056b5b4b0",
                      Previous line is Witness node UUID
```

```
    "nVotes": 3, ← Component has 3 votes
    "isFastCCPEnabled": 1, ← Fast Config-Chang Proposal enabled
    "subFaultDomainId": "585ecbbe-506d-431c-30e1-005056b5b4b0"},
                        Previous line is Witness node UUID Again
    "componentUuid": "37606458-226e-3334-8f16-000c29c1c241",
    "diskUuid": "5250f7cc-08a9-5b7f-6a68-6c5a434e1c11"},
"child-3": {"type": "Witness", ← Nested West FD Witness component
    "attributes":
    {"componentState": 5,
    "componentStateTS": 1483385569,
    "isWitness": 1,
    "faultDomainId": "bf495fc0-48d8-d44b-7f32-536df5cf3930",
                        Previous line is West FD UUID
    "subFaultDomainId": "585472ff-dd82-a3cc-42b7-000c29f69b4e"},
                        Previous line is host 66node7 UUID
    "componentUuid": "37606458-9cef-3334-652f-000c29c1c241",
    "diskUuid": "52725df5-5f6d-74e7-f812-810960cd76d0"},
"child-4": {"type": "Witness", ← Nested East FD Witness component
    "attributes":
    {"componentState": 5,
    "componentStateTS": 1483387164,
    "isWitness": 1,
    "faultDomainId": "a99dc62d-017d-04cf-6726-6593f9c3761e",
                        Previous line is East FD UUID
    "subFaultDomainId": "585472eb-9df5-502c-25f5-000c299e6b3f"},
                        Previous line is host 66node5 UUID
    "componentUuid": "37606458-4066-3434-5fcd-000c29c1c241",
    "diskUuid": "529d41c4-a49d-4122-c337-0c18588f3191"}},
"errorStr": "(null)"
```

In this output, the only component that has the nVotes property defined is the top-level (site) witness component. It has a value of 3. None of the other components have this property defined.

> **NOTE**
>
> Whenever the number of votes assigned to a component is more than one, the nVotes field is listed in cmmd-tool output along with the vote count. When the field is not listed for a given component, the value of one vote is implied.
>
> In contrast, output of the vsan.object_info RVC command output always lists the actual vote count, regardless of its value.

You can also use RVC to list the DOM object's info, using this command while in the `computers` directory of the RVC hierarchy:

```
vsan.object_info [cluster name] [object UUID]
```

Here is an example:

```
vsan.object_info Book-Cluster 37606458-255c-3f33-3c8a-000c29c1c241
```

Figure 22.34 shows the command and its output.

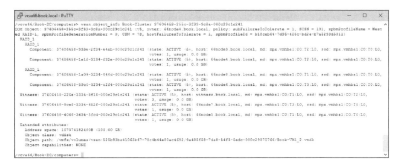

Figure 22.34   Nested RAID 1 object info via RVC

This example shows the following DOM object information:

- UUID

- Version, which is v5 in this example

- Owner, which is `66node4` in this example

- Policy, which includes the following properties:

    - **subFailuresToTolerate**—This is SFTT, which in this example is `1`, or the nested level RAID 1.

    - **SCSN**—This is the state change sequence number. DOM updates this field when it needs to report a state change to CLOM.

    - **spbmProfileName**—This is the storage policy name.

    - **spbmProfileGenerationNumber**—This value is incremented when the policy configuration is changed. This triggers a workflow to reapply the policy to the objects, which can be done automatically at the time of policy modification or deferred to be done manually later.

- **CSN**—This is the configuration sequence number, which indicates the current configuration version. This value is changed when the object configuration is changed (for example, when a new policy is applied that results in reconfiguring the object).

- **hostFailuresToTolerate**—This is the same as PFTT or, in non-nested FD configurations, FTT. It denotes the number of sites whose failure to tolerate. As mentioned earlier, in stretched cluster nested FD, the value 1 is required. If the value is 0, it means the object resides in one site only, which renders the object unprotected from this site's failure.

- **spbmProfileId**—This is the storage policy's profile ID. If you have to rebuild vCenter Server and re-create the old policies, the profile ID of the storage policy will not match the profile ID of the policies applied to the existing DOM objects. Unless you exported the policies using PowerCLI, you will have to re-apply the policies to the DOM objects to resolve their Non-compliant state.

- **RAID_1**, which is the top-level PFTT, which is the site failure to tolerate

  The next RAID_1 listed is for the first site's nested fault domain's configuration. Under it is a list of two components, which are the replicas that make up the RAID 1.

  The following RAID_1 is for the second site's nested fault domain's configuration. Under it is a list of two components. They are the replicas that make up that RAID 1.

- Three witness components:

  - Component placed on the witness node, which is the witness for the site-level failure

  - Component paced on host7, which is a witness for the nested RAID 1 on the West site

  - Component placed on host5, which is a witness for the nested RAID 1 on the East site

  Each component shows the following properties:

  - **Component**—This is the component's UUID.

  - **State**—This is equivalent to componentState listed in the cmmds-tool output. In this example, the state is Active, which is indicated by the value 5.

  - **Host**—This is the host with the disk group on which the component is stored.

  - **MD**—This is the magnetic disk (capacity tier disk) on which the component is stored. (The reference to magnetic is used even when the capacity tier disk type is SSD.)

- **SSD**—This is the cache tier disk on the corresponding host's disk group.

- **Votes**—This is the number of votes assigned to the component. In this example, all components have one vote except for the site witness component, which has three votes.

- At the bottom of the output, the object's extended attributes are listed:

  - **Address space**—This is the object size in bytes and, in parentheses, the size in gigabytes.

  - **Object class**—In this example, it is `vdisk`, which is virtual disk, or VMDK. Other possible classes are `vmnamspace`, `vmswap`, and `vmem`.

  - **Object path**—This is the path to where the object's name is stored. This is not where the object itself is stored. Rather, it is where its namespace-based filename is listed. For example, for the `vdisk` class, the file would be the VMDK's descriptor file within the VM's namespace.

  - **Object capabilities**—No capabilities are listed in this example.

Figure 22.35 is a logical diagram that shows component placements and corresponding vote counts based on the example shown in Figure 22.33 and Listing 22.34.

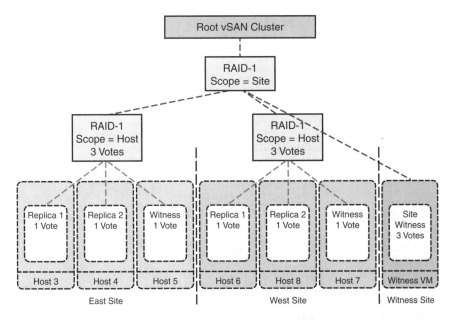

Figure 22.35   RAID 1 component placement in nested FDs

The diagram shows that each component within a data site has a single vote. Adding up the vote counts for the sites gives the top-level RAID 1 configurations three votes each. They therefore have equal weight to the site witness component on the witness VM.

Nested RAID 10 Configuration

For workloads that can benefit from striping while providing a level of availability, RAID 10 can be a good design choice. If the cluster design is a stretched cluster, nested RAID 10 configuration can be used to implement striping.

To demonstrate nested RAID 10 configuration, I applied a corresponding storage policy to one VMDK DOM object. Figure 22.36 shows object placement for a nested RAID 10 FD.

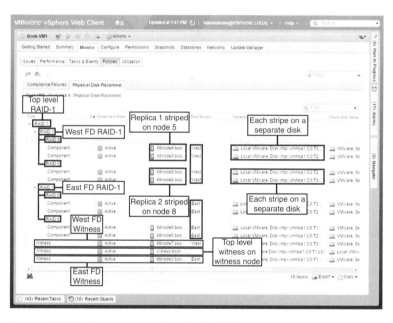

Figure 22.36 Example of nested RAID 10 FDs

In this example, the two top FDs are the East and West sites. Within each site is a nested RAID 10 configuration with the following:

- The top-level FD and the RAID 1 nested configuration are identical to those in the previous example of nested RAID 1 configuration. This example further stripes each RAID 1 configuration into two RAID 0 stripes:
  - The nested RAID 1 configuration on the West FD has one replica on the 66node6 host, which is striped on two separate disks on that host.

- The nested RAID 1 configuration on the West FD has the mirror replica on the 66node8host, which is striped on two separate disks on that host.

- The configuration of the West FD is mirrored on the East FD, with similar distribution on the 66node4 and 66node5 hosts.

- The witness placement is identical to that in the nested RAID 1 configuration discussed earlier in this chapter, in the section "Nested RAID 1 Configuration."

Listing 22.7 shows the content field of the DOM object.

Listing 22.7   Nested RAID 10 DOM object in a nested FD configuration

```
"content": {"type": "Configuration",
 "attributes":
 {"CSN": 62,
 "SCSN": 125,
 "addressSpace": 161061273600,
 "scrubStartTime": 1482976949702377,
 "objectVersion": 5,
 "highestDiskVersion": 5,
 "muxGroup": 495577639488512,
 "groupUuid": "9a485f58-7da8-14f3-5edc-000c29870766",
 "compositeUuid": "b56e6458-bdda-b2a0-c4ff-000c29c1c241"},
 "child-1": {"type": "RAID_1",  ← Top level domain tolerates 1 site failure
   "attributes":
   {"scope": 3},  ← Site Level Replication
      "child-1": {"type": "RAID_1",  ← East FD tolerates 1 host failure
"attributes":
{"scope": 2},  ← Host Level Replication
      "child-1": {"type": "RAID_0",  ← 1st replica of nested East FD's data
is striped
         "attributes":
         {"stripeBlockSize": 1048576},
         "child-1": {"type": "Component",  ← Nested East FD's 1st stripe of
Replica 1
            "attributes":
            {"addressSpace": 80530636800,
            "componentState": 5,
            "componentStateTS": 1483300682,
            "faultDomainId": "a99dc62d-017d-04cf-6726-6593f9c3761e",
            "nVotes": 2,  ← Component has 2 votes
```

            "lastScrubbedOffset": 80530636800,
            "subFaultDomainId": "585472eb-9df5-502c-25f5-000c299e6b3f"},
            "componentUuid": "616f6458-bf0d-1b42-8b05-000c29c1c241",
            "diskUuid": "52768761-0138-5ab2-8151-be75dad6db8b"},
        "child-2": {"type": "Component", ← Nested East FD's 2nd stripe of
Replica 1
            "attributes":
            {"addressSpace": 80530636800,
            "componentState": 5,
            "componentStateTS": 1483300682,
            "faultDomainId": "a99dc62d-017d-04cf-6726-6593f9c3761e",
            "lastScrubbedOffset": 80530636800,
            "subFaultDomainId": "585472eb-9df5-502c-25f5-000c299e6b3f"},
            "componentUuid": "616f6458-95b6-1f42-2723-000c29c1c241",
            "diskUuid": "529d41c4-a49d-4122-c337-0c18588f3191"}},
"child-2": {"type": "RAID_0", ← 2nd replica of nested East FD's data is
striped
            "attributes":
            {"stripeBlockSize": 1048576},
    "child-1": {"type": "Component", ← Nested Wast FD's 1st stripe of
Replica 2
            "attributes":
            {"addressSpace": 80530636800,
            "componentState": 5,
            "componentStateTS": 1483300701,
            "faultDomainId": "a99dc62d-017d-04cf-6726-6593f9c3761e",
            "lastScrubbedOffset": 80530636800,
            "subFaultDomainId": "5854512b-fc8c-e32b-ea7b-000c29c1c241"},
            "componentUuid": "616f6458-7373-2142-19e8-000c29c1c241",
            "diskUuid": "52b98ab8-b006-cf0a-5a74-f99ad934ad1a"},
        "child-2": {"type": "Component", ← Nested East FD's 2nd stripe of
Replica 2
            "attributes":
            {"addressSpace": 80530636800,
            "componentState": 5,
            "componentStateTS": 1483300701,
            "faultDomainId": "a99dc62d-017d-04cf-6726-6593f9c3761e",
            "lastScrubbedOffset": 80530636800,
            "subFaultDomainId": "5854512b-fc8c-e32b-ea7b-000c29c1c241"},
            "componentUuid": "616f6458-8aa7-2342-43f5-000c29c1c241",
            "diskUuid": "52033c1c-61e4-5a48-3083-31fba3f828d8"}}},

```
    "child-2": {"type": "RAID_1", ← West FD tolerates 1 host failure
    "attributes":
    {"scope": 2}, ← Host Level Replication
      "child-1": {"type": "RAID_0", ← 1st replica of nested West FD's data
is striped
        "attributes":
        {"stripeBlockSize": 1048576},
        "child-1": {"type": "Component", ← Nested West FD's 1st stripe of
Replica 1
          "attributes":
          {"addressSpace": 80530636800,
          "componentState": 5,
          "componentStateTS": 1483300682,
          "faultDomainId": "bf495fc0-48d8-d44b-7f32-536df5cf3930",
          "lastScrubbedOffset": 80530636800,
          "subFaultDomainId": "5854730c-c07b-7191-662c-000c2900bdf8"},
          "componentUuid": "616f6458-eed5-2542-2411-000c29c1c241",
          "diskUuid": "52cb33e0-3bb3-c38c-9034-10014a327863"},
        "child-2": {"type": "Component", ← Nested West FD's 2nd stripe of
Replica 1
          "attributes":
          {"addressSpace": 80530636800,
          "componentState": 5,
          "componentStateTS": 1483300682,
          "faultDomainId": "bf495fc0-48d8-d44b-7f32-536df5cf3930",
          "lastScrubbedOffset": 80530636800,
          "subFaultDomainId": "5854730c-c07b-7191-662c-000c2900bdf8"},
          "componentUuid": "616f6458-565d-2742-d276-000c29c1c241",
          "diskUuid": "52906f65-47e1-41bf-ca3e-b2d896030758"}},
      "child-2": {"type": "RAID_0", ← 2nd replica of nested West FDs data
is striped
        "attributes":
        {"stripeBlockSize": 1048576},
        "child-1": {"type": "Component", ← Nested West FD's 1st stripe of
Replica 2
          "attributes":
      "addressSpace": 80530636800,
          "componentState": 5,
          "componentStateTS": 1483156326,
          "faultDomainId": "bf495fc0-48d8-d44b-7f32-536df5cf3930",
          "lastScrubbedOffset": 80530636800,
          "subFaultDomainId": "585472f2-a2fe-b12a-9d88-000c29a9b9c2"},
```

```
            "componentUuid": "616f6458-c4d6-2842-e4de-000c29c1c241",
            "diskUuid": "52c1ddff-031b-2e57-fd72-ef65e108a198"},
        "child-2": {"type": "Component", ← Nested West FD's 2nd stripe of
Replica 2
            "attributes":
            {"addressSpace": 80530636800,
            "componentState": 5,
            "componentStateTS": 1483156326,
            "faultDomainId": "bf495fc0-48d8-d44b-7f32-536df5cf3930",
            "subFaultDomainId": "585472f2-a2fe-b12a-9d88-000c29a9b9c2"},
            "componentUuid": "616f6458-3069-2a42-f26c-000c29c1c241",
            "diskUuid": "5218969d-c772-6e5d-619a-5b8e8f7074aa"}}}},
"child-2": {"type": "Witness", ← Top Level FD's Witness
  "attributes":
  {"componentState": 5,
  "componentStateTS": 1483300682,
  "isWitness": 1,
  "faultDomainId": "585ecbbe-506d-431c-30e1-005056b5b4b0",
  "nVotes": 6, ← Witness (site) Component has 6 votes
  "isFastCCPEnabled": 1, ← Fast Config-Change Proposal enabled
  "subFaultDomainId": "585ecbbe-506d-431c-30e1-005056b5b4b0"}, ← Witness
Node's UUID
  "componentUuid": "636f6458-130a-f591-1fe8-000c29c1c241",
  "diskUuid": "5250f7cc-08a9-5b7f-6a68-6c5a434e1c11"},
"child-3": {"type": "Witness", ← Nested West FD Level Witness
  "attributes":
  {"componentState": 5,
  "componentStateTS": 1483274301,
  "isWitness": 1,
  "faultDomainId": "bf495fc0-48d8-d44b-7f32-536df5cf3930", ← West FD UUID
  "nVotes": 2, ← Witness Component has 2 votes
  "subFaultDomainId": "585472ff-dd82-a3cc-42b7-000c29f69b4e"}, ← Node 7's
UUID
  "componentUuid": "636f6458-9add-f891-9667-000c29c1c241",
  "diskUuid": "52725df5-5f6d-74e7-f812-810960cd76d0"},
"child-4": {"type": "Witness", ← Nested East FD Level Witness
  "attributes":
  {"componentState": 5,
  "componentStateTS": 1483300692,
  "isWitness": 1,
  "faultDomainId": "a99dc62d-017d-04cf-6726-6593f9c3761e", ← East FD UUID
```

```
"nVotes": 2, ← Witness Component has 2 votes
"subFaultDomainId": "5854511c-a92e-62f3-27af-000c29870766"}, ← Node 3's
UUID
"componentUuid": "636f6458-ee01-fa91-3db6-000c29c1c241",
"diskUuid": "527f8c83-430f-36b0-d7e2-1d62a3f9e3e5"}},
```

In this output, each RAID 0 stripe component has a single vote, which gives the corresponding nested RAID 1 parent configuration two votes. Adding up the votes for each nested RAID 1 replica and their witness results in a total of six votes per site. This is the reason the top-level FD's witness is assigned six votes.

Figure 22.37 shows the vote assignments and replication scopes.

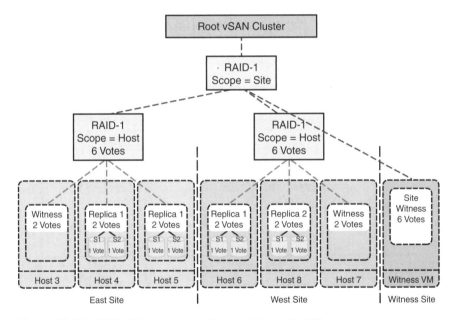

Figure 22.37   RAID 10 component placement in nested FDs

Nested Fault Domain I/O Flow

Bandwidth utilization optimization is one of the objectives of stretched vSAN nested fault domains. To reduce the traffic on the intersite network, vSAN introduced the concept of proxy ownership. As mentioned earlier in this chapter, a DOM object is owned by a single vSAN node, through which I/O to the object is done. All other nodes send I/Os to the object via the DOM client to the DOM owner. In vSAN stretched cluster configuration with nested fault domains, writes are done on the DOM object in each site separately.

However, to maintain coherency, the DOM owner initiates the resync operations when needed. It sends the changes in batches to the DOM proxy, which writes them to the components on the remote site.

Remote Office/Branch Office (ROBO) vSAN Cluster

vSAN 6.1 and later offer a two-node cluster configuration suitable for remote office/ branch office (ROBO). This configuration is a variation on a vSAN stretched cluster with one node in each data site. However, both nodes are placed in the same physical location, in two fault domains.

vSAN 6.5 adds support for direct connect configuration, where the vSAN network between both nodes does not use a switch.

TIP

1Gbps and 10Gbps network interfaces do not require a cross-over cable for direct connect configuration.

---

vSAN 6.6 simplified ROBO cluster configurations licensing. Table 22.4 lists available vSAN 6.6 ROBO licensing options.

Table 22.4 ROBO vSAN 6.6 cluster licensing options

vSAN Feature	ROBO Standard	ROBO Advanced
Flash read/write cache	Yes	Yes
Distributed RAID	Yes	Yes
Storage policy–based management (SPBM)	Yes	Yes
vSphere Distributed Switch (vDS)	Yes	Yes
vSAN snapshots/clones	Yes	Yes
Fault domains (rack awareness)	Yes	Yes
vSphere Replication (VR)	Yes	Yes
iSCSI target service	Yes	Yes
All flash disk group	Yes	Yes
Deduplication and compression	No	Yes
RAID 5/6 erasure coding	No	Yes
Stretched cluster	No	No
QoS IOPS limits	No	No

Configuration requires a witness host, which can be deployed as a virtual appliance from the witness OVA, as discussed earlier, in the section, **"vSAN Stretched Cluster Witness."** The main difference here is that the network requirement for witness-to-site max latency is 500ms RTT, and the minimum bandwidth is 1Mbps on a Layer 3 network. The connection between cluster data nodes requires max latency of 5ms RTT and 1Gbps bandwidth on a Layer 2 network.

vSAN 6.5 introduced support for directly connecting the NICs used for vSAN cluster between the two cluster nodes. If this configuration is used, another vSAN VMKNIC is required in each data node, with uplink connecting to the witness site.

Typical designs consolidate all witness VMs within a data center hosted at a central location (for example, headquarters facilities).

Figure 22.38 shows a logical diagram depicting this design approach.

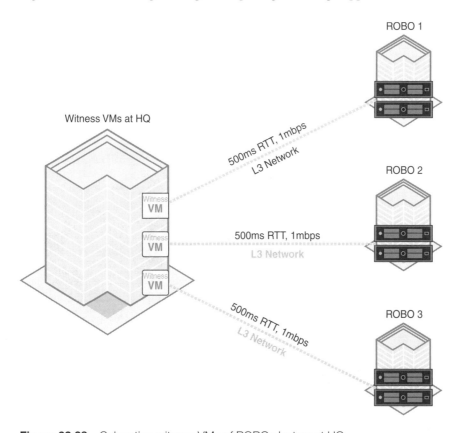

Figure 22.38   Colocating witness VMs of ROBO clusters at HQ

Configuring a ROBO Cluster

Configuring a ROBO cluster involves using a wizard that is a subset of the vSAN Stretched Cluster Configuration Wizard. The difference here is that there is no step for creating the fault domains. The wizard automatically creates two FDs, named `Preferred` and `Secondary`, and sets `Preferred` as the preferred FD. Follow these steps to configure a ROBO cluster:

1. Connect to the vCenter server using the vSphere 6 Web Client as a user with Administrator privileges. This example uses vSAN 6.6.

2. Navigate to the **Hosts and Clusters** view (see Figure 22.39).

3. Right-click the datacenter object and then select the **New Cluster** menu option.

4. Enter the new cluster name (for example, `ROBO-Cluster`).

5. Do not enable any cluster options. Click **OK**.

6. Add the two ESXi hosts, located at the remote site, to the cluster.

7. While the new cluster is selected, select the **Configure** tab. Alternatively, right-click the cluster object and then select **Settings**.

8. Select the **General** option in the Virtual SAN section.

9. Click the **Configure** button.

10. Select the **Configure two host vSAN cluster** radio button.

11. Click **Next**.

Figure 22.39   Configuring a two-node ROBO cluster

12. The configuration wizard validates the network configuration. If no errors are found, click **Next**.

13. The configuration wizard does its best to identify available storage devices and assigns them to the cache and capacity tiers, as appropriate. If it fails to do this properly, select the appropriate cache and capacity tiers. Click **Next**.

14. Select the witness host from the inventory tree. In this example, it is in `witness-DC`. However, it can be a cloud-based nested host or at the HQ datacenter. It would have been deployed from the same OVA usable for vSAN stretched clusters discussed earlier in this chapter.

15. Select the cache and capacity tier disks to be claimed by the witness host and then click **Next**.

16. Review the settings selections. If no changes are required, click **Finish**.

The end result looks similar to that of vSAN stretched cluster, with one node in each of the two fault domains.

Deduplication and Compression

vSAN 6.2 introduced space efficiency features such as vSAN deduplication and compression, which are discussed here. It also introduced the sparse format, discussed later in this chapter.

The concept of deduplication (shortened as *dedupe*) has been around for a while. The basic premise is to identify identical blocks in a file system and collapse them into a single block with multiple pointers from each file that uses them. If any of the deduped blocks is changed in one of the files, the pointer from that file is changed to point to a separate modified block.

vSAN implementation of dedupe and compression requires all-flash configuration and vSAN on-disk format v3 (or v4 in the UI) or higher. Dedupe is done during the process of destaging data from the cache tier to the capacity tier disks. Dedupe domains are within each disk group, which avoids the need for a global lookup table; this reduces resource overhead. In other words, dedupe is disk group centric because it is done on committed write data located in the cache tier of each disk group.

Once the blocks have been deduped, they are compressed.

TIP

Using larger disk groups can result in a better dedupe ratio.

Compression is done using the LZ4 algorithm, which is a lossless data compression algorithm that is focused on compression and decompression speed.

Compression is done during destaging of deduped data from the cache tier. Compression is done on each unique 4KB block of deduped data. Only data that can be compressed into 2KB or less per block gets stored in a compressed state. Otherwise, if the compressed size is larger than 2KB, it is stored uncompressed but is still deduped. This avoids 4KB block misalignment issues and reduces CPU overhead that would be used to decompress data compressed with less than 50% saving (>2KB compressed size).

vSAN neither dedupes hot write data (data that is frequently written) nor compresses uncompressible data. This helps avoid wasting compute resources for such operations.

Deduplication and Compression Licensing

Dedupe and compression are available via vSAN Advanced and Enterprise license editions and ROBO Advanced.

Configuring Deduplication and Compression

You enable dedupe and compression by using the vSAN cluster configuration properties. To enable them, follow this procedure:

1. Connect to the vCenter server using the vSphere 6.0, Update 2 or higher Web Client as a user with Administrator privileges.

2. Navigate to the **Hosts and Clusters** view (see Figure 22.40).

3. Right-click the cluster inventory object and select the **Settings** menu option.

4. In the Virtual SAN (or vSAN) section, select **General**.

5. Click the **Edit** button.

6. In the Edit vSAN Settings dialog, select **Deduplication and Compression** check box. If the on-disk format is not v3 or higher, additional capacity tier disks space will be required during the process of reformatting the disks with the newer version. If there is insufficient space, the only approach to perform this operation is to allow reduced redundancy. In other words, some objects will violate the availability rules of their corresponding storage policies during the upgrade process. To enable this option, proceed to the next step. Otherwise, skip to step 8.

7. If needed, select the **Allow Reduced Redundancy** check box.

8. Click **OK** to compete the configuration changes. The time to complete the process will vary, depending on the starting version of the on-disk format and the amount of data .

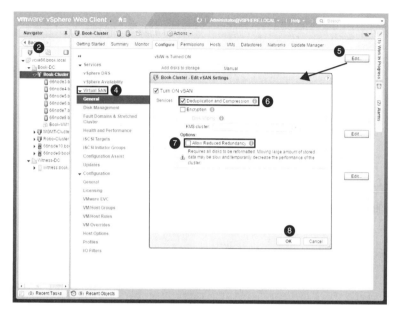

Figure 22.40   Enabling the Dedupe and Compression option

9. Monitor the related tasks in the Recent Tasks pane of the vSphere Web Client. If an on-disk format upgrade will be performed, monitor the progress in the On-disk Format Version section of the vSAN General menu screen (see Figure 22.41).

Figure 22.41   Monitoring progress of an on-disk format upgrade

The upgrade process involves removing one disk group at a time from a given host and then re-creating it and re-adding the disks to it with the upgraded on-disk format.

A successful upgrade results in version 4.0 or 5.0 displayed in the on-disk format version section of the UI. The upgrade process may generate general system errors (see Figure 22.42).

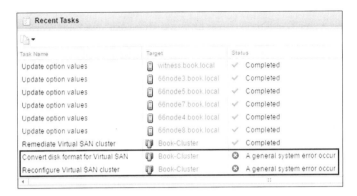

Figure 22.42   Monitoring progress of an on-disk format upgrade

In this example, I chose not to enable the Allow Reduced Redundancy option because my cluster is practically new and has very minimal data. However, I got the general system errors listed in Figure 22.42. These errors resulted in vSAN Health Check reporting a failed virtual SAN cluster configuration consistency test.

Selecting the failed test in the top pane shows the details in the bottom pane.

In the UI, click the button **Remediate inconsistent configuration**. In the confirmation dialog that appears, select the **Allow reduced redundancy** check box and click **OK** (see Figure 22.43).

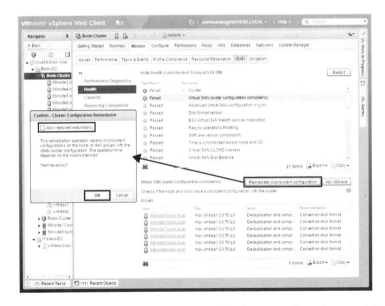

Figure 22.43   Failed Heath Check test for cluster configuration consistency

Successful remediation upgrades the on-disk format, if needed, and enables both deduplication and Compression on each disk in the disk groups on all nodes in the cluster.

Listing 22.8 shows a vSAN disk's properties before and after upgrade, using this command:

```
esxcli vsan storage list
```

This listing shows one disk only for demonstration purposes. The rest of the disks in the disk group reflect the same changes in both cache and capacity tier disks. I inserted highlighted comments with left-pointing arrows to point out relevant properties.

Listing 22.8   vSAN disk properties before and after enabling dedupe/compression

```
[root@66node6:~] esxcli vsan storage list
Before Upgrade:
mpx.vmhba1:C0:T3:L0
   Device: mpx.vmhba1:C0:T3:L0
   Display Name: mpx.vmhba1:C0:T3:L0
   Is SSD: true
   VSAN UUID: 5218969d-c772-6e5d-619a-5b8e8f7074aa
   VSAN Disk Group UUID: 52af39e8-9ccd-e4aa-f9a6-56cd2dddedb9
   VSAN Disk Group Name: mpx.vmhba1:C0:T0:L0
   Used by this host: true
   In CMMDS: true
   On-disk format version: 5 ← Original on-disk format version
   Deduplication: false ← Original dedupe setting
   Compression: false ← Original compression setting
   Checksum: 14465820054401920250
   Checksum OK: true
   Is Capacity Tier: true
   Encryption: false
   DiskKeyLoaded: false

After Upgrade:
mpx.vmhba1:C0:T3:L0
   Device: mpx.vmhba1:C0:T3:L0
   Display Name: mpx.vmhba1:C0:T3:L0
   Is SSD: true
   VSAN UUID: 52346d30-2e14-b1a2-810c-09e8a882e925
   VSAN Disk Group UUID: 525d2bdf-2914-713c-91ce-8060de2e735d
   VSAN Disk Group Name: mpx.vmhba1:C0:T0:L0
   Used by this host: true
```

```
In CMMDS: true
On-disk format version: 5 ← New on-disk format version
Deduplication: true ← New dedupe setting
Compression: true ← New compression setting
Checksum: 7451193732402716298
Checksum OK: true
Is Capacity Tier: true
Encryption: false
DiskKeyLoaded: false
```

In this output, the value of the VSAN UUID field is the disk's UUID.

In this example, the on-disk version was already v5. It could be older than v3 in clusters upgraded from pre-vSAN 6.2 versions, if the format was not upgraded during the vSAN upgrade process.

Both deduplication and compression properties were changed from false to true after the on-disk format upgrade.

Displaying Dedupe and Compression Stats

Dedupe- and compression-related components and cache tier tables occupy 5% of the total vSAN datastore raw capacity. This is a fixed value.

To list the overhead amount as well as dedupe and compression ratios, follow this procedure:

1. Connect to the vCenter server using the vSphere 6.0, Update 2 or higher Web Client as a user with Administrator privileges.

2. Navigate to the **Hosts and Clusters** view.

3. Select the cluster object in the inventory tree.

4. Select the **Monitor** tab.

5. Click the **vSAN** button.

6. Select the **Capacity** section. On the right-hand side, three panes are displayed: Capacity Overview, Deduplication and Compression Overview, and Used Capacity Breakdown (see Figure 22.44).

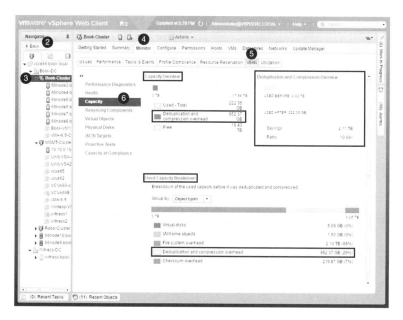

Figure 22.44   Listing dedupe overhead

In this example, the dedupe and compression overhead is 952.37GB, and the vSAN datastore size is 17.58TB. The percentage of the overhead is a bit over 5%.

The Deduplication and Compression Overview pane shows the space used before and after dedupe. In this example, the values are 2.32TB and 222.35GB, respectively. This makes the ratio 10.69%.

If you list the properties of a disk by using `cmmds-tool` to list the `DISK_STATUS` object type, the content field in the output includes a property named `writeConsolidation-Ratio`. This field should show the current dedupe and compression consolidation ratio. The UUID here is of one of the disks in a disk group. Here is the command you can use:

```
cmmds-tool find --format json --type DISK_STATUS --uuid [UUID]
```

Or you can use the abbreviated version:

```
cmmds-tool find -f json -t DISK_STATUS -u [UUID]
```

Listing 22.9 shows this command and its output. I inserted a highlighted comment with a left-pointing arrow to point out the consolidation ratio.

Listing 22.9   Listing `writeConsolidationRatio` of DISK_SATUS

```
cmmds-tool find -f json -t DISK_STATUS -u 52346d30-2e14-b1a2-810c-
09e8a882e925
{
 "entries":
[
 {
   "uuid": "52346d30-2e14-b1a2-810c-09e8a882e925",
   "owner": "585472f2-a2fe-b12a-9d88-000c29a9b9c2",
   "health": "Healthy",
   "revision": "147",
   "type": "DISK_STATUS",
   "flag": "2",
   "minHostVersion": "3",
   "md5sum": "833a29ab2ab9a340fb22c27fcaca99d6",
   "valueLen": "288",
   "content":
   {"capacityUsed": 13266583552,
   "l2CacheUsed": 0,
   "l1CacheUsed": 0,
   "writeConsolidationRatio": 10,  ← Write Consolidation Ratio is 10
   "avgReadsPerSecond": 0,
   "avgWritesPerSecond": 0,
   "avgThroughPutUsed": 8192,
   "avgReadServiceTime": 0,
   "avgReadQueueTime": 0,
   "avgWriteServiceTime": 0,
   "avgWriteQueueTime": 0,
   "avgDiskReadsPerSec": 0,
   "avgDiskWritesPerSec": 0,
   "avgSSDReadsPerSec": 0,
   "avgSSDWritesPerSec": 0,
   "estTimeToFailure": 0,
   "numDataComponents": 2,
   "logicalCapacityUsed": 144003039232,
   "physDiskCapacityUsed": 134949402173},
   "errorStr": "(null)"
 }
]
}
```

In this example, the ratio is 10, which means 10%.

The vSAN Health Check UI

With the introduction of vSAN 6.0, VMware adopted an agile process for the vSAN development cycle. This means that new features and improvements can be shipped with update releases or asynchronously from such releases. A positive effect of this was the first release of the vSAN Health Check user interface (Health Check UI). Initially, all vSAN health monitoring was done via Ruby vSphere Console (RVC), which I cover in the "Ruby vSphere Console (RVC)" section in Chapter 21; however, to simplify the health monitoring process and integrate it with vCenter alerts, the Health Check UI was developed.

The first release of the UI was in the form of an installable package for vCenter (for both Windows and virtual appliances). It involved pushing a health monitoring agent to each node in a vSAN cluster via a rolling update process. This meant that each node had to be placed in maintenance mode and rebooted, which can be disruptive and failure prone. Therefore, the subsequent releases were included with vSphere 6.0, Update 1 and 2. Table 22.5 lists the release history.

Table 22.5 vSAN Health Check release history

Health Check Version	vSphere Version	Release Format
v1 (6.0.0)	6.0 General Availability (GA)	Asynchronous (VIB)
v1.1 (6.0.1)	6.0 GA	Asynchronous (VIB)
v2 (6.1)	6.0, Update 1 (U1)	Included with U1
v3 (6.2, 6.5)	6.0, Update 2 (U2) and 6.5 GA	Included with 6.0, U2 and 6.5
v4 (6.6)	6.5, Express Patch 2	Included with 6.5, Express Patch 2

It is important to know that versions 6.0.0 and 6.0.1 cannot be installed on 6.0, U1 or U2. These versions are compatible only with 6.0 GA release (without any update releases installed).

Configuring Health Check

Configuring Health Check in its first release was cumbersome and required running several RVC commands manually. However, this was significantly improved in the subsequent releases, starting with vSAN 6.1, in which all the configuration is done via the vSphere Web Client UI. That release also avoids the need for rolling updates of vSAN nodes in order to install the vsanhealth.vib file.

On vSAN 6.2 and later, Health Check is enabled by default. It validates cluster configuration at creation time; however, the Health Check Interval option is disabled by default.

To enable it, use the following procedure, which is based on vSAN 6.5 (earlier versions use a slightly different UI):

1. Connect to the vCenter server using the vSphere 6.x Web Client as a user with Administrator privileges.

2. Navigate to the **Hosts and Clusters** view.

3. Locate the cluster inventory object and select it (see Figure 22.45).

4. Right-click the cluster object and select **Settings** option from the context menu.

5. Select **Health and Performance** in the Virtual SAN section (or the vSAN section for vSAN 6.5 and newer).

6. Click the **Edit Settings** button in the Health Service section.

7. In the Edit Periodical Health Check dialog, select the **Turn ON periodical health check** check box.

8. The default time interval is 60 minutes. If you want to use a different interval, adjust the Time Interval value and then click **OK**.

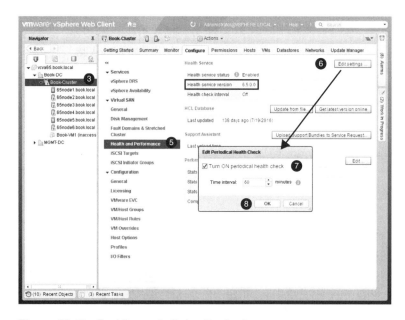

Figure 22.45   Enabling periodic health checks

NOTE

Observe the Health Service Version field's value. In this example, it is 6.5.0.0, which is the version included with vCenter 6.5. If your current vSAN version is 6.2, this field would display 6.2.0.0 instead. If you are upgrading your environment from vSAN 6.2 or an earlier version to vSAN 6.5, vCenter must be upgraded first, before you upgrade the ESXi hosts. This means that at a certain stage of the upgrade process, the environment has mixed versions, and vCenter will report in this field that hosts need to be updated. This is resolved when all nodes in the cluster have been upgraded to ESXi 6.5.

Accessing the Health Check UI

To access all available tests provided by the Health Check UI, follow this procedure:

1. Connect to the vCenter server using the vSphere 6.x Web Client as a user with Administrator privileges. This example is from vSphere 6.5.

2. Navigate to the **Host and Clusters** view (see Figure 22.46).

3. Select the cluster object in the inventory tree.

4. Select the **Monitor** tab.

5. Click the **Virtual SAN** button (or the **vSAN** button in 6.5 or newer).

6. Select the **Health** section. At this point, you should see a list of test name groups and their corresponding test results in two columns.

7. To drill down into a warning, expand the corresponding test name group in the Test Name column.

8. Select the test whose result shows a warning or an error.

9. Inspect the lower pane for test result details. If a remedy is identified, a button is usually displayed in the top-right corner of that pane. There is also an Ask VMware button.

Figure 22.46   Accessing the Health Check UI

In this example, the vSAN Performance Service is not enabled. Clicking the **Enable** button launches the relevant wizard or configuration menu. See the "**vSAN Performance Monitoring**" section, later in this chapter.

Health Check Tests

In the view displayed in the preceding section, all tests are grouped under seven categories:

- **Hardware Compatibility**—This category includes the following tests, based on the version of the Hardware Compatibility List (HCL) database (DB) file currently installed in this configuration and displays a warning in the test results if there are mismatches:

  - **Controller Driver**—Checks whether the current I/O controller driver is on the HCL.

  - **Controller Release Support**—If the I/O controller model is on the HCL, it checks whether the current firmware version is supported.

  - **SCSI Controller on Virtual SAN HCL**—Checks whether the SCSI I/O controller model is on the HCL.

  - **Virtual SAN HCL DB up-to-date**—If this does not pass the test, you can update the DB by clicking the **Get latest version online** button in the Health and Performance configuration UI, shown in Figure 22.45, earlier in this chapter. For this to work, you must enable Internet connectivity in the vSAN cluster configuration. To do that, follow the procedure in the section "Enabling Internet Connectivity of a vSAN Cluster" in Chapter 21. If vCenter does not have access to the Internet, you can download the current HCL DB version from https://partnerweb.vmware.com/service/vsan/all.json and save it to a file and then click the **Update from file** button and select the downloaded file.

- **Virtual SAN HCL DB Auto Update**—Checks whether HCL DB auto-update is enabled. This option is enabled by default and cannot be disabled.

- **Network**—This category includes the following tests:

  - **All hosts have a Virtual SAN VMKNIC configured**—This test checks whether all hosts have the required vSAN network configured by checking for a VMKNIC (vmkernel network interface card) (for example, vmk2 with the vSAN service enabled). For more details, see the section "Network Health Check," later in this chapter.

  - **All hosts have matching multicast settings**—For more details, see the "vSAN Network" section in Chapter 21. This does not apply to vSAN 6.6, which uses a unicast network.

  - **All hosts have matching subnets**

  - **Basic (unicast) connectivity check (normal ping)**

  - **Hosts with connectivity issues**—This test lists all hosts identified to have connectivity issues based on all tests done by the Health Check service.

  - **Hosts with Virtual SAN disabled**

  - **MTU check (ping with large packet size)**—This test runs the following command on each host:vmkping -I vmk2 <IP-Address> -s 9000

  - **Multicast assessment based on other checks**

  - **Unexpected Virtual SAN cluster members**

  - **Virtual SAN cluster partition**—Based on other network connectivity tests, this test identifies whether any cluster nodes lost access to the rest of the cluster. See the example in the "Network Health Check" section, later in this chapter.

- **Physical disk**—This category includes the following tests:

  - Component limit health

  - Component metadata health

- Congestion
- Disk capacity
- Memory pools (heaps)
- Memory pools (slabs)
- Metadata health
- Overall disks health
- Software state health

- **Data**—This category deals with Virtual SAN object health.

- **Cluster**—This category includes the following tests:
  - Advanced Virtual SAN configuration in sync
  - Deduplication and compression configuration consistency
  - Disk format version
  - ESX Virtual SAN Health service installation
  - Software version compatibility
  - Virtual SAN CLOMD liveness
  - Virtual SAN disk balance
  - Virtual SAN Health service up-to-date

- **Limits**—This category includes the following tests:
  - After one additional host failure
  - Current cluster situation
  - Host component limit

- **Performance service**—This category includes the following tests (see the section "vSAN Performance Monitoring," later in this chapter):
  - All hosts contributing stats
  - Performance data collection
  - Stats DB object
  - Stats master election

The test results of certain limits are based on the values listed in Table 22.6

Table 22.6 vSAN limits check

Resource	Green (Okay)	Yellow (Warning)	Red (Danger)
Components	<80%	80–90%	>90%
Free disk space	<80%	80–90%	>90%
Read cache reservation	<70%	70–90%	>90%
Disk components (usually on a witness VM)	<75%	75–95%	>95%

vSAN Health Check via the Host CLI

vSAN Health Check service uses local Python scripts on each node in the cluster to obtain test results from the corresponding host and presents the aggregate values in the UI.

The main script used is `/usr/lib/vmware/vsan/bin/vsan-health-status.pyc`

To run this script manually on one of the vSAN nodes, use this command:

```
python /usr/lib/vmware/vsan/bin/vsan-health-status.pyc
```

The output is too long to list here. However, I share a few sections for illustration purposes. Listing 22.10 shows the `Limits summary` section of the output.

Listing 22.10 `Limits summary` section of the `vsan-health-status.pyc` script's output

```
}
Limits summary:
(vim.host.VsanLimitHealthResult) {
    dynamicType = <unset>,
    dynamicProperty = (vmodl.DynamicProperty) [],
    hostname = <unset>,
    issueFound = false,
    maxComponents = 750,
    freeComponents = 748,
    componentLimitHealth = 'green',
    lowestFreeDiskSpacePct = 99,
    usedDiskSpaceB = 39766196224,
    totalDiskSpaceB = 3050783023104,
    diskFreeSpaceHealth = 'green',
    reservedRcSizeB = 0,
```

```
    totalRcSizeB = 0,
    rcFreeReservationHealth = 'green'
}
```

For example, the UI eventually aggregates the values of the `usedDiskSpaceB` and `totalDiskSpaceB` fields to yield the value listed in the `Disk space utilization` row in the Current cluster situation test results under the Limits group in the UI (for example, `222GB of 17047GB`).

The Health Check service arrived at this value by aggregating the values from all nodes in the cluster and converting it to GiB.

In this example, the `totalDiskSpaceB` is `3050783023104` per host. Six hosts provide 3,050,783,023,104 × 6, or 18,304,698,138,624 bytes. To convert this to GiB, divide by 1024 three times, which results in 17047.57859802246 (approximately 17,047GiB).

Use a similar conversion to calculate the aggregate `usedDiskSpaceB`, which results in 222GiB in this example.

Figure 22.47 shows a screenshot of this example in the UI.

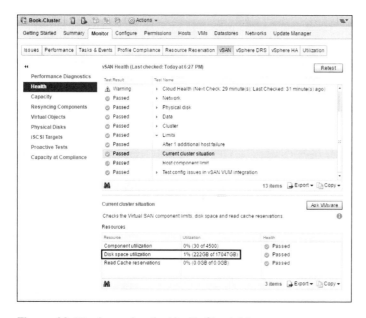

Figure 22.47 Accessing the Health Check UI

Another part of the output is a handy DOM object-to-type/descriptor map. Listing 22.11 shows that section of the output.

Listing 22.11   DOM object mapping section of the `vsan-health-status.pyc` script's output

```
DOM Object to type/descriptor map:
Object: b47f4058-6931-e956-b0da-000c29d918dd - Type: vdisk
   Path: /vmfs/volumes/vsanDatastore/Cluster-VM1/EZT.vmdk
Group uuid: 2e373258-b77c-8509-4e5e-000c292cb974
Object: 56373258-4cf8-04bd-672c-000c292cb974 - Type: vdisk
   Path: /vmfs/volumes/vsan:52a40f74aca1ac06-947769019a0d618b/
2e373258-b77c-8509-4e5e-000c292cb974/Cluster-VM1.vmdk
Group uuid: 2e373258-b77c-8509-4e5e-000c292cb974
Object: e8513a58-e6bc-4594-042b-000c292cb974 - Type: vdisk
   Path: /vmfs/volumes/vsan:52a40f74aca1ac06-947769019a0d618b/
2e373258-b77c-8509-4e5e-000c292cb974/Book-VM1.vmdk
Group uuid: 2e373258-b77c-8509-4e5e-000c292cb974
Object: 506e3b58-e4b5-3ad9-13e2-000c292cb974 - Type: vdisk
   Path: /vmfs/volumes/vsan:52a40f74aca1ac06-947769019a0d618b/
2e373258-b77c-8509-4e5e-000c292cb974/Book-VM1_1.vmdk
Group uuid: 2e373258-b77c-8509-4e5e-000c292cb974
Object: d0373258-cccd-4a77-727d-000c292cb974 - Type: vdisk
   Path: /vmfs/volumes/vsan:52a40f74aca1ac06-947769019a0d618b/
2e373258-b77c-8509-4e5e-000c292cb974/Cluster-VM1_1.vmdk
Group uuid: 2e373258-b77c-8509-4e5e-000c292cb974
Object: 2e373258-b77c-8509-4e5e-000c292cb974 - Type: vmnamespace
   Path: /vmfs/volumes/vsan:52a40f74aca1ac06-947769019a0d618b/
User friendly name: Cluster-VM1
Object: a3d24458-7788-f42a-786b-000c292cb974 - Type: vmswap
   Path: /vmfs/volumes/vsan:52a40f74aca1ac06-947769019a0d618b/
2e373258-b77c-8509-4e5e-000c292cb974/Cluster-VM1-af85b05a.vswp
Group uuid: 2e373258-b77c-8509-4e5e-000c292cb974
Object: 67874458-98c0-bdb4-d375-000c29f08be1 - Type: vmnamespace
   Path: /vmfs/volumes/vsan:52a40f74aca1ac06-947769019a0d618b/
User friendly name: .vsan.stats
```

This output shows the following for each DOM object on the cluster:

- **Object UUID**—This is the unique identifier of the DOM object.

- **Object Type**—In this example, the object types are `vdisk`, `namespace`, and `vmswap`.

- **Path**—The path varies based on the type:

- For objects of `vdisk` and `vmswap` types, this is the path to the descriptor file within the corresponding VM's namespace (VM home).

- For the `namespace` object type, this is the path to where the DOM object is stored.

- **Friendly name**—For `namespace` object types, this is the human-readable name, which is the VM home folder name.

TIP

Run this script on any of the cluster nodes every time new VMs are added or removed. Store the output on your management workstation or some other place where it is handy to use in the unlikely event of data recovery where the VM's namespace object may be inaccessible due to absent components.

The following is another script used by the Health Check service on vSAN nodes:

`/usr/lib/vmware/vsan/perfsvc/VsanLsomHealth.pyc`

This script reports the health status and current details of LSOM health. Because LSOM handles the corresponding node's local vSAN storage, the output provides details of the disk group(s) on the host, the script that ran, and related stats and health status.

Listing 22.12 lists part of the output

Listing 22.12   The first part of the `vsanLsomHealth.pyc` script's output

```
Python /usr/lib/vmware/vsan/perfsvc/VsanLsomHealth.pyc
===========================================================
Node {
    Disk Summary: Diskgroups = 1 / 5 (max), MDs = 3 / 5 (max)
    Component Summary: Opened = 6, Pending = 0, Max = 750
}
===========================================================
Disk {
    UUID: 526c9371-f0c9-a7c4-5f6a-d5fd24671e36
    Capacity: Total = 0 GB, Reserved = 0 GB, Used = 0 GB
    SSD : WB = 614399 MB, Free = 614259 MB
    LLOG: Log = 76 MB, Data = 0 MB
```

```
    PLOG: Log = 41 MB, Data = 140 MB
    Congestion: ssdCongestion = 0, logCongestion = 0, iopsCongestion = 0,
slabCongestion = 0, memCongestion = 0
}
```

The output starts with the `Node` section, which covers LSOM's disk summary. In this example, there is one disk group out of the maximum possible five disk groups on this host.

The next `Disk` section is the first disk in the disk group, which is the cache tier SSD.

Very important stats are listed in this section:

- **SSD**—This is the cache tier's stats:

    - **WB**—Write buffer size in MiB.

    - **Free**—Free WB space.

- **LLOG**—This is the logical log that stores data just arrived in the WB but that has not been assigned capacity tier blocks yet. If the host is rebooted after a crash before this is done, the LLOG is used to recover this data and move it to the PLOG.

    - **Log**—This is the LLOG log size.

    - **Data**—This is the size of data mapped by the LLOG. In this example, it is zero, which means there are no write I/Os pending transfer to PLOG.

- **PLOG**—This is the physical log that references data in WB that has been assigned capacity tier blocks. When the WB data is ready to be evicted (destaged), the data blocks are moved to the mapped capacity tier blocks and then removed from the WB.

    - **Log**—This is the PLOG log size.

    - **Data**—This is the data in the WB that is mapped by the PLOG to the data's final destination on the capacity tier blocks. The size here is 140MiB, which is the difference between the WB size and WB free size. If the LLOG had data, it would reduce the WB free space as well.

Using Health Check for What-If Scenario

One of the vSAN Health Check limits tests is named After 1 Additional Host Failure. This is a what-if scenario that checks the limits of the remaining vSAN resources if one of the current hosts fails. Figure 22.48 shows the UI with results from this test.

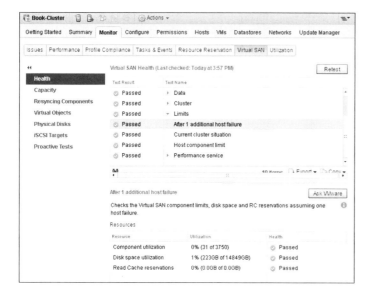

Figure 22.48   Health Check limit if one host fails

This test is similar to running the following RVC command:

```
vsan.whatif_host_failures --num-host-failures-to-simulate 1 [cluster-name]
```

Or you can use the abbreviated version:

```
vsan.whatif_host_failures -n 1 [cluster-name]
```

Here is an example:

```
vsan.whatif_host_failures -n 1 Book-Cluster
```

Listing 22.13 shows this command and its output.

Listing 22.13   Simulating what-if one-host failure scenario

```
vsan.whatif_host_failures  n 1 Book Cluster
Simulating 1 host failures:

+------------------+----------------------------+----------------------------------+
| Resource         | Usage right now            | Usage after failure/re-protection |
+------------------+----------------------------+----------------------------------+
| HDD capacity     | 1% used (17596.79 GB free) | 2% used (14626.81 GB free)       |
| Components       | 1% used (4469 available)   | 1% used (3719 available)         |
| RC reservations  | 0% used (0.01 GB free)     | 0% used (0.00 GB free)           |
+------------------+----------------------------+----------------------------------+
```

In this example, the vSAN datastore is very lightly utilized, and there would be plenty or resources in case of a single host failure.

As of vSAN 6.5, this test is limited to one host failure only. If you try the RVC command using -n 2 for a two-host failure, you get this message:

```
Only simulation of 1 host failure has been implemented
```

The values listed in the Usage Right Now column should be identical to the results of the Current Cluster Situation test.

Network Health Check

vSAN Health Check monitors for network misconfigurations. When it detects them, it shows a white X in a red circle on the cluster object to denote an error. To identify the error details, follow these steps:

1. Connect to the vCenter server using the vSphere 6.x Web Client as a user with Administrator privileges. This example is from vSphere 6.5.

2. Navigate to the **Host and Clusters** view.

3. Select the cluster object in the inventory tree.

4. Select the **Monitor** tab.

5. Click the **Virtual SAN** button.

6. Select the **Health** section.

7. Expand the **Network** test name. It shows Failed under the Rest Result column. In this example, there are two network tests that failed: All Hosts Have Virtual SAN vmknic Configured and Virtual SAN Cluster Partition.

8. Select the **Virtual SAN cluster partition** test name. The lower pane shows the details of the test, listing each node in the cluster and its corresponding partition number. In this example, all hosts are in partition 1 except for the 65node5 host, which is in partition 2.

   Figure 22.49 shows the detected network partition.

Figure 22.49   Health Check detecting network misconfiguration

9. Click the **Ask VMware** button to open a VMware Knowledge Base (KB) article explaining the current state.

10. To identify the root cause of this network partition, click the other failed network test name, **All hosts have a Virtual SAN vmknic configured**. The lower pane shows the host name that failed this test. This means that the identified host needs to have a VMKNIC configured with the vSAN network traffic option. Figure 22.50 shows that the `65node5` host does not have a VMKNIC with this option enabled.

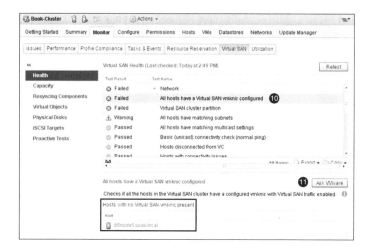

Figure 22.50   Identifying the cause of a network partition

11. Click the **Ask VMware** button to open a VMware KB article that explains the issue and how to resolve it.

In this example, the error was detected upon adding a new host to the vSAN cluster without a vmkernel NIC (VMKNIC) that has vSAN traffic enabled. Actually, the new host was not added to the vDS on which the vSAN distributed port group was configured. I resolved this issue by adding the host to the vDS and configuring an uplink from the host on the vDS vSAN port group. See the "vSAN Network" section in Chapter 21 for details on this procedure.

When the network configuration has been corrected, return to this UI area and click the **Retest** button in the top-right corner of the upper pane. Otherwise, you can wait until Health Check automatically reruns the tests and the test result changes to **Passed**, with a green checkmark.

Figure 22.51 shows another example of a network health event where multiple network tests failed, including the following:

- Basic (unicast) connectivity check (normal ping)
- MTU check (ping with large packet size)
- Virtual SAN partition

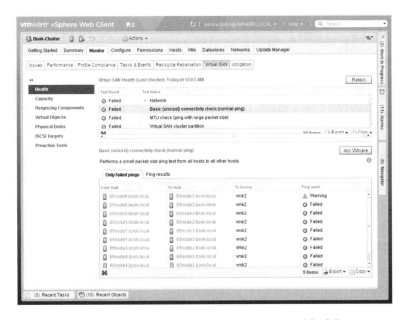

Figure 22.51   Health Check detecting network connectivity failures

In this example, the first test failed to receive normal ping response from nodes listed in the lower pane table, on the Only Failed Pings tab.

This cluster has six nodes. Each row in the table lists the source and destination of each ping test that failed.

The second test that failed is MTU Check (ping with large packet size). This simply means that it was testing for jumbo frame configuration. It failed in this example because I have not configured jumbo frame in my nested vSphere environment.

At the same time, Health Check detected a vSAN partition that was caused by the network connectivity failures.

Running Burn-in Tests

When you purchase a physical storage array, the vendor configures the hardware and firmware and then puts the system through rigorous tests to identify whether there are any hardware or software issues before shipping it. Such tests are commonly referred to as *burn-in tests*.

It is recommended that you do the same with vSAN after building and configuring a cluster. I strongly recommend running these tests before any workload is deployed on the cluster because it will temporarily consume disk space. The extent of the disk space consumption depends on the number of nodes in the clusters and the largest dataset size used by the tests. For example, the largest dataset used is 1TB with 8KB I/O size when a test named Stress Test is run.

To run these tests, follow one of the following approaches:

- In vSAN 6.6, select **Configure**, **Virtual SAN**, **Configuration Assist**.
- In earlier vSAN 6.x versions, select **Monitor**, **Proactive Tests**.

Accessing the Configuration Assist Menu

In vSAN 6.6, a new configuration assist menu was introduced to aid in initial and ongoing vSAN cluster configuration. It is part of the easy install workflow in vSAN 6.6. One of the items checked by this feature is running a burn-in test check. If it was never run, you see a warning.

To run the test, follow this procedure:

1. Connect to the vCenter server using the vSphere 6.x Web Client as a user with Administrator privileges.

2. Navigate to the **Hosts and Clusters** view (see Figure 22.52).

3. Select the cluster inventory object.

4. Select the **Configure** tab.

5. In the Virtual SAN section, select the **Configuration Assist** menu option.

6. In the vSAN Configurations pane, expand the **Burn-in test** group in the Test Name column.

7. Select **Burn-in test check**. Observe the warning listed under the **Burn-in test results** pane at the bottom. The warning in the Issue column says Burn-in test has not been performed.

8. Click the **Run Burn in test** button to go to the Proactive Tests menu, which covered in the next procedure (see Figure 22.53 in the next section).

Figure 22.52 Accessing the vSAN Configuration Assist menu

9. Continue with step 8 of the procedure in the next section.

Accessing the Proactive Tests Menu

On vSAN 6.x versions, use the following procedure to access the Proactive Tests menu:

1. Connect to the vCenter server using the vSphere 6.x Web Client as a user with Administrator privileges.

2. Navigate to the **Hosts and Clusters** view (see Figure 22.53).

3. Select the cluster object in the inventory tree.

4. Select the **Monitor** tab.

5. Click the **Virtual SAN** button.

6. Select the **Proactive Test** menu.

7. Select **Storage Performance test** in the Proactive Tests table.

8. To start the test, click the **Run Test Now** icon (the green video control arrow icon). The Run Storage performance test dialog appears, and in it you can select the test duration, workload, and storage policy.

Figure 22.53 Accessing the vSAN Proactive Tests menu

9. Set the test duration. The default is 10 minutes, which is usually sufficient for most tests.

10. Select the workload. See Table 22.7 for a list of workloads and related details.

11. Select the storage policy to use with this test. The choice of policy depends on the I/O profile your design anticipates for various VMs workloads.

12. Click **OK** to start the test (see Figure 22.54).

Figure 22.54 Starting a vSAN Proactive Test

13. Monitor the progress of the test in the Recent Tasks pane. When the test completes, the test status is reflected in the lower pane of the Proactive Tests table.

Table 22.7 lists workloads available with proactive tests. (See VMware KB 2147074, at http://kb.vmware.com/kb/2147074.)

Table 22.7 vSAN proactive tests workloads

Workload Test Name	Description	Dataset per Host	VMDKs per Host	Read I/O %	OUtstanding IOs (OIOs)	I/O Size	Dataset Size per VMDK	Random I/O?
Low Stress Test	Low-stress test with minimal latency	200MB	1	100	1	4KB	200MB	Yes
Basic Sanity Test (which focuses on the flash cache layer)	Simulates a realistic workload with a 70/30 split using a small 1 GB dataset	1GB	10	70	2	4KB	102MB	Yes
Stress Test	Designed to put a lot of stress on all storage layers (High latency is expected.)	1TB	20	50	4	8KB	51MB	Yes
Performance Characterization—100% Read, Optimal RC Usage	Stress test against read cache capabilities to handle read I/O	10GB	10	100	2	4KB	1GB	Yes
Performance Characterization—100% Write, Optimal WB Usage	Stress test against the write buffer layer ability to handle write I/O	5GB	10	0	2	4KB	512MB	Yes
Performance Characterization—100% Read, Optimal RC Usage After Warmup	Stress test of the read cache layer after it has warmed up	10GB	10	100	2	4KB	1GB	Yes

Workload Test Name	Description	Dataset per Host	VMDKs per Host	Read I/O %	OUtstanding IOs (OIOs)	I/O Size	Dataset Size per VMDK	Random I/O?
Performance Characterization—70/30 Read/Write, Realistic, Optimal Flash Cache Usage	Simulates a realistic workload with a 70/30 split using a 30GB dataset	30GB	10	70	2	4KB	3GB	Yes
Performance Characterization—70/30 Read/Write, High I/O Size, Optimal Flash Cache Usage	Simulates a realistic workload using a 70/30 split but with a focus on performance with large I/O sizes	30GB	10	70	2	64KB	3GB	Yes
Performance Characterization—100% Read, Low RC Hit Rate/All-Flash Demo	Stress test for all-flash vSAN clusters (Not intended for hybrid configurations.)	1TB	10	100	2	4KB	102GB	Yes
Performance Characterization—100% Streaming Reads	Simulates workload of complete sequential read IOPS	1TB	10	100	1	512KB	102GB	No
Performance Characterization—100% Streaming Writes	Simulates workload of complete sequential write IOPS	1TB	10	0	1	512KB	102GB	No

vSAN Performance Monitoring

vSAN performance monitoring is a critical task and must be included in any vSAN cluster design. There are two approaches to monitoring vSAN performance: via the UI and via RVC.

To monitor vSAN performance via the UI, vSAN Performance Service must be enabled first (see the section **"Enabling vSAN Performance Service"**). Over time, the service tracks vSAN performance and store the stats in a dedicated database located on the vSAN datastore.

To monitor vSAN performance via the RVC, use vSAN Observer (see the section **"vSAN Observer,"** later in this chapter).

Enabling vSAN Performance Service

vSAN Performance Service provides a subset of the vSAN Observer feature set. Follow these steps to enable it:

1. Connect to the vCenter server using the vSphere 6.s Web Client as a user with Administrator privileges. This example shows vSphere 6.5.

2. Navigate to the **Hosts and Clusters** view (see Figure 22.55).

3. Select the cluster object in the Navigator pane.

4. For vSphere 6.0, select the **Manage** tab and then click the **Settings** button. For vSphere 6.5, select the **Configure** tab.

5. Select the **Health and Performance** section.

6. Click the **Edit** button in the **Performance Service** pane.

7. Select the **Turn ON Virtual SAN performance service** check box.

TIP

The vSAN performance database is stored on the vSAN datastore as a set of files within their own namespace folder (similar to a VM's home folder). You can apply a custom storage policy to this namespace object to provide availability and performance matching your design requirements. I prefer to apply FTT = 1 and SW = 2 or more. If this is an all-flash cluster, you can also apply RAID 5 or 6 if desired.

---

8. Select a storage policy to apply to the vSAN performance history database.

9. Click **OK**.

Figure 22.55   Enabling vSAN Performance Service

A successful outcome shows a Performance Service pane similar to Figure 22.56.

Figure 22.56   vSAN Performance Service enabled successfully

The performance stats database object is stored on the vSAN datastore in a hidden directory (namespace) named `.vsan.stats`.

Listing 22.14 shows the content of a freshly created vSAN datastore, before vSAN Performance Service is enabled.

Listing 22.14   A freshly created vSAN datastore

```
ls -al /vmfs/volumes/vsanDatastore/
total 0
drwxr-xr-x    1 root      root           512 Oct 23 17:30 .
drwxr-xr-x    1 root      root           512 Oct 23 17:30 ..
```

In this example, the datastore has no visible or hidden content.

Listing 22.15 shows the content of a vSAN datastore after vSAN Performance Service is enabled.

Listing 22.15   A vSAN datastore after Performance Service is enabled

```
ls -al /vmfs/volumes/vsanDatastore/
total 1024
drwxr-xr-x    1 root     root             512 Oct 23 18:32 .
drwxr-xr-x    1 root     root             512 Oct 23 18:32 ..
lrwxr-xr-x    1 root     root              36 Oct 23 18:32 .vsan.stats
-> 28ff0c58-11cb-72d1-686e-000c29d918dd
drwxr-xr-t    1 root     root            1820 Oct 23 18:25 28ff0c58-11cb-
72d1-686e-000c29d918dd
```

To list the content of the .vsan.stats directory, run the following:

```
ls -Al /vmfs/volumes/vsanDatastore/.vsan.stats
```

Listing 22.16 shows this command and its output.

Listing 22.16   Content of .vsan.stats directory

```
ls -Al /vmfs/volumes/vsanDatastore/.vsan.stats
total 792584
-r--------    1 root     root         1441792 Jan 16 05:56 .fbb.sf
-r--------    1 root     root       267026432 Jan 16 05:56 .fdc.sf
-r--------    1 root     root         1179648 Jan 16 05:56 .pb2.sf
-r--------    1 root     root       268435456 Jan 16 05:56 .pbc.sf
-r--------    1 root     root       262733824 Jan 16 05:56 .sbc.sf
drwx------    1 root     root             280 Jan 16 05:57 .sdd.sf
-r--------    1 root     root         4194304 Jan 16 05:56 .vh.sf
-rw-r--r--    1 root     root            7168 Jan 16 05:57 config.db
-rw-rw-rw-    1 root     root               0 Jan 16 05:56 stats.db.lck
-rw-r--r--    1 root     root           88064 Jan 16 05:56 stats.db.tpl
-rw-r--r--    1 root     root          135168 Jan 16 06:07 stats.
db_345600_4295
-rw-r--r--    1 root     root           37664 Jan 16 06:07 stats.
db_345600_4295-journal
```

Accessing vSAN Performance Charts in the UI

After vSAN Performance Service has been enabled, performance stats are stored in the stats database. These stats can be displayed in performance charts in vSphere 6.x Web Client. To see this, follow these steps:

1. Connect to the vCenter server using the vSphere 6.x Web Client as a user with Administrator privileges. This example uses vSphere 6.5.

2. Navigate to the **Hosts and Clusters** view (see Figure 22.57).

3. Select the cluster object in the Inventory pane.

4. Select the **Summary** tab.

5. Click the maximize icon next to the vSAN Performance section.

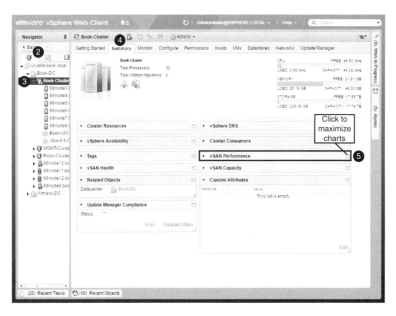

Figure 22.57   Accessing vSAN performance charts

The maximized vSAN performance charts include the following:

- **IOPS**—Read and write

- **Throughput**—Read and write

- **Latency**—Read and write

You need to scroll down to display all the charts.

Running vSAN Performance Diagnostics

New in vSAN 6.6 is the **Performance Diagnostics**. To access this menu, follow this procedure:

1. Connect to the vCenter server using the vSphere 6.x Web Client as a user with Administrator privileges.

2. Navigate to the **Hosts and Clusters** inventory object.

3. Select the cluster object in the Inventory tree.

4. Select the **Monitor** tab.

5. Click the **vSAN** button.

6. Select the **Performance Diagnostics** menu option.

7. Select the diagnostics goal from the pull-down menu. These are the choices:

   - General evaluation

   - Max IOPS

   - Max Throughput

   - Min Latency

8. Select a time range. These are the choices:

   - **Last**—Select this and specify the time range in hours.

   - **Custom**—Select this and specify the date and time range. If proactive performance tests were run, as explained in the section "Accessing the Proactive Tests Menu," earlier in this chapter, the test periods are listed under the custom menu option. You can select one of the saved periods to analyze the test results.

9. Click the **Submit** button to begin the analysis (see Figure 22.58).

Figure 22.58   Running vSAN performance diagnostics

The analysis result is displayed at the bottom when the process is complete.

Displaying Cluster Back-End Performance Charts

You can display vSAN performance charts on the cluster as well as hosts levels. To access a cluster's vSAN back-end charts, continue the procedure from the preceding section:

10. Click the **Performance** button.

11. Select the **vSAN - Backend** option. In the right-hand side pane, there is a time range selection menu at the top. Below that are five charts: IOPS, Throughput, Latency, Congestion, and Outstanding IO. The default time range is the last one hour.

12. To change the time range, enter the number of hours.

13. Alternatively, select **Custom** from the Time Range pull-down menu and specify the date and time ranges.

14. You can save the custom range by selecting the **Save custom date time range** menu option from the Time Range pull-down menu and then enter a name for the custom range and click **OK**.

15. If you have run storage performance tests (see the "Running Burn-in Tests" section, earlier in this chapter), their results are listed in the Time Range pull-down menu as well. You can select any of them to display their corresponding charts.

16. When you're done with the time range selection, click **Refresh** to display the charts.

17. Depending on your screen resolution, some of the charts may not fit in the view, so scroll down to display them. There are five charts in this view: IOPS, Throughput, Latency, Congestion, and Outstanding IO.

See Figure 22.59 for sample charts on vSAN 6.6.

Figure 22.59 Accessing vSAN cluster back-end performance charts

Displaying Cluster-Level VM Consumption Charts

Continuing with the procedure from the preceding section, to display VM consumption charts on the cluster level, proceed with step 18:

18. Select the **vSAN - Virtual Machine Consumption** option.

19. Enter the time range to display (refer to steps 12–15).

20. Click **Refresh** to display the charts. The same stats as for the back-end are displayed for the VM consumption here. You may need to scroll down to display the rest of the stats.

Displaying Host-Level vSAN Performance Charts

Continuing with the procedure from the preceding section, to display host-level vSAN performance charts, proceed with step 21:

21. Select the ESXi host in the Hosts and Clusters inventory tree.

22. Select the **Monitor** tab.

23. Click the **Performance** button.

In this view, there are seven groups available, all prefixed with vSAN - (see Figure 22.60):

- **Virtual Machine Consumption**—This is a host-level subset of the same cluster-level stats.

- **Backend**—This is a host-level subset of cluster-level stats.

- **Disk Group**—At the top of the right side of the pane is a list of disk groups on this host. Selecting the disk group to monitor displays the following charts:

  - **Frontend (guest) IOPS**—This is the cache tier disk IOPS generated by guest I/Os. It includes the following metrics: Frontend Read IOPS, Frontend Write IOPS, Read Cache Read IOPS, and Write Buffer Write IOPS.

  - **Frontend (Guest) Throughput**— This is the cache tier read and write throughput generated by guest I/Os.

  - **Frontend (guest) Latency**—This is the cache tier disk latency of guest-generated I/Os. It includes the following metrics: Frontend Read Latency, Frontend Write Latency, Read Cache Read Latency, and Write Buffer Write Latency.

  - **Overhead IOPS**—This is the cache tier disk's read cache and write buffer overhead IOPS.

  - **Overhead IO Latency**—This is the cache tier disk's read cache and write buffer overhead latency.

- **Reach Cache Hit Rate**—Rate of reading data from cache without fetching the data from capacity tier disks.

- **Evictions**—This includes cache invalidations and evictions metrics.

- **Write Buffer Free Percentage**—Percentage of free write buffer (write cache).

- **Capacity and Usage**—This includes the following metrics: Capacity (Total Cache Tier disk size); Used Capacity; Reserved Capacity; Read Cache Size—in Hybrid disk groups, which would be 70% of a maximum 600GiB cache size—for All-Flash configurations, and is zero because all SSD capacity tier disks are also used for read cache; Write Buffer Size—for All-Flash configuration, which is 100% of the cache size—and the maximum cache size is 600GiB, regardless of the cache tier SSD disk size above that. For hybrid disk groups, it is 30% of the maximum 600GiB cache size.

- **Cache Disk De-stage Rate**—The rate data is moved from the cache tier to capacity tier disks.

  - **Congestions**—This chart tracks congestion of memory, slab, SSD, IOPS, and components. As data is written to the write buffer, an elevator algorithm identifies the oldest and least-written blocks, which then get destaged (moved from the cache tier to the capacity tier). This is done when the write cache space is low. If the destaging operation lags behind new write I/Os, vSAN attempts to throttle the influx of these I/Os by introducing congestion. This means that the writers (VMs) experience higher latencies. Congestion is reduced once destaging catches up with the write I/O rate.

  - **Outstanding IO**—When I/O is issued but not yet completed, it is referred to as outstanding I/O (OIO). This chart tracks both write I/O and recovery write I/O.

  - **Outstanding IO Size**—This chart is the same as the previous chart but for size instead of count.

  - **Delayed IO Percentage**—This chart tracks the percentage of I/Os in vSAN internal queues.

  - **Delayed IO Average Latency**—This chart tracks the average latency of the previous point. This chart tracks the I/O average latency as well as the latency in the following queues: `Namespace`, `Recovery`, `VM`, and `Meta`.

  - **Delayed IOPS**—This chart is the same as the previous chart, but instead of average, it tracks count.

■ **Delayed IO Throughput**—This chart is the same as the previous two charts but tracks the I/O throughput.

■ **Resync IOPS**—This chart tracks the IOPS of resync traffic. It includes the following read and write metrics: `Policy Change`, `Evacuation`, `Rebalance`, and `Repair`.

■ **Resync Throughput**—This chart tracks the resync traffic throughput. It includes the same metrics as the Resync IOPS chart.

■ **Resync Latency**—This chart tracks the average latency of objects resync traffic. It includes the same metrics as the Resync IOPS and Resync Throughput charts.

■ **Disk**—This section includes three charts that trach reads and writes of IOPS, throughput, and latency of the physical/firmware layer of the selected disks. In addition, the Physical/Firmware Layer Latency chart tracks guest average and device average latencies.

■ **Physical Adapters**—This chart shows physical NICs' stats.

■ **VMkernel Adapters**—This chart shows VMkernel adapters (VMKNiC for example vmk2) stats.

■ **VMkernel Adapters Aggregation**—This chart shows the stats for all network I/Os processed in the network adapters used by vSAN.

Figure 22.60 shows vSAN disk throughput and latency of the caching tier disk.

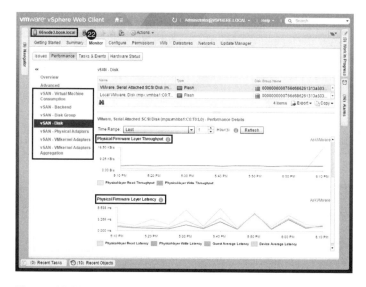

Figure 22.60   Accessing vSAN disk performance charts

Displaying VM-Level vSAN Performance Charts

Much as in the previous two subsections, you can display VM-level vSAN performance charts via vSphere Web Client. Follow this procedure:

1. Select the VM in the inventory tree.

2. Select the **Monitor** tab.

3. Click the **Performance** button.

4. Select **vSAN-Virtual Machine Consumption** or **vSAN-Virtual Disk**.

5. For the latter option, select a virtual disk from the list at the top of the right-hand side pane.

6. You can specify the time range as discussed in the previous two subsections.

The corresponding charts are displayed at the bottom of the right-hand side pane:

- **vSAN-Virtual Machine Consumption** charts track read and write IOPS, throughput, and latency of the VM as a whole.

- **vSAN-Virtual Disk** charts track normalized IOPS and IOPS limits, delayed normalized IOPS, and the following virtual SCSI read and write metrics of the selected virtual disk: `IOPS`, `Throughput`, and `Latency`.

vSAN Observer

The VMware Technical Support team has relied heavily on an RVC tool called vSAN Observer for troubleshooting vSAN performance issues. This tool has existed since vSAN 5.5. However, starting with vSAN 6.6, this tool is being deprecated for end users' consumption. It will remain, though, in RVC for exclusive use by the VMware Technical Support team as needed. A subset of features available in vSAN Observer have been ported to the UI, as discussed in earlier sections of this chapter.

If your vSAN version is pre-6.6 or when instructed by VMware Technical Support, you can follow the procedures in this section to start the tool or to collect a bundle to send to VMware when needed.

Starting vSAN Observer for Live Monitoring

vSAN Observer runs a web server on port 8010 and monitors various vSAN performance metrics. To run it, use the following command while in the computers directory and logged in to the RVC:

```
vsan.observer [cluster-name] --run-webserver --force
```

You can also use the abbreviated version:

```
vsan.observer [cluster-name] -r -o
```

Listing 22.17 shows this command and its output.

Listing 22.17 Running vSAN observer for live monitoring

```
/vcva66/Book-DC/computers> vsan.observer Book-Cluster --run-webserver
--force
2017-01-18 04:34:57 +0000: Spawning HTTPS server
2017-01-18 04:34:57 +0000: Using certificate file: /etc/vmware-vpx/ssl/
rui.crt
2017-01-18 04:34:57 +0000: Using private key file: /etc/vmware-vpx/ssl/
rui.key
[2017-01-18 04:34:57] INFO   WEBrick 1.3.1
[2017-01-18 04:34:57] INFO   ruby 2.3.0 (2015-12-25) [x86_64-linux]
[2017-01-18 04:34:57] INFO
Certificate:
    Data:
        Version: 3 (0x2)
        Serial Number:
            ce:78:a4:f7:ad:5f:46:d2
    Signature Algorithm: sha256WithRSAEncryption
        Issuer: CN=CA, DC=vsphere, DC=local, C=US, ST=California,
O=vcva66.book.local, OU=VMware Engineering
        Validity
            Not Before: Dec 24 02:26:30 2016 GMT
            Not After : Dec 19 02:26:30 2026 GMT
        Subject: CN=vcva66.book.local, C=US
        Subject Public Key Info:
            Public Key Algorithm: rsaEncryption
                Public-Key: (2048 bit)
                Modulus:
                    00:c9:7c:cd:ee:8e:e7:3a:2c:22:4a:8e:92:34:65:
                    97:dc:eb:b8:73:8e:d0:b8:62:1d:04:58:1f:1f:32:
                    3f:d3:ba:8c:05:7c:2b:58:88:48:25:ab:a3:04:e1:
                    23:4b:98:95:aa:81:88:ec:cc:7e:ec:f2:20:3d:5d:
                    8e:0a:e5:9f:3d:55:c7:28:05:38:05:4a:ae:f5:5f:
                    8e:1c:4c:04:71:27:07:72:47:8c:1f:79:66:a6:b8:
                    00:9c:d6:df:28:d7:7d:58:a3:4f:ca:0b:da:47:25:
                    41:49:29:95:d6:63:87:28:ef:47:48:e0:cd:58:a4:
                    d8:08:a6:57:86:95:5e:b0:50:99:a5:2a:83:31:84:
```

```
                  94:a8:12:5b:08:55:ba:1c:e8:ea:20:38:12:a6:e2:
                  ae:9e:12:5c:ca:f5:df:69:ff:95:fe:0f:eb:ce:93:
                  0e:54:f8:9f:de:34:84:65:67:3f:38:df:e5:7c:d5:
                  29:6d:b9:bb:ce:b1:ff:ce:e0:25:75:e3:f9:e4:29:
                  e1:fd:e0:a2:53:3e:25:0f:65:c6:e7:48:d7:48:65:
                  51:31:97:80:77:d4:81:44:9e:07:04:7f:b3:47:46:
                  13:4a:39:dc:14:aa:98:cd:89:ca:d6:1e:89:fc:a5:
                  09:48:43:14:9e:d9:19:d7:54:1a:ef:a2:1a:b7:18:
                  b7:27
            Exponent: 65537 (0x10001)
       X509v3 extensions:
           X509v3 Key Usage:
               Digital Signature, Key Encipherment, Key Agreement
           X509v3 Subject Alternative Name:
               DNS:vcva66.book.local
           X509v3 Subject Key Identifier:
               CC:39:38:03:AF:CB:1D:08:76:EC:4F:3B:68:F3:EC:83:F5:D7:07:9C
           X509v3 Authority Key Identifier:

keyid:CB:38:D1:9E:28:8F:23:00:C7:19:77:27:37:AB:88:3F:39:D5:88:C6


    Signature Algorithm: sha256WithRSAEncryption
         05:ec:fe:09:1f:94:a6:5a:1f:85:9d:a9:73:56:34:35:6d:b8:
         60:38:f6:96:e1:c4:6a:1a:f0:5a:42:a3:30:ff:6d:23:04:6f:
         67:b2:31:1a:c5:dd:15:24:7c:a3:42:52:16:dd:0b:13:a3:00:
         e3:e3:34:d0:44:c7:e7:22:e3:87:66:ff:10:f7:b7:88:78:92:
         e1:31:6f:33:ca:13:f6:d5:25:41:f0:ae:e6:d7:20:ef:78:13:
         73:65:89:9e:78:0e:da:4b:95:5a:7e:8d:d6:15:00:14:74:74:
         1a:bd:a2:54:e9:60:ea:06:1a:84:90:bd:a9:fa:b7:87:5a:19:
         9d:36:8c:cb:ad:9b:c8:f2:85:3c:02:78:6f:88:04:b2:8c:78:
         a1:37:6c:39:9a:61:d7:ea:80:21:ff:bb:7f:3e:ee:32:e7:0b:
         2c:d5:fd:a0:67:82:24:b1:54:e1:cd:95:c2:36:dd:5d:0f:82:
         63:6f:91:e2:47:9c:6d:04:a5:c6:8e:aa:c9:c8:89:67:cf:a6:
         02:11:db:51:fd:73:d2:dd:13:9f:7c:47:1e:7a:7a:23:72:82:
         18:55:7b:23:73:17:23:31:c9:6c:70:2e:97:22:60:a3:02:10:
         ad:e5:6f:79:db:0c:3d:ce:6f:97:1f:42:5f:bb:a4:42:ef:59:
         f2:4d:98:0a
Press <Ctrl>+<C> to stop observing at any point ...


2017-01-18 04:34:57 +0000: Collect one inventory snapshot[2017-01-18
04:34:57] INFO  WEBrick::HTTPServer#start: pid=13495 port=8010
```

The output shows that the web server started and runs on port 8010. It also shows information on the public key assigned to the web server. To stop observing, press **Ctrl+C** to terminate the server.

The URL for this server is https://<VC IP address or hostname>:8010/.

When prompted, enter the vSphere administrator's credentials to log on.

Figure 22.61 shows the landing page after a successful login.

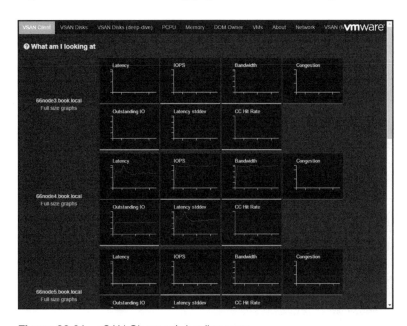

Figure 22.61   vSAN Observer's landing page

The initial page lists all nodes in the cluster, including the witness node if the cluster is stretched. Scroll down to display the rest of the nodes. To navigate to other pages, select their corresponding link at the top of the page.

Each page shows a question at the top-left corner: **What am I looking at?** Click this question to see a summary of what each page includes and for what it is used.

Collecting an Observer Bundle

If a vSAN cluster exhibits possible performance degradation, the VMware Technical Support team may request an Observer HTML bundle. This section provides details on how to collect one.

To capture a vSAN Observer HTML bundle, run this command via the RVC while in the computers directory (for example, /vcva66/Book-DC/computers):

```
vsan.observer [cluster] --run-webserver --force --generate-html-bundle
[path] --interval [interval in seconds] --max-runtime 1
```

Here is an example:

```
vsan.observer Book-Cluster --run-webserver --force --generate-html-bundle /
tmp --interval 30 --max-runtime 1
```

The command runs a web server that captures a performance snapshot every 30 seconds. The web server stops after 1 hour. The HTML bundle is written to the /tmp directory on the vCenter server where RVC is running.

If the performance issue is reproduced before the max runtime is reached, you can interrupt it by pressing **Ctrl+C**. The server is stopped, and the messages listed in Listing 22.18 are displayed.

Listing 22.18   Interrupting vSAN Observer HTML bundle collection

```
2017-01-19 04:16:26 +0000: Press <Ctrl>+<C> to stop observing
2017-01-19 04:16:42 +0000: Execution interrupted, wrapping up ...
[2017-01-19 04:16:42] INFO  going to shutdown ...
[2017-01-19 04:16:42] INFO  WEBrick::HTTPServer#start done.
2017-01-19 04:16:42 +0000: Writing out an HTML bundle to /tmp/
vsan-observer-2017-01-19.04-16-42.tar.gz ...
2017-01-19 04:16:42 +0000: Writing statsdump for system mem ...
2017-01-19 04:16:42 +0000: Writing statsdump for pnics ...
2017-01-19 04:16:42 +0000: Writing statsdump for vmktcpip stack ...
2017-01-19 04:16:42 +0000: Writing statsdump for slabs ...
2017-01-19 04:16:42 +0000: Writing statsdump for heaps ...
2017-01-19 04:16:42 +0000: Writing statsdump for fitness stats ...
2017-01-19 04:16:42 +0000: Writing statsdump for cmmds stats ...
2017-01-19 04:16:42 +0000: Writing statsdump for pcpus ...
2017-01-19 04:16:42 +0000: Writing statsdump for worldlets ...
2017-01-19 04:16:43 +0000: Writing statsdump for helper worlds ...
2017-01-19 04:16:43 +0000: Writing statsdump for DOM ...
2017-01-19 04:16:43 +0000: Writing statsdump for LSOM components ...
2017-01-19 04:16:43 +0000: Writing statsdump for PLOG disks ...
2017-01-19 04:16:43 +0000: Writing statsdump for LSOM disks ...
2017-01-19 04:16:43 +0000: Writing virstoStats for LSOM disks ...
```

```
2017-01-19 04:16:43 +0000: Writing CFStats for LSOM disks ...
2017-01-19 04:16:43 +0000: Writing vsansparse ...
2017-01-19 04:16:43 +0000: Writing vsansparse Open Chains ...
2017-01-19 04:16:43 +0000: Writing statsdump for CBRC ...
2017-01-19 04:16:43 +0000: Writing statsdump for VSCSI ...
2017-01-19 04:16:43 +0000: Writing statsdump for NFS ...
2017-01-19 04:16:43 +0000: Writing statsdump for VSCSI-host ...
2017-01-19 04:16:43 +0000: Writing statsdump for LSOM Congestion ...
2017-01-19 04:16:44 +0000: Writing statsdump for LSOM Host ...
2017-01-19 04:16:44 +0000: Writing statsdump for PhysDisk ...
2017-01-19 04:16:44 +0000: Writing statsdump for SSDs WB ...
2017-01-19 04:16:44 +0000: Writing out CMMDS history ...
2017-01-19 04:16:44 +0000: Done dumping time series stats
2017-01-19 04:16:44 +0000: Generating HTML
2017-01-19 04:16:44 +0000: Generating DOM per-host HTML tabs ...
2017-01-19 04:16:44 +0000: Generating LSOM per-host HTML tabs ...
2017-01-19 04:16:44 +0000: Generating CPU per-host HTML tabs ...
2017-01-19 04:16:44 +0000: Generating Memory per-host HTML tabs ...
2017-01-19 04:16:44 +0000: CBRC wasn't enabled, skipping ...
2017-01-19 04:16:44 +0000: Generating HTML (fill in template)
2017-01-19 04:16:44 +0000: HTML length: 301236
2017-01-19 04:16:44 +0000: Done writing HTML bundle to /tmp/
vsan-observer-2017-01-19.04-16-42.tar.gz
```

The last line in this output states the filename within the path specified on the command line. In this example, it is vsan-observer-2017-01-19.04-16-42.tar.gz. This is the file to send to the VMware Technical Support team.

Browsing vSAN Observer HTML Bundle Stats

To browse the collected vSAN Observer metrics and stats, follow this procedure:

1. Extract the file on your desktop.

2. In a browser, open the stats.html file at the top level of the extracted files. (In my experience, the Firefox browser displays the graphs correctly, while others, like Chrome or Internet Explorer, display them as thumbnail images only.)

3. The initial page displayed should be similar to the page shown earlier, in Figure 22.61.

You can use the navigation links at the top of the page to display the corresponding stats.

vSAN iSCSI Targets (VITs)

Many enterprise business-critical applications require the highest uptime possible, which can be achieved only using application- or guest OS-based clustering technology (for example, Microsoft Windows Server Failover Clustering). Such configurations may require shared storage for quorum and shared data utilizing SCSI3 Persistent Group Reservation (PGR) to arbitrate concurrent access to the shared SCSI LUNs. VMFS5 provides physical mode raw device mappings (RDMs) to facilitate direct access to these LUNs by the VM cluster nodes. However, vSAN lacks the capability to create RDM pointers on the vSAN datastore. vSphere 6.5 introduced vSAN iSCSI targets (VITs) to address this need.

vSAN iSCSI Targets Architecture

VITs are completely different from physical mode RDMs. vSphere 6.5 provides a software layer, ported from FreeBSD, that creates iSCSI targets to which one or more LUNs can be attached. These are actually virtual disks backed by vSAN objects. These virtual disks' descriptor files are stored in special namespace folders, representing the targets, on the vSAN datastore. Another namespace object is used to store VIT configuration. I discuss VIT namespace folder contents in more detail in the section **"The VIT Config Namespace,"** later in this chapter. I also discuss iSCSI target namespace objects in the section "vSAN iSCSI Target Namespaces," later in this chapter.

Configuring a VIT Network

VITs require a VMkernel network adapter (VMKNIC) configured and uplinked to a network accessible by the VMs that will be granted access to the VITs.

TIP

Because the vSAN license includes the vDS license, I prefer using vDS instead of standard vSwitches for vSAN-related networks, including VITs. It ensures consistency of port group naming across all nodes in the cluster and provides enhanced features (as discussed earlier in this chapter). I also prefer to use separate networks for vSAN traffic and VITs. Separation can be achieved by using VLANs when the number of physical NICs is limited. Sharing high-bandwidth NICs with multiple VLANs is a good candidate for using NIOC to guarantee relative shares of the bandwidth to each VMNIC.

To create a dedicated VMNIC for VIT traffic, follow this procedure:

1. Connect to the vCenter server using the vSphere 6.5 Web Client as a user with Administrator privileges.

2. Navigate to **Networking** view (see Figure 22.62).

3. Select the vDS created earlier in this chapter.

4. Right-click the vDS and select the **Add and Manage Hosts** menu option. If you're using 6.5, an icon is now available at the top of the details pane.

Figure 22.62 Accessing the Add and Manage Hosts menu for vDS

5. In step 1 of the Add and Manage Hosts Wizard, select the **Manage host networking** radio button.

6. In step 2 of the wizard, click the **Attached hosts** icon (which is a green plus sign).

7. In the Select Member Hosts dialog that appears, select all hosts in the cluster and then click **OK**.

8. Click **Next**.

9. In step 3 of the wizard, select the **Manage VMkernel adapters** check box and then click **Next**.

10. In step 4 of the wizard, select one of the hosts and then click the **New adapter** icon (a green plus sign). This opens the Add Networking subwizard.

11. In the Select Target Device step, the **Select an existing network** radio button is already selected. Click the **Browse** button.

12. Select the distributed port group that will be used for VIT traffic.

TIP

Create a separate distributed port group for each different class of traffic. This makes it easier to configure different port group settings relevant to the type of traffic.

---

13. In the Port Properties step, leave all available services unchecked.

14. In the IPv4 Settings step, select **Use static IPv4 settings** and enter the IPv4 address and subnet mask. If you must use a different default gateway, you can select the **Override default gateway for this adapter** check box and enter the gateway IP address.

15. Click **Next**.

16. In the Ready to Complete step, review your selections and then click **Finish**.

17. Repeat steps 9–16 for each host. A new vmk(n) adapter is added to each host (in this example, it is vmk3). When you're done, proceed to the next step.

18. Click **Next**.

19. In step 5 of the wizard, if the status of all hosts is **No impact**, click **Next**.

20. In the final step of the wizard, click **Finish**.

Enabling VITs

To enable VITs, follow this procedure:

1. Connect to the vCenter server using the vSphere 6.5 Web Client or vSphere 6.5 HTML5 client as a user with Administrator privileges.

2. Navigate to the **Hosts and Clusters** view.

3. Select the cluster object in the Navigator pane.

4. Select the **Configure** tab.

5. Select **iSCSI Targets** in the Virtual SAN section.

6. Click the **Edit** button.

7. In the Edit Virtual SAN iSCSI Target Service dialog, select the **Enable Virtual SAN iSCSI target service** check box.

8. Select the default ISCSI network from the pull-down list (for example, **vmk3**).

9. Leave the Default TCP Port value at **3260**, which is the standard port used for iSCSI communications.

10. Select the default authentication that meets your design requirements. Available choices are None, CHAP, and Mutual CHAP.

11. Select the storage policy for the home object (for example, **SAN Storage Policy**). This object is where the iSCSI targets' configurations as well as VMDKs backing each LUN will be stored.

12. Click **OK** (see Figure 22.63).

Figure 22.63   Enabling vSAN iSCSI targets

Creating VITs

To create VITs, follow this procedure:

1. Connect to the vCenter server using the vSphere 6.5 Web Client as a user with Administrator privileges.

2. Navigate to the **Hosts and Clusters** view (see Figure 22.64).

3. Select the cluster object in the Navigator pane.

4. Select the **Configure** tab.

5. Select **iSCSI Targets** in the Virtual SAN section.

6. Click the **Add new iSCSI target** icon (a green plus sign) to open the **New iSCSI Target** dialog. A unique IQN is automatically generated and populated in the **Target IQN** field. I prefer to not modify it to ensure its uniqueness.

7. Enter a human-readable target alias.

8. Select **Virtual SAN Default Storage Policy** from the Target Storage Policy pull-down list.

9. Select the VMKNIC to which the target will be bound. This is the VMKNIC created in the section "Configuring a VIT Network," earlier in this chapter.

10. Leave the TCP Port unmodified, at **3260**.

11. Select the authentication method from the Authentication pull-down list.

    At this point, you can finish the process by skipping to step 17. Or you can add the first LUN to the target being created here by proceeding with the next step.

12. Click the **Add your first LUN to the iSCSI target (optional)** check box.

13. Enter the LUN ID (for example, `0`).

14. Optionally, enter an alias (for example, `SQL-data`).

15. Select the LUN storage policy. In this example, I selected a policy named `RAID10`, which provides mirrored replicas with three stripes each.

TIP

The choice of LUN storage policy should be relevant to the expected I/O profile for the LUN. See the section "vSAN Storage Policies" in Chapter 21 for a discussion on matching RAID types to expected I/O patterns.

---

16. Enter the LUN size (for example, `10`) and select the unit of measure (for example, select **GB**).

    The right-hand side of this section shows the vSAN storage consumption resulting from applying the storage policy. In this example, because I am using RAID10, which is mirrored stripes, the storage consumption is double the LUN size to account for the mirror. Striping does not have an impact on storage consumption. Rather, it dictates how many capacity tier disks will be used by the stripes. You can find more details in the "vSAN Storage Policies" section in Chapter 21. In this example, I would specify 100% object space reservation if the LUN will be used as a Windows failover cluster quorum disk. This is similar to creating a thick VMFS VMDK.

17. Click **OK** to conclude this procedure.

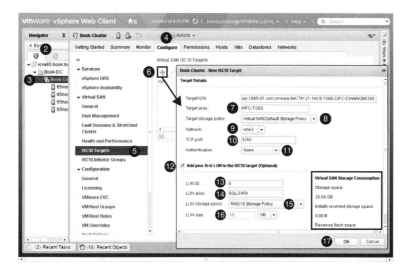

Figure 22.64   Creating a vSAN iSCSI target and the first LUN

Figure 22.65 shows the end result.

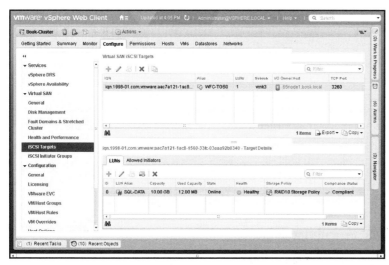

Figure 22.65   vSAN iSCSI target and first LUN created

Creating Initiator Groups

For better security and to control access to VITs and LUNs, you should create initiator groups and assign them to targets and/or LUNs.

> **NOTE**
>
> At this writing, VITs are supported only with physical nodes without multipathing due to the lack of targets' virtual IP addresses.
>
> References to using initiators within VMs in this section will apply after VMware lifts the support restriction.

> **TIP**
>
> You can achieve better load balancing by creating a separate target for each set of clustered nodes. vSphere 6.5 automatically assigns each target to a different owner until all vSAN nodes have been assigned as owners, and then it rotates new targets' ownership on the vSAN nodes again. In other words, if you have a four-node vSAN cluster and you create four targets, each target owner will be one of the four nodes. Additional targets created will be assigned one to each node, in a rotating fashion. There is no need to create multiple targets per set of clustered VMs because vSphere 6.5 does not support LUN assignments to more than one target at a time.
>
> You can then create the LUNs required for each set of clustered VMs attached to their corresponding target. In this example, I created two targets: one for a SQL cluster and the other for an Exchange cluster.

To restrict access of a set of clustered VMs to a specific target, add the VMs' iSCSI initiators to an initiator group and add that target to the Accessible Targets tab of the group. To do so, follow this procedure:

1. Connect to the vCenter server using the vSphere 6.5 Web Client as a user with Administrator privileges.

2. Navigate to the **Hosts and Clusters** view.

3. Select the cluster object in the inventory tree.

4. Select the **Configure** tab (see Figure 22.66).

5. Select the **iSCSI Initiator Groups** option in the Virtual SAN section.

6. Click the **Add a new iSCSI initiator group** icon (a green plus sign).

7. In the dialog that appears, enter the group name.

8. Enter the initiator's IQN of the first VM in the cluster.

9. To add the initiator's IQN from another VM in the cluster, click **Add another member link** in the bottom-right side of the dialog. A blank field is added in the Group Members section.

    Repeat this step until the initiators from all nodes in the VM cluster have been added.

10. Click **OK**.

Figure 22.66   Creating an initiator group

11. Select the newly created initiator group.

12. In the Group Details pane, click the **Accessible Targets** tab.

13. Click the **Add a new accessible target for iSCSi initiator group** icon (a green plus sign).

14. In the dialog that appears, select the check box next to the group or groups associated with the set of clustered VMs.

15. Click **OK** (see Figure 22.67).

16. Repeat steps 11–15 for each initiator group.

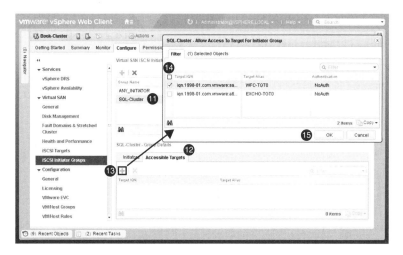

Figure 22.67   Selecting accessible targets

VIT Configuration Under the Hood

The process of enabling and configuring VITs results in creating an `.iSCSI-CONFIG` directory in the vSAN datastore. This directory is the VIT configuration namespace.

The VIT Config Namespace

The VIT config namespace is a vSAN `Namespace` object similar to that used by VMs. The path is /vmfs/volumes/vsanDatastore/.iSCSI-CONFIG, which is a symbolic link to /vmfs/volumes/vsan:[datastore UUID]/[namespace UUID].

The leading dot in the directory name makes it a hidden directory. To list the directory name and its symbolic link, use this command:

```
ls -Al /vmfs/volumes/vsanDatastore/
```

Listing 22.19 shows the path and its corresponding symbolic link

Listing 22.19   The VIT config namespace

```
ls -Al /vmfs/volumes/vsanDatastore/
total 3072
lrwxr-xr-x    1 root     root     36 Oct 29 15:00 .iSCSI-CONFIG ->
8d331158-2a2d-bca6-22f0-000c29d918dd
lrwxr-xr-x    1 root     root     36 Oct 29 15:00 .vsan.stats -> 28ff0c58-
11cb-72d1-686e-000c29d918dd
```

```
drwxr-xr-t    1 root      root      1960 Oct 28 21:29 28ff0c58-11cb-72d1-
686e-000c29d918dd
drwxr-xr-t    1 root      root      1540 Oct 26 22:53 8d331158-2a2d-bca6-
22f0-000c29d918dd
drwxr-xr-t    1 root      root      1540 Oct 27 01:32 a6581158-0e3a-11ee-
2fd8-000c29da46c3
```

The output shows that the .iSCSI-CONFIG directory is a symbolic link to 8d331158-2a2d-bca6-22f0-000c29d918dd, which is the namespace's UUID. This is listed on the second-to-last line in the output (highlighted).

> **TIP**
>
> The permission bit of each namespace listed in the output (for example, drwxr-xr-t), ends with t, which is the sticky bit. This means that the directory can be deleted or renamed only by its owner or root user.

The following is another command to list the namespace objects' UUIDs, using the object store file system tool, osfs-ls:

/usr/lib/vmware/osfs/bin/osfs-ls /vmfs/volumes/vsanDatastore/

Listing 22.20 shows this command and its output.

Listing 22.20   The content of the VIT config namespace

```
/usr/lib/vmware/osfs/bin/osfs-ls /vmfs/volumes/vsanDatastore
8d331158-2a2d-bca6-22f0-000c29d918dd
.iSCSI-CONFIG
28ff0c58-11cb-72d1-686e-000c29d918dd
.vsan.stats
a6581158-0e3a-11ee-2fd8-000c29da46c3
```

This output lists each namespace's UUID followed by the corresponding name.

In this example, the .iSCSI-CONFIG namespace has UUID 8d331158-2a2d-bca6-22f0-000c29d918dd, and the .vsan.stats namespace has UUID 28ff0c58-11cb-72d1-686e-000c29d918dd. (I cover .vsan.stats namespace earlier in this chapter, in the section, "**Enabling vSAN Performance Service**.")

The last UUID in Listing 22.20 belongs to the iSCSI target object, which I discuss later in this section.

To list the attributes of the .iSCSI-CONFIG object, use its UUID with this command:

```
/usr/lib/vmware/osfs/bin/objtool getAttr --uuid [UUID]
```

You can also use the abbreviated version -u instead of --uuid.

Listing 22.21 shows this command and its output.

Listing 22.21   Listing .iSCSI-CONFIG object attributes

```
/usr/lib/vmware/osfs/bin/objtool getAttr -uuid 8d331158-2a2d-bca6-22f0-
000c29d918dd
Object Attributes --
UUID:8d331158-2a2d-bca6-22f0-000c29d918dd
Object type:vsan
Object size:273804165120
User friendly name:.iSCSI-CONFIG
HA metadata:(null)
Allocation type:Thick
Policy:
((\"stripeWidth\" i1)
(\"cacheReservation\" i0)
(\"proportionalCapacity\" (i0 i100))
(\"hostFailuresToTolerate\" i1)
(\"forceProvisioning\" i0)
(\"spbmProfileId\" \"aa6d5a82-1c88-45da-85d3-3d74b91a5bad\")
(\"spbmProfileGenerationNumber\" l+0))
Object class: vmnamespace
Object capabilities: NONE
Object path: /vmfs/volumes/vsan:52d999708422cf21-f4b4b0f762946c2c/
Group uuid: 00000000-0000-0000-0000-000000000000
```

I removed blank lines from the output in Listing 22.21 and wrapped the Policy field's values for readability.

The output shows that the object type is vsan, and its size is 255GB (273804165120 bytes), which is the maximum vSAN component size.

The object is allocated as a thick object. ITs storage policy is the vSAN default storage policy, which includes FTT = 1, SW = 1. This is the policy selected during configuration time. The object's user-friendly name is .iSCSI-CONFIG, and the object class is vmnamespace.

The object's path is the vSAN datastore. The `.iSCSI-CONFIG` namespace includes two directories: /etc and /targets. To list these directories, run the following command:

```
ls -Al /vmfs/volumes/vsanDatastore/.iSCSI-CONFIG/
```

Listing 22.22 shows this command and its output.

Listing 22.22   Listing the content of the VIT config namespace

```
ls -Al /vmfs/volumes/vsanDatastore/.iSCSI-CONFIG/
total 789520
-r--------   1 root      root         1441792 Oct 26 22:51 .fbb.sf
-r--------   1 root      root       267026432 Oct 26 22:52 .fdc.sf
-r--------   1 root      root         1179648 Oct 26 22:52 .pb2.sf
-r--------   1 root      root       268435456 Oct 26 22:52 .pbc.sf
-r--------   1 root      root       262733824 Oct 26 22:52 .sbc.sf
drwx------   1 root      root             280 Oct 26 22:53 .sdd.sf
-r--------   1 root      root         4194304 Oct 26 22:52 .vh.sf
drwx------   1 root      root             420 Oct 27 01:32 etc
drwx------   1 root      root             420 Oct 27 01:30 targets
```

The output in Listing 22.22 shows several hidden files and one hidden directory with the .sf extension. These are VMFS5 metadata system files of the namespace because this namespace, like any other vSAN namespace object, is formatted with VMFS5.

The VIT configuration file vit.conf, is stored in the /etc directory in the `.iSCSI-CONFIG` namespace. Listing 22.23 shows the content of this file with a single target and LUN, as defined earlier in this chapter.

Listing 22.23   Listing the content of the vit.conf file

```
generation 18
initiator-group SQL-Cluster {
        initiator iqn.1991-05.com.microsoft:win2008.book.local
        initiator iqn.1991-05.com.microsoft:win2008-2.book.local
}
initiator-group EXCHG-Cluster {
        initiator iqn.1991-05.com.microsoft:exchange-1.book.local
        initiator iqn.1991-05.com.microsoft:exchange-2.book.local
}
auth-group default {
        auth-type none
}
```

```
auth-group a6581158-0e3a-11ee-2fd8-000c29da46c3 {
        auth-type none
        initiator-group SQL-Cluster
}
auth-group b8cc1658-4f92-66f6-2a9f-000c298ef254 {
        auth-type none
        initiator-group EXCHG-Cluster
}
portal-group default {
        discovery-auth-group no-authentication
        listen vmk3:3260
}
portal-group pg-vmk3-3260 {
        discovery-auth-group no-authentication
        listen vmk3:3260
}
target iqn.1998-01.com.vmware:aac7a121-1ac8-1560-33fc-03aaa92b0340 {
        alias "WFC-TGT0"
        portal-group pg-vmk3-3260
        auth-group a6581158-0e3a-11ee-2fd8-000c29da46c3
        option uuid a6581158-0e3a-11ee-2fd8-000c29da46c3
        option owner-id a6581158-0e3a-11ee-2fd8-000c29da46c3
        lun 0 {
                backend vmdk
                path a6581158-0e3a-11ee-2fd8-000c29da46c3/
f5581158-177a-a4d6-8563-000c29d918dd.vmdk
                size 20971520
                option lun-alias "SQL-DATA"
        }
        lun 1 {
                backend vmdk
                path a6581158-0e3a-11ee-2fd8-000c29da46c3/b6e51658-a6ee-
  322e-ba77-000c29da46c3.vmdk
                size 209715200
                option lun-alias "DB"
        }
}
target iqn.1998-01.com.vmware:a6b59dd0-bc43-3bef-f36a-190eb81f76e0 {
        alias "EXCHG-TGT0"
        portal-group pg-vmk3-3260
        auth-group b8cc1658-4f92-66f6-2a9f-000c298ef254
```

```
        option uuid b8cc1658-4f92-66f6-2a9f-000c298ef254
        option owner-id b8cc1658-4f92-66f6-2a9f-000c298ef254
        lun 0 {
                backend vmdk
                path b8cc1658-4f92-66f6-2a9f-000c298ef254/
d2d01658-2b0e-04ff-131c-000c292cb974.vmdk
                size 20971520
                option lun-alias "EXCHG-QRM"
        }
}
```

This configuration file is in FreeBSD format because the vitd daemon was ported from that distribution.

The first line in the file is generation. The value of this key is incremented each time the configuration is modified, triggering all hosts to refresh the configuration into their memory.

The file includes sections whose settings are wrapped in braces ({ }):

- **Initiator-group**—If defined, this lists the group and the initiators that are members of the group.

- **auth-group default**—This lists the default authentication type, auth-type. In this example, the default authentication type is none.

- **auth-group [UUID]**—The UUID listed here is that of a VIT.

    - The first listing in this section is the authentication type (auth-type).

    - If no authentication is required, the entry would be auth-type none.

    - If an authentication type is specified, it would be listed without the field name auth-type. Two types are possible:

        - **chap**—This type is for Challenge-Handshake Authentication Protocol (CHAP). It requires a user name and a secret word. The initiator authenticates with the VIT, using the credentials defined here. The secret is obfuscated in the vit.conf file.

        - **chap-mutual**—This type is for two-way CHAP authentication, where both the initiator and target authenticate with each other. In this entry, the user and secret word are listed for both directions. The secrets are obfuscated in the vit.conf file.

The next lines in this section are the initiator groups. If no initiator groups are listed here, this would mean that any initiator can access the target.

■ **portal-group default**—This lists the default portal group and the default discovery authentication and the `vmknic:port` combination on which the portal is listening (for example, `vmk3:3260`).

■ **Portal-group**—This defines the iSCSI portal group. In vSAN configuration, it is a single portal per node, which is on the same VMKNIC and port on all nodes (for example, `vmk3:3260`).

■ **Target [IQN]**—The remaining entries in the file are for each target defined on the cluster. The target name is the iSCSI qualified name (IQN). The properties of each target include the following:

  ■ `alias`—This is the friendly name of the target (for example, `WFC-TGT0`).

  ■ `portal-group`—This is the portal group name listed earlier in the file (for example, `pg-vmk3-3260`).

  ■ `auth-group`—This is the authentication group that is the target's UUID. See Listing 22.24 and 22.25 for examples.

  ■ `option uuid`—This lists the target's UUID. It is the same as the DOM object's UUID of the target's directory.

  ■ `option owner-id`—This lists the target's owner UUID, which is the same as the target UUID. It is not the same as the DOM owner.

  ■ The last property of each target is its attached LUN's definitions. Each LUN is listed on its own line (for example, `lun 0`, `lun 1` etc.), with its properties listed within braces:

    ■ `backend`—This is the type of backing device. In vSAN configuration, it is always `vmdk`.

    ■ `path`—This is the path to the VMDK's descriptor file within the target's namespace (see the next section, "vSAN iSCSI Target Namespaces").

    ■ `size`—This is the LUN size, in 512-byte sectors

    ■ `option alias`—This is an optional friendly name given to the LUN.

vSAN iSCSI Target Namespaces

Each VIT has a unique namespace object in which virtual disk descriptor files, representing attached LUNs, are stored. These namespace folders are listed in the /vmfs/

volumes/[vSAN Datastore Name]/.iSCSI-CONFIG/targets directory. To list these namespace folders for a vSAN datastore named vsanDatastore, run this command:

```
ls -Al /vmfs/volumes/vsanDatastore/.iSCSI-CONFIG/targets
```

Listing 22.24 shows this command and its output.

Listing 22.24   Listing content of the VIT `targets` directory

```
ls -Al /vmfs/volumes/vsanDatastore/.iSCSI-CONFIG/targets
lrwxrwxrwx    1 root      root             42 Oct 27 01:30 a6581158-0e3a-
11ee-2fd8-000c29da46c3 -> ../../a6581158-0e3a-11ee-2fd8-000c29da46c3
lrwxrwxrwx    1 root      root             42 Oct 31 04:47 b8cc1658-4f92-
66f6-2a9f-000c298ef254 -> ../../b8cc1658-4f92-66f6-2a9f-000c298ef254
```

In this example, there are two targets defined. The output shows that the `targets` folder actually contains symbolic links to the targets' namespace objects within the vSAN datastore. Notice that the first permission for each entry is a lowercase `l`, which indicates a symbolic link. Each link points to an entry two levels up the directory tree, which in this example is the /vmfs/volumes/vsanDatastore directory.

To list the symbolic links in the directory, run the following command:

```
ls -Al /vmfs/volumes/vsanDatastore/
```

Listing 22.25 shows this command and its output. In it, I highlighted the two namespace folders linked in the previous listing.

Listing 22.25   Listing Namespace Objects' UUID of the VIT targets

```
ls -Al /vmfs/volumes/vsanDatastore/
total 4096
lrwxr-xr-x    1 root      root             36 Nov  3 02:59 .iSCSI-CONFIG ->
8d331158-2a2d-bca6-22f0-000c29d918dd
lrwxr-xr-x    1 root      root             36 Nov  3 02:59 .vsan.stats ->
28ff0c58-11cb-72d1-686e-000c29d918dd
drwxr-xr-t    1 root      root           2240 Nov  3 00:04 28ff0c58-11cb-72d1-
686e-000c29d918dd
drwxr-xr-t    1 root      root           1540 Oct 26 22:53 8d331158-2a2d-bca6-
22f0-000c29d918dd
drwxr-xr-t    1 root      root           1820 Oct 31 06:33 a6581158-0e3a-11ee-
2fd8-000c29da46c3
drwxr-xr-t    1 root      root           1540 Oct 31 05:05 b8cc1658-4f92-66f6-
2a9f-000c298ef254
```

The content of each target's namespace is the virtual disks' descriptor files of the LUNs attached to that target.

Listing 22.26 lists the content of the target whose alias is `WFC-TGT0` and has UUID `a6581158-0e3a-11ee-2fd8-000c29da46c3`, according to the `vit.conf` file discussed earlier.

Listing 22.26   Listing content of a vSAN iSCSI target's namespace

```
ls -Al /vmfs/volume/vsanDatastore/.iSCSI/targets/ a6581158-0e3a-11ee-2fd8-
000c29da46c3
b6e51658-a6ee-322e-ba77-000c29da46c3.vmdk
f5581158-177a-a4d6-8563-000c29d918dd.vmdk
```

In Listing 22.26, I wrapped the output to list one descriptor file per line. In this example, there are two descriptor files, matching the number of LUNs attached to this target.

To identify the vSAN object UUID associated with a given VMDK, run this command:

```
grep vsan /vmfs/volumes/vsanDatastore/[target namespace]/
[descriptor file]
```

Listing 22.27 shows the command and its output for one of the descriptor files.

Listing 22.27   Listing a vSAN iSCSI LUN's object UUID

```
grep vsan /vmfs/volumes/vsanDatastore/a6581158-0e3a-11ee-2fd8-000c29da46c3/
b6e51658-a6ee-322e-ba77-000c29da46c3.vmdk
RW 209715200 VMFS "vsan://b6e51658-a6ee-322e-ba77-000c29da46c3"
```

In this example, the LUN's vSAN object's UUID is `b6e51658-a6ee-322e-ba77-000c29da46c3`.

Monitoring VIT

vCenter provides a facility to monitor vSAN, including iSCSI targets. Follow this procedure to access the VIT monitoring UI:

1. Connect to the vCenter server using the vSphere 6.5 Web Client as a user with Administrator privileges.

2. Navigate to the **Hosts and Clusters** view.

3. Select the cluster object in the inventory tree.

4. Select the **Monitor** tab.

5. Click the **Virtual SAN** button.

6. Select the **iSCSI Targets** section.

7. In the iSCSI Targets pane, select a target's alias.

8. Select the **Physical Disk Placement** tab in the bottom pane (see Figure 22.68).

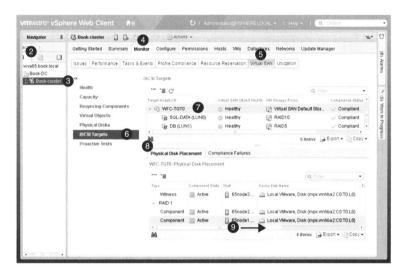

Figure 22.68   Monitoring VITs

In this example, I moved the Cache Disk Name column to the left and positioned it to the right of the Host column.

In the top pane, the target's Virtual SAN Object Health status is `Healthy`, with a green checkmark. This means that all the object's components are available and accessible.

In this example, because the target has the vSAN default storage policy applied to it (FTT = 1, SW = 1), there is RAID 1 (FTT = 1) section listed with two components, which are the mirrored replicas. The third component is the witness. The state for all three components is `Active`.

Each of the three components is placed on a different host, which is the expected placement. This means that if one of the hosts fails or loses network connectivity to the vSAN network, the remaining two hosts host more than 50% (the majority) of the components. The objects remains accessible but in a degraded state. If the failed or disconnected host does not recover within 60 minutes, the missing component, which could be a replica or the witness component, will be created on the fourth node in this cluster by replicating the surviving replica component or creating a witness component—whichever was on the failed host.

9. To see on which disk the corresponding component is placed, scroll the bottom pane to the right so you can see the following additional columns:

- **Fault Domain**—In this case, no fault domains were defined, so this column has no values listed. This means that each node in the cluster is within its own fault domain.

- **Cache Disk UUID**—In this case, with a single disk group per node, each host on the list has a single cache tier disk with a unique UUID for each.

- **Capacity Disk Name**—This is the capacity disk on which the listed component is stored. In this example, each replica is made up of a single component since its size is less than 255GB, and the stripe width is 1.

- **Capacity Disk UUID**—These are the UUIDs of each capacity disk.

The values in these columns help with further troubleshooting of problematic components, including the possibility of a failed or unmounted capacity disk.

To list the target's vSAN object details via the CLI, first obtain the object's UUID. You can locate it in the vit.conf file shown in Listing 22.23 earlier in this chapter. It is the value of the field named `option uuid` in the definition of the target with `alias "WFC-TGT0"`. In this example, the UUID is `a6581158-0e3a-11ee-2fd8-000c29da46c3`. Use this UUID in the following command on the console of any of the vSAN nodes:

```
cmmds-tool find --uuid [Object UUID] --format json
```

You can also use the abbreviated option `-u` instead of `--uuid` and `-f` instead of `--format`.

Then locate in the output the section with `"type": "DOM_OBJECT"` in it. Sections are wrapped with curly braces ({ }), and the properties are separated by commas.

Listing 22.28 shows this command and the relevant section of the output.

Listing 22.28   Listing a VIT's DOM object details

```
cmmds-tool find -u a6581158-0e3a-11ee-2fd8-000c29da46c3 -f json
{
    "uuid": "a6581158-0e3a-11ee-2fd8-000c29da46c3",
    "owner": "57b67c43-71ef-7d94-52b0-000c29d918dd",
    "health": "Healthy",
    "revision": "13",
    "type": "DOM_OBJECT",
```

```
    "flag": "2",
    "minHostVersion": "3",
    "md5sum": "4d5ae9e5851745b511aec59cf2304a39",
    "valueLen": "1400",
    "content": {"type": "Configuration", "attributes": {"CSN": 15, "SCSN": 12,
"addressSpace": 273804165120, "scrubStartTime": 1477531814476796,
"objectVersion": 4, "highestDiskVersion": 4, "muxGroup": 524573769010176,
"groupUuid": "a6581158-0e3a-11ee-2fd8-000c29da46c3", "compositeUuid":
"a6581158-0e3a-11ee-2fd8-000c29da46c3", "objClass": 2}, "child-1":
{"type": "RAID_1", "attributes": {}, "child-1": {"type": "Component",
"attributes": {"capacity": [0, 273804165120], "addressSpace": 273804165120,
"componentState": 5, "componentStateTS": 1477873716, "faultDomainId":
"57b67c43-71ef-7d94-52b0-000c29d918dd", "lastScrubbedOffset": 1900544},
"componentUuid": "a6581158-752d-caee-5aae-000c29da46c3", "diskUuid":
"5273aff0-4473-4adc-69dc-e5cff8572295"}, "child-2": {"type": "Component",
"attributes": {"capacity": [0, 273804165120], "addressSpace": 273804165120,
"componentState": 5, "componentStateTS": 1477852329, "faultDomainId":
"57b67f25-0080-ca9d-77da-000c292cb974", "lastScrubbedOffset": 1835008},
"componentUuid": "a6581158-895a-cdee-1fd5-000c29da46c3", "diskUuid":
"52f7fa8d-de29-88d3-901c-f3f013c905be"}}, "child-2": {"type": "Witness",
"attributes": {"componentState": 5, "componentStateTS": 1477873716,
"isWitness": 1, "faultDomainId": "57b68127-135e-e2a1-dd78-000c298ef254"},
"componentUuid": "46c21358-fbeb-ddbf-f156-000c292cb974", "diskUuid":
"525a0acc-9127-5649-2da2-06f718d3793f"}},
    "errorStr": "(null)"
}
```

To make things easier to explain, Listing 22.29 shows the strings in the content section. In this listing, I wrapped each line at the delimiter, which is a comma. You can append |python -m json.tool to the end of the command to automatically format the output as shown in Listing 22.29.

Listing 22.29 Breakdown of a VIT's DOM object content

```
{"type": "Configuration",
    "attributes": {
        "CSN": 15,
        "SCSN": 12,
        "addressSpace": 273804165120,
        "scrubStartTime": 1477531814476796,
        "objectVersion": 4,
        "highestDiskVersion": 4,
        "muxGroup": 524573769010176,
        "groupUuid": "a6581158-0e3a-11ee-2fd8-000c29da46c3",
        "compositeUuid": "a6581158-0e3a-11ee-2fd8-000c29da46c3",
        "objClass": 2
    },
```

```
"child-1": {
    "type": "RAID_1",  ← This is the RAID1 Object
    "attributes": {},

    "child-1": {
        "type": "Component",  ← First replica component
        "attributes": {
        "capacity": [0, 273804165120],
        "addressSpace": 273804165120,
        "componentState": 5,
        "componentStateTS": 1477873716,
        "faultDomainId": "57b67c43-71ef-7d94-52b0-000c29d918dd",
        "lastScrubbedOffset": 1900544},
        "componentUuid": "a6581158-752d-caee-5aae-000c29da46c3",
        "diskUuid": "5273aff0-4473-4adc-69dc-e5cff8572295"},

    "child-2": {"type": "Component",  ← Second replica component
        "attributes": {"capacity": [0, 273804165120],
        "addressSpace": 273804165120,
        "componentState": 5,
        "componentStateTS": 1477852329,
        "faultDomainId": "57b67f25-0080-ca9d-77da-000c292cb974",
        "lastScrubbedOffset": 1835008},
        "componentUuid": "a6581158-895a-cdee-1fd5-000c29da46c3",
        "diskUuid": "52f7fa8d-de29-88d3-901c-f3f013c905be"}},

    "child-2": {"type": "Witness",  ← Witness component
        "attributes": {
        "componentState": 5,
        "componentStateTS": 1477873716,
        "isWitness": 1,
        "faultDomainId": "57b68127-135e-e2a1-dd78-000c298ef254"},
        "componentUuid": "46c21358-fbeb-ddbf-f156-000c292cb974",
        "diskUuid": "525a0acc-9127-5649-2da2-06f718d3793f"}},
```

All three components show a component state value of 5, which means Active.

Refer to Table 21.7 in Chapter 21 for all the possible component states and what they mean.

10. Select one of the LUNs attached to the iSCSI target.

11. In the bottom pane, select the **Physical Disk Placement** tab (see Figure 22.69).

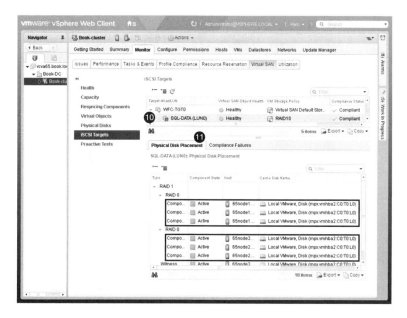

Figure 22.69   Monitoring a VIT's LUNs

In this example, I selected a LUN called SQL-DATA, which is LUN0 attached to the WFC-TGT0 target. The policy applied to this LUN is RAID 10, which includes FTT = 1, SW = 3. In other words, it provides RAID 1 mirrors, where each mirror is striped into three stripes.

The lower pane shows two RAID 0 sets of components. These are the SW = 3 rule in the policy. These two sets represent the RAID 1 replicas. The witness component for both replicas is in the last row of the bottom pane.

All components are in Active state, which means that the LUN's vSAN object is in a healthy state.

You can do the exercise of listing the DOM owner properties of the LUN by using cmmds-tool, as shown earlier for the target object. However, the object UUID in the LUN's case is that of the back-end VMDK's object UUID.

For example, I highlighted the UUID in the relevant lines in the vit.conf file listed here:

```
lun 0 {
                backend vmdk
                path a6581158-0e3a-11ee-2fd8-000c29da46c3/f5581158-177a-
    a4d6-8563-000c29d918dd.vmdk
```

Listing 22.30 shows this command and the text of the content section from the output, which I wrapped at the comma delimiter.

Listing 22.30 Listing a VIT's LUN DOM object details

```
cmmds-tool find -u f5581158-177a-a4d6-8563-000c29d918dd -f json
    "content":
    {"type": "Configuration",
    "attributes": {"CSN": 36,
    "SCSN": 31,
    "addressSpace": 10737418240,
    "scrubStartTime": 1477852347814511,
    "objectVersion": 4,
    "highestDiskVersion": 4,
    "muxGroup": 524573769010176,
    "groupUuid": "a6581158-0e3a-11ee-2fd8-000c29da46c3",
    "compositeUuid": "f5581158-177a-a4d6-8563-000c29d918dd"},

 "child-1": {
    "type": "RAID_1", ← This is the RAID1 Object
    "attributes": {},

  "child-1": {"type": "RAID_0", ← First RAID1 replica component
    "attributes": {
       "stripeBlockSize": 1048576},

    "child-1": {
      "type": "Component", ← First stripe of first replica
      "attributes": {
        "aggregateCapacity": 3579838464,
        "addressSpace": 3579838464,
        "componentState": 5,
        "componentStateTS": 1477873710,
        "faultDomainId": "57b67c43-71ef-7d94-52b0-000c29d918dd"},
```

```
"componentUuid": "0ac21358-6ed3-68ba-5d5b-000c292cb974",
"diskUuid": "5241c49f-007d-b349-f73f-50c07c1dd693"},

"child-2": {
    "type": "Component",  ← Second stripe of first replica
    "attributes": {
        "aggregateCapacity": 3578789888,
        "addressSpace": 3578789888,
        "componentState": 5,
        "componentStateTS": 1477873713,
        "faultDomainId": "57b67c43-71ef-7d94-52b0-000c29d918dd",
        "lastScrubbedOffset": 3578789888},
    "componentUuid": "0ac21358-c1af-70ba-e771-000c292cb974",
    "diskUuid": "52e134bb-e6a6-ec63-2aff-84e5aaefd1c3"},

"child-3": {
    "type": "Component",  ← Third stripe of first replica
    "attributes": {
        "aggregateCapacity": 3578789888,
        "addressSpace": 3578789888,
        "componentState": 5,
        "componentStateTS": 1477873709,
        "faultDomainId": "57b67c43-71ef-7d94-52b0-000c29d918dd",
        "lastScrubbedOffset": 3578789888},
    "componentUuid": "0ac21358-06af-75ba-682c-000c292cb974",
    "diskUuid": "5273aff0-4473-4adc-69dc-e5cff8572295"}},

"child-2": {
    "type": "RAID_0",  ← Second RAID1 replica component
    "attributes": {
        "stripeBlockSize": 1048576},

        "child-1": {
            "type": "Component",  ← First stripe of second replica
            "attributes": {"aggregateCapacity": 3579838464,
            "addressSpace": 3579838464,
            "componentState": 5,
            "componentStateTS": 1477852319,
    "faultDomainId": "57b67f25-0080-ca9d-77da-000c292cb974"},
```

```
        "componentUuid": "f5581158-53f5-14d8-3d5d-000c29d918dd",
        "diskUuid": "52f7fa8d-de29-88d3-901c-f3f013c905be"},

    "child-2": {
        "type": "Component",  ← Second stripe of second replica
        "attributes": {"aggregateCapacity": 3578789888,
            "addressSpace": 3578789888,
            "componentState": 5,
            "componentStateTS": 1477852318,
            "faultDomainId": "57b67f25-0080-ca9d-77da-000c292cb974"},
        "componentUuid": "f5581158-f0a0-15d8-4188-000c29d918dd",
        "diskUuid": "52ef6b09-6bda-897a-41d0-61813cde5144"},

    "child-3": {
        "type": "Component",  ← Third stripe of second replica
        "attributes": {
            "aggregateCapacity": 3578789888,
            "addressSpace": 3578789888,
            "componentState": 5,
            "componentStateTS": 1477852319,
            "faultDomainId": "57b67f25-0080-ca9d-77da-000c292cb974"},
        "componentUuid": "f5581158-d817-16d8-7d82-000c29d918dd",
        "diskUuid": "52e869ee-6a7f-84ef-4cd1-66bafc80ab0d"}}},

"child-2": {
    "type": "Witness",  ← Witness of RAID1 Replica components
    "attributes": {
        "componentState": 5,
        "componentStateTS": 1477873716,
        "isWitness": 1,
        "faultDomainId": "57b68127-135e-e2a1-dd78-000c298ef254",
        "nVotes": 3},  ← Component has 3 votes
    "componentUuid": "0dc21358-e1b9-8d0c-f49d-000c292cb974",
    "diskUuid": "5289fe6f-90e0-6dcb-54c2-cbd8c6f83b68"}},
```

Using ESCXLI to List VITs details

It is sometimes necessary to list VIT details via the CLI. Becoming familiar with the available ESCXLI commands will help you with these tasks.

This is the `esxcli` namespace for VIT:

```
esxcli vsan iscsi
```

Running this command without any options returns the available namespaces. See Listing 22.31 for an example.

Listing 22.31   Listing the vSAN iSCSI namespace with ESCXLI

```
esxcli vsan iscsi
Usage: esxcli vsan iscsi {cmd} [cmd options]

Available Namespaces:
  initiatorgroup        Commands to manipulate Virtual SAN iSCSI target
initiator group
  target                Commands for Virtual SAN iSCSI target configuration
  defaultconfig         Operation for default configuration for Virtual SAN
iSCSI Target
  homeobject            Commands for the Virtual SAN iSCSI target home
object
  status                Enable or disable iSCSI target support, query status.
```

To list all initiator groups, run the following command:

```
esxcli vsan iscsi initiatorgroup list
```

Listing 22.32 shows this command and its output.

Listing 22.32   Listing a VIT's initiator groups via the CLI

```
esxcli vsan iscsi initiatorgroup list
Initiator group
   Name: RAC
   Initiator list: iqn.1991-05.com.microsoft:win2008.book.local
   Accessible targets:
        Alias: RAC-TGT0
        IQN: iqn.1998-01.com.vmware:af9c274e-9e90-f4bb-e7d0-ecf5743f48f9

        Alias: RAC-TGT1
        IQN: iqn.1998-01.com.vmware:56354ed7-4765-cd83-81a4-ed01f947ee74

Initiator group
   Name: WFC
   Initiator list: iqn.1991-05.com.microsoft:win10-work
   Accessible targets:
        Alias: WFC-TGT0
        IQN: iqn.1998-01.com.vmware:1fc77bd9-e0ea-30cc-579b-ca2bedaf44c2
```

This example shows two initiator groups: RAC and WFC. The RAC group has one initiator and two targets, and the WFC group has one of each.

To list the targets, run this command:

```
esxcli vsan iscsi target list
```

The output from this command is too wide to fit on this book's page, so I've split it into two screens. Figure 22.70 shows the command and the left part of the output.

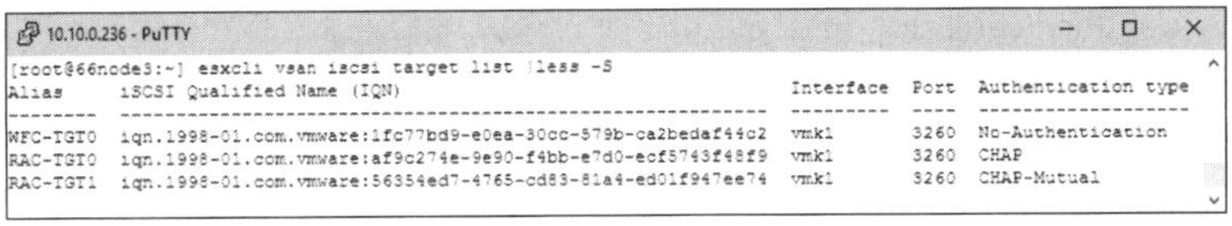

Figure 22.70   Listing vSAN iSCSI targets via the CLI (left half)

Figure 22.71 shows the right part of the output.

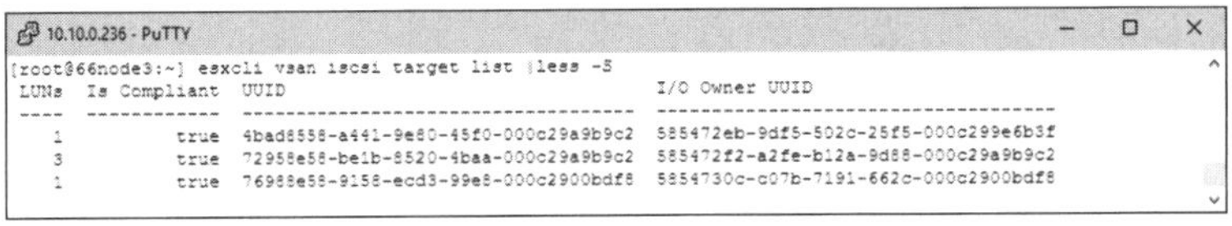

Figure 22.71   Listing vSAN iSCSI targets via the CLI (right half)

In this example, there are three targets: WFC-TGT0, RAC-TGT0, and RAC-TGT1. All targets are on the iSCSI portal on the vmk1 interface and port 3260. The authentication type of each of the three targets is different:

- No-Authentication

- CHAP

- CHAP-Mutual

The right half of the output shows the following:

- The number of LUNs behind each target

- Each target's compliance with the storage policy

- The target's UUID

- The DOM owner of each target, which is the vSAN node through which all I/Os to the target are done

Next I show how to list LUNs attached to a target by using the target's alias via this command:

```
esxcli vsan iscsi target lun list --target [alias]
```

You can also use the abbreviated option -t instead of --target:

```
esxcli vsan iscsi target lun list -t [alias]
```

Figure 22.72 shows this command and its output.

```
10.10.0.236 - PuTTY                                                    —   □   ×
[root@66node3:~] esxcli vsan iscsi target lun list --target RAC-TGT0
ID Alias      Size  UUID                                      Is Compliant  Status
-- -----      ----- ----------------------------------------- ------------  ------
 0 RAC0     102400 MiB 7c958e58-c44e-2704-c9f6-000c29870766        true    online
 1 RAC1     204800 MiB 93b58e58-f3f2-fa73-4345-000c2900bdf8        true    online
 2 RAC2      51200 MiB 02c98e58-a884-35d8-9e57-000c29a9b9c2        true    online
[root@66node3:~]
```

Figure 22.72   Listing vSAN iSCSI LUNs on a target via the CLI

You can drill down a bit deeper into a given LUN by using this command:

```
esxcli vsan iscsi target lun get --id [LUN ID] --target [target alias]
```

You can also use the abbreviated version:

```
esxcli vsan iscsi target lun get -i [LUN ID] -t [target alias]
```

Figure 22.73 shows an example of this command and its output.

```
10.10.0.236 - PuTTY                                                    —   □   ×
[root@66node3:~] esxcli vsan iscsi target lun get -i 0 -t RAC-TGT0
LUN Information
   ID: 0
   Alias: RAC0
   UUID: 7c958e58-c44e-2704-c9f6-000c29870766
   Size: 102400 MiB
   Is Compliant: true
   Policy: (("stripeWidth" i2) ("hostFailuresToTolerate" i1) ("spbmProf
ileId" "af3652fb-a0a4-47c0-b4c0-f8a3b7f99413") ("spbmProfileGenerationN
umber" l+1) ("subFailuresToTolerate" i1) ("CSN" 14) ("spbmProfileName"
"Nested RAID-10"))
   Status: online
[root@66node3:~]
```

Figure 22.73   Listing a vSAN iSCSI LUN's details via the CLI

In this example, the LUN has the following information:

- **ID**—0
- **Alias**—RAC0 (This is the friendly name assigned to the LUN at creation time.)

- **UUID**—The LUN's DOM object's UUID on the vSAN datastore.

- **Size**—The size is listed in MiB.

- **Is Compliant**—This is the storage policy compliance of this LUN. In this example, it is `true`, which means it is compliant.

- **Policy**—These are the details of the storage policy applied to this LUN. In this example, the policy has the following properties:

    - `stripeWidth`—This is the stripe width (SW), which is 2 in this example.

    - `hostFailuresToTolerate`—This is PFTT or Primary FTT, which is the number of site failures to tolerate. In this example, the value is 1.

    - `spbmProfileId`—This is the storage profile ID.

    - `spbmProfileGenerationNumber`—This is the number of times the storage profile was modified. The current value is 1, which means it has not been modified since creation.

    - `subFailuresToTolerate`—This is SFTT or Secondary FTT, which is the intrasite number of failures to tolerate. The value in this example is 1, which means RAID 1. This value combined with the SW value 2 means that the object is configured on each data site as RAID 10 (1+0), where each local mirror has two stripes.

    - `CSN`—This is the configuration sequence number, which is an internal vSAN property.

    - `spbmProfileName`—This is the storage policy name, which in this example is `Nested RAID-10`.

- **Status**—This is the current LUN status, which is `online` in this example.

The next namespace is `defaultconfig`, which can be used to get or set the default configuration of the VIT. To list the default configuration, use this command:

```
esxcli vsan iscsi defaultconfig get
```

Listing 22.33 shows this command and its output.

Listing 22.33 Listing a VIT's default configuration

```
esxcli vsan iscsi defaultconfig get
Default Config Information
   Network Interface: vmk1
```

```
Network Port: 3260
Authentication type: No-Authentication
Authentication user-id:
Authentication mutual user-id:
```

> **TIP**
>
> If your design calls for using CHAP or CHAP-Mutual for all targets presented by VIT,
> change the default configuration by using one of the commands shown next.

To change the default configuration to use CHAP, use this command:

```
esxcli vsan iscsi defaultconfig set --authtype=CHAP --userid=[name]
--secret=[password]
```

You can also use the abbreviated version:

```
esxcli vsan iscsi defaultconfig set -m CHAP -u [name] -s [password]
```

To change the default configuration to use CHAP-Mutual, use this command:

```
esxcli vsan iscsi defaultconfig set --authtype=CHAP-Mutual --userid=
[name] --secret=[password] --mutual-userid=[user to authenticate target
with initiator] --mutual-secret=[initiator's password]
```

You can also use the abbreviated version:

```
esxcli vsan iscsi defaultconfig set -m CHAP -u [name] -s [password] -U
[user to authenticate target with initiator] -S [Initiator's password]
```

This does not change the existing targets' configurations.

The last two command sets apply the same changes that can be done via the UI, as shown
earlier, in Figure 22.63.

To list the VIT home object (namespace), which is one per vSAN cluster, use this
command:

```
esxcli vsan iscsi homeobject get
```

Listing 22.34 shows this command and its output.

Listing 22.34   Listing a VIT's home object

```
esxcli vsan iscsi homeobject get
Namespace Information
   UUID: a6ac8558-b457-67bc-a49b-000c299e6b3f
   Policy: (("stripeWidth" i1) ("cacheReservation" i0)
```

```
("proportionalCapacity" (i0 i100)) ("hostFailuresToTolerate" i1)
("forceProvisioning" i0) ("spbmProfileId" "aa6d5a82-1c88-45da-85d3-
3d74b91a5bad") ("spbmProfileGenerationNumber" l+0) ("CSN" 127) ("SCSN" 125)
("spbmProfileName" "Virtual SAN Default Storage Policy"))
    Is Compliant: true
```

The output in Listing 22.34 shows the namespace's UUID and policy, as well as its compliance with the policy. In this example, the policy in use is the vSAN default storage policy, which is FTT = 1. On a stretched cluster configuration, this translates to PFTT = 1, where one replica of the namespace object is on one data site, and the other replica is on the other data site.

Storage Policy Noncompliance

vSAN regularly monitors all objects for compliance with storage policies applied to them. If any of the components are absent or degraded for any reason, the object is placed in the `Noncompliant` state.

To demonstrate this, I removed a disk group on one of four hosts, using ensure accessibility mode, and then re-created the disk group on that host. The RAID 5 object became noncompliant.

To list such an object, follow this procedure:

1. Connect to the vCenter server using the vSphere 6.x Web Client as a user with Administrator privileges. This example shows vSphere 6.5.

2. Navigate to the **Hosts and Clusters** view and select the cluster object.

3. Select the **Monitor** tab.

4. Click the **Virtual SAN** button (or **vSAN** on 6.5 or newer).

5. Select the **Virtual Objects** section. This option is available on vSAN 6.5 and newer.

6. Select the virtual disk whose compliance status column shows as `Noncompliant`.

7. Select the **Compliance Failures** tab in the bottom pane. The reason for noncompliance shows in this example as follows:

```
Property Name: VSAN - Number of Failures to tolerate
Expected Value: 1
Current Value: 0
```

This means that one component is missing, and if another failure occurs, the object may become unavailable.

Figure 22.74 shows the `Noncompliant` state.

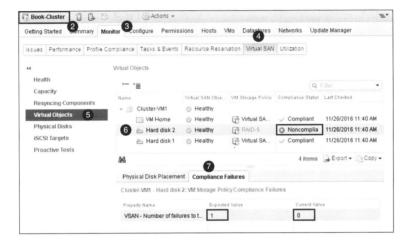

Figure 22.74   Policy noncompliant object

To remediate this state, correct the root cause of the missing component, and then vSAN will resync from a surviving replica (for RAID 1 or RAID 10) or re-create the RAID 5 stripe from parity.

To monitor resyncing of components, vSAN 6.x offers two facilities: the UI and the RVC.

Monitoring Resyncing Components via the UI

To monitor resyncing components via the UI, follow this procedure:

1. Connect to the vCenter server using the vSphere 6.x Web Client as a user with Administrator privileges.

2. Navigate to the **Hosts and Clusters** view (see Figure 22.75).

3. Select the cluster object in the Inventory pane.

4. Select the **Monitor** tab.

5. Click the **vSAN** button.

6. Select the **Resyncing Components** menu option.

Figure 22.75   Monitoring resyncing components via the UI

The right-hand side pane shows the following stats of the resync process on the top:

- **Resyncing components**—The count of component currently resyncing

- **Bytes left to resync**—The total size of components left to resync

- **ETA to compliance**—The estimated time remaining to complete the resync and the objects state become compliant

The bottom part shows the list of components currently resyncing.

7. To refresh the stats, click the **Refresh** icon above the stats. When the resync operation is complete, the Resyncing Components pane becomes blank.

Monitoring Resyncing Components via the RVC

To monitor resyncing component via the RVC, run the following command while in the `computers` directory of the RVC prompt:

```
vsan.resync_dashboard [cluster-name]
```

Here is an example:

```
vsan.resync_dashboard Book-Cluster
```

Listing 22.35 shows this command and its output.

Listing 22.35 Monitoring resyncing components via the RVC

```
/vcva66/Book-DC/computers> vsan.resync_dashboard Book-Cluster
2017-01-16 22:54:18 +0000: Querying all VMs on VSAN ...
2017-01-16 22:54:18 +0000: Querying all objects in the system from 66node3.
  book.local ...
2017-01-16 22:54:19 +0000: Got all the info, computing table ...
+---------------------------------------------------------------+-----------------+---------------+
| VM/Object                                                     | Syncing objects | Bytes to sync |
+---------------------------------------------------------------+-----------------+---------------+
| Book-VM1                                                      | 2               |               |
|    [vsanDatastore] 9a485f58-7da8-14f3-5edc-000c29870766/Book-VM1_2.vmdk |        | 1.00 GB       |
|    [vsanDatastore] 9a485f58-7da8-14f3-5edc-000c29870766/Book-VM1_3.vmdk |        | 2.00 GB       |
+---------------------------------------------------------------+-----------------+---------------+
| Total                                                         | 41              | 237.00 GB     |
+---------------------------------------------------------------+-----------------+---------------+
```

In Listing 22.35, I truncated some of the table rows for readability. To refresh the list, repeat the command (by pressing **Up Arrow** key and then **Enter**).

Resync Throttling

Depending on the volume of data to resync and the available bandwidth, latency may be negatively impacted, which can affect the current I/Os. vSAN 6.5 and later have a feature that you can use to throttle a resync operation and provide I/O relief. However, the prolonged resync operations may increase the window of exposure during which any additional failures may result in some objects becoming inaccessible. Use this facility with caution and only when instructed by VMware Technical Support.

Resync throttling can be done via the UI or the CLI.

Resync Throttling via the UI

To throttle a resync operation via the UI, follow this procedure, which continues from step 7 in the earlier section "Monitoring Resyncing Components via the UI":

8. Click the **Resync Throttling** button (refer to Figure 22.75).

9. In the Set Resync Throttling dialog that appears, select the **Enable throttling for resyncing components traffic** check box (see Figure 22.76).

10. To slow down the process, move the slider to the left to reduce the throughput (lower Mbps). Conversely, to accelerate the process, slide it in the opposite direction to increase the bandwidth (higher Mbps).

11. Click **OK** to apply the changes.

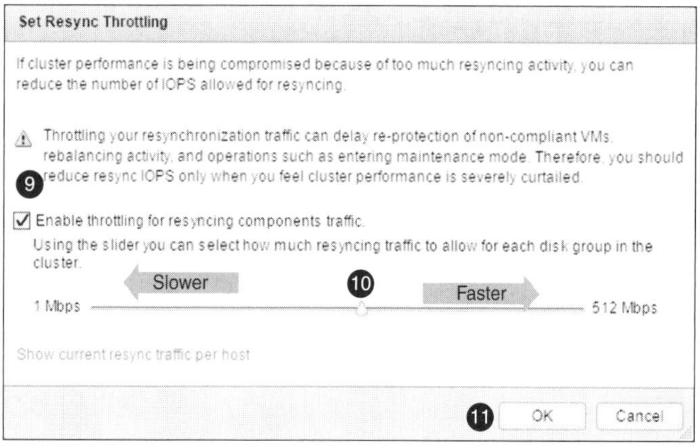

Set Resync Throttling

If cluster performance is being compromised because of too much resyncing activity, you can reduce the number of IOPS allowed for resyncing.

⚠ Throttling your resynchronization traffic can delay re-protection of non-compliant VMs, rebalancing activity, and operations such as entering maintenance mode. Therefore, you should **⑨** reduce resync IOPS only when you feel cluster performance is severely curtailed.

☑ Enable throttling for resyncing components traffic.
Using the slider you can select how much resyncing traffic to allow for each disk group in the cluster.

◄ Slower   **⑩**   Faster ►
1 Mbps —————————————————— 512 Mbps

Show current resync traffic per host

⑪ [OK]   [Cancel]

Figure 22.76   Resync throttling UI

Resync Throttling via the CLI

To throttle a resync operation via the CLI, run the following command at any node in the cluster while logged on as root via SSH or directly on the host:

```
esxcli vsan resync throttle set --level [bandwidth value in Mbps]
```

For example, to throttle resync traffic down to 100Mbps, run the following command:

```
esxcli vsan resync throttle set --level 100
```

If you do not know the current resync bandwidth, run the following command first:

```
esxcli vsan resync throttle get
```

If the output is `Level: 0 Mbps`, it means that throttling has not been set.

After applying the change, the output is `Level: 100 Mbps` instead.

To reset throttling back to `disabled`, repeat the `set` command with `--level 0` instead of the value you previously set.

Sample Object Properties During Resync

To give you an idea of how an object looks in `cmmds-tool` output, Listing 22.36 shows an example of an object with a resyncing component.

Listing 22.36   Sample nested RAID 1 object with a resyncing component

```
{
 "entries":
[
 {
    "uuid": "37606458-255c-3f33-3c8a-000c29c1c241",
    "owner": "585472ff-dd82-a3cc-42b7-000c29f69b4e",
    "health": "Healthy",
    "revision": "379",
    "type": "DOM_OBJECT",
    "flag": "2",
    "minHostVersion": "3",
    "md5sum": "d97e993bbf9287d9b3f78621cfaebcd2",
    "valueLen": "2936",
    "content": {"type": "Configuration",
        "attributes":
        {"CSN": 230,
        "SCSN": 310,
        "addressSpace": 107374182400,
        "scrubStartTime": 1484589797750180,
        "objectVersion": 5,
        "highestDiskVersion": 5,
        "muxGroup": 367906733493248,
        "groupUuid": "9a485f58-7da8-14f3-5edc-000c29870766",
        "compositeUuid": "37606458-255c-3f33-3c8a-000c29c1c241"},
        "child-1": {"type": "RAID_1", ← Site level RAID 1 config
          "attributes":
          {"scope": 3}, ←Replication scope is the top level (cross-sites)
          "child-1": {"type": "RAID_1", ←Nested RAID 1 config
                "attributes":
                {"scope": 2}, ← Replication scope is local site level
                "child-1": {"type": "Component", ←First Replica: nested RAID
1 object
                    "attributes":
                    {"addressSpace": 107374182400,
                    "componentState": 5, ← Healthy replica which is source of
resync
                    "componentStateTS": 1484606195, ←Time stamp newer than
absent comp
                    "faultDomainId": "a99dc62d-017d-04cf-6726-6593f9c3761e",
```

```
                        Previous line is East fault domain UUID
            "subFaultDomainId": "5854511c-a92e-62f3-27af-
000c29870766"},
                        Previous line is 66Node3 host UUID
            "componentUuid": "85eb7258-bd27-2751-a247-000c29c1c241",
            "diskUuid": "52a332c5-847f-0710-e902-10ece89b3899"},
          "child-2": {"type": "Component", ←Second Replica: nested RAID
1 object
            "attributes":
            {"addressSpace": 107374182400,
            "componentState": 6, ← Absent State
            "componentStateTS": 1484603654,← Time stamp Older than
healthy comp
            "staleLsn": 1804, ← Stale Log Sequence Number
            "staleCsn": 218,  ← Stale Config Sequence Number
            "bytesToSync": 1073741824, ← Number of bytes to sync
            "recoveryETA": 3600,← 60 minutes for resync to complete (in
seconds)
            "faultDomainId": "a99dc62d-017d-04cf-6726-6593f9c3761e",
                        Previous line is East fault domain UUID
            "flags": 16777216,
            "subFaultDomainId": "5854512b-fc8c-e32b-ea7b-000c29c1c241",
                        Previous line is 66Node4 host UUID
            "rLsn": 1804},
            "componentUuid": "ff2f7458-df46-bb05-9efe-000c29c1c241",
            "diskUuid": "522a384c-c2b7-1b97-e3c7-b66773156c05"}},
          "child-2": {"type": "RAID_1",
[snipped rest of healthy components for readability]
    "errorStr": "(null)"
  }
]
}
```

In this example, one nested RAID 1 had an absent replica on the 66Node4 host with an intact replica on the 66Node3 host. The timestamps of the components are different, with the absent one being older (earlier timestamp).

Resync from the healthy component on the 66Node3 host to the 66Node4 host has 60 minutes of estimated time to resync, with 1073741824 bytes remaining to resync.

The same concepts apply to other configuration types during resync operation.

NOTE

vSAN 6.6 introduced a new bitmap that tracks surviving components' changes since the mirror became absent. If a component returns before the current resync is complete, vSAN restarts the resyncs, using the bitmap as a reference of which blocks to resync instead of resyncing the whole component from scratch. This can save on resync time for large components.

vSAN Sparse Format

Chapter 13, "Virtual Disks and RDMs," discusses virtual machine snapshots. vSAN 6 introduced support for the VSANSPARSE format for handling these snapshots on vSAN datastores. This format offers improved snapshot performance by caching metadata in memory and efficiently storing the snapshot files on vSAN datastore.

When a snapshot is created for a VM, its virtual disks are placed in read-only mode, and any changes to their data are redirected to the snapshot files, which are children of the read-only virtual disks. This process leaves the parent disk unmodified and creates a point-in-time snapshot. If a second snapshot is taken, a child is created for the first snapshot file, and it is placed in read-only mode.

A snapshot file is sparse in nature. This means that the data contained in the snapshot file is not sequential and represents modified blocks of the read-only parent VMDK. From the VM's perspective, it sees the overlay of the snapshot files on top of the parent disk so that the modified blocks show their current content of the child disk instead of the static content on the parent disk, along with the rest of the unmodified blocks that are located on the parent disk.

Figure 22.77 shows a logical diagram of how the snapshot content is rendered to the VM.

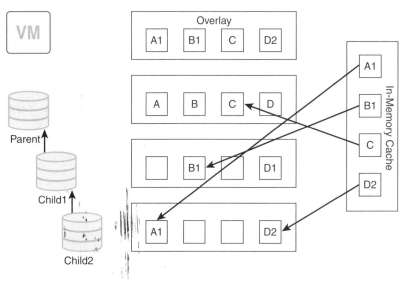

Figure 22.77 Snapshot content logical diagram

In this diagram, the parent disk had blocks A, B, C, and D. In the first snapshot on Child1, blocks B and D were modified to B1 and D1. A second snapshot was taken, which created Child2. In it, blocks A and D were modified to A1 and D2.

The overlay that the VMs see is the latest modified blocks, A1, B1, and D2, along with the unmodified block C.

The snapshot file is not pre-allocated and grows, in 4KiB chunks, as data is written to it. On VMFS datastores, the blocks allocated to the snapshot file are stored in noncontiguous space on the file system. It would be the same on a vSAN datastore if VSANSPARSE format were not used. Using this format stores the blocks on the vSAN objects corresponding to the child disks and updates the in-memory cache with pointers to the blocks in snapshot files corresponding to the overlay in Figure 22.77 in this example.

Current writes always go to the child farthest from the parent. In this example, that would be Child2.

The vSAN sparse format also interoperates with the Content-Based Read Cache (CBRC) used with VMware Horizon View virtual desktop infrastructure (VDI), which significantly improves read performance of linked-clones configurations used by VDI.

Each child snapshot file includes a reference to its parent, as well as the object UUID of itself. Listing 22.37 shows the content of Child1 and Child 2, listed in Figure 22.77.

Listing 22.37   Snapshot descriptor files' content

```
[Child1 content]
root@node1: cat /vmfs/volumes/vsanDatastore/Book-VM1/Book-VM1-000001.vmdk
# Disk DescriptorFile
version=4
encoding="UTF-8"
CID=fffffffe
parentCID=fffffffe
isNativeSnapshot="no"
createType="vsanSparse"
parentFileNameHint="Book-VM1.vmdk"  ← Parent disk name
# Extent description
RW 209715200 VSANSPARSE "vsan://a5959f58-f006-9167-5dd5-00505688b733"


# The Disk Data Base
#DDB


[Child2 content]
[root@node1: cat /vmfs/volumes/vsanDatastore/Book-VM1/Book-VM1-000002.vmdk
# Disk DescriptorFile
version=4
encoding="UTF-8"
CID=fffffffe
parentCID=fffffffe
isNativeSnapshot="no"
createType="vsanSparse"
parentFileNameHint="Book-VM1-000001.vmdk"  ← Parent disk name
# Extent description
RW 209715200 VSANSPARSE "vsan://cf959f58-569a-1176-1347-00505688b733"


# The Disk Data Base
#DDB


ddb.longContentID = "6340bf40043db795a825b10fffffffffe"
```

The descriptor file for each child shows the following fields and sections specific to the
VSANSPARSE files:

- **createType**—This field shows the value as vsanSparse.

- **parentFileNameHint**—The value of this field is the name of this child's parent. For the first snapshot, the parent is the original VMDK. For the second child, the parent is the first child's VMDK.

- **Extent Description**—This section shows the following fields:

  - `RW` (read/write permission), which is the permission allowed when the file is writable.

  - The extent size in 512-byte sectors.

  - `VSANSPARSE`, which means that this file is a vSAN sparse snapshot file. (This is compared to VMFS value for the parent VMDK.)

  - `Vsan://[object UUID]`, which is the URI for the vSAN object UUID of the snapshot file referenced by this descriptor file.

Common vSAN Basic Administrative Tasks

VMware Technical Support may ask you to remove a host from a cluster and then re-add it. The following sections describe the procedures doing these operations.

Removing a Host from a vSAN Cluster

In some scenarios, an ESXi host may need to leave a cluster to be decommissioned or for an extended maintenance period. Removing a host from a vSAN cluster may also be a troubleshooting step when you're working with the VMware Technical Support team.

To accomplish this task, follow this procedure.

1. Connect to the vCenter server using the vSphere 6.5 Web Client as a user with Administrator privileges. This example uses vSphere 6.5, Patch 2.

2. Navigate to the **Hosts and Clusters** view.

3. Select the host to be removed from the cluster.

4. From the Actions pull-down menu, select **Maintenance Mode** and then **Enter Maintenance Mode**. You can also select **Enter Maintenance Mode** icon next to the host name at the top of the display (see Figure 22.78).

Figure 22.78   Accessing the Maintenance Mode menu

5. If the host has any powered-off and suspended VMs registered, leave the **Move powered-off and suspended virtual machines to other hosts in the cluster** check box selected. Otherwise, uncheck this box.

6. Depending on the current state of the ESXi host, select the relevant Virtual SAN data migration mode (see Figure 22.79).

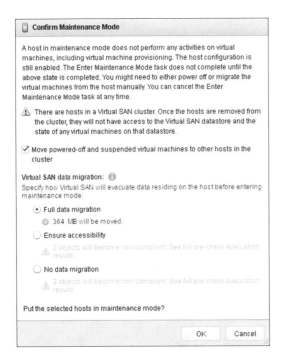

Figure 22.79   Virtual SAN Migration Modes menu

NOTE

vSAN 6.6 provides validation of the effect of each migration mode. It is based on the current state of the LSOM components, the storage policy in effect, and available storage resources.

7. Click **OK** to proceed with entering maintenance mode.

8. Use one of the three approaches for removing the host from the cluster:

    a. Using the mouse, drag and drop the host onto the datacenter inventory object (see Figure 22.80).

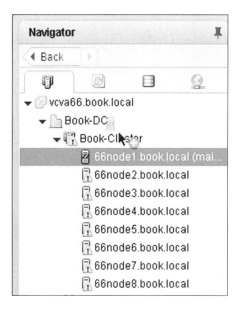

Figure 22.80   Removing a host from a cluster via drag and drop

    b. Right-click the host's inventory object and then select the **Move to** menu option (see Figure 22.81). In the dialog that appears, select the datacenter object and then click **OK**.

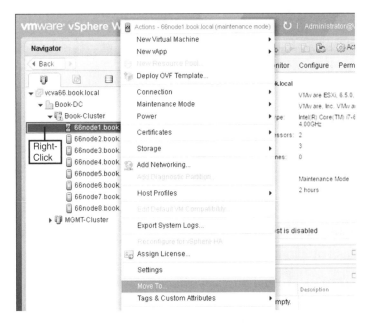

Figure 22.81   Removing a host from a cluster via the Move To menu item

   c. Run the following CLI command while logged on to the host via SSH as root:

```
esxcli vsan cluster leave
```

A successful operation exits silently. Otherwise, an error is returned. If you use the CLI, ensure that the host is in maintenance mode prior to running the command because the CLI does not check for the host being in that state. If a vSAN cluster has DRS and/or HA enabled, the host remains in the cluster while vSAN is disabled on it.

Rejoining a Host to a vSAN Cluster

To add a host back to a vSAN cluster via the UI, repeat, in the reverse directions, steps 8a or 8b in the preceding section, "Removing a Host from a vSAN Cluster."

If the CLI was used to leave the cluster, you can use the following steps to rejoin the cluster:

   1. Obtain the vSAN cluster UUID by running this command on one of the existing vSAN cluster nodes while logged on, as root, to that node via SSH:

```
esxcli vsan cluster get |grep 'Sub-Cluster UUID'
```

The output would be similar to this:

```
Sub-Cluster UUID: 529a3a87-d8c6-f326-c031-65d0746aebb0
```

2. Log on as root to the host you want to rejoin the cluster to via SSH.

3. Run the following command, using the cluster UUID:

```
esxcli vsan cluster join --cluster-uuid [UUID]
```

You can also use the abbreviated version:

```
esxcli vsan cluster join -u [UUID]
```

Here is an example:

```
esxcli vsan cluster join -u 529a3a87-d8c6-f326-c031-65d0746aebb0
```

If the cluster is stretched and this host will be the witness node, you must add two more options: --witness-node (or -t) and --witness-preferred-fault-domain (or -p).

To identify the preferred fault domain, run this command on one of the cluster nodes while logged on to it as root via SSH:

```
cmmds-tool find --type PREFERRED_FAULT_DOMAIN | sed
's/.*content//;s/].*$//'
```

You can also use the abbreviated version:

```
cmmds-tool find -t PREFERRED_FAULT_DOMAIN | sed 's/.*content//;s/].*$//'
```

The following is sample output:

```
= (a99dc62d-017d-04cf-6726-6593f9c3761e "East")
```

This means that the preferred fault domain's name is East, and its UUID is a99dc62d-017d-04cf-6726-6593f9c3761e.

Using the previous output, this would be the full command line to join a witness node to the cluster with abbreviated options:

```
esxcli vsan cluster join -u [Cluster UUID] -t -p East
```

Here is an example:

```
esxcli vsan cluster join -u 529a3a87-d8c6-f326-c031-65d0746aebb0 -t -p East
```

> **TIP**
>
> In rare situations you have to rebuild vCenter from scratch due to data corruption or data loss. vCenter version 6.5, Express Patch 2 or later has a new feature that causes this behavior: After you re-add a host to the vSAN cluster, it shows as network partitioned. This is because the new vSAN cluster you created on the new VC has a different cluster UUID from the original one. To force the hosts to join the cluster, run this command on each host in an SSH session or directly on the server's local console:
>
> ```
> esxcfg-advcfg -s 1 /VSAN/IgnoreClusterMemberListUpdates
> ```

Using `cmmds_tool` to List Various Types

Throughout this chapter and Chapter 21, I have provide `cmmds_tool` command examples. To list a specific CMMDS type, you can use the `--type` option. Table 22.8 lists the various types and what they mean.

Table 22.8 CMMDS types (case sensitive), in order of listing in output

Type	Description
SUB_CLUSTER	Sub-cluster entity
CLUSTER	Cluster or site entity
NODE	Cluster node (owned by CMMDS agent)
DISK	Storage device (owned by DOM)
SUBNET	Network for a sub-cluster
NET_INTERFACE	Network link (owned by CMMDS agent)
HEALTH_STATUS	Health status of an entity
CMMDS_MASTER	Master node for a sub-cluster
CMMDS_BACKUP_MASTER	Backup node for a sub-cluster (owned by CMMDS backup master)
OSFS_NAME	Human-readable name of an OSFS object (This is the name given to a namespace.)
LSOM_OBJECT	LSOM component object (owned by the DOM of the node where object resides)
DOM_OBJECT	Composite object (It may have components that are a mix of LSOM and DOM objects, owned by the DOM that is the composite object owner.)

Type	Description
SUB_CLUSTER_MEMBERSHIP	Generation number (shows as rev=<n> in outputs) and a list of UUIDs for nodes in the current membership of the cluster
DISK_USAGE	Usage status for a disk
DISK_STATUS	Performance status for a disk
DOM_NAME	Human-readable name of a DOM composite object
POLICY	Policy of a composite object
HA_METADATA	HA-specific metadata
CONFIG_STATUS	Performance status of an object
NODE_DECOM_STATE	Decommissioning status of a node
NODE_DECOM_FAILED	Helper announcing failed decommissioning of a cluster node (entering maintenance mode with full data migration)
ACCESS_GENERATION	Object accessibility generation number
NODE_USAGE	Node summary usage and limits
DOM_STALE_OWNER	Stale owner entry (This is published when a component notices that its owner is stale and wants it to yield ownership. The value is the up-to-date configuration the owner should publish and use once it yields ownership.)
HOSTNAME	Cluster node's host name
DISK_INCOMING	Components being relocated to this disk
DOM_OWNER_CANDIDATE	The candidate owner entry that should win the next owner election
NODE_FAULT_DOMAIN	The cluster node's fault domain
DOM_OBJECT_DELETED	The entry published when an owner object is deleted
DISK_DECOM_STATE	Decommissioning status of a disk
DISCARDED_COMPONENTS	List of components that are no longer required and should be deleted
PREFERRED_FAULT_DOMAIN	The preferred fault domain (for witness nodes) in stretched cluster configurations

Type	Description
VSAN_ISCSI_TARGET_CONFIG	Entry for vSAN iSCSI target (VIT) config information (vSAN 6.5 and newer) (It includes the UUID for the namespace where the configuration files are stored.)
VSAN_ISCSI_TARGET_NET_IF_ ADDRESS	Entry to map the VIT network interface name to IPV4 and IPV6 addresses

Listing a Disk's Stats by Using the CLI

While troubleshooting caching and capacity tier disks' hardware issues, it is helpful to list the physical disks' statistics. You can obtain these stats by using this command:

```
esxcli storage core device stats get --device <device-ID>
```

You can also use the abbreviated option -d instead of –device, as in this example:

```
esxcli storage core device stats get -d <device-ID>
```

Listing 22.38 shows this command and its output.

Listing 22.38   Listing a physical disk's stats

```
esxcli storage core device stats get -d naa.644a84202d7a8b001d1d96e209e03e5a
naa.644a84202d7a8b001d1d96e209e03e5a
   Device: naa.644a84202d7a8b001d1d96e209e03e5a
   Successful Commands: 1545293
   Blocks Read: 11556659
   Blocks Written: 141840
   Read Operations: 1523722
   Write Operations: 10653
   Reserve Operations: 0
   Reservation Conflicts: 0
   Failed Commands: 170789
   Failed Blocks Read: 0
   Failed Blocks Written: 0
   Failed Read Operations: 0
   Failed Write Operations: 0
   Failed Reserve Operations: 0
```

If you see that any of the Failed stats are incrementing frequently, there could be a hardware or driver problem with the device. There could also be a problem with the I/O adapter to which the device is attached. In this case, other devices attached to the I/O adapter would exhibit similar issues.

vSphere 6.5 vSAN Health CLI Namespace

When a vCenter virtual appliance is stored on a vSAN datastore, unless it is carefully designed, it runs a risk of being unavailable due to certain vSAN failure modes. For example, when using the default vSAN datastore policy with vCenter, you have protection against a single failure. If double faults occur, one or more of vCenter's virtual disks may become inaccessible, which means you cannot use vCenter to check the cluster's health. To provide an alternative to vSAN Health Service provided on vCenter, vSphere 6.5 added the new `esxcli vsan health` namespace. You can run this command on any node in the cluster by using SSH to check the health status of the whole cluster.

You can list the cluster's health status for all tests by using this command:

```
esxcli vsan health cluster list
```

Listing 22.39 shows this command and its output.

Listing 22.39   Output of the `esxcli vsan health cluster list` command

```
[root@66node4:~] esxcli vsan health cluster list
Health Test Name                                    Status
-------------------------------------------------   --------
Overall health                                      green
Performance service                                 green
  Stats DB object                                   green
  Stats master election                             green
Network                                             green
  Hosts disconnected from VC                        green
  Hosts with connectivity issues                    green
  vSAN cluster partition                            green
  All hosts have a vSAN vmknic configured           green
  All hosts have matching subnets                   green
  vSAN: Basic (unicast) connectivity check          green
  vSAN: MTU check (ping with large packet size)     green
  vMotion: Basic (unicast) connectivity check       green
  vMotion: MTU check (ping with large packet size)  green
  Network latency check                             green
Physical disk                                       green
  Overall disks health                              green
  Metadata health                                   green
  Disk capacity                                     green
  Software state health                             green
  Congestion                                        green
```

```
    Component limit health                          green
    Component metadata health                       green
    Memory pools (heaps)                            green
    Memory pools (slabs)                            green
Data                                                green
  vSAN object health                                green
Cluster                                             green
  ESXi vSAN Health service installation             green
  vSAN Health Service up-to-date                    green
  Advanced vSAN configuration in sync               green
  vSAN CLOMD liveness                               green
  vSAN Disk Balance                                 green
  Resync operations throttling                      green
  Software version compatibility                    green
  Disk format version                               green
Limits                                              green
  Current cluster situation                         green
  After 1 additional host failure                   green
  Host component limit                              green
```

If any of the tests fails, the Status column says red instead of green. If the test result is a warning, the status is yellow.

To identify details of a failed test, run this command:

```
esxcli vsan health cluster get [test name]
```

For example, to list a test named vSAN object health, run this command:

```
esxcli vsan health cluster get --test="vSAN object health"
```

You can also use the abbreviated version:

```
esxcli vsan health cluster get -t "vSAN object health"
```

You can append |less -S to the command for better column formatting of the output.

NOTE

The test names that you can use with this command are the indented tests in Listing 22.39. The group names are not actual test names, and you cannot use them. For example, Overall health, Performance service, Network, and so on are group names. However, each group reflects the failed status of any of the tests within that group. In other words, if any of the tests in a group fails or has a warning, the whole group's status is red or yellow, respectively.

Listing 22.40 shows this command and its output.

Listing 22.40   Listing a single health test output by using the CLI

```
esxcli vsan health cluster get -t "vSAN object health" |less -S

vSAN object health           red

Object health overview
Health/Objects                                          Number      Objects
UUID
reduced-availability-with-no-rebuild                       0
healthy                                                    0
non-availability-related-reconfig                          0
reduced-availability-with-active-rebuild                   0
reduced-availability-with-no-rebuild-delay-timer           8          [object
list]
inaccessible                                               0
datamove                                                   0
non-availability-related-incompliance                      0
```

In the output in Listing 22.40, I replaced the actual list of objects' UUIDs with [object list] for readability. The actual list of UUIDs includes the objects in the reduced-availability-with-no-rebuild-delay-timer state. This means there are eight vSAN objects that are missing some of their components and that resync operation will begin after the default 60 minutes of wait time. This resync re-creates the missing components from the surviving mirrors (replicas).

You can obtain similar output by using the following ESXCLI command:

```
esxcli vsan debug object health summary get
```

Listing 22.41 shows this command and its output.

Listing 22.41   Using `esxcli vsan debug` to list object health summary

```
esxcli vsan debug object health summary get
Health Status                                        Number Of Objects
---------------------------------------------------  ------------------
inaccessible                                                  0
reduced-availability-with-active-rebuild                      0
nonavailability-related-incompliance                          0
data-move                                                     0
```

```
nonavailability-related-reconfig                           0
reduced-availability-with-no-rebuild                       0
reduced-availability-with-no-rebuild-delay-timer           8
healthy                                                    0
```

The output in Listing 22.41 shows only the count of affected objects, while the output in Listing 22.40 shows the count as well as the affected objects' UUIDs.

You can identify on which hosts the absent components are located by running this command:

```
esxcli vsan debug object list|grep -A2 ABSENT
```

This command lists any component with an `Absent` state along with the line after it.

Listing 22.42 shows this command and its output.

Listing 22.42   Listing absent components by using ESXCLI

```
esxcli vsan debug object list|grep -A2 ABSENT
        Component State: ABSENT,  Address Space(B): 0 (0.00GB),  Disk UUID:
523df2b9-1b22-9d99-e308-f292444baf46,  Disk Name: mpx.vmhba1:C0:T1:L0:2
        Votes: 1,  Capacity Used(B): 12582912 (0.01GB),  Physical Capacity
Used(B): 4194304 (0.00GB),  Host Name: 66node9.book.local
--

        Component State: ABSENT,  Address Space(B): 0 (0.00GB),  Disk UUID:
527c7dd7-2f2f-ba23-31e8-7a4bd6943598,  Disk Name: mpx.vmhba1:C0:T3:L0:2
        Votes: 1,  Capacity Used(B): 12582912 (0.01GB),  Physical Capacity
Used(B): 4194304 (0.00GB),  Host Name: 66node9.book.local
--

        Component State: ABSENT,  Address Space(B): 71583137792
(66.67GB),  Disk UUID: 5282daf5-b128-bed4-e5ff-244e9aca6f7e,  Disk Name:
mpx.vmhba1:C0:T2:L0:2
        Votes: 1,  Capacity Used(B): 12582912 (0.01GB),  Physical
Capacity Used(B): 4194304 (0.00GB),  Host Name: 66node9.book.local
        Component: b7ad0a59-f6a2-13be-838c-000c2900bdf8
--

        Component State: ABSENT,  Address Space(B): 0 (0.00GB),  Disk UUID:
5282daf5-b128-bed4-e5ff-244e9aca6f7e,  Disk Name: mpx.vmhba1:C0:T2:L0:2
        Votes: 1,  Capacity Used(B): 12582912 (0.01GB),  Physical Capacity
Used(B): 4194304 (0.00GB),  Host Name: 66node9.book.local
--

        Component State: ABSENT,  Address Space(B): 161061273600
(150.00GB),  Disk UUID: 523df2b9-1b22-9d99-e308-f292444baf46,  Disk Name:
mpx.vmhba1:C0:T1:L0:2
        Votes: 2,  Capacity Used(B): 12582912 (0.01GB),  Physical
```

```
Capacity Used(B): 4194304 (0.00GB),  Host Name: 66node9.book.local
          Component: a2840359-3d69-42aa-b52d-000c29870766
--

        Component State: ABSENT,  Address Space(B): 0 (0.00GB),  Disk UUID:
5282daf5-b128-bed4-e5ff-244e9aca6f7e,  Disk Name: mpx.vmhba1:C0:T2:L0:2
        Votes: 1,  Capacity Used(B): 12582912 (0.01GB),  Physical Capacity
Used(B): 4194304 (0.00GB),  Host Name: 66node9.book.local
--

        Component State: ABSENT,  Address Space(B): 273804165120
(255.00GB),  Disk UUID: 523df2b9-1b22-9d99-e308-f292444baf46,  Disk Name:
mpx.vmhba1:C0:T1:L0:2
        Votes: 1,  Capacity Used(B): 603979776 (0.56GB),  Physical
Capacity Used(B): 595591168 (0.55GB),  Host Name: 66node9.book.local
          Component: a0c4fb58-2c6b-bc81-d0d5-000c29870766
--

        Component State: ABSENT,  Address Space(B): 268435456000
(250.00GB),  Disk UUID: 5282daf5-b128-bed4-e5ff-244e9aca6f7e,  Disk Name:
mpx.vmhba1:C0:T2:L0:2
        Votes: 1,  Capacity Used(B): 12582912 (0.01GB),  Physical
Capacity Used(B): 4194304 (0.00GB),  Host Name: 66node9.book.local
          Component: 35890359-8416-c0cc-19be-000c29e9187e
--

        Component State: ABSENT,  Address Space(B): 268435456000
(250.00GB),  Disk UUID: 527c7dd7-2f2f-ba23-31e8-7a4bd6943598,  Disk Name:
mpx.vmhba1:C0:T3:L0:2
        Votes: 1,  Capacity Used(B): 12582912 (0.01GB),  Physical
Capacity Used(B): 4194304 (0.00GB),  Host Name: 66node9.book.local
          Component: 35890359-654e-c3cc-f1a3-000c29e9187e
        Component State: ABSENT,  Address Space(B): 268435456000
(250.00GB),  Disk UUID: 527c7dd7-2f2f-ba23-31e8-7a4bd6943598,  Disk Name:
mpx.vmhba1:C0:T3:L0:2
        Votes: 1,  Capacity Used(B): 12582912 (0.01GB),  Physical
Capacity Used(B): 4194304 (0.00GB),  Host Name: 66node9.book.local
```

In this example, it is clear that all the absent components, which I highlighted in the listing, are on the 66node9 host, so you can focus your troubleshooting on that host. First, check for network connectivity issues, which most commonly cause this scenario. The output of esxcli vsan health cluster list should show a red status for the network vSAN cluster partition.

If there is no network partition, the next place to look is the physical disk status. This, too, you can identify from the esxcli vsan cluster list output.

You get the idea! Explore the remaining options in the Listings 22.40–22.42 and make yourself familiar with the various combinations. These commands will come in handy.

Summary

This chapter provides details about vSAN advanced features and takes a deep dive into some complex tasks and object property inspections. These skills should aid you in maintaining and troubleshooting vSAN clusters' configurations and data. This chapter also covers creating and configuring vSAN stretched clusters for additional levels of availability. ROBO is a subset of vSAN stretched cluster configuration for smaller remote offices/branch offices. Dedupe and compression details are also covered in this chapter, along with vSAN iSCSI targets.

This chapter also covers component resync operations and how to throttle them as well as vSAN sparse file format, which is used for snapshots and linked clones.

In this chapter I share with you some troubleshooting tips using ESXCLI commands available in vSphere 6.5 and later.

## Chapter 23

Virtual Volumes (VVols)

Block storage has always had the disadvantage of lack of visibility into file systems on devices the storage arrays provide to various environments. This has prevented the implementation of features like native snapshots, linked clones, and many others in the VMware vSphere environment. To address this issue, VMware has developed a new storage integration and management framework, referred to as VMware Virtual Volumes, or VVols for short.

What Are VVols?

VVols virtualize SAN block devices and NFS shares by abstracting the physical resources into logical pools of storage capacity, called VVols storage containers.

I covered vStorage APIs for Storage Awareness (VASA) in Chapter 20, "VASA." VASA separates the data path from the management path by using VASA providers (VPs) to facilitate the management. VMware expanded the reach of VASA to enable both VVols and vSAN (discussed in Chapter 21, "vSAN Core Features," and Chapter 22, "vSAN Advanced Features.")

When a storage vendor implements VASA 2.0, virtual machine–related files, (for example, VMDKs, snapshots, swap files) are created on a storage array as VVols, and the array is aware of where these files are placed on the block devices. NFS filers can also implement VVols, using VASA 2.0 APIs for NAS devices.

VVols Architecture

The VVols implementation on vSphere 6 separates the management plane from the data plane. The management plane facilitates communications between vCenter servers, ESXi hosts, and the storage arrays or NAS filers. This communication is done via VASA providers (also known as vendor providers), which act as proxies between vCenter and ESXi hosts on one end and the storage arrays or NAS filers on the other end.

Figure 23.1 shows a high-level VVols architecture.

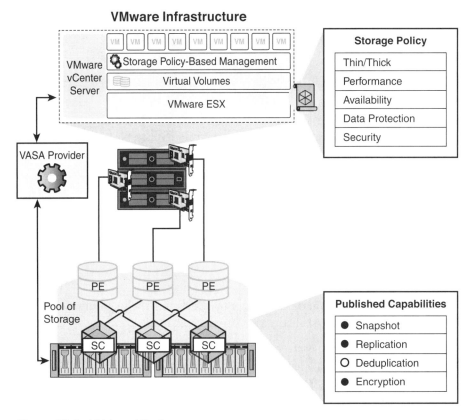

Figure 23.1   VVols architecture

Architectural Elements of VVols

With the high-level architecture diagram in Figure 23.1 in mind, consider this scenario: You, a vSphere administrator, need to create a new VMFS datastore. You would usually follow these steps to accomplish this task:

1. Identify the storage capacity needed for the datastore.

2. Contact the storage administrator to request provisioning of a new LUN.

3. When the device is created and presented to the ESXi hosts, rescan for new devices.

4. Create a VMFS datastore on the newly discovered device and mount it on all hosts in the cluster.

However, when the storage administrator attempts to present the newly created LUN to the host, she finds out that this host already has 256 LUNs presented. Because ESXi 6.0 is limited to a maximum of 256 LUNs, the task cannot be completed.

At this point, the only logical choice is to consolidate two or more datastores to reduce the number of LUNs presented to this host. "Not so fast," you say to the storage administrator. "We should start using VVols instead." The storage administrator scratches her head and asks, "What in the world are VVols?"

That is where you step in to explain that the host needs only a single device, per SCSI storage, presented to it from a VVols-capable storage array. This acts as a protocol entry point for all I/Os issued by that host to the storage array. You no longer need a dedicated LUN for each datastore on that storage array. This is referred to as the protocol endpoint (PE).

The storage administrator still looks puzzled, and asks, "Does this mean the host will have free rein on all available storage resources on the storage array?"

"No, not by a long shot," you say. "The storage resources on the array would be carved out into storage containers (SCs) that logically represent the storage space to allocate to a given datastore."

Assuming that you have done your homework and configured the ESXi host and vCenter server, as described later in this chapter, all you need to do now is rescan for new devices on the host to discover the PE. It shows up on the host as a block device with a LUN ID that is higher than 256. Does this mean that the ESXi host can see more than 256 LUNs? No, not really. The host still has the same old limitation. However, the MaxLUN IDs are no longer limited to 0 to 256. To avoid interfering with legacy storage arrays' LUN ID space, VMware designed the VVols API to require LUN IDs higher than 256.

Back to the VVols story. Now that you have discovered the PE device, you proceed with creating a VVols datastore. The storage administrator is watching you do all this. She interrupts, asking, "Did you mean to say VMFS datastore?" "No!" you say. "The VVols datastore is an abstraction of VMFS. The host mounts the storage container as a datastore. When VMs get created on the datastore, the host uses VASA APIs to communicate with the storage VASA provider (VP) to relay to the array the metadata of the VVols objects associated with the VM."

The moral of the story: Each VMFS datastore needs at least one dedicated block device on which to create the required partition and file system metadata. However, the block VVols datastore needs only one device that acts as a PE for the storage protocol (iSCSI, FC, or FCoE). The PE is the protocol's entry point to the resources on the storage array. Storage resources are allocated to one or more hosts in a logical structure referred to as a storage container (SC). Each SC is then mounted on each ESXi host, to which it is assigned as a VVols datastore. The SC is actually larger than the VVols datastore size. The extra space will be used for certain VVols-specific resources (for example, snapshots, clones and others which), as described in this chapter.

When the need arises to enlarge the datastore, you simply allocate more storage resources to grow the SC on the storage array. The added space becomes available to the VVols datastore immediately, without the need to modify the datastore. Compare that to VMFS, where you have to first grow the LUN on which it resides and then go through the process of growing the datastore into the added LUN space. Another advantage to using VVols is that instead of presenting a number of devices to each host separately, you use a single PE through which the host accesses all SCs assigned to it.

Moreover, VVols enables the storage arrays and NFS servers to utilize native operations such as snapshots, fast clones, and linked clones. This offloads these operations to the storage arrays or NFS filers, and the related resources are created on the SC on which the datastore resides.

> **NOTE**
>
> NAS-based PEs are somewhat different from block-based PEs. Each NAS PE is associated with a single SC, while each block-based PE is specific to a single host. This means that all hosts "see" the same PE for the given NAS SC, while there is one unique PE per host for I/O entry into all block SCs.
>
> In other words, block PEs are one per host to many SCs, while NAS PEs are one PE to one SC. This results in hosts seeing as many NAS PEs as there are NAS SCs and only a single block PE per host for all the SCs on the given storage array. Some storage vendors (for example, Dell EqualLogic PS Series) present the same block PE to all hosts, though. You'll learn more about this later in the chapter.

One more fact I would like to highlight here: When you create a virtual machine on a VVols datastore, each VMDK as well as the VM's home directory (referred to as the namespace) is created on the VVols datastore as a separate virtual volume. This means that each of these files has its own NAA ID assigned by the storage array. This way, when you trigger a VM snapshot operation, the storage array creates a physical snapshot for the VVols corresponding to the relevant VMDKs. I explain how this works later in this chapter.

Configuring the vSphere Environment to Use VVols

In this section, I discuss the high-level steps in configuring storage arrays, NAS servers, and a vSphere 6 environment to present and utilize VVols resources.

Block Device Array Configuration

The high-level steps for configuring a block device storage array for VVols are as follows:

1. Verify that the storage array you plan to use is certified for VVols.

2. Verify that the firmware version on the storage array matches what is listed on the VMware Compatibility Guide (vCG).

3. Create storage pools or aggregates.

4. Configure capability profiles.

5. Add ESXi hosts to the list of authorized hosts or the storage group or similar access control list (ACL) specific to the storage array. For some storage arrays you may need to configure the iSCSI initiators on the ESXi hosts first, with the array's iSCSI target's registration.

6. If the array is not configured with Fibre Channel (FC) ports, configure iSCSI interfaces or equivalent.

7. Create one or more VVols storage containers as the storage design requires and add the ESXi hosts to the access control list (ACL) or equivalent. This process usually results in creating a protocol endpoint (PE) for each host.

NAS Server Configuration

The high-level steps for configuring a NAS server for VVols are as follows:

1. Verify that the NAS server you plan to use is certified for VVols.

2. Verify that the firmware version on the NAS server matches what is listed on the vCG.

3. Create storage pools or aggregates.

4. Configure capability profiles.

5. Register ESXi hosts on the NAS appliance.

6. Configure a VVols-enabled NAS server.

7. Create one or more VVols SC, assigned to one or more storage pools, and then add ESXi hosts to the SC's ACL.

vSphere 6 Configuration

To configure the vSphere 6.x environment to utilize VVols, do the following:

1. Obtain and install the VVols-certified VASA provider specific to the storage array.

2. If the host is equipped with FC HBAs, configure FC fabric zoning as explained in Chapter 2, "Fibre Channel Storage Connectivity." Otherwise, configure iSCSI initiator(s) and then add iSCSI targets of the VVols-capable storage array.

3. Register the VASA provider in vCenter Server.

4. Rescan all HBAs or iSCSI initiators and verify that the device representing the PE is discovered. This device is usually 512 bytes to 4KB in size and has a LUN number above 256.

5. Mount SCs presented from the storage array. The process of mounting the SCs is similar to the process of creating datastores, but with `VVol` type.

6. Create VM storage policies, using the VVols VP.

7. As you deploy new VMs, specify the VVols storage policies relevant to the design requirements. The use of policies would limit the VM components' deployment to VVols datastores that are compliant with the corresponding policies.

In the following sections, I provide detailed procedures for these steps.

Locating VASA-Certified Storage Arrays on the vCG

The VMware HCL has recently been renamed the VMware Compatibility Guide (vCG) because it includes non-hardware as well as hardware listings. Go to www.vmware.com/go/vcg and follow these steps to locate VASA-certified storage arrays on the vCG:

1. In the field What Are You Looking For, select **vSphere APIs for Virtual Volumes (VVols)**.

2. Select the product release version, array type, and partner name.

3. Optionally, select the VASA provider name to narrow down the results.

4. Click the **Update and View Results** button.

5. Scroll down to see the results, which include VVols' certified VASA provider download links, where you can obtain the installation packages and documentations. Clicking a link in the VASA Provider Name column opens a detailed page with a list of storage arrays certified with this provider. See Table 20.1 in Chapter 20 for deliverables and dependencies.

Installing VASA Providers

Installation of VVols-certified VASA providers is similar to the process described in Chapter 20. Refer to the procedures in that chapter for details.

Configuring Block Storage Arrays for VVols

The configuration of block storage array VVols varies by vendor. I cover one example in this chapter.

The block device example for this section is an EqualLogic PS6010 single member with firmware version 8.0.6.

Configuring Dell Virtual Storage Manager (VSM) and Registering the VASA Provider with vCenter

The following are steps for configuring vSphere 6.x Environment with Dell EqualLogic storage arrays for use with VVols:

1. Download the Dell Virtual Storage Manager (VSM) OVA from the Dell EqualLogic support site, at eqlsupport.dell.com. (This site requires a support account to access the downloads.)

2. Deploy Dell VSM from the OVA. (See Chapter 20 for details.)

3. Power on the VSM VM and use vSphere Remote Console to log on as root user. The default password is `eql`.

4. At the welcome screen, select option 1, Configuration.

5. From the Configuration menu, select option 4, Register VMware vSphere Storage APIs for Storage Awareness (VASA), as shown in Figure 23.2.

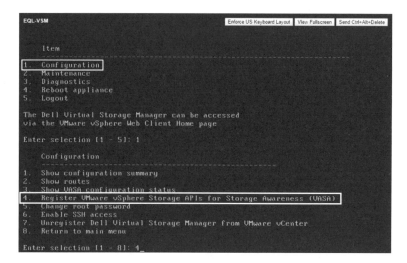

Figure 23.2 Dell VSM initial configuration

6. Enter vCenter credentials with privileges to register the VP (for example, root user). The registration process can take up to two minutes. When it is complete, the following message is displayed: `vCenter registration with the VASA provider was successful press [enter] to continue.`

7. If you are already logged on to vCenter, log out and then log in again to refresh the VSM plug-in configuration in vCenter.

8. Navigate to the **Home** page on vCenter and click the **Dell Virtual Storage Manager** icon in the inventory tree.

9. Select **VSM Home** (see Figure 23.3).

10. Select the **Getting Started** tab.

11. Click **Add Groups**. The Add PS Series Group dialog appears.

12. Enter the group name or IP address.

13. Enter the storage array's user name (for example, `grpadmin`).

14. Enter the user's password.

15. Click **Add**. The group is listed in the table at the bottom of the dialog.

16. Click **OK**.

17. Select **PS Group** in the Dell Storage section. The newly added group should be listed there. Now you are ready to allow the ESXi hosts' iSCSI initiators to access EQL VVols protocol endpoints.

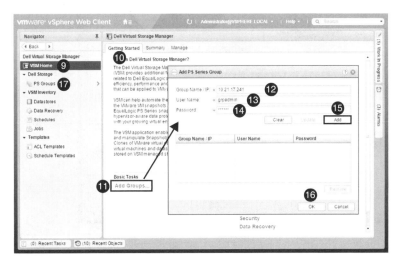

Figure 23.3   Adding an EQL storage group to VSM

Allowing ESXi Hosts' iSCSI Initiators to Access EQL VVols Protocol Endpoints

Before you can access VVols on the EQL storage group, ESXi hosts' iSCSI initiators need to be allowed to access the EQL VVols protocol endpoint. Do the following to accomplish this task, continuing from the previous section:

18. Select the storage group in the PS Groups menu (see Figure 23.4).

19. Select the **Manage** tab.

20. Select **Protocol Endpoints**.

21. Select the vSphere cluster to which you want to allow access.

22. To allow all initiators from all ESXi hosts in the cluster, click the **Allow All** button.

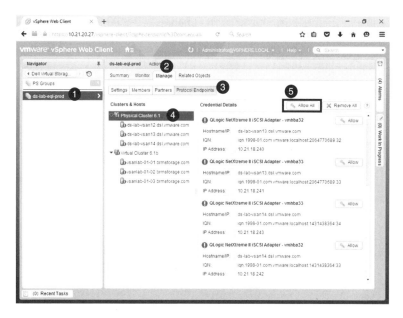

Figure 23.4   Allowing ESXi hosts' iSCSI initiators access to the EQL storage group

Configuring a NAS Server for VVols

As with block storage arrays, the configuration of NAS servers VVols varies by vendor. The NAS server appliance example for this section is an EMC Unity storage simulator with firmware version 4.0. The appliance provides a single storage processor but has the capability of replicating to a second separate simulator. Before you can create a VVols-enabled NAS server on this version of Unity, you need to configure a storage pool that it will use.

Creating Storage Pools for Use by EMC Unity VVols SCs

Storage pools created on EMC Unity can be used for any storage protocol supported by the storage array. You can plan and create these pools in advance, based on the I/O profile that your applications require as well as data availability and recoverability requirements.

To create a storage pool on an EMC Unity storage simulator, follow this procedure:

1. Log in to the EMC Unisphere, using the management port IP address or host name of the EMC Unity storage appliance in a browser.

2. In the STORAGE section, click the **Pools** option.

3. At the Pools page, launch the Create Pool Wizard by clicking the plus sign in the top-left part of the page (see Figure 23.5).

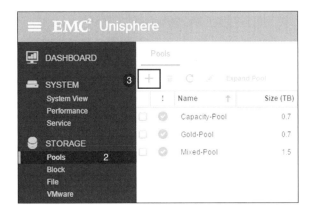

Figure 23.5   Launching the Create Pool Wizard

4. Enter the pool's name and, optionally, a description, and click **Next**.

The Assign Tier to the Virtual Disk page appears. This is where you locate unused virtual disks that are equivalent to RAID sets of NL-SAS, SAS, or SSD disks in the physical appliance. In this screen, you can assign unused virtual disks to their corresponding storage tiers. You do this by clicking the **Edit** icon (which looks like a pencil) to get a pull-down list with the three tiers detailed in Table 23.1.

Table 23.1 EMC Unity storage tiers

Storage Tier	Disk Type	Default RAID Configuration (Physical Appliances)
Extreme Performance	SAS Flash (SSD)	RAID 5
Performance	SAS (Spinning disks)	RAID 5
Capacity	Near-Line SAS (NL-SAS)	RAID 6

5. Select a relevant tier for each disk in the list. You need to assign a tier to at least one disk before you can proceed (see Figure 23.6).

6. Click **Next**.

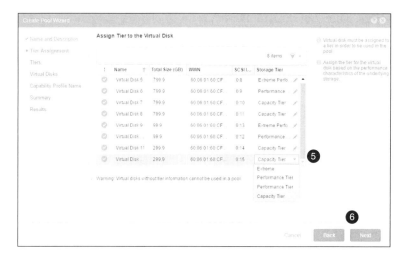

Figure 23.6   Assigning tiers to disks

7. At this point, you can select one or more storage tiers that you just assigned to the disks. If your design calls for utilizing Fully Automated Storage Tiering for Virtual Pools (FAST VP), make sure to select the relevant tier combination. In this example, I select all three tiers (see Figure 23.7).

8. Click **Next**.

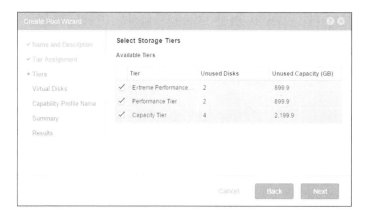

Figure 23.7   Selecting tiers

9. Select how many disks from each tier you want to include in the storage pool. In this example, there are two each in the Extreme Performance and Performance tiers. In addition, there are four disks in the Capacity tier. For this example, I want to have more in the Capacity tier because I anticipate having more cold blocks

(less frequently accessed) than hot blocks (most frequently accessed). In a physical EMC Unity array, I would select a combination of disks to deliver planned capacity. However, because I am using a simulator, pool capacity is limited, so in this case I select the smallest disk in each class, and I select one Extreme Performance, one Performance, and two Capacity tier disks (see Figure 23.8).

10. Click **Next**.

Figure 23.8   Selecting Pool's Disks

11. To be able to utilize the storage pool for VVols, you must create a VMware capability profile, so check the box **Create VMware Capability Profile for the Pool**, enter the capability profile name and description, and then click **Next** (see Figure 23.9).

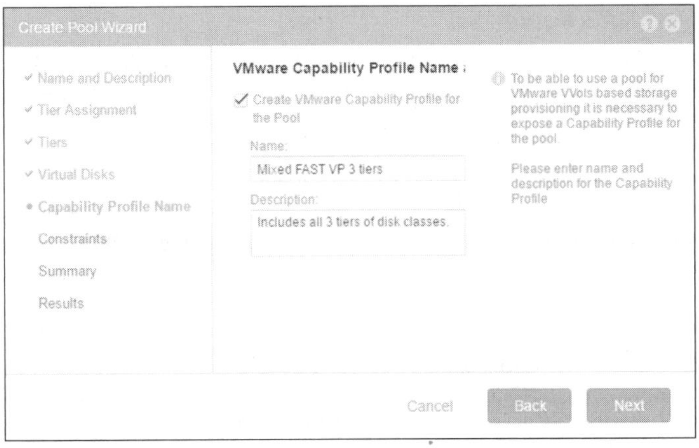

Figure 23.9   Creating a Capability Profile

12. You can add one or more usage tags (for example, SQLDATA) and click the plus sign to add more (see Figure 23.10). To remove a tag, click the X next to it. In this dialog, observe available tiering policies: Start High Then Auto-Tier, Auto-Tier, Highest Tier, and Lowest Available Tier. These are configured in another area of EMC Unisphere.

13. Click **Next**.

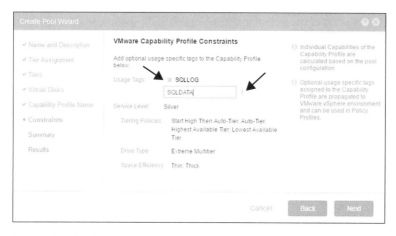

Figure 23.10   Creating Capability Profile Constraints

14. Review your selections and then click **Finish**.

The results step shows the progress of creating the new storage pool as well as the capability profile.

Creating a VVols-Enabled NAS Server

This section details the procedure for creating a VVols-enabled NAS server on EMC Unity. Before proceeding, make sure you have created a storage pool for use with this NAS server. See the previous section for details. Then follow these steps:

1. Log on to EMC Unisphere on the Unity storage appliance's management IP.

2. Click the **Update System Settings** icon (which looks like a gear) in the top-right corner of the page (see Figure 23.11).

3. In the Settings dialog, if it is not already expanded, expand the **Software and Licenses** section and select the **License Information** link.

4. Scroll down the list of licenses in the **License Management** table. Verify that the VMware VASA/VVols license is installed.

5. In the bottom-left corner of the Settings dialog, click the **Initial Configuration Wizard** link.

Figure 23.11   Accessing EMC Unity's Initial Configuration Wizard

6. After the Initial Configuration screen opens, click **Next** until you reach the NAS Servers section.

7. In the Network-Attached Storage (NAS) Servers screen, click the **Create NAS Server** icon (a green plus sign icon), as shown in Figure 23.12.

8. Enter the server name.

9. Click the **Pool** field.

Figure 23.12   Creating a NAS Server on EMC Unity

10. Select a pool from the presented list and then click **Select a pool**.

11. If desired, select the storage processor (SP) on which the NAS server will run. In this example, the Unity virtual appliance is equipped with a single SP, SP A.

12. Click **Next**.

13. In the Configure NAS Server Address window, select which Ethernet port to use with this server (see Figure 23.13).

14. Enter the IP address, subnet mask, and gateway addresses in their respective fields.

15. Edit the VLAN ID, if needed. It is recommended to separate the storage network from the users networks, so enter the storage network's VLAN ID here.

16. Click **Next**.

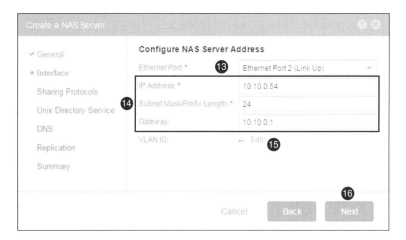

Figure 23.13   Configure NAS Server IP Address

17. In the Configure Sharing Protocols window, select the **Linux/Unix Shares (NFS)** and **Enable VVols** check boxes (see Figure 23.14). VVols requires NFSv3. Do not select the Enable NFSv4 check box for this NAS server. I prefer using a separate NAS server, per SP, for each protocol I include in a design because it makes the troubleshooting process simpler and reduces the complexity of the configuration.

18. Click **Next**.

Figure 23.14   Configuring sharing protocols

19. Because this NAS server will be used for NFS protocol only (that is, no SMB protocol as well), skip the Unix Directory Service step and click **Next**.

20. Configure DNS if you plan on using it with NFS. Otherwise, it is optional. Click **Next**.

21. If your design calls for replicating NFS shares, configure it at this step. Otherwise, click **Next** without selecting the **Enable** check box.

NOTE

Synchronous replication on EMC Unity is available only for block storage. To replicate NFS shares, you have no choice but asynchronous replication.

Replicating a VVols-enabled NFS share works only on a whole SC. Individual VVols are not granularly replicated. In other words, you cannot select specific VVols to replicate. It is all or none. With asynchronous replication being the only available choice, your RPO will be more than zero minutes. If you need to provide synchronous replication, you can use vSphere Replication (VR) instead. For details on VVols Replication, see the section "VVols Replication," later in this chapter.

---

22. Review the summary of your choices and then click **Finish**.

23. The wizard goes through the verification process, and if no errors are found, the procedure completes successfully. Observe that the last step listed in the details is Create VMware NAS PE server and click **Close** (see Figure 23.15).

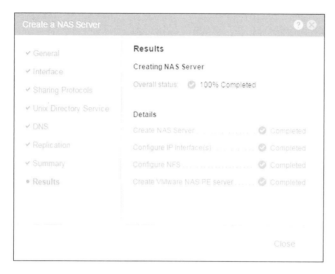

Figure 23.15 Results of creating a NAS server

24. The Initial Configuration Wizard now shows that the NAS server has been added to the list. Click **Next** and then click **Close** to exit the wizard.

25. Close the Settings dialog.

Creating a NAS VVols SC

The final step in creating the NAS VVols resources on the storage appliance side is to create an SC. This is similar to creating an NFS share export but is done using VVols APIs. Follow these steps:

1. Log on to EMC Unisphere on the Unity storage appliance.

2. Navigate to the **VMware** option in the STORAGE section (see Figure 23.16).

3. Click the **Datastores** link at the top of the screen.

4. Click the **Launch the Create VMware Datastore Wizard** icon, which is a plus sign.

Figure 23.16   Launching the Create VMware Datastore Wizard

5. The first step of the wizard is to select the datastore type. Select the **VVol (File)** radio button.

6. Click **Next** (see Figure 23.17).

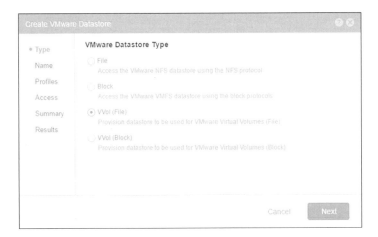

Figure 23.17   Creating a Datastore—Selecting Datastore Type

7. Enter the datastore name and optional description and then click **Next**. The Capability Profiles selection step shows a list of all profiles on this appliance. The list shows the profile name, the storage pool to which it is assigned, the available space, and the subscription percentage (which is the percentage of space subscribed on the storage pool by existing datastores of all types). The last column is Datastore Size (GB), which defaults to the same value in the Available Size column.

    You can select one or more capability profiles to assign to the new datastore. Also, you can edit the value in the Datastore Size (GB) column to specify what you want to allocate to this datastore.

8. Select a capability profile (see Figure 23.18).

9. Specify the datastore size. In this example, I use 400GB.

10. Click **Next**.

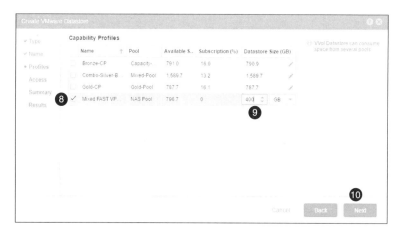

Figure 23.18   Selecting a capability profile for the new SC

11. In the Configure Access step, click the **Select Host Access** icon, which is a plus sign (see Figure 23.19).

12. Select the hosts to which to grant access to this datastore. In this example, I do not provide access to host 10.10.0.197 because it is not part of the cluster I am configuring.

13. Click **OK**.

14. Click **Next**.

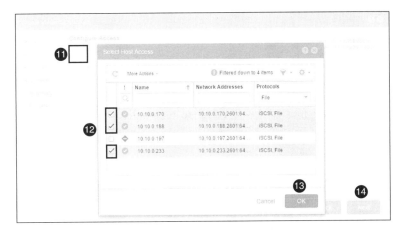

Figure 23.19 Selecting host access for the new SC

15. Review your selections and then click **Finish** (see Figure 23.20).

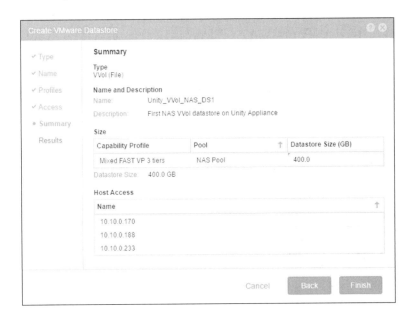

Figure 23.20 Summary of the VMware datastore creation process

The Results step shows the progress of creating the new storage container, adding the capability profile, and modifying the VVols datastore (also known as a storage container).

The Datastores page now shows the newly created VVols (file) datastore, along with the existing mix of VMFS and VVols (block) datastores. Again, the reference to datastores from the storage array perspective is actually to SCs from the VVols API perspective. I show you later in this chapter how to create a datastore on a given SC and mount it on the host's end.

Configuring the vSphere 6 Environment for VVols

Before a vSphere 6 environment can access any VVols resources, it must first register the corresponding storage vendor's VASA provider. VASA 2.0 provides bidirectional communications with the storage arrays. It is the conduit for out-of-band storage management, while the data remains on the storage protocol's specific paths.

Registering VASA Providers

The procedure for registering VVols VASA providers is similar to that for VASA 1.0. For details, see Chapter 20.

The URL for the EMC Unity VASA provider is https://<Unity-management-IP:8443/vasa/version.xml. Because the Unity VP is integrated into the storage appliance, the URL uses the EMC Unity storage appliance's management IP address. The user name to use for registering the VP is either admin or local/admin.

Mounting VVols SCs

To mount a VVols SC, do the following:

1. Connect to the vCenter server using the vSphere 6 Web Client as a user with Administrator privileges.

2. Navigate to the **Hosts and Clusters** view.

3. Select the cluster or datacenter that contains the hosts to which you granted access to the VVols storage container.

4. From the Actions pull-down list, select **Storage** and then select **New Datastore** (see Figure 23.21).

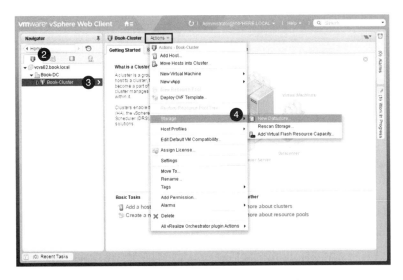

Figure 23.21   Accessing the New Datastore menu option

5. In the Location step, make sure the cluster is already listed as the location and click **Next**.

6. In the Type step, select **VVol**.

7. In the Name and Container selection step, enter the datastore name. This does not have to match the storage container name displayed here. Use the naming convention defined by your design (see Figure 23.22).

The Backing Storage Container section show a list of all SCs presented to this environment. However, there is no way to differentiate NAS from block VVols SCs in this screen. This is why it is critical to adopt an SC naming convention that clearly includes the SC type at creation time. In this example, I have four SCs; one of them is named `Unity_VVol_Block_SC0`, and another is `Unity_VVol_NAS_SC1`. It is easy to tell which type each of these SCs is. However, the other two are just named `Unity_VVol_SC1` and `Unity_VVol_SC3`. I remember creating these as block VVAI SCs. However, I deliberately omitted the `VVol` type from the names to use them as examples of what not to do.

> **NOTE**
>
> If you look closely at the Existing Datastore column, you can see that one of the SCs, `Unity_VVol_SC1`, has a datastore on it named `Unity_VVol_DS1`. This means that this SC was used already to mount as a datastore, possibly on one of the other hosts in the cluster. The remaining SCs do not have datastores name on them yet. This means they have not been mounted since they were created.

If you have multiple VVols storage vendors with their VPs registered in this environment, the listed SCs can be from any of them. To identify which VP provides which SC, click that SC and observe the content of the Backing Storage Container Details section at the bottom of the dialog. This section includes two fields: Storage Array(s) and Storage Provider(s).

8. While EMC Unity supports both block and NAS VVols SCs, I select the `Unity_VVol_NAS_SC1` as an example to create a VVols NAS datastore from that appliance. (The next section covers a Dell EqualLogic block VVols SC example just to provide a variety of vendors.)

9. Click **Next**.

Figure 23.22 Selecting a backing SC

10. In the Select Hosts Accessibility step, select the hosts in the cluster or datacenter on which you want to mount the datastore (see Figure 23.23). The selected hosts should match or be a subset of the list of hosts selected in step 11 in the section "Creating a NAS VVols SC," earlier in this chapter.

11. Click **Next**.

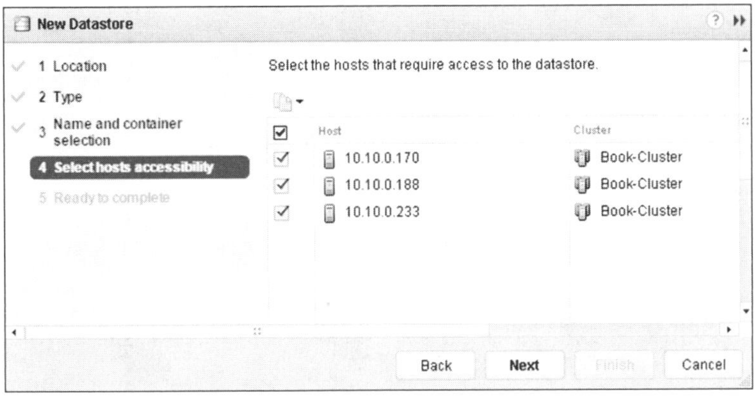

Figure 23.23 Selecting a datastore's host accessibility

12. In the Ready to Complete step, review your choices and click **Finish**.

Listing PEs via the UI

As explained earlier in this chapter, VVols-based datastores are accessed by the host via a protocol endpoint (PE) for a given protocol. This section shows how to use the UI to list the PEs on a given host. Alternatively, you can list the PEs via the CLI. I will show you how to that in the next section, "Listing PEs via the CLI." Follow these steps to list PEs by using the UI:

1. Connect to the vCenter server using the vSphere 6 Web Client as a user with Administrator privileges.

2. Navigate to the **Hosts and Clusters** view.

3. Locate the ESXi host you want to examine in the inventory tree and select it.

4. Select the **Manage** tab.

5. Click the **Storage** button.

6. Select the **Protocol Endpoints** section. The list of PEs known to this host is displayed. In this view, block VVols PEs have the type SCSI, while NAS PEs have the type NFS.

7. Select one of the NFS PEs. The Protocol Endpoint Details section includes two tabs: **Properties** and **Datastores** (see Figure 23.24).

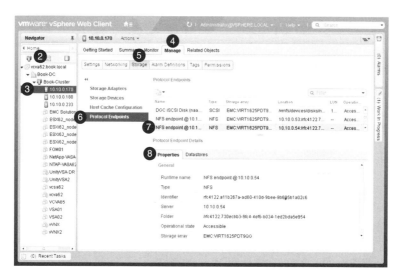

Figure 23.24   Exploring the VVols NAS PE Properties tab

8. Select the **Properties** tab. Here you see the following:

   ■ **Runtime name**—In this example, it is the NFS endpoint at 10.10.0.54. This
   IP address is for the NAS server that was created earlier in this chapter, in the
   section "Creating a VVols-Enabled NAS Server."

   ■ **Type**—In this example, it is NFS.

   ■ **Identifier**—In this example, it is `rfc4122.a11b267a-ad60-`**410d**`-9bee-`
   `9b695b1a02c6`, which is a unique identifier (UUID) that follows the convention of RFC 4122, which is why the UUID is prefixed with `rfc4122`. The
   UUID version is indicated by the first digit of the bytes I highlighted in the
   UUID. In this case, it is version 4, which means RFC 4122 random UUID.

   ■ **Server**—This is the IP address of the NAS server presenting this PE.

   ■ **Folder**—This is the NAS server's folder name that represents this NAS SC.
   It is analogous to an NFSv3 share and is unique per SC.

   ■ **Operational state**—The SC can be accessible or inaccessible.

   ■ **Storage array**—This is the storage array name.

9. Select the **Datastores** tab. While NAS PEs are unique for each datastore, in this
   view, each NAS PE from this storage array lists all NAS VVols datastores on this
   array. Figure 23.25 shows the view of one PE.

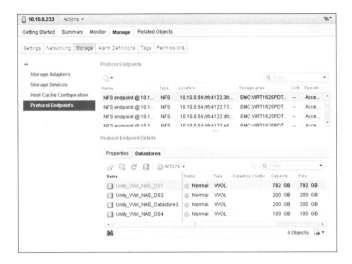

Figure 23.25 Exploring the VVols NAS PE Datastores tab

Figure 23.26 shows the view from another PE. Note that the same datastores are listed in both figures.

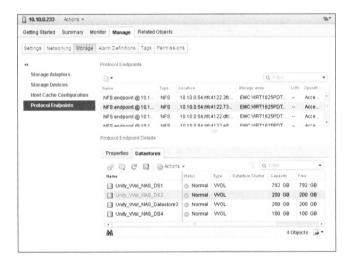

Figure 23.26 Exploring the VVols NAS PE

The same concept applies to the remaining NAS PEs.

If you inspect a block PE on the same array (in this example, the screenshot is from another host in the cluster though), there is a single block PE in contrast to multiple NAS PEs on the host (see Figure 23.27).

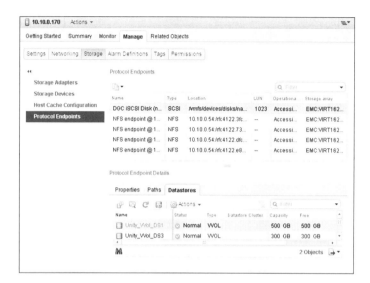

Figure 23.27   Exploring the VVols block PE

In this example, there is a single block PE with the 1023 LUN number and two block VVols datastores. Note that the Protocol Endpoint Details section has a third tab, Paths, which is specific to block devices. If you select this tab, you see a list of paths to the block PE LUN 1023 (see Figure 23.28).

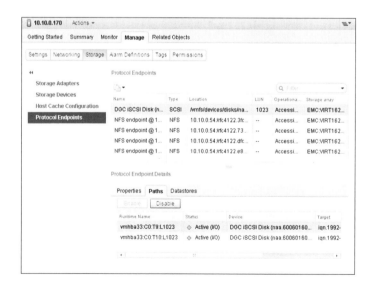

Figure 23.28   Exploring the VVols block PE Paths tab

In this example, the PE is on iSCSI targets T9 and T10.

To complete the comparison between NAS and block VVols PEs, let's now inspect the Properties tab (see Figure 23.29).

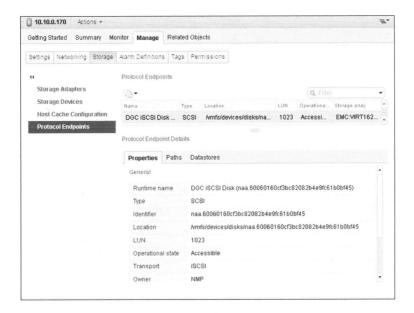

Figure 23.29   Exploring VVols block PE Properties tab—part 1

The fields in common between the PE types are as follows:

- **Runtime name**—This is similar to any block device, which defaults to the vendor name, protocol, and, in parentheses, device ID. The device ID in this case is the NAA ID.

- **Type**—In this case, it is SCSI.

- **Identifier**—In this example, it is the NAA ID, which is identical to the ID used as part of the runtime name.

- **Operational state**—This is the same as the NAS PE's operation state.

- **Storage array**—This is the same as the NAS PE's storage array (displayed in Figure 23.30).

The following are unique properties to block PEs are:

- **Location**—This is the host side path to the disk device node (/vmfs/devices/disk) and the device's NAA ID.

- **LUN**—In this example, it is 1023. Other vendors may have a value of 257 or higher.

- **Transport**—This lists the storage protocol for the device. In this example, it is iSCSI.

- **Owner**—This refers to the multipathing plug-in that claimed the device. In this example, it is NMP (Native Multipathing Plug-in).

To display the remaining properties, scroll down in the Protocol Endpoints section (see Figure 23.30).

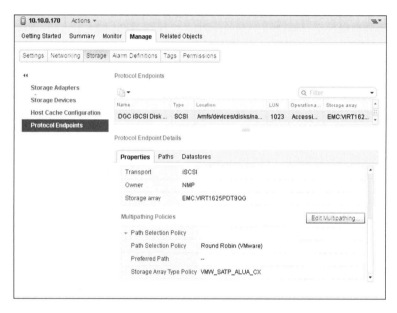

Figure 23.30   Exploring the VVols block PE Properties tab—part 2

The remaining properties are in the Multipathing Policies subsection: Path Selection Policy, Preferred Path and Storage Array Type Policy. I cover these properties in Chapter 5, "vSphere Pluggable Storage Architecture (PSA)."

Listing PEs via the CLI

ESXi provides a command-line interface (CLI) that includes several namespaces. New to vSphere 6 is the vvol namespace, which is part of the storage namespace.

To obtain a list of namespaces, run the following command:

```
esxcli storage vvol
```

This is the output of the command:

```
Usage: esxcli storage vvol {cmd} [cmd options]

Available Namespaces:
  storagecontainer      Operations to create, manage, remove and restore
VVol StorageContainers.
  daemon                Operations pertaining to VVol daemon.
  protocolendpoint      Operations on VVol Protocol EndPoints.
  vasacontext           Operations on the VVol VASA context.
  vasaprovider          Manage VVol VASA Provider Operations.
```

To list PEs, use the `protocolendpoint` namespace.

Follow this procedure to list PEs via the CLI:

1. Log on to the ESXi host console as root user via SSH or directly via the DCUI (Direct Console User Interface). The default host security profile has SSH and EXI Shell disabled. To enable them, see the section "Enabling SSH Host Access" in Chapter 2.

2. Run the following command:

   ```
   esxcli storage vvol protocolendpoint list
   ```

Listing 23.1 shows sample output from this command.

Listing 23.1   Listing PEs via the CLI

```
[root@node2:~] esxcli storage vvol protocolendpoint list
rfc4122.07c733ce-594a-4271-ba6f-3470df261f49
   Host Id:
   Array Id: EMC:VIRT1625PDT9QG
   Type: NFS
   Accessible: false
   Configured: false
   Lun Id:
   Remote Host: 10.10.0.54
   Remote Share: /rfc4122.dfc6ab2f-bbad-4233-9cf7-a242530e8b10
   Storage Containers: 730ecbb3-8fc4-4ef6-b034-1ed2bda5e954

rfc4122.11a3729e-d58f-43ff-9626-f1bffab45936
   Host Id: 8e156024-3cc0857b
   Array Id: EMC:VIRT1625PDT9QG
   Type: NFS
```

```
   Accessible: true
   Configured: true
   Lun Id:
   Remote Host: 10.10.0.54
   Remote Share: /rfc4122.3fcd6b98-ab61-4584-89a9-da4426c70b38
   Storage Containers: 730ecbb3-8fc4-4ef6-b034-1ed2bda5e954

rfc4122.1c5fe4b8-5329-4eb0-be9a-09236c87d9f6
   Host Id: 6724b87a-f4bc0e3d
   Array Id: EMC:VIRT1625PDT9QG
   Type: NFS
   Accessible: false
   Configured: true
   Lun Id:
   Remote Host: 10.10.0.54
   Remote Share: /rfc4122.e82d1444-ca11-4035-88a1-2e60d712f76c
   Storage Containers: 730ecbb3-8fc4-4ef6-b034-1ed2bda5e954

rfc4122.60060160-cf3b-c820-82b4-e9fc61b0bf45
   Host Id: naa.60060160cf3bc82082b4e9fc61b0bf45
   Array Id: EMC:VIRT1625PDT9QG
   Type: SCSI
   Accessible: true
   Configured: true
   Lun Id: naa.60060160cf3bc82082b4e9fc61b0bf45
   Remote Host:
   Remote Share:
   Storage Containers: 371ab5df-fd88-4116-abe5-0374f4b50e8a, 400a35bd-14d2-
4a6b-be36-a668f664f347

rfc4122.a11b267a-ad60-410d-9bee-9b695b1a02c6
   Host Id: 1f33511e-d68b1f4c
   Array Id: EMC:VIRT1625PDT9QG
   Type: NFS
   Accessible: true
   Configured: true
   Lun Id:
   Remote Host: 10.10.0.54
   Remote Share: /rfc4122.730ecbb3-8fc4-4ef6-b034-1ed2bda5e954
   Storage Containers: 730ecbb3-8fc4-4ef6-b034-1ed2bda5e954
```

Let's inspect the output of the first PE in the listing, which is a NAS PE. Remember that there is a NAS PE for each NAS VVols SC. As for block PEs, there is only one per host for all SCs on the given storage array. (Some vendors have a single block PE for all hosts, though). This is the PE Identifier, which is in RFC 4122 format:

```
rfc4122.07c733ce-594a-4271-ba6f-3470df261f49
```

This is an ID assigned to the PE when it is presented to this host:

```
Host Id:
```

In this example, it is blank, which means that this host has not been added to the ACL of the SC associated with this PE. The ID format for NAS PEs uses a hexadecimal value without any prefix, while for SCSI PEs, the NAA ID is used instead.

This is the storage array's name:

```
Array Id: EMC:VIRT1625PDT9QG
```

It was assigned to the simulator's virtual appliance during deployment from OVA. Physical arrays would have their names assigned by EMC and usually start with APM for the VNX array family. Other storage vendors have their own naming conventions.

This is the PE type, which can be NFS or SCSI:

```
Type: NFS
```

This reflects whether this host has been granted access to the SC associated with the PE (that is, added to the SC's ACL):

```
Accessible: false
```

In this example, the host is not on the SC's ACL.

This field's value is set to `false` when the PE is discovered by the host before the PE was added to the associated SC's ACL:

```
Configured: false
```

Until the PE is added to the ACL, the SC associated with this NAS PE is not visible to this host.

When the host is added to the SC's ACL, the value of both the `Accessible` and `Configured` fields changes to `true`, and the `Host Id` field is populated with the ID assigned to the PE for this host.

This field is used by block VVols devices only:

```
Lun Id:
```

The value is usually similar to the value of the `Host Id` field. (For an example, see the fourth PE in Listing 23.1.)

This field is for NAS PEs only:

```
Remote Host: 10.10.0.54
```

The value is the IP address of the NAS server's port. It is blank for block PEs.

This is the NFS export/share name on the NAS server:

```
Remote Share: /rfc4122.dfc6ab2f-bbad-4233-9cf7-a242530e8b10
```

The value is blank for block PEs. This remote share is mounted on ESXi hosts under /vmfs/volumes in a directory using the remote host and remote share as part of its name. For this example, this is the mount point:

```
NFSv3PE_10.10.0.54__rfc4122.dfc6ab2f-bbad-4233-9cf7-a242530e8b10
```

This mount point is symbolically linked to a directory named with the NAS PE host ID, as in this example:

```
NFSv3PE_10.10.0.54__rfc4122.dfc6ab2f-bbad-4233-9cf7-a242530e8b10 ->
9ccc2232-57c9d49a
```

You can obtain this information by using this command:

```
ls -al /vmfs/volumes/NFSv3PE_10.10.0.54__rfc4122.dfc6ab2f-bbad-4233-9cf7-
a242530e8b10
```

> **NOTE**
>
> The mount point is empty while the VMs on NAS SC accessible via that PE are in a powered-off state. When a VM is powered on, a `BIND` request is sent from the object store file system daemon (`OSFSD`) to `vvold`, which in turn sends it to the VP. The VP responds with the PE ID along with a secondary VVol ID. OSFS then binds the VVol to the PE, using the secondary VVol ID. From this point on, all I/O to the VVol is sent to the PE, and the PE issues the I/O on the bound VVol. For more details on VVols binding, see the section "I/O Flow to VVols," later in this chapter.

The following is last field of the first PE's properties in Listing 23.1:

```
Storage Containers: 730ecbb3-8fc4-4ef6-b034-1ed2bda5e954
```

This is the list of all SCs mounted by this host, even though each NAS PE is associated with a single SC. In this example, the SC UUID listed in this field is identical to the value in the remaining three NAS PEs in Listing 23.1. An easy way to tell if this SC belongs to this PE is to compare the value of the `Remote Share` and `Storage Containers` fields. If the value after the prefix /rfc4122 matches the value in the `Storage Containers` field, the SC is associated with this PE.

For the purpose of this demonstration, I added this host to the SC's ACL. I then ran this command:

```
esxcli storage vvol protocolendpoint list --pe rfc4122.07c733ce-594a-4271-
ba6f-3470df261f49
```

This command specifies a single PE to list, using the `--pe` option. You can also use the abbreviated option `-p` instead and use the PE ID displayed on the first line of the first PE listed in Listing 23.1.

TIP

If any of the ESXi hosts hang while running ESXCLI commands, `hostd` may be hung due to an APD state of any of the attached block devices. You can use `localcli` instead as it does not use the `hostd` process.

Listing 23.2 shows the output using `localcli`.

Listing 23.2   Listing a single PE via the CLI after adding a host to the SC's ACL before mounting the datastore

```
localcli storage vvol protocolendpoint list -p rfc4122.07c733ce-594a-4271-
ba6f-3470df261f49


rfc4122.07c733ce-594a-4271-ba6f-3470df261f49:
    Host Id: 9ccc2232-57c9d49a
    Array Id: EMC:VIRT1625PDT9QG
    Type: NFS
    Accessible: true
    Configured: true
    Lun Id:
    Remote Host: 10.10.0.54
    Remote Share: /rfc4122.dfc6ab2f-bbad-4233-9cf7-a242530e8b10
    Storage Containers: 730ecbb3-8fc4-4ef6-b034-1ed2bda5e954
```

Compare this listing with that of the PE prior to adding the host to the SC's ACL. Observe that the value of the fields `Accessible` and `Configured` is now set to `true`. Also note that the `host Id` field now shows a unique value, representing the PE ID for this specific host.

I then mount the datastore represented by the SC and repeat the same command to list the PE properties. Listing 23.3 shows the output.

Listing 23.3   Listing a single PE via the CLI after adding a host to the SC's ACL after mounting the datastore

```
localcli storage vvol protocolendpoint list -p rfc4122.07c733ce-594a-4271-
ba6f-3470df261f49

rfc4122.07c733ce-594a-4271-ba6f-3470df261f49:
   Host Id: 9ccc2232-57c9d49a
   Array Id: EMC:VIRT1625PDT9QG
   Type: NFS
   Accessible: true
   Configured: true
   Lun Id:
   Remote Host: 10.10.0.54
   Remote Share: /rfc4122.dfc6ab2f-bbad-4233-9cf7-a242530e8b10
   Storage Containers: 730ecbb3-8fc4-4ef6-b034-1ed2bda5e954, dfc6ab2f-bbad-
4233-9cf7-a242530e8b10
```

The only difference between this listing and Listing 23.2 is the additional SC UUID (highlighted in the output) listed in the `Storage Container` field. Observe that this new SC UUID matches the UUID in the `Remote Share` field.

The example of the third PE in Listing 23.1 shows the value of `Accessible` as `false` and `Configured` as `true`. This is a special case where the SC was accessible and mounted previously. However, this host was removed from the ACL of the SC.

Table 23.2 compares the combination of these two fields' values and their reflection of the SC status.

Table 23.2 Comparing the `Accessible`/`Configured` combination

Accessible	Configured	Host on SC ACL	SC Mounted on Host
true	true	Yes	Yes
false	false	No	Never mounted
false	true	No; was previously on ACL	Was previously mounted

Next, I list the only block PE separately and examine its properties. To do that, I run this command, based on the list of PEs in Listing 23.1:

```
localcli storage vvol protocolendpoint list --pe rfc4122.60060160-cf3b-
c820-82b4-e9fc61b0bf45
```

Listing 23.4 shows the output of this command.

Listing 23.4   Listing a single block PE via the CLI after adding a host to the SC's ACL

```
localcli storage vvol protocolendpoint list --pe rfc4122.60060160-cf3b-
c820-82b4-e9fc61b0bf45

rfc4122.60060160-cf3b-c820-82b4-e9fc61b0bf45:
   Host Id: naa.60060160cf3bc82082b4e9fc61b0bf45
   Array Id: EMC:VIRT1625PDT9QG
   Type: SCSI
   Accessible: true
   Configured: true
   Lun Id: naa.60060160cf3bc82082b4e9fc61b0bf45
   Remote Host:
   Remote Share:
   Storage Containers: 371ab5df-fd88-4116-abe5-0374f4b50e8a, 400a35bd-14d2-
4a6b-be36-a668f664f347
```

Based on the details provided in Listing 23.1, it is clear that this PE is a block PE because the Type is SCSI. In addition, the host is on the ACL of two block SCs that have been mounted on this host. (Both SCs are listed in the Storage Containers field.)

The LUN ID of the PE for this host is naa.60060160cf3bc82082b4e9fc61b0bf45.

The Remote Host and Remote Share fields are blank because they are specific to NAS PEs only.

Table 23.3 compares NAS PEs to SCSI PEs and their relationships with NAS and block SCs.

Table 23.3 Comparing NAS PEs to block PEs

PE Type	PE Count Per Host	SC Type	SC Count per PE
NAS	Same as the number of SCs accessible by host	NAS	One SC per PE
SCSI	One (Some vendors— for example, Dell[PS Seriesmd]present the same PE to all hosts)	Block	Up to the maximum number of SCs the array supports

Listing Storage Containers via the CLI

As mentioned earlier, SCs are equivalent to VVols datastores. You can list these SCs via the host's CLI by using this command:

```
localcli storage vvol storagecontainer list
```

Listing 23.5 shows the output of this command from an ESXi 6 host.

Listing 23.5   Listing SCs via the CLI

```
esxcli storage vvol storagecontainer list

Unity_VVol_DS1:
   StorageContainer Name: Unity_VVol_DS1
   UUID: vvol:371ab5dffd884116-abe50374f4b50e8a
   Array: EMC:VIRT1625PDT9QG
   Size(MB): 512000
   Free(MB): 512000
   Accessible: true
   Default Policy:

Unity_VVol_NAS_DS1:
   StorageContainer Name: Unity_VVol_NAS_DS1
   UUID: vvol:730ecbb38fc44ef6-b0341ed2bda5e954
   Array: EMC:VIRT1625PDT9QG
   Size(MB): 811008
   Free(MB): 811008
   Accessible: true
   Default Policy:

Unity_VVol_DS3:
   StorageContainer Name: Unity_VVol_DS3
   UUID: vvol:400a35bd14d24a6b-be36a668f664f347
   Array: EMC:VIRT1625PDT9QG
   Size(MB): 307200
   Free(MB): 307200
   Accessible: true
   Default Policy:

Unity_VVol_NAS_DS4:
   StorageContainer Name: Unity_VVol_NAS_DS4
   UUID: vvol:dfc6ab2fbbad4233-9cf7a242530e8b10
   Array: EMC:VIRT1625PDT9QG
   Size(MB): 102400
   Free(MB): 102400
   Accessible: true
   Default Policy:
```

The listing shows the following properties for each SC:

- `StorageContainer Name`—Regardless of the name you gave to the SC on the storage array, what is actually displayed here is the name you gave the datastore the first time you mounted the SC. In my example, an SC name was `Unity_VVol_NAS_SC4`, but I named the datastore `Unity_VVol_NAS_DS4`.

  Some storage vendors mount the datastore on the hosts at the same time the SC is created, using the vendor's vCenter integrated storage management plug-in (for example, Dell EqualLogic's Virtual Storage Manager [VSM]). In this case, the datastore name and SC name are identical. For an example, see the section "Adding a Block VVols Datastore," later in this chapter.

- `UUID`—This is the SC's UUID, which is prefixed with `vvol` and a colon. This is analogous to the VMFS datastore UUID.

- `Size` **and** `Free` **fields**—This is the total logical size, in MB, of the SC and the free capacity. In this case, both values are the same because this is a freshly created SC. The physical size is larger, as you will see in the section "Mounting a VVols Datastore on Additional Hosts," later in this chapter.

- `Accessible`—This means that this host is on the SC's ACL.

- `Default Policy`—If the storage vendor implements this feature, it shows the default capability profile set when more than one CP is associated with the SC. This field is blank when no default policy is set.

Exploring VVols Datastore Properties via the UI

In the previous section, I covered how to examine the NAS and block PE properties. In this section, I do the same for NAS and block VVols datastores (the host's view of mounted SCs)

Even though the datastore is on a NAS server, access to it by the hosts does not follow the same I/O flow as that of a pure NFSv3 datastore. For more details, see Chapter 16, "NFS."

To inspect any VVols datastore properties, NAS or block, you can follow this procedure:

1. Connect to the vCenter server using the vSphere 6 Web Client as a user with Administrator privileges.
2. Navigate to the **Storage** view (see Figure 23.31).
3. Locate the VVols datastore in the inventory tree and select it.
4. Select the **Manage** tab.
5. Click the **Settings** button.

6. Select the **General** section. Here you see the following details:

   - **Default Storage Policy**—I discuss this later in this chapter.

   - **Properties**—This includes the datastore name and type (which in this case is VVol).

   - **Capacity**—This field shows the capacity value as `<size> free out of <size>`. If you expand this section, you get three fields: `Total Capacity`, `Provisioned Space`, and `Free Space`.

   - **Backing Storage Container**—This section includes the following fields:

     - `Name`—This is the SC name. In this example, it is `Unity_VVol_NAS_SC1`.

     - `UUID`—This is the backing storage container's UUID, in the format `vvol:<ID>`, where `<ID>` is the same as the ID listed on the SC properties on the storage array but prefixed there with `rfc4122` and here with `vvol`.

     - `Storage Array(s)`—This is the name of the storage array. It matches the storage array listed in the registered VP details. See Chapter 20 for details.

     - `Storage Provider(s)`—This matches the VP name you specified when you registered the VP.

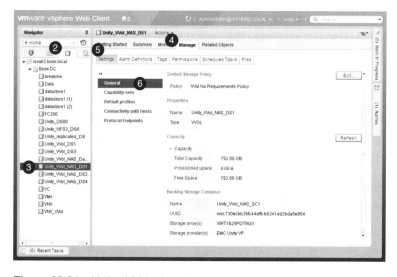

Figure 23.31 Listing VVols datastore properties

7. Select the **Capability sets** section, and you see a list of capability profiles associated with the SC on which this datastore resides. Such sets vary by vendor and by how they were configured on the storage array. When you select the listed set called **Mixed Fast VP 3 tiers**—in this example from an EMC Unity—the lower pane shows three sections:

- **Storage Properties**—Expanding this section shows the following storage capabilities:

  - **Drive Type**—This is set to Extreme MultiTier. This means, for this storage array, that the storage pool on which this datastore resides has multiple types of drives, based on the I/Os per seconds (IOPS) rating, as high as SSD and down the line to SAS and NL-SAS. The second line here shows Any as the drive type. This means that the I/O can be sent to any dive type in this storage pool. See step 7 in the section "Creating Storage Pools for Use by EMC Unity VVols SCs," earlier in this chapter.

  - **Tiering Policy**—Policies listed here are practically all the ones supported by the storage array: Auto Tier-High, Auto Tier, Highest, Lowest, and Any. This means that it is left up to the storage array to select any of the policies and that creating a storage policy with any of these capabilities would list this datastore as compatible.

  - **FAST Cache**—This is a large-capacity secondary cache using SAS flash drives. This is not available only in physical deployments. Where available, the setting values are Enabled or Disabled.

  - **RAID Type**—This is available in physical deployments only, which is why I cannot exhibit it here. Where available, the RAID types provided by EMC Unity are RAID5, 6, 10, and Mixed.

- **Service Level**—Expanding this subsection lists the service levels associated with the storage pool. They can be Platinum, Gold, Silver, or Bronze. Platinum is available in physical deployments only.

- **Usage Tag**—These are the tags added to the capability profile when it was created. If none exist, this section is not listed (see Figure 23.32).

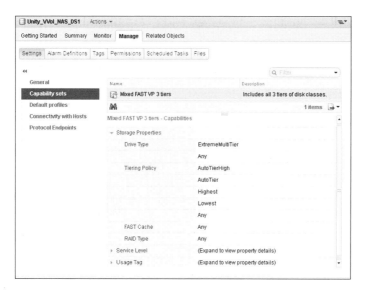

Figure 23.32   Listing VVols datastore capability sets

8. Select the **Default profiles** section. Some storage vendors provide the option to select a default CP when the SC has more than one CP associated with it. This view shows the default CP. Otherwise, all CPs associated with the SC are displayed.

9. Select **Connectivity with Hosts**. This view list the hosts that have this datastore mounted. This tab also shows the datastore mount point on each host. The format of a mount point is `/vmfs/volumes/vvol:<SC UUID>` (for example, `/vmfs/volumes/vvol:730ecbb38fc44ef6-b0341ed2bda5e954`).

10. Select **Protocol Endpoint**. This view lists the protocol endpoints, providing access to this datastore, on all hosts that mounted this datastore. The content differs by protocol and vendor. For example, NAS PEs from EMC Unity show a list similar to the list shown earlier in this chapter, in the section "Listing PEs via the UI." However, this view is database-centric instead of host-centric. For block PEs, depending on how the storage vendor implemented them, there can be multiple PEs listed for the datastore or just a single one. Figure 23.33 shows block PEs for a datastore on an EMC Unity virtual appliance.

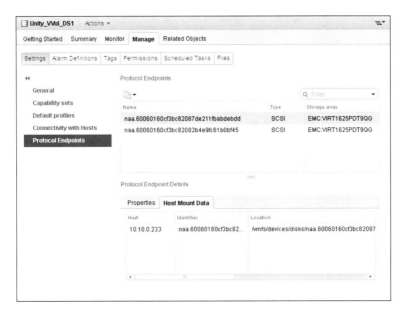

Figure 23.33   Listing VVols datastore Block PEs of an EMC Unity

Here you see two PEs, which matches the count of hosts connected to the datastore. To identify which PE belongs to which host, select a PE and then select the **Host Mount Data** tab in the Protocol Endpoint Details pane. The Host column lists the host name or IP address. The Location column shows the host's block device path, representing the PE on this host. The PE's NAA ID is listed under the /vmfs/devices/disks path. Repeat this for the other PE to identify the host.

In contrast with the EMC Unity, Figure 23.34 shows an example from a Dell EqualLogic PS6000 iSCSI storage array.

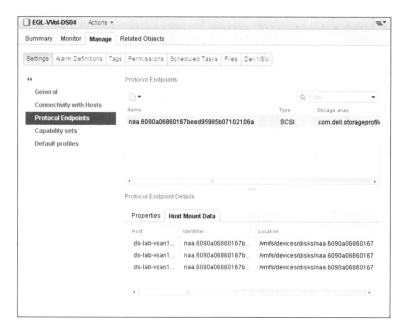

Figure 23.34   Listing VVols datastore Block PEs of a Dell PS Series

In this example, there is a single PE for all hosts with access to the datastore. The Host Mount Data tab shows three hosts sharing the same PE, which also means that the Location column shows the same path on each host.

Adding a Block VVols Datastore

Earlier in this chapter I covered the process of creating and mounting NAS VVols datastores on an EMC Unity simulator. In this section, I go through a similar process for a block VVols datastore on a Dell EqualLogic PS6000 storage array. This procedure assumes that you have already installed and configured Dell EqualLogic Virtual Storage Manager (VSM) and authorized the ESXi host's iSCSI initiators for VVol access. (See the section "Configuring Block Storage Arrays for VVols," earlier in this chapter.)

1. Connect to the vCenter server using the vSphere 6 Web Client as a user with Administrator privileges.

2. Navigate to the **Home** tab.

3. Click the **Dell Virtual Storage Manager** icon in the inventory tree (see Figure 23.35).

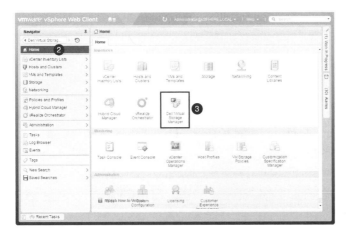

Figure 23.35 Policy compliance validation after selecting the migration target datastore

4. Click the **Create Dell Datastore** icon on the top left of the Datastores pane (a cylinder with a plus sign).

5. Enter the datastore name (see Figure 23.36). If you plan to create identically sized datastores that share the same datastore name prefix, specify the prefix only (for example, EQL-VVol-DS). You will specify the number of datastores to create later, in step 11 of this procedure. A sequential number will be automatically appended to this name.

6. Select the **VVol** radio button.

7. Select the datacenter.

8. Click **Next**.

Figure 23.36 Selecting the datastore name, type, and placement

9. Select the vCenter cluster, host, or a resource pool and then click **Next**.

10. Select the PS group (see Figure 23.37).

11. Select the storage pool.

12. Select the number of datastores to create.

13. Select the datastore size. If you plan on creating datastores of varying sizes, create them one at a time. The pie chart at the bottom of the dialog gives you an idea of the available space on the storage pool.

14. Click **Next**.

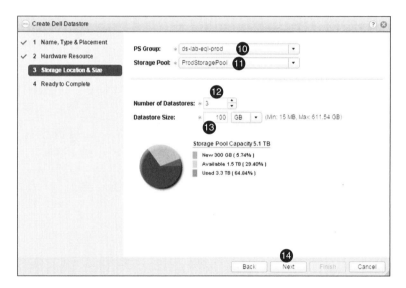

Figure 23.37   Selecting the datastore's storage location and size

15. Review your selections and then click **Finish**.

16. When the process is complete, the newly added datastores are listed in the datastores list (see Figure 23.38).

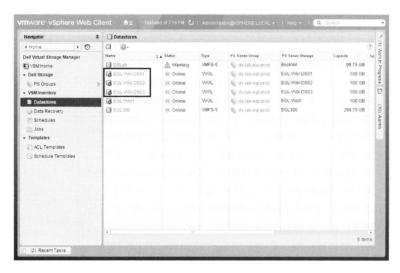

Figure 23.38 Process completed successfully

Mounting a VVols Datastore on Additional Hosts

The procedure just covered is specific to Dell EqualLogic VVols certified PS series storage arrays. The workflow, while simple and easy, does not provide the flexibility of a granular configuration. For example, I had originally configured my environment with a single ESXi host. When I created a VVols datastore, it was presented and mounted on that host only.

Later, I added two new hosts and created a cluster with all three hosts. There is no way that I know to use Dell VSM to mount the datastore on the two newly added hosts.

However, I was able to mount it using the following procedure, which is, up to step 9, identical to that for block SCs on EMC Unity:

1. Connect to the vCenter server using the vSphere 6 Web Client as a user with Administrator privileges.

2. Navigate to the **Storage** view (see Figure 23.39).

3. Locate the existing VVols datastore in the inventory tree and select it. In this example, it is **EQL-VVol1**.

4. Select the **Manage** tab.

5. Click the **Settings** button.

6. Select the **Connectivity with Hosts** section. Notice that a single host is listed here. In this example, it is host 12.

7. Right-click the datastore and select the **Mount Datastore to Additional Hosts** menu option.

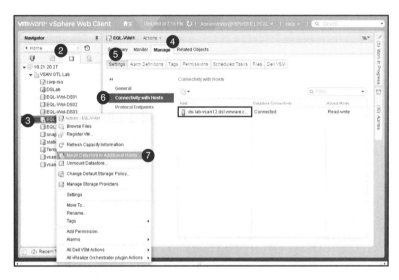

Figure 23.39   Accessing the Mount Datastore to Additional Hosts menu option

8. Select the additional hosts from the list. In this example, they are two hosts that are members of Physical Cluster 6.1 (see Figure 23.40).

9. Click **OK**.

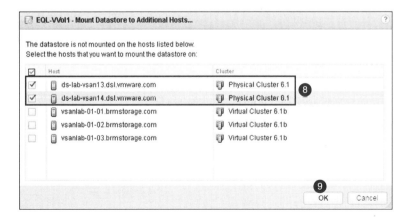

Figure 23.40   Selecting additional hosts

A successful operation would result in all three hosts being listed in the Connectivity with Hosts section (see Figure 23.41).

Figure 23.41   Additional hosts added to datastore connectivity with the host

10. Click the Dell SVM button. The datastore logical and physical space utilization are displayed (see Figure 23.42).

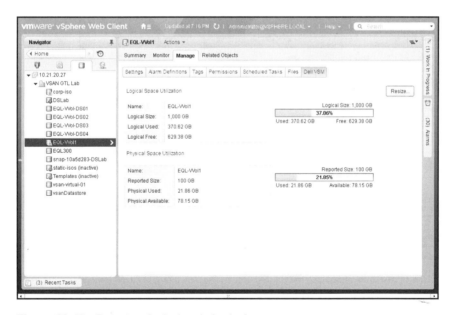

Figure 23.42   Datastore logical and physical space

Note that the logical space and physical space are named after the datastore name. The logical space in this example is 10 times the size of the physical space to accommodate snapshots, clones, and so on created for VVols residing on this datastore. (I cover more details on this topic later in this chapter.)

Mounting an Unmounted VVols Datastore

Another scenario is that I had unmounted a VVols datastore that was previously mounted on a single host. I ended up with a storage container on the storage array with the name of the original datastore.

To utilize this storage container, I would simply follow the workflow of manually creating a VVols datastore without the use of the VSM UI:

1. Connect to the vCenter server using the vSphere 6 Web Client as a user with Administrator privileges.

2. Navigate to the **Storage** view.

3. Right-click the datacenter and select **Storage**.

4. Select the **New Datastore** option (see Figure 23.43).

Figure 23.43 Accessing the New Datastore menu option

5. In the Location step, click **Next**.

6. In the Type step, select the **VVol** radio button and then click **Next**.

7. In the Name and Container Selection step, type the datastore name and select the backing storage container. I had originally named the datastore EQL-VVol3, which is why VSM named the storage container with the same name. This time, I will experiment with using a different datastore name: EQL-VVol-DS04.

8. Click **Next** (see Figure 23.44).

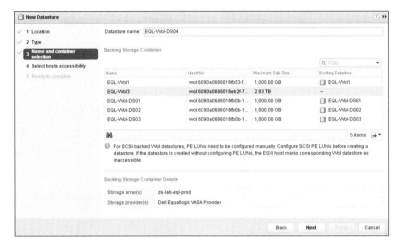

Figure 23.44   Datastore name and container selection

9. Select the hosts in the same cluster to which to mount the VVols datastore.

10. Click **Next** (see Figure 23.45).

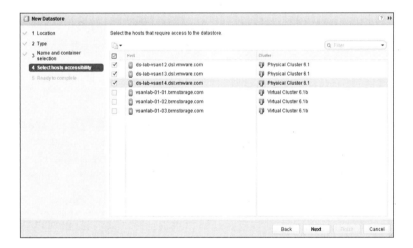

Figure 23.45   Selecting hosts' accessibility

11. In the Ready to Complete step, review your choices and then click **Finish**.

12. Select the datastore with the new name, EQL-VVol-DS04, which shows up now in the inventory tree (see Figure 23.46).

13. Select the **Manage** tab.

14. Click the **Dell VSM** button to display the logical and physical space utilization.

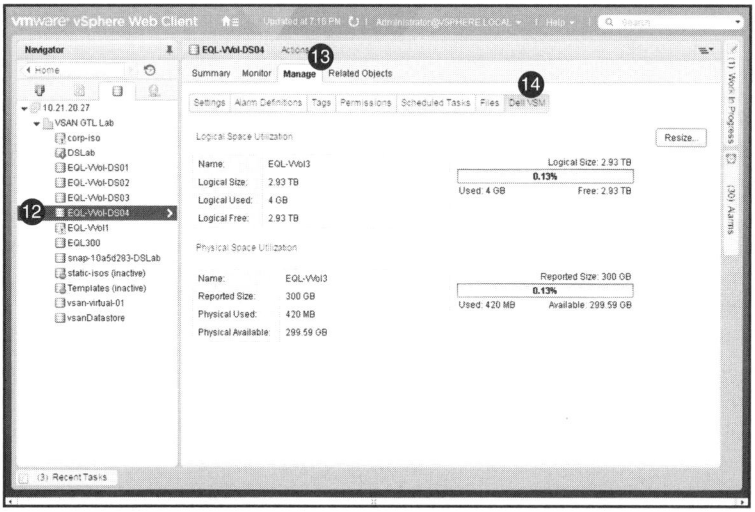

Figure 23.46   Accessing the Dell VSM section in the VVols datastore properties

Compare this to the results from the procedure, in the section "Mounting a VVols Datastore on Additional Hosts," and observe that the logical and physical space kept the original datastore (SC) name, which was created using the Dell VSM UI.

Resizing the VVols Datastore Size

VVols provides the ability to expand the datastore size as the need arises. This is a much simpler process than using the classic VMFS datastore on a block device. In that case, you had to first contact the storage administrator to add space to the backing LUN. Then you had to rescan the HBA to refresh the new LUN size followed by the process of growing the VMFS datastore.

With VVols, all you need to do is resize the datastore in one step. This procedure provides the detailed steps for accomplishing this task:

1. Connect to the vCenter server using the vSphere 6 Web Client as a user with Administrator privileges.

2. Navigate to the **Home** page.

3. Click the **Dell Virtual Storage Manager** icon in the inventory tree.

4. Select the **Datastores** object from the inventory list.

5. Locate the datastore you want to grow in the datastores list and then click the datastore's name in the Name column (see Figure 23.47).

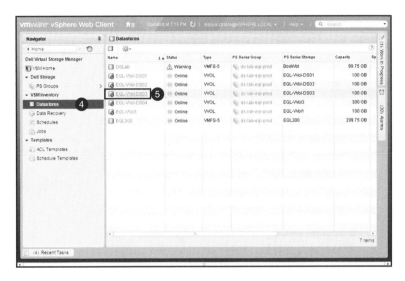

Figure 23.47   Accessing the VVols datastore via the Dell VSM UI

6. You are taken to the **Dell VSM** section of the datastore **Manage** tab. Click the **Resize** button (see Figure 23.48).

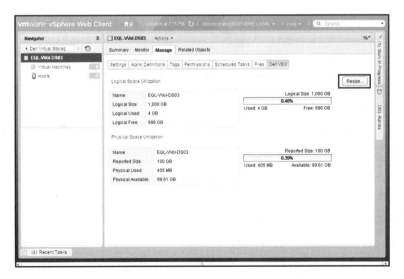

Figure 23.48   Accessing the VVols datastore Resize option

7. In the **Resize Dell Datastore** dialog, enter the new size. The pie chart displayed should help you avoid exceeding the available space on the storage pool.

8. Click **OK** (see Figure 23.49).

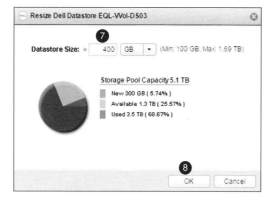

Figure 23.49   Entering a larger datastore size

9. Successful results show the new logical and physical size, which are still in almost a 10:1 ratio. In other words, when the physical space is grown, the logical space follows suit, maintaining the original ratio (see Figure 23.50).

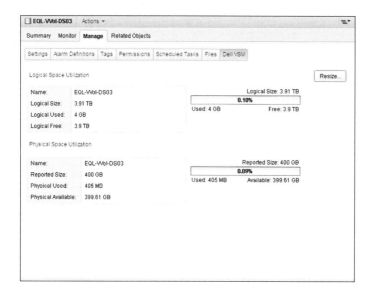

Figure 23.50   VVols datastore resized successfully

Creating Virtual Machine Storage Policies for VVols

Now that you have configured the storage and vSphere environments to communicate with each other, the next step to utilizing the storage capabilities is to create one or more virtual machine storage policies. This assumes that you already have at least one LUN presented to the ESXi hosts and that it has been formatted with a VMFS5 datastore.

The following procedure uses a Dell EqualLogic storage array, but it is similar to other block storage arrays. The only differences is the name of the VASA provider and the exposed capabilities. Follow these steps to create a virtual machine storage policy for VVols:

1. Connect to the vCenter server using the vSphere 6 Web Client as a user with Administrator privileges.

2. Navigate to the **Home** page.

3. Click the **VM Storage Policies** icon in the Monitoring section (see Figure 23.51).

Figure 23.51   Accessing the VM Storage Policies icon

4. Click the **Create New Storage Policy** icon (see Figure 23.52).

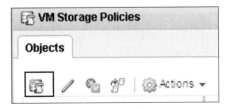

Figure 23.52   Locating the Create New Storage Policy icon

5. If you have multiple vCenter servers, select the relevant one.

6. Enter a name for the policy.

7. Enter a description (optional).

8. In the Rule-Sets overview screen, click **Next**.

9. In the Rules Based on Data Services field, select the VVols VASA 2.0 specific provider. In this example, it is com.dell.storageprofile.equallogic.std, which is the VVols VP for Dell EqualLogic storage arrays (see Figure 23.53).

Figure 23.53   Selecting a storage policy's VASA provider

NOTE

Figure 23.53 shows additional VPs in the pull-down list. The VVols VP for Dell EqualLogic PS Series is the last one on the list, com.dell.storageprofile.equallogic.std. Do not confuse this with com.dell.storageprofile.equallogic.std.VASA10, which is used for VASA 1.0–related policies. See Chapter 20 for more details. A vSAN VP is used with VMware vSAN, covered in Chapters 21 and 22.

10. Once you select the VP, a new <Add rule> dropdown list appears in the dialog (see Figure 23.54). Select the relevant rule from the list. (At the end of this procedure, Table 23.4 outlines the available rule and their corresponding capabilities.) Other VPs have different choices.

Figure 23.54   Selecting a storage policy's rule

11. Now you should have a pull-down list of capabilities exposed by the selected rule. Select the desired capability from the list. Table 23.4 lists capabilities from Dell EqualLogic to demonstrate the available capabilities. Other storage vendors have many other capabilities. In this example, I selected **SAS and RAID 6** capabilities for the DiskType and RaidType rules (see Figure 23.55).

Figure 23.55   Selecting storage capability

12. In this example, I selected two rules: DiskType and RaidType. You can add more rules to Rule-Set 1, depending on the combination of capabilities your design requires. If the storage array supports creating tags, click the **Add tag-based-rule** button and then select a tag from the list that appears. For example, you can create a special combination of resources and tag each with a descriptive tag (for example, SQL-Data, SQL-Logs, and so on). This makes the selection easier for the vSphere administrator. Click **Next**.

13. The storage compatibility list is displayed (see Figure 23.56). On the top you see two groups: compatible and incompatible sets of datastores. Select the **Compatible** row, and the bottom half of the dialog lists the datastores in this group. In this example, I have five datastores that meet the requirements of this policy. Note that the Type column shows that all datastores' type is VVOL, which mean these VVols datastores are compliant with policy. Click **Next**.

Figure 23.56 Listing compatible storage

14. Review your choices in the Ready to Complete screen and then click **Finish**. Now the newly created policy is listed in the VM Storage Policies list.

Table 23.4 lists the various storage capabilities exposed by the Dell EqualLogic VASA provider. The capabilities can be any or a combination of four rules and their corresponding capabilities:

- **RaidType**—The SC is on a storage pool that includes a single RAID type or a mix of RAID types.

- **DiskType**—The SC is on a storage pool that is made up of any or the combination of these disk types.

- **DiskSpeed**—The SC is on a storage pool that is made up of any or the combination of disks with listed disk speeds.

- **Encryption**—Whether disks backing the SC offer on-disk encryption.

Table 23.4 Explanation of VVols storage policy rule types for Dell EqualLogic

Rule Type	Capabilities	Notes
RAIDType	Mixed, RAID 5, RAID 6, RAID 10, RAID 50, RAID 60	This is the RAID type or types configured in a storage pool. Mixed means a single storage pool is configured with more than one RAID type.
DiskType	Best Effort, SATA, SATA SSD, SAS, SAS SSD	This is the type of disks in a storage pool. Best Effort capability tries to locate the best devices available. Some vendors classify these as Best Effort (mixed), Slow (SATA), Fast (SATA or SAS), Faster (Hybrid or SAS), and Fastest (SSD).
DiskSpeed	Best Effort, 5400, 7200, 10000, 15000	This is the disk rotational speed in RPM. Best Effort capability is for storage pools with mixed disk speeds.
Encryption	No, Yes	This is for disks that offer on-disk encryption.

Some storage vendors allow you to combine parts of different storage groups or pools into a VVols storage container. This enables auto-tiering capability, offered by that storage array, to be exposed as a capability of that SC.

Deploying New VMs Using Storage Policies

The final step in utilizing VVols via VASA 2.0 exposed storage capabilities is to create a VM and select a storage policy for the VVols datastore selections. You might notice a lot of similarities between VVols and VASA storage policies. That is due to the fact that VASA provides the underlying APIs for both, with the difference being the VASA version used. However, when you deploy a VM using the VVols storage policy, you see major differences in how VVols capabilities are used.

Let's revisit the example in Chapter 20 of an enterprise application that uses Microsoft SQL Server for a database server. Your design should meet the application's I/O requirements and take advantage of the exposed VVols storage capabilities to better place each virtual disk on the datastore to meet such I/O requirements. For example, a VM storage design for this Microsoft SQL Server would be divided into four types of virtual disks: System disk, Data disk, TempDB disk, and Transaction Logs disk. If you wanted to be even more granular, you could add a fifth virtual disk for the guest OS swap/page file. This VVols storage can also offer data protection service level agreements (SLAs) for only the subset of virtual disks that need such protection. In other words, virtual disk placement on VVols datastores would be dictated by the data protection services provided by the SCs backing these datastores. Because VVols offers some of these services as inherent storage capabilities, it is easy to apply a separate storage policy to each virtual disk so that they get placed on datastores that provide the required I/O profile as well as data protection services. Snapshots is an inherent protection capability that is available on all SCs, without exposing it as a VASA capability. In other words, you get this capability regardless of the storage policy used to place the VMDKs on the VVols datastores.

> **NOTE**
>
> The vSphere 6.0 version of VVols APIs (VASA 2.0) does not expose replication as a supported data protection capability. However, the vSphere 6.5 version of VASA (3.0) introduces support for VVols replication for arrays that support it. Until support is available from your storage vendor, I recommend using the vSphere Replication (VR) feature to mitigate the risk because it works on the VM/VMDK level and is supported on VVols as well as vSAN datastores based VMs. Some storage vendors offer replication of the whole SC (for example, NetApp SnapMirror), but the recovery process for it would not be on a per-VVol basis. (Remember that a VMDK is a virtual volume, just like other VM components.)

Table 23.5 shows the I/O profiles and data protection services required for the virtual disks that comprise a Microsoft SQL Server VM. I then use the content of this table later on for disk placement design decisions and pair them with corresponding storage policies.

Table 23.5 SQL Server VM's virtual disks, I/O profiles, and data protection services requirements

Virtual Disk Class	I/O Profile		RAID Type	Backing Disk Type	Data Protection Services	
	Random/ Sequential	Read/ Write			Snapshot	Replication
Guest OS System Disk	Random	Read	RAID 5 or 10	HDD	Yes	Use VR until supported
Swap/Page File Disk	Random	Read/write	RAID 10	HDD	No	No
Data Disk	Random	Read/write	RAID 10	HDD/SSD	Yes	Use VR until supported

Virtual Disk Class	I/O Profile		RAID Type	Backing Disk Type	Data Protection Services	
	Random/ Sequential	Read/ Write			Snapshot	Replication
Transaction Logs Disk	Sequential	Write	RAID 10	HDD/SSD	Yes	Use VR until supported
TempDB Disk	Random	Read/write	RAID 10	HDD	No	No

In this chapter, I will create a storage policy for each row except for the swap/page file and TempDB disks, which can use the same policy. This means I will have four storage policies to use with this VM. In my environment, I am not planning for a DR site. As a result, I will not consider replication choices.

The storage policy names are as follows:

- VVol System Disk Policy

- VVol SQL TempDB or Swap Disk Policy

- VVol SQL Data Disk Policy

- VVol SQL Logs Disk Policy

Creating a New VM Using Storage Profiles

This process follows the Microsoft SQL Server VM example from earlier in this chapter. It is identical in many aspects to the procedure provided in Chapter 20, with the only difference being using VVol-specific storage policies. You can modify it for other applications according to the number of virtual disks and the I/O profile for each disk. Follow these steps:

1. Connect to the vCenter server using the vSphere 6 Web Client as a user with Administrator privileges.

2. Navigate to the **Hosts and Clusters** view.

3. Locate and select the data center on which the VM will reside.

4. Select the **Actions** pull-down list and then select **New Virtual Machine**, **New Virtual Machine**.

5. In the Select a Creation Type step, select the **Create a new virtual machine** option and then click **Next**.

6. Enter a name for the VM (for example, VVol-SQL-Server01).

7. Select the datacenter and then click **Next**.

8. Select the cluster or ESXi host and then click **Next**.

9. In the Select Storage step, select the storage policy you created for the guest OS system disk placement.

10. Select one of compatible datastores listed at the bottom part of the dialog. Observe the **Compatibility** section at the bottom of the dialog, which should state **Compatibility checks succeeded**.

11. Click **Next** (see Figure 23.57).

Figure 23.57   Selecting a storage policy in a new VM

12. Select the VM compatibility. In this example, it is **ESXi 6.0 and later**. Click **Next**.

13. Select the guest OS family and version. In this example, it is **Windows - Microsoft Windows Server 2012 (64-bit)**. Click **Next**.

   Now comes the tricky part! In the Customize Hardware step, these are the high-level customizations:

   ■ Configure the CPU count (that is, the number of sockets and cores per socket) and any other VM options.

   ■ Configure the system disk's size per your VM design. The default may not always be large enough for the applications to be installed in the guest OS.

   ■ Add the remaining virtual disks per your VM design, using the storage policies created earlier.

I cover only the addition of one of the virtual disks because the process is identical with the exception of selecting the corresponding storage policy for each disk.

14. Add a second SCSI controller to which you will attach the SQL data–related virtual disks. You add it by selecting **SCSI Controller** from the New Device field and then clicking **Add**.

15. If your design calls for using the VMware Paravirtual adapter, scroll down the window and expand the **New SCSI controller** section. Otherwise, skip to step 17.

16. In the Change Type field, select **VMware Paravirtual** from the pull-down list.

17. In the New Device field, select **New Hard Disk** from the pull-up menu.

18. Click **Add**.

19. Scroll the window down and expand the newly added **New Hard disk** section.

20. Select the relevant disk size.

21. In the Virtual Device Node field, select the second listing, **New SCSI Controller**. This is the controller just added in step 14. Notice that the SCSI device node number now changed from SCSI(0:1) to SCSI(1:0). This means that the new disk will be the first disk attached to the new SCSI controller (see Figure 23.58).

Figure 23.58   Customizing an added virtual disk

22. In the Location field, select **Browse**. The Select a Datastore Cluster or Datastore dialog opens.

23. Select the VM storage policy for this virtual disk (see Figure 23.59).

24. Select a datastore from the Compatible section.

25. Click **OK**.

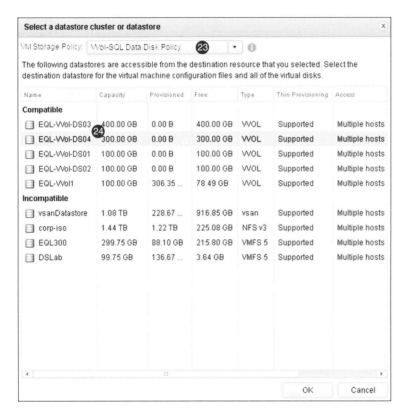

Name	Capacity	Provisioned	Free	Type	Thin Provisioning	Access
Compatible						
EQL-Vvol-DS03	400.00 GB	0.00 B	400.00 GB	VVOL	Supported	Multiple hosts
EQL-Vvol-DS04	300.00 GB	0.00 B	300.00 GB	VVOL	Supported	Multiple hosts
EQL-Vvol-DS01	100.00 GB	0.00 B	100.00 GB	VVOL	Supported	Multiple hosts
EQL-Vvol-DS02	100.00 GB	0.00 B	100.00 GB	VVOL	Supported	Multiple hosts
EQL-Vvol1	100.00 GB	306.35 ...	78.49 GB	VVOL	Supported	Multiple hosts
Incompatible						
vsanDatastore	1.08 TB	228.67 ...	916.85 GB	vsan	Supported	Multiple hosts
corp-iso	1.44 TB	1.22 TB	225.08 GB	NFS v3	Supported	Multiple hosts
EQL300	299.75 GB	88.10 GB	215.80 GB	VMFS 5	Supported	Multiple hosts
DSLab	99.75 GB	136.67 ...	3.64 GB	VMFS 5	Supported	Multiple hosts

Figure 23.59   Browsing for a for policy-compatible datastores

26. Select the Disk Provisioning option per your VM design.

27. Repeat steps 17–26 for the remaining virtual disks. If you will use a separate virtual disk for the guest OS swap/page file, it may be advisable to leave it attached to the SCSI0 controller (that is, SCSI0:1) in step 21.

28. Click **Next**.

29. Review your selections and then click **Finish** to create the VM.

Listing a VM's Policies After Deployment

This example had five virtual disks with four storage policies. To verify that they were deployed correctly, check the virtual machine's policies and verify the compliance with these policies. To do so, follow this procedure:

1. Connect to the vCenter server using the vSphere 6 Web Client as a user with Administrator privileges.

2. Navigate to the **VMs and Templates** view (see Figure 23.60).

3. Locate the VM in the inventory tree and select it.

4. Select the **Manage** tab.

5. Click the **Policies** button.

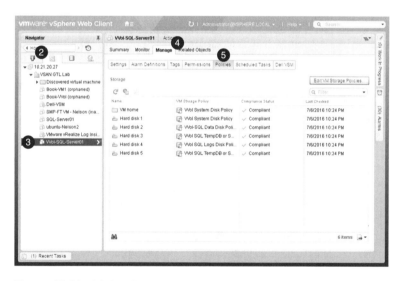

Figure 23.60   Listing the storage policies of a VM

The virtual machine's virtual disks are listed, along with their corresponding storage policies. Note that there is a non-virtual disk item listed here, **VM home**. This is the virtual machine directory. It is on the same datastore as the system disk because I changed the default location for both to **VVol System Disk Policy** instead of the default option, which was **Store with the virtual machine**. Because the I/O profile and data protection service are required for both the VM home and the system disk, they need to apply the same storage policy to each. This choice differs from the policy I used for the similar VM on a non-VVols datastore, which used only VASA 1.0 (see Chapter 20). The reason for this change in design is to make sure that all the VM's files and namespace are stored on a

VVols datastore to take advantage of inherent data protection and availability capabilities such as snapshots and, for other type of VMs, linked clones.

In this view, all items listed are compliant with their corresponding storage policies.

I/O Flow to VVols

To trace the I/O path to a VVol, you need to first understand the VVols binding process. When a VM enters a powered-on state, the host sends a `BIND` request to the VP. The VP binds the VVol to the PE and then returns the PE ID to the host. The process of binding each VVol to the PE creates a secondary ID for each block VVol (for example, `0x3ffe20000000010`) or a file path with a unique ID for each NAS VVol (for example, `0x3200000001/export`). Figure 23.61 shows a simplified diagram of the I/O flow to a NAS VVol and a block VVol.

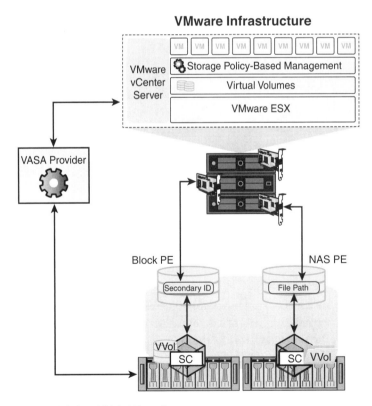

Figure 23.61   VVols I/O path

Block VVols I/O follows this path:

1. The iSCSI/FC/FCoE initiator sends the I/O to the block PE.

2. The PE passes the I/O to the secondary ID bound to the PE.

3. The I/O is then passed to the block VVol object on the SC.

Listing 23.6 shows sample vvold.log events generated by the block VVol binding process.

Listing 23.6   Block VVols binding process events in vvold.log

```
--> VasaOp::BindVirtualVolume [#1578]: ===> Issuing 'bindVirtualVolume' to
VP EMC Unity VP (#outstanding 0/16) [session state: Connected]
--> VasaOp::DoRetry [#1578]: ===> FINAL SUCCESS bindVirtualVolume (VP EMC
Unity VP) retry=false, batchOp=false timeElapsed=868 msecs (#outstanding 0)
vvolInfo = naa.60060160cf3bc8208cdacf47e8062da0 num kv 5
vvold[FFA84B70] [Originator@6876 sub=Default] Meta Keys:
--> [VMW_ContainerId] = [rfc4122.e80c977e-9c80-47c7-ab19-39277c42f7e4]
--> [VMW_CreateTime] = [2016-07-24T16:22:38.535725Z]
--> [VMW_VmID] = []
--> [VMW_VVolName] = [Book-VM7]
--> [VMW_VVolType] = [Config]
--> Binding PE(Type = SCSI, Host Id = naa.60060160cf3bc82082b4e9fc61b0bf45,
secondaryId = 0x3ffe2000000005a, LogicalSize = 4096)
 SI:BindVirtualVolume successful
```

The first log message lists the `Issuing 'bindVirtualVolume'` request to the VP named `EMC Unity VP`. It also states that the session state is `Connected`. This is the session between `vvold` and the VP.

The second line shows that the bind request was successful.

The next line shows the VVol ID and that it has five key/value (KV) pair settings to follow.

The five KV pairs are then listed:

- `ContainerId`—This is the SC ID prefixed with `rfc4122`. In this example, it is `rfc4122.371ab5df-fd88-4116-abe5-0374f4b50e8a`.

- `CreateTime`—This is the time the object was created on the SC.

- `VmId`—This is blank at the time of binding this object but will have the VM UUID when other operations are done on it later.

- `VVolName`—This is the name of the VVol object. In this example, it is the VM home directory or namespace, as evidenced by the next KV pair.

■ VVolType—In this example, it is `Config`, which means the VM namespace. Some logs may list a numeric `objType` KV pair. For example, `objType = 3` indicates the `Config` object type.

Table 23.6 list the VVol object types.

Table 23.6 Types of VVol objects

VVol Object Type	VVol Object Type Number	Notes
Unknown	0	Unknown object (This is very uncommon.)
Data	1	VMDKs and delta disk files
Memory	2	Memory snapshots (also with suspended VMs)
Config	3	VM home directory, also known as the namespace object (It includes the VM's metadata and log files.)
Swap	4	Objects created when the VM is powered on
Other	5	Vendor-specific objects such as VMware vSphere Replication (VR) and Content-Based Read Cache (CBRC)

The next message in the log sequence shows the following `Binding PE` information:

■ Type—`SCSI` means that the PE is a block PE

■ Host Id—This is the PE ID assigned to this host.

■ Secondary Id—This is the VVol's secondary ID, assigned by the binding process (see Figure 23.60, earlier in this section).

■ Logical size—This is the logical size of the VVol being mounted, in megabytes. It is always 4096MB (that is, 4GB).

The last message in the log shows that the binding process succeeded.

NAS VVols I/O follows this path:

1. The Ethernet adapter sends the I/O to the NAS PE.

2. The PE passes the I/O to the file path.

3. The I/O is sent to the NAS VVol object on the SC.

Listing 23.7 shows sample vvold.log events generated by the NAS VVols binding process.

Listing 23.7   NAS VVols binding process events in vvold.log

```
--> VasaOp::BindVirtualVolume [#2498]: ===> Issuing 'bindVirtualVolume' to
VP EMC Unity VP (#outstanding 0/16) [session state: Connected]
--> VasaOp::DoRetry [#2498]: ===> FINAL SUCCESS bindVirtualVolume (VP EMC
Unity VP) retry=false, batchOp=false timeElapsed=410 msecs (#outstanding 0)
vvold[FFA84B70] [Originator@6876 sub=Default] vvolInfo = naa.60060160cf3bc8
20aa6814fdb441afe8 num kv 5
vvold[FFA84B70] [Originator@6876 sub=Default] Meta Keys:
--> [VMW_ContainerId] = [rfc4122.730ecbb3-8fc4-4ef6-b034-1ed2bda5e954]
--> [VMW_CreateTime] = [2016-07-24T21:03:35.349508Z]
--> [VMW_VmID] = []
--> [VMW_VVolName] = [Book-VM7]
--> [VMW_VVolType] = [Config]
--> Binding PE(Type = NFS, Host Id = 1f33511e-d68b1f4c, secondaryId =
0x3200000024/export, LogicalSize = 4096)
SI:BindVirtualVolume successful
```

These log events may appear identical to those of the block VVol at first glance, but they are not. The only thing in common here is that the VVolName value is the same as that of the block VVol object log entries. The reason is that this VM has some VMDKs on a block VVol SC and some VMDKs on a NAS VVol SC. The namespace has to exist on each SC where the VM has any VVol objects.

Here are the log entry details:

- The first two messages are similar to those of the block VVol.

- vvolInfo shows a different VVol ID because this VVol is on a NAS SC, and the other log was showing events for a different block VVol object.

- These are the meta keys:

  - Container ID—This is the NAS SC ID.

  - CreateTime—This is the time this VVol was added to the VM. If you compare this to Listing 23.6, you see that this VVol was created close to 4.5 hours after the VM was created on the block SC.

  - VmID—This is still blank here.

  - VVol Name—This is identical to the name of the block VVol, as explained earlier.

  - VVolType—The type is Config.

- The `Binding PE` message shows the following:
  - `Type`—The type is `NFS`, indicating that this is a NAS VVol.
  - `Host Id`—This is the NAS PE ID assigned to this host.
  - `Secondary Id`—Because this is a NAS VVol, its secondary ID is a file path in the format `<ID>/export`. You'll learn more on this later in this chapter.

- Finally, there is a message that the binding process was successful.

Viewing VVols Binding Details in the UI

Based on the details in the previous section, let's explore the storage array management UI to identify the binding details. This example is on the EMC Unity virtual appliance. Follow these steps:

1. Log on to EMC Unity Unisphere management UI.
2. Navigate to **VMware** in the STORAGE section (see Figure 23.62).
3. Select the **Virtual Volumes** link.
4. Select the VM's Config object in the list that is located on the block SC.
5. Click the edit icon (which looks like a pencil).

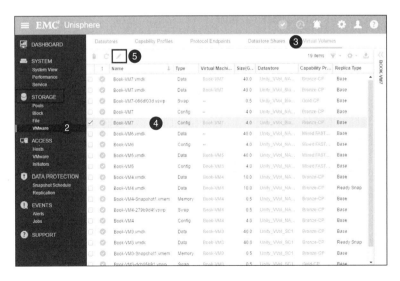

Figure 23.62   Accessing VVols properties

6. In the Properties dialog, select the **Binding Details** tab (see Figure 23.63).

Figure 23.63   Listing block VVol binding details

These are the binding details listed in this example:

- **VMware Protocol Endpoint**—scs_pe_1. This is the PE name on the array's end.

- **Secondary ID**—0x3ffe20000000061. This is the secondary ID assigned to this VVol when bound to the PE. This matches the value in Listing 23.6.

7. Repeat steps 1–6 for the second Config VVol for this VM, located on the NAS datastore. The binding details for that object are shown in Figure 23.64.

Figure 23.64 Listing NAS VVol binding details

These are the binding details:

- **VMware Protocol Endpoint**—nas_pe_4. This is the PE's name on the storage array.

- **Full Path**—10.10.0.54:/rfc4122.730ecbb3-8fc4-4ef6-b034-1ed2bda5e954/0x3200000024/export. This is in the format [NAS Server's port IP]:[SC UUID}/[Secondary ID/export]. The secondary ID matches that in Listing 23.7, earlier in this chapter.

Exploring Datastore Properties via the CLI

It is sometimes beneficial to know your way around the CLI as far as VVols datastores are concerned. This section covers many commands that give you a clearer picture of what goes on under the hood. Follow these steps:

1. Log on to the ESXi host's command console directly or via SSH as root.

2. List the VVols datastore properties via vmkfstools by using this command:

```
vmkfstools -Ph -v10 /vmfs/volumes/<datastore-name>
```

This is the expanded version of this command:

```
vmkfstools    --queryfs    --humanreadable    --verbose    10    /vmfs/
volumes/<datastore-name>
```

Note that in the abbreviated command options, the value of -v may be used with or without a space (for example, -v10 or -v 10). However, the expanded version must have a space. This command's output is the same for NAS and block VVols datastores.

Listing 23.8 shows an example of this command and its output.

Listing 23.8 Listing VVols datastore properties using `vmkfstools`

```
vmkfstools --queryfs --humanreadable --verbose 10 /vmfs/volumes/Unity_VVol_
NAS_DS1
vvol-1.00 file system spanning 1 partitions.
File system label (if any): Unity_VVol_NAS_DS1
Mode: public
Capacity 300 KB, 300 KB available, file block size 4 KB, max supported file
size 0 bytes
UUID: 00000000-00000000-aabb-000000000000
Logical device: vvol:730ecbb38fc44ef6-b0341ed2bda5e954
Partitions spanned (on "notDCS"):

Is Native Snapshot Capable: NO
OBJLIB-LIB: ObjLib cleanup done.
WORKER: asyncOps=0 maxActiveOps=0 maxPending=0 maxCompleted=0
```

This output shows the following:

- **File system type and version**—vvol-1.00. This means the first release of VVols.

- `File system label`—Unity_vvol_NAS-DS1. This is the name assigned to the datastore the first time the SC was mounted on any host.

- `Mode`—public. In the old days of VMFS, there were three modes: public, private, and shared. I cover these modes in Chapter 12, "VMFS Architecture." private and shared modes have been deprecated. (You sometimes see private mode with VisorFS, which I cover in Chapter 19, "VisorFS.")

- `Capacity`—This is not the actual capacity of the datastore. Rather, it is the size of the object that represents the datastore.

- **Max supported file size**—This is not relevant because the file size is not set at the SC level but at the VM namespace level. See the section "Listing Virtual Machine Files on a VVols Datastore via the CLI," later in this chapter. The supported file size is 62.9TB, similar to the max limit of VMFS to maintain compatibility with VMFS5 datastores for features like storage migration (for example, Storage VMotion or cold migration).

- **UUID**—This, too, can be ignored because the volume UUID is that of the SC.

- **Logical Device**—This is the SC's UUID, which I explain earlier in this chapter, in the section "Listing Storage Containers via the CLI."

- **Partitions spanned (on "notDCS")**—The SC, by design, does not have an actual file system on it and, hence, no partitions. The reference to `notDCS` here means "not on Direct Connect Storage." If this were a VMFS5 datastore, it would list (on `"lvm"`) instead, and the line would be followed by the device name and partition number (for example, `naa.600601600d403500367d964a5 2cfe511:1`).

- **Is Native Snapshot Capable**—The value here is `no` because native snapshot capability is enabled on the VM's namespace VVols object. For more details on this, see the section "Native Snapshots on VVols," later in this chapter.

3. List VVols datastores directories linked to the SC UUID by using this command:

```
ls -al /vmfs/volumes/ |grep vvol
```

Listing 23.9 shows this command and its output.

Listing 23.9 Listing symbolic links between datastores' directories and SCs

```
ls -al /vmfs/volumes/ |grep vvol
lrwxr-xr-x    Unity_VVol_DS1 -> vvol:371ab5dffd884116-abe50374f4b50e8a
lrwxr-xr-x    Unity_VVol_DS3 -> vvol:400a35bd14d24a6b-be36a668f664f347
lrwxr-xr-x    Unity_VVol_NAS_DS1 -> vvol:730ecbb38fc44ef6-b0341ed2bda5e954
lrwxr-xr-x    Unity_VVol_NAS_DS4 -> vvol:dfc6ab2fbbad4233-9cf7a242530e8b10
drwxr-xr-x    vvol:371ab5dffd884116-abe50374f4b50e8a
drwxr-xr-x    vvol:400a35bd14d24a6b-be36a668f664f347
drwxr-xr-x    vvol:730ecbb38fc44ef6-b0341ed2bda5e954
drwxr-xr-x    vvol:dfc6ab2fbbad4233-9cf7a242530e8b10
```

I truncated the owner and size columns in Listing 23.9 for readability.

The first four lines show the symbolic links (symlinks) between the datastore names and their corresponding SC UUID. This is evidenced by the l attribute at the beginning of each line. I highlighted the symlink of the datastore I used in the earlier example with vmkfstools.

The second four lines show the directories named after the SC UUIDs. These are actually the mount points of the SCs, with the corresponding SCs' UUIDs. I highlighted the directory of the datastore I used earlier, in the vmkfstools example.

Listing Virtual Machine Files on a VVols Datastore via the CLI

Continuing with the sample VM created in the earlier section "**Deploying New VMs Using Storage Policies**," let's see how its files look on the datastore via the CLI. Follow these steps:

1. While still logged on to vCenter as an administrator, navigate to the VM's **Summary** tab.

2. Identify the name of the host on which the VM is running (see Figure 23.65).

Figure 23.65   Locating the host running the VM

3. Log on to the identified ESXi host's console directly or via SSH as root.

4. Locate the VM's directory by using this command:

   ```
   [root@ds-lab-vsan13:~] vim-cmd vmsvc/getallvms |grep SQL
   ```

   Listing 23.10 shows the output of the command.

Listing 23.10   Locating the VM's directory via the CLI

```
[root@ds-lab-vsan13:~] vim-cmd vmsvc/getallvms |grep SQL
70     VVol-SQL-Server01    [EQL-VVol-DS03] naa.6090a0c8a01aa8fedf77f5d324df
287c/VVol-SQL-Server01.vmx    windows8Server64Guest    vmx-11
```

The highlighted text in the output is the datastore name and the VM's namespace (also known as the VM's home directory), respectively.

5. Run this command to list the VM's namespace symbolic link:

```
ls -al /vmfs/volumes/EQL-VVol-DS03/
```

Make sure to include the trailing / because you want to list the content of that datastore. If you omit the /, the command returns the datastore's symlink instead.

Listing 23.11 shows this command and its output.

Listing 23.11 Listing VM namespace properties on a block VVol SC via the CLI

```
[root@ds-lab-vsan13:~] ls -al /vmfs/volumes/EQL-VVol-DS03/
total 1024
lrwxr-xr-x    VVol-SQL-Server01 -> naa.6090a0c8a01aa8fedf77f5d324df287c
drwxr-xr-t    naa.6090a0c8a01aa8fedf77f5d324df287c
```

I truncated some of the columns in Listing 23.11 for readability.

Observe that the VM's home directory is symbolically linked to a device with an NAA ID similar to what you would see with block devices.

Based on the attribute of the last line in Listing 23.11, this UUID is the name of a directory. (The lowercase d at the beginning of the line indicates a directory.) This is actually the VVols UUID that represents the VM's namespace on the block VVol SC.

If you attempt to locate this NAA ID among the datastore devices on this host (in the /vmfs/devices/disks directory), you will not find it. The reason is that, by design, a VVol is accessible via the VVol's secondary ID when the VVols are bound on the PE accessible by this host as a protocol entry point into the SC.

6. Use vmkfstools to list the properties of the namespace block VVol object. You should get output similar to that in Listing 23.12.

Listing 23.12 Listing VM namespace properties on a block VVol using vmkfstools

```
vmkfstools -Ph -v10 /vmfs/volumes/EQL-VVol-DS03/VVol-SQL-Server01
VMFS-5.61 file system spanning 1 partitions.
File system label (if any): naa.6090a0c8a01aa8fedf77f5d324df287c
Mode: public ATS-only
Capacity 4 GB, 3.2 GB available, file block size 1 MB, max supported file
size 62.9 TB
Volume Creation Time: Thu Jul  7 05:25:04 2016
```

```
Files (max/free): 40704/40677
Ptr Blocks (max/free): 64512/64496
Sub Blocks (max/free): 16384/16379
Secondary Ptr Blocks (max/free): 256/256
File Blocks (overcommit/used/overcommit %): 0/861/0
Ptr Blocks  (overcommit/used/overcommit %): 0/16/0
Sub Blocks  (overcommit/used/overcommit %): 0/5/0
Volume Metadata size: 492175360
UUID: 577de7b0-3fb8ae2c-34aa-90b11c2465b3
Logical device:
Partitions spanned (on "vvol"):
      naa.6090a0c8a01aa8fedf77f5d324df287c
Is Native Snapshot Capable: YES
OBJLIB-LIB: ObjLib cleanup done.
WORKER: asyncOps=0 maxActiveOps=0 maxPending=0 maxCompleted=0
```

In this example, I used the VM's home directory (namespace), which is the same as using the directory's NAA ID because the home directory is symbolically linked to its NAA ID.

If you compare this output to the output in Listing 23.8, you should notice right away that Listing 23.8shows the file system version as `vvol-1.0.0`, while here the file system version is `VMFS-5.61`.

The reason is simple: Each VM's VVol namespace object is formatted with the VMFS5 file system. This is similar to how vSAN namespace objects are also formatted with VMFS5. See Chapter 21 for more details.

This is why the output showing the datastore (that is, SC) properties does not show VMFS, while the namespace object on it does.

Now let's examine some of the interesting VMFS properties of the namespace VVol object:

- `File system label`—This is the same as the VVol's NAA ID.

- `Mode`—`public ATS-only`. This means that the VVol is on a storage array that supports the ATS VAAI primitive and that on-disk locking will not use SCSI-2 reservations (see Chapter 17, "VAAI").

- `Capacity`—This is the capacity allocated to this VVol, which is the namespace. While the VM's virtual disks descriptor files are located within this VVol, their actual capacity resides on their own VVols, as I show you in the next step of this procedure. This line also includes the file block size, which is 1MB and the max supported file size, which is 62.9TB.

- `UUID`—This is similar to the VMFS datastore signature, but here it is for the namespace VVol object.

- `Logical device`—This is always blank for block VVols. For NAS VVols, it lists the file path of the namespace object. For details see step 7.

- `Partitions spanned (on "vvol")`—This is the VVol device that represents the namespace object. It is the same NAA ID for the VVol listed in the volume label. Note that it states `(on "vvol")` compared to `(on "lvm")` for standard VMFS5 datastores or `(on "notDCS")` for the VVols datastore itself. The reason is that the file system on VVols is not handled by VMFS Logical Volume Manager (LVM). Rather, it is handled by the `vvol` vmkernel module.

- `Is Native Snapshot Capable`—This is one of the many advantages that VVols provides. The value here is `YES`. This is not possible on standard VMFS5 datastores. See the section "Native Snapshots on VVols," later in this chapter, for more details.

7. Use `vmkfstools` to list the namespace object properties on the NAS VVol SC. You should get output similar to that in Listing 23.13. This example uses an EMC Unity simulator, whereas the previous block VVol example is on a Dell EqualLogic PS6000 iSCSI array.

Listing 23.13 Listing VM namespace properties on NAS VVol by using `vmkfstools`

```
vmkfstools -Ph -v10 /vmfs/volumes/Unity_VVol_NAS_DS4/Book-VM2 .
NFS-1.00 file system spanning 1 partitions.
File system label (if any): naa.60060160cf3bc820b18ae12b076738b9
Mode: public
Capacity 4.5 GB, 4.5 GB available, file block size 4 KB, max supported file
size 131072 TB
UUID: bdcad441-76e115e7-0000-000000000000
Logical device: 10.10.0.54 /rfc4122.dfc6ab2f-bbad-4233-9cf7-
a242530e8b10/0x3200000015/export
Partitions spanned (on "notDCS"):
        nfs: naa.60060160cf3bc820b18ae12b076738b9
NAS VAAI Supported: NO
Is Native Snapshot Capable: NO
OBJLIB-LIB: ObjLib cleanup done.
WORKER: asyncOps=0 maxActiveOps=0 maxPending=0 maxCompleted=0
```

This output shows that the file system on this object is NFS-1.0.0. This is not a reflection of the NFS protocol version in use, which is NFSv3 in this case. Remember that VVols is only supported on NFS version 3.

The rest of the properties are as follows:

- File system label—naa.60060160cf3bc820b18ae12b076738b9. This is the VVol ID representing the namespace object.

- Mode—public. Why isn't it public ATS-only, as in the previous listing? That is because the VVol is on a NAS SC, and ATS is a block VAAI primitive. NFS handles file locking on the NAS SC, and there is no need for SCSI-2 reservations or ATS.

- Capacity—This is the size of the namespace object, and files stored on it are not very large.

- UUID—This is the NFS device ID assigned to this VVol by the NAS server. Note that the trailing zeros are added here to make the UUID length similar to the UUID length of a VMFS datastore.

- Logical Device—This is the logical device created by the NAS appliance for this VVol and includes the following:

- The NAS server IP address, which is the same as the Remote Host field value listed in the properties of the PE through which this VVol is accessed.

- The mounting point, which is prefixed with the SC ID (RFC4122 format) followed by the file path (which is the secondary ID created when the VVol was bound to the PE). This example shows it as follows:

  10.10.0.54 /rfc4122.dfc6ab2f-bbad-4233-9cf7-a242530e8b10/0x3200 000015/export

- Partitions spanned (on "noDCS")—Because this is a NAS VVol, the VVol UUID listed is prefixed with nfs:, and the rest of the name is the VVol UUID, which is the same as the file system label. Observe that there is no partition number listed after the device because this is not a block device, and there is no actual partition table on it.

- NAS VAAI Supported—In this example, the NAS server does not support NAS VAAI.

- Is Native Snapshot Capable—While this output states that the value is NO, this VVol actually is native snapshot capable, as I show in the section "Native Snapshots on VVols," later in this chapter.

8. List the content of the namespace directory on a NAS SC by using the following:

```
ls -al /vmfs/volumes/Unity_VVol_NAS_DS4/Book-VM4/
```

Listing 23.14 shows this command and its output.

Listing 23.14   Listing VM namespace content on NAS VVol by using the `ls` command

```
ls -al /vmfs/volumes/Unity_VVol_NAS_DS4/Book-VM4/
-rw-------     .naa.60060160cf3bc820869b0887c0bc6e41.lck
-rw-------     .naa.60060160cf3bc820869b0887c0bc6e41.meta
-rw-------     Book-VM4.nvram
-rw-------     Book-VM4.vmdk
-rwxr-xr-x     Book-VM4.vmx
-rw-r--r--     vmware.log
```

I removed some output columns in Listing 23.14 for readability.

The output shows one VMDK files and one hidden .meta files. (Any file prefixed with a period is hidden and can be listed using the `ls -al` command.)

To explain the hidden .meta file, let's first identify the VMDK's data extent VVol ID, using this command:

```
cat /vmfs/volumes/Unity_VVol_NAS_DS4/Book-VM4/Book-VM4.vmdk |awk '/
Extent/||/RW/{print}'
```

The output would be something like this:

```
# Extent description
RW 20971520 VMFS "vvol://dfc6ab2fbbad4233-9cf7a242530e8b10/naa.6006016
0cf3bc820869b0887c0bc6e41"
```

If you compare the NAA ID listed in this output to the file with .meta extension in Listing 23.14, you see that they are the same. This is due to the fact that the .meta file represents VMDK's extent VVol object's metadata. The actual data extent is the VVol object with UUID `naa.60060160cf3bc82 0869b0887c0bc6e41` on SC with logical device ID `vvol:dfc6ab2fbbad4233- 9cf7a242530e8b10`, which represents the SC on which this VM resides.

NOTE

On VMFS datastores, this extent would be a flat file with a name like Book-VM4-flat.vmdk.

What is the function of the .meta file? It informs the VP of the properties of the VMDK that this .meta file represents.

To list the content of this .meta file, use `hexdump` because the file is binary. This is the command to use:

```
hexdump -C /vmfs/volumes/Unity_VVol_NAS_DS4/Book-VM4/.naa.60060160cf3b
c820869b0887c0bc6e41.meta
```

Figure 23.66 shows the output.

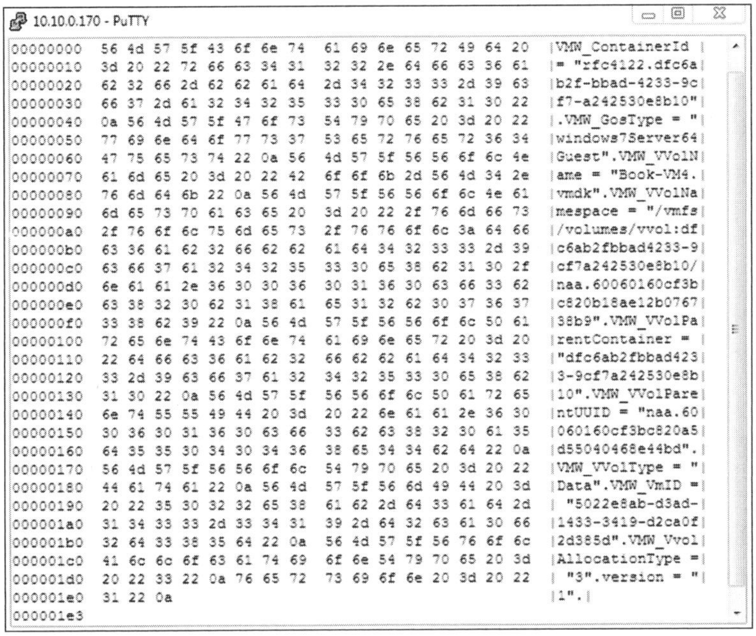

Figure 23.66   Listing Content of a VVol's .meta File

The text in the right column of the output shows the metadata content, which is key/value pairs separated by periods. Listing 23.15 lists these key/value pairs.

Listing 23.15   A virtual disk's extent metadata key/value pairs

```
VMW_ContainerId = "rfc4122.dfc6ab2f-bbad-4233-9cf7-a242530e8b10"
VMW_GosType = "windows7Server64Guest"
VMW_VVolName = "Book-VM4vmdk"
VMW_VVolNamespace = "/vmfs/volumes/vvol:dfc6ab2fbbad4233-9cf7a242530e8b10/
naa.60060160cf3bc820b18ae12b076738b9"
VMW_VVolParentContainer = "dfc6ab2fbbad4233-9cf7a242530e8b10"
```

```
VMW_VVolParentUUID = "naa.60060160cf3bc820a5d55040468e44bd"
VMW_VVolType = "Data"
VMW_VmID = "5022e8ab-d3ad-1433-3419-d2ca0f2d385d"
VMW_VvolAllocationType = "3"
version = "1"
```

These key/value pairs match what you would see in /var/run/log/vvold.log file
events, similar to those in Listing 23.16.

Listing 23.16   Virtual disk's extent metadata key/value pairs from the vvold.log file

```
2016-07-11T06:41:45.134Z info vvold[FFDEFB70] [Originator@6876 sub=Default]
vvolInfo = naa.60060160cf3bc820869b0887c0bc6e41 num kv 9
2016-07-11T06:41:45.134Z info vvold[FFDEFB70] [Originator@6876 sub=Default]
Meta Keys:
--> [VMW_ContainerId] = [rfc4122.dfc6ab2f-bbad-4233-9cf7-a242530e8b10]
--> [VMW_GosType] = [windows7Server64Guest]
--> [VMW_VmID] = [5022e8ab-d3ad-1433-3419-d2ca0f2d385d]
--> [VMW_VVolName] = [Book-VM4.vmdk]
--> [VMW_VVolParentUUID] = [naa.60060160cf3bc820a5d55040468e44bd]
--> [VMW_VVolType] = [Data]
--> [VMW_VVolNamespace] = [/vmfs/volumes/vvol:dfc6ab2fbbad4233-
9cf7a242530e8b10/naa.60060160cf3bc820b18ae12b076738b9]
--> [VMW_VVolParentContainer] = [dfc6ab2fbbad4233-9cf7a242530e8b10]
--> [VMW_VvolAllocationType] = [3]
```

This is an example of how `vvold` informs the VP with the metadata properties of a
VVol after it receives the VVol ID from the array via the VP.

OSFS and Its Role in VVols

Chapter 21 covers object store file system (OSFS) and its role in vSAN. OSFS also has a
major role in VVols.

Simply put, OSFS creates, deletes, binds, unbinds, mounts, and unmounts the VM's
namespace directory and formats it with VMFS (for block VVols) or mounts the NFS share
representing it (for NAS VVols). It also mounts and unmounts VVol objects on these SCs.

Each VVol storage array or NAS server has a catalog of namespaces on each SC. This catalog
allows for getting and setting certain types of metadata associated with each VVol on the
SCs. The storage array responds to VVols query requests from the ESXi hosts, via the VP,
based on this metadata. Such requests are initiated by OSFS, which sends them to the VASA
host module that communicates with the storage VP and from there to the storage array.

All messages generated by OSFS are stored in the /var/run/log/osfs.log file.

Listing 23.17 shows an example of a set of OSFS events.

Listing 23.17 OSFS events in the osfs.log file

```
2016-07-16T19:17:21Z osfsd: VmklinkMPI-LIB : Received request ID 137 of
size 165
2016-07-16T19:17:21Z osfsd: VmklinkMPI-LIB : { : ID: 0x137, bufLen: 165 }
2016-07-16T19:17:21Z osfsd: VmklinkMPI-LIB : Msg received. Calling recv
Handler
2016-07-16T19:17:21Z osfsd: VmklinkMPI-LIB : { : ID: 0x137, bufLen: 165 }
2016-07-16T19:17:21Z osfsd: 34389:DebugDumpVmklinkRequest:1065: {ID: 0x137;
type: LOOKUP; pid: [    vvol]; cid: dfc6ab2fbbad4233-9cf7a242530e8b10;
status: 0; bufLen: 0; mf: 778133870; o: 3474018245700235318 }
2016-07-16T19:17:21Z osfsd: 34389:Provider_Lookup:479: Found matching
driver for ID [    vvol]
2016-07-16T19:17:21Z osfsd: Enqueue a new work item in threadpool osfsd-
nvvol
2016-07-16T19:17:21Z osfsd: Add the new item into the pending list
2016-07-16T19:17:21Z osfsd: Adding a thread to threadpool osfsd-nvvol
2016-07-16T19:17:21Z osfsd: Added a new thread to threadpool (osfsd-nvvol),
numThreadsInPool (1)
2016-07-16T19:17:21Z osfsd: Starting main loop for the worker thread osfsd-
nvvol
2016-07-16T19:17:21Z osfsd: 166455:Lookup:663: Got lookup request for "naa.
60060160cf3bc820b18ae12b076738b9"
2016-07-16T19:17:21Z osfsd: 166455:Provider_Lookup:479: Found matching
driver for ID [    vvol]
2016-07-16T19:17:21Z osfsd: 166455:VVolMount:2245: VVolMount@2245:Lookup
was sent UUID based name naa.60060160cf3bc820b18ae12b076738b9
2016-07-16T19:17:21Z osfsd: 166455:VVOLLIB : VVolLib_Open:8701: container
Id passed: dfc6ab2f-bbad-4233-9cf7-a242530e8b10 Normalized: dfc6ab2f-
bbad-4233-9cf7-a242530e8b10
2016-07-16T19:17:21Z osfsd: 166455:VVOLLIB : VVolLib_Open:8734: created
devFS node 'naa.60060160cf3bc820b18ae12b076738b9' (objType 3)
2016-07-16T19:17:21Z osfsd: 166455:VVOLLIB : VVolLib_BindVVol:4106:
Bind on Config VVol naa.60060160cf3bc820b18ae12b076738b9 successful:
logicalSizeInMB = 4096 (NFS, 9ccc2232-57c9d49a:0x3200000015/export)
2016-07-16T19:17:21Z osfsd: 166455:VVOLLIB : VVolLibSoapToVVolInfo:3163:
VVolLib_BindVVol got vvol naa.60060160cf3bc820b18ae12b076738b9 keys 4
2016-07-16T19:17:21Z osfsd: 166455:VVOLLIB : VVolLibSoapToVVolInfo:3171:
VVolLib_BindVVol kv 0 key VMW_ContainerId value rfc4122.dfc6ab2f-bbad-
4233-9cf7-a242530e8b10
2016-07-16T19:17:21Z osfsd: 166455:VVOLLIB : VVolLibSoapToVVolInfo:3171:
VVolLib_BindVVol kv 1 key VMW_VmID value 5022e8ab-d3ad-1433-3419-
d2ca0f2d385d
```

2016-07-16T19:17:21Z osfsd: 166455:VVOLLIB : VVolLibSoapToVVolInfo:3171: VVolLib_BindVVol kv 2 key VMW_VVolName value Book-VM4

2016-07-16T19:17:21Z osfsd: 166455:VVOLLIB : VVolLibSoapToVVolInfo:3171: VVolLib_BindVVol kv 3 key VMW_VVolType value Config

2016-07-16T19:17:21Z osfsd: 166455:VVOLLIB : VVolLib_Open:8996: Bound VVol naa.60060160cf3bc820b18ae12b076738b9 to (9ccc2232-57c9d49a, 0x3200000015/ export)

2016-07-16T19:17:21Z osfsd: 166455:VVolOsfs_Mount:978: VVolOsfs_ Mount@978:Trying to probe NFS VVOL object (uuid: naa.60060160cf3bc820b18a e12b076738b9, container: vvol:dfc6ab2fbbad4233-9cf7a242530e8b10)

2016-07-16T19:17:21Z osfsd: 166455:VVolOsfs_Mount:1033: VVolOsfs_ Mount@1033:Using option string (nfs 256 65,36 10.10.0.54 10.10.0.54 / rfc4122.dfc6ab2f-bbad-4233-9cf7-a242530e8b10/0x3200000015/export naa.6006 0160cf3bc820b18ae12b076738b9 0 hidden)

2016-07-16T19:17:21Z osfsd: 166455:VVolOsfs_Mount:1046: VVolOsfs_ Mount@1046:Using mntFlags (0x3)

2016-07-16T19:17:21Z osfsd: 166455:VVolOsfs_Mount:1066: VVolOsfs_ Mount@1066:Successfully probed NFS VVol object naa.60060160cf3bc820b18ae1 2b076738b9

2016-07-16T19:17:21Z osfsd: 166455:VVOLLIB : VVolLib_UserUnlockVVol:9482: Successfully released user lock on VVol naa.60060160cf3bc820b18ae12b0767 38b9

2016-07-16T19:17:21Z osfsd: 166455:LookupCompletion:701: lookup completion: buf = naa.60060160cf3bc820b18ae12b076738b9

2016-07-16T19:17:21Z osfsd: 166455:PostVmklinkSendEvent:355: Create ordered event to send response.

2016-07-16T19:17:21Z osfsd: 166455:DebugDumpVmklinkRequest:1065: {ID: 0x137; type: LOOKUP; pid: [vvol]; cid: dfc6ab2fbbad4233- 9cf7a242530e8b10; status: 0; bufLen: 37; mf: 778133762; o: " 3474018245700235318 }

2016-07-16T19:17:21Z osfsd: 34389:Event_Pump:301: PumpEvents: Interrupted system call, continuing

2016-07-16T19:17:21Z osfsd: VmklinkMPI-LIB : VmklinkMPILib_Send called for 0x137,

2016-07-16T19:17:21Z osfsd: VmklinkMPI-LIB : Matching request found for 0x137,

2016-07-16T19:17:21Z osfsd: VmklinkMPI-LIB : Send got req = 1F022BD8 (ID: 137)

2016-07-16T19:17:21Z osfsd: VmklinkMPI-LIB : Vmklink send sent total: 223 bytes of 223 needed

2016-07-16T19:17:21Z osfsd: VmklinkMPI-LIB : Sent request ID 137 size 202

2016-07-16T19:17:21Z osfsd: VmklinkMPI-LIB : { : ID: 0x137, bufLen: 202 }

2016-07-16T19:17:21Z osfsd: 34389:OSFSVmklinkResourceAvailableCBHandler: 522: resource available callback received

2016-07-16T19:17:26Z osfsd: Completed main loop for the worker thread osf sd-nvvol

Here is a summary of these events: OSFS received a lookup request for a VVol storage container with ID `dfc6ab2fbbad4233-9cf7a242530e8b10`. It identified the VP type as `VVol`.

> **NOTE**
>
> The reason OSFS has to identify the VP type is that OSFS handles both vSAN and VVols operations.

It sent a lookup request for the VVol mount point with the container ID `dfc6ab2f-bbad-4233-9cf7-a242530e8b10`. This maps to the SC named `Unity_VVol_NAS_SC4` (which is a mounted datastore named `Unity_VVol_NAS_DS4`).

It then created a `devFS` (file system device) named after the VVol ID `naa.60060160cf3bc820b18ae12b076738b9` with VVol object type `3` (which means namespace).

It then binds the VVol to the `Config VVol` with the same ID and enumerates the logical size (`4096`), protocol (`NFS`), and PE:secondary ID/mount point combination (`9ccc2232-57c9d49a:0x3200000015/export`).

> **NOTE**
>
> Config VVol is another name for a namespace object.

It then lists four key/value pairs for that object:

- `VMW_ContainerId`, with value `rfc4122.dfc6ab2f-bbad-4233-9cf7-a242530e8b10`

- `VMW_VmID`, with value `5022e8ab-d3ad-1433-3419-d2ca0f2d385d`

- `VMW_VVolName`, with value `Book-VM4`

- `VMW_VVolType`, with value `Config`

These four key/value pairs mean that this object is for a namespace called `Book-VM4`. In other words, this is the home directory for a VM called `Book-VM4`.

Finally, it successfully bound that object to the NAS VVol PE whose host ID is `9ccc2232-57c9d49a`. The secondary ID and NFS mount point is `0x3200000015/export`.

Such `devFS` would show in the /vmfs/volumes/Unity_VVol_NAS_DS4 directory as `Book-VM4 -> naa.60060160cf3bc820b18ae12b076738b9`, which is a symbolic link between the VVol name and its `devFS` device name.

User locks on the VVol were then released. This cleared any stale locks that may have been left on the NFS VVol.

Eventually, OSFS announced that the mounted resource was available.

Storage Array's View of VVols

All VM VVol objects are visible to the storage array. Storage vendors have various ways to list these VVols. In this section, I provide examples from the EMC Unity simulator and Dell EqualLogic PS6000 iSCSI physical storage array.

Listing VVols on EMC Unity UI

To list VVols on the EMC Unity user interface, follow these steps:

1. Log on to the EMC Unisphere UI as an admin user via the EMC Unity management port IP address or host name in a browser.

2. Navigate to the **VMware** option in the Storage section (see Figure 23.67).

3. Select the **Virtual Volumes** link in the top-right part of the screen.

In this view, you see a list of all VVols on this storage array for both block and NAS protocols.

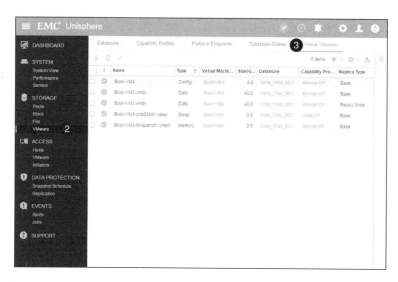

Figure 23.67   Listing VVols on EMC Unity UI

This view shows the following columns:

- **Health Status**—The column label is an exclamation point. A green checkmark indicates a healthy status. When you hover the mouse over it, a bubble says `The component is operating normally. No action is required.`

- **Name**—This is the VVol component filename.

- **Type**—This is the VVol component type. Refer to Table 23.6 for details.

- **Virtual Machine**—This is the VM to which the VVol belongs. This is a hyperlink in the UI. Clicking it takes you to the VM details (see Figure 23.64).

- **Size(GB)**—This is the total size of the VVol, in gigabytes.

- **Datastore**—This is a storage container that contains the VVol. This, too, is a hyperlink, and when clicked, it opens the SC details.

- **Capability Profile**—This is the CP for this VVol, which is based on the SC's CPs. Again, this is a hyperlink that takes you to the CP details.

- **Replica Type**—This shows whether the VVol is a snapshot or a fast clone of another VVol. Table 23.7 lists the EMC Unity replica types of VVols.

Table 23.7 EMC Unity replica types of VVols

VM Type	VVol Object	VVol Type	Replica Type	Notes
Powered-on VM with no snapshots or clones	Namespace	Config	Base	
	VMDK file	Data	Base	
	vswp file	Swap	Base	
Powered-on VM with a snapshot	Namespace	Config	Base	
	VMDK file	Data	Base	
	VMDK snapshot	Data	Ready Snap	On the same storage policy as parent
	vmem file	Memory	Base	When memory snapshot is taken while VM is powered on
	vswp file	Swap	Base	

VM Type	VVol Object	VVol Type	Replica Type	Notes
Powered-on linked clone (fast clone)	Parent VMX file	Config	Base	
	Parent VMDK file	Data	Base	Parent VMDK is read-only
	Child VMX file	Config	Base	On same storage policy as parent
	Child VMDK file	Data	Ready Snap	On same storage policy as parent
	Child vswp file	Swap	Base	
Powered-on full clone (with source powered off)	Source VMX file	Config	Base	
	Source VMDK file	Data	Base	Source remains read/write
	Clone VMX file	Config	Base	
	Clone VMDK File	Data	Base	Can be on different storage policy from source
	Clone vswp file	Swap	Base	

EMC Unity leverages VAAI to offload snapshot and clone operations to the array. The type of snapshot created on it is a native snapshot, which I cover in the next section. Fast clones are also native, which means they are pointer based on the array.

Native Snapshots on VVols

Chapter 15, "Snapshot Handling," discusses virtual machine snapshots on non-VVol datastores. It explains how VAAI primitives can help improve the performance of the process of creating VM snapshots. For quite a while, snapshots created on certain vendors' NFS datastore have enjoyed the luxury of utilizing native snapshots. What are native snapshots?

Using VASA 2.0 APIs, storage vendors implement VVols on their storage arrays, as discussed throughout this chapter. A storage array becomes aware of the VMDK data placement on disk as a VVol and knows when a block is modified within that VVol. When a native snapshot is created, a snapshot VVol object is created on the storage array. That snapshot VVol object has records of all the parent's VVol's unmodified file blocks (FBs). These records are referred to as pointer blocks (PBs) or pointer records. This means that the snapshot VVol object represents the parent VMDK in its original state, as of the time of taking the snapshot. This also means that the snapshot object occupies no physical space on the SC because it is only pointers to the parent VVol. From that point on, when any FB that gets modified on the VMDK, that FB gets marked for copy-on-write (COW), which triggers the process of copying the original FB to the snapshot VVol object first before writing the change to the original FB. This process modifies the snapshot's PB to point to the FB copy on the snapshot VVol object. This is how most storage vendors handle physical LUN snapshots, which they leverage to implement VVol-based native snapshots. Because the VMDK is a VVol with its own NAA ID, the storage array can treat it like a LUN for the purpose of native snapshot operations.

Some storage vendors, such as EMC Unity, implement snapshots a bit differently on the back end. However, the end result of creating native snapshots is more or less the same. In this section, I show how to take VVol-based native snapshots on an EMC Unity 4.0 virtual appliance.

A snapshot of a VM is done exactly the same way as legacy VM snapshots, and the VASA 2.0 API enables the EMC Unity to create the snapshots as native on the array. Figure 23.67 in the previous section shows a list of VVols of a VM with a single VMDK after one snapshot was taken. In that figure, you see two VVol objects with the same name. However, the Replica Type column shows one of them as Base and the other as Ready Snap. The Ready Snap object is the native snapshot file.

This procedure is the same for VMs located on NAS SCs or block SCs.

To dig a bit deeper into that object's properties, follow these steps:

1. Select the check box at the beginning of the row with the Ready Snap replica type (see Figure 23.68).

2. Click the edit icon, which looks like a pencil.

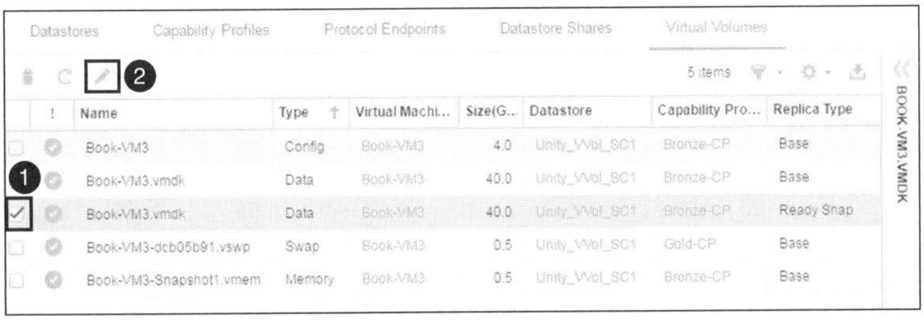

Figure 23.68 Accessing the VVol properties icon on EMC Unity UI

The object properties include several fields. The following fields are relevant to this section (see Figure 23.69):

- **Type**—This is the VVol object type for a VMDK or its snapshot. In this case, it is Data.

- **VMware UUID**—This is the VVol's NAA ID. Take note of this ID because it comes up in a couple steps.

- **Capacity**—This field shows a bar representing the VVol capacity, which can grow to the max size of the parent disk. I just created this snapshot, and the VM is idle, so it is still at zero.

- **Datastore**—This is the SC name. In my example, the SC is named similarly to the datastore, with the datastore using DS<n> suffix and the SC using SC<n>.

- **Thin**—Snapshots are always thin provisioned by design, so this is Yes.

- **Replica Type**—This is the state of the snapshot, in this case Ready Snap.

- **Parent**—In this example, the parent is Book-VM3.vmdk.

- **Virtual Machine Name**—In this example, the VM name is Book-VM3.

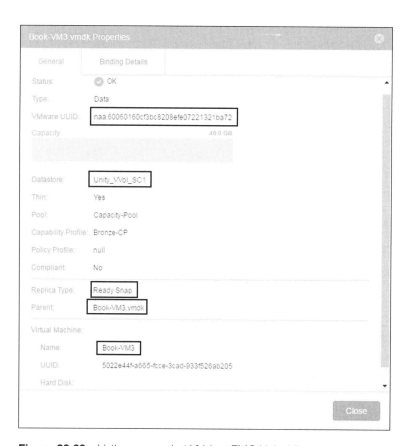

Figure 23.69 Listing a snapshot VVol on EMC Unity UI

3. Click **Close** to dismiss this dialog.

4. Repeat steps 1–3 for the parent disk whose Replica Type field is Base. Figure 23.70 shows a cropped Properties dialog for the parent disk.

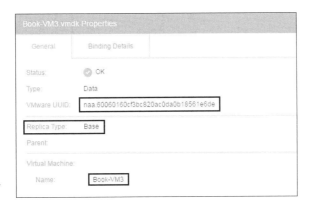

Figure 23.70   Listing the parent VVol on EMC Unity UI

The relevant information from both objects' properties are listed in Table 23.8

Table 23.8 EMC Unity replica types of VVols

Field	Value
Parent VMDK	
Virtual Machine Name	Book-VM3
VVol UUID	naa.60060160cf3bc820ac0da0b18561e6de
Datastore	Unity_VVol_SC1
Snapshot VMDK	
VVol UUID	naa.60060160cf3bc8208efe07221321ba72
Parent VMDK	Book-VM3.vmdk

5. List files in the VM home directory on the datastore via ESXi host. The command and output are shown in Listing 23.18.

Listing 23.18   Listing the VM's home directory content on the ESXi host

```
[root@node2:~] cd /vmfs/volumes/Unity_VVol_DS1/Book-VM3/
[root@node2:/vmfs/volumes/vvol:371ab5dffd884116-abe50374f4b50e8a/naa.600601
60cf3bc82082bd1ba0ca58416b] ls -al
    628 Jul 11 00:43 Book-VM3-000001.vmdk
```

```
    153 Jul 11 00:43 Book-VM3-Snapshot1.vmem
1265003 Jul 11 00:44 Book-VM3-Snapshot1.vmsn
    289 Jul 11 00:40 Book-VM3-dcb05b91.vswp
      0 Jul 11 00:40 Book-VM3-dcb05b91.vswp.lck
   8684 Jul 11 00:44 Book-VM3.nvram
    684 Jul 11 00:43 Book-VM3.vmdk
    391 Jul 11 00:43 Book-VM3.vmsd
   2746 Jul 11 00:43 Book-VM3.vmx
      0 Jul 11 00:40 Book-VM3.vmx.lck
   2739 Jul 11 00:43 Book-VM3.vmx~
 171470 Jul 11 00:51 vmware.log
192937984 Jul 11 00:40 vmx-Book-VM3-3702545297-1.vswp
```

Listing 23.18 includes the parent VMDK descriptor file `Book-VM3.vmdk` and the snapshot delta descriptor file `Book-VM3-000001.vmdk`.

6. List the content of the parent disk's descriptor file. Listing 23.19 shows this output.

Listing 23.19   Listing the parent disk's descriptor file content

```
cat Book-VM3.vmdk
# Disk DescriptorFile
version=4
encoding="UTF-8"
CID=fffffffe
parentCID=ffffffff
isNativeSnapshot="no"
createType="vmfs"

# Extent description
RW 83886080 VMFS "vvol://371ab5dffd884116-abe50374f4b50e8a/naa.60060160cf3b
c8208efe07221321ba72"

# The Disk Data Base
#DDB

ddb.adapterType = "lsilogic"
ddb.geometry.cylinders = "5221"
ddb.geometry.heads = "255"
ddb.geometry.sectors = "63"
```

```
ddb.longContentID = "09d272cbabc4966c15e7114afffffffe"
ddb.nativeDeltaBytes = "0"
ddb.objectParentUri = "vvol://371ab5dffd884116-abe50374f4b50e8a/naa.6006016
0cf3bc820ac0da0b18561e6de"
ddb.thinProvisioned = "1"
ddb.uuid = "60 00 C2 91 e1 33 0a fc-a1 88 07 c4 d5 7c 5d bf"
ddb.virtualHWVersion = "11"
```

7. List the content of the snapshot delta disk's descriptor file. Listing 23.20 shows this output.

Listing 23.20   Listing the delta disk's descriptor file content

```
cat Book-VM3-000001.vmdk
# Disk DescriptorFile
version=4
encoding="UTF-8"
CID=fffffffe
parentCID=ffffffff
isNativeSnapshot="yes"
createType="vmfs"

# Extent description
RW 83886080 VMFS "vvol://371ab5dffd884116-abe50374f4b50e8a/naa.60060160cf3b
c820ac0da0b18561e6de"

# The Disk Data Base

#DDB
ddb.adapterType = "lsilogic"
ddb.geometry.cylinders = "5221"
ddb.geometry.heads = "255"
ddb.geometry.sectors = "63"
ddb.longContentID = "09d272cbabc4966c15e7114afffffffe"
ddb.nativeParentCID = "fffffffe"
ddb.nativeParentHint = "Book-VM3.vmdk"
ddb.thinProvisioned = "1"
ddb.uuid = "60 00 C2 91 e1 33 0a fc-a1 88 07 c4 d5 7c 5d bf"
ddb.virtualHWVersion = "11"
```

In Listing 23.19 and 23.20 I highlighted the relevant properties. It is clear that Listing 23.20 is for a native snapshot because the value of `IsNativeSnapshot` is yes.

Using Listings 23.18–23.20 and Table 23.8, I compiled Table 23.9 to list the NAA IDs for the corresponding descriptor file from both sources.

Table 23.9 Parent and snapshot disks' NAA IDs from host and array outputs

	From VMDK Descriptor Files	From Array VVol Properties
Parent VVol UUID	naa.60060160cf3bc8208efe0722 1321ba72	naa.60060160cf3bc820ac 0da0b18561e6de
Snapshot VVol UUID	naa.60060160cf3bc820ac0da0b1 8561e6de	naa.60060160cf3bc8208e fe07221321ba72

Wait a minute! Did I get these backward? No!

I just copied them from their corresponding outputs. If you compare Table 23.9 to Table 23.8, the NAA IDs do seem reversed.

What's going on here? Everything is where it belongs. To explain this paradox, let me remind you of something you learned in Chapter 15. There, I explained that in the VMware environment has the snapshot process backward compared to storage vendors' physical snapshot implementation. VMware keeps the parent disk frozen and redirects all the changes to the snapshot disk (also known as the delta disk). To reconcile that, VMware implemented the native snapshot-related functions in VMware's `disklib` so that the storage array snapshot's VVol ID is used as the VMware parent disk's UUID and vice versa, where the storage array parent disk's VVol ID is used as VMware snapshot disk's UUID. This maintains each side's snapshot implementation without requiring anyone to reinvent the wheel.

Putting It All Together

At this point, you may feel a bit lost about who does what for VVols to function. Figure 23.71 shows all the software elements and protocols that work together to make the magic happen.

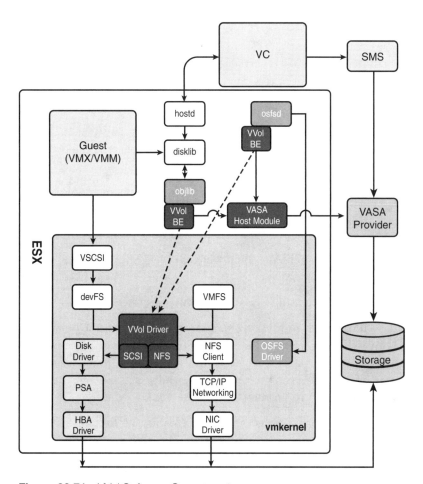

Figure 23.71   VVol Software Components

vCenter uses Storage Management Service (SMS) to communicate with the storage via the Storage VP.

vCenter communicates with `hostd` (via `vpxa`, which is not shown here) for all operations vCenter does on the host, such as creating, modifying, or deleting a VM and informing the host of the registered VP's URL.

`hostd` interfaces with many of the CLI-based tools, such as `esxcli`, to pass the command on to the relevant component. This is why when you use `esxcli` or `vmkfstools` while `hostd` is hung, the host appears to freeze for a short while. As mentioned in a tip earlier, if you are in this situation, you can use `localcli` instead of `esxcli`.

Say that the operation requested by vCenter is to take a VM snapshot. `hostd` calls `disklib`, which formulates the content of the parent disk and delta disk descriptor files so that the parent disk uses the snapshot VVol object, and the delta disk uses the VVol object that was assigned to the parent disk prior to this operation.

`disklib` calls `objlib` to handle the VVol object's operations.

`objlib` has a VVol back-end (BE) function attached to it. `objlib` asks the VP about the current metadata. It then tells the `VVol driver`, which lives in the vmkernel, the details of each VMDK.

If the datastore (SC) is a block SC, the SCSI part of the driver is used to communicate with the disk driver.

If the datastore is a NAS SC, the NFS part of the driver communicates with the NFS client.

Each protocol's path goes through the relevant components to eventually reach the storage.

When the operation is completed successfully, `hostd` relays the status to vCenter.

On the sidelines, `osfsd` communicates with `VASA host module` on the host to get VVol information from the array via VP. `osfsd` communicates with `OSFS driver` in the host's kernel directly. It also communicates, via its `VVol BE`, with `VVol driver` in the host's kernel. The `VVol driver` gives `osfsd` access to the storage, while `OSFS kernel driver` handles the operations related to the VM's namespace and the VMDKs within it.

If the need arises to troubleshoot any of these components, VMware has logs for that. All components running within the vmkernel log their events in /ver/run/log/vmkernel.log.

TIP

You may want to start with a log called vmkwarning.log in the /var/run/log directory, and, if you find messages relevant to the operation you are troubleshooting, you may then look them up in the vmkernel.log file and see surrounding events for the bigger picture.

Some of the components running in the user space (outside vmkernel) have separate logs:

- The guest, which is handled by VMX and VMM processes (user worlds), writes events in vmware.log file located in the VM's home directory (namespace).

- `hostd` writes its events to `/var/run/log/hostd.log`.

- `osfsd` writes to `/var/run/log/osfsd.log`.

- `vvold` writes to `/car/run/log/vvold.log`.

All logs rotate, and the older files are compressed with gzip and named `<log-name>.<n>.`
gz (for example, vmkernel.0.gz, vmkernel.1.gz). The most recent compressed file has the
lowest prefix number.

Most of the messages are self-explanatory. If a message from a user world log has more
details in its corresponding vmkernel peer, it advises you to look up the vmkernel log for
more information. For example, vvold.log shows the following:

```
2016-07-16T19:22:32.507Z error vvold[FFCFFB70] [Originator@6876
sub=Default] HostManager::MountNFSPEs NFS PE configure failed: Sysinfo
error on operation returned status : NFS has reached the maximum number of
supported
```

This was the related message in vmkernel.log:

```
2016-07-16T19:22:32.506Z cpu0:34074)NFS: 202: NFS mount 10.10.0.54:/
rfc4122.0faec917-bfa6-471e-bf4b-7f84baea359d failed: NFS has reached the
maximum number of supported volumes.
```

The timestamp in both messages is the same, which means I found the associated message
in both logs.

This happens to be a common issue, where the ESXi host defaults to a maximum of eight
NFS mounts per host. (I explained this in Chapter 16.)

All you need to do is set the following options to settings that do not exceed their corresponding values:

- `NFS.MaxVolumes`—Up to 256
- `Net.TcpipHeapSize`—Up to 32
- `Net.TcpipHeapMax`—Up to 1536

TIP

Certain VVol configuration properties are stored on ESXi hosts in the /etc/vmware/esx.conf
file (for example, the VP, PE, and SC properties). Listing 23.21 shows examples of these
properties. I added highlighted text to identify relevant information.

Listing 23.21   VVol-related properties in the esx.conf file

```
/nas/NFSv3PE_10.10.0.54__rfc4122.730ecbb3-8fc4-4ef6-b034-1ed2bda5e954/
enabled = "true"
/nas/NFSv3PE_10.10.0.54__rfc4122.730ecbb3-8fc4-4ef6-b034-1ed2bda5e954/share
= "/rfc4122.730ecbb3-8fc4-4ef6-b034-1ed2bda5e954"
```

```
/nas/NFSv3PE_10.10.0.54__rfc4122.730ecbb3-8fc4-4ef6-b034-1ed2bda5e954/host
= "10.10.0.54"
/nas/NFSv3PE_10.10.0.54__rfc4122.730ecbb3-8fc4-4ef6-b034-1ed2bda5e954/isPE
= "true"
/nas/NFSv3PE_10.10.0.54__rfc4122.e82d1444-ca11-4035-88a1-2e60d712f76c/
enabled = "true"
/nas/NFSv3PE_10.10.0.54__rfc4122.e82d1444-ca11-4035-88a1-2e60d712f76c/share
= "/rfc4122.e82d1444-ca11-4035-88a1-2e60d712f76c"
/nas/NFSv3PE_10.10.0.54__rfc4122.e82d1444-ca11-4035-88a1-2e60d712f76c/host
= "10.10.0.54"
/nas/NFSv3PE_10.10.0.54__rfc4122.e82d1444-ca11-4035-88a1-2e60d712f76c/isPE
= "true"
```

[PE info]

```
/nas/NFSv3PE_10.10.0.72__NAS_PE2/isPE = "true"
/nas/NFSv3PE_10.10.0.72__NAS_PE2/host = "10.10.0.72"
/nas/NFSv3PE_10.10.0.72__NAS_PE2/share = "/NAS_PE2"
/nas/NFSv3PE_10.10.0.72__NAS_PE2/enabled = "true"
/nas/NFSv3PE_10.10.0.54__rfc4122.3fcd6b98-ab61-4584-89a9-da4426c70b38/isPE
= "true"
/nas/NFSv3PE_10.10.0.54__rfc4122.3fcd6b98-ab61-4584-89a9-da4426c70b38/host
= "10.10.0.54"
/nas/NFSv3PE_10.10.0.54__rfc4122.3fcd6b98-ab61-4584-89a9-da4426c70b38/share
= "/rfc4122.3fcd6b98-ab61-4584-89a9-da4426c70b38"
/nas/NFSv3PE_10.10.0.54__rfc4122.3fcd6b98-ab61-4584-89a9-da4426c70b38/
enabled = "true"
/nas/NFSv3PE_10.10.0.54__rfc4122.dfc6ab2f-bbad-4233-9cf7-a242530e8b10/isPE
= "true"
/nas/NFSv3PE_10.10.0.54__rfc4122.dfc6ab2f-bbad-4233-9cf7-a242530e8b10/host
= "10.10.0.54"
/nas/NFSv3PE_10.10.0.54__rfc4122.dfc6ab2f-bbad-4233-9cf7-a242530e8b10/share
= "/rfc4122.dfc6ab2f-bbad-4233-9cf7-a242530e8b10"
/nas/NFSv3PE_10.10.0.54__rfc4122.dfc6ab2f-bbad-4233-9cf7-a242530e8b10/
enabled = "true"
/nas/NFSv3PE_10.10.0.54__rfc4122.0faec917-bfa6-471e-bf4b-7f84baea359d/isPE
= "true"
/nas/NFSv3PE_10.10.0.54__rfc4122.0faec917-bfa6-471e-bf4b-7f84baea359d/host
= "10.10.0.54"
/nas/NFSv3PE_10.10.0.54__rfc4122.0faec917-bfa6-471e-bf4b-7f84baea359d/share
= "/rfc4122.0faec917-bfa6-471e-bf4b-7f84baea359d"
/nas/NFSv3PE_10.10.0.54__rfc4122.0faec917-bfa6-471e-bf4b-7f84baea359d/
enabled = "true"
```

[VP Info]

```
/vvol/domainId = "4cfceb1a-bda2-4794-b90a-c22d194e4d0f"
```

```
/vvol/vp[0003]/vpName = "EMC Unity VP"
/vvol/vp[0003]/url = "https://10.10.0.184:8443/vasa/version.xml"
/vvol/vp[0003]/arrayids[0000]/arrayId = "EMC:VIRT1625PDT9QG"
/vvol/vp[0003]/arrayids[0000]/active = "true"
/vvol/vp[0003]/arrayids[0000]/priority = "0"

[SC Info]
/vvol/container[0002]/storageArrayIds[0000]/storageArrayId =
"EMC:VIRT1625PDT9QG"
/vvol/container[0002]/containerId = "730ecbb3-8fc4-4ef6-b034-1ed2bda5e954"
/vvol/container[0002]/containerName = "Unity_VVol_NAS_DS1"
/vvol/container[0003]/storageArrayIds[0000]/storageArrayId =
"EMC:VIRT1625PDT9QG"
/vvol/container[0003]/containerId = "e80c977e-9c80-47c7-ab19-39277c42f7e4"
/vvol/container[0003]/containerName = "Unity_VVol0"
/vvol/container[0004]/containerName = "Unity_VVol_DS1"
/vvol/container[0004]/containerId = "371ab5df-fd88-4116-abe5-0374f4b50e8a"
/vvol/container[0004]/storageArrayIds[0000]/storageArrayId =
"EMC:VIRT1625PDT9QG"
/vvol/container[0005]/containerName = "Unity_VVol_DS3"
/vvol/container[0005]/containerId = "400a35bd-14d2-4a6b-be36-a668f664f347"
/vvol/container[0005]/storageArrayIds[0000]/storageArrayId =
"EMC:VIRT1625PDT9QG"
/vvol/container[0000]/containerName = "Unity_VVol_NAS_DS4"
/vvol/container[0000]/containerId = "dfc6ab2f-bbad-4233-9cf7-a242530e8b10"
/vvol/container[0000]/storageArrayIds[0000]/storageArrayId =
"EMC:VIRT1625PDT9QG"
/vvol/container[0001]/containerName = "Unity_VVol_NAS_DS0"
/vvol/container[0001]/containerId = "0faec917-bfa6-471e-bf4b-7f84baea359d"
/vvol/container[0001]/storageArrayIds[0000]/storageArrayId =
"EMC:VIRT1625PDT9QG"
```

In Listing 23.21, there is a VP property that I did not mention before: domainId field. It is vCenter's instance UUID. The VP settings listed here come from vCenter when VP is registered on it.

VVols Interoperability with Other vSphere Features

At this writing, VVols can interoperate and coexist with many vSphere features but not some others. Table 23.10 shows VVols interoperability status.

Table 23.10 VVols interoperability with vSphere 6.0 features and related products

Feature	Interoperable?	Notes
vSphere 6 Feature		
High Availability (HA)	Yes	Including datastore heartbeat
Linked clones	Yes	With VMware View/Horizon
Native snapshots	Yes	
Thin provisioning	Yes	Default
Content-Based Read Cache (CBRC)	Yes	
vSphere auto-deploy	Yes	
NFSv3	Yes	
vMotion, xvMotion, and Storage vMotion	Yes	
vSAN	Yes	Coexist because OSFS handles both vSAN and VVols
vSphere APIs for I/O (VAIO) filtering	Yes	Certified solutions only
VM fault tolerance (FT)	No	Neither legacy FT nor SMP-FT
IPv6	No	
NFSv4.1	No	
Windows Server Failover Clustering (WSFC)	No	
RDMs	No	Neither physical nor virtual mode RDMs
Storage DRS	No	
Storage I/O Control (SIOC)	No	
vSphere-Related Solutions		
vSphere Replication 6.0	Yes	
VMware Site Recovery Manager (SRM) 5.x–6.1.0	No	
VMware vRealize Automation (vRA) 6.2.x	Yes	
VMware Horizon 6.1.x	Yes	
VMware vRealize Operations Manager (vROPS) 6.0–6.1	No	
VMware vSphere Data Protection (vDP) 5.x–6.1.0	No	
VMware vCloud Director 5.x	No	

VVols Replication

vSphere 6.5 has introduced a long-awaited feature for VVols, which enables storage arrays to replicate whole VMs or certain VMDKs along with the VM's namespace. This feature, called VVols Replication, is enabled by VASA 3.0, introduced with vSphere 6.5. The storage vendor provides a new VP based on VASA 3.0 and certifies the corresponding storage arrays for that version.

VVols Replication is available when both vCenter and ESXi hosts have been upgraded to version 6.5, along with VPs that implements VASA 3.0 protocol.

The concept of replicating the whole VM is enabled by replication groups. These groups are created on the storage array and specify the source and target storage pools, SCs, and PEs. vCenter discovers the newly created replication groups as a storage policy rule, based on data services, and makes them available in vSphere 6.5 Web Client and SPBM. This assumes that the storage array's failover workflow implements failover orchestration software compatible with VVols.

The high-level replication workflow is as follows:

1. Create replication groups on the storage array pairs.

2. Create VM storage policies that include the replication capability. After creating such policies, vCenter discovers the replication groups' names.

3. Assign the storage policy to existing VMs or at the time of deploying new ones.

4. Select the replication group or use automatic assignment. This can be done on the Namespace and Data VVol object only. The remaining objects inherit the configuration. Data VVol objects do not inherit the policy from the Namespace object and must explicitly have the policy assigned to them. If they don't, the VMDKs are excluded from replication.

vSphere 6.5 adds the replication-related details to the metadata of the corresponding Namespace, Data, Memory, and CBRC digest VVol objects. Metadata key/value pairs include the following:

```
VMW_ContineId
VMW_VVolPerentUUID
VMW_VVolNamespace
VMW_VVolParentContainer
```

NOTE

Swap VVol objects are not included because they are created on the target SC upon powering on the failed over VMs.

Replication preserves snapshot history. Replicating snapshots enables you to recover application consistent states.

VPs replicate the metadata unmodified, and vSphere handles modifications on the target upon failover. Think of it as VMFS volume resignature but at a more granular level. The changes to the metadata involve the target storage–specific details, such as the VVol UUID of the replica replacing the one included in the replicated object's metadata and descriptor files.

You should be able to replicate VMs from multiple SCs to a single SC on the target storage array. If there is a conflict with VM namespace VVol object names, vSphere handles renaming them to avoid data corruption. This is kind of similar to VMFS volume renaming after it has been resignatured.

If the source VM is a linked clone, unless the parent VM is replicated along with it, the target VM will be a full clone.

Creating a Storage Policy to Enable Replication Groups

The VVols management plane utilizes SPBM to facilitate VVol object placement and data service assignment via VM storage policies. One of the data services is VVols Replication. This section outlines the procedure of creating VM storage policy components and adding them to VM storage policies. Follow these steps:

1. Log on to vCenter using the vSphere 6.5 Web Client.

2. Navigate to **VM Storage Policies** (see Figure 23.72).

3. Select the **Storage Policy Components** tab.

4. Click the **Create Storage Policy Component** icon.

Figure 23.72   Accessing the Create Storage Policy Component menu

5. Enter the component name and optionally a description (see Figure 23.73).

6. Select **Replication** from the Category pull-down list.

7. Select the relevant storage provider. In this example, I am using the sample VMware VP 3.0. This results in the addition of a new **<Add rule>** pull-down list.

8. Select a rule from the pull-down list (in this example, **RPO**).

9. Enter the number of hours, which is the replication interval. If you need to set it in minutes, change the time unit to minutes from the corresponding pull-down list. In this example, the design calls for an RPO of one hour.

10. Click **OK**.

Figure 23.73 Assigning the storage policy and replication group

11. Repeat steps 4–10 to create additional components, as needed.

12. Select the **VM Storage Policies** tab.

13. Click the **Create VM Storage Policy** icon.

14. Enter the policy name and, optionally, a description.

15. Click **Next** until you reach step 2b Rule-Set 1.

16. Select the VP from the <Select provider> pull-down list (see Figure 23.74).

17. Select a relevant rule from the <Add rule> pull-down list. These rules vary by vendor. In this example, I select a read latency rule and set the value to `15` (the unit is in milliseconds in this example).

18. Click the **Add component** icon.

19. Select **Replication**, **Hourly Replication** (or one of the components you created earlier in this procedure).

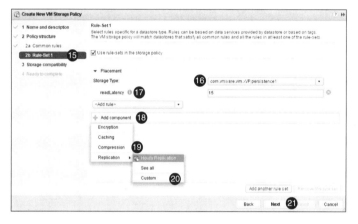

Figure 23.74   Defining a VM storage policy for replication

20. If you want to change the predefined RPO value at the time of adding the component, you can select **Custom** from the Add Component menu and then select the rule from the now visible **<Add rule>** pull-down list. The value of the component is now editable. Set it to the new value (see Figure 23.75).

Figure 23.75   Defining a VM storage policy for replication with a custom component

21. Click **Next**.

22. At the Storage compatibility step, review the list of compatible datastores and make sure they meet your design requirements. Click **Next**.

23. Review the values displayed in the Ready to Complete step and then click **Finish**.

I created these additional policies:

- **Production - Database (OLTP)**—RPO = 2

- **Production - Standard/OS**—RPO = 4

These names match the VMware beta lab I used to obtain the screenshots for this section and the next one.

Now you are ready to assign these policies to new and existing VMs.

Assigning a Replication Group Policy to a New VM

Once the storage policy has been created with the replication capability rule added, you can follow this procedure to assign it during initial VM deployment:

1. Follow the procedure in the section "Creating a New VM Using Storage Profiles," earlier in this chapter, using vSphere 6.5 Web Client. However, in step 10, select the policy you created here and then move to step 2 below 0.

2. Select a replication group from the Replication Group pull-down list (see Figure 23.76).

Figure 23.76 Assigning the storage policy and replication group

You can select the **Automatic** replication group or a preconfigured one. If you want to select a preconfigured one, select it from the list of replication groups to apply the policy to the VM-related VVol objects. If you want to assign certain virtual disks to a different replication group, select a preconfigured replication group and then, after the VM is created, follow the steps in the following procedure.

3. Continue with the rest of the procedure from the "Creating a New VM Using Storage Profiles" section.

> **NOTE**
>
> If the VM was assigned to an Automatic replication group, keep in mind that individual virtual disks cannot be assigned manually to preconfigured replication groups.

Assigning a Replication Group Storage Policy to an Existing VM

To assign a replication group storage policy to an existing VM, follow these steps:

1. Log on to vCenter using vSphere 6.5 Web Client.

2. In the Operations and Policies section, select the **VM Storage Policies** icon.

3. Select the storage policy currently assigned to the VM.

4. Select the **VMs** tab.

5. Click the **Virtual Machines** button if it is not already selected.

6. Select the VM.

7. Right-click the VM.

8. Click **Edit VM Storage Policies**. Figure 23.77 shows the dialog that appears.

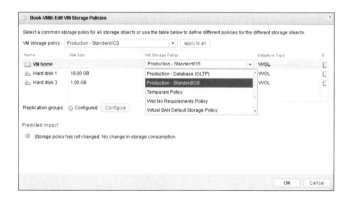

Figure 23.77   Assigning a different storage policy

9. To apply a different policy to all of a VM's objects, select one from the **VM storage policy** pull-down list at the top of the dialog and then click **Apply to all** button.

10. Otherwise, to apply a different policy for each object, select each object and then select the policy from the pull-down list in the VM Storage Policy column.

11. Click **Configure** to open the Configure VM Replication Groups dialog.

12. To assign all of a VM's objects to the same replication group, select **Common replication group** and then select one of the preconfigured groups or **Automatic** from the pull-down list (see Figure 23.78). Otherwise, skip to the next step.

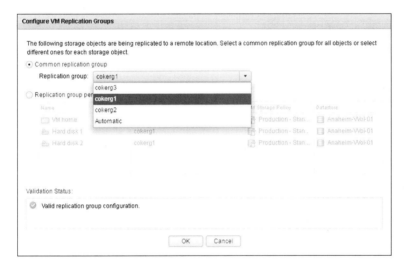

Figure 23.78 Configuring replication groups

13. To assign a different replication group to each VM object, select **Replication group per storage object**, select the object to modify, and then select a replication group from the pull-down list in the Replication Group column (see Figure 23.79).

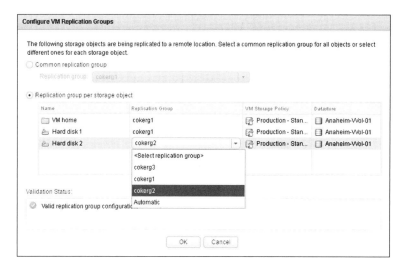

Figure 23.79   Configuring the replication group for each object

14. Click **OK** to save the replication group changes.

15. Click **OK** to save the VM storage policy changes.

Unfortunately, at the time of this writing, 2 storage vendors have VVols Replication–certified arrays available to provide failover orchestration procedures. These vendors are HP and Nimble Storage. I do not have access to their products, which is why I am unable to demonstrate the feature on their devices. However, they should work as follows:

1. You use the storage array management UI to select the option to fail over to the replica.

2. The VP notifies vCenter and, in turn, the ESXi hosts, about the failover.

3. `vvold` and `osfsd`, along with `disklib` and `objlib`, modify the VVols' metadata to reflect the replica VVols', SCs', and PEs' UUIDs on the recovery storage array.

4. HA powers on the VMs on the replica VVols.

Summary

This chapter provides details about Virtual Volumes, which separates the storage data paths from the management out-of-band path. It represent VMDKs as abstract objects, VVols, managed by the storage arrays. The storage array gains full control over VMDK content, layout, and management. The datastores are abstracted as SCs that are also managed by the storage array. Access to VVols is done via one or more protocol endpoints. VVols enable data services such as native snapshots at the individual VMDK level. SPBM enables creating policies for initial placement of VVols on SCs, according to the CPs associated with the SCs.

This chapter also covers sample configurations from a block device storage array and a NAS server.

This chapter provides under-the-hood details on VVols software architecture and the major role that OSFS plays.

VVols Replication is new to vSphere 6.5, and it requires VASA 3.0. At the time of this writing, no arrays or NAS servers are certified except from two vendors; HP and Nimble Storage.

Index

D

Q

R

T

W